Coordination Theory and Collaboration Technology

Computers, Cognition, and Work

A series edited by

Gary M. Olson, Judith S. Olson, and Robert E. Kraut

Bloom et al. (Eds.) • *Facilitating the Development and Use of Interactive Learning Environments*

Finn et al. (Eds.) • *Video-Mediated Communication*

Fox • *The Human Tutorial Dialogue Project: Issues in the Design of Instructional Systems*

Hoschka (Ed.) • *Computers as Assistants: A New Generation of Support Systems*

Koschmann (Ed.) • *CSCL: Theory and Practice of an Emerging Paradigm*

Moran/Carroll (Eds.) • *Design Rationale: Concepts, Techniques, and Use*

Olson/Malone/Smith (Eds.) • *Coordination Theory and Collaboration Technology*

Oppermann (Ed.) • *Adaptive User Support: Ergonomic Design of Manually and Automatically Adaptable Software*

Smith • *Collective Intelligence in Computer-Based Collaboration*

Coordination Theory and Collaboration Technology

Edited by

Gary M. Olson
University of Michigan

Thomas W. Malone
Massachusetts Institute of Technology

John B. Smith
University of North Carolina—Chapel Hill

2001

LAWRENCE ERLBAUM ASSOCIATES, PUBLISHERS
Mahwah, New Jersey London

Lawrence Erlbaum Associates, Inc., Publishers
10 Industrial Avenue
Mahwah, New Jersey 07430

Cover design by Kathryn Houghtaling Lacey

Library of Congress Cataloging-in-Publication Data

Coordination theory and collaboration technology / edited by Gary M. Olson, Thomas W. Malone, John B. Smith.
p. cm.
Includes bibliographical references and index.
ISBN 0-8058-3403-6 (cloth : alk. paper)
1. Group work in research—United States. 2. Research—United States—Methodology. 3. Information technology—United States. I. Olson, Gary M. II. Malone, Thomas W. III. Smith, John B., 1940-

Q180.55.G77 C66 2001
001.4'068—dc21

2001018986

Books published by Lawrence Erlbaum Associates are printed on acid-free paper, and their bindings are chosen for strength and durability.

Printed in the United States of America
10 9 8 7 6 5 4 3 2 1

This volume is dedicated to the memory of Laurence Rosenberg, whose enthusiasm and leadership inspired many researchers to take on the difficult task of building and evaluating information systems in relation to their social, organizational, and economic contexts.

Contents

Introduction

The global revolution in human interconnectedness goes back at least to the last century. By the turn of the century, we had telegraphy and telephony that started us on the path to a wired world, networked transportation (e.g., railroads) that fundamentally altered how we organized our communities (e.g., Stilgoe, 1985), and office technology that began altering the ways we were able to organize ourselves (Yates, 1989). Throughout the 20th century the pace of innovation and change accelerated, with each generation lauding the next apparent steps toward a better world.

However, by the latter decades of the 20th century we began to realize that the technologies of interconnectedness were not by themselves a panacea. Rather, the century was full of surprises. When new technologies of connectedness emerged the initial inclination was to think of possible gains, such as efficiency gains in speed or accuracy (Sproull & Kiesler, 1991). But repeatedly we are surprised by second-order effects that no one had predicted. For instance, electronic mail provides what seems like an effective asynchronous communication medium of considerable flexibility, making it possible for people anywhere on a relevant network to communicate easily. But new problems arise. First, making it easy to communicate makes it too easy to become flooded with information, resulting in efforts to filter the message stream to reasonable levels (e.g., Malone, Grant, Turbak, Brobst, & Cohen, 1987). Second, something about the medium itself appears to make users of email cast their messages in ways that come across as hostile or negative to recipients (Sproull & Kiesler, 1991), adding a further unpleasant dimension to email usage. To be sure, email use is flourishing as this century comes to a close, but it is a more complex and surprising medium than first thought.

Repeated surprises of these sorts have led many to call for multidisciplinary research that would bring together experts on human cognitive, social, and organizational behavior with the technologists who are designing and deploying the new tools. Indeed, the 1980s witnessed the birth of numerous new conferences to explore the issues involved, such as CHI, CSCW, ECSCW, and INTERACT. Numerous smaller workshops and seminars further accelerated the pace of multidisciplinary discussion.

It was in this context that the National Science Foundation (NSF) announced a funding program in the area of Coordination Theory and Collaboration Technology (CTCT, or CT squared). This initiative was announced in calls for proposals issued in 1989 and 1990. It grew out of a series of workshops funded by NSF that began the process of defining this area of research and creating a community of researchers whose work might be funded.

Two workshops on Coordination Science were held at MIT (June 1987 and February 1988) under the leadership of Thomas Malone, and one on Open Systems at Xerox PARC (June 1988) that was organized by Bernardo Huberman. These workshops gave strong indication that the questions about coordination asked in many disciplines are similar and that ideas and methods from each could inform the other.

Two workshops were sponsored by NSF on issues of technology and cooperative work, one organized by Jolene Galagher at the University of Arizona (February 1988), the other at New York University (June 1988) under the leadership of Margrethe Olson. These workshops focused on the behavioral science aspects of coordination and collaboration relating to the interaction of individuals, small groups, and formal organizations and on computer-based systems and software design for collaboration. Two influential books came from these workshops (Galegher, Kraut & Egido, 1990; M. Olson, 1989).

The 1988 announcement of the CTCT initiative captures many of the themes explored in these anticipatory workshops.

> The initiative focuses on processes of coordination and cooperation among autonomous units in human systems, in computer and communication systems, and in hybrid organizations of both systems. . . . This initiative is motivated by three scientific issues which have been the focus of separate research efforts, but which may benefit from collaborative research. The first is the effort to discover the principles underlying how people collaborate and coordinate work efficiently and productively in environments characterized by a high degree of decentralized computation and decision-making. The second is to gain a better fundamental understanding of the structure and outputs of organizations, industries and markets which incorporate sophisticated,

> decentralized information and communications technology as an important component of their operations. The third is to understand problems of coordination in decentralized, or open, computer systems. [NSF 88-59, p. 2]

Two rounds of CTCT competition were held, one in 1988 (with results announced in June of 1989) and a second in 1990. From these two rounds of competitions, 20 projects were funded out of 136 applications. In subsequent years, additional projects were funded out of the regular NSF unsolicited proposal competition, so that by the time the CTCT group held a series of three grantee workshops in 1991, 1992, and 1993, nearly 30 different projects participated. These annual workshops gave the investigators in this program an extended opportunity for interdisciplinary exchange.

A closely related activity took place in March 1989, several months after the submission deadline for the first CTCT Initiative. A major workshop on scientific collaboration was held at Rockefeller University under the direction of Joshua Lederberg and Keith Uncapher. This workshop focused on the feasibility of designing network dependent multi-purpose systems to support remote scientific collaborations in specific disciplines. The components of such systems would include multimedia communications, remote access to instrumentation, digital journals and libraries, and a variety of services to support science. This initial workshop led to a series of follow-on meetings that by 1993 resulted in an influential National Research Council report on "collaboratories" (cf. NAS report). Several of the original CTCT projects clearly fit into this "collaboratory" concept, and additional projects were included in the CTCT workshops described earlier. A recent review showed that collaboratories were becoming an increasingly widespread form of sociotechnical support for distributed team science (Finholt & Olson, 1997).

Laurence Rosenberg of the National Science Foundations was a key player in all of these activities. Throughout this period he was manager of the Information Technology and Organizations program, and a deputy director of the Division of Information, Robotics, and Intelligent Systems (IRIS) in the directorate for Computer and Information Science Engineering (CISE). He was primarily responsible for funding these various workshops that led to the CTCT initiatives, and was also active in the closely related collaboratory arena. In particular, he served as the NSF program manager for the nearly 30 projects funded under the CTCT initiative.

In the spring of 1994 Larry Rosenberg died of cancer after a relatively brief illness. The three editors of this volume decided that a fitting tribute to Larry's efforts at NSF would be for those of us who had been funded through his interdisciplinary CTCT initiatives to put together a book that reported on the work we had done. This effort was facilitated by the fact that those of us so funded had come to know each other quite well through the annual workshops of the CTCT program in the 1991–1993 period. We had become familiar with each other's work, and had explored a number of themes and cross-connections among the projects. These links are reflected in a number of ways in the individual chapters in this volume.

The multiyear projects funded by the CTCT program were all invited to submit chapters for this volume, and almost all of those invited agreed. The initial drafts of chapters were carefully reviewed by other authors, and revisions were obtained. Thus, we used the collegiality established by Larry in the program and its annual workshops to facilitate the production of this volume. We offer these chapters to honor the memory of his efforts on all of our behalf.

Special thanks must go to Sue Schuon, Deborah Jahn and Dawn Nugent for their diligent assistance in bringing this volume to completion.

—Gary M. Olson
—Thomas W. Malone
—John B. Smith

REFERENCES

Finholt, T. A., & Olson, G. M. (1997). From laboratories to collaboratories: A new organizational form for scientific collaboration. *Psychological Science, 8*, 28–36.

Galegher, J., Kraut, R. E., & Egido, C. (1990). *Intellectual teamwork: Social and technical foundations of cooperative work.* Hillsdale, NJ: Lawrence Erlbaum Associates.

Malone, T. W., Grant, K. R., Turbak, F. A., Brobst, S. A., & Cohen, M. D. (1987). Intelligent information-sharing systems. *Communications of the ACM, 30*, 390–402.

Olson, M. H. (1989). *Technological support for work group collaboration.* Hillsdale, NJ: Lawrence Erlbaum Associates.

Stilgoe, J. R. (1985). *Metropolitan corridor.* New Haven, CT: Yale University Press.

Sproull, L., & Kiesler, S. (1991). *Connections: New ways of working in the networked organization.* Cambridge, MA: MIT Press.

Yates, J. (1989). *Control through communication: The rise of system in American management.* Baltimore: Johns Hopkins University Press.

PART I

THEORETICAL APPROACHES TO COORDINATION AND COLLABORATION

CHAPTER

1

The Interdisciplinary Study of Coordination*

Thomas W. Malone
Kevin Crowston
Massachusetts Institute of Technology

1. INTRODUCTION

In recent years, there has been a growing interest in questions about how the activities of complex systems can be coordinated (e.g., Bond & Gasser, 1988; Huberman, 1988b; Huhns & Gasser, 1989; Johansen, 1988; NSF, 1991; NSF-IRIS, 1989; Rumelhart, et al., 1986; Winograd & Flores, 1986). In some cases, this work has focused on coordination in parallel and distributed computer systems; in others, on coordination in human systems; and in many cases, on complex systems that include both people and computers.

Our goal in this chapter is to summarize and stimulate development of theories that can help with this work. This new research area—the interdisciplinary study of coordination—draws upon a variety of different disciplines including computer science, organization theory, management science, economics, linguistics, and psychology. Many of the researchers whose efforts can contribute to and benefit from this new area are not yet aware of each other's work. Therefore, by summarizing this diverse body of work in a way that emphasizes its common themes, we hope to help define a community of interest and to suggest useful directions for future progress.

There is still no widely accepted name for this area, so we will use the term *coordination theory* to refer to theories about how coordination can

*Reprinted (with permission) from *ACM Computing Surveys*, Vol. 26, No. 1, March 1994, 87–119.

occur in diverse kinds of systems. We use the term *theory* with some hesitation because it connotes to some people a degree of rigor and coherence that is not yet present in this field. Instead, the field today is a collection of intriguing analogies, scattered results, and partial frameworks. We use the term *theory*, however, in part to signify a provocative goal for this interdisciplinary enterprise, and we hope that this chapter will help us move closer toward that goal.

1.1. A Motivating Question

We begin with one of the questions that coordination theory may help answer: *How will the widespread use of information technology change the ways people work together?* This is not the only possible focus of coordination theory, but it is a particularly timely question today for two reasons.

First, in recent years, large numbers of people have acquired direct access to computers, primarily for individual tasks like spreadsheet analysis and word processing. These computers are now beginning to be connected to each other. Therefore, we now have, for the first time, an opportunity for vastly larger numbers of people to use computing and communications capabilities to help coordinate their work. For example, specialized new software has been developed to (a) support multiple authors working together on the same document, (b) help people display and manipulate information more effectively in face-to-face meetings, and (c) help people intelligently route and process electronic messages (see detailed references in Section 3.3).

It already appears likely that there will be commercially successful products of this new type (often called "computer-supported cooperative work" or "groupware"), and to some observers these applications herald a paradigm shift in computer usage as significant as the earlier shifts to time-sharing and personal computing. It is less clear whether the continuing development of new computer applications in this area will depend solely on the intuitions of successful designers or whether it will also be guided by a coherent underlying theory of how people coordinate their activities now and how they might do so differently with computer support.

Second, in the long run, the dramatic improvements in the costs and capabilities of information technologies are changing—by orders of magnitude—the constraints on how certain kinds of communication and coordination can occur. At the same time, there is a pervasive feeling in businesses today that global interdependencies are becoming more critical, that the pace of change is accelerating, and that we need to create more flexible and adaptive organizations. Together, these changes may soon lead us across a threshold where entirely new ways of organizing human activities become desirable.

For example, new capabilities for communicating information faster, less expensively, and more selectively may help create what some observers (e.g., Toffler, 1970) have called "adhocracies"—rapidly changing organizations with highly decentralized networks of shifting project teams. As another example, lowering the costs of coordination between firms may encourage more market transactions (i.e., more "buying" rather than "making") and, at the same time, closer coordination across firm boundaries (such as "just in time" inventory management).

1.2. How Can We Proceed?

If we believe that new forms of organizing are likely to become more common, how can we understand the possibilities better? What other new kinds of coordination structures will emerge in the electronically connected world of the near future? When are these new structures desirable? What is necessary for them to work well?

To some extent, we can answer these questions by observing "leading edge" organizations as they experiment with new technologies. But to understand the experiences of these organizations, we may need to look more deeply into the fundamental constraints on how coordination can occur. And to imagine new kinds of organizational processes that no organizations have tried yet, we may need to look even further afield for ideas.

One way to do both these things—to understand fundamental constraints and to imagine new possibilities—is to look for analogies in how coordination occurs in very different kinds of systems. For example, could we learn something about tradeoffs between computing and communicating in distributed computer systems that would illuminate possibilities for coordination in human organizations? Might coordination structures analogous to those used in beehives or ant colonies be useful for certain aspects of human organizations? And could lessons learned about coordination in human systems help understand computational or biological systems, as well?

For these possibilities to be realized, a great deal of cross-disciplinary interaction is needed. It is not enough just to believe that different systems are similar; we also need an intellectual framework for "transporting" concepts and results back and forth between the different kinds of systems.

In the remainder of this chapter, we provide the beginnings of such a framework. We first define coordination in a way that emphasizes its interdisciplinary nature and then suggest an approach for studying it further. Next, we describe examples of how a coordination perspective can be applied in three domains: understanding the effects of information technology on human organizations and markets, designing cooperative work tools, and designing distributed and parallel processing computer systems. Finally, we briefly suggest elements of a research agenda for this new area.

2. A FRAMEWORK FOR STUDYING COORDINATION

2.1. What Is Coordination?

We all have an intuitive sense of what the word *coordination* means. When we attend a well-run conference, when we watch a winning basketball team, or when we see a smoothly functioning assembly line we may notice how well coordinated the actions of a group of people seem to be. Often, however, good coordination is nearly invisible, and we sometimes notice coordination most clearly when it is lacking. When we spend hours waiting on an airport runway because the airline can't find a gate for our plane, when the hotel where we thought we had a reservation is fully booked, or when our favorite word processing program stops working in a new version of the operating system, we may become very aware of the effects of poor coordination.

For many purposes, this intuitive meaning is sufficient. However, in trying to characterize a new interdisciplinary area, it is also helpful to have a more precise idea of what we mean by coordination. Appendix A lists a number of definitions that have been suggested for this term. The diversity of these definitions illustrates the difficulty of defining coordination, and also the variety of possible starting points for studying the concept. For our purposes here, however, it is useful to begin with the following simple definition:

Coordination is managing dependencies between activities.[1]

This definition is consistent with the simple intuition that, if there is no interdependence, there is nothing to coordinate. It is also consistent with a long history in organization theory of emphasizing the importance of interdependence (e.g., Galbraith, 1973; Hart & Estrin, 1990; Lawrence & Lorsch, 1967; Pfeffer, 1978; Roberts & Gargano, 1989; Rockart & Short, 1989; Thompson, 1967).

As the definition suggests, we believe it is helpful to use the word *coordination* in a fairly inclusive sense. For instance, it is clear that actors performing interdependent activities may have conflicting interests and that what might be called "political processes" are ways of managing them (e.g., Ciborra, 1987; Kling, 1980; Schelling, 1960; Williamson, 1985). Furthermore, even though words like "cooperation," "collaboration," and "competition"

---

[1]This definition was particularly influenced by Rockart and Short (1989) and Curtis (1989). The importance of coordination in this very general sense was perhaps first recognized by Holt (1980, 1988).

each have their own connotations, they can each be viewed, in part, as ways of managing dependencies between activities.

It should also be clear that coordination, as we have defined it, can occur in many kinds of systems: human, computational, biological, and others. For instance, questions about how people manage dependencies among their activities are central to parts of organization theory, economics, management science, sociology, social psychology, anthropology, linguistics, law, and political science. In computer systems, dependencies between different computational processes must certainly be managed, and, as numerous observers have pointed out, certain kinds of interactions among computational processes resemble interactions among people (e.g., Fox, 1981; Hewitt, 1986; Huberman, 1988a, 1988b; Miller & Drexler, 1988; Smith & Davis, 1981). To give a sense of the approaches different fields have taken to studying coordination, we summarize in Appendix B examples of results about coordination from computer science, organization theory, economics, and biology.

Even though we believe there are more similarities among these different kinds of systems than most people appreciate, there are obviously many differences as well. One of the most important differences is that issues of *incentives, motivations*, and *emotions* are usually of much more concern in human systems than in other kinds of systems. In computer programs, for example, the "incentives" of a program module are usually easy to describe and completely controlled by a programmer. In human systems, on the other hand, the motivations, incentives, and emotions of people are often extremely complex, and understanding them is usually an important part of coordination. Even in human systems, however, analogies with other kinds of systems may help us understand fundamental constraints on coordination and imagine new kinds of organizations that might be especially motivational for people.

2.2. Basic Coordination Processes

A primary vehicle for facilitating transfer among these different disciplines is identifying and studying the basic *processes* involved in coordination: Are there fundamental coordination processes that occur in all coordinated systems? How can we represent and analyze these processes? Is it possible to characterize situations in a way that helps generate and choose appropriate coordination mechanisms for them?

One of the advantages of the definition we have used for coordination is that it suggests a direction for addressing these questions. If coordination is defined as managing dependencies, then further progress should be possible by *characterizing different kinds of dependencies and identifying the coordination processes that can be used to manage them.*

Table 1.1 suggests the beginnings of such an analysis (see Malone, Crowston, Lee, & Pentland, 1992, for more details). For example, one possible kind

TABLE 1.1
Examples of Common Dependencies Between Activities and Alternative Coordination Processes for Managing Them

Dependency	*Examples of Coordination Processes for Managing Dependency*
Shared resources	"First come/first serve," priority order, budgets, managerial decision, market-like bidding
Task assignments	(same as for "Shared resources")
Producer–consumer relationships	
Prerequisite constraints	Notification, sequencing, tracking
Inventory	Inventory management (e.g., "Just In Time"; "Economic Order Quantity")
Usability	Standardization, ask users, participatory design
Design for manufacturability	Concurrent engineering
Simultaneity constraints	Scheduling, synchronization
Task–subtask	Goal selection, task decomposition

Note. Indentations in the left column indicate more specialized versions of general dependency types.

of dependency between different activities is that they require the same (limited) resources. The table shows that shared resource constraints can be managed by a variety of coordination processes such as "first come/first serve," priority order, budgets, managerial decision, and market-like bidding. If three job shop workers need to use the same machine, for instance, they could use a simple first come/first serve mechanism. Alternatively, they could use a form of budgeting with each worker having preassigned time slots, or a manager could explicitly decide what to do whenever two workers wanted to use the machine at the same time. In some cases, they might even want to "bid" for use of the machine and the person willing to pay the most would get it.

The lists of dependencies and coordination processes in Table 1.1 are by no means intended to be exhaustive. It is important to note, however, that many specific processes that arise in particular kinds of systems (such as "design for manufacturability") can be seen as instances of more generic processes (such as managing "usability" constraints between adjacent steps in a process). In fact, we believe that one of the most intriguing possibilities for coordination theory is to identify and systematically analyze a wide variety of dependencies and their associated coordination processes. Such a "handbook" of coordination processes could not only facilitate interdisciplinary transfer of knowledge about coordination; it could also provide a guide for analyzing the coordination needs in particular situations and generating alternative ways of fulfilling them (see Malone, Crowston, Lee, & Pentland, 1992).

One question that arises immediately is how to categorize these dependencies and coordination processes. Table 1.1 provides a start in this direction. Crowston (1991) suggested a more structured taxonomy based on all the possible relationships between "tasks" and "resources."

To illustrate the possibilities for analyzing coordination processes, we discuss in the remainder of this section the coordination processes listed in Table 1.1 and how they have been analyzed in different disciplines.

2.2.1. Managing Shared Resources

Whenever multiple activities share some limited resource (e.g., money, storage space, or an actor's time), then a *resource allocation* process is needed to manage the interdependencies among these activities. Resource allocation is perhaps the most widely studied of all coordination processes. For example, it has received significant attention in economics, organization theory, and computer science.

Economics. Much of economics is devoted to studying resource allocation processes, especially those involving market-like pricing and bidding mechanisms. As economists have observed, for instance, markets have a number of interesting properties as resource allocation mechanisms (Simon, 1981). For one thing, they can be very *decentralized*: Many independent decision-makers interacting with each other locally can produce a globally coherent allocation of resources without any centralized controller (e.g., Smith, 1776). For another thing, markets have a built-in set of *incentives*: When all participants in a perfect market try to maximize their own individual benefits, the overall allocation of resources is (in a certain sense) globally "optimal" (e.g., Debreu, 1959).

Organization Theory. Organization theory has also paid great attention to resource allocation issues. For instance, control of resources is intimately connected with personal and organizational power: those who control resources have power and vice versa (e.g., Pfeffer & Salancik, 1978). In general, organization theorists emphasize hierarchical resource allocation methods where managers at each level decide how the resources they control will be allocated among the people who report to them (e.g., Burton & Obel, 1980a, 1980b). In practice, however, resource allocation in organizations is much more complex than a simple hierarchical model suggests. For instance, managers may try to increase their own power by attracting resources (e.g., employees and money) away from other possible activities (Barnard, 1964) or by using their resources in a way that is very suboptimal from the point of view of the whole organization.

How can we choose between different resource allocation methods? Recent work in *transaction cost theory* addresses part of this question by analyzing the conditions under which a hierarchy is a better way of coordinating multiple actors than a market (e.g., Williamson, 1975, 1985). For example, if there are extra costs associated with a market transaction (such as extensive legal and accounting work), then the costs of internal transactions within a hierarchical firm may be lower and therefore preferable. A related question involves the conditions under which it is desirable to use market-like resource allocation mechanisms (such as transfer pricing) within a hierarchical organization (Eccles, 1985).

Computer Science. Resource allocation issues also arise in computer systems and much work has been done on these topics (e.g., Cytron, 1987; Halstead, 1985). For instance, operating systems require algorithms for allocating resources—such as processors and memory—to different processes and for scheduling accesses to input/output devices, such as disks (e.g., Deitel, 1983). As we see shortly, there have already been examples of cross-fertilization of ideas about resource allocation between computer science and other fields. For example, in Section 2.3.3, we see how ideas about distributed computer systems helped understand the evolution of human organizations, and in Section 3.4, we see how analogies with human markets have generated novel resource allocation schemes for computer systems.

Task Assignment. One very important special case of resource allocation is task assignment, that is, allocating the scarce time of actors to the tasks they will perform. An insight of the approach we are taking here, therefore, is that all the resource allocation methods listed in Table 1.1 are potentially applicable for task assignment, too.

For instance, in trying to imagine new coordination processes in a human organization, one might consider whether any given situation requiring task assignment could be better managed by managerial decision, by prior assignment according to task type, or by a pricing mechanism. To illustrate the surprising ideas this might lead to, consider Turoff's (1983) suggestion that employees within a large organization should be able to "bid" for the internal projects on which they wish to work, and that teams could be selected using these bids. There are obviously many factors to consider in determining whether such an arrangement would be desirable in a particular situation, but it is interesting to note that one potential disadvantage—the significantly greater communication required—would be much less important in a world with extensive computer networks.

2.2.2. *Managing Producer/Consumer Relationships*

Another extremely common kind of relationship between activities is a "producer/consumer" relationship, that is, a situation where one activity produces something that is used by another activity. This relationship clearly occurs in all physical manufacturing processes, for instance, where the output of one step on an assembly line is the input to the next. It also occurs with information whenever one person in an organization uses information from another or when one part of a computer program uses information produced by another.

Producer/consumer relationships often lead to several kinds of dependencies:

Prerequisite Constraints. A very common dependency between a "producer" activity and a "consumer" activity is that the producer activity must be completed before the consumer activity can begin. When this dependency exists, there must at least be some *notification* process to indicate to the consumer activity that it can begin. For instance, when an automobile designer delivers a completed drawing of a part to the engineer who will design the manufacturing process for that part, the arrival of the drawing in the engineer's in-box "notifies" the engineer that her activity can begin.

Managing prerequisite dependencies also often involves explicit *sequencing* and *tracking* processes to be sure that producer activities have been completed before their results are needed. For instance, techniques from operations research, such as PERT charts and critical path methods, are often used in human organizations to help schedule large projects with multiple activities and complex prerequisite structures. These and other project tracking systems are also often used by managers to identify activities that are late and then use their authority to "motivate" the people responsible for the late tasks.

What alternatives can we imagine for managing this dependency? One possibility would be computer-based tracking systems that made it easy for everyone in the project to see status information about all the other activities and their dependencies. In this case, late tasks could be visible to everyone throughout the project, and "authoritarian" motivation by managers might become less important.

Sequencing problems arise frequently in computer systems, as well. For instance, one of the key issues in taking advantage of parallel processing computers is determining which activities can be done in parallel and which ones must wait for the completion of others (Arvind & Culler, 1986; Holt, 1988; Peterson, 1977, 1981). Some of these ideas from computer science have also been used to help streamline processes in human organizations by taking advantage of their latent parallelism (e.g., Ellis, Gibbons, & Morris, 1979).

Inventory. Satisfying a prerequisite constraint means that the producer activity is not too *late*. But in some cases, the producer activity might also be too *early* (e.g., if the item produced is perishable or there is no place to store it). When it is important for an item to be neither too late nor too early, we call this an "inventory dependency." One way of managing an inventory dependency is to carefully control the timing of both activities so that items are delivered "*just in time*" to be used. This technique, for example, is becoming increasingly common in manufacturing environments (Schonberger, 1982, 1986). A more common approach is maintain an *inventory* of finished items, ready for the second activity to use, as a buffer between the two activities. Operations researchers, for instance, have developed techniques for determing at what stock levels and by how much to replenish an inventory in order to minimize costs (e.g., the "*economic order quantity*"; McClain, Thomas, & Mazola, 1992).

Managing this dependency is also important in certain parts of computer science. For example, in parallel processing systems, the rate of execution of processes must sometimes be regulated to ensure that the producer does not overwhelm the consumer or vice versa (e.g., Arvind et al., 1986). As our framework would suggest, a common approach to this problem is to place a buffer between the two processes and allocate space in the buffer to one process or the other. Network protocols manage similar problems between communicating processes that do not share any memory (Tannenbaum, 1981).

Usability. Another, somewhat less obvious, dependency that must often be managed in a producer/consumer relationship is that whatever is produced should be usable by the activity that receives it. One common way of managing this dependency is by *standardization*, creating uniformly interchangeable outputs in a form that users already expect. This is the approach on assembly lines, for example. Another approach is to *ask users* what characteristics they want. For instance, in human organizations this might be done by market research techniques such as surveys and focus groups (Kinnear & Taylor, 1991).

A third, related, alternative is *participatory design*, that is, having the users of a product actively participate in its design (Schuler & Namioka, 1992). This is a widely advocated approach to designing computer systems, for example, and it is interesting to note that the increasingly common practice of "concurrent engineering" (Carter & Baker, 1991) can also be viewed as a kind of participatory design. In concurrent engineering, people who design a product do not simply hand the design "over the transom" to those who design its manufacturing process. Instead, they work together concurrently to create designs that can be manufactured more easily.

In computer systems, the usability dependency occurs whenever one part of a system must use information produced by another. In general, this dependency is managed by designing various kinds of interchange languages and other standards.

2.2.3. *Managing Simultaneity Constraints*

Another common kind of dependency between activities is that they need to occur at the same time (or cannot occur at the same time). Whenever people schedule meetings, for instance, they must satisfy this constraint.

Another example of this constraint occurs in the design of computer systems in which multiple processes (i.e., instruction streams) can be executed simultaneously. (These systems may have multiple processors or a single processor which is shared between the processes.) In general, the instructions of the different processes can be executed in any order. Permitting this indeterminancy improves the performance of the system (e.g., one process can be executed while another waits for data to be input) but can cause problems when the processes must share data or resources. System designers must therefore provide mechanisms that restrict the possible orderings of the instructions by synchronizing the processes (i.e., ensuring that particular instructions from different streams are executed at the same time; Dubois, Schuerich, & Briggs, 1988).

Synchronization primitives can be used to control sharing of data between a producer and consumer process to ensure that all data is used exactly once (the *producer/consumer* problem) or to prevent simultaneous writes to a shared data item (the *mutual exclusion* problem). For example, if two processes simultaneously read and then update the same data (adding a deposit to an account balance, say), one process might overwrite the value stored by the other.

One example of interdisciplinary transfer involving this concept is the work of Singh and colleagues in using computer science concepts about synchronized interactions to model process in human organizations (Singh & Rein, 1992).

2.2.4. *Managing Task/Subtask Dependencies*

Top-down Goal Decomposition. A common kind of dependency among activities is that a group of activities are all "subtasks" for achieving some overall goal. As discussed in more detail shortly, there is a sense in which some overall evaluation criteria or "goals" are necessarily implied by the definition of coordination. The most commonly analyzed case of managing this dependency occurs when an individual or group decides to pursue a goal, and then decomposes this goal into activities (or subgoals) which together will achieve the original goal. In this case, we call the process of choosing the goal *goal selection,* and the process of choosing the activities *goal decomposition.*

For example, the strategic planning process in human organizations is often viewed as involving this kind of goal selection and goal decomposition process. Furthermore, an important role for all managers in a traditionally conceived hierarchy is to decompose the goals they are given into tasks that they can, in turn, delegate to people who work for them. There are, in general, many ways a given goal can be broken into pieces, and a long-standing topic in organization theory involves analyzing different possible decompositions such as by function, by product, by customer, and by geographical region (Mintzberg, 1979). Some of these different goal decompositions for human organizations are analogous to ways computer systems can be structured (e.g., Malone & Smith, 1988).

In computer systems, we usually think of the goals as being predetermined, but an important problem involves how to break these goals into activities that can be performed separately. In a sense, for example, the essence of all computer programming is decomposing goals into elementary activities. For instance, programming techniques such as subroutine calls, modular programming, object oriented programming, and so forth can all be thought of as techniques for structuring the process of goal decomposition (Liskov & Guttag, 1986). In these cases the goal decomposition is performed by a human programmer. Another example of goal decomposition in computer systems is provided by work on planning in artificial intelligence (e.g., Allen, Hendler, & Tate, 1990; Chapman, 1987; Fikes & Nilsson, 1971). In this case, goals are decomposed by a planning program into a sequence of elementary activities, based on knowledge of the elementary activities available, their prerequisites, and their effects.

In some cases, techniques for goal decomposition used in computer systems may suggest new ways of structuring human organizations. For example, Moses (1990) suggested that human organizations might sometimes be better off not as strict hierarchies but as multilayered structures in which any actor at one level could direct the activities of any actor at the next level down. This multilayered structure is analogous to successive layers of languages or "virtual machines" in a computer system (see Malone, 1990).

Bottom-up Goal Identification. Even though the most commonly analyzed cases of coordination involve a sequential process of goal selection and then goal decomposition, the steps do not necessarily happen in this order. Another possibility, for instance, is that several actors realize that the things they are already doing (with small additions) could work together to achieve a new goal. For example, the creation of a new interdisciplinary research group may have this character. In human systems, this bottom-up process of goal selection can often engender more commitment from the actors involved than a top-down assignment of responsibility.

2.2.5. *Managing Other Dependencies*

As noted before, the dependencies discussed so far are only a suggestive list of common dependencies. We believe there are many more dependencies to be identified and analyzed. For instance, when two divisions of a company both deal with the same customer, there is a *shared reputation* dependency between their activities: What one division does affects the customer's perception of the company as a whole, including the other division. As another example, when several people in the same office want to buy a new rug, a key problem is not how to *allocate* the rug, but what color or other *characteristics* it should have. We might call this, therefore, a *shared characteristics* dependency (another special case of the shared resource dependency).

In general, there may be many ways of describing different dependencies, coordination processes, and their relationships to each other, and we suspect that there are many opportunities for further useful work along these lines.

2.2.6. *Summary of Basic Coordination Processes*

Table 1.2 loosely summarizes our discussion so far by listing examples of how common coordination processes have been analyzed in different disciplines. The key point of this table, and indeed of much of our discussion, is that the concepts of coordination theory can help identify similarities among concepts and results in different disciplines. These similarities, in turn, suggest how ideas can be transported back and forth across disciplinary boundaries and where opportunities exist to develop even deeper analyses.

2.3. Example: Analyzing the Task Assignment Process

So far, the examples we have described have mostly involved a single field or analogies that have been transported from one discipline to another. To illustrate the possibilities for developing abstract theories of coordination that can apply simultaneously to many different kinds of systems, let us consider the task assignment process as analyzed by Malone and Smith (Malone, 1987; Malone & Smith, 1988; see also related work by Baligh & Richartz, 1967; Burton & Obel, 1980a). As we have described in more detail elsewhere (Malone, 1992), these analyses illustrate the kind of interdisciplinary interaction that our search for coordination theory encourages: The models grew originally out of designing distributed computer systems, they drew upon results from operations research, and they led eventually to new insights about the evolution of human organizations.

TABLE 1.2
Examples of How Different Disciplines Have Analyzed Coordination processes

Coordination Process	*Computer Science*	*Economics and Operations Research*	*Organization Theory*
Managing shared resources (including task assignments)	techniques for processor scheduling and memory allocation	analyses of markets and other resource allocation mechanisms, scheduling algorithms and other optimization techniques	analyses of different organizational structures; budgeting processes, organizational power, and resource dependence
Managing producer–consumer relationships (including prerequisites and usability constraints)	data flow and Petri net analyses	PERT charts, critical path methods; scheduling techniques	Participatory design; market research
Managing simultaneity constraints	synchronization techniques, mutual exclusion	scheduling techniques	meeting scheduling, certain kinds of process modeling
Managing task–subtask relationship	modularization techniques in programming; planning in artificial intelligence	economics of scale and scope	strategic planning; management by objectives; methods of grouping people into units

2.3.1. A Generic Task Assignment Problem

Consider the following task assignment problem: A system is producing a set of "products," each of which requires a set of "tasks" to be performed. The tasks are of various types, and each type of task can only be performed by "server" actors specialized for that kind of task. Furthermore, the specific tasks to be performed cannot be predicted in advance; they only become known during the course of the process and then only to actors we will call "clients." This description of the task assignment problem is certainly not universally applicable, but it is an abstract description that can be applied to many common task assignment situations. For instance, the tasks might be (a) designing, manufacturing, and marketing different kinds of automobiles, or (b) processing steps in different jobs on a computer network.

2.3.2. Possible Coordination Mechanisms

One (highly centralized) possibility for solving this task assignment problem is for all the clients and servers to send all their information to a central decision maker who decides which servers will perform which tasks and then notifies them accordingly. Another (highly decentralized) possibility is suggested by the competitive bidding scheme for computer networks formalized by Smith and Davis (1981). In this scheme, a client first broadcasts an *announcement* message to all potential servers. This message includes a description of the activity to be performed and the qualifications required. The potential servers then use this information to decide whether to submit a *bid* on the action. If they decide to bid, their bid message includes a description of their qualifications and their availability for performing the action. The client uses these bid messages to decide which server should perform the activity and then sends an *award* message to notify the server that is selected.

Malone and Smith (Malone, 1987; Malone & Smith, 1988) analyzed several alternative coordination mechanisms like these, each of which is analogous to a mechanism used in human organizations. In particular, they developed formal models to represent various forms of *markets* (centralized and decentralized) and various forms of *hierarchies* (based on products or functions). Then they used techniques from queuing theory and probability theory to analyze tradeoffs among these structures in terms of *production costs, coordination costs,* and *vulnerability costs*. For instance, they showed that the centralized schemes had lower coordination costs, but were more vulnerable to processor failures. Decentralized markets, on the other hand, were much less vulnerable to processor failures but had high coordination costs. And decentralized hierarchies ("product hierarchies") had low coordination costs, but they had unused processor capacity which led to high production costs.

2.3.3. Applying These Models to Various Kinds of Systems

Even though these models omit many important aspects of human organizations and computer systems they help illuminate a surprisingly wide range of phenomena. For instance, as Malone and Smith (1988) showed, the models are consistent with a number of previous theories about human organizational design (e.g., Galbraith, 1973; March & Simon, 1958; Williamson, 1985) and with major historical changes in the organizational forms of both human organizations (Chandler, 1962, 1977) and computer systems. These models also help analyze design alternatives for distributed scheduling mechanisms in computer systems, and they suggest ways of analyzing the structural changes associated with introducing new information technology into organizations (see Section 3.2 of this chapter; Crowston, Malone, & Lin, 1987; Malone & Smith, 1988).

2.4. Other Processes Needed for Coordination

In addition to the processes already described for managing specific dependencies, two other processes deserve specific attention: *group decision making* and *communication*. It is sometimes possible to analyze these processes as ways of managing specific dependencies. For instance, communication can be viewed as a way of managing producer/consumer relationships for information. However, because of the importance of these two processes in almost all instances of coordination, we describe them separately here.

2.4.1. Group Decision Making

Many coordination processes require making decisions that affect the activities of a group. For instance, in sharing resources a group must somehow "decide" how to allocate the resources; in managing task/subtask dependencies, a group must decide how to segment tasks. In all these cases, the alternative ways of making group decisions give rise to alternative coordination processes. For example, any group decision can, in principle, be made by authority (e.g., a manager decides), by voting, or by consensus (resulting from negotation).

Because of the importance of group decision making in coordination, answers to questions about group decision making (e.g., Arrow, 1951; Simon, 1976) will be important for developing coordination theory. For instance, what are the decision-making biases in groups (e.g., Janis & Mann, 1977) as opposed to individuals (Kahneman & Tversky, 1973)? How do computer-based group decision-making tools affect these processes (e.g., Dennis, Joey, Jessup, Nunamaker, & Vogel, 1988; Kiesler, Siegel, & McGuire, 1984; Kraemer & King, 1988)? Can we determine optimal ways of allocating tasks and sharing information for making group decisions (Miao, Luh, & Kleinman, 1992)? How do (or should) decision-making processes change in situations where both rapid response and high reliability are required (Roberts, Stout, & Halpern, 1994).

2.4.2. Communication

As with decision making, there is already a great deal of theory about communication, both from a technical point of view (e.g., Shannon & Weaver, 1949) and from an organizational point of view (e.g., Allen, 1977; Rogers & Agarwala-Rogers, 1976; Weick, 1969). One obvious way of generating new coordination processes, for example, is by considering alternative forms of communication (synchronous vs. asynchronous, paper vs. electronic) for all the places in a process where information needs to be transferred.

A coordination framework also highlights new aspects of these problems. For example, when we view communication as a way of managing producer/consumer relationships for information, we may be concerned about how to make the information "usable." How, for instance, can actors establish common languages that allow them to communicate in the first place? This question of developing standards for communication is of crucial concern in designing computer networks in general (Dertouzos, 1991) and cooperative work tools in particular (e.g., Lee & Malone, 1988). The process by which standards are developed is also of concern to economists, philosophers, and others (e.g., Farrell & Saloner, 1985; Hirsch, 1987).

A related set of questions arises when we are concerned about how a group of actors can come to have "common knowledge," that is, they all know something, and they also all know *that* they all know it. There is a growing literature about this and related questions in fields as diverse as computer science, economics, and linguistics (Aumann, 1976; Cohen & Levesque, 1991; Gray, 1978; Halpern, 1987; Milgrom, 1981; Shoham, 1993).

3. APPLYING A COORDINATION PERSPECTIVE

3.1. Approaches to Analyzing Coordination in Different Kinds of Systems

Any scientific theory (indeed, any statement about the world) must neglect some things, in order to focus on others. For example, Kling (1980) described how different perspectives (such as rational, structural, and political) on the use of information systems in organizations each illuminate aspects of reality neglected by the others. In some situations, one or another of these perspectives may be most important, and all of them are involved to some degree in any real situation. In applying coordination theory to any particular system, therefore, it may be necessary to consider many other factors as well.

For instance, in designing a new computer system to help people coordinate their work, "details" about screen layout and response time may sometimes be as important as the basic functionality of the system, and the reputation of the manager who introduces the system in a particular organization may have more effect on the motivation of people to use it in that organization than any incentive structures designed into the system. Similarly, in designing a distributed processing computer system, the failure rates for different kinds of communications media and processors may be the primary design consideration, overwhelming any other considerations about how tasks are allocated among processors.

3.1.1. Parametric Analysis Versus Baseline Analysis

There are at least two ways an interdisciplinary theory can help deal with differences like these among systems: *parametric analysis,* and *baseline analysis.*

Parametric Analysis. In parametric analysis, the abstract theories include parameters which may be different for different kinds of systems. For instance, the principles of aerodynamics apply to both birds and airplanes, even though parameters such as size, weight, and energy expenditure are very different in the two kinds of systems. Similarly, abstract models of coordination may include parameters for things like incentives, cognitive capacities, and communication costs which are very different in human, computational, and biological systems. Examples of models that have been applied to more than one kind of system in this way are summarized in Sections 2.3 and 3.4.2.

Baseline Analysis. In baseline analysis, one theory is used as a baseline for comparison to the actual behavior of a system, and deviations from the baseline are then explained with other theories. For example, in behavioral decision theory (e.g., Kahneman & Tversky, 1973), mathematical decision theory is used to analyze the ways people actually make decisions. In the cases where people depart from the prescriptions of the normative mathematical theory, new theories are developed to explain the differences. Even though the original mathematical theory does not completely explain people's actual behavior, the anomalies explained by the new theories could not even have been recognized without a baseline theory for comparison. This suggests that an important part of coordination theory will be *behavioral coordination theory* in which careful observations of actual coordination in human systems are used to develop, test, and augment abstract models of coordination.

3.1.2. Identifying the Components of Coordination in a Situation

In order to analyze a situation in terms of coordination, it is sometimes important to explicitly identify the components of coordination in that situation. According to our earlier definition, coordination means "managing dependencies between activities." Therefore, because activities must, in some sense, be performed by "actors," the definition implies that all instances of coordination include *actors* performing *activities* that are *interdependent.*[2] It is also often useful to identify *evaluation criteria* for judging how well the dependencies are being "managed." For example, we can often identify some overall "goals" of the activity (such as producing automobiles or printing a report) and other dimensions for evaluating how well those goals are being met (such as minimizing time or costs). Some coordination

[2]See Baligh (1986); Baligh and Burton (1981); Barnard (1964); Malone (1987); Malone and Smith (1988); McGrath (1984); and Mintzberg (1979) for related decompositions of coordination.

processes may be faster or more accurate than others, for instance, and the costs of more coordination are by no means always worthwhile.

It is important to realize that there is no single "right" way to identify these components of coordination in a situation. For instance, we may sometimes analyze everything that happens in a manufacturing division as one "activity," while at other times, we may want to analyze each station on an assembly line as a separate activity. As another example, when we talk about muscular coordination, we implicitly regard different parts of the same person's body as separate "actors" performing separate "activities."

Conflicting Goals. One important case of identifying evaluation criteria occurs when there are conflicting goals in a situation. In analyzing coordination in human organizations, it is often useful to simply ask people what their goals are and evaluate their behavior in terms of these criteria. However, some amount of *goal conflict* is nearly always present (e.g., Ciborra, 1987; Schelling, 1960; Williamson, 1985), and people may be unable or unwilling to accurately report their goals, anyway. To understand these situations, it is often useful to try to identify the conflicting goals and also to analyze the behavior of the system in terms of some overall evaluation criteria. For instance, different groups in a company may compete for resources and people, but this very competition may contribute to the company's overall ability to produce useful products (e.g., Kidder, 1981).

Another important example of conflicting goals occurs in market transactions: As we saw earlier, all participants in a market might have the goal of maximizing their own individual benefits, but we, as observers, can evaluate the market as a coordination mechanism in terms of how well it satisfies overall criteria such as maximizing consumer utilities (e.g., Debreu, 1959) or "fairly" distributing economic resources.

3.1.3. Preview of Examples

In the remainder of this section, we describe examples of how concepts about coordination have been applied in three different areas: (1) understanding the new possibilities for human organizations and markets provided by information technology, (2) designing cooperative work tools, and (3) designing distributed and parallel computer systems. The early examples use very general notions of coordination; the later ones are more explicit in their identification of specific components of coordination.

This list is not intended to be a comprehensive list of all ways that theories of coordination could be applied. In fact, most of the work we describe here did not explicitly use the term *coordination theory*. We have chosen examples, however, to illustrate the wide range of applications for interdisciplinary theories about coordination.

3.2. Understanding the Effects of Information Technology on Organizations and Markets

Managers, organization theorists, and others have long been interested in how the widespread use of information technology (IT) may change the ways human organizations and markets will be structured (e.g., Leavitt & Whisler, 1958; Simon, 1976). One of the most important contributions of coordination theory may be to help understand these possibilities better.

To illustrate how the explicit study of coordination might help with this endeavor, we begin with a very general argument that does not depend on any of the detailed analyses of coordination we have seen so far in this chapter.[3] Instead, this argument starts with the simple observation that coordination is itself an activity that has costs. Even though there are many other forces that may affect the way coordination is performed in organizations and markets (e.g., global competition, national culture, government regulation, and interest rates), one important factor is clearly its cost, and that is the focus of this argument. In particular, it seems quite plausible to assume that information technology is likely to significantly reduce the costs of certain kinds of coordination (e.g., Crawford, 1982).

Now, using some elementary ideas from microeconomics about substitution and elasticity of demand, we can make some simple predictions about the possible effects of reducing coordination costs. It is useful to illustrate these effects by analogy with similar changes in the costs of transportation induced by the introduction of trains and automobiles:

1. A "first order" effect of reducing transportation costs with trains and automobiles was simply some substitution of the new transportation technologies for the old: People began to ride on trains more and in horse-drawn carriages less.
2. A "second order" effect of reducing transportation costs was to increase the amount of transportation used: People began to travel more when this could be done more cheaply and conveniently in trains than on foot.
3. Finally, a "third order" effect was to allow the creation of more "transportation-intensive" structures: People eventually began to live in distant suburbs and use shopping malls—both examples of new structures that depended on the widespread availability of cheap and convenient transportation.

Similarly, we can expect several effects from using new information technologies to reduce the costs of coordination:

[3] See Malone (1992) and Malone and Rockart (1991) for more detailed versions of the argument in this section.

1. A "first order" effect of reducing coordination costs with information technology may be to substitute information technology for some human coordination. For instance, many banks and insurance companies have substituted automated systems for large numbers of human clerks in their back offices. It has also long been commonplace to predict that computers will lead to the demise of middle management because the communication tasks performed by middle managers could be performed less expensively by computers (e.g., Leavitt & Whisler, 1958). This prediction was not fulfilled for several decades after it was made, but many people believe that it finally began to happen with large numbers of middle management layoffs in the 1980s and 1990s.

2. A "second order" effect of reducing coordination costs may be to increase the overall amount of coordination used. In some cases, this may overwhelm the first order effect. For instance, in one case we studied, a computer conferencing system was used to help remove a layer of middle managers (see Crowston et al., 1987). Several years later, however, almost the same number of new positions (for different people at the same grade level) had been created for staff specialists in the corporate staff group, many of whom were helping to develop new computer systems. One interpretation of this outcome is that the managerial resources no longer needed for simple communication tasks could now be applied to more complex analysis tasks that would not previously have been undertaken.

3. A "third order" effect of reducing coordination costs may be to encourage a shift toward the use of more "coordination-intensive" structures. In other words, coordination structures that were previously too "expensive" will now become more feasible and desirable. For example, as noted before, information technology can facilitate what some observers (e.g., Mintzberg, 1979; Toffler, 1970) have called *adhocracies*. Adhocracies are very flexible organizations, including many shifting project teams and highly decentralized networks of communication among relatively autonomous entrepreneurial groups. One of the disadvantages of adhocracies is that they require large amounts of unplanned communication and coordination throughout an organization. However, technologies such as electronic mail and computer conferencing can help reduce the costs of this communication, and advanced information sharing tools (e.g., Lotus, 1989; Malone, Grant, Turbak, Brobst, & Cohen, 1987) may help make this communication more effective at much larger scales.

What might these new coordination-intensive structure be like? Let us consider recent work on two specific questions about the effects of information technology on organizations and markets: (1) How will IT affect the size of organizations? and (2) How will IT affect the degree of centralization of decision making in organizations? This work does not focus explicitly on any specific dependencies. Instead, it compares two pairs of general coordination mechanisms that can manage many such dependencies: (1) market transactions vs. internal decision making with firms, and (2) centralized vs. decentralized managerial decisions.

3.2.1. Firm Size

Malone, Yates, and Benjamin (1987) have used ideas from transaction cost theory to systematically analyze how information technology will affect firm size and, more generally, the use of markets as a coordination structure. They conclude that by reducing the costs of coordination, information technology may lead to an overall shift toward smaller firms and proportionately more use of markets—rather than internal decisions within firms—to coordinate economic activity.

This argument has two parts. First, because market transactions often have higher coordination costs than internal coordination (Malone, Yates, & Benjamin, 1987; Williamson, 1985), an overall reduction in the "unit costs" of coordination should lead to markets becoming more desirable in situations where internal transactions were previously favored. This, in turn, should lead to less vertical integration and smaller firms.

For example, after the introduction of computerized airline reservation systems, the proportion of reservations made through travel agents (rather than by calling the airline directly) went from 35% to 70%. Thus, the function of selling reservations was "disintegrated" from the airlines and moved to a separate firm—the travel agents. Preliminary econometric analyses of the overall U.S. economy in the period 1975–1985 are also consistent with these predictions: The use of information technology appears to be correlated with decreases in both firm size and vertical integration (Brynjolfsson, Malone, Gurbaxani, & Kambil, 1989).

If we extrapolate this trend to a possible long-run extreme, it leads us to speculate that we might see increasing use of "firms" containing only one person. For instance, Malone and Rockart (1991) suggest that there may someday be electronic marketplaces of "intellectual mercenaries" in which it is possible to electronically assemble "overnight armies" of thousands of people who work for a few hours or days to solve a particular problem and then disband. Flexible arrangements like this might appeal especially to people who had a strong desire for autonomy—the freedom to choose their own hours and working situations.

3.2.2. Centralization of Decision Making

Gurbaxani and Whang (1991) have used ideas from agency theory to systematically analyze the effects on centralization of the reductions in coordination costs enabled by IT. They conclude that IT can lead to either centralization or decentralization, depending on how it is used. Although this conclusion may not be surprising, the structure of their analysis helps us understand the factors involved more clearly: (1) When IT primarily reduces *decision information costs*, it leads to more centralization. For instance, the Otis elevator company used IT to centralize the reporting and dispatching functions of their customer service system, instead of having these functions distributed to numerous remote field offices (Stoddard, 1986). (2) On the other hand, when IT primarily reduces *agency costs,* it leads to more decentralization. As used here, agency costs are the costs of employees not acting in the interests of the firm. For instance, when one insurance company developed a system that more effectively monitored their salespeople's overall performance, they were able to decentralize to the salespeople many of the decisions that had previously been made centrally (Bruns & McFarlan, 1987). Overall, this bidirectional trend for IT and centralization is consistent with empirical studies of this question (Attewell & Rule, 1984).

An alternative approach to this question is provided by (Danziger, Dutton, Kling, & Kraemer, 1982). In a sense, this work can be considered a kind of "behavioral coordination theory." In studies of computerization decisions in 42 local governments in the United States, they found that changes in centralization of power were not best explained any of the formal factors one might have expected. Instead, they found that because people who already have power influence computerization decisions, the new uses of computers tend to reinforce the existing power structure, increasing the power of those who already have it.

3.3. Designing Cooperative Work Tools

There has recently been a great deal of interest in designing computer tools to help people work together more effectively (e.g., Ellis, Gibbs, & Rein, 1991; Greif, 1988; Johansen, 1988; Peterson, 1986; Tatar, 1988, 1990; additional references in Table 1.3). Using terms such as *computer-supported cooperative work* and *groupware* these systems perform functions such as helping people collaborate on writing the same document, managing projects, keeping track of tasks, and finding, sorting, and prioritizing electronic messages. Other systems in this category help people display and manipulate information more effectively in face-to-face meetings and represent and share the rationales for group decisions.

In this section, we describe how ideas about coordination have been helpful in suggesting new systems, classifying systems, and analyzing how these systems are used.

3.3.1. Using Coordination Concepts From Other Disciplines to Suggest Design Ideas

One way of generating new design ideas for cooperative work tools is to look to other disciplines that deal with coordination. For instance, even though the following authors did not explicitly use the term *coordination the-*

ory, they each used ideas about coordination from other disciplines to help develop cooperative work tools.

Using Ideas From Linguistics and Philosophy About Speech Acts. Winograd and Flores (Flores, Graves, Hartfield, & Winograd, 1988; Winograd, 1987; Winograd & Flores, 1986) have developed a theoretical perspective for analyzing group action based heavily on ideas from linguistics (e.g., Searle, 1975). This perspective emphasizes different kinds of speech acts, such as requests and commitments. For example, Winograd and Flores analyzed a generic "conversation for action" in terms of the possible states and transitions involved when one actor performs a task at the request of another. An actor may respond to a request, for instance, by promising to fulfill the request, declining the request, reporting that the request has already been completed, or simply acknowledging that the request has been received. The analysis of this conversation type (and several others) provided a primary basis for designing the Coordinator, a computer-based cooperative work tool. For example, the Coordinator helps people make and keep track of requests and commitments to each other. It thus supports what we might call the "mutual agreeing" part of the *task assignment process*.

Using Ideas From Artificial Intelligence and Organization Theory About Blackboards and Adhocracies. Malone (1990) described how ideas from artificial intelligence and organization theory combined to suggest a new tool for routing information within organizations. In the "blackboard architecture," program modules interact by searching a global blackboard for their inputs and posting their outputs on the same blackboard (Erman, Hayes-Roth, Lesser, & Reddy, 1980; Nii, 1986). This provides very flexible patterns of communication between different program modules: Any module can communicate with any other module, even when this interaction is not explicitly anticipated by the program designer. In adhocracies, as we saw earlier, just this kind of unplanned, highly decentralized communication is essential for rapidly responding to new situations (Mintzberg, 1979; Toffler, 1970). Stimulated, in part, by this need for an "organizational blackboard," Malone and colleagues designed the Information Lens system (Malone, Grant, Turbak, Brobst, & Cohen, 1987). A central component of this system is an "anyone server" that lets people specify rules about what kinds of electronic messages they are interested in seeing. The system then uses these rules to route all non-private electronic messages to everyone in the organization who might want to see them. (To help people deal with large numbers of messages, another part of the system uses a different set of rules to sort and prioritize the messages people receive.)

Using Ideas From Philosophy and Rhetoric About Decision Making. Two cooperative work tools, gIBIS (Conklin & Begeman, 1988) and Sibyl (Lee, 1990) are designed to help groups of people make decisions more effectively. To do this, they explicitly represent the arguments (and counterarguments) for different alternatives a group might choose. Both these systems are based on ideas from philosophy and rhetoric about the logical structure of decision making. For example, the basic elements in the gIBIS system (issues, positions, and arguments) are taken from a philosophical analysis of argumentation by Rittel and Kunz (1970). The constructs for representing arguments in Sibyl are based on the work of philosophers like Toulmin (1958) and Rescher (1977).

Using Ideas From Computer Science About Parallel Processes. Holt (1988) described a theoretical language used for designing coordination tools that is based, in part, on ideas about Petri nets, a formalism used in computer science to represent process flows in distributed or parallel systems (Peterson, 1981, 1977). This language is part of a larger theoretical framework called "coordination mechanics" and has been used to design a "coordination environment" to help people work together on computer networks.

Summary of Examples. Clearly, using ideas about coordination from other disciplines provide any guarantee of developing useful cooperative work tools. However, we feel that considering these examples within the common framework of coordination theory provides two benefits: (1) it suggests that no one of these perspectives is the complete story, and (2) it suggests that we should look to previous work in various disciplines for more insights about coordination that could lead to new cooperative work tools.

3.3.2. A Taxonomy of Cooperative Work Tools

As shown in Table 1.3, the framework we have suggested for coordination provides a natural way of classifying existing cooperative work systems according to the coordination processes they support. Some of these systems primarily emphasize a single coordination-related process. For instance, electronic mail systems primarily support the message transport part of communication, and meeting scheduling tools primarily support the synchronization process (i.e., arranging for several people to attend a meeting at the same time). There is a sense, of course, in which each of these systems also support other processes (e.g., a simple electronic mail system can be used to assign tasks), but we have categorized the systems here according to the processes they explicitly emphasize.

Some of the systems also explicitly support several processes. For example, the Information Lens system supports both the communication routing

TABLE 1.3
A Taxonomy of Cooperative Work Tools Based on the Processes They Support

Process	*Example Systems*
Managing shared resources (task assignment and prioritization)	Coordinator (Winograd & Flores, 1986) Information Lens (Malone, Grant, Turbak, Brobst, & Cohen, 1987)
Managing producer–consumer relationships (sequencing prerequisites)	Polymer (Croft & Lefkowitz, 1988)
Managing simultaneity constraints (synchronizing)	Meeting scheduling tools (e.g., Beard et al., 1990)
Managing task–subtask relationship (goal decomposition)	Polymer (Croft & Lefkowitz, 1988)
Group decision making	gIBIS (Conklin & Begeman, 1988) Sibyl (Lee, 1990) electronic meeting rooms (e.g., Dennis et al., 1988; DeSanctis & Gallupe, 1987; Stefik et al., 1987)
Communication	Electronic mail, Computer conferencing (e.g., Lotus, 1989) electronic meeting rooms (e.g., Dennis et al., 1988; DeSanctis & Gallupe, 1987; Stefic et al., 1987) Information Lens (Malone, Grant, Turbak, Brobst, & Cohen, 1987) collaborative authoring tools (e.g., Ellis et al., 1990; Fish, Kraut, Leland, & Cohen, 1988; Neuwirth, Kaufer, Chandhok, & Morris, 1990)

process (by rules that distribute messages to interested people) and a form of resource allocation process (by helping people prioritize their own activities using rules that sort messages they receive). And the Polymer system helps people decompose goals into tasks and sequence the tasks (e.g., to prepare a monthly report, first gather the project reports and then write a summary paragraph).

One possibility raised by this framework is that it might help identify new opportunities for cooperative work tools. For instance, the Coordinator focuses on supporting one part of the task assignment process (mutual agreement on commitments). However, it does not provide much help for the earlier part of the process involving selecting an actor to perform the task in the first place (see Section 2.3). New tools, such as an "electronic yellow pages" or bidding schemes like those suggested by Turoff (1983) and Malone (1987) might be useful for this purpose.

Another intriguing possibility suggested by this framework is that it might be possible to implement "primitives" for a number of different coordination-related processes in the same environment, and then let people combine these primitives in various ways to help solve particular coordination problems. This is one of the goals of the Oval system (Lai, Malone, & Yu, 1988; Malone, Lai, & Fry, 1992).

3.3.3. Analyzing Incentives for Using Cooperative Work Tools

Another use for coordination theory in designing cooperative work tools can be to help systematically evaluate proposed or actual systems. For example, Markus and Connolly (1990) systematically analyzed how the payoffs to individual users of a cooperative work system depend on how many other people are using the system. They did this by using an economic model from Schelling (1978) to extend Grudin's (1988) insights about the incentives to use cooperative work systems. For instance, online calendars and many other cooperative work applications involve "discretionary databases" which users can view or update as they see fit. For each individual user, however, the benefits of viewing the database can be obtained without contributing anything. Thus, it is often in the interests of each individual user to use the database without making the effort required to contribute to it. Unfortunately, the equilibrium state of a system like this is for no one to ever contribute anything!

An interesting empirical illustration of this phenomenon occured in a study of how one large consulting firm used the Lotus Notes group conferencing system. In this study, Orlikowski (1992) found that there were surprising inconsistencies between the intended uses of the system and the actual incentives in the organization. For instance, Orlikowski observed that this organization (like many others) was one in which people were rewarded for being the "expert" on something—for knowing things that others did not. Should we be surprised, therefore, that many people were reluctant to spend much effort putting the things they knew into a database where everyone else could easily see them?

These observations do not, of course, mean that conferencing systems like this one cannot be useful in organizations. What they do mean, however, is that we must sometimes be sensitive to very subtle issues about things like incentives and organizational culture in order to obtain the full benefits of such systems. For instance, it might be desirable in this organization to include, as part of an employee's performance appraisal, a record of how often their contributions to the Notes database were used by other people in the organization.

3.4. Designing Distributed and Parallel Processing Computer Systems

Much recent activity in computer science has involved exploring a variety of distributed and parallel processing computer architectures. In many ways, physically connecting the processors to each other is easy compared to the difficulty of coordinating the activities of many different processors working on different aspects of the same problem.

In this section, we describe examples of work that have addressed these issues in an explicitly interdisciplinary way, drawing on insights from other disciplines or kinds of systems to design or analyze distributed or parallel computer systems. In particular, we consider examples of analogies with social and biological systems as a source of design ideas, and quantitative tools for analyzing alternative designs.

3.4.1. Analogies With Social and Biological Systems as a Source of Design Ideas

Competitive Bidding Markets for Resource Allocation. One of the basic problems in designing distributed or parallel computer systems is how to assign tasks to processors, and several distributed computer systems have addressed this problem with competitive bidding mechanisms based on analogies with human markets. For example, the Contract Nets protocol (Davis & Smith, 1983; Smith & Davis, 1981) formalizes a sequence of messages to be exchanged by computer processors sharing tasks in a network. The "contracts" are arbitrary computational tasks that can potentially be performed by any of a number of processors on the network, the "clients" are machines at which these tasks originate, and the "contractors" are machines that might process the tasks (i.e., the servers). The sequence of announcement, bid, and award messages used by this protocol was already described in our analysis of the task assignment process (Section 2.3). One of the desirable features of this system is its great degree of decentralization and the flexibility it provides for how both clients and contractors can make their decisions. For instance, clients may select contractors on the basis of estimated completion time or the presence of specialized data; contractors may select tasks to bid on based on the size of the task or how long the task has been waiting.

Using these or similar ideas, a number of other bidding systems have been developed (e.g., Kurose & Simha, 1989; Stankovic, 1985). For instance, several bidding systems have been developed to allow personal workstations connected by a local area network to share tasks (Malone, Fikes, Grant, & Howard, 1988; Waldspurger, Hogg, Huberman, Kephart, & Stornetta, 1988). In this way, users can take advantage of the unused processing capacity at idle workstations elsewhere on the network. Furthermore, the local bidding "negotiations" can result in globally coherent processor scheduling according to various priorities (e.g., Malone et al., 1988). (For a review of several related systems and an analysis of a variety of bidding algorithms, see Drexler & Miller, 1988; Miller & Drexler, 1988.)

The notion of competitive bidding markets has also been suggested as a technique for storage management by Miller and Drexler (1988; Drexler &

Miller, 1988). In their proposal, when object A wishes to maintain a pointer to object B, object A pays "rent" to the "landlord" of the space in which object B is stored. These rents are determined by competitive bidding, and when an object fails to pay rent, it is "evicted" (that is, garbage collected). Their proposal includes various schemes for how to determine rents, how to pass rents along a chain of references, and how to keep track of the various costs and payments without excessive overhead. They conclude that this proposal is not likely to be practical for small scale storage management (such as garbage collection of individual Lisp cells), but that it may well be useful for sharing large objects in complex networks that cross "trust boundaries" (e.g., interorganizational networks). The scheme also appears useful for managing local caching and the migration of objects between different forms of short-term and long-term storage.

"Scientific Communities" for Information Routing and Resource Allocation. Another central problem that arises in distributed and parallel processing systems is how and when to route information between processors. For instance, one interesting example of this problem arises in artificial intelligence programs that search a large space of possibilities, the nature of which is not well known in advance. It is particularly useful, in this case, for processors to exchange information about intermediate results in such a way that each processor can avoid performing work that is rendered unnecessary by work already done elsewhere.

One solution to this problem is suggested by the Scientific Community Metaphor embodied in the Ether system (Kornfeld, 1982; Kornfeld & Hewitt, 1981). In this system, there are a number of "sprites," each analogous to an individual scientist, that operate in parallel and interact through a global database. Each sprite requires certain conditions to be true in the global database before it is "triggered." When a sprite is triggered, it may compute new results that are added to the global database, create new sprites that await conditions that will trigger them, or stifle a collection of sprites whose work is now known to be unnecessary. In one example use of this system, Kornfeld (1982) showed how sharing intermediate results in this way can dramatically improve the time performance of an algorithm (even if it is executed by time-sharing a single processor). He calls this effect "combinatorial implosion."

This system also uses the scientific community metaphor to suggest a solution to the resource allocation problem for processors. Each sprite is "supported" by a "sponsor," and without a sponsor, a sprite will not receive any processing time to do its work. For instance, a sponsor may sometimes support both work directed toward proving some proposition and also work directed toward proving the negation of the proposition. Whenever one of these lines of work is successful, support is withdrawn from the other.

3.4.2. Analyzing Stability Properties of Resource Allocation Algorithms

Another way of applying coordination concepts is to help evaluate alternative designs of distributed and parallel processing computer systems. For instance, Huberman and his colleagues (Huberman & Hogg, 1988; Lumer & Huberman, 1990) applied mathematical techniques like those used in chaos theory to analyze the dynamic behavior of distributed computer networks. In one case they analyze, for example, heavily loaded processors in a network transfer tasks to more lightly loaded processors according to a probabilistic process. When any processor in such a system can exchange tasks with any other processor, the behavior of the system is unstable for large numbers of processors (e.g., more than 21 processors in a typical example). However, when the processors are grouped hierarchically into clusters that exchange tasks frequently among themselves and only occasionally with other clusters, the system remains stable for arbitrarily large numbers of processors. This hierarchical arrangement has the disadvantage that it takes a long time to reach stability. In an intriguing analogy with human organizations, however, Huberman and his colleagues find that this disadvantage can be eliminated by having a few "lateral links" between different clusters in the hierarchy (Lumer & Huberman, 1990).

3.5. Summary of Applications

As summarized in Table 1.4, the examples we have described show how a coordination perspective can help analyze alternative designs, and suggest new design ideas. In each case, these applications depended upon interdisciplinary use of theories or concepts about coordination.

4. RESEARCH AGENDA

We have seen how a number of different disciplines can contribute to answering the questions about coordination, and how theories of coordination can, in turn, be applied to the concerns of several different disciplines. What is needed to further develop this interdisciplinary study of coordination?

As we suggested earlier, a central concern of coordination theory should be identifying and analyzing specific coordination processes and structures. Therefore, a critical item on the agenda for coordination research should be developing these analyses. For example, the following kinds of questions arise.

4.1. Representing and Classifying Coordination Processes

How can we represent coordination processes? When should we use flowcharts, Petri nets, or state transition diagrams? Are there other notations that are even more perspicuous for analyzing coordination? How can we classify

TABLE 1.4
Sample Applications of a Coordination Perspective

Application Area	*Examples of Analyzing Alternative Designs*	*Examples of Generating New Design Ideas*
Organizational structures and information technology	Analyzing the effects of decreasing coordination costs on firm size, centralization, and internal structure	Creating temporary "intellectual marketplaces" to solve specific problems
Cooperative work tools	Analyzing how the payoffs to individual users of a system depend on the number of other users	Designing new tools for task assignment, information routing, and group decision making
Distributed and parallel computer systems	Analyzing stability properties of load sharing algorithms in computer networks	Using competitive bidding mechanisms to allocate processors and memory in computer systems.
		Using a scientific community metaphor to organize parallel problem solving

different coordination processes? For instance, can we usefully regard some coordination processes as "special cases" of others? How are different coordination processes combined when activities are actually performed?

4.1.1. How General Are Coordination Processes?

Another set of questions has to do with how generic coordination processes really are: How far can we get by analyzing very general coordination processes, and when will we find that most of the important factors are specific to coordinating a particular kind of task? For example, are there general heuristics for coordination that are analogous to the general problem-solving heuristics studied in cognitive science and artificial intelligence?

4.1.2. Analyzing Specific Processes

At least as important as these general questions are analyses of specific processes. For example, how far can we go in analyzing alternative coordination processes for problems such as resource allocation? Can we characterize an entire "design space" for solutions to this problem and analyze the major factors that would favor one solution over another in specific situations? Could we do the same thing for other processes such as goal selection or managing timing dependencies? Are there other processes (such as managing other kinds of dependencies) that could be analyzed systematically in ways that have not yet been done?

In analyzing alternatives processes for specific problems, we might consider various kinds of properties: Which processes are least "expensive" in terms of production costs and coordination costs? Which processes are fastest? Which processes are most stable in the face of failures of actors or delays of information? Which processes are most susceptible to incentive problems? For instance, how does the presence of significant conflicts of interest among actors affect the desirability of different resource allocation methods? How do information processing limitations of actors affect the desirability of different methods? For example, are some methods appropriate for coordinating people that would not be appropriate for coordinating computer processors, and vice versa? What new methods for coordinating people become desirable when human information processing capacities are augmented by computers?

4.1.3. Applications and Methodologies

A critical part of the research agenda for this area is developing coordination theory in the context of various different kinds of systems. For instance, in Section 3, we suggested numerous examples of these possibilities for human organizations and computer systems.

In some cases, this work may involve applying previously developed theories to these application areas. In many cases, however, we expect that new systems or new observations of these systems will stimulate the development of new theories. For example, all of the following methodologies appear likely to be useful in developing coordination theory: (a) empirically studying coordination in human or other biological systems (e.g., field studies, laboratory studies, or econometric studies), (b) designing new technologies for supporting human coordination, (c) designing and experimenting with new methods for coordinating distributed and parallel processing computer systems, and (d) formal modeling of coordination processes (e.g., mathematical modeling or computer simulation).

5. CONCLUSIONS

Clearly, the questions we have just listed are only the beginning of a set of research issues in the interdisciplinary study of coordination. However, we believe they illustrate how the notion of coordination provides a set of abstractions that help unify questions previously considered separately in a variety of different disciplines and suggests avenues for further exploration.

Although much work remains to be done, it appears that this approach can build upon much previous work in these different disciplines to help solve a variety of immediate practical needs, including: (1) designing computer and communication tools that enable people to work together more effectively, (2) harnessing the power of multiple computer processors working simultaneously on related problems, and (3) creating more flexible and more satisfying ways of organizing collective human activity.

ACKNOWLEDGMENTS

This work was supported, in part, by Digital Equipment Corporation, the National Science Foundation (Grant Nos. IRI-8805798 and IRI-8903034), and other sponsors of the MIT Center for Coordination Science.

Parts of this chapter were included in three previous papers (Malone, 1988; Malone & Crowston, 1990; Malone & Crowston, 1991). We are especially grateful to Deborah Ancona, John Carroll, Michael Cohen, Randall Davis, Rob Kling, John Little, and Wanda Orlikowski for comments on earlier versions of the paper, and to participants in numerous seminars and workshops at which these ideas have been presented.

APPENDIX A: PREVIOUS DEFINITIONS OF COORDINATION

"The operation of complex systems made up of components." (NSF-IRIS, 1989)

"The emergent behavior of collections of individuals whose actions are based on complex decision processes." (NSF-IRIS, 1989)

"Information processing within a system of communicating entities with distinct information states." (NSF-IRIS, 1989)

"The joint efforts of independent communicating actors towards mutually defined goals." (NSF-IRIS, 1989)

"Networks of human action and commitments that are enabled by computer and communications technologies." (NSF-IRIS, 1989)

"Composing purposeful actions into larger purposeful wholes." (A. Holt, personal communication, 1989)

"Activities required to maintain consistency within a work product or to manage dependencies within the workflow." (Curtis, 1989)

"The intergration and harmonious adjustment of individual work efforts towards the accomplishment of a larger goal." (Singh, 1992)

"The additional information processing performed when multiple, connected actors pursue goals that a single actor pursuing the same goals would not perform." (Malone, 1988)

"The act of working together." (Malone & Crowston, 1991)

APPENDIX B: RESULTS ABOUT COORDINATION FROM SELECTED FIELDS

Even though use of the term *coordination theory* is quite recent, a great deal of previous work in various fields can contribute to the interdisciplinary understanding of coordination. In this appendix, we briefly describe examples of such work from several different disciplines. These examples focus on cases where coordination has been analyzed in ways that appear to be generalizable beyond a single discipline or type of actor. We have not, of course, attempted to list all such cases; we have merely tried to pick illustrative examples from several disciplines.

Computer Science

Sharing Resources. Much research in computer science focuses on how to manage activities that share resources, such as processors, memory, and access to input/output devices (e.g., Deitel, 1983). Other mechanisms have been developed to enforce resource allocations. For example, semaphores, monitors, and critical regions for mutual exclusion are programming constructs that can be used to grant a process exclusive access to a resource (e.g., Dijkstra, 1968; Hoare, 1975). Researchers in database systems have developed numerous other mechanisms, such as locking or timestamping, to allow multiple processes to concurrently access shared data without interference (e.g., Bernstein & Goodman, 1981).

Managing Unreliable Actors. In addition, protocols have been developed to ensure the reliability of transactions comprising multiple reads or writes on different processors (e.g., Kohler, 1981). In particular, these protocols ensure that either all a transaction's operations are performed or none are, even if some of the processors fail.

Segmenting and Assigning Tasks. One of the important problems in allocating work to processors is how to divide up the tasks. For example, Carriero & Gelernter (1989) discuss three alternative ways of dividing parallel programs into units: according to the type of work to be done, according to the subparts of the final output, or simply according to which processor is available.

Managing Information Flows. Another important set of issues involves managing the flow of information. For instance, researchers in artificial intelligence and particularly in distributed artificial intelligence (DAI; e.g., Bond & Gasser, 1988; Huhns & Gasser, 1989) have used "blackboard architectures" to allow processes to share information without having to know precisely which other processes need it (Erman et al., 1980; Nii, 1986), and "partial global plans" to allow actors to recognize when they need to exchange more information (Durfee & Lesser, 1987).

Economics and Operations Research

In a sense, almost all of economics involves the study of coordination, with a special focus on how incentives and information flows affect the allocation of resources among actors. For example, *classical microeconomics* analyzes how different sources of supply and demand can interact locally in a market in ways that result in a globally coherent allocation of resources. Among the major results of this theory are formal proofs that (under appropriate mathematical conditions) if consumers each maximize their individual "utilities" and firms each maximize their individual profits, then the resulting allocation of resources will be globally "optimal" in the sense that no one's utilities can be increased without decreasing someone else's (e.g., Debreu, 1959).

Some more recent work in economics has focused on the limitations of markets and contracts for allocating resources. For instance, *transaction cost theory* analyzes the conditions under which a hierarchy is a better way of coordinating multiple actors than a market (e.g., Williamson, 1975). *Agency theory* focuses on how to create incentives for some actors (agents) to act in a way that advances the interests of other actors (principals) even when the principals cannot observe everything their agents are doing (Ross, 1973). One result of this theory is that there are some situations where no incentives can motivate an agent to perform optimally from the principal's point of view (Jensen & Meckling, 1976).

Finally, some parts of economics focus explicitly on information flows. For example, *team theory* and its descendants analyze how information should be exchanged when multiple actors need to make interdependent decisions but when all agents have the same ultimate goals (e.g., Hurwicz, 1973; Marschak & Radner, 1972; Reiter, 1986). *Mechanism design theory* also analyzes how to provide incentives for actors to reveal information they possess, even when they have conflicting goals. For example, this theory has been applied to designing and analyzing various forms of auctions. In a "second price auction," for instance, each participant submits a sealed bid, and the highest bidder is only required to pay the amount of the second highest bid. It can be shown that this mechanism motivates the bidders to each reveal the true value they place on the item being sold, rather than trying to "game the system" by bidding only enough to surpass what they expect to be the next highest bid (Myerson, 1981).

Operations research analyzes the properties of various coordination mechanisms, but operations research also includes a special focus on developing optimal techniques for coordination decisions. For instance, operations research includes analyses of various scheduling and queueing policies and techniques such as linear programming and dynamic programming for making resource allocation decisions optimally (e.g., Dantzig, 1963).

Organization Theory

Research in organization theory, drawing on disciplines such as sociology and psychology, focuses on how people coordinate their activities in formal organizations. A central theme in this work has involved analyzing general issues about coordination (e.g., Galbraith, 1977; Lawrence & Lorsch, 1967; March & Simon, 1958; Simon, 1976; Thompson, 1967; summarized by Malone, 1990, and Mintzberg, 1979). We can loosely paraphrase the key ideas of this work as follows:

All activities that involve more than one actor require (1) some way of dividing activities among the different actors and (2) some way of managing the interdependencies between the different activities (Lawrence & Lorsch, 1967; March & Simon, 1958). Interdependencies between activities can be of (at least) three kinds: *pooled*, where the activities share or produce common resources but are otherwise independent; *sequential*, where some activities depend on the completion of others before beginning, and *reciprocal*, where each activity requires inputs from the other (Thompson, 1967). These different kinds of interdependencies can be managed by a variety of coordination mechanisms, such as: *standardization*, where predetermined rules govern the performance of each activity; *direct supervision*, where one actor manages interdependencies on a case-by-case basis, and *mutual adjustment*, where each actor makes on-going adjustments to manage the interdependencies (Galbraith, 1973; March & Simon, 1958; Mintzberg, 1979).

These coordination mechanisms can be used to manage interdependencies, not only between individual activities, but also between groups of activities. One criterion for grouping activities into units is to minimize the difficulties of managing these intergroup interdependencies. For example, activities with the strongest interdependencies are often grouped into the smallest units, then these units are grouped into larger units with other units with which they have weaker interdependencies. Various combinations of the coordination mechanisms, together with different kinds of grouping, give rise to the different organizational structures common in human organizations, including functional hierarchies, product hierarchies, and matrix organizations. For instance, sometimes all activities of the same type (e.g., manufacturing) might be grouped together in order to take advantage of economies of scale; at other times, all activities for the same product (e.g., marketing, manufacturing, and engineering) might be grouped together to simplify managing the interdependencies between the activities.

Biology

Many parts of biology involve studying how different parts of living entities interact. For instance, human physiology can be viewed as a study of how the activities of different parts of a human body are coordinated in order to keep a person alive and healthy. Other parts of biology involve studying how different living things interact with each other. For instance, ecology can be viewed as the study of how the activities of different plants and animals are coordinated to maintain a "healthy" environment.

Some of the most intriguing studies of biological coordination involve coordination between different animals in a group. For example Mangel and Clark (1988) discusses the optimal hunting pack size for lions, who trade the benefit of an increased chance of catching something against the cost of having to share what they catch. Deneubourg and Gross (1989) point out that the interaction between simple rules—such as "do what my neighbour is doing"—and the environment may lead to a variety of collective behaviors.

The most striking examples of such group behaviors are in social insects, such as honey bees or army ants, where the group displays often quite complex behavior, despite the simplicity of the individuals (e.g., Franks, 1989; Seeley, 1989). Using a variety of simple rules, these insects "allocate" individual workers at economically efficient levels to a variety of tasks—including searching for new food sources, gathering nectar or pollen from particular sources (bees), carrying individual food items back to the bivouac (ants), guarding the hive (bees) and regulating the group temperature. For example, in honey bees, the interaction of two simple local rules controls the global allocation of food collectors to particular food sources. First, nectar storing bees unload nectar from foraging bees returning to the hive at a rate that depends on the richness of the nectar. Second, if bees are unloaded rapidly, they recruit other bees to their food source. The result of these two rules is that more bees collect food from better sources. Seeley (1989) speculates that this decentralized control may occur because it provides faster responses to local stresses (Miller, 1978), or it may be simply because bees have not evolved any more global means of communication.

REFERENCES

Allen, J., Hendler, J. and Tate, A. (Eds.). (1990). *Readings in Planning.* San Mateo, CA: Morgan Kaufmann.

Allen, T. J. (1977). *Managing the Flow of Technology*. Cambridge, MA: MIT Press.

Arrow, K. J. (1951). *Social Choice and Individual Value* (Vol. 12). New York: Wiley.

Arvind and Culler, D. E. (1986). Dataflow architectures. *Annual Reviews in Computer Science* (Vol. 1). Palo Alto, CA: Annual Reviews, Inc.

Arvind, Nikhil, R. S. and Pingali, K. K. (1986). I-Structures: Data structures for parallel computing. In *Proceedings of the Graph Reduction Workshop*. Santa Fe, NM, October.

Attewell, P. and Rule, J. (1984). Computing and organizations: What we know and what we don't know. *Communications of the ACM, 27*, 1184–1192.

Aumann, R. J. (1976). Agreeing to disagree. *Annals of Statistics, 4,* 1236–1239.

Baligh, H. H. (1986). Decision rules and transactions, organizations and markets. *Management Science, 32*, 1480–1491.

Baligh, H. H. and Burton, R. M. (1981). Describing and designing organizational structures and processes. *International Journal of Policy Analysis and Information Systems, 5*, 251–266.

Baligh, H. H. and Richartz, L. (1967). *Vertical Market Structures*. Boston, MA: Allyn & Bacon.

Barnard, C. I. (1964). *The Functions of the Executive*. Cambridge, MA: Harvard University.

Beard, D., Murugappan, P., Humm, A., Banks, D., Nair, A. and Shan, Y. -P. (1990). A Visual Calendar for Scheduling Group Meetings. In D. Tatar (Ed.), *Proceedings of the Third Conference on Computer-supported Cooperative Work* (pp. 279–290). Los Angeles, CA: ACM Press.

Bernstein, P. and Goodman, N. (1981). Concurrency control in distributed database systems. *ACM Computing Surveys* (June).

Bond, A. H. and Gasser, L. (Eds.). (1988). *Readings in Distributed Artificial Intelligence*. San Mateo, CA: Morgan Kaufman.

Bruns, W. J. and McFarlan, F. W. (1987). Information technology puts power in control systems. *Harvard Business Review* (Sept.–Oct.), 89–94.

Brynjolfsson, E., Malone, T., Gurbaxani, J. and Kambil, A. (1989). *Does Information Technology Lead to Smaller Firms?* (Technical report 106). Center for Coordination Science, MIT.

Burton, R. M. and Obel, B. (1980a). A computer simulation test of the M-form hypothesis. *Administrative Science Quarterly, 25*, 457–466.

Burton, R. M. & Obel, B. (1980b). The efficiency of the price, budget, and mixed approaches under varying *a priori* information levels for decentralized planning. *Management Science, 26*.

Carriero, N. and Gelernter, D. (1989). How to write parallel programs: A guide to the perplexed. *ACM Computing Surveys, 21*(3), 323–357.

Carter, D. E. and Baker, B. S. (1991). *Concurrent Engineering: The Product Development Environment for the 1990's*. Reading, MA: Addison-Wesley.

Chandler, A. D., Jr. (1962). *Strategy and Structure: Chapters in the History of the American Industrial Enterprise*. Cambridge, MA: MIT Press.

Chandler, A. D. (1977). *Administrative coordination, allocation and monitoring: Concepts and comparisons* (Working paper 77-21). Brussels: European Institute for Advanced Studies in Management.

Chapman, D. (1987). Planning for conjunctive goals. *Artificial Intelligence, 32*, 333–377.

Ciborra, C. U. (1987). Reframing the role of computers in organizations: The transaction costs approach. *Office: Technology and People, 3*, 17–38.

Cohen, P. and Levesque, H. J. (1991). *Teamwork* (Technote No. 504). Menlo Park, CA: SRI International.

Conklin, J. and Begeman, M. L. (1988). gIBIS: A hypertext tooling for exploratory policy discussion. In *Proceedings of CSCW '88 Conference on Computer-Supported Cooperative Work* (pp. 140–152). Portland, OR: ACM Press.

Crawford, A. B., Jr. (1982). Corporate electronic mail—A communication-intensive application of information technology. *MIS Quarterly, 6*(September), 1–13.

Croft, W. B. and Lefkowitz, L. S. (1988). Using a planner to support office work. In R. B. Allen (Ed.), *Proceedings of the ACM Conference on Office Information Systems* (pp. 55–62). Palo Alto, CA.

Crowston, K. (1991). *Towards a Coordination Cookbook: Recipes for Multi-Agent Action*. Ph.D. Dissertation, MIT Sloan School of Management, Cambridge, MA.

Crowston, K., Malone, T. W. and Lin, F. (1987). Cognitive science and organizational design: A case study of computer conferencing. *Human Computer Interaction, 3*, 59–85.

Curtis, B. (1989). Modeling coordination from field experiments. In *Organizational Computing, Coordination and Collaboration: Theories and Technologies for Computer-Supported Work.* Austin, TX.

Cytron, R. (1987). Limited processor scheduling of doacross loops. In *Proceedings of the 1987 International Conference on Parallel Processing* (pp. 226–234) Pennsylvania State University, University Park, Pennsylvania.

Dantzig, G. B. (1963). *Linear Programming and Extensions.* Princeton, NJ: Princeton University Press.

Danziger, J. N., Dutton, W. H., Kling, R. and Kraemer, K. L. (1982). *Computers and Politics: High Technology in American Local Governments.* New York: Columbia University Press.

Davis, R. and Smith, R. G. (1983). Negotiation as a metaphor for distributed problem solving. *Artificial Intelligence, 20,* 63–109.

Debreu, G. (1959). *Theory of value: An axiomatic analysis of economic equilibrium.* New York: Wiley.

Deitel, H. M. (1983). *An Introduction to Operating Systems.* Reading, MA: Addison-Wesley.

Deneubourg, J. L. and Gross, S. (1989). Collective patterns and decision-making. *Ethology, Ecology & Evolution, 1,* 295–311.

Dennis, A. R., Joey, F. G., Jessup, L. M., Nunamaker, J. F. and Vogel, D. R. (1988). Information Technology to Support Electronic Meetings. *MIS Quarterly, 12:4*(December), 591–619.

Dertouzos, M. L. (1991). Building the Information Marketplace. *Technology Review* (January), 29–40.

DeSanctis, G. and Gallupe, R. (1987). A foundation for the study of group decision support systems. *Management Science, 33*(5), 589–609.

Dijkstra, E. W. (1968). The structure of the T. H. E. operating system. *Communications of the ACM, 11*(5), 341–346.

Drexler, K. E. and Miller, M. S. (1988). Incentive engineering for computational resource management. In B. A. Huberman (Ed.), *The Ecology of Computation* (pp. 231–266). Amsterdam: Elsevier.

Dubois, M., Scheurich, C. and Briggs, F. A. (1988). Synchronization, coherence, and event ordering in multiprocessors. *IEEE Computer, 21*(2), 9–21.

Durfee, E. H. and Lesser, V. R. (1987). Using partial global plans to coordinate distributed problem solvers. In *Proceedings of the Tenth International Joint Conference on Artificial Intelligence (IJCAI-87)* (pp. 875–883).

Eccles, R. G. (1985). *The Transfer Pricing Problem: A Theory for Practice.* Lexington, MA: Lexington Books.

Ellis, C. A., Gibbons, R. and Morris, P. (1979). Office streamlining. In *Proceedings of the International Workshop on Integrated Offices.* Versailles, France. Institut de Recherche d'Informatique de d'Automatique.

Ellis, C. A., Gibbs, S. J. and Rein, G. L. (1990). Design and use of a group editor. In G. Cockton (Ed.), *Engineering for Human-Computer Interaction* (pp. 13–25) North Holland/Elsevier, Amsterdam.

Erman, L. D., Hayes-Roth, F., Lesser, V. R. and Reddy, D. R. (1980). The HEARSAY-II speech understanding system: Integrating knowledge to resolve uncertainty. *ACM Computing Surveys, 12*(2), 213–253.

Farrell, J. and Saloner, G. (1985). Standardization, compatibiity, and innovation. *Rand Journal of Economics, 16*(Spring), 70–83.

Fikes, R. E. and Nilsson, N. J. (1971). STRIPS: A new approach to the application of theorem proving to problem solving. *Artificial Intelligence, 2,* 198–208.

Fish, R., Kraut, R., Leland, M. and Cohen, M. (1988). Quilt: A collaborative tool for cooperative writing. In *Proceedings of the Conference on Office Information Systems* (pp. 30–37). Palo Alto, CA.

Flores, F., Graves, M., Hartfield, B. and Winograd, T. (1988). Computer systems and the design of organizational interaction. *ACM Transactions on Office Information Systems, 6*(2), 153–172.

Fox, M. S. (1981). An organizational view of distributed systems. *IEEE Transactions on Systems, Man and Cybernetics, 11*(1), 70–79.

Franks, N. R. (1989). Army ants: A collective intelligence. *American Scientist, 77*(March–April), 139–145.

Galbraith, J. R. (1973). *Designing Complex Organizations*. Reading, MA: Addison-Wesley.

Galbraith, J. R. (1977). *Organization Design*. Reading, MA: Addison-Wesley.

Gray, J. (1978). *Notes on data base operating systems* (Research Report RJ 2188). IBM.

Greif, I. (Ed.). (1988). *Computer Supported Cooperative Work*. Los Altos, CA: Morgan Kaufmann.

Grudin, J. (1988). Why CSCW applications fail: Problems in the design and evaluation of organizational interfaces. In D. Tatar (Ed.), *Proceedings of the Second Conference on Computer-supported Cooperative Work* (pp. 85–93). Portland, OR: ACM Press.

Gurbaxani, V. and Whang, S. (1991). The Impact of Information Systems on Organizations and Markets. *Communications of the ACM, 34*(1), 59–73.

Halpern, J. J. (1987). Using reasoning about knowledge to analyze distributed systems. In *Annual Review of Computer Science* (Vol. 2; pp. 37–68). Palo Alto, CA: Annual Reviews Inc.

Halstead, R. H. (1985). Multilisp: A language for concurrent symbolic computation. *ACM Transactions on Programming Languages and Systems, 7*, 4, 501–538.

Hart, P. and Estrin, D. (1990). Inter-organization computer networks: Indications of shifts in interdependence. In *Proceedings of the ACM Conference on Office Information Systems*. New York: ACM.

Hewitt, C. (1986). Offices are open systems. *ACM Transactions on Office Systems, 4*(3), 271–287.

Hirsch, E. D. (1987). *Cultural Literacy: What Every American Needs to Know*. Boston, MA: Houghton Mifflin.

Hoare, C. A. R. (1975). Monitors: An operating systems structuring concept. *Communications of the ACM, 17*(10), 549–557. Corrigendum, *CACM, 18*(2): 95.

Holt, A. W. (1980). *Coordinator Programs* (Unpublished technical report). Wakefield, MA: Massachusetts Computer Associates, Inc.

Holt, A. W. (1988). Diplans: A new language for the study and implementation of coordination. *ACM Transactions on Office Information Systems, 6*(2), 109–125.

Huberman, B. A. (Eds.). (1988a). *The Ecology of Computation*. Amsterdam: North-Holland.

Huberman, B. A. (1988b). *Open systems: The ecology of computation* (PARC working paper P88-00074). Palo Alto, CA: Xerox PARC.

Huberman, B. A. and Hogg, T. (1988). The behaviour of computational ecologies. In B. A. Huberman (Ed.), *The Ecology of Computation* (pp. 77–116). Amsterdam: Elsevier.

Huhns, M. N. and Gasser, L. (Eds.). (1989). *Distributed Artificial Intelligence* (Vol. 3). San Mateo, CA: Morgan Kaufmann.

Hurwicz, L. (1973). The design of resource allocation mechanisms. *American Economic Review Papers and Proceedings, 58*(May), 1–30.

Janis, I. L. and Mann, L. (1977). *Decision-making*. New York: Free Press.

Johansen, R. (1988). *Groupware: Computer Support for Business Teams*. New York: The Free Press.

Kahneman, D. and Tversky, A. (1973). On the psychology of prediction. *Psychological Review, 80*, 237–251.

Kidder, T. (1981). *The Soul of a New Machine*. Boston: Little, Brown.

Kiesler, S., Siegel, J. and McGuire, T. W. (1984). Social psychological aspects of computer-mediated communication. *American Psychologist, 39*, 1123–1134.

Kling, R. (1980). Social analyses of computing: Theoretical perspectives in recent empirical research. *ACM Computing Surveys, 12*(1), 61–110.

Kohler, W. (1981). A survey of techniques for synchronization and recovery in decentralized computer systems. *ACM Computing Surveys, 13*(2), 149–183.

Kornfeld, W. A. (1982). Combinatorially Implosive Algorithms. *Communications of the ACM, 25*(10), 734–738.

Kornfeld, W. A. and Hewitt, C. (1981). The scientific community metaphor. *IEEE Transactions on Systems, Man and Cybernetics, SMC-11*, 24–33.

Kraemer, K. and King, J. L. (1988). Computer-based systems for cooperative work and group decision-making. *ACM Computing Surveys, 20*(2), 115–146.

Kurose, J. F. and Simha, R. (1989). A microeconomic approach to optimal resource allocation in distributed computer systems. *IEEE Transaction on Computers, 38*(5), 705–717.

Lai, K. Y., Malone, T. and Yu, K.-C. (1988). Object Lens: A spreadsheet for cooperative work. *ACM Transactions on Office Information Systems, 6*(4), 332–353.

Lawrence, P. and Lorsch, J. (1967). *Organization and Environment.* Boston, MA: Division of Research, Harvard Business School.

Leavitt, H. J. and Whisler, T. L. (1958). Management in the 1980's. *Harvard Business Review, 36*(November/December), 41–48.

Lee, J. (1990). Sibyl: A qualitative decision management system. In P. Winston (Ed.), *Artificial Intelligence at MIT: Expanding Frontiers* (Vol. 1). Cambridge, MA: MIT Press.

Lee, J. and Malone, T. W. (1988). How can groups communicate when they use different languages? Translating between partially shared type hierarchies. In R. B. Allen (Ed.), *Proceedings of the ACM Conference on Office Information Systems* (pp. 22–29). New York: ACM.

Liskov, B. and Guttag, J. (1986). *Abstraction and Specification in Program Development.* Cambridge, MA: MIT Press.

Lotus. (1989). *Lotus Notes Users Guide.* Cambridge, MA: Lotus Development Corp.

Lumer, E. and Huberman, B. A. (1990). *Dynamics of resource allocation in distributed systems* (SSL-90-05). Palo Alto, CA: Xerox PARC.

Malone, T. W. (1987). Modeling coordination in organizations and markets. *Management Science, 33*, 1317–1332.

Malone, T. W. (1988). *What is coordination theory?* (Working paper #2051-88). Cambridge, MA: MIT Sloan School of Management.

Malone, T. W. (1990). Organizing information processing systems: Parallels between organizations and computer systems. In W. Zachary, S. Robertson and J. Black (Eds.), *Cognition, Computation, and Cooperation* (pp. 56–83). Norwood, NJ: Ablex.

Malone, T. W. (1992). Analogies Between Human Organization and Artificial Intelligence Systems: Two Examples and Some Reflections. In M. Masuch (Ed.), *Distributed Intelligence: Perspectives of Artificial Intelligence on Organization and Management Theory.* Amsterdam: Elsevier.

Malone, T. W. and Crowston, K. (1990). What is coordination theory and how can it help design cooperative work systems? In D. Tatar (Ed.), *Proceeding of the Third Conference on Computer-supported Cooperative Work* (pp. 357–370). Los Angeles, CA: ACM Press.

Malone, T. W. and Crowston, K. G. (1991). *Toward an interdisciplinary theory of coordination* (Technical report #120). Cambridge, MA: Massachusetts Institute of Technology, Center for Coordination Science.

Malone, T. W., Crowston, K., Lee, J. and Pentland, B. (1992). *Tools for inventing organizations: Toward a handbook of organizational processes* (Unpublished Working Paper). Cambridge, MA: MIT Center for Coordination Science.

Malone, T. W., Fikes, R. E., Grant, K. R. and Howard, M. T. (1988). Enterprise: A market-like task scheduler for distributed computing. In B. Huberman (Ed.), *The Ecology of Computation.* New York: North-Holland.

Malone, T. W., Grant, K. R., Turbak, F. A., Brobst, S. A. and Cohen, M. D. (1987). Intelligent information-sharing systems. *Communications of the ACM, 30*, 390–402.

Malone, T. W., Lai, K.-Y. and Fry, C. (1992). Experiments with Oval: A radically tailorable tool for cooperative work. In *Proceedings of the ACM Conference on Computer-Supported Cooperative Work (CSCW '92).* Toronto, Ontario.

Malone, T. W. and Rockart, J. F. (1991). Computers, networks, and the corporation. *Scientific American, 265*(3, Sept.), 128–136.

Malone, T. W. and Smith, S. A. (1988). Modeling the performance of organizational structures. *Operations Research, 36*(3), 421–436.

Malone, T. W., Yates, J. and Benjamin, R. I. (1987). Electronic markets and electronic hierarchies. *Communications of the ACM, 30*, 484–497.

Mangel, M. and Clark, C. W. (1988). *Dynamic Modeling in Behavioral Ecology*. Princeton, NJ: Princeton University Press.

March, J. G. and Simon, H. A. (1958). *Organizations*. New York: Wiley.

Markus, M. L. and Connolly, T. (1990). Why CSCW applications fail: Problems in the adoption of interdependent work tools. In D. Tatar (Ed.), *Proceedings of the Third Conference on Computer-supported Cooperative Work* (pp. 371–380). Los Angeles, CA: ACM Press.

Marschak, J. and Radner, R. (1972). *Economic Theory of Teams*. New Haven: Yale University Press.

McClain, J., Thomas, L. J. and Mazola, J. (1992). *Operations Management* (3rd ed.). Englewood Cliffs, NJ: Prentice-Hall.

McGrath, J. E. (1984). *Groups: Interaction and Performance*. Englewood Cliffs, NJ: Prentice-Hall.

Miao, X., Luh, P. B. and Kleinman, D. L. (1992). A normative-descriptive approach to hierarchical team resource allocation. *IEEE Transactions on Systems, Man and Cybernetics, 22*(3), 482–497.

Milgrom, P. (1981). An axiomatic characterization of common knowledge. *Econometrica, 49*(1), 17–26.

Miller, J. G. (1978). *Living Systems*. New York: McGraw-Hill.

Miller, M. S. and Drexler, K. E. (1988). Markets and computation: Agoric open systems. In B. A. Huberman (Ed.), *The Ecology of Computation* (pp. 133–176). Amsterdam: North-Holland.

Mintzberg, H. (1979). *The Structuring of Organizations*. Englewood Cliffs, NJ: Prentice-Hall.

Moses, J. (1990). *Organization and Ideology* (Unpublished manuscript). Cambridge, MA: Department of Electrical Engineering and Computer Science, Massachusetts Institute of Technology.

Myerson, R. B. (1981). Optimal auction design. *Mathematics of Operations Research, 6*, 58–73.

Neuwirth, C. M., Kaufer, D. S., Chandhok, R. and Morris, J. H. (1990). Issues in the design of computer-support for co-authoring and commenting. In *Proceedings of the Third Conference on Computer Supported Cooperative Work (CSCW 90)* (pp. 183–195). Los Angeles, CA: ACM Press.

Nii, H. (1986). The blackboard model of problem solving. *AI Magazine* (Spring), 38–53.

NSF. (1991). *Coordination Theory and Collaboration Technology Workshop Summary*. Washington, DC: Available from NSF Forms & Publications Unit.

NSF-IRIS. (1989). *A report by the NSF-IRIS Review Panel for Research on Coordination Theory and Technology*. Washington, DC: Available from NSF Forms & Publications Unit.

Orlikowski, W. (1992). Learning from Notes: Organizational Issues in Groupware Implementation. In *Proceedings of the Conference on Computer Supported Cooperative Work (CSCW 92)*. Toronto, Canada: ACM.

Peterson, D. (1986). *Proceedings of the Conference on Computer-Supported Cooperative Work*. Austin, TX: ACM.

Peterson, J. L. (1977). Petri nets. *ACM Computing Surveys, 9*(3), 223–252.

Peterson, J. L. (1981). *Petri Net Theory and the Modeling of Systems*. Englewood Cliff, NJ: Prentice-Hall.

Pfeffer, J. (1978). *Organizational Design*. Arlington Heights, IL: Harlan Davidson.

Pfeffer, J. and Salancik, G. R. (1978). *The External Control of Organizations: A Resource Dependency Perspective*. New York: Harper & Row.

Reiter, S. (1986). Informational incentive and performance in the (new)^2 welfare economics. In S. Reiter (Ed.), *Studies in Mathematical Economics (Studies in Mathematics, Volume 25)*. Mathematical Assocation of America.

Rescher, N. (1977). *Dialectics: A Controversy-Oriented Approach to the Theory of Knowledge*. Buffalo, NY: State University of New York Press.

Rittel, H. and Kunz, W. (1970). *Issues as elements of information systems* (Working paper 131). Stuttgart, Germany: University of Stuttgart, Institut fur Grundlagen der Planung I.A.

Roberts, K. H. and Gargano, G. (1989). Managing a high reliability organization: A case for interdependence. In M. A. V. Glinow and S. Mohrmon (Eds.), *Managing complexity in high technology industries: Systems and people* (pp. 147–159). New York: Oxford University Press.

Roberts, K. H., Stout, S. K. and Halpern, J. J. (1994). Decision dynamics in two high reliability military organizations. *Management Science, 40,* 614–624.

Rockart, J. F. and Short, J. E. (1989). IT and the networked organization: Toward more effective management of interdependence. In M. S. Scott Morton (Ed.), *Management in the 1990s Research Program Final Report.* Cambridge, MA: Massachusetts Institute of Technology.

Rogers, E. and Agarwala-Rogers, R. (1976). *Communication in organizations.* New York: Free Press.

Ross, S. (1973). The economic theory of agency. *American Economic Review, 63,* 134–139.

Rumelhart, D. E., McClelland, J. L. and PDP Research Group. (1986). *Parallel Distributed Processing: Explorations in the Microstructures of Cognition.* Cambridge, MA: MIT Press.

Schelling, T. C. (1960). *Strategy of Conflict.* Cambridge, MA: Harvard University Press.

Schelling, T., C. (1978). *Micromotives and Macrobehavior.* New York: Norton.

Schonberger, R. (1982). *Japanese Manufacturing Techniques.* New York: Free Press.

Schonberger, R. (1986). *World Class Manufacturing.* New York: Free Press.

Schuler, D. and Namioka, A. (Eds.). (1992). *Participatory Design.* Hillsdale, NJ: Lawrence Erlbaum Associates.

Searle, J. R. (1975). A taxonomy of illocutionary acts. In K. Gunderson (Ed.), *Language, Mind and Knowledge* (pp. 344–369). Minneapolis: University of Minnesota.

Seeley, T. D. (1989). The honey bee colony as a superorganism. *American Scientist, 77*(November–December), 546–553.

Shannon, C. E. and Weaver, W. (1949). *The mathematical theory of communication.* Urbana: University of Illinois Press.

Shoham, Y. (1993). Agent Oriented Programming. *Artificial Intelligence, 60,* 51–92.

Simon, H. A. (1976). *Administrative Behavior* (3rd ed.). New York: Free Press.

Simon, H. A. (1981). *Sciences of the Artificial* (2nd ed.). Cambridge, MA: MIT Press.

Singh, B. (1992). *Interconnected Roles (IR): A coordination model* (Technical Report No. CT-084-92). Austin, TX: Microelectronics and Computer Technology Corp. (MCC).

Singh, B. and Rein, G. L. (1992). *Role Interaction Nets (RIN): A process description formalism* (Technical Report No. CT-083-92). Austin, TX: MCC.

Smith, A. (1776). *The Wealth of Nations* (1986 ed.). London: Penguin Books.

Smith, R. G. and Davis, R. (1981). Frameworks for cooperation in distributed problem solving. *IEEE Transactions on Systems, Man and Cybernetics, 11*(1), 61–70.

Stankovic, J. (1985). An applicaiton of Bayesian decision theory to decentralized control of job scheduling. *IEEE Transactions on Computers, C-34*(2), 117–130.

Stefik, M., Foster, G., Bobrow, D. G., Kahn, K., Lanning, S. and Suchman, L. (1987). Beyond the chalkboard: Computer support for collaboration and problem solving in meetings. *Communications of the ACM, 30*(1), 32–47.

Stoddard, D. (1986). *OTISLINE* (Case 9-186-304). Harvard Business School.

Tannenbaum, A. S. (1981). *Computer Networks.* Englewood Cliffs, NJ: Prentice-Hall.

Tatar, D. (Ed.). (1988). *Proceedings of the Second Conference on Computer-supported Cooperative Work.* Portland, OR: ACM Press.

Tatar, D. (Ed.). (1990). *Proceedings of the Third Conference on Computer-supported Cooperative Work.* Los Angeles, CA: ACM Press.

Thompson, J. D. (1967). *Organizations in Action: Social Science Bases of Administrative Theory.* New York: McGraw-Hill.

Toffler, A. (1970). *Future Shock.* New York: Bantam Books.

Toulmin, S. (1958). *The Uses of Argument.* Cambridge, England: Cambridge University Press.

Turoff, M. (1983). *Information, value, and the internal marketplace.* Unpublished manuscript. New Jersey Institute of Technology.

Waldspurger, C. A., Hogg, T., Huberman, B. A., Kephart, J. O. and Stornetta, S. (1988). *Spawn: A distributed computational ecology* (Unpublished working paper). Palo Alto, CA: Xerox PARC.
Weick, K. E. (1969). *The social psychology of organizing*. Reading, MA: Addison-Wesley.
Williamson, O. E. (1975). *Markets and Hierarchies*. New York: Free Press.
Williamson, O. E. (1985). *The Economic Institutions of Capitalism*. New York: Free Press.
Winograd, T. (1987). A language/action perspective on the design of cooperative work. *Human Computer Interaction, 3*, 3–30.
Winograd, T. and Flores, F. (1986). *Understanding computers and cognition: A new foundation for design*. Norwood, NJ: Ablex.

CHAPTER

2

Communication and Collaboration in Distributed Cognition

Richard J. Boland, Jr.
Case Western Reserve University

Ramkrishnan V. Tenkasi
University of Southern California

Our research is concerned with the processes of collaboration that are required by organizations as they increasingly adopt more network-like organization structures (Drucker, 1988; Huber, 1984; Malone, Yates, & Benjamin, 1987). We want to understand the kinds of communication that are needed and design information technologies to support them (Boland & Tenkasi, 1995; Boland, Tenkasi, & Te'eni, 1994). By network-like organizations we mean those that resemble open systems as described by Hewitt (1985, 1986).Open systems are composed of decentralized, autonomous units, each with different and inconsistent knowledge bases. Open systems are characterized by distributed cognition (Hutchins, 1996; Norman, 1993) in which the task of the organization is achieved by individuals and technologies acting independently within their own domains on parts of the overall problem, but taking each other and their interdependencies into account in their actions. In a network-like, open system organization, coordination emerges within this process of distributed cognition.

Emergent coordination in an open system of distributed cognition differs sharply from coordination based on a command and control structure, in which a hierarchical system coordinates activity by exchanging messages to and from a central point. Managers at the apex of the hierarchy use their understanding of the whole organization and its task to guide the activities and logics employed in its subunits. In an open system of distributed cognition, by contrast, coordination is immanent within the network of interactions and is dependent on the members of the organization to communicate among themselves. We refer to this communication process as one of perspective making and perspective taking—meaning the ability to develop one's own understanding of a situation and the ability to recognize and appreciate others' distinctive ways of understanding the same situation. Dougherty (1992), for example, found that successful new product development in multidisciplinary teams was associated with the creation of communication practices that encouraged appreciation of each other's perspectives and their mutual interdependencies. Unsuccessful teams were those where members failed to take each other into account in their individual decisions.

We began our research with the assumption that each autonomous unit in an organization has a complex understanding of its environment, technologies and constraints that determines its interpretations and actions. This understanding of its situation is unique and generally unavailable to other units. Yet the actions of all the units are interdependent, each relying to some extent on assumptions as to how other units will respond to changes, threats or opportunities in their environment. When the environment is placid and relatively stable, such autonomous units could build suitably reliable images of how others were making sense of their situation and taking action within it. The logic of interpretation and action used by others could be learned from observed behaviors and a tradition of expectations could be built up by working together over time. Brown and Duguid (1991) referred to this process as the development of "communities of practice."

As economic, political, and market environments become more turbulent, and as technologies affecting design, production, and distribution begin to change more rapidly, the diverse elements of a decentralized, networked organization face increasingly differentiated environments and develop unique local logics that could change rapidly. In circumstances of heightened uncertainty and complexity, it becomes more and more difficult to reliably take others into account in our independent actions, so that coordinated outcomes emerge.

Knowledge intensive firms (Alvesson, 1995; Starbuck, 1992) such as those in the computer, pharmaceutical, and biotechnology industries, rely on the synthesis of highly specialized expertise and knowledge domains (Purser, Pasmore, & Tenkasi, 1992). The need to integrate distinctive knowledge domains has resulted in the development of new organizational forms based on network or open system models, most notably the lateral–flexible form of organization (Galbraith, 1994; Galbraith & Lawler, 1993). Our research concerns the way information technologies can mediate and support collaboration in environments of distributed cognition such as those found in knowledge intensive firms, and lateral–flexible forms of organizing.

Our findings to date indicate the importance of recognizing and supporting the process of inquiry individuals employ to strengthen their distinctive ways of knowing, which we refer to as perspective making, and the process of communicating about their perspectives with others, which we refer to as perspective taking (Boland, Schwartz, Tenkasi, Maheshwari, & Te'eni, 1992; Boland, Tenkasi, & Te'eni, 1994; Boland & Tenkasi, 1995). Creatively managing the dynamic tension between making strong perspectives within a community of knowing, and being open to taking the perspective of another community of knowing, is essential for collaboratively developing organizational knowledge. We find that the interdependent, dynamic processes of perspective making and perspective taking are achieved through reflection and conversations that involve the narrativization of experience as well as explicit rational analytic procedures.

THE ROLE OF PERSPECTIVES IN DISTRIBUTED COGNITION

Actors in an organizational setting have their own unique perspectives through which they identify and interpret the salient features of their situation, understand the values and goals of the organization, and employ a logic of action. For the individual, Boulding (1956) referred to this perspective as an "image," Pepper (1942) referred to it as a "world hypothesis," and Bartlett (1932) referred to it as a "schema." In parallel with this, a number of scholars have commented on the unique cognitive repertoires that can develop at the group level. Fleck (1935/1979) referred to a group's perspective as a "thought world," Fish (1980) referred to it as an "interpretive community," and Barnes (1983) called it a "context of learning."

People in organizations do not have many opportunities to actively and openly reflect upon the ways in which they or their group interpret a situation or display a theory-in-use in their organizational practice (Argyris & Schon, 1978). This lack of reflection upon their interpretive practices has been identified as a potent reason for organizational failure (Nystrom & Starbuck, 1984; Starbuck & Milliken, 1988). Achieving significant change in the understanding of group members requires them to reflect upon existing assumptions, processes, and structures. Making representations of those perspectives and placing them open for discussion is one way of doing so (Bartunek & Moch, 1987). Our research question was how to enable individuals to make their understandings of a situation visible and how to exchange them with others. We have approached this question as one of enabling perspective making and perspective taking through the visualization of understandings with cause maps.

Much of social behavior is predicated upon assumptions an actor makes about the knowledge, beliefs, and motives of others. This process of perspective taking is fundamental: In coming to know ourselves and in communicating with others, the knowing of what others know is a necessary component (Bakhtin, 1981; Clark, 1985; Clark & Marshall, 1981; Festinger, 1954; Garfinkel, 1967; Krauss & Fussell, 1991; Mead, 1934). As Brown (1981) observed, effective communicating requires that the point of view of the other be realistically imagined. This reflects the fundamental distinction between a signal which, by convention, indicates a specified action or object, and a symbol, which always carries a surplus of metaphorical referent and possible meanings (Giddens, 1979). Others such as Rommetveit (1980) have affirmed this point: "An essential component of communicative competence in a pluralistic social world . . . is our capacity to adopt the perspectives of different *others*" (p. 126).

Individuals utilize a variety of inference heuristics to estimate what others know. Such heuristics can induce systematic errors and biases (Kahneman, Slovic, & Teversky, 1982). For example, the *availability heuristic* means that a person's own perspective may lead that person to overestimate the likelihood that the perspective will be shared by others. This *false consensus* effect, in which people assume that others are more similar to themselves than is actually the case (Ross, Greene, & House, 1977), is a form of bias particularly relevant to the perspective taking process. Steedman and Johnson-Laird (1980) proposed that "the speaker assumes that the hearer knows everything that the speaker knows about the world and about the conversation, unless there is some evidence to the contrary" (p. 129). That speakers overestimate the extent to which their knowledge is shared by others is supported in studies by Mead (1934), Garfinkel (1967), and Dougherty (1992).

These biases and heuristics imply that the way humans communicate in organizations is based on implicit understandings of the beliefs, values, and knowledge of others that are for the most part untested and assumed to be the same as one's own. Dougherty (1992) provided detailed case studies of communication in product development teams, and shows how unsuccessful teams failed to identify and reconcile qualitative differences in their perspectives. As a result, they did not attribute the same importance to elements in the environment, did not take the activities and priorities of others into account, and did not appreciate the differences between their "thought worlds" and the unique insights each had to offer. The communication that was needed, however, was not a message about those differences, but an appreciation of the way each group had a total and coherent view that was different from the others. As Dougherty (1992) put it, "Nor is the problem like the proverbial set of blind men touching a different part of the elephant. It is more like the tales of eye witnesses at an accident or of individuals in a troubled relationship—each tells us a 'complete' story, but tells a different one." (p. 191)

In summary then, we see the problem of integrating knowledge in distributed cognition not as the sending of a message or the joint access to the same data, but as a problem of: (a) making the unique knowledge and meanings of each individual more accessible by helping them to represent their perspective visually, and (b) exchanging and discussing those representations with others. It is a problem of perspective making and perspective taking in which the ability of individuals in distinct communities of knowing to elaborate, differentiate, and complexify their own perspective is balanced with the ability to engage in conversation among themselves about those perspectives.

EXPERIENCE WITH A TOOL FOR VISUALIZING PERSPECTIVES

We have developed a software system name Spider[1] that enables individuals to visualize their perspective on a situation in the form of a cause map, showing their beliefs about the factors and their causal relations that influence their sphere of concern. A cause map is a directed graph whose nodes represent measurable factors in the individual's decision domain, and whose arcs represent beliefs about cause–effect relations between source and destination nodes. We have employed the Spider system in several different settings of distributed cognition. Individuals first made a map of their own causal understandings of the situation they face and then exchanged cause maps with others to discuss the similarities and differences. We have found that, just as Weick and Bougon (1986) suggested, building a cause map is highly evocative for the map maker as well as surprisingly informative to the colleague who discusses it with her. Because the map-making process confronts a person with explicating personal beliefs as to cause and effect in the organizational setting, it is an occasion to think carefully and deliberately about a situation in a way that is quite different from an everyday organizational experience. Similarly, discussing one's map with others almost always raises awareness of differences in perspectives that had gone undetected, sometimes for many years.

Traditionally, researchers themselves have constructed cause maps of decision makers for the researcher's own purposes. They typically assume the maps to be a rather stable representation (Axelrod, 1976; Huff, 1990). Our use of cognitive maps emphasizes that individuals are responsible for constructing their own maps. They then exchange them with others, critique them, and modify them.

In our research, we have found that map making is a more creative experience than we had anticipated. Initially, we saw cause mapping as a way of

---

[1]The Weatherhead School of Management makes the Spider cause mapping software available without cost for educational use. Access it through the research heading at http://info.cwru.edu/spidermap

depicting an understanding that an individual already possessed. We assumed that a well developed perspective was resident in the person's memory, ready to be portrayed as a map. What we found instead was that individuals started making a map by putting up several factors, along with some causal relations. They then shifted to a mode of discovery rather than representation. In discovery mode, factors would be put up, relations would suddenly be seen, and new factors would be suggested. Typical comments made after the first few elements had been added to a map were: "Look what's emerging here," or "Oh, this is interesting." The map maker would be actively constructing an understanding while engaging with the tool. This suggests that individuals did not have well formulated causal understandings in the first place, and that the opportunity for reflexivity in the construction of maps was itself an innovation in their practice.

That individuals were experiencing a sense of discovery during map making and that they were actively constructing an understanding through reflecting upon the map as it was being developed, was a challenge to our original assumptions. We had thought our project was about communication in the sense of a conduit model, in which the problem was to provide an efficient, convenient channel for the representation and transmission of a message in the form of a map. But we have come to see that it was really about reflexivity and interpretation, both in the construction and in the reading of maps. We have come to see communication of perspectives in distributed cognition as a series of conversations—first with oneself while constructing an understanding in the form of a cause map, and then with another while exchanging and discussing those cause maps. The communication is in these conversations of perspective making and perspective taking, not in the map as a transmitted message.

A second challenge to our initial assumptions came from listening to what people said when they were constructing a map. They did not only use the abstract categories of causal factors and relations to think through the construction of the map, but also relied on storytelling. Instead of identifying a factor to include in a map by generalizing it through inductive reasoning, and instead of linking factors with a paradigmatic statement of their causal relationships (if x increases, then y increases), our map makers would put a factor into a map and link it with other factors while recounting a dramatic incident with a customer, a competitor, or another manager. This suggests that the map makers way of thinking through a situation was not so much an exploration of a problem space using logical operators as suggested by Simon (1977) and others, as it was a narration of their experience of being in that situation. Through narrating their experience, they identified important factors and explored how they were linked together.

Subsequently, we have drawn upon the work of Bruner (1990) who posited that narrative is a fundamental mode of human cognition, equal in importance to the paradigmatic, information processing mode of cognition that dominates cognitive science. We have found his work very helpful in understanding how people coordinate activities not only through exchanging messages about states and actions, but also through narrativizing real and hypothetical events in conversations with self and other (Boland & Tenkasi, 1995). We even found this narrative mode of cognition to be evident when managers analyzed the seemingly abstract and unambiguous representations of an accounting budget record (Boland, 1993). There, we observed that managers interpreted budget and performance reports by bringing to life the persons behind the accounting numbers, endowing those persons with motivations and intentions, and narrating a sequence of events which produced the numbers.

AN EXAMPLE: MAPPING CAUSES OF QUALITY IN MEDICAL CARE

As an example of how Spider can support perspective making and perspective taking in open system, we review a process of causal mapping by physicians in the neurology department of a large teaching hospital. The objective was to improve the department's ability to collaborate and to increase the quality of medical care. The map makers were neurologists who were long time members of the department's quality assurance committee. The cause maps of three physicians (A, B, and C) are shown in Figs. 2.1, 2.2, and 2.3. The physicians first worked individually with one of the authors, using the Spider mapping tool to make a personal map of the causes of quality in medical care. After making their individual maps, they studied the maps made by the other physicians to identify similarities and differences. Finally, they met as a group to discuss the possibility of a synthesis.

In constructing a map, each physician would first put down three to five factors and some of the relations between them. In Fig. 2.1, for example, Physician A started with the factors "Technical Quality of Medicine" and "Social Quality of Medicine." These factors were introduced with a story about the physician's long-standing argument with institutional leaders in neurology about the lack of attention to the social quality of medicine. He then added the factor "Time Spent with Patient" along with a story about a patient who required a long series of questions and seemingly off point discussions before the important symptoms and background knowledge needed for a correct diagnosis emerged. The factor "Pressure to Cut Costs" was then added, noting how insurance companies and Medicare were leading the hospital to think in terms of patients per hour and to pressure physicians to reduce the time spent with each patient.

Then, Physician A began drawing the causal relations among those factors, beginning with the negative relation between "Pressure to Cut Costs" and

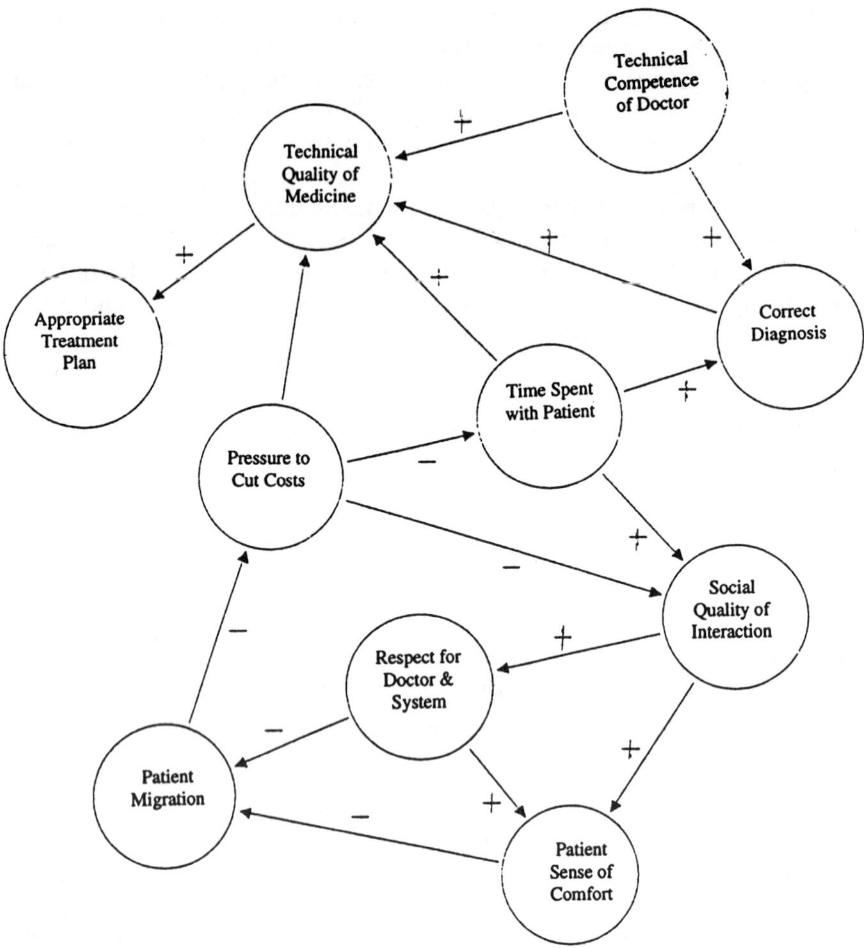

FIG. 2.1. Map of the causes of quality in medical care prepared by Physician A.

"Time Spent With Patient." After a period of identifying causal relations, he was prompted to begin a process of considering each factor and asking, "what other factors affect this one?" and "what other factors does this one affect"? Most of the time, these new factors and their relation to the map came from a story about a patient who was "doctor shopping" and migrating through the system, or a patient who had lost respect for a one of his colleagues. Once the map reached the stage of Fig. 2.1, he used a feature of the Spider system to probe it for cycles. This revealed several cycles, all related to the way that cost cutting pressure feeds back upon itself in a vicious cycle.

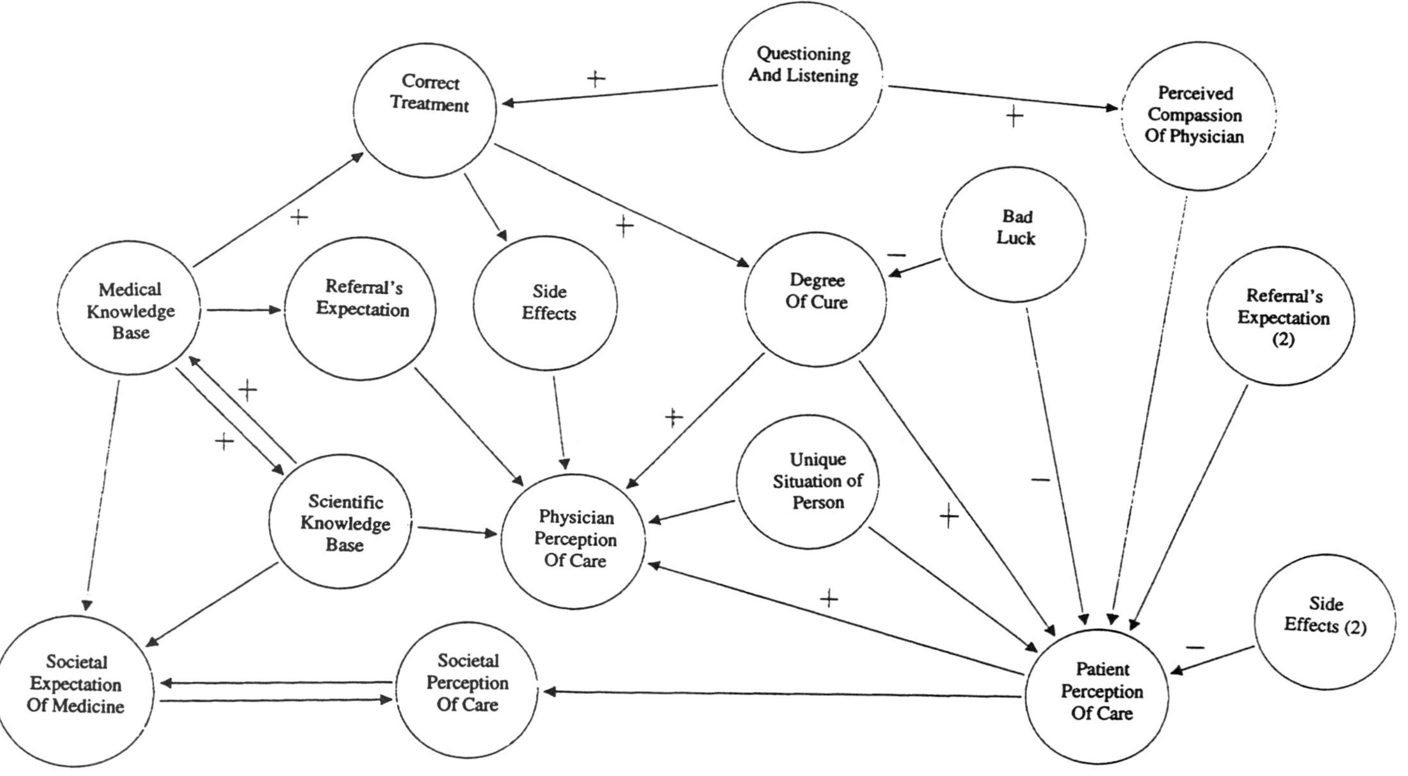

FIG. 2.2. Map of the causes of quality in medical care prepared by Physician B.

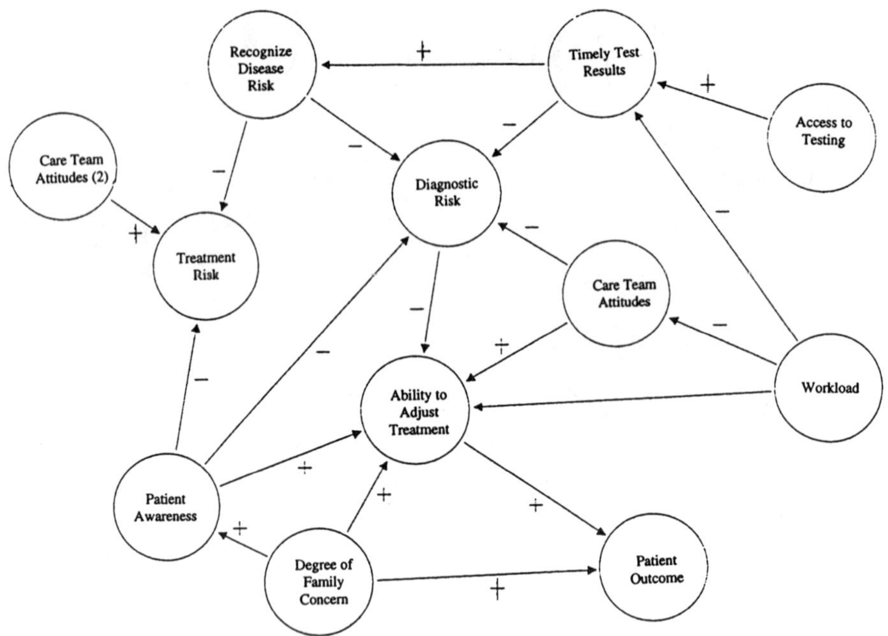

FIG. 2.3. Map of the causes of quality in medical care prepared by Physician C.

Figure 2.4 shows such a cycle, in which cost cutting pressures leads to reduced time with a patient, which hurts the social quality of interaction and eventually results in the patient migrating through the health care system, creating increased costs and further pressure to cut costs. This vicious cycle was not in Physician A's initial description of the situation, nor was it in his unfolding discussion of it. Rather, a self-reflective awareness of the cycle emerged through the process of mapping itself and its discovery was a pleasant surprise, "confirming" Physician A's initial insight that social quality was a key factor. This kind of discovery is not to be taken as a new "truth," but instead as a stage in the perspective making of Physician A. In his perspective making, his way of understanding quality of medical was being systematically elaborated, refined, and strengthened.

In Fig. 2.2, we see that Physician B sees the problem of quality in healthcare somewhat differently. As with Physician A, social interaction and the patient's perception of the physician are present in this map, but they do not play as central a role. Instead, the role of science in driving not only the degree of cure that is possible, but also the perceptions of care by society, by physicians and by patients become the focal points for defining quality of care.

In Fig. 2.3, Physician C raises a different set of issues, in which risks from the disease, the diagnosis, and the treatment as well as the ability to adjust

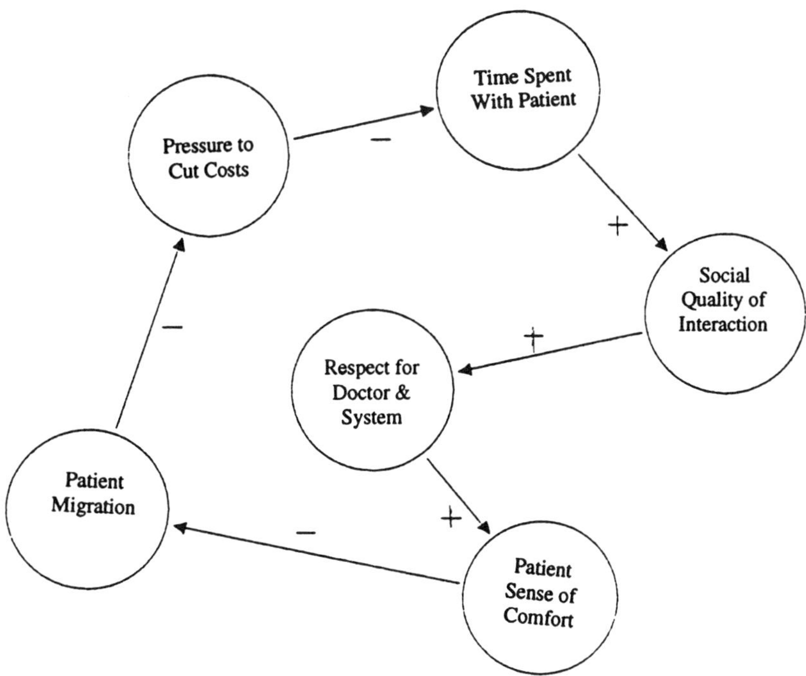

FIG. 2.4. Examples of a cycle in cause map of Physician A.

treatment become focal points. The role of the family in helping the patient understand his or her condition and follow through with treatment (especially as the treatment is adjusted) is highlighted. In addition, Physician C recognizes the workload on the system and the attitudes of the care team as important in affecting the way that treatment can be dynamically adjusted. The "Ability to Adjust Treatment" then becomes the focal point for defining quality of care, which can be seen from the number of factors leading into it.

As each of these physicians is shown the maps of the others, the first response invariably is "this map is very similar to mine." The physician will begin by identifying factors that seem similar, such as "Social Quality of Interaction" (Fig. 2.1) and "Questioning and Listening" (Fig. 2.2), or "Side Effects" (Fig. 2.2) and "Treatment Risk" (Fig. 2.3). After a while, though, the tone shifts and an awareness of the differences between their map and that of another begins to emerge. The awareness of differences grows, and leads to a realization such as: "This person sees things very differently than I do!". This realization of fundamental perceptual difference between oneself and others is the beginning of a perspective taking process, in which the individual explores what those differences and their implications are. The recognition of difference and the process of perspective taking, however, required a prior episode of perspective making in which one's own understanding was constructed and reflected upon. Perspective making in the form of a cause map provides the condition of possibility for recognizing differences with others through close examination of their maps.

In this group of neurologists, the analysis and synthesis of a dozen maps led the department leader to express, "I had been thinking about quality much too simplistically." The maps were intended to reveal different ways of thinking about the cause of quality in medical care, but ended up revealing different definitions of what quality of medical care means. The synthesis map that the group produced contained multiple definitions of quality, dominating different areas of the map, including perceptions of relevant groups, costs versus risks, and technical outcomes on an absolute scale.

The important point for our purpose here is the way that collaboration on improving quality of medical care was not primarily a question of communicating existing understandings with a communication model of encode, transmit, and decode. Instead, it involved a process of perspective making, or the visual construction of an understanding in the first place, and a process of perspective taking, made possible by reflecting upon similarities until a realization of differences was achieved. Only then could they engage in a discussion on how they might coordinate their group efforts in the future.

RETHINKING COMMUNICATION IN DISTRIBUTED COGNITION

Based on our work in this and other projects, we now see the process of communication and coordination in environments of distributed cognition much differently than we did at the outset. We had thought of communication as a problem of representing and transmitting a message in the form of a directed graph. That way of thinking about communication assumed that shared meanings and a resulting coordination can be achieved when the cognitive maps (or schemas) more or less coincide among members of the firm.

The notion of schemas and shared meanings now seems much more problematic. If a cause map is developed through a creative, constructive process—if it is not "just there" to be recorded and exchanged with others—what could it mean to say that managers do or should have "shared meanings"? When each actor must, in a sense, invent an understanding, how can one speak about people sharing something that they have yet to inventively construct? One possibility is to return to one of the origins of our use of terms like *schemas, cause maps*, and *frames*, namely the work of Bartlett (1932) who adopted the notion of schema from Sir Henry Head to interpret his own studies of remembering. A review of his classic study shows that Bartlett was not intending to suggest that a schema was a well-formed structure or that it was somewhat stable. Instead, he used the term to express an active process of interpretation that was continuously being constructed, interpretively extended, and creatively revised. In fact, he refers to the way subjects in his experiments appeared to simultaneously employ multiple schemas and to inventively make associations among them in a constructing a remembrance.

With this in mind, we now think of communication and coordination in distributed cognition as a skill for reflexively narrativizing ongoing experience in a way that constructs and reconstructs understandings of a situation, and of engaging in conversation with others about these narrativized representations. We believe that information technology can support this process by enabling the construction of visual images, such as cause maps and other representations that "mirror" the notion of schema, including diagrammatic depictions of a story, pictures, or graphic designs, among others (Boland & Tenkasi, 1995). We find Star's (1989) description of the role of a 'boundary object' in doing science work to be useful here. A boundary object is not a message being transmitted between people with different expertise on a scientific team, but something that can be put out between them and used as a focus for a conversation among them in which they explore its possible meanings and implications. It is an occasion for conversation, not a self-contained message for transmitting and decoding by a recipient.

Using the idea of boundary objects, we are now exploring how cause maps, narrative maps, graphic images, and other forms of representation can be used in distributed cognition to improve organizational practices of communicating and coordinating. We are interested in how communities develop distinct ways of knowing through their ways of narrativizing experience and engaging in conversation about boundary objects.

CONCLUSIONS

We see the task of information technology to be one of supporting the subjective process of perspective making and perspective taking. This is an interpretive process of inquiry in which an individual constructs a visual "reading" of the situation he or she is in, makes that reading available to others, and engages in conversation with them, seeking to extend her own horizon of meaning (Gadamer, 1975). What is required from information technology in distributed cognition are facilities of self indication, reflection, and interpretation—an environment for active sense making in which individuals can construct representations of their changing understandings and can explore them in conversation with others.

In addition to specialized software such as the Spider cause mapping tool, groupware systems provide an ideal infrastructure to support perspective making and perspective taking. Boland and Tenkasi (1995) identified a number of ways that the discussion forums provided by group technologies can be used to strengthen knowledge structures within a distinctive community of knowing, and also to enable conversation on the perspectives of others. Such forums can allow for narrative as well as calculative forms of reasoning, can include cause maps as well as maps of narratives, and can structure conversations about such maps along with their implications for collaboration in knowledge work. We see communication and coordination as an ongoing process of interpretation through conversation. We are excited about the prospects for designing tools of visualization, organizational structures, and group processes that better enable such interpretive conversations.

ACKNOWLEDGMENTS

Support for this research was provided by the National Science Foundation Program on coordination Theory and Collaboration Technology (Grant #IRI-9015526) by the Digital Equipment Corporation (Grant #111), by the TRW Foundation and by the Kay Star Foundation. The authors give special thanks to Susan Leigh Star and Ulrike Schultze for helpful suggestions on an earlier version of this manuscript.

REFERENCES

Alvesson, M. (1995) *Management of Knowledge-Intensive Companies.* New York: De Gruyter.

Argyris, C. and Schon, D. (1978) *Organizational Learning, a Theory of Action Perspective.* Reading, MA: Addison Wesley.

Axelrod, R. (1976) *Structure of Decision: The Cognitive Maps of Political Elites.* Princeton, NJ: Princeton University Press.

Bakhtin, M. M. (1981) Discourse in the Novel. In M. Holquis (ed.), *The Dialogic Imagination.* Austin: University of Texas Press.

Barnes, B. (1983) The Conventional Character of Knowledge and Cognition. In *Science Observed.* London: Sage.

Bartlett, F. C. (1932) *Remembering: A Study in Experimental and Social Psychology.* London: Cambridge University Press.

Bartunek, J. and Moch, M. K. (1987) First-order, Second-order and Third-order Change in Organization Development Interventions: A Cognitive Approach. *Journal of Applied Behavioral Science, 23*(4), 483–500.

Boland, R. J. (1993) Accounting and the Interpretive Act. *Accounting, Organizations and Society, 18*(2/3), 125–146.

Boland, R. J., Schwartz, D., Tenkasi, R. Maheshwari, A. and Te'eni, D. (1992) Sharing Perspectives in Distributed Decision Making. *ACM Conference on Computer Supported Co-operative Work,* Toronto, 306–313.

Boland, R. J. and Tenkasi, R. V. (1995) Perspective Making and Perspective Taking in Communities of Knowing. *Organization Science, 6*(4), 350–372.

Boland, R. J., Tenkasi, R. V. and Te'eni, D. (1994) Designing Information Technology to Support Distributed Cognition. *Organization Science, 5*(3), 456–475.

Boulding, K. E. (1956) *The Image: Knowledge in Life and Society.* Ann Arbor: University of Michigan Press.

Brown, J. S. and Duguid, P. (1991) Organizational Learning and Communities-of-Practice: Toward a Unified View of Working, Learning and Innovation. *Organization Science, 2*(1), 40–57.

Brown, R. (1981) *Social Psychology.* New York: The Free Press.

Bruner, J. S. (1990) *Acts of Meaning.* Cambridge, MA: Harvard University Press.

Clark, H. H. (1985) Language Use and Language Users. In G. Lindzey and E. Aronson (eds.), *Handbook of Social Psychology.* New York: Random House.

Clark, H. and Marshall, C. (1981) Definite Reference and Mutual Knowledge. In A. Joshi, I. Sag, and B. Weber (eds.), *Elements of Discourse Understanding.* Cambridge, England: Cambridge University Press.

Dougherty, D. (1992) Interpretive Barriers to Successful Product Innovation in Large Firms, *Organization Science, 3*(2), 179–202.

Drucker, P. (1988) The Coming of the New Organization. *Harvard Business Review*, Jan–Feb, 45–53.

Festinger, L. (1954) A Theory of Social Comparison Processes. *Human Relations, 7*, 117–140.

Fish, S. (1980) *Is There a Text in This Class?* Cambridge, MA: Harvard University Press.

Fleck, L. (1979) *Genesis and Development of a Scientific Fact.* In T. Trenn and R. K. Merton (Eds.), Chicago: University of Chicago Press. (Originally published in 1935)

Gadamer, H. G. (1975) *Truth and Method.* New York: Seabury.

Galbraith, J. R. (1994) *Competing with Lateral-Flexible Organizations.* Reading, MA: Addison Wesley.

Galbraith, J. R. and Lawler, E. E. (1993) *Organizing for the Future.* San Francisco, CA: Jossey-Bass.

Garfinkel, H. (1967) *Studies in Ethnomethodology.* Englewood Cliffs, NJ: Prentice-Hall.

Giddens, A. (1979) *Central Problems in Social Theory.* Berkeley: University of California Press.

Hewitt, C. (1985) The Challenge of Open Systems. *Byte*, pp. 223–242.

Hewitt, C. (1986) Offices are Open Systems. *ACM Transactions on Office Information Systems, 4*(3), 271–287.

Huber, G. P. (1984) The Nature and Design of Post Industrial Organizations. *Management Science, 30*, 928–951.

Huff, A. S. (1990) *Mapping Strategic Thought,* Chichester, England: Wiley.

Hutchins, E. (1996) *Cognition in the Wild.* Cambridge, MA: MIT Press.

Kahneman, D., Slovic, P. and Teversky, A. (1982) *Judgment Under Uncertainty: Heuristics and Biases*, New York: Cambridge University Press.

Krauss, R. and Fussell, S. (1991) Perspective Taking in Communication: Representation of Others' Knowledge in Reference. *Social Cognition, 9*(1), 2–24.

Malone, T., Yates, J. and Benjamin, R. (1987) Electronic Markets and Electronic Hierarchies. *Communications of the ACM, 26*, 430–444.

Mead, G. H. (1934) *Mind, Self and Society.* Chicago: University of Chicago Press.

Norman, D. A. (1993) *Things that Make Us Smart.* Reading, MA: Addison Wesley.

Nystrom, P. C. and Starbuck, W. H. (1984) To Avoid Organizational Crisis, Unlearn. *Organizational Dynamics, 12*(4), 53–65.

Pepper, S. C. (1942) *World Hypotheses.* Berkeley, University of California Press.

Purser, R. E., Pasmore, W. and Tenkasi, R. (1992) The Influence of Deliberations on Learning in New Product Development Teams. *Journal of Engineering and Technology Management, 9*, 1–28.

Rommetveit, R. (1980) On Meanings of Acts and What is Meant by What is Said in a Pluralistic World. In M. Brenner (ed.), *The Structure of Action.* Oxford: Blackwell and Mott.

Ross, L., Greene, D. and House, P. (1977) The False Consensus Phenomenon: An Attributional Bias in Self-Perception and Social Perception Processes. *Journal of Experimental Social Psychology, 13*, 279–301.

Simon, H. A. (1977) *The New Science of Management Decision* (2nd rev.). Englewood Cliffs, NJ: Prentice-Hall.

Star, S. L. (1989) The Structure of Ill-Structured Solutions: Boundary objects and heterogeneous Distributed Problem Solving. In M. Huhns and L. Gasser (eds.), *Readings in Distributed Artificial Intelligence 2.* Menlo Park, CA: Morgan Kaufmann.

Starbuck, W. H. (1992) Learning by Knowledge Intensive Firms. *Journal of Management Studies, 29*(6), 713–740.

Starbuck, W. H. and Milliken, F. J. (1988) Executives' Perceptual Filters: What They Notice and How They Make Sense. In D. Hambrick (ed.), *The Executive Effect: Concepts and Methods for Studying Top Managers.* Greenwich, CT: JAI Press.

Steedman, M. and Johnson-Laird, P. (1980) The Production of Sentences, Utterances and Speech Acts: Have Computers Anything to Say? In B. Butterworth (ed.), *Language Productions: Speech and Talk.* London: Academic Press.

Tenkasi, R. V. and Boland, R. J. (1993) Locating Meaning in Organizational Learning: The Narrative Basis of Cognition. In R. W. Woodman and W. A. Pasmore (Eds.), *Research in Organizational Change and Development* (Vol. 7, pp. 77–103). Greenwich, CT: JAI Press.

Weick, K. E. and Bougon, M. K. (1986) Organizations as Cognitive Maps: Charting Ways to Success and Failure. In H. Sims and D. Goia (eds.), *The Thinking Organization.* San Francisco: Jossey-Bass.

CHAPTER

3

Coordination as Distributed Search

Edmund H. Durfee
University of Michigan

Daniel Damouth
Orincon Corporation, San Diego, CA

Piotr J. Gmytrasiewicz
University of Texas at Arlington

Marcus J. Huber
Intelligent Reasoning Systems, Oceanside, CA

Thomas A. Montgomery
Ford Motor Company, Dearborn, MI

Sandip Sen
University of Tulsa

A variety of tasks and problems become apparent when investigating a broad interdisciplinary field such as coordination theory and collaboration technology. Among them is the problem of characterizing the field in some way. Because our work, and the work reported in this book as a whole, emerged from a program in computer and information science and engineering, we can begin by characterizing computational tools for supporting coordination. A simple characterization of tools for supporting human collaboration has been seen in the computer-supported cooperative work (CSCW) literature, where different tools are identified with different time and place[1] characteristics

[1]For the purposes of this chapter, "place" connotes a locus of attention. Thus, different places could be geographically separated, but they could also be conceptually separated. The key issue is that decisions need to be made in the context of various physical and/or mental "places."

(Johansen, 1988). The result is a lattice as in Fig. 3.1, where we have placed representative entries in each of the matrix elements (many other entries can and have been made in the literature).

Although the question being addressed in the entries of this matrix is implicit in the CSCW endeavor, for our purposes it is important to make it explicit. What the matrix is categorizing are "tools that support collaboration on a particular task among multiple participants who are in the *x* and *y*," where *x* and *y* are values along the different matrix indices. Broadly construed, therefore, the kinds of technologies that fit into this type of matrix are collaboration technologies, which assume that participants *want* to collaborate on a particular task. This perspective abstracts away issues of conflict, in order to pay attention to the details of achieving coherent collaboration among participants (see, e.g., the CTCT-supported work on collaboratories such as that of Schatz, Atkins et al., Fischer, Olson, and so forth).

Conflict, however, can arise whenever there are multiple agents and multiple tasks. To get to the point where the question associated with Fig. 3.1 makes sense, the agents must initially establish (negotiate) the goals to which the participants are committed (e.g., the CTCT-supported work of Kraus and Wilkenfeld). Moreover, in many applications, agents will contend over resources (including each other's attention) as different combinations of agents pursue different tasks. Resource allocation thus becomes a critical concern (see, e.g., the CTCT-supported work of Pasquale).

Our work assumes that a sophisticated agent—such as a person—is too dear to be dedicated to only a single task, and thus an agent must be able to pursue multiple tasks at the same time. From this perspective, then, we use the same matrix as in Fig. 3.1 but ask a different (although just as important) question. Because most if not all participants in a collaboration are also participating in other collaborations, let us use the matrix to categorize "tools that support collaborations on multiple tasks by a *single* participant, when the collaborative tasks are in the *x* and *y*" (see Fig. 3.2).

	Same Time	Different Times
Same Place	Electonic Whiteboards	Electronic Bulletin Boards
Different Places	Teleconferencing	Electronic Mail

FIG. 3.1.

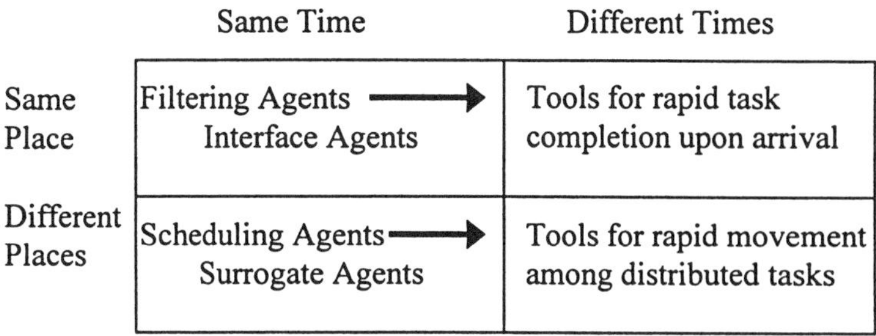

FIG. 3.2.

A person can face tasks at the same place and different times, as visitors (email messages) arrive periodically at the person's office (mail program) in the course of a day. Or the tasks might be at different places at different times, so that the person must travel (perhaps electronically) from task to task during a day. Either way, computational tools such as advanced interfaces and networking software can support the person in his or her collaborations by allowing the person to move more quickly among tasks (to switch physical or mental contexts better) and to complete each task faster.

Often, however, tasks for various collaborations should be done at the same time. For such tasks, there are two general approaches to providing computational support. One approach is to use computer processes to *prioritize* tasks, which serves to conceptually push the problem back into the "different times" column. These processes can, for example, filter and sort email (Malone, Grant, Turbak, Brobst, & Cohen, 1987), and can solve scheduling problems to help the user navigate among competing tasks so as to attend to them one at a time in the proper order. Hence, this approach performs "triage" on the tasks, but the user should still eventually attend to them all personally.

The other general approach is to *delegate* responsibility for tasks so that they can indeed be handled in parallel. The idea here is to generate, to some degree, processes for the user that act on the user's behalf when he or she is otherwise occupied. Thus, in this approach, the user might never have to attend to some of the tasks. In the case of "same place, same time," these processes could reside at the user–machine interface, intercepting tasks meant for the user and completing them semiautonomously (such as filing incoming email messages). Much of the recent work in building "agents" into interfaces has been directed toward this problem. In the case of "different places, same time," the processes could reside (geographically or conceptually) remotely from the user, acting on his or her behalf with little if any supervision on the part of the user. Thus, while interface agents could be monitored and continuously tailored by the user, remote surrogate agents cannot be. A user employing surrogate agents must therefore have confidence in his or her decision making, and the agents must have the ability to act and interact flexibly and adaptively as circumstances change, based on well-founded criteria when at all possible.

Our work is to develop theories and mechanisms for creating such surrogate agents, and in particular for giving such agents the ability to coordinate. Coordination, as we define it, can be in support of collaboration, but need not be. We construe coordination broadly as the process of considering the likely decisions/actions of others when deciding what to do. If such considerations lead to concerted activity for mutual benefit, then the coordination process supports a cooperative outcome. But such considerations can also occur in noncooperative situations, where a successful competitor could be one who coordinates its decisions most effectively against those of others. Implicit in the matrix of Fig. 3.2 is that competition will exist, at least competition for the attention of a participant in an interaction. Thus, for us, Fig. 3.2 captures aspects of coordination theory, while Fig. 3.1 is more focused on collaboration technologies.

The work on coordination theory that we summarize in this chapter addresses only a small subset of problems that arise in developing computational mechanisms for coordinating surrogate agents. The problems we particularly concentrate on are:

- How to analyze, understand, and represent an application domain in such a way that an agent can make quantitatively based adaptations to its multiagent environment when carrying out tasks on behalf of a human user.
- How an agent can generate, communicate about, and make commitments to models of itself and of others so as to get an adequate appreciation of the multiagent environment with which it must coordinate its decisions.
- How protocols for communication and interaction can arise in an arbitrary system of agents, despite the agents having differing objectives and capabilities.

In this chapter, we describe some of our results in investigating these problems. We begin with the first problem, and outline a methodology that has allowed us to develop quantitative predictions of performance that can be used by an agent in the application domain of distributed meeting scheduling. We then turn to the second problem, where, unlike meeting scheduling where mutual agreement on a meeting time is a shared objective, we consider the possibility that agents are not necessarily desirous of collaboration. Instead, coordination might be geared toward avoiding conflicts rather than reaching detailed agreements, and so might require agents to make fewer commitments to each other. Next, we turn to the question of the emergence of protocols in agent populations, and consider how basic knowledge and assumptions on the part of agents might give rise to a rich variety of situation-dependent modes of interaction. We conclude by summarizing what we have done, and outlining some of the challenges remaining for the future.

TRUSTABLE SURROGATE AGENTS

Researchers who have been developing artificial agents have taken a variety of tacks in realizing them. Some researchers have focused on the notion of building "believable" agents, that act in and react to their environment (including humans) in a manner that appears to mimic how natural agents would behave (Maes, 1994). In a similar vein, some researchers have been investigating "learning" agents that can, in some way or another, observe the behavior of a human and learn from that behavior to act in a similar manner in similar future situations (Mitchell, Carvana, Freitag, McDermott, & Zabowski, 1994). Other researchers have developed more "instructable" agents, that can be given explicit instructions about how to behave under different circumstances (Malone et al., 1987).

Our emphasis has been on building agents that can be physically and conceptually distant from the humans they represent, and therefore we have shied away from assuming that an agent can observe its corresponding human or that a human can supervise his or her agents. We have thus concentrated more on designing agents that fall closer to the instructable category, although we have been particularly concerned about the degree to which the instructions for the agents can be well-founded and quantitative, rather than heuristic and qualitative. Agents with such detailed models of their application domain and available strategies, even if not "believable" (they might not act like humans—who could well lack or ignore such models) nor "instructable" (improving the model in a principled way would require more effort than simply providing an instruction), are expected to be "trustable" (they would make principled decisions based on quantitative analyses).

Our particular domain of inquiry has been the meeting–scheduling application, and within this domain we have analytically developed and experimentally verified quantitative predictions of performance for various strategies involved in scheduling meetings (Sen, 1993; Sen & Durfee, 1991, 1992, 1994b), including strategies for deciding how many possible meeting times to propose, strategies for rejecting or counterproposing meeting times, strategies for committing to and canceling meetings, and strategies for deciding which possible meeting times to (counter)propose at any given time.

For example, the choice of strategy for deciding which time intervals to consider next for a meeting will have numerous effects, including effects on the density of meetings in different parts of the calendar, the likelihood of scheduling future meetings of different types, the costs of scheduling, and the time needed to schedule meetings. More importantly, given targets for calendar densities and limited costs and time for scheduling, a calendar management agent should adapt its strategy choice based on the larger context of what it expects to schedule in the future and what it knows of the calendars of the other agents. These adaptations might not be under the constant supervision of the user, and thus (we argue) should be made by embedding domain knowledge (a rigorous model of the task) into the agent, rather than trying to capture a superficial model of the user acting in a small sample of cases.

Distributed Meeting Scheduling

The agents in a Distributed Meeting Scheduling (DMS) system exchange relevant information to build local schedules that fit into a globally consistent schedule. To facilitate information exchange, the agents need a common communication protocol for negotiating over meeting times. For our agents, we have chosen to adapt the multistage negotiation protocol (Conry, Kuwabara, Lesser, & Meyer, 1991), which is a generalization of the contract net protocol (Smith, 1980). In our protocol, each meeting has a particular agent who is responsible for it, called the host. The host contacts other attendees of the meeting (who are called invitees) to announce the meeting, and collects bids (availability information). This process could be repeated several times before a mutually acceptable time interval is found, or it is recognized that no such time interval exists. Other meetings could be undergoing scheduling concurrently; in general, an agent can simultaneously be involved in scheduling any number of meetings, acting as a host for some and an invitee for others.

How well this protocol performs in efficiently converging on good schedules is strongly impacted by heuristic strategies about what information to exchange and how to model tentatively scheduled meetings. In order to decide what to propose for a meeting, the agents have to search their calendars in a systematic manner using some appropriate search bias. Strategies for communication must balance demands for privacy (which lead to exchanging less information) with demands for quickly converging on meeting times (which can be sped up by exchanging more information). Strategies for modeling tentatively scheduled meetings can range from blocking off tentative time(s) for a meeting unless and until the arrangements fall through, to ignoring tentative commitments about a meeting when scheduling other meetings. We have embarked on research to develop, analyze, and verify a formal model of DMS to formulate rigorous, quantitative predictions of the performance of the following types of heuristic strategies:

Search Biases determine the order in which the calendar space is searched to find acceptable time intervals for a meeting. Here, we consider linear early (LE) where agents try to schedule a meeting as early as possible, and hierarchical (H), where agents build a temporal abstraction hierarchy over the calendar space. At each node in the hierarchy, agents keep a record of the number of intervals of different lengths free below that node in the hierarchy. The calendar space lends itself to a very natural hierarchy of hours, days, weeks, and so on, and the agents participating in a meeting can first identify a good week to meet in, then identify a good day within that week, and finally an actual interval within that day. Given a meeting of some particular length to schedule, the host obtains information about the invitees regarding how many intervals of that length are open at each node (e.g., at each week) at the highest level of the hierarchy. It multiplies the numbers together for corresponding nodes, ranks the nodes, elaborates the best one, and proceeds to repeat the process for the next level of the hierarchy under the elaborated node.[2] Backtracking occurs if a particular portion of the ground level being elaborated contains no solution to the scheduling problem.

Announcement Strategies determine how a meeting is announced, and usually involve proposing some number of possible times. We specifically consider the options called *best* (where only the best meeting time from the host's perspective, ranked by some heuristic like being the earliest, is communicated) and *good* (where several times preferred by the host, 3 by default, are communicated).

Bidding Strategies determine what information an invitee sends back based on an announcement. We consider the options called yes–no (where an invitee says yes or no to each proposal sent by the host) and alternatives (where an invitee proposes other time(s) when it can meet).

Commitment Strategies are *committed* (when a time is proposed by a host or invitee agent, that agent tentatively blocks it off on its calendar so no other meetings can be scheduled there) and *noncommitted* (times are not blocked off until full agreement on a meeting time is reached).

Adaptive Scheduling

Our analysis of various strategy options (Sen & Durfee, 1992) show that no one strategy combination dominates another over all circumstances. Changing environmental factors like system load, organization size, and so on, can produce a change in the strategy combination that will produce the best results on any given performance metric. If there is a way to predict the best

---

[2]Although some of this information could be obtained indirectly, we assume in this chapter that agents will directly communicate about the densities of various intervals, with a resulting decrease in privacy.

strategy combination for a given performance metric and given environmental and system conditions, we would like our automated scheduler to take advantage of that. Such a scheduler would be adaptive to changes in the system and the environment, providing us with the most desirable performance as measured by certain performance metrics. In this chapter, we concentrate on adapting the search bias to adjust to environmental and performance needs. More details, as well as discussion on other aspects of the design of an adaptive meeting scheduler, can be found elsewhere (Sen, 1993; Sen & Durfee, 1994a, 1994b).

As mentioned earlier, a search bias sorts the available meeting times according to some metrics; a scheduling agent will use the results of the bias to order the proposals it makes for meeting times, from best to worst. There are a variety of factors that could go into ordering proposals. For example, because a scheduler must consider that meeting requests will arrive continuously, one factor in deciding where in the calendar to schedule a meeting will be the expectations the scheduler has about the demands of future meetings.

For example, some users might be subject to receiving high priority meeting requests that arrive on short notice. These HPSN meetings demand that the calendar have open slots on a relatively frequent (e.g., daily) basis. In turn, then, an appropriate search bias should try to spread meetings out, so as to leave some uncommitted time every day. The hierarchical (H) search bias does precisely this: By first concentrating on portions of the calendar that are most likely to accommodate a meeting, the bias tends to place meetings evenly in the calendar. Our simulation studies have verified this behavior (Sen, 1993).

But the tradeoff with scheduling meetings evenly is that it tends to fragment the calendar. A user who is subject to receiving infrequent requests for long-duration meetings might be better off trying to pack meetings into the calendar as densely as possible, so as to leave larger chunks of time free for, for example, spending a day at a remote site. The linear early (LE) search bias does precisely this, giving top priority to scheduling meetings as early as possible, and thus leaving later portions of the calendar relatively empty. Again, we have empirically verified this behavior (Sen, 1993).

Typically, the scheduling climate of a user will vary over time, at times having more HPSN meetings and at other times having more long-duration meetings. An adaptive meeting scheduler should be sensitive to the changing character of meeting requests, and change appropriately so as to maximize the chances of successfully scheduling current and anticipated future meetings.

But other factors, beside the changing meeting environment, can also influence the selection of strategies, such as the expected cost and delay in scheduling a meeting. For example, if agents use the H search bias and have schedules that are about evenly dense, then the criterion that the H search bias counts on, of differentiating portions of the calendar based on the density of meetings, becomes less discriminating. Because all parts of the calendar are equally likely to yield a good meeting time, switching to the LE search bias can actually reduce the cost (number of iterations required) to arrive at a meeting time, as it does not require passing messages about the inner nodes of the temporal abstraction of the calendar space as the H search bias does.

But, if the LE search bias is used for a while to schedule meetings, there will be considerable density variations along the length of the calendar; when a meeting is being scheduled for a large number of attendees, such variations can combine to give very different success probabilities at different parts of the calendar. Additionally, if the host is more free than invitees, and the latter are using a yes–no bidding strategy, a savings can be obtained by using the H search bias. Hence, after a while there will be sufficient mismatch between the schedules of agents to warrant the switch back to the hierarchical search bias. The selling point of adaptive search bias is that the scheduling agent can choose the most appropriate bias for any meeting based on the current states of the attendee calendars.

Building adaptive scheduling agents requires that these qualitative expectations be mapped to rules of behavior for strategy adaptation, which in turn means that we need to provide quantitative measures to the agents to help them decide. The following probabilistic analysis will assume the availability of the density profile characteristics (or DPCs, which depict the variation of meeting densities over the length of agent calendars) for the desired meeting length for the attendees of the meeting.

Search Bias Analyses. Consider the LE search bias with the invitee agents responding with acceptance or rejection messages (no counterproposals). In this scenario, a host agent is trying to schedule a meeting with A invitees. Let $K = L - l + 1$ be the number of places in which a meetings of length l can start on a working day of length L. For invitee x, let $n_x \leq K$ be the number of these intervals open on the day in question. If the host was using one proposal per iteration, the probability that it will take I iterations to schedule the meeting is given by (Sen, 1993): $P_{i,1} = \sum_{j=0}^{i-1} (-1)^j \binom{i-1}{j} \frac{\prod_{x=1}^{A} \binom{K-j-1}{n_x - j - 1}}{\prod_{x=1}^{A} \binom{K}{n_x}}$. If the host was proposing N intervals per iteration, the probability that it will take i iterations to schedule the meeting is given by $P_{i,N} = \sum_{j=N(i-1)+1}^{N*i} P_{j,1}$.

Now we analyze the H search bias. Let us assume M agents (numbered 1, . . . ,M) are involved in scheduling a meeting of length l, and that they have constructed identical temporal abstraction hierarchies over the base calendar space (the linear ordering of calendar hours). For any internal node in the hierarchy, we will calculate the probability that one or more common intervals are free in the base space of the calendars under that node, for every attendee of the meeting. Let x be the node in question. Because the hierarchies formed by the agents are identical, every agent has $a(l,x)$ intervals of length l below this node of its abstraction hierarchy. Let the number of intervals of length l currently free under node x for agent i be $f_i(l,x)$. We can then calculate the following (see Sen, 1993, for details):

P{At least one interval is free in each attendees calendar under node x}

$$= \sum_{j=1}^{a(l,x)} (-1)^{j+1} \binom{a(l,x)}{j} \frac{\prod_{i=1}^{M} \binom{a(l,x)-j}{f_i(l,x)-j}}{\prod_{i=1}^{M} \binom{a(l,x)}{f_i(l,x)}}.$$

Given a two-level hierarchy (days and hours), for example, we can use this equation to compute the probabilities for scheduling under each day. The days are then sorted by these probabilities, and the agents negotiate over days in decreasing order of this probability until a mutually free interval is found.

Moreover, for a particular situation, we can develop probability mass functions and probability distribution functions of the random variable corresponding to the iteration at which scheduling is complete, using the previous equations for the LE and H search biases. This information can be used to calculate the expected number of trials to schedule a meeting, and thus give a measure of the expected scheduling cost. If this is a predominant concern, then the adaptive scheduler will adopt the bias that minimizes expected cost.

Sample Experiments. In the following, we consider two different sets of DPCs (see Fig. 3.3). Each set involves a host trying to schedule a meeting of length $l = 2$ hours with 2 invitees. All the agents are assumed to be managing calendars divided into 10 blocks of 5 hours each. We assume, in the case of the hierarchical search bias, that the temporal abstraction hierarchy is comprised of calendar hours, which are grouped into these blocks. The hierarchical negotiation mechanism, used by the host, first gathers information from the invitees about their respective calendar densities in each of the blocks, orders these blocks by the probability of successfully scheduling a meeting in each of the blocks, and negotiates over one block at a time going down the ordered list. As the first iteration involves exchanging information

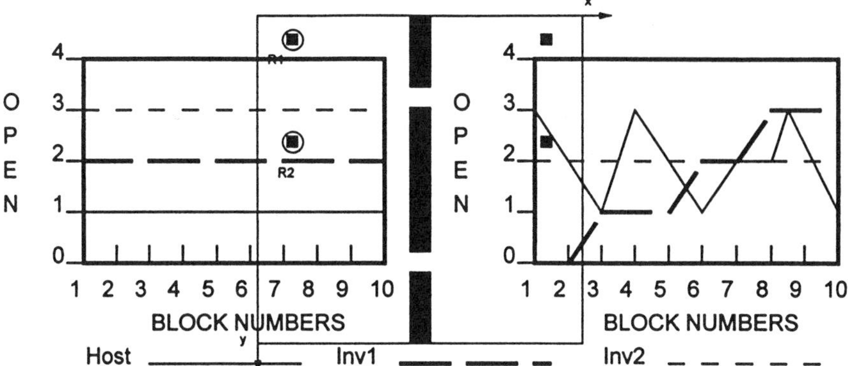

FIG. 3.3. Some example density profile characteristics. Three participants in the meeting, with indicated number of OPEN intervals for each of the time blocks indicated.

about the internal nodes of the abstraction hierarchy, meetings can only be scheduled starting from the second iteration only.

Assuming meetings cannot straddle blocks, there are four intervals in each block that could have accommodated the meeting if the calendars were empty. So, the constant K in the LE equation, and terms $a(l,x)$ $\forall x \in \{1, \ldots, 10\}$ in the H equation, are equal to 4. The n_x and the $f_i(l,x)$ terms are obtained from the DPCs.

Consider the following two cases (for more details, see Sen & Durfee, 1994a). In the case of the first set of DPCs, assume that the host has the curve labeled DPC1, with one interval open per block. In this case, the expected number of iterations to schedule the new meeting given the LE strategy (when announcing the single *best* or the three *good* intervals) can be contrasted with the H strategy. In this case, the LE strategy with either announcement strategy is expected to be less costly than the H strategy (Table 3.1). Note, however, that the DPCs in this case are nice and level—the kind of DPCs that arise from the even meeting distribution attained by the H strategy. Thus, whereas these DPCs indicate the H strategy has been in use, the quantitative cost predictions indicate that a shift over to the LE strategy is in order.

The second case presents a contrary example. The second set of DPCs is much less uniform, as would be expected if the schedulers had been using the LE strategy. In this case, if we compare the expected cost (number of iterations) of using the LE strategy with that of the H strategy, we see that switching to the H strategy is expected to yield a considerable savings (Table 3.1).

Finally, let us revisit the notion of privacy. The analysis that we just presented captures a subset of the strategies and performance metrics that are more generally of interest (see Sen & Durfee, 1994a, for a fuller discussion).

TABLE 3.1
Expected Iterations for Scheduling the Meeting

Case	*LE (best)*	*LE (good)*	*H*
Case1	2.575	1.294	3.575
Case2	10.68	3.836	2.193

For the case of privacy, the amount of information revealed is related to the number of iterations and the announcement strategy for the linear announcement cases. Thus, the expected number of intervals that the host reveals in LE(best) equals the number of iterations, while the intervals for LE(good) is the number of iterations times the number of intervals proposed per iteration (in our Example, 3). Thus, not surprisingly, LE(best) retains more privacy than LE(good) because it reveals information more slowly—leading to more time spent iterating. Choosing among these strategies thus depends on the relative importance of privacy versus the delays and costs associated with more iterations. The hierarchical strategy is less easily comparable, because the first iteration in H exposes information about larger portions of the agents' calendars, albeit at an abstract level such that others still will not know precisely when another agent is free. So, for Case 2 in Table 3.1, deciding whether H preserves privacy better than other strategies depends on the degree to which the abstract exposure is of concern. Certainly, H involves many fewer precise intervals being revealed.

Summary

In this section, we have briefly described how an application domain can be modeled such that a surrogate agent can make quantitatively based decisions about adapting its strategy, even if the agent's associated user is not available to train it. This kind of analysis can form the basis for developing trustable surrogate agents that can be adaptive over a variety of environmental and performance needs. Our ongoing work in this area includes developing design strategies for such agents, with particular emphasis on the intertwined adaptive design decisions about the various strategies that a meeting scheduling agent can employ (see Sen & Durfee, 1994a).

COMMITMENTS TO MODELS

The DMS domain demonstrated how, during its activity on behalf of a user, an agent might desire to modify the strategies (or behaviors) it employs. In the DMS domain, for example, being able to change between hierarchical (H) and linear early (LE) strategies for selecting proposed meeting times allows an agent to maximize its chances of success while minimizing its costs as its schedule evolves. But some of the benefits of a strategy might only be accrued if an agent can depend on the strategy choices of others. For example, if an agent receives a counterproposal from another agent that is known to be employing the LE strategy, then it knows that it is useless to propose any time intervals earlier than the counter proposal (those intervals must not be free for the other agent, or it would have proposed them). In fact, if a group of agents were to commit to using the LE bias, then they all might take advantage of this to schedule their meetings more efficiently. But, if an agent can unilaterally change its bias, these advantages might not be achieved.

Obviously, there are some things about another agent that are important to know, and other things that are less important. In the DMS domain, a strong amount of cooperation is expected: All participants want to successfully schedule a meeting. Moreover, agreement of fairly precise details are needed (although it is possible to arrange a meeting in terms of "I'll look for you in the lab tomorrow afternoon," such arrangements introduce inefficiencies in searching and context switching for the agents). Many kinds of coordination might require much less specific commitment on the part of the agents. For example, mobile agents who wish to avoid collision need to make commitments, but possibly commitments about where they will *not* be, rather than where they will be, at particular times.

Commitments of a less detailed nature not only avoid overcommitment in the face of uncertainty for an agent, but they are often longer lived as well, meaning that the overhead of coordinating—of finding strategies/behaviors that are sufficiently compatible—need be done less often. The tradeoffs between the precision, flexibility, cost, and longevity of different levels of commitment have led to a variety of models in the multiagent systems literature, including: compiled conventions and social laws (Dijkstra, 1965; Hoare, 1978; Shoham & Tennenholtz, 1992); agent/module specifications (Nii, 1986); organizational structuring (Corkill & Lesser, 1983); distributed planning/scheduling (Durfee & Lesser, 1991; Ephrati & Rosenschein, 1994); contracting (Smith, 1980); and observation (Huber & Durfee, 1995; Tambe, 1995). (For a more complete discussion of these various kinds of models, see Durfee, Damouth, Huber, Montgomery, & Sen, 1994.)

None of these modeling strategies is clearly better than the others. Although, in our ordering, the models become increasingly precise and timely (relevant to the current situation), they also may become increasingly incomplete, uncertain, or inconsistent. What constitutes an appropriate model of another agent depends on how that model will be used, and on what needs to be stressed in the model. In essence, an agent's model of another represents expectations about that other agent. Is it important that the expectations abstractly describe the other agent over a long period of time (perhaps forever), or is it more important to have very specific predictions about the immediate future? The answer to this question depends on how the agents are interacting. For example, in DMS, the model was very much like the contracting model: An agent knew exactly about the availability of a particular interval for another, but that did not give it insight about other intervals, and the knowledge it had could be short-lived as other agents try to schedule with it as well. Moreover, the specific model in the DMS domain can represent a commitment that the agent generating the model—saying "I am free at this particular time"—might prefer not making. So how an agent presents itself to others in the model it projects can impact its predictability and flexibility.

In short, effective coordination usually implies that an agent know just enough about others to achieve its goals (such as avoiding conflict) without knowing any more (which can waste memory, computation, and communication). Similarly, an agent should only make the most minimal commitments it can to others to achieve the coordination, so as to retain as much flexibility for itself as possible.

Coordination Search

A fundamental objective of developing a theory of coordination is that the theory should support the process of determining the right level of modeling that agents should use to maximize performance while minimizing overhead. This determination is typically only found through search: The interacting agents in a society must find, often with many failed attempts, the appropriate level of modeling and coordination reasoning to get the benefits of coordination without incurring excessive costs. For example, when there were very few automobiles on the road, interactions among them were infrequent enough, and the characteristics of the roads were varied enough, that allowing drivers to develop models of each other and negotiate over the road made sense. As encounters increased and roadways became more uniform, coordinating interactions on a case-by-case basis became less efficient compared to enacting traffic laws. In a sense, the traffic laws generalized and codified how past encounters had been negotiated.

We turn shortly to an example of coordination search for controlling traffic in a simple robotics environment. First, however, let us consider the components of coordination search more abstractly. The need to represent actions and interactions at different levels of generality leads to the first abstract element of a framework for viewing coordination as distributed search:

Element 1: The ability to model yourself, others, and collections of agents as a hierarchy of more or less abstracted behaviors.

What this means is that an agent must be capable of representing itself—its goals, plans, expectations, and so on—in many different ways simultaneously. A courier, for example, represents itself as delivering packages overnight to its customers without giving details of the routes that packages will travel. At the same time, a courier also might give a more detailed model of package movement needs when contracting with an airline to carry packages.

Next, in order to specify information about interactions, it is necessary that an agent be able to identify relationships among the activities (goals, plans, etc.) of agents, and the (dis)utilities of those related activities:

Element 2: The ability to compare models to identify relationships and measure their desirability.

Of course, detailed comparisons and measures of desirability are going to be very domain dependent; we see an example with the robot delivery task shortly. But the quality of the comparisons and measures depends on what level of abstraction they are (or can be) seen. Finding the right level of abstraction to find, evaluate, and modify relationships requires:

Element 3: The ability to search through a space of models, typically using communication protocols because the space will be distributed among agents, to find relationships at the right level of detail.

And once relationships are found, the agents need the ability to modify those relationships. For example, if the anticipated activities of two drivers leads to a collision relationship, the drivers generally should search for alternative activities with less dire interactions, such as having one driver delayed until the other passes by. This means the agents need:

Element 4: The ability to locally search for modifications of models at the right level of detail to change relationships.

Finally, the search process itself represents actions that the agents are taking, and they cannot afford to necessarily search for all possible abstractions, relationships, and alternatives. What they need is:

Element 5: The ability to apply (often heuristic) control knowledge to avoid unnecessary work/overhead in the local and distributed search process.

Elsewhere, we have argued that viewing coordination as a search in a hierarchical space allows us to treat previously distinct coordination techniques, such as organizational self-design, multiagent planning, and distributed resource scheduling, in a uniform way (Durfee, 1993; Durfee & Lesser, 1991).

Search Reduction in Hierarchical Distributed Problem Solving

Thinking of the coordination process as a distributed search allows us to put into perspective some of the ideas regarding models and commitment. We said before that cost-effective coordination implies that an agent have models of others only to the degree of detail necessary to coordinate with them successfully. Thus, part of the distributed search that agents must engage in is a search for the right level of detail to model each other.

To realize such a search process, our research has investigated the use of a protocol for coordination when agents have hierarchical representations of their behaviors. The basic idea is simple. When an agent encounters one or more other agents with which it is unfamiliar, the agents should engage in a dialogue to coordinate adequately. They begin by exchanging very abstract models of their behavior. This might suffice to discover that the agents, in fact, have no need to coordinate at all: They know enough about each other to know that they do not need to coordinate. If, at an abstract level, it appears there could be reason to coordinate, they can exchange selected elaborations of their abstract model, only including information that is expected to be relevant. They can keep doing this kind of exchange, providing more detailed and narrow modeling information, until they have sufficient models to coordinate their decisions.

This kind of hierarchical protocol was seen in the meeting scheduling application, where agents could incrementally narrow down possible meeting times, only concentrating on areas of their calendars that were most promising. However, notice that the goal of distributed meeting scheduling required the agents to eventually get down to the level of talking about specific time intervals. This need not be the case for all types of coordination. Our hierarchical protocol, in fact, is based on the assumption that it might often be the case that agents break off elaborating their models in favor of resolving conflicts at an abstract, inexact level.

For example, we have been investigating the domain of multiple mobile robots that share a common workspace (see also the CTCT-supported work of Arkin for a similar application domain). Each has its own goals (deliveries to make) and is capable of achieving them alone. However, to succeed, a robot must avoid colliding with other robots. Thus, the process of coordinating need not lead to a detailed plan of where each robot is at every instant of time. Instead, it need only arrive at a set of commitments that assure that collisions will be avoided.

For example, consider the two-robot case shown in Fig. 3.4. Each robot has multiple packages to take from its source location (in left room) to its destination (in right room). The shortest route for both robots is through the upper doorway, but there is another doorway that is more distant. How should they coordinate?

If they begin with their most abstract views, each sees that the other wants to use the doorway for the foreseeable future, and this could lead them to collide at the door. At this level of detail, they could coordinate: If Robot 2 does all of its deliveries through the distant door, collision avoidance is assured (Fig. 3.5). This is at a price, of course, as there might be many times when

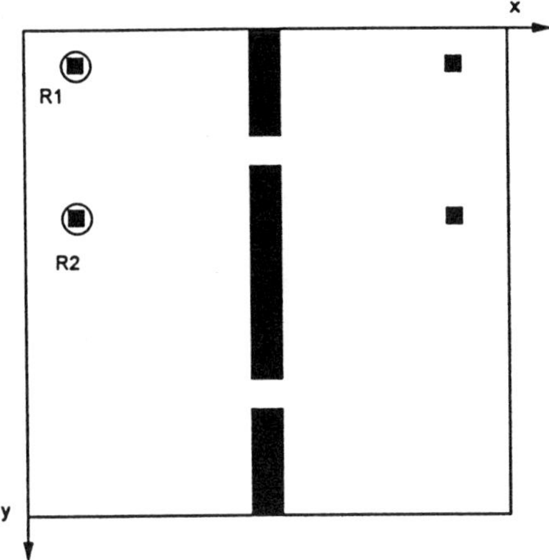

FIG. 3.4. Two robots delivering color-coded objects from source (left room) to destination (right room).

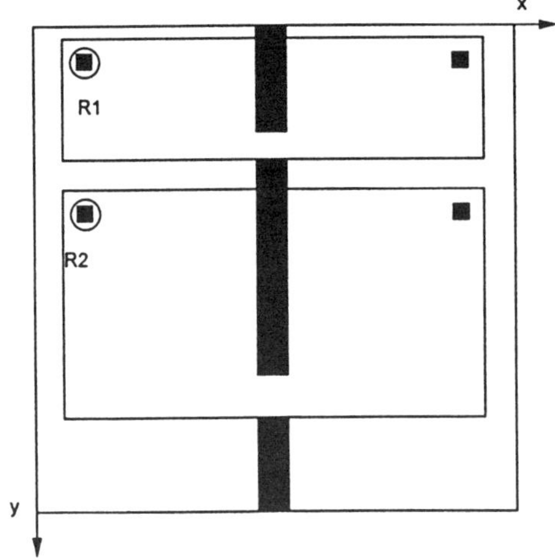

FIG. 3.5. Robots permanently divide area to avoid collisions.

Robot 2 could have safely used the closer door (and thus made its deliveries more efficiently), but such opportunities will not be discovered.

So, perhaps the robots should coordinate over individual deliveries. Figure 3.6 shows the possible conflict over their first delivery, where the area around the door is suspect during the delivery time. At this level, they could resolve the conflict. They could commit to behaviors that they have moved

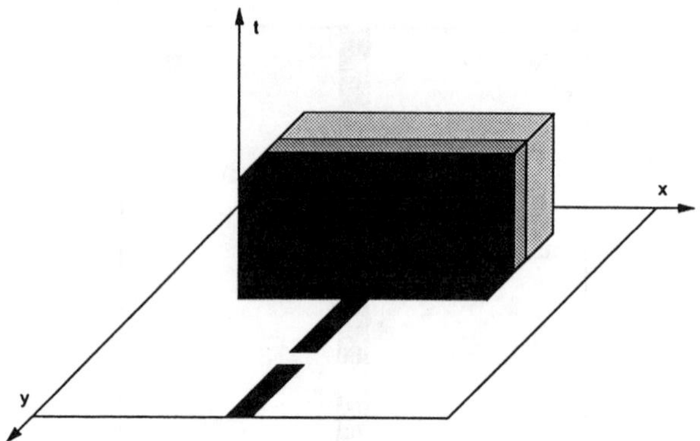

FIG. 3.6. Spatiotemporal volumes with overlap for first deliveries.

apart spatially (Fig. 3.7) as Robot 2 again uses the distant door, or they could move their behaviors apart temporally (Fig. 3.8) Robot 2 waits until Robot 1 is done before beginning its activity.

By communicating at even deeper levels of detail, the robots could break their behaviors into portions constituting moving to the door, through the door, and beyond the door. Doing so will not change the spatial approach to removing the conflict, but it can improve the temporal solution (Fig. 3.9), where now Robot 2 waits until Robot 1 has made it through the door and then begins. Thus, there is some amount of parallel activity. Finally, they could communicate at a very detailed level about where they will be and when, such that they can both begin moving and Robot 2 waits, at the last second, for Robot 1 to go through the door first. The time to complete both deliveries is much shorter because the robots are essentially working in par-

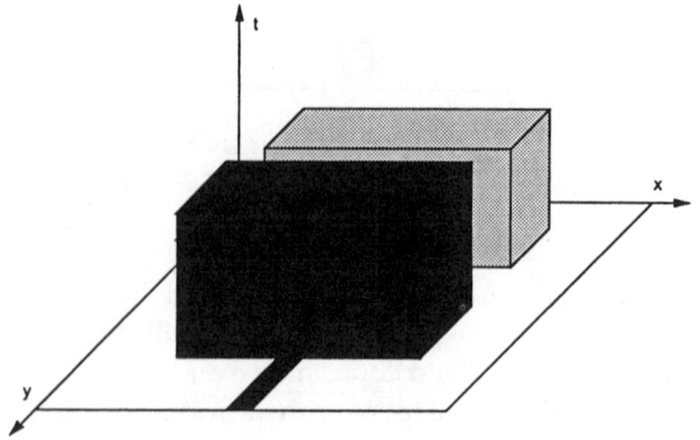

FIG. 3.7. Conflict removed by changing spatial behavior.

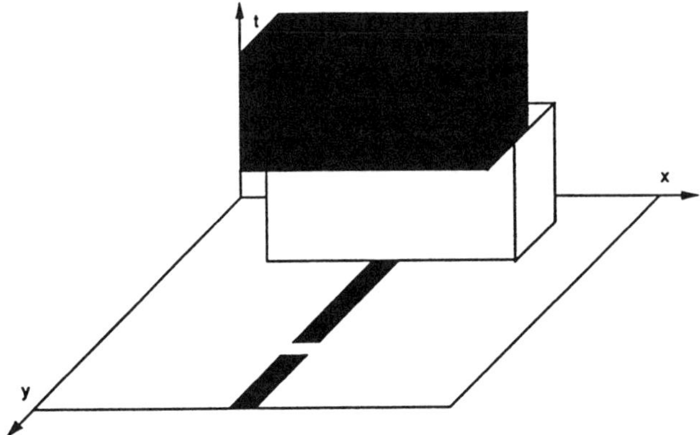

FIG. 3.8. Conflict removed by changing temporal aspects of a behavior.

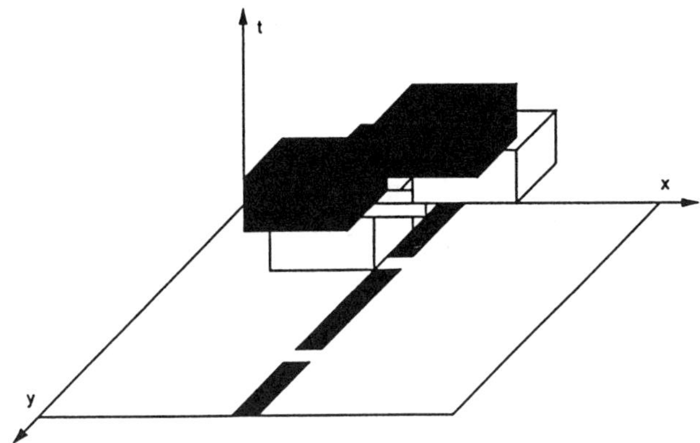

FIG. 3.9. Temporal conflict resolution at an intermediate level of detail.

allel. But is this the best method for coordination? The amount of information exchanged to get to this solution is quite high. Moreover, the solution commits robots to being in certain places at certain times, which they might have trouble living up to. Perhaps coordination at more abstract levels would be more cost effective and flexible!

Our simulation experiments have investigated these tradeoffs (Durfee & Lesser, 1991), and we do not detail them here. Instead, let us consider more analytically the role of abstraction in a distributed search to gain insights from that. Knoblock (1991) and Korf (1987) have looked at how the use of abstraction can, in principle, reduce search within an agent from exponential to linear complexity by dividing a large problem into a number of smaller problems. Now let us consider what happens when the smaller problems can be solved by different agents (see Montgomery, & Durfee, 1993, for more detailed derivations of the results summarized here).

Consider a problem (such as a planning problem) that has a solution length (such as the number of plan steps in the solution plan) of n. Let us say that there is an abstraction hierarchy of height l, where the first abstraction level divides the initial problem of length n into n/k subproblems of length k. At each abstraction level above, k subproblems are abstracted into one subproblem of length k, until the top level is reached, at which point there is one problem left of length $\frac{n}{k^{l-1}}$. If each problem is solved sequentially, then the overall complexity is: $f(\frac{n}{k^{l-1}}) + \frac{n}{k^{l-1}} f(k) + \frac{n}{k^{l-2}} f(k) + \cdots + \frac{n}{k} f(n)$. If we assume that each subproblem is solved by a separate agent, then after the most abstract problem is solved, its $\frac{n}{k^{l-1}}$ subproblems can be solved in parallel, after which the next $\frac{n}{k^{l-2}}$ subproblems can be solved in parallel, and so on. In effect, all the coefficients in the complexity expression are eliminated, giving: $f(\frac{n}{k^{l-1}}) + (l-1)f(k)$. Since k is assumed constant for a given problem space, and since $l = \log_k n$, this yields a complexity which is $O(\log_k n)$. Therefore, concurrent processing can potentially reduce an exponential search problem to logarithmic complexity.

Of course, this analysis is based on some pretty strong assumptions, which are satisfied in certain simple problems (such as the Towers of Hanoi, Montgomery & Durfee, 1993), but which may not be met in other problems. Yet, even though the logarithmic speedup is in general beyond reach, the speedup from parallelism thanks to abstraction can result in significant practical improvements in coordination performance.

For example, let us once again consider the domain of mobile robots performing deliveries. As the number of robots grows, so does the complexity of coordinating them. For example, given the hierarchical protocol previously described, coordinating 20 robots could require all 20 to share with each other their abstract behaviors, and then incrementally elaborating downward until they resolve all the conflicts. This can be extremely time consuming, and the combinatorics of detecting and resolving the conflicts can make such an approach infeasible.

Rather than abandoning the notion of using abstractions within a protocol, however, a useful method for dealing with such larger problems is to extend the application of abstraction. Specifically, consider what happens if the 20 agents coalesce into several teams, such as four teams of 5. Now, if each team "captain" abstractly represents the behaviors of its team, the captains can resolve interteam conflicts, while intrateam conflicts can be resolved in parallel within the teams.

Our empirical studies have shown that the use of higher level "team" abstractions can significantly improve coordination among larger numbers of agents without introducing excessive additional overhead (Montgomery

& Durfee, 1993). This is true despite the fact that many of the assumptions for our more formal analysis do not hold in this case. Among these are that the delivery tasks (randomly) assigned to different teams are generally not of equal difficulty, and that the "downward refinement property" (Bacchus & Yang, 1991) generally does not hold because information must flow both up (a team captain must generate an abstraction of the team based on information from the team members) and down (after negotiating with other captains, a team captain must supply team members with the commitments that have been agreed to).

Knowledge-Based Abstraction

As we have seen, the use of abstraction can be critical for efficiently searching for coordinated behaviors. If adjacent levels of abstraction in a hierarchical protocol provide nearly the same amount of detail, then the protocol will lead to excessive overhead because too many rounds of communication will be needed. On the other hand, if the levels are too far apart, then agents might not have just the right level of abstraction to optimally model each other. Decisions about how to construct the abstraction hierarchy thus have important ramifications to the costs and benefits of coordination search.

In the delivery domain, for example, our early experiments were based on decomposing delivery paths based on the path generation algorithm. This algorithm worked by line of sight, such that the level of abstraction between the entire delivery and the individual robot movements was comprised of a series of movement vectors. For many of our experiments, this worked well, because usually we were talking about robots moving through doors such that they approached the door, and left the door, on an angle, resulting in the three "to the door, through the door, beyond the door" components of the plan. However, when delivery sources and destinations line up straight through the door, or when robots are doing deliveries in a big open room, the "line-of-sight" method yields an abstraction that is no different from that of the full delivery. That is, the "intermediate" level of the abstraction hierarchy is identical to the most abstract level, and thus (as our experiments showed) the gap between the intermediate and the most detailed levels was too large, and expensive coordination resulted.

The decomposition of a delivery into portions such as "to the door, through the door, beyond the door" should not be an artifact of the path planning algorithm. Rooms and doorways are important features of an indoor spatial environment, as are corridors and even "corners" of large rooms. We thus considered how explicitly encoding the hierarchical structure of a spatial region could be used by our hierarchical protocol. Our empirical results (described in Durfee, Damouth, et al., 1994) illustrated that, indeed, having explicit knowledge to guide the development of abstractions could overcome the previously seen limitations of our approach. They allowed resolution of conflicts at more appropriate levels than were possible before, and they provided decomposition knowledge that focused the exchange of more detailed information when that was desired. Thus, an important future avenue of research is to identify methods for automating the construction of explicit abstraction knowledge; we have shown that the hand-crafted knowledge that we supplied for the indoor delivery application works well. Our results in the domain of distributed meeting scheduling using a hierarchy of abstractions over time also showed the promise of this approach. But applying these techniques to arbitrary domains requires new methods for generating such knowledge.

More generally, our research in the construction and exchange of agent models at varying levels of abstraction has helped put in concrete, computational terms the conceptual arguments about the costs and benefits of building, using, and committing to different agent models as outlined in the beginning of this section. Much work remains in various facets, including the development of abstraction hierarchies for the models, improving on the metrics for evaluating coordination quality, and extending the repertoire of local search methods and distributed search protocols. Pursuing this last avenue requires a deeper understanding of the building blocks of protocols, and the motivations for constructing different kinds of protocols.

TOWARD EMERGING PROTOCOLS AMONG AUTONOMOUS AGENTS

Understanding how protocols emerge among agents which are, by nature, self-interested is an ongoing concern. Articulating the "first principles" of protocol construction is important when developing artificial agents, because the arsenal of protocols that we might provide them with might still not suffice for novel multiagent situations. Rather than falling back on standard, but inappropriate, protocols, we should provide agents with the ability to devise communication strategies on the fly, and these strategies might lead to new protocols.

Our efforts along this front have begun by considering a single, rational agent that is trying to choose its next action to take in a multiagent world. Obviously, it should choose the action that it expects will be most to its benefit, but the consequences of its actions (the payoffs) could well depend on the actions that other agents might be taking at the same time. Thus, to choose its best action, an agent should try to predict the actions of others. Of course, if the others are also supposedly rational, then they will be going through the same process. An agent thus needs to think about what the other agents expect the other agents to do. In fact, this nesting could continue on, into deeper recursively nested models of the decision situations that agents believe the others face.

We have developed methods for representing and solving such nested models, called the Recursive Modeling Method (RMM; Gmytrasiewicz & Durfee, 1993, 1995). Rather than go through the details of RMM here, we focus on one aspect of RMM, namely, RMM's ability to allow an agent to compute the expected utility of sending a message. A message contains information, and the information can change the state of knowledge of a recipient. In considering whether to send a message, therefore, a speaker should model the expected effects that the message will have on the hearer. In RMM, this amounts to the expected changes in the nested models of agents, which in turn could affect the likely choice of actions of the hearer. A speaker will consider how the change in the hearer's likely actions would impact its own (the speaker's) expected payoffs. If the expected payoffs rise, the message could be sent; the expected utility of the message is precisely the difference between the expected payoff after sending the message and the expected payoff before sending the message.

This works fine for individual messages, but can it explain dialogues between agents? For example, consider the simple dialogue of one agent asking a question, and another agent answering the question. The seemingly simple protocol rule of "respond to a question with an answer" is actually not all that simple when agent autonomy is considered. Why should an agent answer a question? What is in it for the agent?

Using RMM, we have shown how assigning cost to communication and computation can cause an agent that would otherwise share particular information to refrain from doing so if it believes that a hearer might already know the information (Durfee, Gmytrasiewicz, & Rosenschein, 1994). Thus, asking a question amounts to an "admission of ignorance" directed toward an agent that the question-asker believes will see utility in supplying the desired information. This not only requires the question-asker to develop a nested model of the potential answerer, but also means that the question-asker must assign utility to the outcome of the complete dialogue (in this case the two messages) rather than to a single message.

Of course, such reasoning about nested models of agents' decision-making situations, especially across a series of messages, can be quite costly. This is why it should only be done when the pre-established protocols no longer seem suitable. After performing the recursive reasoning about communication, moreover, an agent could cache the result and use feedback from the environment to determine whether, in fact, it was a good decision. By generalizing the circumstances that triggered the message dialogue, moreover, the agent(s) could over time construct a new protocol. An open problem is taking these preliminary ideas and investigating whether, in fact, they can lead to the emergence of protocols.

CONCLUSIONS

In this chapter, we have outlined the conceptual framework for our work on collaboration technology and, more centrally, coordination theory, and we have grounded that framework in terms of describing computational mechanisms that embody aspects of it. For the most part, we have kept to a fairly high level of discussion, pointing to (rather than presenting) the more detailed technical treatments in favor of trying to illuminate the broader problems and solution strategies in this niche of coordination theory. Our understanding of how coordination is accomplished in dynamic systems comprised of complex agents is still far from complete, and the computational embodiment of the understanding we have so far seems to raise more questions than it answers. Nonetheless, our efforts have shown that it is possible to develop quantitative models of multiagent application domains that allow principled decisions about strategies to be made by surrogate agents. As surrogate agents need to interact in more diverse ways with different kinds of other agents, moreover, the kinds of information they should exchange, and the different commitments they should make, will require them to be much more flexible about modeling themselves and others. Abstraction becomes crucial, therefore, when agents engage in a distributed search for sufficiently coordinated behaviors. The rules for conducting this search, in terms of how abstractions are formulated and how information is passed, are currently rather primitive, but the foundation is in place for a wider variety of mechanisms to be explored, including exploring how new protocols and other rules of interaction might emerge for new applications.

ACKNOWLEDGMENTS

A number of colleagues have influenced the work reported here, and we gratefully acknowledge their input, including input from the various CTCT workshops, and colleagues such as Victor Lesser, Jeffrey Rosenschein, and Keith Decker. Ideas in this chapter have appeared before (Durfee, Damouth, et al., 1994; Sen & Durfee, 1994a).

This research has been sponsored, in part, by the National Science Foundation under Coordination Theory and Collaboration Technology grant IRI-9015423, under grant IRI-9010645, and under a Presidential Young Investigator Award IRI-9158473.

REFERENCES

Agre, P. E., & Chapman, D. (Sept. 1988). *What are plans for?* Technical Report AI Memo 1050, MIT. ftp://publications.ai.mit.edu/ai-publications/1000-1499/AIM-1050A.ps

Bacchus, F., & Yang, Q. (August 1991). The downward refinement property. In *Proceedings of the Twelfth International Joint Conference on Artificial Intelligence* (pp. 286–292), Sydney, Australia.

Conry, S. E., Kuwabara, K., Lesser, V. R., & Meyer, R. A. (Dec. 1991). Multistage negotiation for distributed constraint satisfaction. *IEEE Trans on Systems, Man, and Cybernetics, 21*(6), 1462–1477.

Corkill, D. D., & Lesser, V. R. (August 1983). The use of meta-level control for coordination in a distributed problem solving network. In *Proceedings of the Eighth International Joint Conference on Artificial Intelligence* (pp. 748–756), Karlsrugh, Germany.

Dijkstra, E. W. (Sept. 1965). Solution of a problem in concurrent programming control. *Communications of the ACM, 8*(5), 569.

Durfee, E. H., & Lesser V. R. (Sept. 1991). Partial global planning: A coordination framework for distributed hypothesis formation. *IEEE Trans. on Systems, Man, and Cybernetics, 21*(5), 1167–1183.

Durfee, E. H., & Montgomery, T. A. (Dec. 1991). Coordination as distributed search in a hierarchical behavior space. *IEEE Transactions on Systems, Man, and Cybernetics, 21*(6), 1363–1378.

Durfee, E. H. (1993). Organisations, plans, and schedules: An interdisciplinary perspective on coordinating AI systems. *Journal of Intelligent Systems* (Special Issue on the Social Context of Intelligent Systems), *3*(2–4).

Durfee, E. H., Damouth, D., Huber, M., Montgomery, T. A., & Sen, S. (1994). The search for coordination: Knowledge-guided abstraction and search in a hierarchical behavior space. In C. Castelfranchi & E. Werner (Eds.), *Artificial social systems* (pp. 187–206). New York: Springer-Verlag.

Durfee, E. H., Gmytrasiewicz, P. J., & Rosenschein, J. S. (July 1994). The utility of embedded communications: Toward the emergence of protocols. In *Proceedings of the Thirteenth International Distributed Artificial Intelligence Workshop* (pp. 85–93), Seattle, WA.

Ephrati, E., & Rosenschein, J. S. (July 1994). Divide and conquer in multi-agent planning. In *Proceedings of the Twelfth National Conference on Artificial Intelligence* (pp. 375–380), Seattle, WA.

Gmytrasiewicz, P. J., & Durfee, E. H. (1993). Toward a theory of honesty and trust among communicating autonomous agents. *Group Decision and Negotiation, 2*, 237–258 (Special issue on Distributed Artificial Intelligence).

Gmytrasiewicz, P. J., & Durfee, E. H. (June 1995). A rigorous, operational formalization of recursive modeling. In *Proceedings of the International Conference on Multi-Agent Systems* (pp. 125–132), San Francisco, CA.

Hoare, C. A. R. (August 1978). Communicating sequential processes. *Communications of the ACM, 21*(8), 666–667.

Huber, M. J., & Durfee, E. H. (June 1995). Deciding when to commit to action during observation-based coordination. In *Proceedings of the International Conference on Multi-Agent Systems* (pp. 163–169), San Francisco, CA.

Johansen, R. (1988). *Groupware: Computer support for business teams*. New York: Free Press.

Knoblock, C. A. (July 1991). Search reduction in hierarchical problem solving. In *Proceedings of the Ninth National Conference on Artificial Intelligence*, Anaheim, CA.

Korf, R. E. (1987). Planning as search: A qualitative approach. *Artificial Intelligence, 33*(1), 65–88.

Maes, P. (1994). Agents that reduce work and information overload. *Communications of the ACM, 37*(7), 30–40.

Malone, T. W., Grant, K. R., Turbak, F. A., Brobst, S. A., & Cohen, M. D. (1987). Intelligent information-sharing systems. *Communications of the ACM, 30*(5), 390–402.

Mitchell, T., Caruana, R., Freitag, D., McDermott, J., & Zabowski, D. (1994). Experience with a learning personal assistant. *Communications of the ACM, 37*(7), 80–91.

Montgomery, T. A., & Durfee, E. H. (1993). Search reduction in hierarchical distributed problem solving. *Group Decision and Negotiation, 2*, 301–317 (Special issue on Distributed Artificial Intelligence).

Nii, H. P. (Summer 1986). Blackboard systems: The blackboard model of problem solving and the evolution of blackboard architectures. *AI Magazine, 7*(2), 38–53.

Sen, S., & Durfee, E. H. (November 1991). A formal study of distributed meeting scheduling: Preliminary results. In *ACM Conference on Organizational Computing Systems* (pp. 55–68), Atlanta, GA.

Sen, S., & Durfee, E. H. (February 1992). A formal analysis of communication and commitment in distributed meeting scheduling. In *Working Papers of the 11th International Workshop on Distributed Artificial Intelligence* (pp. 333–342), Glen Arbor, MI.

Sen, S. (October 1993). *Predicting tradeoffs in contract-based distributed scheduling*. Doctoral thesis, University of Michigan.

Sen, S., & Durfee, E. H. (March 1994a). On the design of an adaptive meeting scheduler. In *Proceedings of the Tenth IEEE Conference on AI Applications*, San Antonio, TX.

Sen, S., & Durfee, E. H. (1994b). The role of commitment in cooperative negotiation. *International Journal of Intelligent and Cooperative Information Systems, 3*(1), 67–81.

Shoham, Y., & Tennenholtz, M. (July 1992). On the synthesis of useful social laws for artificial agent societies (preliminary report). In *Proceedings of the Tenth National Conference on Artificial Intelligence*, San Jose, CA.

Smith, R. G. (Dec. 1980). The contract net protocol. *IEEE Transactions on Computers, 29*(12), 1104–1113.

Tambe, M. (June 1995). Recursive agent and agent-group tracking in a real-time dynamic environment. In *Proceedings of the International Conference on Multi-Agent Systems* (pp. 368–375), San Francisco, CA.

CHAPTER

4

Strategic Negotiation in Multiagent Environments

Sarit Kraus
Bar Ilan University, Ramat Gan
University of Maryland, College Park

Jonathan Wilkenfeld
University of Maryland, College Park

This chapter reports on ongoing work in the development of a strategic model of negotiation. The model is applied to a range of environments in which negotiation can be utilized to resolve conflicts in two domains: access to resources, and cooperative task performance. These situations include both intelligent agents in multiagent environments, and human applications in multilateral crisis situations. Our focus on Distributed Artificial Intelligence (DAI) has facilitated the joining of two usually distinct areas: the development of autonomous agents in computer science, and crisis bargaining in decision science/political science. In both cases, negotiations are employed in situations where time is critical to some or all parties, resources are scarce, and tasks may require cooperative behavior. The significance of this work lies in its ability to provide a method whereby time spent on negotiation among the agents is minimized, and agreements involving mutual benefit are assured.

The work reported here represents progress made over 5 years by a computer scientist and a political scientist, whose collaborative work has been very much in the tradition of the initiative on Coordination Theory and Collaborative Technology of the National Science Foundation. This interdisciplinary collaboration has resulted in new insights in both realms, in ways which would not have been possible within the confines of single disciplines.

The discussion begins with a presentation of the strategic model of negotiation. This is followed by a discussion of several applications of the model in both robotics and human environments. We conclude with a review of the relevant literature and compare it with our approach.

I. STRATEGIC MODEL OF NEGOTIATION

The strategic model of negotiation is a modification of Rubinstein's Alternative Offers model (Rubinstein, 1982, 1985). We utilize modified definitions from Kraus, Wilkenfeld, and Zlotkin (1995).[1] We assume here that there is a set of n agents denoted by $\mathcal{A}$ that negotiates the division of M units of a resource. We present a formal definition of an agreement.

Definition 1 Agreement. *An* agreement *is a tuple* $(s_1, \ldots, s_n)$, *where* $s_i \in$ *IN and* $s_1 + \ldots + s_n = M$. s_i *is agent i's portion of the resource or task.*

The negotiation procedure is as follows. The agents can take actions only at certain times in the ordered set $\mathcal{T} = \{0, 1, 2 \ldots\}$. In each period $t \in \mathcal{T}$ one of the agents, say i, proposes an agreement to one of the other agents. That agent (j) either accepts the offer (chooses Yes) or rejects it (chooses No), or opts out of the negotiation (chooses Opt). The other agents which neither received nor made an offer may opt out of the negotiation (chooses Opt), or they can choose not to do anything (chooses Nop). We require that the agents always make offers in the same order, and an agent's negotiation strategy in general is any function from the history of the negotiations to its next move.

We assume that each agent has preferences or utility functions (denoted by U) over agreements reached at various points in time, and for opting out at various points in time. The *time preferences* and the preferences between agreements and opting out are the driving force of the model. In situations of incomplete information, we will assume that there is a finite set of agent types characterized by their capabilities (e.g., their disk space, computational power, payment agreements). These characterizations produce a different utility function for each type of agent. We also assume that in such situations each agent has some probabilistic beliefs about the other agents' types. Thus, although the set of possible types of agents is known, and the utility function of each type is also known, the agent has incomplete information about the precise type of the other agent(s).

In order to find strategies that contribute to the stability of the environment, we use different notions of equilibrium. If there is full information, we employ the notion of (subgame) perfect equilibrium (P.E.) (see Rubinstein, 1982; Selten, 1975) which requires that the agents' strategies induce a Nash

---

[1]See Osborne and Rubinstein (1990) for a detailed review of the bargaining game of Alternative Offers.

equilibrium[2] at any stage of the negotiation. That is, in each stage of the negotiation, assuming that an agent follows the P.E. strategy, the other agent has no strategy which is better than to follow its own P.E. strategy. Subgame perfect equilibrium is essentially a backward induction argument, using the rationality of agents at each stage of the game to decide what a good choice is and then rolling backward (Tan & Werlang, 1988). So, if there is a (unique) perfect equilibrium, and if it is known that an agent is designed to use this strategy, no agent will prefer to use a strategy other than this one in each stage of the negotiations.

When there is incomplete information, there is no proper subgame. In such situations we use the concept of *sequential equilibrium* (S.E.) instead (Kreps & Wilson, 1982). A sequential equilibrium includes a system of beliefs (Kraus et al., 1995), in addition to a profile of strategies (as in P.E.). At each negotiation step t, the strategy for agent i is optimal given its current belief (at step t) and its opponent's possible strategies in the S.E. Each agent's belief (about its opponent's type) is consistent with the history of the negotiation. That is, the agents' belief may change over time, but only consistent with the history. We assume that each agent in a negotiation interaction has an initial probability belief about its opponent's type.

The strategic model of negotiation has been developed as a way of reaching mutual benefit, while avoiding costly and time-consuming interactions that might increase the overhead of coordination. That is, we have provided a model in which agents can avoid spending too much time negotiating an agreement and therefore are better able to stick to a timetable for satisfying their goals.

In the process of developing and specifying the strategic model of negotiation, we have examined bilateral negotiation as well as multiagent negotiation, single encounters and multiple encounters, situations characterized by complete as well as incomplete information, and the differing impact of time on the payoffs of the participants (Kraus, 1997; Kraus & Wilkenfeld, 1993b; Kraus et al., 1995; Kraus & Zlotkin, 1992; Schwartz & Kraus, 1997). Although some combinations of these factors can result in minor delays, the model nevertheless reveals an important capacity for reaching agreement in early periods of the strategic negotiation. In all the situations that we consider the strategic-negotiation protocols that we suggest satisfy the following criteria: symmetrical distribution (no central unit or agent), simplicity (process simple and efficient), stability (distinguishable equilibrium point) and satisfiability or accessibility (access to the resource or task completed). If there is complete information, conflict is always avoided.

---

[2]A pair of strategies (σ, τ) is a Nash Equilibrium if, given τ, no strategy of Agent 1 results in an outcome that Agent 1 prefers to the outcome generated by (σ, τ) and similarly for Agent 2 given σ.

2. COOPERATION AMONG AUTOMATED AGENTS

We examine the problems of resource allocation and task distribution among autonomous agents which can benefit from sharing a common resource or distributing a set of common tasks.

2.1. The Resource Allocation Problem

The first situation we examine consists of agents that must share a joint resource; the resource can only be used by one agent at a time. Under these circumstances, an agreement is a schedule that divides usage of the resource among the agents.[3] It is desirable that all agents that need the resource will gain access to it.

Typical examples of joint resources include: communication lines, printers, disks, bridges, road junctions, fresh water, clean air, and so forth. Other work in the DAI community dealing with the resource allocation problem includes a multistage negotiation protocol that is useful for cooperatively resolving resource allocation conflicts arising in distributed networks of semi-autonomous problem solving nodes (Conry, Meyer, & Lesser, 1988; Kuwabara & Lesser, 1989); tradeoffs in resource allocation and real-time performance, with mechanisms for resource allocation based on the criticality of tasks (Lesser, Pavlin, & Durfee, 1988); resource allocation using specialist "sponsor" agents (Kornfeld & Hewitt, 1981); and resource allocation via resource pricing (Chandrasekn, 1981).

A particularly good example of a shared resource is a communication satellite, due to the high costs associated with its launching and continued maintenance. The only way a company may be able to afford access to such a resource is by sharing it with other companies. Even competing companies may find it mutually beneficial to participate in such a joint project.

When a common resource is to be shared, a coordination mechanism will be required to manage usage of the resource. Discussion of such a coordination mechanism should begin (and may even conclude) prior to discussion of other technical aspects of the joint project. There is always a cost associated with the elapsed time between when the agent needs the resource and when it actually gains access, and the cost will depend on the internal state of the agent (i.e., task load, disk space, and so on). In the following sections, we demonstrate the application of the strategic model of negotiation to the resource allocation problem in several different settings.

---

[3]Our model is also applicable in the case where the resource itself can actually be divided between the agents. This case does not differ significantly from the case where only the resource usage time can be divided.

2.1.1. One Agent Uses the Resource While the Other Waits for Access

We assume that there is one agent currently using a resource (A symbolizing "access"), and a second agent that also wants to use it (W symbolizing "waiting"). W wishes to gain access to the resource during the next M time periods. The agents begin a negotiation process on the re-division of the resource between them. A continues to use the resource as the negotiation proceeds.

We now present a number of assumptions concerning the utility functions of the agents. We denote A's utility function by U^A and W's by U^W. First we assume that the least preferred outcome for both agents is disagreement (Disagreement).[4]

A0. Disagreement is the worst outcome: For each $i \in \mathcal{A}$, $x \in \{\{S \cup \{Opt\}\} \times \mathcal{T}\}: U^i(x) > U^i(\text{Disagreement})$.

The next two conditions ($A1$), ($A2$) concern the behavior of the utility function U^i on agreements reached in different time periods. Condition ($A1$) requires that among agreements reached in the same period, Agent i prefers larger portions of the resource.

A1. The resource is valuable: For all $t \in \mathcal{T}$, $r, s \in S$ and $i \in \mathcal{A}$: $r_i > s_i \Rightarrow U^i((r, t)) > U^i((s, t))$.[5]

For agreements that are reached within the same time period, each agent prefers to get a larger portion of the resource.

The next assumption states that although time is valuable to W, A prefers to prolong the negotiation.

A2. Costs of agreements over time: Each Agent $i \in \{W, A\}$ has a number c_i such that: $\forall t_1, t_2 \in \mathcal{T}, s, \bar{s} \in S$, $U^i((s, t_1)) \geq U^i((\bar{s}, t_2))$ iff $(s_i + c_i t_1) \geq (\bar{s}_i + c_i t_2)$, where $c_W < 0$ and $c_A > 0$.

We assume that agent A gains over time ($c_A > 0$) and that Agent W loses over time ($c_W < 0$), that is, Agent W prefers to obtain any given number of units sooner rather than later, while Agent A prefers to obtain any given number of units later rather than sooner.

---

[4]In Kraus et al. (1995) we assume that for Agent A disagreement is the most preferred outcome. If negotiating is costly to A also, disagreement is the worst outcome also for A. The results of the negotiations when assumptions A1–A5 hold do not depend on A's attitude toward disagreement.

[5]For all $s \in S$ and $i \in \mathcal{A}$, s_i is Agent i's portion of the resource. Throughout the rest of the chapter, A's portion in an agreement is written first.

A3. Cost of opting out over time: for any $t \in \mathcal{T}$, $U^W((\text{Opt}, t)) > U^W((\text{Opt}, t+1))$ and $U^A((\text{Opt}, t)) < U^A((\text{Opt}, t+1))$.

W prefers opting out sooner rather than later, and A always prefers opting out later rather than sooner. This is because A gains over time while W loses over time. For this reason, A would *never* opt out. In the worst case, A would prefer for Agent W to opt out in the next period.

Even though Agent A is gaining over time, an agreement will be reached (after a finite number of periods). The reason for this is that Agent W can threaten to opt out at any given time. This threat is the driving force of the negotiation process toward an agreement. If there is some agreement s that A prefers at time t over W's opting out in the next period $t + 1$, then it may agree to s.

So the main factor that plays a role in reaching an agreement is the worst agreement for Agent W in a given period t which is still preferable to W than opting out in time period t. We will denote this agreement by $\hat{s}^{W,t} \in S$. If Agent A will not agree to such an agreement, its opponent has no other choice but to opt out.

Agent A's loss from opting out is greater than that of W. This is because A's session (of using the resource) is interrupted while in progress. This is stated in the following assumption.

A4. Range for Agreement: For every $t \in \mathcal{T}$ $U^W((\hat{s}^{W,t}, t)) > U^W((\hat{s}^{W,t+1}, t + 1))$, $U^W((\text{Opt}, t)) > U^W((\hat{s}^{W,t+1}, t + 1))$, and if $\hat{s}_A^{W,t} \geq 0$ then $U^A((\hat{s}^{W,t}, t)) > U^A((\text{Opt}, t + 1))$ and $U^A((\hat{s}^{W,t+1}, t + 1)) > U^A((\hat{s}^{W,t}, t))$.

If there are some agreements that Agent W prefers over opting out, then Agent A also prefers at least one of those agreements over W's opting out even in the next period. An additional assumption is necessary to ensure that an agreement is possible at least in the first period. That is, there is an agreement that both agents prefer over opting out.

A5. Possible agreement: For all $i,j \in \mathcal{A}$, $U^i((\hat{s}^{j,0}, 0)) \geq U^i((\hat{s}^{i,0}, 0))$
$\hat{s}^{i,0}$ is the worst agreement for Agent i in Period 0 which is still better than opting out.

We consider two cases. In the first case, an agent loses less per period while waiting than it can gain per period while using the resource. In the second situation, an agent loses more while waiting for the resource than it can gain while using the resource. For this second agent, sharing a resource with others is not efficient. Therefore, it prefers to have its own private resource if possible. However, in some cases the agents don't have any choice but to share a resource (like a road junction or another expensive resource).

We first consider the case where *W loses less over time than A can gain over time.* In such a case for any offer, if it is big enough, it is possible to find an offer in the future that will be better for both sides (i.e, both agents have positive total gain). Although it might appear that such an assumption will cause long delays in reaching an agreement, we have proven that, in fact, the delay will be at most one period since W may opt out. However, because better agreements for both parties can be found in the future, the agreement that is reached is not *Pareto Optimal* over time.

The intuition behind this proof is as follows. First, an agreement won't be achieved when it is W's turn to make an offer and there is still the possibility of an agreement in the next period, since A is gaining over time and would like to delay reaching an agreement. Second, A will always offer W at Time T an agreement that will prevent W from opting out (i.e., $\hat{s}^{W,t}$). Because W won't get anything better in the future and because it loses over time, it will accept such an offer. So, if W is the first agent to make an offer (this is a reasonable assumption because A is using the resource and does not have a motive to start the negotiations), the agreement will be reached in the second period with $\hat{s}^{W,1}$. If A is the first one, agreement will be reached in the first period with $\hat{s}^{W,0}$.

The second case considers the situation where *Agent W's losses over time are greater than Agent A's gains.*[6] In this model, for any agreement in period $t \in \mathcal{T}$, there is no other agreement in the future that *both* agents will prefer over this agreement. On the other hand, if an agreement s in period t is small enough, one can find an agreement in a period earlier than t which both agents prefer over s in Period t. According to our assumptions, this property will cause the agents to reach an agreement in the first period.

We demonstrate the case where W loses less over time than A can gain over time, in the following example.[7]

Example 1. *The United States and Germany have embarked on a joint scientific mission to Mars involving separate mobile labs launched from a single shuttle in orbit around the planet. Each country has contracts with a number of companies for the conduct of experiments. These experiments were preprogrammed prior to launch. Arrangements were made prior to launch for the sharing of some equipment to avoid duplication and excess weight on the mission. Instructions to begin each experiment must be sent from Earth.*

The U.S. antenna was damaged during landing, and it is expected that communications between the United States and its lab on Mars will be down for repairs for one day (1,440 minutes) of the planned 5-day duration of the mission. The United States can use a weaker and less reliable backup line, but this

---

[6]Additional conditions consider the borderline cases: $\hat{s}_A^{W,t} + |c_W| \leq M$.

[7]Examples 1, 2, and 3 also appear in Kraus et al. (1995).

involves diverting this line from other costly space experiments, and thus the expense of using this line is very high to the United States. The United States would like to share use of the German line during the 1-day period so that it can conduct its planned research program. Only one research group can use the line at a time, and that line will be in use for the entire duration of the particular experiment.

A negotiation ensues between the two labs over division of use of the German line, during which time the Germans have sole access to the line, and the United States cannot conduct any of its experiments (except by use of the very expensive backup). By prearrangement, the Germans are using some of the U.S. equipment for their experiments, and are gaining $5,000 per minute. Whereas the Germans cannot conduct any of their experiments without some U.S. equipment, the United States could conduct some of its experiments without German equipment. The United States is losing $3,000 per minute during the period in which they must rely on their backup communications line. An agreement between the United States and Germany to share the communications line will result in a $1,000 gain per period (minute) for each group.

If an agreement on sharing the line is not reached, the United States can threaten to opt out of the arrangement. In this case, the United States will be able to conduct a small portion of its experiments by using all of its equipment and no German equipment, and by using the backup communications line. The overall U.S. gain will be $550,000, but it will lose $1,000 per any minute of the negotiation. If the United States opts out, the Germans will not be able to continue their experiments (without the U.S. equipment) and their gain will be restricted to whatever they had gained at the point the United States opted out. If the Germans opt out, they will need to pay the United States $100,000 for use of the U.S. equipment up to that point. Note that the Germans play the role of A (attached to the communication line) and the United States plays the role of W (waiting for the line). A dollar is the smallest unit of currency in this example.

Formally,

- $U^g((s, t)) = 1000s_g + 5000t$, $U^g((\mathrm{Opt}_u, t)) = 5000t$, $U^g((\mathrm{Opt}_g, t)) = 5000t - 100000$
- $U^u((s, t)) = 1000s_u - 3000t$, $U^u((\mathrm{Opt}_u, t)) = 550000 - 1000t$, $U^u((\mathrm{Opt}_g, t)) = -1000t$
- $M = 1440$

The Germans prefer any agreement over opting out.

$\tilde{s}_u^{u,t} = 551 + 2t$

An agreement will be reached in the second period (Period 1) with ($887,553).

It should be noted that there are agreements in the future that both agents prefer over reaching the agreement ($887,553) *in the second period. This is because the Germans gain more over time than the United States loses over time. For example, the agreement* ($879,561) *in the fourth time period (Period 3) is better for both agents than* (\$887,553) *in the second time period. The problem is that there is no way that the United States can be sure that when the fourth time period arrives, the German will offer them* (\$879,561). *In that time period the Germans need to offer only* (\$885,555) *in order to prevent the United States from opting out, and they don't have any motivation to offer more.*

2.1.2. Incomplete Information

In some automated agent interaction situations, the agents do not have complete information about each other and about the environment. The incompleteness of information may be the result of different factors. For example, an agent may hide its actions from the other agents; an agent may not be able to explore the environment and may be missing information about the environment; the resources that are available to one agent are not known to the others; or one agent is not familiar with its opponent's utility function.

We have considered situations when the agents have incomplete information about each other's utility functions (Kraus & Wilkenfeld, 1993b; Kraus et al., 1995). The situation of incomplete information becomes even more interesting when we can expect recurring encounters between the same two agents. The agents can use information obtained in one encounter in a subsequent one. So, we will assume that there is a set of agents whose members negotiate with each other, from time to time, on sharing a resource. However, we still assume that in a given period of time no more than two agents need the same resource. When there is an overlap between the time segments in which two agents need the same resource, these agents will be involved in a negotiation process.

We assume that there is a finite set of types of agents in the environment ($Type = \{1, \ldots, k\}$), and each has a different utility function that depends on its resource usage. The different distributions of resource usage among the agents can be due to different tasks that the agents are executing, or different configurations. For example, if all the agents are communications servers that share a common communication line then an agent that has smaller disk space will use the resource more frequently than an agent that has larger disk space.

When $j \in Type$ plays the role of W (waiting for the resource) we denote it by W_j, and when it plays the role of A (attached to the resource) we denote it by A_j. We also assume that each agent maintains some probability belief concerning its opponent's type. We denote by ϕ_j^i, where $i \in \{A, W\}$, $j \in Type$, i's probability of its opponent being of Type j. We assume that $\forall i \in \{A, W\}\ \Sigma_{j=1}^{k}\ \phi_j^i = 1$. This probability belief changes over time. We denote by $\mathcal{A}$ the set of all possible configurations of agents (i.e., $\mathcal{A} = \{W_1, W_2, \ldots, W_k, A_1, \ldots, A_k\}$).

The assumptions of the previous section are still valid, but we add additional requirements to ($A2$). We assume that each agent has utility with a constant cost of Time c_i. We will concentrate on the cases where Agent A_i $i \in$ *Type* gains over time ($c_{A_i} > 0$) and Agent W_i loses over time ($c_{W_i} < 0$). Agent W prefers any given portion of the resource sooner rather than later, while Agent A prefers any given portion of the resource later rather than sooner. The exact values, c_{A_i} and c_{W_j} are private information. That is, Agent A_i knows its private gain c_{A_i}, but may not know c_{W_j}, although it knows that it is one of k values.

Furthermore, we will consider the situation where it is common knowledge that $|c_{W_k}| < c_{W_{k-1}}| < \ldots < |c_{W_1}| < |c_{A_k}| < \ldots < |c_{A_1}|$. That is, Agent W_k loses less than agent W_1 loses while waiting for the resource. Agent A_k also gains less than A_1 while using the resource. Both agents lose less while waiting than they can gain while using the resource. We also assume that for any time period t, $\hat{s}_A^{W_k,t} < \hat{s}_A^{W_{k-1},t} < \ldots < \hat{s}_A^{W_1,t}$. That is, W_k is more willing to opt out (compared with reaching an agreement) than W_1. In addition, we assume that $\hat{s}_A^{W,t} + |c_W| \leq M$. We show that in situations that satisfy our conditions, there exists a sequence of strategies that are in sequential equilibrium which have the following properties.

1. In general, W_i will not offer A_j anything better than its possible utility from opting out in the next iteration, with the addition of W_i's loss over time (i.e., $\hat{s}_A^{W_i,t+1} + |c_{W_i}|$), since it can always wait until the next iteration and opt out.

2. If A_j receives such an offer, it may realize that its opponent is no stronger than Type i. This is because a stronger agent will not offer $\hat{s}_A^{W_i,t+3} + |c_{W_i}|$. If it realizes that its opponent is at most of Type i, it can wait until the next iteration and offer W $\hat{s}^{W_i,t+3}$. Since A_j gains more than W loses $|c_{W_i}| < c_{A_j}$, A_j will prefer it over W's current offer.

3. It is better for W_i to "pretend"[8] to be the strongest type by offering only $\hat{s}_A^{W_k,t+3} + |c_{W_k}|$. This offer will be rejected, but in this way it will not convey any information about W's type to A_j.

4. In the next iteration, if W_i gets an offer that is worth less than opting out (less than $\hat{s}^{W_i,t+3}$), then it will really opt out. That is, if A_j offers $\hat{s}^{W_l,t+3}$ and W is of a stronger type than l it will opt out. This is because W_i knows that in any future time period t', it will not reach an agreement better than $\hat{s}^{W_i,t+3}$, *and* W_i would prefer to opt out over that possibility. Therefore, A_j computes its expected utility for offering $\hat{s}^{W_i,t+3}$, for any $i \in$ Type, according to its beliefs, and offers the one where its expected utility is maximal. After receiving the offer, W will either accept it or opt out according to its type.

---

[8]When we say that an Agent B pretends to be Agent C in a given situation, we mean that Agent B will take the same action as Agent C, regardless of its expected utility in this situation.

This means that, if the agents use sequential equilibrium strategies, the negotiation will end in the second iteration and the agents will reach an agreement in this period with high probability. The exact probability and the details of the agreement depend on Agent A_j's initial belief.

Example 2. *We return to the example of the mission to Mars. Suppose that neither of the labs (agents) on Mars knows the exact details of the contracts the other has with companies. There are two possibilities for the contracts: high (h) and low (l). If the type of contracts the German's hold is h, then their utility functions are similar to those of Example 1. They gain $5,000 per minute during the negotiation and gain $1,000 per minute when they share the line with the United States. If the United States also holds contracts of Type h, then their utility functions are also similar to those of Example 1. The United States loses $3,000 per minute during the negotiation period and gains $1,000 per minute when sharing the line with the Germans. If the United States opts out the overall U.S. gain will be $550,000, but they will also lose $1,000 per minute during the negotiation.*

However, if the German contracts are of Type l, then they only gain $4,000 per minute while using the line by themselves. The United States losses while negotiating if their contracts are Type l are only $2,000 per minute. But if the United States opts out, their overall gain is only $450,000. They still negotiate for the usage of the German line in the next 24 hours (i.e., $M = 1440$) from the time the negotiation ends.

Formally, let $s \in S$, $t \in \mathfrak{T}$,

Type h	*Type l*
$U^{g_h}((s,t)) = 1000s_g + 5000t$ $U^{g_h}((\mathrm{Opt}_u, t)) = 5000t$ $U^{g_h}((\mathrm{Opt}_g, t)) = 5000t - 1000$	$U^{g_l}((s,t)) = 1000s_g + 4000t$ $U^{g_l}((\mathrm{Opt}_u, t)) = 4000t$ $U^{g_l}((\mathrm{Opt}_g, t)) = 40t - 1000$
$U^{u_h}((s,t)) = 1000s_u - 3000t$ $U^{u_h}((\mathrm{Opt}_u, t)) = 550000 - 1000t$ $U^{u_h}((\mathrm{Opt}_g, t)) = -1000t$ $\hat{s}^{u_h,t} = (889 - 2t, 551 + 2t)$	$U^{u_l}((s,t)) = 1000s_u - 2000t$ $U^{u_l}((\mathrm{Opt}_u, t)) = 450000 - 1000t$ $U^{u_l}((\mathrm{Opt}_g, t)) = -1000t$ $\hat{s}^{u_l,t} = (989 - t, 451 + t)$

Let us assume that Germany (playing the role of A) is of Type h and the United States (playing the role of W) is of Type l. We denote them by g_h *and* u_l. *We will consider two cases. Suppose* g_h *believes that with probability* 0.5 *its opponent is of Type h and with probability* 0.5 *its opponent is of Type l (i.e.,* $\phi_l^g = 0.5$ *and* $\phi_h^g = 0.5$). *According to our results (Kraus et al., 1995), and in the first period,* u_l *will pretend to be of Type h and will offer* g_h $(\hat{s}_g^{u_h,1} + |c_{u_h}|, \hat{s}_u^{u_h,1} - |c_{u_h}|) = (\$890{,}550)$. g_h *will reject the offer. In the second time period,* g_h *compares between offering W* ($887,553), *which will be accepted by both types, and offering* ($988,452) *which will be accepted by Type l, but after such an offer, if W is of Type h, it will opt out.*

Because its expected utility from offering ($887,553) *is higher, it makes this offer, which is accepted by* u_l.

However, suppose g_h *believes only with probability* 0.1 *its opponent is of Type h, and with probability* 0.9 *its opponent is of Type l. The behavior of* u_l *in the first period is similar to the previous case. It pretends to be h. However, in the second period,* g_h*'s expected utility from* ($988,452) *is higher than* ($887,553) *and therefore it makes this offer to W, which is accepted by* u_l.

2.2. The Task Distribution Problem

Our second situation involves a set of autonomous agents which needs to satisfy a common goal. In order to satisfy any goal, costly actions must be taken. In addition, an agent cannot satisfy the goal without reaching an agreement with the other agents. Each of the agents wants to minimize its costs (i.e., prefers to do as little as possible).

We note that even though the agents have the same goal (under our simplified assumptions), there is actually a conflict of interests. The agents try to reach an agreement over the division of labor. We assume that each step of the negotiation takes time, and the agents have preferences for reaching agreements in different time periods. Research on the task distribution problem in the area of Distributed Problem Solving systems includes Davis and Smith's work on the Contract Net (Smith & Davis, 1983); Cammarata et al.'s work on strategies of cooperation that are needed for groups to solve shared tasks effectively in the context of collision avoidance in air traffic (Cammarata, McArthur, & Steeb, 1983); Lesser and Erman's model of a distributed interpretation system that is able to function effectively even though processing nodes have inconsistent and incomplete information (Lesser & Erman, 1980); and Carver et al.'s work on agents with sophisticated models that support complex and dynamic interactions between the agents (Carver, Cvetanovic, & Lesser, 1991).

The "delivery domain" is a good example of the task distribution problem (Fischer & Kuhn, 1993; Sandholm, 1993; Wellman, 1992; Zlotkin & Rosenschein, 1993). A group of delivery companies can reduce their overall and individual delivery costs by coordinating their deliveries. Each delivery requirement is a single task. Delivery coordination is actually the exchanging of tasks. One company, for example, that needs to make a delivery from A to B and a delivery from C to D can execute other deliveries from A to B with no extra cost. Therefore, it may agree to exchange its C to D delivery for another A to B delivery. The application of the strategic model to the delivery domain allows multiple delivery companies to reach an efficient agreement on task distribution without delay, that will be mutually beneficial.

Example 3. *There are three agents that are responsible for the delivery of electronic newsletters of two different companies. The delivery is done by phone (either by fax machines or electronic mail). The expenses of the agents depend only on the number of phone calls. Therefore, if there is a subscriber who subscribes to all companies' newsletters, the three newsletters may be delivered to it by one of the agents for the price of only one phone call. The agents negotiate over the distribution of the common subscriptions. Each of the agents can opt out of the negotiations and deliver all of its own newsletters by itself.*

We assume that there are three electronic newsletters (N1, N2, and N3) that are delivered by separate delivery services (D1, D2, and D3). The payment arrangements to the delivery services are as follows. The publisher of N1 pays D1 \$200 per delivery of one edition; similarly, the publisher of N2 pays D2 \$225, and the publisher of N3 pays D3 \$250. Each delivery to a given subscriber (i.e., a phone call to this subscriber's server) also cost \$1, and each agent loses \$1 for each time period that it is late in making a delivery. There are M subscribers with subscriptions to all newsletters (i.e., N1, N2, and N3), and there are substantial savings to a delivery service if one of the agents can deliver all newsletters to the same subscribers. If an agreement among D1, D2, and D3 for joint deliveries to the M joint subscribers is reached, then the publisher of N3 will pay D3 only \$215 per delivery of an edition, and in such an event the publisher of N1 will pay D1 \$170, and the publisher of N2 will pay D2 \$200 (the lower prices reflect the fact that there are competing advertisers in the two newsletters, and consequently their joint delivery may detract from the sales impact of each newsletter). They must pay \$1 per phone call to the server, and will lose \$2 for any time spent in negotiation. Notice that in this example, only the number of phone calls to the subscribers made by a delivery agent plays a role in its payments and not the distribution of the rest of the subscribers between the other two agents.

Formally,

$U^1((\text{Opt}, t)) = 200 - M - t$ *and* $U^1((s, t)) = 170 - s_1 - 2t$
$U^2((\text{Opt}, t)) = 225 - M - t$ *and* $U^2((s, t)) = 200 - s_2 - 2t$
$U^3((\text{Opt}, t)) = 250 - M - t$ *and* $U^3((s, t)) = 215 - s_3 - 2t$
Suppose $M = 100$. *Then* $\hat{s}_1^{1,t} = 69 - t$, $\hat{s}_2^{2,t} = 74 - t$ *and* $\hat{s}_3^{3,t} = 64 - t$. *Note that for all* $i \in \{1, 2, 3\}$, $\hat{s}^{i,t}$ *is not unique in this case.*

$\hat{T} = 36$ *and it is D3's turn to make an offer in the time period prior to* $\hat{T}$. *In this period, D1 is willing to deliver up to 34 newsletters, if an agreement will be reached (i.e.,* $\hat{s}_1^{1,35} = 34$*) and D2 is willing to deliver up to 39 newsletters (i.e., =* $\hat{s}_2^{2,35} = 39$*). So,* $x^{35} = (34, 39, 27)$. *It is easy to compute, that whenever it is D1's turn to make an offer (t is divided by 3),* $x^t = (31, 38, 31)$, *when it is D2's turn to make an offer,* $x^t = (35, 36, 29)$ *and when it is D3's turn to make an offer (prior to time period 35),* $x^t = (33, 40, 27)$. *Therefore, in the first time period (0), D1 will offer (31, 38, 31), and its opponents will accept its offer.*

2.3. Document Allocation in Large Knowledge Bases

Given the enormous volume of data stored in modern information retrieval systems, searching a database of documents requires vast computational resources. To meet these computational demands, various researchers have developed parallel information retrieval systems (e.g., Aalbersberg & Sijstermans, 1991; Frieder & Siegelmann, 1991; Stone, 1987)). As efficient exploitation of parallelism demands fast access to documents, data organization and placement significantly affect the total processing time. We assume a distributed database environment, in which sites are owned by different independent agents. Thus, a good response time for queries and, in particular, a good allocation, are measured subjectively by the different sites, and no one global cost is defined. In addition, we do not want to assume a fixed database but rather a dynamic one. At one end, new documents are arriving all the time, and at the other end, the subjects of the queries to a specific site are also changing dynamically; thus the agents may benefit from dynamic allocation of documents.

The strategic model can be applied as a dynamic data placement strategy for distributed memory and distributed I/O multicomputers, where the sites are owned by different agents. Both existing and new documents will be swapped among the agents via a negotiation, where each agent measures its priorities using local estimation functions and local learning/prediction algorithms.

An example of an information center where our techniques may be useful is the Earth Science Data and Information System (ESDIS) which is a segment of the Earth Observing System.

Earth Science Data and Information System

The Earth Science Data and Information System is comprised of several earth science data centers, each of which includes large amounts of earth observation data from NASA and other correlative research missions in upper atmosphere, atmospheric dynamics, and global biosphere (Hughes STX Corporation, 1994). Each data center provides access to, manipulation of, or distribution of datasets (including supporting information and expertise) for a wide community of users. Data centers also provide selection and replication of data and needed documentation and, often, the generation of user tailored data products.

The search for data can be done using the ESDIS V0 Information Management System (IMS). In this system, from one user interface, a scientist is able to search the Global Change Master Directory for directory information about datasets, search and locate datasets at seven NASA and NASA-affiliated Data Archive Centers (DAACs), view sample browse granules[9] from datasets, and order data products offered by the DAACs.

The ESDIS V0 IMS system consists of an IMS Server at each DAAC that responds to requests for services from the V0 IMS Client, the user interface (Hong, 1994). Each ESDIS V0 DAAC is independent and implements its dataset holdings independently of any other DAAC. However, the messages that are passed between the V0 Client and the V0 IMS Servers describe datasets as various parameter valid values. Each dataset is defined in the V0 IMS system with different values for the parameters of source, sensor, geophysical, and dataset name. The minimal field that must be specified to be a valid V0 IMS search is one of the following fields: sensor, geophysical, or dataset name, and geographical area. A prototype version of the V0 IMS Client was released in August, 1994 to the scientific community.

Negotiation Over the Allocation of Documents

Currently the allocation of documents to the ESDIS centers is done statically. Each center stores and maintains data by specific subjects or by specific collection sources. When a user in a given data center needs a document that is stored at a different data center, the document is transferred to the user's local machine.

Because the system was released to the scientific community quite recently, there is still not enough information on its performance. But it is already clear that one of the bottlenecks of ESDIS is the network and the volume of large documents that need to be transferred (mainly using FTP).

We have developed a dynamic strategic-negotiation protocol for document allocation. We assume that each data center will have some estimation of which scientists intend to use its services in the near future and what their main interests are. Using this information it is useful to store the related documents as close as possible to the location where they will be needed most frequently, and thus when a user asks for specific documents, the data center will be able to provide them much faster than in the static approach. However, these preferences may conflict with preferences of other data centers. We propose to resolve these conflicts through strategic negotiation, and show that using this method, the servers have simple and stable negotiation strategies that result in efficient agreements without delays (Schwartz & Kraus, 1997).

---

[9]A *browse* is a representation of a dataset or data granule used to prescreen data as an aid to selection prior to ordering. For example: a browse image might be a reduced resolution version of a single channel from a multichannel instrument. A *granule* is the smallest aggregation of data which is independently managed (i.e., described, inventoried, retrievable). Granules may be managed as logical granules or physical granules.

In particular, we prove that in the case of simultaneous responses to an offer, there are a large number of possible stable negotiation strategy profiles. These strategies depend on the specific settings of the environment and cannot be provided to the agents in advance. We propose that the agents choose strategy profiles which are optimal with respect to a given social criterion. We proved that the problem of finding the optimal solution which maximizes the social criterion is itself NP complete, and therefore propose using a heuristic method for obtaining a near-optimal solution. We prove that such methods yield better results than the static allocation policy currently used for data allocation for servers in distributed systems. We develop three types of heuristic algorithms for obtaining the near-optimal solution: a backtracking algorithm, a genetic algorithm, and a random-restart hill-climbing algorithm. We implement these algorithms, and compare them for several environments. We found that the hill-climbing algorithm provides, in general, the best results.

In situations where agents have incomplete information, a revelation process was added to the protocol, after which a negotiation takes place, as in the complete information case. Using negotiation efficiency by self-motivated servers demonstrates the benefits of using a negotiation mechanism in real world, multiagent environments.

3. THE HOSTAGE CRISIS SIMULATION

The theoretical work on a strategic model of negotiation has also been applied to a typical problem in multilateral international negotiation. In the following sections we describe a hostage crisis scenario (Section 3.1), link it back to the basic assumptions of the strategic model (Section 3.2), and provide an overview of a decision support system designed to support experimental work in negotiation theory and the training of crisis negotiators (Section 3.3).

3.1. Scenario

In the field of international relations, the hostage crisis situation was chosen as a typical case of multiparty negotiation. The scenario is based on the hypothetical hijacking of a commercial airliner enroute from Europe to India and its forced landing in Pakistan. The passengers are predominantly Indian and the hijackers are known to be Sikhs. The hijackers demand the release from Indian security prisons of up to 800 Sikh prisoners (see Kraus & Wilkenfeld, 1990a)).[10] The three parties must consider several possible

[10]The original specification of the model was based on a Middle East setting involving Israel, Egypt, and Palestinian hijackers. The experimental results reported in this chapter used the India–Pakistan–Sikh model in order to minimize participants bias during the course of the experiments (see Section 3.3.1).

outcomes: India or Pakistan launch military operations to free the hostages; the hijackers blow up the plane with themselves aboard; India and the Sikhs negotiate a deal involving the release of security prisoners in exchange for the hostages; Pakistan and the Sikhs negotiate a safe passage agreement; and the hijackers give up. The specific issues to be negotiated are the following:

India-Sikhs:

- Number of security prisoners to be released by India in exchange for release of all of the hostages.

India-Pakistan:

- Indian request for logistical information to enhance the probability of success of an Indian military operation.
- Indian request for assistance (or at least neutrality) during an Indian operation, to enhance the probability of success.
- Indian request that Pakistan deny the hijackers press access in order to prevent them from publicizing their message.
- Pakistani request for Indian assistance during a Pakistani operation, to enhance probability of success.
- Pakistani request that India accept a Sikh offer.

Pakistan-Sikhs:

- Hijackers' request for press access to publicize their cause.
- Pakistani request that the hijackers give up or reach an agreement for safe passage.
- Pakistani request that the hijackers accept an Indian offer.

In the simulation setting, actors negotiate these issues until an agreement is reached or a player opts out of the negotiations by launching a military operation (India or Pakistan) or by blowing up the plane (Sikhs).

Each party to the negotiation has a set of objectives, and a certain number of utility points is associated with each (see Kraus & Wilkenfeld, 1990a). Utility points were assigned in order to express a complex set of preferences in such a way that subtle distinctions can be made among them. In combining the range of utility points associated with each objective with the possible outcomes, a matrix is generated which yields a point output total for each outcome. We note that these payoff points are not utility functions (in the decision theory sense), but rather our description of the crisis. Each player will develop his or her set of preferences for the outcomes based on these utility points (see Doyle, 1989). Time is incorporated into the model both as a reference point for the calculation of utilities and probabilities, and as a differential factor for the three parties. In general, time works in favor of the hijackers, and against India and Pakistan. Time impacts on the probability of success and failure of an operation to free the hostages (whether it is day or night, whether there is time to train a rescue team, and so on), on publicity for the Sikh's cause (regardless of whether direct press access is granted), and deterioration over time in India and Pakistan's internal and external images. For more detail on the Hostage Crisis Simulation, see Kraus and Wilkenfeld (1990b).

3.2. The Strategic Negotiation Model Applied to the Hostage Crisis Situation

We assume that there are three players: the "Initiator" of the crisis–the Sikh hijackers (*Sik*); the "Participant" (against its will) in the crisis–India (*Ind*); and a "Third Party"–Pakistan (*Pak*). There exists a set of possible agreements between all possible pairs of players.[11] The negotiation procedure that follows is as described in Section 1. In the Hostage Crisis, the hijackers opt out by blowing up the plane. India or Pakistan opt out by launching military operations. In this case the set of agents is defined to be: $\mathcal{A} \stackrel{\text{def}}{=} \{sik, ind, pak\}$. We assume that the set $S_{i,j}$, $i, j \in \mathcal{A}$, $i \neq j$ includes the possible agreements between players i and j. We also assume that $S_{i,j} = S_{j,i}$ and denote the set of all possible agreements by S.

In analyzing the Hostage Crisis case, we identified special conditions on the sets of possible agreements. In our case $S_{ind,pak} = \emptyset$, that is, there is no possible agreement between India and Pakistan that can end the crisis. There is only one possible agreement between the hijackers and Pakistan (hostages are freed and hijackers are granted free passage).

We assume that India holds M Sikh security prisoners and an agreement between the hijackers and India is a pair (s_{sik}, s_{ind}) where $s_{sik}, s_{ind} \in IN$, $s_{sik} \geq 1$ and $s_{sik} + s_{ind} = M$. That is, an agreement between the hijackers and India is the division of the M prisoners between them. In the hostage crisis situation $M = 800$ (Sikh prisoners in Indian jails). We also assume that player $i = sik, ind, pak$ has a utility function $U^i : \{\{S \cup \{\text{Opt}\}\} \times \mathcal{T}\} \cup \{\text{Disagreement}\} \to IR$.

We have identified several conditions that the utility function of the players in the Hostage Crisis satisfy. We assume that these conditions are known to all players. That is, we have developed a model of complete information.

---

[11]In the formal model, we have concentrated on the negotiation process. We haven't incorporated the possible actions of Pakistan (e.g., providing information) into the model.

A0. Disagreement is the worst outcome.

A1. The prisoners are desirable: For any $(s_{sik}, s_{ind}),(r_{sik}, r_{ind}) \in S_{sik,ind}$ and $t \in \mathcal{T}$, if $r_i \geq s_i$, $(i = sik, ind)$ then $U^i((r_{sik}, r_{ind}), t) \geq U^i((s_{sik}, s_{ind}), t)$.

A2. Agreement's cost over time: Pakistan and India prefer reaching a given agreement (either Pakistan/Sikh or India/Sikh agreement) sooner rather than later. In particular, India prefers to release any given number of prisoners sooner rather than later, while the hijackers, through Period 10, prefer to obtain any given number of prisoners later rather than sooner.

India has a number $c_{ind} < 0$ such that:[12]

For any $(s_{sik}, s_{ind}), (r_{sik}, r_{ind}) \in S_{sik,ind}$ and $t_1, t_2 \in \mathcal{T}$, $U^{ind}((s_{sik}, s_{ind}), t_1) \geq U^{ind}((r_{sik}, r_{ind}), t_2)$ iff $(s_{ind} + c_{ind} * t_1) \geq (r_{ind} + c_{ind} * t_2)$.

The hijackers, through Period 10, prefer any agreement later rather than sooner. In particular, the hijackers have two constants $c_{sik} > 0$ and $c'_{sik} < 0$ such that:

let $t_1, t_2 \in \mathcal{T}$, and we will assume that for $i = 1, 2$, $t_i = t_i^1 + t_i^2$ where if $t_i \geq 10$, $t_i^1 = 10$, otherwise then $t_i^2 = 0$. For any $(s_{sik}, s_{ind}),(r_{sik}, r_{ind}) \in S_{sik,ind}$, $U^{sik}((s_{sik}, s_{ind}), t_1) \geq U^{sik}((r_{sik}, r_{ind}), t_2)$ iff $(s_{sik} + c_{sik} * t_1^1 + c'_{sik} * t_1^2) \geq (r_{sik} + c_{sik} * t_2^1 + c'_{sik} * t_2^2)$.

A3. Opting out over time: India and Pakistan prefer to opt out sooner rather than later. The hijackers, through Period 10, prefer opting out later rather than sooner.

We note that assumption (A2) does not hold for Opt and the preferences of the players for opting out in different periods of time do not change in a stationary way. Furthermore, the preferences of a player for opting out versus an agreement fluctuate across periods of time in a nonstationary fashion. In the case of the Hostage Crisis this is due to different rates of change over time in the probabilities associated with success or failure of the actions taken when opting out.

A4. Preferences for agreements: Whereas the Sikhs prefer any agreement between themselves and India (victory for the Sikhs) to any agreement between themselves and Pakistan (i.e., defeat for the Sikhs), both India and Pakistan prefer a Sikh/Pakistan agreement at any time to any Sikh/India agreement or opting out.

A5. Possible agreement: The hijackers and Pakistan prefer any possible agreement over opting out. In the first period there is at least

[12]This is a model of constant cost of delay (Rubinstein, 1982) and not of time constant discount rates which is more common in economic models (Binmore, Rubinstein, & Wolinsky, 1986).

one agreement between the hijackers and India which all players prefer over opting out.

The foregoing assumptions (especially A2 and A3) demonstrate that time is an important element in the strategic model (Kraus & Wilkenfeld, 1993a). Specifically, we propose that although the hijackers gain utility over time, there is a point at which the process is reversed and the hijackers begin to lose over time (in the Hostage Crisis, this can be due to factors such as a shift in media sympathy from the plight of the Sikh prisoners to the deteriorating circumstances of the hostages on board the aircraft).

There are several similarities between the Hostage Crisis situation and the case of resource allocation in automated multiagent environments, where one agent has use of the resource while the other waits for access (Section 2.1.1). They are reflected in parallel numbering of the assumptions here (A0–A5) and in Section 2.1.1. In both cases there are two parties that negotiate over the division of M units. In the Hostage Crisis the players negotiate the division of the M prisoners, and in the automated agents case the division of M units of a resource. In the Hostage Crisis there is a third party, Pakistan, that plays an important role in the negotiation; however, the other assumptions are similar.

- In both cases disagreement is the worst outcome (assumptions A0).
- Agents A and W in the automated agents situation, and India and the Sikhs in the Hostage Crisis, would each like a larger portion of the M units. This is reflected in assumptions (A1) in both cases: The prisoners are desirable and the resource is valuable.
- In the first ten time periods agreement costs over time are the same in both cases. Agent A and the Sikhs gain over time, and Agent W, India and Pakistan, lose over time (Assumptions A2). In the Hostage Crisis, the Sikhs begin to lose from the eleventh time period on.
- The preferences for opting out over time through Period 10 are similar in both cases. W, India and Pakistan prefer to opt out sooner rather than later, and Agent A and the Sikhs prefer to opt out later rather than sooner.
- In both cases there is a possibility for a beneficial agreement to all agents (A5), although the preferences of the agents are different (A4).

Although the cases are similar, the results of the two negotiations differ. This is due to the participation of a third party in the Hostage Crisis situation and the fact that in the Hostage Crisis from the eleventh time period, all agents are losing over time, whereas in the automated agents case agent A always gains over time. Whereas in the automated agents case agreement on the division of the resource is reached without a delay, in the Hostage Crisis we have formally shown (Kraus & Wilkenfeld, 1991, 1993a) that if there is a time period in which the hijackers start to lose over time, and if the players use perfect equilibrium strategies, then agreement will be reached in this time period (Period 10 in the Hostage Crisis scenario) between the hijackers and Pakistan.

3.3. GENIE: A Decision Support System for Multilateral Crisis Negotiation

The specific implementation of the GENIE Decision Support System (DSS) that has been explored in our research to date contains a knowledge base and interface modules tailored to the Hostage Crisis scenario described in Section 3.1.

Decision Support Systems can play a crucial role in the crisis decision-making process such as the one described earlier by allowing the decision-maker to navigate large amounts of information quickly and to explore interrelationships between factors that may influence the decision. A DSS can also facilitate the simultaneous evaluation of multiple positions in crisis negotiation. This can play a decisive role in real time negotiations by allowing the supported parties to rapidly formulate dynamic strategies and quickly evaluate their opponents' proposals. GENIE falls in the category of support for individual negotiators, in that it is designed to aid one party to a negotiation in determining a successful course of action vis-à-vis the other parties (for a complete description of GENIE and its theoretical base, see Kraus and Wilkenfeld (1991, 1993a); Kraus et al. (1995); Wilkenfeld et al. (1995).

By employing GENIE, a negotiator can explore various negotiation positions simultaneously. It provides the negotiator with a mental picture of the negotiation model through problem structuring and knowledge organization. Its function is to present a complex negotiation model to the user in an easily understandable and organized manner. To achieve this, GENIE uses an interactive outline which presents the types of data in the model as outline topics and allows the user to interactively select the topics of interest. The flexibility which this approach provides allows the negotiator to investigate the consequences of various positions almost instantly. This allows forward, backward, or random evaluation of positions during the formulation of a negotiating strategy. It also allows a negotiator to quickly evaluate opponent proposals during actual negotiations. Simultaneous viewing of a number of negotiating positions facilitates comparative analysis and the optimization of choices.

GENIE was designed in three basic modules. The *knowledge base module* consists of data on the utility functions of each of the parties to the negotiation, and a series of structural equations that define the relationships among critical variables, thus allowing for the calculation of the utility point totals associated with various outcomes across various time periods. The *interface module* features a menu-driven interactive outline that combines data management and modeling capability in a screen which enables a negotiator to quickly set parameters for the viewing of information, allowing the user to form a quick mental picture of the entire simulation. Use of the interface allows the user to brainstorm and experiment with different options to form a personalized strategy for utility maximization. Finally, the *display module* provides the negotiator with graphic output options, consisting of either a time static bar chart representation of the comparative utilities of various outcomes (different agreements, military operations, and so on), or time series graphs that allow the negotiator to observe changes in utility points associated with various outcomes over time. In all cases, because this is a full-information model, the individual negotiator can compare his or her projected utilities with those of the other two parties for specific outcomes.[13]

3.3.1. Summary of Research Findings to Date

During the past 3 years, we have used the GENIE Decision Support System to conduct a series of pilot experiments designed to explore several aspects of both the behavioral and instrumental characteristics of the negotiation process. We provide a sampling of these experimental results, and point the reader to more complete discussions of the findings.

Behavioral Findings. An early set of experiments focused on the types of communications patterns most conducive to the achievement of negotiated agreements, versus those associated with the adoption of violent means for resolving the crises. Among the results isolated thus far are findings pertaining to the pivotal role of third party mediation in crisis: By maintaining open and balanced communications channels with each of the engaged parties, a greater number of agreements is produced than when the third party acted in a more biased manner. For additional details on these experimental results, see Kraus, Wilkenfeld, Harris, and Blake (1992).

Instrumental Findings. A series of preliminary experiments has confirmed the following hypotheses:

1. DSS-supported users are more likely to identify utility maximization as their primary objective in a crisis situation, whereas non-DSS-supported users are more likely to identify deeply held principles as the primary motivating factor.

[13]Additional capabilities of GENIE include the projection of mutually beneficial resolutions and calculation of reservation price.

2. DSS-supported users will achieve higher utility scores than will non-DSS-supported users.
3. Simulations with a DSS-supported user present among the parties will produce higher overall scores than experiments without DSS-supported users.
4. Simulations with DSS-supported users are more likely than simulations without DSS support to end in negotiated agreements.

For additional details on these experimental results, see Wilkenfeld et al. (1995); Holley and Wilkenfeld (1994).

4. RELATED WORK

We conclude with a discussion of related work in the fields of distributed artificial intelligence and crisis decision making.

4.1. Related Work in Distributed Artificial Intelligence

Researchers examining agent interaction differ over the basic assumption of the degree of control that the designer should have over individual agents, and over their social environment (i.e., interaction mechanisms). We present a two-dimensional classification of these studies. On the first dimension we have the degree of control over the *social layer* of the agents. It ranges from a highly structured interaction mechanism to a totally unstructured interaction (see Table 4.1).

TABLE 4.1
Degree of Control on the Social Layer

	Structured	*Unstructured*
PS	Moses & Tennenholtz (1993); Shoham & Tennenholtz (1992); Smith & Davis (1993); Malone, Files, Grant, & Howard (1988); Lesser (1991); Conry, Meyer, & Lesser (1991); Durfee (1988)	
MA	Rosenschein & Zlotkin (1994); Wellman (1992); Ephrati & Rosenschein (1991) *Strategic-Model Applied to Automated Agents*	Sycara (1990); Kraus & Lehmann (1995); Lochbaum, Grosz, & Sidner (1990); Gasser (1993) *Hostage Crisis Simulation*

Note. The rows indicate degree of control on the social layer. The columns indicate degree of control on other agents in the domain

On the second dimension we have the degree of autonomy of the individual agents. It ranges from the case where all agents cooperate in achieving joint goals and each agent tries to maximize some system global utility (those systems are known as Distributed Problem Solving [DPS]), to the case where autonomous agents, each with their individual motivation to achieve their own goal and to maximize their own utility, try too coordinate their actions and cooperate (those systems are known as Multiagent systems [MA]; Bond & Gasser, 1988). DPS environments are usually characterized by centrally designed agents, whereas in MA systems the agents are usually heterogeneous and possibly designed for different purposes.

In the upper left corner of Table 4.1 we find the work of Shoham, Tennenholtz, and Moses on Social Laws (Moses & Tennenholtz, 1993; Shoham & Tennenholtz, 1992) which shows that "precompiled" highly structured "social laws" are able to coordinate agent activity and to restrict online conflict. Agents are assumed to follow the social laws since they were designed to, and not because they individually benefit from the social laws. The same approach could have been applied in an MA system in the case where the social laws are "stable" (i.e., it is in each agent's individual interest to follow the law). In our research, we assume that the agents are individually motivated and therefore the issue of stability plays an important role in the design of the interaction mechanism.

Even in DPS systems it may be useful to incorporate pure competition among the agents. Davis and Smith's work on the Contract Net (Smith & Davis, 1983) introduced a form of simple negotiation among cooperative agents, with one agent announcing the availability of tasks and awarding them to other bidding agents. Malone refined this technique considerably by overlaying it with a more sophisticated economic model (Malone et al., 1988). In the general contract net approach, and also in the economics oriented refinements, the main underlying assumption is that agents are "benevolent" and are motivated to help each other. Such an assumption is not feasible when agents are self-motivated.

Another more experimentally based approach for interagent collaboration in DPS is presented in the on-going research of Lesser, Durfee, and their colleagues using the "Functionally Accurate, Cooperative, (FA/C)" paradigm. For example, the "Partial Global Planning" architecture has been implemented and evaluated in the vehicle monitoring domain (DVMT; Decker & Lesser, 1993; Durfee, 1988; Durfee & Lesser, 1987). The agents iteratively exchange tentative partial solutions to construct global solutions. Multiagent planning in the communication network domain was treated as a distributed constraint on satisfaction and was implemented by using a multistage negotiation (Conry et al., 1991). The multistage negotiation provides each agent sufficient information to enable it to make local decisions that are globally correct. These researchers approach the issue of global efficiency and performance more directly in real-world working systems, whereas we are analyzing the use of formal tools and general mechanisms in more idealized domains.

We are unfamiliar with work that belongs in the upper right corner (Table 4.1) where agents are working together toward achieving some joint goals, but use unstructured communication protocols. This is, of course, due to the fact that because structured communications protocols usually provide more efficient cooperation, and if agents are designed especially to achieve some joint goals, the designers can incorporate a structured communication protocol in the agents to make the DPS system more efficient. In the lower right corner autonomous agents without structured communications protocols try to cooperate. This is usually the case in domains where humans are interacting with each other and with autonomous agents. For example, in the case of labor negotiation, Sycara (1987, 1990) presented a model of negotiation that combines case-based reasoning and optimization of the multiattribute utilities. In her work agents try to influence the goals and intentions of their opponents. Kraus and Lehmann developed an automated Diplomacy player that negotiates and plays well in actual games against human players (Kraus & Lehmann, 1995; Kraus, Ephrati, & Lehmann, 1991). Researchers in discourse understanding develop formal models to support communication in human–machine interaction (see Grosz & Sidner, 1990; Lochbaum, Grosz, & Sidner, 1990). There, models of individual and shared plans are used for understanding nonstructured communication.

Gasser (1993) focused on the social aspects of agent knowledge and action in multiagent systems ("communities of programs"). As in real-world societies, social mechanisms can dynamically emerge. Communities of programs can generate, modify, and codify their own local languages of interaction. Gasser's approach may be most effective when agents are interacting in unstructured domains, or in domains where their structure is continuously changing. In our research, we choose to predesign the social layer of multiagent systems by creating a structured interaction mechanism (i.e., a model of alternating offers).

Our research on the Hostage Crisis simulation falls in this category. Because we want it to be a training tool for real-life negotiation situations, where negotiators can usually communicate freely with each other, we allow nonstructured negotiations during the simulation. Therefore, the strategic model serves only to predict what a rational player would do and to provide advice as to which strategy to adopt.

In most of the unstructured negotiation scenarios, there is no guarantee that agreement will be reached, and the negotiation may take a long time. In the Hostage Crisis situation, the strategic model predicts that an agreement will be reached in Period 10. In the automated agents case, the negotiation always ends at the latest in the second stage of the negotiation.

Our work on applying the strategic model to automated agents resides in the lower left corner (see Table 4.1). It assumes that there is full control over the agent interaction mechanism by bounding the agents to highly structured public behavior (like negotiation protocols, voting procedures, bidding mechanisms, and so on). However, our work is concerned with problems in developing agents in *Multiagent Systems*. That is, each agent tries to maximize its own utility. The agents cooperate because we have carefully adjusted the interaction mechanism such that it will be stable. Using a stable mechanism, it is to the benefit of each individual agent (that wishes to maximize its own private utility) to adopt a given private behavior. When those private behaviors (strategies) are in equilibrium, then the designers of the interaction protocols can assume that the individual agents will be designed to have those private behaviors, which yield cooperation.

Ephrati and Rosenschein (1991) used the Clarke Tax voting procedure as a consensus mechanism. The mechanism assumes an explicit utility transferability (i.e., a kind of monetary system). In the problem of task distribution and resource allocation, there is no explicit way to transfer utility. There is an *implicit* way to transfer utility (e.g., by executing one of your tasks, I may transfer some utility I could have been getting, to you). However, this implicit utility transfer is not sufficient for the implementation of the Clarke Tax procedure. The Clarke Tax mechanism assumes that agents are able to transfer utility out of the system (the taxes that are being paid by the agents). The utility that is transferred out of the system is actually wasted and reduces the efficiency of the consensus that is reached. This is the price that needs to be paid to ensure stability.

Zlotkin and Rosenschein (1991, 1993; Rosenschein & Zlotkin, 1994) analyzed the relationship between the attributes of the domain in which the agents are operating and the availability of interaction mechanisms to satisfy the efficiency, simplicity, symmetry, and stability conditions. They have classified interaction domains as task oriented domains, state oriented domains, and worth oriented domains. In all of the foregoing domains time plays no explicit role in the agent's utility functions. It may be appropriate when negotiation time can be neglected relative to plan execution time. However, in highly dynamic systems, negotiation time plays an important role in the evaluation of the performance of the system and cannot be neglected. Our approach focuses precisely on this kind of domain and provides coordination mechanisms that ensure efficient agreements with no delay. Within the MA-structured group of researchers, it is the first attempt to treat the temporal aspect of negotiation explicitly.

To summarize, our work is characterized by providing a formal strategic model of negotiation that takes the passage of time during the negotiation process itself into account. In automated agent domains, it can be used for both resource allocation and task distribution, without side payments. The only assumptions that we made in these cases relate to the negotiation protocol, which is a protocol of alternating offers. However, we make no assumptions about the offers the agents make during the negotiation as is the case in some other work (e.g., Zlotkin & Rosenschein, 1989). In particular, the agents are not bounded to any previous offers that have been made. Nevertheless, the negotiation ends with no delay. When the strategic model is applied to the Hostage Crisis scenario, delay in reaching an agreement is expected. However, the DSS helps human players to increase their utility.

4.2. Related Work in Crisis Decision Making

Decision theorists have dealt quite extensively with the development of negotiation and bargaining strategy (for an excellent review of this literature, see Thompson, 1990). The analysis of negotiation and bargaining behavior in crisis situations has fallen predominantly in the domain of political science. Studies in this area include a focus on deterrence (George & Smoke, 1974), the bargaining process itself (Snyder & Diesing, 1977), cross-national models of crisis decision making (Brecher, 1978; Stein & Tanter, 1980), cognitive closure and crisis management (Lebow, 1981), quantitative analysis of bargaining (Leng, 1988) and studies of crisis prevention (George, 1983). Comprehensive statistical analysis of the behavior of states in crises is reported (Brecher & Wilkenfeld, 1989, 1997; Brecher, Wilkenfeld, & Moser, 1988; Wilkenfeld, Brecher, & Moser, 1988).

Our approach in the development of a model of strategic negotiation has been guided most directly by two studies. According to Snyder and Diesing (1977), the three types of bargaining in crisis are *accommodative*, *coercive*, and *persuasive*. In the accommodative approach, we note a convergence of the bargaining positions of the parties toward a settlement through a sequence of bids or proposals for settlement, involving demands, offers, and concessions. Coercive bargaining is a process of showing firmness, involving threats and warnings, and in general exerting pressure to influence the other party to accept one's position. Coercion includes the threat of harm. Persuasion also attempts to influence the other party to accept one's position, but does not involve threatening harm. Both coercive and accommodative moves (threats and concessions) present the adversary with a choice between a pair of outcomes, one certain and the other uncertain. Persuasion involves moving the choice to one's own advantage (Snyder & Diesing, 1977, pp. 195–198).

A second typology with relevance to behavior patterns in crisis bargaining is proposed by Leng (1987; see also Leng & Gochman, 1982).) Unlike Snyder and Diesing, Leng's typology is based on the joint behavior of the crisis dyad. Among the relevant behaviors examined are: *Fight*: The antagonists employ mutually coercive influence strategies, with the level of conflict spiraling upward to very high levels of conflictive behavior (1967 Six Day War); *Resistance*: One antagonist pursues a coercive strategy while the other stands firm. This produces a relatively moderate rate of escalation (Italy-Ethiopia 1935); *Standoff*: Both parties demonstrate firmness through threats, and neither is willing to retreat from its stand, but neither is willing to increase the level of tension beyond a certain point. This usually ends in compromise or stalemate (Berlin Wall 1961); *Dialogue*: Both sides pursue accommodative bargaining strategies. Escalation is low and reciprocity is high (Morocco Crisis 1905–1906); and *Prudence*: One party is assertive, leading to rapid submission by the other (Austria Anschluss 1938) (Leng, 1987, pp. 182–194).

Although none of these approaches is directly incorporated into the strategic model of negotiation, they have helped sharpen our conception of the process and helped us distill its central elements.

5. CONCLUSIONS

The results presented in this chapter contribute to the development of autonomous agents that are capable of reaching mutually beneficial agreements efficiently and without delay. They have also contributed to the creation of a decision support system designed to provide an environment in which crisis decision makers can be trained and in which experiments can be conducted.

As the research in intelligent systems has progressed steadily over the past decade, it has become increasingly clear that there are classes of complex problems that cannot be solved by a single system in isolation; they require several systems to work together interactively in a cooperative framework. Furthermore, there are heterogeneous intelligent systems that were built in isolation, and their cooperation is necessary to achieve a new common goal. In situations where multiple agents are acting on different goals in the same environment, cooperation may be beneficial to all agents.

The theoretical part of this research, the strategic model of negotiation, provides a negotiation framework that explicitly accounts for the passage of time during the negotiation process itself. Therefore, it provides the autonomous agents with efficient strategies. The model provides a unified solution to a wide range of problems, and thus is appropriate for agents acting in dynamic real-world domains.

Since the end of 1995, when this chapter was written, the research on automated negotiation and crisis bargaining has advanced significantly. Our recent results have been published in Santmire et al. (1998); Schwartz and Kraus (1998); Azulay-Schwartz and Kraus (2000). For surveys on related issues in DAI please consult Weiss (1999); O'Hare and Jennings (1996); Huhns and Singh (1997). For surveys on recent related advances in political science, see Dixit and Nalebuff (1991); Hopmann (1996); Starkey, Boyer, and Wilkenfeld (1999).

ACKNOWLEDGMENTS

This chapter is based on continuing work supported by the National Science Foundation and the U.S. Institute of Peace. Some of the work discussed here was also reported in Kraus, Wilkenfeld, and Zlotkin (1995); Kraus and Wilkenfeld (1993a); Wilkenfeld, Kraus, Holley, and Harris (1995).

REFERENCES

Aalbersberg, I. and F. Sijstermans. 1991. High-quality and high performance full-text document retrieval: the parallel InfoGuide System. In *Proc. of the IEEE Conference on Parallel and Distributed Information Systems*.

Azulay-Schwarts, R. and S. Kraus 2000. Negotiation on data allocation in multi-agent environments. *Autonomous Agents and Multi-Agent Systems*.

Binmore, K., A. Rubinstein, and A. Wolinsky. 1986. The Nash bargaining solution in economic modeling. *Rand Journal of Economics*, 17(2):176–188.

Bond, A. H. and L. Gasser. 1988. An analysis of problems and research in DAI. In A. H. Bond and L. Gasser, editors, *Readings in Distributed Artificial Intelligence*. Morgan Kaufmann, San Mateo, California, pages 3–35.

Brecher, M., editor. 1978. *Studies in Crisis Behavior*. Transaction Books, New Brunswick, New Jersey.

Brecher, M. and J. Wilkenfeld. 1989. *Crisis, Conflict and Instability*. Pergamon Press, Oxford, England.

Brecher, M. and J. Wilkenfeld. 1997. *A Study of Crisis*. University of Michigan Press, Ann Arbor, MI.

Brecher, M., J. Wilkenfeld, and S. Moser. 1988. *Crises in the Twentieth Century: Vol. I. Handbook of International Crises*. Pergamon Press, Oxford, England.

Cammarata, S., D. McArthur, and R. Steeb. 1983. Strategies of cooperation in distributed problem solving. In *Proceedings of IJCAI-83*, August, Morgan Kaufmann, Chambery, France, pages 767–770.

Carver, N., Z. Cvetanovic, and V. Lesser. 1991. Sophisticated cooperation in FA/C distributed problem solving systems. In *Proc. of AAAI-91*, Anaheim, California, pages 191–198.

Chandrasekn, B. 1981. Natural and social system metaphors for distributed problem solving: Introduction to the issue. *IEEE Transaction on Systems Man and Cybernetics*, 11(1):1–5.

Conry, S. E., R. A. Meyer, and V. R. Lesser. 1988. Multistage negotiation in distributed planning. In A. H. Bond and L. Gasser, editors, *Readings in Distributed Artificial Intelligence*. Morgan Kaufmann, San Mateo, California, pages 367–384.

Conry, S. E., K. Kuwabara, V. R. Lesser, and R. A. Meyer. 1991. Multistage negotiation for distributed satisfaction. *IEEE Transactions on Systems, Man, and Cybernetics, Special Issue on Distributed Artificial Intelligence*, 21(6):1462–1477, December.

Decker, K. and V. Lesser. 1993. A one-shot dynamic coordination algorithm for distributed sensor networks. In *Proc. of AAAI-93*, July, Washington, DC, pages 210–216.

Dixit, A. K. and B. Nalebuff. 1991. *Thinking Strategically: The Competitive Edge in Business, Politics, and Everyday Life*. W. W. Norton, New York.

Doyle, J. 1989. Reasoning, representation, and rational self-government. In *Proc. of the 4th International Symposium on Methodologies for Intelligent Systems*, North-Holland, Amsterdam, pages 367–380.

Durfee, E. H. 1988. *Coordination of Distributed Problem Solvers*. Kluwer Academic Publishers, Boston.

Durfee, E. H. and V. R. Lesser. 1987. Global plans to coordinate distributed problem solvers. In *Proc. of IJCAI-87*, pages 875–883.

Ephrati, E. and J. S. Rosenschein. 1991. The Clarke tax as a consensus mechanism among automated agents. In *Proc. of AAAI-91*, July, Anaheim, California, pages 173–178.

Fischer, K. and N. Kuhn. 1993. *A DAI approach to modeling the transportation domain*. Technical Report RR-93-25, Deustsches Forschungszentrum fur Kunstliche Intelligenz GmbH.

Frieder, O. and H. T. Siegelmann. 1991. On the allocation of documents in information retrieval systems. In *Proceedings of the ACM Fourteenth Conference on Information Retrieval (SIGIR)*, Chicago, Illinois.

Gasser, L. 1993. Social knowledge and social action. In *IJCAI-93*, August, Morgan Kaufmann, Chambery, France, pages 751–757.

George, A. L. 1983. *Managing US-Soviet Rivalry: Problems of Crisis Prevention*. Westview Press, Boulder, CO.

George, A. L. and R. Smoke. 1974. *Deterrence in American Foreign Policy*. Columbia University Press, New York.

Grosz, B. J. and C. L. Sidner. 1990. Plans for discourse. In P. R. Cohen, J. L. Morgan, and M. E. Pollack, editors, *Intentions in Communication* (pp. 417–444). Bradford Books at MIT Press, Cambridge, MA.

Holley, K. and J. Wilkenfeld. 1994. The use of decision support systems in international education. In *Annual Meeting of the International Studies Association*, Washington DC.

Hong, S. 1994. *IMS server cookbook*. Unpublished manuscript.

Hopmann, P. T. 1996. *The Negotiation Process and the Resolution of International Conflicts*. University of South Carolina Press, Columbia, SC.

Hughes STX Corporation. 1994. *EOSDID, information management system*. Technical Report IMSV0-OP-GD-001 v1.2 940426, NASA.

Huhns, M. and M. Singh, editors. 1997. *Readings in Agents*. Morgan Kaufmann, San Mateo, California.

Kornfeld, W. and C. Hewitt. 1981. The scientific community metaphor. *IEEE Transaction on Systems Man and Cybernetics*, 11(1):24–33.

Kraus, S. 1997. Beliefs, time and incomplete information in multiple encounter negotiations among autonomous agents. *Annals of Mathematics and Artificial Intelligence*, 20(1–4):111–159.

Kraus, S., E. Ephrati, and D. Lehmann. 1991. Negotiation in a non-cooperative environment. *J. of Experimental and Theoretical AI*, 3(4):255–282.

Kraus, S. and D. Lehmann. 1995. Designing and building a negotiating automated agent. *Computational Intelligence*, 11(1):132–171.

Kraus, S. and J. Wilkenfeld. 1990a. An automated strategic model of negotiation. In *AAAI-90 Workshop on Reasoning in Adversarial Domains*, July, Boston.

Kraus, S. and J. Wilkenfeld. 1990b. *Modeling a hostage crisis: Formalizing the negotiation process*. Technical Report UMIACS TR 90-19 CS TR 2406, Institute for Advanced Computer Studies, University of Maryland.

Kraus, S. and J. Wilkenfeld. 1991. Negotiations over time in a multiagent environment: Preliminary report. In *Proc. of IJCAI-91*, Sydney, Australia, pages 56–61.

Kraus, S. and J. Wilkenfeld. 1993a. A strategic negotiations model with applications to an international crisis. *IEEE Transaction on Systems Man and Cybernetics*, 23(1):313–323.

Kraus, S. and J. Wilkenfeld. 1993b. The updating of beliefs in negotiations under time constraints with uncertainty. In *Proc. of IJCAI-93 workshop on Artificial Economics*, August, Chambery, France, pages 57–68. Also presented in BISFAI93.

Kraus, S., J. Wilkenfeld, M. Harris, and B. Blake. 1992. The hostage crisis simulation. *Simulations and Games*, 23(4):398–416.

Kraus, S., J. Wilkenfeld, and G. Zlotkin. 1995. Multiagent negotiation under time constraints. *Artificial Intelligence*, 75(2):297–345.

Kraus, S. and G. Zlotkin. 1992. Resource allocation among agents with incomplete information: An on-line negotiation approach. In *AI Track of the Ninth Israeli Symposium on Artificial Intelligence*, Tel-Aviv, Israel.

Kreps, D. and R. Wilson. 1982. Sequential equilibria. *Econometrica*, 50:863–894.

Kuwabara, K. and V. Lesser. 1989. Extended protocol for multistage negotiation. In *Proc. of the Ninth Workshop on Distributed Artificial Intelligence*, September, Washington, pages 129–161.

Lebow, R. N. 1981. *Between Peace and War*. Johns Hopkins University Press, Baltimore.

Leng, R. 1987. Structure and action in militarized disputes. In C. Hermann, C. Kegley, and J. Rosenau, editors, *New Directions in the Study of Foreign Policy*. Allen and Unwin, Winchester, MA.

Leng, R. 1988. Crisis learning games. *American Political Science Review*, 82, 1.

Leng, R. and C. Gochman. 1982. Dangerous disputes: A study of conflict behavior and war. *American Journal of Political Science*, 26(4):664–687.

Lesser, V. R. and L. D. Erman. 1980. Distributed interpretation:a model and experiment. *IEEE Transaction on Computers*, 29(12):1144–1163.

Lesser, V. R., J. Pavlin, and E. H. Durfee. 1988. Approximate processing in real time problem solving. *AI Magazine*, 9(1):49–61.

Lochbaum, K. E., B. J. Grosz, and C. L. Sidner. 1990. Models of plans to support communication: An initial report. In *Proceedings of AAAI-90*, July, Boston, pages 485–490.

Malone, T. W., R. E. Fikes, K. R. Grant, and M. T. Howard. 1988. Enterprise: A marketlike task schedule for distributed computing environments. In B. A. Huberman, editor, *The Ecology of Computation*. North Holland, Amsterdam, pages 177–205.

Moses, Y. and M. Tennenholtz. 1993. Off-line reasoning for on-line efficiency. In *Proc. of IJCAI-93*, Chambery, France, pages 490–495.

O'Hare, G. M. P. and N. R. Jennings, editors. 1996. *Foundations of Distributed Artificial Intelligence*. Wiley, New York.

Osborne, M. J. and A. Rubinstein. 1990. *Bargaining and Markets*. Academic Press, San Diego, California.

Rosenschein, J. S. and G. Zlotkin. 1994. *Rules of Encounter: Designing Conventions for Automated Negotiation Among Computers*. MIT Press, Boston.

Rubinstein, A. 1982. Perfect equilibrium in a bargaining model. *Econometrica*, 50(1):97–109.

Rubinstein, A. 1985. A bargaining model with incomplete information about preferences. *Econometrica*, 53(5):1151–1172.

Sandholm, T. 1993. An implementation of the contract net protocol based on marginal cost calculations. In *Proc. of AAAI-93*, July, Washington, DC, pages 256–262.

Santmire, Tara E., Jonathan Wilkenfeld, Sarit Kraus, Kim M. Holley, Toni E. Santmire, and Kristian Gleditsch. 1998. The impact of cognitive diversity on crisis negotiations. *Political Psychology*, 19(4):721–748, December.

Schwartz, R. and S. Kraus. 1997. Negotiation on data allocation in multi-agent environments. In *Proc. of AAAI-97*, July, Providence, Rhode Island, pages 29–35.

Schwartz, R. and S. Kraus. 1998. Bidding mechanisms for data allocation in multi-agent environments. In Munindar P. Singh, Anand S. Rao, and Michael J. Wooldridge, editors, *Intelligent Agents IV: Agent Theories, Architectures, and Languages*. Springer-Verlag, New York, pages 61–75.

Selten, R. 1975. Re-examination of the perfectness concept for equilibrium points in extensive games. *International Journal of Game Theory*, 4:25–55.

Shoham, Y. and M. Tennenholtz. 1992. On the synthesis of useful social laws for artificial agent societies. In *Proc. of AAAI-92*, July, San Jose, California, pages 276–281.

Smith, R. G. and R. Davis. 1983. Negotiation as a metaphor for distributed problem solving. *Artificial Intelligence*, 20:63–109.

Snyder, G. H. and P. Diesing. 1977. *Conflict Among Nations: Bargaining, Decision Making and System Structure in International Crises*. Princeton University Press, New Jersey.

Starkey, B., M. Boyer, and J. Wilkenfeld. 1999. *Negotiating a Complex World: An Introduction to International Negotiation*. Rowman and Littlefield, Boulder, CO.

Stein, J. G. and R. Tanter. 1980. *Rational Decision Making: Israel's Security Choices 1967*. Ohio State University Press, Columbus.

Stone, H. 1987. Parallel querying of large databases. *IEEE Computer*, 20(10).

Sycara, K. P. 1987. *Resolving Adversarial Conflicts: An Approach to Integrating Case-Based and Analytic Methods*. Ph.D. thesis, School of Information and Computer Science, Georgia Institute of Technology.

Sycara, K. P. 1990. Persuasive argumentation in negotiation. *Theory and Decision*, 28:203–242.

Tan, T. and S. Werlang. 1988. A guide to knowledge and games. In *Proc. of the Second Conference on Theoretical Aspects of Reasoning about Knowledge*, March, Pacific Grove, California, pages 163–177.

Thompson, L. 1990. Negotiation behavior and outcomes: Empirical evidence and theoretical issues. *Psychological Bulletin*, 108(3):515–532.

Weiss, G., editor. 1999. *Multiagent Systems: A modern approach to Distributed Artificial Intelligence*. MIT press, Cambridge, MA.

Wellman, M. 1992. A general-equilibrium approach to distributed transportation planning. In *Proc. of AAAI-92*, July, San Jose, California, pages 282–289.

Wilkenfeld, J., M. Brecher, and S. Moser. 1988. *Crises in the Twentieth Century, Vol. II: Handbook of Foreign Policy Crises*. Pergamon Press, Oxford, England.

Wilkenfeld, J., S. Kraus, K. Holley, and M. Harris. 1995. Genie: A decision support system for crisis negotiations. *Decision Support Systems*, 14:369–391.

Zlotkin, G. and J. S. Rosenschein. 1989. Negotiation and task sharing among autonomous agents in cooperative domains. In *Proc. of IJCAI-89*, August, Detroit, Michigan, pages 912–917.

Zlotkin, G. and J. S. Rosenschein. 1991. Cooperation and conflict resolution via negotiation among autonomous agents in noncooperative domains. *IEEE Transactions on Systems, Man, and Cybernetics, Special Issue on Distributed Artificial Intelligence*, 21(6):1317–1324, December.

Zlotkin, G. and J. S. Rosenschein. 1993. A domain theory for task oriented negotiation. In *Proc. of IJCAI-93*, August, Chambery, France, pages 416–422.

CHAPTER

5

Two Design Principles for Collaboration Technology: Examples of Semiformal Systems and Radical Tailorability*

Thomas W. Malone
Kum-Yew Lai
Kenneth R. Grant
Massachusetts Institute of Technology

In reflecting upon our experiences in designing collaboration technologies over the past 10 years, two key design principles have struck us repeatedly, and we believe their importance is still not widely appreciated. We call these two principles the principles of *semiformal systems* and *radical tailorability*. In this chapter, we describe the history of our work and how it illustrates the application and importance of these two principles.

Both these design principles are based on the premise that computers are not likely, in the foreseeable future, to have the cognitive capabilities that humans do. It is, of course, true that computers can already do many things that humans cannot, and it is certainly possible that someday computers may be able to do so many human-like things that this premise will no longer be a useful basis for design. For the foreseeable future, however, it seems safe to assume significant limitations on the cognitive capabilities of computers.

The question this raises, therefore, is what role computational agents can play in the world of human activities. It is, of course, tempting to think of "intelligent agents" as being much like intelligent humans. We would like them to be able to perform important tasks by themselves, communicating

---

*Reprinted (with permission) from J. Bradshaw (Ed.), *Software Agents*, AAAI Press/The MIT Press, Menlo Park, Calif., 1997, 109–143. Copyright © 1997 American Association for Artificial Intelligence. Portions of this chapter are copyright © 1987, 1988, 1989, 1992 Association for Computing Machinery (see acknowledgments for detailed list) and are reprinted here with permission.

with humans using natural human languages when necessary, and inferring as many things as possible without ever being told (e.g., Maes, 1997).

But to the extent computers are unable to do these things in the ways that humans do, we may be led astray by models of computer systems that are based too closely on how humans behave. For instance, computational agents that try to communicate using natural language but have severely limited capabilities for doing so may be much less useful than agents that simply use a restricted artificial language which is easily understandable by humans. Similarly, agents that attempt to infer things without ever being told may cause more trouble than they save if they take actions based on seriously incorrect inferences.

Our experience has convinced us that a certain amount of humility is desirable in proceeding toward the goal of building truly useful collaboration technology. In particular, there are two kinds of unrealistic expectations to which software designers are often vulnerable: First, it is often easy for software designers to overestimate their own ability to anticipate and predefine all the ways in which people will want to use collaborative systems. Second, it is easy for many designers to overestimate the ability of their "intelligent" computational agents to understand and act effectively in the complex world of human collaboration.

To help prevent these two kinds of unrealistic expectations, we have found the following two design principles to embody useful forms of humility:

1. Don't try to formally define all the ways a system can be used, and don't build computational agents that try to solve complex problems all by themselves. Instead, build systems where the boundary between what the systems do and what the humans do is a flexible one. We call this the principle of *semiformal systems* because it involves blurring the boundary between formally represented information acted upon by computational agents and informally represented information acted upon by humans.

2. Don't try to predetermine all the formal structure in a system, and don't build agents that try to figure out for themselves things that humans could easily tell them. Instead, try to build systems that make it as easy as possible for humans users to see and modify the information and reasoning processes their systems are using. We call this the principle of *radical tailorability* because one way of applying this principle is to create "tailoring languages" with which people who are not skilled programmers can easily "tailor" new applications for themselves.

In recounting the history of our work, we will attempt to illustrate the implications of these two design principles. We proceed as follows: First, we describe the Information Lens system, an early intelligent tool for helping people find, filter, sort, and prioritize electronic messages. In addition to describing the design of the system, we briefly report on empirical studies of the use of this system. Next, using this early work as a basis, we describe in more detail the two design principles of semiformal systems and radical tailorability. Then, we describe the Oval system, a much more general tool for supporting information sharing and collaboration. The Oval system can be thought of as a radically tailorable, semiformal environment in which communities of intelligent agents and humans can interact. Finally, we describe a number of examples of agent-oriented applications we have developed in the Oval environment.

INFORMATION LENS: AN INTELLIGENT TOOL FOR MANAGING ELECTRONIC MESSAGES

In late 1984, we began work on the original version of the Information Lens (see Malone, Grant, Turbak, Brobst, & Cohen [1987] and Malone, Grant, Lai, Rao, & Rosenblitt [1987] for complete descriptions). The system was motivated by a desire to help people cope intelligently with the increasingly common problem of having large amounts of electronic mail: It helped people filter, sort, and prioritize messages that were already addressed to them, and it also helped them find useful messages they would not otherwise have received. In some cases, the system responded automatically to certain messages, and in other cases it suggested likely actions for human users to take.

Key Ideas

The Information Lens system was based on four key ideas:

1. A rich set of semistructured message types (or frames) can form the basis for an intelligent information sharing system. For example, meeting announcements can be structured as templates that include fields for "date," "time," "place," "organizer," and "topic," as well as any additional unstructured information. These templates can help people compose messages in the first place (e.g., by reminding them of what information to include). More importantly from our present point of view, by putting much of the essential information in special fields, these templates also enable computational agents to automatically process a much wider range of information than would be possible with simple keyword methods or automatic parsing.

2. Sets of "if–then" rules can be used to conveniently specify automatic processing for these messages. These rules may include multiple levels of reasoning, not just Boolean selection criteria.

3. The use of semistructured message types and automatic rules for processing them can be greatly simplified by a consistent set of display-oriented

editors for composing messages, constructing rules, and defining new message templates.

4. The initial introduction and later evolution of a group communication system can be much easier if there is an incremental adoption path, that is, a series of small changes, each of which has the following properties: (a) individual users can continue to use their existing system with no change if they so desire, (b) individual users who make small changes receive some immediate benefit, and (c) groups of users who adopt the changes receive additional benefits beyond the individual benefits.

System Overview

In order to provide a natural integration of this system with the capabilities that people already used, the system was built on top of an existing electronic mail system. Users could continue to send and receive their mail as usual, including using centrally maintained distribution lists and manually classifying messages into folders. In addition, the Information Lens provided four important optional capabilities: (1) people could use structured message templates to help them compose their messages; (2) receivers could specify rules to automatically filter and classify messages arriving in their mailbox; (3) senders could include as an addressee of a message in addition to specific individuals or distribution lists, a special mailbox (named "Anyone") to indicate that the sender was willing to have this message automatically redistributed to anyone else who might be interested; and (4) receivers could specify rules to find and show messages addressed to "Anyone" that the receiver would not otherwise have seen (see Fig. 5.1). Our primary implementations of this system were in the Xerox Interlisp environment.

Messages

Figure 5.2 shows a sample of the highly graphical interaction through which users could construct messages using semistructured message templates. After selecting a field of a message by pointing with a mouse, the user could point with the mouse again to see the field's default value, an explanation of the field's purpose, or a list of likely alternatives for filling in the field. If the user selected one of these alternatives, that value was automatically inserted in the message text. The user could also edit any fields directly at any time using the built-in display-oriented text editor. Users who did not want to take advantage of these message construction aids could simply select the most general message type ("Message") and use the text editor to fill in the standard fields ("To," "From," and "Subject") just as they would have done in the underlying mail system. The templates for different types of messages were arranged in an "inheritance hierarchy" with some message types

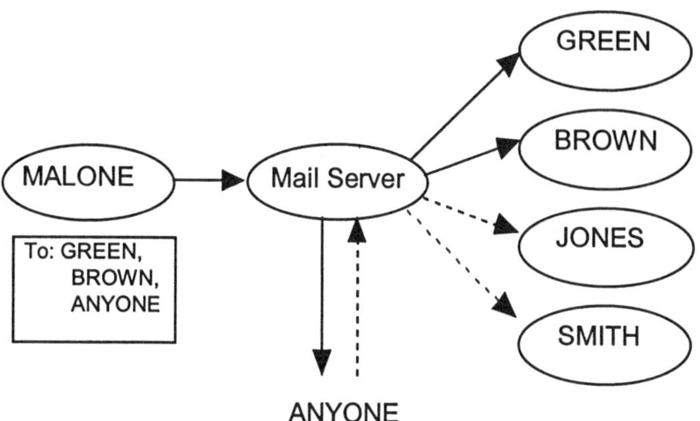

FIG. 5.1. The Information Lens system includes components in the users' workstations and in a central server (called "Anyone"). Messages that include "Anyone" as an addressee are automatically distributed (via the dotted lines) to all receivers whose interest profiles select the messages as well as to the other explicit addressees.

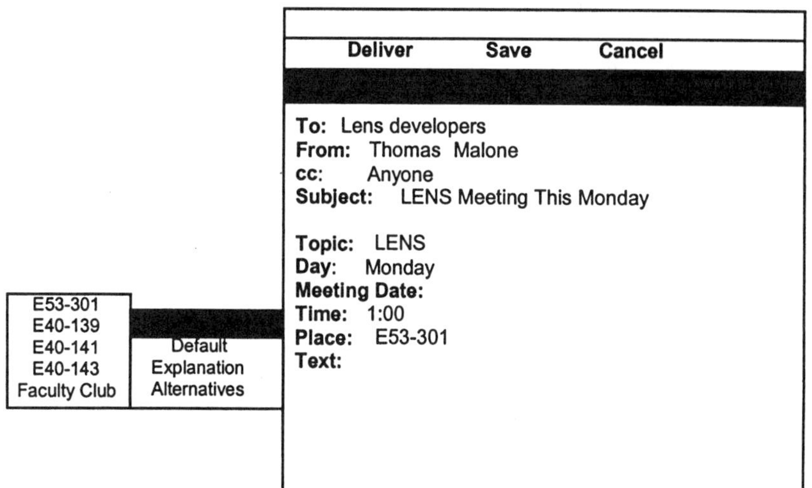

FIG. 5.2. Messages are composed with a display-oriented editor and templates that have pop-up menus associated with the template fields. (Note: The format of screen displays in this figure and others throughout the chapter differ in minor ways because different figures are taken from different generations of the systems described.)

being specializations of others (e.g., see Fikes & Kehler, 1985). For example, the "Seminar Announcement" template was a specialization of the "Meeting Announcement" template, and it included an additional field for speaker that was not present in "Meeting Announcements."

Rules

Just as the structure of messages simplified the process of composing messages, it also simplified the process of constructing rules for processing messages. For instance, Fig. 5.3 shows an example of the display-oriented editor used to construct rules in the Information Lens system. This editor used rule templates based on the same message types as those used for message construction, and it used a similar interaction style with menus available for defaults, alternatives, and explanations.

Figure 5.4 shows some sample rules for performing actions such as moving messages to specific folders (Fig. 5.4a), deleting messages (Fig. 5.4b), and automatically "resending" messages to someone else (Fig. 5.4c). "Resending"

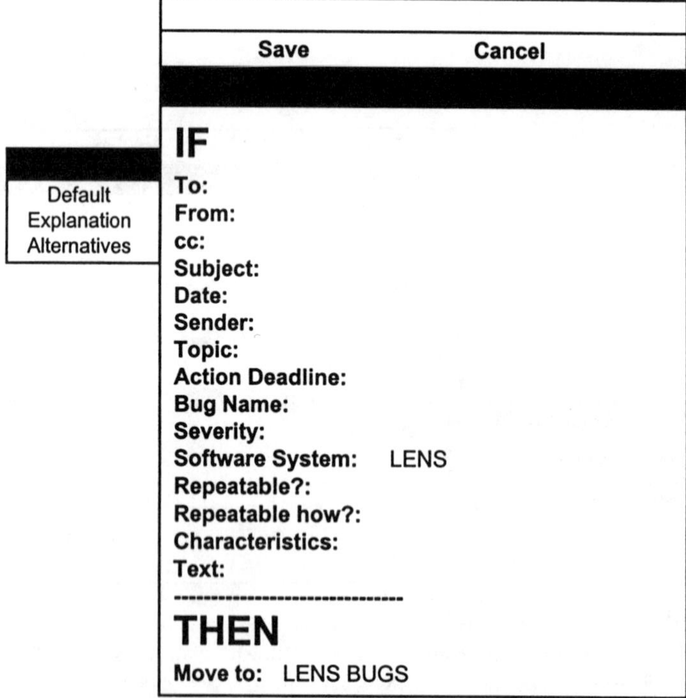

FIG. 5.3. Rules for processing messages are composed using the same kind of editor and the same templates as those used for composing messages in the first place.

(a)	IF	Message type:	Action request
		Action deadline:	Today, Tomorrow
	THEN	Move to:	Urgent
(b)	IF	Message type:	Meeting Announcement
		Day:	Not Tuesday
	THEN	Delete	
(c)	IF	Message type:	Meeting proposal
		Sender:	Not Axsom
	THEN	Resend:	Axsom
(d)	IF	From:	Silk, Siegel
	THEN	Set Characteristic:	VIP
	IF	Message type:	Action request
		Characteristics:	VIP
	THEN	Move to:	Urgent
(e)	IF	Message type:	Request for information
		Subject:	AI, Lisp
	THEN	Show	

FIG. 5.4. Sample rules.

a message is similar to "forwarding" it, except that instead of copying the entire original message into the body of a new message, the new message preserves the type and all but the "To" and "cc" fields of the original message. Rules could also "set characteristics" of a message that could then be tested by later rules (Fig. 5.4d).

When the local rules finished processing all incoming messages, the numbers of new messages that had been automatically moved into different folders since the last time the folder was viewed were shown on a hierarchical display of the folder names. In order to help users understand and modify their rules, a simple explanation capability allowed users to see a history of the rules that fired on a given message.

In addition to the local rules applied when messages were retrieved to a user's workstation, an individual user could also specify central rules to select messages addressed to "Anyone" that the user wanted to see (see Fig. 5.4e).

Group Use of Message Types

Users of systems like the Information Lens can take advantage of simple sorting rules, even if they do not use any of the specialized message templates the system provides. But, to the extent that a group of people all use the same message templates, they can benefit even more from rules based on the shared message structures.

One of the important questions, therefore, is how groups of people can develop and evolve a shared language of common message types. One simple solution is to require everyone to use the same message types, perhaps determined by some central administrator or standards committee. Another, more complicated, solution is to let anyone create new message types as long as they also write "translation rules" that translate these types into and out of the common language.

Lee and Malone (1990) described one way of categorizing all possible solutions to this translation problem and propose a hybrid solution called "Partially Shared Views" that combines many of the best features of the different schemes. Essentially this solution lets different (and possibly overlapping) groups of people develop and use shared sets of message type definitions (called "views"). When someone adopts a view, they can receive messages directly from other users of the view. When someone receives a message created in a view they have not adopted, the message is translated automatically into one of the message types they have adopted.

The most interesting case of this automatic translation occurs when the "foreign" message type is a specialization of one already known to the receiver. In this case, the foreign message type is automatically translated into the "nearest common ancestor" type known to both groups. For instance, if you received a "Seminar Announcement" message, and you had not adopted a definition for this type of message, then the message would be automatically translated into the nearest "parent" type, say "Meeting Announcement," which you had adopted. Information from any fields not present in "Meeting Announcements" (e.g., "Speaker") would simply be added into the "Text" field of the "Meeting Announcement" message. Then all the rules you had defined for "Meeting Announcements" would be applied to the incoming message.

Users' Experiences With Information Lens

In order to see how people outside our own group would actually use a system like the Information Lens, we worked for several years (approximately 1985–1988) with a corporate test site to implement a version of the system in their environment and observe their usage experience. These studies are described in detail by MacKay (1988) and MacKay, Malone, Crowston, Rao, Rosenblitt, and Card (1989). In this section we summarize some of the key results.

Can Nonprogrammers Use Rules?

One of the most important questions we had was whether non-programmers would be able to use rules effectively. The test site we studied was very advanced in its use of computer technology, and a number of our test users were skilled computer programmers. However, our test sample also included secretaries, managers, and other non-computer scientists. We were happy to find that no one at the test site had trouble understanding how to create and use rules. Even users who had never had any computer programming experience at all told us they found the template-based method of constructing rules to be quite easy to use. For instance, one user, with no computer training, described his first experience with the rule editor as follows: "It's obvious. You just go into the [fields] and type whatever you want."

When Do Users Run Rules?

When we designed the Information Lens system, we expected that people would use rules to sort and process their messages before reading the messages. However, it was also possible for users to read all their messages first and then apply the rules to sort the messages into folders. To our surprise, we found that a number of users preferred to use rules in this way. These users said they liked to feel "in control" by seeing all their messages before any rules moved them, and then they could use the rules to file the messages in folders for later retrieval. We called the first kind of users "prioritizers," and the second kind of users "archivers" (MacKay, 1988).

What Kinds of Rules Do Users Write?

In the sample of people we studied most carefully, users created an average of 15 rules each (with a range from 2 to 35 rules per person). The most common kind of rules sorted messages based on the distribution lists to which the messages were addressed. For instance, users often used rules to move messages addressed to a particular distribution list into a folder with the same name, thus creating a kind of computer conferencing system based on electronic mail.

Another important observation was that some of the users who reported the most satisfaction with the system had only a few rules. For instance, one user who was on the verge of being overwhelmed (with more than 30 messages per day), created only two rules: One rule moved messages into a special folder if their "Subject" field contained the name of a conference this person was organizing. The other rule moved messages into a different folder if they were addressed to this person by name (rather than simply to a distribution list of which this person was a member). This person said that these two rules "changed her life!"

SEMIFORMAL SYSTEMS AND RADICAL TAILORABILITY

In reflecting upon our experience with Information Lens, we had the feeling that there were some underlying–but largely inarticulate–design principles that contributed to its apparent success and that could be useful in designing many other kinds of systems. Eventually we were able to articulate two of these principles using the terms *semiformal systems* and *radical tailorability*.

Semiformal Systems

One of the things that struck us most strongly about our experience with Information Lens was the usefulness of letting people structure their messages to a certain degree (e.g., by putting some information in special fields), but still letting them include other unstructured information. For instance, there may well be times when people want to put "I don't know yet" in the "Place" field of a "Meeting Announcment" message. In this case, the system can still be useful, even though perhaps not as useful as it would be if the field contained the expected kind of information.

More generally, the agents in the Information Lens system operate in a very complex human-centered environment of interpersonal messaging. In this complicated environment, the agents "understand" very little of what is actually going on, but they can still be useful. This usefulness is possible, we believe, because the agents do simple things with the bits of structure they do understand and then "degrade gradefully" (e.g., by doing nothing) when there is not enough recognizable structure for them to take any sensible action. These observations led us to become more reflective about the benefits of systems that formalize certain things for automatic processing by computers, while leaving other things informal for processing by humans.

Definition of Semiformal Systems

We eventually came to call such systems *semiformal systems*, and we defined a semiformal system as a computer system that has the following three properties:

1. it represents and automatically processes certain information in formally specified ways;
2. it represents and makes it easy for humans to process the same or other information in ways that are not formally specified; and
3. it allows the boundary between formal processing by computers and informal processing by people to be easily changed.

In the past, computer systems have almost always been at one extreme or the other. At one extreme are very highly structured systems like conventional databases and knowledge bases with strict requirements about the contents of different kinds of fields and with structured procedures for processing the information represented in the system. At the other extreme are very unstructured systems like conventional electronic mail and word processing where the computer's role is primarily to record, store, and transmit information that is to be understood only by people, not to understand or otherwise process the information it stores. The concept of semiformal systems opens up a vast middle ground between these two extremes and suggests how computers can be useful in a much wider range of ways than we have previously come to expect.

Semistructured Information. One important consequence of this definition is that information in a semiformal system is "semistructured" with some structured elements such as named fields and some unstructured elements such as free text, voice, or images. It is also often useful for a semiformal system to be "tolerant" of unstructured or unexpected information, even in places where some kind of structured information might usually be expected.

Visible Reasoning. Another important attribute of semiformal systems that is implied by this definition is that the reasoning processes used by the system are often accessible to their human users. In other words, rather than creating intelligent agents whose operations are "black boxes," designers should try to create "glass boxes" where the essential elements of the agents' reasoning can be seen and modified by users.

A serious risk, for example, of "learning agents" like those described by Maes (1997) is that agents will infer incorrect rules (or fail to infer correct ones) when users could have easily described the rules they actually wanted to use. A semiformal approach to designing such systems would suggest that any attempts to have agents automatically "learn" from observing users' behavior should occur only *after* the system already provides a way for users to directly specify what they want.

Of course, this does not mean that unsophisticated computer users should be exposed to details of low level programming languages. It does mean, however, that designers should try to create user interfaces where the essence of what is going on in a system is exposed to users in a form that is meaningful and understandable to them. One approach to part of this problem is suggested by the "explanation" facilities in traditional knowledge-based systems. Another approach is suggested by the principle of radical tailorability described shortly.

When Are Semiformal Systems Useful?

Semiformal systems are most useful when we understand enough to formalize in a computer system some, but not all, of the knowledge relevant to acting in a given situation. We believe that this includes almost all of the real-world situations in which agents might be used. A number of commentators, for example, have pointed out that there is, in some sense, an essentially infinite amount of potential complexity in any real situation (e.g., Suchman,

1983). On the other hand, there are also clearly many situations where patterns and structural knowledge can be useful.

The trick, we believe, is to design flexible systems that allow us to exploit the patterns and knowledge we understand when they are useful without getting in the way when they are not. And this is precisely the goal of the design principle we have called semiformal systems.

Radical Tailorability

Another aspect of the Information Lens system that struck us as being particularly important was the ability of users to change the formal structures that the system supported for them.

The most important example of this was the ability of users to create and modify their own mail processing rules. It would, of course, have been possible to build a system with a few "pre-canned" and generally useful rules. It would also be possible (though not usually economically feasible) to have skilled programmers modify the rules used by people whenever the people's mail processing needs changed. Neither of these alternatives, however, is as desirable as having a system that is easy enough to use that most people can understand their own mail processing rules and can change them whenever the need arises.

A second example of how people could change the formal structure of the Information Lens system was by modifying the message types. By adding new message types to their own system, individual users could simplify the creation of messages they frequently sent. And by agreeing upon new message types to be shared in a group, users could make possible more powerful filtering rules for these new types of messages.

Both of these ways of modifying Information Lens are examples of how people can shape the formal structure in their systems to fit the situations in which the systems are used. This process of letting end users modify their own systems is often called "end user programming," and Information Lens embodied—in rudimentary form—a kind of end user programming we have since come to call *radical tailorability*.

Definition of Radical Tailorability

Loosely speaking, we call a system *radically tailorable* if it allows end users to create a wide range of different applications by progressively modifying a working system. Radically tailorable systems are not new; perhaps the best known examples of existing radically tailorable systems are spreadsheets. However, we believe it is useful to articulate two desirable properties of such systems in order to help create more systems with these properties.

First, we use the term *tailorable* to mean that these systems can be changed without ever "really programming." More specifically, by tailorable, we mean that *end users* (not skilled programmers) can progressively modify a working system (such as a spreadsheet) without ever having to leave the application domain and work in a separate underlying "programming" domain. With conventional programming languages, it is, of course, possible to change a working application. Doing so, however, requires that someone (usually a trained programmer) modify instructions that are related in potentially very complex ways to what the end user of the application sees on the screen. In radically tailorable systems, on the other hand, changes are made directly in the context of a working application, usually on the same screens. In this way, radically tailorable systems can help reduce the "cognitive distance" between using an application and designing it (Hutchins, 1986).

Second, we use the term *radically* to suggest that very large changes can be made by tailoring. Radically tailorable systems, therefore, differ from "ordinary" tailorable systems (such as word processing programs with "Preferences" parameters) in the degree to which users can create a wide range of substantially different applications. For instance, starting with the same blank spreadsheet, users can create applications ranging from personal budgeting to sales forecasting to corporate finance.

When Are Radically Tailorable Systems Useful?

As the continuing needs for "maintenance" and "systems integration" of nearly all computer systems demonstrates, the need for adapting computer systems to the situations in which they are used is very pervasive.

One of the critical questions in determining whether a radically tailorable approach to system modification is feasible, however, is whether a designer can create a set of building blocks at the *right* level of abstraction. That is, the building blocks should not be so low level that they require significant effort to do anything useful, nor so high level that they require significant modification whenever the users' needs change (diSessa, 1985).

Fortunately, our experiences with Information Lens led us toward a set of building blocks that turned out to be widely useful. To begin with, we were genuinely surprised at how useful the semistructured messages turned out to be. For instance, in one of our papers (Malone, Grant, Lai, Rao, & Rosenblitt, 1987), we described how adding a few specialized action types to certain kinds of messages greatly simplified the process of designing a variety of different applications such as computer conferencing, task tracking, and calendar management.

Even though simple versions of these new applications were relatively easy to program using the basic architecture in Information Lens, there were some obvious limitations to them. For instance, it was possible to automatically sort "Action Request" messages into a "To do" folder, but like any other folder, the table of contents format for messages in the folder would show only the "From," "Date," and "Subject" fields of the messages. To see other information (such as the "Due Date" or "Requestor"), we would have to display each message individually. Clearly this application called for a more general display format for the contents of objects in folders.

As we continued along this line of thinking, we felt ourselves inexorably drawn toward generalizing the Information Lens to include more types of objects (besides just messages), more types of display formats for collections of objects (besides the tables of contents for messages), and more types of agents (besides those used to sort and route messages). As described in the next section, the result of these generalizations became the system we called Oval.

OVAL: A RADICALLY TAILORABLE TOOL FOR INFORMATION MANAGEMENT AND COOPERATIVE WORK

In 1987, we began work on the first version of the Oval system[1] system (Lai, Malone, & Yu, 1988). The name "Oval" is an acronym for the four key components of the system: Objects, Views, Agents, and Links. Unlike the Information Lens system, which was focused exclusively on electronic messaging, we wanted Oval to be a much more general tool for supporting many kinds of cooperative work and information management applications. In particular, we had two primary goals in designing this system that differed from the goals of many previous systems to support similar tasks:

1. *Integration.* The system should combine many different kinds of formal and informal information and many different applications into a single integrated environment where people use a simple and consistent interface for everything from reading mail to querying databases and where these applications can interact with each other.
2. *Tailorability.* The system should let ordinary people create and modify these applications for themselves without requiring the help of professional programmers.

---

[1]The early versions of Oval were called "Object Lens" (Lai et al., 1988; Malone, Yu, & Lee, 1989). However, we eventually changed the name to "Oval" to reduce the widespread confusion between Information Lens and Object Lens. In this chapter, therefore, we will use the name Oval to refer to all versions of the system, including those that were originally called "Object Lens." A detailed description of the differences between the system originally called Object Lens and the later versions of Oval is included as an appendix to this chapter.

In order to achieve these goals, the system helps people keep track of and share knowledge about various "objects" such as people, tasks, projects, companies and many other things with which they work. For example, people can use hypertext links to represent relationships between a message and its replies, between people and their supervisors, and between different parts of a complex product.

The system also lets people create various kinds of "intelligent agents" to help them organize and respond to this knowledge. For instance, people can use intelligent agents to find electronic messages in which they are interested, to notice overdue tasks, and to notify others of upcoming deadlines.

A key aspect of the system, for our purposes here, is that both the people and their agents use and modify the same knowledge base of linked objects. Among other things, this means that information people maintain in the system for their own purposes can also be used by their agents to be more helpful. For instance, information people store in the system about hierarchical reporting relationships and task assignments might also be used by their agents to select problem reports about projects for which people in a particular group are responsible.

In order to make it feasible for people to maintain many different kinds of information in the system, it must be both easy and useful for them to do so. By designing Oval as a radically tailorable system, we have tried to accomplish both these goals.

Overview of Oval

Oval is based on four key building blocks: *objects, views, agents,* and *links*. In the next four subsections, we provide an overview of how these four components allow us to expose semiformal knowledge to users in a way that is both visible and changeable. Much more detailed descriptions of the system features can be found in Lai et al. (1988) and Malone et al. (1989).

Objects

Semistructured *objects* represent things in the world such as people, tasks, messages, and meetings. Each object includes a collection of fields and field values and a set of actions that can be performed upon it. For example, Fig. 5.5 shows a template for an object of type "Task." These objects are semistructured in the sense that users can fill in as much or as little information in different fields as they desire and the information in a field is not necessarily of any specific type (e.g., it may be free text, a link to another object, or a combination of text and links). Users see and manipulate these objects via a particularly natural form of template-based interfaces.

These object types are arranged in a hierarchy of increasingly specialized types with each object type inheriting fields, actions, and other properties

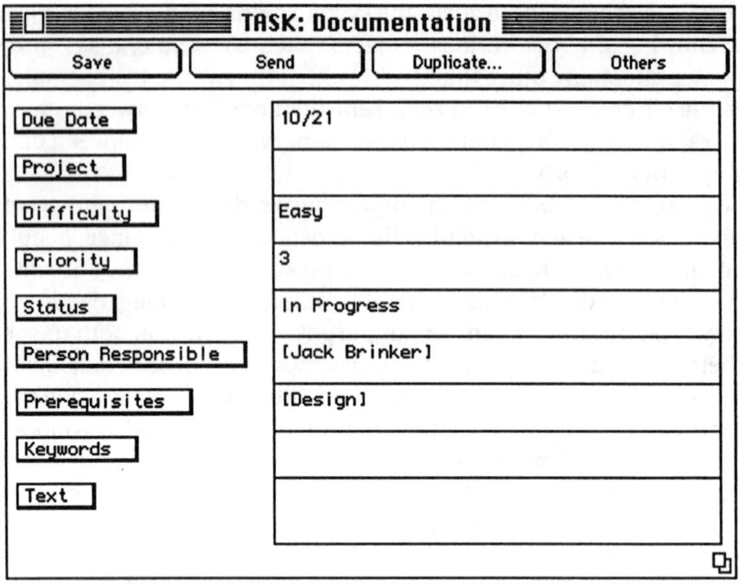

TASK: Documentation

Save | Send | Duplicate... | Others

Due Date	10/21
Project	
Difficulty	Easy
Priority	3
Status	In Progress
Person Responsible	[Jack Brinker]
Prerequisites	[Design]
Keywords	
Text	

FIG. 5.5. Objects can be edited with a simple template editor. Fields can include text, graphics, or links to other objects.

from its parents in the hierarchy. For example, objects include fields for "Name," "Keywords," and "Text" and standard actions (like "Save," "Send," and "Add Link") which can be performed on them. In addition, some object types have other specialized actions that are appropriate only for that kind of object. For instance, messages have actions like "Reply" and "Forward" and agents (see below) have a "Trigger" action that triggers them to start running.

Views

User customizable *views* summarize collections of objects and allow users to edit individual objects. For instance, Fig. 5.6a shows a "table" view that includes the values of selected fields from the tasks in the folder pertaining to a specific project. Users can easily tailor the format of these displays by selecting from a menu the fields they want to have included in the table.

In cases (like this one) where the objects in a folder are related to each other, Oval can also display these relationships in a "network" format. For instance, Fig. 5.6b shows the same folder, but with the display format changed to show the relationships represented by links in the "Prerequisites" field. In this case, the display resembles a simple PERT chart. Figure 5.6c shows the same folder of task objects with a third view, the "calendar" format, which places objects in a calendar according to the dates shown in their "Due Date" fields.

a

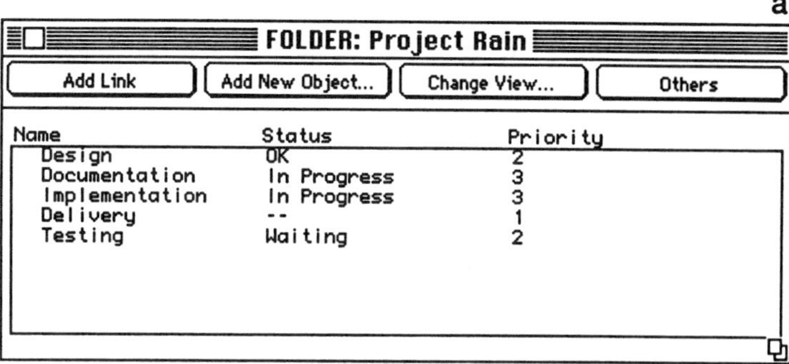

b

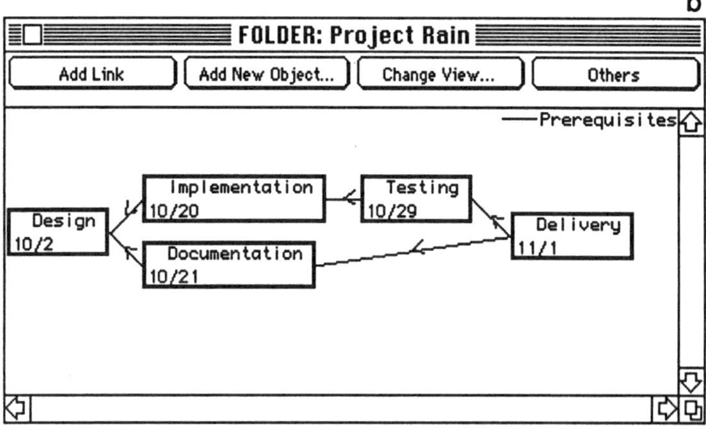

c

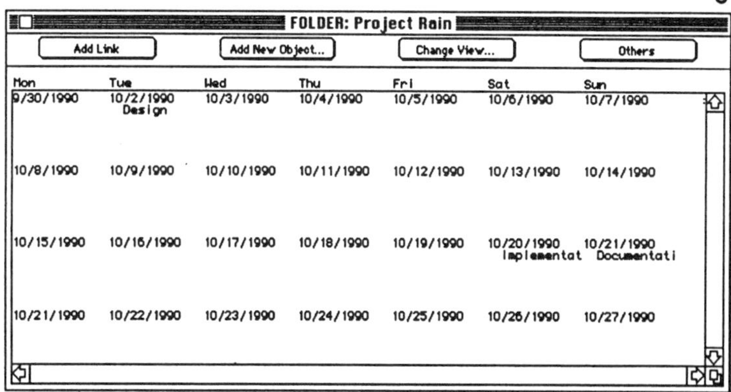

FIG. 5.6. In (a), users can select which fields to display in tables that summarize a collection of objects. In (b), users can choose which fields to be used as edges in a network that summarize the relationships among objects. Finally, in (c), users can choose a field containing dates that will be used to display the objects in a calendar.

Users can select any view format (e.g., table, network, or calendar) for any collection of objects. In keeping with the semiformal philosophy, the system will do its best to apply the view, even if it doesn't make sense for all the objects. For instance, if a calendar view contains objects for which there is no recognizable date in the appropriate field, those objects will be shown in a calendar cell called "No date."

Agents

Rule-based *agents* perform active tasks for people without requiring the direct attention of their users. Agents can be triggered by events such as the arrival of new mail, the appearance of a new object in a folder, or the arrival of a prespecified time. For instance, Fig. 5.7 shows an example of a simple agent designed to help a user keep track of tasks to be done. This agent is triggered whenever a task is added to the "New Tasks" folder or when a task already in the folder is changed.

When an agent is triggered it applies a set of rules to a collection of objects. Rules contain descriptions of the objects to which they apply and actions to be performed on those objects. For instance, the agent shown in Fig. 5.7 includes several rules, one of which is shown. This rule finds any tasks with a "Due Date" less than today and copies them to the "Late Tasks" folder. Some other possible actions include moving and deleting objects from folders and mailing them to other users.

Embedded Descriptions. With the capabilities we have described so far, all rules must depend only on information contained in the objects to which they are being applied. For instance, a rule about a message can depend only on information contained in the message itself. It is often desirable, however, to be able to specify rules that also depend on other information contained elsewhere in the knowledge base. For instance, in the Information Lens system, if a user wanted to specify a rule that applied to all messages from vice presidents, the rule would have to include the names of all the vice presidents in the "From" field.

In Oval, it is possible to draw upon other information by having descriptions embedded within other descriptions. For instance, the rule shown in Fig. 5.8 is satisfied if the message is from any person with a job title that includes "vice president." To apply this rule, the system checks to see whether the string in the "From" field of the message is the same as the "Name" of any "Person" object in the knowledge base that satisfies the description.

Other Agent Actions. For users who can (and want to) write programs more complex than the sequences of rules described so far, it is a simple matter conceptually for systems like Oval to include "escapes" to more powerful scripting or programming languages. The current prototype of Oval

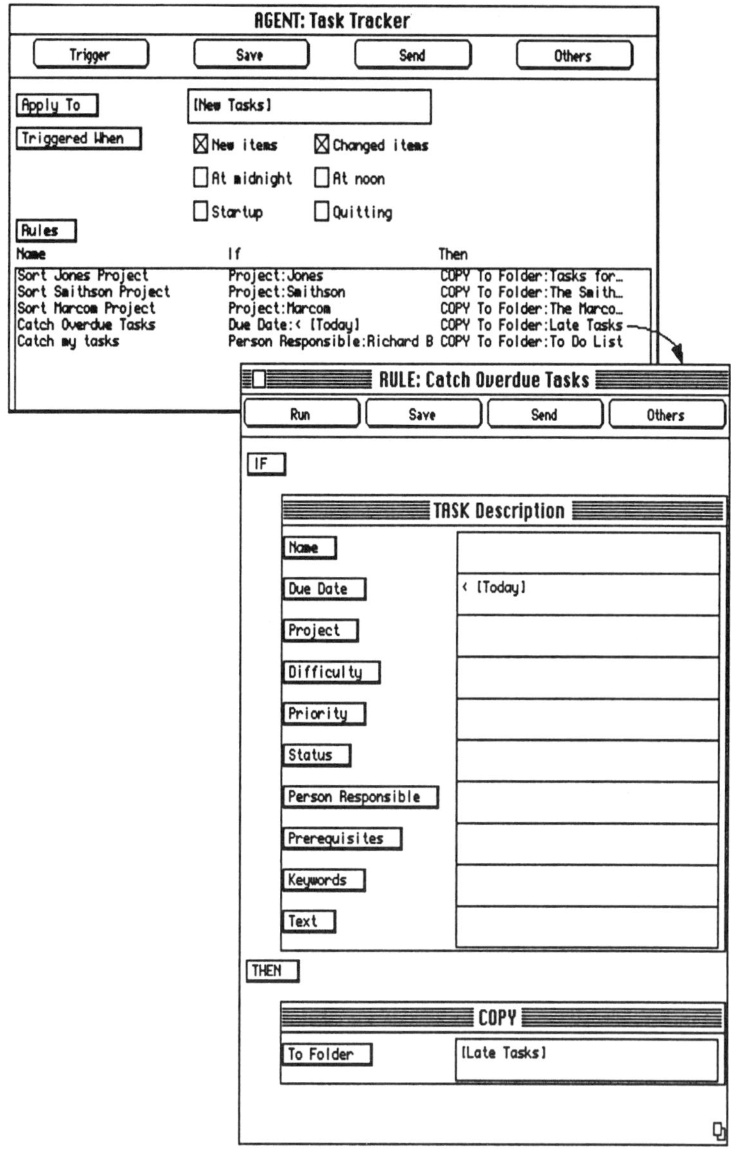

FIG. 5.7. Agents include a collection of rules and specifications for when and where to apply them. Rules describe the objects that satisfy them and specify what action to perform on those objects.

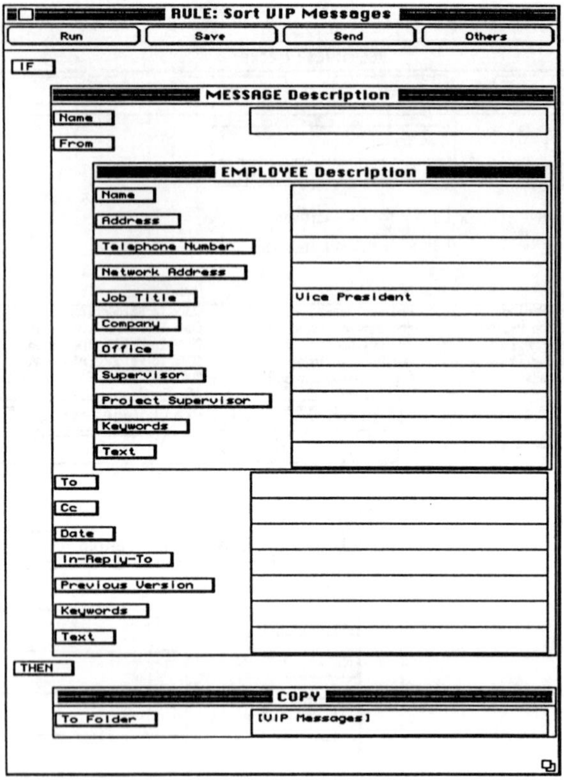

FIG. 5.8. Rules can use embedded descriptions to create complex queries.

illustrates this possibility by allowing users to invoke any arbitrary program (written in Lisp, the language in which Oval is implemented) as the action of a rule. It would also be possible (though not implemented in our current prototype) for an agent itself to be any arbitrary program that is triggered by some specified condition.

Links

Users of Oval can easily see and change the relationships among objects by inserting and deleting *links* between the objects. For example, by inserting in the fields of some objects links (or "pointers") to other objects, users can represent relationships between messages and their replies, between people and their supervisors, or between different parts of a complex product. Users can then follow these hypertext links by clicking on them. In addition to this "manual" navigation using links, the knowledge represented by the links can also be tested by agents and used in creating displays that summarize relationships.

For instance, Fig. 5.5 contains a link to two objects: (1) a "Person" object called "Jack Brinker" that represents the person responsible for the task, and (2) a "Task" object called "Design" that is a prerequisite to documentation.

User Tailoring

The primary user level modifications to the system include: (a) defining new object types, (b) adding fields to existing object types, (c) selecting views for objects and collections of objects (from a prespecified set of display formats), (d) specifying parameters for a given view (such as which fields to show), (e) creating new agents and rules, and (f) inserting new links.

Implementation Environment

The primary implementations of Oval were as a proof-of-concept prototype in Macintosh Common Lisp on networked Apple Macintoshes. This implementation of Oval was not robust enough for daily use in most environments, and therefore, we have not done formal empirical tests of the the usability of the system in real-world situations. The implementation was, however, sufficiently robust for rapid prototyping and demonstration of many applications. For instance, more than 100 copies of the software were distributed to other researchers and developers for demonstration purposes.[2]

Sharing Information

Even though the low-level systems issues involved in data sharing were not the primary focus of this project, we implemented three primary ways for people to save and share information in Oval:

1. *Mailing objects.* Users can mail any collection of objects back and forth to each other in messages. For instance, all the objects linked (directly or indirectly) to a given object can be automatically collected and mailed. This is done by inserting a link to the object in a message and then choosing the option of mailing "all levels" of other objects linked to the first object.

When users receive a message containing objects, the identity of the objects is preserved (i.e., preexisting links will point to the newest versions of the objects and the previous versions will be stored as "previous ver-

---

[2]For information on how to obtain a copy of the software for research purposes at no charge, contact Heather Mapstone, MIT Technology Licensing Office, E32-300, 28 Carleton Street, Cambridge, MA 02139 (Telephone: (617) 253-6966. Fax: (617) 258-6790. Email: mapstone@mit.edu.)

sions"). Users are notified of these changes, and if they desire, can undo them in specific cases.

This method of explicitly mailing objects is sometimes more awkward than having a shared database. However, many applications can be supported quite satisfactorily in this way for groups of people who are connected only by email gateways, without the necessity of shared databases.

2. *Sharing databases.* We also implemented a rudimentary version of "live" sharing of objects stored on remote databases. To do this, we used a remote relational database and mapping functions to translate between Oval objects and records in the relational database. Even though we did not do so, it would also be quite consistent with the overall Oval framework to use an object-oriented database for data storage and sharing.

3. *Sharing files.* Finally, users can save any collection of Oval objects in a file which they (or other people) can load later. These files can, of course, be shared in all the ways other files can be shared: on a file server, on floppy disks, and so forth. This is, in many ways, the least interesting way of sharing objects, but it is, in practice, the way we have used most often so far.

A key issue that arises when people share information in Oval is how to share definitions of new object types. As mentioned earlier, Lee and Malone (1990) discussed this issue in detail and propose a general solution called "partially shared views" which involves grouping type definitions into "views," explicitly sharing these views, and automatically translating unknown types into the nearest "ancestor" type in a view shared by both the sender and the receiver. In the current version of the system, we implemented the following special case of this general solution: When users save or mail objects not defined in the basic system, the type definitions are saved or mailed along with the objects themselves.

What's New Here?

Because the novel contribution of Oval is a subtle one, it is useful to be explicit about what we believe the contribution to be. The individual components of Oval (objects, views, agents, and links) are not new; each of them has been used before in at least some (and sometimes many) previous systems.

What we believe is novel about the Oval system is the choice of this set of building blocks and the particular way of combining them that is both simple and surprisingly powerful. That is, we believe the primary innovation in Oval is a user interface that has two important properties: (a) It is simple and intuitive for users to understand, and (b) It provides users a surprisingly large amount of functionality for creating and modifying a wide range of applications.

It would, of course, be no surprise to say that we could implement many applications in a general purpose programming language or that primitives like objects, views, agents, and links were helpful in doing so. The surprising thing, we believe, is that so many applications can be implemented using only the extremely restricted and simplified tailoring language provided by Oval.

EXAMPLES OF APPLICATIONS AND AGENTS IN OVAL

To test our hypothesis that Oval is radically tailorable, we used the system to try to implement the functionality of a variety of cooperative work applications. The applications we used for these tests included well-known systems such as gIBIS (Conklin & Begeman, 1988), Coordinator (Winograd, 1987), Notes (Lotus, 1989), and Information Lens (Malone, Grant, Turbak, Brobst, and Cohen, 1987). With a few exceptions described in detail by Malone, Lai, and Fry (1995), we found that it was possible to emulate the basic functionality of each of these systems, using only the user-level tailoring facilities of Oval described before. We also implemented a number of more generic applications for tasks such as project management, software maintenance, and workflow management.

In this section, we briefly describe several of these examples, emphasizing the use of agents in these applications. Because an important focus of our work was on making a system that would be easy for users to tailor, we describe the construction of the first application in somewhat more detail than the others. Based on this description, readers can get some sense of the ease of tailoring new applications.

It is important to note, by the way, that, we were concerned primarily with whether the overall user interface paradigm and user-level capabilities provided by Oval could accommodate in a "natural" way the primary functionality of the applications we tried to emulate. Because our system is only a research prototype, we did not attempt to replicate the level of attention to robustness, speed, live sharing of data, access controls, and so forth present in the commercial products we analyzed. These attributes are clearly essential in creating widely usable software systems, but they were not the primary focus of our work.

It is also important to realize that these applications provide a kind of "stress test" for the tailorability of the system. We would not expect beginning users of a system like Oval to be immediately able do all the tailoring needed for these applications. For instance, some of the applications require the use of tailoring features (such as defining new object types) that we would expect only of experienced users. In general, we had, as a rough goal, the notion that the kinds of people who could use spreadsheets should be able to use Oval.

Also, just as spreadsheets are used by people at many different levels of sophistication, we expect that radically tailorable systems like Oval will be used in very different ways by end users, by power users, and by programmers (Mackay, 1990; Nardi & Miller 1990). Because the system provides a wide spectrum of tailoring options, we believe that many users would make only minimal changes to applications developed by others, although some power users would develop applications for other people, and programmers would use the system to dramatically reduce the time and effort required to develop completely new applications.

gIBIS—Argumentation Support

gIBIS (Conklin & Begeman, 1988) is a tool for helping a group explore and capture the qualitative factors that go into making decisions. Elements of a policy analysis in gIBIS are represented as a network containing three types of nodes: Issues, Positions, and Arguments. Each Issue may have several Positions that "Respond to" it, and each Position, in turn, may have various Arguments that "Support" or "Object to" it. Users can create new nodes of any type, and they can browse through a network by following the hypertext links between nodes or by looking at summary views that graphically display the different kinds of nodes and their relationships.

Defining New Object Types and Creating Examples of Them

To emulate gIBIS in Oval, we first defined the three types of objects used by gIBIS: Issues, Positions, and Arguments. For instance, to define the new type of object called "Argument," we performed the actions illustrated in Fig. 5.9. First, we selected the basic object type called "Thing" and then chose the "Create Subtype" action (Fig. 5.9a). To create individual examples of this type, we selected the new type and chose the "New object" action. The new Arguments have the fields "Name," "Keywords," and "Text" by default, as these fields are present in all Things. To add the fields (like "Supports," "Objects to," and "Entered by") that are present in Argument objects but not in all Things, we used the "Add Field" action on one of the new Argument objects (Fig. 5.9b). Finally, we filled in the fields of this (and other objects) by typing and by adding links (Fig. 5.9c).

As an example of the kind of "shortcuts" that Oval includes to enhance the convenience of users, consider how new fields were added in Fig. 5.9b. In designing a way for users to add fields to an object type, a common reaction for programmers who have worked with object-oriented systems would be to have an operation that is performed on a "type definition" somewhere in the system. In some early versions of the Oval system, this is exactly what we did. However, in working with Oval, we realized that nearly every time a user wants to perform a "type operation" (such as adding fields, setting default values for a field, and so forth) the user is already in the context of a specific instance of

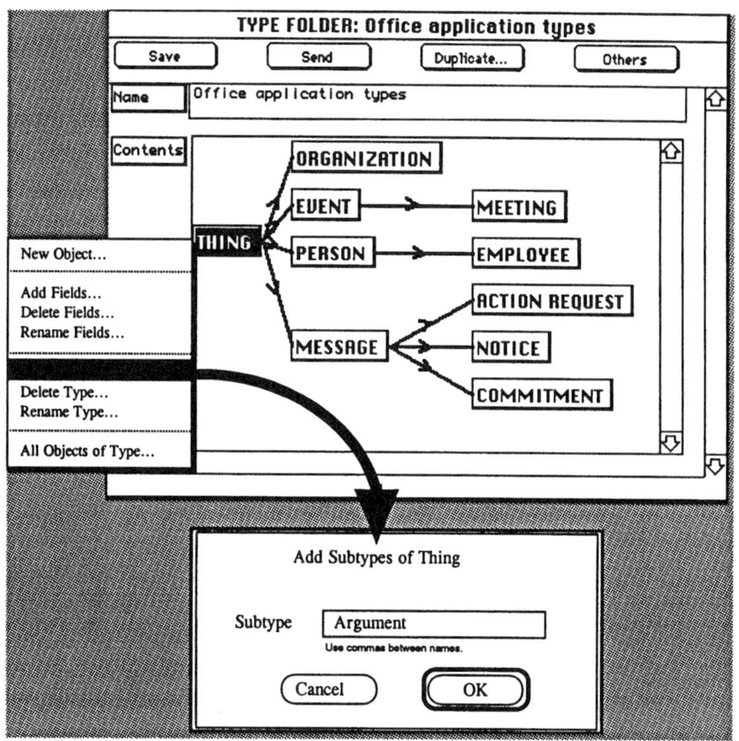

FIG. 5.9(a). To define a new type of object, users create it as a subtype of some existing object type. (Note: In this and subsequent figures, the heavy curved arrow is added for clarity. It is not part of the actual screen display.)

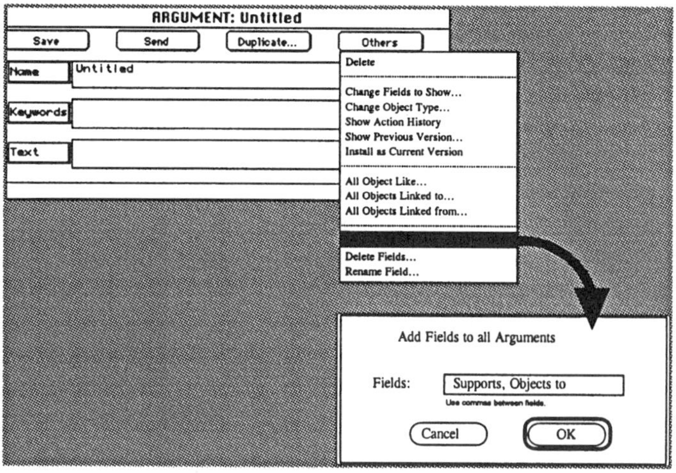

FIG. 5.9(b). Users can add fields to an object type with the "Add Fields" action on any instance of that type. The fields then appear in all objects of that type.

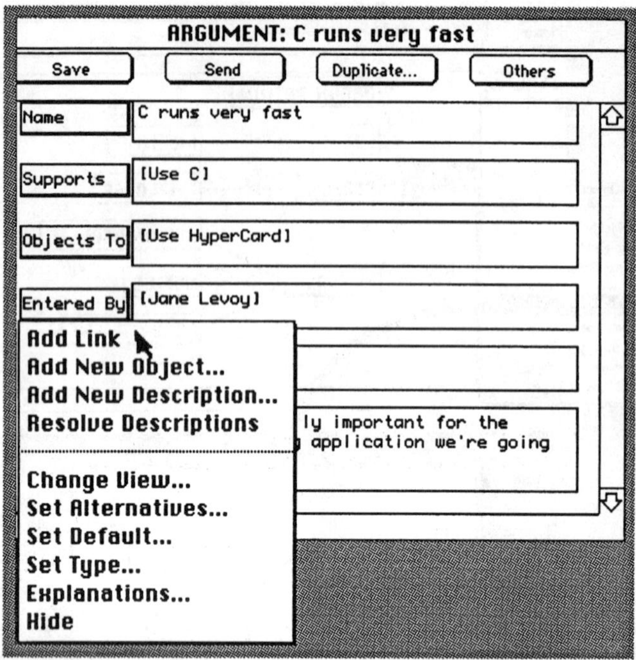

FIG. 5.9(c). Users can fill in the fields of an object by typing or by inserting links to other objects.

the type. Therefore, we made all these type operations accessible from the instances themselves. This seems to significantly enhance the "immediacy" of using the system; instead of making changes indirectly to an abstract type definition, users are directly changing a specific object that is of interest to them.

Linking Objects

The square brackets in Fig. 5.9c indicate "live" links to other objects that can be traversed by clicking on them. To add these links in the first place, the user selects the "Add link" action in a field and then points to the object to which the link goes. It is also possible to use the "Add New Object" action on a field as a shortcut to both create a new object and insert a link to that object into the field.

Viewing Collections of Objects

When a field in an Oval object contains links to other objects, users can tailor views to specify how they wish to have these objects displayed. For instance, in Fig. 5.10, the objects in the "Contents" field of the Folder are ini-

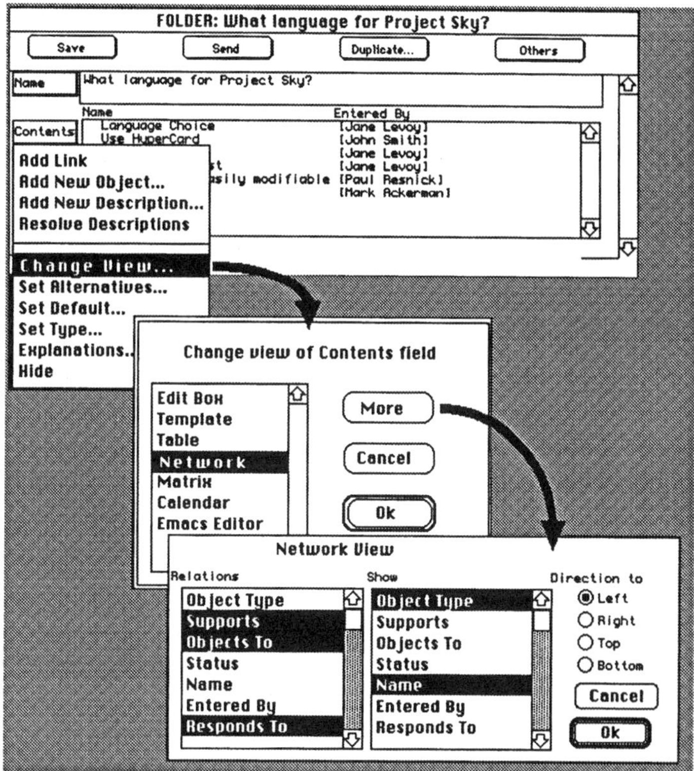

FIG. 5.10. Users can "Change View" on any field. Here, the "Network" view was selected. Then, two other choices were made: (1) the fields from which links will be used to construct the network, and (2) the fields to be shown in the nodes of the network.

tially displayed in a "Table" view, with the "Name" and "Entered by" fields shown in the table.

In the original gIBIS system, users can also view the relationships between the nodes in an argument network graphically. To do this with Oval, we selected the "Change View" action for a field containing the nodes and then chose the "Network" display format (see Figs. 5.10 and 5.11). This format allows us to choose the fields from which links will be shown in the network. For example, in Fig. 5.10, we chose to show links from three fields, "Supports," "Objects to," and "Responds to." We also chose to display in each node the "Name" and "Object Type" fields. The result is shown in Fig. 5.11.

In one sense, of course, there is nothing new about this notion of using general display formats for many kinds of objects. We have been genuinely surprised, however, at how widely useful and powerful this feature is when

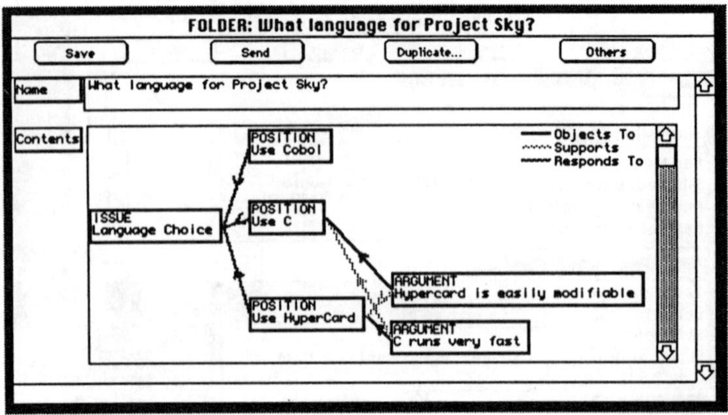

FIG. 5.11. This network view, the result of the choices made in Fig. 5.10, shows the relationships between Issues, Positions, and Arguments as in the gIBIS system.

users can apply it themselves to create new applications. For instance, it makes it possible for end users to create in seconds specialized displays like organization charts, PERT charts, and part explosion graphs that might otherwise require days or weeks of programming.

Coordinator—Conversation Structuring and Task Tracking

The Coordinator is an electronic mail-based system that helps people structure conversations and track tasks (Action Technologies, 1988; Winograd & Flores, 1986). For instance, a typical "Conversation for Action" begins with a "Request" message from Person A to Person B, explicitly requesting Person B to do something by a certain date. Person B is then prompted to respond with a "Promise" message (promising to perform the action), with a "Decline" message (declining to perform the action), or with a "Counteroffer" message (offering to perform the action by a different date or to perform a different action). If B promises to do the action, then a typical conversation might continue with B eventually sending a "Report completion" message (indicating that the action has been performed) and A replying with a "Close" message (indicating that the action was performed satisfactorily).

In addition to this prototypical conversational sequence, a variety of other message sequences are possible when, for instance, A is not satisfied with B's performance or when the conversation begins with B "offering" to do something rather than with A "requesting" something. In all these cases, the system automatically groups all messages for a single conversational "thread" together, and allows users to easily see the status of various conversations. For example, users can easily see all the outstanding requests they have made to other people or all the things they have promised to do for others (along with their due dates).

This system was originally implemented without any components called "agents." However, to emulate this system, we found it useful to create a number of agents to sort messages into appropriate folders based on their contents. As described in more detail by (Malone et al., 1995), we created 23 folders (such as "Open Matters" and "My promises"), and 14 agents with 47 rules that move messages into and out of these folders. For instance, Fig. 5.12 shows an agent that moves conversations with promises from the user into two folders: "My Promises" and "All Open Promises and Offers."

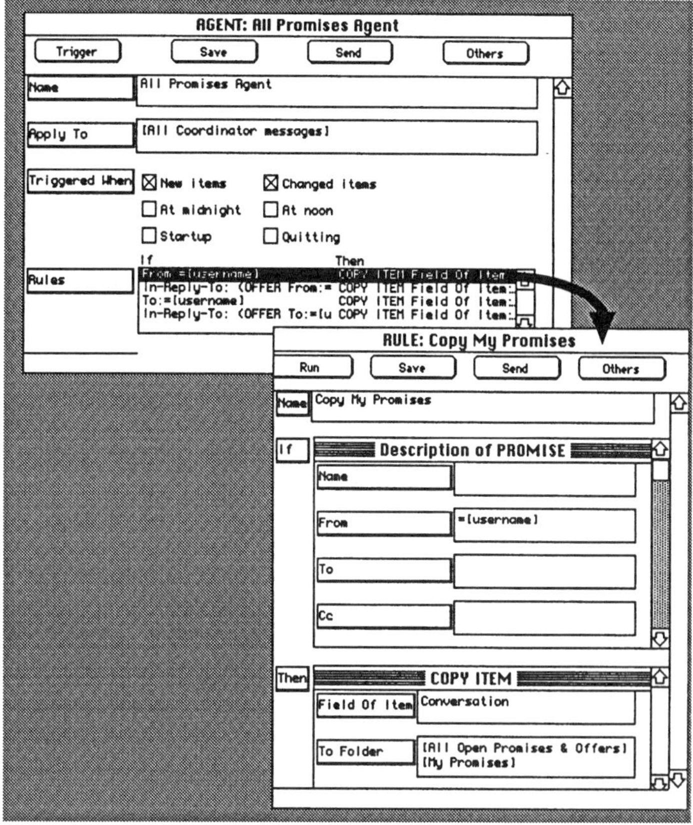

FIG. 5.12. An agent that tracks conversations involving promises. The rule shown puts conversations that include Promise messages from the user into the appropriate folders.

Notes—Semistructured Information Sharing

Of the other systems analyzed here, Lotus Notes (Lotus, 1989) is the most similar to Oval. It was developed independently and announced soon after the basic ideas of Oval were first published (Lai et al., 1988). Notes is also similar to earlier computer conferencing systems with the important additions that the documents in a database are semistructured templates (with optional "hot links" to other documents), and the documents in a database can be filtered and summarized according to various user-definable views.

For example, a typical Notes application might help a company keep track of information, gleaned from various sources, about it's competitors. Such an application might include a template that includes fields for which competitor the information is about, which customer(s) are involved (if any), and how important the creator of the item feels the information is. The template could also include a field for unstructured text describing the information in detail. The application might also include customized views of the data that, for example, show only high priority reports or sort reports by what competitors and customers are involved.

As this example illustrates, Notes—like Oval—can be used to create many different applications. Thus, we did not literally tailor Oval to emulate Notes itself, but rather we can tailor Oval in different ways to emulate different Notes applications. For instance, Fig. 5.13 shows a simple application for competitive information tracking like the one just described. It requires the definition of a new object type ("Competitive Information Report") and a table view for a folder containing objects of this type.

In general, the primitives that Notes provides for creating applications have equivalents in Oval, and thus the kinds of applications that can be created in Notes can also be emulated in Oval. For instance, the templates in Notes are equivalent to object types in Oval; the databases in Notes are equivalent to folders in Oval; and the views in Notes are equivalent to views of collections of objects in Oval. Notes views are all variations of a kind of "outline" display format that does not currently exist in Oval, but is similar to the table format display that does exist (see Fig. 5.13).

In certain ways, however, Notes is significantly more limited than Oval. For instance, Notes does not include any of the other folder display formats in Oval such as networks and calendars. More importantly from our point of view in this chapter, Notes does not have active agents like those in Oval. If agents were integrated into Notes, they could help users do all of the kinds of things described in the other examples in this chapter.

One useful way of thinking about the relationship between Oval and Notes, therefore, is to view Oval as illustrating an integrated user interface paradigm and a number of additional features that Notes could, in principle, be extended to include.

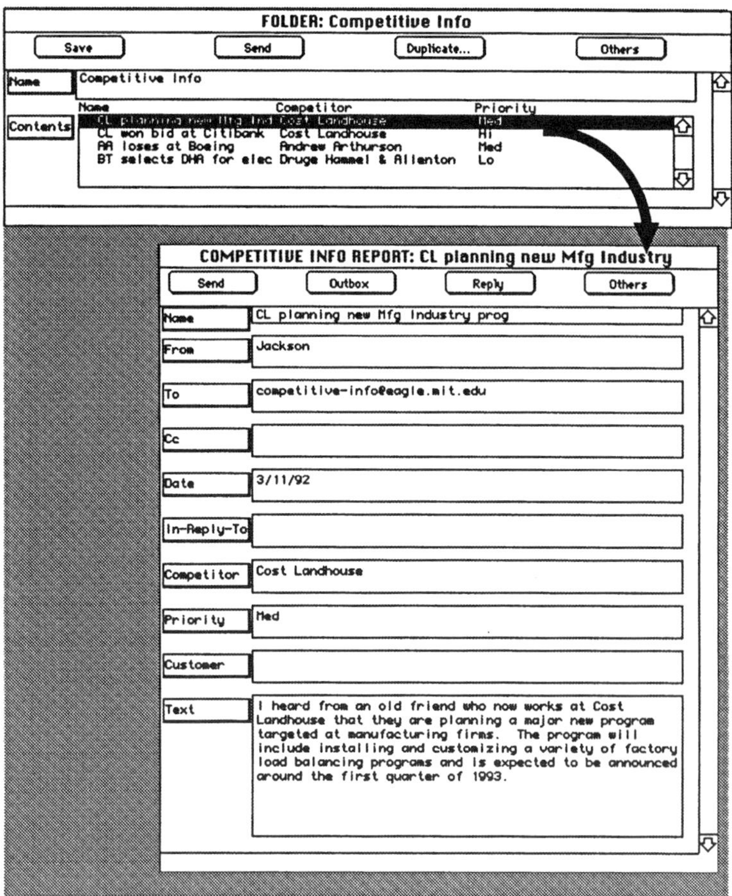

FIG 5.13. A table format display summarizing documents like those in a Notes database.

Information Lens—Intelligent Mail Sorting

Implementing Information Lens in Oval is quite straightforward. For instance, users can define new message types as subtypes of Message in the object type hierarchy and create rules to filter and sort messages (see Fig. 5.14).

Other Applications

In addition to the applications described in detail before, we have developed a number of other applications using the Oval system. The range of these applications provides a further demonstration of the tailorability of Oval, and this section briefly summarizes a sample of these other applications. All

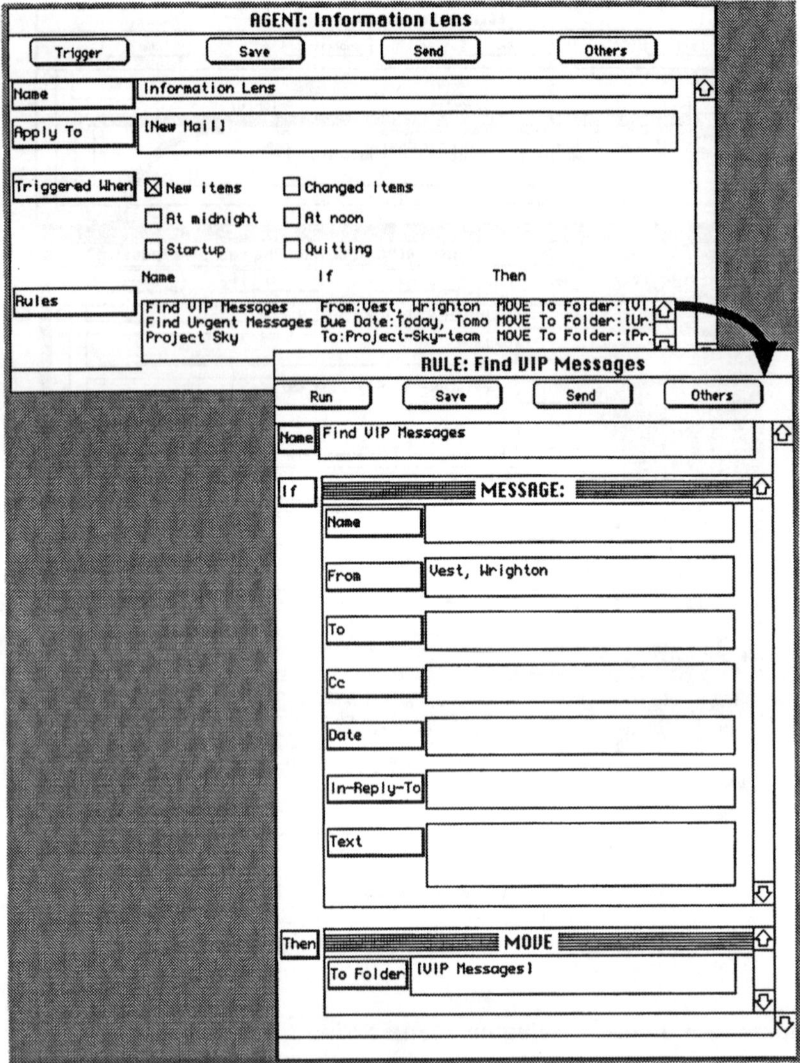

FIG. 5.14. Examples of an agent and a rule like those in Information Lens.

of these applications, except (1), are included with the demonstration version of Oval that is available to other researchers. They are described further in documentation that accompanies that system (Lee, 1992):

1. a project management system that tracks the tasks to be done, people responsible, prerequisites, overdue tasks, and so forth. This system was created by defining a new type of object called "Task" and viewing collections

of these tasks using different views. For instance, a network view is used to summarize the links in the "prerequisite" fields (thus creating a PERT chart) and a calendar view is used to display objects according to the date in their "Due date" field. An agent finds overdue tasks (using a rule that looks for tasks whose "Due date" is less than today) and moves them to a special folder. It is also possible for people to mail tasks back and forth to each other. For example, a project manager can mail new tasks to people responsible for performing them, and they can then mail back new versions of the tasks as the status of the tasks changes.

2. a system for tracking software bug reports and automatically routing them to appropriate people. For instance, the demonstration includes agents that route bug reports to the programmers responsible for modules in which the bugs occur. Other agents route bug reports to programmers responsible for modules that call the ones containing bugs (on the theory that programmers may be interested in knowing about bugs in modules they use, even if they are not responsible for fixing them). This system is based, in part, on field studies of support "hot lines" in software companies (Pentland, 1991, 1992) and of engineering change processes in manufacturing organizations (Crowston, 1991).

3. a workflow system for order approval. This application is not a complete workflow system, but it demonstrates how rule-based agents can be used to route forms to appropriate people. For instance, the demonstration includes an agent with rules that route purchase requests to different managers for approval depending on the dollar amount of the purchase request.

CONCLUSIONS

Our experience with all the systems described has strengthened our belief in the importance of using semiformal systems—where computer systems can gradually support more and more of the knowledge and processing involved when humans work together, without ever having to "understand" it all.

Our experience has also strengthened our belief in the importance of trying to design radically tailorable systems which end users (not skilled programmers) can modify to suit the needs of the changing situations in which they find themselves. Such systems, we believe, will make it feasible for many more people to maintain in computer systems information that is useful for themselves, for other people, and for their computational agents. These systems will also make it feasible for many people to directly tell their agents what to do, rather than having to depend on the limited abilities of their agents to figure out what needs to be done or to depend on skilled programmers to program the agents.

We were also struck by the the usefulness of the particular "tailoring language" (composed of objects, views, agents, and links) that we used. We suspect that these building blocks may provide a surprisingly powerful basis for creating a wide variety of information management and cooperative work applications.

As we look to the future, we can imagine a world (e.g., perhaps on the Internet) in which people share massively interconnected databases containing the kinds of semistructured objects we have seen here. The people in this world will be assisted by armies of computational agents that work constantly on their owners' behalf: searching for relevant information, notifying their owners when important things change, and responding automatically to certain conditions in the database.

A variety of technical challenges remain before such a world can come to pass. Among the most important of these technical challenges are issues of scaling: How can we manage globally distributed databases with millions of interconnected objects shared by hundreds of thousands of users and agents? How can we help numerous, partially overlapping communities of users collectively evolve shared definitions for different types of objects and shared understandings about what these objects mean?

Perhaps even more important than these technical challenges, however, are social and organizational questions: What kinds of information do people want to share in the first place? What kinds of incentives would lead people to contribute to and maintain these knowledge bases? Can systems like these help reduce the tiresome details of successful collaboration without leading people to feel overwhelmed by computerized "red tape"? And, for that matter, what makes work satisfying for people in the first place, and how can systems like these increase those satisfactions?

APPENDIX:

Relationship Between Oval and Object Lens

As noted earlier, we have used the name "Oval" in this chapter to include versions of the system that we originally called "Object Lens" (Lai et al., 1988). We eventually changed the system name from "Object Lens" to "Oval" to avoid confusion with the Information Lens system.

The primary differences between later versions of Oval and the system that was originally called Object Lens are the following: (1) Later versions of Oval were implemented in Macintosh Common Lisp on Macintoshes; Object Lens was implemented in Interlisp-D on Xerox 1100 workstations. (2) Later versions of Oval included two new kind of views that were not implemented in Object Lens: calendars and matrices. (3) Later versions of Oval included the capabilities described above for mailing objects around in a way that preserved instance identity. These capabilities were not present in Object Lens. (4) Later versions of Oval included several "user convenience" features which were not present in Object Lens. For instance, in later versions of Oval, type operations could be performed on instances (see text for more detailed description.)

ACKNOWLEDGMENTS

Most of this chapter is reprinted from Malone, Lai, and Grant (1997). The reprinted portions are copyright © 1996, American Association for Artificial Intelligence. All rights reserved. Parts of the chapter also appeared previously in Malone et al. (1987), Malone et al. (1987), Lai et al. (1988), Malone et al. (1989), MacKay et al. (1989), Malone and Lai (1992), and Malone et al. (1995).

The work described here was performed by many people over a number of years. Here is a partial list of the people who contributed to these projects: Steven Brobst, Stu Card, Michael Cohen, Kevin Crowston, Christopher Fry, Jintae Lee, Wendy MacKay, Ramana Rao, David Rosenblitt, Franklyn Turbak, and Keh-Chiang Yu.

Financial support for the development of the Oval system was provided by the National Science Foundation (Grant No. IRI-8903034) under the program on "Coordination Theory and Collaboration Technology" headed by Larry Rosenberg. Additional financial support for Oval and the other work described here was also provided by Digital Equipment Corporation, Apple Computer, Xerox Corporation, Wang Laboratories, General Motors/Electronic Data Systems, Bankers Trust Company, and by the corporate sponsors of the Center for Coordination Science, the Management in the 1990s Research Program and the International Financial Services Research Center at the Sloan School of Management, MIT.

REFERENCES

Action Technologies, Inc. (1988). *The Coordinator, Version II, User's Guide*. Emeryville, CA: Action Technologies, Inc.

Conklin, J. and Begeman, M. (1988). gIBIS: A Tool for Exploratory Policy Discussion. *ACM Transactions on Office Information Systems, 6*, 4 (October).

Crowston, K. (1991). *Towards a Coordination Cookbook: Recipes for Multi-Agent Action.* Ph. D. thesis, Sloan School of Management, Massachusetts Institute of Technology.

diSessa, A. A. (1985). A Principled Design for an Integrated Computational Environment. *Human Computer Interaction, 1,* 1–47.

Fikes, R. and Kehler, T. (1985). The Role of Frame-based Representation in Reasoning. *Communications of the ACM, 28*(9), 904–920.

Hutchins, E. L., Hollan J. D., and Norman, D. A. (1986). Direct Manipulation Interfaces. In D. Norman & S. Draper (Eds.), *User-Centered System Design* (pp. 87–124). Hillsdale, NJ: Lawrence Erlbaum Associates.

Lai, K.-Y., Malone, T. W., and Yu, K.-C. (1988). Object Lens: A Spreadsheet for Cooperative Work. In *ACM Transactions on Office Information Systems, 6*(4), 332–353.

Lee, G. (1992). *Oval Applications Catalog* (September). Cambridge, MA: MIT Center for Coordination Science.

Lee, J. and Malone, T. W. (1990). Partially Shared Views: A Scheme for Communicating Among Groups That Use Different Type Heirarchies. *ACM Transactions on Information Systems, 8*(1), 1–26.

Lotus. (1989). *Lotus Notes Users Guide.* Cambridge, MA: Lotus Development Corp.

MacKay, W. E. (1988). More Than Just a Communication System: Diversity in the Use of Electronic Mail. In *Proceedings of the ACM Conference on Computer-Supported Cooperative Work,* 26–28. Portland, OR: ACM Press.

MacKay, W. E. (1990). Patterns of Sharing Customizable Software. In *Proceedings of the CSCW 1990 Conference on Computer-Supported Cooperative Work*, 209–222. Los Angeles: ACM Press.

MacKay, W. E., Malone, T. W., Crowston, K., Rao, R., Rosenblitt, D., and Card, S. K. (1989). How Do Experienced Information Lens Users Use Rules? In *ACM Conference on Human Factors in Computing Systems*, K. Bice & C. Lewis (Eds.), 211–216. Austin, TX: ACM SIGCHI.

Maes, P. (1997). Agents that Reduce Work and Information Overload. In J. M. Bradshaw (Ed.), *Software Agents,* Cambridge, MA: AAAI/MIT Press.

Malone, T. W., Grant, K. R., Lai, K.-Y., Rao, R., and Rosenblitt, D. (1987). Semi-structured Messages are Surprisingly Useful for Computer-Supported Coordination. *ACM Transactions on Office Information Systems, 5,* 115–131.

Malone, T. W., Grant, K. R., Turbak, F. A., Brobst, S. A., and Cohen, M. D. (1987). Intelligent Information Sharing Systems. *Communications of the ACM, 30*(5), 390–402.

Malone, T. W., and Lai, K. Y. (1992). Toward intelligent tools for information sharing and collaboration. In R. P. Bostrom, R. T. Watson, & S. T. Kinney (Eds.) *Computer Augmented Teamwork: A Guided Tour* (pp. 86–107). New York: Van Nostrand Reinhold.

Malone, T. W., Lai, K. -Y., and Fry, C. (1995). Experiments With Oval: A Radically Tailorable Tool for Cooperative Work. *ACM Transactions on Information Systems, 13*(2), 177–205.

Malone, T. W., Lai, K.-Y., and Grant, K. R. (1997). Agents for information sharing and coordination: A history and some reflections. In J. M. Bradshaw (Ed.), *Software Agents* (pp. 109–143). Cambridge, MA: AAAI/MIT Press.

Malone, T. W., Yu, K.-C., and Lee, J. (1989). *What Good are Semistructured Objects? Adding Semiformal Structure to Hypertext.* Working Paper 102. Cambridge, MA: MIT Center for Coordination Science.

Nardi, B. A. and Miller, J. R. (1990). An Ethnographic Study of Distributed Problem Solving in Spreadsheet Development. In *Proceedings of the CSCW 1990 Conference on Computer-Supported Cooperative Work*, 197–208. Los Angeles: ACM Press.

Pentland, B. (1991). *Making the Right Moves: Toward a Social Grammar of Software Support Hot Lines.* Ph. D. thesis, Sloan School of Management, Massachusetts Institute of Technology.

Pentland, B. (1992). Organizing Moves in Software Support Hotlines. *Administrative Science Quarterly, 37*(4), 527–548.

Suchman, L. A. (1983). Office Procedure as Practical Action: Models of Work and System Design. *ACM Transactions on Office Information Systems*, *1*(4), 320–328.

Winograd, T. (1987). A Language/Action Perspective on the Design of Cooperative Work. In *HCI, 3*, 3–30.

Winograd, T. and Flores, F. (1986). *Understanding Computers and Cognition: A New Foundation for Design*. Norwood, NJ: Ablex.

CHAPTER

6

On Economies of Scope in Communication

Thomas Marschak*
University of California, Berkeley

This chapter grew out of the sort of interdisciplinary research that, I believe, Larry Rosenberg had in mind when he developed NSF programs in the area of Coordination. It is not easy for persons in one discipline to share ideas with those in another, and even harder to conduct joint research. But when investigators are stimulated by the goals of a well-run program of research support, then such joint efforts sometimes occur. In this case the disciplines were theoretical Computer Science on the one hand and Economic Theory on the other. The economist (Marschak) was introduced to the relevant Computer Science specialty, namely the theory of Communication Complexity, by Umesh Vazirani, a computer scientist. (Both were receiving support from a multiinvestigator NSF grant). The economist noticed that one could give the Communication Complexity problem an interesting organizational interpretation, in which processors become people. An ancient economic puzzle about decreasing returns to scale in organizations, could be viewed as the question of "subadditivity" in communication complexity. The first result of the collaboration was a joint piece by Marschak and Vazirani (1991) in *The Journal of Organizational Computing.* The present chapter, in which Marschak pursued the ideas further, was the second result. Whatever its merits, the chapter would not exist without the interdisciplinary stimulus of the NSF program.

---

*From "On Economics of Scope in Communication," by T. Marschak, 1996, *Economic Design, 2*, pp. 1–31. Copyright 1996 by Springer-Verlag. Reprinted with permission.

1. INTRODUCTION

The economic theory of the firm has long sought a fundamental reason for decreasing returns to scale. A plant producing X units of product at a cost of C can, in principle, be replicated as often as one wants. If that is so, then rX units of product should never cost more than rC, where r is any positive integer. Unlimited constant (or increasing) returns are, however, not observed in reality. There seems to be agreement that in many industries the empirical evidence is consistent with constant or even increasing returns over some range of output, but eventually cost goes up faster than output. While the expanding firm may face rising input prices (a rising price of capital, in particular), a more fundamental reason for the inevitability of decreasing returns is supposed to be the classic one: "some input is always fixed—it cannot, by its very nature, be replicated". The fixed non-replicable input is a person or group of persons, whom we may call the Top Manager. If there were not such a non-replicable person or group of persons 'in charge of' the firm, then there would not *be* a firm in the first place. As the firm expands, more and more of a burden is placed on the Top Manager, and to cope with the increased burden new quantities of certain variable inputs have to be hired. Eventually further expansion requires a more than proportionate increase in those input quantities. Such an explanation of (eventually) decreasing returns to scale goes back at least as far as a paper by Kaldor early in the 1930s.[1]

What has remained a mystery is the precise nature of the 'burden' which is placed on the fixed managerial entity when the firm acquires r independent plants and makes them divisions of the firm. One could call it the 'burden of coordinating the divisions.' That label hardly solves the mystery, since it is not clear why the r plants need to be 'coordinated' just because they have become divisions of a single firm. In one class of models that might resolve the matter, the Top Manager knows something that the r division managers—previously the independent plant managers—do not know. The private information of the Top Manager, together with certain pieces of the private information of each division manager, determine the task each division manager ought to perform (e.g., the output quantity he ought to produce) if the entire firm is to perform well (if it is to maximize profit, for example). As more and more divisions are added, more private information has to be collected by

[1]Kaldor (1934). "In order to determine the optimum size of the combination [of factors] it is necessary to assume that the supply of at least one of the factors . . . should be fixed. . . . It has been suggested that there is such a 'fixed factor' for the individual firm even under long-run assumptions—namely the factor alternatively termed 'management' or 'entrepreneurship'. . . . [A] firm cannot have two entrepreneurs, and as the ability of only one entrepreneur is limited, the costs of the individual firm must be rising, owing to the diminishing returns to the other factors when applied in increasing amounts to the same unit of entrepreneurial ability."

the Top Manager from the divisions. In addition to that steadily growing *communication* effort, the top manager has to engage in a growing *computing* effort; he has to compute a new set of divisional tasks, using the divisional information he has collected as well as his own private information. It is a loose but plausible conjecture that the Top Manager's communication and computing burdens grow more than proportionately as we increase r, the number of independent plants that are turned into divisions.

To make formal sense of this conjecture one would need (a) a natural and workable measure of the information-processing effort faced by each of the r plants as it performs its task; (b) a way of aggregating the r individual efforts to obtain the total effort of the r plants; (c) a measure of the total effort expended by the r plants when they become divisions of the firm and carry out the tasks assigned to them by the Top Manager; (d) a measure of the Top Manager's own information-processing effort. The conjecture would then take the form: when r starts to exceed some value, then (c) + (d) exceeds the total effort of the previously independent plants—as measured by (b)—and that excess grows faster than r. If it should turn out that (c) may in fact be *less than* (b), then to explain decreasing returns one relies solely on (d) outpacing r.

In the present chapter we pursue one special but widely studied approach to the measurements (a), (b), and (c); we model the information processing of the r independent organizations, and of the large organization which results when they merge, as a 'mechanism' in which messages are exchanged. We take the size of the set of possible messages as the central measure of information-processing effort. We find that in certain cases (c) may indeed be less than (b): placing the independent organizations 'under one roof,' and letting them share a common mechanism, may bring a quite unexpected saving, even if their tasks remain exactly what they were when they were separate and even if those tasks are completely independent of each other. We develop conditions that rule out such disturbing cases. We do not pursue the remaining elements of a decreasing-returns-to-scale explanation; no Top Manager appears in the discussion. Rather the chapter is a small step toward clarifying such an explanation for one class of information-processing models.

The 'Top Manager' decreasing-returns-to-scale explanation will not be understood until it has been explored for a variety of models, including models in which all the efforts that make up information processing—communicating, computing, and others—are simultaneously assessed. That is a tall order. Probably it lies far in the future. The present chapter concentrates on communication effort. On the other hand, a new approach to the modelling of computing effort has been developed by Radner and Van Zandt (1992; Radner, 1993). In their model the organization receives n real numbers and its task is to compute a function of those numbers. The function has to have the associative property: it is the sum of the n numbers, for example, or their maximum. The task is performed by a collection of processors. In the case of the adding task, it takes a processor one time unit to add one number to the sum stored in its memory and to replace the old stored sum with the resulting new sum. Any network of processors can be chosen; in particular they may be arranged hierarchically—so that each adds sums received from the processors below and the top processor obtains the final sum of the n numbers. No time is required for inter-processor communication itself and no separate charge is made for that communication. One studies the trade-off between delay (time until the task is complete) and number of processors. The model does not lend itself to exploration of the Top Manager conjecture sketched above.[2] Instead, another class of returns-to-scale questions can be fruitfully studied: as we vary n, the size of the organization's task, what happens to the efficient combinations of delay and number of processors? It is found, for example, that one cannot keep delay fixed while arbitrarily increasing n, no matter how many processors are used.

It may turn out that the decreasing-returns-to-scale explanation sketched above can be studied by incorporating both computational-effort measures of the Radner/Van Zandt variety, and communication-effort measures, into a single model containing division managers and a Top Manager.

A substantial literature in economics, and in computer science as well, considers mechanisms and their message spaces. In economics the literature began in an attempt to understand the informational efficiency of the competitive mechanism among resource-allocating procedures, and much of it has continued to pursue that agenda.[3] In computer science, the literature goes by the name of Communication-complexity Theory.[4] The vocabu-

---

[2]"Our interest ... has been the returns to scale of firms as unified organizations, not the returns to scale of holding companies" (Radner & Van Zandt, 1992, p. 270).

[3]The literature began with Mount and Reiter (1974) and Hurwicz (1977), where the message-space minimality of the competitive mechanism among all mechanisms achieving Pareto optimality was shown. Jordan (1982) showed that the competitive mechanism is unique among mechanisms that achieve Pareto-optimality and individual rationality with a minimal message space. Minimality of the Lindahl mechanism when public goods are introduced was argued by Sato (1981). Calsamiglia (1977) studied the required message-space size when increasing returns are introduced, and Calsamiglia and Kirman (1993) studied it when fairness is added. Reichelstein and Reiter (1988) consider message-space size when certain incentive properties are required, and Jordan (1987) considered it when the mechanism is required to have a convergence property. Message-space requirements for inter-period efficiency in infinite-period economies were studied by Hurwicz and Weinberger (1990). In Marschak and Reichelstein (1993, 1995) mechanisms with individually addressed messages (rather than messages broadcast to everyone) are studied and message-space size becomes the total number of individually addressed message variables; in that setting an analogue of the 'replication-is-best' conjecture which is the concern of the present chapter can be stated but remains open. There are a number of other contributions. For a survey, see Hurwicz (1986).

[4]For a survey see Lovasz (1990).

laries in the two fields are somewhat different; for example, a 'mechanism' becomes a 'protocol' in the communication-complexity literature. Each literature, however, considers a group of n agents. Agent i has the private information e_i, which lies in a set E_i. A mechanism, or protocol, defines at least one sequence of message announcements—possibly a one-element sequence—for every $(e_1, \ldots, e_n)$. That sequence has the property that it is 'acceptable' to each agent i, given i's private information e_i. (For example, certain elements of the sequence may be messages sent by i; if the sequence is to be acceptable to i given e_i, then each message that i sends must be a certain specified function of e_i and of what i has heard in the sequence up to that point.)

Thus the mechanism/protocol defines a covering of every E_i. Each set in the covering corresponds to one of the protocol's possible message sequences; for every e_i in the set, i finds that message sequence to be acceptable. The protocol also defines a covering of $E \equiv E_1 \times \cdots \times E_n$. Every set of that covering again corresponds to some message sequence; and for each e in the set, the message sequence is acceptable to *every* agent. The set corresponding to a given message sequence is therefore a *rectangle*. It is the Cartesian product of its n projections. Its ith projection belongs to that set in the covering of E_i which corresponds to the given message sequence.

To complete the specification of a mechanism/protocol, one associates a final *action* with any given message sequence. That action is taken for every e that lies in the rectangle associated with that message sequence. The possible actions belong to a set Z. One seeks mechanisms/protocols that perform a *task* given—to put it in the most general way—by a correspondence F from E to Z. The mechanism/protocol performs the task if for every message sequence and for every e in the rectangle associated with that sequence, the action associated with the rectangle lies in $F(e)$. In many problems F becomes a function.

In both literatures the information-processing (communication) cost of a mechanism is measured by the size of the set of rectangles. In the communication-complexity literature that set is finite. The task to be performed is defined by a finite valued (often a two-valued) function F. A winner in the class of protocols performing the task has the smallest possible number of rectangles. The winner therefore has the property that if each message in a message sequence is a binary string, and if sending one bit takes one time unit, then the longest time ever required to find an action that equals $F(e)$—i.e., the time required for the 'worst possible' e—is as short as it can be.[5]

In the economic literature the set of rectangles defined by a mechanism is typically an infinite set. Moreover the message sequence associated with

[5]The 'worst possible' time is given by the logarithm (to the base 2) of the number of rectangles.

a rectangle may usually be viewed as containing a single message, which all agents find acceptable for every e in the rectangle. The rectangles are indexed by the set of possible messages—the 'message space'—and regularity conditions on the candidate mechanisms imply that the indexing is 'smooth.' A winning mechanism among all those that perform the task defined by some F is one for which the message space is as small as possible; dimension is often the measure of the message space's size. If the number of rectangles is infinite, one can not easily interpret the message space size as the worst possible time until an action is found. Rather the information-processing cost captured in message-space size is perhaps best interpreted as the cost of having the n agents master, once and for all, the *language* that is required to carry out the mechanism. But the same language-mastering interpretation can also be given to the size of the set of rectangles when that set is finite. It is therefore, an interpretation that unites the two literatures. It costs more to master a six-dimensional language than a five-dimensional one; and it costs more to master a six-thousand-element language than a five-thousand-element language.[6]

Returning now to the returns-to-scale issue, the present chapter takes the point of view that information processing goes on within the 'small' organizations that may be assembled to form a large one. The large organization can then let them continue to engage, quite separately, in exactly the same information processing as before, so as to achieve exactly the same tasks as before. Or they can jointly engage in a new information processing procedure, which also achieves the same tasks as before, but requires (for example) that members of one of the previously separate organizations communicate directly with members of another. Our central question will be: *When the tasks that have to be achieved remain exactly as they were before, can such a new joint procedure ever improve on simple replication of the previously separate procedures?* We shall find that for the mechanism/protocol model there may indeed be a joint procedure that improves on pure replication with regard to language size, even though the tasks are unchanged, provided the collection of possible acceptable message sequences (rectangles) is finite. If the language is not finite but instead is a continuum, then this odd and unexpected phenomenon cannot occur. If the cost of learning (a finite) language is sufficiently important relative to the other information-processing costs that form part of the 'Top Manager' explanation, then there might indeed be *increasing* returns to scale or scope for organizations that use a finite language. 'Scope' is a more appropriate term than 'scale,' since the model per-

[6]There are other interpretations of message-space dimension, and of size of a finite set of rectangles. Consider a class of mechanisms/protocols for which higher message-space dimension, or higher rectangle-set size, implies a larger set of E_i-projections of the rectangles for every agent i. Then larger dimension, or larger rectangle-set size, implies more effort on the part of i in categorizing his private information so as to judge whether a given message sequence is acceptable.

mits the 'small' organizations to perform quite different tasks (unlike the classic story, where they are all producers of the same product).

Our core model starts with two separate organizations, A and B, each composed of just two persons. The propositions we shall obtain have straightforward counterparts for the case of many separate organizations, each with an arbitrary number of members, but we shall not pursue those counterparts here. In organization A, Person i, $i = 1, 2$, privately observes a variable e_i, called i's *local environment* and lying in a set E_i of possible local environments. Organization A's task, given the private observations of its two members, is to find (compute) the *action* $F_A(e_1, e_2)$. Organization B is analogous. Its two members are Person 3 and Person 4, and its task is to compute the action $F_B(e_3, e_4)$, where $e_3 \in E_3$, $e_4 \in E_4$.

When A and B merge, so that their members become a new four-person organization, they face the joint task of finding $F(e_1, e_2, e_3, e_4) \equiv (F_A(e_1, e_2), F_B(e_3, e_4))$. Organizations A and B, and the merged organization as well, achieve their tasks by again using a mechanism/protocol. There is no Top Manager, with his own private information, in the merged organization, although a fifth person, who has no private information, may be called in to assist the four members with their information-processing.

We confine attention to the study of what we shall call the *replication-is-best conjecture*. That conjecture says that for the merged organization a 'cheapest' procedure for achieving its task is to replicate the separate procedures that A and B followed before the merger, provided those separate procedures were themselves 'cheapest.'

In Section 2 we provide the mechanism/protocol framework in which the conjecture can be stated precisely and studied. We interpret the mechanism model, and the size-of-the-set-of-rectangles cost measure, by considering several 'scenarios.' In one main scenario a protocol prescribes, for any value of the members' private information, a conversation among them. The protocol may be 'non-deterministic'—a member may sometimes have several choices when it is his turn in the conversation. Or it may be 'deterministic'—there is always just one choice. In Section 3 we state a 'continuum' version of the conjecture (all mechanisms used have a language that is a continuum), and in Section 4 a finite version. In Section 5 we sketch a proof of the continuum conjecture, under the assumption that mechanisms satisfy a suitable 'smoothness' condition, and we present our unexpected counterexample to the finite conjecture. In Section 6 we interpret the failure of the finite conjecture, relating the failure to the scenarios in Section 2. In Section 7 we show that the finite conjecture holds if the rectangle covering associated with the mechanism/protocol has a 'bisection' property; that property insures that the protocol is deterministic. In Section 8 we show that the finite conjecture also holds if we require finite mechanisms/protocols to satisfy a property called 'adjacency,' which might perhaps be interpreted as a finite analogue of the smoothness conditions that are needed for the continuum conjecture to hold. Concluding remarks are made in Section 9.

2. A FRAMEWORK FOR THE STUDY OF THE REPLICATION-IS-BEST CONJECTURE: MECHANISMS AND THEIR MESSAGE SPACES

Consider an n-person organization; A, B and the merged organization are examples. Person i repeatedly observes a *local environment* e_i in a set E_i of possible local environments. In response to the current *environment* $e = (e_1, \ldots, e_n) \in E \equiv E_1 \times \ldots \times E_n$, the organization has to choose an *action* z in a set Z of possible actions. To perform this task the organization uses a *mechanism* $\langle M, (g_1, \ldots, g_n), h\rangle$ *on* E. Here M is a set which we call the *message space* when a name is needed, though the name does not fit equally well all of the scenarios we shall consider. The set may be finite or it may be a continuum. Each g_i is a function from $M \times E_i$ to some $\Re^{k_i}$, to be called, when appropriate, *an agreement function for i*; h is a function from M to Z, called an *outcome function* or an *action function*. An element (message) m of M is *acceptable* for $e = (e_1, \ldots, e_n)$ if and only if $g_i(m, e_i) = 0$, $i = 1, \ldots, n$. For $\langle M, (g_1, \ldots, g_n), h\rangle$ to qualify as a mechanism on E, it must be the case that

$$\text{for every } e \in E, \text{ there is an } m \in M \text{ which is acceptable for } e.$$

When the mechanism has obtained an m which is acceptable for e, then the action $h(m) \in Z$ is taken. The organization chooses a particular mechanism $\langle M, (g_1, \ldots, g_n), h\rangle$ because those actions meet some goal. We suppose the goal to be defined by a correspondence F from E to Z. For the environment $e \in E$, the actions in the set $F(e) \subseteq Z$ meet the goal. Often that set will be a singleton for every e, so that F becomes a function from E to Z. We say that the mechanism $\langle M, (g_1, \ldots, g_n), h\rangle$ *realizes* the goal defined by F if

$$h(m) \in F(e)$$

whenever m is acceptable for e.

We will use g as an abbreviation for $(g_1, \ldots, g_n)$ and '$g(m, e) = 0$' as an abbreviation for '$g_i(m, e_i) = 0$, all i.'

Note that for each m in M, the set

$$\sigma_m \equiv \{e \in E \mid \text{for all } i, g_i(m, e_i) = 0\}$$

is a *rectangle*: it is the Cartesian product of the n projections $\sigma_m^i \equiv \{e_i \in E_i \mid g_i(m, e_i) = 0\}$. Moreover, the collection $\{\sigma_m \mid m \in M\}$ is a *covering* of E. A covering of E whose sets are rectangles will be called a *rectangle covering*. An alternative and equivalent definition of mechanism is the *Rectangle Definition*. Here a mechanism on E is composed of

1. an index set M,
2. a covering $\Sigma = \{\sigma_m \mid m \in M\}$ of E, where each set σ_m is a rectangle,
3. an action function $h: M \to Z$.

Given $\langle M, \Sigma, h\rangle$, one can restate the mechanism so that it takes the previous '$\langle M, g, h\rangle$' form by defining functions $g_1, \ldots, g_n$ such that $g_i(m, e_i) = 0$ if and only if $e_i \in \sigma_m^i$.

To say that '$\langle M, \Sigma, h\rangle$ realizes the goal correspondence F' means that for every m in M and every e in σ_m, we have $h(m) \in F(e)$. Note that if F is a *function*, then F is *constant on every rectangle in* Σ. Every level set $\{e \in E \mid F(e) = K\}$ is covered, or 'tiled,' by some of the rectangles in Σ; each rectangle lies in one and only one level set. It will be convenient to say that Σ is a *tiling of the function F*.

The '$\langle M, g, h\rangle$' abstraction is quite versatile. We consider three scenarios which the abstraction fits. In each case we consider measures of the mechanism's costs.

2.1. The 'Proposer,' 'Coordinator,' or 'Card Displayer'

There is a proposer, who holds up a sequence of trial cards, seen by everyone. Each card exhibits one and only one m in M (or one and only one rectangle in the covering Σ). Person i says YES if and only if i's current local environment satisfies $g_i(m, e_i) = 0$ (or e_i is in the E_i-projection of the displayed rectangle). When an m^* has been found to which all say YES, then the action $h(m^*)$ is taken.

If M is a differentiable manifold, then the dimension of M is a natural cost measure in this scenario. If M is finite, then the corresponding cost measure is $|M|$, its cardinality. We may think of these measures as the size of the language that has to be mastered once and for all by the members of the organization if the organization is to use the mechanism; each member has to be able to recognize every element of M. In the differentiable-manifold case, the dimension measure is silent on the question of how long it takes until the organization finds its action. It might take forever. But in the finite case, the measure $|M|$ gives the *maximum* time *if* we specify that one card can be displayed (one proposal made) per time unit.

2.2. Simultaneous Shouting

At each step $t \geq 1$ of a sequence of steps, *every* Person i shouts (sends) *to everyone* the message

$$m_i^t = f_i(m^{t-1}, e_i),$$

chosen from a set $M^i \subseteq \Re^{k_i}$, in response to the message n-tuple $m^{t-1} = (m_1^{t-1}, \ldots, m_n^{t-1}) \in M^1 \times \ldots \times M^n \equiv M$, previously shouted. A fixed message m^0 starts the procedure; i's first message is $m_i^1 = f_i(m^0, e_i)$. An n-tuple m^* is *stationary for e* if and only if

$$0 = f_i(m^*, e) - m_i^* \equiv g_i(m^*, e_i),\ i = 1, \ldots, n.$$

When such a stationary m^* is reached, the action $h(m^*)$ is taken.

Again natural cost measures are dim M when M is a differentiable manifold and $|M|$ when M is finite.

2.3. A Conversation With One Speaker at a Time

Persons $1, \ldots, n$ speak in sequence; all the others hear the speaker's announcements and can identify the speaker. If it is person i's turn at step t, then person i's announcement m_i^t either belongs to a message set M_i or else is an element z of the action set Z. In the latter case the conversation is *complete* and the action z is taken. Each person always remembers everything that has been said.

We permit the protocol which governs the conversation to be 'non-deterministic.' That means Person i's announcement, when it is i's turn, is selected from a *set*. Unless the set is a singleton, we cannot be sure of i's choice. The set depends on i's memory and on i's current local environment e_i according to a set-valued function d_i, defined on the Cartesian product of E_i with the set of all finite sequences having the following property: for any $j \in \{1, \ldots, n\}$, and any integer $t > 1$, the tth member of the sequence belongs to M_j if and only if it is j's turn to speak at step t, i.e. if and only if $j \equiv t \bmod n$. We now let m^t denote the message sent at step t; if $i \equiv t \bmod n$, then we define $m_i^t \equiv m^t$. Thus

$$m_i^t \in d_i[(m^1, \ldots, m^{t-1}), e_i], \tag{†}$$

where $d_i[.]$ is a subset of M_i or of Z. The initial announcement $m^1 = m_1^1$ is chosen (by Person 1) from a set $d_1(e_1)$. The (set-valued) functions d_i satisfy the requirement that for every $e = (e_1, \ldots, e_n)$ in E, a completed conversation is obtained no matter what choices are made from the sets $d_i[.]$. Call the triple $\pi = \langle (M_1, \ldots, M_n), d_1, \ldots, d_n, Z \rangle$ a *protocol* on E. Call the conversation $m = (m^1, \ldots, m^{\bar{t}}, z)$ a *π-conversation for e* if it starts with $m^1 \in d_1(e_1)$, continues with choices that obey (†), and ends with a member of Z.

Let $C(\pi)$ denote the set of all π-conversations for all e in E. Since the only component of e that enters i's function d_i is the component e_i, the set

$$\sigma_m(\pi) \equiv \{e \in E \mid m \text{ is a } \pi\text{-conversation for } e\}$$

is a rectangle. For the π-conversation $m = (m^1, \ldots, m^{\bar{t}}, z)$, the rectangle's projection with respect to E_i is

$$\sigma^i_m(\pi) \equiv \{e_i \in E_i \mid m^1 \in d_1(e_1);\ m^t_i \in d_i[(m^1, \ldots, m^{t-1}), e_i]$$

$$\text{for } i \equiv t \bmod n \text{ and } 1 < t < \bar{t};\ z \in d_i[(m^1, \ldots, m^{\bar{t}}), e_i]$$

$$\text{for } i \equiv \bar{t} \bmod n\}.$$

To interpret a protocol π as a mechanism $\langle M, g, h\rangle$, we have to start with a definition of the set M. We consider two alternative definitions. In the first definition, $M \equiv C(\pi)$. In the second definition, we take M to be a subset of $C(\pi)$ which (i) contains a π-conversation for e, for every e in E; and (ii) is smallest—in a suitable sense—among all such subsets. For either definition of M, the functions g_i are defined as follows:

$$\text{for } m \in M,\ g_i(m, e_i) = 0 \text{ if and only if } e_i \in \sigma^i_m(\pi).$$

As for the outcome function h, we have

$$h(m) = z, \text{ where } z \text{ is the final announcement of } m.$$

It is clear that if we are given any rectangle covering of E, say Σ, then there is *some* protocol π such that every rectangle in Σ equals $\sigma_m(\pi)$ for some m in $C(\pi)$.[7] Conversely, for any protocol π and for either of our two definitions of M, the set $\Sigma_\pi \equiv \{\sigma_\pi(m) \mid m \in M\}$ is a rectangle covering of E.

One possible cost measure for the mechanism defined by π is the size of M as defined in the first way. A more 'optimistic' cost measure is the size of M as defined in the second way. To interpret these measures, one can first imagine a completed conversation being *proposed* (by a Center) to all n persons; person i says Yes if and only if he finds (given e_i) that the function d_i indeed requires him to make the announcements in the proposed conversation. The first cost measure is the size of the set of conversations that the agents must stand ready to recognize. Each of those conversations occurs for some e and some sequence of choices from the sets $d_i[.]$. In the second measure that set is narrowed. We let the set of possible conversations be a

---

[7]We may, for example, construct π as follows. Person 1 announces an arbitrary rectangle in Σ. Person 2 announces Yes if e_2 lies in the E_2-projection of that rectangle and announces No otherwise. Person 3 proceeds analogously, and so on. If all n persons announce Yes, then an action z is chosen. If not, then 1 announces a second rectangle and a new round begins.

minimal subset of $C(\pi)$. The conversations in that subset define a subset, say Σ^*_π, of the rectangle covering Σ_π; Σ^*_π covers E and is not larger, in a suitable sense, than any other subset of Σ_π that covers E.[8]

If one now supposes that conversations are in fact carried out rather than being centrally proposed, then only with luck will the choices made at each step comprise a conversation that belongs to our subset of $C(\pi)$. Only with luck will the rectangle defined by that conversation belong to Σ^*_π. In that sense the second measure is optimistic.

Associated with the two size measures are two 'time' measures. Suppose that M is finite and that every announcement is a binary string. Suppose sending one bit takes one time unit. If r_M is the smallest integer r such that $2^r \geq |M|$, then r_M is the longest time ever required to complete a conversation. Given the chosen definition of M, r_M is the associated time measure.

The following example illustrates these concepts. There are two persons, each with three possible local environments, and three possible actions: $E_1 = \{1, 2, 3\}$, $E_2 = \{1, 2, 3\}$, $Z = \{A, B, C\}$. Consider the protocol π which has message sets $M_1 = \{m^*, m^{**}\}$, $M_2 = \{\bar{m}, \bar{\bar{m}}\}$ and is described by the tree in Fig. 6.1. The set $d_1(e_1)$ contains two possible announcements when $e_1 = 2$—namely m^* and m^{**}. All other sets $d_1(.)$ and $d_2(.)$ are singletons.

There are six possible conversations: (m^*, C), (m^{**}, C), (m^*, m, A), $(m^{**}, \bar{m}, B)$, (m^*, m, C), and $(m^{**}, \bar{m}, C)$. The six associated rectangles are shown in Fig. 6.2. Our first size measure is 6; that is the total number of possible conversations. Our second, 'optimistic,' size measure is 4. That is the number of possible conversations in the lucky case where person 1 chooses m^* when $e_1 = 2$ and $e_2 = 3$, and chooses m^{**} when $e_1 = 2$ and $e_2 = 1$. Then the conversations (m^*, m, C) and $(m^{**}, \bar{m}, C)$ do not occur.

Now suppose the sets $d_i(.)$ are all singletons. The protocol π is then 'deterministic.' Every person has only one choice in forming the announcement he makes. For every point e, there is a unique π-conversation. The rectangles that correspond to the possible π-conversations now comprise a *partitioning* of E. Moreover, it is a partitioning which has an important property that we shall call the *bisection property*: the rectangles must be generated by a sequence of bisections. Person 1's starting announcement $m^1 = d_1(e_1)$ divides E into two disjoint subsets, namely $\{e \in E \mid d_1(e_1) = m^1\}$ and its complement. The next announcement, by Person 2, is $m^2 = d_2(m^1, e_2)$, and that announcement divides the first subset into two disjoint subsets; and so on.[9] Given any rectangle partitioning with the bisection property, we can construct a deter-

[8]If Σ_π is finite, than 'not larger than' is immediately defined. If Σ_π is not finite but is smoothly indexed (in a sense defined in Section 5 below) by an open set in a finite-dimensional Euclidean space, then 'not larger than any other subset of Σ_π covering E' should be restated more precisely as 'smoothly indexed by an index set having no larger dimension than the index set of any other smoothly indexed subset of Σ_π that covers E.'

[9]We provide a more formal definition of a partitioning with the bisection property in Section 7.

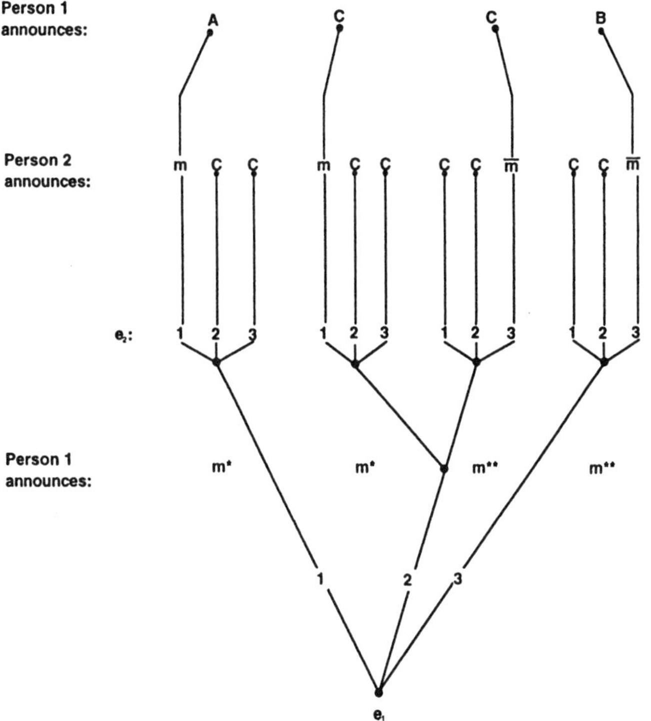
Person 1
announces:
A
C
C
B
Person 2
announces:
m C C
m C C
C C $\overline{m}$
C C $\overline{m}$
e_2:
1 2 3
1 2 3
1 2 3
1 2 3
Person 1
announces:
m*
m*
m**
m**
1
2
3
e_1

FIG. 6.1.

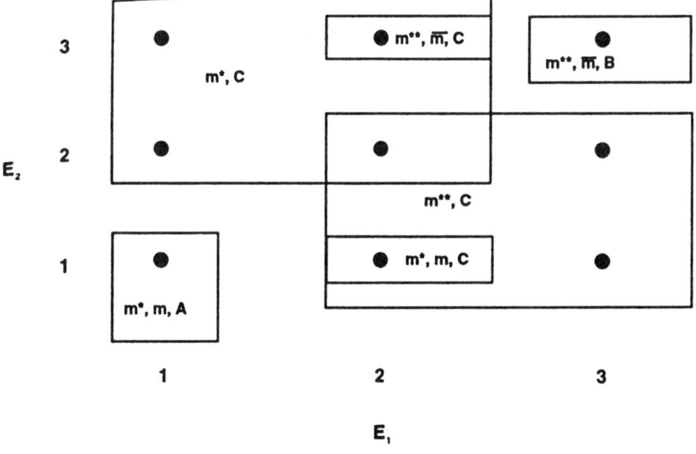
3
2
1
E_2
m*, C
m**, $\overline{m}$, C
m**, $\overline{m}$, B
m**, C
m*, m, C
m*, m, A
1
2
3
E_1

FIG. 6.2.

ministic protocol π such that each rectangle corresponds to some π-conversation and each π-conversation corresponds to some rectangle. Figure 6.3 shows a partitioning of a 16-point set $E = E_1 \times E_2$. The partitioning lacks the bisection property.

The partitioning of E shown in Fig. 6.3 becomes a partitioning with the bisection property if we divide the lower left rectangle into two rectangles, one containing the point on the left and the other containing the two remaining points.

In Fig. 6.4 the four-rectangle covering of a nine-point set $E = E_1 \times E_2$ has the bisection property. The three solid lines show a sequence of *three* bisections (labelled i, ii, iii). The tree shown in Fig. 6.5 defines a deterministic protocol, with actions *A, B, C,* which follows the bisection sequence and provides four conversations, one for each rectangle.

3. A CONTINUUM VERSION OF THE REPLICATION-IS-BEST CONJECTURE

We are now ready to consider a 'continuum' version of the replication-is-best conjecture for our two two-person organizations, *A* and *B*. There is an obvious generalization of the conjecture to an arbitrary number of organizations, each with arbitrarily many members, but we shall not consider it. Recall that *A*'s goal is given by F_A, which is a *function* (not a correspondence) from the environment set E_A to the action set Z_A. We suppose that E_A and the set $F_A(E_A)$ of goal-fulfilling actions are continua. Specifically, $E_A = E_1 \times E_2$, and E_1, E_2 are, respectively, open subsets of $\Re^{\ell_1}, \Re^{\ell_2}$. In addition, Z_A is an open subset of a finite dimensional Euclidean space and F_A is continuous on E_A. We make exactly analogous assumptions for Organization *B*. Finally, we suppose

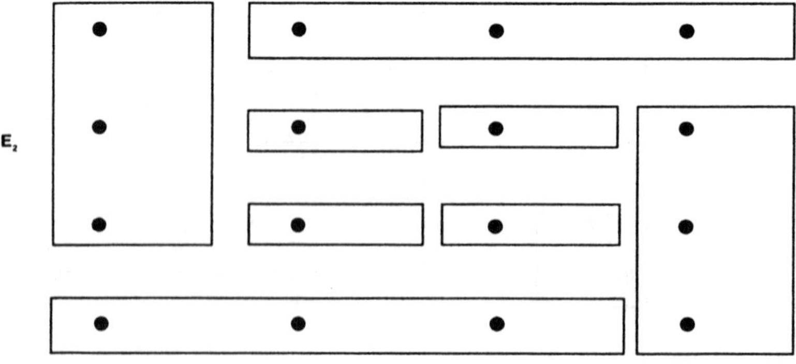

FIG. 6.3.

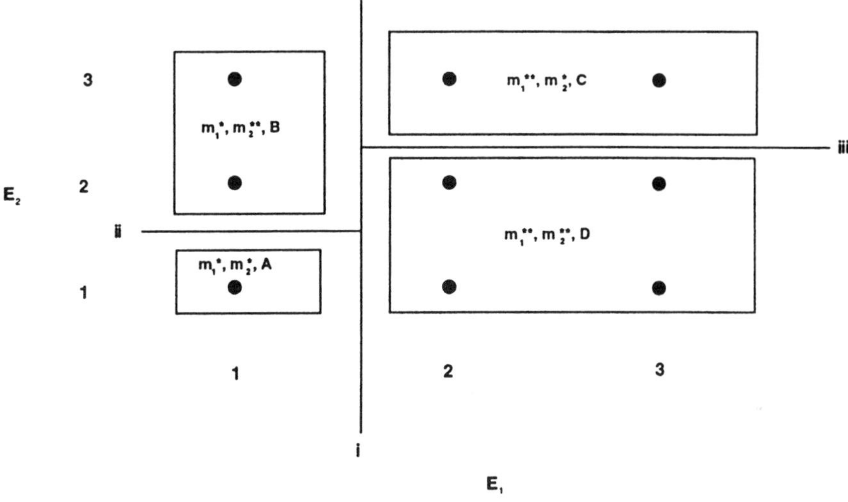
3
2
1
E2
ii
iii
i
m1*, m2**, B
m1*, m2*, A
m1**, m2*, C
m1**, m2**, D
1
2
3
E1
FIG. 6.4.

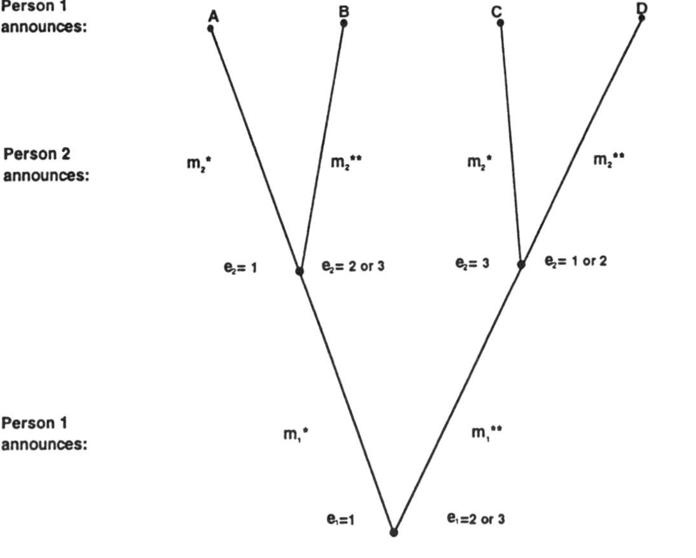
Person 1
announces:
A
B
C
D
Person 2
announces:
m2*
m2**
m2*
m2**
e2= 1
e2= 2 or 3
e2= 3
e2= 1 or 2
Person 1
announces:
m1*
m1**
e1=1
e1=2 or 3
FIG. 6.5.

that all three of our organizations–A, B and the merged organization–have to use *regular* mechanisms, defined in the following way.

Definition. A mechanism $\langle M, (g_1, \ldots, g_n), h\rangle$ on $E = E_1 \times \ldots \times E_n$ is *regular* if

1. M is a differentiable manifold.
2. Every function g_i is continuously differentiable with respect to all its arguments.
3. For every $\bar{e}$ in E, there exists a neighborhood $N_{\bar{e}}$ containing $\bar{e}$ such that for all e in $N_{\bar{e}}$, and for all m in a neighborhood of some $\bar{m}$ satisfying $g(\bar{m}, \bar{e}) = 0$:
   3.1. the matrix $D_m g(m, e)$ has full rank,
   3.2. for every i, the matrix $D_{e_i} g_i(m, e_i)$ has full rank.

For such mechanisms dim M will be our cost measure. The replication-is-best conjecture is as follows when A and B each have just two persons. (Persons 1 and 2 in A and Persons 3 and 4 in B):

Suppose $\langle M_A, (g_1, g_2), h_A\rangle$ with $h_A : M_A \to Z_A$, is a regular (two-person) mechanism realizing the goal function F_A on a neighborhood of a point $\bar{e}^A$ in $E^A \equiv E_1 \times E_2$ (an open subset of $\Re^{\ell_1 + \ell_2}$), and suppose that for every sufficiently small neighborhood of $\bar{e}^A$, all regular mechanisms realizing F_A on that neighborhood have message-space dimension not less than dim M_A. *Suppose $\langle M_B, (g_3, g_4), h_B\rangle$ with h_B: $M_B \to Z_B$, is a regular (two-person) mechanism realizing F_B on a neighborhood of $\bar{e}^B$ in $E^B \equiv E_3 \times E_4$ (an open subset of $\Re^{\ell_3 + \ell_4}$), and suppose that for every sufficiently small neighborhood of $\bar{e}^B$, all regular mechanisms realizing F_B on that neighborhood have message-space dimension not less than* dim M_B. *Suppose $\langle M, (\bar{g}_1, g_2, \bar{g}_3, g_4), (\bar{h}_A, \bar{h}_B)\rangle$ is a regular (four-person) mechanism realizing (F_A, F_B) on $E = E^A \times E^B = E_1 \times E_2 \times E_3 \times E_4$ where $\bar{h}_A : M \to Z_A, \bar{h}_B : M \to Z_B$. Then*

$$\dim M \geq \dim M_A + \dim M_B.$$

Without regularity conditions like (2) and (3), the functions F_A, F_B, and $F = (F_A, F_B)$ can be realized with a message space M of dimension *one*,[10] so that the conjecture fails, but in a vacuous way. Once we let dim M_A and dim M_B be our measures of the communication effort in the two separate mechanisms, the sum of the two dimensions is the natural measure of their total effort. We can trivially construct a merged mechanism realizing (F_A, F_B). Its message

[10]By smuggling many numbers into one number. For example, two messages, each a real number, can be encoded into a single decimal whose odd-numbered digits are the first message and whose even-numbered digits are the second message. Suitable regularity conditions rule out this and other smuggling devices.

space is $M_A \times M_B$, whose dimension is dim M_A + dim M_B; that merged mechanism simply replicates the two separate ones. The question is whether we can do better than that, and the conjecture says No.

4. A FINITE VERSION OF THE REPLICATION-IS-BEST CONJECTURE

This time the goal functions F_A, F_B are *finite-valued* and every mechanism considered has a *finite* message space M. Consider a finite mechanism on $E^A = E_1 \times E_2$, say $\langle M_A(g_1, g_2), h_A\rangle$, which realizes F_A. The mechanism defines a tiling of F_A, i.e., a finite collection of rectangles covering E^A, where F_A is constant on each rectangle. Similarly, for F_B and for $F \equiv (F_A, F_B)$. We shall state the conjecture, in fact, in the following 'rectangle' form,

Suppose the finite-valued goal function $F_A : (E_1 \times E_2) \to \Re$ can be realized by a mechanism with Q_A rectangles but not by a mechanism that has fewer rectangles. Suppose the finite-valued function $F_B : E_3 \times E_4 \to \Re$ can be realized with Q_B rectangles but not with fewer rectangles. Suppose the finite-valued function $F : E_1 \times E_2 \times E_3 \times E_4 \to \Re^2$, where $F \equiv (F_A, F_B)$, can be realized by a mechanism with Q rectangles in $E_1 \times E_2 \times E_3 \times E_4$. (Each rectangle is the Cartesian product of its four projections.) Then

$$Q \geq Q_A \cdot Q_B.$$

From a mathematical point of view, this conjecture appears to be the natural analogue of the continuum conjecture. For the three mechanisms that 'minimally' realize F_A, F_B, and F, respectively, $|M_A| = Q_A$, $|M_B| = Q_B$, and $|M| = Q$. The product $|M_A| \cdot |M_B|$ is the analogue of dim M_A + dim M_B. Analogously to the continuum conjecture, F can be realized with $Q_A \cdot Q_B$ rectangles by using the *product covering* $\Sigma_A \cdot \Sigma_B$ of E, where Σ_A, Σ_B are the coverings realizing F_A, F_B, respectively. The product covering is $\{(\sigma_A \times \sigma_B) | \sigma_A \in \Sigma_A, \sigma_B \in \Sigma_B\}$. The conjecture says that we cannot improve on the product covering.

5. THE CONTINUUM CONJECTURE HOLDS BUT THE FINITE CONJECTURE IS FALSE

5.1. Proving the Continuum Conjecture

Given a differentiable manifold M and a rectangle-covering $\Sigma = \{\sigma_m = \sigma_m^1 \times \ldots \times \sigma_m^n | m \in M; \sigma_m^i \subseteq E_i$, all $i\}$ of $E_1 \times \cdots \times E_n$, we shall say that Σ is *smoothly indexed by M* if there are functions $g_i : M \times E_i \to \Re^{k_i}$, satisfying (2), (3) of the regularity definition, such that $\sigma_m^i = \{e_i \in E_i | g(m, e_i) = 0\}$.

The central step in proving the continuum conjecture is to show the following:

(*) *Suppose a covering of* $E = (E_1 \times E_2) \times (E_3 \times E_4) = E^A \times E^B \subseteq \Re^{\ell_1+\ell_2+\ell_3+\ell_4}$ *is composed of rectangles (with respect to the four projections), and is smoothly indexed by a set M. Then for every sufficiently small neighborhood* $\bar{E} = \bar{E}^A \times \bar{E}^B \subset E$, *one can select from the* E^A*-projections of the rectangles a covering of* $\bar{E}_A$, *smoothly indexed by a set* M_A, *and one can select from the* E^B*-projections a covering of* $\bar{E}^B$, *smoothly indexed by a set* M_B, *where* $\dim M_A + \dim M_B = \dim M$.

Suppose we have established (*). Suppose we have a regular mechanism—written $\langle M_A, \Sigma_A, h_A\rangle$ in 'rectangle' form—that realizes F_A on a neighborhood of $\bar{e}^A \in \bar{E}^A$. Suppose that

1. for every neighborhood of $\bar{e}^A$, every regular mechanism that realizes F_A on that neighborhood has a message space (index set) whose dimension is at least $\dim M_A$.
   Similarly suppose that the regular mechanism $\langle M_B, \Sigma_B, h_B\rangle$ realizes F_B on a neighborhood of $\bar{e}^B \in E^B$ and
2. for every neighborhood of $\bar{e}^B$, every regular mechanism that realizes F_B on that neighborhood has a message space whose dimension is at least $\dim M_B$.

Finally, suppose that the regular mechanism $\langle \bar{M}, \bar{\Sigma}, (\bar{h}_A, \bar{h}_B)\rangle$, where $\bar{\Sigma} = \{\bar{\sigma}_m = \bar{\sigma}_m^1 \times \bar{\sigma}_m^2 \times \bar{\sigma}_m^3 \times \bar{\sigma}_m^4 | m \in M\}$, realizes (F_A, F_B) on $E^A \times E^B$ and has $\dim \bar{M} < \dim M_A + \dim M_B$. Then (*) guarantees that we can use $\bar{\Sigma}$ to construct a *regular* 'A-projection' mechanism $\langle \bar{\Sigma}_A, \bar{M}_A, h_A^*\rangle$ on a neighborhood of $\bar{e}^A$, where $\bar{\Sigma}_A \subset \{\sigma_1^m \times \sigma_2^m | m \in \bar{M}\}$. The function h_A^* in that mechanism assigns, to every 'rectangle' $\bar{\sigma}_1^m \times \bar{\sigma}_2^m$ of $\bar{\Sigma}_A$, the same 'A-action' as does the mechanism $\langle \bar{M}, \bar{\Sigma}, (h_A, h_B)\rangle$, namely $\bar{h}_A(m)$; the mechanism therefore realizes F_A on all sufficiently small neighborhoods of $\bar{e}^A$. Similarly we can construct a regular '*B*-projection' mechanism $\langle \bar{\sigma}_B, \bar{M}_B, h_B^*\rangle$ which realizes F_B on all sufficiently small neighborhoods of $\bar{e}^B$. But (*) guarantees that we can choose $\bar{\Sigma}_A, \bar{\Sigma}_B, \bar{M}_A, \bar{M}_B$ so that $\dim \bar{M}_A + \dim \bar{M}_B = \dim \bar{M}$. Since (by hypothesis) $\dim \bar{M} < \dim M$, we therefore have $\dim \bar{M}_A < \dim M_A$, or $\dim \bar{M}_B < \dim M_B$. That contradicts the minimality hypotheses (i), (ii). The continuum conjecture is proved.

A proof of (*) is given in Marschak and Vazirani (1991).

5.2. Attempting to Prove the Finite Conjecture

The natural attempt is to mimic the continuum proof. To do so, it will be useful first to define a general property of finite coverings.

Definition. A finite covering Σ of a set $V \times W$ will be called *normal with respect to* (V, W) if there exists a covering T_V of V, each of whose sets is a V-projection of a set in Σ, and a covering T_W of W, each of whose sets is a W-projection of a set in Σ, such that

$$|T_V| \cdot |T_W| \leq |\Sigma|.$$

Then the natural analogue of $(*)$ is:

$(* *)$ *If Σ is a finite covering of the set $E^A \times E^B$, and every set in Σ is a rectangle with respect to (E^A, E^B), then Σ is normal with respect to (E^A, E^B).*

If $(* *)$ were true, then we could prove the finite conjecture by supposing that $Q < Q_A \cdot Q_B$. We then construct from the E^A-projections of the given Q-rectangle covering of $E^A \times E^B$ a Q_A^*-rectangle covering of E^A; *any* such covering of E^A must realize F_A on E^A, since the Q-rectangle covering realizes $F = (F_A, F_B)$. We construct a Q_B^*-rectangle covering of E^B, using some of the E^B-projections of the given Q rectangles; that covering realizes F_B on E^B. It follows from $(* *)$ that we can do all this while satisfying $Q_A^* \cdot Q_B^* \leq Q$. Since (by assumption) $Q < Q_A \cdot Q_B$, we have that either $Q_A^* < Q_A$ or $Q_B^* < Q_B$. That would contradict the hypothesis of the finite conjecture and would complete the proof.

Assertion $(* *)$ is, however, false—a strong hint that the finite conjecture might also be false. Here is a counterexample.[11] We let E_2 and E_4 be single points. E_1 and E_3 each consist of three points. Thus $E_1 \times E_2 \times E_3 \times E_4$ is the same as $E_1 \times E_3$ as far as the testing of $(* *)$ is concerned. $E_1 \times E_3$ is an array of nine points which we cover with the three rectangles shown in Fig. 6.6. One rectangle is indicated by single lines; another rectangle by double lines; and the third rectangle, indicated by broken lines, consists of four separated points. If $(* *)$ were true, then we would be able to select from the three rectangles' E_1-projections a one-set covering of E_1; or we would be able to select from the E_2-projections a one-set covering of E_2. But in fact we need two of the E_1-projections to cover E_1 and we need two of the E_2-projections to cover E_2.

5.3. A Counterexample to the Finite Conjecture

Figure 6.6 is a counterexample to $(* *)$, but it does not provide us with a direct counterexample to the finite conjecture itself. There is, however, a surprisingly simple counterexample to the finite conjecture.

---

[11] I am very grateful to a referee for this counterexample. It improves on a previous counterexample, which was substantially more cumbersome.

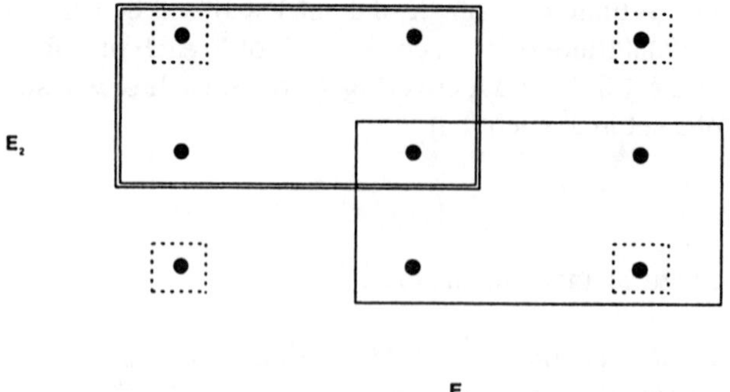

FIG. 6.6.

In the counterexample, there are four points denoted Q, R, S, T, in E_i, $i = 1, 2, 3, 4$. The function $F_A(e_1, e_2)$ takes the values zero or one. The function is given by the following figure:

e_2	Q	R	S	T
T	1(1)	1(2)	0	1(11)
S	1(3)	1(4)	1(5)	0
R	0	1(6)	1(7)	1(8)
Q	1(12)	0	1(9)	1(10)

For organization B, the definition of F_B is portrayed by the same figure, with e_3 the horizontal variable and e_4 the vertical variable. The twelve *one* points have been numbered for reference. The *one* points can be tiled with the three rectangles shown—numbered [1], [2], [3]—together with a fourth rectangle, to be labeled [4], namely:

1	11
12	10

It is easily verified that they cannot be tiled with fewer than four rectangles. The *zero* points can be tiled with four rectangles and not with fewer. *So a tiling of F_A requires eight rectangles and so does a tiling of F_B.*

We will also need two more rectangles composed of *one* points. They are

[5]:	3	5	[6]:	2	11
	12	9		6	8

Now consider the 144 (*one, one*) points in $E_1 \times E_2 \times E_3 \times E_4$. They can be tiled with just *twelve* of the 36 products obtainable from the rectangle system. Each of the 36 ordered pairs obtained from rectangles 1 to 6 defines a rectangle in $E_1 \times E_2 \times E_3 \times E_4$. For example, 3×1 denotes a rectangle (the product of Rectangle 1 and Rectangle 3) with E_1-projection $\{S, T\}$, E_2-projection $\{Q, R\}$, E_3-projection $\{Q, R\}$, and E_4-projection $\{S, T\}$.

The 36 rectangles comprise a tiling of the (*one, one*) points in $E_1 \times E_2 \times E_3 \times E_4$. But *we can discard all but twelve of the 36* while still tiling the (*one, one*) points. The following twelve rectangles suffice:

rectangle in $E_1 \times E_2 \times E_3 \times E_3$	E_1-projection	E_2-projection	E_3-projection	E_4-projection
1×1	$\{Q, R\}$	$\{S,T\}$	$\{Q, R\}$	$\{S,T\}$
3×1	$\{S,T\}$	$\{Q, R\}$	$\{Q, R\}$	$\{S,T\}$
1×3	$\{Q, R\}$	$\{S,T\}$	$\{S,T\}$	$\{R,Q\}$
2×5	$\{R,S\}$	$\{R,S\}$	$\{Q,S\}$	$\{Q,S\}$
5×2	$\{Q,S\}$	$\{Q,S\}$	$\{R,S\}$	$\{R,S\}$
6×2	$\{R,T\}$	$\{R,T\}$	$\{R,S\}$	$\{R,S\}$
2×6	$\{R,S\}$	$\{R,S\}$	$\{R,T\}$	$\{R,T\}$
3×3	$\{S,T\}$	$\{Q, R\}$	$\{S,T\}$	$\{Q, R\}$
4×5	$\{Q,T\}$	$\{Q,T\}$	$\{Q,S\}$	$\{Q,S\}$
5×4	$\{Q,S\}$	$\{Q,S\}$	$\{Q,T\}$	$\{Q,T\}$
4×6	$\{Q,T\}$	$\{Q,T\}$	$\{R,T\}$	$\{R,T\}$
6×4	$\{R,T\}$	$\{R,T\}$	$\{Q,T\}$	$\{Q,T\}$

It takes a few moments to verify that each of the 144 (*one, one*) points lies in at least one of these twelve rectangles.

For the (*zero, zero*), (*one, zero*), and (*zero, one*) points, we use the corresponding 'product' tilings, without discarding any of the pairs. Each of those three product tilings has $4 \times 4 = 16$ rectangles. We have, then, constructed a tiling of the function (F_A, F_B) which has only $(3)(16) + 12 = 60$ rectangles. *The Finite Conjecture says that we need* $8 \times 8 = 64$.[12]

[12]If it were not for the fortuitous discovery of the preceding counterexample, we would have to rely on a probabilistic argument, showing that counterexamples to a *generalized* version of the conjecture must exist. Such probabilistic existence proofs are common in combinatoric settings. In the generalized version of the Finite Conjecture, Organization A consists of Persons 1 and 2, as before, and A's task is (as before) to find $F_A(e_1, e_2)$, where F_A is again a zero/one function. But B is arbitrarily large. It consists of Persons 3, 4, . . . ,$2k$ and its task is to find

$$F_B(e_3, \ldots, e_{2k}) \equiv [F_A(e_3, e_4), F_A(e_5, e_6), \ldots, F_A(e_{2k-1}, e_{2k})].$$

6. INTERPRETING THE FAILURE OF THE FINITE CONJECTURE

How one interprets the failure of the Finite Conjecture depends on the scenario and the cost measure that one selects. Consider first the case in which organizations A and B operate with a *card displayer* or *proposer*. A requires Q_A cards and B requires Q_B cards. The merged organization uses a single card displayer, which in itself constitutes a 'saving.' (That saving might disappear in a model in which the single displayer is more expensive than either of the two displayers in the unmerged situation, since the single displayer is responsible for a larger card collection than were the two unmerged displayers.) The responders have no memory. Person i responds *Yes* or *No* to the card currently displayed. Person i's response is based only on the private information e_i and is uninfluenced by anyone's prior responses. The displayer can distinguish only between *at least one 'No'* and *no 'No's at all.*

The argument shows that for k sufficiently large there exists, with probability one, a counterexample to the finite conjecture. Unfortunately, the argument only guarantees a counterexample for ludicrously large k. The argument is therefore worth summarizing, in order to emphasize how extremely fortunate is the discovery of the preceding small counterexample, in which $k = 2$.

The building block of the probabilistic argument is a (two-dimensional) array of Zeros and Ones, defining the function $F_A(e_1, e_2)$. The array has the following properties: (i) the *ones* can be tiled with T rectangles and no fewer; (ii) the *ones* can *also* be covered with another system of rectangles; (iii) we can give each rectangle in the second system a nonnegative weight, with the weights adding up to $W < T$, where W is rational; (iv) every *one* is covered by rectangles of the second system with weights summing to at least one. An example of such a building block is the preceding sixteen-point zero/one array, where the *ones* are covered with $T = 4$ rectangles, numbered 1 to 4. The second system of rectangles consists of those four rectangles *plus* rectangles 5 and 6. We can give each of those six rectangles the weight 1/2, so that $W = 3 < 4 = T$. Every *one* lies in two of the second system's rectangles, so that the weights of the rectangles covering the point add up to one.

The merged organization could duplicate what A and B were doing separately by tiling all the points in k-space on which (F_A, F_B) takes a given value, with the k-fold product of the two-space tiling that Organization A used before the merger. But in fact, because, of the building block's properties, *for k large enough*, the merged organization can do better than that for the (*one, one, one, . . . ,one*) points and can do as well (by using the product tilings) for the other points.

Suppose there are D (*one, one*) points in the building block. The merged organization could, if it replicated what A and B did separately, tile the (*one, one, . . . ,one*) points with T^k rectangles. Suppose, however, that we are given the following urn:

The urn contains a number of '($2k$)-space' tiles. Each of the D^k points (*one, one, one, . . . ,one*)—a vector with $2k$ '*one*'s—is covered by at least one of the tiles. There is a weight attached to each tile. Every point is covered by tiles whose weights sum to one or more and the sum of the weights over all the tiles in the urn is W^k. There may be several copies of a given tile in the urn. *The frequency of a given tile in the urn equals its weight divided by W.*

Now the separate work of the two card displayers that A and B use could instead be performed by a *single* displayer even if A and B *do not* merge. Such a single displayer would have to be observable to all four persons. The displayer needs $Q_A \cdot Q_B$ cards. Each card has a left half (the only half that A's members examine) and a right half (the only half that B's members examine). If the visibility of the displayer to all four persons can be achieved with

---

The argument now proceeds in several steps.
Step 1. The probability that a given point (out of our D^k (*one, one, . . . ,one*) points) is covered in a single draw from the urn is

$$\geq \frac{1}{W^k} \geq \frac{1}{\lceil W^k \rceil}.$$

[The symbol $\lceil x \rceil$ denotes the smallest integer $\geq x$].
Step 2. The probability that a given point is not covered in one draw is

$$\leq 1 - \frac{1}{\lceil W^k \rceil}.$$

Step 3. We now study the probability that a given point is not covered in H_k drawings with replacement, where

$$H_k \equiv \lceil \log_e D^k \rceil \cdot \lceil W^k \rceil.$$

That probability is

$$\leq \left(1 - \frac{1}{\lceil W^k \rceil}\right)^{H_k} = \left[\left(1 - \frac{1}{\lceil W^k \rceil}\right)^{\lceil W^k \rceil}\right]^{\lceil \log_e D^k \rceil} < \left(\frac{1}{e}\right)^{\lceil \log_e D^k \rceil} \leq \left(\frac{1}{e}\right)^{\log_e D^k} = \frac{1}{D^k}$$

Step 4. The probability that *at least one* of the D^k points is not covered in H_k drawings with replacement is

$$\leq \sum_{\text{all points } i} (\text{probability that point } i \text{ is not covered}) < \left(\frac{1}{D^k}\right) \cdot D^k = 1.$$

(The second inequality is strict by Step 3).
Step 5. For large enough k, $H_k < T^k$.
To see this, note that

$$\begin{aligned} H_k &\leq (\log_e D^k + 1) \cdot (W^k + 1) \\ &= (k\log_e D + 1) \cdot (W^k + 1). \end{aligned}$$

But since $T/W > 1$,

$$k\log_e D + 1 < \frac{T^k}{W^k + 1} \text{ for large enough } k.$$

Hence for large enough k, $H_k < T^k$.
Conclusion. For sufficiently large k, there is some number of drawings, *less than* T^k, which yield tiles for which the probability that at least one point is not covered is *less than one*.

negligible cost, then $Q_A \cdot Q_B$ is a lower bound to the total displayer effort for which the two separate organizations have to pay.

If the two organizations now merge, and if we have a counterexample to the Finite Conjecture, then the single displayer whom the merged organization requires costs less than that lower bound. Only a Q-card displayer is now required, and Q is less than $Q_A \cdot Q_B$. The cheaper displayer's Q cards are not just simple pairings of the original cards. Thus in the counterexample of the preceding section, the cheap displayer uses Rectangles 5 and 6, which are not used before the two separate organizations merge.

Now consider the *nondeterministic* conversation scenario. A counterexample to the finite conjecture would mean the following: In the unmerged situation we have selected a Q_A-rectangle covering of E^A, a nondeterministic protocol, and Q_A conversations, one for each rectangle. We suppose that for every e^A, Persons 1 and 2 engage in the conversation assigned to the rectangle containing e^A (or if e^A lies in several rectangles, then they engage in one of the associated conversations). Sometimes—as at the point (3, 2) of Fig. 6.2—this means that someone makes a 'lucky' choice out of the sets given by the protocol. Under that supposition the longest time ever required is approximately log Q_A if every message is a binary string; that longest time cannot be reduced by using another nondeterministic protocol. The quantity log Q_B has an analogous interpretation for Organization B. In the unmerged situation, the longest time required for both actions to be found is approximately max (log Q_A, log Q_B).

The merged organization saves on 'conversation facilities'—a single facility, housing a four-person conversation, is required instead of two facilities. (The saving might disappear if there are sufficiently strong scale diseconomies for such facilities). Its longest action-finding time is longer than in the unmerged situation (unless log $Q <$ max(log Q_A, log Q_B)). In a counterexample the merged organization does *not* replicate the two separate protocols if it wants to achieve the (F_A, F_B) goal while minimizing the number of possible conversations. Its best protocol is *not* one in which 1 and 2 send exactly the same messages to each other as they did before the merger and 3 and 4 do the same. For a counterexample, we can argue a 'language' saving. If the 'lucky' choices are always made, then the four pre-merger members of A and B need the capacity, between them, to recognize $Q_A \cdot Q_B$ distinct conversations. If we have a counterexample, then after the merger they only need the capacity to recognize $Q < Q_A \cdot Q_B$ distinct conversations.

In either of the two preceding scenarios, one might reject as too fanciful our interpretation of the finite counterexample's 'language' saving. Yet if there were a counterexample to the *continuum* conjecture—if A required 4 message variables (a message space of dimension 4) to compute F_A, B required 5 to compute F_B, but the merged organization required only 8 to compute (F_A, F_B)—then it would be quite natural to say that number of message variables (language size) is a major component of the three organizations' information-processing costs and the merged organization indeed achieves a saving. We suggest the stories of the single card displayer, and of the conversation-recognizing capacities, as the best candidates for analogous interpretations of the finite counterexample.

Once we turn to the *deterministic* protocol scenario, there is no counterexample to worry about. A deterministic protocol, as we noted above, gives a rectangle covering which is a partitioning *and* has the bisection property. We now show that under that restriction the Finite Conjecture indeed holds.

7. THE FINITE CONJECTURE HOLDS WHEN THE MECHANISMS USED BY ALL THREE ORGANIZATIONS ARE REQUIRED TO HAVE THE BISECTION PROPERTY

First we need a general formal definition.

Definition. A sequence of finite partitionings of a set S, say $\Sigma_1, \ldots, \Sigma_t, \ldots$, is a *bisection sequence* if (i) $\Sigma_1 = S$; and (ii) for all $t > 1$, Σ_t contains two elements σ^*, σ^{**}, each a subset of S, such that $\Sigma_{t-1} = (\Sigma_t \backslash \{\sigma^*, \sigma^{**}\}) \cup \{\sigma^* \cup \sigma^{**}\}$. Given k sets $U_1, \ldots, U_k$, we shall call a t-element partitioning Σ of $U_1 \times \cdot \times U_k$ a *rectangle bisection partitioning* (*rbp*) if Σ is the tth member of a bisection sequence and each partitioning in that sequence is composed of rectangles with respect to $(U_1, \ldots, U_k)$.[13]

We next prove a general lemma. Its statement uses the term 'normal' defined in Section 5.

Lemma. Suppose the Q-element set Σ is an rbp of $U_1 \times \cdots \times U_k$. If $\{I, J\}$ is a partitioning of $\{1, \ldots, k\}$, and $V \equiv \times_{\ell \in I} U_\ell$, $W \equiv \times_{\ell \in J} U_\ell$, then Σ is normal with respect to (V, W).

Proof. The proof is by induction on Q. The proposition holds trivially for $Q = 1$ and $Q = 2$.

If we examine the first two members of the bisection sequence that yields a given rbp Σ of $V \times W$, we see that either there is a partitioning of V, say $\{\bar{V}, \bar{\bar{V}})$ and a partitioning of Σ, say $\{\bar{\Sigma}, \bar{\bar{\Sigma}}\}$, such that $\bar{\Sigma}, \bar{\bar{\Sigma}}$ are, respectively, rbp's of $\bar{V} \times W$, and $\bar{\bar{V}} \times W$; or there is a partitioning $\{\bar{W}, \bar{\bar{W}}\}$ of W and a partitioning $\{\tilde{\Sigma}, \tilde{\tilde{\Sigma}}\}$ of Σ such that $\tilde{\Sigma}, \tilde{\tilde{\Sigma}}$ are, respectively, rbp's of $\bar{V} \times W$ and $\bar{\bar{V}} \times W$. Without loss of generality, we may suppose that the former statement holds.

[13] I.e., each set in the partitioning is the Cartesian product of its projections with respect to $U_1, \ldots, U_k$.

Now suppose that the assertion of the Lemma holds for all $\bar{Q}$ with $2 < \bar{Q} < Q$. Since $|\bar{\Sigma}| < Q$ and $|\bar{\bar{\Sigma}}| \leq Q$, the induction hypothesis says that $\bar{\Sigma}$ and $\bar{\bar{\Sigma}}$ are normal with respect to $(\bar{V}, W)$ and $(\bar{\bar{V}}, W)$ respectively. That means there exists a covering $T_{\bar{V}}$ of $\bar{V}$ whose sets are $\bar{V}$-projections of sets in $\bar{\Sigma}$, and a covering T_W of W whose sets are W-projections of sets in $\bar{\Sigma}$, such that

$$|T_{\bar{V}}| \cdot |T_W| \leq |\bar{\Sigma}|. \tag{1}$$

Similarly, we have coverings $T_{\bar{\bar{V}}}$, $\tilde{T}_W$, of $\bar{\bar{V}}$ and W, respectively, such that

$$|T_{\bar{\bar{V}}}| \cdot |\tilde{T}_W| \leq |\bar{\bar{\Sigma}}|. \tag{2}$$

Without loss of generality we may suppose that

$$|T_W| \leq |\tilde{T}_W|. \tag{3}$$

Since $\bar{\Sigma} \cap \bar{\bar{\Sigma}} = \varnothing$, the collection $T_{\bar{V}} \cup T_{\bar{\bar{V}}}$ is a covering of V with $|T_{\bar{V}}| + |T_{\bar{\bar{V}}}|$ sets, each a V-projection of a set in Σ. The collection T_W is a covering of W, each of whose sets is a W-projection of a set in Σ. In view of (1)–(3), we therefore have

$$|\Sigma| = |\bar{\Sigma}| + |\bar{\bar{\Sigma}}| \geq |T_{\bar{V}}| \cdot |T_W| + |T_{\bar{\bar{V}}}| \tilde{T}_W| \geq |T_{\bar{V}} + T_{\bar{\bar{V}}}| \cdot |T_W|.$$

Thus Σ is normal with respect to (V, W) and the induction is complete.

Now suppose that the covering Σ_A of $E^A = E^1 \times E^2$ is (i) an rbp, (ii) a tiling of F_A, and (iii) minimal among all coverings with those two properties. Suppose that the analogous statement holds for the covering Σ_B and the function F_B. Suppose that the covering Σ of $E^A \times E^B$ is an rbp, a tiling of (F_A, F_B), and minimal among all coverings with those two properties. Then

$$|\Sigma| \geq |\Sigma_A| \cdot |\Sigma_B|. \tag{4}$$

That is the case since the Lemma guarantees the existence of rbp's $\tilde{\Sigma}_A$, $\tilde{\Sigma}_B$ of E^A, E^B, with $|\tilde{\Sigma}_A| \cdot |\tilde{\Sigma}_B| \leq |\Sigma|$. Since the sets in those rbp's are, respectively, A-projections and B-projections, they are tilings of F_A, F_B, respectively. So if (4) were false, we would have a contradiction.[14]

Thus if number of rectangles is our cost measure for mechanisms, then replication is indeed best when the rectangles have to comprise a partitioning with the bisection property. Since a deterministic protocol yields a rectangle partitioning with the bisection property, we also conclude that repli-

[14]It is not known whether the conclusion of the Lemma holds if the rectangle-covering Σ is a partitioning but does *not* have the bisection property. No counterexample has been found.

cation is best for the deterministic-conversation scenario, with each announcement being a binary string, when we take maximum conversation-completion time as our cost measure. For a positive integer J, let $\rho(J)$ denote the smallest integer d such that $2^d \geq J$. Then our cost measures for three mechanisms with brp's Σ_A, Σ_B, Σ become $\rho(|\Sigma_A|)$, $\rho(|\Sigma_B|)$, and $\rho(|\Sigma|)$. Since the function ρ is nondecreasing, we see that no (F_A, F_B)-realizing deterministic protocol for the merged organization can have a shorter maximum completion time than a protocol which corresponds to the product partitioning obtained from the rectangles that the two organizations were using before the merger.

8. THE FINITE CONJECTURE HOLDS WHEN A REGULARITY CONDITION IS IMPOSED ON THE MECHANISMS USED

It is natural to seek a regularity condition on finite mechanisms—a condition that is, in some sense, analogous to our regularity condition for continuum mechanisms—and that rules out counterexamples to the Finite Conjecture. The bisection requirement is not such a condition, since for a continuum mechanism the covering Σ is generally *not* a partitioning and yet the continuum version of the conjecture is true. Instead, the regularity condition we consider is suggested by the situation in Fig. 6.6, where a *non-normal* rectangle covering is portrayed. One of the rectangles in that covering—the rectangle indicated by broken lines—is not a 'proper' rectangle but rather consists of disjoint pieces with parts of other rectangles intruding between the pieces. If we required the rectangles to be 'proper,' then would non-normality be ruled out? If so, then what condition on the mechanisms used by A, B and the merged organization would yield proper rectangles, and hence a normal covering, and therefore the validity of the Finite Conjecture?

Before proceeding, we note that no generality is lost if we henceforth let $E^A = E_1 \times E_2$ and $E^B = E_3 \times E_4$ be finite sets.[15]

Next, given a finite mechanism (in rectangle form) on the finite set $E^A \times E^B$, say $\langle M, \Sigma, (h_A, h_B)\rangle$, with $\Sigma = \{\sigma_m \mid m \in M\}$, we define a *two-dimensional portray-*

[15]The Finite Conjecture only deals with functions F_A, F_B which are not only finite valued but which can be tiled with a finite number of rectangles. (That rules out, e.g., the case in which E_1 and E_2 are each the real line and F_A equals zero when $e_1 \geq e_2$ and one otherwise). Now suppose E_1 and E_2 are continua and suppose the smallest number of rectangles on each of which F_A is constant is, say, L. We can select a finite number of points from each of those L rectangles to obtain $\tilde{E}^A$, a finite subset of E^A. We can select the points, moreover, in such a way that (i) the points in a given one of the original continuum rectangles comprise a new rectangle (a subset of $\tilde{E}^A$), and (ii) the L new rectangles comprise a minimal tiling of $\tilde{F}^A$ where $\tilde{F}^A$, denotes the restriction of F^A to the set $\tilde{E}^A$.

al (TDP) of Σ. Let ν_A be a *numbering function* for $E^A = E_1 \times E_2$, i.e., a one-to-one function from E^A onto $\{1, 2, \ldots, J_A\}$, where $J_A = |E^A|$. Define ν_B to be a J_B-valued numbering function for E^B, where $J_B = |E^B|$. Let $A \equiv \{1, 2, \ldots, J_A\}$, $B \equiv \{1, 2, \ldots, J_B\}$. For each m in M, define

$$\tau_m \equiv \{(a, b) \in A \times B \,|\, a = \nu_a(e^A),\, b = \nu_b(e^B),\, (e^A, e^B) \in \sigma_m\}.$$

Then the triple $[\nu_a, \nu_b, \{\tau_m | m \in M\}]$ is a TDP of Σ.

It is easy to check that $\{\tau_m | m \in M\}$ covers $A \times B$, and that τ_m is a rectangle in $A \times B$: it is the product of τ_m^A (its A-projection) and τ_m^B (its B-projection). Notice, moreover, that the projection τ_m^A itself defines a rectangle in $E_A = E_1 \times E_2$. If we *decode* the points a in τ_m^A, we obtain precisely the rectangle $\sigma_m^1 \times \sigma_m^2$ in E^A. Thus a Q_A-element covering of A defines a Q_A-rectangle covering of $E^A = E_1 \times E_2$. Figure 6.7 provides an illustration. Now define an outcome function h_A which assigns to each of those Q_A rectangles–say to the rectangle comprising the decoded elements of τ_m^A—the action $h_A(m)$ in Z_A. That outcome function together with those Q_A rectangles (suitably indexed) comprise a mechanism on $E^A = E_1 \times E_2$. If, moreover, our original (four-person) mechanism $\langle M, \Sigma, (h_A, h_B)\rangle$ realizes (F_A, F_B) on $E_A \times E_B$, then the (two-person) mechanism we have just constructed realizes F_A on E^A.

Now suppose the sets in a covering of $A \times B$ are not only rectangles but *proper rectangles* as well (i.e., each projection of every rectangle is a set of *adjacent* points). Then we can use the following *correct* 'two-space' version of the claim denoted (* *) in Section 5.

(* * *) *Consider $A \times B$ in $\Re^2$, where A is a finite set of points on a horizontal axis and B is a finite set of points on a vertical axis. Let S be an ℓ-set covering of $A \times B$ each of whose sets is a proper rectangle. Then S is normal with respect to (A, B).*

Before proving (* * *) we note its implications. Suppose we know that (i) F_A can be realized (tiled) with Q_A rectangles in E^A but not with fewer, (ii) F_B can be realized with Q_B rectangles in E^B but not with fewer. Suppose we nevertheless had a mechanism which realizes (F_A, F_B) on $E_A \times E_B$ with $Q < Q_A \cdot Q_B$ rectangles and *has a TDP consisting of proper rectangles*. Consider the Q rectangles in the covering of $A \times B$ given by the TDP. (* * *) tells us that we can construct a Q_A^*-set covering of A from the A-projections and a Q_B^*-set covering of B from the B-projections, so that $Q_A^* \cdot Q_B^* \le Q$ (i.e., it tells us that a situation like the example in Fig. 6.6—which has an 'improper' rectangle—can be ruled out). Then we have a Q_A^*-rectangle mechanism on E^B realizing Q_B, and (since $Q < Q_A \cdot Q_B$) either $Q_A^* < Q_B$ or $Q_B^* < Q_B$, contradicting the assumed minimalities.

A TDP of a Mechanism on $E_1 \times E_2 \times E_3 \times E_4$

The mechanism:

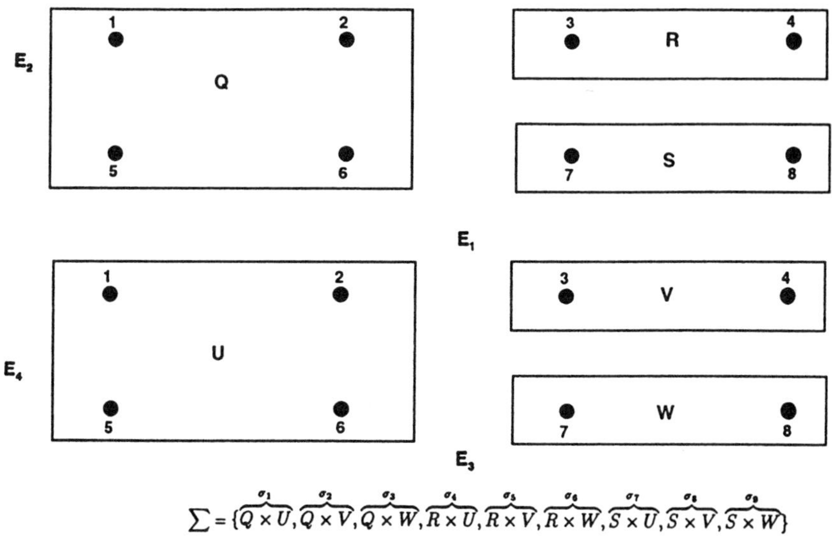

The two-dimensional portrayal:

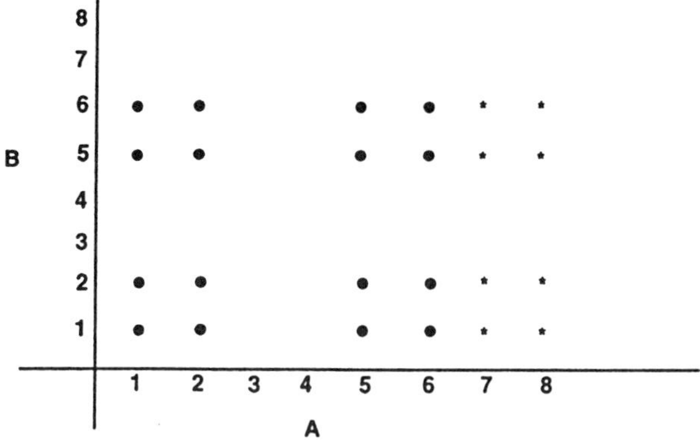

FIG. 6.7. The points shown as *dots* are a portrayal of σ_1. The points show as *asterisks* are a portrayal of σ_7. (Note that each of those portrayals is a rectangle but not a proper rectangle). The portrayals of the other rectangles in Σ are not shown.

To summarize:

Let us say that a finite (four-agent) mechanism on the finite set $E^A \times E^B$ has the *adjacency property* if the mechanism has a TDP consisting entirely of proper rectangles. Suppose $(* * *)$ is correct. Then the finite conjecture holds for four-agent mechanisms with the adjacency property.

Proof[16] of $(* * *)$. Let $\ell \equiv |S|$. Suppose that the smallest covering of A whose sets are A-projections of the rectangles in S has ℓ_A elements. Suppose that the smallest covering of B whose sets are B-projections has ℓ_B elements. Suppose S is not normal with respect to (A, B), i.e., $\ell < \ell_a \cdot \ell_b$. We shall then obtain from the B-projections a covering of B with fewer than ℓ_b sets, which is a contradiction.

To construct the required covering of B, consider the bottom row of points in $A \times B$. Find a *tallest* rectangle (a rectangle with the most points in its B-projection), among all rectangles that contain points in the bottom row. *By assumption, there must be at least ℓ_A rectangles containing points in the bottom row.* Since all rectangles are proper, 'tallest' is well-defined. Let H denote the height of the tallest rectangle (the number of points in its B-projection) and let the bottom H points in B be the first set in the covering of B that we are constructing. If $H > 1$, proceed to the points in the horizontal line given by $b = H$ and if $H = 1$ proceed to the line $b = H + 1$. On that line again find the tallest rectangle among the rectangles—there are again at least ℓ_A of them—whose numbers are attached to the points on the line. Note that none of these rectangles are among those encountered in the first step (along the bottom line). Let the B-projection of the new tallest rectangle be the second set in our covering of B. Proceed in this manner until B has been covered. At each step at least ℓ_A rectangles have been accounted for and those rectangles are never encountered at a later step. Consequently, there can be no more than ℓ/ℓ_A steps, each step providing a set in our covering of B. By assumption, $\ell/\ell_A < \ell_B$, so we have indeed constructed a covering of B with fewer than ℓ_B sets. That concludes the proof.

9. CONCLUSION

We have found two ways to 'salvage' the finite conjecture. We can impose the adjacency condition on all the mechanisms used. That is, perhaps, analogous to imposing smoothness conditions in the continuum case (where we do it in order to rule out the smuggling of many numbers into one number). Or we can insist on the bisection property for the coverings that the mechanisms define. That means that if we confine attention to the deterministic-conver-

[16]A slightly different version of this proof appeared in Marschak and Vazirani (1991).

sation scenario, then the merged organization can indeed do no better than to replicate what the two organizations were doing before the merger.

The 'proposal' scenario, however, seems quite plausible and is a standard scenario in the literature on continuum mechanisms. It is quite surprising that in a finite example, where the goal functions F_A, F_B are not particularly 'exotic', the merged organization does *not* replicate the two separate ones even though it wants to achieve exactly the same tasks as the two separate organizations. One may react to this discovery, of course, by saying 'This just shows that number of possible proposals is not a good cost measure,' or 'It shows that additional elements of a mechanism's information-processing costs (computation for example) need to be modelled as well.' Those are natural reactions and it would certainly be useful if such comments led to new modellings, for which the unexpected phenomenon disappears.

On the other hand, the mechanism/message-space model of information-processing is the only one to have been studied widely in both economics and computer science. If we seek to resolve the decreasing-returns puzzle by incorporating precise models of information processing into the 'Top-Manager-with-private-information' explanation, then the mechanism/message space model has to be a serious candidate. Finite mechanisms are more realistic than continuum mechanisms. The failure of the finite replication-is-best conjecture is therefore quite disruptive, since it suggests that for certain elements of information-processing cost there may even be *increasing* returns. To clear the decks for the Top-Manager explanation it would certainly be helpful to rule out such disturbing counterexamples. Should we accept the somewhat artificial adjacency constraint? Or should we insist on a scenario in which members converse in strict accordance with a shared protocol that never gives a member more than one choice when it is that member's turn to speak?

ACKNOWLEDGMENTS

Support from National Science Foundation grant IRI9120074 is gratefully acknowledged. Much of the chapter suggestions from U. Vazirani, who is absolved from any responsibility for errors or unusual interpretations. I am particularly grateful to C. B. McGuire, who wrote a computer program that discovered the critical 16-point example in Section 5.

REFERENCES

Calsamiglia, X., 1977, Decentralized resource allocation and increasing returns, Journal of Economic Theory.

Calsamiglia, X. and A. Kirman, 1993, A unique informationally efficient and decentralized mechanism with fair outcomes, Econometrica.

Hurwicz, L., 1977, On the dimensional requirements of informationally decentralized Pareto-satisfactory adjustment processes, In: K. J. Arrow and L. Hurwicz, eds., Studies in resource allocation processes (Cambridge University Press, Cambridge).

Hurwicz, L., 1986, On informational decentralization and efficiency in resource allocation mechanisms, In: S. Reiter, ed., Studies in mathematical economics (Mathematical Association of America, Washington, DC).

Hurwicz, L. and H. Weinberger, 1990, A necessary condition for decentralization and an application to intertemporal allocation, Journal of Economic Theory.

Jordan, J., 1982, The competitive process is informationally efficient uniquely, Journal of Economic Theory.

Jordan, J., 1987, The informational requirements of local stability in decentralized allocation mechanisms, In: T. Groves, R. Radner and S. Reiter, eds., Information, incentives, and economic mechanisms (University of Minnesota Press, Minneapolis, MN).

Lovasz, L., 1990, Communication complexity: A survey, In: B. H. Korte, ed., Paths, flows, and VLSI layout (Springer Verlag, Berlin).

Kaldor, N., 1934, The equilibrium of the firm, Economic Journal.

Mount, K. and S. Reiter, 1974, The informational size of message spaces, Journal of Economic Theory.

Marschak, T. and S. Reichelstein, 1993, Network mechanisms, informational requirements, and hierarchies, Working paper.

Marschak, T. and S. Reichelstein, 1995, Communication requirements for individual agents in networks and hierarchies, In: J. Ledyard, ed., The economics of informational decentralization: Complexity, efficiency, and stability (Kluwer Publishing Company, Dordrecht).

Marschak, T. and U. Vazirani, 1991, Communication costs in the performance of unrelated tasks: Continuum models and finite models, Journal of Organizational Computing.

Rather, R., 1993, The economics of decentralized information processing, Econometrica.

Radner, R. and T. Van Zandt, 1992, Information processing and returns to scale, Annales d'Economie et de Statistique.

Reichelstein, S. and S. Reiter, 1988, Game forms with minimal strategy spaces, Econometrica.

Sato, 1981, On the informational size of message spaces for economies with public goods, Journal of Econometric Theory.

CHAPTER

7

Knowledge, Discovery, and Growth

Stanley Reiter
Northwestern University

1. INTRODUCTION

The aim of the work reported in this chapter is to build a formal model of technology in which technological change can be studied. Technological change takes place by invention, or discovery. It proceeds by finding new ways of doing things, by finding new things to do, or new uses for things already known. These things typically involve a creative act. Something previously unknown or nonexistent becomes known or comes into existence.

A formal model of the growth of technology or knowledge must therefore accommodate creative acts. It must do so without pretending to be a model that predicts specific creations, inventions, or discoveries, because, to do that would be in effect to make them. That is, a model that predicts the fruits of creative acts would itself be an engine for making creative acts—for short, a Promethean machine.[1]

A model of knowledge, including technological knowledge, and its growth is potentially useful in connection with a number of different problems in economics. Among these is the theory of economic development. There appears to be wide agreement among economists, and others, that technological change is perhaps the most important driver of economic development.[2] This chapter does not contain a theory of economic development. The model presented is a partial model intended, like a modular component in a stereo sound system, to be embedded in or linked to a more general economic model. The present model contains functions that can serve as connectors to a broader economic model. In that model they would be endogenously determined, whereas in the present model they are exogenous parameters.

In economics technology is modeled in a number of different ways. In almost all of them the concept of a commodity is used. Technology is modeled, for example, as a relation between input commodities and output commodities expressed by a function, the production function. In some cases processes of production are explicitly introduced in terms of variables called activity levels or process intensities.[3] Then production possibilities are expressed by a mapping, which may be linear or nonlinear, between the space of activity levels and the commodity space. Although there are many different models of technology appropriate to specific purposes, the simplest and perhaps most general is the production set model. The production set is a subset of the commodity space consisting of all input–output combinations that economic agents know how to produce. "Commodity" and "production set" are primitive concepts in economics. The commodities and the production set are regarded as exogenously given.

Part 2 presents a model of technology in which technology is, as is conventional, viewed as knowledge of how to produce things. However, in contrast to conventional models of technology in economic theory, knowledge of how to produce things is represented explicitly. Technology is therefore a special category of knowledge. Commodities and production sets are derived in the present chapter from technological knowledge.

Because technological knowledge depends on other knowledge, such as scientific knowledge, technology is embedded in a more general model of knowledge. Although that model, presented in Part 3, should logically come before the model of technology, the intuitive, informal discussion in Part 2 of modeling technology serves to motivate and clarify the model of knowledge presented in Part 3.

Knowledge resides in the mind of a person. It may have several representations. It is modeled in this chapter as a finite subset of the set of all possible statements in a natural language, say, English. The English language is based on a finite alphabet. That alphabet may be augmented by appending a finite number of other symbols. The collection of sentences of finite length, (i.e., finite strings of symbols from the alphabet, well-formed according to the rules or usage of the language) is countably infinite. It contains a representation of every item of knowledge that can conceivably be expressed in English. In this way we avoid on the one hand, models that implicitly bound what might be known in the future, but is not now known, and on the other, introducing aggregates that are not well-defined sets.

The *knowledge of Person i at Time t* is represented as a finite subset of the set of possible English sentences. Formally, that set is a primitive of the model; its interpretation is the knowledge in the mind of a Person i at Time t.

Thus, in an application of the model the representation of what is in the mind of the person whose knowledge is being modeled is the task of the applier. It cannot be expected that there will be a unique representation. In these circumstances, and in view of the use to be made of the model in this chapter, it is desirable to have an economical, or parsimonious representation. Therefore, an equivalence relation on the set of sentences is introduced in Part 3, so that a knowledge set consists of equivalence classes of sentences, or of representative sentences, each representing the class of sentences equivalent to it. A representative sentence may be interpreted as an "idea."

A knowledge set may also be given additional structure. For instance, different areas of knowledge may be recognized formally. This model of knowledge is presented and discussed further in Part 3.[4]

The main focus of this investigation is on the growth of knowledge. This takes place by two processes, by learning from others, and by the discovery (creation or invention), of new knowledge. Knowledge has the property that its acquisition by one person does not diminish what is available for others to acquire. This is sometimes extended to the idea that knowledge once in existence is a public good, freely available to all. The latter proposition is clearly not true. Although one can borrow Von Neuman's book on quantum mechanics from a library without charge, that does not automatically transfer the knowledge represented in it into the mind of the borrower. Acquiring knowledge, even if it is already known to others, entails the expenditure of effort and resources, and also entails private acts of discovery. It is not so different in this respect from creating new knowledge. This matter is discussed further in Part 4.

Discovery takes place when new ideas (representative sentences) are added to someone's stock of knowledge. Whether discovery is of socially new knowledge or of privately new knowledge, discovery typically involves a creative act on the part of the discoverer. Hence, a model of the growth of knowledge must rest ultimately on a theory of the process(es) of creation. Part 4 presents a view of acts of creation that provides the basis for the model of the growth of knowledge presented in the following Part 5.[5] Briefly summarized, that view is:

i. Discovery results from interaction between an individual mind and a body of knowledge;
ii. More knowledge facilitates discovery, but does not guarantee it; (Discoveries are almost always made by people with knowledge of the area in which the discovery is made, for example, discoveries in game theory are usually made by people who know a lot of game theory–in chemistry, by chemists);
iii. There is no penalty in the form of inhibition of discovery from having more (adequately structured) knowledge;

iv. There are individual differences in cognitive and other skills and abilities relevant to making discoveries;
v. Discovery is a purposeful activity—intensity of effort and resources devoted to that activity have an effect;
vi. Creative acts typically involve bringing together disparate ideas, often from different frames of reference.

It seems clear that understanding the ideas that an inventor worked with in the process of making a particular discovery or creation is necessary to understanding the process of coming to that discovery. Descriptions of that process for particular inventions make up much of the content of books dealing with the history of science or technology. That sort of understanding is, of course, retrospective.

But, to recapitulate a point made earlier, a theory of discovery or creation cannot reasonably attempt to predict from a specific set of ideas the particular creation(s) they will give rise to when subjected to the effort of a particular person, (who may not be the theorist). If there were such a theory, and if it were a good one, the theory would itself make the discoveries.[6] Furthermore it would do so without the abilities, skills, effort, and resources of *any* person other than the theorist.

Fortunately, to analyze the economic role of discovery it is not necessary to have a model that predicts or explains specific discoveries. It is enough to explain:

i. a measure of the flow of discoveries,
ii. the dependence of that flow on economic and social parameters, and,
iii. the economic effects of a flow of discoveries, measured in some average sense.

In addition, a model can provide *ex ante* for discoveries whose specific nature is unknown, for example, new processes of production or new commodities, which are to be included *ex post*, after their specific nature is known. Such a model can permit *ex ante* analysis of economic consequences of discoveries.

To model the growth of knowledge without attempting to make what I have called a Promethean machine, it is useful to have some concept of *amount of knowledge*. In this model the amount of knowledge is a measure of the size of the set of sentences that constitutes knowledge. Such a measure would generally be multidimensional, corresponding to distinctions among different kinds of knowledge. The simplest case is that of a one-dimensional measure. Although this is from some viewpoints evidently a gross oversimplification, it is one that connects naturally with existing models of production in which technological change is considered. In those models, technological knowledge is represented by a (real) parameter, as, for example, a coefficient multiplying a Cobb-Douglas or CES production function, and technological change is expressed as a change, usually an increase, in the value of that parameter. The one-dimensional measure we use here is the number of sentences in the knowledge set being measured (after due allowance for nonuniqueness of representation), and its growth is the change over time of the number of sentences that embody knowledge. This is analogous to the one-dimensional measure of a heterogeneous collection of objects used in production called "amount of capital." Although these are clearly oversimplifications, such a measure can be useful as a starting point in addressing some questions.

Part 5 presents a mathematical model of the growth of knowledge based on the view summarized earlier. A "prepared mind" is stimulated by a combination of ideas to conceive a new idea. In terms of sets of sentences, several subsets of knowledge come together to stimulate the conjecture and exploration of a candidate new sentence. Thus, the possibilities of cross-fertilization are given by the power set of the knowledge set being considered. But, because a subset of sentences can be considered to be a compound sentence, and as such an element of the knowledge set under consideration, the size of the knowledge set itself measures the number of potential cross-fertilizings.

These ideas can be expressed in different mathematical structures. We have at present no clear basis for choosing among them. In order to avoid merely mathematical complexities, I give these ideas a very simple mathematical expression. Starting with an isolated person, this leads to a first order linear difference equation in the size of the set representing the knowledge of that person at Time t. For mathematical convenience this difference equation is replaced by the analogous differential equation, in continuous time and with the amount of knowledge treated as a continuous variable—a real number. Because the size of knowledge sets is typically very large, and the changes relatively small, this does not appear to be a heinous simplification.

Next I consider a community of persons engaged in research or R&D activities (i.e., in the attempt to produce new knowledge). Such a community consists of persons in communication with one another through various means. The model of an isolated person is extended to one of an interacting community. The result is a system of differential equations that characterizes the simultaneous growth of the knowledge of each person in the community. This system of equations is the basis for analyzing the growth of the subset of knowledge that is technology.

The growth of knowledge, and of technology, can be exponential, depending on the values of the parameters that represent ability, skill, resources, and effort applied to discovery and learning. This means that there can be (exponentially) increasing returns in the production of knowledge, and exponential growth in the amount of knowledge. Is this consistent with what can be observed?

Part 5 presents some data on the growth of knowledge in computer science from 1958 to 1990. The size of the body of knowledge in that field is measured in two ways, first, the number of pages published each year from 1958 to 1990 in the field of computer science, and second, the number of articles published in those years. Of course, the underlying assumption is that the number of ideas per paper, or per sentence, is on average, not too far from constant. The results are that knowledge so measured grew exponentially at about 10% per year over that period. The rate of growth is probably somewhat understated, because papers that properly belong in computer science were not found, because they were published in journals not primarily devoted to computer science, and this is more likely to be the case in later than in earlier years.

Through the introduction of a (time varying) commodity space and a (time varying) attainable production set, both defined in terms of the underlying technology, the growth of the attainable production set and its dependence on the underlying parameters can be analyzed.[7] This is done in Part 6, in the context of a Leontief model of production. Exponentially increasing returns in knowledge and technology translate into exponentially increasing returns in the production set. In examples analyzed in Part 6 a fixed amount of the primary resource yields an exponentially increasing amount of outputs over time as knowledge grows, because the output coefficients grow exponentially.[8] Can this result be consistent with the physical laws governing relations between matter and energy?

First, growth of knowledge may lead not to growth of a given set of output coefficients, but to new ways of satisfying economic wants via different substances and processes not now known in such a way as to remain well inside the fundamental constraints imposed by physical laws.[9]

Learning curves in manufacturing are a well-observed phenomenon usually attributed to increase of knowledge by those engaged in production. So, learning curves ought to be derivable from a model of the growth of knowledge. Part 7 presents derivations of two forms of learning curves from the model of the growth of knowledge.

As noted before, the model presented in this chapter is a partial one. Insofar as application to economic development is concerned, it is intended that it will ultimately be linked with or embedded in a model in which a general dynamic economic analysis of its implications for economic growth or development can be carried out, and in which the effects of instruments of social and economic policy can be studied. The paper by Arrow (1962) on learning-by-doing and that of Lucas (1988) contain analyses to which this model might be linked. In connection with development, this chapter can be viewed as an attempt to provide a model of the growth of knowledge and technology that can be connected to and support such analyses.[10]

2. A MODEL OF TECHNOLOGY

2.1. Technology and Knowledge

The effects of discovery or invention on economic life come mainly through changes in technology and ultimately changes in production of goods and services. Among the many ways of representing technology used in economic models, the production set model is perhaps the simplest and most general. In that representation, we postulate a commodity space, usually a (finite dimensional) Euclidean space, and a subset of it, called the production set, which contains all the input–output vectors that are technologically feasible (i.e., for which there is knowledge of a process or processes which if carried out would produce the specified outputs from the specified inputs).[11] An act of production is a choice of a point from the production set.

I propose to use a somewhat different model of technology, in which the commodity space and the production set are constructed from technological knowledge, rather than given exogenously. To motivate this model and to clarify its interpretation it is useful to have an example of a technology in mind. There is a wide choice of examples available, for instance, agriculture, steelmaking, aircraft manufacturing, pharmaceuticals. Unfortunately, these examples are complicated. Knowledge about any one of them is described in an extensive and complex literature not readily accessible to nonspecialists. An example drawn from any of these unfamiliar areas of technology might be more confusing than illuminating.

However, there is an example that is likely to be familiar to most people—the art of cooking—which, in other words, is the knowledge of how to produce edible dishes from raw materials. For the sake of the example I take this body of knowledge, as of today, to be what is recorded in cookbooks now in existence.

Typically, a cookbook contains (i) recipes, and (ii) discussions, that may or may not be part of a recipe, of matters relevant to the preparation of food. A recipe can be viewed as consisting of four parts:

First, a description of what will be produced if the recipe is carried out, including not only the name of the product (e.g., *Cheese Bites*), but perhaps also other aspects of the use of the product—in this case, that it is "interesting, attractive, and not messy," and therefore good to serve at cocktail parties;

Second, a list of ingredients and outputs, with the quantities specified;

Third, a list of statements describing the actions to be taken in order to execute the recipe (i.e., to carry out the act of production specified by the recipe);

Fourth, a statement to the effect that the recipe works. A statement to this effect in the form of the claim that "All the recipes in this book have been tested under a variety of relevant conditions," is often found in the Introduction to a cookbook. This may be thought of as a statement attached to each recipe. Otherwise, in the absence of an explicit claim, I take it that testimony to the reliability of the contents is implicit in publication.

The standard models of technology in economics focus on the list of ingredients and products, which are modeled as input–output vectors in the commodity space, and abstract from everything else.[12]

The model I use incorporates *all* the elements of a recipe. Knowledge of how to produce a product or service, not restricted to preparation of food, is thought of as embodied in *recipes*. Each recipe is a list of statements in a natural language, say English, that describe what is to be done, including at each step how much of each substance, equipment, or labor is involved in that step.[13] The ingredients, substances, and procedures involved are described and identified—named—in the natural language. Whatever details are necessary in order to identify the elements required are given. The use of natural language descriptions permits denumerably many distinctions among entities (substances, objects, laborious procedures) to be made, without specifying them once and for all in advance.

For a list of statements to constitute a recipe it must also contain a description of what *uses* are fulfilled by it,[14] and a statement certifying that it *works*. Thus, all four parts of a cookbook recipe are modeled as a list of English sentences, where the list of ingredients and products may or may not be displayed separately, but may appear dispersed in the sentences that specify the actions to be taken.[15]

This model of technology does not so far use the concept of a commodity. The objects, substances, or other entities that appear in a recipe can be anything that can be given a name in the natural language. Although the collection of names of entities in the language is a given finite set, a new name can be coined at any time to refer to a substance or entity hitherto unknown, or to make new distinctions among substances or objects. Furthermore, there can be more than one name for the same thing, and there is no assumption that the equivalence of these names is recognized.

For each named substance or object there is also given some way of representing its quantity, for instance by elements of an additive group, like the integers, or the rational numbers.

Different cookbooks may each contain a recipe for the same dish, and these recipes may have different descriptions. For example, one can find recipes for beef stew in many cookbooks. Furthermore, these recipes may not prescribe exactly the same steps in preparation, or may not specify exactly the same ingredients, or the same quantities. They may give different names to the product, or may describe slightly different uses for the product. In any of these cases, the recipes would be different. And yet the differences may be small enough that they may be considered to be minor variations of the "same recipe." It is natural in situations like this to regard all these descriptions as equivalent.

As already mentioned, a cookbook, and more generally a body of technological knowledge, may also contain statements of a general nature embodying knowledge. For example, some cookbooks discuss the chemical composition and the modes of action of various baking powders.[16] Although statements about the action of baking powders may be common to cooking and to chemistry, it would not be hard to find statements about chemistry that are never found in cookbooks, and to find a graduated collection of statements that are 'between' them in the sense that they go from statements more relevant to cooking to statements increasingly remote from it. This illustrates a situation in which the line separating technological knowledge from other areas of knowledge is somewhat arbitrary. In the present model, the certification of tested recipes makes an unambiguous distinction between technology and other knowledge.

I propose to embed the model of technology in a larger model of a *body of knowledge*, and where necessary make distinctions among fields of knowledge as needed. The larger model would include tested recipes, but could also include partially specified recipes. For example, it might include recipes that have the first three parts, but lack the fourth. That is, they may be regarded as conjectured, but as yet untested recipes. It could also include statements about properties of entities involved in recipes, or about entities related to such entities, or about statements about such statements, and so on. And it could include the contents of books and journal articles on food chemistry, human physiology, and more remote areas of knowledge chosen according to the use to be made of the model.

Thus, technological knowledge is a special case of knowledge. The discussion of modeling technology presented in this Part can serve as a motivation for a model of more general knowledge that follows in Part 3.

3. A MODEL OF KNOWLEDGE

To begin with let the set of persons at any time, t, be a given finite set, denoted

$$\mathbf{A} = \{1,2,\ldots,N\}.^{17}$$

Knowledge Resides in the Mind of a Person. What a person "knows" can be described in natural language, as a finite collection of sentences in that language—English, for example.[18] Let **E** denote the set of English sentence (i.e., finite strings of symbols from the English alphabet), possibly augmented with a finite number of other symbols.[19]

The availability of quantifiers, such as "for all," and "for some," which are, of course, English words, makes the language rich enough to include mathematics. It also includes self-referential sentences. Thus the set **E** includes undecidable propositions, because of Godel's theorem. Because the use to be made of this model does not require the set of sentences to include only those that are either *true* or *false*, or to be free of the problems of self-reference, there is no need to restrict it further.[20]

$$\text{For } i \in \mathbf{A} \text{ let } K'(i,t) \text{ be a subset of } \mathbf{E}.$$

The set K′(i,t) is interpreted as Person i's knowledge at Time t. It includes any recipes that Person i knows at t, together with any other knowledge that i has. Thus,

$$K'(i,t) \supseteq K'^{*}(i,t),$$

where $K'^{*}(i,t)$ is the set of recipes known by i at t.

The set K′(i,t) may include the rules of logic, the rules of the calculus of probability, or of other systems of thought. However, it is possible for Person i to know some sentences, and to know the rules of logic, and yet not to know a sentence, which is implied by what he or she does know, or one that is logically equivalent to what he knows.

Here, in contrast to other possible usage, the word *knowledge* refers to sentences (or structures of them) that may or may not be true, or whose truth may be unknown, as well as to sentences that Person i is aware of, and to which he may attach some degree of belief. Because the credence that Person i attaches to a sentence can be expressed by a sentence, there is no difficulty in expressing this in the model.[21]

Let I(i,t) be an equivalence relation on the set K′(i,t). Sentences are equivalent according to I(i,t) if Person i at t regards them as expressing the same thing. In particular, the relation I(i,t) expresses the equivalence of recipes that would be so considered in the discussion of equivalent recipes in Part 2.

The relation I(i,t) can be extended from K′(i,t) to all of **E**. One such extension results from letting the equivalence classes be singletons on $E \setminus K'(i,t)$, but others might also be possible.

Now, let

$$K(i,t) = K'(i,t)/I(i,t),$$

namely, the quotient set of K′(i,t) with respect to the relation I(i,t). The elements of K(i,t) are representatives of the equivalence classes of I(i,t), and may be called *ideas*. (Here the term *ideas* must be understood broadly, for instance, to include the canonical or basic recipes discussed in Part 2.) Each of these may be represented by a canonical sentence that expresses the idea. From now on, an element of the knowledge set K(i,t) is understood to be a canonical sentence (i.e., a representative of an equivalence class of sentences that express the same thing).

As in the case of technology in Part 2, it is useful to have an example of knowledge in mind. Examples that have the virtue of familiarity are Economics, or Game Theory (or a subfield of specialization, such as Economic Theory). In these fields existing knowledge is for the most part written in the form of books, journal articles, or preprints. However, the set K(i,t) is interpreted as including only what i has in his or her head at Time t. Thus, if Person i bought Myerson's book on game theory at Time t-1 and has it on his shelf unread, its contents are not included in K(i,t), unless i has acquired this knowledge through other sources.

The sets K(i,t) for $i \in \mathbf{A}$[22] have the possibility of being organized further with many different structures. In the example of economic theory, general equilibrium theory might be distinguished from principle–agent theory. Or, a sentence that states, say, that one theorem is a special case of another, might be included in a structure consisting of relations defined on a subset of sentences in K(i,t), expressing the depth of knowledge in an area.

We introduce a measure of the amount of i's knowledge at t, denoted,

$$k(i,t)$$

called the *size of K(i,t)*.

A natural candidate is the measure of K(i,t), which, since K(i,t) is finite, is the number of elements in K(i,t).[23,24]

Then,

$$k(i,t) = |K(i,t|.$$ [25]

Distinctions of substance among different ideas or knowledge can be introduced formally. Let

$$\mathbf{L} = \{L_q,\ q = 1,2, \ldots\}$$

be a partition of $\mathbf{E}_i/I(i,t)$[26] and let

$$K_q(i,t) = L_q \cap K(i,t),$$

and let

$$k_q(i,t) = |K_q(i,t)|, \qquad \text{for } q = 1,2, \ldots .$$

The partition **L** classifies knowledge, the elements in Lq being considered of the same kind. The sets L_q can be called *areas of knowledge*, or *subfields*. Since K(i,t) is finite, only a finite number of the sets $K_q(i,t)$ can be nonempty.

If the partition **L** is the finest possible, then to know that a statement (idea, or recipe) is in the set Lq′ for some q′ identifies that statement up to the equivalence relation I(i,t) (i.e., the statement is uniquely identified as a particular idea).

In this model new knowledge consists of new statements appended to an existing knowledge set. This involves a creative act. The next Part, Part 4, discusses the creative process.

4. CREATIVITY AND DISCOVERY

4.1. Creative Power and Knowledge

Person i makes a *discovery* (or an *invention*) when he adds a new sentence or list of sentences to his knowledge, perhaps describing a new product or process of production, or a new theorem.[27] Discovery or invention involves a creative act—something that *was not* before a certain time *is* afterwards. The aim of this Part is to develop an understanding of the act of discovery sufficient to justify and support the model presented in Part 5. That model is intended not as a model of the creative act itself, but *a model of the growth of knowledge as a result of discovery*, a model that can be used to analyze the economic significance of discovery.

Plato, through the mouth of Socrates, speaking about the creative powers of poets, states that the poets create by "... divine power...."[28] Since then people have sought in different ways to understand this power. Some have studied the lives of "obviously" gifted creators, such as Einstein, or Picasso, with the aim of detecting how they differ from people who have not made such remarkable discoveries or creations. Although it is clear that there are individual differences in intellectual abilities, and in creative powers, whatever they may be, it is also clear that human beings have created, discovered, and invented in every time and place where human beings lived. The divine power seems to have been distributed generally to humanity. Whatever abilities facilitate creative achievements, originality, discovery and invention, they are part of the human genetic endowment.[29,30]

It is evident that discoveries are almost always made by people who have knowledge of the field in which the discovery is made. Most discoveries in mathematics are made by mathematicians, in chemistry by chemists, and so on. In earlier times, when technology was further removed from science than it appears to be now, discoveries and inventions were made by people without academic or professional credentials, but rarely by those who had little knowledge of the field to which the inventions belong. Even today many "small" discoveries, leading to improved technology, are made by those who carry out production. Of course, it is not the credentials of the person that matter, but the fact of working intensively in that field. At one time many medical discoveries were made by practicing physicians. Nowadays medical discoveries are overwhelmingly made by researchers who may be biologists, biochemists, and the like, or MDs, who are focused on research. They are more rarely made by physicians who are exclusively in clinical practice, or whose activity and experience are removed from the areas which now spawn discoveries.

This suggests that the *knowledge of* and *attention to* a field play important roles in discovery in that field.

It is useful at this point to have in mind a more concrete situation. Consider the performance of a graduate student and an experienced faculty member (in economics) in reading and understanding a new paper. The student typically will have to work hard to follow the contents of the paper, and is likely to do so in a limited way.[31] He can be expected to be able to summarize the contents and perhaps to supply some missing steps in the arguments, but not usually to be able to see and evaluate the contents in the context of the broader literature.

The faculty member typically will absorb the contents more quickly, and will relate them to other work in the field. He will be able to form a judgment about the significance of the paper in light of his knowledge of the literature. He is also more likely to see other applications of the methods used, or think of other methods that could be used either with or in place of the ones in the paper.

A few years later when the student has become an experienced faculty member himself, his performance will be very like that of the faculty member now. On the other hand, if the faculty member should choose to read a paper in a field he is not familiar with, such as computer science, he is likely to have the same difficulties as the student, perhaps mitigated by his knowledge and experience in those aspects of his field that are related to the material he is reading.

One important difference between the student and the faculty member is the difference in their knowledge. The knowledge of a novice most typically consists of relatively isolated pieces rather than of a richly interconnected integrated structure of thought.[32]

The task of understanding the paper involves making what are subjectively discoveries. It is not essentially different from that of making other discoveries.[33]

It is important to note that commanding a large body of knowledge does not in itself lead to difficulties that offset the benefits of knowledge, provided that knowledge about the structure of knowledge is also large.[34] This is typically the case when the knowledge under consideration is that of an experienced specialist.

Another aspect of the facility that goes with expertise and experience involves the distinction between knowing and knowing how, mentioned in Part 3, footnote 16. One aspect of knowing how to do something is captured by the description of the process that must be carried out to produce the specified something, as in the representation of technology by recipes. A second aspect of knowing how is not so convincingly captured by verbal representation of knowledge. Such knowledge, which might better be called skill, may not involve language at all.[35] The student may also have lesser skills than the more experienced faculty member. The model presented in Part 5 deals with both aspects of knowledge.

Although knowledge exists in the mind of an individual, it is rare that a single person operates in isolation. It is typically the case that an individual is part of a community of those with overlapping interests in a subfield of knowledge. The community uses a number of means of formal and informal communication to share knowledge. It seems clear that knowledge of persons in a community grows more rapidly than does that of persons working in isolation. Moreover, the product of persons who function in isolation often shows signs of that isolation.[36]

4.2. The Act of Discovery

Hadamard states, "Indeed, it is obvious that invention or discovery, be it in mathematics or anywhere else, takes place by combining ideas."[37] This conception is not unique to Hadamard, but is frequently, if not universally, mentioned by students of creativity. Koestler, in his book *The Act of Creation*[38] makes it the central element in his understanding of creation. In his view, normal thought takes place within a frame of reference, or an associative context, a type of logic, universe of discourse, or a particular code or matrix. In ordinary life we may use many different frames of reference, usually one at a time, switching from one to another according to the situation. According to Koestler, creating involves bringing together otherwise independent frames of reference. Koestler gives this process the name *bisociation*.[39]

The term may be understood to identify either a property of the *process* of creation, or a property of the creative *product*. It is possible, as Perkins argued, to hold the view that the creative product does involve the joining of different frames of reference, while maintaining that ordinary mental processes are capable of and do accomplish the work of bisociation (i.e., there is no special process of bisociation).[40]

Bringing together ideas from different domains, or combining different frames of reference, suggests that the potential for discovery or for creative acts afforded by a given knowledge base is related to the set of *combinations* of ideas or of frames of reference in that knowledge base. In this way a state of knowledge can be said to generate a set of potential discoveries—discoveries waiting to happen. Indeed, the history of science provides many examples of roughly simultaneous and independent discovery of the same thing.[41]

It is not necessary to go deeply here into the processes by which an act of creation or discovery comes about, (even if, as is doubtless not the case, they were fully known), because the aim here is not to model those processes as such, but rather to focus on certain salient characteristics of them that provide the basis for a quantitative model of the growth of knowledge, including the knowledge we call technology, and to enable us to assess its economic significance.

One of these salient ideas is that the knowledge base itself contains the seeds of discoveries "waiting to happen." These seeds are in the form of combinations of ideas that will sooner or later stimulate a *prepared mind* to conceive the new idea and make the new discovery.

In this context a prepared mind has four properties:

it is one in command of the relevant knowledge base;

it is one that has sufficient command of the skills relevant to the task at hand;

it is one that is intensely focused on the specific knowledge in question; and,

it is one that is suitably disposed to the discovery to be made.[42]

The first three properties do not require further comment, but perhaps the fourth does. The act of discovery is an interaction between elements of knowledge of different kinds. Some are of the kind that make up knowledge in the field of specialization, and others are rather more general ideas that can be seen as integral and perhaps unchangeable aspects of the personality of the investigator.[43] "Thus, discovery or creation of new knowledge is not just a matter of "ripeness," of discoveries waiting to happen, but must also involve a contribution from the discoverer(s) that goes beyond knowledge and effort.[44]

There are cases of important discoveries made by an "outsider" whose knowledge of the field was limited relative to that of the established authorities. It can be argued that ignorance of established ideas tends to free the mind to see from a different perspective, or to make connections that others would not see. It can also be argued that it is the personality of the discoverer that is crucial here, rather than ignorance of the subject matter of the field. In any field at any time there are a certain number of people who see things from one or another kind of unconventional viewpoint. And this is not necessarily due to ignorance. In most cases the product of the unique perspective is dismissed, and does not contribute to knowledge in a significant way. In some cases the investigators are dismissed as cranks, usually correctly. But in rare cases discoveries of value are made. How should this be modeled? In this chapter, these phenomena are part of what is meant by a "prepared mind" (i.e., a property of the individual distinct from, but interacting with, the body of knowledge he or she commands).

Because the focus here is not on the individual discoverer, these considerations can enter the model in Part 5 in a way that does not require going in detail into the mental processes involved.

A related consideration is the role of chance in discovery. It is evident, and has been much discussed both in general terms,[45] and with reference to specific examples of serendipitous discoveries, such as Fleming's discovery of penicillin, that chance plays a role in individual discoveries. However, the model presented in Part 5 is not stochastic. It could be modified, as indicated in Part 5, so as to make it stochastic. This has not been done, mainly because the use made of the model here avoids technical complexities associated with a stochastic model, so in the interests of clarity and simplicity stochastic elements are omitted. Beyond this, although chance no doubt plays a role in discovery, it is not so clear what that role is and how it should enter in a formal analysis. Is the role of chance more significant than noise in determining *whether* a particular discovery is made, or *when* it is made, or *who* makes it?[46] The model presented in Part 5 does not address these questions, but rather is intended to facilitate analysis of the economic consequences of an ongoing process of discovery. In any case, that model of discovery can be modified to include stochastic elements.

Discoveries differ in importance. Some, such as the theory of relativity, or the discovery of the mode of action of the genetic code, appear to change existing knowledge in a fundamental way, while others appear to be small additions or modifications. The model presented in Part 5 does not make a formal distinction between "big" and "small" discoveries. The need to make this distinction depends on the use to be made of the model. For some purposes the model will have to be given more structure, but for present purposes one can assume that the flow of discoveries consists of a "typical" mixture of big and small ones.[47]

The model presented in Part 5 attempts to formalize the considerations discussed in this Part. To summarize these considerations, they are:

1. Discovery grows out of the existing structure of knowledge;
2. It does so as the result of the application of effort, resources, skill, and talent by individuals to the existing structure of knowledge;

3. Individuals do not operate in isolation, but exist in communities. They learn from one another; their interaction facilitates the growth of knowledge of all of them;
4. Discovery proceeds by combining ideas.

The main aim of Part 5 is to make these considerations the basis for a dynamic model of the growth of knowledge, of technology, and of production possibilities.

5. GROWTH OF KNOWLEDGE

5.1. Remarks on Modeling Growth of Knowledge

We begin with a class of models of the growth of knowledge in the case of an isolated person, i, as follows.

Recall from Part 3 the partition

$$\mathbf{L} = \{L_q, q = 1,2,\ldots\}$$

of $\mathbf{E}/I(i,t)$, and recall that

$$K_q(i,t) = L_q \cap K(i,t)$$

and

$$k_q(i,t) = |K_q(i,t)|.$$

The partition **L** classifies knowledge, the elements in Lq being of the same kind. The sets L_q can be called *areas of knowledge*, or *subfields*. Since $K(i,t)$ is finite, only a finite number of the sets $K_q(i,t)$ can be nonempty.
Then,

$$k_q(i,t+1) - k_q(i,t)$$

gives the change in the (amount of) knowledge of person i in the qth subject area in the Period t to t + 1.

A model that at Time t determined the values of the variables $k_q(i,t+1)$ would thereby predict the number of discoveries in the subfield q. If the partition **L** of **E** /I(t) were the finest possible, then the model would predict the discoveries up to I-equivalence.

If the sets L_q were fine enough, say in the extreme case singletons, the determination of $k_q(i,t+1)$ amounts to predicting a specific discovery. There is a gradation of specificity from this Promethean theory at one extreme, to the other extreme at which Q = 1 and discoveries are counted without making any distinctions based on substance.

For the uses to which the model is put in this chapter, the model with Q = 1, or 2 is sufficient. Furthermore, discoveries are treated as deterministic. The situation may be likened to modeling the occurrence of fires. There are fires of many kinds. It may be for certain purposes necessary to distinguish chemical fires from forest fires, and both from house fires. Nevertheless, for other purposes it may be desirable to ignore distinctions among types of fires, and to treat the total number of undifferentiated fires per year as if it were deterministic, perhaps interpreting that number as the expected number of fires that would come out of a stochastic model. And it may be possible to relate that number usefully to certain characteristics of the preexisting situations that tend to give rise to fires, in spite of the impossibility of predicting individual fires.

The motivation for the choices made here is twofold. First, to explore a model from which a one-dimensional measure of the growth of knowledge can arise, and second, to keep the technicalities of the model as simple as possible, while allowing the effect of the growth of knowledge on technology and production possibilities to be analyzed.

We turn now to the formal model of the growth of knowledge.

5.2. Individual Characteristics

The discussion in Part 4 sees discovery as the result of an interaction between a person, the agent of discovery, and a body of knowledge she or he commands. A person's characteristics play a role in facilitating or impeding discovery. These characteristics are in part innate, and in part the result of decisions made by the agent himself, such as decisions to invest in the acquisition of skills, say through education or apprenticeship, and social decisions, such as how much society invests in its educational system, and its research institutions. Another important decision is how to allocate effort and resources to particular areas of knowledge. In a more complete model, of which the present model would form a part, these decisions would be endogenous. In this model, these decisions are formalized by exogenously determined functions of time.

The first step in the construction of the model is to introduce four functions that characterize the persons in the set **A**.[48] These are:

$$a(i,t) = (a_1(i,t),\ a_2(i,t)) \text{ for } i \in \mathbf{A},\ t = 1,2,\ldots. \tag{1}$$

Here $a_1(i,t)$ is to be interpreted as a measure of Person i's endowment of creative abilities. These include the qualities of mind or personality that might predispose someone to make a particular kind of discovery as discussed in Part 3.2. The parameter $a_2(i,t)$ represents the level of skill that Person i has attained at Time t. Creative abilities may, of course, be no different from cognitive abilities generally;[49]

$$e(i,t) \text{ for } i \in \mathbf{A},\ t = 1,2,\ldots, \tag{2}$$

to be interpreted as the intensity of effort put forth by Person i at Time t;

$$r(i,t) \text{ for } i \in \mathbf{A},\ t = 1,2,\ldots, \tag{3}$$

to be interpreted as the resources i has available to use at t;
and finally,

$$d(i,t) = f(e(i,t), r(i,t), a(i,t)) \text{ for } t = 1,2,\ldots, \tag{4}$$

where $d(i,t)$ is to be interpreted as a measure of i's *fertility or productivity* in discovering.

It is assumed that the function f is nonnegative and is increasing in all its arguments. That is, more effort increases i's fertility in discovery, more resources also does, and more skill and ability do too.[50]

Choice of the functions $e(i,t)$ and $r(i,t)$ would in general depend on incentives of Person i to expend effort and resources in the attempt increase his or her knowledge. These incentives would in turn depend at least in part on the economic returns to such knowledge, such as reputation and consequent salary and working conditions in the case of an academic, or profit in the case of an investor in R&D. In general, these functions would be strategies, or decision functions. But in order to keep the model simple and focused on knowledge and technology, the demand side is omitted. Therefore, the elements necessary to make decisions about how to allocate effort and resources to discovery and learning are not endogenous. Instead they are treated as exogenous parameters. The dependence of the growth of knowledge, and of technology and production on these parameters can be studied by a kind of "comparative dynamics" analysis. This aspect of the analysis is discussed further in Part 6.[51]

To simplify notation, define

$$e(i,t) = (e(i,t), r(i,t)),$$

and write

$$d(i,t) = f(e(i,t), a(i,t)). \tag{4'}$$

5.3. Growth of Knowledge of an Isolated Person

Hadamard's observation previously referred to that "it is obvious that invention or discovery . . . takes place by combining ideas," is one among many expressions of the same notion. Indeed, if there is anything universally agreed upon by students of creative activity it is this idea. Valery's statement of the idea seems particularly apt.[52] According to Valery, the discoverer plays two roles, one as knower of his body of knowledge, in which capacity he makes up combinations of ideas which he presents to himself in his second role, that of the one who recognizes the value of what is before him.

This idea suggests that the products of discovery or creative activity are the result of an interaction between the potential discoverer and his knowledge, in which potential discoveries are generated in the mind of the discoverer by combinations of existing ideas. In this view the body of knowledge can be seen as a population (of ideas) that breeds new ideas, and requiring the intervention of a discoverer to bring them to awareness.

This idea suggests a model in which every combination of elements of K(i,t) is a potential stimulant for, or seed of, a new idea in the mind of i. Therefore the number of subsets of K(i,t) is the number of opportunities for discovery presented to Person i at Time t. Then, Person i's fertility parameter, determined by the intensity of effort and resources devoted to discovery, and by i's skill and ability, determine the yield of discoveries from the potential ones.

Modeling this would seem to require that combinations of subsets make up the breeding population (i.e., subsets of the power set of K(i,t)). However, the power set of K(i,t) is determined by K(i,t) itself and so is its size. Indeed, as was pointed out earlier, a subset of K(i,t) can be uniquely described by a compound sentence (i.e., an element of K(i,t)). Thus, the set K(i,t) itself can be used in place of its power set, and considered to be the "breeding population." The use of the size of K(i,t) instead of that of its power set amounts to a (nonlinear) change of units. The larger the set K(i,t) the more combinations of statements it permits, and therefore the greater the opportunity for a combination to stimulate a new idea in the mind of person i.[53] The more person i's mind is a 'prepared mind', the more will be his productivity in discovery from a given body of existing knowledge.

Because, as discussed in Part 4.1, there is no inhibitory effect on discovery from more knowledge, the relationship between knowledge and discovery is increasing in knowledge. And because more effort, or more resources, skill or ability produces more discovery from a given body of knowledge, the relationship between discovery and the parameters that represent these characteristics is also increasing in the parameter d(i,t).[54]

Perhaps the simplest, but not the only, mathematical expression of these considerations is the following.

Let K(t) denote some body of knowledge and d(t) the parameter measuring the fertility or productivity of a potential discoverer who commands the knowledge K(t) at t. Let k(t) be the size of K(t). Then, the equation

$$k(t+1) - k(t) = d(t)k(t), \qquad t = 1,2,\ldots, \tag{5}$$

describes the growth of knowledge over time that the process of discovery described before would generate.

Thus, the growth of knowledge is the result of two factors, one is the number of "breeding parent" statements in the population of statements constituting the relevant body of knowledge at t, and the other is a measure, namely d(t), of the discoverer's fertility or productivity in finding something new and interesting among the potentially new statements or ideas "waiting to be discovered."[55]

Equation (5) is a difference equation in discrete variables, and as such somewhat inconvenient to work with. The set K(t) would typically be very large, and the difference in the size over a short interval of time comparatively small. It is a convenient and perhaps acceptable idealization to replace (5) by its continuous analog, in which the variables k(t) and t are continuous.[56] Here k(t) is a continuous measure of the size of K(t). Then, the differential equation analogous to (5) is

$$\dot{k}(t) = \delta(t)k(t), \qquad t \geq 0. \tag{6}$$

where

$$\dot{k}(t) = \frac{dk(t)}{dt}.$$

This is an ordinary differential equation with variable coefficient. Since the focus here is on the basic ideas underlying the model it is desirable to carry out the analysis in the simplest mathematical setting in which it makes sense. For this reason, suppose that for all t,

$$d(t) = d(0) = d.$$

Then equation (6) has the form

$$\dot{k}(t) = \delta k(t). \tag{6'}$$

This familiar differential equation for k(t) has the solution

$$k(t) = C\exp(\delta t). \tag{7}$$

In the continuous model with Q > 1, the time derivative

$$\partial k_q(i,t)/\partial t$$

replaces the time difference $k_q(i,t+1) - k_q(i,t)$, and gives the change in the knowledge (in isolation) of person i in the qth subject area in the period t to t + 1.

It will now be assumed that for each $i \in A$ and all t, the partition $\mathbf{L}, = \mathbf{L}(i,t)$, of E/I(i,t) contains only a finite number, Q, of subsets. Then

$$K(i,t) = K_1(i,t) \cup K_2(i,t) \cup \ldots \cup K_Q(i,t),$$

and, because the sets Kq(i,t) are pairwise disjoint,

$$k(i,t) = \Sigma k_q(i,t). \tag{8}$$

The counterpart of equation (6) applied to these knowledge sets is,

$$\begin{pmatrix} \dot{k}_1(i,t) \\ \vdots \\ \dot{k}_Q(i,t) \end{pmatrix} = \begin{pmatrix} \delta_{11}(i,t) & \cdots & \delta_{1Q}(i,t) \\ \vdots & \vdots & \vdots \\ \delta_{Q1}(i,t) & \cdots & \delta_{QQ}(i,t) \end{pmatrix} \begin{pmatrix} k(i,t) \\ \vdots \\ k(i,t) \end{pmatrix}, \tag{9}$$

where the coefficient d_{qr} (i,t) represents, for r = q, i's fertility in discovery arising from allocating effort, resources and skills relevant to the subfield q, and innate ability, and, for $r \neq q$, d_{qr} (i,t) represents serendipitous discovery arising from effort devoted to r that results in finding something in q. The same k(i,t) appears on the right in every row, because any ideas that i knows at t can combine to suggest a discovery in any subfield. The effect of i's interests and the allocation of effort and resources that i makes among the fields of knowledge 1, . . . , Q are expressed by the matrix of coefficients in equation (9).

For some purposes it would be desirable to preserve the distinctions among subfields when there is more than one person. But, because of (8), equation (9) implies

$$\dot{k}(i, t) = \delta(i, t) k(i, t), \tag{10}$$

where

$$d(i,t) = \Sigma d_{qr}(i,t),$$

the sum being taken over all q and r. Therefore, the distinctions among subfields disappear, and, when it is assumed that the coefficients are constants, (10) is the same as (6′) with k(t) = k(i,t) and d = d(i,0) = d(i).

For simplicity, unless otherwise stated, it is assumed that Q = 1. This amounts to making no distinctions among the discoveries the model attempts to predict. If Q > 1 is assumed, then the functions k(i,t) must be replaced by the vector of functions (k_1(i,t), . . . ,k_Q(i,t)), and the coefficients d(i,t) by d_{qr}(i,t).

When d(i,t) is a step function, representing one or more changes in the allocation of effort and resources to discovery, perhaps as a result of policy decisions, the solution of (10) is a piecing together of exponentials at rates determined by the effort and resources i devotes to discovery, and on i's skill and ability. A change in the values of these parameters results in a change in the value of d (i,t), and therefore those changes have the effect of changing the rate at which i's knowledge grows. If, for example, i decided to reduce to zero the effort devoted to exploring K(i,t), then i's knowledge would cease to grow altogether.[57] If any of the parameters were to change from time to time, then so would d(i) and the solution would be a concatenation of exponentials with different rates of growth, corresponding to the changes in d(i,t).

5.4. Growth of Knowledge in a Community

Although knowledge is always knowledge held by some person, discovery and invention generally do not occur in isolation from the knowledge in the minds of others. There is typically a community of persons who communicate their ideas and results among themselves by various means. The existence of this community enriches knowledge and accelerates the process of discovery.[58]

Let **A** be the set of persons in the community under consideration. Each person in the community **A** has access to the knowledge of others, through publications or various forms of direct communication. But knowledge in the minds of others, or written down in papers, does not enter into the mind of Person i without effort. Person i therefore must allocate his effort between acquiring knowledge from others and working to discover new knowledge—between reading papers and writing them.

Let

$$e^1(ii)$$

denote the effort i devotes to discovery, and

$$e^2(ij)$$

the effort given to acquiring knowledge from j. Then, for i,j in **A**,

$$d(ij) = f(e^1(i,j), e^2(ij), r^1(ij), r^2(ij), a(i)),$$

is the parameter measuring i's productivity in discovery, when j = i, and in acquiring knowledge from j otherwise.

It is assumed, similarly to what was assumed in the case of an isolated person, that[59] for all i and j in {1, . . . , N}

$$d(ij) \geq 0, \tag{11}$$

where not all $d(ii) = 0$.
It is sometimes convenient to assume that for all i, $d(ii) > 0$.

When $Q > 1$ (i.e., when more than one subfield of knowledge is distinguished), the coefficients $d(ij)$ are replaced by

$$\delta_{q_1 q_2 \cdots q_Q}(ij).$$

Equation (10), characterizing the growth of i's knowledge in isolation, must be modified to take account of the fact that i's knowledge can grow in two ways, the first by discovery and the second by learning from others. Thus, for i = 1,2, . . . ,N, where N is the number of people in **A**,[60]

$$\begin{aligned}
\dot{k}(1,t) &= \delta(11)k(1,t) + \cdots + \delta(1N)k(N,t) \\
\dot{k}(2,t) &= \delta(21)k(1,t) + \cdots + \delta(2N)k(N,t) \\
&\vdots \\
\dot{k}(N,t) &= \delta(N1)k(1,t) + \cdots + \delta(NN)k(N,t).
\end{aligned} \tag{12}$$

Equation (12) can be written more compactly in matrix form as[61]

$$\dot{k}(t) = \Delta k(t), \tag{13}$$

where

$$\dot{k}(t) = \begin{pmatrix} \dot{k}(1,t) \\ \vdots \\ \dot{k}(N,t) \end{pmatrix},$$

$$\Delta = ((\delta(ij))), i, j = 1, \cdots, N,$$

$$k(i,t) = \begin{pmatrix} k(1,t) \\ \vdots \\ (k(N,t) \end{pmatrix}.$$

There are several different processes of interaction among people in the community that are represented by equations (12) or (13). These include the following special cases.

First, suppose that each member of the community publishes or otherwise communicates to the others knowledge that she or he regards as new. We may suppose that ∂k(i,t)/∂t is the amount of new knowledge Person i chooses to add to his knowledge set at Time t. If Person i should encounter at t some piece of knowledge already in K(i,t), then it would not be added to K(i,t). If a person's judgment of what is new is a competent judgment, then, at least to a first approximation, these time derivatives measure what is put into the communication network among the agents at Time t. Each agent then extracts from those inputs knowledge added to his or her own knowledge set at Time t. This leads to the following equations.

$$\begin{aligned}
\dot{k}(1,t) &= \delta'(11)k(1,t) + \delta'(12)\dot{k}(2,t)\cdots + \delta'(1N)\dot{k}(N,t) \\
\dot{k}(2,t) &= \delta'(21)\dot{k}(1,t) + \delta'(22)k(2,t)\cdots + \delta'(2N)\dot{k}(N,t) \\
&\vdots \\
\dot{k}(N,t) &= \delta'(N1)\dot{k}(1,t) + \cdots + \delta'(NN-1)\dot{k}(N-1,t) \\
&\quad + \delta'(NN)k(N,t).
\end{aligned}$$

This is a linear system that in vector form is

$$\Delta'\dot{k}(t) = \delta k(t),$$

where

$$\Delta' = \begin{pmatrix} 1 & -\delta_{12} & \cdots & -\delta_{1N} \\ -\delta_{21} & 1 & \cdots & -\delta_{2N} \\ \vdots & \vdots & \ddots & \vdots \\ -\delta_{N1} & -\delta_{N2} & \cdots & 1 \end{pmatrix},$$

and

$$\delta = \begin{pmatrix} \delta_{11} \\ \delta_{22} \\ \vdots \\ \delta_{NN} \end{pmatrix}.$$

In general, D′ is invertible. Hence, the system reduces to

$$\dot{k}(t) = \hat{\Delta}^{-1}k(t), \tag{13a}$$

where

$$\hat{\Delta}^{-1} = \Delta'^{-1}\delta$$

is the inverse of D′, with the ith row multiplied by d(ii), i = 1, . . . , N. The entries in $\hat{\Delta}^{-1}$ are functions of the d(ij) defined at the beginning of this Part, and hence are functions of the parameters representing ability, skill, resources and effort.

Another special case of equations system (12) or (13) of interest is obtained if for each i and j ≠ i,

$$d(ij) = d(i).$$

Still another special case particularly relevant to economic development is that in which the knowledge of the agents is nested. That is, everything that is known to the least knowledgeable agent is also known to the next least knowledgeable one and so on to the agent whose knowledge set at time t includes all the others. Without loss of generality let them be

$$K(1,t), K(2,t), \ldots, K(N,t).$$

In this case, one view of the process of transfer of knowledge leads to the conclusion that the matrix D in equation (13) is a (lower) triangular matrix, all of whose entries are nonnegative, and whose diagonal elements are d(ii), i = 1, . . . ,N, which may be assumed to be positive and distinct. In this view i's access to j's knowledge leads to discoveries just as i's access to i's knowledge set does, but perhaps with different yields.

A refinement of this view is that person i only works on that part of K(j,t) that is not already in K(i,t).

Then, under the assumption that knowledge is nested,

$$\begin{aligned}
&\dot{k}(1,t) = \delta(11)k(1,t) \\
&\dot{k}(2,t) = \delta(21)k(1,t) - k(2,t)) + \delta(22)k(2,t) \\
&\vdots \\
&\dot{k}(N,t) = \delta(N1)k(1,t) - k(2,t) + \\
&\qquad\qquad \delta(22)(k(2,t) - k(3,t)) + \cdots + \\
&\qquad\qquad \delta(NN)(k(N-1,t) - k(N,t)),
\end{aligned}$$

Which can also be written as,

$$\dot{k}(t) = \Delta'' k(t), \tag{14}$$

where

$$\Delta''$$

$$\begin{pmatrix} \delta(11) & 0 & 0 & \vdots & 0 \\ \delta(21) & \delta(22)-\delta(21) & 0 & \vdots & 0 \\ \delta(31) & \delta(32)-\delta(31) & \delta(33)-\delta(32) & \vdots & 0 \\ \vdots & \vdots & \vdots & \vdots & \vdots \\ \delta(N1) & \delta(N2)-\delta(N1) & \cdots & & \delta(NN)-\delta(NN-1) \end{pmatrix}.$$

Here there is a boundary condition, namely that

$$k(j+1,t) - k(j,t) \geq 0.$$

The set K(i,t)\K(i+1,t) contains what i knows at t, but i+1 does not know at t.

If we assume that effort, and resources of i devoted to learning from Person 1 is always at least as productive as the same effort and resources allocated to learning from any other person, where $i \neq 1$, then

$$\Delta'' = \begin{pmatrix} \delta(11) & 0 & \cdots & 0 \\ \delta(21) & \delta(22)-\delta(21) & 0 & 0 \\ \vdots & \vdots & \vdots & \vdots \\ \delta(N1) & 0 & 0 & \delta(NN)-\delta(N1) \end{pmatrix} \tag{15}$$

In this case i does not allocate different amounts of resources and effort to acquiring knowledge from different people. Because everything that i can learn from others i can learn from Person 1, it is equivalent under the stated assumption for i to learn everything from Person 1 or to learn separately items that Persons i-1, i-2, . . . , 1, know that i does not. As before, these equations are valid for $k(1,t) - k(j,t) \geq 0$ for all $j = 2, \ldots, N$.

Note that if

$$d(j\,j) \leq d(j\,1)$$

then Agent j can use d(j 1) on the entire set K(1,t), including K(j,t). We suppose therefore that for all $j = 2, \ldots, N$,

$$d(j\,j) > d(j\,1).$$

If the dynamics are described by equation (14), and if $d(11) > 0$, then there is at least one eigenvalue that is real and positive.

We now examine the solutions of (13) more explicitly, under the *assumption that D has N linearly independent eigenvectors.*
Under that assumption, the solutions to (13), or (14), or (14) when (15) holds, consist of linear combinations of pure exponentials.

Let the (N linearly independent) eigenvectors of D be

$$S = (S_1, \cdots, S_N).$$

Let S be the matrix whose columns are the eigenvectors of D. Then the matrix L, given by.

$$S^{-1} \Delta S = \Lambda, \tag{16}$$

where,

$$\Lambda = \begin{pmatrix} \lambda_1 & & & \\ & \lambda_2 & & \\ & & \ddots & \\ & & & \lambda_N \end{pmatrix}$$

is the diagonal matrix whose (diagonal) elements are the eigenvalues of D.[62]

Under these conditions (i.e., when (16) is valid), the vector differential equation (13) has the following general solution.

$$\begin{aligned} k(t) &= \exp(\Delta t) k(0) \\ &= S \exp(\Lambda t) S^{-1} k(0) \\ &= c_1 \exp(\lambda_1 t) s_1 + \cdots + c_N \exp(\lambda_N t) s_N. \end{aligned} \tag{17}$$

Thus, the general solution is a linear combination of pure exponentials,[63] and the constants c_i are determined by the initial conditions, that is,

$$c_i = S^{-1} k(0).$$

Note that when distinctions among subfields are made equation (12) takes the form given in equation (18)

$$\begin{aligned} \dot{k}_1(1,t) &= \delta_{11}(11) k_1(1,t) + \cdots + \delta_{1Q}(11) k_Q(1,t) + \cdots + \delta_{1Q}(1N) k_Q(N,t) \\ &\vdots \\ \dot{k}_Q(1,t) &= \delta_{Q1}(11) k_1(1,t) + \cdots + \delta_{QQ}(11) k_Q(1,t) + \cdots + \delta_{QQ}(1N) k_Q(N,t) \\ &\vdots \\ \dot{k}_Q(N,t) &= \delta_{Q1}(N1) k_1(1,t) + \cdots + \delta_{QQ}(N1) k_Q(1,t) + \cdots + \delta_{QQ}(NN) k_Q(N,t) \end{aligned} \tag{18}$$

which can be written

$$\dot{k}(t) = \tilde{\Delta} k(t),$$

where $\tilde{\Delta}$ is an NQ □ NQ matrix and $\dot{k}(t)$ and $k(t)$ are NQ vectors. Assumptions about the structure of $\tilde{\Delta}$ can be imposed in order to address specific questions about the interaction among different subfields.

5.5. Aggregation of Knowledge

Consider an economy in which the research sector consists of a set A of people partitioned into two groups, the first denoted A_1, consisting of N_1 people, and a second denoted A_2, consisting of N_2 people. For the entire group

$$A = A_1 \cup A_2,$$

consisting of

$$N = N_1 + N_2$$

people, when no distinctions are made among subfields, equation (13) of Part 5 is the system

$$\begin{aligned}
\dot{k}(1,t) &= \delta(11)k(1,t) + \cdots + \delta(1N)k(N,t) \\
&\vdots \\
\dot{k}(N_1,t) &= \delta(N_1 1)k(1,t) + \cdots + \delta(N_1 N)k(N,t) \\
\dot{k}(N_{1+1},t) &= \delta(N_{1+1} 1)k(1,t) + \cdots + \delta(N_{1+1} N)k(N,t) \\
\dot{k}(N,t) &= \delta(N1)k(1,t) + \cdots + \delta(NN)k(N,t)
\end{aligned} \tag{19}$$

of differential equations governing the growth of knowledge.

Under certain assumptions stated below, this system can be put in the form

$$\begin{aligned}
\begin{pmatrix} \dot{k}_1(t) \\ \dot{k}_2(t) \end{pmatrix} &= \Delta \begin{pmatrix} \bar{k}_1(t) \\ \bar{k}_2(t) \end{pmatrix}, \\
\bar{k}_1(t) &= \left(\sum_{i=1}^{N_2} k(i,t) \right) \\
\bar{k}_2(t) &= \left(\sum_{i=N_1+1}^{N_2} k(i,t) \right)
\end{aligned} \tag{20}$$

where

$$\Delta = \begin{pmatrix} \delta_{11} & \delta_{12} \\ \delta_{21} & \delta_{22} \end{pmatrix}.$$

That is, equations (20) describe the behavior of the first sector and the second sector as aggregates. This equation system is derived from (19) as follows.

Suppose that

$$\delta(ij) = \begin{cases} \delta_i' \text{ for } i, j \in A_1, \\ \delta_i'' \text{ for } i \in A_1, j \in A_2, \\ \delta_i'' \text{ for } i \in A_2, j \in A_1, \\ \delta_i' \text{ for } i, j \in A_2. \end{cases}$$

Then,

$$\begin{aligned} \dot{k}(1,t) &= \delta_1' \sum_{j=1}^{N_1} k(j,t) + \delta_1'' \sum_{J=N_1+1}^{N} k(j,t) \\ \dot{k}(2,t) &= \delta_2' \sum_{j=1}^{N_1} k(j,t) + \delta_2'' \sum_{J=N_1+1}^{N} k(j,t) \\ &\vdots \\ \dot{k}(N_1, t) &= \delta_{N_1}' \sum_{j=1}^{N_1} k(j,t) + \delta_{N_1}'' \sum_{J=N_1+1}^{N} k(j,t) \\ \dot{k}(N_{1+1}, t) &= \delta_{N_1+1}'' \sum_{j=1}^{N_1} k(j,t) + \delta_{N_1+1}' \sum_{j=N_1+1}^{N} k(j,t). \\ &\vdots \\ \dot{k}(N,t) &= \delta_N'' \sum_{j=1}^{N_1} k(j,t) + \delta_N' \sum_{J=N_1+1}^{N} k(j,t). \end{aligned} \tag{21}$$

That is to say, each person learns equally effectively from the others in each group, though perhaps differently from those in the other group than from those in his own group.

It follows that,

$$\begin{aligned} \sum_{i=1}^{N_1} \dot{k}(i,t) &= \sum_{i=1}^{N_1} \delta_i' \left(\sum_{j=1}^{N_1} k(j,t) \right) + \sum_{i=1}^{N_1} \delta_i'' \sum_{j=N_1+1}^{N} k(j,t) \\ \sum_{i=N_1+1}^{N} \dot{k}(i,t) &= \sum_{i=N_1+1}^{N} \delta_i'' \left(\sum_{j=1}^{N_1} k(j,t) \right) + \sum_{i=N_1+1}^{N} \delta_i' \sum_{j=N_1+1}^{N} k(j,t). \end{aligned} \tag{22}$$

Let

$$\bar{\delta}_{11} = \frac{1}{N_1}\sum_{i=1}^{N_1}\delta'_i, \quad \bar{\delta}_{12} = \frac{1}{N_1}\sum_{i=1}^{N_1}\delta''_1,$$
$$\bar{\delta}_{21} = \frac{1}{N_2}\sum_{i=N_1+1}^{N}\delta''_i, \quad \bar{\delta}_{22} = \frac{1}{N_2}\sum_{i=N_1+1}^{N}\delta'_1. \tag{23}$$

Then, for

$$N_1\bar{\delta}_{11} = \delta_{11}, \quad N_1\bar{\delta}_{12} = \delta_{12}$$
$$N_2\bar{\delta}_{21} = \delta_{21}, \quad N_2\bar{\delta}_{22} = \delta_{22}, \tag{24}$$

the system of equations (21) can be written (in vector form) as

$$\begin{pmatrix}\dot{k}_1(t)\\ \dot{k}_2(t)\end{pmatrix} = \Delta\begin{pmatrix}\bar{k}_1(t)\\ \bar{k}_2(t)\end{pmatrix},$$
$$\bar{k}_1(t) = \left(\sum_{i=1}^{N_1}k(i,t)\right),$$
$$\bar{k}_2(t) = \left(\sum_{i=N_1+1}^{N}k(i,t)\right) \tag{25}$$

where

$$\Delta = \begin{pmatrix}\delta_{11} & \delta_{12}\\ \delta_{21} & \delta_{22}\end{pmatrix}.$$

The effort, resources and perhaps also skill and ability that an individual devotes to learning and discovery are likely to vary over his/her lifetime. Most likely the resulting time path of d(i j,t) is one that is concave, perhaps an parabola opening downward. However, it is plausible that the average fertility of a community of researchers is constant over time as young ones enter and old ones retire, leaving the total number constant. Therefore, the aggregate equations (25) lend themselves to a more meaningful analysis of the implications of policies that effect the parameters, in equation (24), namely:

(i) policies that effect the skills with which persons enter the research community;
(ii) policies effecting the allocation of resources and effort to learning and discovery; and
(iii) policies effecting the number of people in the research community.

Policies (i) and (iii) are likely to involve long-run considerations. They would include the size and quality of educational institutions, and of research institutions. Policies (ii) are likely to have shorter horizons, involving current support for research efforts.

It is clear from (24) that analysis of policy instruments can proceed via the effects on the average level of productivity in the research community on the one hand and the total number of researcher on the other.

It is also clear from (17), or the corresponding solution to (20), that resources devoted to increasing the elements of D yield increasing returns to scale in terms of knowledge. In Part 6, it will be clear that this implies increasing returns to scale in production.[63]

5.6. Example I: An Example of the Growth of Knowledge in Two Fields

Consider two fields, say, biology and pharmaceuticals, denoted 1 and 2 respectively.[64] People in biology do basic research; people in pharmaceuticals develop new drugs. Suppose there are N_1 people engaged in biological research and N_2 in developing drugs, where $N = N_1 + N_2$. On the one hand, suppose that the pharmacists use knowledge generated by the biologists, but that the biologists do not learn from the pharmacists. We will compare this with the situation in which neither the biologists nor the pharmacists learn from the other group. Then the aggregation procedure given by equations (20) through (25) applied to (26) yields

$$\begin{pmatrix} \dot{k}_1(t) \\ \dot{k}_2(t) \end{pmatrix} = \Delta \begin{pmatrix} \bar{k}_1(t) \\ \bar{k}_2(t) \end{pmatrix},$$
$$\bar{k}_1(t) = \left(\sum_{i=1}^{N_1} k_1(i,t) \right) \tag{26}$$
$$\bar{k}_2(t) = \left(\sum_{i=N_1+1}^{N} k_2(i,t) \right)$$

where

$$\Delta = \begin{pmatrix} \delta_{11} & \delta_{12} \\ \delta_{21} & \delta_{22} \end{pmatrix},$$

where

$$\delta_{ij} = N_i \bar{\delta}_{ij}.$$

with

$$d_{12} = 0,$$

and

$$d_{11}\text{-}d_{22} > 0, \text{ and } d_{12} > 0.$$

Then,

$$D = \begin{pmatrix} \delta_{11} & 0 \\ \delta_{21} & \delta_{22} \end{pmatrix}$$

has eigenvalues

$$1_1 = d_{11},\ 1_2 = d_{22}.$$

The corresponding eigenvectors are

$$s_1 = \begin{pmatrix} 1 \\ \dfrac{\delta_{21}}{\delta_{11} - \delta_{22}} \end{pmatrix},\ s_2 = \begin{pmatrix} 0 \\ 1 \end{pmatrix}.$$

The matrix S of eigenvectors is

$$S = \begin{pmatrix} 1 & 0 \\ \dfrac{\delta_{21}}{\delta_{11} - \delta_{22}} & 1 \end{pmatrix},$$

and hence

$$S^{-1} = \begin{pmatrix} 1 & 0 \\ \dfrac{-\delta_{21}}{\delta_{11} - \delta_{22}} & 1 \end{pmatrix}.$$

Therefore, the solution is given by

$$\begin{aligned} \bar{k}_1(t) &= C_1 e^{\delta_{11} t} s_{11} + C_2 e^{\delta_{22} t} s_{21} \\ \bar{k}_2(t) &= C_1 e^{\delta_{11} t} s_{12} + C_2 e^{\delta_{22} t} s_{22}, \end{aligned}$$

where

$$\begin{pmatrix} C_1 \\ C_2 \end{pmatrix} = \begin{pmatrix} 1 & 0 \\ \dfrac{-\delta_{21}}{\delta_{11} - \delta_{22}} & 1 \end{pmatrix} \begin{pmatrix} \bar{k}_1(0) \\ \bar{k}_2(0) \end{pmatrix}$$

$$= \begin{pmatrix} \bar{k}_1(0) \\ -\bar{k}_1(0)\dfrac{\delta_{21}}{\delta_{11} - \delta_{22}} + \bar{k}_2(0) \end{pmatrix}.$$

Therefore

$$\bar{k}_1(t) = \bar{k}_1(0)e^{\delta_{11}t}$$
$$\bar{k}_2(t) = \bar{k}_1(0)e^{\delta_{11}t}\frac{\delta_{21}}{\delta_{11} - \delta_{22}} + \left(\bar{k}_2(0) - \bar{k}_1(0)\frac{\delta_{21}}{\delta_{11} - \delta_{22}}\right)e^{\delta_{11}t}, \tag{27}$$

These equations can be used to compare the effects on the growth of pharmaceutical knowledge of varying the parameters d_{ij}. It is interesting that the parameter d_{21} enters linearly, while d_{11} and d_{22} enter exponentially. It is evident that increasing d_{11} or d_{22} increases the growth rates of $\bar{k}_1(t)$ and $\bar{k}_2(t)$, respectively. Since d_{21} enters linearly into the equation for $\bar{k}_2(t)$, it may not be so evident that increasing d_{21} from the value 0 has the effect of increasing the growth of $\bar{k}_2(t)$ exponentially. The second case holds when $d_{21} = 0$.

In the second case, where the pharmacists do not learn from the biologists,

$$d'_{12} = d'_{21} = 0;$$

here primes denote the corresponding variables in the second case. It is immediately evident that

$$\bar{k}'_1(t) = \bar{k}'_1(0)e^{\delta'_{11}t}$$
$$\bar{k}'_2(t) = \bar{k}'_2(0)e^{\delta'_{22}t}.$$

If we assume that $d'_{ii} = d_{ii}$ for i = 1,2, then

$$\frac{\bar{k}_1(t)}{\bar{k}'_2(t)} = \frac{\bar{k}_1(0)}{\bar{k}'_2(0)},$$

and,

$$\begin{aligned}\frac{\bar{k}_2(t)}{\bar{k}_2'(t)} &= \frac{\bar{k}_1(0)e^{\delta_{11}t}\rho + (\bar{k}_2(0) - \bar{k}_1(0)\rho)e^{\delta_{11}t}}{\bar{k}_2'(0)e^{\delta_{22}t}} \\ &= \frac{\bar{k}_1(0)}{\bar{k}_2'(0)}\rho e^{(\delta_{11}-\delta_{22})t} + \frac{(\bar{k}_2(0) - \bar{k}_1(0)\rho)}{\bar{k}_2'(0)}.\end{aligned} \tag{28}$$

Because the relevant quantities in this expression are positive, the ratio grows exponentially at the rate $d_{11} - d_{22}$. Thus, while both $\bar{k}_1(t)$ and $\bar{k}_2(t)$ increase exponentially in isolation, $\bar{k}_2(t)$ increases much faster when transfer of knowledge from 1 to 2 is possible than it does in isolation.

5.7. Evidence of Exponential Growth of Knowledge

The model just presented predicts that in fields in which positive effort, resources, skill, and ability are applied, knowledge grows exponentially. Is this at all consistent with what can be observed?

The following data were collected for the field of computer science, broadly defined. The number of pages published annually in a sample of 21 journals of computer science, and separately, the number of articles published annually in those journals were collected for the period 1958 to 1991. If the number of ideas per article, or the number of journal pages per idea, is not too variable, these quantities would be good approximations to the measure $\bar{k}_q(t)$, where q labels the field of computer science.

Table 7.1 shows the data collected, and Table 7.2 exhibits the regression of the natural logarithm of number of pages and number of articles, respectively, on time.[65] These regressions show that the number of pages grew exponentially at the rate of about 9% per annum, and the number of articles at about 11% per annum. These regressions seem to be very close fits.

6. GROWTH OF TECHNOLOGY AND THE PRODUCTION SET

The technological significance of the growth of knowledge derives ultimately from its effect on production. The next step in the analysis is to use the dynamics of discovery and growth of knowledge to derive the growth of production possibilities. This might be carried out without introducing the concept of commodity into the model of technology. As the number of recipes grows, the number of different products, or useful substances would in general grow, or new recipes might give more efficient ways of producing existing things.

In order to connect the model with standard models of production the commodity and production set are introduced, and the analysis carried out

TABLE 7.1
The Number of Pages and the Number of Articles Published Annually in a Sample of Computer Science Journals From 1954 to 1991

Year (time)	*Pages (P)*	*Articles (A)*
1954	380	48
1955	558	42
1956	750	72
1957	1038	96
1958	1080	154
1959	1490	186
1960	1298	182
1961	1992	204
1962	1692	190
1963	1960	242
1964	1628	220
1965	1956	236
1966	2844	316
1967	3158	322
1968	3440	352
1969	2862	274
1970	3414	324
1971	3094	356
1972	5014	428
1973	4700	426
1974	5678	498
1975	7302	688
1976	7302	632
1977	8630	720
1978	8560	722
1979	10036	1188
1980	11400	880
1981	12338	994
1982	15126	1108
1983	18376	1260
1984	23042	1508
1985	21982	1636
1986	24572	1732
1987	24956	1672
1988	24498	1644
1989	27234	1768
1990	27218	1888
1991	29686	1958

in that framework. In the interest of clarity and simplicity, this is done in a simple Leontief model of production.

Research and Development (R&D) refers to the step that converts knowledge, including conjectured recipes, into tested recipes. In the present model there is so far nothing that distinguishes this step from any other act of discovery. However, it is plausible in this connection to think of an attempt by an individual to develop a new recipe (which includes the invention of a new product, or a new use for an existing product as well as a new

TABLE 7.2
Regressions of the Natural Logarithms of the Number of Pages (LP) and the Number of Articles (LA) on Time (TIME)

1. REGRESSION OF THE LOG OF THE NUMBER OF PAGES IN COMPUTER SCIENCE (LP) ON TIME:

LP = 6.361 + 0.11 TIME

(107.65 (41.64)

R SQUARE = .979 RBAR SQUARE = .979

2. REGRESSION OF THE LOG OF THE NUMBER OF ARTICLES IN COMPUTER SCIENCE (LA) ON TIME

LA = 4.301 + 0.09 TIME

(56.21) (29.24)

R SQUARE = .954 RBAR SQUARE = .952

Note. The numbers in parenthesis are T-statistics

way of making something from existing materials), as primarily motivated by the anticipation of an economic return. Therefore, analysis of decisions to invest in R&D projects would require that the problem be embedded in a model in which anticipated returns could be expressed. This remains to be done. For the present, the model incorporates effort and resources devoted to R&D as parameters. It therefore allows analysis of the effect of R&D decisions on the technology K*. This is done in Part 6.3.

6.1. Research and Development

General knowledge leads to new technology through the application of effort, and resources to R&D. In this process a potential innovator finds a project that seems sufficiently promising in technical and economic terms, and commits resources to its development into a tested recipe and ultimately into production. The model as it stands does not include the economic structures, such as, markets and prices and consumers' demand, or other institutions, on which decisions to invest in the development of a particular area or project turn. Hence the analysis of expected or potential returns to investment in an R&D prospect is not endogenous. Suppose instead that this economic analysis is done in a different model (ultimately to be integrated with this one) and leads to the selection of a certain fraction of the prospects for investment and to the allocation of effort and resources to their development. The part of this process dealt with in the present model is as follows.

Suppose to begin with that every person in **A** is a potential innovator or participant in R&D. The knowledge K(i,t) of Person i at Time t consists of two parts, one containing tested recipes and the other containing the rest, so that

$$K(i,t) = K^*(i,t) \cup K(i,t) \backslash K^*(i,t). \tag{1}$$

Then

$$k(i,t) = k^*(i,t) + k^{**}(i,t), \tag{2}$$

where k*(i,t) is the size of K*(i,t) and k**(i,t) is the size of K(i,t)\K*(i,t).

Suppose that the yield of new recipes from the knowledge of Person i at t depends on the size of the knowledge base, and the effort and resources put into development by Person i. Then, let

$$w(i) = x(e^*(i), a(i)), \tag{3}$$

where, for all values of a(i),

$$x(0,a(i)) = 0.$$

Then, the yield of new recipes from the knowledge base K(i,t) given (3) is

$$k^*(i,t) = H(w(i), k(i,t))$$

The simplest form of H is that given in (4), where the coefficient w(i) is the *productivity of i in R&D*. (If Person i is not engaged in R&D, then e*(i) = 0.) Then, for all i and t,[66]

$$k^*(i,t) = w(i)k(i,t). \tag{4}$$

Let W = I w,

where w = (w(i), . . . ,w(N)), and I is the identity matrix. It follows from (17) of Part 5 that

$$\begin{aligned} k^*(t) &= Wk(t) = W\exp(\Delta t)S^{-1}k(0) \\ &= W\exp(\Lambda t)S^{-1}k(0) \end{aligned}$$

$$k^*(t) = \begin{pmatrix} w(1)(c_1 e^{\lambda_1 t} s_{11} + c_2 e^{\lambda_2 t} s_{21} + \cdots + c_N e^{\lambda_N t} s_{N1}) \\ \vdots \\ \vdots \\ w(N)(c_1 e^{\lambda_1 t} s_{1N} + c_2 e^{\lambda_2 t} s_{2N} + \cdots + c_N e^{\lambda_N t} s_{NN}) \end{pmatrix} \tag{5}$$

6.2. Growth of the Production Set in the Commodity Space

6.2.1. Knowledge, Technology and the Production Set. The classical economic model of production (the production set in the commodity space) can be derived from the model of technology presented in Part 2 as follows.

Given a collection of recipes, a commodity space can be defined. Let

$$K^* = K^*(t) = \cup K^*(i,t)$$

$$i \in A$$

denote the recipes known by the persons i in A at time t, and let

$$M(K^*)$$

denote the list of names of entities that appear in K*. I.e., a name is in M(K*) if and only if there is some recipe in K* in which that name appears.[67] The list M(K*) is well-ordered in some arbitrary way, from 1 to m(K*), the index of the last item on the list.

An *input–output array for a recipe r* is a function from M(K*) to Z, where Z is the set of possible measurements of substances on the list M(K*), say Z is an additive group. Let F(r) be a function whose value at the recipe r is the set of input–output arrays for r.

$$F(r) = \{f \in Z^{M(K^*)} \mid f \text{ is an input-output array for } r\}.$$

This function can be given the following representation. Each name n in M(K*) can be identified with its position on the list. A function

$$f \in F(r)$$

can be represented as the array

$$^{z} = (^{z}1, \ldots {}^{z}m(K^*)),$$

where

$$z_j = 0$$

if the name in position j is not mentioned in recipe r.

Let Z* denote the space of m(K*)-tuples, z.

Commodities can now be defined.

6.2.2. Commodities. A commodity is a set of names of objects from the list M(K*) that are regarded as equivalent in the model. Thus, let

$$\mathbf{P} = \{Mc\}_{c=1,2,\ldots,C},$$

be a partition of M(K*).

Each subset in the partition is a *commodity* and is given a name. For present purposes, the name of the commodity Mc can be identified with c.

For example, a set of names of objects consisting of "Taurus," "Oldsmobile," "Buick" ... might be given the name "full-sized American-made car," defined to be a commodity and identified as the third commodity. If Ford Motor Co. should introduce a newly designed full-sized car next year, it could be included as an instance of the commodity "full-sized American-made car" next year.

For each commodity, c, let y_c denote the *quantity of* c, where y_c is an element of an additive group, G_c.[68] Then, the commodity space is

$$Sp(p) = G = \prod_{c=1}^{C} G_c$$

The elements of Sp(**P**) are vectors

$$y = (y_1, ,y_C,)$$

where the cth component of y is a quantity of the cth commodity Also, there is a mapping, Y,

$$Y : Z^* \to Sp(\mathbf{P}),$$

The function Y translates quantities of objects into quantities of commodities. Thus, let M_1 consist of the objects 1, 2, ... ,p with measurements z_1, z_2, ..., z_p. Then, $Y(z_1)$, $Y(z_2)$, ..., $Y(z_p)$ are the corresponding quantities of commodity 1, and the total amount of commodity 1 corresponding to z_1, z_2, ..., z_p of the objects 1, ..., p is $\sum Y(z_j)$. The mapping Y therefore determines an aggregation rule for the partition **P**.

For example, suppose the objects in M_1 are sea-going vessels of different types and speeds. They appear on the list M(K*) as different objects, but the partition **P** defining commodities puts them in one class, M_1, called "ship." The measurements associated with the original objects might be linear dimensions of the vessel, parameters that characterize the shape, and the speed. These constitute a multidimensional quantity and would differ from vessel to vessel. The quantity of the commodity *ship* might be "ton-miles per hour of transport capacity," computed from the measurements z_j of the individual vessels via the function Y.

6.2.3. *Production Set.* The production set determined by K* is a subset, Y(K*), of the commodity space Sp(**P**).defined by the condition that

$$Y(K^*) = \{ y \in Sp(P) \mid \exists\, r \in K^* \text{ such that } z \in F(r) \text{ and } Y(z) = y\}$$

$$= \{ y \in Sp(P) \mid \exists\, r \in K^* \text{ such that } Y^{-1}(y) \cap F(r) \neq \varnothing \}.$$

That is, the production set determined by K* consists of all commodity vectors y such that y corresponds to an input–output array produced by some recipe in K*.[69]

Assumptions can be imposed on K* that imply the familiar properties (e.g., convexity, or linearity), assumed about the production set in models where it is a primitive.

If there is technological change, so that K*(t+1) . . . K*(t),[70] then the commodity space may change and the production set determined by K*(t+1) may be different from that determined by K*(t). If a new recipe produces a new product, then either that product can be classified as an instance of an existing commodity, or as a new commodity.

The commodity space associated with a given technology K*, is not unique. Different choices of **P** and of the mappings F and Y lead to different commodity spaces. The distinctions among substances and objects that are made for the purposes of knowledge may or may not be preserved in the distinctions that economic institutions make, and the distinctions made by economic institutions may not be preserved by economic models, each designed to serve a different purpose. However, in both the case of economic institutions and models, the classification expressing the distinctions that are recognized is made with knowledge of the technology K*(t). Therefore, the commodity space can change after a new recipe enters K*.

Although the description, properties, and name of a new product cannot be known in advance of its invention or discovery, it can in advance be assigned the number m(K*) + 1 in the list of names M(K*(t+1)) and, if the new product is to be classified as a new commodity, assigned the number $C + 1$ in the list of commodities. A similar convention would apply to the case in which a new use for some object or substance is discovered, a use that leads to a distinction being drawn between objects or substances that were hitherto regarded as indistinguishable.[71]

6.2.4. *The Attainable Production Set in the Commodity Space.* Turning to the production set, (and suppressing the time index, t, temporarily), let the commodity space be (as in 6.2.3)

$$Sp(p) = G = \prod_{c=1}^{C} G_c$$

and suppose that Y, a subset of G, is the production set determined by the technology K*(t) = K*(1,t)x . . . xK*(N,t), and the partition **P**. Suppose that element y □ G ,where

$$y = (y_1, \ldots, y_C).$$

can be written in the form

$$y = (y^1, y^2),$$

where y^1 is the vector of *produced commodities*, and y^2 is the vector of *unproduced or primary commodities* whose amounts are given from nature.[72] Suppose the produced commodities are 1, . . . ,C_1 and the unproduced ones are C_1+ 1, ... , *C*.

Let

$$v \in G$$

denote the endowment vector. Only the components of v that are unproduced commodities can be different from 0. Then the set

$$\{y \in G \mid y \geq v\}$$

consists of commodity vectors that do not use more than the available amounts of unproduced commodities. Let

$$\hat{Y} = Y \cap \{y \in G \mid y \geq v\},$$

denote the set of *attainable productions*, where Y is the production set.[73,74]

The focus of this model is on the relationship between discovery and invention and economic growth. Therefore, it is appropriate to assume that other possible causes of growth are absent. These include growth deriving from increasing returns and externalities, from trade, and from growth in the supply of unproduced resources. Therefore, the model of production considered is one with constant returns and no substitution possibilities, and the endowment of primary commodities is held constant. In that case, in the absence of technological change, $\hat{Y}$ would be constant over time.

Because Y, and therefore $\hat{Y}$, depend on the functions F and Y, analysis of the effect of new knowledge on production sets must involve properties of those functions. However, instead of specifying F and Y directly and deriving the production set through them, I consider a familiar simple model of production, and let F and Y be defined implicitly, determined by "reverse engineering."

Assume that Y is given by a Leontief input–output model with no joint production. Then,

$$Y = \{ y \in G \mid y = Ax, x \geq 0,$$

where A is an $L \times L_1$ matrix

$$\text{and } x = (x_1, \ldots, x_{C_1})\}.$$

It is assumed that each produced commodity has one activity (industry) that produces only that commodity.[75]

Under standard conditions on the matrix A the efficient frontier of $\hat{Y}$ is the intersection of a hyperplane determined by the column vectors of A, and therefore by the coefficients of A, with the non-negative orthant of the commodity space. In that case, the points at which the efficient frontier intersect the coordinate axes characterize the efficient frontier. Moreover, they also characterize the set $\hat{Y}$, since it is the convex hull of those points and the origin.

The coefficients of A depend on the recipes in K*, and hence as K* changes over time, so does the matrix A. The effect of discovery or invention on production possibilities is expressed in the change over time of the attainable production set $\hat{Y}$ and its efficient frontier. Because K* changes by including new recipes, we first model the relation between recipes and the coefficients of A.

Because of the underlying linearity it is plausible to suppose that the relation between recipes in K*(t) and the coefficients of Y is homogeneous linear. The coefficients of $\hat{Y}$ are the same as those of Y, and are denoted a_{pc} Thus, for $p = 1, \ldots, L_1$, and $c = 1, \ldots, L$,

$$a_{pc}(t) = b^1_{pc} k^*(1,t) + \cdots + b^N_{pc} k^*(N,t). \tag{2.1}$$

The coefficient b^i_{pc}, $i = 1, \ldots, N$, measures the effect of technological knowledge of person i on the coefficient a_{pc}. Since the sets K*(i,t) consist of tested recipes, the effect of knowledge in any one of them on the technical coefficients is self-contained. This justifies the assumption that the relation between knowledge of agents and technical coefficients is, to a first approximation, linear. Recipes that effect any particular coefficient can be in the knowledge set of any person. According to (2.1), the total effect is the sum of the effects from each person. Interactions among the knowledge sets of different persons are already captured in the underlying equations that determine the sets K*(i,t).

Substituting from (5) the solutions for the functions k*(i,t) in the case where D has N linearly independent eigenvectors,[76] gives the following equation for $a_{pc}(t)$.

$$
\begin{aligned}
a_{pc}(t) &= b_{pc}^{1}k^{*}(1,t) + \cdots + b_{pc}^{N}k^{*}(N,t) \\
&= b_{pc}^{1}w(1)k(i,t) + \cdots + b_{pc}^{N}w(N)k(N,t) \\
&= b_{pc}^{1}w(1)(C_1e^{\lambda_1 t}s_{11} + C_2e^{\lambda_2 t}s_{2N} + \cdots + C_Ne^{\lambda_N t}s_{NN}) \\
&\quad + \cdots + \\
&\quad b_{pc}^{N}w(N)(C_1e^{\lambda_1 t}s_{1N} + C_2e^{\lambda_2 t}s_{2N} + \cdots + C_Ne^{\lambda_N t}s_{NN}) \\
&= C_1e^{\lambda_1 t}(b_{pc}^{1}w(1)s_{11} + \cdots + b_{pc}^{N}w(N)s_{N1}) \\
&\quad + \cdots + \\
&\quad C_Ne^{\lambda_N t}(b_{pc}^{1}w(1)s_{N1} + \cdots + b_{pc}^{N}w(N)s_{NN}) \\
&= \sum_{j=1}^{N} C_je^{\lambda_j t}\sum_{i=1}^{N} b_{pc}^{i}w(i)s_{ji}.
\end{aligned}
\tag{2.1'}
$$

If the impact of recipes on a technical coefficient is independent of the source, then

$$b_{pc}^{i} = b_{pc}, \tag{2.2}$$

It follows that

$$a_{pc} = b_{pc}\sum_{j=1}^{N} C_je^{\lambda_j t}\sum_{i=1}^{N} w(i)s_{ji}. \tag{2.3}$$

If further, the productivity in R&D of agents is the same, then for all i,

$$\mathrm{w(i) = w},$$

and

$$a_{pq} = b_{pq}w\sum_{j=1}^{N} c_je^{\lambda_j t}\sum_{i=1}^{N} s_{ji}. \tag{2.4}$$

Let

$$\frac{1}{N}\sum_{i=1}^{N} s_{ji} = \overline{s}_j.$$

Then, (2.4) can be written

$$a_{pc} = b_{pc}wN\sum_{j=1}^{N} C_je^{\lambda_j t}\overline{s}_j. \tag{2.5}$$

Notice that the same conditions yield the corresponding expression for the sum of the components of k*(t), namely,

$$\sum_{i=1}^{N} k^*(i,t) = wN\sum_{j=1}^{N} C_j e^{\lambda_j t}\bar{s}_j. \tag{2.6}$$

The next step in the analysis is to find the rate of growth of the attainable production set $\hat{Y}$, and its efficient frontier. This is done in the context of a low dimensional example.

6.2.5. Growth of the Attainable Production Set. Consider an example in which there are 2 produced commodities and 1 primary commodity (i.e., $C = 3$, and $C_1 = 2$). Let the initial endowment vector be

$$v = (0, 0, 1),$$

and the matrix A be,

$$A = \begin{pmatrix} a_{11} & -a_{21} \\ -a_{12} & a_{22} \\ -1 & -1 \end{pmatrix}. \tag{2.7}$$

Figure 7.1 shows the projection of the set $\hat{Y}$ into the plane given by $y_3 = -1$, and the points $\hat{y}_1$ and $\hat{y}_2$ at which the line determined by the two columns of A intersect the y_1 and y_2 axes respectively.[77]

Then the equations

$$y = Ax$$

are

$$y_1 = a_{11}x_1 - a_{21}x_2 \tag{3.1}$$

$$y_2 = -a_{12}x_1 + a_{22}x_2 \tag{3.2}$$

$$-1 = -x_1 - x_2 \tag{3.3}$$

From 3.3), $x_1 = 1 - x_2$.

Substituting in (3.1) and (3.2) gives

$$y_1 = -x_2(a_{11} + a_{21}) + a_{11} \tag{3.5}$$

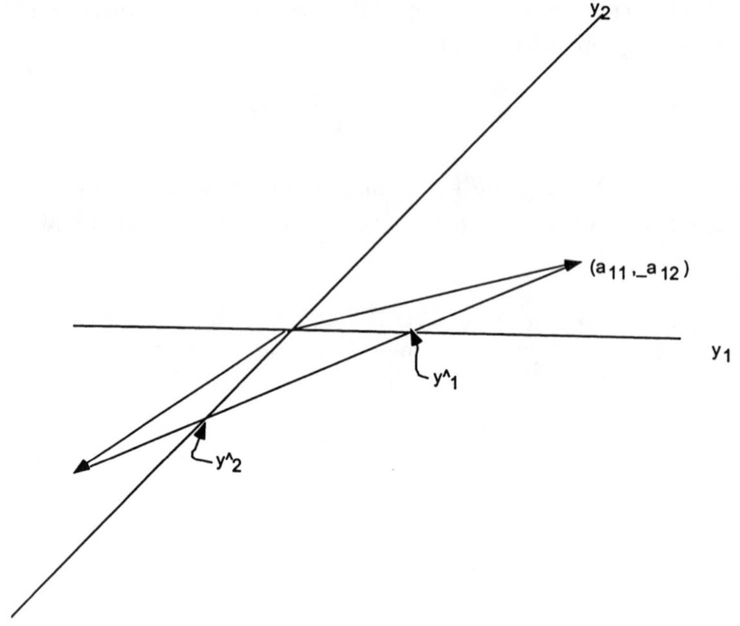

FIG. 7.1.

and

$$y_2 = x_2(a_{12} + a_{22}) - a_{12}. \tag{3.6}$$

Solving (3.5) for x_2 in terms of y_1 yields

$$x_2 = \frac{a_{11} - y_1}{a_{11} + a_{21}}. \tag{3.7}$$

Substituting in (3.6) gives,

$$y_2 = \frac{a_{11}(a_{12} + a_{22}) - a_{12}(a_{11} + a_{21})}{a_{11} + a_{21}} - y_1 \frac{a_{12} + a_{22}}{a_{11} + a_{21}}. \tag{3.8}$$

Let

$$B = \frac{a_{11}(a_{12} + a_{22}) - a_{12}(a_{11} + a_{21})}{a_{11} + a_{21}},$$

and

$$C = \frac{a_{12} + a_{22}}{a_{11} + a_{21}}.$$

Then equation (3.8) can be written as

$$y_2 = B - C\,y_1.$$

To find the points $\hat{y}_1$ and $\hat{y}_2$ where the efficient frontier of $\hat{Y}$ intersects the y_1- and y_2-axes respectively, set $y_2 = 0$ and solve (3.8) for $\hat{y}_1$, and then carry out the corresponding procedure for $\hat{y}_2$. Thus, setting $y_2 = 0$ gives,

$$\begin{aligned} \hat{y}_1 &= \frac{B}{C} \\ &= \frac{a_{11}(a_{12} + a_{22}) - a_{12}(a_{11} + a_{21})}{a_{12} + a_{22}} \\ &= \frac{a_{11}a_{22} - a_{12}a_{21}}{a_{12} + a_{22}} \end{aligned} \tag{3.9}$$

Setting $y_1 = 0$, yields

$$\begin{aligned} \hat{y}_2 &= B \\ &= \frac{a_{11}a_{22} - a_{21}a_{12}}{a_{11} + a_{21}} \end{aligned} \tag{3.10}$$

Substituting from (2.1) and (2.2) into equations (3.9) and (3.10) respectively yields equations (3.11) and(3.12) which give the time paths $\hat{y}_1(t)$ and $\hat{y}_2(t)$, in the special case when equation (2.2) is valid

$$\begin{aligned} \hat{y}_1(t) &= \frac{b_{11}\bar{k}^*(t)b_{22}\bar{k}^*(t) - b_{12}\bar{k}^*(t)b_{21}\bar{k}^*(t)}{b_{21}\bar{k}^*(t) + b_{22}\bar{k}^*(t)} \\ &= \frac{\bar{k}^*(t)(b_{11}b_{22} - b_{12}b_{21})}{b_{21} + b_{22}}, \end{aligned} \tag{3.11}$$

and,

$$\hat{y}_2(t) = \frac{b_{11}\bar{k}^*(t)b_{22}\bar{k}^*(t) - b_{12}\bar{k}^*(t)b_{21}\bar{k}^*(t)}{b_{11}\bar{k}^*(t) + b_{12}\bar{k}^*(t)}$$

$$= \frac{\bar{k}^*(t)(b_{11}b_{22} - b_{12}b_{21})}{b_{11} + b_{12}}, \tag{3.12}$$

where

$$\bar{k}^*(t) = \sum_{i \in A'} k^*(i,t). \tag{3.13}$$

It follows that

$$\hat{y}_1(t) = wN\, B_1 \sum_{j=1}^{N} C_j e^{\lambda_j t} \bar{s}_j, \tag{3.14}$$

where

$$B_1 = \frac{(b_{11}b_{22} - b_{12}b_{21})}{b_{21} - b_{22}},$$

and

$$\hat{y}_2(t) = wN\, B_2 \sum_{j=1}^{N} C_j e^{\lambda_j t} \bar{s}_j \tag{3.15}$$

where

$$B_2 = \frac{(b_{11}b_{22} - b_{12}b_{21})}{b_{11} + b_{12}}.$$

The set of commodity vectors attainable with one unit of the third commodity, is the convex hull of the three points, 0, $\hat{y}_1(t)$, and $\hat{y}_2(t)$. Hence the growth of $\hat{Y}(t)$ is determined by $\hat{y}_1(t)$ and $\hat{y}_2(t)$. As equations (3.14) and (3.15) make clear, their growth is exponential in t (when there is a positive eigenvalue) at a rate that depends on the number of people, their abilities and the resources allocated to their respective areas, and to the effort expended on R&D in those areas, and on the pursuit of knowledge in the areas they rest on.

Figure 7.2 shows the attainable production set at two points in time under the assumption that B_1 is greater than 2.[78]

In this example, under the assumptions made, the set of attainable productions grows exponentially over time.[79] Therefore so would production.

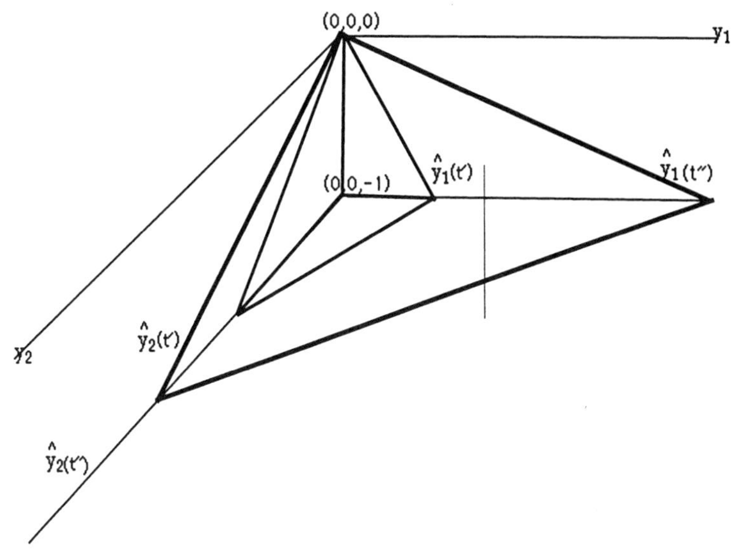

FIG. 7.2.

If the model of production were, say a linear activity analysis model, the attainable production set could be characterized by the points at which the rays in the commodity space generated by the basic activities intersect the resource constraints. Of course, the analysis of the growth of the attainable set would be more complicated, because the direction of a ray determined by a basic activities could change over time.

If a recipe involving a new product were discovered, then it is either included in the set Mc of some existing commodity c, or the classification **P** is changed so that a new commodity is introduced. In that case, it is commodity $C_1 + 1$, and the differential equation for the growth of that commodity determines its trajectory starting from the initial condition

$$y_{L_1+1} = 0.$$

If the set of potential developers is a subset A of the set **A** of persons, then the sum in equation (3.15) is taken over the subset A. If the set of developers is specialized by industry, so that there is a set, $A_{p'}$ whose knowledge is relevant to the coefficients a_{pq} if an only if $p = p'$, then the sum in equation (2.1) is taken over $i \in A_{p'}$.[80]

6.3.1. Growth of the Attainable Production Set in Example I. Recall that in Example 1 of Part 5.6, in which biologists and pharmacists do research and R&D, the parameters d_{ij} depend on the skills and abilities of the members of the respective groups, and on the effort and resources they devote to discovery and to learning from others (i.e., on the parameters e(i) and a(i)).

Recalling equation (4), for all i and t,

$$k^*(i,t) = w(i)k(i,t),$$

where, from (3), w(i) depends on the effort and resources e*(i) that i devotes to R&D, and on i's ability and skill parameters a(i).

To compare the growth of attainable production sets of different economies, characterized by different complexes of parameter values, involves comparing the time paths of the attainable production sets. In the present example, the attainable production set is determined by the point $\hat{y}_i(t)$ defined in 6.2.4. Using equations (3.11) and (3.12), we see that

$$\hat{y}_1(t) = w(2)B_1\bar{k}_2(t)$$

and

$$\hat{y}_2(t) = w(2)B_2\bar{k}_2(t),$$

since the biologists do not directly contribute any new recipes.

Substituting the solution for $\bar{k}_2(t)$ from equation (29) Part 5, yields,

$$\hat{y}_1(t) = w(2)B_1\left(\bar{k}_1(0)e^{\delta_{11}t}\frac{\delta_{21}}{\delta_{11}-\delta_{22}} + \left(\bar{k}_2(0) - \bar{k}_1(0)\frac{\delta_{21}}{\delta_{11}-\delta_{22}}\right)e^{\delta_{11}t}\right)$$

and,

$$\hat{y}_2(t) = w(2)B_2\left(\bar{k}_1(0)e^{\delta_{11}t}\frac{\delta_{21}}{\delta_{11}-\delta_{22}} + \left(\bar{k}_2(0) - \bar{k}_1(0)\frac{\delta_{21}}{\delta_{11}-\delta_{22}}\right)e^{\delta_{11}t}\right)$$

Comparing this situation with the one in which $d_{21} = 0 = d_{12}$, we see that

$$\frac{\hat{y}_1(t)}{\hat{y}_1'(t)} = \frac{w(2)B_1\left(\bar{k}_1(0)e^{\delta_{11}t}\frac{\delta_{21}}{\delta_{11}-\delta_{22}} + \left(\bar{k}_2(0) - \bar{k}_1(0)\frac{\delta_{21}}{\delta_{11}-\delta_{22}}\right)e^{\delta_{22}t}\right)}{w(2)B_1(\bar{k}_2(0)e^{\delta_{22}t})}$$

$$= \frac{\bar{k}_1(0)}{\bar{k}_2'(0)}\frac{\delta_{21}}{\delta_{11}-\delta_{22}}e^{(\delta_{11}-\delta_{22})t} + \frac{\bar{k}_2(0) - \bar{k}_1(0)\frac{\delta_{21}}{\delta_{11}-\delta_{22}}}{\bar{k}_2'(0)}.$$

This is the same expression as for the growth of $\bar{k}_2(t)$ relative to $\bar{k}_2'(t)$ as in equation (30) of Part 5. The same result applies to the ratio $\frac{\hat{y}_2(t)}{\hat{y}_2'(t)}$. Thus, the addition to the relative rate of growth of knowledge due to communication between the basic research community and the R&D community carries over to the relative rate of growth of the attainable production set for given resources.

6.3.2. Remarks on Development. Consider an example in which there are two countries each with a single sector that does both basic research and R&D. Suppose that Country 1 is underdeveloped compared to Country 2. That is, K(1,0) is very small compared to K(2,0), where K(i,0) is the present state of knowledge in Country i. Then k(1,0) is much smaller than k(2,0). The disparity between the states of knowledge in the research sector between the two countries reflects the backwardness of the current technology in Country 1 and the lack of knowledge of more basic subjects as well. Example I can be reinterpreted to represent the growth of two countries, one of which, Country 2, is less developed than is Country 1. We may assume that everything known in Country 2 is also known in Country 1. In that case, the matrix D′ has the form

$$\Delta' = \begin{pmatrix} \delta'_{11} & 0 \\ \delta'_{21} & \delta'_{22} - \delta'_{21} \end{pmatrix}.$$

Let

$$\begin{aligned} \delta_{11} &= \delta'_{11} \\ \delta_{12} &= 0 \\ \delta_{21} &= \delta'_{21} \\ \delta_{22} &= \delta'_{22} + \delta'_{21} \end{aligned}$$

Then, for

$$\Delta = \begin{pmatrix} \delta_{11} & 0 \\ \delta_{21} & \delta_{22} \end{pmatrix}$$

so defined, the analysis of Example I, with d_{22} replaced by d'_{22}-d'_{21}, applies.

Country 1 may contain people whose innate abilities are the equal of those in Country 2, but lack of education and of training and experience with an advanced technology leads to the skill component of the parameter a(1) being much smaller than a(2). Similarly, resources are scarce in Country 1, so that r(1) is small and hence so are e(1) and e*(1). Therefore, both d(11) and d(12) are small compared to Country 2, and so is w(1), that is, what Country 1 can learn from 2 is small and what Country 1 can develop on its own is small. If this situation persists, the analysis of a more general version of equation (28) suggests that Country 1 will fall further and further behind relative to Country 2.

The fact that knowledge available in Country 2 is a public good and in principle also available to Country 1 is inconsequential if the acquisition of that knowledge requires ability, skill, effort, and resources that Country 1 doesn't have or can't afford.

To change this outcome, Country 1 can adopt policies that increase the parameters d(11), d(12), or w(1). For example, if it is cheaper and easier to imitate than to discover, Country 1 could try to increase d(12) and w(1) If Country 2 chooses a policy of growth by imitation, making $d'_{22} = 0$, and devoting its available persons and resources to learning from Country 1, even then its knowledge and attainable production set will increase exponentially. It will eventually (in the limit as time goes to infinity) have its rate of growth catch up with that of Country 1.

This seems to have been the course followed by Japan during its early period of industrialization.[81] It seems to be the case that even today the Japanese research community is more heavily concentrated in R&D than in basic research.

Because of the nature of human capital, investment in Country 1's human capital is not necessarily attractive to Country 2 investors, even if the social return to investment in human capital in Country 1 is higher than it is in Country 2. Moreover, it is not clear that the marginal social return to human capital is higher in Country 1 than in Country 2, or even if it were, whether the fraction of it that could be captured by an investor is therefore higher in Country 1 than in Country 2.

It seems that it would not be difficult to augment the present model with economic and social institutions in which the economies of initially advanced and initially backward countries grow further apart under some conditions, and initially backward countries catch up with and even surpass the initially advanced ones under other conditions.

7. LEARNING CURVES

Learning curves are examples of an economic effect of the growth of knowledge. They appear in the context of manufacturing. The two important properties of learning curves are:

(i) that the number of *direct labor hours* required to produce a unit of product decreases as the *cumulative number produced* increases, and;
(ii) that the *rate of reduction of hours* declines with cumulative output.

According to Argote and Epple,[82] the form of the learning curve conventionally assumed is

$$\gamma = ax^{-b} \qquad (7.1)$$

where a is the number of direct labor hours required to produce the first unit; x is the cumulative number of units produced; and b is a parameter measuring the rate at which labor hours are reduced as cumulative output increases. Cumulative output, x, is interpreted as a proxy for knowledge acquired through production.[83] Thus, learning curves ought to be derivable from the model of the growth of knowledge presented in Part 5. Such a derivation follows.

It is useful to have an example in mind, say, the assembly of an aircraft being built by some organization A. The aircraft to be assembled has already been designed, and the processes by which its parts are manufactured, and by which the assembly of them is to be carried out are also specified. The volumes of blueprints, or computer generated graphics, and other descriptions of the steps to be taken in assembling the aircraft exist. In short, a complete recipe, r, for the assembly of the aircraft is known and is to be followed by those doing the assembly. Moreover, a facility has been constructed and equipped with all tools and machinery needed to execute the recipe, and the required labor force is in place.

Let z denote this fixed combination of inputs, and suppose that the rate of output, denoted y(t) at Time t, is determined by a linear relation

$$y(t) = n\, z, \qquad (7.2)$$

where n is a positive scalar. This relation states that if the given recipe were carried out precisely as designed, the number of aircraft assembled per unit time would be the constant given by (7.2).

However, the labor force starts out with the knowledge of the prescribed recipe as embodied in the documents that specify it. Thus, the initial knowledge of the N people who make up the organization A is collectively

$$K(i,0) = K(A,0) = \{r(0)\}, \qquad (7.3)$$

$$i \in A$$

but, as a result of the experience of producing, they find out things about the recipe that they didn't know at the beginning. This knowledge allows them to improve on the way things are done—to produce from the fixed z a higher rate of output per unit time. Thus, n is not a constant, but depends on K(A, t). The recipe actually being used to assemble aircraft at t is r(t) rather than r(0) = r, r(t) being the modified version of r based on the knowledge acquired in the experience of production.

There are at least two ways of specifying the group's knowledge, corresponding to different assumptions about the way learning-by-doing occurs.

First, suppose that each worker learns equally from himself and the others. This is expressed by the condition that, for each i and j in A,

$$d_{ij} = d_i. \tag{7.4}$$

In that case the differential equation system (10) is,

$$\begin{pmatrix} \dot{k}(1,t) \\ \vdots \\ \dot{k}(N,t) \end{pmatrix} = \begin{pmatrix} \delta_1 & \cdots & \delta_1 \\ \vdots & \vdots & \vdots \\ \delta_N & \cdots & \delta_N \end{pmatrix} \begin{pmatrix} k(1,t) \\ \vdots \\ k(N,t) \end{pmatrix}, , \tag{7.5}$$

and so

$$\begin{aligned} \frac{\partial \sum_{i=1}^{N} k(i,t)}{\partial t} &= \sum_{i=1}^{N} \dot{k}(i,t) \\ &= \sum_{j=1}^{N} \delta_j \sum_{i=1}^{N} k(i,t) = N\bar{\delta} \sum_{i=1}^{N} k(i,t), \end{aligned} \tag{7.6}$$

where,

$$\sum_{j=1}^{N} \delta_j = N\bar{\delta}.$$

This is equivalent to the differential equation

$$\dot{k}(t) = N\bar{\delta}\bar{k}(t). \tag{7.6'}$$

Now,

$$v(t) = b\sum_{i=1}^{N} k(i,t),$$

where b is the coefficient b_{11} from equation (2.1), and k*(i,t) = k(i,t), (because the only knowledge involved here is of the recipe(s) actually being used). It follows from (7.6′) that

$$v(t) = b\bar{k}(t) = bce^{N\bar{\delta}t}. \tag{7.7}$$

Let y(t) be the number of aircraft assembled per unit time, say, per day. Then $\frac{1}{y(t)}$ is the number of days it takes to assemble one aircraft, and some fixed fraction of $\frac{N}{y(t)}$ is the number of hours of direct labor per aircraft. Then the number of hours of direct labor per aircraft at Time t is given by

$$\gamma = \frac{c}{y(t)}. \tag{7.8}$$

For simplicity assume that

$$\mathrm{b} = 1,$$

that is,

$$\nu(\bar{k}(t)) = \bar{k}(t), \tag{7.9}$$

and

$$\mathrm{c} = 1.$$

Denote by x(t) the accumulated output at Time t. Then,

$$\begin{aligned} x(T) &= \int_0^T y(t)dt = \int_0^T Ce^{N\bar{\delta}t}dt \\ &= \frac{1}{N\bar{\delta}}(e^{N\bar{\delta}T} - 1). \end{aligned} \tag{7.10}$$

Solving equation (7.10) for T in terms of x yields

$$\mathrm{T} = (1/N\bar{\delta})\ \ln(\mathrm{x(T)} + 1).$$

Writing t = T, substituting from (7.10) into (7.2) and using (7.9), gives the rate of production y as a function of cumulative production x. Namely,

$$\mathrm{y} = \ \mathrm{z}\ \exp(\ln(N\bar{\delta}\mathrm{x} + 1).$$

Hence, equation (7.8) gives the direct labor per aircraft as a function of cumulative output.

$$\gamma = \frac{1}{y} = \frac{z}{N\bar{\delta}x + 1}. \tag{7.11}$$

The function defined by (7.11) is a learning curve in the sense that it has the two essential properties (i) and (ii) above—direct labor hours decline with cumulative output, and the rate of decline diminishes with cumulative output.

However, it is not the learning curve conventionally assumed, according to Argote and Epple. That curve can be obtained by the second way of characterizing the group's knowledge at t. This is done as follows.

It follows from (12) of Part 5 or (2.1) of Part 6, that

$$\bar{k}^*(t) = \begin{pmatrix} (c_1 e^{\lambda_1 t} s_{11} + c_2 e^{\lambda_2 t} s_{21} + \cdots + c_N e^{\lambda_N t} s_{N1}) \\ + \\ + \\ (c_1 e^{\lambda_1 t} s_{1N} + c_2 e^{\lambda_2 t} s_{2N} + \cdots + c_N e^{\lambda_N t} s_{NN}) \end{pmatrix}$$

Or, under the assumptions made,

$$\bar{k}(t) = N \sum_{j=1}^{N} c_j e^{\lambda_j t} s_j. \tag{7.12}$$

Equation (7.12) represents the function $\bar{k}(t)$ as a superposition of exponentials. Let

$$\mu(t) = \ln\left(N \sum_{j=1}^{N} c_j e^{\lambda_j t} s_j \right).$$

Then,

$$Ce^{\mu(t)} = N \sum_{j=1}^{N} c_j e^{\lambda_j t} s_j.$$

Consider the following differential equation for $\bar{k}(t)$.

$$\frac{\partial \bar{k}(t)}{\partial t} = \beta(t)\bar{k}(t), \tag{7.13}$$

which is an equation with a variable coefficient that is satisfied by $\bar{k}(t)$ for b = m. Broaden the class of differential equations to include (7.13). The function

$$\beta(t) = d \ln t, \tag{7.14}$$

yields an equation in this class. Then, the following is among the solutions of (7.13), (7.14), but not all solutions can be guaranteed to be increasing.

$$\bar{k}(t) = ct^d.$$

Therefore,

$$y = zct^d,$$

Furthermore,

$$x(T) = zc\int_0^T t^d dt = \frac{C}{d+1}T^{d+1}.$$

Solving for T in terms of x, we get

$$T = \left(\frac{x(d+1)}{C}\right)^{\frac{1}{d+1}}.$$

Then, substituting in the equation for y gives

$$y(x) = C\left(\frac{x(d+1)}{C}\right)^{\frac{d}{d+1}}.$$

It follows that

$$\gamma(x) = \frac{1}{y(x)} = ax^{-b}, \tag{7.15}$$

where

$$b = \frac{d}{d+1},$$

and

$$a = \frac{1}{C}\left(\frac{d+1}{C}\right)^{\frac{-d}{d+1}}.$$

Equation (7.15) is the commonly used form of the learning curve.

ACKNOWLEDGMENTS

I am indebted to Itzhak Bilboa, Leo Hurwicz, Joel Mokyr, Roger Myerson, Scott E. Page, and Rob Porter for helpful comments and references. This research was supported by NSF Grant No. IRI-9020270/01.

ENDNOTES

1 This matter is discussed further in this Introduction, and in Part 4 below, which contains a discussion of creative process(es) that serves as the basis for the model of the growth of knowledge (discovery) in Part 5.

2 Lucas (1988) calls for the formulation of formal models of economic development addressing what he calls the mechanics of the subject. The model presented in this chapter would be a step in that direction, if it is satisfactory.

3 See for example Koopmans (1957).

4 The word *knowledge* is used in this chapter to refer to statements that the person whose knowledge is being modeled is aware of and believes to be valid. Thus, someone who believes he has seen a flying saucer would have in his knowledge set the sentence, "I saw a flying saucer." Another usage common among those working in a Bayesian framework, and among those who study knowledge as an operator in a modal logic, would regard this as a statement of belief, and reserve the term *knowledge* for statements that are absolutely true. Knowledge in the latter sense is hard for human beings to come by. Even mathematical theorems, which provide perhaps the best candidates for absolutely true statements, are proved by human beings, whose operations are subject to error, (or by machines whose operations are also subject to error). There does not seem to be a better term for the conglomeration of beliefs, convictions and structures of information that make up what is in common usage what someone knows. These and other distinctions applying to knowledge are discussed in Part 3.

5 The terms *discovery, invention, creative act* are used interchangeably in this chapter. This seems natural in a model in which new knowledge is a sentence (as yet unknown) waiting to be found in the set of sentences complementary to the current knowledge of the discoverer. Fuller discussion of these matters can be found in Part 4.

6 Some work in Artificial Intelligence goes in this direction. For example, Newell and Simon (1956), and Newell, Shaw, and Simon (1957), wrote a computer program designed to prove given theorems in a given mathematical setting. (There is also a program, called BACON, that "inferred" certain physical laws, for example, Boyle's Law, from given data.) A program that successfully came up with proofs of theorems would seem to constitute a Promethean machine, at least in a limited area of operation. Whether Simon's ideas about creative thinking generally, or computer programs embodying them, constitute a theory of discovery that is capable of predicting discoveries not yet made is a question that goes well beyond the scope of this chapter. Whatever the answer turns out to be, it is fair to say that in the present state of knowledge there is no theory capable of being used to predict specific discoveries relevant to economic growth.

It may be possible to predict a direction in which discovery may be expected, without thereby making the discoveries themselves. A decision by an investigator to devote effort and resources to an area of research is often based in part on the conviction that the area is important and researchable (i.e., that significant results are likely).

7 Unlike some models of technology used in economics, the production set is not a primitive of the model, but a defined entity.

8 This is the case under the assumptions about how knowledge translates into technology and production. If decreasing returns of a sufficiently (but implausibly) high order were introduced at this step, exponential growth in knowledge might be cancelled in the translation into production.

9 This matter is discussed more fully in Part 6, especially in footnote 79.

10 Literature on the subjects of creativity, discovery, invention, and learning is diverse and large. I do not claim to provide adequate references to it, but I have tried to indicate rela-

tionships to that literature of ideas on which the model is based. Because these matters have been the subject of studies in economic history, in the history of science, in individual and social psychology, in philosophy, logic and computer science, and my knowledge of these areas is limited, I have no doubt overlooked things I should have known and acknowledged.

11 In some models, such as infinite horizon models or models with uncertainty, and infinitely many states, the commodity space is infinite dimensional. There are also (hedonic) models in which the commodity space is replaced by a Euclidean space whose coordinates refer to qualities or properties. In that case a commodity is regarded as a bundle of qualities. In such models the list of qualities is fixed, and the commodity space is again Euclidean, but possibly of different dimension than the space of qualities. Although there is provision for new bundles of qualities, there is no provision for new qualities.

12 Some of these standard models introduce assumptions about the structure of the collection of recipes (e.g., constant returns to scale).

13 Statements describing the actions to be taken are typically imperatives, not propositions in the sense of formal logic, that is, neither true or false. If it is desirable to describe the actions in the form of logical propositions, rather than merely natural language sentences, the list of steps that constitute the third part of a recipe can be replaced by a compound conditional statement of the form: If the following actions are taken (a list of actions), then the outcome will be (a statement describing the outcome). In this form, the third part of a recipe is just a (compound) statement.

14 A patent application is required to contain a description of the use of the technology for which a patent is sought.

Two otherwise identical recipes that differ only in the use part of the recipe are different. For example, consider recipes that describe medical treatments. One is the prescription of a daily dose of aspirin to relieve symptoms of arthritis. The "use" part of this recipe is "reduce arthritic pain." Another recipe is the prescription of a daily dose of aspirin to prevent heart attack. The "use" portion of this recipe is different and the technological knowledge expressed in these recipes is also different.

15 In practice, a recipe is typically an incomplete specification of what must be done to produce the intended result. A recipe typically relies on information to be supplied by those who execute it to resolve ambiguities or otherwise complete it. Computer software manuals provide many examples of this. This practice arises in part from the difficulty of writing down a full description of any complicated process. This kind of ambiguity seems to be inherent in natural language, as modern philosophers have pointed out. This phenomenon makes transfer of technology difficult and costly even between groups that have a common background, and even more so between groups in different cultures.

16 In a book dealing with large-scale preparation of foods, such as commercial baking, the role of chemistry would be even more obvious.

17 The set of persons might vary over time with the growth of population, or as result of decisions that result in persons entering or leaving the community of those seeking to discover. Here it is assumed that the set is constant over time.

18 Consider the statement "Adam knows how to ride a bicycle." Although the act of riding a bicycle can be described, it is clear that knowing the description may not in itself constitute being able to ride a bicycle. In modeling technology *knowing how* to produce something was equated with knowing the recipe for it. But to carry out a recipe may require the kind of knowledge that might better be called skill. Polanyi (1958, p. 49) has made this distinction.

When it is desired to maintain a distinction between *knowing* and *knowing how* in the sense of skill, an appropriate modification of the model must be made. This distinction is expressed in the formal model in Part 4.

19 More generally, the set **E** may change over time, if new symbols are added to the alphabet.

20 The set of strings over a finite alphabet is countably infinite. But this is not essential to the analysis carried out with the model presented here (see Part 6). Therefore, augmenting the alphabet, for instance with symbols that permit quantifiers is not troublesome.

21 The following are examples of such statements. "I think that the sentence 'The moon is made of green cheese.' is false." "The probability that Fermat had a proof for his famous theorem is less than one half."

22 It may be convenient sometimes to have a notation for the knowledge held by a group, although this is used in this chapter only occasionally in Parts 6 and 7 and could be dispensed with there.

If A is a subset of **A**(t), then what the persons in A together know at Time t may be denoted

$$\bigcup_{A} K(i,t) = K(A,t).$$

The knowledge that constitutes the technology known by the group A(t) is known by somebody. A recipe may be known by some person, or a group of people together may know it. Let

$$K^*(A,t)$$

denote the set of recipes (the technology) known by A at Time t. Then,

$$K(A,t) \supseteq K^*(A,t).$$

Furthermore, if r is a recipe in K*(A,t) then there is a subset **A**(r) of A which together know r. I.e.,

$$r \in \bigcup_{i \in \mathbf{A}(r)} K(i,t).$$

And,

$$\bigcap_{A} K(i,t)$$

is the *common specialization* of the group A.

23 The possibility that the cardinality of K(i,t) exaggerates person i's knowledge at t may arise if the set contains several statements that describe "the same knowledge," while person i knows that to be the case. The sets K'(i,t) and the relation I(i,t) are primitives of the model. Together they determine K(i,t). The interpretation given above and illustrated in Part 2 makes clear that in any interpretation of the formal model, elements of K(i,t) are to be distinct ideas. Double counting should not arise.

24 The motivation and justification for introducing this measure of knowledge is indicated in Part 1, the Introduction, and is discussed more fully in Part 4.

25 The knowledge of i at t can include sentences to which i attaches no credibility. "The moon is made of green cheese", as well as the sentence "I think the sentence, 'The moon is made of green cheese.' is false", can both be in i's knowledge set, K'(i,t). The number of such sentences can be arbitrarily increased without any real change in i's knowledge. In order to avoid notational complexity, the set K'(i,t) will be understood not to contain sentences to which i gives no credibility, and therefore the sets K(i,t) will not contain ideas which i regards as incredible.

26 The partition L may depend on i and t, in which case it is interpreted as person i's classification of knowledge at Time t. In that case the partition is restricted to consist of only a finite number of sets. The notation suppresses this dependence.

27 The word "discover" is sometimes used to refer to the bringing to light of something that already exists, whereas "invent" is used to refer to bringing into existence something that did not previously exist (see Hadamard [1945, p. xi], for instance). "Columbus discovered America." "Edison invented the electric light bulb." I prefer a usage that permits us to say "Arrow discovered the Impossibility Theorem of Social Welfare." without affirming the "existence" of that theorem before Arrow's statement of it, even though it is in the list of statements that constitute **E**.

28 "For not by art do they speak these things, but by divine power. . . ." (Plato, p. 19.)

29 This does not exclude the possibility that individuals with the same genetic endowment end up with different creative abilities because of different developmental histories. The point here is that there does not seem to be a special faculty of "creativeness."

The view that creative faculties are part of the human endowment would be supported by the existence of some continuity between man and our evolutionary ancestors, or even by the existence of some rudimentary form of creative powers in creatures not directly in our evolutionary line. Such a continuity would be suggested by the following observation. A colony of macaque monkeys was established by a Japanese laboratory on an island, where they could be observed from concealment. The monkeys were fed potatoes, which "appeared" from time to time on the sandy beach where they lived. The monkeys spent considerable time in brushing the sand off the potatoes before eating them. One young female monkey "discovered" that sandy potatoes could be cleaned by washing them in a stream, and later in the salt water that lapped on their beach.

The practice of washing potatoes did not spread immediately to all of the colony. Older monkeys, no doubt set in their ways, were highly resistant to the new way, while young ones were quicker to adopt it.

The macaque genius who discovered washing potatoes also discovered swimming in the water, a practice hitherto unknown among the monkeys. Again some old macaques refused to venture into the water, while most of the young ones swam and played with evident enthusiasm. See Itani and Nishimara (1973).

30 Campbell (1974) "Suggests that the ways humans have of learning and knowing are a result of evolution. This influential paper has engendered a substantial literature exploring evolutionary theories of mind, rationality, and related matters.

31 This observation must be qualified. Matters of ability aside, the student may bring with him knowledge from another relevant field of which the faculty member knows little.

32 This point is related to how knowledge is stored and accessed. This is discussed further in footnote 35.

33 Hadamard (1945, p. 75) observed that there is no essential difference for him between trying to build up a mathematical argument or trying to comprehend a given one.

34 "Contrary to popular belief it is not possible to have too much knowledge about a task domain." The author, Amabile (1990, p. 82), commented that what is important is ". . . the way in which that knowledge is stored, and the ease with which it can be accessed . . . [If information is stored] in wide categories with easy access to association, increased information should only lead to increased creativity." See also footnote 35.

35 Polanyi (1958) emphasized this distinction. Recent research on brain functioning strongly suggests that the brain uses a variety of different mechanisms, which together interact to carry out certain complex functions. One recent example reported in the *New York Times* science pages, Sept. 13, 1992, may serve to illustrate. A brain-injured person could not say whether an elephant is bigger than a dog, but had no difficulty in making the comparison

when shown a picture of an elephant and of a dog. Since the pictures are the same size, the comparison is made by access to knowledge of the relative sizes of elephants and dogs, and not by direct perception of the pictures.

36 However, it should be noted that one of the "signs of isolation" is the persistent pursuit of an idea outside the conventional mainstream. There are examples where this has resulted in pathbreaking discoveries.

37 Hadamard (1945, p. 29) quotes Paul Valery: "It takes two to invent anything. The one makes up combinations; the other chooses, recognizes what is important to him in the mass of things which the former has imparted to him.

"What we call genius is much less the work of the first than the readiness of the second one to grasp the value of what has been laid before him and to choose it" (p. 30).

38 Koestler (1964).

39 *Science News*, Vol. 141, June 6, 1992 reports that two British scientists discovered a new way of shaping ceramic materials. They brought the knowledge of how cars are now painted into a new context, that of shaping ceramic materials. Car painting involves lowering the alkalinity of the car surface so that polymers settle and coat the car, where they are cured to form a permanent paint. "It suddenly struck me that if we can generate a base at an electrode, then we could precipitate [ceramic] materials from solution," recalls Philip J Mitchell, an electrochemist at Loughborough (England) University of Technology. In the June 4 *Nature*, he and Loughborough University materials scientist Geoffrey D. Wilcox described an electrochemical process that creates such a basic environment. They reported they used this approach to make a variety of ceramic films in different shapes, including hair-width ceramic tubes. The story includes a statement by a materials scientist, James H. Adair, at the University of Florida to the effect that "It [the discovery] could really have an impact on how we make complex ceramics."

40 Perkins (1981, p. 96) pointed out the following. "Besides such considerations, there is another sense in which ordinary thinking contains bisociative potential. Thinking within a frame of reference requires sensitivity to the rules of the game, and events may occur that challenge the rules. Just by functioning within a frame, you are in a position to notice or more generally recognize the unexpected. Time and again in the history of science, investigators have accidentally encountered phenomena that should not have occurred, recognized them as anomalies, and gone on to revise or devise frames of reference to accommodate them. Of course, such recognition does only half the work of bisociation, challenging the established frame of reference but not relating it to another one. Nonetheless, it's important to grasp that the work of bisociation—if bisociation is the ultimate outcome—has in a sense begun already when an anomaly in the prevailing frame of reference is observed."

41 One such example is the independent discovery of evolution by Darwin and Wallace. Darwin (1911, p. 68) described his moment of insight as follows.

"In October 1838, that is, fifteen months after I had begun my systematic enquiry, I happened to read for amusement 'Malthus on Population,' and being well prepared to appreciate the struggle for existence which everywhere goes on from long-continued observation of the habits of animals and plants, it at once struck me that under these circumstances favorable variations would tend to be preserved, and unfavorable ones to be destroyed."

Alfred Russell Wallace (1905, pp. 361–362) described his arrival at the theory thusly. "One day something brought to my recollection Malthus' 'Principles of Population' which I had read about twelve years before. I thought of his clear exposition of 'the positive checks to increase'—disease, accidents, war, famine—which keep down the population of savage races to so much lower an average than that of more civilized peoples. It then occurred to me that these causes or their equivalents are continually acting in the case of animals also; and as animals usually breed much more rapidly than does mankind, the destruction every year from these causes must be enormous in order to keep down the numbers of each species, since they evidently do not increase regularly from year to year, as otherwise the world would long ago have been densely crowded with those that breed most quickly. Vaguely thinking over the enormous and constant destruction which this implied, it occurred to me to ask the question, Why do some die and some live? And the answer was clearly, that on the whole the best fitted live. From the effects of disease the most healthy escaped; from enemies, the strongest, the swiftest, or the most cunning; from famine, the best hunters or those with the best digestion; and so on. Then it suddenly flashed upon me that this self-acting process would necessarily *improve the race*, because in every generation the inferior would inevitable be killed off and the superior would remain—that is, the *fittest would survive*."

In addition to being an example of independent arrival at the same discovery, this provides an example of an insight generated by the "cross-fertilization" accompanying the combining of ideas from different frames of reference. One might think after the fact that human populations and animal populations are not such different frames of reference, but it is clear from the quoted passages that they were so regarded by both Darwin and Wallace.

It should also be noted that the existence of simultaneous and independent discoveries has been disputed. Smith (1981, p. 384) argued that nearly all cases of apparently independent invention can be explained by communication (cited in Mokyr, 1990).

42 Commenting on Einstein's early work, Clark (1971, p. 52) wrote "Thus even at this early stage, when dealing with a subject far removed from the new concept of space and time to be embodied in relativity, Einstein revealed two aspects of his approach to science which became keys to his work: the search for a unity behind disparate phenomena, and the acceptance of a reality apart from the direct visible truth." Clark in discussing one of the famous four 1905 papers, "On a Heuristic Viewpoint Concerning the Production and Transformation of Light," said, "It contained Einstein's first implied admission of the duality of nature which was to haunt his life and an early hint of the indeterminacy problem which drove him," as de Broglie has put it, "to end his scientific life in sad isolation and—paradoxically enough—apparently far behind the ideas of his time" (p. 63).

Einstein's belief in the underlying unity of nature, which may have been a motivating force behind the undoubted intensity and persistence of his thought, was well-suited to the "discoveries waiting to be made" in relativity and allowed him to be the one who made them. These same values and beliefs were a handicap to scientific discovery later in his scientific life. Einstein was in this respect not unique. There are numerous examples of this kind.

43 Examples of the latter include Einstein's often quoted conviction that "God does not play at dice," or Kepler's view of the planetary system, which he attributed to ". . . physical reasons or, if you prefer, metaphysical reasons." Those reasons are exposed in the following statement by Kepler. "My ceaseless search concerned primarily three problems, namely, the number, size, and motion of the planets—why they are just as they are and not otherwise arranged. I was encouraged in my daring inquiry by that beautiful analogy between stationary objects, namely, the sun, the fixed stars, and the space between them, with God the Father, the Son, and the Holy Ghost. I shall pursue this analogy in my future cosmographical work." Quoted in Koestler (1971, p. 125).

44 It is often pointed out that important discoveries in science have been made by people who did not have "too much knowledge." Having a fresh point of view uncontaminated by conventional ideas is thought to make it easier to come up with something new. In the present model, discoveries are the result of an interaction between a person and a body of knowledge. I may be the case that ability to bring together in the mind ideas from different fields is facilitated by ignorance of one of the fields, but it seems more likely that the abilities of the discoverer, the intensity of her interest in the problem and the existence in her knowledge of the relevant ideas are more important than whether those ideas are concealed in a

body of other ideas. In the present model, the ability of the investigator plays an explicit role, while the possibility of confusion resulting from knowing too much does not.

45 Hadamard (1945) mentioned the view of the French psychologist Souriau that invention occurs by pure chance and cites Souriau *Theorie de l'Invention* (Paris, 1881). Hadamard also mentions the opinion of the biologist Nicolle, *Biologie de l'Invention* (pp. 5–7) to the effect that "The act of discovery is an accident." Hadamard rejects these views of the role of chance in discovery on philosophical grounds, and on the basis that it flies in the face of experience. How can that view explain the fact that some individuals, such as Poincare, make a stream of important discoveries over a lifetime, while others do not?

46 More recently Donald Campbell in a well-known paper (1960), put forward the idea that discovery proceeds by selection from randomly generated ideas. This view of discovery and invention as an evolutionary process driven by blind chance is interesting as an attempt to see how widely an evolutionary model can be applied, but in my view it is not a satisfactory explanation of discovery and invention, or creative activity. To elaborate on Hadamard's cogent objections, one has only to consider the experience of those who engage in research and write papers. One wonders whether Campbell's paper was the outcome of a process in which Campbell's mind was bombarded by a rain of randomly generated ideas that he screened to select the idea of evolution as an explanation of creativity?

Mokyr (1990, pp. 273–299) discussed an analogy between technological change and evolution.

The idea that random search can be a useful procedure in certain types of problems or situations is no doubt valuable. See for example, Reiter and Sherman (1965).

Mokyr gives examples of a few inventions made during the 19th century that might have appeared at any time. He argues that the rare ability of the discoverer played a role in determining when they appeared, and that this is a matter of chance.

47 In a stochastic version of the model in Part 5, the distribution of the significance of discoveries might be a primitive of the model.

48 These parameters are initially presented as functions of time. It will usually be assumed that they are constant. The model presented here is intended ultimately to be embedded in a general equilibrium model in which the values of many of these parameters are determined endogenously, by investment decisions such as those required to acquire skills, or those that allocate resources to certain activities. Allowing these parameters to be functions of time still permits them to be exogenous in the present model.

49 Perkins (1981), among others, would hold this view.

50 This is in keeping with the idea that creative powers are to be found in all persons.

51 If person i's knowledge at t is partitioned, as in Part 2, and 5.1, so that

$$K(i,t) = K_1(i,t) \cup K_s(i,t) \cup \ldots \cup K_Q(i,t),$$

then the parameters $\varepsilon(i,t)$, $\rho(i,t)$, and perhaps also $\alpha(i,t)$, and hence $\delta(i,t)$ should all be made functions of $q = 1,2,\ldots,Q$, so that $\varepsilon(i,t)$ is replaced by $e_q(i,t)$, etc. In this case certain constraints on the total effort and resources available would apply.

52 See footnote 37.

53 It might be thought that the task of sorting through a large body of knowledge would be overwhelming. In addition to what casual observation of the functioning of those who command a large body of knowledge, which suggests the contrary of this idea, and to what the psychological research referred to earlier suggests, current understanding of how the brain stores knowledge and has access to it seem to be consistent with the view that more knowledge does not inhibit discovery, and that combinatorial complexity may not cause over-

whelming difficulties. Two recent summaries of the present state of knowledge suggest that the acquisition of knowledge changes the structure of the brain. "One way of looking at tuning, adaptive filtering, and associative processes is that they provide means of incorporating 'knowledge' into the structure of the brain. . . . Sustained activation provides a means for working with his incorporated knowledge, when the original information is no longer present" (Desimone, 1992, p. 246). The paper by Kandel and O'Dell (1992) describes functional and anatomical changes in the brain that result from learning and storing memories. The paper describes how mechanisms used for neural development are also used to make activity-dependent changes in the brain.

If knowledge is incorporated into the structure and functioning of the brain, then perhaps the image of shuffling through a stack of cards on which ideas are written is not a useful metaphor for the mental processes of associating combinations of ideas, especially when deep and persistent thought is involved.

Minsky (1985) presented a related view of Mind in a cognitive-artificial intelligence framework.

54 It is also assumed that knowledge once acquired is never forgotten. But, apparently the recipe for making Stradivarius violins has been lost to us, though Stradivarius himself and his proteges no doubt did not forget it while they lived. Similarly, some technologies of preliterate cultures have to be rediscovered, if they are not to be lost. Nevertheless, in light of the availability and cost of memory devices nowadays, this seems not too restrictive an assumption. It should be recalled that the existence of a record of a piece of knowledge does not in itself constitute knowledge. Someone must acquire that information to make it his or her knowledge. The deciphering of Mayan gliphs is one of a number of examples that come to mind.

55 If one of the roads mentioned in 5.1 above, but not taken, namely a stochastic model, were to be followed, it would seem natural here to say that the interaction between a person of given abilities, who is making a given effort, and a body of knowledge that allows certain combinations of ideas would result in a *probability* of discovering something new.

56 With this transition the set K(i,t) may as well be a subset of an uncountable set, such as a set indexed by the real numbers, or a Euclidean space. In such a case the sets K(i,t) would be required to be measurable and the size of K(i,t) might be, in the case of a subset of a Euclidean space, its Lebesgue measure.

57 Viewing effort and ability as parameters whose values may be changed is a special case in which δ(i) is a step function (i.e., a function of time). E.g.,

$$\delta(i,T)=\begin{cases}\delta'(i) & if\ t\le t'\\ \delta''(i) & if\ t>t'\end{cases}$$

The variable coefficient case arises in an example in Part 7.

58 See, for example, Mokyr's (1990) account of invention in the Industrial Revolution in Europe.

59 This allows the possibility that δ(ij) = 0 for some i and j. This is consistent with cases in which knowledge may grow but without having any effect on technology, as would be the case in a society that channeled human creative powers exclusively into the study of religious texts, or certain types of philosophical investigations. However it is consistent with the view expressed in Part 4 that creative powers are ubiquitous.

60 The multiplicity of intellectual communities corresponding to the partition of K(i,t) into subfields and the links among them, can be represented in the structure of Δ.

61 In the variable coefficients case, where Δ is a function of time, the solution may be found in Gantmacher (1959, Vol. II, pp. 133–136).

62 It is often assumed that the eigenvalues of Δ are distinct, since this is a sufficient condition for Δ to be diagonizable. This condition is not necessary, and the condition given is both sufficient and more natural in this problem.

63 Under the assumption expressed in (11) some growth of knowledge is assured. Nevertheless, this model could apply to a society in which there is growth of knowledge, but not growth of technology, and therefore no economic growth derived from technology. A culture that channeled all creative activity into religious or abstract philosophical study cut off from the economic sphere would provide an example. See Mokyr (1990) for a discussion of such societies in a global historical context.

64 This example is further developed in Part 6. It has several interpretations.

65 Tables 7.1 and 7.2 were prepared by Sangeeta Kasturia.

66 This equation can be interpreted as saying that a tested recipe appears in K*(i,t) when all development work has been completed. That is, a tested recipe is transferred from K(i,t)\K*(it) to K*(i,t) when it is completed.

67 Suppose there is a recipe that calls for some substance that is not an instance of a commodity. Then either the recipe could not be recognized in the model, or the collection of sets corresponding to the list of commodities would not be a covering, still less a partition, of the set of existing names.

68 E.g., y_c might be restricted to integer values, in which case c is considered to be indivisible, or a real number if c is regarded as divisible. Of course, other measures of 'quantity of c' are possible.

69 It should be clear from the definition that the production set determined by K* also depends on the way commodities are defined and measured (i.e., on **P**, Φ and Ψ).

70 Recall that it is assumed that there is no forgetting of previously known technology.,

71 For example, the discovery of rH factors led to the introduction of more blood types than were recognized before. The discovery that aspirin is effective in preventing heart attacks is the basis of a new use for an existing substance. It constitutes a new recipe, but does not require a new commodity.

72 Commodities are dated. Therefore the vector of produced commodities includes those currently produced, and y^2 includes those inherited from the past as well as those given from nature.

73 A more explicit notation would show the dependence of Y and $\hat{Y}$ on K*, **P**, the functions Φ and Ψ, as well as v and t. Note that $y \geq v$ is equivalent to $-y \leq -v$.

74 Under any of a number of standard assumptions about the technology, $\hat{Y}$ is compact.

75 The structure underlying this production set can be sketched as follows. Each commodity has an equivalence class of objects involved in recipes in K*. It is assumed that for each such class of objects there is a recipe, called *basic*, such that whatever nonnegative multiple of its input–output array is specified, there is another recipe in K* whose input–output array is equivalent to it in the given commodity classification. These basic recipes correspond to the industry input–output vectors in the commodity space. An additional linearity property assures the addition property for commodities.

76 This assumption is made for simplicity. In the general case the solution would be a linear combination of functions $\exp(\lambda_i t)\, t^k$, which would further complicate the notation without changing the situation qualitatively.

77 A necessary and sufficient condition that the line determined by the columns of A intersect the non-negative quadrant is that $a_{11} \geq a_{21}$, and $a_{22} \geq a_{12}$.

78 In higher dimensions the changes in the attainable production set can be more complex.

79 The existence of fixed factors of production is not incompatible with increasing returns to scale in the "knowledge sector," and therefore not with exponential growth of the production set over time. On the other hand, fundamental physical constraints, such as the laws of thermodynamics, together with finite bounds on the amount of matter or energy in the world ultimately set limits on growth of the attainable production set. However, the relevance of these bounds is unclear, because at any particular time knowledge of the possibilities of new substances or new forms of energy is limited. Therefore, calculations of ultimate limits of growth must be relative to knowledge existing at that time. Experience shows that those calculations can be far from the truth.

An example of this is provided by the calculation of Lord Kelvin of the age of the sun. Kelvin based his calculation on the idea of Helmholtz that the sun's energy came from gravitational contraction. Kelvin calculated that the age of the sun was at most 500 million years. This was inconsistent with Darwin's theory of evolution, something that both Darwin and Kelvin recognized. Neither man was willing to accept the conclusions unreservedly. Kelvin was aware that the calculation was based on the accuracy of Helmholtz's theory of gravitational contraction as the source of solar energy, and to his credit Kelvin stated that "I do not say that there may not be laws which we have not discovered." See Ferris (1988, pp. 247–248).

80 Recall from footnote 22 that $A_{p'}$ denotes the set of agents whose knowledge is relevant to the coefficients where $p = p'$.

81 Mokyr (1990) points out that the British in the period of the Industrial Revolution, borrowed freely from European knowledge, while other European societies were closed to outside knowledge for a variety of reasons. He attributes to this fact part of the difference in the growth of British technology and of the economy as compared to Europe.

82 Argote and Epple (1990). They give extensive references to the literature on Learning Curves.

83 See, ibid.

REFERENCES

Amabilie, T. M. (1990). Within You, Without You: The Social Psychology of Creativity, and Beyond. In M. A. Runco & R. S. Albert (Eds.), *Theories of Creativity*. Newbury Park, CA: Sage Publications.

Argote, L., & Epple, D. (1990). Learning Curves in Manufacturing. *SCIENCE*, Vol. 247, 23 February, pp. 920–947.

Arrow, K. J. (1962). The Economic Implications of Learning by Doing. *Review of Economic Studies, 29*, 155–173.

Campbell, D. (1960). Blind Variation and Selective Retention in Creative Thought as in Other Knowledge Processes. *Psychological Review, 67*(6), 380–400.

Campbell, D. (1974). Evolutionary Epistemology. In P. A. Schilpp (Ed.), *The Philosophy of Carl Popper*, Vol. 14, I and II LaSalle. Chicago: Open Court.

Clark, R. W. (1971). *Einstein The Life and Times*. New York: World Publishing, Times Mirror.

Darwin, C. (1911). *The Life and Letters of Charles Darwin* (Vol. 1). Francis Darwin (Ed.), New York: Appleton.

Desimone, R. (1992). The Physiology of Memory: Recordings of Things Past. *Science*, Vol 258, 9 October, pp. 245–246.

Ferris, T. (1988). *Coming of Age in the Milky Way*. New York: William Morrow.

Gantmacher, F. R. (1959). *The Theory of Matrices*. New York: Chelsea Publishing Company.

Hadamard, J. (1945). *An Essay on The Psychology of Invention in the Mathematical Field.* Princeton, NJ: Princeton University Press.

Itani, J., & Nishimara, A. (1973). The study of infrahuman culture in Japan. *The Fourth International Congress of Primatology* (Vol. 1). E. W. Menzel, Jr. (Ed.). Basel: Karger.

Kandel, E. R., & O'Dell, T. J. (1992). Are Adult Learning Mechanisms Also Used for Development? *Science*, Vol. 258, 9 October, pp. 243–245.

Koestler, A. (1964). *The Act of Creation.* Hutchinson of London.

Koopmans, T. C. (1957). *Three Essays on the State of Economic Science.* New York: McGraw-Hill.

Lucas, R. E. Jr. (1988). On the Mechanics of Economic Development. *Journal of Monetary Economics, 22,* 3–42.

Minsky, M. (1985). *The Society of Mind.* New York: Simon and Schuster.

Mokyr, J. (1990). *The Lever of Riches: Technological Creativity and Economic Progress.* New York: Oxford University Press.

Newell, A., Shaw, J. C., & Simon, H. A. (1957). Empirical explorations of the logic theory machine. *Proceedings of the Western Joint Computer Conference, 11,* 218–39.

Newell, A., & Simon, H. A. (1956). The logic theory machine. *IRE Transactions on Information Theory* IT-2. *3,* 61–79.

Perkins, D. N. (1981). *The Mind's Best Work.* Cambridge, MA: Harvard University Press.

Plato, I. (   ). *Great Dialogues of Plato.* Trans. W. H. D. Rouse, Eds. E. H. Warmington & P. G. Rouse. New York: New American Library.

Polanyi, M. (1958). *Personal Knowledge: Toward a Post-Critical Philosophy.* Chicago: University of Chicago Press.

Reiter, S., & Sherman, G. R. (1965). Discrete Optimizing. *Journal of the Society for Industrial and Applied Mathematics*, Vol. 13, No. 3.

Rivera-Batiz, L. A., & Romer, P. A. (1991). Economic Integration and Endogenous Growth. *The Quarterly Journal of Economics*, May.

Science News. (1992). Vol. 141, June 6.

Simon, H. A. (1977). *Models of Discovery.* Dordrecht, Holland: D. Reidel.

Simonton, D. K. (1988). Creativity, Leadership and Chance. In R. J. Steinberg (Ed.), *The Nature of Creativity.* New York: Cambridge University Press.

Smith, C. S. (1981). *A Search For Structure.* Cambridge MA: MIT Press.

Stokey, N. L. (1991). Human Capital, Product Quality, and Growth. *The Quarterly Journal of Economics*, May.

Wallace, A. R. (1905). *My Life* (Vol. 1). New York: Dodd, Mead.

PART

II

COLLABORATION TECHNOLOGY FOR SPECIFIC DOMAINS

CHAPTER

8

Infrastructure and Applications for Collaborative Software Engineering

Prasun Dewan
University of North Carolina, Chapel Hill

Vahid Mashayekhi
John Riedl
University of Minnesota

1. INTRODUCTION

In this project, we are researching two closely related areas of collaboration technology: collaborative applications and infrastructures. The area of collaborative applications is investigating better computer support for cooperative work than what has been offered by traditional applications. Researchers are exploring computer support for a variety of collaborative activities including group decision making [38], writing [49], and budget planning [26].

We are investigating support for distributed collaborative software engineering. This research direction is both important and promising. It is important because software engineering costs are constantly increasing as a percentage of the cost of large systems and research has shown that the cost of interaction among team members is a significant part of the total cost of these systems [24].

It is promising because collaborative applications have the potential for cutting down these costs. For instance, an application allowing distributed users to gather software requirements both synchronously and asynchronously could reduce travel cost, as they could interact with each other from their offices; time spent in meetings, as they could do more work asynchronously; and documentation and maintenance costs, as the tool could automatically keep logs of events and the rationale behind design decisions.

Similarly, a program editor offering: fine-grained locking could allow programmers to work more concurrently; implicit locking–unlocking could reduce the overhead of checking-in–checking-out data; fine-grained access control could decrease the likelihood of programmers not responsible for some program component erroneously modifying the component; and collaborative undo–redo could reduce the effort required to recover from team errors and allow newcomers to playback the history. Previous research has shown that some of these benefits do, in fact, occur in other collaborative activities such as group decisions and also in some phases of collaborative software engineering such as design [55, 52, 23].

It is very likely that these benefits will also occur in other phases of software engineering. For these reasons, our first hypothesis is:

> *Software Engineering Hypothesis:* It is possible to develop collaborative applications that cut down on team interaction costs in distributed collaborative software engineering: requirements analysis, design, inspection, programming, debugging, and testing.

The area of collaborative infrastructures is exploring software abstractions and architectures for supporting the implementation of distributed collaborative applications. The implementations of collaborative applications are difficult because, in addition to single-user interaction tasks, these applications must perform collaboration tasks such as: dynamically making and breaking connections with (possibly remote) users, multiplexing input from and demultiplexing output to multiple users, coupling the input–output of the users, providing concurrency and access control, and offering collaborative undo–redo [21, 60, 51].

Researchers have designed several different kinds of software abstractions (and associated architectures) for supporting collaborative applications. These include abstractions that allow distributed sharing of a message bus [35, 57], screen bitmaps [60], windows [39], widgets [59], and text buffers [37].

Our own previous work has explored sharing of "active variables." Active variables were originally used to show a program variable changing over time during a debugging session [63]. They were extended to "editable active variables" [19] to provide a user model in which editing actions by the user trigger arbitrary actions in the program. Editable active variables capture structural, syntactic, and semantic information about application data, which is needed to support several requirements for collaborative applications such as variable-grained concurrency and access control.

Therefore, our second hypothesis is:

> *Infrastructure Hypothesis:* It is possible to create an extension of the abstraction of an editable active variable that, in comparison to other sharing abstractions, offers programmers more automation and flexibility for implementing

collaborative applications. It is also possible to implement this new abstraction on state-of-the art workstations and local-area networks without introducing noticeable delays (1/10th sec) [67] for user-interface operations.

Our project is investigating these two hypotheses. We have stated them separately because they are independent and can, in fact, be explored separately. We are studying them together because of the leverage the research of one gives to the other. An infrastructure based on active variables makes it easy to prototype the collaborative software engineering applications needed to test the first hypothesis. Conversely, our experience with the implementation and use of the collaborative software engineering applications provides us with the data needed to test the second hypothesis.

The rest of this chapter is an overview of the work we have done so far to test these hypotheses. All of the individual results we mention here have been described in detail in previous conference and journal papers. The purpose of this chapter is to outline the infrastructure and software engineering components of our work, showing the relationship between them. Because this chapter is an overview, we use an informal, conversational style in the presentation, leaving more precise, detailed descriptions to the individual papers referenced.

The chapter is organized as follows. Section 2 outlines our overall research method for designing and evaluating the infrastructure and applications. Section 3 addresses the infrastructure part of our work, overviewing the various components of this research. Similarly, Section 4 addresses the collaborative software engineering applications. Finally, Section 5 gives conclusions and directions for future research.

2. RESEARCH METHOD

Our research method is described by the following sequence of steps. These steps describe an iterative process wherein results from a higher level step are used in a lower level step and feedback from a lower level step is used in a higher level step.

1. Decompose the application sharing functionality into individual collaboration functions that can be researched individually. For each of these of these functions do the following steps.
2. Identify collaboration scenarios that exercise the function.
3. Create taxonomies that classify the scenarios into various categories.
4. Based on the scenarios and taxonomies, identify requirements for specific applications and the general infrastructures.

5. Design an interaction model for the function that meets the infrastructure requirements. By an interaction model, we mean a description of the semantics of the function from the users' point of view.

6. Design programming abstractions that support the interaction model.

7. Design an overall architecture for the implementation of the abstraction.

8. Implement the architecture in an infrastructure.

9. Use the infrastructure to implement the function in the collaborative applications desired.

10. Evaluate how well the infrastructure applications perform the function. Several kinds of evaluations can be performed. (a) *Inspections:* The design of an application–infrastructure can be inspected to determine how many of its requirements are met. (b) *Simulations:* The relative flexibility of an interaction model–abstraction can be evaluated by determining which of the existing interaction models–abstractions can be simulated by it. The amount of effort (e.g., lines of code) required to do the simulations is a measure of the relative automation provided by the system. (c) *Usage, Programming, and Performance Data:* The usability of the collaborative applications and infrastructure in practice can be measured through studies evaluating their usability, extensibility, and performance.

11. Derive general principles that are independent of the particular scenarios, models, abstractions, architectures, and thus can be applied to other projects in collaboration tools and infrastructures.

Thus, the contributions of this research include a set of principles, scenarios, application designs, models, abstractions, architectures, and implementations that enable an assessment of the hypotheses. In the next two sections, we discuss some of the actual contributions of our work in these areas. The research method overviewed here is motivated and discussed in more depth in [14].

3. INFRASTRUCTURE SUPPORT

3.1. The Concept of a Groupware Generator

Our goal is to abstract out the functionality that is common to collaborative applications and implement it in the infrastructure, much as research in databases has abstracted common functionality in database systems and implemented it in database management systems. What we would like to build is a "groupware generator," a system that automatically generates an implementation of a collaborative application from its specification (Fig. 8.1).

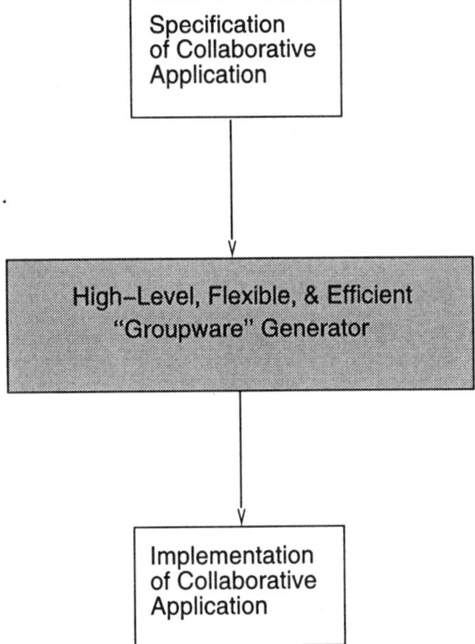

FIG. 8.1. Generating collaborative applications.

The system must support high-level specifications, be flexible enough to implement arbitrary collaborative applications, and give the performance necessary to support acceptable response times.

We have used the term *groupware generator* to draw the analogy with a parser generator. Like a parser generator, a groupware generator will not implement all aspects of a collaborative application. Just as a parser generator implements only the parser component of a compiler, a groupware generator implements only the group aspects of a collaborative application.

3.2. Functional Decomposition

Returning to the compiler analogy, the notion of a parser generator required the decomposition of the functionality of a compiler into separate subfunctions such as scanning, parsing, and semantics that could be implemented independently. We need a similar decomposition of the functionality of a collaborative application into functions that can be investigated separately. So far, we have identified the following such functions: (a) *Session Management* allows users to start, terminate, join, and leave sessions with collaborative applications. (b) *Single-User Interaction* determines the effect of users' commands on their displays. (c) *Coupling* determines which of the edits made by a user are shared with another user and when they are shared. (d) *Remote Undo* determines the effect of user undos on the displays of other users. (e) *User Awareness* makes users aware of the activities of other users. (f) *Access Control* prevents unauthorized user commands. (g) *Concurrency Control* prevents inconsistent concurrent user commands. (h) *Differencing* points out the differences between two different display states created by asynchronous coupling between users. (i) *Merging* merges two different display states into a single state.

We refer to all of these functions other than single-user interaction as collaboration functions because they are invoked only when multiple users are sharing the application. These are the functions that a collaboration infrastructure–groupware generator must support. This dimensionalization of the design space of collaborative applications addresses collaboration at the lowest, "common object perception" level in Malone and Crowston's collaboration hierarchy of coordination, group decision making, communication, and common object perception [42].

We have chosen the lowest level because it is the most flexible level one in that solutions at this level apply at the levels above it. The particular technical dimensions we have chosen at this level are consistent with the ones used in most of the collaboration literature today [60, 21, 51]. These dimensions are discussed in more depth in [18]. In the rest of the section, we overview how these functions may be supported automatically by a groupware generator.

3.3. Generalized Single-User Editing

To build a groupware generator, we first need a general model of multiuser interaction, which, in turn, requires a general model of single-user interaction. We have used an editing-based model of single-user interaction [19]. Figure 8.2 shows the main properties of this model.

According to this model, an application can be considered as an editor of a display of its data structures. A user interacts with the application by editing the display using text–graphics editing commands. Thus, interaction with an interactive application is similar to interaction with a text or graphics editor. The difference is that the display is "active," that is, changes to it can trigger computations in the application when the value is committed to the application. The dial in Fig. 8.2 shows that users–applications have control over when changes are committed to the application. For instance, commitment can occur on each incremental change, when a sequence of changes to the data structure are completed, or when the user explicitly executes the *Accept* command [11].

This is a simple and general model of single-user interaction. It models the single-user applications found in contemporary interactive systems: A text or

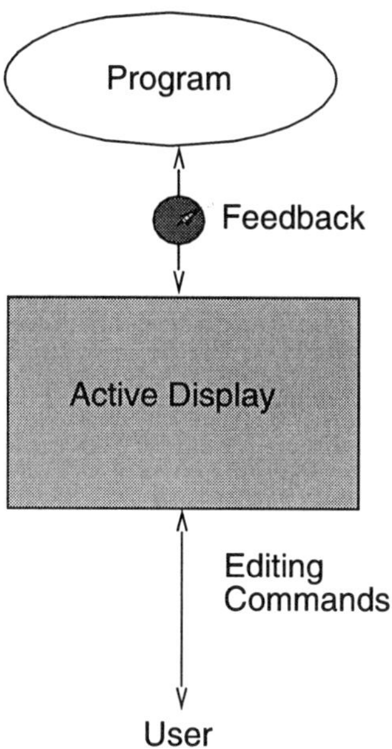

FIG. 8.2. Generalized single-user editing.

graphics editor can be considered an editor of a text or graphics file; a language-oriented editor can be considered an editor of a program syntax tree; a spreadsheet can be considered an editor of a matrix that responds to an editing of an entry in the matrix by updating related entries; and a debugger can be considered an editor of a debugging history that responds to the insertion of a new command in the history by computing the command and appending the output to the history. At some level of abstraction, any single-user interactive application can be considered a single-user generalized editor.

3.4. Collaborative Editing

Figure 8.3 shows how collaboration is added to the model. As in Fig. 8.2, a user interacts with an application by editing an active display of the data structures of the application. Different users edit different versions of the active display and linkage between the displays allows them to share their editing changes without violating consistency and authorization constraints. The arrow within the linkage circle represents a user–application–controlled dial and indicates that the sharing and control functions are performed flexibly.

How should the various settings of this dial be designed? It is important to identify principles that can be used to guide the design of these settings.

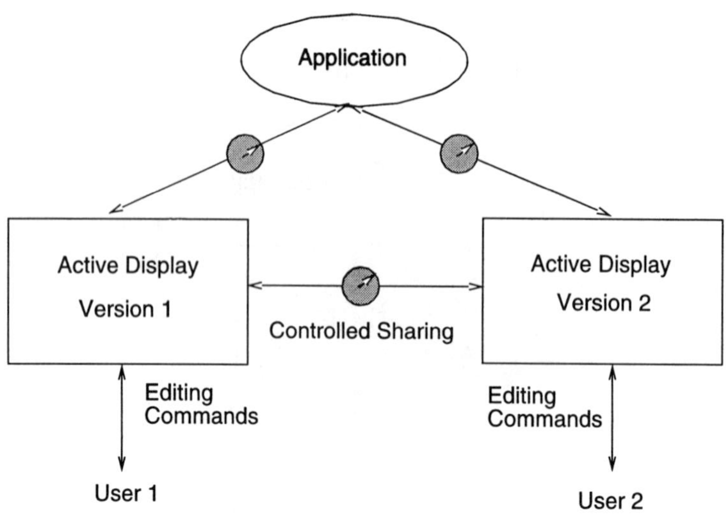

FIG. 8.3. Collaborative editing.

Here are two of the principles we have identified so far, which apply to the coupling component of the collaboration model:

> *Sharing principle:* Local editing changes sent to remote users should contain the intersection of the information the local and remote users want to send and receive, respectively.
>
> *Communication principle:* Local changes should be seen by remote users at the later of the times the remote and local users want to send–receive the contained information.

If these principles are not followed then either the receivers are misled (if they receive information that the senders did not mean to send them), or they get information overload (if they receive information they did not want) or some useful collaboration among the senders and receivers want is prevented (if the information exchanged is less than the intersection of the information the senders–receivers want to send–receive respectively). Other principles we have identified for access control, concurrency control, and undo are given in [18].

These principles, advocating flexibility, are easy to state but hard to follow because, as designers of collaboration models, we do not know exactly how particular users would like to collaborate. For instance, for the coupling function, we do not know what particular users would like communicated and when they would like the communication to occur. We have used two methods to determine how flexible the collaboration model should be:

Cover existing designs: We have tried to cover the collaboration semantics of existing applications and infrastructures.

Anticipate designs: We have also tried to anticipate useful collaboration semantics that have not so far been provided in collaborative systems, based on scenarios of how people collaborate without the computer. Some of these semantics were, in fact, implemented in collaborative applications developed independently of our work [28].

We have developed a paramaterized model of collaboration, which defines a whole design space of collaboration semantics. A particular application that follows this model may choose to support a single point in this space or allow its users to dynamically switch among different points. The various dimensions of this space are motivated and described in detail in [17, 62, 48].

3.5. Framework

Before we describe our framework for implementing the collaboration model, let us first consider existing systems that can be be used to implement collaborative applications.

Perhaps the first kind of system that comes to mind when we consider multiuser interaction is a database management system (DBMS). By a DBMS, we mean a traditional relational DBMS offering no support for triggers. It is possible to use such a system to implement a collaborative application. For each user of the application, a separate DBMS client is created, which manages the interaction with the user. When a user changes a shared value, its client stores the new value in the DBMS, from where the clients of other users sharing the value can retrieve it and display it to their users. This approach has some advantages. It provides automatic support for concurrency control and access control. Moreover, from a coupling point of view, it is flexible since clients can use arbitrary criteria to decide which values are deposited–retrieved from the DBMS and when these values are deposited–retrieved. On the other hand, it offers no automation for coupling since clients must manually deposit and retrieve data from the database system. This task is difficult, specially when the data are complex, as these data must be "flattened" into relations and then "unflattened" from relations. This approach also does not offer good performance for various reasons. Unflattening–flattening of complex data can involve expensive joins. Moreover, traditional DBMS are disk-resident, therefore clients must pay the cost of accessing the disk for retrieving–storing data. Furthermore, it requires that clients poll the DBMS to check whether shared data have changed. As a result, it is unsuitable for supporting real-time collaboration. Finally, this approach does not provide automatic support for awareness, diffing, or merging; and its support for access control, concurrency control, and undo is too restrictive for several applications [18].

These disadvantages of DBMS are not surprising as they were not designed to support collaboration. Let us now consider a technology that was designed to support collaboration: a shared window system.

A shared window system is an extension of a single-user window system that offers the same programming interface as the latter. It allows multiple users to share physical copies of a logical window created by a client. It also usually supports some form of floor control that ensures that, at any time, only one user can provide input to the client. A client window can be considered an "active in-core database" because it is stored in-core and the system automatically keeps its physical replicas consistent. Thus, this approach can offer the performance needed for supporting real-time collaboration. Moreover, because the programming interfaces of shared and single-user window systems are the same, the client is "collaboration-transparent," that is, completely unaware it is being used by multiple, collaborating users. From the automation point of view, it is not possible to do better, because a collaborative implementation is generated by the system without requiring the programmer to write any specification code. On the other hand, because no collaboration specifications are allowed, the approach supports no flexibility, allowing only WYSIWIS (What You See Is What I See) coupling, and coarse-grained concurrency control based on the notion of a unique floor holder.

The distributed system technology gives applications the required flexibility and performance. As in the DBMS case, separate processes can be created for different users, which can directly communicate with each other to implement arbitrary collaboration functions. Unlike the DBMS approach, this approach does not require the overhead of retrieving and storing data in a database. However, like the DBMS approach, it offers no automation because the application must implement all aspects of collaboration, and is, thus, "collaboration-opaque."

These are only three of the possible technologies for implementing collaborative applications. In [13] we survey and evaluate other frameworks for implementing collaborative applications. None of these frameworks, however, meets our goal of a high-level, flexible, and efficient groupware generator. Therefore, we have developed a new framework to meet this goal. The basic ideas in our framework are outlined next.

3.6. Abstractions

Suite defines three main abstractions: shared active variables, interaction variables, and value groups. A shared active variable is an ordinary program variable that is "exported" to the users of the program. For each user interacting with the variable, another kind of data structure, called an interaction variable, is created, which contains a version of the value of the active variable and additional attributes. A user may edit an interaction variable using type-specific editing commands, which can trigger changes in the active variable and corresponding interaction variables created for different users. Interaction variables have attributes that implement the coupling, access control, and other parameters of our collaboration model. Together, these parameters ensure that the values of peer interaction variables can be flexibly coupled, merged, protected, undone, and kept consistent. Theses parameters are set by the application programmer–user and implemented by the system. Figure 8.4 illustrates these abstractions.

The abstractions of shared active variables and interaction variables can be understood from multiple viewpoints. From a programming language point of view, they are simply program variables that can be manipulated by multiple users using type-specific editing commands. From a database point of view, they can be considered as replicas with multiple consistency constraints. From a software engineering view, they are different versions that can exchange values. From a user-interface point of view, active variables corresponds to models [54] and interaction variables correspond to views [54] that the system automatically generates and keeps consistent. Thus,

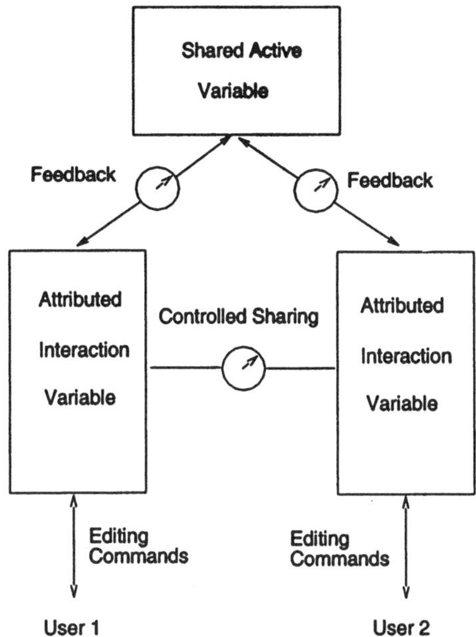

FIG. 8.4. Shared active variables and interaction variables.

these abstractions integrate and extend properties of a variety of existing abstractions.

We treat every program variable as a first class object that can be made a shared active variable. Thus, active and interaction variables can be both simple values such as integers and strings and complex values such as records, arrays, and sequences. Moreover, each component of a structured active variable is itself an independent active variable associated with its own attributed interaction variables. As a result, each simple value in the display of a user can be shared differently with its peers in the displays of other users. A problem with this approach is that a typical display may contain a large number of simple values and a large number of coupling and other attribute values must be defined for each of these values.

We introduce the notion of value groups to solve this problem. A value group unites a group of related interaction variables that are expected to share attribute values. It is a first class attributable object in that it is associated with its own set of attributes, which are inherited by members of the groups. Moreover, it is also a first class couplable object in that it can be linked with corresponding value groups created for other users. This results in a powerful facility for defining common attributes that allows attributes to be shared among interaction variables–value groups of a particular user (through inheritance) and those of different users (through coupling). For instance, a particular user can set an attribute of a value group that determines if the variable is public or private. Through coupling, this attribute value can be propagated to the corresponding value groups created for other users; and then, through inheritance, it can be propagated to the members of these groups at each user's site. Thus a single attribute definition can be shared by O(N*M) interaction variables, where N is the number of users and M is the number of interaction variables created for a user. The notion of coupled value groups is similar to the concept of prototype delegation in object-oriented languages with the main difference that coupling is birectional while delegation is unidirectional.

3.7. Architecture

We have now seen three new abstractions, shared active variables, interaction variables, and value groups. How should they be placed in a distributed environment? Figure 8.5 shows three alternatives, centralized, replicated, and hybrid.

In the centralized case, a single process manages all shared active variables, interaction variables, and value groups. In the replicated case, a separate process is created for each user, which stores the interaction variables and value groups of that user and replicas of the shared active variables. These two cases are duals of each other, in the centralized case the output

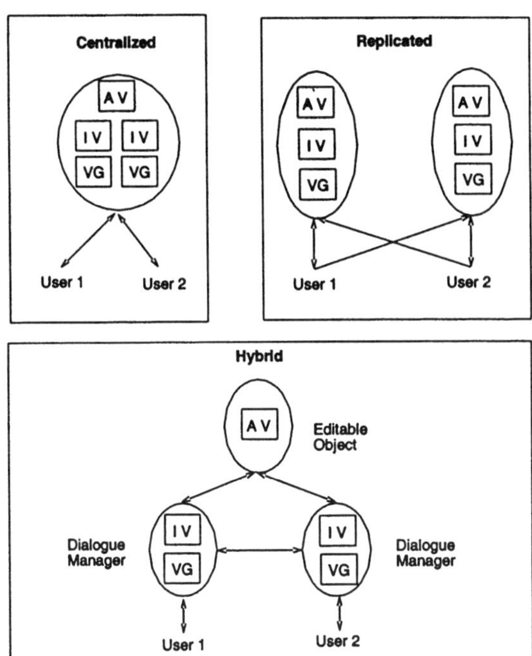

FIG. 8.5. Architectural alternatives.

of the centralized process is broadcast to all users sharing it whereas in the replicated case the input is broadcast to all replicas [40].

These two architectures correspond to the centralized and replicated database systems and offer similar advantages: The centralized architecture reduces update cost whereas the replicated architecture decreases retrieval cost. The update cost in this case is the cost of transmitting input to the application and the retrieval cost is the cost of transmitting output to the users. An important difference is that centralization–replication in the database case is applied to pure data and in the application case it is applied to both data and code. As a result, centralization–replication of applications leads to new kinds of consequences which are similar to those found in process migration.

A replicated architecture performs the application computations multiple times, once for each user. This may lead to several problems. Consider the case where the application accesses a file. Not all sites that replicate it may have access to a common file system. Let us assume that the different sites do indeed have a common file system. Now consider the case where the application reads the file. All replicas will try to read the file at the same time, leading to an I/O bottleneck. Worse, if the application code writes to a file, all replicas will write the same value to the file, leading to undesired semantics. The problems caused by read and write can be solved by a replicated file system but not the problems caused by arbitrary side effects. For instance, consider an application that sends a mail message or prints a check–the message will be mailed or the check will be printed multiple times, once for each user. Even if the computations have no side effects, there is still the problem of performing potentially expensive computations multiple times. The centralized case does not have these problems but does not give the desired performance because of the cost of broadcasting potentially large amounts of output.

We have devised a new, hybrid architecture that combines the benefits of these two architectures and is based on the distinction between active and interaction variables. The active variables of an application are managed by a single central process, called the editable object, and each user's interaction variables and value groups are managed by a separate local process, called a dialogue manager. This architecture gives the benefits of the replicated architecture inasmuch as output is computed locally by the dialogue manager. However, it does have the drawbacks of the latter because all semantic computations such as file accesses are done once in the central object. The idea of a local dialogue manager is similar to the notion of a local X server except that the former is a higher level user-interface agent performing additional input–output processing. It is also similar to the idea of local caching except that an interaction variable is not an exact replica of an active variable. It contains a version of the active variable and several additional attributes, which do not have to be transmitted over the network.

3.8. Communication Between Objects and Dialogue Managers

The (editable) object is implemented by the application programmer whereas the dialogue managers are provided by the system. Figure 8.6 shows the nature of the procedural interface provided to an object to communicate with its dialogue managers.

The interface contains both collaboration-transparent and collaboration-aware components, and allows the incremental addition of collaboration-awareness in the object. The details of this interface are given in [11, 10, 16].

Figure 8.6 also shows the layer of the dialogue manager that implements collaboration. In general, a user-interface layer can be divided into three categories of increasing levels: window system, toolkit, and user interface management system (UIMS). As Fig. 8.6 shows, we have taken the approach of implementing collaboration at the highest application-independent user-interface layer–the UIMS. This is the converse of the approach taken by shared window systems of implementing collaboration at the lowest user-

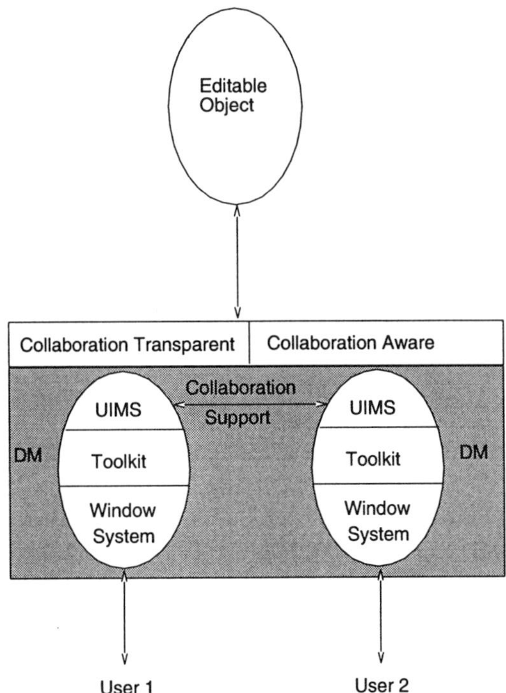

FIG. 8.6. The structure and programming interface of dialogue managers.

interface layer—the window system. A higher layer has more information regarding the application semantics and can thus support more collaboration parameters automatically. On the other hand, a lower layer provides automatic collaboration for not only direct clients of it but also indirect clients that use the higher layers. Thus, although our approach was necessary for supporting flexible collaboration, the shared-window system approach is more general in that it allows sharing of the large number of direct and indirect clients of an existing window system.

3.9. The Suite Implementation

We have implemented the abstractions and architecture described earlier in a software system called Suite. Figure 8.7 shows some of the components of the implementation.

We have used the X windows system, the Unix operating system, and the C programming languages as the bases for our implementation. The object precompiler extends a C program to a distributed object that communicates with other objects using a high-level remote procedure interface, while the dialogue precompiler extends a distributed object into an editable object.

Figure 8.7 also shows the structure of the dialogue manager source code. The bottom-most layers of the program are clients of the Unix operating system and the X window system. The program contains our own user-interface toolkit and single-user UIMS, and higher level layers to implement coupling and other collaboration functions. As mentioned before, this program is provided by the system and can be considered a cross between a UIMS and a DBMS.

3.10. Evaluation of Infrastructure

We have done four kinds of evaluations of our work in collaboration:

Simulations. We have used our abstractions to simulate, using very few parameter specifications (less than 30) coupling, access control, and other collaboration functions implemented in existing applications including the traditional application such as talk applications and contemporary collabo-

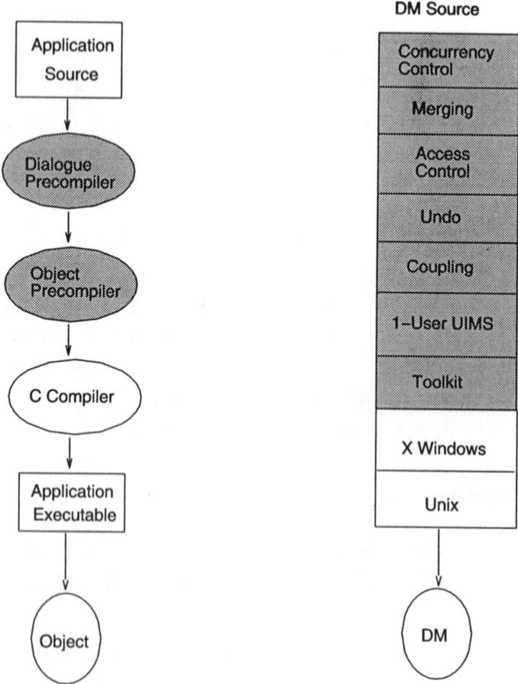

FIG. 8.7. The Suite implementation. The shaded regions represent software components provided by Suite.

rative applications such as CES [27]. Some of these simulations are given in [16, 62, 48].

Programming Data. The simulations give information regarding the effort required to implement existing applications. They do not indicate how flexible it is for creating new kinds of applications and how much effort is required to implement such applications. The experience of a variety of programmers who have used Suite to create new kinds of applications sheds some light on this issue. Most of these applications are part of the FLECSE environment described in the next section. Other significant applications such as a visitor scheduling application [12] and a multiuser TeX editor were also developed. Some of these applications such as the collaborative debugger are multiuser extensions of existing applications whereas others such as the inspection application are new applications that have no counterparts in the single-user case. The programmers who implemented these applications can be divided into several categories: (a) Suite creators–the first author and his gradate students who helped design and implement the system; (b) target clients–the third author and his graduate students working on this project whose needs were explicitly supported by the Suite creators, (c) supervised programmers–students at the universities of the first and third authors who could consult with experienced Suite programmers on how to program Suite, (d) unsupervised programmers–researchers at other institutions, who did not consult existing Suite programmers on how to use Suite. We do not have complete information regarding the experience of these different kinds of programmers. The information we have indicates: (a) The current version of Suite is flexible enough to implement the collaboration requirements of the applications designed by the various programmers who used it. Earlier versions of Suite did have limitations found by the creators and target clients, but once the initial limitations were overcome, few programmers reported new limitations regarding coupling and other functions we had addressed in our work. They do, however, find limitations regarding other issues such as awareness and concurrency control, which we are currently researching. (b) The absolute effort required to learn Suite and program applications using it is small. Typically, a (supervised) programmer implemented a Suite application as a semester project. Most of the semester, however, was taken in learning about Suite and designing the application. Once these two tasks were over, the amount of time and code required to specify collaboration parameters was insignificant. Experienced programmers such as the authors can specify these parameters in minutes. (c) The relative effort required to use Suite is small. The third author supervised projects that implemented the same multiuser application using Suite, Lotus Notes, and the Web, and found that Suite offered significantly higher level support to implement these applications. We have not made a major effort to target Suite to a wider set of programmers, but the fact that programmers not in our target set are using Suite is evidence that such an effort would be worthwhile. We are planning a variation of Suite implemented on top of the Web and plan to support its use by the internet community.

Usage Data. The programming data gives information regarding the effort required to implement new kinds of multiuser applications but does not indicate whether these applications were, in fact, perceived by users to be useful. Collecting usage data is a difficult task as it requires applications that have been debugged to the extent that they can be used by others and careful experiments to test their usage. Most of the Suite applications implemented so far have been demonstrational applications that do not meet the robustness requirement. Some were used by its designers in real work–an example is the multiuser Tex editor, which was used by its two implementors to collaboratively write the paper describing their application. Given our resources, we focused on one application for user studies, deciding that if these experiences were positive, we would focus on additional applications. The application we selected was the software inspection application. Our user experiments with it show that users found the ability to move between synchronous and asynchronous collaboration offered by the Suite coupling model useful in increasing their productivity because they could work individually when possible and meet in synchronous collaborations only when necessary. Synchronous collaboration was typically simulated by transmitting each change incrementally and coupling selections, whereas asynchronous collaboration was typically simulated by transmitting each change on explicit execution of a special transmit command and decoupling the selections. Both collaborations were non-WYSIWIS because the scrollbars and views were decoupled. The next section gives details regarding some of these experiments.

4. APPLICATIONS SUPPORT

4.1. Hypotheses for Applications Research

FLECSE, for *FLexible Environment for Collaborative Software Engineering*, is an on-going research project in which we are investigating the development of a software engineering toolset that explicitly supports collaboration. Tools we have developed to date include a *collaborative software inspector (CSI)* [45], which allows multiple users to collaboratively evaluate a document; a *collaborative debugger*, which allows multiple users to enter transactions of debugging commands; CTool, a simple tool that supports collaboratively browsing and testing of a module; RCSTool, a visual and collaborative interface to RCS [65]; VoteTool, a tool enabling software engineers to determine majority decisions on various issues, and SplitJoin, a tool that supports split and join transactions [56] and uses heuristics to determine when a transaction should be split. These tools cover several of the phases of the software life cycle (Table 8.1) and will form a testbed for testing the performance, usability, and extensibility of our collaborative models and infrastructures.

The applications research presented here focuses on the effects of collaborative support for software inspection. We have chosen software inspection as our representative software engineering task because it is widely practiced and highly structured. Software inspection is peer review of a software artifact, aimed at detecting and resolving faults. The traditional model of inspection has a large synchronous component, requiring participants to attend the inspection meeting at the same time and place. The time and space constraints make inspection meetings costly and consequently suitable for distribution and asynchronization.

Our prototype development research is intended to explore the ability of collaborative applications to increase the flexibility of software engineers by enabling them to work in a distributed and asynchronous fashion. From the Software Engineering Hypothesis we generate two Software Inspection Hypotheses:

Software Inspection Hypothesis 1: Distributed software inspection can replace face-to-face software inspection.

Software Inspection Hypothesis 2: Asynchronized software inspection can replace face-to-face software inspection.

We have designed and implemented prototypes for distributed and asynchronous inspections of software artifacts. We believe the collaboration requirements and design elements we identify for the software inspection can contribute to our understanding of collaboration requirements and design elements for other software engineering tasks. We have performed initial user studies to compare our prototypes with face-to-face inspection to

TABLE 8.1
FLECSE Collaborative Tools and the Software Life Cycle

Tool	*Requirements*	*Design*	*Code*	*Test*
CSI	X	X	X	X
Debugger				X
Ctool			X	X
RCSTool	X	X	X	X
VoteTool	X	X	X	X
SplitJoin			X	

evaluate our hypotheses. Our motivation for comparing distributed and asynchronous inspections with face-to-face inspection is to establish the feasibility of these models when compared with the traditional inspection model. We believe our solutions in software inspection are applicable to other software engineering tasks and can act as a first step in addressing our main application hypothesis. However, the scope of this section is limited to studying the problems of distributed and asynchronized software inspection. Further studies covering a wider range of software engineering tasks are required to assess the feasibility of the application hypothesis in general. Moreover, our user studies only present evidence for or against our hypotheses. User studies that can statistically show the correctness of our hypothesis are beyond the scope of our work at this point.

4.2. Traditional Software Inspection

Software inspection is a detailed review of a small amount of material by technically competent peers with the goal of detecting faults [22]. Boehm includes software inspection in his list of the 10 most important approaches for improving the quality of software, saying, "Walkthroughs (inspections) catch 60 percent of the errors (faults)" [2]. Yourdon and Humphrey both developed widely used techniques for inspection [29, 69]. In both approaches, team members have specific roles: Reviewer, moderator, producer, and recorder. Participants individually prepare for the inspection, attend the inspection meeting, and find faults that result in action items. The preparation stage differs in the two techniques. In Yourdon's technique, the reviewers read the target material and informally note faults and concerns. Reviewers are also encouraged to note positive aspects of the target material. In Humphrey's technique, each reviewer creates a fault list and gives the list to the producer before the meeting. The producer correlates the faults and prepares to address the faults in the inspection meeting. Humphrey also adds an optional introductory meeting to his model. The introductory meeting introduces background material or inspection criteria. We have chosen to follow Humphrey's model because it is more structured and provides intermediate results through the individual and correlated fault lists.

4.2.1. Requirements and Design Elements

We identify a number of user-level collaboration requirements for conducting face-to-face inspections that must also be conserved in distributed and asynchronous inspection:

Train of Thought: Participants must be able to follow the progression of ideas during the meeting. Train of thought is sustained in face-to-face inspection meetings since only one discussion takes place at a time. In the course of each discussion, participants listen to comments made by other participants and therefore are able to follow the development of ideas.

Sharing of Information: Participants must be able to share inspection information with one another. This information consists of the target material, correlated fault list, in-meeting inspection artifacts, postmeeting summaries, and actions items. In a paper-based face-to-face meeting, producers and recorders duplicate and distribute the target material among participants, capture the meeting proceedings, and enter this information into permanent storage for later retrieval.

Visual Cues: Participants must be able to direct the attention of other participants to areas of interest in the information space. In face-to-face meetings, speakers often achieve this goal by using pointers or visual cues to provide a common focus for the group and guide the participants through the inspection material.

Reaching a Consensus: Participants must be able to arrive at decisions for resolving differences. In face-to-face meetings, once a discussion has matured, a potential resolution is identified and is placed before the group as a proposal. The participants must decide whether they collectively agree with a proposal either informally by a "show of hands" (or saying aye), or more formally by balloting.

Coordination: Participants must be able to communicate with one another in an effort to coordinate their activities and ensure that the group's objectives are met. In face-to-face meetings, participants use verbal communication for moving through the meeting agenda and ensuring that project deadlines are satisfied.

From analyzing this set of requirements we arrive at three basic design elements for face-to-face inspections: *Shared information space*, *group decision making*, and *communications*. The shared information space satisfies the "Sharing of Information" requirement; group decision making satisfies the "Reaching a Consensus" requirement; and communications satisfies the "Train of Thought," "Visual Cues," and "Coordination" requirements. In face-to-face inspections, participants are responsible for meeting all the foregoing requirements: An experienced moderator can effectively lead the group through the meeting, mediate differences, and ensure that the meeting is on schedule; the producer ensures that inspection material is ready for review, distributes it among reviewers, and discusses any problems with the reviewers in an objective manner; reviewers prepare for the discussions by studying the inspection material thoroughly, concentrate on discussions, offer suggestions, and arrive at general agreements for resolving issues; recorder writes down all issues raised, gathers all relevant inspection data, produces the action item list, and commits a complete copy of the proceedings to permanent records.

We will re-visit the above requirements and design elements in Sections 4.5 and 4.6, where we apply them to distributed and asynchronous software inspection models and examine their transformation in each case.

4.3. Time and Space Axes

In general, collaborative meetings can be categorized by the two dimensions of space and time [21]. A *same-time, same-place* meeting is the current board-room type meeting where everyone congregates at a table, using pointers, overhead projectors, and handouts as meeting tools. A *different-time, same-place* environment might be a bulletin board in a publicly accessible room used for posting announcements. An example of a *same-time, different-place* meeting would be a teleconferencing system supporting audio and video, allowing the meeting to take place with members in different locations [58, 66]. Conceptually, a *different-time, different-place* meeting would enable participants to work together at the time and place of their choosing. An example is the e-mail systems, but existing implementations of structured activities are scarce.

Ideally, to provide complete flexibility for the software development teams, support for dissimilar meeting modes must be available for the diverse set of constraints, requirements, and participation styles possessed by the different inspection teams. Their meeting tools must be able to supply as many of these meeting modes as possible.

The software inspection process consists of two distinct meeting modes: fault collection and inspection meeting. These modes are denoted in Fig. 8.8 by the bottom and top halves of the cube. During fault collection (bottom half), individuals review the documents independently and are not restricted by place and time. Therefore, the fault collection activity spans the time and space axes and consists of all the parallel planes across the bottom half of the cube. The inspection meeting process (top half), consists of all participants discussing the correlated fault list generated by the reviewers. Traditional centralized inspection meetings cover the back left octant (same-time, same-place). We are exploring the potential for distributed inspection, denoted by the shaded section (same-time, different-place) in Fig. 8.8 [45], and asynchronous inspection, denoted by the cube directly in front of the shaded section (different-time, different-place) in Fig. 8.8 [46]. A tool that combines distributed software inspection with asynchronous software inspection would give complete flexibility in time and space for the software inspection process.

In our implementation, we used Suite to create semiautomatically generated software inspection applications with support for distribution and asynchrony. Suite explicitly supports distribution and asynchrony. Suite dialog managers support distributed access to objects. Each dialog manager contains a replica of the syntactic component for interaction with the object, while the semantic component is shared among all users of the object. Coupling between dialog managers supports a wide range of interaction styles, from purely synchronous, in which keystrokes are propagated in real-time,

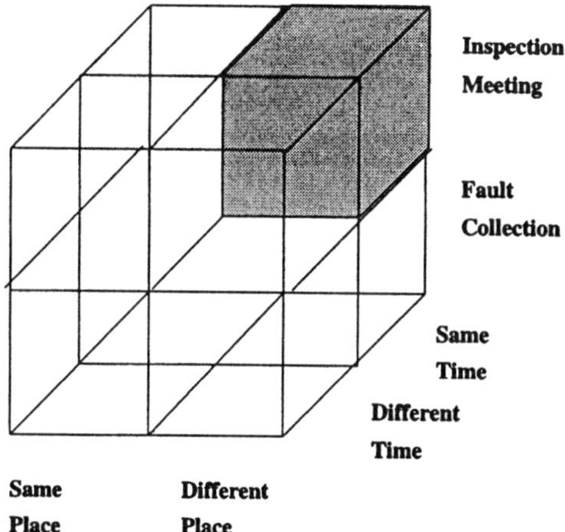

FIG. 8.8. Distributed software inspection, denoted by the shaded section, refers to activities performed during the inspection meeting from different places at the same time.

to purely asynchronous, in which users explicitly execute a commit command to transmit changes.

As we study asynchrony and distribution in inspection meetings, it could be that eliminating face-to-face meetings is neither possible nor desirable. For instance, social interaction is regarded to be critical to the task of software inspection as currently formulated [4], and this may be true for many types of meetings. Presently, our focus is on technical issues in distributed and asynchronous inspection. If our work is successful, it will make it possible for further investigation of the social changes introduced by distributed and asynchronous meeting models. Our expectation is that face-to-face meetings may turn out to be critical for team building and for resolving particularly different issues. However, we expect that, with suitable support, many day-to-day activities can be performed completely distributed and asynchronously.

4.4. Related Work in Software Inspection

Research in the area of software inspection has resulted in the introduction of new inspection processes and computer-supported tools. The formal inspection techniques include Active Design Reviews, *N*-phase inspection, and phased inspection. Active Design Reviews is a new approach for reviewing design documents, where a small group of reviewers use questionnaires to study the design artifact and record both positive and negative comments [53]. The questionnaires are provided by the producers and are meant to enable the reviewers to take a more active role in the inspection process and focus their attention on a particular aspect of the design. The *N*-fold inspection technique replicates the formal inspection method using *N* independent teams working in parallel under the control of a single moderator [43]. Each team is provided with a checklist and asked to analyze the software artifact. A fault may be detected by several teams, but the moderator gathers and records only the independent faults. The authors observe that independent inspection results do not tend to overlap and therefore more faults can be found if more than a single inspection team is used. Empirical evidence of the authors' observation is reported in a subsequent experimental evaluation [61]. In the phased inspection method, reviewers examine the work in a series of small inspections (also called phases), each of which aims at verifying that the product satisfies some desirable properties [36]. The properties examined are ordered such that each phase can assume the existence of properties checked in the earlier phases.

The computer-supported tools include InspeQ, ICICLE, CIA, and CSRS. InspeQ is a prototype that has been developed to provide computer support for the phased inspection process. The tool provides windows for displaying the work product, inspection checklist, and participants' comments. ICICLE [4] is a system intended to support the set of tasks performed during code inspection. ICICLE assists individual users in the comment-preparation phase of code inspection. It provides a synchronous environment in the inspection meeting phase, with computer support providing a paper-less meeting. Collaborative Inspection Agent (CIA) is a document inspection tool [25]. CIA uses ConversationBuilder [34] to develop a tool for synchronous inspection of all work products at various stages of the life cycle. It supports collaborative work by simultaneously displaying information on multiple user's screens, and allowing participants to play inspection roles. Collaborative Software Review System (CSRS) [32] aims to decrease the required human effort in reviews, conduct inspection incrementally during the software development, and provide online capabilities to collect metrics on the inspection process and software artifacts. The system is implemented on top of EGRET [31], a multiuser, distributed, hypertext environment for asynchronous collaboration. The CSRS process model involves phases for generating information nodes, providing training sessions for the reviewers, conducting individual and group reviews, consolidating the various views and proposals, holding a face-to-face group review meeting, and correcting the detected faults in the software using external support. Empirical studies of the CSRS system suggest that its use improves the breadth and depth of information captured by each reviewer in the inspection [33].

Our work builds on past research by exploring the effectiveness of collaborative inspection tools at supporting distribution and asynchrony. We build on the best known software inspection methods, rather than developing new methods. We extend the techniques used in existing tools to include support for distributed and asynchronous meetings.

4.5. Collaborative Software Inspection

Face-to-face meetings are described as "communication activities in which all participants are physically and simultaneously present" [7]. Bringing all participants together at the same time and place is expensive, but in the past face-to-face meetings were the only method for effective collaboration. The addition of distributed collaborative meeting environments changes this constraint [45]. In distributed software inspection, participants can "meet" with people in other cities through workstations at their desks. The benefits of distributed collaborative software inspection are:

Distribution: People who are geographically distributed can participate in the inspection. The participants can use a workstation or in their offices and meet with people in other cities. This reduces travel cost and increases the feasibility of inspections. The workstation-based tools the software engineers use daily are available during the meeting.

Online Capabilities: The current version of all material is accessible online. The results of the inspection are created online and therefore no secondary data entry into permanent records is necessary. The inspection information is available for metric collection, eliminating unnecessary note-taking and duplication.

Added Structure: Automated support adds structure and consistency to the software inspection process. Humphrey states that a consistent and uniform review is a criterion for developing a high quality software process [29]. Enforcing the structure of the inspection process results in repeatable and measurable results. The tools can also monitor the inspection process, to assure high quality [32].

We propose to distribute software inspection by providing a public workspace for individuals to share information, supporting audio conferencing for participants' interaction, and introducing structure to the software inspection meeting activities.

4.5.1. Design and Implementation

This section applies the face-to-face inspection requirements and design elements we identified in Section 4.2.1 to distributed inspection, and describes the structure of our prototype for distributed inspection, called Collaborative Software Inspection (CSI) [45].

The primary goal of distributed inspection is to support a group of distributed reviewers in inspecting software artifacts. For distributed software inspection, we can divide the set of requirements for face-to-face inspections (see Section 4.2.1) into two distinct classes:

1. Requirements that can be effectively met by distributed participants, without a need for computer support. Only "Train of Thought" is in this category.
2. Requirements that can be effectively met by distributed participants, with proper computer support. These are "Sharing of Information," "Visual Cues," "Reaching a Consensus," and "Coordination."

Similar to the face-to-face inspection case, the requirements in the first class can be satisfied by a trained, disciplined group of inspectors who impose the proper structure onto the meeting. Members of the group are connected through the shared CSI workspace, and through an audioconferencer running on SuiteSound [58]. The group discusses each fault individually by exchanging comments and ideas. Once a decision is made to resolve differences in views, the group moves on to the next discussion. The meeting closes when all faults are discussed or time expires. Although this class of requirements can benefit from computer support, an experienced group of inspectors can perform their inspection tasks without the need for computer support.

The second class of requirements for distributed inspection demands computer support. We group and discuss the related requirements from this class separately.

Sharing of Information and Visual Cues. The inspection artifacts must be placed online and made available to the distributed participants. Participants must be able to view, add, modify, and share this information with one another. What You See Is What I See (WYSIWIS) displays can bring up the same view of the information for all participants to see. Also, during the discussions, distributed participants must be able to direct the group's attention to items of interest by navigating through the information space. A participant can usher other participants through the information space by following links between interrelated pieces of information.

Reaching a Consensus and Coordination. Inspection participants must be able to verbally communicate with one another to perform their tasks, such as discussing faults and making group decisions. This communication may take on a visual form, such as using the UNIX ytalk program that allows multiple distributed users to write in real-time onto a screen seen by all participants, or an audible form, such as an audio teleconferencer that can support the verbal communication of distributed participants.

Based on our earlier requirements, we can group and discuss our design elements for building distributed inspectors of software artifacts.

Shared Information Space. The shared information space in distributed inspection provides a common focus for the group, presents the inspection material to the group, supports linking of interrelated pieces of information, and captures the meeting outcome, the action item list. This design element satisfies the Sharing of Information and Visual Cues requirements.

Group Decision Making and Communications. Supporting the verbal interaction of the participants in distributed inspection provides the needed support for discussion of faults, identification of resolutions, and group decision making. These design elements satisfy the Reaching a Consensus and Coordination requirements.

CSI supports both asynchronous and synchronous inspection tasks.

Asynchronous Tasks. The two main asynchronous activities of software inspection are the individual reviews and the producer's correlation of faults. The process starts with the producer making the target material available to the reviewers. Once the target material is available, the reviewers browse through it, annotating it appropriately. CSI supports annotations by creating hyperlinks between lines of the document and the reviewers' annotations. Both text and audio annotations are possible [58]. After sufficient time for thorough reviews, the producer terminates the review phase, and reviews and categorizes the annotations, integrating them into one list. During fault collection, Suite coupling is set to "transmit on commit" to assure independence of the fault discovery efforts. While the producer is integrating faults reviewers cannot access the inspection objects.[1] Early prototypes only supported fault discovery during the asynchronous phase, but user feedback was strongly in favor of also supporting fault discovery during the synchronous phase, so in the current implementation participants can add additional comments synchronously during the meeting.

Synchronous Tasks. The synchronous activities of inspection include discussion of correlated faults, reaching a consensus on the faults, recording the action items, and determining the meeting status. CSI supports discussion among the participants with a teleconferencing tool named Teleconf [58]. CSI brings the target material online in a window on all participants' screens. Figure 8.9 shows schematically what the user sees during the synchronous part of software inspection. The producer leads the group through the correlated fault list. The producer orders the list as she desires (e.g., by severity of fault or by sequential order in the target material). Participants

[1]In the existing implementation access is prevented by *ad hoc* code in the fault collection object. Now that Suite access control is available [62], a better solution would be to automatically generate the access control.

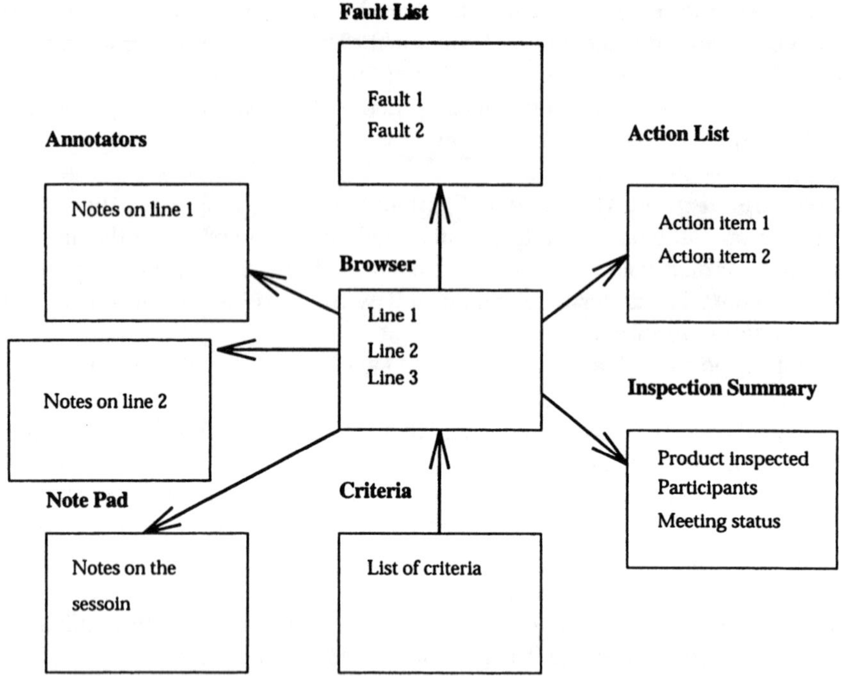

FIG. 8.9. Synchronous activities of software inspection include examining the target material, discussing faults, recording action items, and deciding the meeting status.

can also examine the original annotations at this stage to better understand the faults. The recorder lists the results of these discussions as action items. Each action item describes the fault, and gives its location, a severity rating, and what was decided. This process continues until participants address all the faults on the fault list.

During the synchronous phase, the default coupling is purely synchronous. All events, including scrolling, selection, and keystrokes, are propagated in real-time, so all users can see and discuss the same on-screen images. Periodically participants will wish to look at different sections of the document on their own. To do this they dynamically uncouple scrolling, browse on their own, and recouple scrolling to return to the group. When participants wish to perform a more asynchronous task, such as entering a newly discovered fault, they dynamically uncouple the annotation object to perform the task on their own. When the task is complete they commit the update, and restore coupling to return to the group. CSI's match of coupling modes to interactions styles helps users work together and eliminates unnecessary communication overhead.

On the basis of fault quantity and severity, the participants arrive at consensus on the meeting's status, which may be to accept the target material as is, accept it with the suggested modifications, or reject it. The recorder enters the status in the inspection summary, which also records the team members, their roles, the attendance, and the date and time of the meeting.

CSI has the capability of collecting metrics, such as the number of faults, severity of faults, status of inspection, and number of times people served on an inspection team. We have added a background monitoring module that records events as they occur in a CSI meeting. Although recording events is not part of software inspection, the monitoring makes it possible to investigate interesting research questions, such as the average time it takes for the participants to discover faults.

Eight Suite objects make up CSI: Browser, Annotator, Note Pad, Action List, Inspection Summary, Criteria, Fault List, and History Log. Each object contains a specific piece of information used in inspection and provides the access the inspection team requires. The most important objects are:

Browser displays the target material and supports hyperlinks from the target material to the Fault List and Action List. A line number precedes each line of text in the target material. When the user selects a line number, an annotation window pops up that lets the user record comments about that line.

Fault List lets the producer group the faults found by the reviewers during the individual reviews into a single list. It automatically adds summaries of the individual faults to the integrated Fault List. The Fault List helps the producer categorize faults for presentation at the inspection meeting. The producer can also accept or reject faults, sort on multiple keys, including category, disposition, time of creation, line number, and producer-specific groupings. CSI places the accepted faults at the top of the list and the rejected faults at the bottom. Rejected faults are available during the inspection meeting, so reviewers can negotiate with the producer to upgrade a fault's status to an accepted state.

Action List represents the result of the inspection meeting. The Action List includes a detailed list of faults sorted by severity, disposition, and line number, reducing the work required in the postinspection cleanup.

History Log captures CSI activities. For our study, we modified the History Log to compile data to evaluate CSI's performance versus that of a manual meeting. History Log time-stamps actions performed by all objects and writes them to a log. The data collected includes the number and severity of faults, the time taken to find a fault, and the length of the software inspection meeting.

Figure 8.10 shows the Browser containing the portion of the design document that was inspected in the case study. When a reviewer finds a fault, she opens an Annotator by clicking on the line number. The "Category" and "Dis-

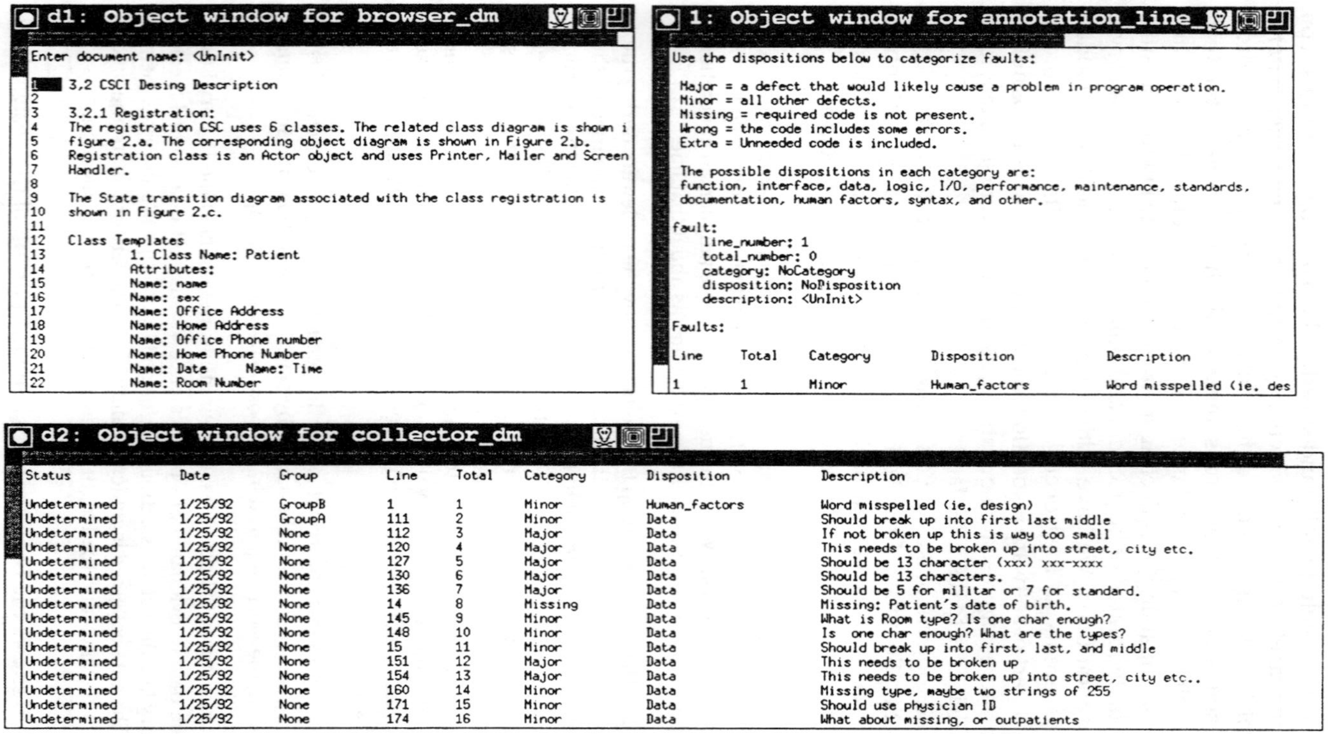

d1: Object window for browser_dm

```
Enter document name: <UnInit>

1  3.2 CSCI Desing Description
2
3  3.2.1 Registration:
4  The registration CSC uses 6 classes. The related class diagram is shown i
5  figure 2.a. The corresponding object diagram is shown in Figure 2.b.
6  Registration class is an Actor object and uses Printer, Mailer and Screen
7  Handler.
8
9  The State transition diagram associated with the class registration is
10 shown in Figure 2.c.
11
12 Class Templates
13         1. Class Name: Patient
14         Attributes:
15         Name: name
16         Name: sex
17         Name: Office Address
18         Name: Home Address
19         Name: Office Phone number
20         Name: Home Phone Number
21         Name: Date      Name: Time
22         Name: Room Number
```

1: Object window for annotation_line_

```
Use the dispositions below to categorize faults:

 Major = a defect that would likely cause a problem in program operation.
 Minor = all other defects.
 Missing = required code is not present.
 Wrong = the code includes some errors.
 Extra = Unneeded code is included.

 The possible dispositions in each category are:
 function, interface, data, logic, I/O, performance, maintenance, standards,
 documentation, human factors, syntax, and other.

fault:
    line_number: 1
    total_number: 0
    category: NoCategory
    disposition: NoDisposition
    description: <UnInit>

Faults:
```

Line	Total	Category	Disposition	Description
1	1	Minor	Human_factors	Word misspelled (ie. des

d2: Object window for collector_dm

Status	Date	Group	Line	Total	Category	Disposition	Description
Undetermined	1/25/92	GroupB	1	1	Minor	Human_factors	Word misspelled (ie. design)
Undetermined	1/25/92	GroupA	111	2	Minor	Data	Should break up into first last middle
Undetermined	1/25/92	None	112	3	Major	Data	If not broken up this is way too small
Undetermined	1/25/92	None	120	4	Major	Data	This needs to be broken up into street, city etc.
Undetermined	1/25/92	None	127	5	Major	Data	Should be 13 character (xxx) xxx-xxxx
Undetermined	1/25/92	None	130	6	Major	Data	Should be 13 characters.
Undetermined	1/25/92	None	136	7	Major	Data	Should be 5 for militar or 7 for standard.
Undetermined	1/25/92	None	14	8	Missing	Data	Missing: Patient's date of birth.
Undetermined	1/25/92	None	145	9	Minor	Data	What is Room type? Is one char enough?
Undetermined	1/25/92	None	148	10	Minor	Data	Is one char enough? What are the types?
Undetermined	1/25/92	None	15	11	Minor	Data	Should break up into first, last, and middle
Undetermined	1/25/92	None	151	12	Major	Data	This needs to be broken up
Undetermined	1/25/92	None	154	13	Major	Data	This needs to be broken up into street, city etc..
Undetermined	1/25/92	None	160	14	Minor	Data	Missing type, maybe two strings of 255
Undetermined	1/25/92	None	171	15	Minor	Data	Should use physician ID
Undetermined	1/25/92	None	174	16	Minor	Data	What about missing, or outpatients

FIG. 8.10. The participants can view the target material in the Browser object (top left) and enter faults into the Annotator object (top right). The Collector object shows the list of entered faults this far.

position" fields in the Annotator object provide a selection of values through pop-up windows.

4.5.2. Pilot Study

To assess the effectiveness of inspection in our distributed collaborative environment and compare it with face-to-face meeting, we used a case study approach with replication logic [68]. The case study is repeated by different groups and we look for the same phenomena to occur in multiple cases to confirm our observations. Here are the selected results of our case study, with our original research questions serving as a framework.

Are collaborative software inspection meetings as successful as manual software inspection meetings? Our results suggest that the CSI meetings can be as effective as face-to-face meeting. The teams performed consistently independent of the form of the meeting. Team 1 continually found more faults than Team 2 and Team 2 always found more faults than Team 3. We also compared the number of faults found in individual reviews with the number of faults reported on the action item list and found consistent performance within the teams independent of the form of the meeting. These results suggest that CSI and face-to-face meetings have similar results.

Answers to survey questions indicate the participants found CSI slightly more difficult to use than face-to-face meetings. The participants found it slightly more difficult to concentrate in the CSI meetings. Also, they felt helpful discussion was less using the CSI and Teleconf than in the face-to-face meeting.

Does the manual process fit automated software inspection? In this version of CSI, reviewers created a joint list from the individual inspections. For example, when the first reviewer found a fault, it was recorded. When the second or third reviewer found the same fault, he or she would find a fault already existed on that line and would not record the fault. This brings up a question: Do we lose fault finding capability because a fault is recorded from the viewpoint of only one person? A second person may view the fault differently leading to the detection of additional faults. At the same time, if the participants do see the the faults the same way, we enjoy a reduction in efforts by having only one person record a fault. A potential solution to this problem is to use a loose coupling mode for participants' interactions, where recorded faults are not transmitted to other participants until after fault collection has concluded. The tradeoff between recording faults single and multiple times in individual review deserves further study.

4.6. Collaborative Asynchronous Inspection of Software

Distributed software inspection frees participants from having to meet in the same place, but they are still bound to work at the same time. We find the concurrent participation in the meeting phase of software inspection to be a significant component of the total inspection cost. The time required from the meeting participants and the problem of scheduling the meeting can make the synchronous meeting the bottleneck for the inspection.

We hypothesize that asynchronizing the meeting phase will help reduce the cost of inspection. Asynchronous collaboration enables interaction without requiring all participants to be present at the same time. Relaxing the time constraint allows the participants to work at a time of their choosing, providing a greater degree of freedom in their actions.

In addition to enhancing flexibility for the participants, we hypothesize that asynchronous meetings will alleviate some of the problems that have been reported in synchronous meetings [8, 30]:

Limited Air Time: Only one person can speak at a time, limiting the time each person can contribute.

Production Blocking: Individuals have to withhold their contributions until they get a chance to report them. During the holding time, they are not producing new ideas and contributions, and may subsequently forget or decide not to offer their ideas.

Serial Thread of Execution: Because ideas are pursued serially, fewer ideas may be pursued.

Asynchronous meetings might reduce these problems by providing a structured context for the on-going meeting. Participants have an equal opportunity for airing their views, alleviating the production blocking and limited air time problems experienced in same-time, same-place meetings. Moreover, discussions may proceed in parallel, allowing several ideas to be pursued concurrently.

We propose to asynchronize software inspection by structuring the ongoing meeting activities, furnishing group decision-making capabilities for resolving issues, and providing means of communication among participants to coordinate with one another and ensure timely completion of their tasks.

4.6.1. Design and Implementation

This section applies the face-to-face inspection requirements and design elements we identified in Section 4.2.1 to asynchronous inspection, and describes the structure of our prototype for asynchronous inspection, called Collaborative Asynchronous Inspection of Software (CAIS) [46]. These ideas are presented with an eye toward their evolution and refinement as the result of lessons learned in our earlier user studies.

The primary goal of asynchronous inspection is to support a group of reviewers in inspecting software artifacts nonconcurrently. For asynchronous inspection, all the requirements identified for face-to-face inspection (see Section 4.2.1) must be met through proper computer support. We discuss each requirement separately.

Train of Thought. When asynchronizing the software inspection meeting, the serial thread of discussion of a single fault needs to be kept. This ordering allows everyone to follow the sequence of comments as they are made and subsequently add new comments. Without reviewing the earlier comments, the participants may pursue defunct lines of reasoning or make duplicate comments, and consequently disrupt the flow of a conversation. Discussions on disjoint faults, however, may occur in parallel threads. Parallelism is possible when interdependencies among disjoint faults are limited so participants can contribute to one discussion independently of the others.

The train of thought requirement also suggests a customized view for each participant, where only those discussions that are active and relevant to each individual participant are displayed. For instance, if a participant is the last person to add a comment to a discussion, the participant's customized view of the meeting should skip this discussion until there are new comments added by others.

Sharing of Information. In an asynchronous inspection meeting, participants must be able to access the inspection material, add information to it, and share their additions with other participants. For instance, the reviewers must be able to access the target material, record faults, and provide a list of their recorded faults to the producer for correlation.

Visual Cues. In an asynchronous inspection meeting, a network of links between related inspection materials can provide the visual cues necessary for participants to perform their tasks. For instance, during the discussion of a fault, the participants require access to the target material to examine a fault within the context that it occurs. By linking a fault to its place of occurrence in the target material and automatically displaying and highlighting the area of interest in the target material, the meeting participants can refamiliarize themselves with the relevant part of the target material and proceed with the discussion of the fault.

Reaching a Consensus. Asynchronous inspection meetings must provide the means for putting forth a proposal, voting on it, tallying the votes, and determining the status of the proposal.

Coordination. Asynchronous inspection meetings must support coordination of participants' activities by notifying them of the events that have occurred since their last visit and informing them of what they need to do in the present to meet the objectives of the group.

Based on our requirements above, we can discuss our design elements for building asynchronous inspectors for software artifacts:

Information Space. The information imposes a structure onto the meeting activities and artifacts, and captures and organizes the additions participants make to the information space. The components of the information space are:

Annotations: During the fault collection phase, annotations are attached to the document being inspected. During the inspection phase, the annotations are organized into a set of discussions, with hyperlinks to lines in the original document. The annotations help satisfy the Visual Cues and Sharing of Information requirements.

Discussions: Each asynchronous discussion pertains to a single fault and is comprised of any number of comments regarding that fault. The participants engage in a dialogue in an attempt to resolve their differences. Their dialogue is captured in a structured manner to allow each participant to pursue the line of reasoning offered by the other participants. Our initial implementation maintained all discussions as a single sequence, requiring the participants to visually scan the sequence to find the discussion of interest. A pilot study of that implementation revealed that users preferred to have each discussion shown separately to make locating the discussions of interest easier. In the present design, we show only the active discussions (i.e., the ones that are not decided yet) one at a time. The asynchronous discussions satisfy the Sharing of Information, Train of Thought, and Visual Cues requirements.

Proposals: The exchange of comments during the discussion phase ends when a participant puts forth a proposal to the group. Further discussion of the fault is disallowed until the status of the proposal is determined. The text of the proposal and its status are saved as part of the history of the fault, satisfying the Sharing of Information requirement.

Group Decision Making. The participants vote on a proposal. The outcomes of their votes include accepting the proposal as a resolution for their differing views, requesting continued discussion of the fault in the asynchronous meeting, abstaining from evaluating the proposal, and sending the fault to the synchronous meeting. Our choice of a voting protocol in CAIS is only one possibility in a rich voting protocol space. We have based our decision on simplicity and repeatability of results. Users can choose to make decisions based either on the unanimous or majority consensus methods. Voting satisfies the Reaching the Consensus requirement.

Communications. In a synchronous meeting, the participants can use verbal communication to inform one another of their individual and group activities. Asynchronous collaboration closes this line of communication to its users.

In a different-time meeting, computer support must provide the necessary awareness of the participants' activities and report on the state of the task.

One way to provide awareness is through a notification subsystem. A notification subsystem can help by keeping the users aware of the most urgent matters, reducing the information volume, processing and presenting the information in a digestible form, and offering advice on how to coordinate participants' activities to better complete the task. Our first asynchronous inspection prototype did not support an event notifier. Users had to visit the meeting to find out whether any new work was done since their last visit and had no idea about how much of the task was left to be done. Our current design provides participants with information on what has been done by others since their last visit, and what is needed from them to help contribute towards the conclusion of the meeting. The notification subsystem satisfies the Coordination requirement.

We define an asynchronous software inspection meeting to consist of a sequence of discussions. A discussion, in turn, is a sequence of comments, terminated by vote taking. If the result of vote taking is inconclusive, the sequence of comments is extended to accommodate more discussion of the fault. A discussion is closed when consensus is reached regarding that fault. The asynchronous meeting is closed when either all faults are addressed or the allotted time has expired. In case time has expired and there are still faults remaining to be discussed, a synchronous meeting is scheduled to complete the inspection (see Fig. 8.11).

There exist a wealth of software infrastructures for developing asynchronous inspectors [1, 3, 9, 64, 34, 41, 49]. In [46, 47, 44] we describe how three selected platforms, namely Electronic Mail, the World Wide Web, and Lotus Notes can be fruitfully explored for developing asynchronous inspectors. In this section, we detail the implementation of our prototype, called Collaborative Asynchronous Inspection of Software (CAIS), in the Suite environment.

We have chosen Suite as our application development platform foremost because of our success in building other multiuser applications in it, including CSI [45]. In the following subsection, we present the CAIS implementation in Suite by introducing the CAIS objects, presenting the group decision-making support and communications in CAIS, and demonstrating asynchronous inspection in CAIS through a scenario.

We use CSI (see Section 4.5) for the individual reviews and fault collection [45]. The correlated faults are sent to the asynchronous meeting, where CAIS is used for the discussion and resolution of the collected faults. CAIS consists of three objects (see Fig. 8.12).

Browser Object contains the document under review, with each line numbered. When a hyperlink is traversed from the fault list to the browser object, the browser is automatically scrolled to the appropriate line of the document, and the line is highlighted to aid the user in locating it.

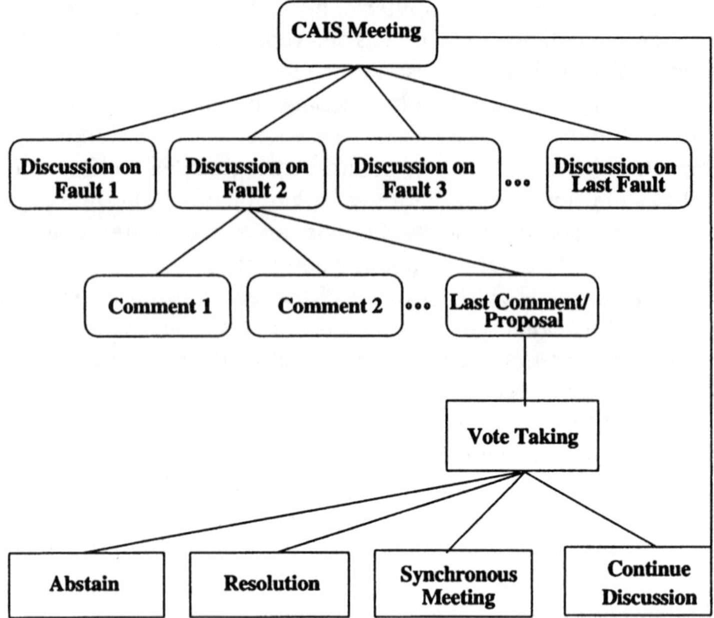

FIG. 8.11. The participants of an asynchronous inspection meeting discuss faults, with each discussion consisting of any number of comments. Once a discussion has matured, a proposal is put forth for resolving the various views, and votes are taken to determine its status. If enough votes are registered in support of the proposal, the discussion is closed. Otherwise, the discussion is reopened.

History Log Object records and time stamps the user activities for later analysis and review. The data collected include the total meeting time, participants' visitation schedules, time spent in discussions and votes, and number of comments and votes entered.

Meeting Object provides a hierarchy of faults, discussions, and comments. This structure is based loosely on a common meeting framework: A person introduces a fault, any number of people comment on it, a proposal is made to end the discussion, and a vote is taken.

In a different-time, different-place meeting, users are presented with a window in which they can enter their votes. Each CAIS participant can vote in the following ways:

Accept indicates that the inspector agrees with the proposal.

Send to Synchronous Meeting indicates that the fault is better set aside for discussion in a synchronous meeting.

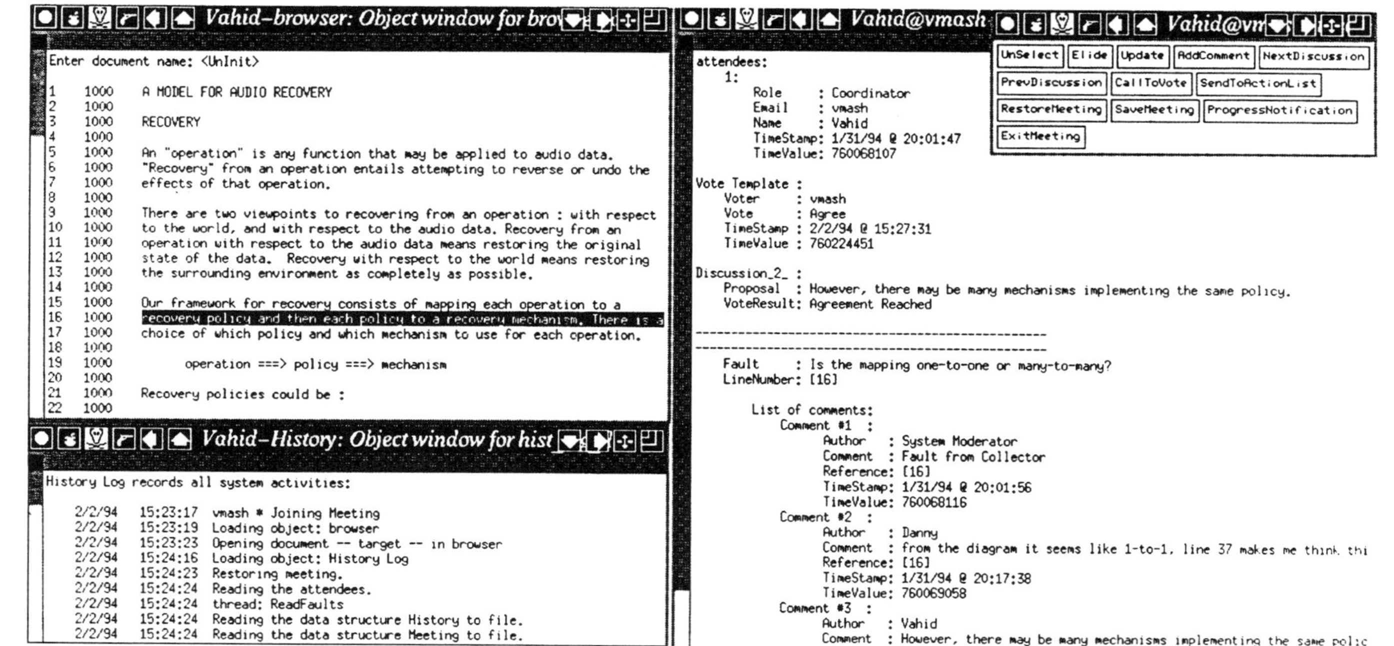

FIG. 8.12. The target material is shown in the Browser object (top left), with the area of active discussion highlighted. The Meeting object (right) displays the participant information, the vote template, and the discussion of the active fault. The History Log object (bottom left) monitors and logs the participant's activities.

Continue Discussion indicates that the call for vote might have been pre-mature and more discussion of the fault is required.

Abstain indicates that the voter wishes to stay out of decision-making process for this fault.

At the conclusion of a CAIS visit, notifications are sent to the participants using the mail delivery system. These notifications include a detailed listing of comments and votes entered by the current participant, a summary of all participants' work in their most recent visit, and an evaluation of how much of the total task has been completed up to this point. The notifications make each user aware of individual and group progress.

During a standard face-to-face meeting, the meeting protocol can change dynamically. Time limits may be imposed, new members may get to vote, or the voting method may change. These properties are also desirable for asynchronous meetings. The owner or meeting manager should be allowed to dynamically change these options based on their own preferences. For CAIS, several of these properties have been fixed for the users in order to be able to take consistent measurements for the pilot study. These options are:

1. A majority vote in agreement is sufficient to end a discussion.
2. One vote of *Send to Synchronous Meeting* ends the discussion and puts it on the agenda for the synchronous meeting. This voting option is reserved for hard problems that may be better handled face-to-face.
3. A vote of *Continue Discussion* opens the discussion of a fault again and informs the participants who have already registered votes that the discussion has been extended. This decision follows the face-to-face meeting model where a discussion may continue as long as participants are interested in it.
4. All faults not acted upon during the asynchronous meeting are sent to the synchronous meeting. This voting option is also for hard problems for which time expires, and that may be better completed face-to-face.

4.6.2. Pilot Study

The primary goal of our pilot study is to assess the feasibility of distributing the software inspection meeting across time by comparing the manual inspection meetings with CAIS meetings. We include both quantitative measurements that include time measurements and comment counts, and qualitative measurements that include feelings about the meetings, and usability issues. Here are the results of our pilot study.

Number of Faults Discussed. Participants discussed all the faults noted during the review phase of the manual and computer-supported meetings. More faults were recorded, however, when participants used CAIS. Approximately 15% of the faults discussed in the CAIS meetings were difficult to resolve asynchronously. These faults were set aside for synchronous meetings that were carried out at the conclusion of the CAIS meetings. Our analysis of the faults shows that all the faults sent to the synchronous meeting were categorized as *major* by the reviewers, indicating that it may be possible to filter out such faults prior to the CAIS meeting and send them to the synchronous meeting directly.

Number of Comments and Votes. The number of comments and votes recorded were comparable between the two meetings, with the producers having a larger share of the total.

Time for Individual Fault Collection. On the average, the participants spent less than an hour in fault collection for both meeting types. This time was spread over a 2-day period for the computer-supported meetings, and limited to a single day for the manual meetings.

Total Meeting Time. The manual meetings lasted an average of 50 minutes, with 20% spent on non-task related activities. The CAIS meetings averaged around 66 minutes, with an undeterminable percentage of time spent on non-task related activities. This total is derived from the summation of all CAIS sessions, measured from the time a user starts up the CAIS software until the user quits. We believe that the additional time spent in the asynchronous meeting is due to four factors: (a) Typing is generally slower than speaking, (b) The reading speed from the screen is about 30% slower than the reading speed from the paper [50], (c) In asynchronous collaboration, a participant is required to read the previous comments for each fault every time to familiarize herself with the context of the discussion up to that point before contributing new ideas, and (d) Because the participants had the freedom of working from home in a relaxed environment, they spent some time checking e-mail, talking to family members, and the like. This time was included as part of the reported time for the asynchronous meetings. Further studies are needed to understand the time requirements of asynchronous meetings better.

Visitation Schedules. Different participants chose to participate in the inspection at very different times. Visitation schedules ranged from early morning to late evening times. Most participants preferred to visit CAIS consistently around one time period, generating a personal meeting pattern.

Midmorning and early evening show the highest traffic, whereas early morning and late nights the lowest.

Postmanual Questionnaire. Participants were generally satisfied with the manual meeting and agreed with its structure. Scheduling a diverse work group was found to be a difficult task, requiring many rounds of negotiation before a common time was found. The amount of time spent on non-task related issues was small and limited to the exchange of pleasantries at the start and occasional friendly remarks during the meeting.

Post-CAIS Questionnaire. Participants were generally satisfied with the CAIS experience and were not hindered by their distribution across time. They found the CAIS meeting structure acceptable and were able to maintain their train of thought from one CAIS meeting to the next. CAIS matched the participation schedule of each individual participant, allowing them the freedom to meet at a time of their choosing. The notification subsystem helped the participants in coordinating their visits, but most participants preferred fewer and less detailed messages.

4.7. Evaluation of Applications Hypotheses

We have introduced distribution and asynchrony as abstractions in the domain of software engineering and have applied them to a representative software engineering task, namely software inspection. Distributed software inspection relaxes the constraint that meeting participants travel to the meeting site and physically attend the meeting. Asynchronous software inspection relaxes the constraint that all participants work together at the same time. We have designed and implemented prototypes for distributed and asynchronous inspections of software artifacts. To assess the feasibility of our hypotheses, we have performed pilot studies of our prototypes and will use their results as evidence for and against our hypotheses.

In Section 4.1 we introduced hypotheses we wished to test. Based on our experience designing, implementing, and performing experiments on software inspection, we now evaluate our hypotheses.

Our experience in designing, implementing, and conducting pilot studies suggests that distributed inspection can be as effective as face-to-face inspection. Distributed software inspections are feasible by providing a public workspace for individuals to share information, satisfying the coordination requirement of the participants by using an audio teleconferencer, and guiding participants through the inspection activities by introducing structure for the meeting. Although the distributed meeting tool was deemed more difficult to use than the face-to-face meeting, it did not hinder the participants' efforts in performing their inspection.

Hypothesis 1: Distributed software inspection can replace face-to-face software inspection. We believe distributed software inspection can replace face-to-face software inspection. Our participants preferred working from their offices and homes, and not having to travel to the inspection meeting place.

In our pilot studies, we successfully inspected software artifacts in an asynchronous environment. Our pilot studies suggest that in some cases asynchronous inspection can be as effective as face-to-face inspection, but that asynchronous discussion of some faults is inefficient. Our overall assessment is that asynchronous software inspection can be used for many faults, but some faults are best resolved synchronously.

Hypothesis 2: Asynchronized software inspection can replace face-to-face software inspection. We believe asynchronous inspection cannot replace face-to-face inspection, but can complement it by resolving a significant portion of the faults asynchronously. Although some inspections may be completely done asynchronously, there are others that require a subsequent synchronous meeting to address difficult faults left unresolved from the asynchronous meeting. When asynchronous inspection is possible, participants are likely to appreciate being able to work at a time of their choosing, and not having to deal with scheduling difficulties.

5. CONCLUSION

In the first part of this chapter, we outlined some of the principles and mechanisms that take us toward our goal of a flexible, high-level, and efficient groupware generator. The principles include:

- Generalized editing is a good basis for the design of a groupware generator.
- The sharing and communication coupling principles defined earlier.
- Functionally specify the user-interface components of an application so that an architecture offering the benefits of both the centralized and replicated architecture can be defined.
- Programs should be able to export to users data structures of arbitrary types.

The mechanisms include:

- The collaboration parameters we have designed.
- The abstractions of active variables, interaction variables, and value groups.

- Our hybrid architecture based on these abstractions.
- The Suite implementation of these abstractions and architecture.

We have separated our contributions into principles and mechanisms because the former are more general and can be expected to have a much longer lifetime. We have identified one set of mechanisms to satisfy these principles. It is possible that there are other such sets with different advantages and disadvantages.

In the second half of this chapter, we have explored the success of this infrastructure in meeting the needs of a specific collaborative application: collaborative software inspection. We have learned that the Suite infrastructure effectively supports both synchronous and asynchronous software inspection of textual documents. Further, we have demonstrated through our design, implementation experience, and pilot tests, that collaborative software inspection makes it possible for software engineers to collaborate more flexibly across time and space. Specifically, we found that:

Distributed Inspection Works: Through our implementation and in our pilot studies we learned that tools that support distributed inspection are feasible, and that participants are effective doing inspections through such a tool. Participants find the tool harder to use than face-to-face inspection, but benefit from the convenience. However, participants still found it a limitation that they all had to be online at the same time for the inspection meeting.

Asynchronous Inspection Works Partially: In our pilot studies, we successfully performed software inspection meetings, as well as fault discovery, asynchronously. Participants resolve faults effectively, and benefit from the more flexible scheduling. However, not all faults could be resolved asynchronously. Asynchrony is therefore best used as an addition to traditional inspection meetings, rather than a replacement. Asynchronous meetings fit the participation schedules of all participants, which may lead to more participation in inspection.

Automation Is Valuable: We have recently completed implementation of another software inspection tool, called AISA for Asynchronous Inspection of Software Artifacts. AISA was developed on the World Wide Web platform. AISA supports asynchronous inspection using many of the techniques used in CAIS, but goes further by providing support for inspection of images, such as software design documents. The World Wide Web automates the development of a user interface to a document, but does not provide automation for multiuser interfaces. In contrast with our experience with Suite, the World Wide Web implementation was more difficult and required many more lines of code. Furthermore, it was much easier to debug the collaboration features using Suite because most of the multiuser interface was generated automatically. A Suite-like system for automating the development of multiuser editing applications including images would be very helpful.

We have sampled here a subset of our work in this area. Other components of our work include persistent, distributed objects [20, 15], an audio server for moving sound through distributed, discrete objects [58, 6], access control [62], merging, [48] and undo–redo [5]. In addition, we have ongoing efforts to address concurrency control and extend our work on access control, undo, and merging. We are also planning to supporting collaborative editing of graphical and audio representations of active variables.

Our research has shown the benefits of simultaneously working on infrastructure and applications. The lessons learned from the applications inform the infrastructure, and the principles discovered in infrastructure research suggest new approaches to applications. For instance, by constructing collaborative applications for supporting software inspection, we have learned about the characteristics of distribution and asynchrony when applied in a particular software engineering task. This work can help us in understanding how these abstractions should be supported in general infrastructures for building collaborative applications. If distribution and asynchrony are shown to be feasible across a number of software engineering tasks, future collaborative infrastructures can integrate them as part of their offered services.

Additional research is needed in creating and studying collaborative applications, and in integrating the new abstractions into collaborative infrastructures.

ACKNOWLEDGMENTS

We thank Larry Rosenberg for the nourishment he gave the young field of collaborative systems.

We also wish to express our gratitude to anonymous referees of our proposals for their insightful comments and suggestions. We thank members of the Suite research group at Purdue University and the University of North Carolina, and the FLECSE research group at the University of Minnesota for their valuable contributions to our efforts over the years.

This research was supported in part by National Science Foundation grants IRI-9015442, IRI-9208319, IRI-9208546, IRI-9496184, and IRI-9408708, in part by a grant from the Software Engineering Research Center at Purdue University, a National Science Foundation Industry/University Cooperative Research Center (NSF Grant No. ECD-8913133), and the research funds of the Graduate School of the University of Minnesota.

REFERENCES

[1] S. R. Ahuja, J. R. Ensor, D. N. Horn, and S. E. Lucco. The Rapport multimedia conferencing system: A software overview. In *Proceedings of the Second IEEE Conference on Computer Workstations*, pages 52–58, March 1988.

[2] Barry Boehm. Industrial software metrics top 10 list. In *IEEE Software*, September 1987.

[3] Nathaniel Borenstein. Computational mail as network infrastructure for Computer-Supported Cooperative Work. In *Proceedings of the ACM Computer Supported Cooperative Work Conference*, pages 67–74. Association for Computing Machinery, November 1992.

[4] L. Brothers, V. Sembugamoorthy, and M. Miller. ICICLE: Groupware for code inspection. In *Proceedings of Computer-Supported Cooperative Work*, pages 169–181, October 1990, Los Angeles, CA.

[5] Rajiv Choudhary and Prasun Dewan. Multi-user undo/redo. Technical Report SERC-TR-125-P, Software Engineering Research Center, Purdue University, August 1992.

[6] Mark Claypool and John Riedl. Silence is golden?—The effects of silence deletion on the CPU load of an audio conference. In *Proceedings of the 1994 IEEE Multimedia Conference*, pages 9–18, Boston, May 1994.

[7] P. Cook, C. Ellis, M. Graf, G. Rein, and T. Smith. Project Nick: Meeting augmentation and analysis. *ACM Transactions on Office Information Systems*, 5(2), pages 132–146, April 1987.

[8] A. R. Dennis, J. S. Valacich, and J. F. Nunamaker, Jr. An experimental investigation of the effect of group size in an electronic meeting environment. *IEEE Transactions on Systems, Man, and Cybernetics*, 20, pages 1049–1057, 1990.

[9] P. Dewan and R. Choudhary. Flexible user interface coupling in a collaborative system. *Proceedings of the ACM CHI 91 Conference*, pages 41–49, April 1991.

[10] Prasun Dewan. A guide to Suite. Technical Report, SERC-TR-60-P, Software Engineering Research Center at Purdue University, February 1990.

[11] Prasun Dewan. A tour of the Suite user interface software. In *Proceedings of the 3rd ACM SIGGRAPH Symposium on User Interface Software and Technology*, pages 57–65, October 1990.

[12] Prasun Dewan. Designing and implementing multi-user applications: A case study. *Software-Practice and Experience*, 23(1):75–94, January 1993.

[13] Prasun Dewan. Tools for implementing multiuser user interfaces. *Trends in Software: User Interface Software*, 1, 1993.

[14] Prasun Dewan. A structured approach to designing and evaluating collaborative systems. In *Schaerding Conference on Interdisciplinary Approaches to System Anaylsis and Design*, May 1994.

[15] Prasun Dewan and Rajiv Choudhary. Experience with the Suite distributed object model. In *Proceedings of IEEE Workshop on Experimental Distributed Systems*, pages 57–63, October 1990.

[16] Prasun Dewan and Rajiv Choudhary. A high-level and flexible framework for implementing multiuser user interfaces. *ACM Transactions on Information Systems*, 10(4):345–380, October 1992.

[17] Prasun Dewan and Rajiv Choudhary. Coupling the user interfaces of a multiuser program. *ACM Transactions on Computer Human Interaction*, 2(1), 1–39, May 1995.

[18] Prasun Dewan, Rajiv Choudhary, and HongHai Shen. An editing-based characterization of the design space of collaborative applications. *Journal of Organizational Computing*, 4(3):219–240, 1994.

[19] Prasun Dewan and Marvin Solomon. An approach to support automatic generation of user interfaces. *ACM Transactions on Programming Languages and Systems*, 12(4):566–609, October 1993.

[20] Prasun Dewan and Eric Vasilik. Supporting objects in a conventional operating system. In *Proceedings of the San Diego Winter '89 Usenix Conference*, pages 273–286, February 1989.

[21] Clarence Ellis, Simon Gibbs, and Gail Rein. Groupware: Some issues and experiences. *Communications of the ACM*, 34(1), pages 39–56, January 1991.

[22] Michael Fagan. Advances in software inspections. *IEEE Transactions on Software Engineering*, 12(7):744–751, July 1986.

[23] G. Fischer, J. Grudin, A. C. Lemke, R. McCall, J. Ostwald, and B. N. Reeves. Supporting indirect, collaborative design with integrated knowledge-based design environments. *Human Computer Interaction*, 7(3):281–314.

[24] Gene Forte and Ronald Norman. A self-assessment by the software engineering community. *Communications of the ACM*, 35(4):28–32, April 1992.

[25] John Gintell and Gerard Memmi. CIA: Collaborative Inspection Agent experience: Building a CSCW application for software engineering. In *Workshop on CSCW Tools*, October 1992.

[26] Irene Greif. Design group-enabled applications: A spreadsheet example. In *Readings in Groupware and Computer-Supported Cooperative Work*, pages 621–631. Morgan Kaufmann, San Mateo, CA, 1993.

[27] Irene Greif, Robert Seliger, and William Weihl. Atomic data abstractions in a distributed collaborative editing system. In *Conference record of POPL*, January 1986.

[28] Jurg M. Haake and Brian Wilson. Supporting collaborative writing of hyperdocuments in sepia. In *Proceedings of the Conference on Computer-Supported Cooperative Work*, pages 138–146, Toronto, October 1992.

[29] Watts Humphrey. *Managing the Software Process*. Addison Wesley, Boston, 1989.

[30] Charles McLaughlin Hymes and Gary M. Olson. Unlocking brainstorming through the use of a simple group editor. In *CSCW 92 Proceedings*, November 1992.

[31] Philip M. Johnson. Supporting exploratory CSCW with the EGRET framework. In *Proceedings of the Conference on Computer-Supported Cooperative Work*, pages 298–305, Toronto, October 1992.

[32] Philip M. Johnson and Danu Tjahjono. Improving software quality through computer supported collaborative review. In *Proceedings of the Third European Conference on Computer Supported Cooperative Work*. Association for Computing Machinery, September 1993.

[33] Philip M. Johnson, Danu Tjahjono, Dadong Wan, and Robert S. Brewer. Experiences with CSRS: An instrumented software review environment. In *Software Quality*, October 1993.

[34] Simon Kaplan, William Tolone, Douglas Bogia, and Celsina Bignoli. Flexible, active support for collaborative work with ConversationBuilder. In *Proceedings of the ACM Computer-Supported Cooperative Work Conference*. Association for Computing Machinery, Toronto, October 1992.

[35] Simon M. Kaplan, William J. Tolone, Douglas P. Bogia, and Celsina Bignoli. Flexible, active support for collaborative work with conversationbuilder. In *Proceedings of CSCW'92*, November 1992.

[36] John C. Knight and E. Ann Myers. An improved inspection technique. *Communications of the ACM*, 36(11):51–61, November 1993.

[37] Michael J. Knister and Atul Prakash. Distedit: A distributed toolkit for supporting multiple group editors. In *Proceedings of ACM Conference on Computer-Supported Cooperative Work*, pages 343–356, October 1990.

[38] Kenneth L. Kraemer and John Leslie King. Computer-based systems for cooperative work and group decision making. *ACM Computing Surveys*, 20(2), June 1988.

[39] Keith A. Lantz. An experiment in integrated multimedia conferencing. In *Proceedings of the Conference on Computer-Supported Cooperative Work*, pages 267–275, December 1986.

[40] J. C. Lauwers and K. A. Lantz. Collaboration awareness in support of collaboration transparency: Requirements for the next generation of shared window systems. In *Proceedings of ACM CHI'90*, pages 303–312, April 1990.

[41] Lotus Development Corporation. *Lotus Notes: The Groupware Standard*, release 3 edition, 1993.

[42] Thomas W. Malone and Kevin Crowston. Towards an interdisciplinary theory of coordination. Technical Report CCS-TR-120, MIT Center for Coordination Science, April 1991.

[43] Johnny Martin and Wei-Tek Tsai. *N*-Fold inspection: A requirements analysis technique. *Communications of the ACM*, 33(2):225–232, February 1990.

[44] Vahid Mashayekhi. *Distribution and Asynchrony in Concurrent Software Engineering*. PhD thesis, University of Minnesota, Minneapolis, MN, March 1995.

[45] Vahid Mashayekhi, Janet Drake, Wei-Tek Tsai, and John Riedl. Distributed, collaborative software inspection. *IEEE Software*, 10(5), September 1993.

[46] Vahid Mashayekhi, Chris Feulner, and John Riedl. CAIS: Collaborative Asynchronous Inspection of Software. In *The Second ACM SIGSOFT Symposium on the Foundations of Software Engineering*, December 1994.

[47] Vahid Mashayekhi, Bob Glamm, and John Riedl. *AISA: Asynchronous Inspection of Software Artifacts*. Technical report, University of Minnesota, 1995.

[48] Jon Munson and Prasun Dewan. A flexible object merging framework. In *Proceedings of the ACM Conference on Computer-Supported Cooperative Work*, pages 231–242, October 1994.

[49] Christine Neuwirth, David Kaufer, Ravinder Chandhok, and James Morris. Computer support for distributed collaborative writing: Defining parameters of interaction. In *Proceedings of the ACM Computer-Supported Cooperative Work Conference*, pages 145–153. Association for Computing Machinery, October 1994.

[50] Jakob Nielsen. *Hypertext and Hypermedia*. Academic Press, San Diego, 1990.

[51] Gary M. Olson, Lola J. McGuffin, Eiji Kuwanan, and Judith S. Olson. Designing software for a group's needs. *Trends in Software: Special Issue on User Interface Software*, pages 129–196, 1993.

[52] J. S. Olson, G. M. Olson, M. Storrosten, and M. Carter. How a group editor changes the character of a design meeting as well as its outcome. In *Proceedings of the ACM Conference on Computer Supported Cooperative Work*, pages 91–98, October 1992.

[53] David L. Parnas and David M. Weiss. Active design reviews: Principles and practices. *Journal of Systems and Software*, 7:259–265, 1987.

[54] Stephen T. Pope. A cookbook for using the model-view-controller user interface paradigm in smalltalk-80. *Journal of Object-Oriented Programming*, 1(3):26–49, August/September 1988.

[55] Brad Quinn Post. Building the business case for group support technology. In *Proceedings of the Hawaii System Sciences Conference*, pages 34–45, January 1992.

[56] Calton Pu, Gail E. Kaiser, and Norman Hutchinson. Split-transactions for open-ended activities. In *Proceedings of the 14th VLDB Conference*, Los Angeles, 1988.

[57] Steven P. Reiss. Connecting tools using message passing in the field environment. *IEEE Software*, 7(4):57–66, July 1990.

[58] John Riedl, Vahid Mashayekhi, Jim Schnepf, Mark Claypool, and Dan Frankowski. SuiteSound: A system for distributed collaborative multimedia. *IEEE Transactions on Knowledge and Data Engineering*, August 1993.

[59] Mark Roseman and Saul Greenberg. Groupkit: A groupware toolkit for building real-time conferencing applications. *Proceedings of the ACM Conference on Computer-Supported Work*, pages 43–50, November 1992.

[60] Sunil Sarin and Irene Greif. Computer-based real-time conferencing systems. *IEEE Computer*, 18(10):33–49, October 1985.

[61] G. Michael Schneider, Johnny Martin, and Wei-Tek Tsai. An experimental study of fault detection in user requirements documents. *ACM Transactions on Software Engineering and Methodology*, 1(2):188–204, April 1992.

[62] Honghai Shen and Prasun Dewan. Access control for collaborative environments. In *Proceedings of the ACM Conference on Computer-Supported Cooperative Work*, pages 51–58, November 1992.

[63] M. J. Stefik, D. G. Bobrowand, and K. M. Kahn. Integrating access-oriented programming into a multiparadigm environment. *IEEE Software*, 3(1):10–18, January 1986.

[64] Robert H. Thomas, Harry C. Forsdick, Terrence R. Crowley, Richard W. Schaaf, Raymond S. Tomlinson, Virginia M. Travers, and George G. Robertson. Diamond: A multimedia message system built on a distributed architecture. *IEEE Computer*, 18(3), December 1985.

[65] Walter Tichy. RCS—A system for version control. *Software Practice and Experience*, 15(7):637–654, July 1985.

[66] Kazuo Watabe, Shiro Sakata, Kazutoshi Maeno, Hideyuki Fukuoka, and Kazuyuki Maebara. A distributed multiparty desktop conferencing system and its architecture. In *Proceedings of the Ninth Annual International Phoenix Conference on Computers and Communications*, pages 386–393, March 1990.

[67] W. E. Woodson. *Human Engineering Guide*. University of California Press, Berkeley and Los Angeles, 1954.

[68] Robert Yin. *Case Study Research: Design and Methods*. Sage Publications, Newbury Park, CA, 1989.

[69] Edward Yourdon. *Structured Walkthrough*. Prentice-Hall, Englewood Cliffs, NJ, 1989.

CHAPTER

9

Cooperative Support for Distributed Supervisory Control

Christopher A. Jasek
Patricia M. Jones
University of Illinois at Urbana-Champaign

Distributed supervisory control systems consist of a group of agents (humans or computers) that control a complex, dynamic, event-driven system (e.g., nuclear power plants, satellite ground control). The control is *distributed* in the sense that each of the agents has a particular responsibility in the control process. For example, agents may be responsible for controlling a single subsystem or for managing and coordinating other agents. The control is *supervisory* in that the agents supervise a highly automated process; their major duties typically include system configuration, monitoring, occasional control actions to fine-tune the system, the execution of standard operating procedures, scheduling and preplanning of future activities, and diagnosis and compensation for abnormal system conditions (e.g., Hollnagel, Mancini, & Woods, 1988; Jones & Mitchell, 1995; Sheridan & Johannsen, 1976).

Distributed supervisory control environments are complex, dynamic, and event driven. By *complex*, we mean that the controlled system (e.g., the nuclear power plant or the satellite and its ground control system) consists of many parts that interact in complex ways. The effects of control actions taken by human operators may be delayed or have nonintuitive consequences due to the characteristics of the process being controlled. By *dynamic* and *event-driven*, we mean that the environment "changes by itself" as well as a result of agents' control actions. Such *operations* environments are much different from the self-paced, artifact-centered environments (e.g., design, scientific visualization and analysis, collaborative writing) in many

CSCW studies (Reeves & Shipman, 1992; Smith & Smith, 1991). (Similar distinctions in taxonomies of knowledge are discussed in Harel & Pnueli, 1985; Larson & LaFasto, 1989; Leitch & Gallanti, 1992; also see Jones, 1995.) In particular, rather than the cooperative creation, study, and revision of a shared artifact (e.g., a design or a document), cooperative work in distributed supervisory control involves timely coordination of control actions, verification of the effects of control actions, and ongoing situation assessment and diagnosis. In artifact-centered environments, people debate, negotiate, and can "undo" their actions. In operations environments, there is usually no time to debate and often actions cannot be undone. Action is constrained by time and system dynamics and thus the smooth and timely coordination of activity is vital. Routine negotiation in these environments primarily occurs "off-line."

This chapter describes a particular distributed supervisory control environment (flight operations at NASA Goddard Space Flight Center) and proposes a software architecture to support cooperative work in real-time flight operations. In Section 1, the flight operations environment is described with respect to the types of cooperation identified in a field study. Section 2 describes how we modeled cooperative work in flight operations and thus how we designed the software architecture named ISAM (Intelligent Support for Activity Management). Section 3 describes the graphical interface to ISAM for the flight operations team; this ISAM client is named Cooperative Support for Mission Operations (CoSMO). Section 4 discusses an evaluation study that compared ISAM as a *mediator* (shared visualization only) to ISAM as an *associate* (shared visualization plus the ability to allocate activities to ISAM). In other words, ISAM as mediator provides a shared visualization that mediates the interaction between members of the flight operations team; ISAM as associate is in a sense "another team member" to which activities can be allocated as well. Section 5 indicates directions for future research.

1. COOPERATION IN SAMPEX FLIGHT OPERATIONS

Flight operations is the task of monitoring and commanding a scientific spacecraft after it is in orbit. A field study of the Solar Anomalous Magnetospheric Particle Explorer (SAMPEX) mission operations room at NASA Goddard Space Flight Center was conducted in August of 1992 (Jones & Goyle, 1993). The study focused on identifying the cooperation that occurs between the members of the Flight Operations Team. A brief summary of that study follows.

1.1. Background on SAMPEX Flight Operations

The scientific mission of SAMPEX is to measure the "elemental and isotopic composition of solar energetic particles, anomalous cosmic rays, and galactic cosmic rays" (SAMPEX FLOP, p. 2-1) via a collection of sophisticated scientific instruments. The SAMPEX Flight Operations Team is responsible for the day to day operations of the SAMPEX spacecraft. The team's mission is to ensure the health and safety of the spacecraft and to transmit scientific data to mission scientists. On a typical day, four *passes* (or real-time contacts) with the SAMPEX spacecraft occur. Each pass is preplanned to accomplish certain routine activities (e.g., calibrate the clock onboard SAMPEX or to download data from SAMPEX) with certain routine outputs (e.g., standard reports or data files). Two examples of standard reports are pass plans and anomaly reports. The *pass plan* summarizes the activities that occurred during the pass and the numeric values of critical spacecraft parameters, and an *anomaly report* describes a problem that occurred during the pass, its possible cause, and its solution.

A pass can be also be described in terms of three sequential stages: prepass (before spacecraft data transmission to the ground), on-pass (during data transmission), and post-pass (after data transmission). Pre-pass activities include configuration of ground equipment and verification of communications with other facilities. On-pass activities include the concurrent management of monitoring and commanding functions. Post-pass activities include filling out reports and transmitting data files to scientists.

The SAMPEX Flight Operations Team uses four networked UNIX workstations to receive and display data and to send commands to SAMPEX. The computer hardware and software that the SAMPEX team uses—a specialized computer called a front-end processor and the four UNIX workstations and their graphical user interface environment—is the first example of the so-called Transportable Payload Operations Control Center (TPOCC, pronounced *tee-pok*). TPOCC represents a significant advance in ground control room technology because of its reliance on portable and generic computing hardware and software (e.g., UNIX workstations and Motif-based graphical user interfaces). A critical feature of the TPOCC environment is its flexibility. All members of the Flight Operations Team are trained on how to customize displays and write software procedures. Thus, as the mission requirements change over time, the team can adapt its software environment to support those new requirements. When the team is not engaged in real-time contact with the spacecraft, they continually work to routinize the activities that will be accomplished in real time (e.g., with the use of scripted software procedures or "procs"; see Jones, 1995, for a detailed example).

1.2. Cooperative Work in SAMPEX Flight Operations

Two members of the Flight Operations Team are present in the mission operations room; one assumes the role of command controller (i.e., monitors status of ground systems and performs spacecraft commanding) and the other the role of spacecraft analyst (i.e., monitors details of spacecraft health and safety; Jones, 1995; Jones, Patterson, & Goyle, 1993). These roles are not defined explicitly at the organizational level, but rather are a usual convention among NASA flight operations teams to structure their work. Usually the more experienced team member serves as the spacecraft analyst because of the more complex and detailed nature of knowledge necessary to monitor spacecraft effectively.

As noted before, in the current TPOCC environment, four UNIX workstations are utilized in routine operations. Team members use two workstations each and configure their own displays in accordance with their particular role. Although there are some individual differences in how members configure displays (see Jones & Goyle, 1993), frequently display configuration is largely routinized, even to the point of some team members writing custom software procedures to do this configuration.

During the stages of a pass, the command controller and spacecraft analyst each perform different tasks (Jones, Patterson, & Goyle, 1993; see Table 9.1). During pre-pass, the command controller typically configures the system, which is a prerequisite for the spacecraft analyst to configure displays. The command controller also performs verification with the groundstation, while the spacecraft analyst continues to configure displays and also collects forms to be filled out for the upcoming support. During the on-pass stage, both the command controller and spacecraft analyst participate in monitoring. This activity is mostly distributed; the command controller monitors ground systems and the spacecraft analyst monitors the spacecraft. Occasionally, however, the team members do look at each other's displays. Spacecraft commanding is a more tightly coupled activity. During this function, the spacecraft analyst will often read the commands to be typed by the command controller; both will double-check the syntax, and then the command controller will uplink the command to the spacecraft. During post-pass, coordination again becomes distributed. The command controller and spacecraft analyst both prepare different reports and occasionally collaborate to verify information. The command controller is typically responsible for the transmission of scientific data to the mission scientists and other file management tasks. Furthermore, during fault detection, planning, and recovery, the command controller and spacecraft analyst coordinate explicitly (verbally) and negotiate throughout the process of problem solving.

TABLE 9.1
Tasks of the Command Controller and Spacecraft Analyst During Different Stages of a Pass.

Stage	*Function*	*Command Controller*	*Spacecraft Analyst*
Pre-Pass	Configuration	Configures equipment and displays	Configures displays
	verification	coordinates with groundstation on voice and data lines	collects paperwork
On-Pass	monitoring	monitors ground systems	monitors spacecraft health and safety
	commanding	executes commands, and verifies consequences	verifies input and consequences
	bookkeeping	prepares clock check	begins filling out pass plan
Post-Pass	bookkeeping	performs file management tasks and prepares ground anomaly reports if necessary	prepares pass plan, solid state recorder log, and spacecraft anomaly reports if necessary

Note. The shaded regions indicate a more tightly coupled interaction between the command controller and spacecraft analyst. From Patterson (1993). Adapted with permission.

1.2.1. Schmidt's Taxonomy of Cooperative Work. A taxonomy of reasons for cooperative work distinguishes between augmentative (more than one individual is needed to accomplish a "high workload" task), integrative (the integration of technique-based specializations), or debative (the integration of perspective-based specializations; Schmidt, 1991). In the case of flight operations, cooperation is dynamic, exhibiting varying degrees of augmentative and integrative cooperation in different circumstances. Cooperation is augmentative during emergency or abnormal situations in which more than one person is needed for effective system control (i.e., redundancy is important in complex systems to cope with unanticipated variability in the future). Cooperation is integrative in that the command controller and spacecraft analyst have somewhat specialized roles during a pass. The spacecraft analyst generally has more experience with the SAMPEX spacecraft system and monitors these systems during the pass. The command controller is responsible for the configuration and monitoring of the TPOCC ground systems.

Furthermore, cooperation can be classified according to location (proximate [same place] or remote [different place]), time (synchronous [same time] or asynchronous [different time]), direct (face-to-face) or machine-mediated; and degree of coupling (distributed or semiautonomous vs. collective cooperation; Ellis, Gibbs, & Rein, 1991; Johansen & Swigart, 1994; Schmidt, 1991). In real-time flight operations, cooperation occurs proximately and synchronously (same time, same place) and directly (face-to-face interaction). Operators also cooperate remotely and synchronously over voice links with other facilities, synchronously and proximately between shifts through verbal reports, and also asynchronously and remotely via a whiteboard, logbook, and bookkeeping artifacts. As described earlier, the cooperation between the command controller and spacecraft analyst is mostly distributed during routine operations but is more collective during high-critical tasks and in abnormal situations.

1.2.2. Other Taxonomies of Cooperative Work. With respect to other well-known taxonomies of group work, the flight operations environment is largely same time–same place (Johansen & Swigart, 1994) and is "high" both on the dimensions of common task and shared environment (Ellis et al., 1991). The "Arizona Groupware Grid" (Briggs & Nunamaker, 1994) distinguishes between individual, coordination, and collaboration work and communication, thinking, and information availability. With respect to this framework, real-time flight operations is largely a "thinking and coordination" function. McGrath (1990) distinguished between production, member support, and group well-being functions and four general stages of problem solving (inception [goal choice], problem solving [means choice], conflict resolution [political choice], and execution [goal attainment]). In a related formulation, McGrath and Hollingshead (1994) proposed generate, choose, negotiate, and execute as four basic categories of activity. Most of real-time flight operations is routinized and procedural; thus, in terms of this framework, generally activity can be viewed as straightforward moves from inception/generation to execution, although most of "generation" takes place offline. A similar but more natural characterization of real-time operations is the "management of the flow of events" (Rasmussen, Brehmer, & Leplat, 1991); this emphasizes the cyclic, ongoing coping with a dynamic environment. Temporal constraints have a large influence on group processes (McGrath, 1990); certainly in the case of real-time operations, activity is coordinated at a relatively high tempo to achieve goals, and the pacing of required activity means that operators focus on smoothly coordinating activities with relatively little verbal interplay. However, critical activities and unexpected events exhibit more explicit verbal behavior and "choosing and negotiating" functions as noted earlier.

2. MODELING AND SUPPORTING COOPERATION IN REAL-TIME FLIGHT OPERATIONS

The four "conceptual primitives" that we used to model the flight operations task and to build our software architecture are Activities, Information, Artifacts, and System Objects. We argue that an activity-centered representation is crucial for real-time operational tasks (hence the primacy of Activity Objects) and that part of the context of activity relates to the transient sources of information in the environment (Information Objects) which in turn provide "snapshots" of the state of the real world (System Objects). Also, Artifact Objects represent critical resources that act as inputs, outputs, and guides to activity. These conceptual primitives are organized into a software architecture named ISAM (Intelligent Support for Activity Management).

2.1. Modeling Activity

The notion of activity is central to any task, but is especially important in cooperative distributed supervisory control environments because these environments are dynamic and event driven, involve much preplanning, and involve the coordination of activity between multiple agents. The normative modeling of activity is important in supporting cooperative work in flight operations because it is necessary to know what activities should occur, when (in response to what event or situation) they should occur, and who should perform them.

The operator function model (OFM) offers a structure that accounts for the management of multiple concurrent activities in dynamic event-driven worlds (Jones, Chu, & Mitchell, 1995; Mitchell, 1987). It is represented as a hierarchic network of nodes which represents activities at various levels of abstraction (e.g., function, subfunction, task, and action). Directed arcs that connect the nodes at the same level represent system triggering events or the successful completion of the originating activity. The OFM is an attractive modeling framework for developing computer support for distributed supervisory control because it is normative (i.e., specifies requirements for activity) and computational (i.e., can be straightforwardly mapped into software; Jones et al., 1995). It has been used as the basis for display design and intelligent support concepts in a variety of supervisory control applications (e.g., Bushman, Mitchell, Jones, & Rubin, 1993; Chu, Mitchell, & Jones, 1995; Cohen, 1990; Jones & Mitchell, 1995; Mitchell & Saisi, 1987; Verfurth, 1991). All of this work has focused on modeling the behavior of a single human operator. However, the OFM can be straightforwardly extended to account for multiple agents (Jones & Goyle, 1993; Jones & Mitchell, 1995) by adding another property to activities in the OFM that specifies who (what agent) is performing them.

A portion of the OFM for SAMPEX flight operations is shown in Fig. 9.1. This part of the model shows the activity requirements for Solid State Recorder operations. These operations involve manipulating the memory on the spacecraft which contains data about the spacecraft's subsystems and instruments. During certain designated passes, the Flight Operations Team is required to perform a set of activities known collectively as "SSR Operations" as partially described in Fig. 9.1. These activities include the downlink or "dump" of portions of the memory (e.g., those containing information about "significant events," system diagnostics, and instrument history). These subfunctions are furthermore decomposed into tasks which commonly involve initiating the subfunction and verifying that it was executed properly. Operator actions which support tasks are represented in the lowest level of the model (e.g., looking at the Events display page supports the task of verifying the correct downlink of the significant events).

The arrows in Fig. 9.1 represent the events that "trigger" a particular activity. For example, the arrow entering the "SSR Operations" activity is labeled with "AOS" (Acquisition Of Signal from the spacecraft by the groundstation); thus, the "SSR Operations" activity should be performed by the operators when "AOS" occurs. Nonlabeled arrows denote completion of an activity.

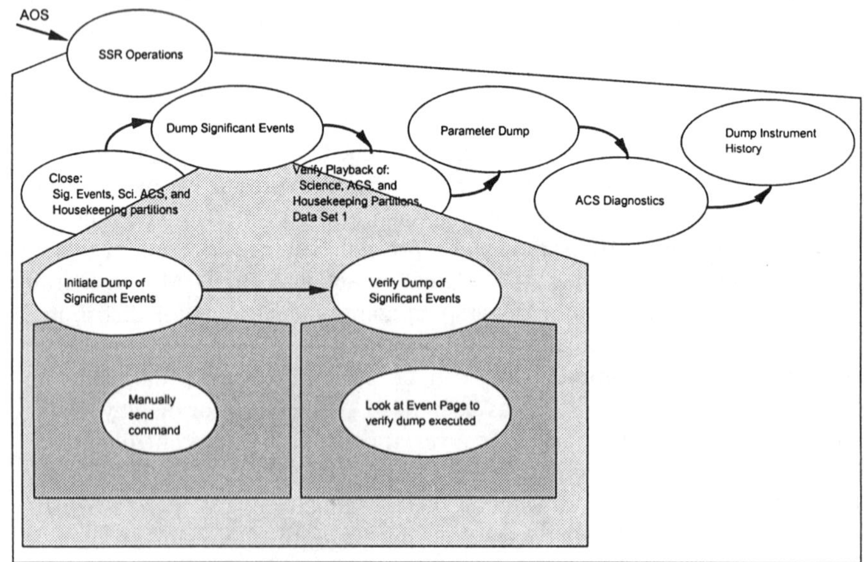

FIG. 9.1. Example portion of SAMPEX OFM. From Jones and Jasek (1997). Reprinted with permission.

The representation of activities in the original formulation of the OFM as described earlier is insufficient to model important aspects of cooperative work. An activity model that supports cooperation also needs to explicate the interdependencies between activities (e.g., temporal and resource constraints; Fox, Chionglo, & Fadel, 1993; Malone & Crowston, 1990). There are many temporal constraints in flight operations. For example, certain activities occur at an absolute time relative to the beginning of the pass; passes themselves provide a fixed time window in which to accomplish activities; and operators cannot verify the results of a command until after it has been uplinked to the spacecraft (i.e., prerequisite constraints). For effective performance, it is critical for such constraints to be taken into account. Resource constraints, such as those associated with computer usage, are also present but have been managed over time to be nearly invisible for most real-time operational tasks in the SAMPEX flight operations environment. Thus, another important extension of the OFM to support distributed supervisory control is to explicitly model such interdependencies. Hence, the notion of triggering events is broadened to consider both "preconditions" and "postconditions" of activity that include temporal, prerequisite, and resource constraints as well as references to artifact and information objects.

In particular, the representation of Activity Objects in the ISAM architecture is as follows. *Activities* correspond directly to nodes within the OFM. Each activity has a *name*, *purpose*, and *level* in the OFM hierarchy. The hierarchic relationships among activities are represented with *parent* and *child* attributes. Activities also have *preconditions* and *postconditions*. Preconditions describe the conditions that must be true for an activity to occur and correspond to triggering events in the OFM. For example, in SAMPEX, an anomaly report is written if a spacecraft parameter is outside the limits of its normal value; therefore, the "write anomaly report" activity has the precondition of a parameter being out of limits. Postconditions represent the conditions that are true when an activity is complete. These allow the completion of an activity to be verified. For example, when the "write anomaly report" activity is complete, the anomaly report artifact will be completely "filled-in." The *priority* of an activity represents the activity's importance in the system. For example, activities that involve fault repair are more critical to system operation than writing reports. Temporal information about an activity is represented by its *status*, *expected start time*, *expected duration*, and *percent completion*. This information describes the interdependencies between activities and also provides planning information. Activities also have a *who* attribute that describes what agent is performing the activity. Finally, activities have links to relevant *system objects*, *artifacts*, and *information objects*. Links are provided to these objects to allow operators to view the data and information relevant to this activity, and also to provide them with a different perspective to the cooperation occurring in the system.

2.2. Other Elements of Coordination: Artifacts and Information Objects

The focus on activities and their interdependencies is only one perspective of cooperation. A focus on the flow of data through a system provides an additional view of how activities are related to each other and forms part of the context in which activities are being performed. In particular, data are modeled as artifact and information objects.

Artifacts are persistent objects that evolve and get "filled in" as activities within the system are accomplished. They serve as input to an activity, guidance for the accomplishment of an activity, and output of an activity. Examples of artifacts are documents or forms that guide and record the accomplishment of activities (e.g., pass plan).

Information objects are temporary structures that hold information as it is created and transmitted through the system. They represent the information content being sent, its source and destination, whether the information was requested or not and by whom, the priority of the information, the time the information was created, and modality of the information (e.g., auditory or visual). Computer displays and the telephone calls are examples of information objects.

Information flow can be modeled with a data flow diagram. A data flow diagram is a software engineering tool that is used to describe the functioning of a software system in detail. Traditionally, the data flow diagram technique (Kowal, 1992) focuses on specifying the data flowing into and out of program modules; however, we use the technique to model information flowing into and out of activities. In this sense, we are expanding what is considered to be data in the original technique to include computer displays, paper reports, and operational documentation.

Figure 9.2 shows an example of a data flow diagram for SAMPEX flight operations. In this diagram, a rectangular, numbered box represents an activity. The activities are hierarchically decomposed (e.g., activity 1.0 is decomposed into activities 1.1, 1.2, and 1.3 which are not shown), and this is shown graphically as a shadow around the activity box. Labeled arrows entering an activity box from any direction indicate the specific information inputs or preconditions of the activity. Labeled arrows exiting an activity box indicate the information outputs or postconditions of the activity. Arrows may also originate from or point to the other graphical symbols described next.

Horizontal boxes that are open at the right end are called data stores and are permanent stores of information (i.e., artifacts). Some common data stores in the flight operations domain are operations manuals, flight logs, computer reports, pass plans, and computer files. Rectangular, "torn page" icons represent temporary information that is created "on the fly" for a particular activity to use (i.e., information objects). Examples of temporary

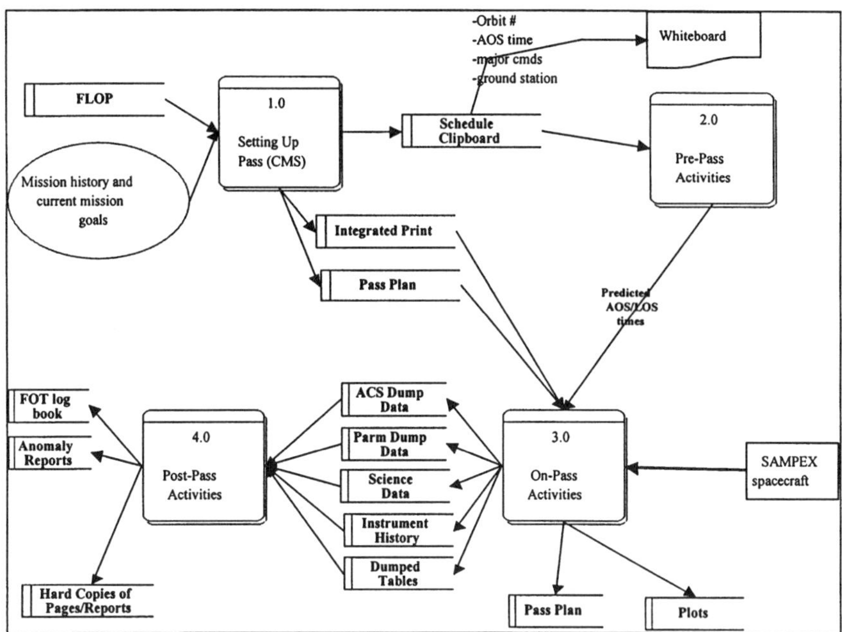

FIG. 9.2. Portion of the data flow diagram for SAMPEX mission operations. From Jones and Jasek (1997). Reprinted with permission.

information are whiteboards, telephone calls, and computer displays. Finally, ovals represent other categories of information (e.g., historical information) that are also inputs to activity.

In the ISAM architecture, Artifact and Information Objects are represented simply in a common, generic format as a collection of slots (parameters). For example, a pass plan artifact contains parameters such as time of the pass, orbit number, and groundstation name.

2.3. Domain Knowledge (System Objects)

The final element needed to be modeled to support cooperation in complex systems is the controlled system itself (i.e., the real-world system that is being monitored and controlled). In monitoring, diagnosis, and control, detailed knowledge of the system aids operators in understanding the complex relationships between different system components. This knowledge is represented as *system objects* that represent a hierarchical decomposition of the components of the controlled system. For example, the SAMPEX spacecraft consists of many subsystems: power, attitude control, communications, and data storage. The subsystems in turn can be described as collections of interrelated components. For example, two components of the power subsystem are the battery and the bus. Furthermore, the components are characterized by parameter values (e.g., a battery is characterized by its voltage and temperature). In ISAM, System Objects are represented simply as a collection of parameters. For example, a spacecraft battery system object contains parameters such as voltage, current, and temperature.

2.4. ISAM System Architecture

The two main parts of the ISAM architecture, as shown in Fig. 9.3, are the object knowledge base and the current context representation. The object knowledge base contains all the activity objects, system objects, information objects, and artifact objects for a particular application. The current context representation contains the current instantiation (or current state)

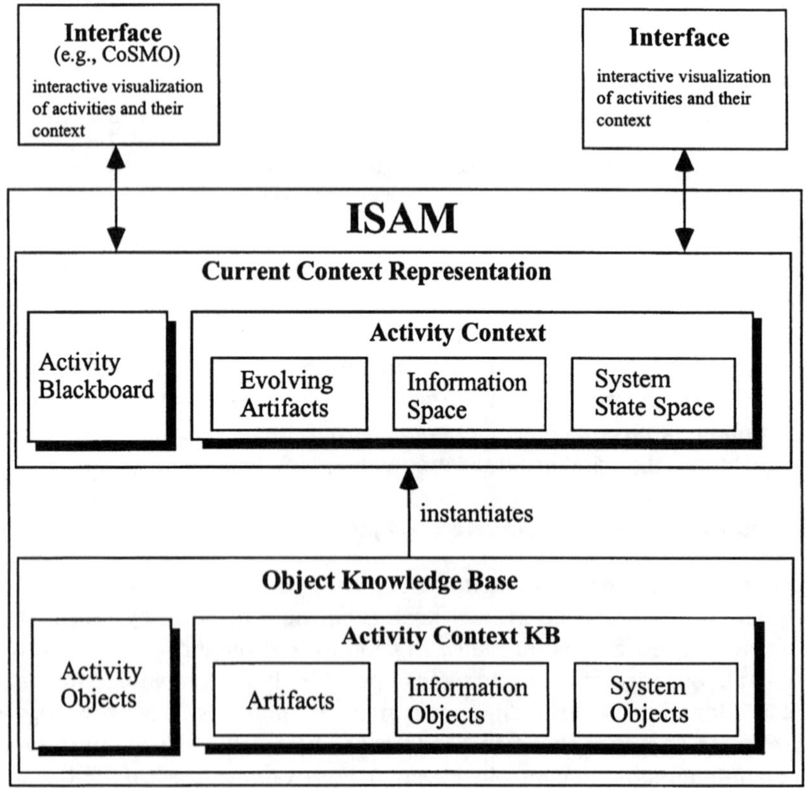

FIG. 9.3. ISAM system architecture. From Jones and Jasek (1997). Reprinted with permission.

of activities and other ISAM objects. These are represented by a current set of evolving artifacts, information space, system state space, and the activity blackboard. Evolving artifacts represent the current state of relevant artifacts. The information space consists of the current information objects. The system state space consists of the current value or status of each system object in the object knowledge base.

The activity blackboard represents the current state of activities (i.e., if they are complete, who is performing them, and when they began). Only the activities that are relevant to the current situation (according to their preconditions) appear on the blackboard. In the case of SAMPEX, for example, an activity to write an anomaly report would only appear if a fault was detected during the pass. Thus, activities on the blackboard represent the current context of work and can be used to interpret operator actions (and also to generate advice and reminders if expected actions do not occur).

A note on what we mean by a *blackboard* is in order here. The blackboard method of problem solving (Nii, 1986) is a well-known artificial intelligence approach to problem solving. It is a flexible model in which a central repository or *blackboard* maintains a current best hypothesis about some evolving situation. The blackboard's state changes as independent *knowledge sources* place, delete, or modify information or knowledge on the blackboard. ISAM's blackboard is based on the OFMspert architecture (Jones & Mitchell, 1995; Jones, Mitchell, & Rubin, 1990; Rubin, Jones, & Mitchell, 1988). In OFMspert, the blackboard data structure corresponds to levels of the operator function model, and knowledge sources post and interpret representations of operator activity on that blackboard. Thus, at any point in time, the state of the blackboard reflects expectations about what the human operator needs to do as well as the extent to which those expectations have been met by operator actions. In other words, OFMspert provides infrastructure for dynamic activity tracking or intent inferencing—a critical resource for providing context-sensitive support in real time.

Client interface applications can be connected to ISAM that allow the operators to visualize the current context representation from various perspectives. Multiple interfaces can be connected simultaneously to the current context in ISAM, allowing several operators to view the current system state simultaneously and thus creating a shared information space. An example of a client interface for the flight operations domain is CoSMO (Cooperative Support for Mission Operations), as described next.

3. CoSMO APPLICATION

CoSMO (Cooperative Support for Mission Operations) is the ISAM application interface to support flight operations for SAMPEX. Because of the prominence of activities in real-time flight operations, the CoSMO interface is "activity-driven." Essentially, CoSMO's interface is direct visualization of the activity blackboard. Activities on the interface are arranged temporally by *expected start time* as in a Gantt-Chart. Time increases from left to right across the screen, and the current time with respect to the beginning of the pass is displayed on a time bar at the bottom of the screen. Activities toward the left of the screen are expected to occur at the beginning of a pass, and activities toward the right occur at the end of a pass. The width of an activity box indicates the *expected duration* of the activity. Activities are also arranged hierarchically along the vertical dimension. Figure 9.4a shows an example of the CoSMO interface. The children of activities as specified in the OFM appear inside the activity box of their parent. These activities have the sequential constraints suggested by their visual representation on the interface.

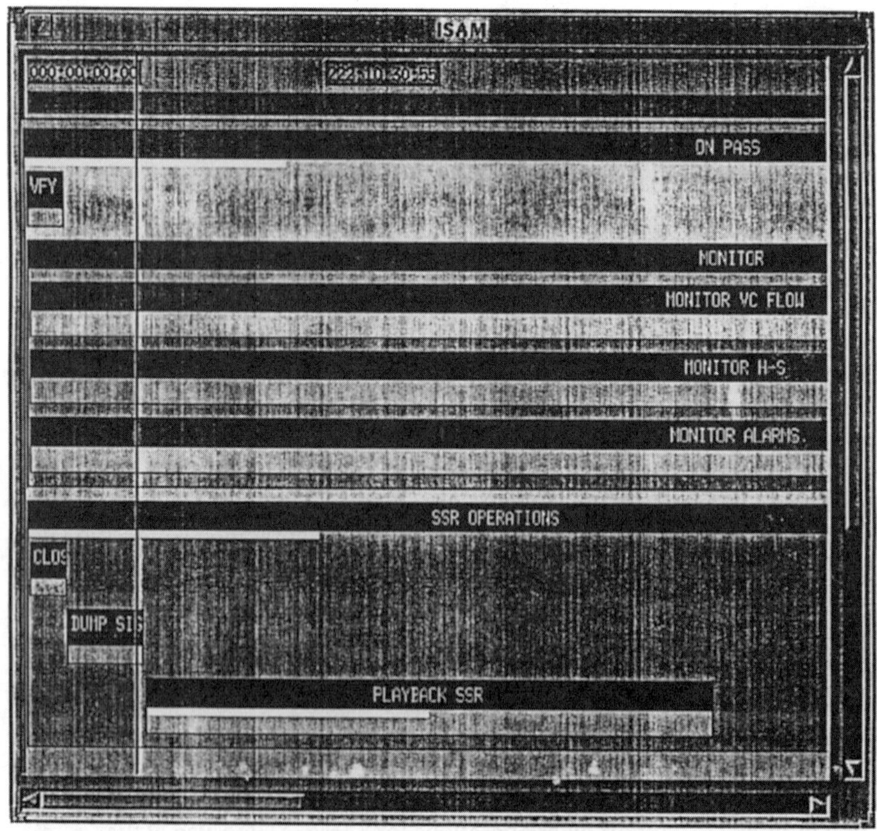

FIG. 9.4a. Example of the CoSMO interface.

Figure 9.4b provides a detailed view of an activity box. One important feature of the visual representation is the "completion bar" that shows the degree of completion of an activity. These bars are graphically "filled-up" as actions to accomplish that activity are completed. Also, the color of the bar indicates status: white means an action was performed but not yet verified, green means an action was performed and verified, red means an action failed (i.e., it was performed but its expected post-conditions are not true), and yellow means late (i.e., expected actions have not yet occurred). This simple color-coding scheme is consistent with regular NASA practice (green = OK, yellow = marginal problem, red = serious problem). The completion bar assists the operators in planning for future activities by providing information as to what activities are currently being performed and how complete those activities are. Furthermore, this completion information propagates to higher level activities, as shown in Fig. 9.4.

The agents responsible for an activity are indicated by the color of the activity's name. In CoSMO, the command controller is represented by blue, the spacecraft analyst by orange, the CoSMO associate by pink (see later discussion), and a "shared" activity (i.e., one in which subactivities belong to different agents) by white.

The activity boxes are also interactive. When the operator clicks on an activity box, the activity menu appears. This menu allows the operator to

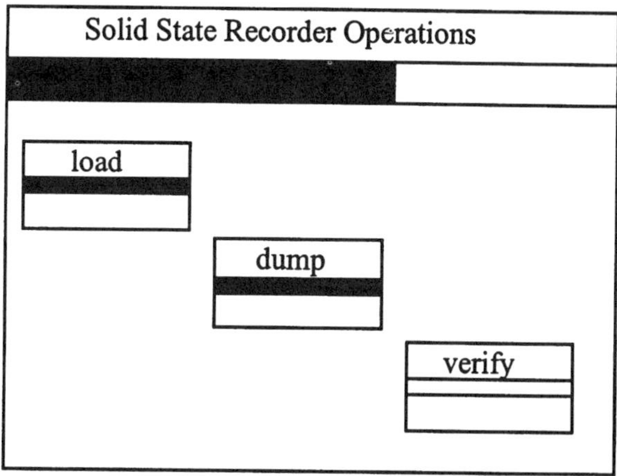

FIG. 9.4b. Detailed sketch of an activity box. This is a simplified sketch rather than a screendump from CoSMO. In this example, the activity "Solid State Recorder Operations" has three subactivities: to load, dump, and verify the solid state recorder. The load and dump activities have been accomplished and the verify activity has not. Thus the completion bars for "load" and "dump" are filled in (actually they would be green, not black) and the completion bar for "Solid State Recorder Operations" is two thirds filled in.

zoom into and out of an activity, view more information, obtain a checklist, and follow links to related artifacts, information objects, and system objects. Zooming allows the operator to view activities at different levels of abstraction. Zooming *in* will display a more detailed view of the activity model (i.e., move one level down in the OFM), and zooming *out* will display the activity at a higher level of abstraction (i.e., move one level up in the OFM). This allows flexibility; the operators can choose to hide unnecessary details or to focus in detail on a particular activity of interest. More information about an activity includes the *purpose* of the activity, *who* is performing the activity, and its *preconditions* and *postconditions*. An activity checklist provides a list of actions that need to be performed in order for the activity to be completed. The checklist provides a detailed view of what actions have already been completed, and what actions still need to be finished. Also in the context of querying an activity object, the operator may choose to view related artifact, system, or information objects associated with that activity. Artifacts are displayed as electronic forms that can be edited and saved (see Fig. 9.5 for an example). Information objects and system objects can be displayed but not modified.

When two (or more) operators are sharing control with ISAM, they each have their own CoSMO client. The substance of the activity requirements (i.e., what activities are displayed), their responsibility (which agent is performing the activity) and the activity status (verified, late, and so forth) are shared; the individual uses of the interface (zooming, querying) are not. Thus, the activity blackboard itself provides the shared context of activity and mediates coordination among the two operators. Within this shared representation, operators may have their own private views that vary in terms of level of detail and requests for further information.

3.1. How CoSMO Supports Cooperative Work

The design of CoSMO supports the supervisory control task of flight operations by providing a flexible, integrated view of evolving activity requirements. The need to maintain "situation awareness" in a dynamic environment is well-recognized as an important feature of effective problem solving (e.g., Bainbridge, 1993; Norman, 1988). Given the procedural and time-critical nature of real-time flight operations, activity-based displays are a natural solution. Furthermore, the ability to flexibly "zoom" into different levels of abstraction supports a variety of coordination strategies. The ability to move between context-dependent links that relate activities to their contextual elements (i.e., related system, information, and artifact objects) is a means of supporting smooth transitions between multiple perspectives. For example, operators can view the system as an evolving set of activity requirements or as a collection of evolving information and artifact objects.

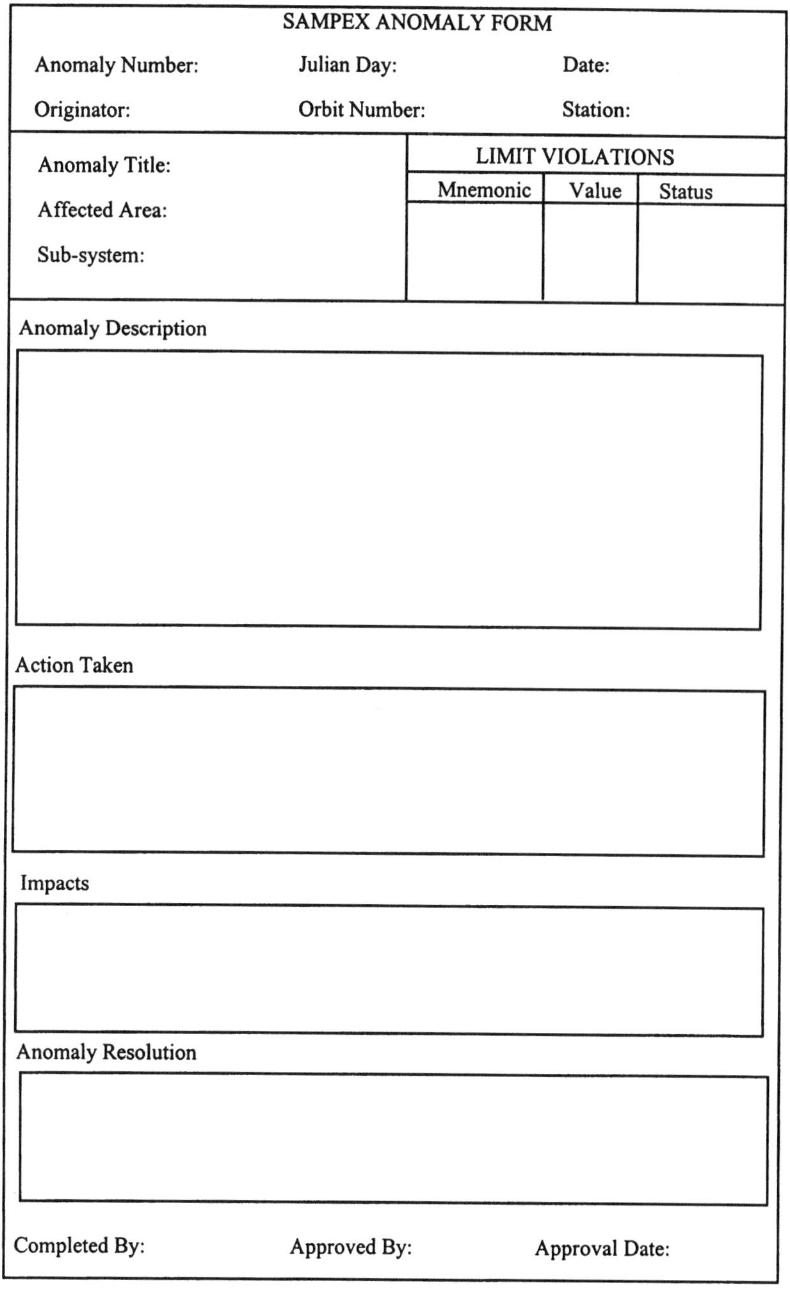

SAMPEX ANOMALY FORM

Anomaly Number: Julian Day: Date:

Originator: Orbit Number: Station:

Anomaly Title:

Affected Area:

Sub-system:

LIMIT VIOLATIONS		
Mnemonic	Value	Status

Anomaly Description

Action Taken

Impacts

Anomaly Resolution

Completed By: Approved By: Approval Date:

FIG. 9.5. A sketch (not a screendump) of an anomaly report artifact.

CoSMO supports cooperation by providing a shared information space (Bannon & Schmidt, 1992; Clark & Brennan, 1991; Robinson, 1993). It also embodies one means of providing a model as a resource for situated action in that it makes such a model visible and interactive yet does not constrain activity to follow that model (Gronbaek, Kyng, & Mogensen, 1993; Schmidt & Bannon, 1992; Suchman, 1987). However, because it is embedded in a same-time, same-place context for cooperative work, CoSMO currently does not support mechanisms of articulation work such as pointing or annotation (Schmidt, 1991). As we note at the end of this chapter, supporting such mechanisms is a direction for future research.

3.2. How ISAM and CoSMO Relate to Other CTCT Projects

The structure and components of ISAM are similar to those of other cooperative systems. One example is the OVAL system (Malone, Lai, & Fry, 1992), a "radically tailorable" tool used to support cooperative work. The building blocks of OVAL (objects, views, agents, and links) are similar to the structures found in ISAM; in fact, many of ISAM's elements can be viewed as specializations of the constructs defined in OVAL. Objects in OVAL are generic and semi-structured; ISAM provides more structured objects in its distinctions between artifacts, information objects, system objects, and activities. Views in OVAL correspond to interface applications like CoSMO that allow the viewing of selected collections of information. Agents in OVAL perform active tasks for people and are event triggered. ISAM provides infrastructure that such agents could use; however, the question of how a tool based on ISAM would provide cooperative support for operators (e.g., by performing delegated tasks) is a research question that will be addressed later in this paper. In OVAL, links define a relationship between objects. ISAM objects are also linked by various relations, but such links are not represented as an explicit construct.

A variety of cooperative work tools have been implemented using OVAL (Malone et al., 1992). These demonstration applications have focused on remote, asynchronous, "conversational" interaction. In contrast, ISAM focuses on supporting direct and synchronous interaction in complex, dynamic, and time-critical environments. Furthermore, the goal of OVAL was to provide a "toolkit" for users to tailor their applications. The current ISAM provides no such infrastructure, but a "workbench" mode for ISAM is currently being implemented so that users can change the contents and structure of the activity model and its context.

Another cooperative tool is the Artifact-Based Collaboration System (ABC) (Smith & Smith, 1991). ABC is a collaborative architecture incorporating a hypermedia database, browsers, applications, and conferencing tools.

Collaboration in ABC occurs around an artifact, a graph structure representing concepts and their interrelations. The general notion of a web or network of interrelated concepts to support collaboration is present in ISAM as well. A browser in ABC is similar to the CoSMO interface connected to ISAM; both allow the viewing of information as represented by objects.

ABC allows users to work in and share a common information space. It supports synchronous and asynchronous modes of cooperation. This environment is very flexible and powerful in that the main artifact can be altered and changed easily over time by adding new nodes and links. Hyperlinks also allow the additional interconnection of different nodes in the artifact. As noted earlier, the ability to dynamically reconfigure the model or artifact around which work is organized—a "workbench" to support users in the continual redesign of their system—is an important facet of flexibility that we are currently grappling with in ISAM.

4. ROLE OF COSMO IN FLIGHT OPERATIONS: THE MEDIATOR-ASSOCIATE EXPERIMENT

ISAM provides infrastructure for the development of cooperative problem solving tools for complex, real-time environments, and CoSMO is an example of such a tool used in flight operations. A question of interest is the appropriate role that an intelligent resource such as CoSMO should play in a real-world dynamic environment. Two possibilities are "mediator" and "associate" roles (Jones, 1995). As a *mediator*, CoSMO serves as a resource for interaction between other agents. CoSMO provides information about the current situation to other agents through the activity-driven interface and also facilitates coordinated activity between the command controller and spacecraft analyst through a shared information space. As an *associate*, CoSMO has the same functionality as a mediator and is also able to perform activities delegated to it by human operators. In this case, the command controller and spacecraft analyst are still in control of the system, but they can choose to delegate certain activities to CoSMO. In this sense, CoSMO becomes another member of the Flight Operations Team that can be instructed what to do by the human operators.

Thus, we operationalize the definition of mediator and associate systems to mean that both provide a shared, evolving view of the current situation vis-à-vis activity requirements and that the associate in addition supports dynamic task allocation by the human operators. The differences between these two levels of automation was investigated in an experimental evaluation of CoSMO, using actual NASA Flight Operations Team members in the context of a high-fidelity interactive simulation of the flight operations environment. In addition to examining system performance measures to quantify the relative benefits of these approaches (e.g., with respect to reaction time, errors), we were also interested in examining the details of the operators' verbal interactions in order to characterize the nature and evolution of cooperative work strategies (as reflected in verbalizations).

In the same way that level of communication can be justified as indicative of either "good" or "bad" coordination (i.e., "we talk a lot and so we are well-coordinated" versus "we are so well-coordinated that we don't have to talk"), one of our interests was simply to observe whether operators talked more or less in the associate mode. On the one hand, a good deal of verbal negotiation could take place on the appropriate use of the automation and on coordinating delegation activities. On the other hand, if operators used the same strategy as in previous experiments (Jones & Mitchell, 1995), they might simply delegate everything, watch the automation perform actions, and therefore talk very little. Second, the level of abstraction of the talk might vary with the level of automation. In particular, one might expect that in the associate mode where operators are actively delegating to CoSMO, they may talk about the work at higher levels of abstraction (e.g., goals and functions) rather than at low levels of actual actions (e.g., display pages, individual commands).

Because of the wide variance in individual differences, we chose to use a within-subjects design. The planned sequence of conditions was: training on baseline simulation and CoSMO, using CoSMO in mediator mode, and using CoSMO in associate mode. Scenarios varied in difficulty and the same scenario mix was used in both the mediator and associate conditions. Two pairs of subjects participated in the study. Subject pair #1 consisted of two experienced operators who had a combined total of 16 years of mission operations experience and had previously worked together. Subject pair #2 consisted of one operator who had 12 years of mission operations experience and one "confederate" researcher familiar with the flight operations domain

Subject pair #1 spent five 1-hour sessions doing the evaluation. In the first session, a background questionnaire and baseline simulation training were conducted. In the second session, the subjects were trained on CoSMO. The remaining three sessions were data collection sessions in which subjects ran four scenarios in mediator mode and four in associate mode. Subject pair #2 spent three 1-hour sessions doing the evaluation. The first session was background questionnaire and training. The next two sessions were data collection: three scenarios of mediator mode and two scenarios of associate mode.

4.1. Task Performance Measures

The first question of interest is the difference in task performance in associate and mediator modes. Several measures of performance are discussed next.

One measure of performance is the number of early, on time, and late activities. An activity is early if it was completed before its expected start time, on time if it was completed after its expected start time but before its expected end time, and late if it was completed after its expected end time. Figure 9.6 shows the percentages of early, on time, and late activities between associate and mediator modes. In associate mode, the percentage of late activities was found to be significantly less by the Mann–Whitney U test ($U = 7, p < .05$). Consequently, the percentage of on time and early activities in associate mode was found to be higher. Thus the subjects' performance was better in associate mode because on average they had significantly fewer late activities and more early and on time activities.

A second performance measure is how many failures were noticed by the subjects. Two types of failures were part of the simulated scenarios: Command failures (when commands sent to the spacecraft were unsuccessfully transmitted) and Out-of-limits telemetry failures (when spacecraft data were outside of expected normal conditions). Figure 9.7 shows the percentage of failures noted by the subjects in associate and mediator modes. A failure is considered noted when the operators wrote an anomaly report for the failure or noted it on the pass plan. As Fig. 9.7 shows, more failures of both types were noted in associate mode. The Mann–Whitney U test showed only the out-of-limits telemetry comparison to be significant ($U = 0, p < .01$). This result suggests that with the help of CoSMO in associate mode, the operators were better at finding failed telemetry.

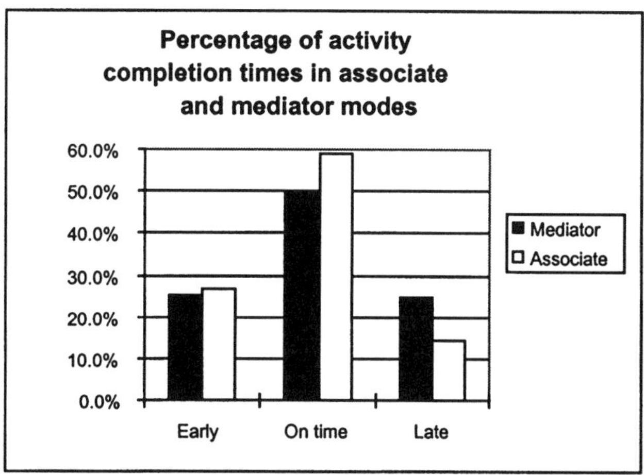

FIG. 9.6. Percentage of activity completion times in associate and mediator modes.

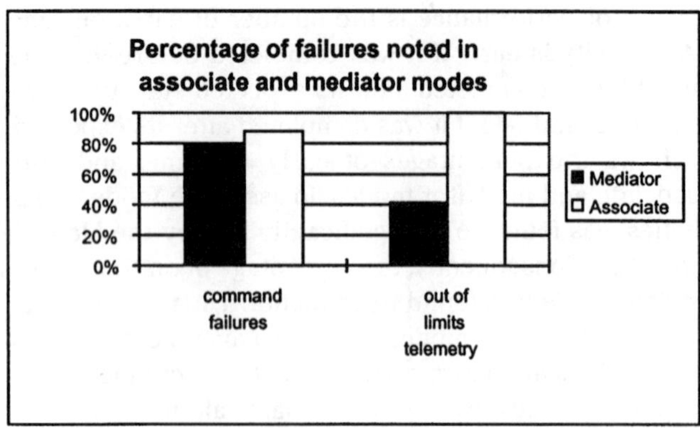

FIG. 9.7. Percentage of failures noted in associate and mediator modes.

Another measure of performance is reaction time to a failure. This is measured as the difference between the time a failure occurred and the time one of the operators performed an action to correct the failure. No significant difference was found for mean reaction times between mediator and associate conditions. This result could possibly suggest that an activity's status, as shown by the color of the completion bar on the interface, does a sufficient job of informing the operator of failures in any mode. Overall, however, the operator teams were more effective in associate mode. Activities were completed on time and more failures were detected.

4.2. Ratings of Usefulness

At the end of the study, subjects were given an extensive questionnaire that asked them to rate and rank the usefulness of the CoSMO features. The full set of results are presented in Jasek (1995); here we focus on the rankings. Kendall's coefficient of concordance was used to assess the degree of agreement among ranks for the ten main features of CoSMO (see Table 9.2). The coefficient computed was .543 ($p < .05$); therefore, the null hypothesis that the operators disagreed on rankings is rejected. Given this result, a "true preferential ordering" of features can be calculated by summing the ranks of each feature (Gibbons, 1985). This true preferential ordering for CoSMO features is shown in Table 9.2.

4.3. The Nature of Talk and Articulation Work

Verbal protocols was collected using a hand-held cassette recorder during each scenario. These data were transcribed and coded into four statement types: notification, verification, inquiry, and delegation. Notification state-

TABLE 9.2
Preferential Ranking of ISAM-CoSMO Features

Rank	*Feature*
1	ability to delegate and undelegate activities
2	color codes representation of activity status
3	timeline
4	links to electronic reports
5	percentage completion bar
6	ability to see last action of an agent
7	links to display pages
8	more information box
9	zooming
10	color coded representation of who is responsible for an activity

ments are used with the intent of notifying the other operator about what activity one or both of the operators should do or are doing (e.g., “I'm doing X now,” “You do X”). Verification statements are used with the intent of communicating the status of an activity to the other operator (e.g., “X is failed,” “X is yellow,” “X was successful”). Inquiry statements pose a question about an activity to the other operator (e.g., “Should I do X now?”, “Is X red?”, “Are you doing X?”). Finally, delegation statements refer to delegating, undelegating, or redelegating an activity (e.g., “I will delegate X,” “Did you redelegate X?”). All statements that refer to delegation are considered to be of this last type even though they may also be notifications or inquiries. Note that all of these statements is some way refer to activities. In analyzing the transcripts, the number of task relevant utterances spoken by the command controller and spacecraft analyst were also counted. The transcripts were coded separately by two individuals; the resulting interrater reliability was significantly high.

Figure 9.8 shows a comparison of the average number of utterances and statement types in associate and mediator modes. The Mann–Whitney U test found that there were significantly more utterances, more notification statements, more verification statements, and fewer delegation statements in mediator mode.

The analysis of the transcripts shows that in mediator mode the operators do a lot of verbal communication. They are constantly talking to each other about what they are doing and what the status of activities are (i.e., they are constantly notifying, verifying, and inquiring). A very common exchange found in the mediator mode transcripts is:

Command controller: “Dumping science.”

Spacecraft analyst: “OK.”

Spacecraft analyst: (after verifying the operation) “Good.”

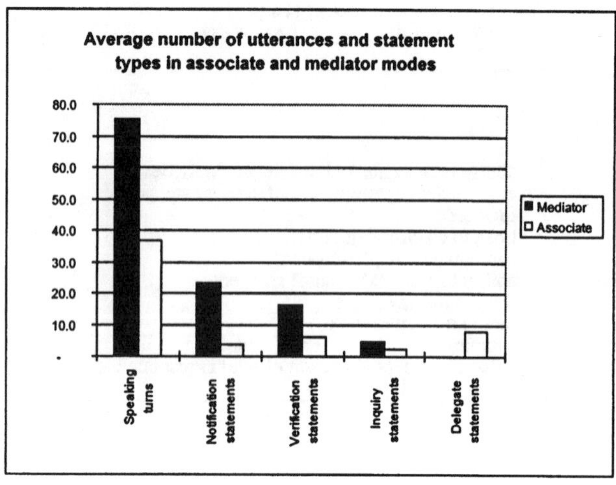

FIG. 9.8. Average number of utterances and statement types in associate and mediator modes.

Thus, as the command controller sends commands, the spacecraft analyst watches and verifies them.

On the other hand, in associate mode there is significantly less dialogue about activity and more dialogue about delegation. As described by one subject, because activities have been delegated to CoSMO, the operators "know when things will happen and just watch." In this mode, the operators delegate everything and watch as CoSMO performs activities (i.e., they are monitoring automation and working at a higher level of supervisory control).

Characterizing articulation work is an important part of the study of cooperative work (Schmidt & Bannon, 1992). In this domain, activity is articulated primarily by standard operating procedures and by explicit verbal communication between the operators. The CoSMO interface itself can be viewed as an artifact that stipulates and mediates the articulation of activities (Jones & Jasek, 1995).

The verbal protocol analysis shows that there are more notification, verification, and inquiry statements in mediator mode. This result suggests that more explicit articulation work is necessary in this mode. In associate mode, the operators give CoSMO the responsibility to perform activities, and CoSMO handles many of the details of the substantive work; hence, there is less need for explicit communication between the operators. In mediator mode, the operators must handle all the details of substantive and articulation work; therefore, they need to communicate.

However, it should be noted that the increased talking about activities in mediator may not be due to the need for the operators to articulate activity.

The subjects might have done more explicit communication because CoSMO was a new tool or because they had never worked with each other before. As subjects gain experience with CoSMO and get used to working with each other, their communication about activities might decrease.

On one hand, it seems natural that there is less articulation work done by the operators in associate mode because CoSMO, which is acting as an automated agent, is doing all the work. On the other hand, it also seems natural that adding an agent would increase the amount of articulation work necessary because there are additional communication paths and the work is more distributed. This raises many questions about how articulation work can be measured and how the articulation of work is affected by adding agents or by automation.

5. SUMMARY AND DIRECTIONS FOR FUTURE RESEARCH

Based on a field study of cooperative work in flight operations, the operator function model framework, and an adapted data flow diagram, the Intelligent Support for Activity Management architecture has been developed. This architecture is centered around the representation of activities and includes artifacts, information objects, and system objects that describe the context in which activity occurs. ISAM represents a normative model of evolving activity requirements that provides the basis for real-time intelligent support. CoSMO is an client interface application developed to support cooperative distributed supervisory control in flight operations. CoSMO supports the supervisory control nature of this task by providing visualization of activity requirements to support "global activity awareness" and provides integrated resources through which operators can navigate. Multiple CoSMO clients connected to the ISAM server provide support for cooperation in a distributed environment by creating a shared information space between multiple operators. An evaluation comparing mediator and associate modes of CoSMO found that operator teams performed better in associate mode, and in associate mode they took advantage of the ability to delegate tasks to CoSMO—in fact, by delegating everything!

Several issues remain to be explored in the context of this particular study. First, CoSMO (and thus ISAM) need to be extended to support mechanisms of articulation work (e.g., pointing, annotation) so as to support asynchronous and distributed interaction. This is not only relevant for flight operations teams themselves, but also to support interaction with the other stakeholders in the process (e.g, groundstation personnel, mission scientists). Second, CoSMO needs to be exercised in simulation scenarios in which activities are not premodeled and thus cannot be delegated. Questions relating to the limits of automation capabilities and how teams work around those limits form a critical set of issues. Finally, in the current framework, there are many interesting questions of visualization and representation and how different interface designs support different varieties of shared reasoning.

A set of longer term issues is relevant as well. The world of flight operations is constantly changing, and one issue is how cooperative technologies can adapt to dynamic environments. A primary source of change is in how work is done by flight analysts. Through the use of reconfigurable software in the current control rooms, analysts can create new displays and procedures and thus are constantly "routinizing" their work during real-time operations. Second, mission requirements evolve over time (e.g., spacecraft component failures, new data collection procedures proposed by mission scientists). Third, another source of change lies in the high turnover rate among personnel and hence the problem of knowledge attrition. Fourth, flight operations is becoming an even more complex environment. Human operators will soon be required to control mission clusters rather than individual missions, command more complex and "smarter" spacecraft systems, and manage a more tightly coupled relationship between science and flight operations. These factors are sources of complexity in trying to characterize a fairly stable set of assumptions about cooperative work practices.

The current representations and reasoning in ISAM need to be extended in several important ways to handle these real-world requirements. First, as previously mentioned, a "workbench" mode to support extensibility and adaptability to future mission requirements is needed. Second, to provide a more complete representation of activity and thus better support for planning and reasoning, we are currently exploring the integration of temporal reasoning and control models with ISAM's Activity Objects. Third, to provide a more complete representation of system state and thus better support for situation assessment and response planning, we plan to extend the System Objects to support causal reasoning and also to represent and reason about uncertainty. In short, by exploiting many intelligent technologies in the concept of supporting activity management, we aim for ISAM to provide a rich testbed for the exploration of human–machine joint cognitive systems in complex dynamic environments.

ACKNOWLEDGMENTS

This material is based on the work supported by the National Science Foundation under Grant No. IRI-9210918 and the National Aeronautics and Space Administration under Grant NAG5-2244. Thanks to Emily Patterson, Colleen Sebald, Eric Brunick, Walter Frei, and Mike Cohen. Thanks to Jim Jacobs for the name CoSMO. Special thanks to NASA Goddard Space Flight Center, especially Bill Stoffel, Matt Fatig, and the SAMPEX Flight Operations Team. We are also grateful to Gary Olson and two anonymous reviewers for their comments on previous versions of this manuscript.

REFERENCES

Bainbridge, L. (1993). The change in concepts needed to account for human behaviour in complex dynamic tasks. *Proceedings of the 1993 IEEE International Conference on Systems, Man, and Cybernetics*, Vol. 1, pp. 126–131.

Bannon, L. J., & Schmidt, K. (1991). CSCW: Four characters in search of a context. In *EC-CSCW '89, Proceedings of the First European Conference on Computer-Supported Cooperative Work.* Reprinted in R. Baecker (Ed.). (1993). *Readings in groupware and computer-supported cooperative work.* San Mateo, CA: Morgan Kaufmann.

Briggs, R. O., & Nunamaker, J. (1994). Getting a grip on groupware. In P. Lloyd (Ed.), *Groupware in the 21st century* (pp. 61–72). Westport, CT: Praeger.

Bushman, J. B., Mitchell, C. M., Jones, P. M., & Rubin, K. S. (1993). ALLY: An operator's associate for cooperative supervisory control systems. *IEEE Transactions on Systems, Man, and Cybernetics, 23*(1), No. 1, 111–128.

Chu, R. W., Mitchell, C. M., & Jones, P. M. (1995). Using OFM/OFMspert as the basis for an intelligent tutoring system: Towards a tutor/aid paradigm for operators of supervisory control systems. *IEEE Transactions on Systems, Man, and Cybernetics, 25*(7), 1054–1075.

Clark, H. H., & Brennan, S. E. (1991). Grounding in communication. Reprinted in R. M. Baecker (Ed.). (1993). *Readings in groupware and computer-supported cooperative work* (pp. 222–233). San Mateo, CA: Morgan Kaufmann.

Cohen, S. (1990). *A model of troubleshooting in electronics assembly manufacturing.* M.S. thesis, Center for Human-Machine Systems Research, School of Industrial and Systems Engineering, Georgia Institute of Technology.

Ellis, C. A., Gibbs, S. J., & Rein, G. L. (1991). Groupware: Some issues and experiences. *Communications of the ACM, 34*(1), January 1991, 38–58.

Fox, M. S., Chionglo, J., & Fadel, F. G. (1993). A common-sense model of the enterprise. Department of Industrial Engineering, University of Toronto, June 1993. (A short version appears in *Proceedings of the Second Industrial Engineering Research Conference*, Los Angeles, May, 1993.)

Gibbons, J. (1985). *Nonparametric statistical inference* (2nd ed.). New York: Dekker.

Gronbaek, K., Kyng, M., & Mogensen, P. (1993). CSCW challenges: Cooperative design in engineering projects. *Communications of the ACM, 36*(4), 67–77, June.

Harel, D., & Pnueli, A. (1985). On the development of reactive systems. Weizmann Institute of Science Report C585-02, Rehovot, Israel. Cited in Davis, A. M. (1990). *Software requirements: Analysis and specification.* Englewood Cliffs NJ: Prentice-Hall.

Hollnagel, E., Mancini, G., & Woods, D. D. (Eds.). (1988). *Cognitive engineering in complex dynamic environments.* New York: Academic Press.

Jasek, C. A. (1995). *Cooperative support for supervisory control: Aiding flight operations teams in satellite ground control.* MS thesis, Department of Mechanical and Industrial Engineering, University of Illinois at Urbana-Champaign.

Jasek, C. A., & Jones, P. M. (1994). Modeling and supporting cooperative work in mission operations: The development of the ISAM system (Tech. Rep. ICC-UIUC-9406). Engineering Psychology Research Laboratory, Department of Mechanical and Industrial Engineering, University of Illinois at Urbana-Champaign.

Johansen, R., & Swigart, R. (1994). *Upsizing the individual in the downsized organization.* Reading, MA: Addison-Wesley.

Jones, P. M. (1995). Cooperative work in mission operations: Analysis and implications for computer support. *Computer Supported Cooperative Work: An International Journal, 31*, 130–145.

Jones, P. M., Chu, R. W., & Mitchell, C. M. (1995). A methodology for human-machine systems research: Knowledge engineering, modeling, and simulation. *IEEE Transactions on Systems, Man, and Cybernetics, 25*(7), 1025–1038.

Jones, P. M., & Goyle, V. (1993). A field study of TPOCC missions operations: Knowledge requirements and cooperative work (Tech. Rep. 93-05). Engineering Psychology Research Laboratory, Department of Mechanical and Industrial Engineering, University of Illinois at Urbana-Champaign.

Jones, P. M., & Jasek, C. A. (1995). Evaluating levels of automation in cooperative supervisory control: The mediator-associate experiment. *Proceedings of the 1995 IEEE International Conference on Systems, Man, and Cybernetics*, Vancouver, British Columbia, Canada, October 1995.

Jones, P. M., & Jasek, C. A. (1997). Intelligent support for activity management (ISAM): An architecture to support distributed supervisory control. *IEEE Transactions on Systems, Man, and Cybernetics, 27*(3), 274–288.

Jones, P. M., & Mitchell, C. M. (1995). Human-computer cooperative problem solving: Theory, design, and evaluation of an intelligent associate system. *IEEE Transactions on Systems, Man, and Cybernetics, 25*(7), 1039–1053.

Jones, P. M., Mitchell, C. M., & Rubin, K. S. (1990). Validation of intent inferencing by a model-based operator's associate. *International Journal of Man-Machine Studies, 33*, 177–202.

Jones, P. M., Patterson, E. S., & Goyle, V. (1993). Modeling and intelligent aiding for cooperative work in mission operations. *Proceedings of the 1993 IEEE International Conference on Systems, Man, and Cybernetics*, Le Touquet, France.

Kowal, J. A. (1992). *Behavior models–Specifying user's expectations*. Englewood Cliffs, NJ: Prentice-Hall.

Larson, C., & LaFasto, F. (1989). *Teamwork: What must go right, what can go wrong*. Newbury Park, CA: Sage.

Leitch, R., & Gallanti, M. (1992). Task classification for knowledge-based systems in industrial automation. *IEEE Transactions on Systems, Man, and Cybernetics, 22*(1), 142–152.

Malone, T. W., & Crowston, K. (1990). What is coordination theory and how can it help design cooperative work systems? *CSCW '90 Proceedings*, pp. 357–370.

Malone, T. W., Lai, K. Y., & Fry, C. (1992). Experiments with OVAL: A radically tailorable tool for cooperative work (Tech. Rep. #132). Cambridge, MA: Center of Coordination Science, Massachusetts Institute of Technology.

McGrath, J. E. (1990). Time matters in groups. In J. Galegher, R. E. Kraut, & C. Egido (Eds.), *Intellectual teamwork: Social and technological foundations of cooperative work* (pp. 23–62). Hillsdale NJ: Lawrence Erlbaum Associates.

McGrath, J. E., & Hollingshead, A. B. (1994). *Groups interacting with technology*. Newbury Park, CA: Sage.

Mitchell, C. M. (1987). GT-MSOCC: A research domain for modeling human-computer interaction and aiding decision making in supervisory control systems. *IEEE Transactions on Systems, Man, and Cybernetics*, SMC-17, 553–570.

Mitchell, C. M., & Saisi, D. L. (1987). Use of model-based qualitative icons and adaptive windows in workstations for supervisory control systems. *IEEE Transactions on Systems, Man, and Cybernetics, SMC-17*, 573–593.

Nii, H. P. (1986). Blackboard systems. *The AI Magazine*, Vols. 2 and 3.

Norman, D. A. (1988). *The psychology of everyday things*. New York: Basic Books.

Patterson, E. S. (1993). TPOCC mission operations: Modeling cooperative work in distributed supervisory control (Tech. Rep. 93-11, Engineering Psychology Research Laboratory, Department of Mechanical and Industrial Engineering, University of Illinois at Urbana-Champaign.

Rasmussen, J., Brehmer, B., & Leplat, J. (Eds.). (1991). *Distributed decision making: Cognitive models for cooperative work*. Chichester: Wiley.

Reeves, B., & Shipman, F. (1992). Supporting communication between designers with artifact-centered evolving information spaces. *Proceedings of the 1992 Conference on Computer-Supported Cooperative Work*, 394–401, Toronto Canada.

Robinson, M. (1993). Computer supported co-operative work: Cases and concepts. In R. M. Baecker (Ed.), *Readings in computer-supported cooperative work* (pp. 29–49). San Mateo, CA: Morgan Kaufmann.

Rubin, K. S., Jones, P. M., & Mitchell, C. M. (1988). OFMspert: Inference of operator intentions in supervisory control using a blackboard architecture. *IEEE Transactions on Systems, Man, and Cybernetics, 18*(4), 618–637.

Schmidt, K. (1991). Cooperative work: A conceptual framework. In J. Rasmussen, B. Brehmer, & J. Leplat (Eds.), *Distributed decision making: Cognitive models for cooperative work*. Chichester: Wiley.

Schmidt, K., & Bannon, L. (1992). Taking CSCW seriously: Supporting articulation work. *Computer-Supported Cooperative Work: An International Journal, 1*(1–2), 7–40.

Sheridan, T. B., & Johannsen, G. (Eds.). (1976). *Monitoring behavior and supervisory control*. Amsterdam: North-Holland.

Smith, J. B., & Smith, F. D. (1991). ABC: A hypermedia system for artifact-based collaboration. *Proceedings of Hypertext '91*, San Antonio, TX, pp. 179–192.

Suchman, L. (1987). *Plans and situated actions: The problem of human-machine communication*. Cambridge, England: Cambridge University Press.

Verfurth, S. C. (1991). *Modeling the pilots and constructing an intent inferencer for a Boeing 727 cockpit*. Unpublished M.S. thesis, Center for Human-Machine Systems Research, School of Industrial and Systems Engineering, Georgia Institute of Technology, Atlanta, GA.

CHAPTER

10

Trellis: A Formally Defined Hypertextual Basis for Integrating Task and Information

Richard Furuta
Texas A&M University

P. David Stotts
University of North Carolina, Chapel Hill

1. INTRODUCTION

The Trellis project is investigating the structure and semantics of hypertextually described interaction [23, 26]. As the work has developed over a number of years, we have broadened our scope from the study of hyperdocuments to encompass *hyperprograms.* A hyperprogram associates user-manipulatable information (the hypertext) with user-directed execution behavior (the process). Consequently a hyperprogram can be said to integrate task with information.

Generalizing, the hyperprogram's execution behavior can be defined by the collective actions of a group of entities, not only the direction of a single user. Such actions can be generated by, and can coordinate the activities of, a collection of human users, computer-based processes, and indeed reflect and are driven by the intentions of the hyperprogram's author. The structural characteristics of a *hyperdocument* permit the specification and documentation of a concurrent protocol and the characteristics of the specification's definition potentially enable the protocol's verification. It is the dynamic characteristics of the *hyperprogram* that permit the prototyping and deployment of the resulting specification.

The Trellis model is defined formally using timed, colored Petri nets. Consequently, hypertexts specified in Trellis describe the traditional hypermedia collection of data objects and relationships among the objects, but also define the process by which the objects are used. In hypertext, "browsing" denotes the traversal of the hypertext, and so we define the hypertext's "browsing semantics" as the process by which the traversal occurs.

As in many modern hypertext research projects, Trellis' notion of "hypertext" is very broad, encompassing all forms of computer representable "media." In addition to static content, such as text and graphics, this definition includes active content, such as video and audio, and procedural content, such as computations and embedded hypertexts.

Trellis implementations are based around a distributed client-server architecture. There is not necessarily a one-to-one correspondence between "user" and "client"—a single user's interface can be formed from the efforts of multiple clients, classes of users may be grouped together and represented by a single client, and clients may be communicating with computer processes rather than human users.

Thus a Trellis document defines an environment in which the constituent objects may be dynamic and in which the state of the document also is changing dynamically. The document's state can be, but is not required to be, related to the actions taken by the human user or users of the environment. However, a central precept is that the state changes are intentional—have, in essence, been "programmed" by an author.

A number of authors have noticed the interesting effect that as information presentation interfaces become more powerful they encompass the abilities of a interface specification system. For example, structured document preparation/presentation systems are being used to specify and implement general user interfaces [3, 7, 8] (i.e., active documents). Creation of an interface in such an environment can, if appropriate, call on the capabilities of the original application. In particular, the specification of user interfaces using active document systems can be seen to be an authoring task. The experience, techniques, and skills developed over time to organize and write traditional documents can be reused directly into the new application domain.

We have examined similar applications of Trellis in our investigations of protocol specification and prototyping [26]. The formal basis of the Petri net permits the development of automatic verification tools. Because Trellis is dynamic, the specifications can be used directly in prototyping the protocol in application. The client–server implementation architecture permits distributed application of the protocol and permits the development of specialized, tuned interfaces that can be run simultaneously with more general development and debugging-oriented interfaces. Because Trellis specifications are interpreted rather than being hard-wired into the application, developers can make modifications "on the fly" as needs arise and can examine how the modifications change the behavior in a continuously running environment.

Hybrid implementation environments retain the characteristics and capabilities of the parent environment. Consequently the hypertextual basis permits the natural incorporation of system documentation into the implementation–in essence the protocol implementation is self-documenting.

A unifying focus in hypertext research is the identification, definition, and development of commonalities with previously orthogonal areas of study. Hypertext has been suggested as an important component of systems supporting the software engineering process [4, 19] and computer-supported cooperative work (CSCW) [12, 26]. Hypertext can be generalized even further; systems such as Apple's HyperCard [1, 2] are used to implement general-purpose computer applications.

A characteristic of these investigations is the central nature of *protocol specification* in addressing the domain's requirements. Software engineering protocols include formal and semiformal artifacts that provide, for example, requirements specifications. The relationships among these artifacts and the procedures that are followed in their manipulation are in turn defined by higher level protocols. In the CSCW domain, the coordination of the interactions among humans and between human and computer can be formalized and refined through the expression of protocols [13, 29].

We have examined the applicability of protocol-centric specification in Trellis within many of these contexts [11, 12]. In the applications we have studied we have found that the ability to rapidly prototype, self-document, incrementally modify, develop verification techniques for, and use the authoring metaphor in the creation of the protocol's specification are of significance.

In this chapter we first give a little more detail about Trellis and its prototype implementations. We then examine a series of example applications of Trellis illustrating its application in hyperprogram specification. An important opportunity presented by the use of a specification mechanism based on a formally defined automaton is the ability to consider automated verification of properties of the specification. Section 4 reviews our efforts along those lines. Section 5 concludes the presentation.

2. TRELLIS: MODEL AND PROTOTYPE ARCHITECTURE

The Trellis project [10, 23, 24] has investigated for the past several years the structure and semantics of human computer interaction, in the context of hypertext (hypermedia) systems, program browsers, visual programming notations, and process models.

In the following sections we summarize the Trellis model and semantics, and then describe the distributed architecture of our Trellis implementations. To illustrate the capabilities of the model, we give specific examples of how Trellis hyperprograms are used as information repositories (image browsing indexes), as parallel program browsers, and as general process models. We conclude with a description of our methods of analyzing the task that is encoded into a Trellis hyperprogram.

2.1. Place/Transition Nets and Browsing Semantics

The Trellis model treats a hyperprogram as an annotated, timed, place/transition net (PT net) that is used both as a graph (for static information) and as parallel automaton (for dynamic behavior). For complete understanding of the example in following sections, we very briefly explain here the syntax and semantics of PT nets, also called Petri nets.[1]

An example PT net is shown in the graphics window on the right side of Fig. 10.1 (the software system itself is discussed in more detail later). PT nets are graphically represented as bipartite graphs in which the circular nodes are called *places* and the bar nodes are called *transitions.* A dot in a place is called a *token*, and it represents activity, or the realization of some logical condition associated with the place. A place containing one or more tokens is said to be *marked.* When each place incident on a transition is marked that transition is *enabled.* An enabled transition may *fire* by removing one token from each of its input places and putting one token into each of its output places. The full token distribution among places is the *state* of the net and is termed a *net marking.* A state change in the net marking that results by firing an enabled transition.

The places of the net are annotated with fragments of information (text, graphics, video, audio, executable code, other hyperprograms); these annotations are termed the *content* elements of the hyperprogram. A hierarchy is created by allowing the content element of a place to be itself an independent hyperstructure.

To use a Trellis model as hypertext, for example, we provide visual interfaces to give a user a tangible interpretation of the PT net and its annotations. When a token enters a place during execution, the content element for the place is presented for viewing (or for other user consumption). Any enabled transitions leading out of the place are shown next to the displayed content element as selectable *buttons*, or hot spots in the interface. Selecting a button (with a mouse, usually) will cause the net to fire the associated transition, moving the tokens around and changing the visible content elements.

We mentioned that a hyperprogram integrates task with information. If one takes the graph view of a PT net, then the content elements and the arcs

[1]Readers unfamiliar with basic net theory can find a thorough exposition in the books by Reisig [18] and Peterson [17], and in the survey paper by Murata [16].

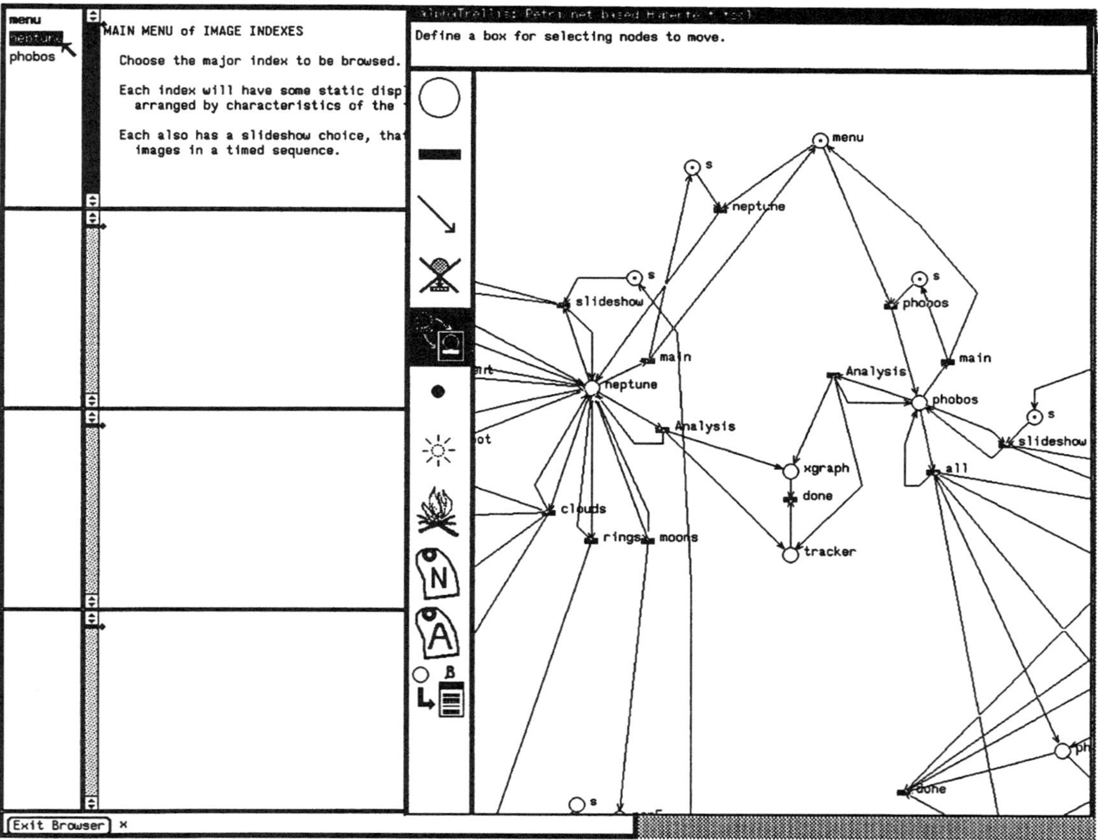

FIG. 10.1. Screen from αTrellis showing an image browsing index.

among them collectively comprise a linked information base; if one considers the parallel automaton view of a PT net, then its execution behavior defines a task composed of concurrent control threads running throughout the information base. The dual nature of a PT net is the integration.

2.2. Client/Server System Architecture

Figure 10.2 shows the high-level structure of a Trellis-based system. The components illustrate the essential features that make Trellis inherently extensible, making it customizable by an organization using it for modeling. The models are basically information servers. The information contained in a model (quality metrics, design structure, reliability models, documentation network) can be accessed and used for varying purposes, depending on the particular interface clients that are written to access the information servers.

The heart of a Trellis system is an information engine, which is a process allowing construction and execution of a Trellis model (annotated, timed PT net as discussed previously). An engine (model) has no visible interface, but does respond to remote procedure call (RPC) requests for its services. Services provided include those operational ones mentioned above, as well as basic functions such as constructing or altering the model's components. The current Trellis engine is implemented in C++ and has over 50 methods comprising its services.

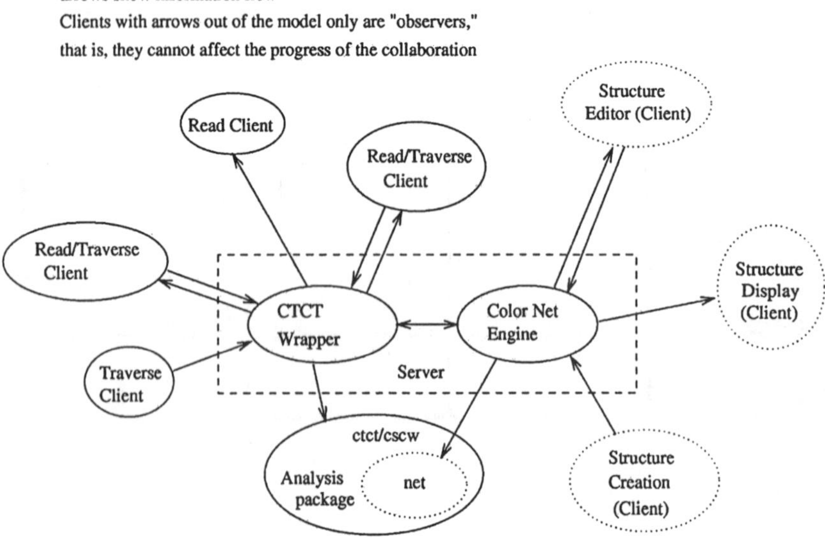

FIG. 10.2. Trellis client/server system architecture.

A client in a Trellis system executes as a separate process (perhaps remotely), communicating with an engine via RPC. Clients provide visible interfaces for models (engines). Different interface clients might be written, for example, to

- operate in different window systems;
- provide different views or present different aspects of a model;
- structure models for specific purposes or, by conventions of different
- application domains;

or for numerous other reasons. All clients, however, interact with the same models, using the RPC API provided by the engine to add information, add links, add agents, change the state of the model, and so forth.

Although it is not shown explicitly in the figure, multiple Trellis engines (models) can be concurrently active, and each may be accessed by multiple clients concurrently. Any particular client can concurrently access several models. In addition to these forms of concurrency, the engine itself is structured as a parallel automaton (i.e., encodes parallel threads of activity) as previously mentioned.

3. HYPERPROGRAMS

In this section we examine four applications of Trellis in varying domains. The first three are presented using an older prototype, αTrellis, and show Trellis' application in specifying an image browsing index, in representing the message flow in a parallel programming language, and in simulating solutions to classical problems in process synchronization. The presentations will introduce additional characteristics of Trellis implementations.

The fourth example, cast now in our newer prototype, χTrellis, illustrates the implementation of a protocol for managing a collaborative meeting.

3.1. Example: Image Browsing Index

Figure 10.1 shows a screen from αTrellis, an early Trellis prototype implemented for Unix platforms and the SunView window system. Two of the three αTrellis browsing clients are visible, with the graphical editing client on the right, overlapping the windows of the text browsing client on the left. αTrellis was an experimental, proof-of-principle vehicle to demonstrate the utility of the automaton-based view of hyperdocuments; as such, we focused on implementing the net engine functionality and analysis methods rather than developing complex interface clients.

In the αTrellis text browser, the screen shows four text windows. When a net place is marked its content element is displayed in one of these text windows. In this example, the text showing in the top window of the browser is the content of the place "menu," which is showing as marked in the graphical editor window. Each enabled transition is displayed as a selectable button in a menu to the left of the text window (transitions "neptune" and "phobos" in the example net). Selection of a button in a browser menu causes the associated transition to fire in the net, changing the net state and thereby causing a change in the information elements that are displayed in the text windows.

The PT editor client on the right presents a graphical view of the underlying model. With it, a user can build or alter the structure of the net, annotate the net with content element names, and also execute the net. The two clients execute as two independent processes, and the net engine executes as a third process. Each client communicates with the engine by RPC. When one client causes a change in the net (e.g., by firing a transition), the other client will be notified and will reflect the change also.

Figure 10.3 shows a third αTrellis client (displaying on a different monitor with X windows) operating concurrently with the editor and browser clients (Fig. 10.3a). This client (Fig. 10.3b) monitors the execution activity in a hyperprogram and displays graphics images on the X windows screen whenever a marked place has a bit-mapped image as its content. This example shows an image browsing index we constructed as part of a NASA experiment at CESDIS (Goddard Space Flight Center, MD). The images of Neptune and Phobos are linked and cross linked in the net structure according to common characteristics. The net as built concurrently displays all images that share a characteristic. The state shown in Fig. 10.3 results when the "neptune" button highlighted back in Fig. 10.1 is selected, followed by the "spot" button in the text frame in Fig. 10.3a. These two transition firings leave the token in place "neptune," and also place tokens into "nepColor" and "nep3"; the associated content images are displayed remotely by the graphics client as shown in Fig. 10.3b.

The graphics client does not allow a user to alter the net structure like the editor client does; it does not even allow a user to fire transitions like the text browser does; it just sits and listens, acting when necessary according to its purpose. To initiate some engine activity, a user would have to interact with the interface provided by one of the other two clients.

3.2. Example: Parallel Program Browsing

The αTrellis application illustrated in this section shows both the usefulness of the model for representing parallel threads of activity, and the usefulness of our hypertextual interpretation of the PT net for supporting human rea-

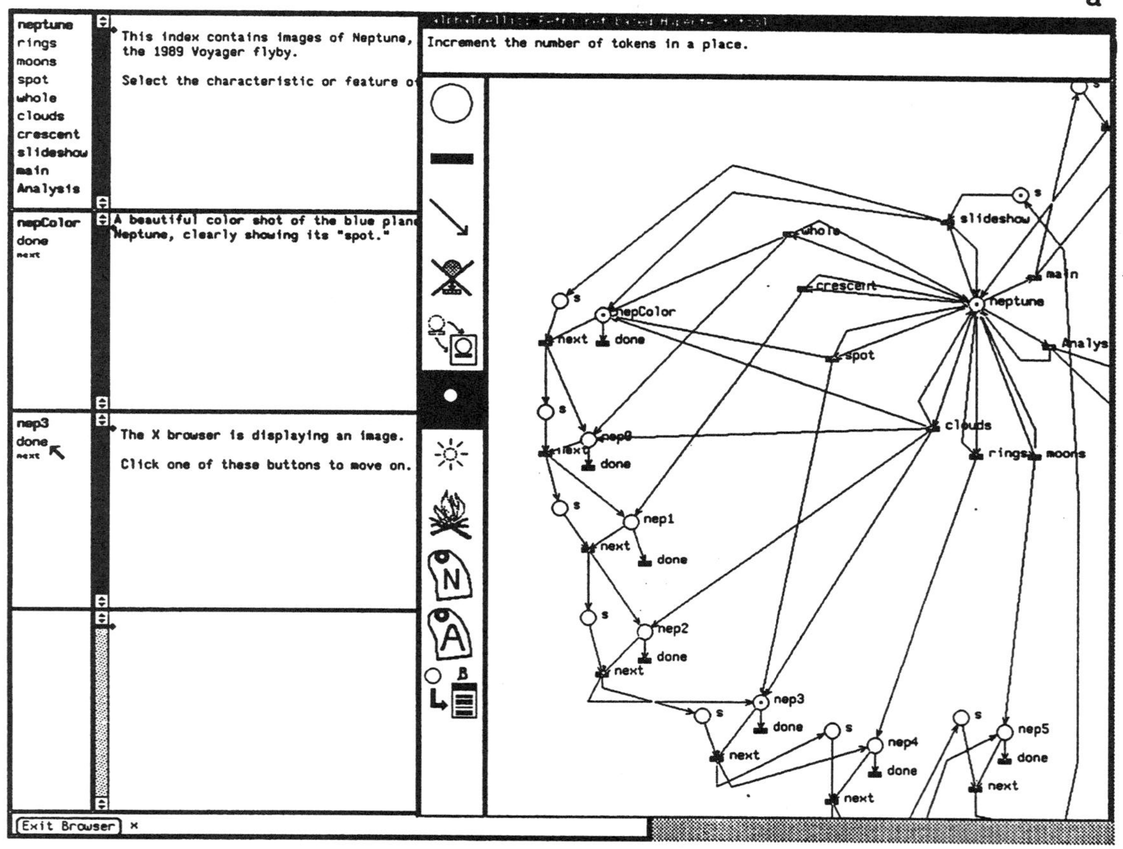

FIG. 10.3. (Continued)

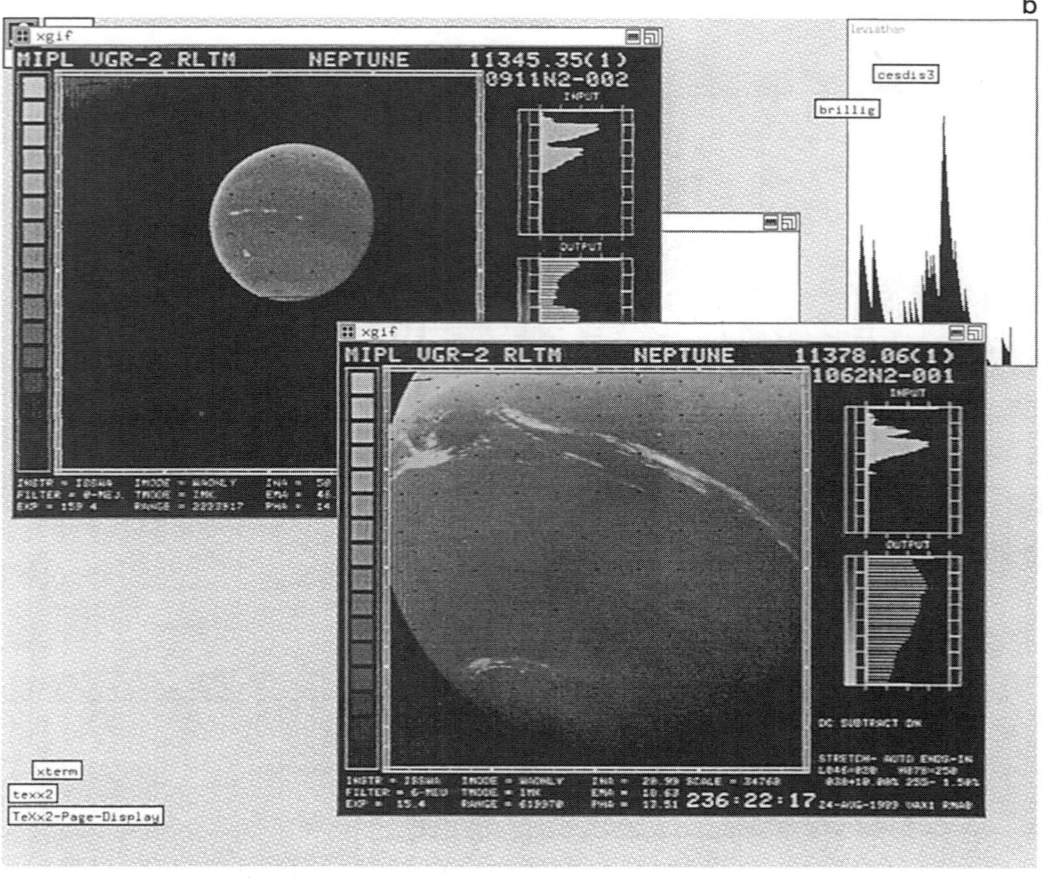

FIG. 10.3. Concurrently displayed Neptune images classified by features.

soning through browsing. A CSP program browser [21] is shown in Fig. 10.4. This specific example uses a CSP program from Hoare's original paper published in the *Communications of the ACM*.

We wrote a translator to parse CSP programs and generate as output the storage format of Trellis hyperprograms. The translation converted the control structures of CSP statements and the message buffers between CSP processes into PT net structures with the appropriate control behaviors. Each place in the PT net represents a statement from the source program. We annotated the places with CSP source code; each place is mapped to a copy of the CSP process that contains its statement, with that statement highlighted (this gives a reader some context for the statement).

The result is a browsing system for simulating the parallel execution of CSP programs. The simulation proceeds by selecting buttons in the text browser to "execute" statements one at a time. The simulation proceeds at user speed and at a user's discretion, following a user's train of thought as browsing progresses.

The first view (Fig. 10.4a) shows the editor client full-screen to illustrate the graphical structure of this particular model. The next view (Fig. 10.4b) shows the editor client with a closeup of the net, with the text browser displaying the CSP code segments that are active at this point in simulated execution.

3.3. Example: Process Simulation in Trellis

We just saw user-directed simulation of processes in Trellis. This section illustrates a facility of the model that allows non-user directed control in a process simulation. The method uses timed transitions in the net, a Lisp interpreter in the αTrellis engine, and chunks of Lisp code (called *agents*) on net transitions [22, 25]. When a transition is fired, its Lisp agent (if one is present) is executed. Trellis in this form is like the concurrent language Linda, in that a sequential kernel language (Lisp) is separate from the parallel control flow language (timed PT nets).

Lisp agents are responsible for, among other things, setting control traps and triggers as the net executes. A transition in a Trellis model has two time values—a minimum and a maximum. By default, the minimum is 0 units and the maximum is ∞. When a transition first becomes enabled, the minimum time must pass before the engine will honor a request to fire it; if the maximum time passes after enabling without any client firing the transition, then the engine will fire it automatically. In effect, the minimum time is a delay, and the maximum time is a time-out. Under these semantics, the "0,∞" default timings cause a transition to behave exactly like an untimed transition (i.e., no delay, never times out).

In the αTrellis engine, the time on a transition can either be a constant or it can be the value of a Lisp variable. Thus execution of a Lisp agent can

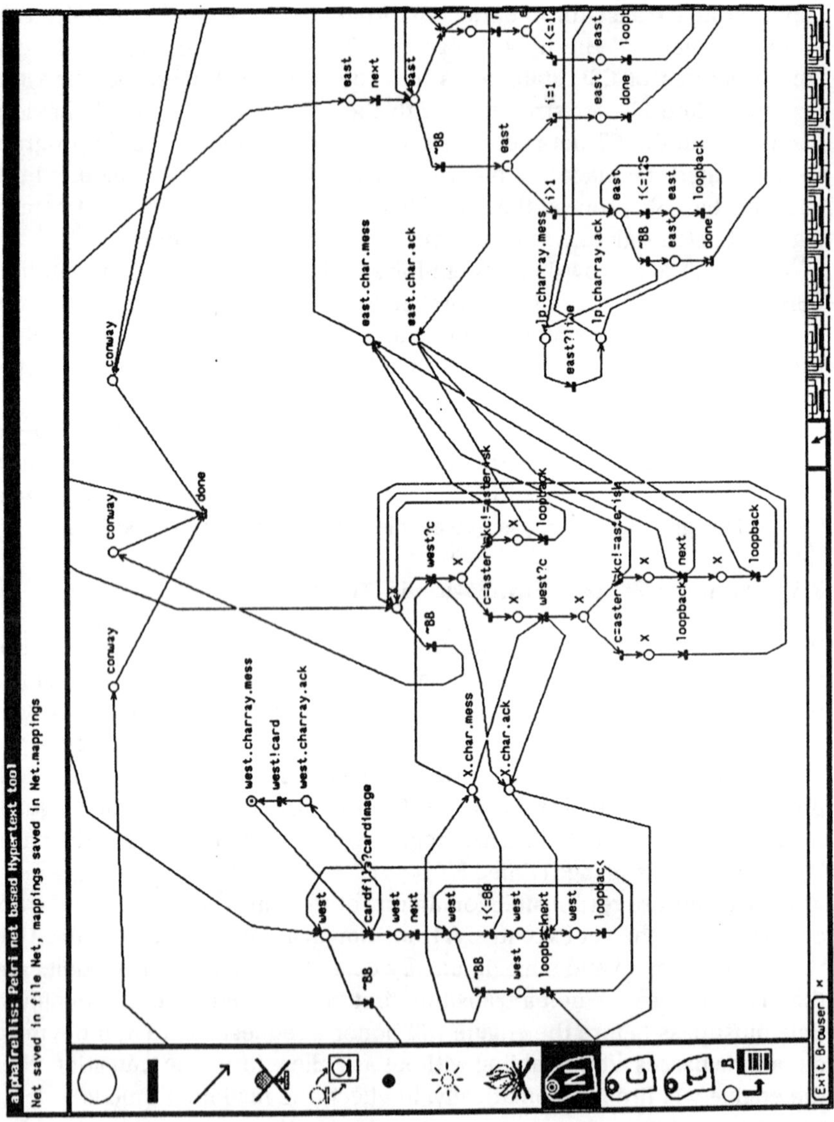

a

alphaTrellis: Petri net based Hypertext tool

Net saved in file Net, mappings saved in Net.mappings

conway
conway
conway
done
west.charray.mess
west!card
west.charray.ack
west
~BB
cardfile?cardimage
west
next
west
~BB
i<=88
west
west
loopback
next
west
loopback
X.char.mess
X.char.ack
~BB
west?c
X
c=aster
kc!=asterisk
X
X
west?c
loopback
X
c=aster
kc!=asterisk
X
X
loopback
next
X
loopback
east.char.mess
east.char.ack
east
next
east
~BB
east
lp.charray.mess
east?line
lp.charray.ack
i>1
i=1
i<=125
east
east
east
done
~BB
i<=125
east
east
loopback
done

Exit Browser

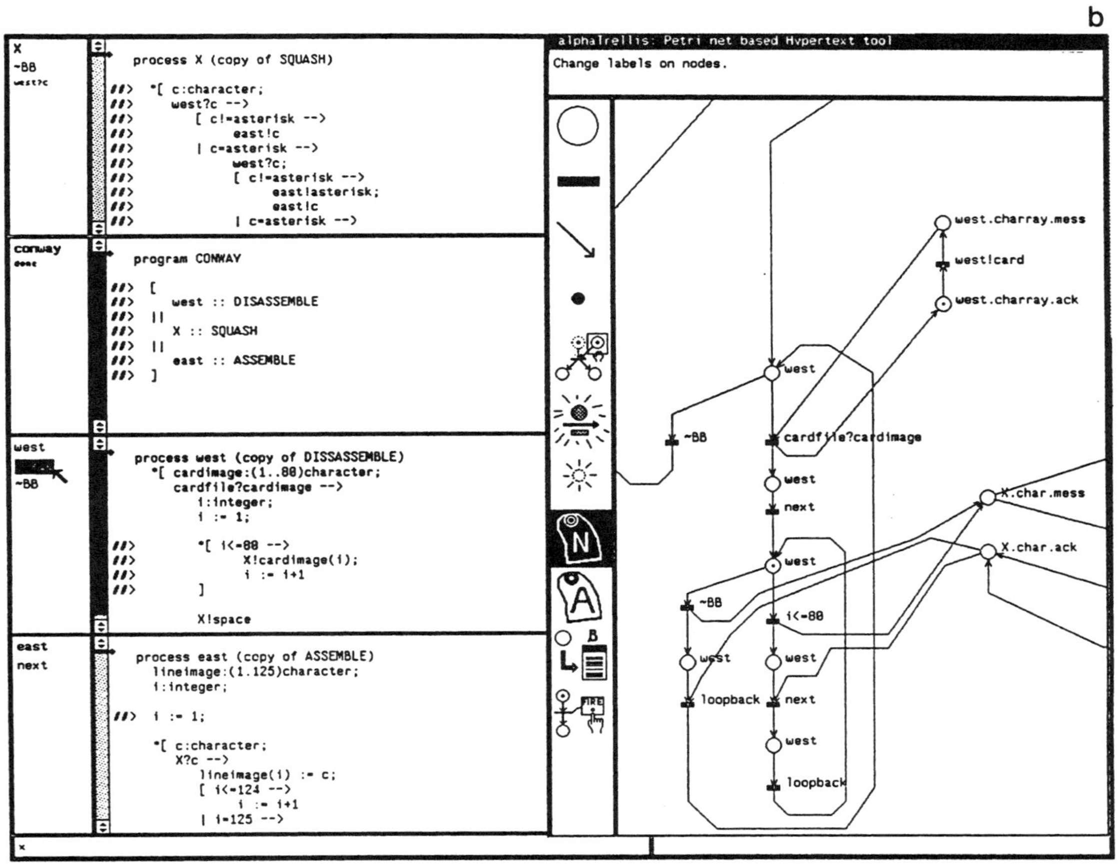

b

alphaTrellis: Petri net based Hypertext tool

Change labels on nodes.

```
X
~BB
west?c

process X (copy of SQUASH)

///> *[ c:character;
///>    west?c -->
///>      [ c!=asterisk -->
///>           east!c
///>      | c=asterisk -->
///>           west?c;
///>           [ c!=asterisk -->
///>                east!asterisk;
///>                east!c
///>           | c=asterisk -->
```

```
conway
done

program CONWAY

///> [
///>    west :: DISASSEMBLE
///> ||
///>    X :: SQUASH
///> ||
///>    east :: ASSEMBLE
///> ]
```

```
west
~BB

process west (copy of DISSASSEMBLE)
  *[ cardimage:(1..80)character;
     cardfile?cardimage -->
        i:integer;
        i := 1;

///>    *[ i<=80 -->
///>          X!cardimage(i);
///>          i := i+1
///>    ]

        X!space
```

```
east
next

process east (copy of ASSEMBLE)
  lineimage:(1.125)character;
  i:integer;

///> i := 1;

  *[ c:character;
     X?c -->
        lineimage(i) := c;
        [ i<=124 -->
             i := i+1
        | i=125 -->
```

west.charray.mess
west!card
west.charray.ack
west
~BB
cardfile?cardimage
west
next
X.char.mess
X.char.ack
west
~BB
i<=80
west
west
loopback
next
west
loopback

FIG. 10.4. αTrellis used for browsing a CSP parallel program.

change transition time values while a hyperprogram is being browsed. To illustrate, consider a net structure that pops up a help window automatically if a reader sits idle for a certain period of time. An author cannot hope to assign an initial time-out value to this popup transition that is comfortable for all readers (for some it will be too fast, for others too slow). However, he can assign a reasonable initial value and then put an *adaptation* agent on transitions in the net. This agent will compute a running average of the time each reader spends looking at each content element. Then, every so many button clicks, the Lisp variable for the popup transition timing is set to some multiple of the reader's average.

The αTrellis engine has a very fine grained internal clock. Individual hyperprograms can contain their own clocks, at their own speeds, by including a place–transition loop with the transition timed to fire at some interval; when it fires, its Lisp agent increments a Lisp variable "clock." Then, the averaging agent will look like this:

```
(setq clicks (+ clicks 1))
(cond ( (eq clicks ccount)
   (setq clicks 0)
   (setq dwell (/ (+ dwell (/ (– clock oclock) ccount)) 2))
   (setq min (* 3 dwell))
   (setq max (* 6 dwell))
   (setq oclock clock) ) )
```

The Dining Philosophers Process. The canonical concurrency example of the Dining Philosophers will further illustrate Lisp agents in Trellis process simulation. An implementation of four philosophers is shown in Fig. 10.5. Shown is the initial screen when the hyperprogram is invoked, with a view giving the names of the various components. Two text browsing clients are executing with the αTrellis editor client; the leftmost browser shows place content elements (which in this example are inconsequential) and the middle browser shows Lisp agents on the enabled transitions.

The internal clock for this hyperprogram is the detached pair of loops visible at the top of the editor window, with transitions labeled "slower" and "faster" to alter the execution speed of dining. Initially, the timings on philosopher fork events are (0,∞), so no action takes place until the user is ready. When the button labeled "init" is selected (and its agent "init.lsp" executed), the timings on transitions are altered to the ones shown in Fig. 10.6. The timings on philosopher fork events then allow a reader two ways to influence process execution. A philosopher can be made to directly pick up a fork by selecting the corresponding button in the text browser (or in the agent brows-

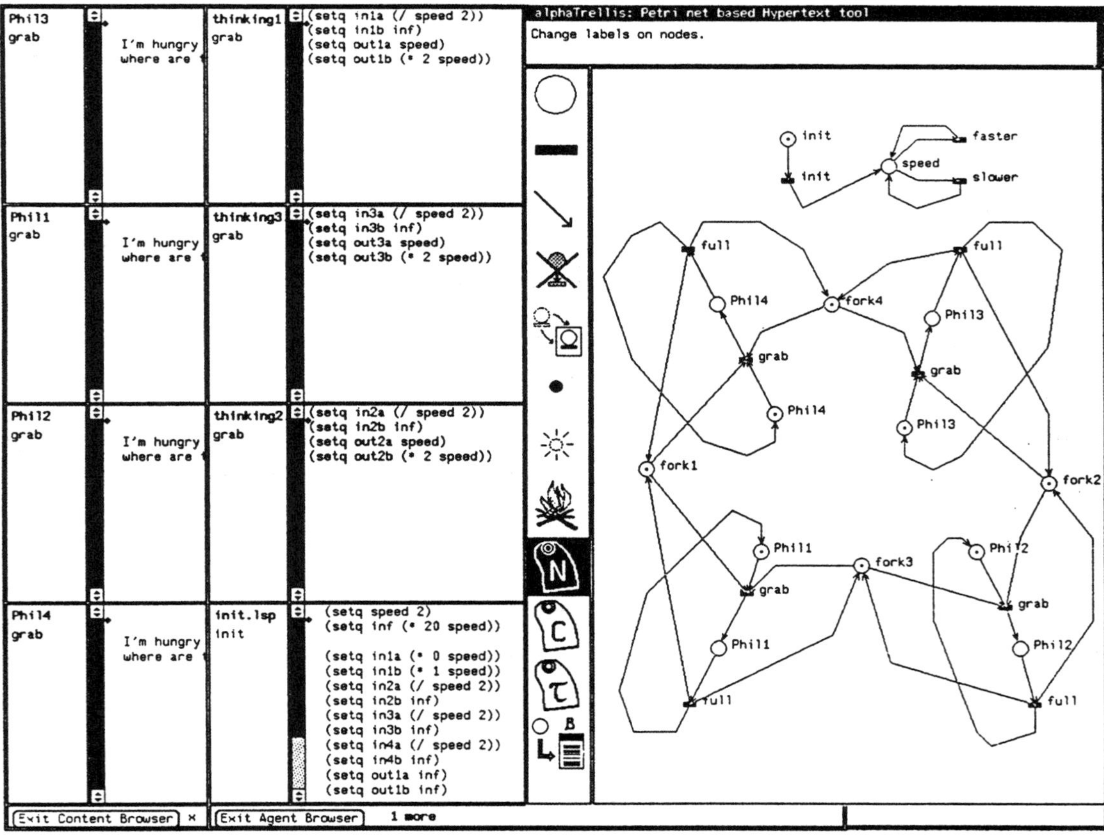

FIG. 10.5. Initial Dining Philosophers screen.

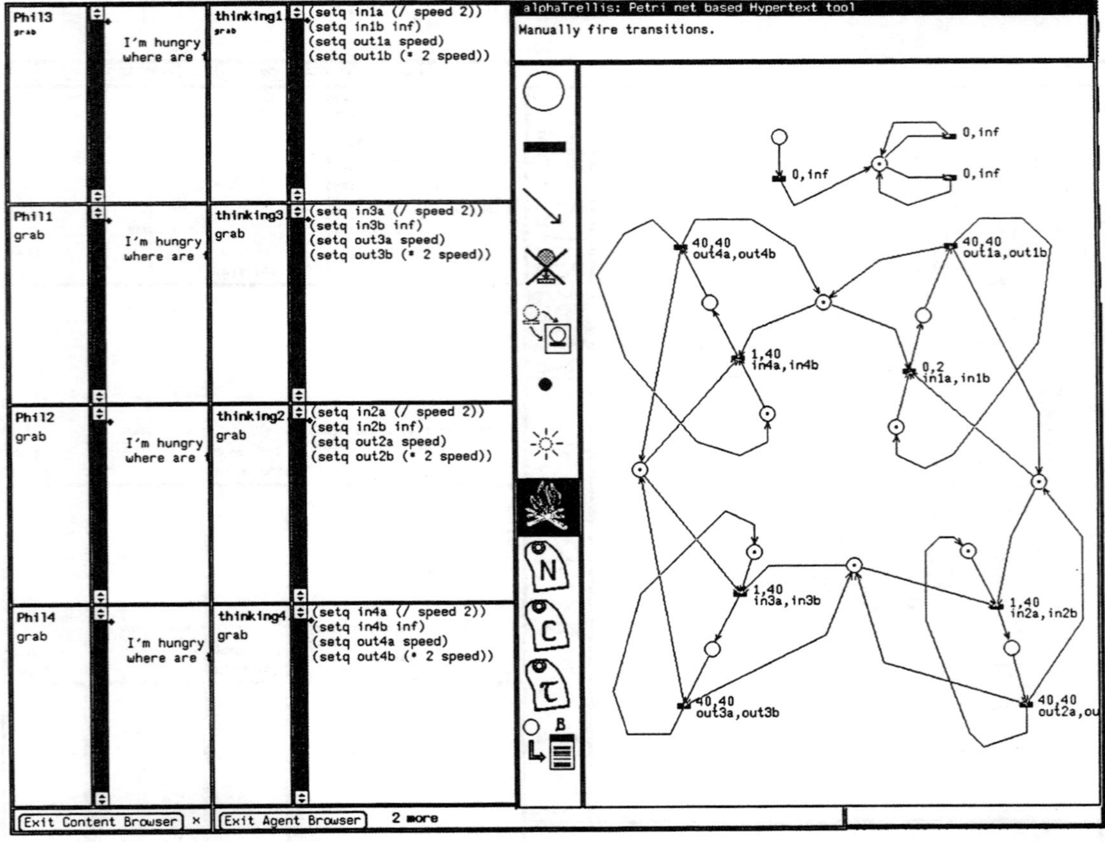

FIG. 10.6. Timings after firing Init button.

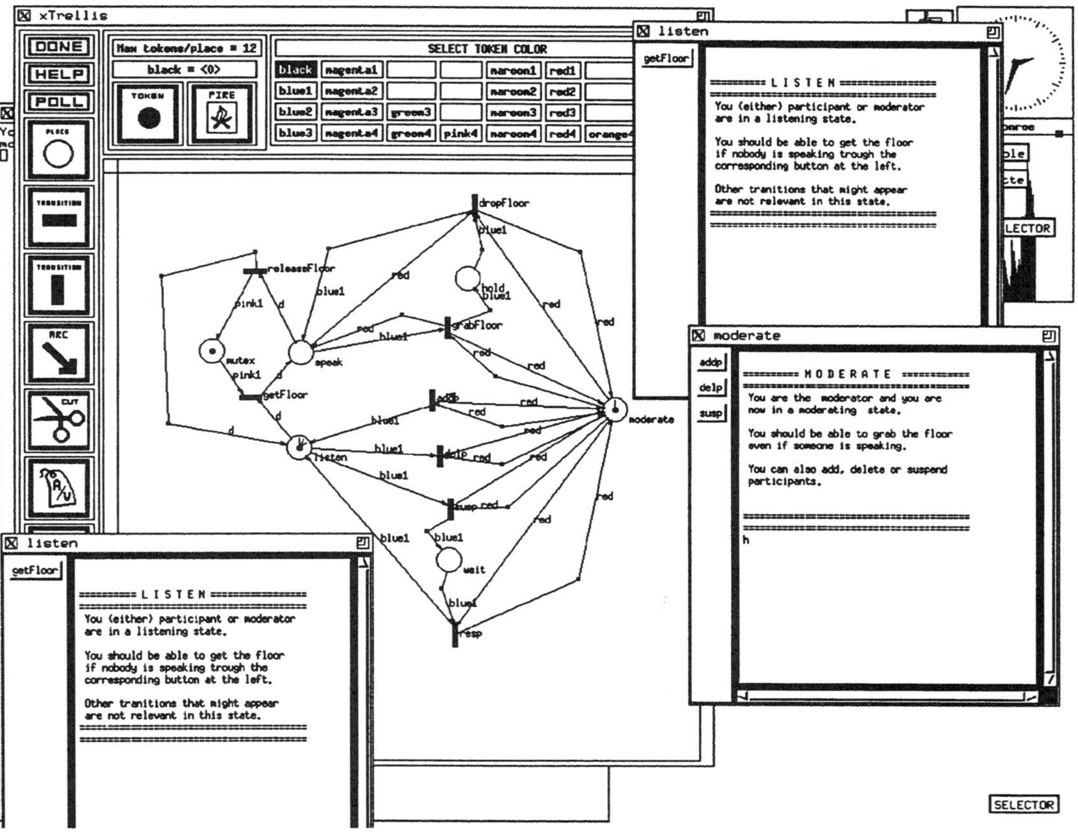

FIG. 10.7. Meeting protocol implementation.

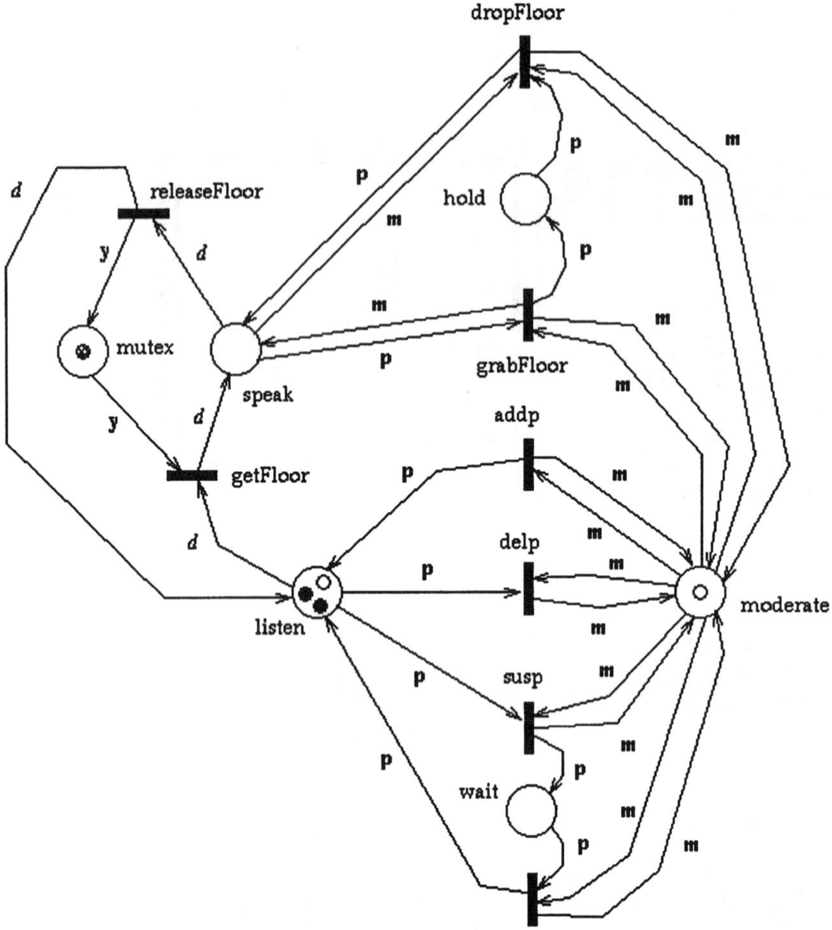

FIG. 10.8. Detail of the meeting protocol specification.

er); however, if the user just sits back and watches, one philosopher (the one with lower timing values) will time out and pick up a fork automatically. Picking up the fork causes execution of a Lisp agent that further alters the timings so the fork will then be put down automatically. Putting the fork down runs a Lisp agent that alters the timings again so the next philosopher picks up a fork, and so on. In this way, the Lisp agents implement a round-robin scheduling policy that will take over whenever the reader does not directly select the execution order. Other scheduling policies can obviously be simulated by writing different agents to adjust the timing triggers appropriately.

3.4. χTrellis: Collaboration Protocols and Hypermedia

The preceding examples introduced the αTrellis prototype in some detail because our early experiments in modeling have been performed with it. Our current efforts are shifting to a newer prototype called χTrellis, which operates in the X-windows environment.

Figure 10.7 shows a snapshot of χTrellis, illustrating the use of Trellis specifications for directing a meeting among several participants. The editor client that shows the related net is in the upper left corner of the screen and client–displays corresponding to the individual participants in the meeting are found around the periphery. More detailed information about this implementation can be found in a separate paper [12]. The Trellis specification, shown in the upper left hand window in the figure, is designed to limit some operations to the moderator and to permit the moderator to override participants if desired. The remaining windows in the display represent the view seen by a meeting participants and by the moderator. In actual use, display of these documents would be distributed over multiple, separated, workstations and would serve as "traffic control" for an ongoing meeting.

Figure 10.8 shows a clearer view of the protocol specification. This represents only a notational convenience over that of αTrellis since specifications in either form can be translated mechanically to the other form. Colored tokens are typed, with different types represented by different colors. Color expressions appear on the arcs of the net, defining which combination of token classes are required for a transition to fire and specifying which tokens classes will be produced when the transition is fired. In Fig. 10.8, these color expressions appear in boldface and italic, representing constants and variables respectively.

In the example of Fig. 10.8, colored tokens are used to distinguish classes of participants. The specific classes of interest that defined in this example are the discussion's moderator and its participants (in addition, some internal classes are defined to implement higher level structures).

As further illustration, consider the fragment of specification shown in Fig. 10.9. This fragment represents two modifications to the original specification. First, it distinguishes the participants from one another by creating a separate class of token for each participant rather than an anonymous pool of participant–class tokens as in Fig. 10.8. Second, it defines a new mechanism by which a moderator can add (addp) and remove (delp) participants from the group listening to the meeting (current listeners are found in place listen). Here, the pool represents a collection of potential meeting participants, all represented by distinct colors. The moderator is represented by an additional color, as seen in the moderate place. Addition of a meeting participant is accomplished by firing the addp transition. As the specification

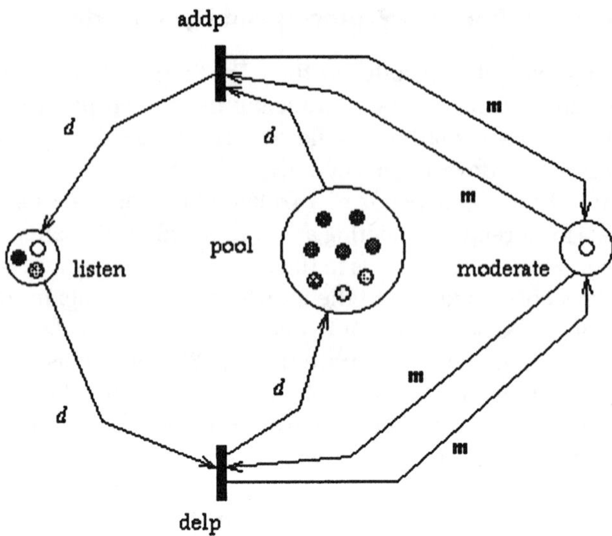

FIG. 10.9. Adding and removing meeting participants.

shows, the expressions on arcs leading into addp require that a moderator (with token of color **m**) be present in place "moderate," and that a new participant be selected from pool, represented by *d.* Firing the transition removes the participant token from the pool, adding one of the same type "listen." Essentially this moves the participant from pool to listen. Additionally, the moderator's token cycles back into moderate.

Note that the color expressions can involve multiple tokens, as in the arcs leading between listen and newMod in the new fragment shown in Fig. 10.10, which shows how to modify the original specification to permit the moderator to exchange roles with a participant. In this fragment, the moderator's token color is represented by a variable rather than a constant as the identity of the moderator may be changed. The expressions leading into newMod require that the variable *m* be bound to the moderator type because of the token found in moderate. Consequently the expression $d + m$ specifies two tokens: one corresponding to the moderator and another corresponding to one of the listeners (we assume no color aliasing so the two tokens' colors are different). The effect of firing newMod, then, is to place the *d* type token into the moderate place (i.e., this participant becomes the moderator), while also restoring both to the pool of listeners.

Figure 10.11 shows a modified specification reflecting the changes described here. Examples like this show that the specification can be modified flexibly to reflect different meeting policies. Because protocols are interpreted, dynamic modifications can be made, either by a person editing the

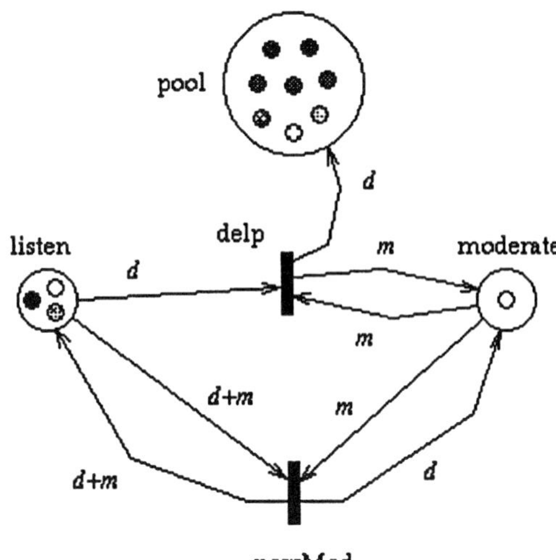

FIG. 10.10. A second modification to the meeting protocol.

specification "on the fly," or through the actions of Trellis dynamic adaptation agents, which could modify the effective appearance of the protocol based on "observation" of the meeting participants' actions.

4. PROCESS ANALYSIS: MODEL CHECKING

Trellis and its implementations provide a formal structure for hyperprograms, and net analysis techniques have been developed for exploiting this formalism. One very promising approach involves our adaptation of automated verification techniques called *model checking* [6] from the domain of concurrent programs. This approach allows verification of browsing properties of Trellis hyperprograms expressed in a temporal logic notation called CTL. An author can state a property such as "no matter how a document is browsed, if Node X is visited, Node Y must have been visited within 10 steps in the past." The model checker efficiently verifies that the PT net structure maintains the validity of the formula denoting the property.

In model checking, a state machine (the model) is annotated with atomic properties that hold at each state (such as "content is visible" or "button is selectable"), and then search algorithms are applied to the graph of the state machine to see if the subcomponents of a formulae hold at each state. By composing the truth values of these subformulae, one obtains a truth value for the entire formula. For PT nets, we obtain a useful state machine from the *coverability graph* explained in an earlier Trellis paper [23].

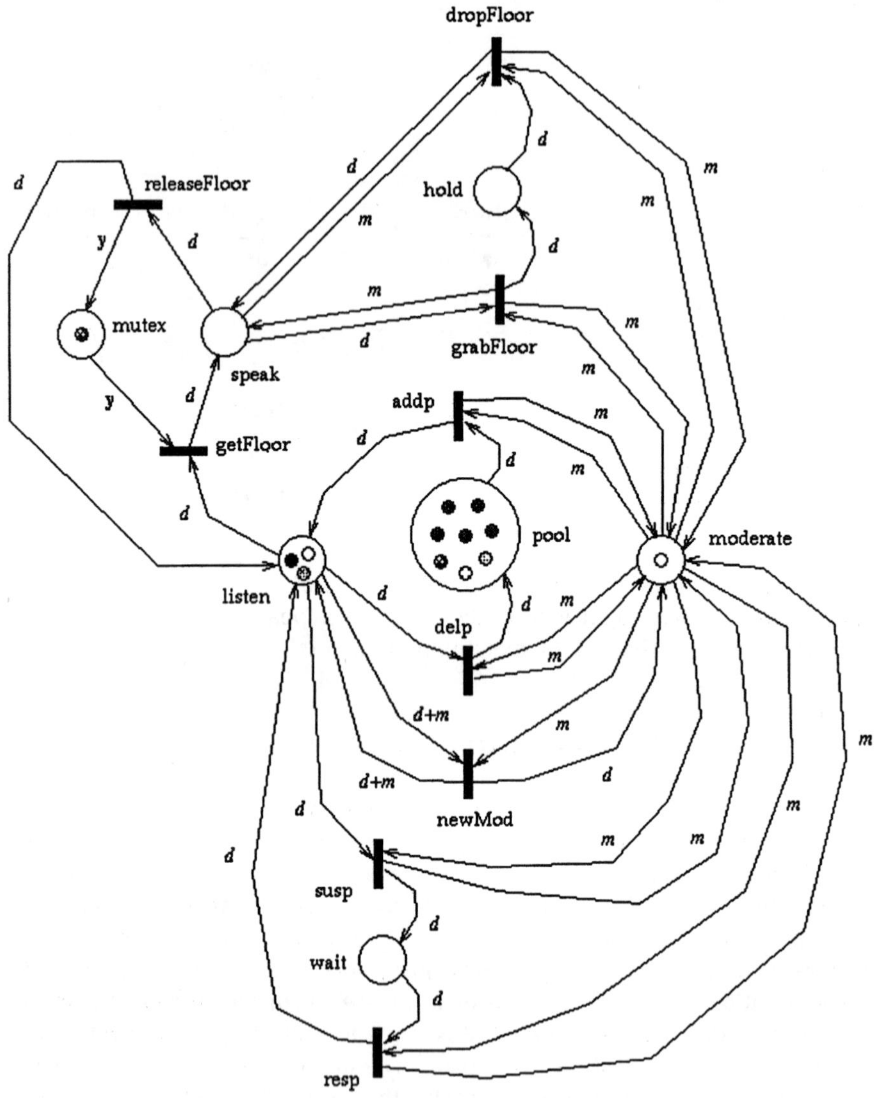

FIG. 10.11. The revised meeting protocol.

The details of our use of CTL are discussed elsewhere [27, 28]. For this rationale, it is sufficient to give an idea of how the method is applied to Trellis (and eventually to IMP/ACT) models. The Trellis document shown in Fig. 10.12 is a small net that expresses the browsing behavior found in some hypertext systems, namely that when a link is followed out of a node, the

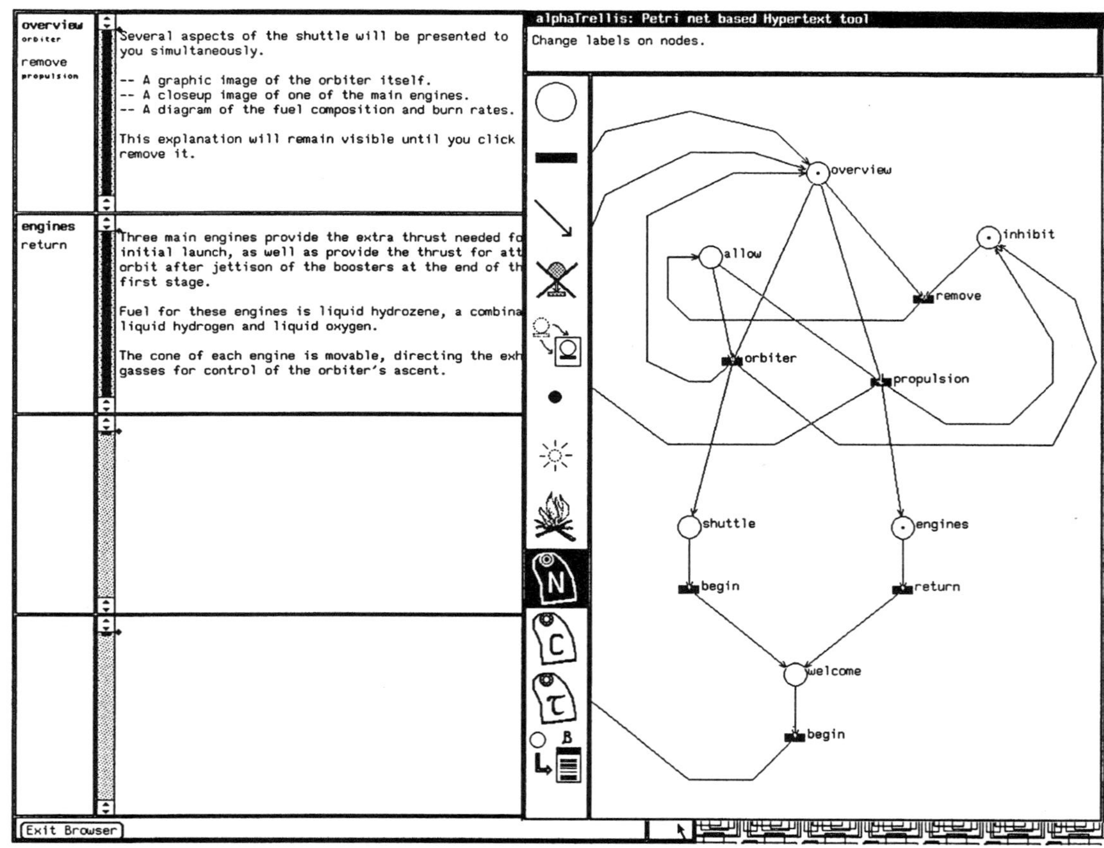

FIG. 10.12. Small Trellis structure with programmed browsing behavior.

source content stays visible and the target content is added to the screen. The source must later be explicitly disposed of by clicking a "remove" button.

After computing the coverability graph and translating it into the input format required by the checking tool, the model can be queried for desired browsing properties. These examples use the syntax of Clarke's CTL model checker, and show its output:

- Is there some browsing path such that at some point both the "orbiter" and "propulsion" buttons are selectable on one screen?

  | = EF(B_orbiter & B_propulsion).
  The formula is TRUE.

- Is it impossible for both the "shuttle" text and the "engines" text to be visible concurrently?

  | = AG(C_shuttle | C_engines).
  The formula is TRUE.

- Can both the "allow" access control and the "inhibit" access control ever be in force at the same time?

  | = EF(C_inhibit & C_allow).
  The formula is FALSE.

- Is it possible to select the "orbiter" button twice on some browsing path without selecting the "remove" button in between?

  | = EF(B_orbiter & AX(A[B_remove U B_orbiter])).
  The formula is FALSE.

This particular Trellis model is very small compared to those encountered in realistic applications. Our checker has also been tested on larger Trellis documents–for example, the one shown back in Fig. 10.4. The state machine derived from this net contains over 6,000 states. Using a DECstation 5000/25, the performance of the model checker on formulae like those above is mostly on the order of a few seconds each, with the most complicated query we tried (not shown) requiring about 15 seconds to answer. We suspect that authors of Trellis models will find such performance not at all unreasonable for establishing the presence or absence of critical browsing properties, and we also expect that future implementations will exhibit improved performance.

5. CONCLUSION

The emergence of hypertext as an authoring-based prototyping mechanism suggests a modification of the view of the role of hypertext in CSCW as one in a set of independent technologies tied together into a collective environment by some metastructuring mechanism. In our work, the hypertext system retains its traditional job of information structuring but also gains the job of process structuring. In the added role, the hypertext structure adopts the role of the environmental metastructuring mechanism and can also fill the role of implementation mechanism for certain of the specific tools found in the environment.

The Trellis net-based representation provides a means for specifying a protocol that can be used directly for verification, training, and simulation. When the hypertextual basis is dynamic, it also provides the means for rapid prototyping of the protocol. On the other hand, the visual presentation of the net requires attention be paid to the complexity of the image, requiring investigation of structuring through abstraction and hierarchy.

The Trellis implementation decision to interpret the underlying net suggests further experimentation with an incremental methodology in protocol development *and* in incremental protocol verification. As prototyping proceeds, more sophisticated behaviors are added, refined, and verified. There is a nice symmetry between this view of protocol development and the worldview of a hypertext as a dynamic web, growing and developing as new paths are encountered and envisioned.

We close by noting that the concepts promoted in Trellis are of utility in other contexts as well, particularly in the context of the World Wide Web. Modifiable browsing semantics specification, particularly the mechanisms of multiheaded links (supporting concurrency) and multitailed links (supporting synchronization), can be found in [5, 15]. Further uses of the Colored-Petri-Net-based specification in support of Web-based collaboration can be found in the CobWeb project [20]. Finally, potential applications for net structures in organizing Web material taken from disparate locations can be found in the Walden's Paths project [9, 14].

ACKNOWLEDGMENTS

This work was primarily supported by the National Science Foundation under grant numbers IRI-9015439, IRI-9007746, IRI-9214046, and IRI-9496187. We also acknowledge support from the Software Engineering Research Center (University of Florida and Purdue University), by the Texas Advanced Research Program under Grants No. 999903-155 and 999903-230, by Northrup Corporation, and by the CESDIS program at NASA.

REFERENCES

1. Apple Computer, Inc. *HyperCard User's Guide*. Apple Computer, Inc., 1987.
2. Apple Computer, Inc. *HyperCard Script Language Guide: The HyperTalk Language*. Addison-Wesley, 1988.

3. Eric A. Bier and Aaron Goodisman. "Documents as user interfaces". In Richard Furuta, editor, *EP90*, pp. 249–262. Cambridge University Press, September 1990. Proceedings of the International Conference on Electronic Publishing, Document Manipulation, and Typography, Gaithersburg, Maryland, September 1990.
4. James Bigelow. "Hypertext and CASE". *IEEE Software, 5*(2):23–27, March 1988.
5. Michael Capps, Brian Ladd, and P. David Stotts. "Enhanced graph models in the web: Multi-client, multi-head, multi-tail browsing". In Computer Networks and ISDN Systems, vol. 28 (Proc. of the 5th WWW Conf., May 6–10, 1996, Paris), pp. 1105–1112. This paper is available online at http://www5conf.inria.fr/fich_html/papers/P19/Overview.html.
6. E. Clarke, E. A. Emerson, and S. Sistla. "Automatic verification of concurrent systems". *ACM TOPLAS, 8*(2):244–263, April 1986.
7. Gil C. Cruz and Thomas H. Judd. "The role of a descriptive markup language in the creation of interactive multimedia documents for customized electronic delivery". In Richard Furuta, editor, *EP90*, pp. 277–290. Cambridge University Press, September 1990. Proceedings of the International Conference on Electronic Publishing, Document Manipulation, and Typography, Gaithersburg, Maryland, September 1990.
8. Paul M. English, Ethan S. Jacobson, Robert A. Morris, Kimbo B. Mundy, Stephen D. Pelletier, Thomas A. Polucci, and H. David Scarbro. An extensible, object-oriented system for active documents. In Richard Furuta, editor, *EP90*, pp. 263–276. Cambridge University Press, September 1990. Proceedings of the International Conference on Electronic Publishing, Document Manipulation, and Typography, Gaithersburg, Maryland, September 1990.
9. Richard Furuta, Frank M. Shipman III, Catherine C. Marshall, Donald Brenner, and Hao wei Hsieh. "Hypertext paths and the World-Wide Web: Experiences with Walden's Paths". In *Hypertext '97: the Eighth ACM Conference on Hypertext*, pp. 167–176. ACM, 1997. Southampton, U.K., April 6–11 1997.
10. Richard Furuta and P. David Stotts. Programmable browsing semantics in Trellis. In *Hypertext '89 Proceedings*, pp. 27–42. ACM, New York, November 1989.
11. Richard Furuta and P. David Stotts. *A hypermedia basis for the specification, documentation, verification, and prototyping of concurrent protocols*. Technical Report TAMU-HRL 94-003, Texas A&M University, Hypertext Research Lab, June 1994.
12. Richard Furuta and P. David Stotts. "Interpreted collaboration protocols and their use in groupware prototyping". In *Proceedings, ACM 1994 Conference on Computer Supported Cooperative Work*, pp. 121–132. Association for Computing Machinery, October 1994.
13. Anatol W. Holt. "Diplans: A new language for the study and implementation of coordination". *ACM Transactions on Office Information Systems, 6*(2):109–125, January 1988.
14. Frank M. Shipman III, Catherine C. Marshall, Richard Furuta, Donald A. Brenner, Hao-Wei Hsieh, and Vijay Kumar. "Using networked information to create educational guided paths". International Journal of Educational Telecommunications, *3*(4):383–400, 1997.
15. B. Ladd, M. Capps, D. Stotts, and R. Furuta. "Multi-head/Multi-tail Mosaic: Adding parallel automata semantics to the Web". In Proceedings of the 4th WWW Conference (WWW Journal, vol. 1), pp. 433–440. O'Reilly and Associates Inc., 1995. Boston, December 11–14, 1995. Also online at http://www.w3.org/pub/Conferences/WWW4/Papers/118/.
16. Tadao Murata. "Petri nets: Properties, analysis and applications". *Proceedings of the IEEE, 77*(4):541–580, April 1989.
17. James L. Peterson. *Petri Net Theory and the Modeling of Systems*. Prentice-Hall, Inc., 1981.
18. Wolfgang Reisig. *Petri Nets: An Introduction*. Springer-Verlag, 1985.
19. Tina Roth and Peter Aiken. *Hypertext support for software development: A retrospective assessment*, 1994. Internal report.
20. David Stotts, Jans Prins, Lars Nylan, and Tianli Fan. *CobWeb: Collaborative web browsing wiht tailorable rules for group interaction*, 1998. Internal report.
21. P. D. Stotts and R. Furuta. "Browsing parallel process networks". *Journal of Parallel and Distributed Computing, 9*(2):224–235, 1990.

22. P. D. Stotts and R. Furuta. "Hypertextual concurrent control of a Lisp kernel". *Journal of Visual Languages and Computing, 3*(2):221–236, June 1992.
23. P. David Stotts and Richard Furuta. Petri-net-based hypertext: Document structure with browsing semantics. *ACM Transactions on Information Systems, 7*(1):3–29, January 1989.
24. P. David Stotts and Richard Furuta. "αTrellis: A system for writing and browsing Petri-net-based hypertext". In *Proceedings of the Tenth International Conference on Application and Theory of Petri Nets*, pp. 312–328, June 1989. Bonn, W. Germany.
25. P. David Stotts and Richard Furuta. "Temporal hyperprogramming". *Journal of Visual Languages and Computing, 1*(3):237–253, 1990.
26. P. David Stotts and Richard Furuta. "Modeling and prototyping collaborative software processes". In Shimon Y. Nof, editor, *Information and Collaboration Models of Integration*, pp. 365–390. Kluwer Academic Publishers, June 1994. Based on the NATO Advanced Research Workshop on Integration: Information and Collaboration Models, Il Crocco, Italy, June 6–11, 1993. Also available as Technical Report TR93-020, Computer Science Collaboratory, University of North Carolina at Chapel Hill, 1993; and as Technical Report TAMU-HRL 93-006, Hypermedia Research Laboratory, Texas A&M University, July 1993.
27. P. David Stotts, Richard Furuta, and J. Cyrano Ruiz. "Hyperdocuments as automata: Trace-based browsing property verification". In D. Lucarella, J. Nanard, M. Nanard, and P. Paolini, editors, *Proceedings of the ACM Conference on Hypertext (ECHT '92)*, pp. 272–281. ACM Press, 1992.
28. P. David Stotts, Richard Furuta, and Cyrano Ruiz Cabarrus. "Hyperdocuments as automata: Verification of trace-based browsing properties by model checking". *ACM Transactions on Information Systems, 16*(1):1–30. January 1998.
29. Willem R. van Biljon. "Extending Petri nets for specifying man-machine dialogues". *International Journal of Man-Machine Studies, 28*:437–455, 1988.

CHAPTER

11

Problems of Decentralized Control: Using Randomized Coordination to Deal With Uncertainty and Avoid Conflicts

Joseph Pasquale
University of California, San Diego

1. INTRODUCTION

Distributed systems based on decentralized control are becoming increasingly important; a good example is the Internet. A well-designed decentralized control system offers the potential of high performance, reliability, and scalability, to a much greater degree than distributed systems with centralized control. However, there are certain significant problems that arise in these systems that inhibit coordination. These problems are fundamental: They are an inherent part of any system where there are multiple decision makers and communication between them takes significant time. These problems can never be eliminated completely; they can only be dealt with by minimizing the damage that results from them, or by lowering the probability that their negative effects will occur. Indeed, it is a tribute to the power of distributed systems that, despite these problems, it is still worth building systems based on decentralized control.

In this chapter we explore the nature of these problems and the value of using *randomization* to attack them. Randomization can support coordination in a number of ways, such as preventing "mutually conflicting" decisions. It can also be used for coordination in cases where it is not known what is the best thing to do, and so you try something (at random), see what happens, and learn so that you do better next time. Finally, randomization is useful when you do not want others to know what you will do, so that they may not take advantage of your decisions for malicious reasons.

As an illustration of the type of problems under study, consider an everyday activity that most of us are familiar with: driving to work. You and many others are driving downtown on a highway during rush hour, on your way to a very important meeting for which you cannot afford to be late. Over the radio, you hear a traffic report that states that there is a major traffic jam a few miles ahead of you. You know of an exit that will allow you to take an alternative route. You have several options:

- You can take the alternate route which, while longer in distance, may take less time because you may be able to travel at a faster speed.
- You can stick with your current route, whose traffic may lessen if many other drivers decide to get off the highway and take alternative routes.

Unfortunately, you must decide quickly what to do, and then stick with whatever route you think is best, because you will not have time to correct a wrong decision later. How can the situation be prevented where all drivers heading to the same destination decide to take, say, the same route, creating congestion? A possible solution is somehow to spread the traffic more or less evenly over all routes. If congestion persists because there are more cars than available capacity over all routes, an additional solution is for some drivers to voluntarily remove their cars from the traffic. This way, at least some fraction of drivers will successfully reach their destinations in time, rather than all drivers being late. If only we could be so cooperative!

What is needed is a method of *coordination*, "the act of managing interdependencies between activities performed to achieve a goal" [1]. Coordination can be achieved by having each driver randomly decide whether or not to get off the highway (to remove their cars from the traffic). If a driver chooses to remain in the traffic, the driver then selects a route at random (to spread traffic over different routes). This use of randomization allows autonomous decision makers (the drivers) that have limited shared information (the level and distribution of traffic) to independently allocate from a shared set of resources (the routes) in a minimally conflicting manner.

The foregoing problem is very common in real distributed systems with decentralized control, where there are many resources and many users of resources, and conflicts between users all trying simultaneously to use the same resources are detrimental to overall performance. Examples include:

- A broadcast communication channel, where a busy station attempts to send when it senses that the channel is free. However, if more than one busy station exists, their transmissions will conflict, resulting in no messages getting through.
- A processor load-sharing system, where the goal is to assign jobs to processors such that no processor is heavily loaded while some are

lightly loaded. Thus, a processor may decide to move a job to the least-loaded processor. However, if many processors select the same processor to move jobs, it will become overloaded, and the load will remain or become even more unbalanced.

- A communication network routing system, where it is desirable to distribute traffic across different routes to avoid congestion. Again, many traffic-generating sources may decide on using the same least-loaded route, resulting in congestion.

We begin by discussing the nature of distributed systems and one of their most important features, their control structure, which may be centralized or decentralized. We analyze the fundamental problems of decentralized control, and how they affect coordination, the central organizing activity of a distributed system that promotes order over chaos. We then analyze the positive role that randomization can play in the coordination process, and we present examples of using randomization in various experiments on decentralized control. Finally, we offer our conclusions.

2. DISTRIBUTED SYSTEMS

Let us begin with some basics: What is a distributed system? Very simply (and informally), a *distributed system* is a set of multiple computing nodes connected by a communication network. A *user* can program a subset of the nodes to solve a computational problem. Each node does some computation, nodes communicate intermediate results between each other, and the final result is communicated to the user.

Distributed systems have become popular because of advances in both hardware and software technology. Hardware components such as processors, memories, storage media, and network transmission media, have become smaller, cheaper, faster, and more reliable, at an ever-increasing rate. Economy of scale favors the construction of computing systems by aggregating commodity parts. The system software infrastructure for taking advantage of the distributed power of these systems has reached a critical level of maturity. In addition to the underlying communication protocols, this includes higher level control–communication programming abstractions such as the remote procedure call, and organizational structures for distributed software such as the client–server model.

In actuality, all systems are *distributed systems*. This is because, at some low-enough level, one has an organization of components that operate and communicate in a structured manner. What really matters, especially in this chapter, is how *control* is distributed in the system. This is generally a function of the speed of communication between the components, relative to the speed at which their states are changing. If communication speed is relatively high, one can have a central state repository that can be kept very current, and a central decision maker operating based on its inputs and the state as recorded in the repository. This is *centralized control*.

Alternatively, it may be best to distribute control over multiple decision makers that can work cooperatively, without necessarily giving up autonomy (at least not completely). This is *decentralized control*. With decentralized control, there is no shared state that is simultaneously available to the decision makers. The period of state change is comparable to communication time; in particular, by the time you receive a message, the state may have changed.

Decentralized control has numerous advantages, including the following:

- *Reliability*: Control can be made redundant so that if any decision maker fails, others can continue to operate and perform its function. This is the principle of avoiding dependence of the system's operation on any single point of failure.
- *Performance*: The parallelism derived from multiple decision-making nodes can increase throughput. This is the principle of avoiding bottlenecks by not tying the system's performance to any particular node (e.g., the slowest node). Furthermore, response is improved by having decision-makers located close to where their decisions are needed. This is the principle of co-locating control and data.
- *Scalability*: Because the system is already designed to support multiple decision-making nodes, adding more should not warrant a change in structure. The degree of scalability especially depends on how flexible the organizational structure is, and whether control relationships are symmetrical and adaptable, rather than hierarchical and fixed.
- *Autonomy*: Because control is not constrained to be centralized, a node need not abandon control of itself to some "master" node. Rather, in systems where control relationships are flexible (part of what the organizational structure defines), a node can maintain control over itself when autonomy is important, or decide to share control when group decision making is most advantageous.

As one might expect, these advantages come at a price.

3. THE FUNDAMENTAL PROBLEMS OF DECENTRALIZED CONTROL

There are two fundamental problems that arise in decentralized control systems:

The State-Information Uncertainty Problem. There is no consistently observable global state describing the entire system because state information is distributed. The state information takes time to collect; the global system state may have changed by the time this happens. Consequently, decision makers must operate under uncertainty, and make decisions based on possibly incorrect, out-of-date, and conflicting, state information.

The Mutually Conflicting Decision Problem. As there are multiple decision makers, many decisions are made in parallel and may conflict. This is due to a number of reasons:

- A decision maker may not know the decision procedure of the other decision makers (a decision procedure is an algorithm that, given a set of inputs and a state, generates a decision, that is, what action to take given the current observations and circumstances).
- The locally optimal decision may not be globally optimal.
- Decision makers may have differing views of the system state.
- Decision makers may have the same view of a system state, which happens to be incorrect.

One can try to solve the state-information uncertainty problem by increasing communication between decision makers. They can exchange their views, and then take part in an agreement protocol to converge on a single system state. However, by the time all this communication happens, the agreed-upon system state may be an outdated view. Furthermore, communication incurs overhead which can itself negatively affect the system and increase response time, which inhibits effective control.

One can try to solve the mutually conflicting decision problem by endowing each decision maker with either the same decision procedure, or different ones appropriate to each one but making all of them known to all decision makers. The decision procedures can be assumed to be common knowledge [2], meaning that everyone (the set of all the decision makers) knows X (the set of all the decision procedures), and everyone knows that everyone knows X, and everyone knows that everyone knows that everyone knows X, *ad infinitum*. However, because they are all working with potentially different information, common knowledge does not ensure the optimal group decision. One can try to resolve this problem by using an agreement protocol to "coordinate" decisions (along with views of the system state), with the same problem of overhead and delayed response as mentioned earlier.

In a real system with autonomous decision makers, the common knowledge assumption and the use of agreement protocols are often not applicable. Real decision makers will be limited in their computational capacity, they may have to operate under real-time constraints, and furthermore, one must consider the possibility that they may act maliciously, for selfish or other reasons.

Despite all this, even if the latter-mentioned problems did not exist, one can see that one can never hope to build decentralized systems where all decision makers make "optimal" decisions. This is because of the two fundamental problems of decentralized control. However, one does not have to give up completely when optimal solutions do not exist. The subject of this chapter shows the value of randomization for efficient coordination in real systems.

4. THE NECESSITY OF COORDINATION

Coordination is the process of decision makers making choices that are harmonious, that "fit together" so that a common goal is achievable, or is better achieved (e.g., with higher efficiency, in less time, at less cost, and so forth). Coordination necessarily requires that the two fundamental problems of decentralized control be addressed.

Let us consider each problem separately. Regarding the state-information uncertainty problem, coordination of decision makers requires mechanisms for directly observing that portion of the system state that is observable, and mechanisms for communicating with others who know that portion of the system state that is not directly observable. A decision maker must be able to decide whether it is best to directly observe or whether to communicate. The manner of communication is important, as indiscriminate communication is bad: Some know more than others, and some communication methods are more effective than others.

State information will not be perfectly accurate; it may be incorrect, incomplete, not timely, and so forth. Consequently, coordination requires methods for determining the *value* of state information. Given state information, how reliable is it? If it describes a past state, what can be said about the current state? If information is missing, can it be inferred from other information?

No single decision maker will know what is going on exactly (i.e., what the complete current system state is). To estimate the complete system state, coordination requires mechanisms for the composition of various sources of state information.

Regarding the mutually conflicting decision problem, coordination requires methods for finding a good "group decision." This may be done dynamically, using a protocol that allows decision makers to agree on a particular group decision. Alternatively, it may be done statically, by having a prearranged agreement on what decisions to make given various circumstances. This requires an assumption that the decision-making algorithms used by all decision makers are common knowledge. Unfortunately, even with this assumption, different decision makers can have different views of the system state (or, they might even have the same, but incorrect view), which can result in a bad group decision.

Because decision makers are autonomous and have limited capabilities, all that can be expected of them is that they "do the best they can" given difficult conditions; any illusions of achieving "optimal" behavior should be dismissed. In a real system, a decision maker must base decisions on multiple pieces of state information, from various sources, and of varying quality. Furthermore, these decisions take into account what others may or may not do.

5. THE USEFULNESS OF RANDOMIZATION

Randomization is a powerful concept that can be used to improve coordination. According to Webster's dictionary [3], randomization is an "arrangement (of samples ...) so as to simulate a chance distribution, reduce interference by irrelevant variables, and yield unbiased statistical data." As indicated by this definition, the concept of randomization is typically applied to the design of experiments. We use randomization for three reasons:

- to dynamically break symmetry in distributed systems without requiring a statically asymmetric control structure
- to reduce the need for complex interactions between decision makers
- to easily incorporate feedback mechanisms

The dictionary definition is worth analyzing in the context of coordination and decentralized decision making. Coordination can itself be considered a series of "experiments." The goal is to make good decisions, or perhaps more important, at least avoid very bad ones. The procedure is to sample the group decision space in an efficient way, and see what works best. One generates the hypothesis that a particular group decision is a good one, and evaluates whether it was indeed good or not.

Let us consider each part of the definition separately.

arrangement so as to simulate a chance distribution

Consider multiple decision makers, where each has a set of possible decisions from which to choose. Each must have some method to make this choice. For the moment, assume that there was some virtual master decision maker, that actually made the choices for all the real decision makers. This master generates an "arrangement" of choices by selecting a choice from each real decision maker's decision set in such a way that this selection process "simulates a chance distribution."

If the randomization process can be distributed, it can be done by multiple separate and independent processes. In this case, the master decision maker is indeed only a virtual requirement; the randomization process can be distributed over all the decision makers, and so no master is really required. The probability distribution defined over all decisions of all decision makers can be partitioned into separate distributions over each decision maker's set of possible decisions. Each decision maker chooses from its own decision set according to its own probability distribution.

After the decisions are made (i.e., selected and carried out), the experiment continues by observing the results of the decisions. Some metric must be used to determine whether the group decision was good or bad. Based on the result, the individual probability distributions may be updated to improve the future likelihood of good decisions and lessen that of bad decisions. That each decision maker agrees to execute this algorithm is an important part of coordination that must not be overlooked.

reduce interference by irrelevant variables

Distributed systems are generally so complicated that it is impossible for the decision procedure(s) to take everything into account that is relevant. More importantly, it is not generally known what is and is not relevant. Fortunately, the randomization process essentially filters out the irrelevant information because it does not rely on it. Furthermore, it introduces "noise" in the decision selection process, consequently lessening the negative effects of relevant bad information (e.g., incorrect views of the system state and bad predictions of what others will do).

There is an assumption here that there are relatively few combinations of decisions that will produce disastrous results. However, these particular combinations often arise exactly in situations where everyone is relying on, say, the same bad information, or that everyone is making the same bad predictions of what others will do. Introducing a little "confusion" can actually help in these situations!

yield unbiased statistical data

The randomization process basically provides a way of searching the decision space in an unbiased way, or biased toward finding good decisions as the experiments are repeated and one learns from the results. In this sense, the procedure is robust. If we lower our expectations, and focus on simply avoiding very bad decisions rather than trying to find the best decision, this general search procedure works generally very well.

Using a distributed randomization process in a decentralized control system also minimizes the biases of any single decision maker. (Compare this to the defining bias of a deterministic master decision maker in a centralized control system.) This is important, not only for the problems discussed earlier, which are the result of the limitations of decision makers due to multiplicity and distribution, but also for problems arising from "malicious" behavior. A malicious decision maker can decide to not play by the rules, and do what is best for itself even if it means that the rest of the system suffers. However, if one does not know exactly what others will do, it is difficult to take advantage of their decisions. This is actually a benefit derived from decentralized control, that one's decision is a small part of the group decision and so its effect is potentially limited, and from randomization, which introduces a nondeterminism that realizes this potential.

6. AVOIDING CONFLICTS AND WORKING TOGETHER

We now discuss a series of problems that illustrate the value of using randomization to coordinate autonomous decentralized decision-making agents. All have elements of the general problem of avoiding mutually conflicting decisions, as was illustrated in the traffic example described in the introduction. The problems all consider coordination for resource allocation where the following basic system model, which we will call *the multiuser multiresource system*, is used. Given n users and r resources, each of the users must allocate one of the resources in order to get its work done. The goal is to avoid the situation where many users try to allocate the same resource. The optimal situation occurs when no resource is allocated by more than one user and all the resources are allocated (assuming $n > r$).

In a real system, the mutually conflicting decisions modeled here correspond to access decisions made at nearly the same time (i.e., less than the time interval to communicate a message) by a set of users regarding the same resource. These decisions may conflict because each user is unaware that it is one of many users trying to access the same resource. The experiments consider various scenarios where communication between users may or may not be possible, and where the users may or may not work together in groups.

6.1. Using Randomization to Select Resources

In this first group of experiments, we focus on how randomization is effectively used to avoid the mutually conflicting decisions of many users selecting the same resource. We first discuss its value when there is no communicated information about the dynamic state of the system, and then we discuss the possible improvements when state information is available.

6.1.1. Resource Allocation Without Communication. In some systems, decision makers do not communicate, either because it is too costly or because it simply may not be possible to do so. Yet, to avoid conflicts, they must find a way of coordinating their decisions. Consider a multiuser multiresource system with no communication between users. All they know are the values of n and r, and they must independently make decisions that do not conflict. A simple approach is to use randomization, in particular, *Time–Space Randomization* (TSR) which works as follows. Each user makes a *time* decision: Should I try to allocate one of the resources (*yes* or *no*)? If the answer is yes, then it makes a *space* decision: Which resource shall I select (1, 2, . . . , r)? Both decisions are decided randomly: The time decision is answered in the affirmative with probability α (called the *access probability*), and each resource is selected with probability $1/r$ (equal likelihood).

After all users make their decisions, a resource will be either wasted (no one allocated it), congested (more than one user tried to allocate it), or utilized (exactly one user allocated it). Performance is measured by the following formula: $G = U - \beta C$, where the gain G is a measure of performance goodness, U is the number of utilized resources, C is the number of congested resources, and β is a parameter used to weigh the importance of congestion relative to utilization. The simple interpretation of this formula is that performance increases linearly with the number of utilized resources, and decreases linearly with the number of congested resources, and the ratio of the rate of decrease with congestion to the rate of increase with utilization is β.

The relevant questions are: What should the value of α be to maximize performance, and, how good is the performance? This problem was analyzed in [4], which we summarize here. It illustrates the value of using randomization to coordinate decision makers to improve performance without the aid of communication, and also indicates the limitations of the improvement.

The complete formulas (and proofs showing their validity) for the optimal access probability and the optimal expected gain are contained in [4]. Here, we present certain simple cases that adequately illustrate the points to be made. Consider a system where performance gain was simply a function of the number of utilized resources (i.e., $\beta = 0$, and that resources are scarce relative to users, i.e., $n > r$). The optimal access probability reduces to the simple formula of $\alpha^* = r/n$; in words, decide to access a resource with a probability based on the ratio of the number of resources to the number of users. For only one resource, the formula is very intuitive: access that resource $1/n$ of the time, as there are n-1 other users trying to access it.

Regarding expected gain, consider a system where there is an extremely large number of users and again with $\beta = 0$. Assuming each user limits it access according to the optimal access probability, how good is the performance? First, note that the maximum possible gain is r (i.e., all the resources are utilized), and the worst is 0 (i.e., all are either wasted or congested). This can be determined by evaluating EG^* as n goes to infinity. The result is surprisingly simple and elegant: $EG^* = r/e$, where e is the base of natural logarithms. This tells us that, by using randomization to coordinate the users, the system achieves approximately 37% of the maximum possible gain. Is this good or bad? It is good in that one can cheaply (i.e., without communication) achieve a positive level of performance, whereas without any coordination the performance can easily degrade to zero utilization. On the other hand, 63% of the potential performance is lost, and so while randomization does provide value, its value is certainly limited. Although this result is based on an infinite number of users, it turns out that EG* quickly approaches the value of r/e for $n >> r$.

A final interesting question is that of pooling versus partitioning: given $r > 1$ resources and $n = kr$ users for some integer $k \geq 1$, is it better for all n users to jointly compete for all r resources by pooling them, or is it better to partition the system *a priori* into r subsystems operating in parallel, each subsystem containing only k users that jointly compete for a single resource? An example is illustrated in Fig. 11.1.

The answer is that if coordination is based on TSR, it is always better to *partition*. One might imagine that pooling resources is always better because there is more opportunity for users finding resources to allocate. However, the potential for congestion dominates. By partitioning the system, an implicit coordination is imposed on the users; they are limited to working in small groups where the potential for mutually conflicting decisions is reduced. This raises the question as to whether there are situations where it is better to work in larger groups. We will see that, if there is sufficient communication, there is value to working in larger groups, whereas if communication is insufficient, it is better to limit the potential interactions (explicit and implicit) of decision-makers as much as possible.

6.1.2. Resource Allocation With Communication. TSR establishes the baseline performance improvement when there is no communicated state information. As one might expect, the availability of state information can

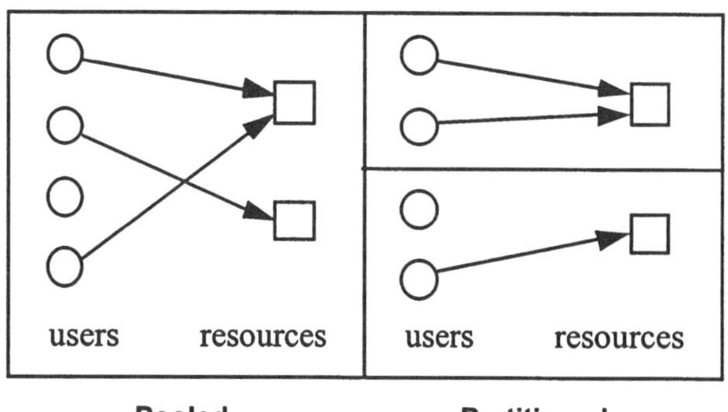

FIG. 11.1. Is it better to pool or to partition?

improve performance; but, one must take its quality and the overhead of communication into account to determine whether, in the end, it is worth it.

To illustrate the value of communicated state information, consider a distributed system of n host computers connected by a network, where the application is load balancing. Each host is composed of a scheduler and a server with a queue. Jobs arrive at each host. When a job arrives, the host's scheduler determines which server should execute the job; this may be the local server, or a remote server. The decision may be based on state information such as the loads (i.e., the number of jobs queued or executing, of the servers, if such information is available). Selecting the server is the key decision here; we evaluate several algorithms below. The job is then sent to the server and is immediately executed if the server is not already executing another job, or is queued for later execution. In the terminology of the multiuser multiresource model, the "users" are the schedulers and the "resources" are the queue-server pairs. See Fig. 11.2.

Note that, unlike the system model for resource access described in the earlier TSR example, congestion is not fatal. If more than one job is assigned to the same server, the additional jobs are simply queued. However, it is still the case that it is better to balance the load across the servers, and in particular, avoid situations where one server has queued jobs while the other server is idle.

We constructed a simulation model of this distributed system. The study is fully described in [5]. Jobs arrive at each host stochastically, with job arrival and service times exponentially distributed. Most important to this example, there is communicated state information: The loads of the servers are communicated to all the schedulers, but with a delay. The delay is a con-

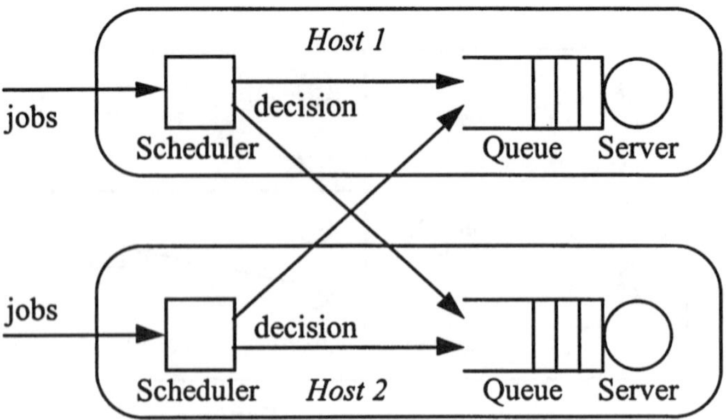

FIG. 11.2. Load balancing.

trol parameter of the experiment to evaluate the sensitivity of the various scheduling algorithms to information quality as affected by different amounts of delay.

We evaluated three different scheduling algorithms:

- Simple Randomization (SR): Select a server randomly, all with equal likelihood. This is like TSR, except that a scheduler always selects some server (rather than possibly abstaining from accessing, as in TSR).
- Weighted Randomization (WR): Select a server randomly, with the likelihood of selecting a server optimally weighted according to relative loads of the servers. A server that is heavily loaded will have a lower weight than one that is lightly loaded.
- Deterministic (DET): Select the server that has the least load.

These are all decentralized control algorithms, and each scheduler executes a copy of the same algorithm. WR and DET make use of the communicated state information, while SR does not. Consequently, one would expect system performance, defined by how quickly jobs are able to be serviced, to be better under WR and DET than under SR because they can take advantage of the additional information. However, WR and DET can also lead to worse performance if the information is unreliable (e.g., because it is not timely).

The results are that when the state information is perfect (i.e., no communication delays), DET is best, followed by WR, followed by SR. This is because DET-based schedulers make the best decisions: the least-loaded server is selected based on completely up-to-date information. WR is better than SR because it effectively incorporates the load information in its decision procedure, whereas SR does not. How much better is WR over SR? On a scale of 0–100%, where 0% and 100% are the respective performances of systems under SR and DET, the performance under WR comes in at 68%. This gives us a quantitative measure of the significant improvement one can obtain when enhancing a randomization-based decision algorithm with communicated state information.

However, if the information is not perfect, the relative performance changes. As communication delay increases, performance under DET degrades rapidly. What was the least-loaded server in the past may be very highly loaded now because all the schedulers are sending jobs to it, all based on out-of-date information. This is a classic case of the mutually conflicting decision problem. For a wide range of non-zero delays, WR does best, followed by SR, followed by DET. Because of randomization, WR and SR avoid always sending to the same server. Finally, when delays are very high, SR does better than WR because it is insensitive to bad (or good) information.

6.2. Using Randomization to Search for Coordinated Decisions

In the previous examples, randomization is used as a defensive coordination mechanism (i.e., to avoid mutually conflicting decisions). We now discuss how randomization can be used as an offensive mechanism, to proactively search for good collective decisions that support coordination.

We describe a series of experiments where decision makers randomly search the joint decision space and, based on feedback they receive, learn over time. The basic decision-making model is as follows:

- Each decision maker has a set of choices to select from, and a probability associated with each choice.
- Each decision is made by randomly selecting one of the choices, weighted according to their respective probabilities.
- After decisions are made, each decision maker is given feedback on whether their decision's overall effect was good or bad.
- Each decision maker adjusts the probabilities of the choices, raising the probability of the selected choice (and lowering those of the others) if its effect was good, or lowering its probability (and raising those of other others) if its effect was bad.

The feedback may be provided by an external source, such as a server in a load-balancing application, or by something internal to the decision maker, such as a model of the system that is kept up-to-date via communications. These feedbacks are not necessarily perfect, as they may be delayed or based on information that is not accurate. We explore how these uncertainties affect coordination next.

The scheme for adjusting the choice probabilities is based on the well-developed theory of learning automata [6]. The probability p of a selected choice is increased to $p + a(1 - p)$ if the choice was determined to be good, or decreased to $p(1 - b)$ if bad, where a and b are learning constants (parameters of the "reward-epsilon-penalty" learning automata scheme). The probabilities of the other choices are proportionally decreased or increased.

It is worth noting that randomization is now being used not only to coordinate the selection of resources, but also to improve the coordination by taking feedback into account. This raises an important point regarding the value of using randomization: Because probabilities are used and can be incrementally modified, randomization methods can conveniently incorporate adaptation.

6.2.1. Learning Optimal Group Decisions. Consider a multiuser multiresource system of two users and two resources, where the users are learning-automata-based decision makers as described before. The optimal decision for each user is to select a different resource. If both users are initialized such that there is an equal probability of selecting either resource, and if they are then allowed to repeatedly make their decisions, rewarding them when they choose different resources and penalizing them when they choose the same ones, we find that they quickly learn to select different resources.

In effect, the users are searching a two-dimensional decision space, where one axis is the probability that User 1 will choose Resource 1 (which also implies that it will choose Resource 2 with the complementary probability), and the other axis is the probability that User 2 will choose Resource 2 (or that it will choose Resource 1 with the complementary probability) see Fig. 11.3. Our studies show that, over time, the search converges on the extreme points of (0, 0), that is, User 1 should select Resource 2 and User 2 should select Resource 1, or (1, 1), that is, User 1 should select Resource 1 and User 2 should select Resource 2. By randomizing their decisions, the users are able to probe the decision space and in effect coordinate their decisions. These results are not surprising, given that the feedback provided is based on perfect state information. However, what happens if the feedback is not perfect?

We devised a simulation model of this two-user two-resource system where we carried out an experiment similar to that just described; however, we incorporated a delay for communicated state information. This study is described in [7], and expands on the results presented here. The state infor-

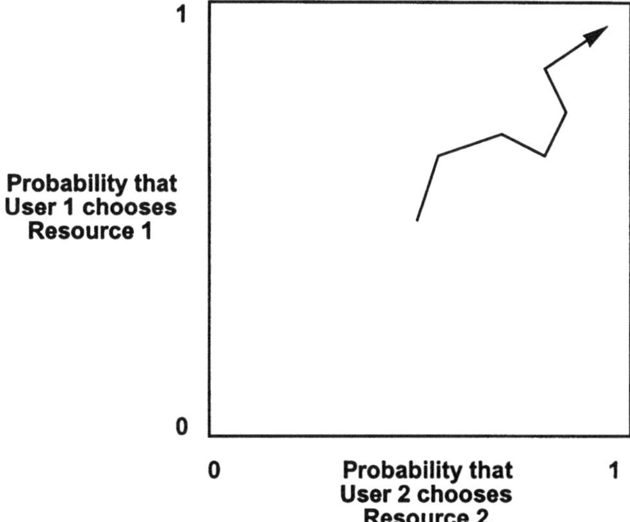

FIG. 11.3. Searching the joint decision space.

mation comprised the current probabilities of a user's choices. If there is no delay for communication, then each user can know the current probabilities of the other user's choices with complete certainty, and can determine whether its choice, made randomly, was the best one given probabilistic expectations. When this experiment is carried out, the results are as described before: Both users learn to make the best joint decisions.

Although communication is used to improve a decision maker's knowledge of the system state, there is generally a cost in that the more communication there is, the more overhead there is. On the other hand, the more communication there is, the more up-to-date the received state information is, and the better the decisions will be that are based on this information. So, there is tradeoff between decision quality and overhead that affects performance. The result is that one will never have perfect state information because one cannot communicate constantly, and even if one could, communication is not instantaneous.

In our simulation model, each user communicates its state with the other every P time units, where P is the period of communication. Consequently, state information can be as old as P time units (and actually more, because we also incorporated a transmission delay). By varying P, we could determine its effect on decision quality, and most important, whether or not the users could learn the optimal decisions as they do under the perfect information scenario.

The main result is that there is a threshold for the communication period whereby, below the threshold the users learn to make optimal decisions (coordination is achieved), and above it coordination breaks down. This threshold, for the simple system described, can be determined analytically (although, despite the simplicity of the system, the analysis is not simple given the complexity of the learning automata probability update scheme), and the analytical results we derived matched the results of the experiments with the simulation model.

Consequently, this study tells us that, even though state information may not be perfect (e.g., because of a non-zero communication period that leads to outdated state information), randomized decisions over the space of resources are still able to not only cope, but eventually produce near-optimal coordinated behavior by learning over time. However, there is a point beyond which the information becomes so bad that such learning is not possible.

We carried out a similar study, described in [8], of a load-balancing application where the distributed system consisted of two hosts, each composed of a scheduler and a server with a queue. The schedulers make randomized decisions and are based on learning automata, as described before. If a scheduler chooses the server with the shorter queue, it is rewarded, otherwise it is penalized. This feedback is provided by "the system," and is not delayed. The result of this study is that the schedulers are able to "co-adapt" to eventually make good decisions. The more one scheduler favors a particular server, the more the other scheduler favors the other server.

However, this system is significantly more complicated than the simple two-user two-resource system already described, because job arrival times and service times in the load-balancing system are stochastic. Consequently, although the decisions the schedulers learn to make are generally good, they are not always optimal, due to these uncertainties. On a scale of 0–100%, where 0% is the performance of a system where no off-loading was possible (i.e., when a job arrives at a host, it is executed on its own server) and 100% is that of a system where the least-loaded server was always selected, the co-adaptive system achieves a performance level of 44%. This shows the significant degree to which uncertainty, which is directly traceable to the two fundamental problems of decentralized control, will degrade performance, despite the randomization-based coordination mechanisms we apply.

6.2.2. Learning to Work Together or Work Alone. In the previous examples, it was determined that with sufficient communication a set of decision makers can learn to make optimal (or at least good) decisions that achieve coordination. Without sufficient communication, coordination breaks down; in this case, it would be better if the system was partitioned to limit interactions between decision makers. However, we can incorporate this problem as yet another decision that must be considered: should a decision maker work in small groups (i.e., partition the system) or should it work as part of one large group? Furthermore, can the optimal choice of working in small groups or in one large group be learned over time?

The smallest possible group is one that includes only a single decision maker; this corresponds to working alone. Consider the value of working alone: Performance is more predictable because one does not depend on the decisions of others. However, by working in a large group (i.e., working together, and accessing all resources from a single shared pool), there is the potential for achieving much higher levels of performance. This is the result of greater opportunities for sharing and better utilization of resources. We saw the value of working alone in the discussion of using randomization without communication: in such a system, despite the implicit coordination achieved by the use of randomization, it is still better to partition resources than to pool them. However, with communication resulting in the availability of timely but not necessarily perfect state information, higher levels of performance are achievable, as shown in the other examples.

To investigate these issues, we constructed a simulation model of a distributed system of two hosts (each composed of a scheduler, and a server with a queue) with the goal of load balancing, where each host decides whether it wishes to work with the other host or not. This study is described in [9]. As in the previous examples, the choices have associated probabilities that are updated according to the learning automata scheme, and the decision is made randomly, weighted according to the probabilities. If both hosts decide to work together, then both servers are accessible to each scheduler, and nonconflicting decisions generate high performance whereas mutually conflicting decisions result in low performance. If either or both hosts decide not to work together, then the system is partitioned into two separate single-host systems, each having "medium" performance (i.e., between the high and low performance of a two-host system). So, should the hosts "play it safe" by working alone, or risk working together to attain the higher potential performance? Uncertainty is introduced by having hosts communicate periodically: The greater the period, the more out-of-date state information can get.

The results of this study are that the hosts learn to do what is best: With sufficient communication, they learn that working together is best and so that is what they do; with insufficient communication, they learn that it is best to work alone. Consequently, the hosts are able to take the value of state information into account. If its value is high, then coordination is possible, and it is attempted; if it is low, coordination is not possible, and so it is not attempted.

6.2.3. Learning How Large Working Groups Should Be. In a follow-up study described in [10], we considered distributed systems of many ($n > 2$) hosts. Now, the decision is not the simple binary one of either working together or working alone. The optimal working group size can range from one (work alone) to n (work together), or any value in between.

We developed the concept of "scope of control." In the context of load balancing, a host controls another host if the former's scheduler is able to send jobs to the latter's server (with possible queueing). A host's scope of control is the set of all hosts it controls. We use randomization to determine the control sets: each Host i maintains a set of probabilities c_{ij} = Prob (Host i controls Host j), for all hosts j. If $c_{ij} = 0$ for all j, we have a partitioned system. Otherwise, we have various degrees of a pooled or shared resource system. See Fig. 11.4.

Load balancing decisions are made as follows. Each time a job arrives at a Host i, a control set is determined: For each Host j, randomly decide if it is in the control set according to its current probability c_{ij}. The scheduler then selects the least-loaded host in the control set, and the job is sent to that host's server.

To learn "optimal" control sets, the control set probabilities are updated according to the learning automata scheme. If the host assignment is a good decision, then the probability of including that host in the control set in the future is increased; a bad decision results in a lowering of the probability. A

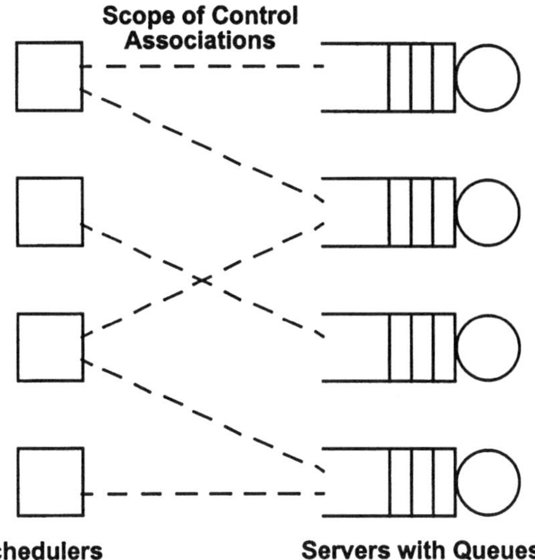

FIG. 11.4. Scope of control.

good decision is defined as one that results in better-than-average performance (i.e., the job completes execution faster than what is expected in a completely balanced system).

The hosts communicate their state information with each other (i.e., they exchange their control set probabilities). A host uses the received probabilities of other hosts to determine whether the decision it makes is expected to be good; this is what is actually used to reward or penalize decisions. Finally, as in our previous experiments, uncertainty is introduced by only periodically communicating state information, so that it becomes less timely until a new update is received.

The main result is that as the communication period increases (i.e., as more uncertainty is introduced), the average sizes of the control sets decrease. When there is very low uncertainty, the hosts learn that it is best to work together in one large group (any host can off-load jobs to any other host). As the uncertainty increases, it is best to work in smaller, but not necessarily singleton, groups (hosts off-load only to other hosts within their group). Finally, when there is high uncertainty, it is best to work alone (no off-loading of jobs).

Consequently, the scope-of-control randomization mechanism provides a way for decision makers to take uncertainty of state information into account. They learn by using randomization to search the group (or control set) space, allowing them to act as a self-organizing system. In fact, the mechanism is very robust. Extending the simulated system by having heterogeneous hosts (i.e., some hosts have faster servers than others, the system self-organizes so that the hosts with faster servers appear more frequently in control sets than those with slower servers). In another related study described in [11], where the distance between hosts is taken into account (the greater the distance, the more communication delay, and hence the greater the uncertainty), the system self-organizes so that hosts prefer to work with those hosts that are in closer proximity than other hosts.

7. CONCLUSIONS

We have shown that randomization can be used to attack the two fundamental problems of decentralized control, that of state-information uncertainty and that of mutually conflicting decisions. These problems inhibit the coordination required to achieve the potentially high levels of performance offered by distributed systems. Using randomization is very appealing because it simplifies the interactions to achieve coordination between decision makers. Randomization can be used as part of defensive mechanisms to prevent mutually conflicting decisions by breaking symmetry. Furthermore, by using randomization, one can easily incorporate adaptive feedback mechanisms to allow a decentralized control system to self-organize into a cooperating whole. This allows randomization to be used to proactively search for good collective decisions that are coordinated, in contrast to its complementary use in defensive mechanisms.

We reviewed a number of studies where randomization was used to improve the performance of various decentralized control systems given different constraints. With no communication, randomization provides a significant but limited performance improvement. The limitation does not make the pooling of resources worthwhile; rather, it is better to statically partition the system. This changes when communication is possible and where the communicated information is of sufficient quality. Where communication of state information is periodic, there is generally a threshold for the communication period whereby, below the threshold, decision makers learn to eventually make optimal decisions (coordination is achieved), and above it coordination breaks down.

Decision makers can learn whether it is worth working together (which requires coordination) or working alone (which does not), based on the quality of the communicated state information. By working together, higher levels of performance are achievable. By working alone, performance is more predictable because decision-makers do not interact, but the performance gain is significantly more modest. In fact, they can learn the optimal size for coordinated groups; this size is directly proportional to the quality of communicated state information.

Yet, despite the power of using randomization, we see very clearly throughout our studies the significant degree to which uncertainty will degrade performance. The two fundamental problems of decentralized control are the roots of this uncertainty; it is only by gaining a deeper understanding of them that we will be able to develop additional methods to realize the potential power of distributed systems.

ACKNOWLEDGMENTS

I am grateful to my students, especially Ted Billard and Alex Glockner, with whom I explored many of these issues. Most importantly, I thank the late Dr. Larry Rosenberg for his support and friendship. Larry's vision and enthusiasm for a research agenda in coordination and collaboration remain an inspiration to me.

This work was supported by the National Science Foundation as part of a Presidential Young Investigator Award, Number IRI-8957603.

REFERENCES

[1] T. W. Malone and K. Crowston, "What is coordination theory and how can it help design cooperative work systems," *Proc. ACM CSCW Conf.*, Los Angeles, October 1990.

[2] J. Halpern and Y. Moses, "Knowledge and common knowledge in a distributed environment," *Journal of the ACM*, Vol. 37, pp. 549–587, July 1990.

[3] *Webster's Ninth New Collegiate Dictionary*. Springfield, MA: Merriam Webster Inc., 1987.

[4] J. Pasquale, "Randomized coordination in an autonomous decentralized system," *Proc. 1st IEEE Intl. Symp. on Autonomous Decentralized Systems (ISADS)*, Kawasaki, Japan, March 93, pp. 77–82.

[5] E. Billard and J. Pasquale, "Utilizing local and global queueing resources with uncertainty in state and service," *Proc. 2nd IEEE Intl. Symp. on Autonomous Decentralized Systems (ISADS)*, Phoenix, April 1995, pp. 258–265.

[6] K. Narendra and M. Thathachar, *Learning Automata: An Introduction*. Englewood Cliffs, NJ: Prentice-Hall, 1989.

[7] E. Billard and J. Pasquale, "Adaptive coordination in distributed systems with delayed communication," *IEEE Transactions on Systems, Man, and Cybernetics*, Vol. 25, No. 4, April 1995, pp. 546–554.

[8] A. Glockner and J. Pasquale, "Coadaptive behavior in a simple distributed job scheduling system," *IEEE Transactions on Systems, Man, and Cybernetics*, Vol. 23, No. 3, May/June 93, pp. 902–906.

[9] E. Billard and J. Pasquale, "Effects of delayed communication in dynamic group formation," *IEEE Transactions on Systems, Man, and Cybernetics*, Vol. 23, No. 5, September/October 93, pp. 1265–1275.

[10] E. Billard and J. Pasquale, "Dynamic scope of control in decentralized job scheduling," *Proc. 1st IEEE Intl. Symp. on Autonomous Decentralized Systems (ISADS)*, Kawasaki, Japan, March 93, pp. 183–189.

[11] E. Billard and J. Pasquale, "Localized decision making and the value of information in decentralized control," *Proc. 7th Intl. Conf. on Parallel and Distributed Computing Systems (PDCS)*, Las Vegas, October 1994, pp. 417–425.

CHAPTER

12

The Architecture and Implementation of a Distributed Hypermedia Storage System*

Douglas E. Shackelford
John B. Smith
F. Donelson Smith
University of North Carolina, Chapel Hill

INTRODUCTION AND MOTIVATION

Future hypermedia systems will integrate diverse information resources, systems, and technologies. They will be based on modular architectures (e.g., Thompson, 1990) that separate orthogonal concerns into plug-compatible components such as change management, query and content search, notification, application-specific concurrency control, computational semantics, and window conferencing. Some of these components, such as change management, may be highly dependent on the semantics of a particular domain, whereas others will provide general support for all applications.

> The key point . . . is that it is modular and open. This modularity is based on the observations that the functions the modules perform are independent of each other, that is *orthogonality implies modularity*. (Thompson, 1990, p. 234)

Orthogonality implies modularity; *modularity implies choice*. The importance of this observation is that every service has a cost associated with it. For example, transactions may be the appropriate concurrency mechanism for one application, while imposing prohibitively high overhead on another.

 This chapter was published previously in the *Proceedings of ACM Hypertext '93*, pages 1–13, and is reprinted here with permission from the Association for Computing Machinery.

Ideally, one should be able to use a service when it is needed without having to pay for it when it is not.

In this chapter, we describe the architecture and implementation of our Distributed Graph Storage (DGS) system. We have designed it in a way that supports modular expansion to add services such as those enumerated earlier. A fundamental requirement has been that the basic hypermedia services for data storage and access should be inexpensive, efficient, and scalable. This is particularly important because the performance of these basic services is an upper bound on the performance of the system as a whole.

The DGS has been developed as a part of a larger program of research that focuses on the process of collaboration and on technology to support that process. We are concerned with the intellectual collaboration that is required for designing software systems or other similar tasks in which groups of people work together to build large, complex structures of ideas. The work of such groups—either directly or indirectly—is concerned with producing some tangible artifact. For software systems, the artifact may include concept papers, architecture, or specification documents, programs, diagrams, reference and user manuals, as well as administrative documents. A subtle but important point is that we view a group's tangible creations as parts of a single artifact.

Our research in the UNC Collaboratory project studies how groups merge their ideas and their efforts to build an artifact, and we are developing a computer system (called ABC for Artifact-Based Collaboration; Smith & Smith, 1991) to support that process. ABC has six key components (Jeffay, Lin, Menges, Smith, & Smith, 1992): the Distributed Graph Storage system, a set of graph browsers, a set of data application programs, a shared window conferencing facility, real-time video and audio, and a set of protocol tools for studying group behaviors and strategies.

REQUIREMENTS FOR THE DISTRIBUTED STORAGE SERVICE

In this section we give a brief summary of key requirements that have shaped our storage service design.

Permanent (persistent) storage: obvious but fundamental.

Sharing with protection: because the artifact effectively constitutes the group's collective memory, it must be sharable by all. There are, however, requirements for mechanisms to authorize or deny access to selected elements of the artifact by individuals or subgroups.

Concurrent access: because collaborators must work together, it is often necessary for more than one user to read or modify some part of the artifact at the same time. Data consistency semantics in these cases should be easily understood and provide minimal barriers to users' access to the artifact.

Responsive performance: sufficient to support interactive browsing of the artifact, is required.

Scalable: we are concerned about scale in two respects: the number of users in a group (and consequent size and complexity of the artifact), and the geographic dispersion of group members. To be scalable, it must be possible to distribute the system over available processing and network resources and to add resources incrementally as necessary. Performance (responsiveness) as perceived by users must not degrade significantly as the system grows in scale,

Available: if data becomes unavailable because of system faults, users may be severely impacted. The system must, therefore, be designed to tolerate most common faults and continue to provide access to most or all elements of the artifact. Replication of data and processing capacity is required to achieve high availability.

User and artifact mobility: users will need to change locations and system administrators will need to move data or processing resources to balance loads and capacity. The system must support this mobility in a way that is transparent to users and application programs. There should be no location dependencies inherent in the storage system.

Private data: these are created by individuals for their own use. Examples include personal notes, annotations on documents, and correspondence. Users must be able to create and protect such data and still establish relationships among them and the public artifact.

Support for applications: many applications used by a group are likely to be existing tools such as editors, drawing packages, compilers, and utilities, which use a conventional file model for persistent storage. The system should make it possible to use such tools on node data-content with no changes.

DATA MODEL CONCEPTS

Attributes and Content

The most basic element of the data model is the *node*, which usually contains the expression of a single thought or idea. Structural and semantic relationships between nodes are represented explicitly as *links* between nodes.[1]

[1]Links to links are prohibited.

The data model provides two mechanisms for storing information within a node: node attributes and node content. *Attributes* are typed, named variables for storing fine-grained information (approximately 1–100 bytes). Some attributes (such as creation time and size) are maintained automatically by the system. There may also be an unlimited number of application-defined attributes.

In comparison to attributes, node *content is* designed to reference larger amounts of information. This content can take one of two forms:

1. a stream of bytes (accessed using a file metaphor)
2. a composite object (accessed using a graph metaphor)

Applications control whether the content of a particular node is of Type l or of Type 2. Because Type I content obeys the standard file metaphor, it can be used to store the same types of information as files (e.g., text, bitmaps, line drawings, digitized audio and video, spreadsheets, and other binary data). Applications that can read and write conventional files can read and write Type I content with no changes. Type I content is stored with the node that contains it.

When a node has Type 2 content, then the content is stored *separately* as a composite object called a subgraph.[2] A *subgraph is* defined as a subset of the nodes and links in the artifact that is consistent with graph-theoretic constraints. For example, all subgraphs satisfy the condition that if a link belongs to a subgraph, then so do the link's source node and target node. Nodes and links may belong to multiple subgraphs at the same time, but every node and link must belong to at least one subgraph. Our data model also provides *strongly typed* subgraphs (e.g., trees and lists) that are guaranteed to be consistent with their type.

Links can have both attributes and content associated with them. Moreover, the data model defines two classes of links: structural and hyperstructural. Structural links (S-links) are used to store the essential structure of an artifact. By contrast, hyperstructural links (HS-links) are lighter weight objects that represent relationships that cut across the basic structure (see Fig. 12.1). Subgraphs containing only structural links are called S-subgraphs; those containing hyperstructural links are called HS-subgraphs.

Using the Data Model to Organize Information

The data model encourages users to compose a large artifact from small subgraphs using subgraph content. This organization can improve human comprehension of the artifact and increase the potential for concurrent

[2]Hereafter, Type 1 content will be referred to as *file* content and Type 2 content will be called *subgraph* content.

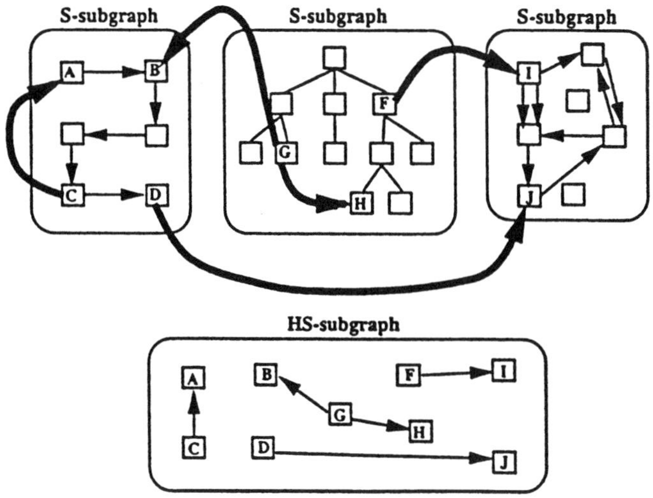

FIG. 12.1. Examples of hyperstructural linking.

access to individual components. The best way to understand these mechanisms is by example.

Figure 12.2 illustrates one way to organize the public and private materials associated with a large research project (node content is indicated by dashed lines). One can observe that Fig. 12.2 subsumes the organization of data in a conventional file system while providing additional mechanisms for storing metainformation about files (in attributes) and for representing semantic and structural relationships between files (in links).

Subgraph SG 9 in Fig. 12.2 is the top-level subgraph of a document. A useful exercise is to compare this graph structure with the way that the conference paper would be stored in a conventional file system. The most striking difference is the number and size of the nodes that compose the document. Whereas a conventional document would normally be stored in a single file or a small number of files, the DGS data model encourages a user to divide documents into many smaller nodes and subgraphs. This maximizes the benefits of hyperstructural linking because each node expresses a single concept or idea. By dividing a document into different subgraphs, collaborators may be able to structure their materials for easier concurrent access.

Fine-Grained Linking Using Anchors

Although nodes are finer grained than traditional files, there are still times when one would like to reference information at an even finer level. For example, an application might want to create a link that points to a specific

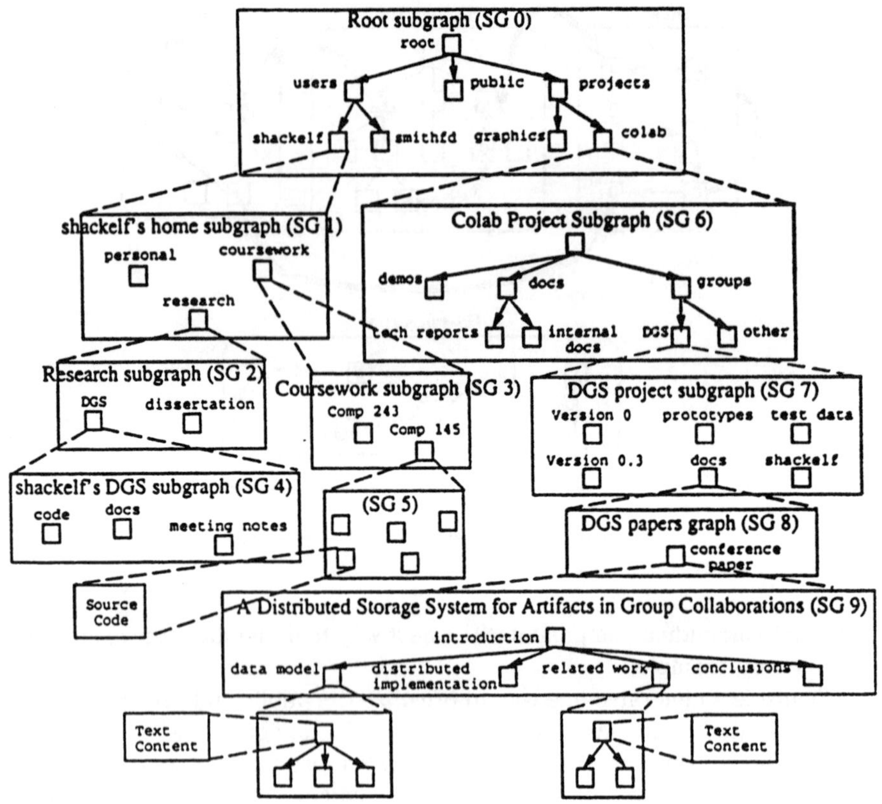

FIG. 12.2. Organizing the public and private pieces of an artifact.

word within a node, rather than to the node itself. To achieve fine-grained linking like this, the data model provides the concept of an anchor within a node. An anchor identifies part of a node's content, such as a function declaration in a program module, a definition in a glossary, or an element of a line drawing. An anchor can be used to focus an HS-link onto a specific place within the content of a node. When an HS-link is paired with one or more anchors in its source or target nodes, it is called an *anchored HS-link*. The relationship between anchors and HS-links is many-to-many.

Common Attributes and Graph Attributes

Some attributes are called *common attributes* because their values are independent of the context from which they are accessed. All objects—nodes, links, and subgraphs—can have common attributes. In addition, nodes and links can have context-sensitive attributes whose value may be different depending on the context from which they are accessed. This second type of attribute is called a *graph attribute* because a subgraph provides the context.

DESIGN AND IMPLEMENTATION

System Architecture

As shown in Fig. 12.3, the DGS has a layered architecture that can be configured in a number of different ways. The *Application Layer* contains the user interface and other code that is application-specific. The top layer of the DGS is the *Application Programming Interface (API)* which exports a graph-oriented data model to applications. An overview of this data model was presented in a previous section. Most of the DGS is implemented in the bottom two layers: the Graph-Cache Manager (GCM) and the Storage Layer. The GCM implements the data model and performs local caching; the *Storage Layer* is responsible for permanently storing results.

Because the API isolates the application from the rest of the DGS, application code is portable across different implementations of the bottom two layers. We currently support two different implementations of the storage layer and two different methods for connecting the API with the GCM. This

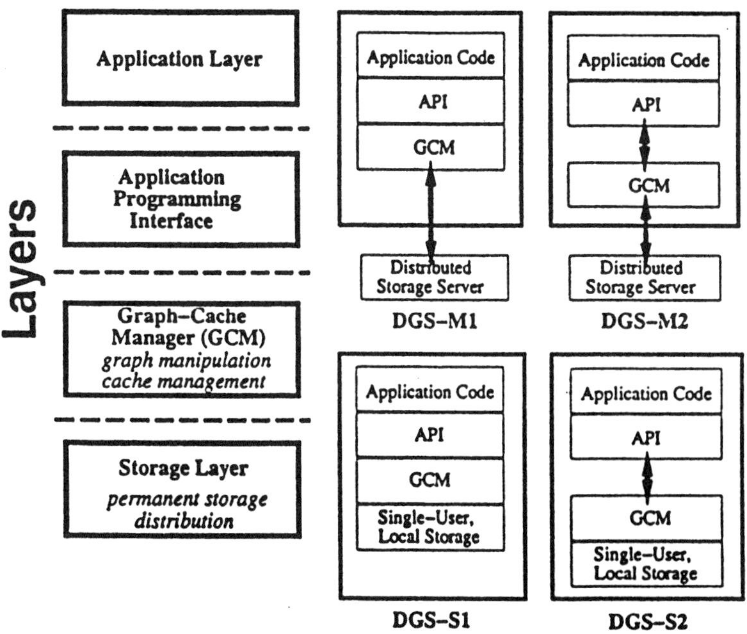

FIG. 12.3. Four implementations of the DGS layered architecture.

yields the four implementations that are shown in Fig. 12.3. In DGS-M2, the application and the GCM run in different processes on the same machine; the Storage Layer is implemented as a multiuser, distributed storage server. DGS-M I is the same except that the GCM is linked with the application to become a single process. The advantage of this design is better local response time due to reduced Interprocess Communication (IPC). A disadvantage is that it increases the size of application executables. DGS-S I and DGS-S2 follow a similar pattern except that the distributed storage server is replaced by a single-user, nondistributed storage layer.

The Object-Oriented API

The API for the DGS is a C++ class library (for a complete description, see Shackelford, 1993). Figure 12.4 shows the major classes in the inheritance hierarchy. The class *Object* defines operations that are common to all objects such as the functions for manipulating the common attributes of an object. Subclasses inherit the API of their parent class and extend the inherited API with more specialized functions.

All node, link, and subgraph objects are identified by an object identifier (OID) that is universal and unique. Once an object is created by the DGS, its OID is never changed and the value is never reused even if the object is deleted. To applications, an OID is an "opaque" (uninterpreted) key that can be used to retrieve the corresponding object. However, we discourage application programmers from making direct reference to OIDs. Most operations can be performed without even knowing that OIDs exist.

Concurrent Access to Objects

Because the DGS data model is object-oriented, the objects of the data model—nodes, links, and subgraphs—exist as distinct entities within the storage system. Before a user's application can access the data within a particular object (see Fig. 12.5), the application must explicitly open the object using its *Open()* function.

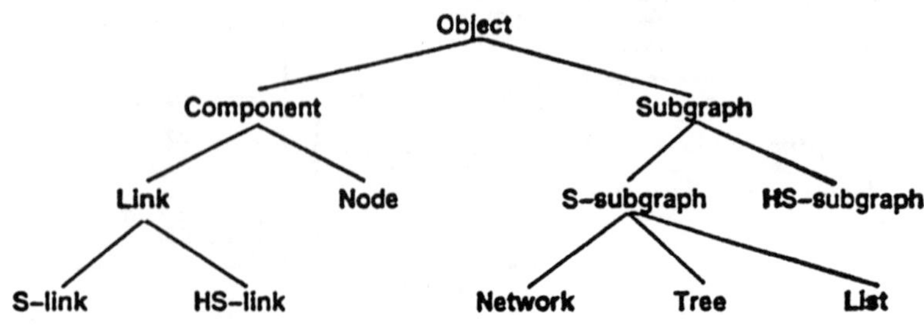

FIG. 12.4. API class hierarchy.

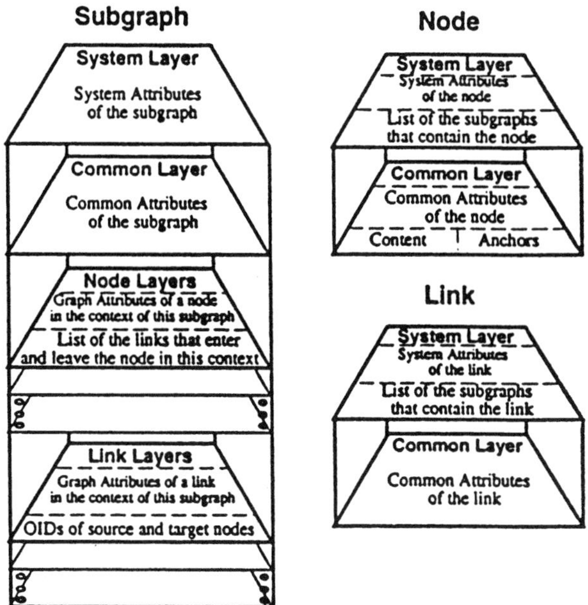

FIG. 12.5. Information stored in nodes, links, and subgraphs.

Open() will fail if the user lacks the proper access authorizations and if the request is in conflict with other requests in progress. Conflict can occur when different users try to access the same object concurrently. To specify allowable concurrent accesses, the API defines three access modes for nodes, links, and subgraphs: DGS-READ, DGS-WRITE, and DGS-READ–NO-ANCHOR. Applications must specify one of these modes as a parameter to *Open()* DGS-READ allows operations that do not change subgraph membership, linking information, or attribute or content values. In the case of nodes, DGS–READ also allows anchor creation and deletion, but only when the application has read–write authorization on the HS-link that is being anchored. DGS-READ–NO-ANCHOR is defined only for nodes and allows all operations of DGS-READ except anchor creation and deletion. DGS-WRITE allows all operations.

The following rules govern concurrent access to an object:

- For links and subgraphs, multiple opens with DGS-READ access and a single open with DGS-WRITE access are allowed concurrently (as is the weaker case of multiple DGS-READ opens alone).
- For nodes, multiple opens with DGS-READ–NO-ANCHOR access and a single open with DGS-WRITE access are allowed concurrently (as is the weaker case of multiple DGS-READ and/or DGS-READ–NO-ANCHOR opens alone).

Thus, for nodes the design supports multiple nonannotating readers and a single writer OR multiple annotating readers. A consequence of this is that a writer is blocked from accessing a node that is being annotated by a reader and vice versa. Changes to an object are not visible to any applications with overlapping opens of the object until it is closed by the writer and then only to applications that open it after the close completes.

Access Control for Objects

Groups can control access to parts of the artifact by specifying access authorizations for node, link, and subgraph objects. Authorizations are expressed in an access control list that is stored with each object. An *access control list* maps names of users or groups of users to categories of operations that they are allowed to perform on the associated object. Two categories of authorizations are defined: access and administer. *Access authorizations* give users permission to access the data associated with a particular object. *Administer authorizations* give users permission to perform operations such as changing the object's access control list. Although the API does not define an explicit annotate permission, a similar effect can be accomplished by restricting the access authorizations associated with HS-subgraphs.

Distributed Implementation

In this section we discuss the distributed implementations (DGS-M1 and DGS-M2 in Fig. 12.3) with emphasis on key design decisions.

Given an artifact composed from small elements and user access via interactive browsers, we believe many characteristics and access patterns of objects will strongly resemble those observed in distributed file systems supporting software teams using workstations (Baker, Hartman, Kupfer, Shirriff, & Ousterhout, 1991; Kistler & Satyanarayanan, 1991). Our design is based on the notion that a scalable implementation can be achieved by applying design principles such as local caching, bulk-data transfer, and minimal client–server interactions pioneered in high-performance, scalable file systems like AFS (Howard et al., 1988), Sprite (Nelson, Welch, & Ousterhout, 1988), and Coda (Kistler & Satyanarayanan, 1991). We also model our approaches to data consistency, concurrency semantics, and replication after these distributed file systems. This provides a sufficient level of function to users without requiring the full complexity of mechanisms (e.g., distributed transactions) used in database systems.

The basic structure of the system is shown in Fig. 12.6. A browser or application process acts on behalf of a user to read and modify objects. Each user's workstation runs a single Graph-Cache Manager (GCM) process that

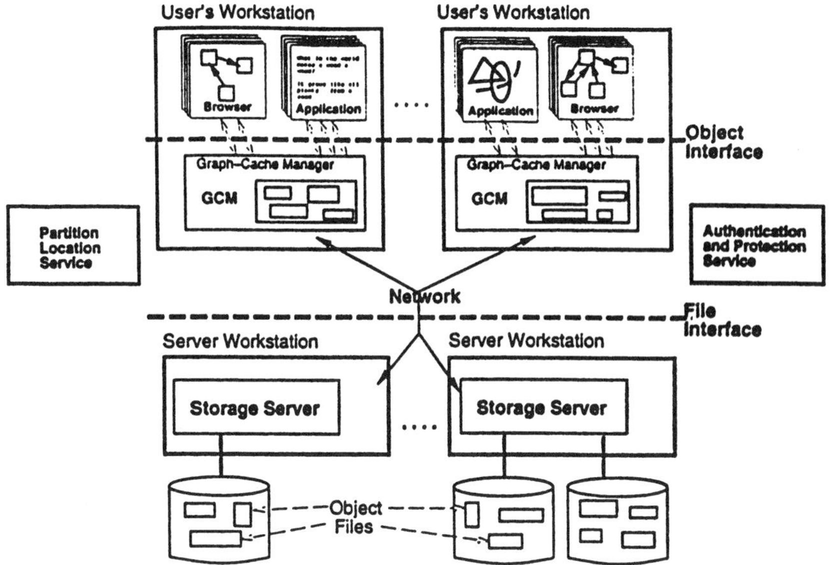

FIG. 12.6. DGS system structure.

services all applications running on that machine. Application requests are directed over local interprocess communication facilities to the GCM. The GCM maintains a local copy of node, link, and subgraph objects used by application processes and is responsible for implementing all operations on objects in the data model except for anchor table merging. The GCM is also responsible for maintaining the consistency of typed S-subgraphs. It is important to note that this design distributes the processing for all complex object operations to the users' workstations and thus minimizes the processing demands on shared (server) resources.

When an application opens an object, the GCM, in turn, opens the object at the storage server and retrieves it using a whole-file transfer. The received object is converted from its representation in a file to an object representation designed for fast access in memory. As the application makes requests, the GCM performs those operations on the copy in its local cache. Write operations are reflected in the storage server only when the GCM closes the object and returns the modified file representation to the storage server. Each file retrieved from the storage server contains either a whole node (including data content, if present), a whole subgraph, or a group of links. An important performance optimization is that context-dependent attributes (graph attributes) and link information for all nodes in a subgraph are stored in one subgraph file. Thus, all of the data needed by a browser to display a subgraph is available from a single request (open) to the storage server. The structure of each type of file is shown in Fig. 12.7. Nodes and subgraphs are stored individually, whereas links are grouped according to the subgraph in which they were created.

The file-oriented interface to the storage server is designed to isolate it as much as possible from the representation and semantics of objects. The primary responsibility of the storage server, therefore, is to store and control access to files indexed by an object's OID. Storage servers are also responsible for maintaining access control lists, enforcing access authorizations, enforcing concurrency semantics, creating unique OIDs and anchor IDs, and merging anchor table information created by concurrent readers of the same node. The storage server must perform several checks before completing an open request. First, it must determine whether the user who is running the application has the correct authorizations to open the object in the requested access mode. Then, the storage server must determine whether the requested access mode is in conflict with any overlapping opens for the same object. An open request will fail if the user lacks proper access authorization or if the open conflicts with other opens in progress.

Each GCM may need to communicate with multiple storage servers, including servers that provide protection services and mappings from an OID to the host system that is the custodian for that object. Object location is based on dividing the artifact store into nonoverlapping collections of nodes, links, and subgraphs called partitions. Each partition is associated with real storage devices. Partitions form boundaries for administrative controls such as space quotas, load balancing among servers, and replication of data. The partition number of an object is embedded in its OID but this substructure is never made visible outside the storage service. An object must (logically) remain in the same partition for its entire lifetime because its OID cannot be changed.

We distinguish the partition number of an object from its absolute physical location(s) and, by introducing a level of indirection (a partition directo-

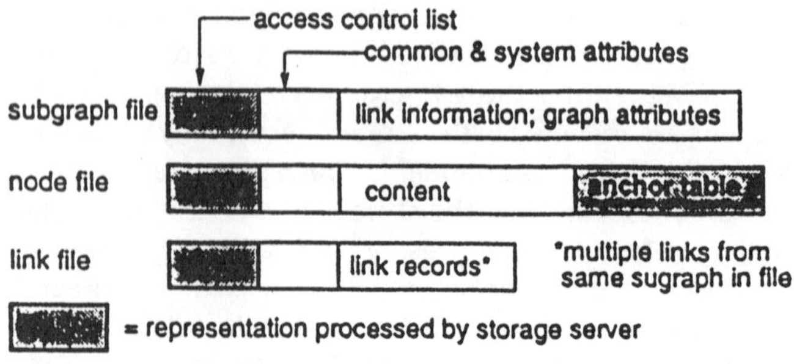

FIG. 12.7. Structure of object files.

ry), it is possible to change the physical location of an object while preserving its OID and, therefore, all its link and composition relationships with other objects (see Fig. 12.8). Partition–location servers maintain a mapping of logical partitions to host(s) running server processes for that partition. The GCM extracts the partition number from the OID of the object and uses the partition location service to find the host running a storage server process maintaining a directory for that partition (the GCM can also cache the partition location information for use in references to other objects). We expect that in most cases one storage server maintains both the partition directory and data storage for an object. Despite their importance, partitions are invisible to users. Only system administrators and system programmers need to understand partitions. An RPC interface to the storage servers is provided for administrative processes to use in creating new partitions, moving objects from one physical partition to another, and performing backup and recovery operations.

Storage servers are responsible for managing partitions on disk, replicating partitions for availability and fault tolerance in case of media or process failures, and for recovering from most failures. The key to our implementation of fault tolerance is the ISIS system developed by Ken Birman and his colleagues at Cornell University (Joseph & Birman, 1986). In particular, we use ISIS process groups to maintain replicated copies of physical partitions and to provide the location independence of logical partitions. Each logical partition corresponds to an ISIS process group.

Performance and scalability are two key requirements for the system. To evaluate the current implementation with respect to these requirements, we

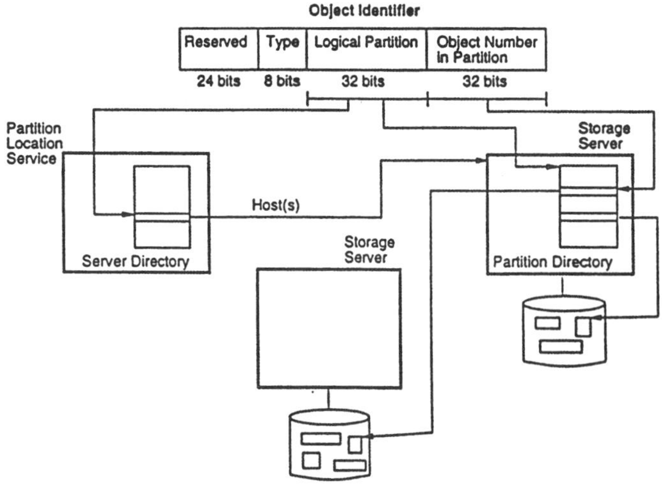

FIG. 12.8. OID and object location.

have begun a series of benchmark experiments similar to those used to evaluate performance and scalability of distributed file systems such as AFS (Howard et al., 1988) and Sprite (Nelson et al., 1988). We have created several benchmark programs designed to stress different aspects of the system. The most interesting of these is a "synthetic browser" program that mimics the requests that result when users search for information in an artifact stored in the system. Load on the storage service is generated by running copies of the synthetic browser on several workstations. This program has parameters that can be used to produce a wide range of browsing behaviors. In our first experiments we are using parameter values that represent the observed behavior of human subjects in a series of experiments we conducted to understand how people would use a hypertext system for problem solving (Smith, 1992). With these values, each instance of the program running on one workstation generates a load on the server corresponding to approximately 10 users working with interactive browsing applications. We have also written an "artifact generator" program that, based on a number of input parameters, creates a structure of subgraphs, nodes, and links to serve as data for the browsing benchmark.

The results of our initial measurements have been very encouraging. The configuration for these measurements consisted of one storage server running on a DECstation 5000/25c and up to seven workstations (DECstation 5000/120s) each running a copy of the synthetic browser program. All workstations were connected by a single ethernet segment. The most significant results are:

- CPU utilization on the server is at most 0.5–1.0% per active user.
- Server response times to requests from 50 users increased by less than 20% over response times to requests from 10 users.

The results show that one server can support at least 50 users. More extensive benchmark experiments are underway to validate this conclusion for a variety of configurations.

We are currently using the DGS for developing browsers and other collaboration support tools. We continue to make enhancements (mostly for operations and administration) and plan to have a version suitable for distribution to other groups by Fall 1993.

COMPARISON WITH RELATED WORK

In this section, we compare our design with several hypertext systems that have significant capability for supporting collaborating groups (i.e., Intermedia; Haan, Kahn, Riley, Coombs, & Meyrowitz, 1992; Yankelovich et al.,

1988), HyperBase/CHS (Schütt & Haake, 1993; Schütt & Streitz, 1990), Augment (Engelbart, 1984), Telesophy (Caplinger, 1987; Schatz, 1987), KMS (Akscyn, McCracken, & Yoder, 1988), and HAM (Campbell & Goodman, 1988; Delisle & Schwartz, 1987). These systems differ widely on factors such as the data model supported, scalability, concurrent reader–writer semantics, and protection.

DGS, HyperBase/CHS, and Dexter (Halasz & Schwartz, 1990) support rich data models that include aggregates (named groups of objects), aggregates of aggregates, and aggregates as endpoints of links. Intermedia, HAM, and Augment do not use aggregates in composition or linking. Telesophy's data model has aggregates but does not give first-class status to links. HB I (Schnase, Leggett, & Hicks, 1991) and Trellis (Stotts & Furuta, 1989) provide strong support for computation within hypertext but do not have aggregates. The DGS data model benefits from the graph-theoretical metaphor on which it is based and is the only system to provide strongly typed aggregate objects.

Other areas in which these systems differ substantially are in the semantics of concurrent reading and writing and in the access protection mechanisms (see Table 12.1). These systems also differ in their capability to scale up to large numbers of users (and objects) while preserving the illusion of location transparency. Both Telesophy and the DGS have made scalability a central issue in their designs. However, the DGS provides more flexibility in its data model and stronger consistency semantics.

SUMMARY AND CONCLUSIONS

Collaborative groups face many problems, but one of the hardest and most important is to meld their thinking into a conceptual structure that has integrity as a whole and that is coherent, consistent, and correct. Seeing that construct as a single, integrated artifact can help. But groups must also be able to view specific parts of the artifact in order to understand and manage it. Our design was guided by these requirements, along with others discussed earlier. The graph-based data model permits us to both partition the artifact and to compose those pieces to build larger components and the whole. The distributed architecture, in turn, permits us to build a system that can scale up in terms of the size of the artifact, the number of users, and their geographic distances from one another.

We observe that most of the academic research in hypermedia is not based on the sort of modular architecture that was described at the beginning of this chapter. Although many communities view hypermedia as an "interesting" application, we take the perspective (also expressed in Schnase et al., 1991) that hypermedia has a broader role to play. In our opin-

TABLE 12.1
Concurrent Reader–Writer Semantics and Object Protect

Hypermedia System	*Concurrent Reader–Writer Semantics*	*Protection of Objects*
Augment	Can have multiple readers of documents that have been submitted to the Journal system	Objects in the Journal are read-only. Access to Journal entries can be restricted at submission time
HAM	Could not be determined	Access Control Lists (Optional): access, annotate, update, and destroy permissions
HyperBase/CHS	Activity markers are provided to warn applications of concurrent activity, but these markers are advisory I nature. All applications are notified when data is changed, so that they can update their view (if desired).	Access control will be based on user roles such as "manager" and "secretary" (not yet implemented).
Intermedia	Supports multiple users reading and annotating, and a single writer. First user to write an object locks out other potential writers.	Provides read, write, and annotate permissions that can be granted to users and groups of users.
KMS	Uses an optimistic concurrency method. When a writer attempts to save a node, he/she may be denied because someone else has concurrently written to the same node. In this case, the human user must manually merge the two conflicting versions.	Owner can protect a frame from modification or read access. In addition, an intermediate form allows users to add annotation items, but not to modify existing items.
Telesophy	Supports multiple concurrent readers and writers. When writes overlap, the last writer completely overwrites the work of others.	could not be determined
DGS	Supports multiple nonannotating readers and a single writer OR multiple annotating readers. Applications must declare their intent at the time that they open an object. Intent can be one of: read and annotate; read-only; read/write and annotate.	Access Control Lists: access (read or read/write) and administer permissions. Rather than associate a single annotate permission with a node, the DGS provides a more flexible mechanism of associating annotate permission with the HS-subgraphs that contain the node. Thus, a user might be allowed to annotate a node within his personal context at the same time that he is denied the ability to annotate the node in a public context.

ion, hypermedia is not just an application, but is a new paradigm for the way we work and collaborate with each other. As such, it will be an essential component of the next generation of operating system support. Our experiences with DGS strongly indicate that it is possible to achieve the richer functions needed for hypermedia storage with cost, performance, and scalability comparable to the best conventional distributed file systems (e.g., AFS).

As we look to the future, additional issues we will explore pertain to wide-area network access, dynamic change notification, graph traversal, and support of a richer set of graph and set operations and queries. Many of these extensions lend themselves to the sort of modular approach that is suggested in the Strawman Reference Model (Thompson, 1990).

ACKNOWLEDGMENTS

A number of individuals and organizations have contributed to this project. Gordon Ferguson and Barry Ellege contributed to a Smalltalk prototype that preceded the DGS. Rajaraman Krishnan, Shankar Krishnan, Xiaofan Lu, Mike Wagner, and Zhenxin Wang have contributed to the implementation of the DGS. This work was supported by the National Science Foundation (Grant # IRI-9015443) and by the IBM Corporation.

REFERENCES

Akscyn, R. M., D. L. McCracken, and E. A. Yoder (1988, July). KMS: A distributed hypermedia system for managing knowledge in organizations. *Communications of the ACM, 31*(7), 820–835.

Baker, M. G., J. H. Hartman, M. D. Kupfer, K. W. Shirriff, and J. K. Ousterhout (1991, October). Measurements of a distributed file system. Operating Systems Review, Special Issue: *Proceedings of the 13th ACM Symposium on Operating Systems Principles* (Pacific Grove, CA), *25*(5), 198–212.

Campbell, B. and J. M. Goodman (1988). HAM: A general purpose hypertext abstract machine. *Communications of the ACM, 31*(7), 856–861.

Caplinger, M. (1987, October). An information system based on distributed objects. In *OOPSLA '87 Proceedings*, pp. 126–137.

Delisle, N. M. and M. D. Schwartz (1987, April). Contexts: A partitioning concept for hypertext. *ACM Transactions on Office Information Systems, 5*(2), 168–186.

Engelbart, D. C. (1984, February). Authorship provisions in AUGMENT. In *Proceedings of the 1984 COMPCON Conference*, San Francisco, CA, pp. 465–472.

Haan, B. J., P. Kahn, V. A. Riley, J. H. Coombs, and N. K. Meyrowitz (1992, January). IRIS hypermedia services. *Communications of the ACM, 35*(1), 36–51.

Halasz, F. and M. Schwartz (1990). The Dexter hypertext reference model. In *Proceedings of the NIST Hypertext Standardization Workshop* (Gaithersburg, MD), pp. 1–39.

Howard, J. H., M. L. Kazar, S. G. Menees, D. A. Nichols, M. Satyanarayanan, R. N. Sidebotham, and M. J. West (1988, February). Scale and performance in a distributed file system. *ACM Transactions on Computer Systems, 6*(1), 51–81.

Jeffay, K., J. K. Lin, J. Menges, F. D. Smith, and J. B. Smith (1992). Architecture of the artifact-based collaboration system matrix. In *Proceedings of ACM CSCW '92 Conference on Computer-Supported Cooperative Work, CSCW Architectures*, pp. 195–202.

Joseph, T. A. and K. P. Birman (1986, February). Low cost management of replicated data in fault-tolerant distributed systems. *ACM Transactions on Computer Systems, 4*(1), 54–70.

Kistler, J. J. and M. Satyanarayanan (1991, October). Disconnected operation in the Coda file system. Operating Systems Review, Special Issue: *Proceedings of the 13th ACM Symposium on Operating Systems Principles* (Pacific Grove, CA), *25*(5), 213–225.

Nelson, M. N., B. B. Welch, and J. K. Ousterhout (1988, February). Caching in the Sprite network file system. *ACM Transactions on Computer Systems, 6*(1), 134–154.

Schatz, B. R. (1987). Telesophy: A system for manipulating the knowledge of a community. In *Proceedings of Globecom '87* (New York), pp. 1181–1186. ACM.

Schnase, J. L., J. J. Leggett, and D. L. Hicks (1991, October). *HBI: Initial design and implementation of a hyperbase management system* (Tech. Rep. TAMU-HRL 91-003). Hypertext Research Lab, Texas A&M University.

Schütt, H. and J. M. Haake (1993, March). Server support for cooperative hypermedia systems. In *Hypermedia '93*, Zurich.

Schütt, H. A. and N. A. Streitz (1990). Hyperbase: A hypermedia engine based on a relational database management system. In *Proceedings of the ECHT'90 European Conference on Hypertext, Databases, Indices and Normative Knowledge*, pp. 95–108.

Shackelford, D. E. (1993, January). *The Distributed Graph Storage System: A users manual for application programmers* (Tech. Rep. TR93-003). Department of Computer Science, The University of North Carolina at Chapel Hill.

Smith, D. K. (1992). Hypermedia vs. paper: User strategies in browsing SNA materials (Tech. Rep. TR92-036). Department of Computer Science, The University of North Carolina at Chapel Hill.

Smith, J. B. and F. D. Smith (1991). ABC: A hypermedia system for artifact-based collaboration. In *Proceedings of ACM Hypertext'91, Construction and Authoring*, pp. 179–192.

Stotts, P. D. and R. Furuta (1989). Petri-net-based hypertext: Document structure with browsing semantics. *ACM Transactions on Information Systems, 7*(1), 3–29.

Thompson, C. W. (1990, January). Strawman reference model for hypermedia systems. In *Proceedings of the NIST Hypertext Standardization Workshop* (Gaithersburg, MD), pp. 223–246.

Yankelovich, N. et al. (1988, January). Intermedia: The concept and the construction of a seamless information environment. *IEEE Computer, 21*(1), 81–96.

PART

III

STUDIES OF COLLABORATION

CHAPTER

13

Communication and Coordination in Reactive Robotic Teams[1]

Ronald C. Arkin
Tucker Balch
Georgia Institute of Technology

1. INTRODUCTION

Coordination theory has most often been considered to be the domain of man–machine interactions. Indeed, throughout most of this volume you will see that the majority of research reported involves computer collaboration with humans to some degree. The research presented in this chapter, however, takes a different tack: It is concerned with the content of information that is necessary for successful cooperation between teams of mobile robots. Most of the communication studies we refer to are at subhuman levels (i.e., derived from animal studies).

At the Georgia Tech Mobile Robotics Laboratory, a robot system design methodology has been developed and refined for both single and multiagent robotic systems. These systems are implemented in both simulation and on mobile robots [3, 13]. The approach relies on two key points: an objective metric of system performance, and an iterative cycle of simulation and instantiation on real systems. Through simulation, the designer can quickly discover which sensors, actuators, and control parameters are most critical. Parameters are varied as performance is measured and compared to that of other configurations. The goal is to find a system that maximizes (or minimizes) the performance metric. Finally, the configuration is ported to a real

[1]A closely related version of this paper appeared in Issue 1.1 of AUTONOMOUS ROBOTS and is reproduced with permission.

robotic system for testing. In this chapter, the approach is applied to communication in reactive multiagent robotic systems.

To discover how communication impacts multiagent robotic system performance, three societal robot tasks were devised. The performance in simulation of a team of robots is measured for each of these tasks for three different types of communication. The experiments are designed so that performance for each type of communication can be compared across different tasks. In all, a six-dimensional space of task, environment, and control parameters was explored including: task, communication type, number of robots, number of attractors, mass of attractors, and percentage of obstacle coverage. The simulation results were supported by porting the control system to a team of Denning mobile robots.

2. RELATED WORK

2.1. Multiagent Robotic Systems

Multiagent robotic systems constitutes a very active area of research. A large body of literature exists regarding systems ranging in size from two to thousands of robots. Dudek et al. [19] provide a taxonomy of these systems classified along the dimensions of group size, reconfigurability, processing ability, and communication range, topology, and bandwidth. The research in this chapter concentrates on relatively small group sizes, typically on the order of two to ten agents. Large-scale swarm robotic systems [27] are not considered. According to the taxonomy cited earlier, our work fits in the categories of LIM-GROUP (small number of robots), COM-NONE, and COM-INF (robots either have no communication or can be heard within the entire range of the simulation), TOP-BROAD (broadcast communication method), BAND-LOW, and BAND-ZERO (have limited bandwidth or no communication), ARR_DYN (robots can reconfigure themselves independently), PROC-FSA (uses finite state automaton processing), and homogeneous (all agents are of the same type).

Fukuda was among the first to study multiagent robotic systems in the context of what he refers to as cellular robotics [24]. This pioneering work is mainly concerned with heterogeneous agents. The research reported in this study is for homogeneous societies, where all the agents are functionally equivalent. Recently, researchers at MIT's AI Laboratory [16, 39] have studied aspects of subsumption-based reactive control using robot societies consisting of up to 20 agents. In particular, learning methods have been evaluated [44]. Applications of multiagent systems are also being investigated in military environments in both the United States and Europe [42, 34]. Extraterrestrial planetary exploration has also been proposed as a useful target domain for these societies [40].

Foraging has been one of the most widely studied tasks to date for multirobot teams. Floreano [21] described nest-based foraging strategies using a neural network architecture. Drogoul and Ferber [20] reported results of simulations of foraging robots demonstrating the spontaneous evolution of structure such as chains from extremely simple agents.

A pressing question, and one that the research described here addresses, is the role of communication in multiagent robotic systems. Arkin [5] previously reported that successful task-achieving behavior can occur even in the absence of communication between agents. It is the goal of the study reported in this chapter to understand what improvements in performance can be gained by adding communication above noncommunicative methods. Along these same lines, Altenburg and Pavicic created a multirobot society consisting of a group of small robots conducting a search and retrieve task (one robot only per object retrieved) using either an infrared or incandescent recruitment signal. The authors reported an approximately 50% improvement in performance for target acquisition using this type of signal. The work as reported in [1] is very preliminary.

Werner and Dyer [51] studied the evolution of communication in synthetic agents and have demonstrated that directional mating signals can evolve in these systems given the presence of societal necessity. MacLennan [37] has also studied this problem and concluded that communication can evolve in a society of simple robotic agents. In his studies, the societies that evolved communication were 84% fitter than those in which communication was suppressed. An order of magnitude better performance was observed when learning was introduced. Franklin and Harmon, in simulation research conducted at ERIM [22], used a rule-based cooperative multiagent system to study the role of communication, cooperation, and inference and how these relationships lead to specialized categories of cooperative systems. Regarding communication, they recognized that information need not be explicitly requested by a receiver for it to be potentially useful to the multiagent system as a whole.

Yanco studied communication specifically in the context of robotic systems. In her research [52], a task was defined requiring communication to coordinate two robots, Ernie and Bert. The robots have a limited vocabulary that self-organizes over time to improve the performance of the task, which involves mimicking the behavior of a leader robot. Noreils [43] described coordinated protocols as a basis for encoding communication signals between robots for navigational tasks. Formal theoretical methods are also being applied in a limited way to this problem. For example, Wang [50] looked at distributed mutual exclusion techniques for coordinating multirobot systems.

The research we report herein is motivated by the desire to create a design methodology for multiagent reactive robotic systems. To effectively design these systems it is important to choose correctly the number of agents and the communication mechanisms of a robot society for a particular task. This goal is decidedly different than the studies reported earlier.

2.2. Biological Systems

Nature offers a wealth of existing successful behaviors that robot designers can often directly apply to their work. Because communication is important in many natural societies it is appropriate to look to them for inspiration. Our strategy for creating multiagent systems has been significantly influenced by biological and ethological studies. In [10], we reported the dimensions by which communication can be described in these systems. Some specific examples of the role of communication in animal societies are reported next.

One of the most commonly studied social biological systems is that of ants. Excellent references on their social organization and communication methods are available [29, 25]. Ants typically use chemical communication to convey information between them. Goss et al. [26] studied foraging behavior in ants, creating computer models that are capable of replicating various species' performance for this task. Franks [23] has looked in particular at the behavior of army ants in the context of group retrieval of prey regarding the relationships of mass to objects retrieved and velocity of return.

Tinbergen's influential work on social behavior in animals [49] described a range of behaviors including: simple social cooperation involving sympathetic induction (doing the same things as others), reciprocal behavior (e.g., feeding activity), and antagonistic behavior; mating behaviors involving persuasion, appeasement, and orientation; family and group life behaviors involving flocking, communal attack (mobs), herding behaviors, and infectious behaviors (alarm, sleep, eating); and fight-related behaviors involving reproductive fighting (spacing rivals), mutual hostility (spacing group individuals), and peck-order (reducing fighting).

An interesting study showing environmental impact on foraging behavior in fish is presented in [18]. The factors considered include food supply, hunger, danger, and competition. Mob behavior and communication in the whiptail wallaby [31] also provides an understanding for the emergent organization of multiple agents and the nature of communication that supports this group behavior. Studies in primates have been conducted regarding the organization of colonies [2] relative to their environment. Finally, research in display behavior in animals [41] provides insights in relation to the state-based communication mechanisms described later in this chapter.

3. THREE TASKS FOR ROBOTIC SOCIETIES

The task a robotic system is to perform dictates to some extent the sensors and actuators required. It is not as apparent how the task impacts control system and communication parameters. Our research focuses on three generic tasks: *Forage*, *Consume*, and *Graze*. Foraging consists of searching the environment for objects (referred to as attractors) and carrying them back to a central location. Consuming requires the robot to perform work on the attractors in place, rather than carrying them back. Grazing is similar to lawn mowing; the robot or robot team must adequately cover the environment. Even more complex tasks can be constructed using these basic tasks as building blocks. This is discussed further in Section 3.5.

3.1. *Forage*

The *Forage* task for a robot is to wander about the environment looking for items of interest (attractors). Upon encountering one of these attractors, the robot moves toward it, finally attaching itself. After attachment, the robot returns the object to a specified home base. Many ant species perform the *Forage* task as they gather food. Robots performing this task would potentially be suitable for garbage collection or specimen collection in a hazardous environment.

Figure 13.1a shows a simulation of two robots foraging for seven attractors and returning them to a home base (the simulation environment is described in Section 6). In the simulation, obstacles are shown as large black circles, attractors are represented as small circles, and the paths of the robots are shown as solid or dashed lines. They leave dashed lines as they

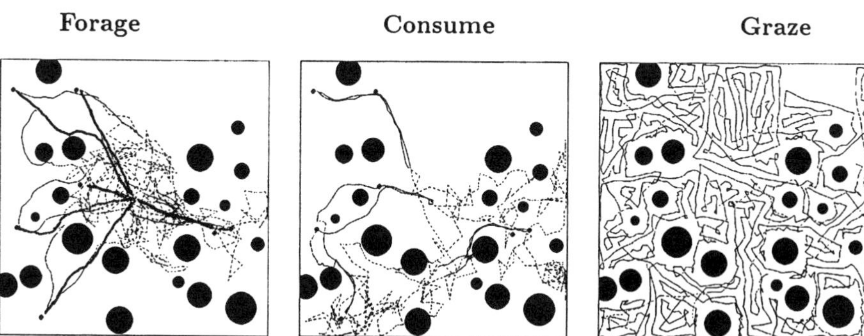

FIG. 13.1. Multiagent simulations of three tasks: (left to right) Forage, Consume, and Graze. The paths of the robots are marked by solid and dashed lines while obstacles are shown as black circles. Each simulation includes two robots and seven attractors.

wander, and solid lines when they acquire, attach, and return the attractors to home base.

The mass of the attractor item dictates how quickly a robot can carry it. The heavier the attractor, the slower the speed. Several robots cooperating can move the attractor faster, but only up to the maximum speed of an individual robot.

3.2. *Consume*

Like *Forage*, the *Consume* task involves wandering about the environment to find attractors. Upon encountering an attractor, the robot moves toward it and attaches itself to the object. Unlike the *Forage* task, however, the robot performs work on the object in place after attachment. The time required to do the in-place work is proportional to the mass of the object. It is not necessary for the robot to carry the object back to home base. Applications might include toxic waste cleanup, assembly, or cleaning tasks.

Figure 13.1b shows a simulation of two robots consuming seven attractors. Note that this task is performed in exactly the same environment as the forage task shown in Fig. 13.1a. The robots leave dashed lines as they wander, and solid lines when they acquire and move to the attractors.

The mass of the attractor item dictates how quickly a robot can consume it. The heavier the attractor, the more time it takes. Several robots cooperating can consume an attractor faster. For this task the rate of consumption is linear with the number of robots and has no ceiling.

3.3. *Graze*

The *Graze* task differs from *Forage* and *Consume* in that discrete attractors are not involved. Instead, the object is to completely cover, or visit the environment. The *Graze* task for a *robot* is to search for an area that has not been grazed, move toward it, then graze over it until the entire environment (or some percentage of it) has been covered. It is assumed that the robot possesses some means to "graze" and that it grazes over a fixed "swath." The size of the task is dictated by the proportion of environment that must be covered before completion. Figure 13.1c shows a simulation of two robots grazing over 95% of the environment. The robots leave dashed lines as they wander, and solid lines when they graze. Grazing robots might be used to mow, plow, or seed fields, vacuum houses [36], or remove scrub in a lumber producing forest.

The size of the swath that a robot can graze, and the percentage of the area that the robot must graze over both affect how long it takes to complete the task. Multiple robots can complete the task faster if they avoid traversing already grazed areas and if they can find ungrazed areas quickly.

3.4. Task Parameters

A number of items contribute to the complete specification of a task, including task factors, environmental factors, and the sensor and motor capabilities of the robots. Table 13.1 enumerates and summarizes the parameters available in our simulation.

We consider these parameters to be the most important:

- *Number of attractors.* Clearly the number of attractors the robots must collect or consume will affect how long it takes to accomplish the task.
- *Mass of attractors.* In general terms, an attractor's mass can be thought of as a "transportability" factor for the *Forage* task, or a "workability" factor for the *Consume* task.
- *Graze coverage.* For the *Graze* task, the total size of the area and the percentage required to be grazed directly impacts the time to cover it.

Sections 7 and 8 report experimental results on how each of these factors affect performance.

3.5. Complex Tasks

For this work, only the three basic tasks and the behaviors necessary for robots to perform them are considered. The results for these tasks are important because more complex tasks are easily described as combinations of simpler ones. Consider a robot removing scrub from a forest; after working for a period of time, it must return to a refueling station. The scrub removal portion of the task is analogous to *Graze*, whereas refueling is similar to *Consume*.

Another complex task, *BoundingOverwatch*, is a movement tactic utilized by Army Scouts. Usually employed by two groups of two ground vehicles, it allows safe penetration into hostile areas. Each group moves forward a short distance, then waits and "covers" the other group as it moves forward. A behavior to perform *BoundingOverwatch* can be built as a more specialized and coordinated *Consume* task. Once appropriate waypoints for each group are selected, virtual attractors can be placed there. The behavior would emerge as each two-element group successively moves from attractor to attractor.

Other research in our laboratory is underway that investigates how complex behaviors may be specified as combinations of basic behaviors [35]. The research includes a language that allows individual robots, and societies of robots to be described formally. Formal operators allow basic, or primitive, behaviors to be grouped into more complex assemblages. These assemblages are further combined to form the overall behavior of the robot. The language includes operators that coordinate individual robots into cooperating groups.

TABLE 13.1
Experimental Parameter Values

Factor	Baseline	Experimental Range
Task Factors		
Number of attractors	—	1 to 7
Mass of attractors	5 avg	1 to 8
Graze Coverage	95%	13% to 95%
Environmental Factors		
Obstacle Coverage	15%	10% to 25%
Obstacle radius	—	1.0 to 4.0
Number of Robots	—	1 to 5
Sensor and Motor Constraints		
Maximum Velocity	2 ft/step	fixed
Attractor Sensor Range	20 ft	fixed
Obstacle Sensor Range	20 ft	fixed
Communication Range	100 ft	fixed
Communication Type	No	No, State, Goal
Graze Swath	2 ft	fixed
Consume Rate	0.01 mass units/step	fixed
Control Parameters		
Obstacle Sphere of Influence	5 ft	fixed
Obstacle Repulsion Gain	1.0	fixed
Robot Repulsion Sphere	20 ft	fixed
Robot Repulsion Gain *(wander)*	0.5	fixed
Robot Repulsion Gain *(acquire)*	0.1	fixed
Robot Repulsion Gain *(deliver, graze)*	0.1	fixed
Move-to-Goal Gain *(acquire)*	1.0	fixed
Move-to-Goal Gain *(deliver)*	1.0	fixed
Consume-Attractor Rate *(consume)*	0.01 mass units/step	fixed
Probe Gain *(graze)*	1.0	fixed

Note. Unless noted otherwise, the values are the same for all three tasks.

For clarity, we describe the robot behaviors somewhat less formally than in this related work, but the same recursive philosophy applies.

4. REACTIVE CONTROL

A schema-based reactive control system is used in this research. To provide the reader appropriate background, a brief summary of reactive control is first provided, followed by some of the special characteristics of schema-based systems.

Reactive control is a paradigm that emerged in the mid-1980s as a new approach to controlling robots. It arose in response to the perceived problems in hierarchical robotic control systems that required a heavy reliance on internal world models. Reactive behavior-based control avoids as much as possible the use of symbolic representations of the world, preferring many tight sensorimotor couplings that ground the robot's perceptions directly.

Reactive control is characterized by several distinct features:

- The basic component is a behavior consisting of a coordinated perceptual and motor process.
- Perception and action are tightly coupled.
- Reliance on explicit world models and representational knowledge is avoided during execution.
- They are particularly well-suited for dynamic and unstructured domains because they rely entirely on immediately perceived sensory data.

Brooks' subsumption architecture is one well-known example of this control paradigm [15]. Other representative examples include [3, 30, 45, 38, 48]. These reactive strategies differ in several significant ways including the organization and nature of the underlying behaviors and whether arbitration, action-selection, or concurrent processing is used to select which of the behaviors are active at any given moment. Space prevents a complete tutorial on reactive systems, so the interested reader is referred to [8] for a more complete review.

Schema-based reactive control has been widely used with success in our laboratory for both simulation studies and real robot implementations [3, 5, 12, 13, 14]. Some features distinguishing schema-based robotic control from other reactive approaches include:

- A dynamic network of processes (schemas) is used rather than a strictly layered system such as found in subsumption.

- Instead of choosing only one behavior (arbitration), several behaviors are allowed to concurrently contribute to the overall action of the robot.
- Potential field techniques [32, 33] are used to encode the robot's behavioral response. Forces analagous to those generated by gravitational or electrical fields repulse or attract the robot as a result of various environmental stimuli.
- Adaptation and learning are facilitated through this flexibility [17, 46, 47] by permitting access to the underlying numeric parameters of the control system.
- Neuroscientific, psychological, and ethological studies provide motivation for schema use. [7]

In schema-based control, each of the active behaviors (motor schemas) computes its reaction to its perceptual stimuli using a method analogous to potential fields [3]. The traditional potential field method computes the attractive forces generated by an attractor and combines them with repulsive forces generated from obstacles, computing a global force field based on potential energy computations drawn from gravitational or electrostatic analogues. It must be noted that unlike traditional potential fields, in our work only the robot's immediate reaction at its current location and its current perceptions of the world is computed. All of the independent behavioral vector force computations are summed and normalized and then sent to the robot for execution. This perceive–react cycle is repeated as rapidly as possible. Problems with local minima, maxima, and cyclic behavior which are endemic to many potential fields strategies are handled by several methods including: the injection of noise into the system [3]; resorting to high-level planning [6]; repulsion from previously visited locales [14]; continuous adaptation [17]; and other learning strategies [46, 47]. The Appendix contains information on the specific computations of the individual schemas used in this research.

Individual schemas are primitive behaviors that are combined to generate more complex emergent behaviors. A group of schemas that together result in a task-achieving behavior is called an *assemblage*. Behavioral assemblages are often arranged in a sequence, so that the overall task is accomplished in a step-by-step manner with each assemblage helping the robot accomplish one step of the task. Assemblages for accomplishing the *Forage*, *Consume*, and *Graze* taskes are described in the next section.

4.1. Baseline Assemblage Parameters

Experimental results were generated for the tasks described in Section 3 by comparing performance of proposed robotic systems to baseline, or control, performance results. The baseline data was computed by first selecting a reasonable set of control parameters, then running a statistically significant number of simulations. Values for these parameters are based on previous research [5]. In this section, the behaviors for executing the three tasks (*Forage*, *Consume*, and *Graze*) and their baseline parameters are described.

At the highest level, the tasks themselves are assemblages that are represented as finite state acceptors (FSAs) consisting of several states. FSAs provide an easy means for both expressing and reasoning about behavioral sets by providing formal semantics [11]. Each state corresponds to a separate assemblage in which a constituent set of motor schemas is instantiated if that particular state is active. *Perceptual Triggers* cause transitions between states. Each active motor schema has a perceptual schema associated with it to provide the information necessary for the robot to interact with its environment.

4.2. *Forage*

For the *Forage* task, the robots can be in one of three states: *wander*, *acquire*, and *deliver*. All robots begin in the *wander* state. If there are no attractors within the robot's field of view, the robot remains in *wander* until one is encountered. When an attractor is encountered, a transition to the *acquire* state is triggered. While in the *acquire* state, the robot moves towards the attractor and when it is sufficiently close, attaches to it. The last state, *deliver*, is triggered when the robot attaches to the attractor. While in the *deliver* state the robot carries the attractor back to home base. Upon reaching home base, the robot deposits the attractor there and reverts back to the *wander* state. Figure 13.2 shows the FSA for *Forage*.[2]

For each state, the active schemas and their parameters are:

- *Wander* State

  noise: high gain, moderate persistence to cover a wide area of the environment.

  avoid-static-obstacle for objects: sufficiently high to avoid collisions.

  avoid-static-obstacle for robots:[3] moderately high repulsion to force individual robots apart and more efficiently cover the environment.

  detect-attractor: perceptual schema that triggers the *acquire* state when the robot senses an attractor.

---

[2]This task was described earlier in [9]. The "forage" state mentioned there corresponds to the "wander" state here.

[3]Avoid-static-obstacle is also used for nonthreatening moving objects. Other schemas such as escape and dodge can be used for noncooperative moving objects when appropriate.

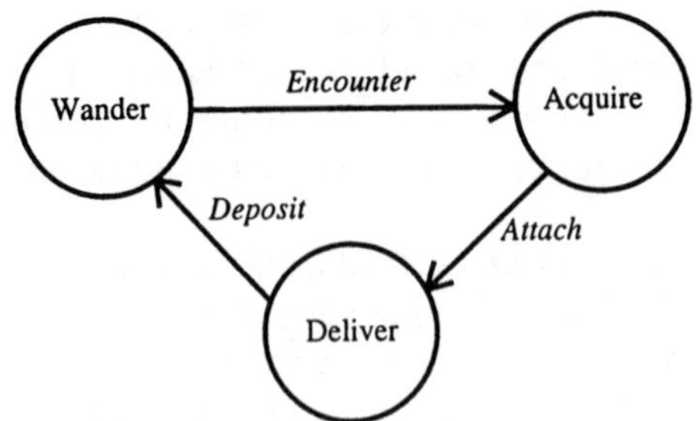

FIG. 13.2. The Forage FSA.

- *Acquire* State

  noise: low gain, to deal with local minima.

  avoid-static-obstacle for objects: sufficiently high to avoid collisions.

  avoid-static-obstacle for robots: very low gain, to allow robots to converge on the same attractor and thus cooperate, but avoid colliding with one another.

  move-to-goal: high gain to move the robot to the detected attractor.

  detect-attachment: a perceptual schema that triggers a state transition to *deliver* when the robot is close enough to attach to the attractor.

- *Deliver* State

  noise: as in *acquire*, low gain to deal with local minima.

  avoid-static-obstacle for objects: as in *acquire*, sufficiently high to avoid collisions.

  avoid-static-obstacle for robots: same as in *acquire*.

  move-to-goal: high gain, with home base as the target.

  detect-deposit: a perceptual schema that triggers a state change when the robot reaches home base.

Specific values used for schema gains and parameters in this study are listed in Table 13.1 in Section 3.4 (see Appendix for additional information on gains and parameters).

4.3. Consume

The FSA and behaviors for the *Consume* task (Fig. 13.3) are similar to those used in *Forage*. In fact, the schemas and their gains are identical in the *wander* and *acquire* states. The *consume* state, however, is unique to to this behavior. In the *consume* state, only one motor schema, consume-attractor is activated. It reduces the mass of the attractor at a fixed rate over time. When the attractor is fully consumed (mass zero) it is deactivated and the robot transitions back to the *wander* state. The only parameter applicable in

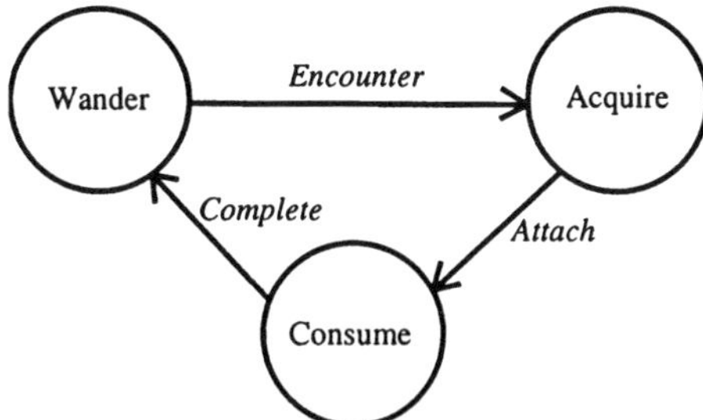

FIG. 13.3. The Consume FSA.

the *Consume* state is the rate at which an attractor is consumed. This value is fixed at 0.01 units/time step for all experiments (Table 13.1 in Section 3.4).

4.4. *Graze*

For the *Graze* task, the *wander* and *acquire* states are again similar to those of *Forage* and *Consume*. The primary difference is that detect-attractor in the *wander* state is replaced with a similar detect-ungrazed-area schema. Detect-ungrazed-area has the same fixed sensor range as detect-attractor, but it detects ungrazed areas instead of attractors. Each robot starts in the *wander* state and searches for ungrazed areas. Upon encountering one, it transitions to the *acquire* state and moves toward it. When the robot arrives at the graze site, it transitions to the *graze* state. The *graze* state is quite different from the corresponding states in the other FSAs. While in the *graze* state, the robot tends to move along its current heading as it "grazes" over a fixed swath of the environment. As long as there continues to be ungrazed areas directly ahead, the robot remains in the *graze* state. The active schemas for this state are:

- noise: low gain, to deal with local minima.
- avoid-static-obstacle for objects: high enough to avoid collisions.
- avoid-static-obstacle for robots: very low, to allow robots to graze close by, but avoid collisions.
- probe: moderate gain, to encourage the robot to keep moving along its current heading towards ungrazed areas.
- graze: performs the actual graze operation over a fixed swath.
- detect-grazed-area: perceptual schema that triggers a state change once the robot has completely grazed the local area.

For simulation purposes, *Graze* is implemented by maintaining and marking a high resolution grid corresponding to the environment. Initially, the entire grid is marked as ungrazed. As robots graze, they mark visited areas on the grid accordingly.

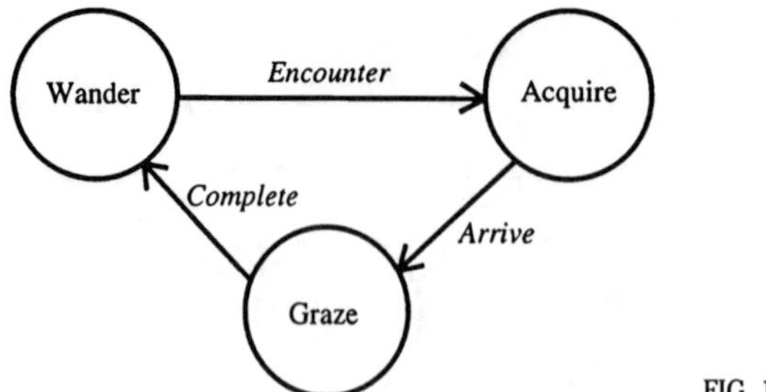

FIG. 13.4. The Graze FSA.

Gains and parameters for each of the schemas active in the graze state are listed in Table 13.1.

5. FORMS OF INTERAGENT COMMUNICATION

Three different types of communication are evaluated in this research. Using a minimalist philosophy, the first type actually involves no direct communication between the agents. The second type allows for the transmission of state information between agents in a manner similar to that found in display behavior in animals [41]. The third type (goal communication) requires the transmitting agent to recognize and broadcast the location of an attractor when one is located within detectable range. Each of these forms of communication is described next.

5.1. No Communication

For this type of multiagent society no direct communication is allowed. The robots are able to discriminate internally three perceptual classes: other robots, attractors, and obstacles. None of this information, however, is communicated to other agents. Each robot must rely entirely on its own perception of the world. Arkin has shown in previous work [5] that this basic information is enough to support cooperation in robot retrieval tasks (*Forage*). Cooperation in this context refers to the observed phenomena of recruitment, where multiple agents converge together to work on the same task. The baseline results (Section 7) show that cooperation also emerges in the *Consume* and *Graze* tasks as well.

5.2. State Communication

When state communication is permitted, robots are able to detect the internal state (*wander*, *acquire*, or *deliver*) of other robots. For the results reported here, the communication is even simpler than that, where only one bit of data is transmitted: with zero indicative of an agent being in the *wander state* and one indicating that it is in any state other than *wander* (i.e., *acquire*, *deliver*, *consume*, or *graze*). In [9], this type of communication was shown to provide a distinct advantage over no communication for performance of the *Forage* task. Communication is often considered a deliberate act, but state communication is not necessarily "intentional" because information can be relayed by passive observation. The sender does not necessarily explicitly broadcast its state, but allows others to observe it. In nature this type of communication is demonstrated when an animal changes its posture or external appearance, such as a dog raising its hackles or exhibiting flight behavior in response to fear.

To take advantage of state information in reactive control, the behavioral assemblages for each task are modified slightly. From a robot's point of view, the most important states to look for in another robot are those where the other robot has found an attractor or an area to graze; that means that the other robot has found useful work. If the robot goes to the same location, it is likely to find useful work as well, or at least be able to assist cooperatively. The appropriate states are *acquire*, *deliver*, *consume*, or *graze*; in the *wander* state the robot has not yet found any work to do.

For all three tasks, the behaviors are modified so that a robot will transition to *acquire* if it discovers another robot in *acquire*, *deliver*, *consume*, or *graze*. Inasmuch as the robot may not yet know the location of the attractor, it follows the other robot instead. Once the attractor is detectable it heads directly for it.

5.3. Goal Communication

Goal communication involves the transmission and reception of specific goal-oriented information. Implementation on mobile robots requires data to be encoded, transmitted, received, and decoded. Goal communication differs from the other two levels in that the sender must deliberately send or broadcast the information. A natural example of this type of communication is found in the behavior of honeybees. When a bee discovers a rich source of nectar, it returns to the hive and communicates the location with a "dance" which encodes the direction and distance from the hive to the source.

For reactive control, goal communication is implemented by modifying the behavioral assemblages in the same manner as described for state communication. However, instead of following the transmitting robot that discovered the attractor, a receiving robot moves directly toward the communicated location of the attractor. The intent is that the agent may now follow a more direct path (beeline) to the attractor.

This very rudimentary form of communication only broadcasts the goal that the transmitting agent is involved with. Another mode of communication, not yet explored, involves the transmission of all detected attractors independent of whether the transmitting agent is already acquiring or delivering one. This would present more options for the receiving agent, perhaps choosing to move to the closest attractor independent of whether or not the transmitting agent would benefit from its help. This additional form of communication is left for future work.

5.4. Explicit Versus Implicit Communication

The implementation of goal and state communication requires explicit signaling and reception of the communicated information. State communication can be implemented simply by mounting a binary signal atop the robot which is either on or off depending on the robot's internal state. This communication, although trivial, is explicit as it requires the deliberate act of invoking the signal.

Information pertinent to cooperation might be gathered by other means as well. The internal state of a robot could be inferred by observing its movement (e.g., recognizing a robot in the *wander* state due to apparent random movements), thereby placing a larger perceptual burden on the receiving agent. Robots can also communicate through their environment. In the graze task, robots leave evidence of their passage since the places they visit are modified. This fact is observable by the other robots. These types of communication are referred to as *implicit* as they do not require a deliberate act of transmission.

Implicit communication was found to be an important mode of cooperation in simulations of the graze task. Because this communication emerges from the interaction of the agent and the environment, it cannot be "turned off." Thus comparative analyses of performance with and without implicit communication are not meaningful.

6. SIMULATION ENVIRONMENT

The simulation environment should provide an accurate estimate of robot performance in the real world. Simulation is important because it offers a means to test many robot system configurations quickly. To be useful, the simulation must report performance in terms of the prescribed performance metric and realistically emulate the environment and the robot's interaction with it. Furthermore, the simulation must allow hardware, control, and environmental variables to be readily manipulated.

Each robot (i.e., agent), is an identical vehicle controlled by one of the task assemblages described before. Each agent's current state, however, is dependent solely on its own perception. The robots execute their tasks in a

64×64 unit environment. The units are dimensionless, but for convenience of comparison to real robot implementations they represent 1 foot. Time is measured in steps. Each step is one iteration of the program that calculates the robots' next positions. The robots are able to sense their location in the environment, and detect obstacles, attractors and other robots within a fixed radius field of view. They are able to grasp and carry attractors, consume attractors, or graze as the task dictates. The simulation automatically enforces the limits and rules set forth in the task specifications, as well as sensor–actuator limits. The robots are allowed to move without restriction within the 64×64 environment, but they may not move outside of it.

6.1. The Performance Metric

What is "performance"? Because one goal of this research is to report the impact of communication on robotic societies, performance must be objectively measurable. Selection of a performance metric is important because these metrics are often in competition (i.e., cost vs. reliability). Some potential metrics for multiagent robotic systems are:

- Cost: Build a system to accomplish the task for the minimum cost. This may be appropriate for many industrial tasks. Use of this metric will tend to reduce the cost of the system and minimize the number of robots used.
- Time: Build a system to accomplish the task in minimum time. This metric will lead to a solution calling for the maximum number of robots that can operate without interference.
- Energy: Complete the task using the smallest amount of energy. This is appropriate in situations where energy stores are limited (e.g., space or undersea applications).
- Reliability–Survivability: Build a system that will have the greatest probability to complete the task even at the expense of time or cost. This may be useful for certain tactical military applications.

The task metric can also be a numeric combination of several measurements. Whatever the metric is, it must be measurable, especially in simulation. For this research, time to complete the task was chosen as the primary performance metric. It is easily and accurately measurable and conforms to what is frequently thought of as performance. No claim is made however that this is the *best* metric; robot path length or energy consumption may be equally useful. In the simulation studies described herein, performance is measured by counting how many iterations the simulation program executes before the task is completed.

There are a few initial conditions for some tasks that prevent the robots from completing it. For example, if an attractor was somehow placed within a circle of obstacles, the robots would never be able to reach it. Such a scenario is not solvable by any robot system without the capacity to move the obstacles. Other scenarios, however, may ultimately be solvable, but may potentially defeat the purely reactive strategies presented here. To provide for these situations, the simulation is allowed to continue for 8,000 steps before failure is declared. As most runs complete in less than 2,000 steps, it is highly likely that the system will *never* complete the task if it does not do so before failure is declared. The objective is to evaluate the impact communication makes on performance, so it is not important to know why the system failed, just to measure how it improves with communication. In cases of failure, the run is recorded as having taken 8,000 steps. This approach reports optimistic performance because the run might never have completed (infinite steps). But, to show improvement over a failure case, the system must actually complete the task *and* in less than 8,000 steps.

6.2. Environmental Factors

As much as can be known about the target system's operating environment should be incorporated into the design process for the control system. If these factors are known a priori, they can be included in the simulation. Important environmental factors include:

- Mobility factors: Is the terrain mountainous or flat? What percent of the environment is served by roadways?
- Obstacle coverage: What percent of the environment is cluttered with obstacles?
- Metric a priori knowledge: Does the robot have a good map of the area or is it completely unknown?
- Static or dynamic: Is the environment filled with moving objects, thus reducing the utility of maps, or is the environment a static one?

For this study, a static flat environment with randomly scattered obstacles is assumed. No a priori knowledge of the obstacles' location is available. Obstacle coverage is varied from 5% to 20% of the total area, with 15% as a baseline.

6.3. Motor and Sensor Constraints

As a step in the robot system design methodology, realistic bounds on the expected motor and sensor capabilities of robots are set. These bounds help reduce the search space for an optimum solution. The affect of communication on performance is the main thrust of this research, so fixed values representing the expected capabilities of the robots were used. If the goal were to determine optimal sensor or motor requirements, those parameters could be varied as well. Table 13.1 (Section 3.4) shows the experimental motor and sensor values used in the simulations.

7. BASELINE RESULTS AND ANALYSIS TOOLS

To build a baseline database of performance measurements, a configuration of environment, control, and task parameters was selected empirically (Table 13.1). The baseline database serves as a control for comparison in the evaluation of the communication experiments described next. The database is generated by running the simulation using the baseline configuration parameters for each of the three tasks: *Forage*, *Consume*, and *Graze*. For each task, the number of robots and the number of attractor objects (or percentage of graze coverage) is varied. For each combination of robots and attractors, a measure of performance is taken by timing runs on 30 different randomly generated scenarios. Overall performance is the average of those 30 runs. For each run, the simulation records the number of steps taken, and whether or not the run timed-out (failed).

The baseline performance measurements were made with no communication allowed between the robots. This control is then compared with the performance in each of the three tasks when state or goal communication is allowed (Section 8). From these comparisons, one can see quantitatively how these modes of communication impact performance.

7.1. Baseline Performance

Performance data is visualized as a 3-dimensional surface with the X axis reflecting the number of robots and the Y axis indicating the number of attractors or percent coverage[4] (see Fig. 13.5). The Z, or height, axis shows the average time to complete the task for that combination of robots and attractors (smaller numbers are indicative of better performance). Each point on the surface represents the the results of 30 simulation runs.

The plots for all three tasks share a similar shape. Notice that the back left corner is the highest point on the three surfaces. This is expected because that location represents the case where one robot by itself must complete the most work (seven attractors for forage and consume, 95% cov-

[4]For *Graze*, the percent of area to be grazed is varied in increments of 13.57%. This allows the difficulty to be varied in seven discrete steps from 13.57% to 95%. Results can be directly compared to *Forage* and *Consume* tasks with one to seven attractors.

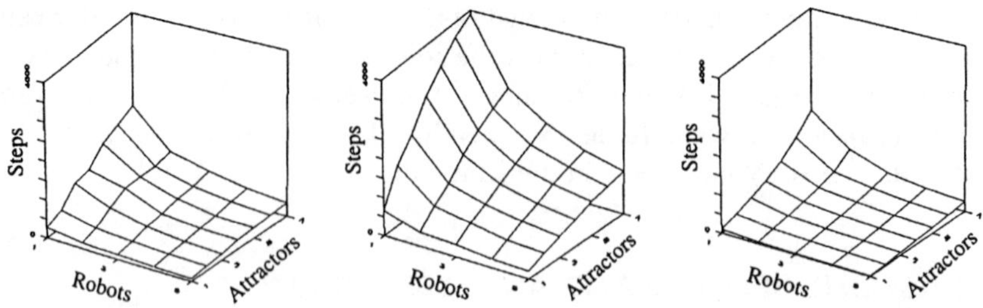

FIG. 13.5. Time to complete a task in movement steps, for one to five robots and one to seven attractors with no communication. From left to right: plots for the *Forage*, *Consume*, and *Graze* tasks. Lower numbers in the height axis (movement steps) indicate better performance. Notice that the shapes of the graphs are similar, indicating that the tasks share a common relationship between performance, numbers of robots and numbers of attractors. The highest point (worst performance), at the back, is the case where only one robot must complete the task alone. The lowest point, at the front, is the case where five robots share the least amount of work.

erage for graze). Similarly, the right front is the lowest point, as the largest number of robots (five) complete the least amount of work (one attractor). It is also apparent for all three tasks that performance initially improves sharply as more robots are added, but then tapers off. In some cases, performance does not improve much at all with more than four robots. This is important if robots are expensive.

To illustrate, suppose a robotic system for the *Forage* task should be both fast *and* inexpensive. Performance is then a combination of the time to complete the task and the cost of the system. Ultimately, the designer must balance the importance of cost versus speed of completion, but one approach is to amortize the cost of the robotic system over its expected lifetime. Thus the cost of one run is the overall cost divided by the expected number of runs. For this example, suppose the amortized cost of each robot per run is valued the same as 300 time steps. Then if N is the number of robots, and T is the time to complete the task, the overall performance is:

$$P = N * 300 + T \tag{1}$$

Using timing measurements taken for *Forage* and adding in amortized cost, a 3-dimensional surface is generated for the new performance metric (Fig. 13.6). A system with two robots is generally best for three or more attractors. If the environment is expected to contain only one or two attractors, one robot is the best choice. Even though more robots may be faster, the overall goals of the designer may call for fewer.

FIG. 13.6. Optimizing in the *Forage* task for time and cost. This graph illustrates a more complex performance metric than time steps alone. Performance here is defined as time to complete the task plus the number of robots times robot cost (300 units). Lower points on the graph indicate better performance. For one or two attractors, overall performance is optimized with one robot, while two robots are better with three or more attractors.

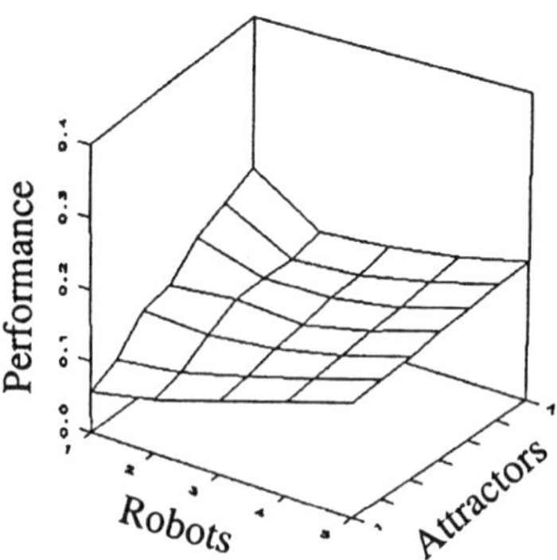

7.2. Speedup

Another effective tool is *speedup* measurement. A plot of speedup reveals how much more efficient several robots are than just one in completing a task. If $P[i, j]$ is the performance for i robots and j attractors, the speedup at that point is:

$$S[i,j] = \frac{\frac{P[1,j]}{i}}{P[i,j]} \tag{2}$$

So, if two robots complete the task exactly twice as fast as one robot, speedup is 1.0 (higher numbers are better). Mataric introduced a similar metric of robot performance in [39]. Anywhere speedup is equal to 1.0, the performance is said to be *linear*. *Superlinear* performance is greater than 1.0, and *sublinear* is less than 1.0. Realize, however, that in some cases more robots will be faster for actual task completion time, but still offer sublinear speedup.

Figure 13.7 shows speedup plots for *Forage*, *Consume*, and *Graze* without communication. Note that speedup for all tasks is generally higher for larger numbers of attractors. Researchers in other branches of computer science have found that randomized search tasks are often completed in superlinear time on parallel systems [28]. Because the *wander* behavior used in all three tasks essentially solves a randomized search task, it is not surprising that performance is superlinear when this behavior is heavily utilized, as is the case when there are large numbers of attractors.

Surprisingly, speedup in the *Consume* task is sublinear at all but one point (Fig. 13.7b). The behavior in the *consume* state can at most offer linear speedup (the limit is set by the specification of the task). So an environment with massive attractors will force the speedup to be limited near 1.0. This

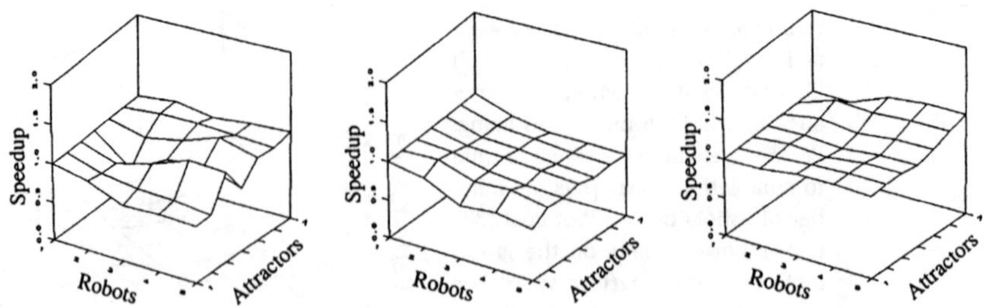

FIG. 13.7. Speedup in a task as the number of robots and attractors are varied with no communication. Left to right: plots for the *Forage*, *Consume*, and *Graze* tasks. Speedup values greater than 1.0 indicate *N* robots perform more than *N* times better than one robot alone in that situation. Of the three tasks, *Graze* shows the best speedup.

hypothesis was tested by reducing the average mass of the attractors, then rerunning the simulations. In the baseline runs, attractor mass varies from 2.0 to 8.0 units, but for these experimental runs, mass was reduced to 1.0 to 4.0 units. Reducing attractor mass allows the robots to spend more time wandering (a superlinear task) instead of consuming (at most linear). The speedup for *Consume* with lower mass attractors is shown in Fig. 13.8. At every point on the surface, speedup is better for low mass attractors than for high mass. In fact, in many cases speedup is superlinear.

Speedup in the *Graze* task is superlinear at all but three points on the surface (Fig. 13.7). In the very worst case, speedup dips to 0.97. Situations requiring a high percentage of graze coverage result in the best speedup; the peak is 1.21 for five robots and 95% coverage. In cases where high graze coverage

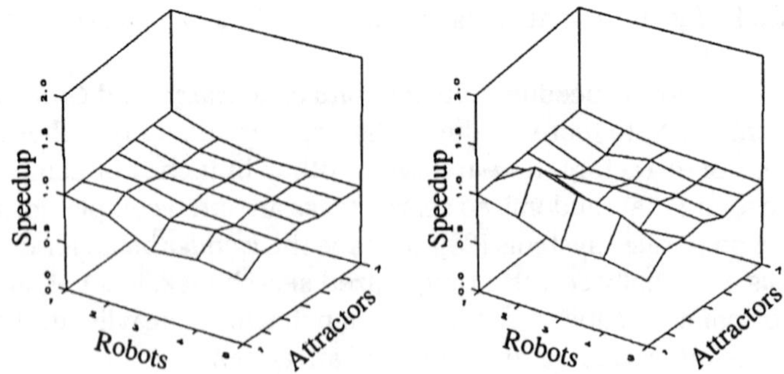

FIG. 13.8. Comparison of speedup in the *Consume* task without communication for attractors of different mass. Speedup when attractors average 5.0 mass units, left, and 2.5 on the right. Overall speedup is better in the case of the lower mass attractors.

is required, robots spend more time in *wander* as they look for the last bit of area to graze. Again, because *wander* is a superlinear time task, the best speedups should be expected for those regimes.

Speedup results are summarized in Table 13.2.

7.3. Timeouts

A *timeout* occurs when a simulation run exceeds a time limit (for these experiments, the limit is 8,000 steps). A timeout mechanism is necessary to avoid lockups in infinite loops in the event the society is unable to complete the task for that particular random world. Frequency of timeouts for each combination of robots and attractors is measured and plotted in Fig. 13.9. The frequency of timeouts serves primarily as a measure of data quality. In situations where timeout frequency is higher, the experimenter cannot know for sure how long the runs would have taken if they were allowed to complete. Some runs may have completed whereas others may have run indefinitely. When there are relatively few timeouts, the performance is known with greater certainty. As would be expected, most timeouts occur when fewer robots must solve a task with more attractors or a higher graze coverage requirement.

7.4. Summary of Baseline Results

Baseline results serve as a control for experimental comparison in assessing the impact of other communication modes on performance. It is important to derive and understand fully these basic results before testing more complex robot configurations. Important results for the baseline configuration are:

- For a given number of attractors, more robots complete a task faster than fewer robots.
- For a given number of robots, it takes longer to complete a task with more attractors.

TABLE 13.2
Summary of Speedup Data for Three Tasks

Task	*Average Speedup*	*Best*	*Worst*
Forage	0.93	1.15	0.64
Consume	0.82	1.01	0.65
Consume (low mass)	0.89	1.26	0.66
Graze	1.07	1.21	0.97

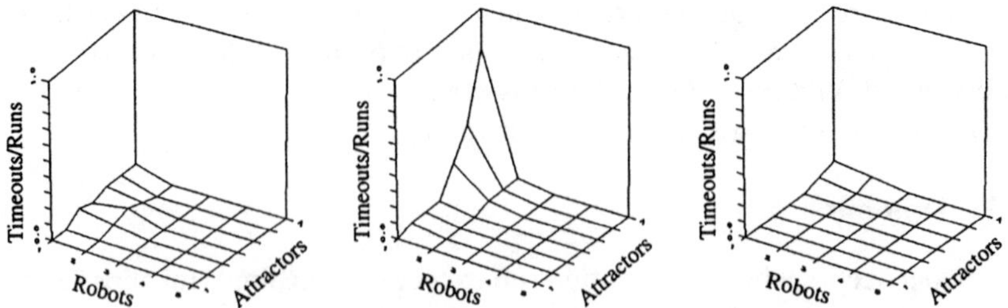

FIG. 13.9. Percentage of runs that end in a timeout for one to five robots and one to seven attractors with no communication. A timeout occurs when the task is not completed within 8,000 timesteps. Lower numbers are better. Timeouts occur more frequently for small numbers of robots with a large numbers of attractors. From left to right: plots for *Forage*, *Consume*, and *Graze* tasks.

- Some performance metrics may result in a system that is optimized with lower numbers of robots than for other metrics.
- Speedup is greater in scenarios where larger numbers of attractors are present.
- Speedup in the *Consume* task is mostly sublinear, but can be superlinear for lower mass attractors.
- Speedup in the *Graze* task is mostly superlinear.
- Timeouts occur more often for low numbers of robots and high numbers of attractors.

8. RESULTS WITH COMMUNICATION

8.1. Communication in the *Forage* Task

Figure 13.10 shows a typical simulation run of two robots foraging for seven attractors with no, state, and goal communication. Inspecting the images from left to right reveals an apparent improvement in the "orderliness" of the robots' paths. The quantitative experimental results summarized in Table 13.3 confirm these qualitative impressions.

Figure 13.5a in Section 7.2 shows a typical performance plot for *Forage*, in this case for no communication (better performance is lower). Each data point represents the results of 30 different simulation runs. The plots for no, state, and goal communication are quite similar in contour but there is improvement in performance evidenced by lower surfaces as the communication becomes more complex. The statistical analysis in Table 13.3 summarizes these observations.

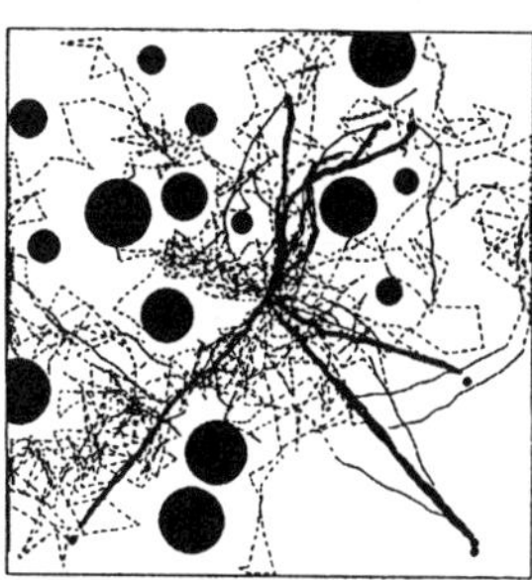

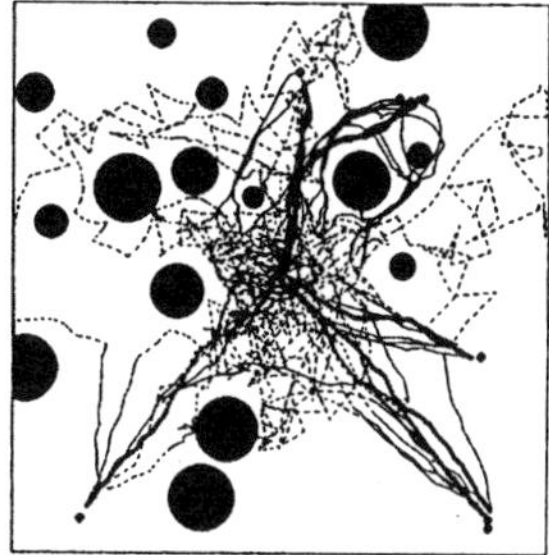

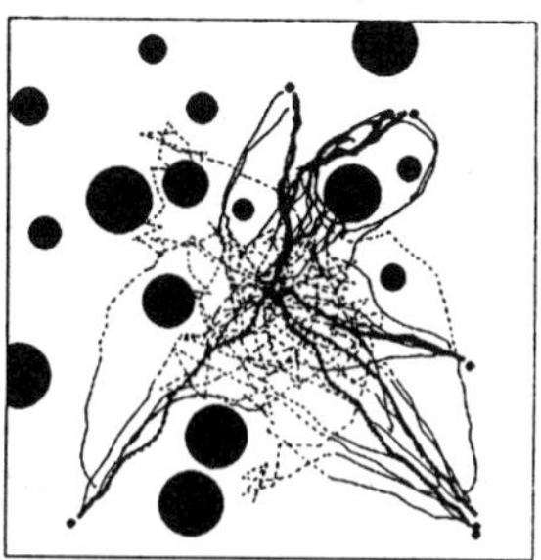

FIG. 13.10. Typical simulation runs of the *Forage* task. From left to right: runs with No, State, and Goal Communication. The overall distance the robots travel, qualitatively apparent as the length of their trails, is reduced as more complex communication is permitted. The simulations required 5,145, 4,470, and 3,495 steps, respectively, to complete.

TABLE 13.3
Summary of Performance Ratios for No, State, and Goal Communication

Task	*Average Improvement*	*Best*	*Worst*
Forage			
State vs. No Communication	16%	66%	-5%
Goal vs. No Communication	19%	59%	-7%
Goal vs. State Communication	3%	34%	-19%
Consume			
State vs. No Communication	10%	46%	-9%
Goal vs. No communication	6%	44%	-16%
Goal vs. State Communication	-4%	5%	-30%
Goal vs. State (low mass attractors)	-1%	23%	-19%
Graze			
State vs. No Communication	1%	19%	0%
Goal vs. No Communication	1%	19%	0%
Goal vs. State communication	0%	0%	0%

To quantify the difference between performance with and without communication, a performance ratio plot is computed (Fig. 13.11). At each point, the performance with communication is divided by the performance without communication. Results greater than 1.0 imply improved performance. For instance, a value of 1.1 indicates 10% improvement. For all the cases tested, State communication improved performance in the *Forage* task an average of 16%. On the average, goal communication is 3% better than state communication in the *Forage* task.

8.2. Communication in the *Consume* Task

The impact of communication on performance of the *Consume* task is similar to that in *Forage*. Figure 13.12 shows a typical simulation of two robots consuming seven attractors with no, state, and goal communication. A surprising result is that the simulation with goal communication actually takes longer than the one with state communication. This slight increase in run time with goal versus state communication is typical for this task.

A representative example of the basic performance data for simulations of the *Consume* task is plotted earlier in Fig. 13.5b, Section 7.2. Again, the contours for all three forms of communication are quite similar. A comparative analysis reveals that on the average, state communication offers a 10% performance advantage over no communication. Goal communication is 4% worse on the average than state communication. Goal communication, however, is still 6% better than no communication at all. Table 13.3 summarizes these results.

Recall that speedup in the *Consume* task is linked to attractor mass (Section 4). Attractor mass may also impact the benefit of communication. Analysis of the data from runs with low mass attractors reveals that goal communication performance is almost indistinguishable from that of state communication (1% worse). Future research may determine if this result is just an anomaly or if environmental and task parameters might shift this trend.

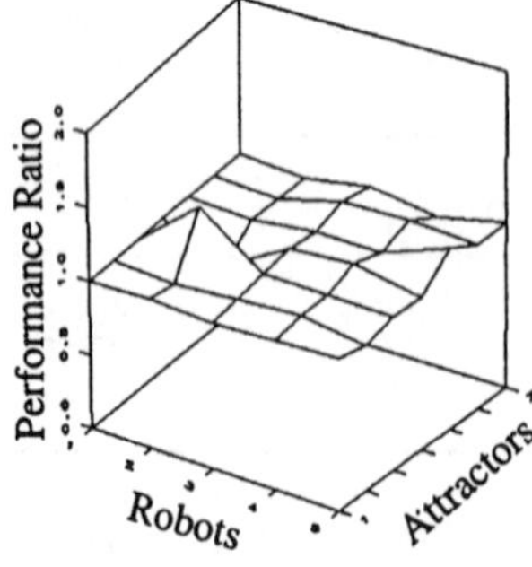

FIG. 13.11. Performance ratio plot for the *Forage* task for Goal versus State communication. A ratio of 1.0 indicates performance is the same. Larger numbers indicate better performance with Goal communication.

No Communication

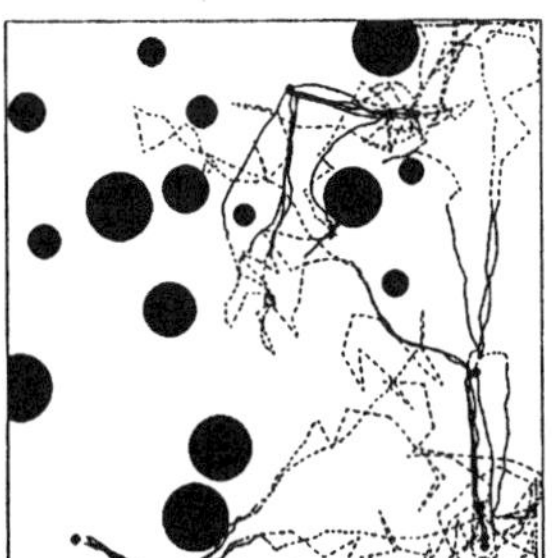

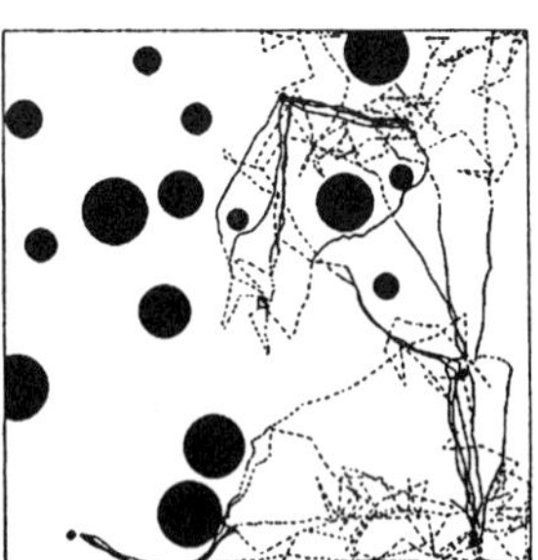

FIG. 13.12. The *Consume* task with No, State, and Goal Communication. The case with State Communication is visibly better than the simulation with No Communication. Performance with State and Goal Communication is about the same. The simulations required 4,200, 3,340 and 3,355 steps, respectively, to complete.

8.3. Communication in the *Graze* Task

The surprising result from Graze task simulations is that communication hardly helps at all. Plots of basic performance data for each of the different levels of communication are not shown because they are visually identical (see Fig. 13.5c for the case with no communication). On average, state communication is only 1% better than no communication. Performance with goal communication is virtually indistinguishable from that with state communication (0% difference). Table 13.3 summarizes these results.

As robots graze they inevitably leave a record of their passage: the graze swath. This physical change in the environment is actually a form of implicit communication. The robots leave marks that advise others where work has or has not been completed. This result is important because it implies that for tasks where such implicit communication is available, explicit communication is unnecessary.

8.4. Summary of Results With Communication

The performance improvement each type of communication offers for each task are summarized in Table 13.3. Several important conclusions may be drawn:

- Communication improves performance significantly in tasks with little implicit communication (*Forage* and *Consume*).
- Communication appears unnecessary in tasks for which implicit communication exists (*Graze*).

- More complex communication strategies (Goal) offer little benefit over basic (State) communication for these tasks (i.e., display behavior is a rich communication method).

9. RESULTS ON MOBILE ROBOTS

The ultimate goal of this research is a working multiagent robotic system; simulation serves only as a development tool. To demonstrate the simulation results, and to move toward a completely functional society, the behaviors for *Forage*, *Consume*, and *Graze* must be instantiated on mobile robots. Our laboratory is equipped with three mobile robots built by Denning Mobile Robotics: George, Ren, and Stimpy. These three-wheeled motorized vehicles are approximately 32 inches in diameter with Ren and Stimpy measuring 3 feet tall and George standing 4 feet. They are equipped with sensors that track their position (shaft encoders), and obstacle detection devices (ultrasonic range sensors).

9.1. *Forage*

The *Forage* task described in Section 4 was ported and tested on Ren and Stimpy. Most of the required schemas had already been coded, but the lack of an existing omnidirectional sensor system for attractor and robot detection complicated matters. The problem was circumvented by simulating the sensor within an embedded perceptual schema utilizing shaft encoder data. Spatial locations of attractors and moving robots are maintained in continuously updated shared files. Fidelity is maintained by coding the perceptual schema so that it does not "reveal" the location of attractors or other robots until they are within sensor range.

A two robot run of the *Forage* task is shown in Fig. 13.13. Most of the parameters are those from the baseline simulation runs, but because the test area is rather small, attractor sensor range was reduced from 20 to 10 feet. The range at which a robot begins to be repulsed from an obstacle (the sphere of influence) was set at 2 feet. There are three attractors (boxes) and one obstacle (chair) in the environment. Both robots were initialized at home base. This run was made without communication. At the beginning of the run (Fig. 13.13), the robots enter the *wander* state, and are repulsed by each other. They immediately detect separate attractors. After tagging their respective attractors, the robots deliver them to home base. Again the robots cycle to *wander*. Only one attractor remains (in the foreground). The attractor is within Ren's sensor range, but outside Stimpy's, so Ren approaches it alone. As Ren returns the attractor to home base, it carries it within Stimpy's sensor range. Stimpy responds by approaching Ren and

FIG. 13.13. Two Denning robots, Ren and Stimpy, demonstrate the Forage task (upper left). Ren tags an attractor (upper right). Stimpy "tags" an attractor (lower left). Ren and Stimpy deliver the attractors to home base (lower right).

helping to deliver the attractor. A (hand-drawn) reconstruction of this run is shown in Fig. 13.14.

9.2. Communication Modes and *Consume*

All three levels of communication for the *Consume* task have been implemented and tested on Ren and Stimpy. A scenario for the two robots with one attractor was used in testing the *Consume* behavior (Fig. 13.15). Although the scenario is simple it serves to illustrate the advantages of and the qualitative differences between the three levels communication described in Section 5. Runs on mobile robots are directly compared with simulations of the same scenario in Fig. 13.15.

In the test scenario, two robots and one attractor are arranged so that one robot is immediately within sensor range of the attractor, whereas the other is just outside sensor range. In the simulations, the attractor is 20 feet from the lower robot. If no communication is allowed, one robot should initially move toward the attractor. The other robot should move away, due to interrobot repulsion. If communication is allowed, both robots should initially move toward the attractor because at least one of them senses it.

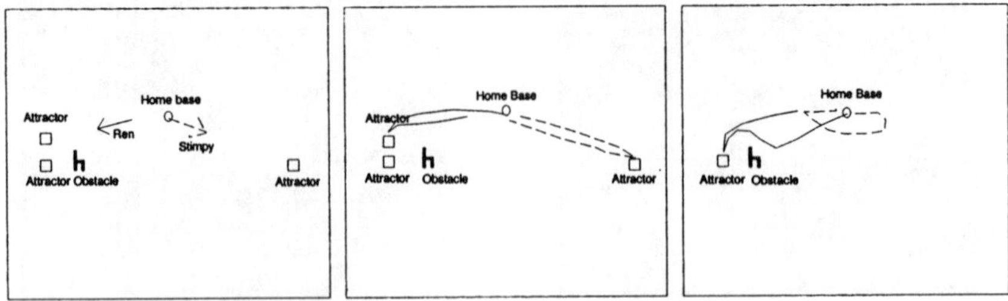

FIG. 13.14. A reconstruction (from above) of the Forage demonstration with two mobile robots. Initially (left) the robots are repulsed from one another and detect separate attractors, which they deliver to homebase (center). Later (right) they cooperate in returning the last attractor to homebase.

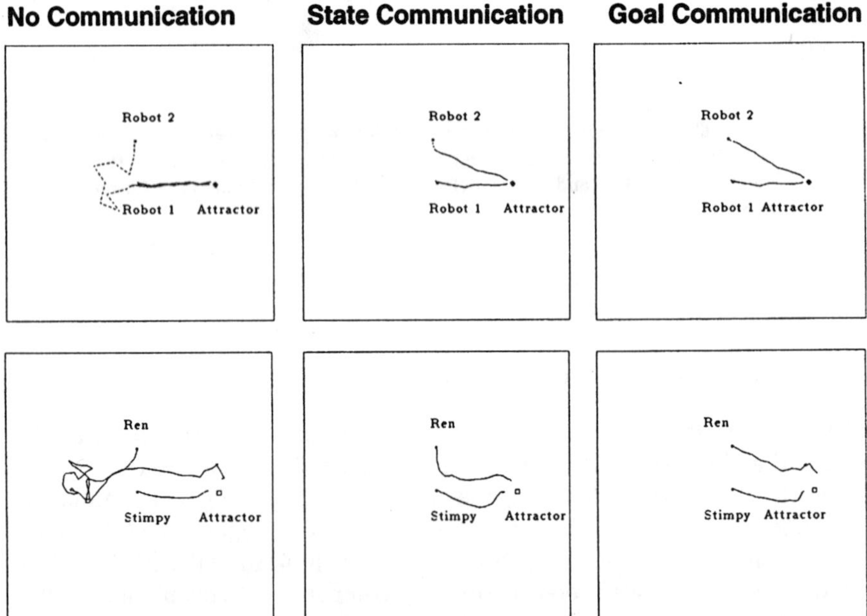

FIG. 13.15. Comparison of simulated *Consume* task runs (top row) with runs on mobile robots (bottom row). The traces made by the simulated and real robots for each level of communication are similar. The differences are primarily attributable to the fact that parameter values used in the robot experiments were adjusted to account for the limited space in our lab.

These predictions are borne out in the simulations shown in the top row of Fig. 13.15. The simulations were run in the environment described in Section 6 using the baseline control parameters (Table 13.1). In the case of No Communication, Robot 1 immediately moves to the attractor and begins consuming it (top left). Robot 2 moves away, and continues to search for attractors in the *wander* state. Eventually it too falls within sensor range of the attractor, moves toward it, and helps consume it. In the case of State Communication (top center), Robot 1 again initially moves toward the attractor. Robot 2 begins to follow it (dotted line), then transitions to the *acquire* state (solid line) when it comes within sensor range of the attractor. Finally, in the case of Goal Communication (top right), both robots immediately move to the attractor and consume it. A qualitative difference between State and Goal Communication is visible in the paths Robot 2 takes to the attractor in Fig. 13.15 (top row). With State Communication, Robot 2, initially outside sensor range of the attractor, makes a curved path to the attractor because it can only follow Robot 1 initially (top center). When Goal Communication is allowed, however, Robot 2 can proceed directly to the attractor (top right).

Now compare the simulations (top row) with runs on the robots Ren and Stimpy (bottom row). Because the sensor range of the robots is set at 10 feet, the scenario was altered for runs on mobile robots so that the attractor is only 10 feet away from the lower robot. The telemetry is shown at half the scale of the simulated runs to account for the smaller scale of the scenario.

Qualitatively, performance for mobile robots with No Communication is quite similar to simulated performance (Fig. 13.15 bottom left). Initially, Ren does not sense the attractor and explores the left side of the laboratory instead. But eventually, it comes within sensor range and moves to the attractor. When State Communication is allowed Ren follows Stimpy to the attractor, making a curved path (bottom center). Finally, when Goal Communication is allowed, Ren travels directly to the attractor (bottom right).

The path of the lower robot for the cases of State and Goal Communication is somewhat different in simulation than on mobile robots. On mobile robots, the lower robot curves away from the upper robot much more than in simulation. This is a result of two factors. First, the scale of the telemetry re-creations are half that of the simulations. Thus, the effects of interrobot repulsion are visually exaggerated. Second, the perceptual process for obstacle detection (a ring of ultrasonic sensors) is not sophisticated enough to ignore robots: Robots are detected as robots and as obstacles. The repulsion between them is further exaggerated. This problem will be resolved as better omnidirectional sensors and perceptual processes are incorporated into our research.

10. SUMMARY AND CONCLUSIONS

The impact of communication on performance in reactive multiagent robotic systems has been investigated through extensive simulation studies. Performance results for three generic tasks illustrate how task and environment can affect communication payoffs. Initial results from testing on mobile robots are shown to support the simulation studies.

Three levels of communication were investigated: no communication, state communication, and goal communication. When state communication is allowed, robots are able to determine the interal state of other robots. When goal communication is allowed, robots transmit goal-oriented information to one another.

To evaluate the impact of communication, a baseline of performance was developed for robots performing *Forage*, *Consume*, and *Graze* tasks without communication. The baseline results were then compared with performance in these tasks when state communication, then goal communication is allowed. Important results established in the baseline experiments include:

- For a given number of attractors, more robots complete a task faster than fewer robots.
- For a given number of robots, it takes longer to complete a task with more attractors.
- Speedup is greater in scenarios where larger numbers of attractors are present.

Principal results when baseline performance is compared with performance in the presence of communication include:

- Communication improves performance significantly in tasks with little environmental communication.
- Communication is not essential in tasks that include implicit communication.
- More complex communication strategies offer little or no benefit over low-level communication.

Future work involves three major research thrusts. The first is concerned with societal performance in fault-tolerant multiagent robotic systems; where unreliable communication may be present and the robotic agents have the potential for failure. The second research thrust involves integrating humans more effectively with the control of a society through teleoperation. The last area includes developing novel methods for formalizing and expressing multiagent robotic systems with the goals of producing tools that will facilitate their use and to establish formally provable properties (i.e., necessary and sufficient conditions) regarding their specifications.

ACKNOWLEDGMENTS

This chapter is dedicated to the memory of Larry Rosenberg who provided support for this research through the National Science Foundation under grant #IRI-9100149.

APPENDIX: MOTOR SCHEMA FORMULAE

This appendix contains the methods by which each of the individual primitive schemas used in this research compute their component vectors. The results of all active schemas are summed and normalized prior to transmission to the robot for execution.

- Move-to-goal: Attract to goal with variable gain. Set high when heading for a goal.

  $V_{magnitude}$ = adjustable gain value

  $V_{direction}$ = in direction towards perceived goal

- Avoid-static-obstacle: Repel from object with variable gain and sphere of influence. Used for collision avoidance.

  $O_{magnitude} =$

  $0 \; for \; d > S$

  $\frac{S-d}{S-R} * G \; for \; R < d \leq S$

  $\infty \; for \; d \leq R$

  where:

  S = Adjustable Sphere of Influence (radial extent of force from the center of the obstacle)

  R = Radius of obstacle

  G = Adjustable Gain

d = Distance of robot to center of obstacle

$O_{direction}$ = along a line from robot to center of obstacle moving away from obstacle

- Noise: Random wander with variable gain and persistence. Used to overcome local maxima, minima, cycles, and for exploration.

$N_{magnitude}$ = Adjustable gain value

$N_{direction}$ = Random direction that persists for $N_{persistence}$ steps ($N_{persistence}$ is adjustable)

- Probe: Used in *Graze* for favoring continued motion in the current directional heading.

$V_{magnitude}$ = adjustable gain value or 0 if no ungrazed areas detected

$V_{direction}$ = Straight ahead along an extrapolated path from the current location only if grazed area ahead. Direction not important if no ungrazed area ahead as gain is 0.

REFERENCES

[1] Altenburg, K. and Pavicic, M., 1993. Initial Results of the Use of Inter-Robot Communication for a Multiple, Mobile Robotic System, *Working Notes of the Workshop on Dynamically Interacting Robots at IJCAI-93*, pp. 95–100.

[2] Altmann, S. 1974. Baboons, Space, Time, and Energy. *American Zoology*, 14:221–248.

[3] Arkin, R. C., 1989. Motor Schema Based Mobile Robot Navigation, *International Journal of Robotics Research*, vol 8(4), pp. 92–112.

[5] Arkin, R. C., 1992. Cooperation without Communication: Multi-agent Schema Based Robot Navigation, *Journal of Robotic Systems*, Vol. 9(3), pp. 351–364.

[6] Arkin, R. C., 1992. Integrating Behavioral, Perceptual, and World Knowledge in Reactive Navigation. *Designing Autonomous Agents*, ed. P. Maes, Bradford-MIT Press, pp. 105–122.

[7] Arkin, R. C., 1992. Modeling Neural Function at the Schema Level: Implications and Results for Robotic Control. *Biological Neural Networks in Invertebrate Neuroethology and Robotics*, ed. R. Beer, R. Ritzmann, and T. McKenna, Academic Press, pp. 383–410.

[8] Arkin, R. C., 1993. Survivable Robotic Systems: Reactive and Homeostatic Control. *Robotics and Remote Systems for Hazardous Environments*, ed. M. Jamshidi and P. Eicker, Prentice-Hall, pp. 135–154.

[9] Arkin, R. C., Balch, T., Nitz, E., 1993. Communication of Behavioral State in Multi-agent Retrieval Tasks, *Proc. 1993 IEEE International Conference on Robotics and Automation*, Atlanta, GA, vol. 1, p. 678.

[10] Arkin, R. C. and Hobbs, J. D., 1992, Dimensions of Communication and Social Organization in Multi-Agent Robotic Systems, *From animals to animals 2: Proc. 2nd International Conference on Simulation of Adaptive Behavior*, Honolulu, HI, Dec. 1992, MIT Press, pp. 486–493.

[11] Arkin, R. C. and MacKenzie, D., 1994. "Temporal Coordination of Perceptual Algorithms for Mobile Robot Navigation", to appear in *IEEE Transactions on Robotics and Automation*.

[12] Arkin, R. C., Murphy, R. R., Pearson, M., and Vaughn, D., 1989. Mobile Robot Docking Operations in a Manufacturing Environment: Progress in Visual Perceptual Strategies, *Proc. IEEE International Workshop on Intelligent Robots and Systems '89*, Tsukuba, Japan, pp. 147–154.

[13] Arkin, R. C., et al., 1993. Buzz: An Instantiation of a Schema-Based Reactive Robotic System, *Proc. International Conference on Intelligent Autonomous Systems: IAS-3*, Pittsburgh, PA., pp. 418–427.

[14] Balch, T. and Arkin, R. C., 1993. Avoiding the Past: A Simple but Effective Strategy for Reactive Navigation, *Proc. 1993 IEEE International Conference on Robotics and Automation*, Atlanta, GA, vol. 1, pp. 678–685.

[15] Brooks, R. A., 1986. A Robust Layered Control System for a Mobile Robot, *IEEE Journal of Robotics and Automation*, RA-2, No. 1, p. 14, 1986.

[16] Brooks, R., Maes, P., Mataric, M., and More, G., 1990. Lunar Base Construction Robots, *IEEE International Workshop on Intelligent Robots and Systems (IROS '90)*, Tsuchiura, Japan, pp. 389–392.

[17] Clark, R. J., Arkin, R. C., and Ram, A., 1992. Learning Momentum: On-line Performance Enhancement for Reactive Systems. *Proc. 1992 IEEE International Conference on Robotics and Automation*, Nice, France, May 1992, pp. 111–116.

[18] Croy, M. and Hughes, R., 1991. Effects of Food Supply, Hunger, Danger, and Competition on choice of Foraging Location by the fifteen-spined stickleback. *Animal Behavior*, 1991, Vol. 42, pp. 131–139.

[19] Dudek, G., Jenkin, M., Milios, E., and Wilkes, D., 1993. A Taxonomy for Swarm Robots. *Proc. 1993 IEEE/RSJ International Conference on Intelligent Robots and Systems (IROS)*. Yokohama, Japan, pp. 441–447.

[20] Drogoul, A. and Ferber, J., 1992. From Tom Thumb to the Dockers: Some Experiments with Foraging Robots. *From Animals to Animals: Proc. 2nd International Conference on the Simulation of Adaptive Behavior*, MIT Press/Bradford Books, Honolulu, HI, pp. 451–459.

[21] Foreano, D., 1993. Emergence of Nest-based Foraging Strategies in Ecosystems of Neural Networks. *From Animals to Animals: Proc. 2nd International Conference on the Simulation of Adaptive Behavior*, MIT Press/Bradford Books, Honolulu, HI, pp. 410–416.

[22] Franklin, R. F. and Harmon, L. A., 1987. Elements of Cooperative Behavior. Internal Research and Development Final Report 655404-1-F, Environmental Research Institute of Michigan (ERIM), Ann Arbor, MI.

[23] Franks, N., 1986. Teams in Social Insects: Group Retrieval of pre by army ants. *Behav. Ecol. Sociobiol.*, 18:425–429.

[24] Fukuda, T., Nakagawa, S., Kawauchi, Y., and Buss, M., 1989. Structure Decision in Self Organising Robots Based on Cell Structures—CEBOT. *IEEE International Conference on Robotics and Automation*, Scottsdale, Arizona, pp. 695–700.

[25] Goetsch, W., 1957. *The Ants*. University of Michigan Press.

[26] Goss, S., Beckers, R., Deneubourg, J., Aron, S., and Pasteels, J., 1990. How Trail Laying and Trail Following can Solve Foraging Problems for Ant Colonies. *Behavioral Mechanisms of Food Selection*, ed. R. N. Hughes, Nato ASI Series, Vol. G. 20, Springer-Verlag, Berlin, pp. 661–678.

[27] Hackwood, S. and Beni, S., 1992. Self-organization of Sensors for Swarm Intelligence, *1992 IEEE International Conference on Robotics and Automation*, Nice, pp. 819–829.

[28] Helmbold, D. and McDowell, C., 1990. Modelling Speedup(n) Greater than n, *IEEE Transactions on Parallel and Distributed Systems*, vol 1(2), pp. 250–256.

[29] Holldobler, B. and Wilson, E., 1990. *The Ants*, Belknap Press, Cambridge Mass.

[30] Kaelbling, L. and Rosechein, S., 1990., "Action and Planning in Embedded Agents", in *Designing Autonomous Agents*, Maes, P. (ed), MIT Press, pp. 35–48.

[31] Kaufmann, J., 1974. Social Ethology of the Whiptail Wallaby, Macropus Parryi, in Northeastern New South Wales. *Animal Behavior*. 22:281–369.

[32] Khatib, O., 1985. "Real-time Obstacle Avoidance for Manipulators and Mobile Robots", *Proc. IEEE Int. Conf. Robotics and Automation*, St. Louis, p. 500.

[33] Krogh, B., 1984. A Generalized Potential Field Approach to Obstacle Avoidance Control, *SME–RI Technical Paper* MS84-484.

[34] Lee, J., Huber, M., Durfee, E., and Kenny, P., 1994. UM-PRS: An Implementation of the Procedural Reasoning System for Multirobot Applications. To appear *AIAA/NASA Conference on Intelligent Robots in Field, Factory, Service, and Space (CIRFFSS '94).*

[35] MaKenzie, D. and Arkin, R. C., 1993. Formal Specification for Behavior-Based Mobile Robots, *Proc. SPIE Conference on Mobile Robots VIII*, Boston, MA, pp. 94–104.

[36] MacKenzie, D. C. and Balch, T. R., 1993. Making a Clean Sweep: Behavior Based Vacuuming. *Working Notes of 1993 AAAI Fall Symposium: Instantiating Real-World Agents*. Raleigh, N.C.

[37] MacLennan, B., 1991. Synthetic Ethology: An Approach to the Study of Communication. In *Artificial Life II*, SFI Studies in the Sciences of Complexity, vol. XI, ed. Farmer et al., Addison-Wesley.

[38] Maes, P., 1991. Situated Agents can have Goals, in *Designing Autonomous Agents*, Maes, P. (ed), MIT Press, pp. 49–70.

[39] Mataric, M., 1992. Minimizing Complexity in Controlling a Mobile Robot Population. *Proc. IEEE International Conference on Robotics and Automation*, Nice, FR, May 1992.

[40] Miller, D., 1990. Multiple Behavior-Controlled Micro-Robots for Planetary Surface Missions. *Proc. 1990 IEEE International Conference on Systems, Man, and Cybernetics*, Los Angeles, CA, November 1990, pp. 289–292.

[41] Moynihan, M., 1970. Control, Suppression, Decay, Disappearance and Replacement of Displays. *Journal of Theoretical Biology*, 29:85–112.

[42] Noreils, F. R., 1992. "Battlefield Strategies and Coordination between Mobile Robots", *Proc. 1992 IEEE/RSJ International Conference on Intelligent Robots and Systems (IROS)*, pp. 1777–1784.

[43] Noreils, F., 1993. Coordinated Protocols: An Approach to Formalize Coordination between Mobile Robots. *Proc. 1992 IEEE/RSJ International Conference on Intelligent Robots and Systems (IROS)*, pp. 717–725.

[44] Parker, L., 1993. Adaptive Action Selection for Cooperative Agent Teams. *From Animals to Animals: Proc. 2nd International Conference on the Simulation of Adaptive Behavior*, MIT Press/Bradford Books, Honolulu, HI, pp. 442–450.

[45] Payton, D. W., 1991. Internalized Plans: A Representation for Action Resources, in *Designing Autonomous Agents*, Maes, P. (ed), MIT Press, pp. 89–103.

[46] Pearce, M., Arkin, R. C., and Ram, A., 1992. The Learning of Reactive Control Parameters through Genetic Algorithsm, *Proc. 1992 International Conference on Intelligent Robotics and Systems (IROS)*, Raleigh, N.C., pp. 130–137.

[47] Ram, A., Arkin, R. C., Moorman, K., and Clark, R., 1992. Case-based Reactive Navigation: A case-based method for on-line selection and adaptation of reactive control parameters in autonomous robotic systems, Technical Report GIT-CC-92/57, College of Computing, Georgia Tech.

[48] Slack, M. G., 1990. Situationally Driven Local Navigation for Mobile Robots, *JPL Publication 90-17*, Jet Propulsion Laboratory, Pasadena, CA.

[49] Tinbergen, 1966. *Social Behavior in Animals*, Methuen & Co., London.

[50] Wang, J., 1992. "Distributed Mutual Exclusion based on Dynamic Costs", *Proc. IEEE International Symposium on Intelligent Control*, Glasgow, UK, pp. 109–15.

[51] Werner, G. and Dyer, M. 1990. Evolution of Communication in Artificial Organisms. *Technical Report UCLA-AI-90-06*, AI Laboratory, University of California, Los Angeles.

[52] Yanco, H. and Stein, L., 1993. An Adaptive Communication Protocol for Cooperating Mobile Robots. *From Animals to Animals: Proc. 2nd International Conference on the Simulation of Adaptive Behavior*, MIT Press/Bradford Books, Honolulu, HI, pp. 478–485.

CHAPTER

14

Seeding, Evolutionary Growth, and Reseeding: The Incremental Development of Collaborative Design Environments

Gerhard Fischer
University of Colorado, Boulder

Jonathan Grudin
Microsoft Research

Raymond McCall
Jonathan Ostwald
University of Colorado, Boulder

David Redmiles
University of California, Irvine

Brent Reeves
TwinBear Research, Boulder, CO

Frank Shipman
Texas A&M University

1. INTRODUCTION

For a number of years we created software-based design environments solely to support individual designers. Recently, however, we turned our attention to the problem of supporting long-term collaboration. This takes place when an artifact functions and is repeatedly redesigned over a relatively long period of time (e.g., many years). Such artifacts are increasingly common in a wide range of domains, including the design of buildings, space-based habitats, software, and computer networks–to name a few that we have looked at.

Our initial plan was to modify our previous architecture of design environments to add more support for the evolutionary development of the design and the knowledge about the design. Because we anticipated this would create "messy" information we proposed a process of seeding, evolutionary growth, and reseeding of the information in the design environment. In the course of working with network designers, building and evaluating prototype systems, and revising our initial theories of collaborative design practice we developed some new outlooks that we think are quite useful. This chapter discusses these results.

This chapter begins by describing our view of design and long-term indirect collaboration. We then discuss the role that knowledge plays in collaborative design. Next the three phases of seeding, evolutionary growth, and reseeding are each described in detail. A discussion section describes experiences from observing and working with network designers and how these experiences affected our system prototypes. After reviewing related work, we conclude with the lessons we learned and believe will be of value to others interested in supporting long-term asynchronous design.

2. LONG-TERM COLLABORATIVE DESIGN

Teamwork is playing a larger role in design projects [DeMarco, Lister 87; Hackman, Kaplan 74; Johansen 88]. Such projects are increasingly large, complex, and long in duration. The design process takes place over many years, only to be followed by extended periods of maintenance and redesign. Specialists from many different domains must coordinate their efforts despite large separations of distance and time. In such projects, constructive collaboration is crucial for success yet difficult to achieve. This difficulty is due in large part to ignorance by individual designers of how the decisions they make interact with decisions made by other designers. A large part of this, in turn, consists of simply not knowing what has been decided and why.

Meetings and other types of direct communication are the commonly used means for coordination and collaboration in design projects, but in many situations–especially ones involving long-term collaboration–these are not feasible. Design projects that extend over many years can involve a high turnover in personnel. Much of the design work on systems is done as maintenance and redesign, and the people doing this work are often not members of the original design team. But to be able to do this work well, or sometimes at all, requires *collaboration* with the original designers of the system. People who are not in the project group at the same time need to collaborate in long-term design.

2.1. Asynchronous Communication

Much research in supporting collaborative work has gone toward supporting synchronous communication (e.g. COLAB [Stefik et al. 87] and GROVE [Ellis, Gibbs, Rein 91]). Earlier, we argued that long-term collaborative design demands support beyond synchronous communication. Even when it is possible for collaborating designers to have direct communication, there is still much potential in providing tools primarily intended for asynchronous use [Hollan, Stornetta 92].

The primary distinctions between synchronous and asynchronous communication are taken from the Computer Supported Cooperative Work field (CSCW), and are represented by the matrix in Fig. 14.1. The following two examples illustrate the benefits of technologically supported asynchronous communication: voice mail and electronic mail.

Consider the installation of voice mail systems in large corporations. Experience suggests that once people become used to the idea of asynchronous communication by phone, they make better use their phone communication. At first people leave messages like:

> Hi, this is Denny, I guess you're out, so call me back.

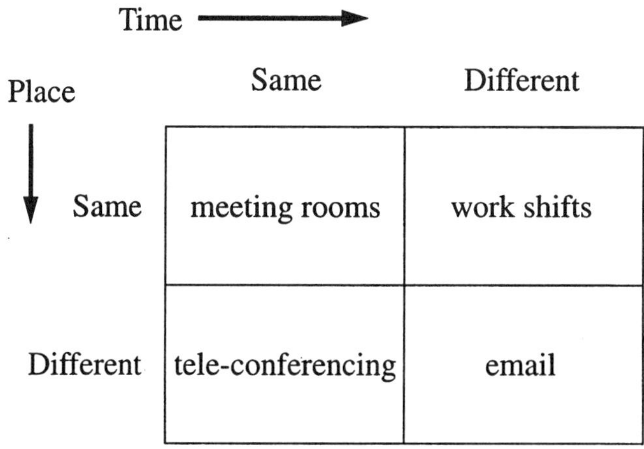

FIG. 14.1. Asynchronous communication. A matrix of CSCW perspectives developed by Johansen [Johansen 88]. Our work focuses on technological support for Asynchronous (i.e., different time, different place) communication. Email is the prototypical example of asynchronous communication.

But after a while, people begin to leave messages that contain more than just, "call me back." For example:

> Hi, this is Denny. I've found a problem with the AR 30 report. The due dates are incorrect for customer number 899902. We need to get these right before Friday's close.

Although it takes time, people learn that it is more efficient to place an item on another person's "electronic stack" or "inbox" than to interrupt what they were doing with a phone call. And although people usually prefer to speak to someone in person, they nevertheless learn how to make good use of the technology. Leaving a detailed message makes more sense for many of the messages and requests. It can be better to give the person time to research the question and call back, rather than surprise him with a problem and expect instant diagnosis.

Asynchronous communication begins to be used where synchronous previously dominated. Although phone mail is at first thought of as an inconvenient backup to the more preferable voice-to-voice, it becomes a useful service in its own right, and more than just a back-up.

In arguing against the assumption that the goal of computational media should be to emulate face-to-face communication, Hollan and Stornetta [1992] cited email as the "paramount success of computationally-mediated informal communication." The interesting aspect related to the point argued here is the statement:

> It meets our critical litmus test of being used by groups even when in close physical proximity. In fact, in our own experience, it is not uncommon to send email to someone in the next adjacent office, or even someone sharing an office.

Like voice mail, in certain situations, email has changed from a tolerable substitute to a preferred medium.

Electronic mail plays an important role as a success model of computer supported communication. Although much CSCW research focuses on providing media that emulate face-to-face meetings, the success of email is a reminder that there is more to good communication support than emulating face-to-face communication. A benefit from a synchronous communication is that it is archived somewhere. Whether this is digital voice recording, or electronic mail, it is available for later retrieval. Clearly this does not solve the problem of information retrieval later, but it is a first step.

The two examples, voice mail and electronic mail, illustrate that asynchronous communication comes to be preferred to synchronous communication for certain types of information. But in this chapter we make the stronger case that not only is asynchronous communication an improvement in some cases, it is absolutely necessary for long-term design. To model design communication only after email or voicemail is to underutilize an important resource for design teams. Careful analysis led us to introduce a key distinction in asynchronous communication, that of predictability.

2.2. Long-Term, Indirect Communication

In long-term collaborative design tasks, communication between designers is not only asynchronous with respect to time and place, but it is also indirect in the sense that the senders and receivers of information are not known a priori. Figure 14.2 introduces predictability into the well-known 2 × 2 matrix of CSCW (compare Fig. 14.1). Also note that predictability pertains to the participants as well. Long-term projects are unpredictable with regard to the team members and users who need to communicate. As we argue later, this attribute caused us to pursue what we describe as embedded communication, where the communication is in a sense "embedded" in the design artifact rather than being stored separately.

Long-term, indirect communication is of particular importance in situations where:

- direct communication is impossible, impractical or undesirable
- communication is shared around artifacts
- designed artifacts continue to evolve over long periods of time (e.g., over months or years)
- designers need to be informed within the context of their work

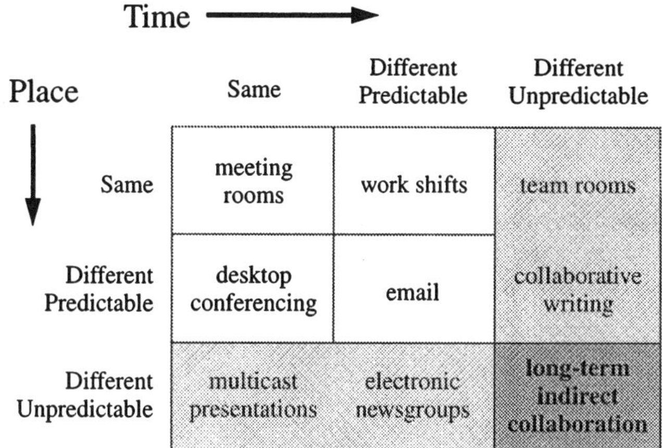

FIG. 14.2. A classification of Different CSCW perspectives. This classification scheme extends the matrix shown in Fig. 14.1. Our focus is on the unpredictable communication that occurs throughout the design life-cycle of complex systems. Not only is the time and place unpredictable: the participants themselves are not always known over the long life-cycles of complex systems [Grudin 94a].

Support for indirect coordination and collaboration must go beyond what electronic mail and most proposed CSCW software could provide. This support should allow team members to work separately—across substantial distances in space and time—but alert them to the existence of potential interactions between their work and the work of others. Where such interactions exist, support should be provided for collaboration and conflict resolution. Designers must be able to interact with design artifacts created by previous designers. Technology enabling this could effectively create virtual cooperation between all designers who ever worked on the project.

These challenges motivated not only a new conceptual model of design environments, but also a new model of the design process.

3. THE EVOLUTION OF KNOWLEDGE IN DESIGN

Our conceptual framework grew from systems augmenting an individual expert solving a problem to support for cooperating experts collaborating over many years and different places.

In the process of our initial research, we formulated a design process model, which we now believe is an important aspect of designing systems for collaboration. The process model is motivated by how large software systems, such as GNU Emacs, Symbolics' Genera, Unix, and the X Window System, have evolved over time. In such systems, users develop new techniques and extend the functionality of the system to solve problems that were not anticipated by the system's authors. New releases of the system often incorporate ideas and code produced by users.

In the same way that these software systems are extensible by programmers who use them, design environments need to be extended by *domain designers* (our term for the users of design environments) who are neither interested nor trained in the (low-level) details of computational environments [Nardi 93].

We illustrate our conceptual framework in the domain of computer network design, which involves complex artifacts that are continuously modified and redesigned. The domain itself is also constantly changing as new technologies are developed.

Knowledge acquisition is a crucial issue in the creation of effective information systems of all types (including expert systems, hypermedia systems, and design environments). There have been two extreme approaches: one is to input information in advance of use, typified by expert systems [Buchanan, Shortliffe 84], and the other is to start with an empty system and allow its information base to grow and become structured as a consequence of use, characterized by initial proposals for argumentative hypertext [Conklin, Begeman 88; McCall, Schaab, Schuler 83]. Neither approach is adequate for the information needs of designers.

The "put-all-the-knowledge-in-at-the-beginning" approach fails for numerous reasons. It is inadequate for domains in which the domain knowledge undergoes rapid changes (the computer network domain being a prime example). Traditional knowledge acquisition approaches that require domain designers to articulate their knowledge outside the context of problem solving or during an initial knowledge acquisition phase fail to capture tacit knowledge [Polanyi 66], because designers know more than they can tell environment developers. Tacit knowledge is a part of human expertise that surfaces only in the context of solving specific problems.

The "just-provide-an-empty-framework" approach requires too much work of designers in the context of a specific project. The difficulties of capturing design knowledge from design projects are well known [Fischer et al. 91]. Documenting interferes with the thinking process itself, disrupting design and requiring substantial time and effort that designers would rather invest in design. Designers typically find it difficult to structure their thoughts in a given format, regardless of the format used [McCall 91]. In addition, domain designers often lack the knowledge and the interest to formalize knowledge so it can be computationally interpreted [Shipman 93].

Our model is between the two extremes of "put-all-the-knowledge-in-at-the-beginning" and "just-provide-an-empty-framework." Designers are more interested in their design task at hand than in maintaining the knowledge base. At the same time, important knowledge is produced during daily design activities that should be captured. Rather than expect designers to spend extra time and effort to maintain the knowledge base as they design, we provide tools to help designers record information quickly and without regard for how the information should be integrated. In our model, knowledge base maintenance is periodically performed by environment developers and domain designers in a collaborative activity.

Our domain-independent design environment architecture plays an important role in the continual development of design environments. It provides a structure for domain knowledge and mechanisms for delivering knowledge as it is needed to support the design task at hand. We have developed our domain-independent architecture through numerous attempts to create domain-oriented design environments [Fischer 92]. The architecture consists of the following five components: (a) a construction component, (b) an argumentation component, (c) a catalog of interesting design examples, (d) a specification component, and (e) a simulation component. The individual components are linked by knowledge-based mechanisms: a construction analyzer (built as a critiquing system [Fischer et al. 93]), an argumentation illustrator, and a catalog explorer [Nakakoji 93]. Design environments contain information encoded using a variety of representational formalities. Construction kits and critics are considered formal representations of design knowledge because they are interpreted by the computer. Argumentation is a semiformal representation in which informal textual and graphic records are linked by formal associations.

Our process model for continual development of design environments from an initial seed through iterations of growth and reseeding is illustrated in Fig. 14.3.

- The seeding process, in which domain designers and environment developers work together to instantiate a domain-oriented design environment seeded with domain knowledge.
- The evolutionary growth process, in which domain designers add information to the seed as they use it to create design artifacts.
- The reseeding process, in which environment developers help domain designers to reorganize and reformulate information so it can be reused to support future design tasks.

To illustrate the evolution of design environments, we discuss seeding, evolution through use, and reseeding in detail in the following three sections.

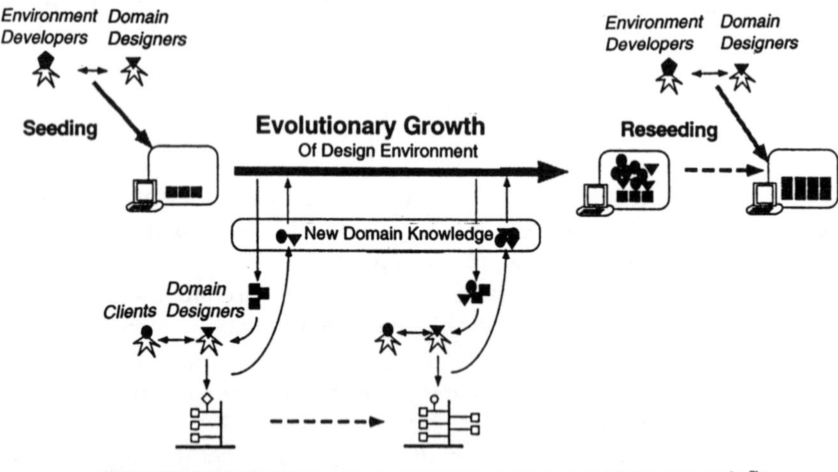

FIG. 14.3. Seeding, evolutionary growth, and reseeding: a process model for domain-oriented design environments. During seeding, environment developers and domain designers collaborate to create a design environment seed. During evolutionary growth, domain designers create artifacts that add new domain knowledge to the seed. In the reseeding phase, environment developers again collaborate with domain designers to organize, formalize, and generalize new knowledge.

NETWORK [Fischer et al. 92; Shipman 93], a design environment supporting computer network design, is used for illustration.

4. THE SEEDING PROCESS

A seed is built by customizing the domain-independent design environment architecture to a particular domain through a process of knowledge construction. Although the goal is to construct as much knowledge as possible during seed building, for complex and changing domains complete coverage is not possible. Therefore, the seed is explicitly designed to capture design knowledge during use [Girgensohn 92].

Domain designers must participate in the seeding process because they have the expertise to determine when a seed can support their work practice. Rather than expecting designers to articulate precise and complete system requirements prior to seed building, we view seed building as knowledge construction (in which knowledge structures and access methods are collaboratively designed and built) rather than as knowledge acquisition (in which knowledge is transferred from an expert to a knowledge engineer and finally expressed in formal rules and procedures). New seed requirements are elicited by constructing and evaluating domain-oriented knowledge structures.

The seeding process for the NETWORK design environment (see Fig. 14.4) was driven by observations of network design sessions, prototypes of proposed system functionality, and discussions centered on the prototypes. In design sessions, a logical map of the network being designed served to ground design meetings, discussions, what-if scenarios, and disagreements. The logical map was chosen as the central representation of the artifact in network design, and a prototype construction kit was implemented based on the logical map [Fischer et al. 92]. Evaluation of the NETWORK seed indicated that designers need support for communication in the form of critiques, reminders, and general comments [Reeves, Shipman 92a]. Pointer, annotation, and sketching tools were integrated into the construction kit so talking about the artifact takes place within the artifact representation space.

An important lesson we learned during the seeding of NETWORK was to base our design discussions and prototyping efforts on existing artifacts. Discussing the existing computer science network at the University of Colorado, Boulder, was an effective way to elicit domain knowledge because it provided a concrete context that triggered domain designers' knowledge (often in the form of "war stories"). We found high-level discussions of general domain concepts to be much less effective than discussions focused on existing domain artifacts.

Information to seed NETWORK was acquired from existing databases containing information about network devices, users, and the architectural

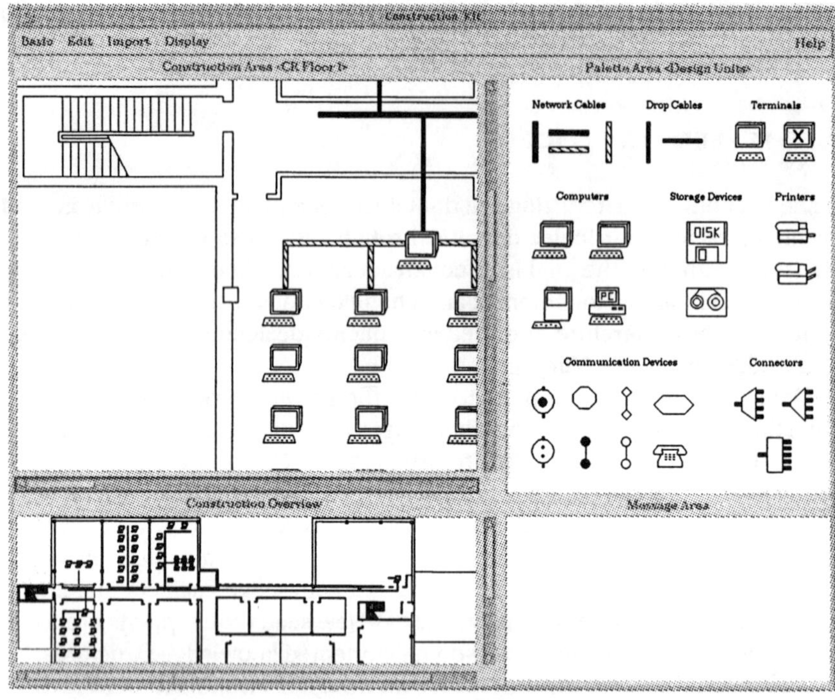

FIG. 14.4. An environment supporting computer network design. A screen image of the NETWORK seed. Shown is a palette of network objects (upper right) and the construction area where logical networks are configured (upper left).

layout of our building. The NETWORK seed contains formal representations of approximately 300 network devices and 60 users. Autocad databases created by facilities maintenance personnel provide architectural details of about 100 rooms. This information is represented in NETWORK's construction kit and in the underlying knowledge representation formalisms. The informal part of the NETWORK seed includes notes from the systems administration class, knowledge about the various research groups, and electronic mail of the network designers.

5. EVOLUTIONARY GROWTH THROUGH USE

During the use phase, each design task has the potential to add to the knowledge contained in the system. New construction kit parts and rules are required to support design in rapidly changing domains [Fischer, Girgensohn 90]. Issue-based information in the seed can also be augmented by each design task as alternative approaches to problems are discovered and recorded. The information accumulated in the information space during this phase is mostly informal because designers either cannot formalize new knowledge or they do not want to be distracted from their design task.

Our approach to this challenge is to view the design environment seed as a medium for communication as well as design. Our critique of current design systems is that they function as "keepers of the artifact," in which one deposits representations of the artifact being designed. But our experience has shown that designers integrate designing and discussing in such a way as to make separate interpretation difficult [Reeves 93]. Talking about an artifact requires talking with the artifact. Therefore, later interpretation of the discussion requires that the discussion be embedded in the context in which it was originally elicited. The most important implication of this view is that design artifacts must not be artificially separated from the communication about them.

This integration was seen in two ways. First, in design sessions videotaped for analysis, deictic references (referring to items by the use of "these," "those," "here," and so forth) were frequent. A long-term study of network designers showed that users took advantage of embedded annotations and made frequent use of deictic references [Reeves 93]. Second, discussion about the artifact guided the incremental design process. Designers took every opportunity to illustrate critiques of each other's work. Only rarely was a detailed comment made and not accompanied by changing the artifact.

The logical map mentioned earlier served not only to represent the real network, but also as a medium through which changes were considered and argued (Fig. 14.5). It focused as well as facilitated discussion. Frequently, in arguing over design artifacts, specific issues led to discussions of larger issues. Collaborating designers preferred to ground discussions in design representations. The logical maps served to point out inconsistencies between an appealing idea and its difficulty of implementation; remind participants of important constraints; and describe network states before and after changes.

6. RESEEDING

Acquiring design knowledge is of little benefit unless it can be delivered to designers when it is relevant. Periodically, the growing information space must be structured, generalized, and formalized in a reseeding process, which increases the computational support the system is able to provide to designers [Shipman, McCall 94].

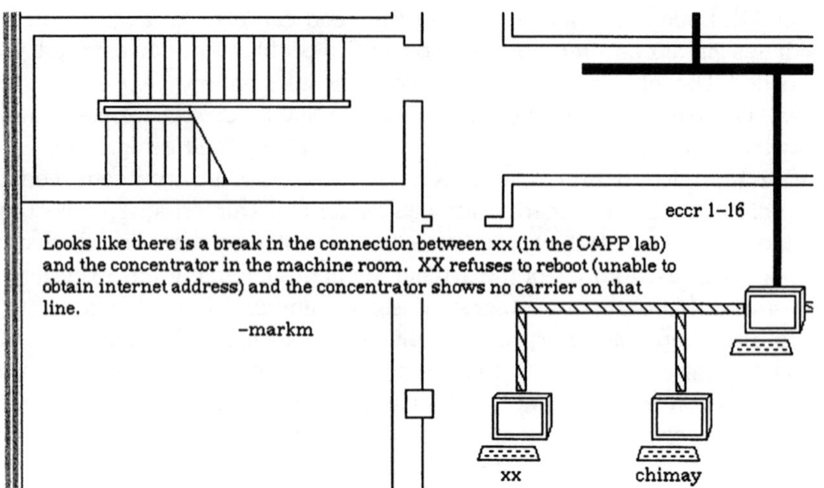

eccr 1–16
Looks like there is a break in the connection between xx (in the CAPP lab) and the concentrator in the machine room. XX refuses to reboot (unable to obtain internet address) and the concentrator shows no carrier on that line.
–markm
xx
chimay

FIG. 14.5. Logical map with embedded discussion. The logical map serves to abstract away low-level details while allowing discussions about the artifact to be embedded in the design.

The task of reseeding involves environment developers working with domain designers. After a period of use, the information space can be a jumble of annotations, partial designs, and discussions mixed in with the original seed and any modifications performed by the domain designers. To make this information useful, the environment developers work with the domain designers in a process of organizing, generalizing, and formalizing the new information and updating the initial seed.

The Need for Reorganization. The organizational aspect of reseeding is necessary because the information space, through modification by designers using the system, eventually becomes inconsistent. For example, as new technology becomes available, informal notes might contradict formal knowledge about network devices.

When an information space is disorganized, it becomes difficult for designers to locate information that they need. This also makes it more difficult to find the "right" place to add new information, thereby compounding the problem. Disorganization can occur when information about the same topic has become located in separate parts of the information space, or when information has been put in a location where designers cannot find it.

The Need for Generalization. Reuse of information between projects requires the generalization of task-specific information entered during use. The goal is to create more generally applicable information by integrating information about specific situations. This is related to the need for reorganization when variations of the same ideas have been added in project-oriented parts of the information space.

An example of generalization in the network domain is that while documenting changes to a design, information concerning the conversion of sections of a network to a new networking standard will likely appear with each conversion of a subnet. In order to bring this information together into a coherent whole, the subnet-specific details need to be abstracted so that the information is of use in new situations.

The Need for Updating Information. As described earlier, systems supporting rapidly changing domains are forced to evolve or become obsolete. Although some of this evolution can occur as evolutionary growth, still there is the need for concerted efforts by environment designers to update domain information.

As an example of the difficulty and potential for support in updating the information consider the problem of updating the initial formal structures created during our seeding of NETWORK. There is frequent change in the number and type of devices, people, and places that the environment needs to represent.

One potential for supporting this process comes from the existence of online sources for some of this information. The sources of online information individually contain only part of the information needed. Also, the sources use a variety of representations and identifiers for the information. As a result, the process of updating turns out to be heuristic. Still, the automation of changes aids the knowledge engineers in their updating of the information space, requiring them to determine and handle exceptional cases and to disambiguate between multiple potential cross-references.

This experience with NETWORK has shown the need to devise semiautomatic methods for updating information from other online sources during reseeding. Although much information in computer network design must be online, such as user and device profiles, other domains are also likely to have potential online sources of information. Support based on these sources can aid both domain designers and environment designers in keeping the design environment up to date.

The Need for Formalizing Information. A final task that is part of reseeding is the formalization of domain information entered during evolutionary growth but not in a format useful for providing knowledge-based support. Experience has shown that in many cases users cannot or will not formalize information on their own [Shipman, Marshall 94].

An example of this is that designers may make comments in notes to themselves or one another about the characteristics of a network device and yet not enter that information into the environment's description of the device. Designers are not being reticent, but cautious in taking time performing tasks which are not necessary to completing their primary task, the design and instantiation of the network.

During reseeding, both because the primary task is the improvement of the information in the design environment and the involvement of the environment designers, the formalization of information entered informally during evolutionary growth becomes possible.

7. DISCUSSION

Experience with the incremental development of the collaborative design environment NETWORK has shown the utility (and perhaps necessity) of using a seeding, evolutionary growth, reseeding process. At the same time it has pointed out the need for further types of support to be provided by design environments for such a process to be successful.

First, the design environment needs to become more than just the storage mechanism for a design, and must start becoming a medium for communication between designers. This leads to the need for embedding communication with the design artifact. Once an artifact and discussion of the artifact develop over some time it becomes necessary to provide prior context to enable the comprehension of comments and design decisions.

Information must be allowed to enter the environment in an informal representation but formal representations are needed to provide knowledge-based support. Thus, computer support for formalization of knowledge is important for successful design environment development. Because of the size of the information space and the potential for missing relevant information entered by other designers, mechanisms are required to help the location and communication of information. This has led to an initial investigation of computational agents which convey design decisions and opinions to other designers.

7.1. Embedded Communication

Analysis of design sessions in several domains (kitchen, architecture, networks) showed that design artifacts ground discussions so strongly that the language itself is difficult to understand without access to video. Deictic references (this, over there, here, that) are frequent, yet computer-based design systems such as CAD, do not support this referencing. This led us to embedded communication: including the discussion about a design artifact in the artifact itself. Though intended to address deixis, this also addressed a shortcoming we see in design rationale systems, namely that the artifact and its rationale are stored separately. This quickly leads to inconsistencies between what was done, and what was supposed to have been done, or what user think should have gotten done.

Competent practitioners usually know more than they can say [Polanyi 66], and conversation leaves many things tacit. One could attempt to overcome these tacit aspects by forcing designers to make more knowledge explicit. Against this approach, which might be labeled the "tyranny of the explicit" [Hill 89], issues of designer attention and desire are seen as motivation for providing computational media in which the designer's natural level of tacit knowledge is respected. The design process suggests the need for a medium in which the design artifact emerges, and which allows the designer to undergo frequent "shifts in stance" [Schoen 83, p. 101].

Observations of collaborating designers using NETWORK show that artifacts serve as medium for communication. Furthermore, discussions about the artifact guide the incremental design process. When communicating asynchronously via textual annotations, network designers integrated the notes and the artifact in ways that made separate interpretation difficult.

7.2. Embedded History

In the same way that evidence of physical history guides cognitive tasks, computational media should provide cues of use which guide design tasks [Hill et al. 92]. For example, as auto parts manuals become worn, they provide visual and tactile cues to guide further use. In the same way that physical wear and tear can be a resource, computational media should embed the history of an artifact in the artifact so that it can serve as guide to further use. Computational media represent the potential to provide history access mechanisms that go beyond what is possible with physical artifacts, such as providing access by various perspectives such as date, user, design change, and relation to other design units.

The approach here was to recognize the fluid nature of the design process and create a computer-based environment in which the artifact is less of an end-product and more of a process. If capturing the design process can be done in a way that does not interfere, then others will be better able to learn from observing the design sequence later. Understanding a complex design is best done by studying the process as well as the product [Kuffner, Ullman 91].

Users draw heavily from past experience in solving current problems [Lee 92]. Computational tools should therefore support this human tendency to reuse previous experience. However, a complicating factor is the tendency for people to "misremember" an event according to plausible inference rather than exact recall [Reder 82]. There is much potential for computer systems to serve as external memory aids in restoring the context surrounding past design decisions [Anderson 85; Reder 82; Suchman 87]. The context becomes all the more important as collaboration increases. In the context of collaborative design, it is not enough to provide user history, there should be artifact history.

Wolf and Rhyne [1992] argued that the process by which information is created and used can be important for understanding of the end product of a work group. In a study done to gain insight into how to facilitate information retrieval in computer-mediated design sessions, they analyzed how group participants used videotape to access meeting information. They found that people searched for information using four main access methods:

- by participant: they remembered person X doing some action
- by communication medium: people recalled what medium was used (e.g., whiteboard, overhead transparency)
- by time: people used relative time ("midway through the meeting"), duration ("25 minutes into the discussion"), and clock time ("we only got through Item 1.2 by 5 o'clock")
- by relation to other events: people used events as markers before or after other events.

These findings of how people use videotape for information retrieval serve as challenges for computational history mechanisms.

Hutchins' [1990] study of team navigation of large ships also motivates history for collaborative artifacts:

> The work a chart does is performed on its surface—all at the device interface, as it were—but watching someone work with a chart is much more revealing of what is done to perform the task than watching someone work with a calculator or a computer. [p. 217]

Asynchronously communicating designers do not have the possibility of "watching someone work with a chart." However, by keeping the artifact history, the interaction is available for watching at a later time. To relate it to Hutchin's study, imagine a chart which could replay the interaction that took place and show the instruments as they were used.

Design history also provides an approach to design rationale. Though design rationale appears to have great promise [Kunz, Rittel 70], there have been few recorded successes [Yakemovic, Conklin 90]. The designers must perceive a benefit for the extra cost of documenting their reasoning [Reeves, Shipman 92b]. History is therefore a potential candidate for an interaction tool, because there is no extra cognitive cost associated with having history support. Yet it provides the benefit of restoring the context of previous work, others' as well as one's own.

The benefit of history related to design rationale is that in domains such as network design, which involve two-dimensional sketches and graphical representations, designers can often deduce rationale by seeing the process of how something came to be [Chen, Dietterich, Ullman 91; Kuffner Ullman 91]. A logical map of the current network hides many tradeoffs and compromises that were made in the past, yet which still affect current decisions. Having the history of the evolution clarifies some of the tacit knowledge that is represented in the static logical map.

One side benefit of some groupware aids is that they also help the individual. For example, one designer said, "What did I do last?" Though the history was primarily viewed as a tool to help one understand other designers' work, it is also useful for reminding oneself of one's own work, called "reflexive CSCW" [Thimbleby, Anderson, Witten 90]. Usually adding multiuser features complicates the system for single users, but history is an example of both kinds of use.

Context Is Important in Reminding. Research in human memory has shown that people are prone to recall by inferring "what is plausible given what they can remember" [Anderson 85]. Memory performance improves the more closely the current context matches the past physical, emotional, and internal context. Much of recall involves plausible inference rather than exact recall [Reder 82].

History tools are needed to support collaborative design. The motivation for this argument lies in the work done in situated cognition relating to context [Carraher, Carraher, Schliemann 85; Lave 88]. Design environments can capture only a portion of the whole context, namely the dates when a given user made certain changes. Yet this small portion can be important in collaborative design.

Each designer on a project team understands only a portion of the overall design artifact. As large projects evolve over time and turnover and attrition take their toll, it will become increasingly important for computer based design environments to help capture the evolution of an artifact and not just its current state. The history serves to remind designers of how the artifact came to be and what the context was when certain decisions were made.

7.3. Computer Support for Formalization of Knowledge

Study of collaborative design projects showed that designers rapidly vary from informal to formal representations. But current CAD systems, for example, only allow the formal representation to be stored. Yet research is showing the importance of "informal sketches" [Gross 96]. These sketches should be part of the system, because they exert enormous influence throughout the development and implementation process. Rather than making arbitrary distinction between formal and informal data, we support a smooth migration from informal representations such as textual notes and sketches, to more formal representation such as OO class diagrams, or standardized graphical items such as palettes.

To address the difficulties involved in formalizing information by both environment developers and domain designers during all phases of design environment development, we have developed tools that support the process of formalization [Shipman 93].

One class of tools suggests possible formalizations that could be added to the information space based on the variety of information that the system already has available from both the seed and information added during use. The formally represented information, along with the placement, textual content, and textual attribute values, can be used by these tools.

For example, one tool in NETWORK looks for vocabulary in textual values of attributes that might relate to other objects and suggests replacement (or augmentation) by a relationship between the two objects. An example of this would be a workstation (c3d2) in the design that has an attribute "disk server" with the value "c3d1" as a text string. This tool would suggest the recasting of this attribute to be a relation, instead of a string, pointing to the object in the design that represents the device c3d1.

Tools can also make use of possible references found in the textual display of objects to suggest new attributes and relations. As an example we discuss the text annotation in Fig. 14.5, which was taken verbatim from an electronic mail message between network designers.

Recognizing some of the references to concepts already formally represented in the system provides domain- and design-specific cues as to the content of the object. Based on the occurrence of these text references, the system suggests new attributes for the mail message, as shown in Fig. 14.6. In this example, the system has recognized references to devices, and places already known to the system. Further, these new attributes can be used later to locate related information.

7.4. Agents to Support Communication

When many designers participate in a project, it is difficult for each to know the whole project. How can each be informed of the changes that affect him, and how can a designer find old knowledge that affects a future modification? The issue of how to make information in group memory available to designers presents formidable challenges.

Our prior work on critics [Fischer et al. 93] and information delivery [Fischer, Nakakoji 91] for individual work has provided the potential solution of creating mechanisms that automatically volunteer information. But

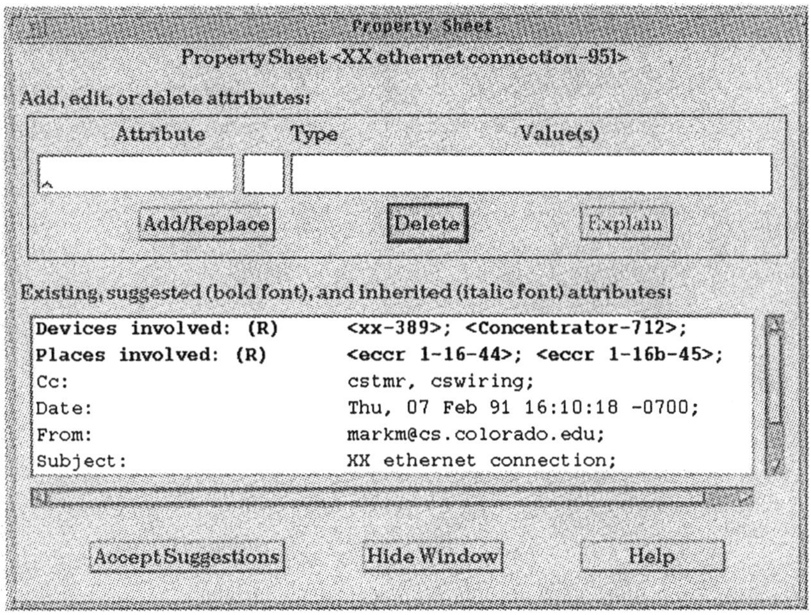

FIG. 14.6. Property sheet with suggested attributes. Suggested attributes for an imported electronic mail message appear in bold in the property sheet. The text of the mail message is shown in Fig. 14.5. When an attribute (e.g., "Devices Involved") is selected by the user, it appears in the top portion of the property sheet, where it may be edited.

having the design environment volunteer information leads to issues such as how to determine what information to volunteer, how to volunteer it, how to let designers interact with the environment to determine what information is volunteered to them and to other designers. In the context of NETWORK, we have begun investigating the use of agents to support communication. Compared to other work on agents providing information we have focused on how designers, rather than text analysis algorithms combined with complex interest profiles, can directly determine what and how information is volunteered. To do this we have focused on how designers can create agents.

As with all the rest of the information in the collaborative design environment, agents are created and evolve through all phases of environment development. An initial set of agents are created during seeding. During the evolutionary growth phase, agents can be created and modified in the agent editor, shown in Fig. 14.7. Finally, like other types of information, agents can be added, edited or removed during reseeding.

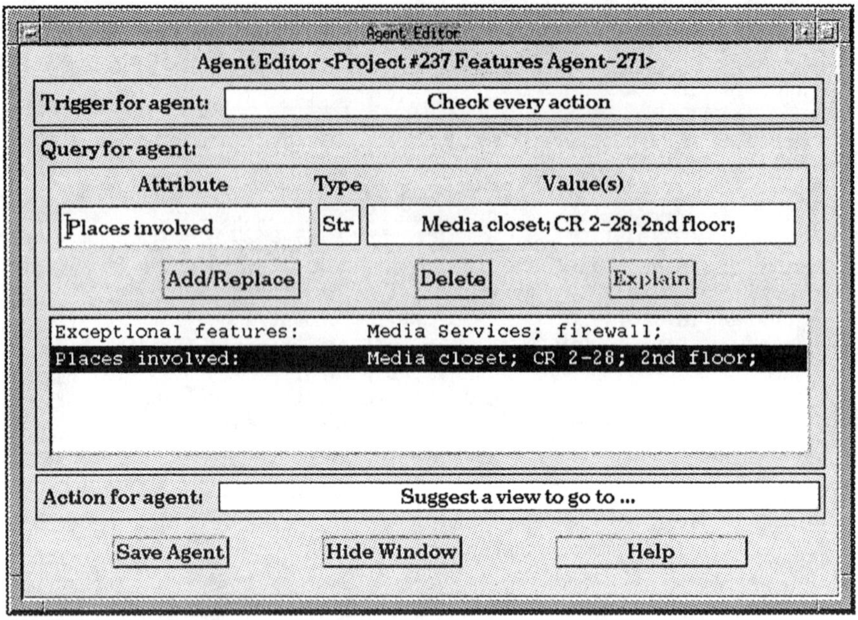

FIG. 14.7. Agent editor showing current status of an agent. Designers can define and edit agents in NETWORK's agent editor. By selecting a trigger, a query, and an action, designers can decide the information to be displayed, the situation in which to display it, and the manner in which to display it.

8. RELATION TO OTHER WORK

We have developed domain-oriented design environments [Fischer 92] to support design in a variety of domains, including user interfaces [Lemke, Fischer 90], buildings [McCall, Ostwald, Shipman 91], computer networks [Fischer et al. 92], and voice dialog systems [Repenning, Sumner 92].

Our previous work on design environments, such as FRAMER [Lemke, Fischer 90], JANUS [Fischer, McCall, Morch 89a], and PHIDIAS [McCall et al. 90] has emphasized systems for individual designers by supporting human problem-domain communication, communicating via abstractions and concepts specific to a domain [Fischer, Lemke 88], and construction kits. Human problem-domain communication and construction kits are necessary but not sufficient for good design. Upon evaluating prototypical construction kits [Fischer, Lemke 88], we found that they do not by themselves assist the user in constructing interesting and useful artifacts in the application domain. To do this they need knowledge to distinguish "good" designs from "bad" designs. Design environments combine construction kits with critics

[Fischer et al. 91]. Critics use knowledge of design principles for the detection of suboptimal solutions constructed by the designer.

One of the challenges for critiquing systems is avoiding work disruption. Our systems accomplish this by making the critics sensitive to the specific design situation [Fischer, Nakakoji 91], incorporating a model of the user [Fischer et al. 91], and giving users control over when and which critics should fire [Fischer, Girgensohn 90]. Part of the JANUS project [Fischer, McCall, Morch 89b] focused on building critics which are useful in spite of not being highly intelligent (i.e., more intelligent than a designer). Simple critics can be informative because they are based on domain knowledge that designers might not have (e.g., network designers are not necessarily familiar with relevant knowledge about fire codes for buildings).

Problems often arise in the use of collaboration technology when some people are required to do additional work to support a system that primarily benefits other users [Grudin 94b]. This is particularly important for systems that would incorporate design rationale information, a very difficult task [Fischer et al. 91]. The system and process we have described addresses this in several ways. By dividing the labor between environment designers and domain designers, between the seeding–reseeding activity and the evolutionary growth, we allow different players to focus on their work on tasks for which they will be rewarded. Also, allowing designers to comment informally during the design process, with formalization of the knowledge postponed until later, minimizes the cost to the designers while permitting others to benefit from the eventual inclusion of the knowledge in the system.

This project gave us an opportunity to build upon our previous design environment work and to broaden these environments to investigate complex issues in long-term collaborative design.

The usefulness of our "seeding–evolutionary growth–reseeding" model has been demonstrated for a variety of systems such as operating systems [Walker et al. 87] and domain-oriented design environments [Fischer et al. 92].

The model successfully addresses a number of important issues. On the one hand, it is an intentional effort to recognize the importance of specialization at the expense of expressive generality [CSTB 90]. By providing a significant seed of knowledge for domain-oriented design environments, specific design projects do not have to recreate domain-oriented abstractions but only have to extend the seed where it is incomplete or inaccurate for their task. New designs can be described using concepts, rules, and examples contained in the seed. The model avoids the pitfalls of expert systems approaches, which are often built on the assumption that all relevant knowledge for a domain can be encoded into a system.

Our model shares many objectives of other group memory projects, including the need for a maintenance activity separate from day-to-day use [Berlin et al. 93; Terveen, Selfridge, Long 93]. However, our emphasis on domain orientation sets our approach apart. In particular, domain orientation is an interesting perspective from which to view two major challenges for shared and evolving information spaces: the development of classification conventions that support information location, and the ability to actively deliver information to users when it is relevant to their task at hand [Fischer et al. 93].

Systems designed for general information storage and retrieval face the difficult task of developing information categories that make sense to the individuals who share the information [Berlin et al. 93]. General categorization schemes are dependent on the group members that develop and use them, and therefore will change as group members come and go. Design domains, on the other hand, are characterized by domain-specific conventions that have relatively precise and stable meaning to domain practitioners. Domain conventions have developed over time to enable designers to conceptualize design problems and to communicate important ideas. The relative stability of domain conventions makes domain-oriented systems less sensitive to turnover in group personnel.

General-purpose information spaces can have only a limited notion of the user's task at hand. Domain-oriented design environments exploit domain semantics and the design context [Fischer et al. 93] to actively notify designers when there is information about which they should know. Active information delivery helps designers to detect inconsistencies early in the design process, and to learn about design concepts of which they were unaware.

9. SUMMARY

This chapter has described a process model for the evolution of domain-oriented design environments through use. We consider design environments as seeds that grow by accumulating design knowledge as they are used to support design tasks. Periodically, a reseeding process is necessary to ensure that new knowledge is accessible to the design environment's computational mechanisms and therefore is accessible to designers using the environment. We claim that such an approach is necessary to support design in complex and open-ended domains, in which new design knowledge surfaces in the context of design tasks.

A seed is a collection of knowledge and procedures capable of growing—of sustaining growth—through interaction with domain designers during day-to-day use. It stimulates, focuses, and mediates discussion—and thus knowledge capture—during the incremental growth phase. The seed must be capable of capturing the information elicited from the use of the system. There is no absolute requirement for the completeness, correctness, or specificity of the information in the seed. In fact, it is often its shortcomings in these respects that provoke input from designers.

Evolutionary growth during system use is a process of adding information related directly or indirectly to the artifact being designed. Thus, the artifact (in our case, the network logical map) is the foundation for evolutionary growth. During the growth phase the designers who use the system are primarily focused on their task at hand. Information input is highly situation specific—tied to a specific artifact and stated in particular rather than in general. For a while, information grows in an orderly manner, but eventually order breaks down and the system begins to degrade in usefulness.

Reseeding is necessary when evolutionary growth stops proceeding smoothly. During reseeding, the system's information is restructured, generalized, and formalized to serve future design tasks. The reseeding process creates a forum to discuss what design information captured in the context of specific design projects should be incorporated into the extended seed to support the next cycle of evolutionary growth and reseeding. Tools contained in design environments support reseeding by making suggestions about how the information can be formalized.

ACKNOWLEDGMENTS

The authors would like to thank the members of the Human–Computer Communication group at the University of Colorado, who contributed substantially to the conceptual framework and the systems discussed in this paper. In particular, Kumiyo Nakakoji provided invaluable assistance. The research was supported by the National Science Foundation under grants No. IRI-9015441 and MDR-9253245, and NYNEX Science and Technology Center (White Plains, N.Y.).

REFERENCES

[Anderson 85] J. R. Anderson, Cognitive Psychology and Its Implications (2nd Edition), W. H. Freeman and Co., New York, 1985.

[Berlin et al. 93] L. Berlin, R. Jeffries, V. L. O'Day, A. Paepcke, C. Wharton, Where Did You Put It? Issues in the Design and Use of a Group Memory, *Human Factors in Computing Systems, INTERCHI'93 Conference Proceedings*, ACM, 1993, pp. 23–30.

[Buchanan, Shortliffe 84] B. G. Buchanan, E. H. Shortliffe, *Rule-Based Expert Systems: The MYCIN Experiments of the Stanford Heuristic Programming Project*, Addison-Wesley Publishing Company, Reading, MA, 1984.

[Carraher, Carraher, Schliemann 85] T. N. Carraher, D. W. Carraher, A. D. Schliemann, Mathematics in the streets and in the schools, *British Journal of Developmental Psychology, Vol. 3*, 1985, pp. 21–29.

[Chen, Dietterich, Ullman 91] A. Chen, T. G. Dietterick, D. G. Ullman, A Computer-Based Design History Tool, *Proceedings of the 1991 NSF Design and Manufacturing Systems Conference*, SME (Society of Manufacturing Engineers), Austin, Texas, January 1991, pp. 985–994.

[Conklin, Begeman 88] J. Conklin, M. Begeman, *gIBIS: A Hypertext Tool for Exploratory Policy Discussion*, Transactions of Office Information Systems, Vol. 6, No. 4, October 1988, pp. 303–331.

[CSTB 90] *Computer Science and Technology Board, Scaling Up: A Research Agenda for Software Engineering*, Communications of the ACM, Vol. 33, No. 3, March 1990, pp. 281–293.

[DeMarco, Lister 87] T. DeMarco, T. Lister, *Peopleware: Productive Projects and Teams*, Dorset, New York, 1987.

[Ellis, Gibbs, Rein 91] C. A. Ellis, S. J. Gibbs, G. L. Rein, Groupware: Some Issues and Experiences, *Communications of the ACM*, Vol. 34, No. 1, 1991, pp. 38–58.

[Fischer 92] G. Fischer, Domain-Oriented Design Environments, *Proceedings of the 7th Annual Knowledge-Based Software Engineering (KBSE-92) Conference* (McLean, VA), IEEE Computer Society Press, Los Alamitos, CA, September 1992, pp. 204–213.

[Fischer et al. 91] G. Fischer, A. C. Lemke, R. McCall, A. Morch, Making Argumentation Serve Design, *Human Computer Interaction*, Vol. 6, No. 3–4, 1991, pp. 393–419.

[Fischer et al. 92] G. Fischer, J. Grudin, A. C. Lemke, R. McCall, J. Ostwald, B. N. Reeves, F. Shipman, Supporting Indirect, Collaborative Design with Integrated Knowledge-Based Design Environments, *Human Computer Interaction*, Special Issue on Computer Supported Cooperative Work, Vol. 7, No. 3, 1992, pp. 281–314.

[Fischer et al. 93] G. Fischer, K. Nakakoji, J. Ostwald, G. Stahl, T. Sumner, Embedding Computer-Based Critics in the Contexts of Design, *Human Factors in Computing Systems, INTERCHI'93 Conference Proceedings*, ACM, 1993, pp. 157–164.

[Fischer, Girgensohn 90] G. Fischer, A. Girgensohn, End-User Modifiability in Design Environments, Human Factors in Computing Systems, *CHI'90 Conference Proceedings* (Seattle, WA), ACM, New York, April 1990, pp. 183–191.

[Fischer, Lemke 88] G. Fischer, A. C. Lemke, Construction Kits and Design Environments: Steps Toward Human Problem-Domain Communication, *Human-Computer Interaction*, Vol. 3, No. 3, 1988, pp. 179–222.

[Fischer, McCall, Morch 89a] G. Fischer, R. McCall, A. Morch, Design Environments for Constructive and Argumentative Design, *Human Factors in Computing Systems, CHI'89 Conference Proceedings* (Austin, TX), ACM, New York, May 1989, pp. 269–275.

[Fischer, McCall, Morch 89b] G. Fischer, R. McCall, A. Morch, JANUS: Integrating Hypertext with a Knowledge-Based Design Environment, *Proceedings of Hypertext'89* (Pittsburgh, PA), ACM, New York, November 1989, pp. 105–117.

[Fischer, Nakakoji 91] G. Fischer, K. Nakakoji, Making Design Objects Relevant to the Task at Hand, *Proceedings of AAAI-91, Ninth National Conference on Artificial Intelligence*, AAAI Press/The MIT Press, Cambridge, MA, 1991, pp. 67–73.

[Girgensohn 92] A. Girgensohn, *End-User Modifiability in Knowledge-Based Design Environments*, Ph.D. Dissertation, Department of Computer Science, University of Colorado, Boulder, CO, 1992, Also available as TechReport CU-CS-595-92.

[Gross 96] M. D. Gross, The Electronic Cocktail Napkin—Computer support for working with diagrams, *Design Studies*, Vol. 17, No. 1, 1996, pp. 53–70.

[Grudin 94a] J. Grudin, Evaluating Opportunities for Design Capture, in T. Moran and J. Carroll (eds.), *Design Rationale: Concepts, Techniques, and Use*, Lawrence Erlbaum Associates, Inc., Hillsdale, NJ, 1994, (in press).

[Grudin 94b] J. Grudin, Computer-Supported Cooperative Work: History and focus, *IEEE Computer*, Vol. 27, No. 5, 1994, pp. 19–26.

[Hackman, Kaplan 74] J. R. Hackman, R. E. Kaplan, Interventions into group process: An approach to improving the effectiveness of groups, *Decision Sciences*, Vol. 5, 1974, pp. 459–480.

[Hill 89] W. C. Hill, The Mind at AI: Horseless Carriage to Clock, *AI Magazine*, Vol. 10, No. 2, Summer 1989, pp. 29–41.

[Hill et al. 92] W. C. Hill, J. D. Hollan, D. Wroblewski, T. McCandless, Edit Wear and Read Wear, *Human Factors in Computing Systems, CHI'92 Conference Proceedings* (Monterrey, CA), ACM, May 1992, pp. 3–9.

[Hollan, Stornetta 92] J. Hollan, S. Stornetta, Beyond Being There, *Proceedings of ACM CHI'92 Conference on Human Factors in Computing Systems*, ACM, New York, 1992, pp. 119–125.

[Hutchins 90] E. Hutchins, The Technology of Team Navigation, in P. Galegher, R. Kraut, and C. Egido (eds.), *Intellectual Teamwork*, Lawrence Erlbaum Associates, Hillsdale, NJ, 1990, ch. 8.

[Johansen 88] R. Johansen, *Groupware: Computer Support for Business Teams*, The Free Press, New York, 1988.

[Kuffner, Ullman 91] T. A. Kuffner, D. G. Ullman, The information requests of mechanical design engineers, *Design Studies*, Vol. 12, No. 1, January 1991, pp. 42–50.

[Kunz, Rittel 70] W. Kunz, H. W. J. Rittel, *Issues as Elements of Information Systems*, Working Paper 131, Center for Planning and Development Research, University of California, Berkeley, CA, 1970.

[Lave 88] J. Lave, *Cognition in Practice*, Cambridge University Press, Cambridge, UK, 1988.

[Lee 92] A. Lee, *Investigations Into History Tools for User Support*, Unpublished Ph.D. Dissertation, University of Toronto, 1992.

[Lemke, Fischer 90] A. C. Lemke, G. Fischer, A Cooperative Problem Solving System for User Interface Design, *Proceedings of AAAI-90, Eighth National Conference on Artificial Intelligence*, AAAI Press/The MIT Press, Cambridge, MA, August 1990, pp. 479–484.

[McCall 91] R. McCall, PHI: A Conceptual Foundation for Design Hypermedia, *Design Studies*, Vol. 12, No. 1, 1991, pp. 30–41.

[McCall et al. 90] R. McCall, P Bennett, P. d'Oronzio, J. Ostwald, F. Shipman, N. Wallace, PHIDIAS: Integrating CAD Graphics into Dynamic Hypertext, *European Conference on Hypertext* (ECHT'90), 1990, pp. 152–165.

[McCall, Ostwald, Shipman 91] R. McCall, J. Ostwald, F. Shipman, Supporting Designers' Access to Information Through Virtually Structured Hypermedia, *Proceedings of the 1991 Conference on Intelligent Computer Aided Design*, Elsevier, New York, NY, 1991, pp. 116–127.

[McCall, Schaab, Schuler 83] R. McCall, B. Schaab, W. Schuler, An Information Station for the Problem Solver: System Concepts, in C. Keren, and L. Perlmutter (eds.), *Applications of Mini- and Microcomputers in Information, Documentation and Libraries*, Elsevier, New York, 1983.

[Nakakoji 93] K. Nakakoji, *Increasing Shared Understanding of a Design Task Between Designers and Design Environments: The Role of a Specification Component*, Unpublished Ph.D. Dissertation, Department of Computer Science, University of Colorado, 1993, Also available as TechReport CU-CS-651-93.

[Nardi 93] B. A. Nardi, *A Small Matter of Programming*, The MIT Press, Cambridge, MA, 1993.

[Polanyi 66] M. Polanyi, *The Tacit Dimension*, Doubleday, Garden City, NY, 1966.

[Reder 82] L. M. Reder, Plausability judgment versus fact retrieval: Alternative strategies for sentence verification, *Psychological Review*, Vol. 89, 1982, pp. 250–280.

[Reeves 93] B. N. Reeves, *Supporting Collaborative Design by Embedding Communication and History in Design Artifacts*, Ph.D. Dissertation CU-CS-694-93, Department of Computer Science, University of Colorado, Boulder, CO, 1993.

[Reeves, Shipman 92a] B. N. Reeves, F. Shipman, Supporting Communication between Designers with Artifact-Centered Evolving Information Spaces, *Proceedings of the Conference on Computer-Supported Cooperative Work* (CSCW'92), ACM, New York, November 1992, pp. 394–401.

[Reeves, Shipman 92b] B. N. Reeves, F. Shipman, *Making it Easy for Designers to Provide Design Rationale*, Working Notes of the AAAI 1992 Workshop on Design Rationale Capture and Use, AAAI, San Jose, CA, July 1992, pp. 227–233.

[Repenning, Sumner 92] A. Repenning, T. Sumner, Using Agentsheets to Create a Voice Dialog Design Environment, *Proceedings of the 1992 ACM/SIGAPP Symposium on Applied Computing*, ACM Press, 1992, pp. 1199–1207.

[Schoen 83] D. A. Schoen, *The Reflective Practitioner: How Professionals Think in Action*, Basic Books, New York, 1983.

[Shipman 93] F. Shipman, *Supporting Knowledge-Base Evolution with Incremental Formalization*, Ph.D. Dissertation, Department of Computer Science, University of Colorado, Boulder, CO, 1993, Also available as TechReport CU-CS-658-93.

[Shipman, Marshall 94] F. M. Shipman and C. C. Marshall, *Formality Considered Harmful: Experiences, Emerging Themes, and Directions*, Technical Report ISTL-CSA-94-08-02, Xerox PARC, 3333 Coyote Hill Road, Palo Alto, CA 94304, 1994.

[Shipman, McCall 94] F. Shipman, R. McCall, Supporting Knowledge-Base Evolution with Incremental Formalization, *Human Factors in Computing Systems, CHI'94 Conference Proceedings*, ACM, 1994, pp. 285–291.

[Stefik et al. 87] M. Stefik, G. Foster, D. G. Bobrow, K. Kahn, S. Lanning, L. Suchman, Beyond the Chalkboard: Computer Support for Collaboration and Problem Solving in Meetings, *Communications of the ACM*, Vol. 30, No. 1, January 1987, pp. 32–47.

[Suchman 87] L. A. Suchman, *Plans and Situated Actions*, Cambridge University Press, Cambridge, UK, 1987.

[Terveen, Selfridge, Long 93] L. G. Terveen, P. G. Selfridge, M. D. Long, From Folklore to Living Design Memory, *Human Factors in Computing Systems, INTERCHI'93 Conference Proceedings*, ACM, April 1993, pp. 15–22.

[Thimbleby, Anderson, Witten 90] H. Thimbleby, S. Anderson, I. H. Witten, Reflexive CSCW: Supporting Long-Term Personal Work, *Interacting with Computers*, Vol. 2, No. 3, 1990, pp. 330–336.

[Walker et al 87] J. H. Walker, D. A. Moon, D. L. Weinreb, M. McMahon, *The Symbolics Genera Programming Environment*, IEEE Software, Vol. 4, No. 6, November 1987, pp. 36–45.

[Wolf, Rhyne 92] C. Wolf, J. Rhyne, Communication and Information Retrieval with a Pen-based Meeting Support Tool, *Proceedings of the Conference on Computer-Supported Cooperative Work* (CSCW'92), ACM, New York, November 1992, pp. 322–329.

[Yakemovic, Conklin 90] K. C. Yakemovic, E. J. Conklin, Report of a Development Project Use of an Issue-Based Information System, *Proceedings of the Conference on Computer-Supported Cooperative Work* (CSCW'90), 1990, pp. 105–118.

CHAPTER

15

Distributed Group Support Systems: Theory Development and Experimentation

Starr Roxanne Hiltz
Donna Dufner
Jerry Fjermestad
Youngjin Kim
Rosalie Ocker
Ajaz Rana
Murray Turoff
New Jersey Institute of Technology

One type of computer-based system to support collaborative work ("groupware"; Johnson-Lenz & Johnson-Lenz, 1982; Ellis, Gibbs, & Rein, 1991) is most often called a Group Support System, or GSS. Other terms that have been used include *Group Decision Support Systems* (GDSS; DeSanctis & Gallupe, 1987) and *Electronic Meeting Systems* (Nunamaker, Dennis, Valacich, Vogel, & George, 1991).

DeSanctis and Gallupe's (1987) seminal paper, "A Foundation for the Study of Group Decision Support Systems" has been extremely influential in providing a common framework for research. They defined GDSS as combining "communication, computer, and decision technologies to support problem formulation and solution in group meetings" (p. 589). Various types of tools or structures for interaction can help a group to avoid process losses and to achieve better decisions or outcomes. For example, the use of the computer as a channel for communication can allow everyone to input simultaneously, thus encouraging greater equality of participation. Failure to quantify preference structures can be overcome by providing appropriate voting scales and tools, whereas failure to efficiently organize and communicate information about ideas and preferences can be overcome by the statistical analysis and display of the results of rating or voting. They also presented a "contingency" theory to help explain why GDSS is not always beneficial; it depends on whether the nature of the technology and structuring provided is appropriate for the group size (smaller vs. larger), the type of task, and the communication mode, of which they identified two: same place (FtF, or "decision room") and different place, or dispersed.

The term *Group Support System* (GSS) has come to be used as more general and inclusive than GDSS, which is often used to imply decision room, same time settings. GSS can apply to many stages and types of group work, not just decision making, and to computer support for groups that are working asynchronously through wide area networks as well as at the same time. *Distributed Group Support Systems* embed GDSS type tools and procedures within a Computer-Mediated Communication (CMC) system to support collaborative work among dispersed groups of people. "Distributed" has several dimensions: temporal, spatial, and technological. The majority of GDSS research has been conducted in "Decision Rooms," where the participants are meeting at the same time and same place. CMC-based systems can be used synchronously (same or different places, but at the same time), or *asynchronously.* The central focus of the program of research reported here is asynchronous groups, in which interaction is distributed in time as well as in space. The group members use the system to work together to reach a decision or complete their cooperative work over a period of time, with each person working at whatever time and place is convenient. In addition, the system used is itself *distributed*; that is, there can be more than one "server" in different places which are linked, and the user interaction may occur on a "user agent" located on the individual PC.

Asynchronous use of computer-based group support tools and processes is a unique mode of communication, different not only from face-to-face (FtF) communication, but even than synchronous use of CMC or other forms of computer support (Rice, 1984, 1993). It leads to different communication behavior (such as the tendency toward much longer entries by participants, and the discussion of many topics at once) and to unique coordination problems and opportunities (Hiltz & Turoff, 1985; Malone & Crowston, 1990; Turoff, Hiltz, Bahgat, & Rana, 1993).

Among the key variables observed to influence the effectiveness of small group decision making in the FtF condition are *leadership* and *process*. For example, imposing certain structures for interaction on small FtF groups, such as a strict agenda that forces "rational" decision making, or brainstorming (Osborn, 1957) or Nominal Group Techniques (Van de Ven & Delbecq, 1974), can improve process and outcomes. Procedures (or structures) for interaction that decrease process losses in the FtF condition may not be the same as those which are helpful in a computer-mediated communication condition, however, particularly in the fully distributed and asynchronous mode.

Many GDSS systems that are decision room based simply include a set of tools and procedures in the "package" that is always provided as part of the system; thus, the effects of medium of communication are confounded with the effects of specific tools and procedures. Our objective has been to isolate specific tools and procedures and explore their effectiveness in the asynchronous environment. Very few other GDSS experiments have looked at the asyncnronous condition. Of the 120 GSS experiments published through the end of 1995 that we have been able to identify (Fjermestad & Hiltz, 1996), besides the three NJIT experiments published to date, only five other experiments have used an asynchronous condition, plus two that compared synchronous and asynchronous conditions, and only one other investigator (Chidambaram, 1989; Chidambaram, Bostrom, & Wynne, 1990) has conducted more than one experiment in the asynchronous mode.

New Jersey Institute of Technology's project is an integrated program of theory building, software tool development and assessment, and empirical studies (both controlled experiments, and as opportunities arise, field studies). The project investigates the effectiveness of different types of tools and procedures for various types of tasks and groups, within the distributed environment. Specific studies also contrast the distributed mode of communication with other modes. This chapter reviews some of the accomplishments of the first 5 years of the program of research, which was partially supported by the National Science Foundation. We first summarize the theoretical framework that was constructed to guide and integrate all of the separate research studies. We then describe the software tools that were developed. Next, the design and results of the first five controlled laboratory experiments are described, each of which was conducted as Ph.D. dissertation research. Several field studies that have been published elsewhere will be briefly alluded to. Finally, we summarize the main findings across the various studies completed thus far, and their implications for theory building and future research directions. In brief, to give a preview, the most important finding is that imposing restricted structures or procedures for interaction in the distributed GSS mode does not have the beneficial effects that have been observed in the FtF or decision room modes of communication.

I. THEORETICAL FOUNDATIONS AND INTEGRATION

A specific GSS is a particular combination of communication mode, tools, and structuring of process (via a facilitator or procedural instructions/agenda). The effects of a GSS on the process and outcomes of collaborative work depend on a number of contingencies. We began with DeSanctis and Gallupe's (1987) framework, which identified three types of contingencies: communication condition (face-to-face or dispersed—we extend this to include synchronous vs. asynchronous); group size and task type. For task type, we currently use McGrath's (1984) "task circumplex." The graphical representation of this typology (not included here) differentiates tasks on two dimensions. The first dimension classifies tasks on the basis of outcome: intellectual (e.g., a decision) or behavioral (e.g., a "product" or action). The second dimension uses the type of behavior of group members (convergent or cooperative, vs. conflicting). We are presently focusing on the four types of cooperative tasks: Generating actions (Type 1: Planning and Type 2: Creative tasks) and Choosing solutions to a specific problem (Type 3: Intellective tasks, which have a "correct" or optimum decision whose quality can be measured; and Type 4: Preference, for which the objective is to reach agreement).

We extended this initial framework to produce a more comprehensive theoretical foundation that will enable us to compare the results of different studies and to compare our results to those of other researchers. One completed paper (Fjermestad, Hiltz, & Turoff, 1993) reviewed the major research models that have been used for studying GSS's and derives and presents an integrated, comprehensive model of the factors that are utilized for their investigation. It shows that in the short time since the publication of the DeSanctis and Gallupe (1987) foundation paper, the number of research dimensions included in various models has more than doubled (from 3 to 7). There has also been a shift in research emphasis from the technology to the interaction among the technology, the task, and the group to produce outcomes. The model organizes all the variables that have been used in GSS research into four dimensions: contextual, intervening, adaptation, and outcomes. A concise overview of the theoretical framework, showing the version we began with, is shown in Table 15.1. There, the contextual factors are shown at the top; the intervening variables, and the outcomes or dependent variables are at the bottom. The model served as the theoretical framework for all individual studies carried out within the program of research.

The Contextual factors are all external or driving variables that comprise the environment or conditions for the decision-making task. For any one experiment, they are (relatively) fixed or controlled. These include characteristics of the group, task, environmental and organizational context, and of the particular technology (GSS) being used.

Intervening factors are related to the emergent structuring of the group interaction, both derived from and adding to the set of conditions created by the context of the group decision sessions. For example, the methods used by the group may vary as to session length, number of sessions, and presence and role of a facilitator. These factors can change from session to session, and thus are dynamic rather than static.

Adaptation, or "modes of appropriation" is an important intervening variable in our model. According to Adaptive Structuration Theory (DeSanctis & Poole, 1991, 1994; Poole & DeSanctis, 1990, 1992; Sambamurthy & DeSanctis, 1989), group outcomes are not determined by the effects of single elements

TABLE 15.1
Theoretical Framework: Distributed Group Support Systems

GDSS

Medium
Tools
Procedures
Synchronous/Asynchronous
Equipment Access
interface
Training

Task

Type
Equivocality
Analyzability
Difficulty
Time
Importance
Enjoyability

Individual

Computer attitudes/skills
Language skills
Demographics
Self-
Consciousness/awareness
Values
Interpersonal Orientation
Initial Quality

Resultant Communication Dimensions

Bandwidth
Social presence
Information richness
Constraints
Ease of Use
Ease of Learning

Group

Size
Leadership
Homogeneity
Structure
Identity/history
Initial consensus

Group/Process Adaptation

1. Level of effort
2. Dropouts/handling
3. Emergent structure/network (equality/dominance)
4. Structuration: Faithful vs. ironic use; Attitudes; Comfort, Respect; Control/reinventions
   Level of consensus

Outcomes

Quality
  Completion (instruction dependent)
  Correctness (task type dependent)
    Absolute
    % Improvement
    Relative
  Collective Intelligence
  Creativity (task type dependent)

Consensus
  Absolute
  Improvement

Subjective Satisfaction with Group,
  Group Solution
Own Performance, Task Facilitator/
  leader performance
GDSS: Tools; Functions; Interface;
  Procedure
Communication Medium
Discussion/Group Process

(such as technology and task characteristics), but by a complex and continuous process in which those elements are appropriated by the group. The four dimensions of the construct (level of use, attitudes toward the GSS, level of consensus, and level of control) are measured in all studies via questionnaire items designed and validated by Scott Poole. For each of these aspects of group appropriation, there can be effective or ineffective modes.

For example, the group may use the GSS facilities little or not at all, even though they are instructed to, or they may use it in a very different manner than was intended.

Finally, the outcomes, or dependent variables, are the result of the interplay of the intervening, adaptation, and contextual factors. They include efficiency measures (e.g., calendar time to decision), effectiveness measures (e.g., number of different ideas generated or decision quality), and subjective satisfaction measures.

It should be noted that work is completed on further developing and applying the integrated framework to a comprehensive comparison of over 100 published experiments on GSS's to date (Fjermestad & Hiltz, 1996). Different outcomes have been observed depending upon the initial set of independent variables and the group processes (influenced by intervening variables) that result in a specific adaptation or "adaptive structuration" (Poole & DeSanctis, 1990) of the technology provided. By focusing on differences in the variables controlled and studied, a foundation is provided for understanding differences in findings.

2. FACILITIES DEVELOPMENT

NJIT's EIES 2 is a CMC enhanced with GDSS tools, that provides the foundation that allows continued evolution and the incorporation of additional functionality (Turoff, 1991). As a result of this capability, we were able to enhance the system and to create a "developer's kit" to allow Ph.D. students, or others, to use a version of Smalltalk to develop their own features or interface characteristics. EIES 2 is based on an object-oriented database and a compiler for the X.409 communication database specification language. This base allows the evolution of new object types as they are needed.

To support group-oriented objectives a CMC system must allow other computer resources to be integrated within the CMC environment. The approach we have chosen uses the metaphor of an "activity" that can be attached to any communication item. "Doing" an activity executes a program or procedure on the host computer or the network of users' computers.

Work has been completed on many kinds of activities. One set, "List" and "Vote," replicate the functionality provided by Minnesota's SAMM (Software Aided Meeting Management) for a group to create and revise a common list of alternatives, and then apply several types of voting procedures to this list: vote for one, vote yes or no on each alternative, and rate or weight each alternative. Another activity, "Poll," allows the construction, response to, and display of results from a poll or survey, within the CMC environment. A third, "Question/Response" Activity, supports processes such as Nominal Group Technique, dialectical inquiry and brainstorming, as well as applications to collaborative learning. Each participant must independently (and possibly anonymously) respond to a problem or question, before seeing the responses of others. Many other activities have been developed to support other kinds of group tasks, including a class "gradebook" activity for the Virtual Classroom™.

It should be noted that the series of studies reported here were conducted between 1990 and 1995 with a VT100 based full screen menu-type interface, rather than a GUI (point and click Graphical User Interface.) The VT100 type interface has the advantage of being usable on any PC or even a "dumb terminal"; whatever the subjects may have had available to use at home or at work would suffice. Later, we completed work on a Web-based GUI that can be used with browsers such as Netscape, for those who have the necessary equipment and prefer this style of interaction.

3. THE FIRST FIVE EXPERIMENTS

Each of these experiments represents an attempt to find appropriate tools and processes to support four different types of task in the McGrath "task circumplex"; they examined:

- Voting tools and sequential procedures for a preference task;
- Conflict vs. Consensus structures plus experience for a planning task;
- The effects of FtF vs. distributed asynchronous CMC as it interacts with a structured design procedure, for a creative task, software design
- Question–Response tool and the Polling tool for an intellective task (peer review)
- Designated leadership and sequential vs. parallel procedures for a mixed task, choosing a stock portfolio.

A concise summary of the methods and findings of the experiments is presented in Tables 15.2 and 15.3. Each group had 1 or 2 weeks to complete each decision (depending on the experiment). This is a relatively long time period, compared to the 10 or 15 minutes that some experimental tasks used in decision room GDSS experiments have taken. Unless otherwise noted, all subjects were undergraduate and graduate students from the Computer Science and Management degree programs at NJIT and Rutgers. Students participated as a course assignment, and were graded; alternate assignments were offered for those who chose not to participate. It should be noted that in asynchronous groups interacting over a week or more, group size cannot be truly controlled. Despite the grade incentive, some students dropped out of the group interaction, perhaps because of illness or computer problems,

TABLE 15.2
Summary of the Experiments: Methods

Authors	*GSS*	*Experimental Design*	*Group Individual*	*Task*	*Sessions*
Dufner et al., 1994	CMC: EIES 2, Level 2, Distributed, Asynchronous, Moderator, Tools: List, Vote, Training: 2.5 hours	2 X 2 Factorial Tools: Tools, no tools Sequential: Sequenced, nonsequenced	31 groups of 3 to 8 subjects per group; 6 to 9 groups per cell, 119 total subjects. Graduates and undergraduates	The Foundation Task, Preference, Type 4 Training task: Paint Vendor Selection	1 FtF training session and 1 asynchronous experimental session over 5 business days. Subjects log-on once/day
Fjermestad et al., 1995	CMC: EIES2, Level 2, Asynchronous, Distributed, Moderator, Leader, Tools: List, Question, Vote, Training: 2 hours	2 X 2 Repeated measures Decision Approach: DI (15), CC (16) Experience: Task 1, Task 2	31 groups of 4 to 7 subjects per group. 160 total subjects, Graduates and undergraduates	PVVI Tasks Type 4	2 asynchronous experimental sessions each up to 12 days
Ocker et al., 1995	CMC: EIES2, Level 2, Distributed, Asynchronous, Tools: Question/Response, IBIS: Facilitator, Training: 1-2 hours, practice task	2 X 2 Factorial Mode: CMC, FtF Structure: Process, no-process	41 groups of 4 to 7 per group; 205 total subjects. Graduates-MBA, MS	Automated Post Office, Type 2	FtF: 2 sessions 2 weeks apart, 1 to 2.5 hours each. CMC: 2 weeks
Rana, 1995	CMC: EIES2, Level 2 Asynchronous, Distributed Moderator: Technical Facilitator only Tools: Question, Poll Training: Printed materials	2 X 2 Factorial: Poll No Poll Question (Q), No Question (No-Q)	33 groups of 2 to 3 subjects per group, 8 to 9 groups per cell, 96 total subjects. Graduates and undergraduates with previous system experience	Peer Review Task, Intellective, Type 3 Training task: None	Asynchronous experimental sessions over 2 weeks
Kim, 1996	CMC: EIES2, Level 2, Asynchronous, Distributed Tools: Question, List Training: 1 hour ftf + 1 week online	2 X 2 Factorial Coordination: Sequential, Parallel Leader: With, Without	47 groups of 3 to 5 subjects per group 212 total subjects, Undergraduates, graduates, & Ph.D	Investment Club Task; Mixed: Intellective + planning + Preference. Training task: leader selection	Training: 1 hour ftf + 1 week online Experiment: CMC: 2 weeks

TABLE 15.3
Summary of the Experiments: Findings

Authors	*Dependent Measures—Outcomes*	*Group Process Adaptation*	*Conclusions*
Dufner et al., 1994	**Perception Measures** Discussion quality Tools > No-tools; Sequence No Diff. Media dimensions Tools > No-tools; Sequence No Diff. Satisfaction Tools > No-tools; Sequence No Diff.	No-tools groups experience more confusion attributed to "log-in" lag than tools groups. The tools (list and vote) provided structure enabling the groups to monitor their progress.	Providing tools in distributed CMC improves perceived group outcomes over no-tools. The presence or absence of sequential procedures has no effects.
Fjemestad et al., 1994	**Group Performance** Number of days: Decision App: DI > CC; Experience No Diff. Number of comments: Decision App: DI > CC; Experience: No Diff. Effectiveness: Decision App/Experience: No Diff. Depth of evaluation: Decision App/Exper: No Diff. **Group Perception** Acceptance: Decision App/Experience: No Diff. Depth of Evaluation: Decision Approach CC > DI; Experience: No Diff. Willingness: Decision App: CC > DI; Experience No Diff.	The DI groups expend a greater effort than CC groups as indicated by the asynchronous meeting time and number of comments, but gain very little in terms of effectiveness and group perceptions. There were no learning effects and no interaction effects reported.	There were no significant differences in decision effectiveness between DI and CC groups. CC groups report greater decision acceptance, depth of evaluation, and willingness to work together again than do DI groups.
Ocker et al., 1995	Quality: Communication Mode: No Diff. Process: No Diff Creativity: Communication Mode: CMC > FtF Process: No Diff.	There wee no interaction effects or effects for process. The task itself may not necessarily be an ill-structured task; it may be a well-structured task; thus the groups were able to proceed to a solution.	The creative task of deciding upon the initial specifications for the design of a software system can benefit from asynchronous CMC. The CMC groups were judged to be considerably more creative in their designs. Quality was judged to be higher, but not significant.

(Continued)

TABLE 15.3
(Continued)

Authors	*Dependent Measures—Outcomes*	*Group Process Adaptation*	*Conclusions*
Rana, 1995	Quality of Review: Poll > no Poll; with low pre-agreement, Q > no Q; Low Pre-agreement > High Pre-agreement Confidence in outcome: High respect and consensus > Low respect and consensus Outcome satisfaction: High comfort and consensus > Low comfort and consensus Decision scheme satisfaction: High respect, comfort, and consensus > Low comfort and consensus Structure in process: High comfort and consensus > Low comfort and consensus Change in understanding: High comfort & Consensus > High or low comfort/consensus; or Low levels of both comfort and consensus Depth of evaluation: Poll and high consensus > No-Poll and low consensus	Group members' subjective perception about various aspects of group process and outcome were affected more by the modes of appropriation than the support tools. In other words, groups that exhibited effective appropriation perceived their group process and outcome to be more effective than the ones that exhibited ineffective modes of appropriation.	The DGSS-supported controlled sharing of individual responses combined with anonymous contribution of opinions and support for consensus management can be used to enhance the state of the referee system.
Kim, 1996	Quality (Obj.): L > NL; Coordination No diff. Quality (Sub.): Coordination mode: Par > Seq; Leader: No Diff. Consensus: Coordination/Leader mode: No Diff. Participation: Coordination/Leader mode: No Diff. Satisfaction: Coordination mode: Par < Seq; Leader: With < Without Process Satisfaction: Coordination mode: Par > Seq; Leader: No Diff. Group Understanding: Coordination mode: Par < Seq; Leader: No Diff.	Too much freedom in group interaction decreases group cohesiveness, which increases the decision cost. A Coordination structure should be somewhat restrictive to maintain a higher level of group cohesiveness.	The degree of restrictiveness of a coordination structure needs to be defined more precisely to generalize the findings of this study. Very little is known about what determines the degree of restrictiveness of a coordination structure in DGSS.

and thus decreased group size below the starting number. When group size is reported, it refers to the ending group size, not the number who were trained and began a task. In all experiments, if this effective group size fell below two, the group was dropped from the analysis.

Most of the studies also used expert judges to rate some aspect of the quality of the group outcomes. In all cases, at least three judges were used. They consisted of faculty members or advanced ("ABD") graduate students with expertise in the area. Coding and rating procedures were developed and refined during pilot studies, and judges were trained with pilot study transcripts before being given the experimental data to rate or code.

The brief overviews that follow are essentially extended abstracts of parts of dissertations that total 300 to 550 pages; obviously, in just a few pages, many details such as a complete list of hypotheses with justifications, and specifics of measurement of variables, must be omitted.

3.1. The Effects of Voting Tools and Sequential Procedures for a Preference Task

This experiment, carried out by Dufner (Dufner, 1995; Dufner, Hiltz, Johnson, & Czech, 1995; Dufner, Hiltz, & Turoff 1994), is a replication (modified for implementation in asynchronous mode) and extension of the doctoral research conducted by Watson (1987) at the University of Minnesota. The study, which was preceded by a full year of pilot studies, extends the Watson research to include an investigation of adaptive structuration, media richness, system and task expectations, and training (Dufner 1989, 1995; Hiltz, Dufner, Holmes, & Poole, 1991).

The Foundation Task, developed at Minnesota and used for this experiment, can be classified as a preference allocation task based on the McGrath Circumplex model (McGrath, 1984). The subjects play the role of a foundation board, and are to reach consensus on how to allocate funds among "applicants" representing very different kinds of objectives, such as cutting local taxes, helping the homeless, or improving the town library.

3.1.1. Procedures and Experimental Design. Individuals were assigned randomly to groups, as much as was possible given time constraints and schedules. These groups were then trained for approximately 3 hours in the use of the medium (EIES 2) and in working together to perform a group decision-making task. All groups were given a suggested agenda ("define the problem," etc.), as used by Watson, and their conferences were seeded with root comments corresponding to each stage in this suggested set of activities. TOOLS groups were also given training in the use of the "List Activity" (an electronic flip table) for group generation and management of lists, and in the use of the "Vote Activity," which provided three forms of voting on the items on the list. Groups assigned to a SEQUENCED condition were instructed as follows: "You must all work on the same agenda item together. The group decides when to move to a new agenda item. You do not have to follow the agenda order. However, you must all work on the same agenda item together. You are asked not to work ahead of or following the group." The "not sequenced" groups were not clearly instructed that they were free to work in parallel; they simply were not given these instructions. After training, each group was given 5 business days to perform the experimental task. Groups were instructed to communicate only through the medium. No formal facilitation was provided to the groups, although technical assistance was given when anyone asked for help. There were a total of 31 groups with 119 subjects; group size varied from 3 to 8 subjects.

3.1.2. Hypotheses and Selected Results. From pilot studies (Dufner, 1989, Hiltz, Dufner, Holmes, & Poole, 1991) we knew that groups in asynchronous mode encounter coordination problems (Dufner, Hiltz, & Turoff, 1994) that cause frustration with the medium. Therefore, we hypothesized that the TOOLS and SEQUENTIAL PROCEDURES would make significant contributions to subjectively reported perceptions of medium richness (Zmud, Lind, & Young, 1990) and satisfaction with the process in the asynchronous environment.

No significant difference in the SEQUENCED versus NOT SEQUENCED groups was found. Re-examining the manipulation, we decided that we could not determine whether this was because imposing a sequenced process truly makes no difference, or whether the manipulation was not strong enough. Therefore, we noted that examining the sequenced vs. parallel process should be tried again in a subsequent experiment.

The TOOLS Groups perceived more media richness, reporting that the medium was significantly more dependable, convenient, flexible, and wide-ranging than did the groups not supported with tools. The TOOLS groups also perceived the system as more personal, more rich, and as providing more feedback and more immediate feedback than did the groups not supported with tools. TOOLS groups were also found to be significantly more likely to recommend the system for future meetings; to have enjoyed their participation in the discussion; and to have a higher opinion of the overall quality of the discussion than did the groups not supported with tools.

These experimental results seem to indicate that user perceptions of media richness and of the quality of group processes can be improved by providing voting tools that support group discussions, at least for preference type tasks, where the primary goal is to reach consensus. This contrasts with the findings by Watson (1987) for the same task and the same type of tools in a synchronous (Decision Room) environment, where tools created few significant differences.

Despite the significant and consistent positive effects of providing the listing and voting tools on subjective perceptions, there were no significant results on other dependent variables measured in this experiment, including changes in level of consensus and the group's equality of influence. Because this experiment did not have decisions that could be rated on quality, the effectiveness of tools such as "List" and "Vote" should be examined for intellective tasks or other tasks for which quality measures can be obtained, in the future.

3.2. Effects of Decision Approach and Experience on Planning Tasks

The basic objective of this longitudinal experiment (Fjermestad, 1994; Fjermestad et al., 1995) was to examine the performance and attitude changes of groups involved with strategic decision making in a computer-mediated-communications (CMC) environment. The two independent variables of interest were decision approach and experience. Decision approach consisted of dialectical inquiry (DI; Schwenk, 1990), which is a structured approach to induce conflict, and constructive consensus, which is a set of instructions telling the group to reach agreement. Experience consisted of working with a group on two related but different tasks, each taking 2 weeks to complete.

Previous research in the field of organizational strategic decision making has demonstrated that structured conflict can improve the quality of decisions (Mason, 1969; Mitroff & Mason, 1981; Schweiger, Sandberg, & Ragan, 1986; Schweiger, Sandberg, & Rechner, 1989; Schwenk, 1990; Tjosvold, 1982) and negatively affect both group perceptions and process outcomes (Schweiger et al., 1986; Schweiger et al., 1989; Turoff, 1991). The two basic structured conflict methods are DI and Devils's Advocate (DA). Schwenk's meta-analysis (1990) indicates that for studies that focus on groups, DI has a slight advantage over the DA.

The tasks were unstructured decision-making tasks, with no right or wrong answers; they are Type 4 (Planning) based on McGrath's (1984) task circumplex, and fit Schweiger et al.'s (1986) requirements for strategic decision making. The three specific tasks used in this study were developed by Chidambaram (1989) and were were modified and updated for use in an asynchronous communications mode instead of a set of discrete FtF meetings. The Threat of Takeover task was used as a training task for all groups and the Issue of Image and Product Line Expansion were the experimental tasks.

3.2.1. Procedures and Experimental Design. The research design is a 2 × 2 factorial repeated measures design. The factors are decision approach and experience. Groups in each decision approach were given 2 weeks (10 business days) to complete each of two tasks.

The 160 subjects used in the study were undergraduate and graduate students in computer science and management information systems at NJIT. They all had some fluency with the use of email and computers and were given course credit and a grade for participation. All subjects were assigned to groups based upon availability and scheduling constraints. The ideal group size was six subjects per group, but due to the subjects' scheduling constraints, the actual group sizes ranged from 4 to 7 (Fjermestad, 1994). Experimental conditions and task orders were randomly assigned to the groups.

The Dialectical Inquiry Approach (DI) is based on the procedures developed by Schweiger et al. (1986; Schweiger et al., 1989) and Tung and Heminger (1993), modified to support asynchronous communication and decision making (Fjermestad, 1994). The DI groups were divided into two subgroups, denoted as the Plan and Counterplan subgroups. These groups were in separate conferences on EIES 2. All members of both groups were to initially develop an individual recommendation (including supporting facts and assumptions) within 2 business days and enter it in a List Activity in the CMC system.

The Plan group then had 2 days to develop a single recommendation. Members read the individual case recommendations and then debated and discussed them in a Question Activity which requires each participant to reply before viewing other's replies. When complete, a case leader organized and entered the subgroup's recommendation. This was then submitted to the Counterplan subgroup, which had 2 days to negate the assumptions and develop a counterplan.

The moderator then created a new conference for the full group and added the plan and counterplan. The full group's objective was to critically evaluate the plan and counterplan through debate and discussion, and to develop a single final group recommendation. A Voting Activity was available if the group chose to use it, in all conditions. The time limit for this task was 4 business days.

The Constructive Consensus Approach (CC) follows the basic method developed by several researchers (Hall, 1971; Hiltz, Johnson, & Turoff, 1991; Nemiroff, Pasmore, & Ford, 1976; Schweiger et al., 1986). The CC groups functioned as one group and were in a single conference for the entire task. Their objective was to reach consensus on a single final recommendation. Each individual group member had 2 days to develop an individual recommendation. The group then had 8 business days to examine the case situations systematically and logically, in order to develop a final recommendation through debate and discussion. A Voting Activity was available if the group chose to use it.

3.2.2. Selected Hypotheses and Results. Based on previous research in FtF conditions cited earlier, it was hypothesized that DI groups would be superior to consensus-structured groups in terms of effectiveness (decision quality), but would be less efficient and express less subjective satisfaction than the consensus structured groups. It was also expected that group performance would improve on the second replication of the use of the assigned decision sturcture, and that furthermore, there would be an interaction. Because DI is an unfamiliar structure, it was expected that the improvement would be more marked for the DI groups.

Contrary to these expectations, there were very few differences between Task 1 and Task 2, and no differences between DI and CC groups in terms of group performance. DI groups required significantly more asynchronous meeting time and communication to complete their recommendations. Depth of evaluation as rated by judges showed no difference; but perceived depth of evaluation was lower in DI than in CC groups. CC groups reported greater decision acceptance and willingness to work together again than DI groups. Relatively few experiential effects were observed. Thus, no advantages were observed for the DI approach as compared to a consensus approach that also carefully structured the interaction, but it took more work and produced less participant satisfaction.

This study of asynchronous strategic decision making and a study using decision room GSS by Tung and Heminger (1993) reported that there are no differences in effectiveness between constructive consensus and dialectical inquiry groups in a GSS environment. Perhaps what is happening is that the GSS technology is significantly improving the consensus groups to the point where the outcomes are as high as the structured conflict processes in a FtF environment. Thus, GSS equalizes consensus groups' performance to that of the Dialectical Inquiry groups without affecting decision and process satisfaction and without any of the process losses.

3.3. Effects of Mode and Structure for a Creative Task: Distributed Software Design Teams

The experiment conducted by Ocker (1995; see also Ocker, Hiltz, Turoff, & Fjermestad, 1995) investigated the effects of distributed asynchronous communication on small groups performing high-level requirements analysis and design work. It is the first experiment to examine the software design process in a fully distributed environment. The experimental task is the Automated Post Office (APO); groups are required to develop and reach consensus on the initial requirements and interface design of an APO and to submit these in the form of a written report. The APO task, as used in this experiment, is a modification of the task used by the University of Michigan (Olson & Olson, 1991; Olson, Olson, Carter, & Storrosten, 1992; Olson, Olson, Storrotsten, & Carter, 1993). It is primarily a creativity type task, but also contains elements of planning and decision making

(McGrath, 1984). The APO task can also be categorized as occurring during the early stages of the innovation process (West, 1990).

3.3.1. Variables and Major Hypotheses. Two variables were manipulated in this experiment. The first variable, an imposed process, pertains directly to the degree of coordination required for the effective performance and satisfaction of groups working on a creative task. Groups in the imposed process conditions followed a sequence of steps adopted from research on argumentation and structured communication (IBIS; Kunz & Rittel, 1970; "Design Space Analysis," MacLean, Young, Bellotti, & Moran, 1991). The imposed process contained three main phases: generation of design alternatives; period of critical reflection and individual evaluation of alternatives; and group evaluation of alternatives and consensus reaching. The second variable is mode of communication (asynchronous computer-mediated communication [CMC] vs. face-to-face). It was expected that asynchronous CMC groups would outperform FtF groups, because of fewer process losses, and the ability of each of the participants to think and work at their own paces. Dependent variables include performance outcome (quality and creativity), and group satisfaction.

> H1: Asynchronous CMC groups will produce solutions of higher quality than face-to-face (FtF) groups.

The problem-solving structure was chosen due to its capability to structure communication and for its fit with the activity of design. It was felt that FtF groups would not need this added coordination, because high-level design has its own inherent structure (Olson et al., 1992), but that it would ease the cognitive burden of distributed asynchronous groups. Therefore, an interaction was hypothesized:

> H2: CMC structured groups and FtF groups will produce solutions of higher quality than CMC unstructured groups and FtF structured groups.

Based on an analysis of the task requirements (e.g. Guindon, 1990; King & Anderson, 1990; Simon, 1973; West, 1990), it was hypothesized that overall, the solutions produced by the asynchronous groups would be more creative than those produced by the face-to-face groups.

> H3. CMC groups will produce more creative solutions than FtF groups.

Again, based on relative coordination requirements, an interaction effect was hypothesized such that the solutions produced by the asynchronous imposed-process groups and face-to-face no-imposed-process groups would be more creative than those produced by asynchronous no-imposed-process groups and face-to-face imposed-process groups. Finally, it was hypothesized that the face-to-face groups would be more satisfied than the asynchronous groups because FtF is a "richer," more personal medium.

3.3.2. Procedures. Subjects were undergraduate students enrolled in an undergraduate upper level systems design course, or graduate students in CIS, MIS, or the MBA program. The majority had coursework and/or job experience directly relevant to systems design.

Groups were required to reach consensus on the initial requirements of the APO and to submit these requirements in a formal report at the end of the experiment. The asynchronous design groups communicated using the EIES 2 computer conferencing system; each of these groups communicated in its own computer conference. The experiment lasted 2 weeks.

The asynchronous groups met together for one 3-hour training session, whereas the face-to-face groups met twice for a total of 6 hours, with the first and second sessions spaced exactly 2 weeks apart. Both the FtF groups and the asynchronous groups in the imposed process condition were trained on the process using the same script. All asynchronous groups were trained on the basic use of the EIES 2 system.

The FtF groups had a PC and word processor available for creating their final reports. (Technical difficulties led two groups to hand write their report; these were among the longer reports, so it does not seem to have negatively affected them. These were later transcribed.)

The computer conferences and FtF meetings were minimally facilitated. The facilitator played the role of a technical assistant, helping groups with equipment problems and answering questions of a technical nature.

All participants completed questionnaires, which was the source of subjective satisfaction data. All groups' final reports were printed using the same word processing package, to mask indications of mode of communication. Quality and creativity of solution were rated by an expert panel of judges, using procedures and scoring adapted from Olson and Olson (1991).

3.3.3. Major Findings. The overall quality of solution was rated by a panel of expert judges to be equally good between the asynchronous groups and the face-to-face groups. (Although the asynchronous groups were rated as consistently higher, the difference was significant only at the .07 level). Contrary to hypotheses, there was no significant interaction effect between mode of communication and the presence or absence of an imposed process in relation to quality of solution.

As for creativity, the solutions produced by the asynchronous groups were judged to be significantly more creative than those produced by the face-to-face groups. Again, there was no interaction effect between mode of communication and the presence or absence of an imposed process.

Contrary to hypotheses, there were no significant differences between CMC and FtF groups on key measures of subjective satisfaction: perceived depth of analysis, solution satisfaction, and decision scheme satisfaction.

3.3.4. Conclusions. The imposed process was hypothesized to benefit asynchronous groups by providing the added coordination that is missing in this form of communication. There are several possible explanations for why this did not occur. Concerning the design of the APO, a strong metaphor is available in the form of automatic teller machines. The problem may have been familiar enough to groups, so that the need for coordination might have been greatly reduced; upon entering the group, group members already knew how to approach the solution to this problem.

The major finding of this experiment is that groups that communicated asynchronously, whether they followed a structured problem-solving approach designed to enhance coordination or were left to their own devices to reach a decision, produced significantly more creative results than the face-to-face groups. A tentative conclusion is that asynchronous communication, in and of itself, leads to higher levels of creativity. Possible explanations for this include a greater amount of communication over an extended period of time, reduced production blocking, and the production of a collective memory.

3.4. Effects of Question and Polling Activities on an Intellective Task: Supporting the Peer Review Process

The task for this experiment consisted of review and decision on publishability of a manuscript submitted to a refereed journal or conference (Rana, 1995). Contrary to the traditional review process, where two or more experts review and rate the quality of a manuscript individually, the distributed group support system based review process as adopted in this experiment called upon reviewers to undertake the task as part of a group, or panel. This new mode for conducting a review involved performance processes that are typical of intellective, decision making, and cognitive conflict tasks (McGrath, 1984). We classify it as primarily intellective, because two criteria for rating the quality of the solution were available: the ratings of the article by the actual reviewers of the paper, and the ratings by a panel of expert judges. The desirability of a system that can support group review activities in a different-time different-place mode was evident. This study being the first to investigate the viability of a DGSS based review process, motivated a research design that would allow the study of independent and interactive effects of support tools from within a DGSS.

Two support tools, Poll and Question activities on EIES2, were made available for this experiment, and utilized in a 2 × 2 factorial design. Poll activity, especially developed for this research, allows reviewers to rate the quality of a manuscript on various scales and enables them to view summary statistics on group ratings. Several scales can be grouped into one Poll. Question activity establishes a structured form of group discussion by requesting the provision of justifications for ratings on individual scales and maintaining an independent chain of discussion on each scale. Group members' responses to Question activity are textual items with no limit on size, whereas Poll activity responses consist of numbers representing scale anchors. One important feature, common to both Poll and Question activities, is that group members cannot view others' responses before having provided their own initial responses.

3.4.1. Procedures. An EIES 2 conference was established for each group. The final data set for this experiment consisted of 33 groups, with 30 groups of Size three and 3 groups that began at Size 3 but ended at Size 2. The majority of subjects were graduate students (73%); all subjects were enrolled in courses that required them to read and critique journal articles, and to use EIES 2 as a regular part of coursework. The mean age of subjects was 30 years with an average full-time work experience of slightly over 5 years. Because some subjects were enrolled in distance sections of courses, the manuscript and training materials instructing them how to use the tools and procedures for their condition were mailed to all subjects, rather than being explained in a face-to-face training session.

Subject groups reviewed a manuscript actually submitted to a refereed source with a pending editorial decision. The selected manuscript met the criteria developed as a result of three rounds of pilot studies and was judged to be commensurate with ability levels of the potential subject population.

Groups in all four conditions were to individually evaluate the manuscript, provide ratings and justifications for the ratings on six scales; share their responses with the group, and finally, discuss and reach agreement on ratings. This four-step process was to be completed over a period of 2 weeks with Steps 1 through 3 completed by the end of the first week. The identities of group members were concealed through the use of pen names.

Three measures for quality of group outcome were adopted: quality of the decision (disposition recommendation); quality of the review; and comprehensiveness of the review. A panel of expert judges independently rated the paper on the same scales as the subjects, and their ratings were compared to those produced by each group. Disposition recommendation categories consisted of Accept as is; Accept with minor revisions; Major revisions; or Reject. The four expert judges were evenly divided on major revisions or rejection. Thus, either of the latter two recommendations were considered "correct" in assessing quality of the decision in terms of the correctness of the disposition recommendation.

The quality of the review was calculated on the basis of the deviation of the group's decision from the judges' decisions on the separate aspects of the manuscript (literature review, methodology, presentation style, and so on). The comprehensiveness measure consisted of counts of the number of lines of discussion associated with each of the separate scales: for example, "substantive emphasis" was the amount of attention paid to critiquing the literature review; methodological emphasis, stylistic emphasis, interpretive emphasis, and wisdom were lines devoted to methodological critiques, and so forth (Cummings, Frost, & Vakil, 1985). Adaptive structuration was measured by a series of questionnaire items.

3.4.2. Hypotheses. Because Question activity imposes a structure for group members to engage in the group proceedings and coordinate their activities, it was expected that Question activity groups would do better than No-Question groups on all three measures of quality (Easton, Vogel, & Nunamaker, 1989; Sambamurthy & DeSanctis, 1989). (Poll activity was expected to be primarily a consensus-enhancing tool, rather than a quality-enhancing tool; these results are not included here.) There were also expected to be some interactions between Poll and Question. In all cases, a moderating variable must be prediscussion level of agreement; if most of the individual reviewers agreed on their initial ratings, one would not expect any of the tools used to make much difference. In addition, many hypotheses were developed with the basic premise that positive forms of Adaptive Structuration (high levels of comfort, consensus, and respect regarding the tools) would be strongly related to favorable outcomes.

3.4.3. Selected Findings and Conclusions. No differences in the quality of decision were detected due to Question or Poll activity. In fact, most groups reached a decision that the paper could not be accepted; thus, there was very little variance from a correct decision in ratings for disposition of the paper, and hence none of the independent and intervening variables were significantly associated with this measure.

With respect to the quality of the review, the results showed that improvement depended upon the level of prediscussion agreement. If groups started with a lower level of initial agreement, then the quality of review was enhanced by the tools. Specifically, at lower levels of initial agreement, groups with the Question activity produced significantly higher quality reviews than No-Question groups. Highly agreed on poor quality ratings before the discussion phase left little or no opportunity for an improvement in the quality of review through discussion. Unexpectedly, the Poll activity showed a marginally significant ($p = 0.0797$) main effect on the quality of the review. This main effect was attributed to the fact that Poll activity groups had significantly lower levels of prediscussion agreement than No-Poll groups. No significant effects on quality of the review were observed due to the modes of appropriation.

In terms of the effects on the measures of comprehensiveness, relatively few effects of the Question activity were supported. One of the significant findings was that groups that used the Question activity had significantly higher wisdom (concern for the paper's contribution and significance) in their reviews than No-Question groups. Mediating effects of the level of pre-discussion agreement similar to those for quality of review were observed on the amount of methodological emphasis. An unexpected, although not surprising, result was that in the absence of the Question activity, the Poll activity had a negative effect on interpretive emphasis.

Mediating effects of the modes of appropriation (DeSanctis & Poole, 1994; Poole & DeSanctis, 1990) on measures of comprehensiveness were rare. The level of challenge was observed to be one of the stronger mediating factors. Additionally, it was observed that a higher level of respect for the system did not always lead to an enhanced level of performance.

Despite the fact that the majority of the hypothesized effects were not observed, the experimental findings offer important implications for the review process. In summary, it was concluded that the strength of the DGSS based review process lies in its ability to allow for (a) disagreement among reviewers before the discussion phase, and (b) the subsequent opportunity for resolution of the disagreements with the use of support tools. These mechanisms combined with anonymous contributions can be profitably used to avoid many commonly noted dissatisfactions with the traditional peer review process (Cole, Rubin, & Cole, 1977; Mahoney, 1977, 1978, 1985; Peters & Ceci, 1982; Rana, Hiltz, & Turoff, 1995).

3.5. Effects of Parallel Versus Sequential Procedures and of a Designated Leader for an Intellective/Mixed (Stock Selection) Task

Silver (1990) defined system restrictiveness as the degree to which and the manner in which a system limits its users' decision-making processes to a subset of all possible processes. The objective of this study is to examine how the use of coordination structures with different degrees of coordination flexibility, or system restrictiveness, affect group performance in a distributed asynchronous GSS (or DGSS for short) environment.

The investment club task, developed for this study, is classified as primarily an intellective task. A group was asked to select at least one, but no more than three stocks from a list of 15 stocks to maximize its portfolio value in 6 months. Six months after the experiment, all portfolio values were calculated and ranked to evaluate decision quality. The task also has aspects of a planning task, as the group had to decide what information to gather and how to evaluate this information, in order to reach a decision; and of a preference task, because the group had to reach agreement, and at the time of the decision, there was no way to actually know what decision would turn out to be best 6 months later.

3.5.1. Experimental Design and Procedures. The experiment (Kim, 1996) was conducted with a 2 × 2 factorial design. There were 212 subjects in 47 groups. The subjects were Rutgers, NJIT, and Fairleigh Dickinson University students enrolled in various degree programs. All subjects in all conditions were given the same basic agenda as a coordinating structure, consisting of root comments in their conferences which requested them to define objectives, decide on criteria, review the candidates (stocks, in the case of the experimental task), evaluate the candidates on the criteria, and reach agreement on selection. Training was given to all subjects in the form of a week long asynchronous conference, which included a practice task, the selection of a leader by following the agenda, ending with the sending of a private message to the experimenter by each member, giving a rank ordering.

Four coordination structures were created with two independent variables. The four coordination structures were different in that each structure restricted interaction in a different way. In parallel communication groups, all discussion items were presented, and discussed concurrently by all members of the group, throughout the experiment. Sequential communication groups discussed one item on the agenda at a time. Once a group moved to the next item, revisiting the previous items was not allowed.

In sequential groups, moving from one discussion item to the next item was made by a leader's decision (in groups with a leader), or by a timetable (in groups without a leader). In sequential groups without a leader, the discussion deadline for each discussion item was announced to the groups at the beginning of the experiment. In sequential groups with a leader, the leader made the summary of the discussion of the item for the group, and opened the next discussion item. In parallel groups with a leader, the only requirement for a leader was to summarize group discussion once in a while.

Groups without a designated leader heard no more about this topic after the training. For those in the Leader conditions, the experimenter used the individual rankings to arrive at the most preferred leader. This was announced in the group's conference, along with the leader's role. The leader was specifically empowered to assign a division of labor, and requested to track and summarize the group's progress. Leaders also were put in a "leadership conference" where they could ask questions about the role.

3.5.2. Major Hypotheses and Findings. It was expected that groups supported with a less restrictive structure would perform better than groups supported with a highly restrictive structure. Previous research on

DGSS indicated that an imposed coordination structure can be overly restrictive due to the limited bandwidth of the interaction medium (Hiltz, Johnson, & Turoff, 1991), and the need to synchronize individual activities. Previous research also demonstrated that a GSS with a high degree of system restrictiveness had negative impacts on group performance (Chidambaram & Jones, 1993; McLeod & Liker, 1992; Mennecke, Hoffer, & Wynne, 1992). GSS's with a high degree of system restrictiveness leave no freedom for the group to adaptively structure the system to its own preferable decision strategy (DeSanctis & Poole, 1991; Poole & DeSanctis, 1990). DGSS, in which coordination of individual activities is one of the major requirements, should not be highly restrictive. Research indicates that individuals come to the group with a relatively inflexible preference for a particular decision making strategy (Putnam, 1982). Therefore, DGSS should be flexible enough to allow the individual freedom to concentrate on aspects of the problem to which he or she can best contribute (Turoff, Rao, & Hiltz, 1993).

A previous experiment with synchronous CMC (Hiltz, Johnson, & Turoff, 1991) found that a designated leader elected by the group could improve the quality of decision for an intellective task. Therefore, it was hypothesized that this would also be true in a distributed environment.

Many of the observed differences in dependent variables were not significantly related to experimental condition. However, objective decision quality, evaluated with actual portfolio values 6 months after the experiment, was significantly better for leader than for no-leader conditions. Parallel groups perceived that their decision quality was better than that of sequential groups. Parallel groups also had higher decision quality as objectively measured, but not significantly so ($p = .14$). The average length of comments in the Leader conditions was longer than in the No Leader conditions; there were no other differences in consensus and participation.

Satisfaction with a coordination process was higher in sequential groups, and higher in groups without a designated leader than groups with a leader. (As in many other studies, these subjective satisfaction results run counter to the objective quality results). Satisfaction with the group, however, was higher in parallel groups. Sequential groups reported more improved understanding of the task structure than parallel groups.

3.5.3. Discussion. It is interesting to notice that sequential groups showed higher satisfaction with the coordination process and more improved task understanding than parallel groups. This is contrary to what was expected, but consistent with some previous research, which indicates that GSS should be designed with some degree of restrictiveness (Dickson, Partridge, & Robinson, 1993). Too much freedom in group interaction decreases group cohesiveness. This, in turn, increases the decision cost either by generating a lower quality decision or taking more time to make a decision. Therefore, a coordination structure in Distributed GDSS (DGSS) should impose some restrictions on interaction to maintain a certain level of group cohesiveness.

In future research, the degree of system restrictiveness of a coordination structure needs to be defined more precisely. In this study, sequential coordination was assumed to be more restrictive than parallel simply because it has more procedural order. However, the findings of this study can not be generalized, or compared to the findings of other research, unless the degree of restrictiveness can be objectively determined. Very little is known about what determines the perceived degree of system restrictiveness.

Although leadership is the process of coordinating the activities of group members (Jago, 1982), there were not many significant findings related to the leader variable. One explanation may be that, though research on leadership explains the variety of leadership styles (House, 1971; Stogdill, 1959), the leader function in this study was too narrowly defined. All leaders were expected to behave exactly the same as they were instructed, regardless of their natural leadership style. Implementing leader's functions in DGSS as process structuring tools is one of the requirements in designing DGSS. The successful implementation of leadership functions in DGSS, however, is dependent on the further understanding of coordination effectiveness of different leadership styles within different contingent factors of DGSS (Turoff et al., 1993). Little research has been done in this area.

4. SUMMARY AND CONCLUSIONS

On the basis of prior studies, several measures were taken to help to assure the effectiveness of the CMC groups in these experiments, regardless of the experimental condition or manipulation which they represented. All received substantial training and practice before being left on their own for a week or two to do their experimental task (with the exception of the Peer Review experiment, in which all subjects were already system users). All were at least technically facilitated, with the facilitator checking in daily to see if there were any problems requiring assistance (some also had designated group leaders). All had a clearly stated task, objective, and deadline, and all subjects considered the task at least minimally important, as it was a graded assignment. If any of these conditions were omitted, we suspect that the results would be negative (Hiltz & Turoff, 1991).

There are three basically different conceptualizations about the nature of CMC, and of asynchronous CMC in particular. One point of view, becoming less prevalent now that millions of people are spending hundreds of millions of hours surfing the net for fun, is that it is a "poverty stricken" and "cold" medium. This point of view focuses on what it is not: it does not have some of the channels of communication of the face-to-face medium.

Most of those scholars who have spent time developing and studying CMC as a support for group interaction share the assumption that it can be an effective and sociable form of communication, but they differ on how this can best come about. One group views such systems essentially as a technological mechanism, feeling that effective CMC must be built into a feature-rich and highly structured and restricted environment. Groups need to have the technology essentially "force" them to behave in what are seen as effective ways to use the medium, in order to minimize process losses and maximize process gains (Johnson-Lenz & Johnson-Lenz, 1991). An example of this approach is the Coordinator (e.g., Flores, Graves, Hartfield, & Winograd, 1988), or software to force a completely sequential mode of coordination of interaction.

The second approach to building CMC systems conceives them as a context for interaction, "containers" so to speak, just as rooms are. This conception is based on a social theory that human systems are self-organizing and arise out of the unrestricted interaction of autonomous individuals. From this perspective, the role of the computer system is to provide a place for people to meet and self-organize (Johnson-Lenz & Johnson-Lenz, 1991).

CMC is a very different form of communication than face-to-face meetings, and it takes some time for individuals to learn to use both the mechanics and the social dynamics of such systems effectively. All of the experiments presented here have included at least one condition in which groups used asynchronous CMC, but without time pressure. They had adequate training and at least a week to complete their discussions and produce their group product or decision. Under these conditions, it appears that groups do not need a restrictive, "mechanistic" approach to coordinating their interaction. They are capable of organizing themselves and will tend to feel frustrated by overly restrictive structures or procedures, and/or to become more inefficient.

Almost all of our attempts at a mechanistic process intervention had no significant positive effects on outcomes. For example, there were no significant differences in the major dependent variables measuring outcomes, between the "imposed sequential" process and the no-process or parallel process groups for the preference task, or for the investment task. Likewise, for a creativity task, there was no difference between groups that followed an imposed procedure, and those that did not; and for a planning task, there was no difference between groups that used Dialectical Inquiry and those that used a consensus approach.

On the other hand, the presence of "tools" that a group can use when it is ready to, does seem to improve the perceived richness of CMC, and can improve process and outcomes. The tools that we have provided in various experiments include the ability to build a common list, a set of voting options, the "question–response activity" that structures the exchange of ideas and opinions similar to Nominal Group Process, the possibility of anonymity, and a "polling" tool which can allow a group to construct any sort of questionnaire type item, and display results of the polling. One must choose the tools made available to the group very carefully, to match them to the nature of the task and the size of the group, we suspect, though we have not experimented with the option of just "throwing" all the available tools at a group and letting it decide on its own what might be appropriate and how to use it. We suspect that even 2 weeks is too short a time to expect a group to deal effectively with this much complexity, but that very long-term groups that interact for months to years, would do perfectly well with such a tool chest at their disposal.

The results of these experiments support the assertion that asynchronous CMC is not like any other form of group communication; not only is it not like face-to-face unsupported meetings, but it also has very different dynamics than a computer-supported meeting in a "decision room." Coordination mechanisms and tools that work or don't work in other media tend to have very different effects in the distributed environment.

Things that *work* in an FtF environment may not help coordination and thus improve outcomes in the distributed environment. For example, DI has generally been found to be very beneficial to FtF groups. On the other hand, things that *do not work* in the FtF or Decision Room mode of communication, may be beneficial in the distributed mode. For example, although Watson (1987) did not find any significant benefits for Listing and Voting tools in a Decision Room, Dufner (1995; results summarized earlier) did observe many aspects of significant enhancement of results associated with the use of these tools.

The results of the experiments also confirm that measures of adaptive structuration are very important in the study of distributed, asynchronous GSS. Particularly since the group has no facilitator physically present to enforce suggested procedures, and because they have so long a period to evolve, they may not behave at all like what was intended and expected in regard to the use of suggested tools and procedures.

5. THE PRESENT AND THE FUTURE

We remain optimistic about the potential benefits of asynchronous, distributed Computer Mediated Communication for supporting groups. The one experiment in this series so far that directly compared CMC and FtF groups, found that CMC groups produced significantly more creative results, for a creativity task (Ocker, 1995, reported earlier). We hope to do many more cross-media comparisons in the future, particularly if we are successful in our quest to obtain the necessary equipment for a state of the art "Decision Room" environment. As a start in this direction, the Ocker research has been extended thus far to examining two additional communication conditions, synchronous CMC groups, and "mixed mode" groups that have 2 hours of FtF meeting, 2 weeks of aysnchronous CMC, and a final face-to-face meeting.

We have concluded that the use of an asynchronous CMC system for GSS allows for a much wider range of possible coordination modes and tool support than is effective for synchronous meetings. All of the experiments to date have confirmed that even the most extreme asynchronous structures do not reduce the quality of the solutions when compared to more classical coordination and group approaches. The reasons for this cannot as yet be confirmed by any of the experiments, but they are hinted at from some of the results:

- All individuals are free to participate as they see fit and as much as they desire to.
- The freedom of participation as an individual seems to encourage:
  - a greater expression of ideas
  - more reflection
  - less inhibition of ideas
  - consideration of more options

To truly understand what is taking place there is a need to have groups deal with more complex and involved problems and to augment the typical statistical analysis with detailed content analysis of the discussions. Though extremely tedious, content analysis could resolve the alternative explanations for our results. In addition, the nature of benefits listed earlier are such that they may make a significant difference in quality only when dealing with fairly complex tasks that also instill a high degree of motivation for the group members.

Although controlled experiments are informative for very specific issues, much of the insight that is needed for the support of asynchronous group communications has and will come from field trials and quasi experiments (Hiltz & Turoff, 1978; Turoff et al., 1993). One key example of this has been our work in the area of collaborative learning (the Virtual Classroom™, Hiltz, 1994; Hsu & Hiltz, 1991, and Worrell, Hiltz, Turoff, & Fjermestad, 1995). Its purpose is to use computer support to increase both access to and the effectiveness of education, at all levels. Rather than being built of steel and concrete, the Virtual Classroom consists of a set of group communication and work "spaces" and facilities that are constructed in software. Thus it is a "virtual" facility for interaction among the members of a class, rather than a physical space. It is "asynchronous," meaning that students and teachers may connect through the networks and participate any time, day or night, seven days a week. The software activities developed for this application stress collaborative learning approaches.

Field trials of various types with collaborative learning have been taking place at NJIT since 1980. Currently NJIT offers complete undergraduate degree programs in Information Systems and in Computer Science and many additional graduate courses through a remote learning program utilizing asynchronous group communications.

What this example and others have taught us, when combined with the experimental work in GSS, is that the key to successful systems is to discard many of the biases that come from making comparisons to face-to-face approaches and trying to adapt an approach of automating the face-to-face environment. Rather, the factors that seem to be crucial to enhancing our understanding of this area and in the future design of the functionality for such systems include:

- Providing a "nonlinear agenda" that allows the individual members of the group to focus on the contributions that each can best make, independent of the work of other members of the group at that moment in time (Turoff, 1991).
- Allowing a group to tailor the relationships structure of comments to fit the application domain as they perceive it. This can only be done by freeing fixed comment relationship structures to provide a full collaborative Hypertext capability (Turoff, Rao, & Hiltz, 1991).
- Providing "reciprocal" coordination structures (Hiltz & Turoff, 1978) that will be able to check on consistency and agreement at the group level and inform participants when they need to reconsider their inputs based on more recent contributions of others. The reason why these factors have not played a significant role in most current GSS work has been the typical lack of complexity of the problem being examined.

The other area that our research is focusing on is the software development process and tools to support that task. Initially, the primary objective of this ongoing project is to increase knowledge about how to create more productive systems to support distributed, collaborative groups, particularly for complex software design and planning type tasks. The subtasks in the software development area span a wide range of critical problem areas:

- The need for enhanced creativity in the design process.
- Greater understanding of requirements between users and designers (e.g., experts who sometimes speak different languages).
- The planning of projects and efforts.

- Complex project management, which includes the tracking and monitoring of what has been accomplished, the detection of potential problems and the handoff and coordination of work between different individuals and subgroups.

Within systems development, it is recognized that the stages of requirements definition and high-level design are important, and even crucial to the development of effective software. Collaborative designers work to achieve some consensus on the general characteristics of the new system in question (Olson & Olson, 1991). Ineffective communication during the requirements definition process is consistently associated with user dissatisfaction and lower quality systems, whereas effective communication is associated with improved productivity and higher quality systems (Curtis, Krasner, & Iscoe, 1988). Additionally, it has been increasingly suggested that the development of information systems and the definition of high-level requirements and design, could benefit from the infusion of creative and innovative solutions (e.g., Couger, Higgins, & McIntyre, 1993; Telem, 1988).

Particularly critical to this area will be the adding of additional tools and processes (such as group hypertext/hypermedia authoring capabilities). Daft and Lengel (1986) were certainly right when they pointed out that the objective of most work meetings is to reduce both uncertainty and equivocality in unstructured problem solving.

Although most work in the Hypertext area appreciates the utility of nonlinear relationships in the content of the material to reduce uncertainty; however, it also seems self-evident that the problem of equivocality can only be handled by allowing people to perceive one another's reactions to the information. This has always been clear in the context of asynchronous communications, where it is critical that each participant needs to know the status of the other members and the group as a whole. Within the context of a collaborative Hypertext environment, it becomes necessary for the individuals to be able to perceive how others traverse the network and how they modify it in a thought process type of temporal sequence.

The concept of utilizing Hypertext to support individuals to integrate the different domains supporting software engineering analysis, design and development is not new (Isakowitz, 1993). However, the equally important concept of supporting group processes and collaboration (Turoff, 1991) has received only a limited amount of attention. The specific goal of our research will be to focus on all the processes associated with software development that may be aided by Collaborative Hypertext Systems (Balasubramanian & Turoff, 1995). There have only been a few specific systems prototyped in this area (Marshall & Shipman, 1993).

The current emergence of a whole new generation of implementation tools means that in the future it will be much easier to develop specific Decision Support functionality and Hypertext capabilities. It also means that there will be a major shift back to more internal development of tailored user software within organizations, rather than the current emphasis on purchased software. An objective of future research in the Group Support Systems area should be to provide a kind of "checklist" of what kinds of tools and procedures are likely to be helpful for different types of tasks, so that organizations can be guided in their self-tailoring of software to fit their needs.

ACKNOWLEDGMENTS

This research was supported by grants from the National Science Foundation program on Coordination Theory and Collaboration Technology (NSF IRI 9015236 and NSF-IRI-9408805). The opinions expressed do not necessarily represent those of the National Science Foundation. Among the many people who have contributed to the program of research, in addition to the coauthors, are Raquel Benbunan, Robert Czech, Kenneth Johnson, Cesar Perez, Ronald Rice, Scott Poole, James Whitescarver, and William Worrell.

REFERENCES

Balasubramanian, V. and Turoff, M. (1995). A Systematic Approach to User Interface Design for Hypertext Systems, *Proceedings, 28th HICSS*, Vol. IV., 241–250, 1995.

Chidambaram, L. (1989). *An Empirical Investigation of the Impact of Computer Support on Group Development and Decision-Making Performance*, Unpublished doctoral dissertation, Indiana University.

Chidambaram, L., Bostrom, R. P., and Wynne, B. E. (1990). A Longitudinal Study of the Impact of Group Decision Support Systems on Group Development, *Journal of Management Information Systems, 7*(3), 7–25.

Chidambaram, L., and Jones, B. (1993). "Impact of Communication Medium and Computer Support on Group Perceptions and Performance: A Comparison of Face-to-Face and Dispersed Meetings, *MIS Quarterly*, December, 465–491.

Cole, S., Rubin, L., and Cole, J. R. (1977). Peer Review and the Support of Science. *Scientific American*, Vol. 237, pp. 34–41.

Couger, J. D., Higgins, L. F., and McIntyre, S. C. (1993). (Un)structured creativity in information systems organizations. *MIS Quarterly*, December, 375–397.

Cummings, L. L., Frost, P. J., and Vakil, T. F. (1985). The manuscript review process: A view from the inside on coaches, critics, and special cases. In L. L. Cummings and P. J. Frost (Eds.), *Publishing in the Organizational Sciences* (pp. 469–508). Homewood, IL: Richard D. Irwin.

Curtis, B., Krasner, H., and Iscoe, N. (1988). A field study of the software design process for large systems. *CACM, 31*, 1268–1287.

Daft, R. and Lengel, R. (1986). Organizational information requirements, media richness and structural design. *Management Science, 32*(5), 554–571.

DeSanctis, G. and Gallupe, R. B. (1987). A foundation for the study of group decision support systems. *Management Science, 33*(5), 589–609.

DeSanctis, G. and Poole, M. S. (1991). Understanding the Difference in Collaborative System Use Through Appropriatation Analysis. *Proceedings of the 24th Hawaii International Conference on System Sciences*, 750–757.

DeSanctis, G. and Poole, M. S. (1994). Capturing the complexity in advanced technology use: Adaptive structuration theory. *Organization Science*, Vol. 5, No. 2, pp. 121–147.

Dickson, G., Partridge, J. L., and Robinson, L. (1993). Exploring Modes of Facilitative Support for GDSS Technology, *MIS Quarterly, 17*(2), June, 173–194.

Dufner, D. K. (1989). *Replication of the Watson Research: Experimental Design and Pre-Research Trials Using Five Student Groups at NJIT*. Unpublished research report, NJIT, Newark, NJ.

Dufner, D. K. (1995). *The Effects of Group Support (Listing and Voting Tools) and Sequential Procedures on Group Decision Making Using Asynchronous Computer Conferences*. Doctoral thesis, Rutgers University Graduate School of Management.

Dufner, D. K., Hiltz, S. R., and Turoff, M. (1994). Distributed Group Support: A Preliminary Analysis of the Effects of the Use of Voting Tools and Sequential Procedures. *Proceedings of the 27th Annual Conference on System Sciences*, Hawaii, 114–123.

Dufner, D. K., Hiltz, S. R, Johnson, K., and Czech, R. M. (1995). Distributed Group Support: The Effects of Voting Tools on Group Perceptions of Media Richness. *Group Decision and Negotiation Journal*, Special Issue on Distributed Communication Systems (Vol. 4, No. 3), pp. 235–250.

Easton, A. C., Vogel, D. R., and Nunamaker, J. F. (1989). Stakeholder identification and assumption surfacing in small groups: an experimental study. *Proceedings of the 22nd Hawaii International Conference on System Sciences* (Vol. 3), pp. 344–352.

Ellis, C. A., Gibbs, S. J., and Rein, G. L. (1991). Groupware: Some issues and experiences. *Communications of the ACM, 34*(1), 39–58.

Fjermestad, J. (1994). *Group Strategic Decision Making in a Computer-Mediated-Communications Environment: A Comparison of Dialectical Inquiry and Constructive Consensus Approaches*. Unpublished doctoral dissertation, Rutgers University.

Fjermestad, J. and Hiltz, S. R. (1996). *An assessment of Experimental Studies of Group Decision Support Systems*. Manuscript submitted for publication.

Fjermestad, J., Hiltz, S. R., and Turoff, M. (1993). An Integrated Theoretical Framework for the Study of Group Decision Support Systems, *HICSS '93, IV*, 179–188.

Fjermestad, J., Hiltz, S. R., Turoff, M., Ford, C., Johnson, K., Czech, B., Ferront, F., Ocker, R., and Worrell, M. (1995). Group Strategic Decision Making: Asynchronous GSS Using Structured Conflict & Consensus Approaches. *Proceedings of the 28th Annual Hawaii International Conference on System Sciences* (Vol. IV), pp. 222–231. Los Alamitos, CA: IEEE Computer Society Press.

Flores, F., Graves, M., Hartfield, B., and Winograd, T. (1988). Computer systems and the design of organizational interaction. *ACM Transactions on Office Information Systems*, April, 153–172.

Guindon, R. (1990). Designing the design process: Exploiting opportunistic thoughts. *Human-Computer Interaction, 5*, 135–344.

Hall, J. (1971). Decision, Decisions, Decisions. *Psychology Today, 5*, pp. 51–54, 86, 88.

Hiltz, S. R. (1994). The Virtual Classroom: Learning Without Limits Via Computer Networks. Norwood, NJ: Ablex.

Hiltz, S. R., Dufner, D. K., Holmes, M. E., and Poole, S. M. (1991). Distributed Group Support Systems: Social Dynamics and Design Dilemmas. *Journal of Organizational Computing, 2*(1), 135–159.

Hiltz, S. R., Johnson, K., and Turoff, M. (1991). Group Decision Support: The Effects of Designated Human Leaders and Statistical Feedback in Computerized Conferences. *Journal of Management Information Systems, 8*(2), 81–108.

Hiltz, S. R. and Turoff, M. (1978). *The Network Nation: Human Communication via Computer*. Reading, MA: Addison Wesley Advanced Book Program. Revised edition MIT Press, 1993.

Hiltz, S. R. and Turoff, M. (1985). Structuring Computer-Mediated Communication Systems to avoid Information Overload. *CACM, 28*(7), 682–689.

Hiltz, S. R. and Turoff, M. (1991). Computer Networking Among Executives: A Case Study. In J. F. Nunamaker, Jr., and R. H. Sprague, Jr. (eds.), *Proceedings HICSS*, pp. 758–769.

House, R. J. (1971). A Path Goal Theory of Leader Effectiveness. *Administrative Science Quarterly, 16*, 321–338.

Hsu, E. Y. P., and Hiltz, S. R. (1991). Management Gaming on a Computer Mediated Conferencing System: A Case of Collaborative Learning through Computer Conferencing. In J. F. Nunamaker, Jr., and R. H. Sprague, Jr. (eds.), *Proceedings HICSS, Vol. IV*, 367–371.

Isakowitz, T. (1993). Hypermedia, Information Systems, & Organizations: A Research Agenda, *Proceedings of the 26th HICSS*, Vol. IV.

Jago, A. G. (1982). Leadership: Perspectives in Theory and Research. *Management Science, 28*, 315–336.

Johnson-Lenz, P. and Johnson-Lenz, T. (1982). Groupware: The process and impacts of design choices. In E. B. Kerr and S. R. Hiltz (eds.), *Computer-Mediated Communication Systems: Status and Evaluation* (pp. 45–55). New York: Academic Press.

Johnson-Lenz, P. and Johnson-Lenz, T. (1991). Post mechanistic groupware primitives: Rhythms, boundaries and containers. *Int. J. of Man-Machine Studies, 34*, 395–417.

King, N. and Anderson, N. (1990). Innovation in working groups. In M. A. West and J. L. Farr (eds.), *Innovation and Creativity at Work*. Chichester: Wiley.

Kim, Y. J. (1996). *Coordination in Distributed Group Support Systems: A Controlled Experiment Comparing Parallel and Sequential Processes*. Doctoral dissertation, Rutgers University Graduate School of Management.

Kunz, W. and Rittel, H. (1970). *Issues as elements of information systems* (Working paper no. 131). Institute of Urban and Regional Development, University of California, Berkeley.

MacLean, A., Young, R., Bellotti, V., and Moran, T. (1991). Questions, options, and criteria: Elements of design space analysis. *Human-Computer Interaction, 6*(4), 201–250.

Mahoney, M. J. (1977). Publication Prejudices: An Experimental Study of Confirmatory Bias in the Peer Review System. *Cognitive Therapy and Research*, Vol. 1, pp. 161–175.

Mahoney, M. J. (1978). Publish and Perish. *Human Behavior*, Vol. 7, pp. 38–41.

Mahoney, M. J. (1985). Open Exchange and Epistemic Progress. *American Psychologist*, Vol. 40, pp. 29–39.

Malone, T. W. and Crowston, K. (1990). What is coordination theory and how can it help design cooperative work systems? *CSCW 90 Proceedings*, 357–370.

Marshall, C. C. and Shipman, F. M. (1993). Searching for the missing link: Discovering implicit structure in spatial hypertext. *Proceedings of Hypertext*, ACM Press, 212–230.

Mason, R. O. (1969). A dialectical approach to strategic planning. *Management Science, 15*(8), B403–B414.

McGrath, J. E. (1984). *Groups: Interaction and Performance*. Englewood Cliffs, NJ: Prentice-Hall.

McLeod, P. L. and Liker, J. K. (1992). Electronic Meeting Systems: Evidence from a Low Structure Environment. *Information Systems Research, 3*(3), 195–223.

Mennecke, B. E., Hoffer, H. A., and Wynne, B. E. (1992). The Implications of Group Development and History for Group Support System Theory and Practice. *Small Group Research, 23*(4), 525–572.

Mitroff, I. I. and Mason, R. O. (1981). *Creating A Dialectical Social Science: Concepts, Methods, and Models*. Boston, MA: D. Reidel.

Nemiroff, P. M., Pasmore, W. A., and Ford, D. L. (1976). The Effects of Two Normative Structural Interventions on Established and Ad Hoc Groups: Implications for Improving Decision Making Effectiveness. *Decision Sciences, 7*, 841–855.

Nunamaker, J. F., Dennis, A. R., Valacich, J. S., Vogel, D. R., and George, J. F. (1991). Electronic meeting systems to support group work. *Communications of the ACM, 34*(7), 40–61.

Ocker, R. (1995). *Computer Support for Distributed Asynchronous Software Design Teams*. Doctoral thesis, Rutgers University Graduate School of Management.

Ocker, R., Hiltz, S. R., Turoff, M., and Fjermestad, J. (1995). Computer Support for Distributed Software Design Teams: Preliminary Experimental Results. *Proceedings of the 28th Annual*

Hawaii International Conference on System Sciences, Vol. IV, pp. 4–13. Los Alamitos, CA: IEEE Computer Society Press, 1995.

Olson, G. M., and Olson, J. S. (1991). User-centered design of collaboration technology. *Journal of Organizational Computing, 1*, 61–83.

Olson, G. M., Olson, J. S., Carter, M., and Storrosten, M. (1992). Small group design meetings: An analysis of collaboration. *Human-Computer Interaction, 7*(4), 347–374.

Olson, J. S., Olson, G. M., Storrosten, M., and Carter, M. (1993). Groupwork close up: A comparison of the group design process with and without a simple group editor. *ACM Transactions on Office Information Systems, 11*(4), 321–348.

Osborne, A. F. (1957). *Applied Imagination* (2nd ed.). New York: Charles Scribner's Sons.

Peters, D. P. and Ceci, S. J. (1982). Peer-review practices of psychological journals: The fate of published articles, submitted again. *The Behavioral and Brain Sciences, 5*, 187–255.

Poole, M. S. and DeSanctis, G. (1990). Understanding the use of group decision support systems: The theory of adaptive structuration. In C. Steinfield and J. Fulk (Eds.), *Organizations and communication technology* (pp. 173–193). Beverly Hills: Sage.

Poole, M. S. and DeSanctis, G. (1992). Microlevel Structuration in Computer-Supported Group Decision Making. *Human Communication Research, 19*(1), 5–49.

Putnam, L. L. (1982). Procedural Messages and Small Group Work Climates: A Lag Sequential Analysis. *Communication Yearbook, 5*, 331–350.

Rana, A. (1995). *Peer Review Process and Group Support Systems: Theory Development and Experimental Validation.* Doctoral thesis, Rutgers University Graduate School of Management.

Rana, A. R., Hiltz, S. R., and Turoff, M. (1995). *Peer Review Process: A Group Support Systems Approach* (Working Paper, NJIT). Newark, NJ.

Rice, R. E. (1984). *The New Media: Communication, Research and Technology.* Beverly Hills, Sage.

Rice, R. E. (1993). Media appropriateness: Using social presence theory to compare traditional and new organizational media. *Human communication Research, 19*(4), 451–484.

Sambamurthy, V. and DeSanctis, G. (1989). An experimental evaluation of DGSS effects on group performance during stakeholder analysis. *Proceedings of the 23rd Annual Hawaii International Conference on System Sciences*, Vol. 3, pp. 79–88.

Schweiger, D. M., Sandberg, W. R., and Ragan, J. W. (1986). Group Approaches for Improving Strategic Decision Making: A Comparative Analysis of Dialectical Inquiry, Devil's Advocacy, and Consensus. *Academy of Management Journal, 29*(1), 51–71.

Schweiger, D. M., Sandberg, W. R., and Rechner, P. L. (1989). Experiential Effects of Dialectical Inquiry, Devil's Advocacy, and Consensus Approaches to Strategic Decision Making. *Academy of Management Journal, 32*(4), 745–772.

Schwenk, C. R. (1990). Effects of Devil's Advocacy and Dialectical Inquiry on Decision Making: A Meta Analysis. *Organizational Behavior and Human Decision Processes, 47*, 161–176.

Silver, M. S. (1990). Decision Support Systems: Directed and Nondirected Change. *Information Systems Research, 1*(1), 47–70.

Simon, H. A. (1973). The structure of ill-structured problems. *Artificial Intelligence, 4*, 145–180.

Stogdill, R. M. (1959). Individual Behavior and Group Achievement. New York: Oxford University Press.

Tjosvold, D. (1982). Effects of Approach on Superiors' Incorporation of Subordinates' Information in Decision Making. *Journal of Applied Psychology, 67*, 189–193.

Telem, M. (1988). Information requirements specification brainstorming collective decision-making approach. *Information Processing & Management, 24*(5), 549–566.

Tung, L. L. and Heminger, A. R. (1993). The Effects of Dialectical Inquiry, Devil's Advocacy, and Consensus Inquiry Methods in a GSS Environment. *Information & Management, 25*, 33–41.

Turoff, M. (1991). Computer-Mediated Requirements for Group Support. *Journal of Organizational Computing, 1*, 85–113.

Turoff, M., Hiltz, S. R., Bahgat, A. N. F., and Rana, A. (1993). Distributed Group Support Systems. *MIS Quarterly*, December, 399–417.

Turoff, M., Rao, U., and Hiltz, S. R. (1991). Collaborative Hypertext in Computer Mediated Communications. *Proceedings of the 24th HICSS*, Vol. IV, 357–366.

Van de Ven, A. H. and Delbecq, A. (1974). The effectiveness of nominal, delphi and interacting group decision making processes. *Academy of Management Journal, 17*, 605–621.

Watson, R. T. (1987). *A Study of Group Decision Support System Use in Three-and-Four Person Groups for a Preference Allocation Decision*. Unpublished doctoral dissertation, University of Minnesota.

West, M. A. (1990). The social psychology of innovation in groups. In M. A. West and J. L. Farr (eds), Innovation and Creativity at Work. Chichester: Wiley.

Worrell, W., Hiltz, S. R., Turoff, M., and Fjermestad, J. (1995). An experiment in collabortive learning using a game and a computer-mediated conference in accounting games. *Proceedings of the 28th Annual Hawaii International Conference on System Sciences*, Vol. IV, pp. 63–71. Los Alamitos, CA: IEEE Computer Society Press.

Zmud, R., Lind, M., and Young, F. (1990). An Attribute Space for Organizational Communication Channels. *Information Systems Research 1*(4), 440–457.

CHAPTER

16

Transforming Coordination: The Promise and Problems of Information Technology in Coordination

Rob Kling
Indiana University

Kenneth L. Kraemer
University of California, Irvine

Jonathan P. Allen
Purdue University

Yannis Bakos
New York University

Vijay Gurbaxani
Margaret Elliott
University of California, Irvine

INTRODUCTION

Information technology (IT) has the potential to change the way organizations coordinate. Because the effective coordination of separate activities within organizations and between organizations plays such a large role in organizational performance, it is important to know how organizations use IT to actually coordinate their activities. What coordination problems does IT solve in practice, and what new coordination problems does it bring to the surface? What is easy about turning technological potential into organizational performance, and what is difficult?

The Advanced Integrated Manufacturing Environments (AIME) project has been a multiyear study of coordination changes in U.S. manufacturing firms implementing new information technologies. AIME project research has confirmed the need for a *behavioral* as well as an *information-processing* view of how IT changes coordination in practice. There is a long tradition of organizational analyses of information systems in organizations—how social forces influence their selective adoption, shape their configurations, enhance or undermine their implementation, and influence their subsequent uses (e.g., Kling, 1980, 1987).

Information-processing views of coordination change show how structural features of IT directly improve organizational performance by simplifying key coordination problems of scheduling, synchronizing, and allocating (e.g., Malone & Crowston, 1994). The information-processing approach has special appeal because it offers a way to think about optimizing organizational structures to reduce coordination costs. Information-processing formulations, such as Malone and Crowston's, emphasize *static*, relatively optimal, solutions to organizational problems. This information-processing view, however, gives us an incomplete understanding of how to cope with *dynamic* organizational problems that arise from changing coordination practices within a world of powerful social and economic logics.

The AIME project has used behavioral theories from organizational sociology and institutional economics to create an understanding of IT as a shifter of potentials and constraints in a world of existing economic and social coordination processes. This chapter identifies some key findings from the project. At the project's inception, the dominant discourse about coordination and information technology was framed in terms of information processing theories of coordination. Although we anticipated that behavioral analyses would add depth to the information-processing analyses, we did not know how much these alternative approaches would be complementary, conflicting, or synergistic. Many observations in this chapter came from detailed empirical field studies of the use of IT to coordinate manufacturing activities.

We did find that IT can sometimes be used to solve many existing coordination problems without any substantial side effects. This is especially the case when the problems and technologies are simple and straightforward. But as the coordination problems become more organizationally complex and interdependent, so often do the information technologies intended to solve them. In such instances, it is more accurate to speak of the use of IT as *transforming* one set of coordination problems into another set of coordination problems. The new set of coordination problems may be more or less tractable for the organization. The "irony" of IT and coordination is that the new kinds of interdependencies created by the sustained use of IT may, in some circumstances, be more difficult to coordinate than the original problems IT use was supposed to address. Much of the difficulty is due to the relative inexperience organizations have in dealing with these new coordination problems. New design techniques and new institutional arrangements for organizational usability have the potential to make these coordination problems much less severe.

Information Technology and Changes in Coordination

Although a distinction is often made between coordination activity and production activity in organizations (e.g., Scott Morton, 1991), coordination itself is an extremely broad term. It is usually defined at a very abstract level, as the alignment of distinct but interdependent activities (Malone & Crowston, 1994). Everything from human communication, to factory scheduling algorithms, to an international currency market can be conceptualized as a coordination problem. To give more concreteness to the kinds of organizational coordination issues the AIME project has focused on, we briefly discuss examples of the difficulty of coordination changes through IT.

One kind of organizational coordination problem arises when the value of a shared information system depends on how different individuals and groups use the system jointly. For example, managers who have acquired group calendar systems that help their subordinates automatically schedule meeting times, or at least be aware of each others schedules, have faced significant organizational difficulties (Bullen & Bennett, 1996; Grudin, 1994). Each person must maintain an accurate, up-to-date personal calendar that publicly defines their appointments and "free time." Maintaining personal calendars on a computer system is a significant amount of work—work done largely for the benefit of other group members, and the clerical staff that schedules meetings. Group calendars—in practice—have a political economy of effort that can make it hard for those who do most of the record keeping to feel that they have gained proportional value (Grudin, 1994; Kling, 1980).

There is also a politics to allocating time and having one's time commitments be publicly visible. The men and women who use the system have to agree on the meaning of free time. Can a person have no free time? Is a person allowed to block off time on his or her calendar for any reason, or only for official company events? The coordination problems of organizational systems such as group calendars are not limited to providing electronic communications and scheduling.

Wagner (1996) found one intriguing challenge when she tried to design a surgical calendar system for a surgical teams that were composed of (typically) male surgeons and (typically female nurses. She noted that:

> If . . . women's (nurses) voices are not heard, the resulting rules and regulations concerning "privacy versus transparency" will reflect a one-sided tendency to protect primarily the needs and interests of surgeons, hereby disre-

> garding the organizational problems created when in an organization characterized by strong dependencies and frequent emergencies one group enjoys a high level of time autonomy (and privacy). (pp. 891–892)

A coordination solution, such as using a temporal database—calendars—to manage commitments and to more efficiently schedule people and resources can be very appealing, especially when it is abstracted from concrete working conditions and social relationships. But it rapidly becomes a problem of managing incentives to keep personal calendars up-to-date, agreeing on the meaning of free time, giving different workers effective voice in scheduling major events, and facing the local politics of temporal privacy.

Another example of organizational coordination difficulties comes from the use of massive, technically complex computer systems that span an entire organization. Whereas a complex system may improve aspects of a firm's coordination, making these systems run smoothly on a daily basis is a huge coordination challenge of its own. In manufacturing, for example, MRPII (Manufacturing Resource Planning) systems have faced significant implementation difficulties (Hayes, Wheelwright, & Clark, 1988; Warner, 1987). As different groups are tightly linked together, the new dependencies between groups have to be coordinated (Attewell, 1991; Kling & Iacono, 1984). The technical capabilities of the system, and any modifications, have to be negotiated by all of the groups relying on the system. The organizational complexity of using MRPII for coordination is shown by the fact that internal politics have been a better predictor of the extent of MRPII use than purely technical factors (Cooper & Zmud, 1990).

These two examples illustrate the kinds of issues organizations face in translating the potential of IT into improved organizational coordination. IT, because of its inherent capability to store, process, and transmit vast amounts of information, has rightly been seen as a powerful enabler of new forms of organizational coordination (e.g., Scott Morton, 1991). However, the specific ways that IT changes organizational coordination in practice cannot be fully described by inherent technological capabilities such as "reducing time and space to zero." These examples are consistent with previous research on computing and organizations, which shows that the use of IT may lead to different coordination outcomes, depending on existing social and economic logics (e.g., Kling, 1996). The actual coordination changes that take place in the presence of IT is a question that has to be answered through empirical, behavioral study.

In the AIME project, we have studied coordination in manufacturing, for both practical and theoretical reasons. Manufacturing is of undeniable practical importance to the U.S. economy, and thus is important to study (Cohen & Zysman, 1987). From a theoretical viewpoint, however, studying coordination in a domain such as manufacturing is particularly interesting because of the harsh technical demands of manufacturing coordination, the rich institutional environment that brings many different groups and activities together, and the constant experimentation taking place with new forms of coordination.

THEORETICAL RESEARCH ON COORDINATION

When individuals and groups specialize, by concentrating their expertise within a narrow range of activities, there is a need for coordination. Coordination among specialized individuals and groups takes place by ordering and arranging the interdependencies among their separate activities (Kling et al., 1992). Manufacturing firms, like all firms, coordinate extensively at many levels. Different groups, such as engineering, marketing, production, and materials each have deep specialized knowledge of their own domains. But their decisions and behavior are frequently interdependent with other activities outside of their domain. Although the skill and attention of these different groups must be focused and choreographed for good organizational performance, conflicts of perspective and practice between any of these groups is common.

To explain this diversity of organizational action, the AIME project used multiple theoretical perspectives to account for actual coordination behavior in IT-using manufacturing firms. This following section describes those theoretical perspectives. It begins with the initial theoretical critiques of a view of manufacturing coordination that depends too heavily on the inherent attributes of the technology, a view that is widespread in the literature on computer-integrated manufacturing. Next, it reviews the theories from organizational sociology the project found useful for studying coordination behavior. Finally, the work on theoretical perspectives from institutional economics is presented as another useful lens for viewing the role of IT in manufacturing coordination.

Basic Critiques of Information-Processing Centered Visions of Coordination

Since the 1980s, discussions of IT's potential for changing manufacturing coordination have taken place under the banner of Computer-Integrated Manufacturing (CIM). CIM is a strongly information-processing centered vision that emphasizes the need for greater computerization, and greater data integration, around a single, enterprise-wide database (e.g., Harrington, 1973; Melnyk & Narasimhan, 1992). The CIM vision argues that the path to more effective coordination is to tightly link together separate areas of the factory through databases and computer-mediated communication—integrating the "islands of automation" to achieve global optimization.

Since the 1990s, practical problems with the CIM vision have been discussed in the research literature, and the popular press. A common observation in popular articles is that the problem of CIM are "more organizational (or cultural) than technical" (e.g., Sheridan, 1992). Social researchers also note the importance of organizational issues, and their elusiveness. In writing about less ambitious incremental changes in manufactuirng systems, Shani, Grant, Krishan, and Thompson (1992) note:

> One result that is abundantly clear is that critical management problems arise not in the adjustment of the technical system, but in the adjustment of the social system. Not only are the time frames required for adjustment much longer (for example, in employee training and in gaining the commitment of managers at different levels and in different functions), but the problems of interpersonal relations and organizational structure are far less transparent and much less easy to define than those of technology. (p. 108)

Analysts who have critiqued U.S. manufacturing computerization make a distinction between computerizing direct (production) activities versus indirect (coordination) activities. Although U.S. manufacturers are seen as not making enough appropriate use of computerization for direct production activities (e.g., Jaikumar, 1986), they have been criticized for excessively computerizing, and overcomplicating, indirect activities such as scheduling, production planning, and production control (e.g., Dertouzos, Lester, & Solow, 1989; Hayes et al., 1988; Roven & Pass, 1992).

The AIME project began its conceptual work by identifying the kinds of organizational issues that were repeatedly being observed in real coordination behavior, but that were not being addressed by the information-processing focus of CIM. From existing research on the impacts of computer technology, the AIME project was aware that organizational change is not dictated solely by the inherent capabilities of a new technology. When an IT system becomes sufficiently large in scope (involving numerous groups), it can be seen as a social and economic institution (Kling & Iacono, 1989) shaped by behavioral as well as technological forces. As a recent National Research Council (1994) study concluded:

> IT alone does not create impacts; its effects reflect a host of decisions made and actions taken—wisely or not—by a range of stakeholders including senior managers, technical professionals, and users. (p. 161)

To understand how manufacturing firms actually use IT to facilitate coordination, the first task of the analyst is to define a set of theoretical concepts that can account for changes in coordination technology, but within a framework of human decision, behavior, belief, and history.

There has been a substantial body of research on common organizational problems with computer systems (Gasser, 1986; Knights & Murray, 1994; Laudon, 1974; Orlikowski, 1993). Our reading of this literature indicates that the appropriate theories would have to account for: the social relationships between participants who influence the adoption and use of computer-based technologies, the infrastructures for supporting systems development and use, and the history of local computing developments (Kling, 1987). Special attention would have to be paid to information-processing views of coordination that assume harmony and cooperation, rather than the possibility of partially conflicting preferences, interests, or values (Kling, 1991; Orlikowski, 1993). Purely technological theories of coordination also tend to overestimate the ability of different subgroups to coordinate quickly and smoothly. The capacity to coordinate can be limited by organizational processes (Beuschel & Kling, 1992; Kling, 1992b; Kling, 1993).

Coordinating manufacturing operations through IT raises important, recurring organizational issues. Addressing these issues requires the use of social and economic perspectives, that assume actors will behave as groups in a social context, or as economic agents (Kling et al., 1992).

The Sociology of Complex Organizations Limits the Possibilities of Coordination Through IT

The first set of behavioral perspectives used by the AIME project comes from organizational sociology (Perrow, 1986; Pfeffer, 1982; Scott, 1992). Sociological theories of coordination assume that groups will conflict over goals and interests. They identify social bases for group differences and interests, such as status, power, and social identification. Sociological theories are pertinent to understanding IT and coordination in manufacturing because such systems tie together organizational units with different occupational cultures and work practices (Kling et al., 1992).

The AIME project used three theoretical perspectives from organizational sociology, each with their own strengths and weaknesses: institutional theory, structural contingency theory, and resource dependency theory. Each of these perspectives has its own language for describing the nature of "alignment" between separate activities. The main concepts from each theoretical perspective, along with key examples from our research, are presented next. More detail on each of these perspectives can be found in Kling et al., 1992.

Institutional Theory. Institutional theory views organizations as groups of people who embody and enact loosely coupled standardized packages of rules, procedures, and beliefs (Powell & DiMaggio, 1991). These standardized packages, or "rationalized myths" (Meyer & Rowan, 1977), are adopted primarily to maintain organizational legitimacy in the eyes of powerful external actors and belief systems. Maintaining organizational legitimacy in the eyes of outside institutions, such as government regulators, professional organizations, and powerful clients, contributes to the survival of the organization. Over time, the institutionalized packages become "taken-for-granted"—organizational actors can no longer think of legitimate alternatives, and the packages become extremely difficult to change.

Our research found institutional theory especially useful for explaining coordination changes in situations where manufacturers face strong external legitimacy demands, and cope with complex sets of technologies that are sensitive to the organizational assumptions embedded within them. We found institutional forces shaping coordination outcomes in both the AIRTECH and DISKCO cases.

We conducted a case study at the Wing Control Division (WCD) of AIRTECH, a Southern California aerospace manufacturer. WCD produces sophisticated control equipment for airplanes, helicopters, and missiles that requires the integration of mechanical, hydraulic, and electronic technologies. WCD's 10–12 product lines are evenly split between commercial and military markets. In terms of market positioning, WCD has a reputation for high-tech design skill, and high prices. As one design engineer said, "we'll win [the contract] on technology if the price doesn't kick us out." Our data collection over the 18-month period consisted of three waves of 22 total individual and team interviews. DISKCO is one division of a multinational computer manufacturing company that manufactures disk drives for mainframes, minicomputers, and workstations. We studied the efforts of DISKCO's manufacturing engineers and IS specialists to develop an effective CIM system to support a new assembly line that manufactures 1–2GB disk drives for workstations.

One of the most potent examples of the power of strong external belief systems comes from the AIRTECH case. AIRTECH used a complex computerized scheduling and logistics system to tightly couple many different factory activities. This Manufacturing Resource Planning (MRPII) system used assumptions about how long it takes to build certain parts, how long it takes to move parts between areas, and how many usable parts are output to tightly coordinate activities. One set of mid-career operations managers, fresh from their professional seminars on "just-in-time" manufacturing, reduced many of these systems assumptions to overly optimistic levels—what their professional ideology told them should be the case. (For example, they reduced the parameters for the times to move materials between work centers to zero.) Short-term schedule improvements turned into long-term chaos, and the operations managers were eventually dismissed (Allen, Bakos, & Kling, 1994).

AIRTECH offers an extreme example of how institutionalized beliefs about ideal forms of managing that are legitimate in managerial worlds can cause coordination difficulty. Another kind of institutional problem is seen in the DISKCO case. A shop floor control system designed to be used by skilled workers who needed little monitoring caused new coordination problems for another DISKCO division that adopted the system (Allen, Kling, & Elliott, 1994). Complex computer systems for manufacturing coordination tightly link groups together. These tight linkages contribute to inertia (Beuschel & Kling, 1992), somewhat reduce local experimentation (Allen, 1992), and create a new set of horizontal coordination and control needs that is open to institutional clash (Allen, 1994b).

These horizontal linkages are complicated by the multiple institutional forces that manufacturers have to answer to, or try to take advantage of, simultaneously. Manufacturers answer to multiple sets of government regulators for labor issues, safety issues, and business law; multiple customers, each with their own requirements for quality and product flexibility; and multiple professional organizations, each with their own growing body of dogma. We found these partially competing logics permeating our two major case sites (Allen, Bakos, & Kling, 1994; Allen, Kling, & Elliott, 1994). Also, as organizations face more intense time and cost pressures, they tend to make more use of available institutionalized packages such as temporary workers, or standardized software (Allen, Kling, & Elliott, 1994). This process leads to a new institutional challenge: trying to effectively fit together fixed packages of organizational procedures from the outside world.

In our research, we also found institutional theory useful for describing how organizational actors initially choose a legitimate new form of coordination. Of the many alternatives, organizational actors tend to repeatedly select from those few options that are publicly visible, and seen as legitimate. Teams are chosen as a popular coordination mechanism, even if their primary purpose is for cost reduction rather than involvement (Allen, Bakos, & Kling, 1994). Groups choose to coordinate others through a computer system, rather than engaging in a process of organizational redesign (Allen, 1992; Allen, Bakos, & Kling, 1994). Understanding the process of choosing coordination methods is an important part of accounting for IT's role in manufacturing coordination.

In sum, institutional theory allowed us to account for how external belief systems could become a significant force in coordination change, the tensions between different external logics that permeated the organizations, and the particular mechanisms used to choose new coordination techniques. Institutional theories expanded our ability to account for coordination issues that lie outside organizational boundaries. Institutional theories also gave us a way of understanding how different groups rely on different logics of coordination, rather than sharing a common unifying logic.

Structural Contingency Theory. Structural contingency theory views organizations as bureaucracies designed to complete tasks. The structure of any particular bureaucracy is determined largely by the uncertainty involved in their formal tasks (Galbraith, 1977). The greater the task uncertainty, the greater the amount of information processing required. Each kind of coordination structure, from standardized rules to cross-functional teams, can cope with a different level of uncertainty at a specific cost to the organization. Structural contingency theory is the behavioral perspective most closely associated with an information-processing view of coordination.

In our research, we found structural contingency theory most useful for characterizing the internal technical needs of manufacturers for coordination. Although institutional theory provided a better explanation of why particular coordination methods were selected and used in the AIRTECH case (Allen, Bakos, & Kling, 1994), structural contingency theory was able to explain the technical reasons why certain coordination choices were able to persist or perish. Structural contingency theory provides the vocabulary—task uncertainty, interdependence, and complexity—for discussing generic technical needs for coordination (Allen, Bakos, & Kling, 1994). It explains the most when there are strong technical demands on interdependent tasks, but (perhaps surprisingly) many manufacturing activities do not have strong technical demands. With its emphasis on information processing in the organization, however, structural contingency theory views can lead to an overemphasis on coordination as formal information exchange, instead of the interconnection of distinct groups (Beuschel & Kling, 1992).

Resource Dependency Theory. Finally, resource dependency theory holds that organizations obtain resources from their environments for survival (Pfeffer, 1982). According to resource dependency theory, organizations respond most readily to the demands of outside organizations that control critical resources. Groups within organizations who manage relations with powerful external organizations gain internal influence. Organizations strive to increase their autonomy relative to powerful organizations in their environment, and organizational subunits seek autonomy from each other.

Resource dependency theory, despite its early promise, was not used much by AIME research. AIME researchers did see some early examples of manufacturing coordination where resource dependency would appear to be an issue. The question of standardized computer systems is a resource dependency issue, both within and between firms. For example, one powerful customer demands the use of a standard CAD package, while another customer demands an entirely different package with different systems needs. Internal groups can be reluctant to become dependent on a shared, centralized system under the control of other groups. Despite this seemingly natural desire for autonomy, what remains to be explained is the incredible extent to which computerized coordination is creating new interdependencies between groups in manufacturing (Allen, 1994a), and the extent to which separate groups have been receptive to this linkage (Allen, 1994b). Autonomy-seeking does not seem to be a powerful explanatory tool across our multiple cases.

IT and the Balance Between Internal and External Coordination Costs: An Institutional Economics Perspective

Theoretical perspectives from institutional economics forms the other, complementary set of theories for AIME project research. Economic theories examine optimal ways to allocate resources under uncertainty and under the assumption that actors are individual utility maximizers. Institutional economic theories seek to identify effective ways to coordination and govern groups of economic agents in their transactions with each other (Kling et al., 1992).

Economic perspectives generally assume that agents behave opportunistically and rationally in their own interests. Organizations, markets, and institutions provide incentive and enforcement mechanisms for governance. The choice among governance mechanisms, as well as their structure and effectiveness, are dependent on the costs of the underlying processes. To the extent that IT affects the governance processes in organization, institutional economics perspectives can show how IT influences changes in organizational structure and performance.

Gurbaxani and Shi (1992) developed a comprehensive theory of the impact of IT on coordination in manufacturing organizations. This theory, based on the institutional economics perspectives of agency theory and transaction cost economics, provides a set of hypotheses about the impact of advanced manufacturing information technologies on coordination, and its resulting influence on organizational structure, processes, and performance.

In the Gurbaxani and Shi framework, manufacturing firms strive to select the incentive and governance structures that maximize economic returns. Manufacturing costs are determined by the sum of internal coordination costs, external coordination costs, and operations costs. Internal coordination costs are the combination costs incurred due to goal differences between economic principals and the agents they hire (agency costs), and the costs of making decisions with less than perfect information (decision information costs). According to agency theory, decision rights in an organization should be located where the total internal coordination costs are minimized. External coordination costs are the sum of costs associated with establishing and maintaining contractual relationships with other parties (contractual costs), and the costs resulting from losses of operational efficiency (operational costs). Operations costs refer to all other noncoordination costs, such as production.

The Gurbaxani and Shi framework predicts the following organizational outcomes from the use of IT for coordination. Coordination through IT will lead to the use of more performance-based compensation schemes. IT use will also lead to a flattening of organizational hierarchy. The reduction in internal coordination costs leads to a larger firm size, especially horizontal firm size. Effects on the location of decision rights are more complicated, because IT-based coordination tends to reduce both agency and decision information costs, potentially leading to increased decentralization or centralization, depending on other contextual factors. Changes in vertical firm size are also contextually dependent, because IT-based coordination leads to a simultaneous reduction in internal coordination costs, and the external coordination costs of using market-based mechanisms.

In practice, however, IT use has been broadly correlated with a decrease in firm size (Brynjolfsson, Malone, Gurbaxani, & Kanbil, in press). The decrease in firm size across a variety of measures—number of employees, revenues, and value-added per firm—suggests a decrease in both horizontal and vertical firm size. According to the Gurbaxani and Shi framework, this appears to make reductions in external coordination costs a more powerful explanation of economy-wide changes in firm size than reductions in internal coordination costs. However, as Brynjolfsson et al. argue, even if both internal and external coordination costs decrease relative to production costs, firms will favor the use of external markets to coordinate rather than their own internal hierarchies.

AIME project research has developed new institutional economy theory to better explain the complexities of reduced coordination costs. For example, a reduction in coordination costs due to IT should lead firms to increase the number of suppliers they use. Although there is evidence of increases in outsourcing, we find that leading firms in many industries are using fewer suppliers (Bakos & Brynjolfsson, 1993a).

The key to understanding this anomaly is to add the problem of incentive to a theory of coordination costs, particularly the supplier's incentive to invest in activities which improve quality (Bakos & Brynjolfsson, 1993a, 1993b, 1993c). By decreasing the number of suppliers, the buyer makes the relationship more permanent by making it more difficult to switch to alternative suppliers. The stability in the relationship gives the supplier the incentive to make "noncontractible" investments in quality, or investments that are difficult to specify and verify in contracts. Because the use of IT has increased the importance of product quality, this theory predicts that many firms will use fewer suppliers even when search and coordination costs are low.

This same analysis of the new importance of reward and incentive can be applied within the firm as well, to the relationship between managers and operators. The initial survey research indicates that the extremely dynamic computer disk drive industry has reduced the relative importance of individual production quantities, and has begun to reward behaviors which are difficult to quantify. As job design moves from individual operators to a more team and process-centered model, firms are most interested in rewarding skill acquisition and retention. This is despite the fact that CIM technologies are providing greater information than ever before on the details of the production process. Firms in these dynamic industries are more likely to make noncontractible investments in their labor force, such as training, and treat operators as less of a commodity.

EMPIRICAL RESEARCH ON COORDINATION

AIME project research has used the theoretical research described above to guide its empirical investigations of how manufacturers use IT to coordinate in practice. The empirical research, which integrates the results from the case studies and the pilot surveys, documents both the potential for IT to solve existing coordination problems, and to create new coordination problems that are sometimes easier, sometimes harder to solve.

How Do Organizations Use IT to Solve Coordination Problems?

There is widespread agreement that IT has the potential to solve important coordination problems. The economy-wide reductions in U.S. firm size (Brynjolfsson et al., in press) suggest that IT use is already enabling new ways of organizing that emphasize the use of network and market based coordination mechanisms.

The ways that IT is used to solve coordination problems in manufacturing are illustrated by the AIME project's long-term study of AIRTECH. In the AIRTECH case, we sought to explain the adoption of new coordination practices that fall under the label "World Class Manufacturing" (Allen, Bakos, & Kling, 1994). Many of these world class manufacturing techniques were being proposed as solutions to the problems of poor coordination in U.S. manufacturing, which had become a leading explanation of poor U.S. manufacturing performance in the 1980s. The ideal descriptions of these techniques, from just-in-time inventory control to concurrent engineering, suggest that they increase the quality of coordination between value-adding production activities.

The case study looked at the adoption of three coordination reforms—lead time reduction through MRPII systems, core competencies through manufacturing cells, and cross-functional teaming. Each of these coordination reforms solved key coordination problems for the organization (Allen, Bakos, & Kling, 1994). The MRPII computer system allowed operations management to quickly modify the assumptions built into the scheduling model across the entire organization. The manufacturing cells allowed AIRTECH to easily identify parts that fell outside of their core competencies, and thus could be outsourced. And the cross-functional teams enabled the early and continuous involvement of many functional areas in group projects. Coordination reforms that help the organization allocate and schedule, identify key products and processes for further improvement, or enhance communications are likely to solve some existing coordination problem. Clearly, information technology has the ability to contribute to all three of these possible kinds of solutions.

In another extended case study of a disk drive manufacturer, DISKCO, IT was able to help the organization coordinate in a different way. DISKCO required substantial improvements in both its production and coordination capabilities because of severe new market demands. The lifetime of products in their industry was being reduced from 5–7 years to 12–18 months. DISKCO's existing means of coordinating design, production, and sales were not intended to deal with this kind of time pressure, and a solution had to be found quickly, under severe resource constraints and a shrinking profit margin. Much like a design engineer might turn to an industry standard part, rather than custom designing in-house, when time is short and costs must be low, DISKCO changed its policy to buy as much standardized software and automated tooling from the outside world, rather than designing them in-house (Allen, Kling, & Elliott, 1994). These standard solutions allowed DISKCO to resolve an important, recurring coordination problem—how to bring up a new assembly line in a fraction of the time and cost of its traditional methods, involving many different functional areas and activities.

What New Coordination Problems Does IT Raise?

Each of the preceding cases revealed a number of fundamental strategies for coordination improvement, the possible role of IT in those improvements, and the actual use of IT for such improvements in selected firms. Although IT use solves some coordination problems, it also raises other new coordination problems. These new coordination problems are sometimes less important than the ones they help solve. However, sometimes they are so new or unconventional that they make the original coordination reform unsustainable (Allen, Bakos, & Kling, 1994). What makes some of these new coordination problems especially difficult is that they are often new types of problems, which conventionally organized manufacturing firms have little experience coping with.

Although specific coordination reforms are often described as changing the amount or quality of coordination, it may be more useful to view them as transformations, or transforming the set of coordination problems faced by the organization (Allen, Bakos, & Kling, 1994). Particularly as coordination problems become more complex and interdependent, transformations from one set of coordination problems to another may result in a new set of issues that may be less tractable for the organization.

In the work on supplier relationships described earlier, the ability of IT use to reduce the coordination problems of outsourcing brings an entirely new kind of coordination dilemma to the surface. How can we ensure that suppliers will participate in necessary, but difficult to verify, mutually beneficial investments? (Bakos & Brynjolfsson, 1993a). The problem of coordinating incentives to invest appears to be more challenging than the old coordination problems of finding suppliers in directories and paying the bills, if for no other reason than firms have less experience with managing this problem.

In the AIRTECH case, each of the coordination reforms created its own new set of coordination problems. In the case of cross-functional teaming, career paths and job performance evaluation were more problematic because both the cross-functional team and the traditional functional area were involved. When conflicts arose between different cross-functional teams, there was not a clear hierarchy for resolving disputes. However, these new problems were less critical than the gains from early cross-functional communication. In the case of the MRPII scheduling system, AIRTECH faced the difficult task of how to coordinate belief systems. The belief systems of operations management worked to unilaterally change the assumptions built into the factory scheduling model, with ultimately disastrous results (Allen, Bakos, & Kling, 1994). Operations management, fresh from a just-in-time seminar, decided to reduce the move and queue times in the scheduling model to zero, in accordance with what they saw as good just-in-time practice. Instead of encouraging reduced cycle times, the changes to the model, without corresponding changes in shop floor practice, made scheduling priorities even more unstable. AIRTECH fell further and further behind schedule.

It was clear that AIRTECH had no developed means of discussing or challenging these assumptions—they could only wait until the daily production situation deteriorated to the point where new operations management people were brought in. Despite the coordination gains of instantaneous, uniform updating of schedules and scheduling assumptions, AIRTECH was much less experienced with the problem of reconciling strong world views, and the effort to reduce lead time by modifying the MRPII systems was scaled back considerably.

The DISKCO case illustrates a new set of coordination dilemmas created by what we refer to as the *off-the-shelf* organization (Allen, Kling, & Elliott, 1994). When the technical demands of a market or key customers increase dramatically, organizations turn to preexisting pieces of institutionalized practices (such as temporary workers) and technologies (such as standardized software packages). The set of coordination problems in this case shifts in emphasis from coordinating traditional production and administration activities to coordinating the combining and fitting of standardized organizational parts, imported from the outside world, that may have partially competing logics (Allen, Kling, & Elliott, 1994).

At DISKCO, both temporary workers and the purchase of sophisticated automated tooling from the outside world were pursued as strategies for ameliorating tough coordination problems, yet their presence together created predictable tensions. A new software package, brought in from another division, made the skills developed on an internally developed system obsolete. DISKCO employees had spent years learning how to do ad-hoc data queries with their homegrown system. The new system, however, used an industry-standard database that DISKCO workers were unfamiliar with. The lack of programmers and users with the skills to use the new system reduced their access to important production data. Although DISKCO reaped tremendous coordination gains from using these standardized organizational pieces, by reducing the time to bring new products to market, they are still inexperienced with the new problems of coordinating the different pieces.

Other new coordination problems associated with IT relate to the infrastructure and skills required to make technology-centered visions of coordination work smoothly. Although a vision such as Computer-Integrated Manufacturing might emphasize coordination through cross-functional database linkage, this linkage requires significant amounts of resources and attention that often are not planned for, talked about, or sometimes even possible in an era where all organizational activities labeled as *support* are being cut from manufacturing budgets. A simple view of computerized coordination as a lower cost replacement for other organizational means of coordination, as in the example of a configuration management committee in the AIRTECH case, unrealistically discounts the amount of continuing human effort needed to coordinate (Beuschel & Kling, 1992). What kinds of coordination are viable depends on the existing institutionalized social arrangements? An increasingly centralized vision of IT-enabled coordination also contributes to inertia and reduced organizational experimentation, when more functional areas have to approve of all changes (Allen, 1992). Changing a particular technology is much faster than changing the skill and experience base that makes a technology useful for the manufacturing organization.

Addressing the New Coordination Dilemmas: Design for Organizational Usability

Some of the new coordination dilemmas posed by IT, such as a society-wide lack of key technical skills or an increase in quality awareness, cannot be solved by the individual manufacturing organization. However, other coordination dilemmas can be anticipated, given an understanding of the organization's history and configuration. Some of IT's coordination dilemmas can be partially managed by involving key organizational actors in a joint process of organizational and technological design, informed by behavioral theory. One method the AIME project has explored to address these problems is "design for organizational usability."

Systems usability refers to how well people can actually exploit a computer system's intended functionality. Usability can characterize any aspect of the ways that people interact with a system, even its installation and maintenance. There are two aspects of IT usability: interface and organizational. Interface usability is centered around an individual's effective adaptation to a user interface, whereas organizational usability is concerned with how computer systems can be effectively integrated into work practices of specific organizations. Although while the Human-Computer-Interaction (HCI) research community has helped pioneer design principles to improve interface usability, organizational usability is less well understood.

Design for organizational usability is a new term that refers to a process of designing computer systems so that organizational usability is the key focus of design (Elliott & Kling, 1997; Kling & Elliott, 1994). It includes, but goes beyond, the focus on user interfaces which is the subject of "design for usability" as currently understood in the HCI community. Design for organizational usability includes designing the infrastructure of computing resources that are necessary for supporting and helping people learn to effectively use systems. It encourages system designers either to accommodate to people's mix of skills, work practices, and resources, or to try to systematically alter them.

Design for organizational usability can be applied to the selection and integration of existing computer systems, or to the design of new systems, to improve the likelihood that people will use them effectively. Coordination issues within an organization's various departments are considered when designing for organizational usability, including: the design of the infrastructure of computing resources that are needed to support and coordinate various groups of users; the appropriate "fit" of computer systems into workers' mix of skills, work practices and resources; and the compatibility of data linkages and architectures between groups within an organization.

The motivation for design for organizational usability comes from the technical and organizational complexity of manufacturing firms we have observed in our AIME project case studies. The collection of computing systems in a medium to large-scale manufacturing firm are likely to be complex, both individually and as linked together. It is common for such systems to be ineffectively used by an organization in a way that does not realize the system's full potential. For example, CIM software may include an end-user database reporting package, but if it physical location in an organization is inaccessible to most employees, then many people who might benefit from this reporting facility are unable to do so. Reasons for ineffective use include poor user interface design; lack of adequate training; missing or unnecessary functionality; and/or a lack of coordination of systems usage by varying groups within an organization such as marketing, engineering, information systems (IS), manufacturing, distribution, and sales. The first two reasons for ineffective use are examples of traditional interface usability. In contrast, the second two are concerned with organizational usability. They involve training, and the facilitation of effective systems use in real working environments. The techniques associated with design for organizational usability are described in more detail in Elliott, Kling, and Allen, 1994.

IT CAN FACILITATE OR COMPLICATE COORDINATION IN SOCIALLY AND ECONOMICALLY COMPLEX SETTINGS

AIME project research has identified many specific kinds of coordination changes in manufacturing firms using IT, and has explored a set of economic and sociological concepts for explaining these changes. In this section, we summarize two main themes of our research. First, the explanations we have found most useful regarding how changes in coordination are actually taking place, and the role of IT in those changes. Second, describing the balance of new coordination opportunities and new coordination problems that are commonly found in IT-using organizations.

Environmental Demands Influence IT in Manufacturing Coordination

The starting point of AIME research was that information technology could play an important role in changing coordination, a role that needs to be investigated and understood. However, changes in coordination behavior are heavily dependent on existing features of the organization, and its environment. Inherent technological capabilities, we find, are selectively invoked and maintained by social and economic logics in the organization. Our research results are consistent with the claim that behavioral theories of coordination activity are needed to cope adequately with the new organizational challenges of coordination change.

AIME project research supports the contention that theories which take seriously the open systems nature of organizations (Kling & Jewett, 1994; Scott, 1992) are indispensable for describing changes in coordination. Both the institutional economics and organizational sociology perspectives foreground the dilemmas of coordinating multiple streams of activity, performed by individuals and groups with conflicting preferences. Despite their differences, institutional economics and organizational sociology share a fundamentally human concern with incentive and payoff, obligation and reciprocity.

Of all the open systems perspectives described, which ones *best* answer the question of how coordination changes? The answer depends, of course, on which question you most want to answer. Each of the theoretical perspectives used by the AIME project focuses on only a few significant parts of the larger coordination picture. The institutional economics perspectives used here are particularly appropriate for questions of incentive, monitoring, and contract enforcement. The organizational sociology perspectives are more useful for questions of group belief and power struggles. The key observation here is that "coordination" is defined so broadly that many different questions can be asked. Even questions that are largely unrelated.

The fundamental assumptions of each type of theory, however, define the limits of their practical usefulness. If a situation can be adequately described by utility maximizing individuals pursuing defined costs and benefits, economic perspectives have insight. If group phenomena, or group membership, is important, a sociological theory opens the possibility for that kind of analysis. These theoretical assumptions also suggest limits in practical use. In the AIRTECH case, the focus on taken-for-granted beliefs in institutional theory was more useful for describing the process of group selection and consensus around a particular reform than the more task-minded structural contingency theory. Structural contingency theory better explained the recurring technical barriers to the sustainability of some of the new coordination reforms (Allen, Bakos, & Kling, 1994).

This observation leads us to the most important tool we have discovered for evaluating the relative explanatory power of these theories: the nature of the environmental demands. Scott and Meyer (1991) defined two different dimensions to environmental demands: technical demands, and institutional demands (Allen, Bakos, & Kling, 1994). All organizations face technical and institutional demands from their environments, although to varying degrees. In technical environments, organizations are rewarded for effective and efficient control of their production systems as their products or services are exchanged in a market. In institutional environments, organizations must conform to an elaborate set of rules and requirements if they are to receive support and legitimacy. Institutional requirements may come from regulatory agencies, professional or trade associations, or from general belief systems held by society. A computer chip manufacturer in a commodity market may face only strong technical demands. A public school may face only strong institutional (regulatory and formal education) demands. A bank in a highly competitive market may face both strong technical demands (from customers) and strong institutional demands (from government regulators).

To the extent that organizations face strong technical demands, rational perspectives on organizations (such as agency theory, transaction cost theory, and structural contingency theory) will have the most explanatory value (Scott, 1992). To the extent that organizations face strong institutional demands, natural perspectives on organizations (such as institutional theory, and resource dependency theory) will have the most explanatory value. This hypothesis is consistent with the results reported in Allen, Bakos, and Kling (1994).

Manufacturing firms are typically seen as having strong technical environments, and relatively weak institutional requirements. Thus, rational theories should have the most explanatory power. AIME research suggests, however, that many manufacturers, particularly high tech manufacturers in industries such as aerospace and health care, also face very strong institutional demands (Allen, Bakos, & Kling, 1994). These surprisingly strong institutional demands, which are increasing, imply that accounting for coordination changes will increasingly require natural, as well as rational, perspectives on organizations. Even in manufacturing industries with only strong technical demands, however, we have found that large increases in the severity of technical demands force organizations to turn to institutionalized coordination methods from the outside world, in a process that is best understood through natural perspectives (Allen, Kling, & Elliott, 1994).

The special role of IT in these coordination choices is best understood in terms of how they tend to shift key parameters in the existing economic and social logics of the situation. In the Gurbaxani and Shi (1992) framework, IT plays a role in shifting internal and external coordination costs. Some of the impacts will likely be unidirectional, such as the increase in output-based compensation schemes. Others, such as the relative decrease in internal vs. external coordination costs, are more dependent on the particular set of choices, previous commitments, and features of the environment in any particular situation. In institutional theory, the role of IT as an embodiment of a particular belief system is essential in describing its coordination impacts. Institutional theory highlights the importance of the inherent attributes of a technology, but in this case it is the ability of IT to embody a particular set of values, and a definition of reality, rather than a generic ability to store, process, and transmit more information (Allen, Bakos, & Kling, 1994). The role of IT in coordination change is a tendency to shift key parameters in important preexisting behavioral logics.

IT Is Most Difficult to Use When Organizations Need It Most: Opportunities and Challenges of IT in Practice

In evaluating the costs and benefits of using IT to change coordination, researchers have understandably emphasized the obvious potential benefits. Many problems of coordination can be framed in terms of formal information exchange, and formal information processing: scheduling, communication, and simulation are a few examples. We have seen in our cases a significant number of opportunities for improving coordination through the application of IT's increased storage, processing, and networking power.

Information technology by its very nature, however, is a technology that opens up significant new coordination challenges. Unfortunately, these costs are often harder to see for those analyzing the problem than the benefits. They are also difficult to manage, because manufacturers typically have less experience with these coordination problems. The practical challenge of IT is to ensure that it solves more important coordination problems than it creates.

The coordination challenges most often mentioned in the context of IT use have to do with issues of infrastructure and skill (Kling, 1987, 1992a). The use of IT, particularly complex sets of multiple ITs joined together, requires a massive infrastructure of support and services that must be coordinated and maintained. Computer hardware and software costs are only a small fraction of the total "costs" of keeping IT running smoothly, and are increasing. Complex IT tends to demand new skills, both conceptual and technical, that are difficult to acquire and maintain. Because these coordination activities are often seen as "indirect," or "support" activities, they are particularly difficult to maintain and coordinate. Manufacturing is no exception to this. Indeed, the hostility toward *support* activities is probably even more intense than in other economic sectors.

Perhaps a more important new coordination challenge found in AIME project research is the problem of coordinating "worldviews." Coordination takes place between different groups, and individuals (Beuschel & Kling, 1992). IT has the potential to embed particular organizational values, both in terms of the resources and skills it requires to be maintained, and in the very design assumptions used in the definition of data models, access rights, and data policies. Through the viewpoint of institutional theory, many groups tightly coordinated through IT must also align the working assumptions built into the system. Through agency theory, the emphasis on tighter output monitoring begs the question of what exactly should be monitored, and how, since people have a strong tendency to work to what is measured, rather than what management intends (e.g., Grant, Higgins, & Irving, 1988). The coordination of assumptions is a particularly difficult coordination problem because it explicitly focuses on differences in purpose. When combined with a dependence on distant technical personnel, and a tight interlinkage with other groups that makes agreement on change difficult, the strong embedding of organizational assumptions makes for a particularly troublesome new category of coordination problems. The AIME project techniques of "design for organizational usability" are intended to address some of these new coordination dilemmas (Elliott & Kling, 1997; Elliott et al., 1994).

CONCLUSION

The AIME project has engaged in a multiyear research study of the role of IT in manufacturing coordination. The role of IT is best seen as introducing powerful new capabilities and constraints to an existing world of strong economic and social logics. Understanding the organizational challenges of these changes is possible with the use of behavioral theories from the social sciences.

Observers are often enthusiastic about the tremendous potential of IT to change manufacturing coordination for the better. This enthusiasm for new technological capabilities is understandable, but history suggests that the design, implementation, use, and impact of IT is shaped in important ways by established patterns of institutional behavior. AIME project research has investigated this process through the use of theoretical perspectives from institutional economics and organizational sociology.

The AIME project research on the role of IT in manufacturing coordination has been exploratory. However, the results from our multiyear study have been strongly consistent with the following claims:

1. *Efforts to improve coordination through IT need for a behavioral as well as an information-processing view of how IT changes coordination in practice.* Information-processing views of coordination change show how inherent attributes of IT directly improve organizational performance by solving key coordination problems of scheduling, synchronizing, and allocating. This information-processing view, however, gives us an incomplete understanding of how to cope with the chronic organizational problems involved in changing coordination practice within a world of powerful social and economic logics.
2. *The explanatory value of different behavioral theories of coordination depends on the nature of the environmental demands faced by an organization.* Rational systems perspectives on organizations, such as agency theory and structural contingency theory, explain coordination behavior in the face of strong technical demands. Natural systems perspectives on coordination, such as institutional theory, explain coordina-

tion behavior in the face of strong institutional demands. We find institutional demands to be surprisingly strong in manufacturing firms.

3. *IT can be used to solve many existing coordination problems without any substantial side effects.* This is especially the case when the problems and technologies are simple and straightforward. For example, IT has played a useful role in communicating production schedules, cross-functional team communications, and the ability to link organizational groups together to reduce new product and process introduction times. Standardized IT systems also allow organizations to dramatically change production processes quickly, at a low up-front cost.
4. *As coordination problems become more complex and interdependent, so often do the information technologies intended to solve them.* In such instances, it is more accurate to speak of the use of IT as *transforming* one set of coordination problems into another set of coordination problems. The new set of coordination problems may be more or less tractable for the organization. The "irony" of IT and coordination is that the new kinds of interdependencies created by the sustained use of IT may, in some circumstances, be more difficult to coordinate than the original problems IT use was supposed to address.
5. *The implementation of IT-based coordination technologies is easier when the new coordination problems do not face strong institutional demands.* IT-based coordination can bring to the surface the difficult problem of coordinating different "worldviews" and incentives, both within the organization and from outside professional and regulatory bodies. For example, centralized databases and close IT-mediated supplier relationships reveal differences in fundamental assumptions that have to be coordinated. Much of the difficulty is due to the relative inexperience organizations have in dealing with these new coordination problems. New design techniques and new institutional arrangements for organizational usability have the potential to make these coordination problems much less severe.
6. *The theoretical flexibility of IT makes it especially attractive when the dynamism of changing organizational practices can benefit from quick changes in information formats and information flows.* However, the actual implementation of IT-based coordination technologies locks in many specific design choices which can require substantial skilled labor time to renovate. Thus, IT use for coordination is more smooth when the formal, technical demands of production are clear, and do not create fundamentally new kinds of social and economic interdependencies. Even in these cases, however, a lack of infrastructural resources for skill-building and support can, and do, hamper technical implementation, given the severe resource constraints manufacturers are facing.

Changing a particular technology is much faster than changing the skill and experience base that makes a technology useful for the manufacturing organization.

7. *The use of IT for coordination is simplest in stable environments, but much more challenging in fast-moving industries.* The more rapidly information changes, the more that manufacturers turn to IT as a coordination solution. However, the time and discipline required for computerization and automation conflicts with the need for short time to market and frequent product changes. Firms in fast-moving industries, such as disk drive manufacturing, are focusing on non-IT changes to cope with the pace of the industry. Specifically, they are changing their reward and incentive systems to encourage skill acquisition, retention, and effective use for continuous improvement. Despite the increase in detailed process information, reward systems are increasingly concerned with encouraging behaviors that are difficult to quantify.

AIME project research has begun the important work of identifying and studying these practical opportunities, and problems. These results have the following implications for manufacturing practice:

1. *Efforts to implement IT for coordination are more likely to succeed if they consider social and economic aspects.* What must be carefully considered is the extent to which proposed information technology fits the organization's coordination problems, solves those problems, and/or creates new coordination problems.
2. *The less the degree of change required by the implementation of new information technologies, the greater the likelihood of successful implementation of the technology.* However, such incremental change might be part of radical organizational change brought about by business reengineering or other broader change in management or operational processes.
3. *The key to success in implementing more advanced IT for coordination is to plan for the greater complexity and organizational impacts brought about by the technology, and to provide social and institutional supports that facilitate the organization's adaptation to these changes.* Chief among the institutional supports are adequate financial resources, effective communication channels, and robust computing infrastructure.

The use of IT for coordination is more complex than much of the academic and practitioner literature suggests. Developing a better understanding of this complexity is the main challenge for scholars and researchers. Coping with this complexity is the main challenge for practitioners. This research is a first but important step in these directions.

ACKNOWLEDGMENTS

Research for this chapter was partially supported by NSF grant IRI 9015 497. We also benefited significantly from our discussions about coordination early in the project with our colleague Professor John King, and with later discussions about manufacturing with Dr. Werner Beuschel. We also appreciate the comments of reviewers, including Gary Olson. This project, as well as NSF's Coordination Theory focus, was enabled by Dr. Larry Rosenberg.

REFERENCES

Allen, J. P. (1992). Enabling Participatory Design in a Hierarchical, Tightly Integrated Setting. In *PDC '92: Proceedings of the Participatory Design Conference.* M. J. Muller, S. Kuhn, & J. A. Meskill (Eds.). Cambridge, MA: Computer Professionals for Social Responsibility.

Allen, J. P. (1994a). *Advanced Manufacturing Technology/Computer Integrated Manufacturing (AMT/CIM): A Review of Organizational Impacts.* Working Paper. Irvine, CA: Center for Research on Information Technology and Organizations, University of California.

Allen, J. P. (1994b). Mutual Control in the Newly Integrated Work Environments. *The Information Society, 10*(2), 129–138.

Allen, J. P., Bakos, Y., & Kling, R. (1994). *Sustaining New Coordination Methods: The Case of World Class Manufacturing.* Working Paper. Irvine, CA: Center for Research on Information Technology and Organizations, University of California.

Allen, J. P., Kling, R., & Elliott, M. (1994). *Technology and Skills in Off-The-Shelf Organizations.* Working Paper. Irvine, CA: Center for Research on Information Technology and Organizations, University of California.

Attewell, P. (1991). Skill and occupational changes in U.S. manufacturing. In P. S. Adler (Ed.), *Technology and the Future of Work* (pp. 46–88). New York: Oxford University Press.

Bakos, Y., & Brynjolfsson, E. (1993a). Why Information Technology Hasn't Increased the Optimal Number of Suppliers. *Proceedings of the 26th Hawaii International Conference on System Sciences*, January.

Bakos, Y., & Brynjolfsson, E. (1993b). Information Technology, Incentives and the Optimal Number of Suppliers. *Journal of Management Information Systems, 10*(2), 37–53, Fall.

Bakos, Y., & Brynjolfsson, E. (1993c). From Vendors to Partners: Information Technology and Incomplete Contracts in Buyer-Supplier Relationships. *Journal of Organizational Computing, 3*(3), 301–328.

Beuschel, W., & Kling, R. (1992). How Coordination Processes Influence CIM Development. In P. Brödner & W. Karwowski (Eds.), *Ergonomics of Hybrid Automation Systems-III: Proceedings of the 3rd International Conference on Human Aspects of Advanced Manufacturing and Hybrid Automation*, Gelsenkirchen, Germany.

Brynjolfsson, E., Malone, T., Gurbaxani, V., & Kanbil, A. (in press). Does Information Technology Lead to Smaller Firms? *Management Science, 40*(12), 1628–1644.

Bullen, C. V., & Bennett, J. L. (1996). Groupware in practice: An interpretation of work experiences. In R. Kling (Ed.), *Computerization and Controversy: Value Conflicts and Social Choices* (2nd edition). San Diego: Academic Press.

Cohen, S. S., & Zysman, J. (1987). *Manufacturing Matters: The Myth of the Post-Industrial Economy.* New York: Basic Books.

Cooper, R. B., & Zmud, R. W. (1990). Information technology implementation research: A technological diffusion approach. *Management Science, 36*(2), 123–139.

Dertouzos, M. L., Lester, R. K., & Solow, R. M. (1989). *Made in America: Regaining the Productive Edge*. Cambridge, MA: MIT Press.

Elliott, M., & Kling, R. (1997). Organizational usability of digital libraries: Case study of legal research in civil and criminal courts. *Journal of the American Society for Information Science, 48*(11), 1023–1035.

Elliott, M., Kling, R., & Allen, J. (1994). *Organizational Usability of Information Systems: Strategies for Assessment*. Working Paper. Irvine, CA: Center for Research on Information Technology and Organizations, University of California.

Galbraith, J. (1977). *Organizational Design*. Reading, MA: Addison-Wesley.

Grant, R. A., Higgins, A., & Irving, R. H. (1988). Computerized performance monitors: Are they costing you customers? *Sloan Management Review, 29*(3), 39–45.

Gasser, L. (1986). The Integration of Computing and Routine Work. *ACM Transactions on Office Information Systems, 4*(3), 205–225.

Grudin, J. (1994). Groupware and social dynamics: Eight challenges for developers. *Communications of the ACM, 37*(1), 92–105.

Gurbaxani, V., & Shi, E. (1992). Computers and Coordination in Manufacturing. *Journal of Organizational Computing, 2*(1), 27–46.

Harrington, J. (1973). *Computer Integrated Manufacturing*. Huntington, NY: Krieger.

Hayes, R. H., Wheelwright, S. C., & Clark, K. B. (1988). *Dynamic Manufacturing: Creating the Learning Organization*. New York: Free Press.

Jaikumar, R. (1986). Post-industrial manufacturing. *Harvard Business Review*, November–December, 69–76.

Kling, R. (1980). Social Analyses of Computing: Theoretical Orientations in Recent Empirical Research. *Computing Surveys, 12*(1), 61–110.

Kling, R. (1987). Defining the Boundaries of Computing Across Complex Organizations. In R. Boland & R. Hirschheim (Eds.), *Critical Issues in Information Systems* (pp. 307–362). London: Wiley.

Kling, R. (1991). Cooperation, Coordination, and Control in Computer-Supported Work. *Communications of the ACM, 34*(12), 83–88.

Kling, R. (1992a). Behind the Terminal: The Critical Role of Computing Infrastructure In Effective Information Systems' Development and Use. In W. Cotterman & J. Senn (Eds.), *Challenges and Strategies for Research in Systems Development* (pp. 153–201). London: Wiley.

Kling, R. (1992b). The AIME Project. *Coordination Theory and Collaboration Technology Workshop Proceedings*. Washington, DC: National Science Foundation.

Kling, R. (1993). The AIME Project. *Coordination Theory and Collaboration Technology Workshop Proceedings*. Washington, DC: National Science Foundation.

Kling, R. (Ed). (1996). *Computerization and Controversy: Value Conflicts and Social Choices* (2nd ed.). San Diego: Academic Press.

Kling, R., & Elliott, M. (1994). Digital design for organizational usability. *Proceedings of Digital Libraries '94 Conference* (pp. 146–155). J. L. Schnase, J. J. Leggett, R. K. Furuta, & T. Metcalfe (Eds.). College Station, TX.

Kling, R., & Iacono, S. (1984). Computing as an occasion for social control. *Journal of Social Issues, 40*(3), 77–96.

Kling, R., & Iacono, S. (1989). The institutional character of computerized information systems. *Office: Technology and People, 5*(1), 7–28.

Kling, R., & Jewett, T. (1994). The Social Design of Worklife With Computers and Networks: An Open Natural Systems Perspective. In M. C. Yovits (Ed.), *Advances in Computers* (Vol. 39, pp. 239–293). Orlando, FL: Academic Press.

Kling, R., Kraemer, K. L., Allen, J., Bakos, Y., Gurbaxani, V., & King, J. (1992). Information Systems in Manufacturing Coordination: Economic and Social Perspectives. *Proceedings of the Thirteenth International Conference on Information Systems*, Dallas, TX.

Knights, D., & Murray, F. (1994). *Managers Divided. Organization Politics and Information Technology Management*. London: Wiley.

Laudon, K. (1974). *Computers and Bureaucratic Reform*. Wiley-Interscience: New York.

Malone, T. W., & Crowston, K. (1994). The interdisciplinary study of coordination. *ACM Computing Surveys, 26*(1), 87–119.

Melnyk, S. A., & Narasimhan, R. (1992). *Computer Integrated Manufacturing: Guidelines and Applications from Industrial Leaders*. Homewood, IL: Business One Irwin.

Meyer, J. W., & Rowan, B. (1977). Institutionalized organizations: Formal structure as myth and ceremony. *American Journal of Sociology, 83*(2), 340–63.

National Research Council, Computer Science and Telecommunications Board (1994). *Information Technology in the Service Sector: A Twenty-First Century Lever*. Washington, DC: National Academy Press.

Orlikowski, W. J. (1993). Learning from Notes: Organizational Issues in Groupware Implementation. *The Information Society, 9*(3), 237–250.

Perrow, C. (1986). *Complex Organizations: A Critical Essay (3rd ed.)*. New York: Random House.

Pfeffer, J. (1982). *Organizations and Organization Theory*. Boston: Pitman.

Powell, W. W., & DiMaggio, P. J. (Eds.). (1991). *The New Institutionalism in Organizational Analysis*. Chicago: University of Chicago Press.

Powell, W. W., & Dimaggio, P. J. (Eds.). (1991). *The New Institutionalism in Organizational Analysis*. Chicago: University of Chicago Press.

Roven, B., & Pass, S. (1992). Manufacturing management information systems require simplification. *Industrial Engineering*, February, 50–53.

Scott, W. R. (1992). *Organizations: Rational, Natural, and Open Systems* (3rd ed.). Englewood Cliffs, NJ: Prentice Hall.

Scott, W. R., & Meyer, J. W. (1991). The organization of societal sectors: Propositions and early evidence. In W. W. Powell & P. J. DiMaggio (Eds.), *The New Institutionalism in Organizational Analysis* (pp. 108–142). Chicago: University of Chicago Press.

Scott Morton, M. S. (Ed.). (1991). *The Corporation of the 1990s: Information Technology and Organizational Transformation*. New York: Oxford University Press.

Shani, A. B., Grant, R., Krishnan, R., & Thompson, E. (1992). Advanced Manufacturing Systems and Organizational Choice: Sociotechnical System Approach. *California Management Review, 34*(4), 91–111.

Sheridan, J. W. (1992). The CIM evolution: Bringing people back into the equation. *Industry Week*, April 20, 29–51.

Wagner, I. (1996). Confronting ethical issues of systems design in a web of social relationships. In R. Kling (Ed.), *Computerization and Controversy: Value Conflicts and Social Choices* (2nd ed., pp. 889–902). San Diego: Academic Press.

Warner, T. N. (1987). Information technology as a competitive burden. *Sloan Management Review*, Fall, 55–61.

CHAPTER

17

Computer Support for Distributed Collaborative Writing: A Coordination Science Perspective

Christine M. Neuwirth
David S. Kaufer
Ravinder Chandhok
James H. Morris
Carnegie Mellon University

GOALS OF THE RESEARCH

The goal of our research is to provide computer support for distributed collaborative writing. Writers can be said to be distributed when they have distributed knowledge and skill, and they share that knowledge and skill in order to develop a draft; or, even when they have significant overlap in knowledge and skill, they distribute the work of producing the draft itself among them. But in this sense, all collaborative writing is distributed. In the sense we use the term here, distributed collaborative writing refers to, additionally, situations in which the writers are distributed in time (i.e., they do not work on the artifact at the same time) or place (i.e., they do not meet face-to-face). The central research questions in distributed collaborative writing are: What does the process of producing a written product look like when it is divided among writers who coordinate to produce it over time and space? and What is the relationship of these processes to success? When the process includes "active agents," the scope of the first question shifts slightly to include not only people, but computers as well. This question is, of course, the central question of "distributed cognition" or "coordination science," applied to collaborative writing. Analogous with the way cognitive scientists (psychologists, AI researchers, and so on) are interested in identifying strategies and representations involved in individual cognition, coordination scientists are interested in identifying the strategies and representations that groups of "agents"—people and computers—use to coordinate their activities (Malone, 1988).

The central question of computer support for distributed collaborative writing is: What are the requirements for supporting distributed collaborative writing processes? This question is related to the previous questions: in order to produce knowledge that is useful in designing computer support, the description of strategies and representations needs to be sufficiently detailed that it yields answers to a set of related questions, including (a) What problems do such writers have and are there ways computers can mitigate them? (b) Are there ways computers can augment the processes? (cf. Olson & Olson, 1991).

There are properties of the process of writing that makes it an interesting, although challenging, application domain for coordination science. Writing is an open-ended design process. A *design* process is one that involves the creation of an artifact. An *open-ended* design process is one in which any existing specifications for the artifact leave many design decisions open, design decisions that nevertheless must be made in order to create it. Moreover, any specifications that might exist are often open to interpretation, and the more heterogeneous the background knowledge and skills of members of the collaborative writing group, the more likely that differences in interpretation will arise (Gabarro, 1987). As a result of these properties, there may be situations in which members of the collaborative writing group do not have shared knowledge, shared goals or criteria, or even a shared representation of how best to proceed with the task (cf. Hewitt, 1986).

OUR RESEARCH STRATEGY

Our research strategy can be outlined by the following steps (Neuwirth & Kaufer, 1992):

- Identifying writers (e.g., novices, experts) and a writing task (e.g., coauthoring). In our research, we have not focused on collaborations in which coauthors or commenters interact face-to-face, although systems that support research into the issues such collaborations raise are clearly valuable (McLaughlin Hymes, & Olson, 1992; Olson, Olson, Storrøsten, & Carter, 1992).
- Building a theory- and research-based model of the task, with a focus on user-centered design (Gould, 1988). Understanding how writers function and hypothesizing the sources of their successes and failures is vital to building tools to support writers. The model draws on techniques, both cognitive and social, for building models of composing processes, but focuses on *problems* that writers—even experienced ones—have with the task. This model informs the design of technology.

- Designing technology to alleviate these problems. This step involves building a theory of the *prima facie* ways computers can augment writers' performance of the task by drawing on a theory of the role of external representations and a theory of task activity. The technology represents a hypothesis about a solution, perhaps a partial solution, to some needs or problems identified by the theory- and research-based model. We have embodied our theories of distributed collaborative writing into a "work in preparation" (PREP) editor, a multiuser environment to support a variety of collaborative and, in particular, coauthoring and commenting relationships for scholarly communication.
- Studying the technology in use, with the aim of building knowledge that will help to refine the model of the task and the design of the technology.

These steps are interconnected and often recursive. For example, studying one of our software tools, the Comments program, in actual use led us to refine our model of the task and to design a new software tool, the PREP Editor (Neuwirth, Kaufer, Keim, & Gillespie, 1988; Neuwirth, Kaufer, Chandhok, & Morris, 1990). Indeed, given that all writing involves technology (e.g., pen and paper), the last step can be thought of as the second step repeated. It is not necessary for the steps to be carried out by the same group of researchers. A study by a group of empirical researchers observing a software tool in use may be relevant to researchers working at other steps, perhaps on the theory of composing or on the design of software. For example, the work of Haas and Hayes (Haas, 1989a, 1989b; Haas & Hayes, 1986), which identified the problems writers have of getting a "sense" of their texts when using word processors, added to our theoretical understanding of the process of composing by identifying an additional subprocess, the subprocess of reading one's own writing, and highlighting its importance. This result stimulated further research into the role of reading during writing, both in print and hypertext environments, and has been used by our research group to inform software design.

Although it is not necessary, then, for the steps to be carried out by the same group of researchers, it is necessary, or at least desirable, that researchers understand the interconnectedness of the steps in order to increase the likelihood that results they produce at one step will be relevant to other steps.

THE PROCESS OF COLLABORATIVE WRITING

In the following, we outline our model of collaborative writing. In its major outlines, we have drawn heavily upon the process model of writing developed by Flower and Hayes (1981a; Hayes & Flower, 1980). Although developed for single authors, the empirically based model is also a useful starting point for characterizing the cognitive processes involved in collaborative writing and, supplemented by observations about actual collaborative writing groups, in deriving design requirements for computer support for those processes. We next introduce the major components of the model: planning, drafting, and reviewing, discuss some implications of the model for design requirements, and provide examples of how our prototype attempts to meet those goals.

In order to make general observations about collaborative writing concrete and to gain further insight into how to support groups, we observed groups of writers working under the following conditions: able to meet face-to-face; able to work at the same time but not face-to-face; and neither able to meet at the same time nor place. The groups, consisting of three writers each, were asked to write a press release, respond to two letters, and write a brief report on their activities.[1] In the following, we describe PREP Editor's support for collaborative writing by drawing on observational data from one of these groups, the group that was neither able to meet at the same time nor place.

Planning

Planning refers to processes of generating (a) criteria for the text (e.g., the purpose of the text, features the text needs in order to meet the needs of its audience, and so on), (b) ideas for the content of the text, (c) plans for how to organize that content, and (d) plans for how to proceed with the process of writing itself (e.g., deciding that particular people will write particular parts of the document or do particular tasks such as review for technical accuracy or style).

When writers work alone, they may not need to articulate the constraints they have imposed and the goals they have set (although studies of experienced writers working alone indicate that they do, indeed, record *some* of their plans). Not surprisingly, coauthors often need to communicate about plans in order to refine their views of the goals that coauthors have generated and increase the likelihood that they will generate compatible products.

From a coordination science perspective, coauthors (or coauthors and reviewers) must manage a producer–consumer relationship—that is, whatever is produced should be usable by the activity that receives it (Malone & Crowston, 1994). This producer–consumer relationship applies not only to the usability of the final draft for readers, but also to the usability of intermediate drafts that coauthors–reviewers exchange among themselves. Communication about plans, goals and constraints may improve usability by sav-

[1]We studied the group's activities and interaction behavior by observing and videotaping their meetings asking subjects working alone to think-aloud. The group members were Ph.D. students in English.

ing coauthors and commenters from having to infer the other's plans. If other coauthors understand the goal, they may be more likely to be able to produce revisions to the draft that are compatible with the first author's goals, and the draft they produce is more likely to be seen as useful by the other author. Or, if another author has a different point of view, it may be more likely to surface and be resolved. Of course, unnecessary communication can also be distracting, leading to a degradation in performance. Research we are currently conducting attempts to relate such patterns of communication to measures such as the time to complete a project and the quality of the product.

When collaborative writers are able to meet face-to-face, they can communicate about plans relatively easily: Face-to-face communication is both highly interactive (e.g., requests for clarification can be answered immediately) and expressive (e.g., facial cues and gestures can also be used to communicate). Even face-to-face communication, however, is not without its problems, and, interestingly, may be augmented by computer support (Olson et al., 1992). But writers seem to experience more difficulties when working over distances. In a study of groups of writers working face-to-face versus at a distance, for example, Galegher and Kraut (1994) reported that writers, working at a distance with traditional computer-mediated communication tools (e.g., email and conferencing tools) and phone, needed to spend more time to achieve the same quality of result and reported less satisfaction with their work and with other members of the group than those working face-to-face. Two recent lines of research represent attempts to mitigate these problems. The first, shared editors supplemented by audio (e.g., phone) and video links, allow writers to communicate at the same time over distances, supported by the ability to see an evolving draft. The PREP Editor prototype can approximate synchronous communication through a set of parameters that allow writers to control how quickly replicated copies are transmitted to others (Neuwirth, Chandhok, Charney, Wojahn, & Kim, 1994). The second line of research focuses on writers working over distances asynchronously. We have extensive experience with our prototype for supporting the latter, and will focus on ways we have seen it used here.

A collaborative writing group can use PREP Editor's column interface to discuss initial design decisions. Figure 17.1 shows a display in which one writer has formulated a set of questions about the writing project as a whole in the leftmost column; the second and third columns, which are linked to the first, depict responses from the other writers. Although collaborative writers can use the PREP Editor interface to discuss such overall design decisions and we have observed them doing so spontaneously, an important outstanding research question remains whether this interface is effective in facilitating such discussions. Some groups we have observed continue to use email to conduct such discussions. Whether this is a matter of adapta-

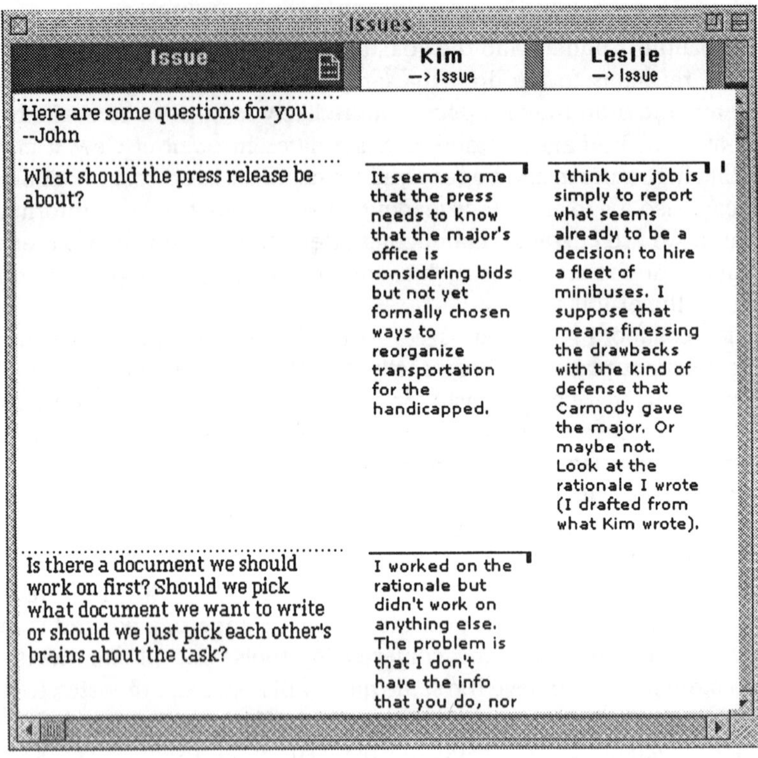

FIG. 17.1. Communication about initial design decisions in the PREP Editor.

tion remains to be seen. The groups we observed were not shown this possible use of the tool, although we are conducting an observational study in which this use will be demonstrated.

Groups of collaborative writers using the PREP Editor over distances use the tool frequently and spontaneously to communicate about plans, goals, and constraints in a way that is grounded in an evolving draft. As an example of such communication, Fig. 17.2 depicts the draft of a letter, together with the author's own comments on the draft, intended for the other writers and explaining the goal of the paragraph. (Note also, the author indicating a judgment about the completeness of, and confidence in, parts of the document).

Although there is a tendency to equate the act of writing with producing the content of the written draft, studies show that experienced writers typically engage in many acts of writing (e.g., jotting down ideas, drawing) that bear no direct relation to the text product, but serve as inexpensive, intermediate external representations to remind writers of their plans for audience, purpose, and procedure, as well as content (Flower & Hayes, 1981b;

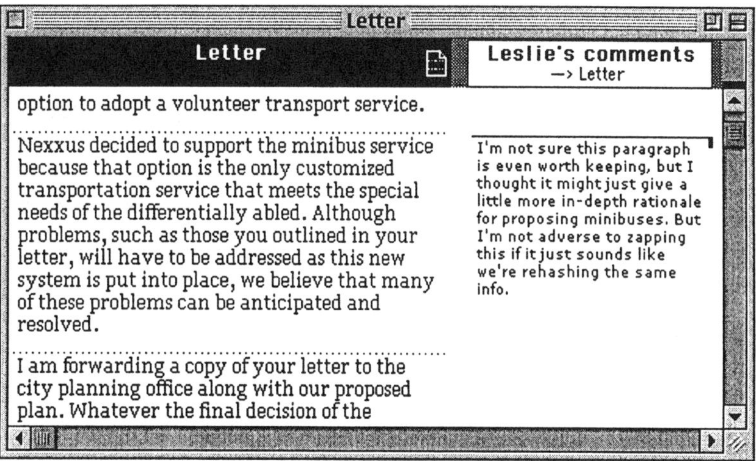

FIG. 17.2. Communication about plans, goals and constraints in the PREP Editor.

Flower, Schriver, Carey, Haas, & Hayes, 1989; Haas, 1990). When working with computer environments that do not support the creation of arrows, boxes, or other diagrams for displaying conceptual relationships among ideas and the suppression of detail, writers report frustration (Bridwell-Bowles, Johnson, & Brehe, 1987) and important planning activity is curtailed (Haas, 1989b). Thus, observations of expert writers at work suggest that supporting the jotting, drawing and note-taking that writers engage in as they write are especially important in writing and that cognitive aspects must be taken into account when designing computer support for coauthoring and commenting tools. There have been some attempts to understand the task-specific activities (e.g., jotting, drawing, writing, gesturing) that occur in collaborative tasks in order to inform the design of specialized tools to support those tasks (Stefik, et al., 1987; Tang & Leifer, 1988). But because there is a tendency to equate the substantive work of writing with a written draft, most text annotators support only communication about the working draft or outlines of a draft. The PREP Editor contains a drawing tool and the objects produced in the drawing can be annotated, but it has not been used extensively to support planning by groups we have observed. An outstanding research question is to what extent this may be due to the fact that the very rough sketches and private jottings that writers working alone produce are less "sharable" artifacts and to what extent it is a deficiency in the tools to facilitate such informal sketching. An interesting research approach might be to provide tools for graphically based idea generation, roughly corresponding to the "network mode" in Smith, Weiss, & Ferguson's Writing Environment (1987), along with pen-based input.

Drafting

Drafting is the process of producing text. Studies of experienced writers indicate that they often set new goals for themselves as they draft, that is, they discover what it is they want to say in the process of saying it (Hayes & Flower, 1980). As a result of this property of writing, a collaborative writer's knowledge of other participants and their actions may be uncertain or changing. This has been confirmed by case studies of collaborative writers at work. For example, Kaye (1993) observed:

"Regardless of the level of detail in a . . . specification . . . , more often than not, the author's ideas only become clear when the extended . . . draft is being written. As a result, colleagues' perceptions of what is being written (based on an earlier draft) may not be an accurate reflection of what any individual team member is in fact writing. Riley (1984) referred to this as the "out-of-step" phenomenon. . . . Various informal tactics are used to minimize the likelihood of [integration] problems arising, and this is obviously fairly straightforward when . . . colleagues work in adjacent offices and see each other regularly, both formally and informally, in between the . . . meetings" (pp. 47–48).

Any system to support collaborative writing needs to accept that any plans made in advance of drafting do not completely control drafting; indeed, that plans will not be made completely in advance of writing and must support communication about changes in plans. Groups using PREP Editor use the interface to discuss evolving plans frequently.

A second property of drafting is that the partially completed product plays an important role in open-ended design processes: The partially completed product becomes part of the task environment and constrains the subsequent course of the design. Writers frequently re-read portions of the text they have produced to provide constraints for another segment of text that they want to produce (Flower & Hayes, 1981a; Kaufer, Hayes, & Flower, 1986). From a coordination science perspective, the draft itself is a "shared resource" that all writers may benefit from accessing, even if they have agreed to work on a particular part.

These two properties of drafting suggest that there will be situations in which collaborative writers could benefit from having parts of the document that others are working on available. This observation must be tempered, however, by noting the need to take the wide variability of writing groups into account. Some writing groups want updates to drafts to be available immediately to all members of the group. Other groups want information about changes delayed until the source has been able to check them for correctness and "commit" to them. For example, Newman and Newman (1993) described a case study of a large group of writers working on a document to support budget allocation decisions within their organization. Different departments had responsibility for different parts of the document, and the outcome of the budget allocation would affect their respective budgets. In this case, departments concealed early drafts from members of other departments, so that the text would not be available to writers outside the department until the political issues had been thought through by writers inside the department. Likewise, individual authors vary considerably in their styles of working (Posner & Baecker, 1992), with some authors anxious to receive immediate feedback on even "half-baked" ideas, whereas other authors, as Kaye (1993) observed, do their writing in concentrated bursts of activity prior to previously agreed deadlines, and, in any case, may not wish to make their developing drafts public (p. 48).

These observations suggest that a system to support collaborative writers should provide authors with the ability to be flexible in making parts of documents visible. We have defined a set of parameters of interaction for the networked version of our prototype, parameters that allow writers flexibility in sharing partial results along the dimensions of who to share with, and what, when, and how quickly to share (Neuwirth et al., 1994). Each user can set these parameters to define his or her own pattern of data exchange. For example, setting parameters for data to flow automatically at a grain size of a keystroke with fast transmission speed approximates synchronous communication. On the other end, setting parameters for data to flow only upon explicit request at a grain size of the column models the situation in which a coauthor requests to see the latest version of another coauthor. By setting these parameters, users can adjust the characteristics of the information flow.

A good deal of the work has been directed at mapping flexible social protocols onto practical communication protocols. Clearly, if social protocols are to be flexible, data exchange protocols (within a system) and network protocols (across systems) must be as well. As far as the flexibility of data exchange within a system is concerned, Dewan and Choudhary (1991) argued that systems must be flexible in their assumptions about data interaction. They proposed a set of system primitives that would allow users to calibrate their assumptions about the exchange of information (not simply data, but views, formats, and windows as well) to other users in a flexible fashion. Our work builds on some of their primitives by allowing for the incremental versus complete exchange of data, but extends it for collaborative writing applications. Future work needs to extend this to sharing views and windows as well.

The fact that different writing situations require integration of asynchronous and synchronous styles of work has also been noted (Dourish & Belotti, 1992; Posner & Baecker, 1992). Minör and Magnusson (1993) presented a system to support an integration of writers' asynchronous and synchronous work strategies. Their model is similar to the one described here, in that it is based on working with copies of a document rather than actually sharing a document. It differs in that, when a user opens a version of a document that is currently being edited by another user, the system attempts to make users aware of each other's activities by showing the differences between two versions of the document. Other parameters of interaction (grain size, flow, and so on) are not defined. The underlying model relies on system knowledge of the hierarchical nature of documents (e.g., sections, subsections). In contrast, the model described here requires minimal interpretation of the document structure per se (import/export algorithms that support reading documents produced in other word processors interpret paragraph breaks as chunks).

Up to this point, we have only discussed collaborators *viewing* sections of documents that are being worked on by others. There is reason to suppose, however, that it can also be useful for collaborators to be able to change sections of documents being worked on by others. Because texts have "texture," that is, coherence relations throughout, a change in one section may require changes in another. That is, although writers may decompose writing the document into subtasks, the decomposition almost always entails interdependencies among subtasks. Although it is possible for an author to suggest a change to an author of another section, it is sometimes more efficient to simply "do it." In our model, coauthors can choose to accept a nonconflicting change automatically or to receive notification of the change with final approval residing with the coauthor responsible for the section.

Reviewing

The process of reviewing consists of two subprocesses: evaluating text and revising text. Often this evaluation and review process takes the form of comments on the text. The problems with comments, that is, critical notes on texts, are well-known and legion: Writers don't understand comments, they think the comments reflect confused readings rather than problems in their texts, they are frustrated by perceived lack of consistency in comments and contradictory comments (Neuwirth et al., 1988). The problems in author–commenter relationships become even more pressing if authors solicit comments from multiple readers. From a coordination science perspective, there is also a consumer–producer relationship that must be managed in the review process.

When collaborative writers can meet face-to-face, this relationship can be managed by communication about the comments. For example, in an observational study of a group of physicists working to produce an article over a period of months, Blakeslee (1992) observed face-to-face meetings in which members of the group discussed and clarified comments that they had made on drafts. This suggests that computer support for distributed collaborative writing should support discussion, not only about plans and drafts, but also about the comments themselves.

A second form that evaluation and review takes, at least among coauthors, is actually making changes to parts of a document that someone else has written. A principal difficulty coauthors face is in coping with those changes, especially understanding why the other person made them. For example, in a study of eight writers' production of an insurance company's two-page annual report, Cross (1990) observed that each writer "omitted, added, highlight or modified" the text to agree with his or her preconception, with unexplained changes causing "considerable frustration" for other writers and an undetected change causing a major problem (p. 193).

This suggests that a system to support collaborative writing should support the detection of changes from one version to another, along with supporting communication about those changes (e.g., annotating the changes with questions about the decision and explanations of changes).

With paper documents, even reviewers often make "changes" in content by marking up the draft. This phenomenon may be due to the fact that many significant problems in texts (e.g., voice, persuasiveness, organization), although easy for an experienced writer to detect, cannot be easily described. For such problems, rewriting is often a more efficient strategy than trying to describe the problem, and writers often choose this strategy when revising others' texts (Hayes, Flower, Schriver, Stratman, & Carey, 1987). Some early systems to support collaborative writing (Comments, Quilt) restricted reviewers to the role of attaching comments to the base document. Although this increases the usability of the commenters' activities from the point of view of the author, it seems to increase the difficulty of the task for reviewers. In our observations of reviewers working with the Comments prototype, writers in the role of commenters often copied a region of the base document into a commenting box and proceeded to rewrite the copy. Writers who worked in this fashion, however, reported difficulties in revising because their revisions were physically separated from the larger body of text. More specifically, they reported needing a "sense of the whole text" even when commenting on a part. One exasperated commenter went so far as to copy an *entire* document into a comment box and to revise it from there. Whether a commenter is able to modify the base document or not should certainly depend on his or her rightful relationship (coauthor, commenter) to the text. Despite potential problems, role specification is likely to be a useful strategy for managing some coordination problems; our design, however, allows new ways of dealing with this interdependency by giving commenters the ability to rewrite his or her *view* of the text and supporting ways for authors to see the changes as proposed changes to the original base document.

Figure 17.3 depicts an interface for detecting changes from one version of a draft to another in the PREP Editor. The comparison interface produces its report in a new column, with the differences linked to the original column for

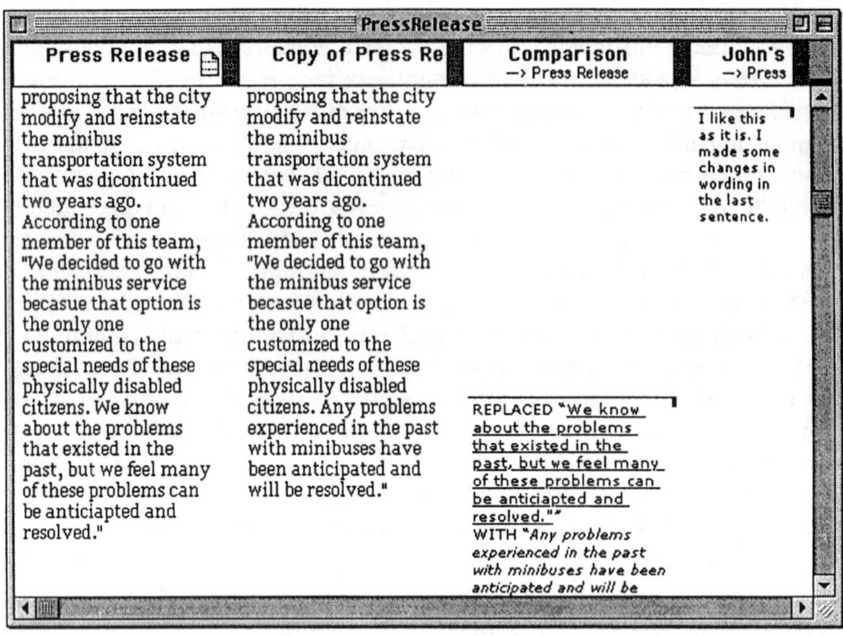

FIG. 17.3. Communicating about changes in drafts.

easy, side-by-side evaluation. To illustrate, Fig. 17.3 depicts four columns: an original draft, its revision, the comparison report, and an evaluation column. An author can "push" particular revisions across the link, as in InterNote (Catlin, Bush, & Yankelovich, 1989). The evaluation column in Fig. 17.3 consists of annotations to the comparison report that a coauthor produced in order to explain some of the changes or to solicit advice about them. An important feature of the interface is the ability of users to annotate changes with explanations of the change or questions to coauthors. Our group's experience with this feature suggests that reviewers will annotate changes selectively in order to draw their coauthors' attention to changes they want to discuss or explain. Likewise, a coauthor can ask a reviewer to explain a change. Our hypothesis is that the ability to annotate changes will greatly alleviate writers' frustrations with undetected and unexplained changes that Cross (1990) observed.

We have experimented with heuristics for automatically generating comparison reports, depending on role relationships among writers. For example, if the annotated draft is from a coauthor, then display changes upon request; if from a reviewer, then display all changes automatically. Apart from generating the comparison before returning the revision (which we, as coauthors, currently sometimes do), the revision's author has little control over how the comparison might be done. As this information might lead to a more productive exchange, we plan to experiment with adding "comparison settings" information to revisions that would serve as hints from the coauthor to anyone who would generate a difference report.

THE PREP EDITOR PROTOTYPE

The PREP editor[2] prototype, then, embodies part of our theory of collaborative writing. It approaches requirements by supporting communication about plans, constraints, drafts, comments, and so on, and by providing a flexible set of parameters for interaction. Central to the PREP editor is a focus on providing a usable, visual representation of the information that will allow new ways of managing interdependencies in open-ended design tasks, in addition to supporting existing patterns.

The Interface

Much of our work has focused on the interface, specifically on the visual representation of the draft and an optimized action grammar. For the visual representation, we have pursued a path that could be called "dynamic glossing," because we support annotation in a style similar to old, glossed scholarly texts. Although in some sense this means that we are mimicking the static annotation process, we are also taking advantage of the dynamic nature of the computer to use visual cues such as shading and spatial relationship to show the interconnections among chunks in the system. To create a visual system that will lend itself to providing and accessing comments easily, the visual grammar must be capable of supporting writers' needs. We have found, for example, that visual alignment of comments is a useful feature for allowing collaborators to see comments "at a glance" (see Fig. 17.1), but in a flexible system, the general case requires a constraint-based layout algorithm that can handle arbitrary shapes and complex interconnections among dynamically selected items (Smolensky, Bell, Fox, King, & Lewis, 1987). We have also worked on the action grammar, optimizing actions that are used frequently. For example, to create a comment, a writer need only click and drag the mouse.

The cognitive needs of collaborative writers are too numerous to detail here. We focus, therefore, on one: accessing comments. Most text annotation systems are based on a hypermedia model and the primary method for

---

[2]The prototype runs on Macs and is available by anonymous ftp at http://eserver.org/software/prep. See also http://www.sixthfloor.com/CS1.html for a commercial product, Common Space, based on this research.

accessing information in hypermedia systems is following link icons from node to node. Typically the user brings a node (e.g., a text node) onto the screen, reads its contents and notes any links, then chooses to traverse some of the links. Such localized link following is adequate for browsing tasks but has been problematic for others (Halasz, 1987). For example, we have found that coauthors and commenters want to visually scan a set of comments quickly and resent the time required by the "search and click" interface to call up each comment, inspect it and put it away. Some researchers have worked to tailor the navigational linking system of hypermedia systems to meet user's writing needs (Catlin et al., 1989; Edwards, Levine, & Kurland, 1986; Fish, Kraut, Leland, & Kurland, 1988; Neuwirth, Kaufer, Chimera, & Gillespie, 1987), but the access problem remains to be addressed. Our approach calls for a tailoring the program to match user's cognitive activities (Norman, 1986).

We have previously analyzed the design features of 12th-century glossed bibles in Cavalier, Chandhok, Morris, Kaufer, & Newirth (1991) and the match to the cognitive needs of commenters. The analysis suggests the following requirements (see Fig. 17.1):

- *The primary text is easily distinguishable from the annotation text.* This requirement allows readers, who may not have seen either the original text or the annotations, to orient themselves to the texts quickly. In glossed bibles, this distinction was usually made by varying type size: the primary text is several points larger than text in the annotations. Of course, other typographic signals such as color could also be used.

- *The annotations are visible "at a glance" while reading the primary text.* This requirement minimizes the problems readers have in accessing annotations. Glossed bibles were usually the result of calligraphic as well as scholarly effort; the annotations were packed in an aesthetically pleasing fashion onto a page, so that all annotations, no matter how dense, are visible. As the corpus of annotations increased over time, the books were recopied with more space for annotations, preserving the easy access by expanding the leading between the lines in the primary text as needed to insure the visual alignment of all annotations.

- *The relationship between the primary text and the annotations is easy to see.* This requirement insures that readers will be able to see which annotations refer to particular portions of text. In glossed bibles, the annotations were typically aligned horizontally to the primary text, so it is possible to scan from the primary text across to the annotation rapidly. Moreover, the scope of the annotation was usually indicated by graphic symbols in the primary text.

- *Different contributors are readily distinguishable.* This requirement aids readers in interpreting annotations by different commentators. The different annotators of glossed bibles are easily distinguishable because each has his or her own column.

The result of all these features of glossed bibles was that *access* to the annotations was superior to most electronic annotation systems. The reader could quickly skim the set of annotations "at a glance." For the scholar, the assignment of marginal "real estate" allowed for quick and easy annotation. A comment could be made as quickly as moving the pen to the adjacent margin. In addition, several scholars often annotated a document side by side, leading to an easy to follow parallel discussion that was the synthesis of both sets of comments. We have embodied these features in the PREP Editor prototype.

Implementation

The PREP Editor utilizes an underlying node–link architecture. This section describes those mechanisms and discusses the features that underlying hypertext engines need to provide to support annotations as they are implemented in PREP. Although the PREP Editor prototype restricts itself to linear texts, the model employed can be applied in those portions of a hypertext applications that provide design objects to support a linear layout of nodes and links, for example, GUIDE, the Rhetorical Space in SEPIA (Haake & Wilson, 1992).

To describe the PREP architecture and interface, we use terms drawn from the Dexter hypertext reference model (Halasz & Schwartz, 1990). The Dexter model divides hypertext functionality into three layers: *the storage layer*—the node–link network structure; *the runtime layer*—the mechanisms supporting the user's interaction with the hypertext (including presentation); and *the within-component layer*—the content and structure *within* nodes and links. The fundamental entity in the Dexter storage layer model is a component, either an atomic component (or node), a link component (or link), or a composite component (or composite node) composed of other components.

The Column: A Composite Component/Linear Presentation Pair. The PREP Editor defines a *column* to be a composite node consisting of atomic or composite nodes with "path" links between them, forming the nodes into a connected graph. The nodes of a column are further constrained in that the "path" links, together with a traversal mechanism defined for them, must allow the hypertext runtime layer to construct a linear ordering for the nodes (i.e., to display the nodes linearly). The structure of links among the nodes does not *have* to be restricted to a directed-acyclic graph (DAG), but the traversal mechanism must include a decision rule for finitely terminating any cycles.

The Annotation Link: A Binary, Directional, Typed Link. "Annotation links" are binary, directional, typed links from a source node to an annotation node. The PREP Editor allows users to create annotation links between columns (i.e., composite nodes).[3] For example, in Fig. 17.1, the two columns on the right are linked to the leftmost column. Such links define a tree of linked columns (although a single PREP document can hold a forest of these trees). Links between columns allow users to create annotations rapidly: A user only has to locate *where* in the primary text to make an annotation and click next to that location in the linked column to make both a link and new node.[4] This user interface allows us to approximate the ease of paper-based annotating by proximal writing in a margin. However, PREP goes one step further than a paper-based metaphor in that PREP annotations remain aligned to their source even as the source text is edited.

The Layout Algorithm. In most hypertext systems, a link, regardless of its type, is represented in the runtime layer layout as a line connecting two squares (in a graph view), or is represented by an icon that is given a "follow it" interpretation when the user clicks on it. The links in the PREP application, however, carry different implications for the runtime–presentation layer. Path links between nodes in a column result in a linear, scrollable display of the nodes that look like an ordinary document in a word processor. Annotation links between columns result in the linked column being allocated (by default) a narrower display and smaller font; unlinked columns, which usually contain a primary text, are allocated (by default) a wider display and larger fonts. Annotation links between nodes result in the nodes being displayed in a side-by-side, horizontal alignment.

An object-oriented constraint-based layout algorithm is at the heart of determining and maintaining side-by-side layout of annotations. Whenever a user changes the screen through some operation on a column or node—creating, moving, deleting, linking, adding to, and so on—constraints from the local objects on the screen whose display is affected by the change are placed in a queue. A constraint solver satisfies the constraints; their satisfaction often leads to the propagation and satisfaction of more constraints. The process of constraint maintenance and propagation continues cyclically until the display is no longer affected. The PREP editor requires dynamic communication between the within-component layer (the content and structure within nodes and links) and the runtime-layer. In particular, the PREP editor requires *component location and size information*, and *size and location change events*. For example, a constraint such as *AlignToptoTop* requires the

[3]When a user creates a new column, if a column is selected, then the new column will be linked to the selected column. If no column is selected, the new column will be unlinked. To link two existing columns, a user selects the "from" column, chooses "Link" from a "Column" menu, and chooses the "to" column.

[4]If the user actually makes a selection in the primary text and clicks in the linked column, then the system puts a link anchor around the selection; otherwise, the system puts a zero-length link anchor in the same line as the primary text.

constraint solver to be able to query an object about its position on the screen. This, in effect, results in querying a link about the location of the component at the other end.

The Storage Model. The storage model presented to users is a database. Whereas a file system presents data in a file as an uninterpreted byte sequence, a database encapsulates substantial information about the types and logical relationships of data items stored within it. A database model allows users to exploit knowledge of the data stored in it (e.g., chunks, linked columns, and so forth) to achieve better performance.

Information Transport Architecture. The abstract system architecture consists of three logical units: a source, a filter, and the receiver(s). In this system, a source agent consults the filter to determine what information to send to which receivers. The work has significant similarities with work in information filtering (cf. ACM Special Issue, 1992). The differences reside in the information source having human agency and thus being able to offer information based on nonformalized models of receivers' interests and states.

Information transport can be done in a variety of ways. We have chosen to emphasize scalability and independence from details of an indigenous network in our implementation. We want the system to support small user groups of two to four individuals, as it has in the past. But we also want it to scale upward gracefully to much larger groups across wide-area networks. A goal, for example, is to have PREP support users of major national research and information networks. As a result, we have chosen stochastic (rather than deterministic) algorithms, of the kind represented in epidemic algorithms (Demers et al., 1987), as having desirable properties of scaleability and independence from many of the details of an indigenous network.

The highly replicated model we are employing has significant implications for consistency. Issues of concurrency control for advanced applications such as cooperation and coordination are just beginning to be studied (Barghouti & Kaiser, 1991). Most work has been done in the context of software development environments and some in CAD systems. It is important, however, to pursue development of protocols for collaborative writing as well, because the consequences of inconsistency are quite different for different domains (e.g., the object code produced by compilation may be invalid, whereas a writer may be able to regain consistency by reversing the effects of some operations explicitly). Thus, we believe that writers may be willing to trade "high availability" for "accuracy," an issue we intend to explore through providing users with a set of parameters that they control.

This strategy turns "consistency" from an accuracy issue into a performance issue. An example of a system that implements a similar policy is the Coda file system (Kistler & Satyanarayanan, 1992). Except for a small number of files that must remain consistent, Coda's strategy is to provide the highest availability at the best performance: The most recent copy that is physically accessible is always used to satisfy a file request. Coda's view is that inconsistency is tolerable if it is rare, occurs only under conditions of failure, is always detected, and is allowed to propagate as little as possible. Kistler and Satyanarayanan (1991) noted that it is the relative infrequency of simultaneous write-sharing of files by multiple users in most file system environments that makes this a viable policy. Unfortunately, the assumption of infrequent simultaneous write-sharing of files sometimes fails to hold for collaborative writing groups. Several users may want to share parts of a document in order to be able to work. For example, in a tight deadline, one person may be working five paragraphs behind another, the first person drafting technical details, the second, adding support from empirical research results. Although this situation could be accommodated by implementing the artifact as a large number of elements implemented as small files, it is easy to imagine situations in which this solution breaks down: For example, a person may, while drafting, discover that he or she needs to make a change to a part of the document currently being worked on by someone else. On the other hand, collaborative writing groups spend large parts of their time engaged in less synchronous activities. A fixed policy that penalizes such groups to accommodate the simultaneous write-sharing case seems inappropriate.

EMPIRICAL STUDIES

To examine the PREP Editor prototype's support for voice modality, we undertook a study with two goals: to compare the nature and quantity of voice and written comments, and to evaluate how writers responded to comments produced in each mode (Neuwirth et al., 1994). Writers were paired with reviewers who made either keyboarded or spoken annotations from which the writers revised. The study provides direct evidence that the greater expressivity of the voice modality, which previous research suggested benefits reviewers, produces annotations that writers also find usable. Interactions of modality with the type of annotation suggest specific advantages of each mode for enhancing the processes of review and revision. This study adds to the previous picture of the utility of the voice modality for supporting collaborative writing activities. The results can be summarized as follows:

1. The mode of production (keyboarded vs. spoken) affected the type of problem that reviewers communicated: Although all reviewers in the study produced more comments on problems of substance than any other type of problem, reviewers in voice mode were likely to produce more comments about purpose and audience than reviewers in keyboard mode, whereas

reviewers in keyboard mode were likely to produce more comments about substance.

It may be that the written text, which more readily permits review of what has been written, reflection upon it, and revision, may facilitate comments that involve complex substantive issues. If production modality does influence the types of problems communicated, then writing tools offering both modes may need to provide guidelines for choosing the most appropriate mode to work in for encouraging evaluation at the appropriate level.

2. The mode of production affected how reviewers characterized problems. Although reviewers in both modalities produced about the same number of annotations overall, the number of words per annotation was far greater in speech. This difference can be accounted for, in part, by the greater frequency of reasons and by the greater number of words used to produce mitigated statements. A higher proportion of the annotations produced in voice contained reasons why the reviewers thought something was a problem and polite language that mitigated the problem.

3. The mode of production affected how writers perceived their reviewers. Writers' evaluations of their reviewers were likely to be less positive when reviewers produced written, rather than spoken, annotations.

4. The study failed to find an overall difference in reviewers' assessments of how responsive writers were to annotations produced or received in the two modalities. Future analyses are planned to examine whether the nature of the annotations and writers' perceptions of reviewers interacted with responsiveness.

5. Despite the previous research findings that spoken annotations would likely be tedious to listen to and more difficult to process, writers using the PREP Editor interface for voice annotations were generally favorably disposed or neutral to voice annotations for most types of comments, except low-level mechanical ones.

In this study, authors chose their reviewers and reviewers were constrained to produce comments in only one modality. More research is needed that varies both conditions of producing annotations and the social relations between the writer and reviewer and looks at annotation interfaces for other sorts of documents (e.g., CAD drawings, blueprints, videos).

CONCLUSION

Our approach has been to draw on the social and cognitive research literature in writing and on our experience with prototype tools to identify social, cognitive and practical issues that we are attempting to address with a formative-evaluation-based prototype.

If we believe that our tool allows writers to create new forms of interaction, we need to understand the possibilities better. What new kinds of coordination structures will emerge? Are these new structures desirable? What is necessary for them to work well? We are conducting studies that chart how the prototype is used, as work teams make progress through realistic document coauthoring and commenting tasks. This should help us come up with better descriptive theories that go beyond the normative theory that currently prevails.

McGrath (1990, p. 54) noted how an increase in the volume of information is related to a decrease in the ability to control and structure it. Similarly, collaborative technologies that increasingly relax the boundaries of who, where, when, and what information will flow across a group network is bound to increase uncertainty. We see our work as split between increasing the technological potential of group interaction and harnessing this potential to satisfactory communication outcomes. Down this second branch, we expect to find some technological solutions, but many social ones as well. Cultures define hundreds of regulatory devices in face-to-face interaction to monitor social behavior. We are still in the earliest stages of establishing cultures for group exchange over networks.

ACKNOWLEDGMENTS

The work reported here has been supported by NSF under grant number IRI-8902891. We thank Dale Miller and Paul Erion for work on programming the PREP editor prototype, and Todd Cavalier for work on graphic design for the PREP editor interface.

REFERENCES

ACM Special Issue on Information Filtering. (1992). *Communications of the ACM, 35*(12), 27–81.

Barghouti, N. S., & Kaiser, G. E. (1991). Concurrency control in advanced database applications. *Computing Surveys, 23*(3), 269–317.

Blakeslee, A. (1992). *Inventing scientific discourse : dimensions of rhetorical knowledge in physics.* Unpublished doctoral dissertation. Carnegie Mellon University, Pittsburgh, PA

Bridwell-Bowles, L. S., Johnson, P., & Brehe, S. (1987). Computers and composing: Case studies of experienced writers. In A. Matsuhashi (Ed.), *Writing in real time: Modeling production processes* (pp. 81–107). Norwood, NJ: Ablex.

Catlin, T., Bush, P., & Yankelovich, N. (1989). InterNote: Extending a hypermedia framework to support annotative collaboration. In *Hypertext'89 Proceedings* (pp. 365–378). Pittsburgh, PA.

Cavalier, T., Chandhok, R., Morris, J., Kaufer, D., & Neuwirth, C. M. (1991). A visual design for collaborative work: Columns for commenting and annotation. J. F. Nunamaker, Jr., (Ed.), *Proceedings of the 24th Hawaii International Conference on System Sciences (HICSS-24)* (pp. 729–738). IEEE Press.

Cross, G. A. (1990). A Bakhtinian exploration of factors affecting the collaborative writing of an executive letter of an annual report. *Research in the Teaching of English, 24*(2), 173–203.

Demers, A., Greene, D., Hauser, C., Irish, W., & Larson, J. (1987). Epidemic algorithms for replicated database maintenance. *Proceedings of the Sixth Annual ACM Symposium on Principles of distributed computing* (pp. 1–12). ACM Press.

Dewan, P., & Choudhary, R. (1991). Flexible user interface coupling in a collaborative system. In *Proceedings of the CHI'91 Conference* (pp. 41–49). New Orleans, ACM SIGCHI.

Dourish, P., & Bellotti, V. (1992). Awareness and coordination in shared workspaces. In *Proceedings CSCW '92 Conference on Computer-Supported Cooperative Work* (pp. 107–114). ACM SIGCHI & SIGOIS, Toronto, Canada.

Edwards, M. R., Levine, J. A., & Kurland, D. M. (1986). *ForComment*. Novato, CA: Broderbund.

Fish, R. S., Kraut, R. E., Leland, M. D. P., & Cohen, M. (1988). Quilt: A collaborative tool for cooperative writing. In *Proceedings of COIS '88 Conference on Office Information Systems* (pp. 30–37). ACM SIGOIS.

Flower, L., & Hayes, J. R. (1981a). A cognitive process of theory of writing. *College Composition and Communication, 32*, 365–387.

Flower, L., & Hayes, J. R. (1981b). The pregnant pause: An inquiry into the nature of planning. *Research in the Teaching of English, 15*, 229–243.

Flower, L., Schriver, K. A., Carey, L., Haas, C., & Hayes, J. R. (1989). *Planning in writing: The cognition of a constructive process*. Technical Report 34, Center for the Study of Writing, Carnegie Mellon University.

Gabarro, J. J. (1987). The development of working relationships. In J. W. Lorsch (Ed.), *Handbook of organizational behavior* (pp. 172–189). Englewood Cliffs, NJ: Prentice Hall.

Galegher, J., & Kraut, R. E. (1994). Computer-mediated communication for intellectual teamwork: An experiment in group writing. *Information Systems Research 5*(2), 110–138.

Gould, J. D. (1988). How to design usable systems. In M. Helander (Ed.), *Handbook of human-computer interaction* (pp. 757–789). Amsterdam, North-Holland: Elsevier.

Haake, J., & Wilson, B. (1992). Supporting collaborative writing of hyperdocuments in SEPIA. In *Proceedings of CSCW'92 Conference on Computer-Supported Cooperative Work* (pp. 138–146). Toronto, Canada.

Haas, C. (1989a). Seeing it on the screen isn't really seeing it: Computer writers' reading problems. In G. E. Hawisher & C. L. Selfe (Eds.), *Critical Perspectives on Computers and Composition* (pp. 16–29). New York: Teachers College Press.

Haas, C. (1989b). How the Writing Medium Shapes the Writing Process: Effects of Word Processing on Planning. *Research in the Teaching of English 23*(2), 181–207.

Haas, C. (1990). Composing in technological contexts: A study of not-making. *Written Communication 7*(4), 512–547.

Haas, C., & Hayes, J. R. (1986). What did I just say? Reading problems in writing with the machine. *Research in the Teaching of English 20*, 22–35.

Halasz, F. G. (1987). Reflections on NoteCards: Seven issues for the next generation of hypermedia systems. In *Hypertext'87 Proceedings* (pp. 345–365). Chapel Hill, NC.

Halasz, F. G., & Schwartz, M. (1990). The Dexter hypertext reference model. In *Proceedings of the Hypertext Standardization Workshop, National Institute of Standards and Technology* (pp. 95–133). NIST Special Publication 500-178. Washington, DC: U.S. Government Printing Office.

Hayes, J. R., & Flower, L. (1980). Identifying the organization of writing processes. In L. Gregg & E. Steinberg (Eds.), *Cognitive processes in writing: An interdisciplinary approach* (pp. 3–30). Hillsdale, NJ: Lawrence Erlbaum Associates.

Hayes, J. R., Flower, L., Schriver, K. A., Stratman, J., & Carey, L. (1987). Cognitive processes in revision. In S. Rosenberg (Ed.), *Advances in applied psycholinguistics, Volume II: Reading, writing, and language processing* (pp. 176–240). Cambridge, England: Cambridge University Press.

Hewitt, C. E. (1986). Offices are open systems. *ACM Transactions on Office Information Systems 4*(3), 271–281.

Kaufer, D. S., & Carley, C. (1993). *Communication at a distance: The influence of print on sociocultural organization and change*. Hillsdale, NJ: Lawrence Erlbaum Associates.

Kaufer, D. S., Hayes, J. R., & Flower, L. (1986). Composing written sentences. *Research in the Teaching of English 20*(2), 121–140.

Kaye, T. (1993). Computer networking for development of distance education courses. In M. Sharples (Ed.), *Computer supported collaborative writing* (pp. 41–69). London: Springer-Verlag.

Kistler, J. J., & Satyanarayanan, M. (1992). Disconnected operation in the Coda File System. *ACM Transactions on Computer Systems, 10*(1), 3–25.

Malone, T. W. (1988, February). What is coordination theory? In *Coordination Theory Workshop*. National Science Foundation, Washington, DC.

Malone, T. W., & Crowston, K. (1994). The interdisciplinary study of coordination. *ACM Computing Surveys, 26*(1), 87–119.

McGrath, J. E. (1990). Time matters in groups. In J. Galegher, R. E. Kraut, & C. Egido (Eds.), *Intellectual teamwork* (pp. 23–61). Hillsdale, NJ: Lawrence Erlbaum Associates.

McLaughlin Hymes, C., & Olson, G. M. (1992). Unblocking brainstorming through the use of a simple group editor. In *Proceedings CSCW '92 Conference on Computer-Supported Cooperative Work* (pp. 99–106). ACM SIGCHI & SIGOIS, Toronto.

Minör, S., & Magnusson, B. (1993). A model for semi-(a)synchronous collaborative editing. In *Proceedings of the Third European Conference on Computer-Supported Cooperative Work* (pp. 219–231). Milan, Italy.

Neuwirth, C. M., Chandhok, R., Charney, D., Wojahn, P., Kim, L. (1994). Distributed collaborative writing: A comparison of spoken and written modalities for reviewing and revising documents. In *Proceedings of the CHI'94 Conference on Computer-Human Interaction* (pp. 51–57). Boston, MA: Association for Computing Machinery.

Neuwirth, C. M., & Kaufer, D. S. (1992). Computers and composition studies: Articulating a pattern of discovery. In G. E. Hawisher & P. LeBlanc (Eds.), *Reimagining computers and composition: Teaching and research in the virtual age* (pp. 173–190). Portsmouth, NH: Boynton/Cook.

Neuwirth, C. M., Kaufer, D. S., Chandhok, R., & Morris, J. H. (1990). Issues in the design of computer-support for co-authoring and commenting. *Proceedings of the Third Conference on Computer-Supported Cooperative Work (CSCW '90)* (pp. 183–195). Baltimore, MD: Association for Computing Machinery.

Neuwirth, C. M., Kaufer, D. S., Chimera, R., & Gillespie, T. (1987). The Notes program: A hypertext application for writing from source texts. In *Hypertext'87 Proceedings* (pp. 345–365). Chapel Hill, NC.

Neuwirth, C. M., Kaufer, D. S., Keim, G., & Gillespie, T. (1988). *The Comments program: Computer support for response to writing*. CECE-TR-3, Center for Educational Computing in English, English Department, Carnegie Mellon University.

Newman, R., & Newman, J. (1993). Social writing: Premises and practices in computerized contexts. In M. Sharples (Ed.), *Computer supported collaborative writing* (pp. 29–40). London: Springer-Verlag.

Norman, D. A. (1986). Cognitive engineering. In D. A. Norman & S. W. Draper (Eds.), *User-centered system design* (pp. 31–61). Hillsdale, NJ: Lawrence Erlbaum Associates.

Olson, G. M., & Olson, J. S. (1991). User-centered design of collaboration technology. *Journal of Organizational Computing, 1*, 61–83.

Olson, J. S., Olson, G. M., Storrøsten, M., & Carter, M. (1992). How a group-editor changes the character of a design meeting as well as its outcome. In *Proceedings CSCW '92 Conference on Computer-Supported Cooperative Work* (pp. 91–98). ACM SIGCHI & SIGOIS, Toronto.

Posner, I. R., & Baecker, R. M. (1992). How people write together. In *Proceedings of the 25th Hawaii International Conference on System Sciences* (Vol. 4, pp. 127–138). Hawaii.

Smith, J. B., Weiss, S. F., & Ferguson, G. J. (1987). A hypertext writing environment and its cognitive basis. In *Hypertext'87 Proceedings* (pp. 345–365). Chapel Hill, NC.

Smolensky, P., Bell, B., Fox, B., King, R., & Lewis, C. (1987). Constraint-based hypertext for argumentation. In *Hypertext'87 Proceedings* (pp. 215–246). Chapel Hill, NC.

Stefik, M., Foster, G., Bobrow, D. G., Kahn, K., Lanning, S., & Suchman, L. (1987). Beyond the chalkboard: Computer support for collaboration and problem solving in meetings. *Communications of the ACM, 30*(1), 32–47.

Tang, J. C., & Leifer, L. J. (1988). A framework for understanding the workspace activity of design teams. In *Proceedings CSCW '88 Conference on Computer-Supported Cooperative Work* (pp. 244–249). ACM SIGCHI & SIGOIS, Portland, OR.

CHAPTER

18

Technology Support for Collaborative Workgroups

Gary M. Olson
Judith S. Olson
University of Michigan

Contemporary organizations are increasingly characterized by more flexible structures that make use of continuing or ad hoc workgroups for accomplishing goals (Peters & Waterman, 1982). A representative workgroup has fewer than 10 members, and works on their task for a period of weeks or months. Although the relationship between workgroup effectiveness and the overall productivity of the organization is complex, it is likely that what makes workgroups effective will contribute to overall organizational effectiveness. Thus, we feel that one promising strategy for exploring the relationship between information technology and the productivity of knowledge workers is to focus on factors that might enhance the effectiveness of workgroups.

There are both practical and theoretical reasons for this focus. First, workgroups are organizationally interesting as well as important. They constitute a key aspect of what have been referred to as "adhocracies" (Bennis, 1968, Toffler, 1980), a more flexible form of organization that is contrasted with bureaucracies. Second, their members are often organizationally and geographically dispersed, and represent several disciplines, meaning that problems of coordination, representation, and communication are central—problems that new collaboration technology might help solve. Third, workgroup activity is both natural and easy to study (McGrath, 1984), making *in situ* research feasible. Many workgroups last only as long as their task takes to complete, making it possible to study their entire life cycle.

Small workgroups can carry out a wide range of tasks. For instance, they might be asked to investigate a set of issues, to set policy on some matter, to formulate a plan for a project or activity, to design something, to implement a plan or design, and so forth. Tools to support these activities differ depending on who is in the group as well as the different kinds of tasks the groups perform. Because we could not possibly take on this whole range of tasks in our research, we have confined our attention to the task of design, in particular the design of software systems.

We have focused on the early stages of system design and specification for several reasons. Much software is designed collaboratively, and at least since Brooks (1975), it has been widely recognized that there are large coordination costs in software design by teams. This seems like a rich domain for the investigation of collaboration technology. Additionally, there are currently very few tools for this stage of software development, even though it is widely recognized as both a difficult and an extremely important stage in the software life cycle.

We are engaged in a program of research to understand how to build appropriate technology to support the work of small groups. We have adopted the approach of user-centered design of these collaborative systems (Olson & Olson, 1991). We use a number of empirical methods to work toward principles and theories that can guide our efforts. We study groups working in their natural environments (e.g., small groups of professionals in companies) and groups working in the laboratory (e.g., observing many small groups engaged in the same task, where the task is a meaningful replica of real work). Our empirical work is guided by a conceptual framework in which we systematically describe the group, the task, and the technology support in standard terms, varying some of these features, keeping others constant. The goal is to develop a theory in which the relationships among these factors can be explained and thus used to guide the design of collaboration technology.

Conceptual Framework. Groupwork is the result of many factors, all of which interact to influence the behavior of the group and the content and form of the eventual product. Many researchers of group work (e.g., Forsyth, 1990; Hackman, 1987; McGrath, 1984, 1990; Pinsonneault & Kraemer, 1989) agree that the major factors include:

> features of the *group's characteristics*, such as size, history, norms, and member characteristics; the *local situation* including the technologies available from which the group gets support, the *task* they have to perform, including its nature and difficulty; the *organizational context* in which they work, including the use of a structured process like those brought in by facilitators.

Figure 18.1, based on this literature, illustrates the range of factors considered important in determining group behavior and the group's eventual success in doing a task as well as how they feel about the experience.

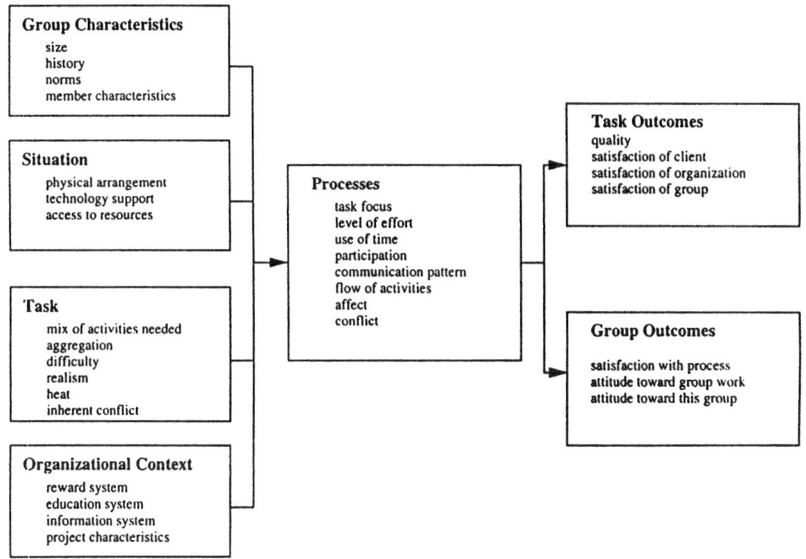

FIG. 18.1. Conceptual framework for collaborative work.

What Fig. 18.1 shows is that conclusions about the behaviors of groups in any particular situation, theories of group behavior, and the implications for technology design, must take into account the constellation of interacting factors. Because the range of factors is large, a research program must be explicit in its focus. Reading down the left-hand side of the figure, we focus on

> small groups (3–7) who know each other and have worked together, and are of nearly equal status, working on a common design task, where the organizational characteristics are held constant and the groups work in real time.

On the other hand, we vary the technology. To date, we have studied people using such tools as whiteboards, paper and pencil, and a group editor called ShrEdit.

The communication channels have varied as well. We have observed groups who are face-to-face, distributed with audio only, or distributed with audio plus high quality video.

Finally, we focus on the following measures: the quality of the work; the satisfaction with the process and the product; and the process by which the groups do their work.

Our near term plans include comparing these results with behavior in tasks involving large amounts of conflictful negotiation and training–mentoring. We are also in the midst of a study comparing people using a pen-based shared drawing tool within Aspects to people using the LiveBoard, a pen based electronic whiteboard–flip-chart. Our next study will include people working with commercially available desktop video systems that show the other group members in less than life-size windows that are digitally transmitted, resulting in a delay and with fuzzy refresh.

Our investigations draw from several disciplines. From the traditional literature on *small group behavior*, we focus primarily on how behavior is affected by the task itself. This is reflected in our work in several ways. First, we chose for our initial focus a complex task, software system design. Because it embodies a wide range of specific activities, it gives us a good view of collaborative problem solving. Second, influenced by the earlier work of Steiner (1972), McGrath (1984) and others, we have developed a taxonomy of tasks and activities that provides a critical framework for guiding our work (Teasley, Olson, & Meader, 1995) and leading to theory development.

We have supplemented the traditional ideas from the study of small groups with some related, but newer ideas. The first of these is the view that small groups at work must be looked at as a system of *distributed cognition* (Hutchins, 1990, 1991, 1995; Norman, 1993; Olson & Olson, 1991). We focus on intellectual work that draws from the minds of the members of the group and from the artifacts they use. These help them remember, focus their attention, and represent the ideas they discuss. This viewpoint leads us to analyze the detailed interactions of the group's joint problem solving and their use of the technology as a coordinating artifact.

Second, where appropriate, we draw from traditional *cognitive* psychology literature to help us understand such factors as the attentional and working memory limits that can come into play as the representational and communicative circumstances of their work vary (Barnard, 1987; Wickens, 1984). This viewpoint has us consider the limits of cognition, in looking both for opportunities for more communication among members through technology as well as for upper limits for such processing.

Third, we draw heavily on the literature of *communication*, both verbal and nonverbal. Our groups engage in lively discussion as they generate ideas, evaluate them, and choose among them.[1] We also look at groups who are either working face-to-face or are distributed with video support. A key aspect of collaborative work is establishing common ground, and carrying out an exchange of information through whatever communication channels are given so that the task can be accomplished (Clark & Brennan, 1991; Daft & Lengel, 1986; Heath & Luff, 1992; O'Conaill, Whittaker, & Wilbur, 1993; Weick & Meader, 1993). These perspectives direct us to analyses that are sensitive to the details of conversation among group members and how it affects their work.

---

[1]In all of our studies we allow groups to engage in unconstrained verbal interactions.

We also have adopted an overall research strategy that we think is critical for doing careful scientific work on processes that are found in real organizations. As shown in Fig. 18.2, we feel it is critical to study such phenomena through a linked approach using both field and laboratory work. Although this strategy is infeasible at the level of entire organizations, it is appropriate for studying workgroups. A key piece of this strategy is demonstrating that there is a homology between work processes found in the field and those found in the equivalent laboratory situations. We construct laboratory versions of the tasks that are done in the field, and study aspects of the same behavior in more controlled settings, using large numbers of groups. This allows us to not only compare quality across conditions of technical support and communication channels, but then to correlate various aspects of the process of group behavior to satisfaction and quality. In both our field and our laboratory work we have made a major investment in developing and using process measures so we can understand not only that work has changed, but how.

In the remaining sections of this chapter we briefly summarize some of our major findings from our program of work studying technology support for collaborative workgroups. First, we describe some of the key findings of our fieldwork on software system design. Second, we describe some of our laboratory work on design, first pointing out its homologies with the field data. We then describe our findings in two studies, one varying technology support in face-to-face meetings, and one in which distributed groups with technology work with open audio or audio plus video. Third, we describe more generally some qualitative results about a philosophy of technology support that may bear significantly on the prospects for enhancing the productivity of workgroups.

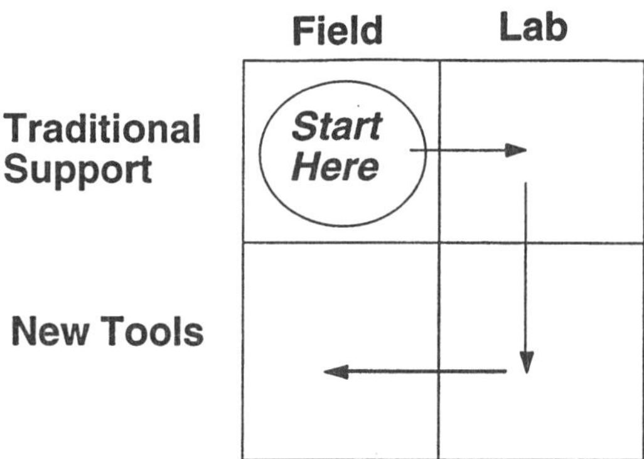

FIG. 18.2. Overall research strategy.

FIELD STUDIES OF SOFTWARE SYSTEM DESIGN

We have carried out extensive analyses of data collected from naturalistic observations of system design being done in field settings. We have reported a number of results of these analyses elsewhere (Olson, Olson, Carter, & Storrøsten, 1992; Olson et al., 1995; Olson, Herbsleb, & Rueter, 1995), and interested readers can pursue details in these other sources. Here we focus in on some aspects of the field data that allow us to discuss the homologies between field and laboratory settings.

The field data were collected at Andersen Consulting (AC) and Microelectronics and Computer Technology Corporation (MCC). We sampled 10 meetings from four different projects for intensive analysis. The meetings ranged in size from three to seven participants, and lasted 1 to 2 hours. Software system design was the principal topic of all of these sessions. The problems were large, requiring many individuals many months to design and code. The systems were both internal products (e.g., an AC systems analysis tool) and prototype ideas for future systems (e.g., a generic architecture for future applications and an exploratory system to edit knowledge bases). In all cases the problem specification was vague at best. The principal focus of the projects during the phase we studied was further development and refinement of the requirements. The major issues discussed included deciding both what features to offer the client and how to implement those features. Because the systems being designed were reasonably large and complex, a variety of expertises were required. Thus, the designers usually had different skills, including in many cases expertise on systems that were similar in some respect to the target system, or on the languages or architectures that the new system built upon. Further details about the groups and the projects are found in Olson, Olson, Carter, and Storrøsten (1992).

Each of the 10 meeting's videotape was transcribed and marked with time stamps. Because we were interested in the moment-by-moment activity in these meetings, we developed a new coding scheme that was a blend of the *design-argument* scheme in Design Rationale (MacLean, Young, & Moran, 1989), the *executive activity* categories of Putnam (1981), Poole and Hirokawa (1986) and Poole and Roth (1989), as well as more standard measures of *participation* (McGrath, 1984).

The analysis we focus on here was based on coding the transcripts into 22 categories that captured the general nature of the design discussions. One set of categories focused on the direct design discussions themselves:

> Various *issues* are raised either implicitly or explicitly, for each issue various *alternative* design possibilities are presented. Eventually a decision among these possibilities must be made by applying various *criteria* that help select the preferred alternatives.

Other categories dealt more with how the groups organized their work. These include such coordination activities as discussion of *goals*, *project management*, and *meeting management* as well as *summaries*, *walkthroughs*, and *digressions*.

We also found substantial amounts of *clarification* in these discussions. This category was defined very strictly as answers to explicit questions. Wherever possible we associated this clarification activity with the other activities, leading to such coding categories as *clarification of issues*, *clarification of goals*, and so forth.

There were two special clarification categories: *Clarification artifact* refers to those occasions when a meeting participant tried to explain some aspect of a drawing, a list, or other meeting artifact, and *clarification general* refers to those remaining clarification episodes that could not be associated with any of the other specific clarification categories. Periods of activity that did not fit into any of our categories were put in a catch-all class called *other*.

We achieved satisfactory degrees of interrater reliability in coding our transcripts with these categories. (See details in Olson, Olson, Carter, & Storrøsten, 1992.)

One of our more striking findings was that the 10 meetings in our sample were all very similar to each other, both in the amount of time spent in these categories and in the patterns of transitions among them. The only obvious difference that emerged was that the meetings varied in the amount of *project management* time they contained, ranging from none to as much as 40%.

Figure 18.3 shows a composite picture based on all 10 design meetings of both the use of time and the pattern of transitions among the coding categories. For each category, the size of the circle represents the amount of time spent in that category. The white areas represent direct time in the category; the black areas represent the associated clarification time. For the transitions, the thickness of the arrows corresponds to the frequency of the transitions. We only show those transitions above a certain minimal threshold in order to keep the diagram simple. The locations of the heads and tails of the transition arrows show explicitly what coding category is involved in the transition.

These discussions were clearly anchored in the design categories. For instance, there were frequent transitions among the core design categories, especially in and out of Criteria. Criteria and Criteria Clarification are involved in 46.1% of all transitions among the 22 categories. Alternatives and their Clarifications account for another large portion of transitions: 40.9% (this includes the transitions with Criteria, so this figure overlaps with the previous one). Together, Alternative and Criteria along with their associated Clarifications accounted for 68.2% of all transitions. In other words, these four categories from the total set of 22 categories are involved in over two thirds of the transitions. This is in contrast to time use: These four cate-

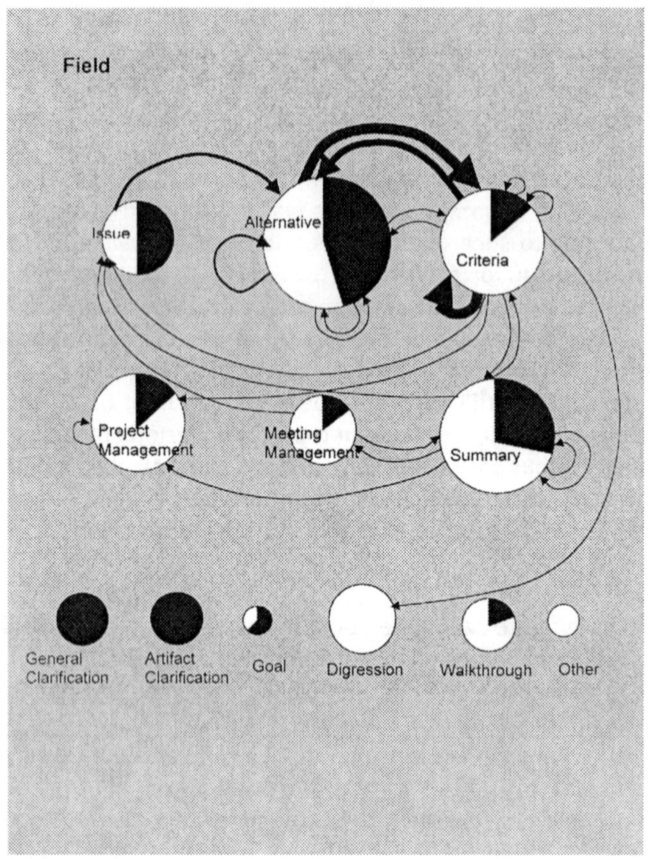

FIG. 18.3. Time use and transitions among coding categories of design activity. From "Small Group Design Meetings: An Analysis of Collaboration," by J. S. Olson, G. M. Olson, M. Carter, and M. Storrøsten, 1992, *Human-Computer Interaction, 7*, pp. 347–374. Copyright by Lawrence Erlbaum Associates. Reprinted with permission.

gories only occupied 36.5% of the total time. Thus, the design meetings we observed had frequent although brief excursions into discussions bearing on design alternatives and criteria for selecting among them.

We discovered through the use of lag sequential analysis (see Olson et al., 1995) that the six design categories above the dashed line in Fig. 18.3 and the remaining 16 categories below the line constitute two functionally distinct categories. We examined the statistically significant sequences in our data for lags up to 5, and we found that there were 25 significant transitions among the 6 design categories of issue, alternative, criterion, and their associated clarifications, but only 2 from these categories to the remaining 16.

Similarly, the remaining 16 categories had 79 significant transitions among themselves but only 11 with the 6 design categories.

To put this finding a bit less technically, it means that these design sessions consisted of interleaved episodes of design discussion (the 6 categories) and of coordination or management discussion (the others). We attempted to characterize the sequential structure of the design discussions by collapsing all 16 nondesign categories into a single category called management, and then exploring in detail the sequential organization of the resulting encoded transcripts.

Again, to our surprise, we found much similarity among the 10 design meetings. Figure 18.4 shows the significant conditional probabilities among the seven categories used in this analysis, and suggests the orderliness of the design discussions. In order to capture higher order sequential dependencies we used an iterative process of rewriting strings of category symbols into higher order categories, writing if you will a grammar of design activity. Interestingly, the same grammar provided an equally good fit of the 10 design meetings. The main differences among the meetings were parametric, in that the MCC meetings tended to have longer sequences of design activity and fewer management activities than the AC meetings. But the important point was that both sets of meetings had the same structure, that is, they could be described by the same grammar. See Olson et al. (1995) for technical details.

These were all very informal, intensely interactive meetings. On the surface they seem to be quite chaotic in organization. But our analyses tell us a different story: Design discussions at the level we described them are quite structured and orderly. There are several reasons why this may be so. First, it may be that design as a task is relatively structured, and that in order to do design at all one must proceed with some degree of sequential orderliness. Second, our designers were quite experienced. The AC designers had

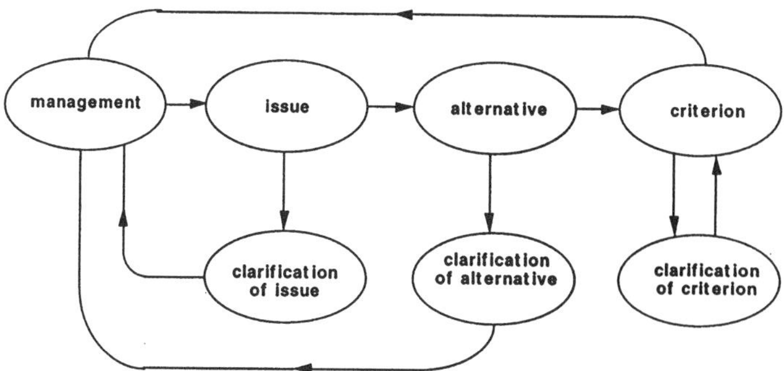

FIG. 18.4. Significant conditional probabilities for transitions among coding categories.

been trained on how to do design and conduct meetings, and the MCC designers had considerable experience in industry prior to coming to MCC. Third, the orderliness may have been due to the high level of our analyses, without concern for who said what or how the issues interplay.

The heart of the design process is the generation of design ideas, discussing their pros and cons, and selecting among these ideas those that are to be potentially included in the final design. We looked at the structure of the arguments that were considered in the design meetings, using the Issues, Alternatives, and Criteria categorization of design primitives to describe the content of the design process of our 10 meetings. We were interested in seeing when and how completely the designers stated the design questions explicitly, listed alternative solutions, and gave reasons why each alternative was good or bad.

For each meeting, we did a complete design rationale graph, a portion of which is shown in Fig. 18.5. Of course, the actual graph from one of the meetings is large, sometimes taking up the better part of a wall. In Fig. 18.5, the issue is noted in the left, the alternatives radiate off the issue, and the criteria are to the right. A criterion stated in support of an alternative is shown by a solid line, as opposed to the dashed line for a negative criterion.

The median number of issues considered in a meeting was 10. There was considerable variation in how many issues were examined in a meeting, ranging from one meeting in which only one design issue was discussed during the entire meeting, to another in which 44 different issues were addressed. The meeting with one issue focused on the feature of the current proposed design that was responsible for the greatest complexity, and six alternative solutions were raised and discussed at length. In the meeting in which there were 44 issues, the participants reviewed several documents that recorded the current state of their part of a design of a very large system architecture. In the process of reviewing the items recorded, new issues and alternatives arose.

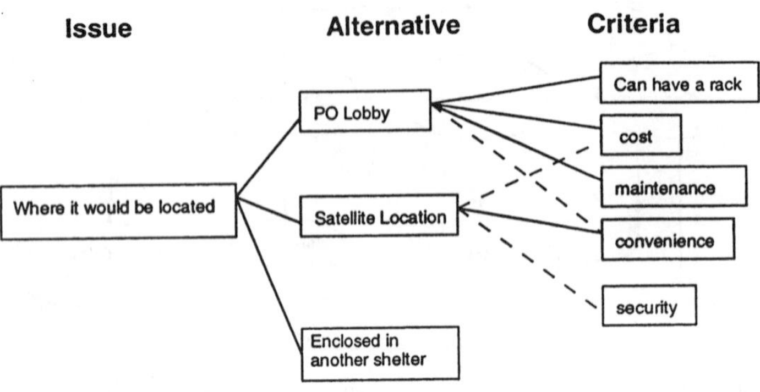

FIG. 18.5. Fragment of a design rationale.

The most typical issue had two alternatives discussed. Twenty-one percent had one or fewer alternatives raised (e.g., "We'll offer only printing of the whole diagram"), whereas 40% of the issues had three or more alternatives. These could be extensive discussions or limited ones. Clearly some issues get lots of attention in terms of an elaborate exploration of alternatives, whereas others are raised and not explored in very much detail. Overall, only 63% of the alternatives raised in the discussion of issues were evaluated at all. Said another way, more than one third of the time, when positions are raised there is no explicit evaluation.

The fact that the 10 design meetings are more similar than different is perhaps our most surprising finding. We expected much less uniformity in the groups' behavior, due to differences in organizations, projects, and participants. Based on our relatively large sample of 10 meetings analyzed in great detail we are inclined to conclude that there is substantial regularity to this behavior in general.

These initial field studies led to two other lines of fieldwork. First, in an examination of what kinds of support designers might need, perhaps in a design database, we examined the kinds of *questions* asked in design meetings (at Andersen Consulting) or questions or issues recorded in detailed minutes (at NTT in Japan) To our surprise, most of the questions had to do with understanding the user's requirements, not the reasons for earlier design decisions, and the patterns were identical in both sites (Herbsleb & Kuwana, 1993; Kuwana & Herbsleb, 1993).

Second, our original field data were collected for teams using traditional software engineering methods. We have used it to help us understand the effects of another engineering method, Object Oriented Design (OOD). This work was comprised of both direct observations of design groups using object-oriented methods in one organization and interview studies of a much wider range of organizations (Herbsleb et al., 1995). The OOD groups that were examined in detail showed that unlike the traditional meetings, they were led by a chief designer, but the design discussions were very much like the traditional ones.

SHREDIT: AN UNSTRUCTURED TOOL TO SUPPORT WORK GROUPS

Qualitative analysis of our field groups' behavior showed that they had difficulty in coordinating the content of their discussions. For example, there were cases where:

> Working on paper copies of a diagram of the system architecture the group members had agreed on to date, the group discussed some significant changes to that architecture and subsequently marked off *different* aspects of the diagram.

> Working on the whiteboard with a list of open issues and people who would be responsible for follow up, a group stopped their meeting when the whiteboard was full, and furthermore had great difficulty discussing potential interactions among the items because the items couldn't be moved.

Based on these and other observations (Olson, Olson, Carter, & Storrøsten, 1992) and our analysis of a variety of extant groupware systems (Olson, Olson, Mack, & Wellner, 1990), we designed and built a group editor called ShrEdit (McGuffin & Olson, 1992). The goal was to provide a simple tool that allowed people to view and edit a shared object (list, diagram, etc.). We began this development effort with the goal of merely exploring architectural issues about speed, concurrency control, and reliability, but in the end we built an easy-to-use, useful tool for the highly interactive phase of early system design.

ShrEdit is a simple text editor that allows all participants to view and edit the same documents. Everyone can type simultaneously within one character position of each other. The individuals' views of the document are independent, but can be coordinated if the discussion requires common focus. We view it as a simple shared electronic workspace, an example of a "permissive" technology (Galegher & Kraut, 1990). This contrasts with a large set of groupware systems that "prescribe" an order of activities, regimes for turn-taking, access control, and so on. We have opted to build and explore permissive technologies because we are interested in how groups adapt to and use flexible tools.

ShrEdit has a close cousin in the commercial product Aspects. Aspects has paragraph locking where ShrEdit has character locking. ShrEdit's small grain locking allows people to work in the same paragraph, often merely cleaning up the spelling and grammar of text as it is written quickly by another. On the other hand, Aspects has a much wider set of formatting functions, and has a telepointer. Both ShrEdit and Aspects offer the group members the ability to either lock their screens together (so that they can coordinate what they are talking about) or be separate (for parallel work). Both of these systems differ from Timbuktu, Point to Point, and Shared-X in that these latter systems allow all parties to see the work, a common view of the work, but only one person at a time cab do the scrolls or edits.

We have taught over 500 people how to use ShrEdit, each in just half an hour, after which they use it successfully in a variety of productive ways. We have also distributed it to more than 80 sites worldwide. Based on our experience with ShrEdit and a number of other comparable systems, we find its simplicity and its ability to allow both focused and parallel work to be key (Olson & Olson, 1992; Olson et al., 1990; Olson, McGuffin, Kuwana, & Olson, 1993).

LABORATORY STUDIES OF DESIGN

Supporting Face-to-Face Work With a Shared Editor: Study I

The field data we have collected and analyzed are rich and interesting. They help us understand the details of the kind of problem solving that constitutes design. Our findings of similarity among meetings and overall structuredness in the activity suggests that some aspects of the process of collaborative design may be somewhat invulnerable to the social and organizational settings in which this work takes place. But we continue also to be interested in whether aspects of the problem solving that constitute collaborative design can be studied under more experimental settings.

There are two key reasons for wanting to bring this task to the laboratory, both related to the traditional virtues of experimental methods. First, in the field it is very difficult to say much about what activity leads to high quality products. It is tricky to evaluate the outcome of group projects as each project has a number of unique features. In contrast, in the laboratory it is possible to give a large number of groups standard problems to work on where the quality of the outcome can be objectively measured.

A second reason for pursuing these issues in the laboratory is that these more controlled settings make it possible to understand what happens when new work technologies are introduced. The technologies themselves can be varied in ways that allow a deeper understanding of what features of the technology contribute to what features of the changes in process and outcome. It is risky to put new technologies into the work setting before their effectiveness is fully understood.

In turning to our laboratory research, we first describe what our lab experiments are like. We then discuss the question of the homologies between the lab and the field before presenting some results about the effects of a simple group technology and communication paths on collaborative design.

We have designed our laboratory studies to preserve as much as we can of the work situation we have studied in the field, while at the same time keeping a bound on complexity so we can run large numbers of groups. We only use groups who already know each other and have worked together before, ideally in a company setting. Such groups are easy to find in a business school, where our lab is located, because over 90% of the incoming students have experience in companies and they all work in groups regularly in their courses. We run groups of three as a compromise between feasibility and realism: The kinds of coordination issues that are so dominant in groups increase dramatically when group size increases from two to three. An intact group of three is much easier to find and recruit than larger groups.

We have also developed a task that is a realistic design task, but does not require any specialized knowledge. Teams of designers from companies have said this task realistically mimics aspects of their work. We embed our task in a scenario about the size of the team available for implementing the design, an overall timetable, and the target audience. We also give the group a specific goal for the 90-minute design session in which they work, so each group knows what kind of output is required at the end of the session. They are to begin the design, assess the features the design will offer to the user, how it will work, equipment needed, and so forth and to make notes on this discussion that are readable by a fictitious group member who was not present at the meeting but would be at the next.

The biggest difference between the field and the lab is the organizational context. In the field our groups are doing work on a project that matters for their company, real company resources are at stake, and the work plays a role in the evolving careers of the group members. We could not study the effects of organizational factors on collaborative work in the laboratory. On the other hand, if there are features of their work that are not much affected by organizational factors, such as the orchestration of their problem solving as revealed in the fieldwork we described earlier, then these features might be amenable to laboratory investigation.

Comparing Field and Laboratory Studies. We look at the problem-solving aspects of design, as revealed through the kind of coding we described in Figs. 18.3 and 18.5. Our claim is that we can demonstrate sufficient homologies between lab and field with respect to these behaviors (which we have already shown in the field are relatively insensitive to organizational setting), and thus study the effect of various laboratory manipulations on the nature of these behaviors. Furthermore, because we can score the quality of the outcomes in the laboratory, we can assess the effect of various factors on the quality of group work.

In all the conditions we report, we have groups of three perform a standard design task that lasts for 90 minutes. Prior to this they have performed several other warm-up tasks so they can adjust to whatever working conditions we give them.

Groups who are working under face-to-face conditions do so in a meeting room called the Collaboration Technology Suite (CTS; Olson, Olson, McGuffin, Mack, Cornell, & Luchetti, 1992) in which computer displays are in units that make up a conference table, with the displays recessed in the table top so as not to interfere with normal eye contact, shown in Fig. 18.6. All sessions are videotaped so we can analyze them in much the same way that we have analyzed our field meetings.

We have run 19 control groups of 3 who work without any new technology. They work in the CTS just like other groups, except we turn off the com-

FIG. 18.6. Collaboration Technology Suite at the University of Michigan.

puters and have them use paper and pencil, and the whiteboards. We transcribed their videotapes and coded these. Figure 18.7 shows a side-by-side plot of the behavior of these lab groups and the field groups. There are a few new categories here that are associated with the specifics of the lab task. The most important is talk about the writing (plan and write) and the actual writing time in which no one is speaking (pause).

The diagrams show that there are some differences. First, as mentioned, the lab groups spend a lot of time writing; we have deleted these pauses and the associated conversation directly about the writing from the diagrams. Another way in which the two differ is on project management time. There is essentially none of this with the lab groups, because there is no real ongoing project at stake. If we exclude project management and writing time, the time spent in the remaining categories correlates .70 between the lab and field groups, suggesting they are using their time similarly. The story is similar for transition times. The only noticeable difference is in the amount of clarification. This is due to the fact that the members of the lab group all were familiar with the problem domain (post offices), while the field groups are often put together because of their complementary expertise. Thus, at the level of behavioral description provided by Fig. 18.7, which focuses on the way in which the groups use their time and structure their activity, the two situations are quite similar.

A comparison of the overall issue–alternative–criteria diagrams shows that the lab groups raised about the same number of issues per hour in the two situations and made similar kinds of evaluative arguments. The lab groups explored the issues more broadly, with 7 alternatives raised per issue in the lab and only 2.5 in the field. Because the laboratory task had people generate *lists* of features, benefits, and costs, it is reasonable that they would consider more such alternatives.

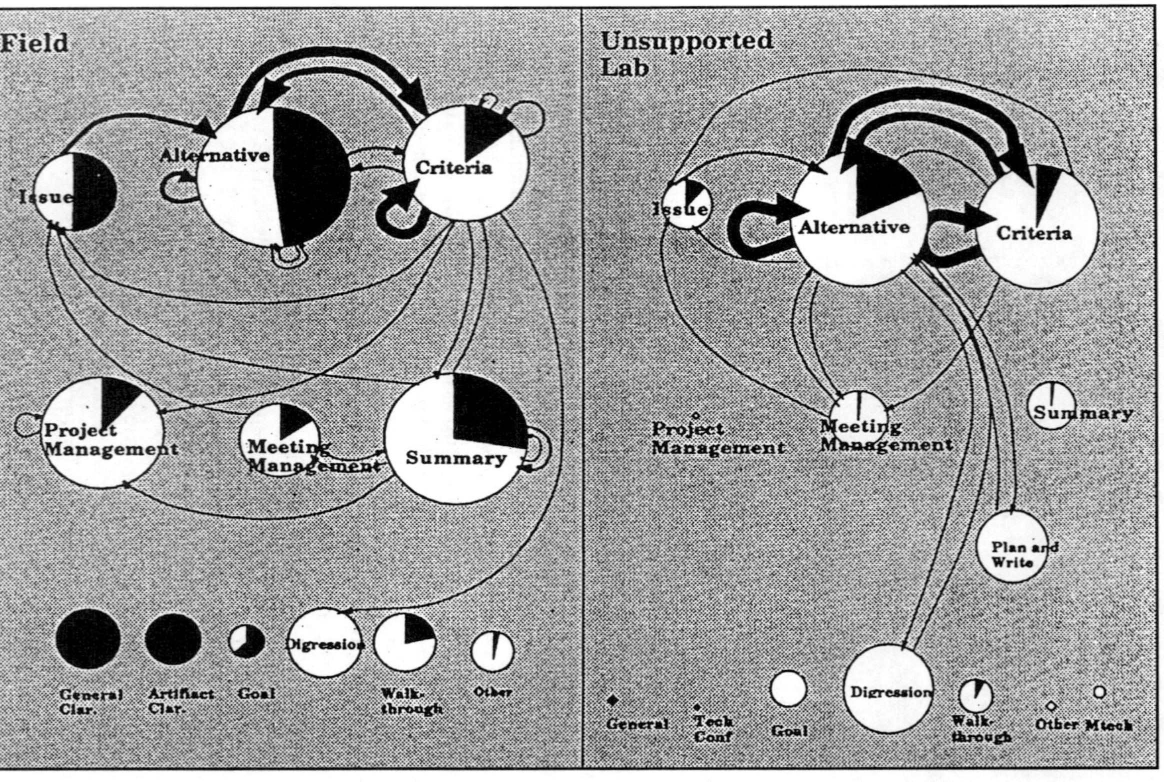

FIG. 18.7. Comparison of the use of time and the transitions among activities in field and unsupported lab conditions. From "Group Work Close up: A Comparison of the Group Design Process With and Without a Simple Group Editor," by J. S. Olson, G. M. Olson, M. Storrøsten, and M. Carter, 1993, *ACM Transactions on Information Systems, 11*, pp. 231–328. Reprinted with permission.

It is important to be clear about what claim we are making. Despite all of the obvious differences between the field and the lab that we described earlier, we have just seen that groups working in the field and the lab organize their activity very similarly. This, of course, focuses on the problem solving they are doing as part of design. It is at this level, and perhaps at none other, that the two kinds of groups are homologous. This encourages us to look at factors that might affect their problem solving, such as new technologies.

Comparing Groups in the Laboratory Using Different Tools. We have run another 19 groups in a condition in which they use ShrEdit to do their design task. These groups were trained in the use of this tool, used it in several warm-up tasks, and then did the same standard design task as the unsupported groups.

There are many results to look at in comparing these two sets of 19 groups, but we focus briefly on only four. (Details are in Olson, Olson, Storrøsten, & Carter, 1993.)

First, the groups working with the new electronic workspace were slightly less satisfied with their process than those working in the more traditional mode. Because this was a new way of working, this is perhaps not surprising.

Second, when we evaluated the final designs of the 38 groups for quality, the groups working with ShrEdit produced designs that were significantly better in quality. Quality was assessed via an objective rating scale that had very high interrater reliability.

Third, an analysis of the flow of activities indicated that the supported groups used their time in ways that were similar to unsupported groups, but with some small differences. An analysis of communication processes in the group shows that they spent more time writing and less time talking. Furthermore, they summarized their work less, likely using the material they had written (the ShrEdit documents) to serve the same purpose. Also, combining the timing data with the content analysis, we found that the unsupported groups repeated their ideas more; for the ShrEdit group, these ideas were already down in the document and even often elaborated on (see Fig. 18.8).

Fourth, we found that the groups using ShrEdit, contrary to our expectations, explored substantially fewer design ideas than the unsupported groups. They considered fewer alternatives and evaluated these alternatives less. Closer examination showed that the larger set of ideas explored by the unsupported groups was "off target"; they explored ideas that were not central to the design task given. When confined to the core design task, both groups were the same.

ShrEdit played a big role in the group process. Ten percent of the time, two or more of the people in the groups with ShrEdit did type simultaneously, with typically sharp bursts of this early (for brainstorming) and late

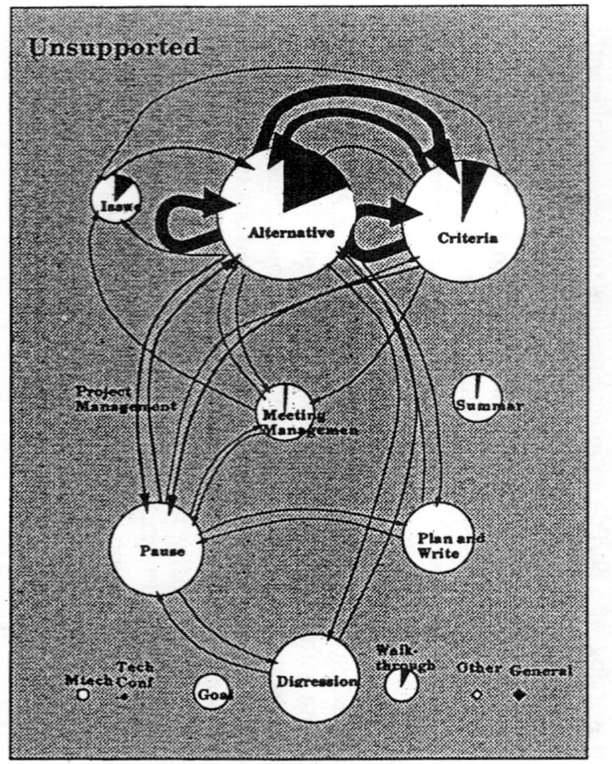

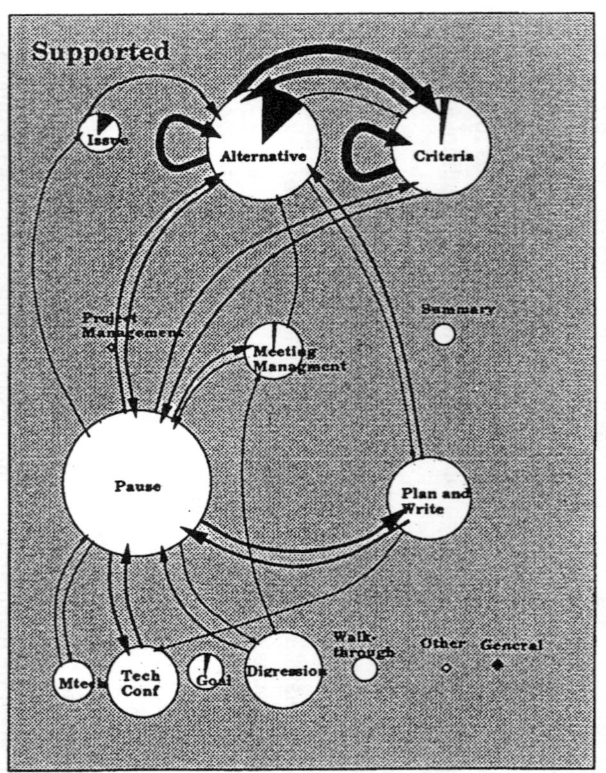

FIG. 18.8. Comparison of the use of time and the transitions among activities in supported and unsupported lab conditions. From "Group Work Close up: A Comparison of the Group Design Process With and Without a Simple Group Editor," by J. S. Olson, G. M. Olson, M. Storrøsten, and M. Carter, 1993, *ACM Transactions on Information Systems, 11*, pp. 231–328. Reprinted with permission.

(finishing up the written text). The middle of the meeting was dominated by discussion and one-at-a-time recording of the ideas discussed. In contrast, the whiteboard groups usually were led by a person at the board, who wrote the ideas as they arose. Then, late in the session, someone wrote a summary of these notes on paper. Whereas in both groups, some of the ideas in the final document were never spoken about, in the ShrEdit groups, all had a chance to see or read them, whereas in the whiteboard group, they were solely authored by the scribe on paper (Storrøsten, 1993).

This study revealed that a very simple collaborative technology can have a very big set of effects on group work. Although groups using it for the first time feel a bit uncomfortable about it, the technology helped them produce better work. And it did so in surprising ways, by apparently encouraging them to focus in on good ideas, and not waste their time exploring a wide range of less effective ideas.

SUPPORTING REAL-TIME WORK AT A DISTANCE: STUDY II

Traditionally, all forms of what we think of as meetings took place face-to-face, in meeting rooms, commons areas, and lunchrooms. But as we all know, groups no longer need to meet in the same location; new technologies are allowing us to relax the constraint of co-location. Modern telecommunications makes an interesting array of options available: teleconferences, video conferences, and synchronous interactions over computer networks. These alternatives to face-to-face interactions have distinctive properties, and have not, in any real sense, replaced what it is possible to do in face-to-face interactions. These new technologies offer the ability of enterprises to organize in new ways and to capitalize on new flexible possibilities. Yet we need to understand better what the opportunities and constraints are that are offered by each mode of synchronous interaction.

Modern networking has brought about the possibility for these small groups to be located in different places while working. A fundamental consideration in ShrEdit's design is that we assumed that the members of a group would always have other communication channels available to them. In a face-to-face setting, of course, the groups can talk and gesture in their usual interactive ways. Indeed, the groups in our studies engaged in extensive discussion while using ShrEdit as a workspace to capture and revise their emerging ideas. So our next step was to investigate the use of ShrEdit by distributed groups, where, as in the face-to-face setting, ShrEdit would be used to share the group's emerging design ideas but we would provide for them other communication channels for talking and interacting.

We decided to provide communication for our groups that was as ideal as we could make it given their distributed set-up. We did this because we wanted a baseline for later studies that looked at other kinds of communication, and in particular digital desktop video. In the present study we focused on how groups of three performed when they have a shared workspace tool and nearly *ideal* communication.

A number of sources indicate that high quality audio is important to synchronous work (e.g., Pagani & Mackay, 1993; Tang & Isaacs, 1993). So half our groups worked with high quality audio in addition to the shared workspace. Our audio was full duplex, directional for both input and output, and of far better quality than found in teleconferencing or most commercial video conferencing systems. More controversial is whether video adds significant value for groups doing distributed problem solving. Although the research record is quite mixed (Egido, 1990; Tang & Isaacs, 1993), many theories (e.g., Daft & Lengel, 1986; Rutter, 1984; Short, Williams, & Christie, 1976; Weick & Meader, 1993) and most people's intuitions are that video should add substantial value to such work.

Thus, the other half of our groups had our good quality audio plus high quality analog video connections to each of their colleagues. The video was arranged in an optimal fashion to create the feeling of sitting around a table with one's colleagues, with the shared workspace in the center as shown in Fig. 18.9. We took more care than usual to create what we felt would be the best possible video conferencing set-up.

We were interested in how these video–audio groups using ShrEdit would compare to face-to-face groups using ShrEdit from our earlier study (Olson, Olson, Storrøsten, & Carter, 1993) on the same range of measures: quality of the work product, satisfaction, and characteristics of the group process. We also compared these audio–video groups to the audio-only groups to assess the added effect of the video. What distinguishes our study from previous investigations is the use of an established workspace tool of known value for sharing the work, the fact that the people in the study comprised intact groups, and the fact that we took a great deal of care to ensure that the audio and video were of the highest quality we could get with present communication technology.

Another function of this study was to establish a baseline from which we could conduct later studies of a variety of less-than-optimal communication technologies. Multimedia desktop conferencing systems that run over the Internet or ISDN lines (e.g., Intel's ProShare, SunSolutions' ShowMe, and AT&T's Vistium) are generally quite constrained in the quality of the audio and video they can provide. With our baseline data we can assess these situations in future investigations.

The subjects were 36 existing groups of three professionals, drawn from the same population as that in our lab study of face-to-face work. As shown

FIG. 18.9. Sketch of the lab set-up for the video-supported condition.

in Fig. 18.9, they worked in three separate rooms, each of which had a workstation with a large screen centered on a desk, with two 13″ video monitors on each side of the screen. A camera and microphone were mounted on each video monitor, with the camera placed at the center of the top of the monitor so that when the participants faced each other, they appeared to each other to be making eye contact.[2] Furthermore, when the other two remote participants were facing each other, their images projected to the receiving participant made them look as if they were looking at each other.

The microphones and speakers were similarly situated to either side of the central screen, corresponding to the person shown on the video screen. They were open full-duplex channels that additionally projected a sense of spatial location. Indeed, in the audio-only condition, group participants often moved their heads to face the speaker boxes of the people they were addressing. The audio condition used the identical microphones and speakers of the video condition; the only difference was that the video monitors were turned off.

As in the earlier study, the groups all used ShrEdit. We trained all groups in ShrEdit in the CTS then took them to the distributed rooms where they worked. The groups performed the same three tasks as in the earlier study, the first two for 20 minutes each and the target design task for 90 minutes. In total, we ran 36 groups. Eighteen of the groups used the full video and audio technologies to communicate; 18 had only the audio. As in the earlier study, we assessed three things: the quality of the product, the participants' satisfaction with the process, and the process of design and coordination. (More details are available in Olson, Olson, & Meader, 1995.)

[2]Eye contact was not perfect. Participants reported that the other person appeared to be looking at their throat when they looked into their eyes.

The results showed that when remote groups work with a flexible, simple shared editor to support their design work and communicate via high quality video (eye contact, spatial relations preserved), the quality of their work is not significantly different from similar groups working without the video, but with high quality, stereo full duplex audio. Furthermore, the video groups are not significantly different from similar groups working face-to-face with the same shared editor. Face-to-face groups are superior to the remote groups without video, however, suggesting there is a small detrimental effect overall when groups work without seeing each other. Figure 18.10 summarizes the quality results for both the face-to-face and remote conditions.

More striking, however, is that the groups working at a distance without video do not like it as much as those who have the video. They reported being less able to tell how their other group members were reacting to things said. They also reported that the communication system got in the way of their being able to persuade others about their ideas or to resolve disagreements. Tang and Isaacs (1993) found that groups in a field setting who were offered video in addition to shared workspace and audio used the system more heavily than those who had audio and workspace tools, suggesting that the preference we saw in our study could be a harbinger of usage patterns when these capabilities were discretionary.

These meetings were then coded for their time use as before. Their patterns were very similar, with the only difference being that the time spent talking about the issue at hand was significantly longer in the audio-only condition, perhaps a measure of grounding. However, in comparing remote work with that face-to-face, people engaged in remote work required more time to manage their work and to clarify what they meant. This suggests that the video we had set up, although intended to duplicate the important aspects of face-to-face, did not succeed in replicating that information. Perhaps there is more sense of what others are doing and what they mean when we are face-to-face than can be presented via even very good video channels.

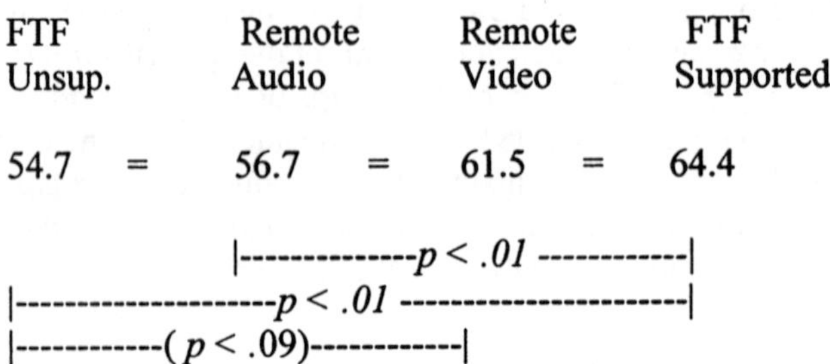

FTF Unsup.
Remote Audio
Remote Video
FTF Supported
54.7 = 56.7 = 61.5 = 64.4
|-------------p < .01 -----------|
|-------------------p < .01 ---------------------|
|-----------(p < .09)-----------|

FIG. 18.10. Means and significant differences for quality scores among the four conditions.

We also coded these meetings for the amount of discussion that was argumentative, thinking that video would bring people "closer" to each other and allow them to engage in this kind of activity. Audio alone was thought to be harder, and thus not good support for the typically difficult but very important activity. However, there was no difference between these conditions; people were equally able to discuss critically. Groups that perceived the medium to be easy to communicate in (regardless of condition) produced better designs (Meader, 1995).

These results are important. Remote work can be done without loss of quality, but it takes extra effort to manage the group and clarify things meant. Video does not seem to change the group's process; time use is the same as without video, and different from face-to-face. But, perceptions are definitely different. People like to see each other. Video makes them feel more able to *communicate* with each other, to persuade and resolve issues. For work that extends over long periods of time, these preferences are very likely to be important.

SIMPLICITY IS A POWER STRATEGY FOR WORKGROUPS

Our research has shown that a very simple groupware tool can have interesting, and in some cases quite positive, effects on the effectiveness of workgroups. We designed ShrEdit deliberately to provide its users with a tool that has as few constraints as possible (Olson & Olson, 1991; McGuffin & Olson, 1992). We did this because we wanted to provide groups with some basic functionality—basically, a shared electronic workspace with as few constraints on its use by individual members as possible—and let them develop their own strategies for working with it. If you look at common collaborative tools like whiteboards or paper and pencil, the tools provide few constraints and groups invent (or are sometimes taught) techniques for making effective use of them in their work. We have watched our groups invent simple techniques for voting and for highlighting and directing attention. We have seen them create tables or parallel lists by using several side-by-side skinny windows. We have watched them organize their work and transition from individual parallel work to a group focus via cutting and pasting of information within and between windows. These were all low overhead, socially created ways of using the possibilities offered by the tool to organize their work in an effective way.

Dourish and Bellotti (1992) have used the data we collected on distributed groups using ShrEdit to analyze the way in which these people used the flexibility of ShrEdit to carry out their work. They noticed in particular that the shared workspace provided an effective though passive form of awareness information about what others were doing. This allowed the groups to move back and forth easily between close and loose collaboration. Furthermore, they could easily assign and coordinate tasks and roles on the fly. They contrasted this with systems that provide active mechanisms for coordination support. In these systems awareness information was provided and controlled separate from or instead of a shared workspace. They claim that these kinds of systems are much more difficult for groups to use, because often the groups' needs or goals are at odds with what the system allows them to do. In contrast, with passive awareness support of the sort provided through a shared workspace like ShrEdit the group can easily adapt the workspace features to their own style of coordination.

We have tried to bring out our integrated approach to studying the effects of new collaborative technologies on workgroups carrying out intellectual tasks. We feel that the blend of field and laboratory research as described in Fig. 18.2 is a critical element to this strategy, and are pursuing a program of research consistent with this. In this chapter we have summarized some of our findings that suggest there may be real leverage in new, simple technologies for enhancing the productivity of such groups.

Of course, workgroups of the kind we have been studying represent only one component of large, knowledge-intensive organizations. Whether enhancing their effectiveness can contribute in any meaningful way to the overall effectiveness of such organizations can only be determined by field studies where workgroups adopt whatever tools or methods make them more effective.

ACKNOWLEDGMENTS

This work was supported by the National Science Foundation (grants IRI-8902930 and IRI-9320543), Intel, the AT&T Foundation, Andersen Consulting, the Ameritech Foundation, and Steelcase.

REFERENCES

Barnard, P. J. (1987) Cognitive resources and learning of human-computer dialogs. In J. M. Carroll (Ed.), *Interfacing thought: Cognitive aspects of human computer interaction*. Cambridge, MA: MIT Press.

Bennis, W. G. (1968) The temporary society. In W. G. Bennis & P. E. Slater (Eds.), *The temporary society*. New York: Harper & Row.

Brooks, F. P., Jr. (1975) *The mythical man month: Essays on software engineering*. Reading, MA: Addison-Wesley.

Clark, H. H., & Brennan, S. (1991) Grounding in communication. In L. B. Resnick, J. M. Levine, & S. D. Teasley (Eds.), *Perspectives on socially shared cognition* (pp. 127–149). Washington, DC: American Psychological Association.

Daft, R. L., & Lengel, R. H. (1986) Organizational information requirements, media richness, and structural design. *Management Science, 32*, 554–571.

Dourish, P., & Bellotti, V. (1992) Awareness and coordination in shared workspaces. *Proceedings of the Conference on Computer Supported Cooperative Work*. New York: ACM.

Egido, C. (1990) Teleconferencing as a technology to support cooperative work: Its possibilities and limitations. In J. Galegher, R. E. Kraut, & C. Egido (Eds.), *Intellectual teamwork: Social and technological foundations of cooperative work* (pp. 351–371). Hillsdale, NJ: Lawrence Erlbaum Associates.

Forsyth, D. (1990) *Group dynamics*. Pacific Grove, CA: Brooks/Cole.

Galegher, J., & Kraut, R. (1990) Computer-mediated communication for intellectual teamwork: A field experiment in group writing. *Proceedings of the Conference on Computer Supported Cooperative Work*, pp. 65–78, New York: ACM.

Hackman, J. R. (1987) The design of work teams. In J. W. Lorsch (Ed.), *Handbook of organizational behavior*. Englewood Cliffs, NJ: Prentice-Hall.

Heath, C., & Luff, P. (1992) Media space and communicative asymmetries: Preliminary observations of video-mediated interaction. *Human Computer Interaction, 7*(3), 315–346.

Herbsleb, J. D., Klein, H., Olson, G. M., Brunner, H., & Olson, J. S. (1995) Problems and object-oriented solutions: An empirical study of OOD. *Human Computer Interaction, 10*, 249–292.

Herbsleb, J. D., & Kuwana, E. (1993) Preserving knowledge in design projects: What designers need to know. *Proceedings of InterCHI '93*, April 1993, Amsterdam.

Herbsleb, J. D., & Kuwana, E. (1993) Preserving knowledge in design projects: What designers need to know. *Proceedings of InterCHI '93*, April 1993, Amsterdam.

Hutchins, E. (1990) The technology of team navigation. In J. Galegher, R. E. Kraut, & C. Egido (Eds.), *Intellectual teamwork: Social and technological foundations of cooperative work* (pp. 191–220). Hillsdale, NJ: Lawrence Erlbaum Associates.

Hutchins, E. (1991) The social organization of distributed cognition. In L. B. Resnick, J. M. Levine, & S. D. Teasley (Eds.), *Perspectives on socially shared cognition* (pp. 283–307). Washington, DC: American Psychological Association.

Hutchins, E. (1995) *Cognition in the wild*. Cambridge, MA: MIT Press.

Kuwana, E., & Herbsleb, J. (1993) Representing knowledge in requirements engineering: An empirical study of what software engineers need to know. *Proceedings of IEEE International Symposium on Requirements Engineering*, January, San Diego, CA.

MacLean, A., Young, R. M., & Moran, T. P. (1989) Design rationale: The argument behind the artifact. *Proceedings of CHI'89, Human Factors in Computing Systems*, Austin, TX, pp. 247–252.

McGrath, J. E. (1984) *Groups: Interaction and performance*. Englewood Cliffs, NJ: Prentice-Hall.

McGrath, J. E. (1990) Time matters in groups. In J. Galegher, R. E. Kraut, & C. Egido (Eds.), *Intellectual teamwork: Social and technical foundations of cooperative work* (pp. 23–78). Hillsdale, NJ: Lawrence Erlbaum Associates.

McGuffin, L. S., & Olson, G. M. (1992) *ShrEdit: A shared electronic workspace* (CSMIL Tech. Rep. No. 45). The University of Michigan.

Meader, D. K. (1995) *Supporting distributed design discussions: A study of video effects on engagement and critical discussion in desktop, multimedia conferencing*. Unpublished doctoral dissertation, Business Administration, The University of Michigan.

Norman, D. A. (1993) *Things that make us smart*. Reading, MA: Addison-Wesley.

O'Conaill, B., Whittaker, S., & Wilbur, S. (1993) Conversations over video-conferences: An evaluation of the spoken aspects of video mediated communication. *Human-Computer Interaction, 8*(4), 389–428.

Olson, G. M., Herbsleb, J. D., & Rueter, H. H. (1994) Characterizing the sequential structure of interactive behaviors through statistical and grammatical techniques, *Human-Computer Interaction, 9*, 427–472.

Olson, G. M., McGuffin, L. S., Kuwana, E., & Olson, J. S. (1993) Designing software for a group's needs: A functional analysis of synchronous groupware. In L. Bass & P. Dewan (Eds.), *User interface software* (pp. 129–148). New York: Wiley.

Olson, G. M., & Olson, J. S. (1996) The effectiveness of simple shared electronic workspaces. In S. Greenberg, S. Hayne, & R. Rada (Eds.) *Real time group drawing and writing*. New York: McGraw-Hill.

Olson, G. M., & Olson, J. R. (1991) User-centered design of collaboration technology. *Journal of Organizational Computing, 1*, 61–83.

Olson, G. M., & Olson, J. S. (1992) Defining a metaphor for group work. *IEEE Software, 9*(3), 93–95.

Olson, G. M., Olson, J. S., Carter, M., & Storrøsten, M. (1992) Small group design meetings: An analysis of collaboration. *Human-Computer Interaction, 7*, 347–374.

Olson, G. M., Olson, J. R., McGuffin, L., Mack, L. A., Cornell, P., & Luchetti, R. (1992) Flexible facilities for electronic meetings. In S. Kinney, R. P. Bostrom, & R. T. Watson (Eds.), *Computer augmented teamwork: A guided tour* (pp. 183–196). New York: Van Nostrand Reinhold.

Olson, G. M., Olson, J. S., Storrøsten, M., Carter, M., Herbsleb, J., & Rueter, H. (1995) The structure of activity during design meetings (pp. 217–239). In T. Moran & J. Carroll (Eds.), *Design rationale*. Hillsdale, NJ: Lawrence Erlbaum Associates.

Olson, J. S., Olson, G. M., Mack, L. A., & Wellner, P. (1990) Concurrent editing: The group's interface. In D. Diaper (Ed.), *INTERACT '90—Third IFIP Conference on Human-Computer Interaction* (pp. 835–840). Cambridge, England: Elsevier.

Olson, J. S., Olson, G. M., & Meader, D. K. (1995) What mix of video and audio is useful for remote real-time work? *Proceedings of CHI '95*, ACM SIGCHI, 362–368.

Olson, J. S., Olson, G. M., Storrøsten, M., & Carter, M. (1992) How a group editor changes the character of a design meeting as well as its outcome. *Proceedings of the Conference on Computer Supported Cooperative Work*, pp. 91–98. New York: ACM.

Olson, J. S., Olson, G. M., Storrøsten, M., & Carter M. (1993) Group work close up: A comparison of the group design process with and without a simple group editor. *ACM Transactions on Information Systems, 11*, 321–348.

Pagani, D. S., & Mackay, W. E. (1993) Bringing media spaces into the real world. In G. DeMichelis, C. Simone, & K. Schmidt (Eds.), *Proceedings of ECSCW '93*. Milan: Kluwer Academic, 341–356.

Peters, T. J., & Waterman, R. H., Jr. (1982) *In search of excellence: Lessons from America's best-run companies*. New York: Harper & Row.

Pinsonneault, A., & Kraemer, K. L. (1989) The impact of technological support on groups: An assessment of the empirical research. *Decision Support Systems, 5*, 197–216.

Poole, M. S., & Hirokawa, R. Y. (1986) *Communication and group decision making*. New York: Sage.

Poole, M. S., & Roth, J. (1989) Decision development in small groups IV: A typology of group decision paths. *Human Communication Research, 15*(3), 323–356.

Putnam, L. L. (1981) Procedural messages and small group work climates: A lag sequential analysis. *Communication Yearbook 5* (pp. 331–350). New Brunswick, NJ: Transaction Books.

Rutter, D. R. (1984) *Looking and seeing: The role of visual communication*. New York: Wiley.

Short, J. A., Williams, E., & Christie, B. (1976) *The social psychology of telecommunications*. New York: Wiley.

Steiner, I. D. (1972) *Group processes and productivity*. New York: Academic Press.

Storrøsten, M. N. (1993) *Supporting collaboration: Impacts of using a group editor*. Unpublished doctoral dissertation, Business Administration, The University of Michigan.

Tang, J. T., & Isaacs, E. (1993) Why do users like video? Studies of multimedia-supported collaboration. *Computer Supported Cooperative Work, 1*, 163–196.

Teasley, S. D., Olson, J. S., & Meader, D. (1995) *Tasks for CSCW: An analysis of task characteristics*. Unpublished manuscript.

Toffler, A. (1980) *The third wave*. New York: Morrow.

Weick, K., E., & Meader, D. K. (1993) Sensemaking and group support systems. In L. Jessup & J. Valacich, (Eds.), *Group support systems*. New York: Macmillan.

Wickens, C. D. (1984) *Engineering psychology and human performance*. Columbus, OH: Charles E. Merrill.

PART

IV

ORGANIZATIONAL MODELING

CHAPTER

19

Central Coordination of Decentralized Information in Large Chains and Franchises

Toby Berger
Nicholas M. Kiefer
Cornell University

I. INTRODUCTION

Chains and franchise operations in service industries often are organized so that individual operators have substantial local control over their activities and pricing, whereas a central administration coordinates advertising, research, and supply. Consider, for example, a quick-service restaurant chain. Here, it is necessary to have many distributed locations for the convenience of customers. Each location is subject to idiosyncratic unique conditions—a competitor across the street, local demographics affecting menu choice, and so on. However, all units share a basic menu of popular items. Therefore, it is reasonable to assume that the information content of the experience of all the units would be useful to individual units in choosing prices and promotions. In a system with many units it is not feasible for the operators to get together and communicate with one another. However, each unit can communicate with the central administration, which can coordinate and summarize information and broadcast useful conclusions back to the units. Of course, the administration is busy and usually is unable or unwilling to process detailed reports from each of the many units.

We study a model of this situation in which many units communicate with the center subject to an overall rate constraint reflecting the ability of the center to receive and process information. The information of interest is the vector of prices and the associated joint probability distribution of the demands for a list of menu items. The hope of the center is to ascertain the underlying demand function that holds on average for the units in the chain and the temporal and statistical fluctuations around that average. With this information in hand, prices can in principle be chosen so as to maximize profits. Each store in each period sees only a noisy observation of a single point on the demand function. All stores with the same prices see noisy observations of the same point; hence, by combining information over time across stores with the same prices, once could estimate the individual point on the demand function via the sample mean of these observation and could gather knowledge about the nature of the statistical fluctuations around this mean. By comparing the profits of stores operating with different pricing strategies, it should be possible to recommend *best* prices. Our approach is not limited to the estimation of average demand functions. It is natural to expect that stores in markets with difference characteristics may be less similar in the demands they face than stores with like characteristics. An example: stores located on interstate exits or highway exchanges may face demands different in important ways from stores in rural or metro markets. Our results are relevant for the problem of identifying and sorting out these distinct markets.

Toward gaining insight into these questions, we consider a stylized model of a related coordination problem known as the CEO problem [1]. Relevant results from the CEO problem are sketched and interpreted in Section 2. In Section 3 applying insights gained from the CEO problem to the chain problem is discussed. Section 4 is devoted to potentially useful lines of future inquiry.

2. A STYLIZED MODEL

A firm's CEO is interested in a discrete memoryless finite alphabet data sequence $\{X(t)\}_{t=1}^{\infty}$. This data sequence cannot be directly observed by the CEO. Information about the data sequence is obtained by a group of L agents who observe independently corrupted versions of $\{X(t)\}_{t=1}^{\infty}$. These agents are the individual stores in the chain problem. Note that $X(t)$ is typically a vector with components corresponding to the demands for each menu item at a given price. Stores can gather only corrupted, or noisy, observations of these demands. The $X(t)$ can, of course, be broken up into demands for different store types with each store collecting information only on its own type. Price and cost information can also be included in $X(t)$. In the abstract formulation we adopt, these considerations are irrelevant. In practice, it probably is unwise to use up agents and data rate sending information that varies little if at all.

The agents are not allowed to convene; that is, for $1 \leq i \leq L$, Agent i has to send data based solely on his own discrete memoryless noisy observations $\{Y_i(t)\}_{t=1}^{\infty}$, which are the quantities sold in our chain problem application. The agents are required to send the encoded versions of their observed data through noiseless communication channels with a total rate R. The aim is to determine the behavior of minimal error frequency as a function of L and R. The L agents are assumed to be statistically exchangeable with common observation matrix $W(y|x)$. Realism in the chain problem suggest that there be several types of agents (e.g., corresponding to North/South or urban/rural markets). Results are given in [2] for an extension of the CEO problem to multiple agent types, with all agents of Type j characterized by a common observation matrix $W_j(y|x)$. Further, endogenous sorting of agents into types is permitted in our setup.

This chapter furthers the tradition of investigating mathematical ties between statistics and information theory as propounded in the works of Kullback [3], Blahut [4], [5], Cover and Thomas [6], and Barron [7], [8], with special emphasis on decentralized hypothesis testing and estimation with constrained data rates as promulgated by Berger [9], Ahslswede and Csiszár [10], Han [11], Zhang and Berger [12], Han and Kobayashi [13], Amari and Han [14], and Shalaby and Papamarcou [15], [16].

There is an associated body of literature dealing with systems in which subdecisions made by individual agents are fused either centrally or heirarchically. This work was pioneered by Tenney and Sandell [17], with the paper by Tsitsiklis [18] being particularly relevant to the problem we consider here. Tsitsiklis' formulation differs from ours in that we do not assume the agents necessarily communicate equal-cardinality functions of their observations. More importantly, Tsitsiklis' distributed decision-making team is tasked with making a single, instantaneous decision about one X_k whereas ours is tasked with making a sequence of such decisions about succesive X_k's based on sequences of observations by each agent. Accordingly, our team can and does use coding over time to reduce errors.

Let $\{X(t), Y_1(t), \ldots Y_L(t)\}$ be temporally memoryless with instantaneous joint probability distribution

$$Pr(x,y_1,\ldots y_L) = p(x)\prod_{i=1}^{L} W(y_i|x),$$

where $p(x)$ is the common probability distribution of the random variables $X(t)$. From the form of the joint distribution, it is clear that the observations of the agents $Y_i(t)$ for $i = 1, 2, \ldots L$ are conditionally independent given $X(t)$.

For $i = 1, \ldots L$, Agent i encodes a block of length n from his observed data $\{y_i(t)\}_{i=1}^{\infty}$ using a source code C_i^n of rate $R_i^n = \frac{1}{n}\log_2|C_i^n|$. The code words from the L agents, $c_1^n, \ldots c_L^n$, are sent to a central estimator whose task is to recover the source message $x^n = (x(1), \ldots x(n))$ as accurately as possible for the CEO. Loss is measured in terms of the expected bit error frequency defined as

$$P_e^n = \frac{1}{n} Ed_H(X^n, \hat{X}^n), \qquad (1)$$

where $\hat{X}^n$ is the CEO's estimate of the random message $\hat{X}^n$ and d_H is the Hamming distance. This distance function allows sharp results and has the property thgat it is minimized when the estimate is equal to the true value, but it may not be the one most applicable to the chain problem; see below.

Denote the CEO's estimate by

$$\hat{X}^n = \Phi_L^n(C_1^n, \ldots C_L^n), \tag{2}$$

where C_i^n denotes the code word selected by agent i; C_i^n is random because of the joint randomness of the observation noise and the source word.

We study the tradeoff between the total rate, $R = \sum_{i=1}^{L} R_i^n$, and the expected error frequency P_e^n in the following format. For given codes C_i^n, $i = 1, \ldots L$, of block length n, let

$$P_e^n(C_1^n, \ldots, C_L^n) = \min_{\Phi_L^n} \frac{1}{n} E d_H(X^n, \Phi_L^n(C_1^n, \ldots, C_L^n)), \tag{3}$$

the minimum expected error attainable for given codes. Define

$$P_e^n(L,R) = \min_{\sum_{i=1}^{L} R_i^n \le R} P_e^n(C_1^n, \ldots, C_L^n) \tag{4}$$

$$P_e(L,R) = \min_n P_e^n(L,R) \tag{5}$$

and

$$P_e(R) = \lim_{L\to\infty} P_e(L,R). \tag{6}$$

Letting the number of agents get large should smooth out noise, so it makes sense to compare this function with the standard rate-distortion function corresponding to a noiseless observation channel.

We show that $P_e(R)$ decays exponentially with increasing R and determine the decay rate,

$$\alpha(p,W) = \lim_{R\to\infty} \frac{-\log P_e(R)}{R}. \tag{7}$$

The result is stated in Theorem 1 in the next section.

3. THE CODING THEOREM

Theorem 1. Let X and Y be r.v. with $P_{X,Y}(x,y) = p(x)W(y|x)$, and let J be an auxiliary r.v. independent of (X,Y) with probability distribution $P_J(j)$ on an alphabet $\mathcal{J}$ having cardinality

$$|\mathcal{J}| = \binom{|\mathcal{X}|}{2} + 2.$$

Let $\mathcal{U}$ be an alphabet with cardinality

$$|\mathcal{U}| = (\binom{|\mathcal{X}|}{2} + |\mathcal{Y}|)|\mathcal{J}| + 1,$$

let $Q(u\,|\,y, J = j)$ be any conditional distribution on $\mathcal{U}$, and let

$$\tilde{Q}(u|x, J = j) = \sum_y W(y|x)Q(u|y, J = j).$$

Then, where

$$D(Q\|Q') = \sum_u Q(u)\log\frac{Q(u)}{Q'(u)}$$

denotes the Kullback–Leibler discrimination functional (see [5] or [6]), the maximum error decay rate is given by

$$\alpha(p,W) = \max_{Q,P_J}\frac{\min_{x_1,x_2\in X}\mathbf{E}[D(\tilde{Q}_{\lambda,J}\|\tilde{Q}(u\,|\,x_1, J))]}{I(Y;\,U\,|\,X, J)}, \tag{8}$$

where

$$\mathbf{E}D(\tilde{Q}_{\lambda,J}\|\tilde{Q}(u\,|\,x_1,J)) = \sum_{j\in\mathcal{J}} P_J(j)D(\tilde{Q}_{\lambda,j}\|\tilde{Q}(u\,|\,x_1,j))$$

and $\tilde{Q}_{\lambda,j} = \tilde{Q}_{\lambda,j,x_1,x_2}$ is defined as

$$\tilde{Q}_{\lambda,j} = \frac{\tilde{Q}^{1-\lambda}(u\,|\,x_1, j)\tilde{Q}^{\lambda}(u\,|\,x_2, j)}{\Delta_\lambda(x_1, x_2\,|\,j)}$$

with

$$\Delta_\lambda(x_1, x_2\,|\,j) = \sum_u \tilde{Q}^{1-\lambda}(u\,|\,x_1, j)\tilde{Q}^{\lambda}(u\,|\,x_2, j)$$

and $\lambda = \lambda(x_1,x_2)$ selected such that

$$\mathbf{E}[D(\tilde{Q}_{\lambda,J}\|\tilde{Q}(u\,|\,x_1, J))] = \mathbf{E}[D(\tilde{Q}_{\lambda,J}\|\tilde{Q}(u\,|\,x_2, J))].$$

An alternative formula for $\alpha(p,W)$ that does not involve the discrimination functional explicitly is

$$\alpha(p,W) = \max_{Q,P_J}\frac{\min_{x_1,x_2\in X}\sup_\lambda \mathbf{E}[-\log\Delta_\lambda(x_1, x_2|\,J)]}{I(Y;\,U\,|\,X, J)}, \tag{9}$$

The proof of the theorem, which is lengthy, is given in [1]. The proof that α is at least as big as the right-hand side of (9) is based on random code selection. Despite the fact that the agents are statistically exchangeable, it is not optimum for them all to use the same encoding rule. However, at most $\binom{|\mathcal{X}|}{2}$ coding schemes need to be used among all the agents. The codewords of all the agents corresponding to a given source word are in general correlated. A second stage of entropy coding of the Slepian–Wolf [19] variety is done to reduce the required rates. The central estimator first decodes the codewords and then does elementwise multiple hypothesis testing to estimate the source word $(X(1), \ldots, X(n))$. The converse that α cannot exceed the right-hand side of (9) is proved in [1] via a genie-aided argument involving a lengthy string of sophisticated inequalities.

4. INTERPRETATION

First, we provide some interpretation of the theorem. If the agents were allowed to convene before communicating to the central administration, then they could smooth out the observation noise by averaging as $L \to \infty$ and send at the distortion-rate function $D(R)$ corresponding to the probability distribution of the source. This distortion-rate function is zero for all $R > H$, where H is the source entropy rate. Theorem 1 says, contrastingly, that the error frequency decays to zero at most exponentially in R when the agents are mutually isolated; in particular, isolated agents require infinite combined data rate in order to drive the headquarters' error rate to zero. Thus, there is significant performance degradation in the case of agents who must remain isolated as opposed to that of agents who may convene. Perhaps this provides partial justification for occasional, expensive meetings of the franchisees or operators.

It is possible to say more about the optimum coding scheme appearing in the theorem. The available agents are divided into groups each of which specializes in a pairwise decision problem corresponding to a particular source letter pair. The total rate is distributed among the agents with a view toward preventing the error decay rate associated with any one pairwise decision problem from dominating the others. The flavor of this result probably extends to other loss functions as well, implying that data should be collected so that the expected loss associated with each pairwise decision should be the same (given that the cost associated with refining each decision is the same).

At the level of abstraction to asymptotic decay of expected loss for large L and large R at which we have been able to analyze the CEO problem, the detailed structure of the loss function is not essential provided the alphabet $\mathcal{X}$ is finite and the loss function equal to zero at the truth and only at the truth. Thus, we are encouraged that results concerning the CEO problem are germane to the chain problem in which big errors probably are worse than small errors. This feeling is reinforced by results obtained recently regarding the Gaussian case [2] that are similar in terms of the lessons learned. However, in order to gain meaningful insights into the analaysis and design suitable data collection schemes for practical applications characterized by a large yet distinctly finite numbers of agents and by tightly constrained data rates, it will be necessary to find means for taking into account the finer-grained distinctions inherent in a suitable loss function.

5. CONCLUSION

Here are two areas for additional work. 1. The proper loss function for the chain problem would take into account the center's objective function: maximization of profit. In practical applications this is likely to result in the desire to achieve equal marginal expected loss across all pairwise decisions, in turn implying that more effort should be allocated toward more important decisions. We have mentioned that this is a focus of ongoing work. 2. We have sidestepped the issue of prices, implicitly allowing natural variation in prices across units to identify demand. Designed experiments would lead to efficient learning of the demand function. Some theoretical work on this is given in [20], and an application in a one-unit setting in [21]. Incorporating optimal experimentation into the rate-constrained coordination problem seems difficult. Current practice uses a few units as "labs" and coordinates "accurate" information on these units with remaining information. This is deserving of further study.

ACKNOWLEDGMENT

This work, supported by the National Science Foundation under Grants IRI-9005849 and IRI-9310670, is dedicated to the memory of Larry Rosenberg.

REFERENCES

[1] T. Berger, Z. Zhang and H. Viswanathan. The CEO Problem. *IEEE Trans. on Inform. Theory*, vol. 42, pp. 887–902, May 1996.

[2] H. Viswanathan, *Variations on the CEO Problem*, M.S. thesis, Cornell University School of Electrical Engineering, Ithaca, NY, January 1995.

[3] S. Kullback, *Information Theory and Statistics*. Wiley, New York, 1959.

[4] R. E. Blahut, Hypothesis testing and information theory, IEEE Trans. Inform. Theory, vol. 20, pp. 405–417, July 1974.

[5] R. E. Blahut. *Principles and Practice of Information Theory*. Addison-Wesley, New York, 1987.

[6] T. M. Cover and J. A. Thomas. *Elements of Information Theory*. Wiley, New York, 1991.

[7] A. R. Barron, The strong ergodic theorem for densities: Generalized Shannon McMillan–Breiman theory, *Annals of Probability*, vol. 13, 1985.

[8] A. R. Barron, Entropy and the central limit theorem, *Annals of Probability*, vol. 14, pp. 336–342, 1986.

[9] T. Berger, Multiterminal estimation and decision theory, *IEEE Shannon Theory Workshop*, Mt. Kisco, NY, September 12–14, 1979.

[10] R. Ahlswede and I. Csiszár, Hypothesis testing with communication constraints, *IEEE Trans. Inform. Theory*, vol. 32, pp. 533–542, July 1986.

[11] T. S. Han, Hypothesis testing with multiterminal data compression, *IEEE Trans. Inform. Theory*, vol. 33, pp. 759–772, November 1987.

[12] Z. Zhang and T. Berger, Estimation via compressed information, *IEEE Trans. Inform. Theory*, vol. 34, pp. 198–211, March 1988.

[13] T. S. Han and K. Kobayashi, Exponential-type error probabilities for multiterminal hypothesis testing, *IEEE Trans. Inform. Theory*, vol. 35, pp. 2–14, January 1989.

[14] S. I. Amari and T. S. Han, Statistical inference under multiterminal rate restrictions; A differential geometric approach, *IEEE Trans. Inform. Theory*, vol. 35, pp. 217–227, March 1989.

[15] H. M. H. Shalaby and A. Papamarcou, Multiterminal detection with zero-rate data compression, *IEEE Trans. Inform. Theory*, vol. 38, pp. 254–267, March 1992.

[16] H. M. H. Shalaby and A. Papamarcou, Error exponents for distributed detection of Markov sources, *IEEE Trans. Inform. Theory*, vol. 40, pp. 397–408, March 1994.

[17] R. R. Tenney and N. R. Sandell, Jr., Detection with distributed sensors, *IEEE Trans. Aerospace Electron. Systems*, vol. 17, pp. 501–510, 1981.

[18] J. N. Tsitsiklis, Decentralized detection by a large number of sensors, *Math. of Control, Signals, and Systems*, vol. 1, no. 2, pp. 167–182, 1988.

[19] Csiszár and J. Korner, *Information Theory: Coding Theorems for Discrete Memoryless Systems*. Budapest, Hungary: Akademiai Kiado, 1981.

[20] N. M. Kiefer. A value function arising in the economics of information. *Journal of Economic Dynamics and Control, 13*, 201–223, 1989.

[21] N. M. Kiefer, T. J. Kelly and K. Burdett. Menu pricing: an experimental approach. *Journal of Economic Business Statistics, 12*(3), 329–338, 1994.

CHAPTER

20

Organizational Performance, Coordination, and Cognition

Kathleen M. Carley
Carnegie Mellon University

Organizations can be viewed as collections of intelligent agents who are cognitively restricted, task oriented, and socially situated. Accordingly, the behavior of the organization is affected by the behavior of the agents and by how the agents are coordinated. Coordination can be achieved passively through the extant organizational structure. This structure limits agent behavior by determining who has access to what information, who must make which decisions, and who must report what to whom.

Carley and Prietula (1994) referred to this perspective as ACTS theory and described it in detail. Central to this perspective is the idea that organizational performance is jointly affected by coordination and cognition. The thesis is that organizational performance should change, given a particular coordination structure, as you replace the agents with agents of differing cognitive abilities. Replace people by robots or rocks and the organizational performance should change. Similarly, organizational performance should change, given a particular type of agent, as you alter the coordination structure. Change the organizational structure from an democratic team to a more hierarchical structure and organizational performance should change. Similar arguments have been made at the interorganizational level (Malone, 1986; Williamson, 1975).

These arguments seem obvious, yet much of organization theory has looked at organizational performance as being dependent on the coordination structure sans agent cognition. For example, structuralism, institutionalism, and population ecology suggest that organizational performance is largely determined by factors other than human cognitive and affective behavior. In contrast, much of the research in organizational behavior has focused on the impact of cognition sans coordination. We have only a limited understanding of the organization as a collection of coordinated intelligent agents. Recent advances have been made, however, using meso-level models in which macrolevel organizational behavior emerges from the microlevel agent actions (Carley, 1991, 1992; Carroll, 1984; Masuch & LaPotin, 1989). In these models, organizations are formed as collections of intelligent adaptive agents. The models of the agents are based on reasonable assumptions about human behavior, generally predicated on decades of research. The complexity of these agents is sufficient that recognizable, and important, organizational behaviors emerge. In this way, these models have increased our understanding of organizational performance and demonstrated the value of meso-level adaptive agent modeling for building organizational theory. All this being said, there has been little attention as to whether the cognitive nature of the agent alters organizational performance and whether there is an interaction effect between cognition and coordination.

Clearly, organizations composed of agents with different features behave differently. Cohen, March, and Olsen (1972) found that the amount of effort agents expended affected the quality of organizational decisions. Carroll (1984) found that organizations composed of agents with different cultural biases perform differently. Carley, Park, and Prietula (1993) found that whether or not agents lied affected the degree to which the organization wasted time. Lin and Carley (1993) found that organizations of proactive agents tended to outperform organizations of reactive agents. Numerous other examples exist. In all these analyses, and many others, we find that agent features make important differences in organizational performance. However, none of these analyses indicates whether or not increasing the cognitive realism of the agent models, so that they more closely approximate the human agent, alters organizational performance.

Organizations employing different coordination structures may also vary in their performance. Mackenzie (1978) and Roberts (1989) argued that hierarchy is linked organizational efficiency and reliability. Galbraith (1973, 1977) discussed the relative importance of centralization and decentralization. Thompson (1967), Mintzberg (1979), La Porte and Consolini (1991), and Roberts (1990), argued that loosely coupled or structural redundant organizations are high performers in stressful conditions. Numerous other examples exist. In all these analyses, and many others, we find that organizations who coordinate through the use of different designs exhibit different performance. Collectively these studies demonstrate that there is no one best organizational design. However, none of these analyses indicate whether or not the performance attributable to a particular coordination structure will remain constant as the agent model is altered.

Understanding whether the degree of agent veridicality interacts with structural changes in the organization or the task in important ways is important for advancing organizational theory. If we find that the veridicality of the agent model does not interact with the organizational structure or task, that the performance of the coordination structures and task are constant regardless of the agent model, then macro theoretical approaches that ignore the agent gain support. In contrast, if we find that organizational performance, and particularly the relative performance of the different coordination structures, is dependent on the realism of the agent model then these theoretical approaches are called into question.

In this chapter we address this issue directly by contrasting the performance of organizations with different coordination structures, different task complexities (from the agent's perspective), and composed of different "types" of agents. The performance of organizations composed of simple adaptive agents (ELM agents), complex adaptive agents (Soar agents), and humans is examined. As we move from ELM to Soar to humans, presumably the realism of agents is increasing. At issue is how this realism interacts with organizational and task constraints in affecting organizational performance. Similarly, the performance of organizations with teams and hierarchies, blocked and distributed information are examined. For each organization performance is measured. Using this data the relative impact of, and interactions among, cognition and coordination on organizational performance is explored relative to a simple ternary classification–choice task.

THE TASK

The task faced by each organization, regardless of its coordination scheme or the cognitive architecture of its agents, is a ternary classification–choice task. Without loss of generality we can think of this task as a highly stylized radar task. There is a range of physical air space surrounding the radar equipment. This airspace can be scanned by the radar equipment and information about the flying object can be gathered. Within the airspace there is a single object. This object has a true state that is either: FRIENDLY; NEUTRAL; or HOSTILE. This object has nine features. These are: speed (mph); direction (indicating degrees of deflection by which the flight path deviates from a direct route); range (miles); altitude; angle; corridor status (in, edge, out); identification (friendly, civilian, unknown); size (feet; small, medium, large); radar emission type (weather, none, weapons; Carley & Lin, 1992). Each feature has a value of either: 1, 2, or 3. The interpretation of these values depends on the feature (e.g., if the feature is "speed," the Value 1 means speed is low, Value 2 means speed is medium, and Value 3 means speed is high). Initially agents in the organization do not know whether having a low or high value on one feature or another is associated with the object being truly FRIENDLY, NEUTRAL, or HOSTILE. Agents must learn these associations.

The true status of the aircraft is defined external to the organization and is not manipulatable by the organization. This is the characteristic of the design for the task. The true status of the aircraft is manipulated by the experimental designer. By changing the rule relating a pattern of aircraft characteristics to an outcome the researcher can examine different types of tasks. In this chapter, the true status of aircraft is generated by using decomposable and unbiased scheme for defining the task.[1]

In an unbiased environment all three possible outcomes are equally likely. In a decomposable environment each piece of information is equally important. Consequently no analyst plays a more important role than any other simply on the basis of seeing a certain type of information. The task has a complexity level of nine; that is, there are nine pieces of information F1 through F9. Each piece of information can take on one of three values, FRIENDLY = 1, NEUTRAL = 2, and HOSTILE = 3. The true state of the aircraft is defined on the basis of the sum of these nine features. If the sum of the values for these features for a specific aircraft is less than 17 the true state is friendly, if this sum is greater than 19 the true state is hostile, otherwise the true state is neutral. This defining rule establishes which true state is associated with which pattern of information. The members of the organization do not know apriori how the true state is calculated from the set of features. Consequently, the agents in the organization do not know apriori how to relate a particular pattern of information to a particular outcome. Because there are nine pieces of information each of which can take on three values there are 19,683 possible patterns that the organization needs to learn. The organizational design limits the organization's ability to learn these patterns.

Each analyst must decide which one of three states (FRIENDLY, NEUTRAL, HOSTILE) the passing object is, based on the information (the features of the object) he or she can access. The information known by each agent is a subset of the total information, and how many pieces of information in each subset is dependent on the organization's resource access structure. After seeing the information, each agent has to make a decision and deliver a recommendation. How these recommendations are processed

---

[1]In a decomposable task each component has a separable, identifiable, and additive effect in determining the problem solution. Each piece of information contributes equally to the final decision. No agent has greater "power" simply by virtue of having access to a more powerful or more important piece of information. In an unbiased environment approximately one third of the 19683 aircraft are friendly and one third of the aircraft are hostile. This is an environment where all the possible outcomes are equally likely to be true (Carley & Lin 1992).

or combined by the organization depends on the organizational structure. After each analyst has made its recommendation it receives feedback on the true state of the aircraft. The feedback can be considered as part of the training procedure.

This radar task is based on a real-world problem, and variations of it have been widely examined (Carley, 1990, 1991, 1992; Hollenbeck, Sego, Ilgen, & Major, 1991; Mallubhatla, Pattipati, Tang, & Kleinman, 1991). Two features of this task make it appropriate for our present purpose. First, the true state of the object is known. Thus feedback can be provided and issues of training (and hence differences in learning procedures) can be addressed. Second, this task is complex enough that it can be solved in a distributed environment where information is shared by different agents, and multiple agents can be used to work on different aspect of the task.

MODELS OF COORDINATION

The organizational design can serve as a passive coordination scheme defining who does what when. Herein, two aspects of organizational design are considered: the organizational structure and the resource access structure. The organizational structure defines who reports to whom and how the organization makes its decision. The resource access structure defines who has access to what information or resources. Regardless of the organizational design there are nine analysts. Each analyst, regardless of the organization it finds itself in, has access to three pieces of information on each task, makes a recommendation based on this information, and passes on this recommendations as its decision. For each analyst each of the three pieces of information can take on three different values. If there is a manager in the organization then the manager takes these nine recommendations and makes a decision based on them. If there is no manager the organizational decision is simply the majority vote. In principle, each manager has the possibility of seeing nine different pieces of information each of which can take on three different values.

Two organizational structures are examined (see Fig. 20.1): the team with manager and the team with voting. Within the team with manager structure, the organizational decision is made by the CEO who makes this decision after it receives all nine analysts' decisions. Within the team with voting structure, the organizational decision is the majority decision given the separate decisions provided by the nine analysts. We focus on team structures as previous research has demonstrated that teams learn more quickly and are typically more "disturbed" by any type of internal or external stress such as turnover or missing information than are other organizational structures (Carley, 1990, 1991, 1992). The two team structures examined differ, however, in their centralization. The team with voting is a decentralized structure, whereas the team with manager is a centralized structure. By focusing on these structures we will be able to see whether slight changes in the cognitive makeup of the agents make major differences in organizational performance when the decisions made by these agents are combined in different ways. Such an analysis would be more difficult with more complex organizational structures although later work should examine such structures.

Two resource access structures are examined (see Fig. 20.1): distributed and blocked. Within the blocked resource access structure, multiple agents see exactly the same information. In this case, three analysts see the same three pieces of information on each task. Within the distributed resource access structure, no two agents see exactly the same information and each piece of information is seen by more than one person. Specifically, each piece of information is seen by three different analysts. In both resource access structures each analyst sees the same number of pieces of information (three). Thus, regardless of the structure, all analysts are facing tasks with the same complexity and so their information load is the same. All managers, regardless of the resource access structure, see nine pieces of information and so are facing the same information load. Differences in "learning" at the analyst level can only be attributable to differences in the cognitive realism of the agents and not to differences in information loads. Differences

BLOCKED DISTRIBUTED

TEAM WITH VOTING

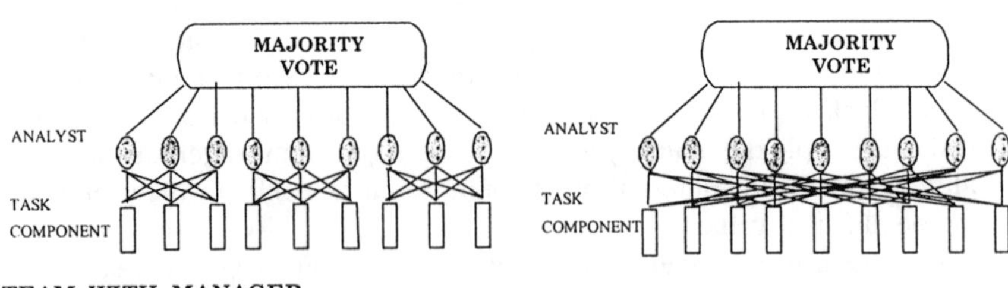

TEAM WITH MANAGER

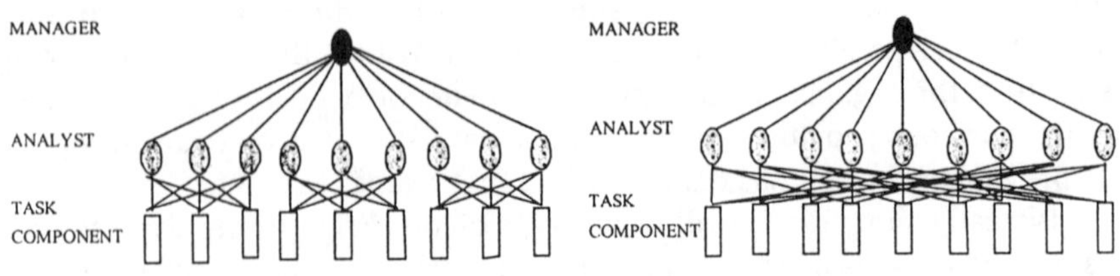

FIG. 20.1. Organizational coordination schemes.

in learning at the managerial level can only be attributable to the extent to which the information they have is consistent and to the cognitive realism of the agents. By focusing on these resource access structures we will be able to see whether slight changes in the cognitive makeup of the agents exacerbate differences due to the level of similarity in different agents' mental models.

For analysts, since they see three pieces of information each of which can take on three values, there are 27 possible patterns. For managers, since they see nine pieces of information each of which can take on three values there are 39 or 19,683 possible patterns. Not all of the patterns are equally likely to occur. The likelihood of a specific pattern is a function of the set of tasks that the organization sees and, for managers, it is also a function of the resource access structure. In this study, the tasks were chosen randomly such that all patterns are equally likely. Thus, for analysts, all patterns are equally likely. For managers, however, the resource access structure determines the likelihood of specific patterns. If the agents are in an organization with a blocked resource access structure then the manager may potentially see only 27 of the possible 19,683 patterns; however, the number actually seen depends on the type of agent. Whereas, a manager in an organization with a distributed resource access structure has a greater likelihood of seeing all 19,683 patterns (if the organization faces that many tasks). How many patterns the manager actually sees depends on the model of cognition. Whether these differences in the number of possible patterns, the probability that certain patterns will occur, and the number of potentially observable possible patterns will affect learning or the speed of making a decision depends on the agent's cognitive capabilities. Regardless of the agent's cognitive makeup the number of patterns affects the resolution of the information available to the decisionmaker and so may affect the quality of the decision maker's decision. For the environment being examined there are 19,683 unique aircraft; hence, 19,683 patterns relating the aircrafts nine features to its true state. The fewer patterns an agent can see the less resolution the agent has on the overall problem.

MODELS OF COGNITION

Three different agent "models" are considered: ELM agents, Soar agents, and human agents. Both ELM (Carley, 1991, 1992; Carley & Lin, 1992) and Soar (Papageorgiou & Carley, 1992; Carley, Kjaer-Hansen, Prietula, & Newell, 1992; Carley, Park, & Prietula, 1993) agents have been used in models of organizations composed of artificial adaptive agents; however, their performance has not been contrasted. Further, there is no research demonstrating how the behavior of these artificial agents actually compare with the behavior of human agents given the specific task we employ. ELM agents are based on a simple experiential learning model using an incremental adaptive algorithm similar in intent to those used in classic learning theory (Bush & Mosteller, 1955). Soar agents are knowledge intensive agents who are capable of employing the various common search algorithms for problem solving (Newell, Yost, Laird, Rosenbloom, & Altmann, 1991).[2] The important point here is that ELM agents are task specific in nature and employ a learning and decision procedure that reflects only a little of what is known about human cognition. In contrast, Soar agents are not task specific and the learning and decision procedures in Soar have been shown to be consistent with much of what is known about human cognition (Laird, Newell, & Rosenbloom, 1987; Rosenbloom, Laird, Newell, & McCarl, 1989). Clearly Soar agents are much closer to humans than are ELM agents in terms of individual behavior. We ask, does this closeness matter when it comes to examining organizational behavior.

Both the specific ELM (Carley & Lin, 1997; Lin & Carley, 1997) and Radar-Soar (Ye & Carley, forthcoming) agents that we employ have been described in detail elsewhere.[3] Soar itself has been described in numerous reports (Laird, Newell, & Rosenbloom, 1987; Laird, Rosenbloom, & Newell, 1986). We limit our description of these models to a brief overview of how these models work, mainly to highlight differences in their assumptions about human problem solving behavior as it relates to the ternary task used in this analysis.

Regardless of how the agents are modeled they make their decisions on the basis of the same incoming information. How the agents are modeled affects how they access, use, recall, and make decisions on the basis of this information. In this study, all analysts see three pieces of information which are the raw task information (about the aircraft). If the agent is a manager he or she sees nine pieces of information which are the decisions of the nine analysts. Each piece of information can take on one of three values: FRIENDLY (=1), NEUTRAL (=2), and HOSTILE (=3). The values for the set of information seen by the agent is referred to as a pattern. For example, an agent might see the pattern 111, meaning that the agent sees three pieces of information for which all three have a value of one. What specific pieces of information the agent sees depends on his or her position in the organization's coordination scheme; specifically, in the organizational structure and the resource access structure.

Regardless of how the agents are modeled they all receive the same feedback in the same way. During training, after each agent has reported his or her decision, he or she is told what the true answer is for the entire problem. That

---

[2]For general discussions of Soar see Mitchell (1988a, 1988b).

[3]See also Carley (1992) for a description of the ELM agents when faced with a binary task. See also Carley and Newell (1994) for a detailed description of Soar as a model of the human agent.

is, each agent is told the true state of the aircraft. Agents are not told how well the organization or they themselves are doing. They have to infer that information from the feedback they receive about the aircraft's true state.

ELM Agents

The Experiential Learning Model (ELM) is a simple model of agent learning and decision making in which the agent incrementally adapts its behavior on the basis of feedback. This model is similar in kind to Bush and Mosteller's (1955) type learning models. This model has been used within various organizational simulation test beds, such as CORP (Carley & Lin, 1997; Lin & Carley, 1977). Such testbeds have been used to examine the relative performance of organizations which place different sociocultural–historical constraints on the agents. ELM employs a simple situated-cognition model of individual action in which agents learn from experience. What information agents have access to and what action they can take are dependent on their social situation in the organization and specific task assigned to them. In ELM the social situation is defined by the agent's position in the organizational design (Carley & Prietula, 1994).

ELM agents are boundedly rational in the sense that: (a) they are not omniscient, (b) they can act only on the information available and their historical knowledge; (c) their historical knowledge is limited to information about the distribution of previous events; and (d) their knowledge is task specific and there are no built in procedures for transferring knowledge between tasks. ELM agents are adaptive in the sense that they change their memories over time.

ELM agents' memories can be thought of as a series of rules of the form "if pattern *x* is seen then report *y*." Each agent has an information load equal to the number of possible patterns that it can possibly see. This information load is affected by the organizational design. In the designs examined the information load for all analysts is 27 and for all managers is 19,683. The higher the load the slower the agent loads and the longer is takes to make a decision. It does not necessarily affect the accuracy of the agent's decision.

The agent reports whether he or she thinks that the aircraft is FRIENDLY (=1), NEUTRAL (=2), or HOSTILE (=3). Each ELM agent has in its memory information for each pattern as to the number of times that he or she saw this pattern and the true answer was FRIENDLY, NEUTRAL, or HOSTILE. The agent then selects as its decision for an observed pattern that event that was most likely in the past. Thus, when faced with the pattern 111, the agent will recall the distribution of true states associated with this pattern, that is, FRIENDLY occurred 6 times, NEUTRAL occurred 4 times, and HOSTILE occurred 2 times. Then the agent will provide as its answer the most likely event, in this case, FRIENDLY.

During training, while the agent is learning, the agent builds up these distributions incrementally. Thus, agents who observe different sets of patterns will actually learn different behavior. If all patterns are equally likely then the analysts and managers will, in the limit, learn to act approximately as majority classifiers (given the task being examined).

For a specific number of tasks, managers in a blocked resource access structure, because they see at most 27 of the possible patterns, will build up more information on how those 27 patterns relate to the three possible outcomes. For those same tasks, managers in a distributed resource access structure have the potential to see 19,683 and so are less likely to build up information on any one pattern. Whether having more information on fewer patterns or less information on more patterns will lead to better decisions is the issue at the managerial level when comparing these resource access schemes for the ELM agents.

Radar–Soar Agents

Radar–Soar agents are complex adaptive agents built on top of the Soar architecture. Following is a brief description of Soar. This is followed by a brief description of the Soar agents.

Soar. Soar is a general-purpose program for solving problems. It incorporates specific knowledge about the world as a set of rules that guide it in solving problems. Soar agents learn from experience by remembering how they solve problems—this is referred to as chunking. Within Soar all cognitive behavior is considered to be symbolic and goal oriented. Soar is considered to be unified theory of cognition as it is a single, integrated set of information processing mechanisms that try to explain every aspect of human thought, not one or two experimental results (Newell, 1990).

Soar characterizes all cognitive behavior as search in problem spaces and serves as an architecture for general intelligent behavior (Laird et al., 1987). Soar's structure is built in levels, starting with memory and proceeding to decisions and goals. A learning procedure (chunking) and default knowledge are also incorporated into the system, but need not be used (Rosenbloom et al., 1989). In this chapter the chunking mechanism is not employed.

- *Memory:* All Soar's long-term knowledge is stored in a single production memory composed of if–then rules. Memory access consists of the execution of these productions. As these productions are executed information is retrieved into a global working memory. The working memory is a temporary memory which roughly corresponds to the set of things that the agent is attending to at any given moment. A special type of working memory structure is the preference. Preferences encode control knowledge about the acceptability and desirability of actions. Acceptability preferences determine which action should be considered as a candidate action. Desirability preferences define a partial ordering on the candidate actions.

• *Decision:* The decision cycle requires two phases: elaboration and decision. During the elaboration phase, the long-term (production) memory is accessed repeatedly (effectively in parallel), until no more productions can execute. This can result in a set of preferences being established. During the decision phase, these preferences are interpreted. This can result in changes in the agent's goal, state, actions, etc. This decision cycle ensures that Soar will make its decisions after all the rules have been fired; consequently, Soar will use the most powerful knowledge it has available. When there is little knowledge in long-term memory, Soar will behave in ways that resemble general problem-solving techniques such as hill climbing, or means–ends analysis. When there is lots of knowledge in long-term memory, Soar will behave as an expert as it will have clear preferences about what to do next.

• *Goals:* Goals are set whenever a decision cannot be made; that is, when an impasse is reached during the decision phase. Impasses include: ties; conflicts; no-changes; constraint failures. When an impasse occurs, Soar creates a subgoal to resolve the impasse and a corresponding performance context. This results in a hierarchical goal structure. A subgoal is terminated when either its impasse is resolved or a higher impasse in the stack is resolved. This architectural feature is called *universal subgoaling* (Laird et al., 1986). Goals are functions on behavior (i.e., agents prefer some actions to others). An agent's behavior is determined by the *principle of rationality*; that is, if the agent knows that one of its actions leads to a preferred situation according to its goal, then it will intend the preferred action, and this action will then occur if it is possible (Newell et al., 1991). Agents exhibit goal-directed behavior, because all actions intend to attain the agent's goal. Agent's are rational, because everything the agent knows serves the agent's interest.

Radar–Soar

Developing task-related agents in Soar requires determining for each agent its initial task knowledge, possible actions, and problem spaces. This task knowledge is instantiated as productions in the agent's long-term knowledge base. The actions are instantiated as operators within problem spaces (which are the arenas for action). As productions are fired the agents solve problems by moving through a series of problem spaces and within each space taking those actions that are preferred. A task is formulated using a problem space by: determining which problem space to adopt; setting a goal which determines which desired state is adopted; and determining the initial state. The formulated task is accomplished by: attempting state-operator pairs; applying operators; and terminating the current state when the desired state is reached.

Analysts and managers differ in the problem spaces and actions they used for communication. Both analysts and managers move between problem spaces by taking actions in one space which then move the agent to a subsequent space. Regardless of whether the agent is an analyst or a manager the agent makes its decision within a make-decision space.

The make-decision space is critical to the subject of this chapter. In this space the agent compares the newly observed information with each of the models currently in its knowledge base and calculates the level of match for each model. A model is a description of aircraft features and the values they take on (a pattern) and a predicted outcome. Each model is represented as a rule of the form "if pattern X is seen then report Y." (These patterns are equivalent to the patterns in ELM.) The match is the number of features in the observed aircraft and the model that have identical values. For example, for analyst, if the model is that all three features are FRIENDLY and the observation is that one of the three features is FRIENDLY and the other two are not, then the match is one. If the agent has *N* models then *N* matches are calculated. The agents preference for a model is based on the match. Specifically, agents prefer models with higher matches and are indifferent among those with the same level of match. After the matches have been calculated the agent chooses that model that has the highest match. If there are several such models the agent randomly chooses among them. Among the equally preferred models, which model is chosen is determined randomly. Because the agent stores a model for each problem that it observes, this results in the agent's decision having a probability associated with it proportional to the number of times the agent has observed this type of aircraft with this type of outcome. The more models the agent has the longer it takes for the agent to make a decision (without chunking). When a model is chosen the agent makes as its decision the choice recommended by this model.

When the current situation is beyond the agent's knowledge, he or she will make a decision based on reasoning and not simply by guessing. If an agent sees an aircraft he or she will compare the features of that aircraft to the models available (to start with this will only be the initial knowledge). Then the agent will choose the model that has the closest match to the current aircraft. For example, imagine that the agent sees only three aircraft features and that the first aircraft seen has the features high, high, medium. The agent will calculate the match with the existing models. The match with the first model (all high) is 2, the match with the second model (all medium) is 1, and the match with the third model (all low) is 0. These matches set up a preference ordering among outcomes such that the first model is preferred to the second, which is preferred to the third. Thus the agent will choose the first model and make whatever decision it suggests.

A second critical space for this model is the update knowledge space. The update knowledge space is the space where the agent creates new models. In this space the agent takes its observation and the feedback it has received and creates a new model. Feedback is of the form the aircraft's true status is FRIENDLY (or NEUTRAL, or HOSTILE). Each observation results in a new model. Each time the agent receives feedback during training it creates a new model linking the observed pattern with the true state of the aircraft.

- *Analysts:* Overall, the analyst's goal is to resolve all commands forwarded by the manager. The analyst sees a sequence of commands and responds to these, and stops when all commands are resolved. These commands direct the analyst in the observation of the airspace and the making of decisions on the information observed. Each Radar–Soar analyst is implemented with 11 problem spaces connected hierarchically. The top problem space contains the initial states and the desired state (the goal state). The goal state is where all commands are resolved. This connects to the communication problem space. In the communication problem space, three operators are sequentially proposed: the get-command operator; the report operator; and the get-feedback operator. Each operator in turn calls the corresponding problem space. Within the get-command problem space, there are two kinds of commands from the manager: "observe" and "tell-me," which when accepted by the analyst lead to two different problem spaces, the observe air-space problem space and the make-decision problem space. In the observe air-space problem space, two operators are raised. One is the parse information operator which the analyst uses to analyze the signal captured from the air-space about the flying object; another is the interpret operator which the analyst uses to convert each signal to the attribute it represents. Each operator calls up their corresponding problem space. In the make-decision problem space, two operators are also proposed, one is the model-select operator which compares the information of the aircraft to all the different models in an analyst's long-term memory, then makes a decision based on the maximum match; the other operator is the write-decision operator which the analyst uses to record his or her decision so that it can be reported to the manager later. Each of these operators also creates their own problem spaces in which the operators are enacted.

Each analyst sees exactly three pieces of information or features. The three initial productions (or initial models) are:

If feature-1 = feature-2 = feature-3 = FRIENDLY then decision = FRIENDLY
If feature-1 = feature-2 = feature-3 = NEUTRAL then decision = NEUTRAL
If feature-1 = feature-2 = feature-3 = HOSTILE then decision = HOSTILE

Within the make-decision space the analyst's goal is to suggest a decision about the true state of the aircraft. Initially the analyst can only compare the observation with these three models. Thus, initially the analyst will act as a majority classifier. Over time as new models are built the analyst's behavior will come to emulate the lessons of history. However, to the extent that multiple models are equally valid the analyst will choose between them stochastically.

- *Managers:* Managers are conceptually similar to analysts. The main difference is that they have additional communication actions, can command other agents, and their initial models are based on nine rather than three pieces of information. The Radar–Soar manager is implemented using six problem spaces connected hierarchically. The top problem space contains the initial states and the desired state for the manager. The top problem space, as with the analyst connects to the communication problem space. Within the communication problem space four operators are sequentially proposed: the give-command operator; the receive-response operator; the make-organizational decision operator; and get-feedback operator. These four operators in turn lead to four problem spaces in which the manager carries out its actions.

The manager's goal is to make the best possible organizational decision for each of the problems it faces. Each manager sees exactly nine pieces of information, one for each analyst. The three initial productions are:

If agent-1 = agent-2 =. . . agent-9 = FRIENDLY then organizational decision = FRIENDLY

If agent-1 = agent-2 =. . . agent-9 = NEUTRAL then organizational decision = NEUTRAL

If agent-1 = agent-2 =. . . agent-9 = HOSTILE then organizational decision = HOSTILE

The manager will build up models at the same rate as the analysts. A manager in a blocked resource access structure will build up more models with similar left hand sides than will managers in distributed resource access structures. Hence, when a new aircraft is observed there will, on average, be more models with equivalent matches to the new data. Hence the manager's preference ordering will be less likely to suggest a unique outcome and the manager will be more likely to be indifferent among a wider variety of models. Consequently, stochastic factors may play a greater role in the organizational outcome when the resource access structure is blocked.

Because Radar–Soar agents act in a stochastic fashion, two agents who see the same information may respond differently. Thus, in a blocked resource access structure, even though three analysts see the same information they may not respond in a similar fashion. Consequently, the manager in a Radar–Soar organization, even when the resource access structure is blocked, may potentially see more patterns than the ELM manager in the same situation. Whether the potential lack of consensus among analysts despite common incoming information, in the Radar–Soar situation, will lead to better decisions is the issue when comparing Radar–Soar and ELM organizations with blocked resource access structures. Whether the lack of consensus among analysts caused by interpretation (differences caused by analysts in a blocked resource access structure stochastically making different choices) or caused by different information (differences caused by analysts in a distributed resource access structure making different choices) leads to better or worse performance is the issue in contrasting Radar–Soar organizations under the different resource access structures.

Human Agents

A series of experiments were run by Carley and Prietula to examine the effect of structure. These organizations duplicate the organizations examined via simulation by Carley.[4] In the human experiments subjects were run as either analysts or managers; managers and analysts are not present at the same time.

Each analyst (subject) was given a series of simple "radar classification problems." Each problem involves two simple steps. Step 1, each analyst receives three parameter readings about an aircraft in the air space, such as: SPEED = Low, RANGE = Short, SIZE = Small. Step 2, on the basis of this information, each analyst classifies the aircraft as either: HOSTILE, NEUTRAL, or FRIENDLY. Information was given to the subjects and collected from them electronically. In Fig. 20.2 an illustrative display is shown. After the subject makes his or her decision, he or she is asked to provide an estimate of confidence in that decision. The subject's decision, speed, and confidence are stored.

The same procedure is repeated for the subjects acting as managers. There are two differences between the analyst and managerial condition. First, in the analyst condition the subjects receive raw information on the aircraft. Whereas, in the managerial condition the subjects receive the decisions of a set of nine human subjects. Second, in the analyst condition the subjects are told that their decision is not the final organizational decision, that they are working as part of a team, and that they are receiving reduced information about aircraft from scanners. In contrast, the subjects acting as

[4]The human experimental data reported on here is a subset of that collected by Carley and Prietula. The automated data collection procedure was written by Prietula.

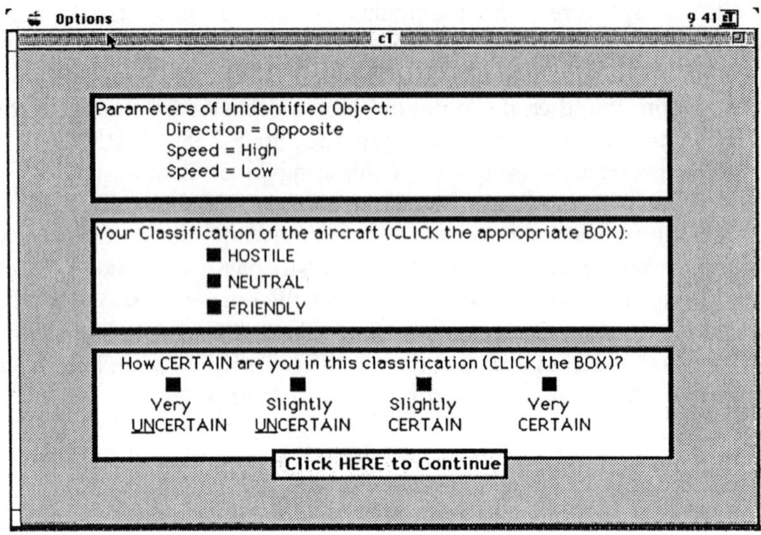

FIG. 20.2. Illustrative data collection screen.

managers are told that their decision is the final organizational decision, that they are receiving information from a set of nine analysts as to what those analysts think is the true state of the aircraft.

PERFORMANCE

Performance is measured at the organizational level. Each organization for each problem makes a single decision. For teams with voting the organizational decision is the majority vote of the group. For teams with manager the organizational decision is the decision made by the manager. For each problem there is a "correct" answer, the true state of the aircraft. Performance is measured in terms of the number of times the organizational decision is the correct decision.

Overall performance is defined as the percentage of decisions made by the organization that match the true state of the aircraft. For example, a match occurs if the organizational decision is that the aircraft is FRIENDLY and the true state of the aircraft is FRIENDLY. A second measure is "slight error"—the percentage of decisions that are one step different from the true state of the aircraft. This can happen, for example, when the true state of the aircraft is NEUTRAL, and the organization thinks it is either FRIENDLY or HOSTILE. A third measure is "severe error"—the percentage of the decisions that are two steps different from the true state of the aircraft. This can happen, for example, when the true state of the aircraft is FRIENDLY and the organization thinks it is HOSTILE. Table 20.1 shows the mapping between organizational decision, true state, and these measures. These three measures are calculated separately for each phase. Thus, the percentage in each phase is based on 30 decisions.

RESEARCH DESIGN

A series of organizations varying in their coordination structure and the cognitive structure of the agent were analyzed. A total of 12 organizations were examined, four coordination schemes (two organizational structures by two resource access structures) by three types of agents. All agents, regardless of the organization or cognitive abilities are pretrained on a random sample of 10 problems. Each organization was then faced with a series of 60 problems/aircrafts. These 60 cases are divided into two phases, each of which has 30 cases. The difference between the first phase and second phase is that during the first phase the agents are learning and during the second phase the agents are not learning. During the first phase the agents receive feedback and during the second phase they do not. The 60 problems are drawn randomly from the possible 19,683, with the constraint that for each set of 30 one third of them have a true state of FRIENDLY, another one third have a true state of NEUTRAL, and the final one third have a true state of HOSTILE. All organizations get the same set of problems. Analyses using ELM reveal that these problems are typical of the overall set of 19,683 problems; that is, performance is not significantly different on this set than it is for the overall set. This suggests that the results should generalize to others sets of problems for this task.

TABLE 20.1
Definition of Organizational Performance Measures

Organizational Decision	*True State*		
	FRIENDLY	NEUTRAL	HOSTILE
NEUTRAL	correct	one away	two away
NEUTRAL	one away	correct	one away
HOSTILE	two away	one away	correct

RESULTS

Overall the organizations examined make the correct decision 58.1% of the time. Further, these organizations make slight errors (off by one) 34.7% of the time, and a severe error (off by two) 7.2% of the time. The agent's nature does affect the organization's performance (see Table 20.2). First, all agents do better than simply guessing. Secondly, ELM agents are more similar to Human agents than are Soar agents. Further, cognitively sophisticated agents tend to make fewer severe errors. On the one hand, what these results are suggesting is simply that humans are not particularly well suited to this task, in general, and that information aids that admit keeping track of past performance (as is done in ELM or Soar) improve organizational performance. A supporting point is that ELM agents who were trained not just on the training set, but on all 19,683 possible tasks, have higher performance than any of the agents shown here. A corroborating point is made by researchers interested in technology to support group decision making (Olson, 1989). However, these information aids may aid in overall performance but they may serve to mask critical failures that humans appear to pick up on. On the other hand, and more to the point of this chapter, what these results are suggesting is that organizational performance can be dramatically affected by how the agents in the organization are modeled.

In Table 20.2 we see that organizations of Soar agents tend to outperform organizations of either ELM or Human agents. This is true even though there is no transference of learned productions among Soar agents. The reason has to do with the variance among the individual agents. Soar agents, because they are choosing among rules in a stochastic fashion, can see exactly the same information and yet make slightly different decisions. ELM agents, on the other hand, given similar experiences, will make exactly the same deci-

TABLE 20.2
Agents and Organizational Behavior

		Organizational Behavior	
Agent	*Overall Performance*	*Light Error (One Away)*	*Severe Error (Two Away)*
ELM	0.567 (0.497)	0.338 (0.474)	0.096 (0.295)
Soar	0.654 (0.477)	0.317 (0.466)	0.029 (0.169)
Human	0.521 (0.501)	0.388 (0.488)	0.092 (0.289)

Note. The number in parentheses is the standard deviation. *N* is 240 in each cell.

sion given the same information. Human agents, see exactly the same information and yet can make very different decisions. Thus, these results are suggesting that slight variations in individual response given the same information can lead to improved organizational decisions; whereas, extreme variation in individual response can lead to worse organizational decisions.

Overall, these results suggest that researchers interested in exploring organizational behavior resulting from agent behavior need to be careful about how they model the agents. Such a conclusion is of little import, however, if the difference in organizational behavior is simply scaled by agent type. In other words, if regardless of the type of coordination scheme or of whether or not the agents are undergoing training, organizational performance for organizations of Soar agents was always proportionally higher than that for ELM agents, which was in turn always proportionally higher than that for Human agents, the impact of the agent model would be less critical to the study of organizational behavior. Whereas, if there are interaction effects among agent cognition, coordination, and training, then in fact the model of the agent is critical to the study of organizational behavior.

In fact, there are interaction effects. All organizations, regardless of the agents' cognitive capabilities exhibit poorer performance when there is a manager (see Fig. 20.3). This is due largely to the fact that as decisions move up the hierarchy information is lost. This effect is quite robust and has been discussed by numerous organizational theorists using terms such as *infor-*

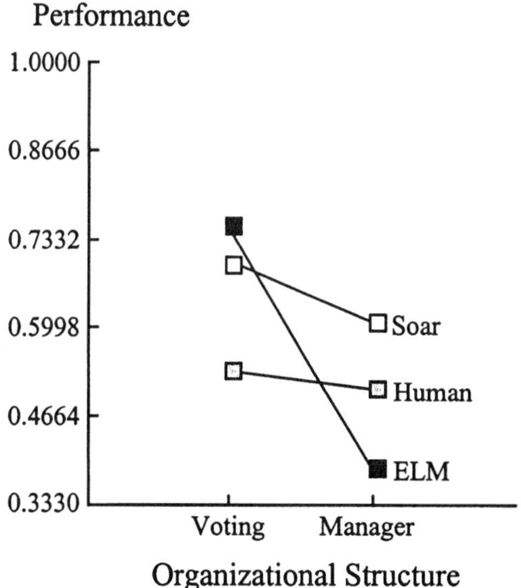

FIG. 20.3. Interaction between organizational structure and cognition.

mation condensation (Jablin, Putnam, Roberts, & Porter, 1986) and *uncertainty absorption* (March & Simon, 1958). Additionally, this analysis shows that organizations of ELM agents are relatively more disadvantaged by the manager than are Soar organizations which are relatively more disadvantaged than are human organizations. Part of ELM's relative disadvantage comes from the fact that the managers have rarely observed the patterns before and so are often guessing. However, organizations of ELM agents where the managers have seen all possible patterns still exhibit a greater reduction in performance when they have a manager than do organizations of other types of agents. The more cognitively sophisticated managers, Soar and human, do relatively better at this task than the ELM managers because they are not overcommitted to the lessons of history and can respond in a stochastic or "strategic" fashion. This ability, to overcome history through the fortuitous guess, causes organizations of these agents to be less disadvantaged by the information loss inherent in more hierarchical structures.

There are also interaction effects between the resource access structure and agent cognition. In particular, while the organizations of artificial agents tend to exhibit lower performance when information is distributed, organizations of humans tend to do better. Soar organizations are less disadvantaged by a distributed structure than are ELM organizations. The potential lack of consensus among analysts despite common incoming information results in worse decisions for Radar–Soar and ELM organizations; but, better decisions for human organizations. Further, Soar organizations are less

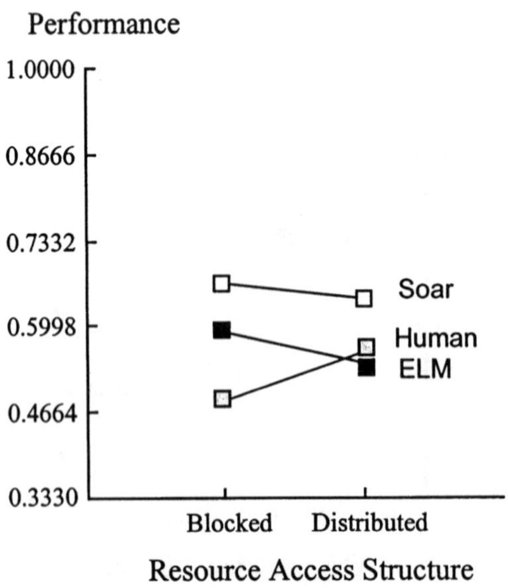

FIG. 20.4. Interaction between resource access structure and cognition.

disadvantaged by this lack of consensus, than are ELM organizations, as it occurs in both resource access structures. In the blocked structure the lack of consensus among Radar–Soar analysts is caused by interpretation (analysts seeing the same information but stochastically making different choices). In the distributed structure the lack of consensus among Radar–Soar analysts is caused by different information (analysts see different information and make different choices). For Soar agents the lack of consensus, coupled with the ability to respond stochastically results in overall better performance. For ELM, who learn slowly and respond consistently, the low level of training results in worse performance in a distributed environment because on average, more of the agents in the organizations will be guessing. In fact, had the ELM agents been fully trained (not shown) then the ELM organization, like the human organization, would have had an increase in performance when the resource access structure was distributed. Humans can take advantage of the greater resolution afforded by the distributed structure as can more fully trained ELM organizations.

Now consider these impacts only in organizations with managers. In Fig. 20.5, the relative impact of the different types of cognitive agents under these resource schemes for just teams with managers are shown. As note previously, ELM organizations when they have managers, the managers have less to learn in a blocked than in a distributed structure. As a result,

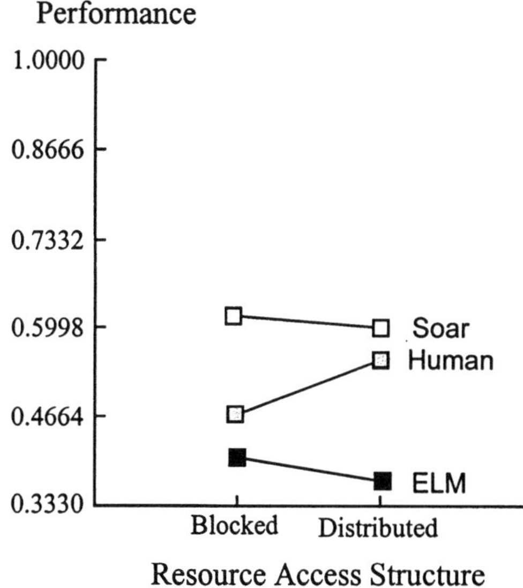

FIG. 20.5. Interaction between resource access structure and cognition in teams with managers.

they should and do, do better in this structure when they are only minimally trained as in this experiment. This lowering in performance for the ELM organizations is due simply to lack of training. Soar and human organizations can overcome this in two ways. First, differences in agent interpretation by the analysts (which should lead to the problem being "harder" from the manager's standpoint as it increases the number of patterns actually improves performance as the organization does not get trapped by an erroneous understanding of historical precedence as do the ELM organizations.

TRAINING

Now consider the impact of training. Both ELM and Soar organizations do better in Phase two when they are not receiving feedback than they did in Phase one when they did receive feedback. This is caused, not by some perverse ability to do better in the absence of feedback but simply because the only impact feedback to these artificial organizations into alter what decisions they have made. During phase one, the individuals in all organizations are learning. Feedback moves the agents, whether human, Soar, or ELM, out of the realm of guessing and improves their accuracy. Soar and ELM organizations do better in phase two as they remember the lessons of phase one and are less likely to guess during the second phase than the first. The

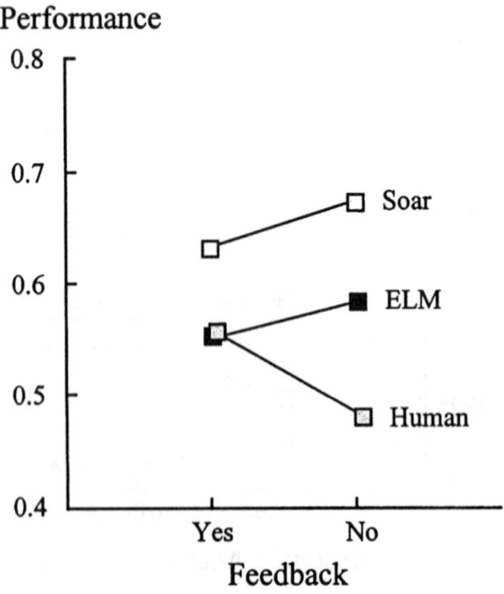

FIG. 20.6. Impact of training.

absence of feedback keeps them from learning more but does not inhibit them from applying the lessons of history. In contrast, within human organizations feedback appears to be necessary both for learning and for convincing the humans to continue to apply the lessons of history.

DISCUSSION

In interpreting the foregoing results the reader should keep in mind the following caveats. First, these results are based on only 30 problems per phase where the 30 problems were chosen at random from a set of 19,683 possible problems. This is a very small proportion of the possible problems. Future work should consider increasing the sample size, or running the overall study multiple times with different sample problems.

Second, the results for each type of agent are based on a single organization. For ELM, this is not a problem as all ELM organizations faced with the same set of problems in the same order will respond in the same way. For Soar, this is more of a problem as the stochastic nature of the decision making will lead to slight differences in performance across different Soar organizations. For Humans, this is yet more of a problem. That is, we expect that there is even greater variance in the behavior of individual humans than there is in behavior of Soar agents and certainly more than in the behavior of ELM agents. Future studies should run a Monte-Carlo analysis for Soar organizations and should average the behavior for multiple Human organizations.

Third, the results presented have been at the organizational level. They provide no insight into whether at the individual level Soar agents acts more like Human agents than do ELM agents. Future work should explore this issue through a more detailed analysis of individual action. Such an exploration could look at both individual performance, and also at the impact of the order of decisions on the specific learning pattern achieved by the various types of agents. Such analyses would provide greater insight into how agent level actions change in response to cognition and coordination.

Fourth, the radar task that we used is highly stylized and differs from a real radar task in interesting ways. For example, there is no autocorrelation among aircraft features. Whereas, in reality these features tend to clump. For example, aircraft with weapons emission signals also are often traveling very fast. At issue is whether this lack of clumpiness makes the problem relatively more difficult for humans than for the simulated agents. The data we have collected cannot completely address this question. However, when the presence of features is not uniform (as in this study) and when sets of features tend to go together in predicting some outcome the problem is "easier" for humans. Certainly, for ELM agents, such clumpiness or bias reduces uncertainty and increases performance (Carley & Lin, 1995). Given the Soar agent model, it will also be the case that for Soar agents clumpiness will improve performance. Because the performance of all agents will improve in such a situation, it is not clear whether in fact humans will be relatively more advantaged. Future research might address this question.

All these caveats aside, the import of this study is that it demonstrates that the model of cognition affects organizational performance results in complex and interesting ways, and that interactions between the organizational structure and the model of cognition are important in determining overall organizational performance. This research on coordination using computational models differs from other work in this venue in two ways. First, studies of coordination that employ computational models of agents rarely contrast the behavior of the simulated agents with humans (Durfee, 1988). Such a contrast is important when the goal is predicting actual organization behavior. Herein, a basic attempt at making such comparisons is made. Second, many of the computational studies of coordination employ large models that emulate the organizations in question (Gasser & Majchrzak, 1992, 1994; Levitt et al., 1994) rather than examine the behavior of highly stylized coordination schemes such as those examined here. The models examined herein are less "accurate" in describing organizational coordination, but are better models of individual cognition. Important advances in understanding organizational performance can be made by contrasting the results from the two styles of computational modeling. Future studies should consider extending these results by contrasting alternate models of individual behavior and by attending to the limits of the current study.

CONCLUSION

This research suggests that complex adaptive agent models can be fruitfully applied to the study of organizations. Two different complex adaptive agent models of humans were constructed, these agent models were placed within models of organizational coordination, and the resulting organizational performance was examined. These simulated results were compared with the actual performance of humans engaged in the same coordination structures. This combination of simulation and human experiments is particularly valuable in understanding the veridicality of the computational models. Moreover, this combination is valuable in understanding how the veridicality of the agent model interacts with structural and task changes in affecting organizational performance. Consider the following two examples.

Clearly, the forgoing analysis supports previous research that teams outperform hierarchies (regardless of the type of agent) and that organizations of artificial agents often outperform organizations of humans. More importantly, this analysis refines these points by pointing to important interactions between structure and cognition. For example, for managers, the ability to respond stochastically, to make "strategic" decisions, improves performance. The result of these "guesses," is that differences in performance due to the organizational structure are minimized when the agents in the organizations are more cognitively capable. The fortuitous guess has advantages. This compliments earlier work by Carley and Lin (1995) showing that factors facilitating managerial decision making, such as bias in the task, serve not only to improve performance but to mitigate the impact of structure. Ouchi (1980) suggested that as task complexity and information uncertainty increases new forms of coordination may be needed. This chapter, in contrast, suggests that new coordination qua mechanisms for linking individuals together, may have little impact as the agents in these organizations are generally intelligent. Performance should become not just a function of the coordination scheme linking individuals (Malone, 1986); but also, the specific messages being communicated among linked positions. Thus improvements in coordination might be achievable not through structure, but through content.

Previous research suggested that specialization, much as we see in the blocked structure, is disadvantageous. For instance, in blocked structures agents develop unique skills, perspectives, and ways of thinking (Brewer & Kramer, 1985) that can reduce the group's flexibility in a crisis (Carley, 1991) and exacerbate conflict when it occurs (Dearborn & Simon, 1958; Jablin, 1979; Monge, Rothman, Eisenberg, Miller, & Kirste, 1985). This suggests that consensus is valuable to the organization. In this chapter, however, it was found that for organizations the lack of consensus among agents caused by interpretation (different decision on same information) results in improved performance; but the lack of consensus among agents caused by resolution (seeing different information) tends to degrade performance. In other words a shared perspective, whether or not it results in consensus seems to be important in increasing performance. However, whether the observed results are actually the result of having a shared perspective, or a function of the degree of disagreement, needs further study.

Complex interactions among agent cognitive capacity, task complexity, and organizational design affect overall organizational performance. The implication of this finding is that researchers must be very careful in interpreting results of studies of organizational performance based on modeling organizations as collections of intelligent adaptive agents as such results maybe highly dependent on the agent model.

ACKNOWLEDGMENT

This work was supported in part by Grant No. IRI-9111804 by the National Science Foundation.

REFERENCES

Brewer, M. B. and R. M. Kramer (1985). The psychology of intergroup attitudes and behavior, *Annual Review of Psychology, 36*, 219–243.

Bush, R. R. and F. Mosteller (1955). *Stochastic Models of Learning*, New York: Wiley.

Carley, K. M. (1990). Coordinating for Success: Trading Information Redundancy for Task Simplicity. *Proceedings of the 23rd Annual Hawaii International Conference on System Sciences.*

Carley, K. M. (1991). Designing Organizational Structures to Cope with Communication Breakdowns. *Industrial Crisis Quarterly, 5*(1), 19–57.

Carley, K. M. (1992). Organizational Learning and Personnel Turnover. *Organization Science, 3*(1), 2–46.

Carley, K. M. and J. Harrald (1993). Organizational Learning Under Fire: Theory and Practice. *American Behavioral Scientist, 40*(3), 310–332.

Carley, K., J. Kjaer-Hansen, M. Prietula, and A. Newell (1992). Plural-Soar: A Prolegomenon to Artificial Agents and Organizational Behavior. In M. Masuch & M. Warglien (Eds.), *Artificial Intelligence in Organization and Management Theory* (pp. 87–118). Amsterdam, The Netherlands: Elsevier.

Carley, K. M. and Z. Lin (1995). Organizational Designs Suited to High Performance Under Stress. *IEEE Systems, Man and Cybernetics, 25*(1), 221–230.

Carley, K. M. and Z. Lin (1997). A Theoretical Study of Organizational Performance under Information Distortion. *Management Science, 43*(7), 976–997.

Carley, K. M. and A. Newell (1994). The Nature of the Social Agent. *Journal of Mathematical Sociology, 19*(4), 221–262.

Carley, K. M., D. Park, and M. Prietula (1993). Agent Honesty, Cooperation and Benevolence in an Artificial Organization. *Proceedings of AI and Theories of Groups and Organizations: Conceptual and Empirical Research*, Eleventh National Conference on Artificial Intelligence, Washington, DC.

Carley, K. M. and M. J. Prietula (1994). ACTS Theory: Extending the Model of Bounded Rationality, In K. M. Carley and M. J. Prietula (Eds.), *Computational Organization Theory* (pp. 55–87). Hillsdale, NJ: Lawrence Erlbaum Associates.

Carroll, G. R. (1984). Organizational Ecology. *Annual Review of Sociology, 10*, 71–93.

Cohen, M. D., J. B. March, and J. P. Olsen (1972). A Garbage Can Model of Organizational Choice. *Administrative Science Quarterly, 17*(1), 1–25.

Dearborn, D. C. and H. A. Simon (1958). Selection Perception: A Note on the Departmental Identification of Executives. *Sociometry, 21*, 140–144.

Durfee, E. H. (1988). *Coordination of Distributed Problem Solvers*. Boston, MA: Kluwer.

Galbraith, J. (1973). *Designing Complex Organizations*. Reading, MA: Addison-Wesley.

Galbraith J. R. (1977). *Organization Design*. Reading, MA: Addison-Wesley.

Gasser, L. and A. Majchrzak (1992). HITOP-A: Coordination, Infrastructure, and Enterprise Integration. *Proceedings of the First International Conference on Enterprise Integration*. Boston: MIT Press.

Gasser, L. and A. Majchrzak (1994). ACTION Integrates Manufacturing Strategy, Design, and Planning. In P. Kidd and W. Karwowski (Eds.), *Ergonomics of Hybrid Automated Systems IV*. Netherlands: IOS Press.

Hollenbeck, J. R., D. R. Ilgen, D. J. Sego, J. Hedlund, D. A. Major, and J. Phillips (1995). The Multilevel Theory of Team Decision Making: Decision Performance in Teams Incorporating Distributed Expertise. *Journal of Applied Psychology, 80*, 292–316.

Jablin, F. M. (1979). Superior-subordinate communication: The state of the art. *Psychological Bulletin, 86*, 1201–1222.

Jablin, F. M., L. L. Putnam, K. H. Roberts, and L. W. Porter (Eds.). (1986). *Handbook of Organizational Communication: An Interdisciplinary Perspective*. Beverly Hills, CA: Sage.

Laird, J. E., P. S. Rosenbloom, and A. Newell (1986). *Universal Subgoaling and Chunking: The Automatic Generation and Learning of Goal Hierarchies*. Boston, MA: Kluwer.

Laird, J., A. Newell, and P. Rosenbloom (1987). Soar: An Architecture for General Intelligence. *Artificial Intelligence, 33*, 1–64.

La Porte, T. R., and P. M. Consolini (1991). Working in Practice But Not in Theory: Theoretical Challengers of 'High-Reliability Organizations'. *Journal of Public Administrative Research & Theory, 1*(1), 19–47.

Levitt, R. E., G. P. Cohen, J. C. Kunz, C. I. Nass, T. Christiansen, and Y. Jin (1994). A Theoretical Evaluation of Measures of Organizational Design: Interrelationship & Performance Predictability. In K. M. Carley & M. J. Prietula (Eds.), *Computational Organization Theory* (pp. 1–18). Hillsdale, NJ: Lawrence Erlbaum Associates.

Lin, Z. and K. M. Carley (1993). Proactive or Reactive: An Analysis of the Effect of Agent Style on Organizational Performance. *International Journal of Intelligent Systems in Accounting, Finance and Management, 2*, 271–288.

Lin, Z. and K. M. Carley (1997). Organizational Response: The Cost Performance Tradeoff. *Management Science, 43*(2), 217–234.

Mackenzi, K. D. (1978). *Organizational Structures*. Arlington Heights, IL: AHM Publishing Corporation.

Malone, T. W. (1986). Modeling Coordination in Organization and Markets. *Management Science, 33*(10), 1317–1332.

Masuch, M. and P. LaPotin (1989). Beyond Garbage Cans: An AI Model of Organizational Choice. *Administrative Science Quarterly, 34*, 38–67.

Mintzberg, H. (1979). *The Structure of Organizations*. Englewood Cliffs, NJ: Prentice-Hall.

Mitchell, W. M. (1988a). Toward a Unified Theory of Cognition. *Science, 241*, 4861, 27–29.

Mitchell, W. M. (1988b). Soar: A Unified Theory of Cognition? *Science, 241*, 4863, 296–298.

Monge, P. R., L. W. Rothman, E. M. Eisenberg, K. L. Miller, and K. K. Kirste (1985). The dynamics of organizational proximity. *Management Science, 31*, 1129–1141.

Newell, A., G. Yost, J. E. Laird, P. S. Rosenbloom, and E. Altmann (1991). Formulating the Problem-Space Computational Model. *25th Anniversary Commemorative of Computer Science*, Carnegie Mellon University.

Newell, A. (1990). *Unified Theories of Cognition*. Cambridge, MA: Harvard University Press.

Olson, M. (Ed.). (1989). *Technological Support for Work Group Collaboration*. Hillsdale, NJ: Lawrence Erlbaum Associates.

Ouchi, W. G. (1980). Markets, bureaucracies, and clans. *Administrative Science Quarterly, 25*, 129–140.

Papageorgiou, C. P. and K. M. Carley (1992). A Cognitive Model of Decision Making: Chunking and the Radar Detection Task. *CMU-CS Technical Report*.

Roberts, K. (1989). New Challenges to Organizational Research: High Reliability Organizations. *Industrial Crisis Quarterly, 3*(3), 111–125.

Roberts, K. (1990). Some Characteristics of One Type of High Reliability Organizations. *Organization Science, 1*(2), 160–176.

Rosenbloom, P. S., J. E. Laird, A. Newell, and R. McCarl (1989). A Preliminary Analysis of the Soar Architecture as a Basis for General Intelligence. *Proceedings of the workshop on Foundation of Artificial Intelligence*, Cambridge, MA: MIT Press.

Thompson, J. (1967). *Organizations in Action*. New York: McGraw Hill.

Williamson, O. E. (1975). *Market and Hierarchies: Analysis and Antitrust Implications*. New York: Free Press.

Ye, M. and K. M. Carley (1995). Radar-Soar: Towards An Artificial Organization Composed of Intelligent Agents. *Journal of Mathematical Sociology, 20*(2–3), 219–246.

CHAPTER

21

Computational Enterprise Models: Toward Analysis Tools for Designing Organizations

Raymond E. Levitt
Stanford University

Yan Jin
University of Southern California

Gaye A. Oralkan
McKinsey Co.

John C. Kunz
Stanford University

Tore R. Christiansen
StudentUniverse.Com

I. INTRODUCTION

Since 1989, the Virtual Design Team (VDT) research group at Stanford has been conducting research to develop a theoretical framework and computational simulation model to predict the impact of changes in organization structure on the performance of project-oriented organizations engaged in knowledge work. The long-range goal of this research program is to formalize theories and develop computational analysis tools that can support the systematic (re)engineering of organizations engaged in a variety of project-oriented and ongoing enterprises. The research was initially directed toward large and complex but routine design projects like design of power plants and oil refineries. For such design projects, both goals and means are clear and agreed upon by a majority of participants; coordination of large numbers of interdependent activities is the principal organizational issue to be addressed. This chapter:

1. Discusses some abstractions we chose to make in the representation and reasoning of VDT-2 that permitted rapid progress in modeling complex but routine design projects;
2. Presents results from a case study in which we used this organization and work process framework and computational model to predict aggregate and detailed performance of a team engaged in a challenging, real-world engineering project; and
3. Provides a view of how the representation and reasoning assumptions of VDT-2 can be extended in a number of ways to create a simulation tool that can be used to test virtual prototypes (i.e., to do real "organizational" (re)engineering), and to run new kinds of computational, "virtual" experiments for project-oriented enterprises engaged in less routine knowledge work.

1.1. The Need for New Enterprise Modeling Tools

In the face of increasingly competitive global markets and tight-fisted taxpayers, many private and public organizations are now "(re)engineering" their organizations to improve their products or services significantly and to reduce the time between the conceptual design of a new product or the receipt of a new order, and the delivery of the product or service to a satisfied customer. Business Process Reengineering is a time-consuming and costly undertaking that can pose potentially fatal risks to organizations in making significant changes in their operations and structures. Thus, before implementing changes aimed at improving a process, managers would like to be able to predict the specific performance consequences of alternative task breakdowns, organization structures, and investments in information systems and communications technologies. But how well do extant organization theory or engineering management techniques help managers in making such predictions?

Organizational "contingency theory" (Galbraith, 1977; Mintzberg, 1979; Thompson, 1967), which aims to address these questions, models environment, technology, and structure as monolithic variables and can thus provide only aggregated and qualitative predictions about how process or structural changes aimed at reducing time to market and increasing quality—and which typically increase subtask interdependency dramatically as a side effect—will impact cost, schedule, and quality.

Project management tools such as the Critical Path Method (CPM) have been widely used to predict duration of project-oriented tasks such as construction, aerospace, and pharmaceutical product development. In many of today's product development projects, however, managers are striving to shrink time to market toward zero, so that interdependent activities that were previously executed sequentially are now often executed concurrently, or with considerable overlap. A fundamental limitation of the CPM model is that it assumes that parallel activities are independent of one another. Thus the CPM model underestimates the added complexity, coordination effort, and potential for rework created by "high velocity" projects with many concurrent but interdependent activities. It thus makes predictions that have turned out to be consistently optimistic. Moreover, CPM assumes resources needed by activities are one-dimensional stacks that can be assigned to any activities that require them, thus ignoring organizational structure, roles, or differing actor skill levels associated with human resources that can significantly impact performance in knowledge work projects.

Thus, neither extant organization theory nor engineering management techniques currently provide reliable and detailed predictions of organizational performance for product development teams. Our motivation for pursuing the VDT research program was a perceived need for a new "micro-contingency theory of organizations," and for a computational modeling tool based on this richer theoretical base, to answer questions about the effects of specific changes in task requirements, actor capabilities, project organization structure and policy, or communication tools on a range of project cost, schedule, and quality performance measures.

1.2. A Computational Organization and Process Modeling Approach

The development of social science and "social systems engineering" has been severely hampered by the lack of appropriate mathematical or computational analysis tools. Organizational theorists generally model the behaviors of interest to researchers or managers in terms of discrete, nominal, or ordinal variables. Thus, there is a mismatch between their theories and the continuous, numerical mathematical tools that have served so well to model physical systems. During the 1980s, artificial intelligence researchers developed techniques for representing discrete, nonnumerical variables and for reasoning about relationships among them (Clancey, 1989; Kunz, Stelzner, & Williams, 1989). These nonnumerical reasoning techniques have provided researchers with a powerful new set of tools to begin developing rigorous computational models of problem domains using qualitative simulation with discrete, nonnumerical variables.

The authors believed that qualitative simulation approaches could be used to augment numerical modeling techniques such as discrete event simulation in developing computational analysis tools for social systems. The Virtual Design Team (VDT) is a computational analysis tool for modeling large, multidisciplinary design organizations, consisting of human actors supported by increasingly sophisticated information processing and communication tools. Although others have proposed the use of computational models to simulate microorganizational behavior (Bushnell, Senfarty, & Kleinman, 1988; Carley, Kjar-Hansen, Newell, & Prietula, 1992; Cohen, March, & Olson, 1972; Masuch & LaPotin, 1989), the Virtual Design Team is a pioneering effort to employ ideas from artificial intelligence for modeling the aggregate behavior of full-scale organizations engaged in realistic tasks—an approach that our colleague, James March, has termed "organizational wind tunnel research" (Cohen, 1992).

VDT models organizations as information-processing structures—a view of organizations that dates back to Max Weber's work in the early 1900s, and that is elaborated in the work of March, Simon, and Galbraith (Galbraith, 1977; March, 1988; March & Simon, 1958; Simon, 1973, 1976). In this view—which seems especially applicable to organizations of "knowledge workers" like engineers or software developers—an organization is an information-processing and communication system, structured to achieve a specific set of tasks, and comprised of boundedly rational information-processing actors. Actors exchange information (termed *communications* in VDT) along specified channels (e.g., formal lines of authority, or informal communication paths) using communication tools (e.g., memos, voice mail, meetings, CAD file sharing) with limited bandwidth for information of various kinds (e.g., text, schematics, geometry). To represent these organizational entities, their attributes, relationships, and constraints, VDT employs explicit descriptions of tasks, communications, actors, communication tools, and structure. A detailed description of VDT is beyond the scope of this chapter and can be found in (Levitt et al., 1994a; 1994b). We provide an overview of VDT in Section 2.

1.3. The Virtual Design Team as an Extensible Enterprise Modeling Platform

We believe that projects will become increasingly common as a way of organizing knowledge work. Authors like Savage (1990) argue that knowledge workers of the 21st Century will be organized into "virtual networked teams"—temporary organizations with many of the characteristics of projects. Moreover, the most widely used current approaches to Business Process Reengineering (e.g., Hammer & Champy, 1993), can be viewed as attempts to transform ill-defined, ongoing work processes into a series of "miniprojects" each of which has a defined beginning and end point, a clear customer, its own suppliers (for whom the subject process is the customer), performance standards against which it can be measured, and a "process owner"—cf. project manager—responsible for it.

The trend toward projects as organizing metaphors for knowledge work argues strongly for using an organization and work process modeling language like VDT that has been validated as a model of routine, project-oriented design work as a starting point for the development of work process models in other industries. However, some of the abstractions that made the initial domain so tractable (e.g., abstract task content, motivated actors, static structures) need to be re-evaluated in the context of potentially greater uncertainty in both goals and means of actors and work processes, and longer time spans of the modeled work processes. We assert that the abstractions that served to model routine design processes reliably and parsimoniously can now be enriched or extended as needed to address the modeling requirements of less routine work.

In the following section we provide an overview of VDT framework, and present results from its application in the construction and aerospace industries. We then discuss the most important abstractions in the representation and reasoning of VDT that currently limit its applicability to routine, project-oriented enterprises, and discuss planned or completed efforts to implement and test extensions to this framework on a wider range of work processes and organizations.

2. AN OVERVIEW OF THE VIRTUAL DESIGN TEAM SYSTEM (VDT-2)

VDT-2 (Christiansen, 1993) explicitly incorporates information processing and communication models from organization theory that allow qualitative predictions of organizational performance. The implementation of VDT combines qualitative pattern matching with discrete event simulation of the design process for a given set of product requirements. Given a description of the product to be designed, the design team organization, and the design process, the simulation produces predictions of the efficiency and effectiveness of the design process through explicitly simulating design actions of and interactions among design actors. VDT calculates organizational efficiency and effectiveness as aspects of the performance of design teams. Measures of efficiency include the simulated critical path duration and the sum of all activity durations (a surrogate for design labor cost). Measures of effectiveness are obtained from considering how coordination items are dealt with during project execution. Coordination activity includes *communication* and *verification* tasks, and thus design process effectiveness is measured by the relative number of corrected exceptions (the verification quality) and the relative number of attended communications (the communication quality).

2.1. Organizational Concepts in VDT

The basic premise of the VDT model is that organizations are fundamentally information-processing structures (Galbraith, 1977). To operationalize the information processing model, VDT employs explicit descriptions of *tasks, communications, actors, tools*, and *structures*.

Task. Our goal is to analyze engineering design teams carrying out routine designs. We, therefore, view the task of a design team as the completion of a set of predetermined activities (e.g., design, review, and approve a series of components or subsystems of the artifact to be designed). Each activity has a name, a work-item size that defines the minimum work volume within the activity that can be tested and found to have failed, skill requirements, a responsible actor, and three kinds of interdependence relationships with other activities:

- *Sequential dependence*, as in CPM (i.e., the start or finish of one activity follows the start or finish of the other by a specified time interval),
- *Information dependence* (i.e., two actors need to communicate to resolve interdependence between the activities to which they are assigned), and
- *Failure dependence* (i.e., one activity provides specifications for the design of the other, and if its specifications change, the design of the other must be modified accordingly).

To complete the activity, the responsible actor must process an amount of information defined as the *work volume* of the activity, communicate with interdependent design team participants and resolve "exceptions" that arise in completing the activity. Activities are characterized by their complexity and uncertainty. The more complex an activity, the more likely exceptions (such as failures) will occur as each work item is completed; and the more uncertain the activity, the greater the need for communication between its responsible actor and actors responsible for parallel, information-dependent activities.

Communication. A communication in VDT is an elementary packet of information sent from one actor through a specified channel to another actor, using a single communication tool. Communications can be information exchange, exceptions, decisions, and noise. Completion of each activity involves processing the number of "work items" specified by the activity's work volume. Each communication has attributes of: time stamp, author, recipient, work volume, distribution list, ranking of natural idioms, variability of the associated task, and priority.

Actors. Actors include managers, designers and design subteams from various disciplines, such as electrical, process, and mechanical engineering. The actor description includes role characteristics, such as position in the team hierarchy; authority for design, approval, and coordination tasks; and preferred communication patterns (hierarchical vs. peer-to-peer contact). The actor description also includes individual attributes, such as a skill set made up of user-defined skills (e.g., high skill in mechanical engineering, medium skill in baton twirling); task experience (high, medium, or low). VDT explicitly simulates actors' *attention allocation, information processing, decision making*, and *communication* behavior.

Communication Tools. Each communication is transmitted via a tool selected by an actor. The VDT framework represents communication tools in terms of values on a set of variables that are theorized to affect both the choice of tool and the results of that choice. The adoption and behavior of tools is then defined in terms of the relationships among the tool variables and the characteristics of the task, actors, and organizational structure. Tools are characterized in VDT by their: synchronicity (synchronous, partial, asynchronous); cost (low, medium, or high); recordability (whether or not a permanent record of the communication is available routinely); proximity to user (close or distant); capacity (number of messages that can be transmitted concurrently); and bandwidth (low, medium, or high for each of the natural idioms supported, i.e., spoken words, text, schematics, geometry).

Organization Structure. Structure in VDT is defined by a set of organizational relationships among actors, and levels of authority of actors in specific roles. Organizational relationships among actors delimit the channels along which tools can be used to send communications. Relationships modeled in VDT include: *supervised-by* to implement hierarchical structure; and *coordinates-with* to implement lateral relations among information-dependent actors. A set of project-specific coordination policies assigns decision-making authority to actors in particular roles (e.g., *project manager*) for reviews and approvals. A centralized structure is implemented by policies that increase the proportion of exceptions to be resolved by high-level managers (e.g., the *project manager*); decentralized structures refer most exceptions to lower level managers (e.g., the *subteam leaders*).

2.2. Simulation Environment

VDT operationalizes Galbraith's information processing model of organizations by: explicitly incorporating specific tasks; modeling actors with attention allocation, information processing and communication capabilities; and simulating coordination behaviors at the microlevel in terms of explicit interaction among team participants. The VDT simulation environment performs qualitative pattern matching among attributes of the objects discussed in Section 2.1 (e.g., How closely does an actor's skill set match the skill requirement of an activity to which the actor has been assigned?). Depending on the result of the qualitative match, VDT assigns numerical values of cutoff points in a Monte Carlo style discrete event simulation of information processing and throughput.

Two examples will help to illustrate the interplay between nonnumerical pattern matching and numerical discrete event simulation in VDT.

- If an actor has a medium skill level in the required skill for an activity, the actor's processing speed and error rate will remain at nominal values. If the actor has a low or zero level of skill in the required skill for an activity, the actor's processing speed is reduced and its error rate is increased by a factor (say 20%) that is read from an external file used by VDT termed the "behavior matrix."
- When an exception is detected by an actor in VDT, the actor initiates an exception communication to itself, or to a supervisor located one, two, or more levels up the hierarchy, depending on the organization's level of centralization. The actor to whom the exception is sent makes a decision about whether to rework, correct (i.e., do 50% rework), or ignore the portion of the activity that generated the exception. The probabilities of each of these decisions are determined by a matrix that relates the decision-maker's role (project manager, subteam leader, or subteam) in the rows of the matrix to a probability for each decision option in the columns of the matrix. In engineering organizations we have found through observation that more senior managers tend to be more likely to direct that rework be done, whereas in software development teams that we studied, managers are less likely to want to rework every known bug compared to programmers. The behavior matrix can be set to reflect either of these two cultures about how to react to known errors, or other rework cultures such as: "All roles always select rework."

Although it is not accessible through the graphical user interface, the behavior matrix is a text file that can be edited by a knowledgeable user of VDT to reset default values of parameters in VDT's discrete event simulation to values that correspond more closely to the characteristics of a particular organization and process domain such as software engineering or power plant design. Figure 21.1 shows the architecture of the VDT system.

VDT is a formal model in that it includes basic concepts from, and predicts behavior based on, a set of widely accepted microbehavioral theories of attention allocation, decision making, and communication of organizational actors—and it relies on our own empirical observations, where we could not find theory or data about key process parameters in the literature

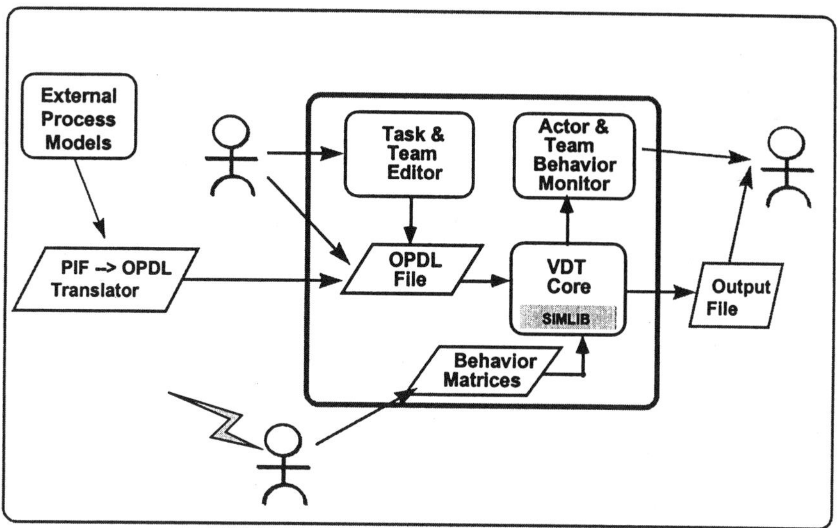

FIG. 21.1. Architecture of VDT system. VDT accepts input via an Organization and Process Description Language (OPDL) text file. This can be generated with a text editor, with VDT's graphical user interface (see Fig. 21.2) or by automatic translation of any work process and organization model that follows the Process Interchange Format (PIF) standard. Knowledgeable "power" users of VDT can modify many default values of system parameters by editing the text-based "behavior matrix." VDT outputs include detailed text files and several graphical displays such as the one shown in Fig. 21.3. VDT runs on PCs under the MS Windows operating system.

such as attention allocation behavior by engineers (Christiansen, 1993; Cohen, 1992). VDT simulates this "canonical" microbehavior of actors, and their interactions with other actors, in performing specific activities in an organization with specific structure, policies, and culture. VDT's simulation generates emergent behavior in the form of both aggregate (project level) and detailed (actor and activity level) performance predictions.

VDT was implemented on a Sun Microsystems SparcStation using Kappa, an object-oriented programming environment from IntelliCorp, and the SIMLIB, a discrete event simulation system we developed on top of Kappa. VDT runs under MS Windows 3.11, 95 or NT. It has a graphical user interface that permits rapid modeling of process and organizational attributes and relationships and intuitive visualization of simulation results (see Figs. 21.2, 21.3). Both VDT and Vité Project,® the commercial implementation of VDT (Vité, 1996), have been used to teach organization design classes at Stanford, and at several other universities in the United States and Europe.

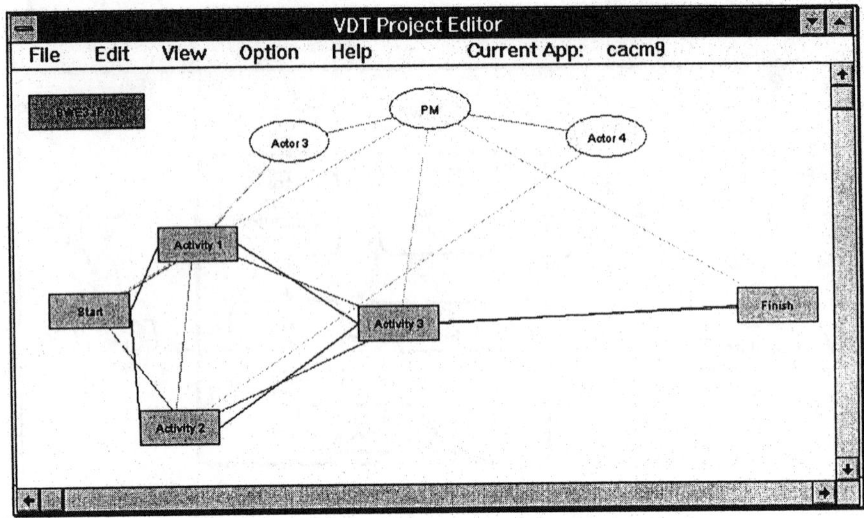

FIG. 21.2. VDT graphical user interface. The VDT model links the organization chart (ellipses) and the activity diagram (rectangles) of a project. Relationships shown by lines include Reports-to among actors, Responsible-for among actors and activities, and Successors, Reciprocal-Information-Dependence and Failure-dependence among activities. Attributes such as activity work volume or actor skill set can be edited through dialog boxes accessed from an activity or actor.

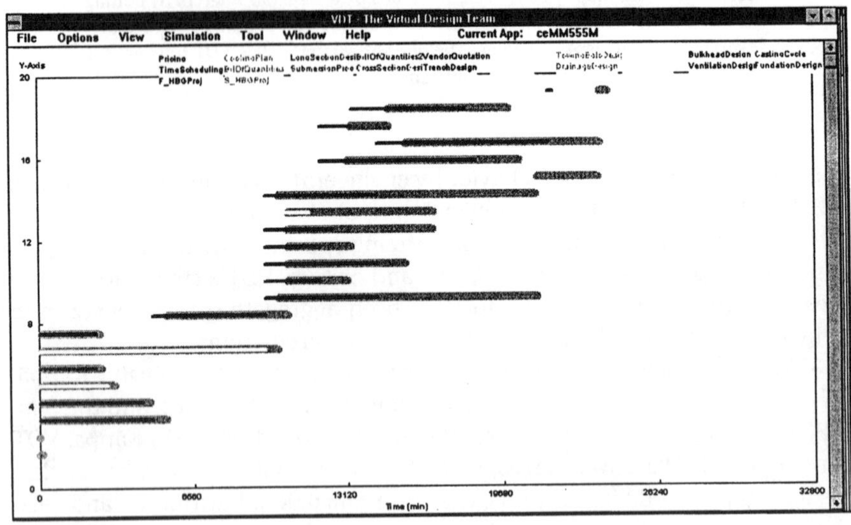

FIG. 21.3. VDT vs. CPM activity schedule predictions. The VDT simulation produces a Gantt chart for an example project. Thin solid bars show the traditional Critical Path Method time projection. The thicker gray bars show the more realistic VDT prediction considering both planned direct work and additional predicted rework and coordination among actors.

3. THE SATELLITE LAUNCH VEHICLE: A CASE STUDY IN THE USE OF VDT FOR ORGANIZATIONAL ANALYSIS IN THE AEROSPACE DOMAIN

An aerospace company has done carefully regulated design and manufacture of a military launch vehicle since the 1970s. The company is now adapting the design for commercial use as a launch platform for commercial satellites. The time available for design and delivery of the commercial platform can be as low as 20% of what was available for the defense versions, and fixed price commercial proposals must frequently be tendered in a keenly competitive global marketplace. For these reasons, the company is simultaneously changing its processes to become more "agile." Specific objectives in this defense conversion process are to outsource design and manufacture of major subsystems and to substantially decentralize engineering decision making.

The purposes of our modeling and analysis were, first, to predict the effects of different levels of decentralization on product delivery time, cost and quality; and second, to predict the effects of different levels of design engineering support on performance of new design and manufacturing subcontractors.

The model predicted that, because of the number of interdependencies between its activities and many other parallel activities in the project, one of the firm's design subteams would incur an unusually high coordination "load" to support a new vendor, and would become heavily backlogged. The predicted effect was that the total time and effort to complete the particular activity would be significantly greater than estimated. In addition, because the at-risk activity was on the critical path of the project, the model predicted that the project would exceed its budgeted cost and duration. Quality concerns associated with this backlogged actor's work were also evident from our analysis. Several months after these predictions were discussed with managers, the project encountered the predicted cost and schedule overruns (i.e., the aggregate predictions were confirmed) and the actor we had predicted would become backlogged was indeed severely backlogged, and needed considerable help from a group of experienced designers to "dig out" of its backlogged state (i.e., VDT's detailed predictions were also confirmed in this case).

Using "what-if" studies conducted with different input values to VDT, the model predicted that the activity and project duration impacts could have been managed with use of additional staff with more appropriate skill sets. The what-if studies also predicted significant changes in project performance given a change in centralization of decision making. Finally, the organization model predicted effects on project performance of additional variables such as degree of formalization of communications among organizational participants and resequencing of activities in the engineering process.

VDT-2 has been commercialized and used to model more than 20 large engineering projects in a variety of product development domains. In these cases, VDT's aggregate predictions have been validated against predictions of experienced project managers and found to be in good agreement (Christiansen, 1993; Cohen, 1992). In every case VDT's predictions of activity and project duration and cost were more realistic than the overly optimistic predictions made by CPM techniques, for the reasons stated in Section 1.1. Figure 21.3 shows a typical set of VDT schedule predictions for activities in a given project, versus activity schedules computed by CPM analysis of the same project (Vité, 1996).

4. ENTERPRISE MODELING FOR RE-ENGINEERING

A typical enterprise is composed of multiple business, management, and production units that operate in the same or different locations. In *Structure in Fives* (Mintzberg, 1983), Mintzberg presents a flexible conceptual framework for thinking about enterprises. He classifies organizational forms into five generic types each containing five generic components in different configurations. The five basic components of an organization include (1) Strategic Apex, (2) Middle Line, (3) Operating Core, (4) Technostructure, and (5) Support Staff. Mintzberg also discusses five coordination mechanisms for integrating the work of specialized units in an organization. This view of organizations synthesizes much of the contingency theory literature and provides the basis for more recent attempts to employ contingency theory findings for organization design (see Burton & Obel, 1994).

Mintzberg's book provides a high-level framework for analyzing organizations through categorization and models how organization structure can impact performance through coordination mechanisms. However, his framework does not predict the effect on performance of detailed and specific changes in organization design, such as communication techniques, training, and organizational learning. Furthermore, contemporary organizations, driven by advanced technology and globalization, tend to be more network oriented, and the boundaries between his five components become less visible. As a result, it becomes difficult and subjective to model contemporary enterprises in this way.

Burton and Obel's (1998) superb synthesis of the contingency literature in a book that is sold with the included OrgCon expert system provides an excellent vehicle for diagnosing and designing organizations. Because it is based on the contingency theory literature, OrgCon functions at a single, aggregated level of analysis—the entire organization. OrgCon and related, static diagnostic tools can be used to diagnose organizational subunits, but the meaning of words such as "environment" or "senior management" can become unclear. More seriously, the validity of the contingency theory underlying the tools can then be called into question, as it was, by and large, developed at the level of the entire organization.

The goal of of the Process Handbook research (Malone, Crowston, Lee, & Pentland, 1993) is to provide a set of theories, methodologies, and tools, to enable the modeling and redesign of processes and organizations in a more systematic way. The Process Handbook approach to enterprise engineering or re-engineering adopts a process-oriented perspective. It views processes as definitions and prescriptions of organizational activities and views systematic process design and innovation as a driving force to reach more efficient organizations. A key element of this work is a novel approach to representing processes, which uses ideas from computer science about inheritance, and ideas from coordination theory about managing dependencies.

The goals of this representation are to improve understanding of complex processes, to assist in the identification of process inefficiencies, and to facilitate generation and comparative evaluation of alternative processes. The Process Handbook thus provides a systematic methodology for synthesizing the design of processes and organizations; however, the analysis and evaluation of the process design are left to users.

The *Enterprise Modeling* research effort at the University of Toronto (Fox & Gruninger, 1998) aims at formalizing the knowledge found in Enterprise Engineering perspectives such as Time-based Competition, Quality Function deployment, and so forth; integrating the knowledge into a software tool that will support the enterprise engineering function by exploring alternative organization models spanning organization structure and behavior; and providing a means for visualizing the enterprise from many of the perspectives already described (Fox & Gruninger, 1998). The TOVE enterprise ontology developed in this research provides a rich and precise representation of generic knowledge, such as, activities, processes, resources, time, and causality, and of more enterprise oriented knowledge such as cost, quality, and organization structure. Again, from the enterprise re-engineering point of view, this enterprise modeling research is focused on enterprise design rather than on providing an organization analysis tool to support the synthesis–analysis–evaluation cycle of organizational design.

As described earlier, modern organizations tend to be less hierarchical and their participants more extensively networked. Both information and control boundaries among traditional enterprise sectors become blurred. Tom Peters presented a series of case studies in which companies have adopted project organizations. He said, "Almost all of tomorrow's work will be done in project configurations. Functional staffs will all but disappear . . ." (Peters, 1992, p. 10). Organizing dynamically for specific tasks will become a new trend for competitive enterprises.

Our *VDT* approach to enterprise modeling conceptualizes enterprise re-engineering as a process of transforming ill-defined, ongoing work processes into a series of "miniprojects" each of which has a defined beginning and end point, a clear customer, its own suppliers for which the process is the customer, performance standards against which it can be measured, and a "process owner" responsible for it. Based on this conceptualization, we are in the process of extending our VDT-2 framework, developed and validated for modeling single project organizations, into a model of project-oriented enterprises. The limitations of VDT-2 for this purpose and our ongoing and proposed conceptual extensions to address these limitations are presented in the next two sections.

5. LIMITATIONS OF VDT

VDT2 models an engineering design team in terms of tasks, communication, actors, and organization structure. It simulates planned design activities and their implicit coordination requirements by assuming that: all activities and their assignment to actors can be predefined; actors are fully motivated; and organization structures are static. Although the assumptions have proved acceptable for modeling single design project teams, they cause significant limitations for VDT-2 when applied to modeling enterprises.

Routine Tasks. The size and complexity of multiproject enterprises create significant uncertainties about the composition and assignment of tasks (or subprojects). Interactions among multiple projects contribute further to their unpredictability. VDT-2 models "routine" design work for which activities are known in advance and are preassigned to appropriate actors. A great deal of work in enterprises is not routine by this definition. Modeling nonroutine tasks requires both a richer ontology for task description to represent nonroutine task situations, and a richer actor description (Jin & Levitt, 1993) to reason about the uncertain task situations, and to generate and assign tasks dynamically as the need for them arises.

Single Organization With Congruent Goals. VDT assumes that all actors belong to a single organization and are positively motivated toward achieving project objectives. It abstracts teams of 10 to 20 discipline-based specialists into compound, "subteam" actors that behave just like other actors except that they process information and exceptions at a rate that is a multiple of the single actor rate.

For enterprise modeling, multiple subteams whose members owe their primary allegiance to a variety of different parent organizations must work sequentially and in parallel on the same or different subprojects. In this case, modeling organizations or even subteams as actors with congruent goals is clearly too abstract. Interorganizational issues such as goal conflicts and competition for scarce resources along with devices to deal with these conflicts, such as contracts, incentives and development of trust between parties, must be explicitly addressed. To address this characteristic, we will need to explicitly represent economists' notions of agency (i.e., self-serving behavior and ways to regulate it, for both subteams and actors; Milgrom & Roberts, 1992).

Static Actor Attributes and Organization Structure. VDT2 models only static actors and organizations. VDT2 actors do not learn from their own experience or from others. As a result, organization structure and policies (e.g., centralization) remain the same throughout the simulation. Modern enterprises, however, must adapt themselves in order to compete in the changing world market and dynamic environment. Thus, for enterprise modeling, static assumptions about attributes of both actors and organizations are invalid. Actors (and consequently organizations) must adapt themselves through their own experience and their observation of others. To model this kind of dynamic organizational adaptation, VDT must explicitly represent and reason about internal and external performance feedback to actors and adaptation of goals, skills relationships, and other parameters of organization structure (Oralkan, Jin, & Levitt, 1994).

Simple Actor Behavior. As a result of routine task and single project team assumptions, VDT actors have rather simple, primarily statistical, behaviors. Because project activities and their assignment to team actors are predefined, actors in VDT2 do not need to reason about task situations to infer activity generation and assignment. VDT models exceptions and their resolution in routine projects using Monte Carlo simulation events for which frequency parameters on possible outcomes are set by qualitative inferences.

The static actor assumption, and the limited statistical decision-making capabilities of VDT actors are bottlenecks to modeling nonroutine tasks, where a variety of decisions must be made by actors in response to various task situations. The same limitations render VDT ineffective for modeling heterogeneous project teams, where agency issues among multiple actors and subteams can be critical to predicting overall enterprise performance.

Limited Representation of Decision Support Technology. Galbraith (1977) described organizations in terms of node capacity and communication channel capacity. In case of routine tasks, because decisions are mostly uniform, the impact of changing node decision-making capacity on team performance can be abstracted by changing actor processing speed. However, the impact of information technology on channel capacity and on the ability of actors to prioritize communications awaiting their attention remains important even for routine design work.

VDT was able to capture these impacts by modeling only the communications capabilities of tools like spreadsheets and 3-D CAD, not their decision support capabilities. However this limits its usefulness as an organizational analysis tool even in that domain, because it cannot address questions about how the decision support capabilities of proposed new tools might effect organizational performance, except as instantaneously accelerating the performance of work by each actor in isolation.

A richer model of work processes and of agent decision making implemented to address some of the limitations raised earlier should allow us to enrich our model to include, for example, groupware tools, including the rate at which actors learn to use these tools, and the ways in which they can effect the quality of coordination through sharing of knowledge and information in an integrated decision-support mode. Gaye Oralkan's (1996) research on adaptation by actors in response to new information technologies provided an interesting first step in this direction.

6. FROM VDT-2 TO PROJECT-ORIENTED ENTERPRISE MODELS

Figure 21.4 shows how we are currently working to extend VDT's scope to meet the requirements of enterprise modeling. We start from the existing VDT-2, an organization model of a single engineering design team working on a single project. We then expand the scope of VDT-2 in two directions: from routine design tasks to nonroutine production management tasks; and from single project to multiple concurrent projects. Finally, our experience with modeling nonroutine tasks, and interactions between multiple projects and teams will allow us to address full-scale enterprise modeling where multiple and different kinds of projects and teams are involved. We have defined a set of research projects to pursue these extensions. We are, at present, in the process of extending VDT-2 to model nonroutine tasks, multiple teams, and adaptive organizations. The remainder of this section describes the organization modeling issues that arise in making these extensions, and the agent-oriented approach we are employing to address these issues.

6.1. Modeling Specific Nonroutine Projects

In our VDT research, we chose to focus initially on modeling organizations engaged in routine design of complex facilities like fossil power and petrochemical process plants. This strategy has been successful to date. The abstraction of task content and task-oriented actor behavior that could be assumed for the organizations engaged in routine project-oriented work facilitated rapid development and testing of our initial modeling framework.

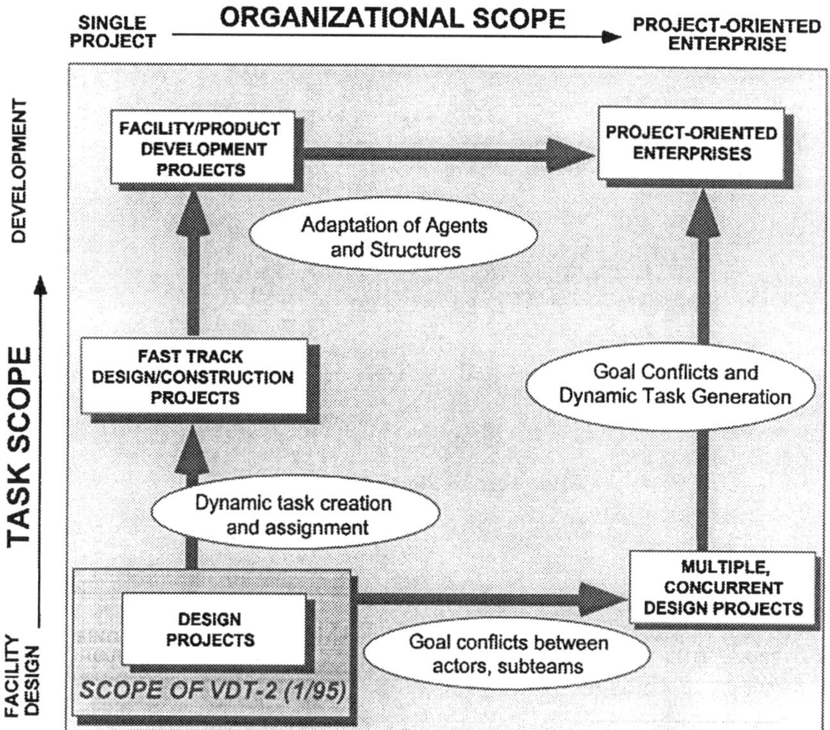

FIG. 21.4. From VDT-2 to enterprise modeling. We start in the lower left corner with the existing VDT-2 framework and expand it in several dimensions. Modeling goal conflicts allows incorporation of actors from different organizations with potentially conflicting goals; providing actors with knowledge and authority to generate new tasks and assign actors to them allows modeling of less routine work (e.g., medical clinics); combining these two capabilities with ways to model adaptation of actors' goals, preferences, and competence will permit us to model a wide range of project-oriented enterprises.

To model enterprises, however, these abstractions are no longer valid, as tasks and actor behaviors for an enterprise can be highly unpredictable.

We propose the following operational definition of "routine" work:

> *The activities needed to execute routine work, along with estimates of their duration, sequence and assignment to responsible actors, can all be prespecified with a reasonable degree of confidence, based on prior experience.*

Many projects, and most enterprises do not fit this definition. Exposure to environmental vagaries, immature technologies and other factors can reduce the predictability of activities, durations, sequences and task assignments to the point that they cannot be meaningfully prespecified. Such organizations have to learn to adapt rapidly in the face of both endogenous and exogenous changes. For the reasons set out in Section 5, we believed that the logical first step in enlarging the coverage of VDT toward enterprise modeling was to address how to model work processes and actors in nonroutine projects.

From an organization modeling point of view, the unpredictability or nonroutineness of tasks may be reflected by complex exceptions, of the sort characterized by Galbraith (1977). During the execution of preplanned tasks, exceptions may arise as a result of information uncertainty, environmental disturbance, or random errors of actors. In response to exceptions, preplanned tasks must be modified or replaced; new activities introduced; and assignments of tasks to actors revised. In order to model such nonroutine tasks, we first need information about what kinds of exceptions might arise in each task and environmental situation, and how actors might respond to each kind of possible exception, given their functional, organizational, and social positions. Second, we need a framework or ontology to represent the context of exceptions and decisions made in response to the exceptions.

We have been developing a model of nonroutine project work for construction projects—a class of projects that can be highly unpredictable. Based on our detailed analysis of work and exceptions in two kinds of construction projects—tunnel construction and building construction—we have achieved a better understanding of several kinds of generic exceptions that might arise during construction, and of the different ways construction managers choose to deal with different exceptions (Sugihara, 1994).

Based on this understanding, we have extended VDT's exception generation and decision-making process to model several different kinds of exceptions besides the "task failure" exception modeled in VDT-2. We have also modeled different kinds of decisions in response to exceptions. For example, beyond specifying "rework," "correct," or "ignore" to an existing activity as in VDT-2, a project manager in this VDT-Enterprise (VDT-E) framework may also decide to add a new set of activities and assign them to particular team members based on rules about current work load, skill match, and so forth, when a serious exception has arisen.

To support this context-based exception–decision process, we have developed an extended process ontology which treats activities and exceptions as instances of a higher level "exception" class, and allows them to be instantiated dynamically by reasoning about context (Nasrallah, 1995). Our enterprise task model will thus provide a rich framework to describe nonroutine tasks. To make use of the framework in organization modeling, we will need a more sophisticated actor model that can reason about task situations like the agents in Carley, Kjaer-Hansen, Newell, & Prietula, PluralSoar (1992) framework, and make decisions about what has to be done to resolve given kinds of exceptions in different task and environmental situations. Section 6.4 describes how our agent-oriented framework for enterprise modeling will address these requirements.

6.2. Modeling Multiple Projects and Teams

There are two basic issues involved in modeling multiple projects and teams. The first issue is how to model dependencies between activities in different projects explicitly; the second is how to model interactions among multiorganization teams explicitly. Two modest extensions to VDT task model appear to provide much of the required functionality for modeling both precedence relationships and actor relationships more realistically in enterprises.

In our enterprise model, we will treat dependencies among activities that belong to different projects in a more sophisticated way than we do for activities in VDT-2 (Levitt, Christiansen et al., 1994). In addition to the strict precedence relationships that exist in VDT-2, we will model a relationship we call "prerequisite" in which we can specify a minimum level of required completion for the prerequisite activity before the constrained activity can be started. Violating the minimum completion status of a prerequisite activity is possible, but only at the cost of a higher expected failure probability for the constrained activity. In addition, we will model dependencies between interdependent projects at the project level through aggregating activity dependencies.

For example, concurrency is one of the dependency measures we introduced to model project relationships. Assume we have two projects, Project P1 and Project P2. We can measure the concurrency of the two projects by the proportion of the total amount of work of one project that must be completed before the second project can start. This proportion of work can be calculated based on the prerequisite relationships between the activities of the two projects.

Second, as mentioned before, project-oriented enterprises are structured as dynamic networks of relationships between their participants, rather than as inverted tree structures that exist in one-dimensional hierarchies or the orthogonal, intersecting tree structures found in matrix organizations. Moreover, project teams may have members who belong to different parent organizations with different goals, and may work in diverse locations. The interactions, including control and communication, among such teams can thus depend in large part on the extent to which team members are able to develop shared goals for the project and mutual trust (Poole & DeSanctis, 1992).

The level of goal incongruency between actors was ignored in VDT-2 with its single organization, and task-oriented "engineering nerd" view of agents.

From an enterprise design point of view, understanding the impact of agency, and designing better contracting approaches, monitoring systems, reward systems, and reporting systems become critical for successful modeling and prediction. In our ongoing enterprise modeling research, we have begun to represent agency of project teams and their members through introducing new organizational attributes to represent goal incongruency between agents and new measuring instruments to capture the levels of goal incongruency between actors and their peers and supervisors–subordinates. We have also added new microbehaviors for VDT's organizational actors, based on the level of goal incongruency between each actor and his–her–their subordinates and peers. These new behaviors include: selective delegation of decision making, sending monitoring and reporting communications, responding selectively to communications, and changing probabilities of error generation and detection based on the level of monitoring, reporting, and communication between agents with potentially incongruent goals (Levitt, Thomsen et al., 1999; Thomsen, 1996).

6.3. Modeling Adaptive Organizations/Teams

The final research issue we discuss in extending our VDT framework to model enterprises is the adaptive nature of organizational action. To model ongoing enterprises, we need to represent and reason about: nonroutine projects that cannot be executed with predefined tasks and assignments; multiple projects that make attention processes more complex; multiple teams that need to learn to interact given their differences in goals and culture; and simulation time that spans multiple projects for several cycles of organizational action. Organizational learning or adaptation becomes a key issue for building realistic models in this domain. We view this as the most challenging research issue in the path of extending a static model like VDT toward reliable enterprise modeling.

In addition to the internal complexity of full-scale enterprise organizations, there are two major reasons why modeling the learning organization is necessary. First, large enterprises face complex organizational environments that change over time. We are modeling multiple projects over long periods of time with multiple teams participating, and over long enough periods that changes occur in the environment. The interpretations of these changes by the teams involved, and the responses constructed by actors based on these interpretations, thus become more important. Teams and the enterprise learn from their past responses to the environment and the feedback they get from the environment, and they adapt their future interpretations and responses based on these past experiences in each new cycle of action.

There is also a second kind of organizational learning or adaptation that takes place in response to a top-down change in the organization. This could be a change in organizational structure, contractual structure between multiple participants in a project, a newly introduced technology, or a new task structure. These kinds of top-down changes embedded in existing structures have both intended and unintended consequences. Intended consequences (which are first-order and relatively easier to predict in the short term) may, in the long term, be mediated by the unintended consequences of top-down changes. The unintended consequences of a top-down change can be studied by modeling the organization as an adaptive system that operates within a structural context. The responses of individuals, teams, or enterprise organizations to these top-down changes provide the second half of an adaptive organizational model.

Our view of organizational learning is based on a "structuration" view of organizations. "Structuration Theory" (Giddens, 1984; Sewell, 1992) treats structure as both the medium and outcome of organizational action; the organizing principle of Weick (1979, 1990). Weick and Roberts (1993) emphasizes structuring over structure, organizing over organization. Both reflect a dynamic view of the context within which action takes place. Context or conceptual structures constrain and facilitate action, but they get enacted, selected, and retained through action. The structure which is conceived of in various ways in each individual's beliefs gets enacted through individual action, and becomes observable as a systematic pattern, as individual action aggregates into organizational action. This dynamic is created by the concept of agency, the ability and power of agents to interpret conceptual structures, enact them, communicate with other agents, and monitor both their own and others' performance in order to modify their beliefs and actions. At the core of this view of agency lies adaptation, which enables system adaptation to emerge as the result of interactions among adaptive agents. Modern theories that view communication networks as "Public Goods" (Monge & Contractor, in press) provide an alternative view of structural evolution that is applicable to virtual organizations or communities of practice. Gaye Oralkan (1996) has completed and tested the Explorer model of organizational learning, an important first step in this direction. Explorer models single-agent learning in a structuration framework in which actor's goals, targets, preferences, and rule beliefs coevolve in response to changing environments. We hope to extend her work to a multiagent learning model that could be the basis for an adaptive future version of VDT.

6.4. Our Proposed Agent-Oriented Modeling Approach

So far we have described a set of planned and ongoing extensions to VDT in the form of modeling nonroutine tasks with more detailed task content; enterprises that work on multiple projects simultaneously; intra or interorganizational project teams that consist of subteams with multiple subcultures and goals; and organizational adaptation to a changing environment or to a top-down organizational change. In order to support each of these extensions, there are two fundamental modeling issues that must be addressed. First, we need a richer ontology for task and task environment description so that nonroutine tasks and interactions among them can be described. Second, we need a sophisticated actor model that can reason about task situations, infer the needs for task generation and assignment, and learn in order to adapt all of these behaviors to a changing environment. As described earlier, our ongoing work on modeling construction projects has made a significant extension to VDT task ontology to cover the context-based exception and decision process—one important feature of nonroutineness of engineering projects (Nasrallah, 1995). In this subsection, we provide an overview of our agent-oriented approach to modeling more sophisticated actors.

We are developing a framework, called *O-Agents*, to model organizational agents, based on *i-Agents*, an agent-oriented framework developed in our previous research on intelligent agents (Jin & Levitt, 1993). An important difference between an O-Agent and an i-Agent is that while an i-Agent is designed to solve problems, including coordination problems, in the most effective and efficient way possible, an O-Agent is designed to mimic human behavior at abstraction levels which eliminate as much domain knowledge as possible for reasons of modeling parsimony. Despite the differences in agent rationality implicit in the goals of these two systems, we have found that the architecture of i-Agents is sufficient to model O-Agents. Thus, O-Agents will employ the basic i-Agents architecture but will change the knowledge or "character" of its agents to change them into organizational modeling building blocks.

An O-Agent has two types of attributes; those that describe its "character," which is modified over time through learning; and those that describe its current mental state, which represents its view of task and organization status, and can thus change dynamically as the situation changes. In terms of character there are three attributes that we consider for our enterprise modeling framework: Capabilities (i.e., competencies); Values (i.e., motivations); and Strategy. *Capability* of an agent refers to the area(s) of expertise held by the agent. It should match the level of detail in our task requirements, and should be comparable to the capabilities that are provided by technologies with which agents cooperate.

Capabilities are not static in an adaptive organization, agents may expand their expertise by working with other agents, and by using technologies such as expert systems. The capabilities attributed to an agent are connected to a set of knowledge sources which are applied by the agent to reason about task situations and to infer needs for task generation, task assignment, and several kinds of learning.

Values define what the agent considers important at an abstract level, and guide most choices of agent action. Agents may, for example, value efficiency, power, personal competence, autonomy, or cooperation. The ranking of values changes from agent to agent, but is greatly influenced by the culture of an organization that chooses individuals with values consistent with its organizational culture and rewards them for developing and maintaining appropriate values over time. The *values* of an agent are sets of criteria that are used by the agent to decide whether or not to choose a certain action. By modeling different values for different groups of agents we can start addressing issues like the effect of socialization, incentive structures, culture, and hierarchy on creating cooperation or conflict in multiple team situations.

The *strategy* attribute refers to the tactics agents use in interacting with other agents, and in adapting to the organizational environment. Strategies are guided by values. Agents may have strategies about communication with other agents, or selection of tasks and technologies. We use the strategy attribute, together with the values attribute, to model agents' (economic) agency and coordination behavior. For example, agents may have a strategy of responding to supervisors in a timely fashion, but delaying their responses to peers' and subordinates' communications. From a learning perspective, values and strategies adapt to agent's experience. From a structuration point of view both values and strategies are constrained by existing organizational structures, and are used in turn to reshape these structures.

In terms of *mental state*, agents have capacities, commitments, beliefs, and knowledge about others that change over time. *Capacity* of an agent refers to the resource constraints (i.e., time, tool) an agent is facing at a given point in time to perform his or her task although he or she is normally capable of doing that task given the resources. *Commitment* is what the agent has volunteered or been assigned to do within a given time period. This could be a task with a time deadline. Commitments become more problematic when task structures are not predefined but are created in real-time. In this situation, commitments to allocate one's capacity (e.g., among multiple projects) are greatly influenced by one's beliefs about the world.

Beliefs are agent's view of the world (e.g., status of the multiple projects). Beliefs may be shaped differently depending on the amount of information agents can get about the world and on their values and capabilities. This difference complicate the organization's behavior by introducing conflicts among agents. Rational agents make their decisions (e.g., to select a strategy for action) through reasoning about the current state of the world, including task and organization situations, and the potential effects of applying various action strategies in the current situation to achieve outcomes consistent with their goals. Boundedly rational agents in O-Agents, however, have limited access to information and limited time to examine the consequences of a decision. Through restricting agents' view of the world and limiting the kinds of knowledge attached to agents, we can model different kinds of boundedly rational agents found in enterprise organizations.

As described earlier, agents' knowledge about task processing and coordination is attached to Capabilities and Strategies, respectively. Another type of knowledge—knowledge about other agents—is represented as part of agents' beliefs. Nonroutine tasks and learning project teams involve extensive interactions among agents, such as task assignment, information exchange, learning from others' experience, and so on. Agents' knowledge about others is a key factor that affect the interactions. Through varying the level of knowledge about others for different agents in a given enterprise setting, we can model different organizational situations in which we can study the effect of different incentive systems, task generation policies, and organization structures.

A major issue in setting microlevel agent attributes is that of distribution. An intradepartmental project team may have a relatively homogenous population of agents; whereas a project team that crosses hierarchical levels, and departmental or even organizational boundaries will have a much more heterogeneous agent population. The amount and kind of heterogeneity (i.e., conflicting vs. complementary) will create interesting results in terms of adaptation, cooperation and overall performance of the project.

O-Agents is being developed based on lessons learned from both VDT and i-Agents research. The success of VDT applications in modeling routine project teams and of i-Agents applications to modeling distributed construction planning has led us to develop O-Agents. We believe that inserting the more sophisticated O-Agents into VDT's task, actor and structure framework will provide VDT with significantly enhanced potential and flexibility for modeling project-oriented enterprises.

7. RECAPITULATION

In a previous work on computational organizational modeling (Levitt, Cohen et al., 1994) we described our VDT framework for modeling project organizations engaged in complex but routine design work. Since then, VDT has been refined, tested, and validated against more than 100 real-world projects. The routine design project version of VDT designed by Christiansen (1993), "VDT-2," has been found to make predictions that agree both with the aggregate predictions of the underlying theory and with the specific predictions of experienced project managers. In the strongest test of its predictive ability to date, VDT-2 was validated by comparing its aggregate and detailed predictions to the outcome of an aerospace defense conversion project and performed unusually well at both levels (Kunz et al., 1996). VDT-2 is currently being commercialized for use in high velocity new product development projects of all kinds (Vite, 1996).

This chapter has set out our view of the challenges in extending VDT-2 toward a framework that will ultimately provide the same kind of reliable organizational wind tunnel for organizational engineers and scientists to analyze the performance of enterprise organizations. We have argued that enterprises engaged in knowledge work are rapidly adopting project organizational forms, so that the VDT framework, which combines qualitative inference with Monte Carlo simulation to model abstract tasks and actors involved in routine project work, represents a reasonable starting point for developing an enterprise modeling framework. At the same time, we have tried to show that VDT's current framework has several inherent limitations as a model of less routine work in complex and dynamic enterprises.

Through a discussion of these limitations in the VDT framework and the issues involved in overcoming them, we have attempted to make a case for using an expanded ontology of tasks, actors, and structure to represent nonroutine work; and a rich, agent-oriented model of actor behavior to model adaptive enterprises engaged in a variety of project-oriented work.

REFERENCES

Bushnell, L. G., Serfarty, D., and Kleinman, D. L. (1988). In *Science of Command and Control: Coping with Uncertainty* (pp. 62–72). In S. E. Johnson and A. H. Lewis (Eds.). AFCEA International Press, London.

Burton, R. M., and Obel, B. (1998). *Strategic Organizational Diagnosis and Design: Developing Theory for Application* (2nd ed.). Boston, MA: Kluwer.

Carley, K. M. C., Kjaer-Hansen, J., Newell, A., and Prietula, M. (1992). Plural-Soar: A Prolegomenon to Artificial Agents and Organizational Behavior. In *Artificial Intelligence in Organization and Management Theory* (pp. 87–118). M. Masuch and M. Warglien (Eds.), North-Holland, Amsterdam.

Christiansen, T. R. (1993, September). *Modeling Efficiency and Effectiveness of Coordination in Engineering Design Teams.* Dissertation in partial fulfillment of Ph.D., Department of Civil Engineering, Stanford University.

Clancey, W. J. (1989). Viewing Knowledge Bases as Qualitative Models, *IEEE EXPERT*, Vol. 4, No. 2.

Cohen, G. P. (December, 1992). *The Virtual Design Team: An Information Processing Model of Design Team Management.* Dissertation in partial fulfillment of Ph.D., Department of Civil Engineering, Stanford University.

Cohen, M. D., March, J. G., and Olsen, J. P. (1972). A Garbage Can Model of Organizational Choice, *Administrative Science Quarterly*, Vol. 17, No. 1, 1–25.

Fox, M. S., Gruninger, M. (1998, Fall). Enterprise Modelling, *AI Magazine*, AAAI Press, pp. 109–121.

Galbraith, J. R. (1977). *Organization Design*. Addison-Wesley, Reading, Massachusetts.

Giddens, A. (1984). *The Constitution of Society*. Berkeley: University of California Press.

Hammer, M., and Champy, J. (1993). *Re-engineering the Corporation: A Manifesto for Business Revolution.* New York: Harper Business.

Jin, Y., and Levitt, R. E. (1993). i-AGENTS: Modeling Organizational Problem Solving in Multiagent Teams. *International Journal of Intelligent Systems in Accounting, Finance and Management*, Special Issue on Mathematical and Computational Models of Organizations: Models and Characteristics of Agent Behavior, Vol. 2, No. 4, 247–270.

Special Issue on Mathematical and Computational Models of Organizations: Models and Characteristics of Agent Behavior, Vol. 2, No. 4, 247–270.

Kunz, J. C., Stelzner, M. C., and Williams, M. D. (1989). In *Topics in Expert System Design* (pp. 87–110). G. Guida and C. Tasso (Eds.). North-Holland, Amsterdam.

Kunz, J., Christiansen, T., Cohen, G., Jin, Y., and Levitt, R. (1996). *The Virtual Design Team: A Computational Simulation Model of Project Organizations.* Transactions of ACM.

Levitt, R. E., Christiansen, T. R., Cohen, G., Jin, Y., Kunz, J., and Nass, C. (1994). *The Virtual Design Team: A Computational Simulation Model of Project Organizations* (Working Paper #29). Center for Integrated Facility Engineering, Stanford University.

Levitt, R. E., Cohen, G. P., Kunz, J. C., Nass, C. I., Christiansen, T., and Jin, Y. (1994). The Virtual Design Team: Simulating How Organization Structure and Information Processing Tools Affect Team Performance. In K. M. Carley and M. J. Prietula (Eds.), *Computational Organization Theory.* Hillsdale, NJ; Lawrence Erlbaum Associates.

Levitt, R. E., Thomsen, J., Christiansen, T. R., Kunz, J. C., Jin, Y., and Nass, C. (1999, November). Simulating Project Work Processes and Organizations: Toward a Micro-Contingency Theory of Organizational Design. *Management Science*, Vol. 45, No. 11, 1479–1495.

Malone, T. W., Crowston, K., Lee, J., and Pentland, B. (1993). Tools for Inventing Organizations: Toward a Handbook of Organizational Processes. CCS WP#141, Sloan School WP#3562-93.

March, J. G. (1988). *Decisions and Organizations.* Oxford: Basil Blackwell.

March, J. G., and Simon, H. A. (1958). *Organizations.* New York: Wiley.

Masuch, M., and LaPotin, P. (1989). Beyond Garbage Cans: An AI Model of Organizational Choice. *Administrative Science Quarterly, 34*, 38–67.

Milgrom, P., and Roberts, J. (1992). *Economics, Organization and Management.* Englewood Cliffs, NJ: Prentice-Hall.

Mintzberg, H. (1979). *Structuring of Organizations.* Englewood Cliffs, NJ: Prentice-Hall.

Mintzberg, H. (1983). *Structure in Fives: Designing Effective Organizations.* Englewood Cliffs, NJ: Prentice-Hall.

Monge, P. R., and Contractor, N. S. (in press). Emergence of communication networks. In L. Putnam and F. Jablin (Eds.), *New Handbook of Organizational Communication.* Newbury Park, CA: Sage.

Nasrallah, W. (1995, January). *Virtual Construction Management Model.* Dissertation in partial fulfillment of degree of Engineer, Dept. of Civil Engineering, Stanford University.

Oralkan, G. A. (1996, September). *Explorer: A computational model of organizational learning in the presence of new technology.* Dissertation in partial fulfillment of Ph.D, Department of Civil Engineering, Stanford University.

Oralkan, G. A., Jin, Y., and Levitt, R. E. (1994). *Modeling Organizational Change in Response to Information Technology*, Working Paper #26, Center for Integrated Facility Engineering, Stanford University.

Peters, T. (1992). *Liberation Management: Necessary Disorganization for the Nanosecond Nineties*, Columbine, NY.

Poole, M. S., and DeSanctis, G. (1992). Microlevel Structuration in Computer-Supported Group Decision Making, *Human Communication Research*, Vol. 19, No. 1.

Savage, C. M. (1990). *Fifth Generation Management: Integrating Enterprises Through Human Networking*, Bedford, MA: Digital Press.

Sewell, W. H. (1992). *A Theory of Structure: Duality, Agency, and Transformation, American Journal of Sociology*, Vol. 98, No. 1, 1–29.

Simon, H. A. (1973). Applying Information Technology to Organization Design, *Public Administration Review*, Vol. 33, 268–277.

Simon, H. A. (1976). *Administrative Behavior: A Study of Decision-Making Processes in Administrative Organization.* New York: Free Press.

Sugihara, K. (1994, May). *Strategies for Human Resource Management at a Construction Site: The Virtual Construction Team.* Dissertation in partial fulfillment of degree of Engineer, Dept. of Civil Engineering, Stanford University.

Thomsen, J. (1996). *Modeling goal incongruency between actors in VDT.* Unpublished Ph.D. proposal, department of civil engineering, Stanford University.

Thompson, J. D. (1967). *Organizations in Action*. New York: McGraw-Hill.

Vité (1996). URL: www.vite.com.

Weick, K. E. (1979). *The Social Psychology of Organizing*, Reading, MA: Addison-Wesley.

Weick, K. E. (1990). Technology as Equivoque: Sensemaking in New Technologies. In Goodman and Sproull (Eds.), *Technology and Organizations* (pp. 1–45). San Francisco, CA: Jossey-Bass.

Weick, K. E., and Roberts, K. H. (1993). Collective Mind in Organizations: Heedful interrelating on flight deck. *Administrative Science Quarterly*, Vol. 38, 357–381.

CHAPTER

22

Extending Coordination Theory to Deal With Goal Conflicts

Clayton Lewis
Rene Reitsma
University of Colorado, Boulder

E. Vance Wilson
California Polytechnic State University at San Luis Obispo

Ilze Zigurs
University of Colorado, Boulder

1. INTRODUCTION

Malone and Crowston (1990, 1994) proposed coordination theory as a framework for understanding and promoting *smooth working* in settings with multiple actors (and those in which a single actor may perform actions with complex interrelationships). They offer as models a winning basketball team and a smoothly functioning assembly line. They provide a broad definition of coordination, "the act of working together harmoniously," and a narrower one, "managing dependencies between activities." Coordination theory offers an understanding of the nature of various kinds of dependencies among activities and how they can be managed to avoid problems, such as unsatisfied prerequisites for important tasks.

Malone and Crowston's development of this framework has concentrated on situations in which the goals of participants are shared, although they note that situations where participants have conflicting interests are included in the intended coverage of the theory. Our intent in this chapter is to pursue this suggestion.

Our analysis of goal conflicts shares two features with existing coordination theory. First, it emphasizes efficiency of process, smooth working, rather than quality of outcomes. Second, it aims to support design and intervention rather than only post hoc analysis. That is, our central aim in developing our analysis is to suggest how goal conflicts can be transformed so as to promote smooth working, not, for example, to predict what outcome of a goal conflict is likely.

We begin by presenting a simple framework in which to represent and analyze goal conflicts, in terms of which we can make more precise what we mean by harmony and its opposite, disharmony. Consistent with coordination theory, we point out that identical or compatible goals for participants do not guarantee harmony. But our main argument concerns the converse: Do differing goals guarantee disharmony? The answer is no, and we identify a number of ways of promoting harmony in the presence of conflicting goals.

Some approaches to harmony fall in the emerging field of dispute systems design (Ury, Brett, & Goldberg, 1989), in which a process is established for settling conflicts efficiently. We describe an example of this approach, the process used for allocating water in the Colorado River basin each year. Whereas dispute systems design presumes disputes will occur on a regular basis, and seeks to moderate them, other approaches to harmony transform goal conflicts in such a way as to eliminate disputes altogether. To illustrate this class of approaches we analyze the development of the cash register, whose introduction substantially eliminated a serious conflict between cashiers and proprietors of retail establishments. We suggest that the cash register exemplifies a potentially valuable alternative to dispute resolution that offers a new role for technology in promoting harmony in the presence of goal conflicts.

2. A REPRESENTATION OF GOAL CONFLICT

2.1. Trajectories in State Space

Starting with a traditional game theoretic view (following Von Neumann & Morgenstern, 1953) we think of all the conflict situations we will consider as involving a set of participants who are traversing a state space. Their trajectory through the space is determined by actions that they take; the available actions differ from state to state and are usually different for different participants. We will not assume that the state space is discrete or that the actions available are finite (see Basar & Olsder, 1982 for a discussion of game theoretic treatments of dynamic infinite games).

We will also not assume that the participants' trajectory through the state space has a definite end, with payoffs assignable to the participants at the end. Rather, we assume that the states in the space have *values* for each participant, with these values usually being different for the different participants. In the finite case such a structure might be formalized as a stochastic game (Luce & Raiffa, 1957) but an informal view is adequate for our purposes (and does not require knowledge of the detailed structure of the situation and its contingencies that we lack in most cases.)

2.2. Opposing Actions and Harmony

Often participants have available actions that are in opposition, meaning that some action by A may move toward some state, but some action by B may move away from that state. We can define harmonious and disharmonious processes by examining the trajectory of the participants. The trajectory of a harmonious process is free of opposing actions, whereas a disharmonious trajectory includes actions by one participant that oppose those of another.

An example may clarify our suggested analysis. Imagine two people riding in a car in which each person can reach the steering wheel. As they drive along they necessarily share the same trajectory, but they may have very different ideas about where they want to go. In *disharm*onious working they are fighting for the wheel: when A tries to turn in at Burger King, B fights back; at the entrance to Pizza Hut B's efforts to get into the parking lot are thwarted by A. In harmonious working A and B agree on which way to turn the wheel as they motor along.

The intuitive notion of opposing actions, which is critical to our definition of harmonious working, resists easy formalization in general. In simple situations opposing actions may simply be inverses of one another, so that applying both in succession produces no change of state. But this doesn't cover all cases; for example, it might take two applications of some action of B's to cancel a single action of A's. Another complication is that opposing actions may not completely cancel: In a conflict over the temperature of a room, turning on the heater and the air conditioner at the same time might leave the temperature unchanged, but not the noise level.

We propose the following treatment to capture the basic intuition while dealing with these complications. A sequence of actions, leading from some state S0 to another state S1, is disharmonious if there is a shorter sequence of actions leading from S0 to some state S1' whose value for both parties is the same as S1.

Note that this definition meshes with the concern of coordination theory for economical attainment of goals. In harmonious working the participants get where they are going with a minimum of activity, while in disharmonious working they waste actions.

2.3. Choosing Actions Based on Supposed Values of States

We assume that each participant chooses actions in such a way as to direct the trajectory to states that have high value for them, and from which the trajectory is unlikely to lead onward to states of low value for them. This treatment presumes that values represent participants' *beliefs* about states, not actual payoffs as in game theory. We specifically allow that values may be inaccurate, so that a participant may direct the trajectory into states that are objectively bad for them.

To help in analyzing choices based on values we distinguish two aspects of the value of a state. A state's *intrinsic value* corresponds to the participant's belief about the payoff in the standard game theoretic sense: it represents the supposed value to the participant of being in that state. A state's *tactical value* for a participant reflects the participant's judgment of the likely future consequences of being in that state. For example, a state will have a low tactical value for Participant A if being in that state allows an opposing Participant B to select an action that leads to a state with a high value for B and a low value for A.

Tactical value generalizes the idea of backed-up value in game tree search (e.g., Rich & Knight, 1991, p. 310). In ordinary game tree search participants take alternate moves. In that case the best state for A is the one that maximizes the value for A of the state reached by B's best next move. In our situation, where we do not assume participants "play" alternately, A may also have the possibility of choosing an action before or simultaneous with B's next choice, so a state can have a high tactical value for A because of the options is opens up for A as well as because of the options it leaves for B.

Both components of values can be inaccurate, as occurs in real situations (but not in classical game theory; see Von Neumann & Morgenstern, 1953, p. 30). It is possible for people to be wrong in judging the desirability of future states of affairs, in part because their ability to predict what state of affairs will actually result from some action is limited. People are even more likely to misjudge tactical values, as these depend in part on knowledge of other participants' values.

2.4. Unstable Harmony

Inaccurate values can lead to trajectories that are harmonious but unstable, in the sense that participants' actions would be different if they were aware of the actual value to them of the states traversed. The children's swindle in which an older child gives a nickel (worth 5 cents) to a younger child in exchange for a dime (worth 10 cents, but smaller than a nickel) provides an example: the younger child attaches a higher value to having the nickel than to having the dime, because the nickel is larger. Both children are pleased with the deal, but only as long as the younger child does not wise up. The trajectory of their interaction, at least until the younger child becomes enlightened, is free from disharmonious, opposing actions, because the younger child is guided by an inaccurate valuation of the relevant states.

Our analysis of such a trajectory describes it as unstable harmony: A harmonious trajectory is unstable if it would be avoided if the participants had more accurate values for some states. We suggest that the design of processes should aim to promote not just any harmony but stable harmony, because of the likelihood that unstable harmony will collapse into conflict.

3. STABLE HARMONY IN THE PRESENCE OF GOAL CONFLICTS

3.1. Identical Goals Do Not Guarantee Harmony

Participants' overall goals are represented by the true instrinsic values of states. It might appear that when participants have the same goals, harmony will be assured, because participants will agree on the states they wish to seek or avoid. But in real situations disharmony can easily occur even when the true value of states is the same for all participants, because participants choose actions not based on the true value of states, but instead on their *beliefs* about values, including tactical values. It is easy to see that participants who do not understand each others' valuations will assign inaccurate tactical values. These inaccurate tactical values, in turn, could lead the participants to take a round-about route to a state both are happy with.

Even when participants understand that they share goals, disharmony can easily arise. In fact, this case is the province addressed by current coordination theory. In situations of any complexity participants may be unable to assign an accurate value to states, and may not be able accurately to predict and evaluate the effects of available actions. Under these conditions participants may agree on inappropriate actions, or may fail to agree on what to do.

The difficulty in coordinating a collection of interdependent processes can be represented in just this way. Work is wasted or delayed because participants cannot work out the true value of completing one subtask rather than another. Coordination technology aims to clarify such evaluations by exposing to participants key components of value, such as the effects of tying up scarce resources or supplying prerequisites for other processes.

3.2. Different But Reconcilable Goals

The fact that participants have different goals, that is, that they do not agree on the values of all states, does not mean that they cannot agree perfectly on a trajectory. Suppose A likes hamburgers and B likes pizza. If A steers for Burger King conflict will arise, as it will if B steers for Pizza Hut. But there may be an eatery that offers both hamburgers and pizza, toward which they can harmoniously steer.

This is an illustration of the contrast between *position*-based and *interest*-based negotiation (Fisher & Ury, 1981). A position is a state or family of states that a participant may select as a target, directing his or her efforts toward that end. An interest is an underlying characteristic of states that determines its intrinsic valuation. Commonly, the particular positions parties choose will conflict, even when there are states that satisify their underlying interests. As long as A and B try to work toward the specific destinations of Burger King and Pizza Hut, conflict results. If they recognize an underlying interest not in these particular restaurants but in the kinds of food available there, a harmonious solution is possible, a restaurant they agree on, even though their interests are plainly different.

Note that harmony depends not only on the shift of perspective from positions to interests but also on A and B sharing some knowledge of each others' interests. If A and B identify their respective interests in hamburgers and pizza but do not communicate them, neither party can propose a destination they can agree on, except by chance. Once one party understands what determines the other's valuation, agreement becomes easier.

In our analysis interest-based negotiation works by adjusting participants' tactical valuations. If B realizes that A's values are based on a desire for burgers, rather than on a desire to go to Burger King, B's tactical valuation of states leading to an alternative restaurant will change. In particular, these states will look more attractive tactically than those leading to Pizza Hut, for which B has to anticipate counteraction from A.

3.3. Dealing With Directly Conflicting Goals by Dispute Management

Some conditions must be met for interest-based harmony to be possible. In particular, the conflict between A and B must not be so direct that there are no states whose intrinsic value is high for both. Division of resources is a common source of such opposition, in which A's interest in having the whole pie is directly incompatible with B's interest in having it all. What are the prospects for harmony in the common case in which participants' goals are unavoidably opposed?

Dispute systems aim to change the actions that participants resort to so as to minimize opposition and promote harmony. Dispute resolution seeks to replace power confrontations like strikes or wars by determination of right and wrong, as in a legal proceeding, and to replace legal proceedings by attempts to reconcile underlying interests (Ury et al., 1989). Each such replacement reduces the cost of the overall process.

The premise of dispute systems design is that provisions can be made that will constructively transform not just a particular dispute but "the stream of disputes that arise in nearly all relationships, organizations, and communities" (Ury et al., 1989, p. 357). Thus a dispute system is a standing arrangement for handling disputes as they arise in some setting, like a government agency or corporation.

As part of a study of the role of computer models in policy determination we examined one such dispute system, the Annual Operating Plan (AOP) procedure for the Colorado River. In this section we present an account of the AOP as recorded in 3 years (1992–1994) of successive AOP meetings and negotiations (USBR, 1994) and interpret the AOP process in the framework of our analysis of harmony. McKinney (1992) described a somewhat similar dispute system created to manage water issues for the State of Montana.

The AOP process is one of the developments in a long and often bitter contest for Colorado River water between states in the Colorado River Basin. That the water from the Colorado River is highly contested is easy to understand. The Colorado is the only major river in the semiarid and arid southwestern United States, and as such it provides many millions of people, farms, industries, and its own natural communities of animals and plants with water, often transported along an intricate infrastructure of reservoirs, river reaches, tunnels, and aqueducts.

The water serves many purposes, often categorized as *consumptive* and *nonconsumptive* uses. Consumptive uses divert water from the river and physically consume it, for drinking, irrigation, or use in industrial processes. Some of this water may ultimately return to the river, but will usually be charged with dissolved salts or other pollutants. Nonconsumptive uses leave the water more or less where it is, as for example rafting, hydroelectric generation, or support of animal life in the river.

Needs for different nonconsumptive uses may not conflict, because (for example) water used to generate hydropower upstream can be used again for rafting downstream. Conflict often does occur even among these uses, however, because (again, for example) the desired timing or size of the release of water for power generation may not be what is wanted for rafting.

As can readily be understood, conflicts among consumptive uses are more powerful. There is only so much water available; lots of people want it; who gets it? Reisner (1987) provided an account in vivid detail of the century-long struggle for this water, with participants employing a full range of economic, political, and criminal means. Another view of the contest is presented in "Updating the Hoover Documents 1978" (USBR, 1980), which lays out the long series of legal actions and agreements that punctuate the dispute.

The historical trend in this story is the gradual replacement of active, sometimes violent struggle by political and legal action. The AOP process represents a further step: replacement of legal action by an administrative process. It fits very well Ury et al.'s (1989) statement of objectives for dispute resolution, just cited.

3.3.1. The AOP Process.

> On January 1, 1972, and on January 1 of each year thereafter, the Secretary of the Interior shall transmit to the Congress and to the Governors of the Colorado River Basin States a report describing the actual operation under the adopted criteria for the preceding compact water year and the projected plan of operation of the current year. The plan of operation shall include such detailed rules and quantities as may be necessary and consistent with the criteria herein, and shall reflect appropriate consideration of the uses of the reservoirs for all purposes, including flood control, river regulation, beneficial consumptive uses, power production, water quality control, recreation, enhancement of fish and wildlife, and other environmental factors. The projected plan of operation may be revised to reflect the current hydrologic conditions, and the Congress and the Governors of the Colorado River Basin States shall be advised of any changes by June of each year. (USBR, 1980, Appendix VII)

This first article of the 1970 "Criteria for Coordinated Long-Range Operation of Colorado River Reservoirs Pursuant to the Colorado River Basin Project Act of September 30, 1968 (P.L. 90-537)" established the Colorado River AOP process. The process consists of an annual series of meetings, held by the United States Bureau of Reclamation (USBR), in order to establish the monthly operations for the Colorado River basin for the coming water year.

The AOP meetings begin early in the year, always at McCarran Airport in Las Vegas, and are open to the public. Invitations for and minutes of the meetings are distributed to people and organizations who have expressed interest in Colorado River operations. Meetings are separated by periods of 4 to 6 weeks.

At the first meeting of the year the USBR presents background data and an initial draft of the operating plan. Comments on the current draft are collected between meetings and reflected in a modified draft, also prepared by USBR, and presented at the next meeting. The meetings continue until a final plan is passed on to the Secretary of the Interior for issuance, as called for in the legislation quoted earlier.

We now examine the AOP process from the perspective of our analysis of conflict and harmony. Participants in the AOP process have sharply conflicting goals, but the process is quite harmonious in our sense. Very little time is spent dealing with confrontations or threats, and the tone of the discussion, in meetings and in correspondence, is civil and constructive. We believe the harmonious character of the process is attributable to two features whose effects are clear in our analysis: severe restriction on the space of admissible states, and severe restrictions on the available actions.

3.3.1.2. Limiting the State Space. Plans that can be considered in the AOP negotiations are constrained by a dizzying array of court decrees and agreements, collectively known as "the law of the river" (USBR, 1980). Examples of these are the Colorado River Compact of 1922, the Mexican Water Treaty of 1945, the Upper Colorado River Basin Compact of 1948, the Colorado River Storage Project Act of 1956, the Supreme Court Decree in Arizona vs. California of 1964, and the Colorado River Basin Project Act of 1968 (USBR, 1980).

Of particular interest for our discussion is the effect of many of these constraints in limiting the state space within which AOP participants are allowed to act. Specifically, some of these constraints exclude regions of the state space in which conflict among the participants would be especially acute. One example of this is the Supreme Court Decree of 1964, originating from a dispute between California and Arizona over the division of water in the Lower Colorado Basin (see map in Fig. 22.1). In its decree, the Court established a formula governing the division of water between those two states within the limits set by the 1922 Colorado River Compact. The formula requires that all of the normally available water in the river be evenly divided between two groups of states: those in the Lower Basin (CA, AZ, and NV) and those in the Upper Basin (CO, WY, UT, and NM).

The effect of this decree is to eliminate from consideration in the AOP a whole class of plans in which water would not be divided equally between these groups. Regardless of how strongly either group might wish to increase its consumption at the expense of the other, there is no way to accomplish this within the constraints set by the Supreme Court decree.

Many other provisions in the law of the river impose similar constraints. There are constraints governing the equalization of amounts of water stored in the Upper and Lower Basins by the end of the water year, constraints governing the allocation of possible surplusses or shortages of water among the states, and constraints governing other matters such as rights held by Native American tribes or the needs of fish species threatened with extinction.

All of these constraints limit the scope of debate in the AOP process. Time is not wasted exploring a vast range of possibilities, all of which would be sure to provoke bitter opposition. Referring to our earlier image of the drivers sharing a steering wheel, constraints like these can be thought of as guardrails that prevent the drivers from straying into regions of the state space where their preferences are so divergent that fighting for the wheel would be inevitable.

3.3.1.3. Elimination of Direct Action. Another striking feature of the AOP process that contributes to harmonious working is that the participants in the AOP have no formally defined power. The people who attend the hear-ings and submit written comments on draft versions of the AOP possess neither vote nor veto, not even when they officially represent their states or other powerful entities. In fact, there exists no legal requirement that interested parties be consulted or that their views should influence the AOP. Even USBR personnel preparing the AOP draft have no formal powers, because technically it is the Secretary of the Interior who ultimately issues the AOP for the coming water year. The AOP, therefore, is simply a process called into being by USBR representatives as a means to realize USBR's obligation laid down in Article 1 of the 1970 "Criteria for Coordinated Long-Range Operation. . . ."

Due to the absence of formal power the AOP process often appears to lack focus. Options are proposed, discussed, ignored, and re-discussed, until they either disappear or get incorporated into the AOP for the coming year. On the other hand, the lack of power does much to eliminate conflict, as inevitably it must. Harmony in our technical sense is guaranteed if participants have no actions available that can oppose one another. The AOP process approaches that state of affairs. Participants can (and often do) present views that argue against the positions expressed by others. But they cannot, for example, veto a position advanced by another party, or join a voting bloc to oppose another bloc.

This elimination of direct action is especially interesting in the historical context of conflict over water in the arid West. When water use was governed by direct action, as by a farmer opening a gate to divert water from the river onto a field, direct counteractions like sabotage or even murder were not unknown, as Reisner (1987) recounted. The AOP process is remarkable in that it represents a transformation on a very large scale of this kind of intense conflict into a largely amicable albeit very serious routine.

It is important to note that this transformation has not been accomplished by changing participants' underlying valuations. The issues involved are as important as they ever have been. What has been done instead is to limit the actions available to participants so as to exclude sharply opposing actions. Just as the constraints governing the AOP have eliminated regions within the state space in which conflict would be especially acute, so the restriction of participants' actions reduces the incidence of conflict in the remaining regions of the state space.

One can ask why the participants are prepared to accept these restrictions. One possible reason is that participants may recognize the ability of other participants to take effective counteractions if they break the restrictions. In other words, if the price of nonconformance is higher than the expected benefits, conformance is the preferred alternative.

A second, more complex, consideration concerns the availability of actions outside the AOP framework. A participant could attempt to press legislation in Congress, for example, that would alter the terms of the AOP, or might take court action, such as that which led to the Supreme Court decree mentioned earlier. But the perceived costs and risks of this kind of action seem to be high. Small states may be reluctant to press a conflict with populous California in the political arena, whereas California may not wish to repeat its unsuccessful court battle with Arizona. On balance, the participants seem to feel that the costs of the AOP restrictions are acceptable when compared to the alternatives.

These characteristics correspond well with aspects of what is known as the theory of plural incrementalism (Braybrooke & Lindblom, 1963; Brenner, 1973; Lindblom, 1959, 1968). According to this theory, the quality of decisions rests entirely in the quality of the decision-making process; there is need neither for objectives nor their evaluation. All that matters is that in a dynamic field of political forces, an agreed-upon process for negotiation exists. As long as parties comply with the rules of this process, the process goes forward in directions determined in a complex way by the shifting interests of the parties and their influence. The resultant process is stable in that its structure changes only occasionally. Representation of parties reflects many different interests (pluralism) and changes and decisions encompass only small, incremental modifications to a larger, self-propagating process (incrementalism). For now the AOP process seems to be coping robustly with a wide range of conflicting interests, but it is certainly possible that it will be seriously affected in the future by long-term shifts in these interests, such as the all but inevitable increase in demand for water.

3.3.1.4. The Character of Conflict in the AOP Process. We have argued that the AOP process is remarkably harmonious, but it is not free of all conflict. Proposals are made and opposed, and effort is expended. We present two examples to give a sense of how these residual conflicts play out.

Frequently, discussions center on positions, not interests. This is perhaps not surprising in view of the importance of directly opposed interests among the participants; there is little to be gained by attempting to reconcile them. At the same time, positions, but not interests, may be easier to defend by legal arguments, which are potent in a process like the AOP that is explicitly embedded in a nest of legal constraints.

An example from the 1994 AOP illustrates this. In the July 14, 1993 Draft Revision of this AOP, the USBR proposed that a "high steady release for research purposes may be scheduled from Glen Canyon Dam for one to two weeks during water year 1994, possibly in early April.... This research release will be designed to facilitate the study of effects of high steady releases on backwaters, beaches, vegetation and wildlife" (USBR, 1994). One of the many objections to this research release was submitted by the State of Colorado on July 27, 1993 (USBR, 1994). The State "strongly objects" to the release, but does so exclusively by reference to provisions in the law which allegedly would prevent the USBR from implementing the proposed release. The objection makes no reference at all to any interest of the state that might be harmed by the release, although there was at least one: loss of revenue from hydropower generation from the water released.

The State of Colorado engaged here in purely positional negotiation. By revealing nothing about how it saw its interests being affected by the proposed research release, it foreclosed any possible compromise. No party favoring the release could make a modified proposal that could respond to Colorado's concerns, because its concerns were not revealed.

In this particular situation it appears that Colorado's positional approach actually promoted a harmonious resolution. The proposed release was dropped from consideration with very little effort expended on it. Had Colorado been more forthcoming in its response, a great deal of work could well have gone into framing and considering alternative proposals, with the same result in the end. The fact that the proponents of the research release did not challenge Colorado to reveal its interests suggests that their motivation was not strong enough to have made a successful compromise likely.

A dispute in the 1993 AOP process illustrates the important role of tactical valuations even within the severe limits on participants' actions. The crux of the conflict was the interplay of two seemingly unrelated matters: a legal requirement that equalizes stored water in the Upper and Lower Basins, and the construction of a new reservoir in Arizona.

A part of the law of the river called the "Equalization Criteria" or "Section 602(a) Storage" says (stated simply) that by the end of the water year (September 30th), storage in Lake Powell (Upper Basin) must be equal or lower than that in Lake Mead (Lower Basin). If, at any time after January, it appears that Powell will contain more water than Mead by September 30th, releases from Powell must be made to move water from Powell to Mead, equalizing their contents. The aim of the provision is to keep the Upper Basin from stockpiling water in Lake Powell at the expense of users downstream.

The 1993 AOP raised an issue regarding the filling of the newly constructed New Waddell Reservoir, part of an important new water project in Arizona. The question was how to account for the water, to be drawn from the Colorado system, needed to fill New Waddell. A straightforward approach would have been simply to count the New Waddell water against Arizona's annual apportionment of 2.8 million acre-feet. But this could be considered unfair, because Arizona would not actually be using the water. Instead, it would remain in storage. A creative alternative approach would be to consider the water stored in New Waddell as still being in the Colorado and not charge it to Arizona's apportionment at all.

At this point it is important to realize that although this issue seems to concern Arizona's supply of water for 1993, it was in fact California's water supply that was at stake. The reason for this is that the law of the river permits states to use each other's "unused apportionments." Historically, California has used more water than its regular apportionment and it could do so by virtue of the fact that Arizona never used its full apportionment. Therefore, any water used for filling New Waddell, and charged against Arizona' apportionment, would in effect be unavailable for California, as it would no longer be part of Arizona's unused apportionment! So California had an interest in not counting the New Waddell water against Arizona's apportionment.

In a letter of June 5, 1992, the Upper Colorado River Commission (a consortium of Upper Basin states) endorsed the spirit of the proposal not to count the water against Arizona's apportionment. However, the commission noted that the proposal could establish an undesirable precedent from the point of view of the Upper Basin states.

Here is its reasoning: "This alternative would require Lower Basin bookkeeping, before equalization releases from Powell were made, to reflect system water at places 'other than' Mead. While this alternative looks attractive, its greatest risk is that the Lower Basin might insist on equalization based on *Powell and all other Upper Basin system storage* when we insist on *Mead and all other Lower Basin system storage*" (emphasis added; USBR, 1994). That is, the Commission detected the horns of a dilemma. If the New Waddell water was not considered as part of the Lower Basin storage when equalization releases were determined, this would entitle the Lower Basin to a larger equalization release, at the expense of water stored in the Upper Basin. On the other hand, if the New Waddell water were to be considered part of Lower Basin storage for purposes of determining equalization, even though it would not be in Lake Mead, this would open the way to arguments that Upper Basin water outside Lake Powell should be considered as well. Any inclusion of Upper Basin water outside Lake Powell when equalization was determined would also lead to a larger equalization release.

Notice that this whole argument rests entirely on tactical valuations, in the terms of our framework. There was no argument about who would get what water in the short term. Rather, the Upper Basin states were concerned about the future lines of action that would be opened up for Lower Basin states, even within the limited scope of actions in the AOP process, by creating a precedent in the New Waddell case.

Respecting the fears of the Upper Basin, it was determined in the AOP that the filling of New Waddell was to be charged against Arizona's apportionment. As it happened, the spring of 1993 was unusually wet, so there was plenty of water in the river and no state had to worry about its apportionment. And no precedent that could complicate equalization was established.

Could the residual conflicts illustrated in these examples be reduced still further? It is hard to see how. The present AOP process allows no more than argument, and without the ability to offer arguments participants would feel they had no scope whatever for influencing river operations. The AOP process has to give the participants enough representation to make breaking out of the process seem relatively unattractive, as argued above.

Given the role of the equalization constraint in the New Waddell issue, it could be argued that the guardrail constraints actually increase low-level conflict, or the time and effort invested in conflict, by making decisions more complex and interrelated. Conceivably, the constraints might be tuned to reduce this effect. But given that the constraints originate outside the AOP process, it is doubtful that the analysis necessary to do this would ever be done, if such an analysis is even possible. The physical linkages inherent in the river system (water consumed for one purpose cannot be consumed for another, water stored in one place cannot be stored at another, etc.) are sufficient to give even simple constraints far-reaching and hard to trace consequences.

3.4. Averting Disputes: The Cash Register

The AOP, and other dispute systems, work by processing disputes harmoniously. The disputes are still there, but participants' handling of them is largely free of overt conflict and opposing actions. Positive though this result is, it is sometimes possible to do even better: disputes can be eliminated altogether, even in situations of direct goal conflict. Of particular interest from the perspective of the role of technology in coordination, technological innovation can have this effect. The cash register is an example.

In the pre-cash register era the proprietors of retail establishments (e.g., bars), found themselves in direct conflict with their employees who handled money. At the end of the day the bartender, having collected payment for so many drinks, was expected to tender the money to the proprietor, but in fact very often kept some share of it. In the long term the proprietor would determine that the bartender was holding back, because the inventory of liquor would decrease more rapidly than was consistent with the reported rate of sales. But in the short run the proprietor had no way to detect and counteract the theft.

Exactly this situation led to the invention and subsequent refinement of the cash register (Marcosson, 1945). In our analysis we see either overtly disharmonious working, with the proprietor and bartenders engaging in various activities intended to reveal and conceal the pilferage, or, if the proprietor never becomes aware of the holdback, at best an *unstable* harmony based on the proprietor's ignorance of what is happening. The root of the conflict is the sharply differing values for the two participants of states in which the cashier turns over all proceeds (high intrinsic value for the proprietor and low for the bartender) and states in which the cashier holds back (low intrinsic value for the proprietor and high for the bartender).

The function of the original cash register, devised to improve this situation from the proprietor's point of view, was to change the tactical value of some of the hold-back states. The cash register makes a record of each sale, which the proprietor can use to check the amount tendered by the clerk. If the bartender uses the cash register, and then holds back, the bartender must anticipate punitive action by the proprietor. So states in which the bartender has used the cash register for sales, but then holds back money, still have their high intrinsic value for the bartender. But when their strongly negative tactical value is taken into account they become states which the bartender will avoid.

The effect of this change in value is to bring about agreement between bartender and proprietor on the value of some states. Both bartender and proprietor now wish to avoid states in which the bartender holds back and has used the cash register. But (as experience soon showed) conflict continued because the participants still had strongly differing values for states in which the bartender held back and *had not used* the cash register. Dishonest bartenders continued to hold back by just not using the register for some sales.

The first cash register accepted as providing reasonable security to proprietors (Marcosson, 1945) was developed in the light of this experience. It had a bell fitted which sounded when a sale was registered (the origin of the phrase "ring up a sale"), so that a proprietor in another area of the establishment could hear if the register was being used or not. A locked cash drawer was linked to the register so that it opened only when a sale was recorded, so that the clerk could not make change without using the register.

These changes do nothing to change the value for the bartender of states in which money is held back and the register has not been used. But trajectories leading to such states are blocked because they pass through earlier states in which the proprietor misses the sound of the bell and the bartender cannot make change. These states have very low tactical valuation for the bartender and are therefore avoided.

The cash register does not entirely prevent holding back. For example, in a flurry of sales a clerk could safely ring up only some and make change for more than one sale when the cash drawer is open. But it does greatly reduce the incidence of hold-backs, making stable harmony between proprietor and clerk much more common. Note that it does this without changing the intrinsic value of states (money held back would still be valuable to the clerk) or directly restricting the actions available to either participant. Its action is more subtle: It changes the likely response by the proprietor to actions of the clerk, and thereby imposes negative tactical values on otherwise attractive states for the clerk.

A subsequent development in the cash register for general retail sales illustrates further possibilities. It provides better security and convenience for the proprietor by engaging the interests of a third party, the customer. Most registers now print a receipt, so that a clerk who does not ring up a sale cannot provide a receipt. Assuming that customers want receipts, and will take action if they do not get them, the clerk has further reason to avoid states in which the register is not used.

If the desire of customers for receipts is strong and consistent enough, the proprietor need no longer monitor register use at all, and the bell can be dispensed with. But it now becomes important that customers be made to want receipts. Thus a store that alters its return policy so as not to require receipts will be undermining, to some extent, the security of its system of recording sales. If the goods sold by a store are such that customers are unlikely to need to return them, a store may offer a direct reward to customers who are not offered receipts, thus recruiting customers to monitor the use of the register in that way.

The cash register profoundly alters the landscape of states that participants in retail transactions traverse. States in which the clerk pockets the cash are now subdivided into those in which the sale was recorded and those in which it was not, and the former states now have a large negative tactical valuation for the clerk. Because the register links the recording of sales with other effects, such as making change, states in which the register is not used acquire negative tactical valuations for the clerk. These valuations depend in part on the role of another participant, the customer, who can be relied upon to complain if change is not provided, or a receipt is not given. In the case of receipts, the customer's part in the affair is also subject to manipulation by the proprietor, who can to some extent control the tactical valuation by the customer of states in which they fail to get a receipt. Making receipts important to the customer in any way makes it more likely that customers will play their unwitting role of preventing unregistered sales.

In summary, the introduction of the cash register promotes harmonious working between clerk and proprietor. It does this by altering the state space being traversed in such a way as to change the value of some courses of action and to introduce some new ones. In its latest forms it artfully weaves together the values of clerk, proprietor, and customer to create a space in which stable harmony is highly likely.

Many other examples can be cited of innovations that have restructured potential conflict situations, including several variant cash registers devised for special purposes described in Marcosson (1945). A lower tech example is the use of tickets for admission to events. When properly organized, ticket sales are handled separately from the collection of tickets at the gate, and tickets are numbered to simplify accurate inventory checks. Customers demand tickets, because they know they will not be admitted without one. Ticket sellers cannot hold back money because a check on their ticket supply directly reveals how many they have sold. Note that combining ticket sales with ticket collection makes the system vulnerable; a ticket seller might simply collect money from patrons and wave them through, without removing tickets from inventory. Note also that tickets must be marked in some way to prevent their being returned to inventory and resold after being collected. By making customers want ticket stubs, the proprietor can enlist the aid of customers in ensuring that tickets are mutilated when collected.

As these examples show, many business practices are shaped, sometimes in subtle ways, in such a way as to bring the potentially conflicting values of participants, especially proprietors and employees, into alignment. Such arrangements promote stable harmony in the presence of sharp conflicts in the intrinsic values of states for the participants. Some of the examples also show that technology can play an important role in enabling such arrangements, a matter to which we will return.

4. DISCUSSION

4.1. Incorporating Goal Conflicts in Coordination Theory

We have proposed an analysis of harmony in the presence of goal conflicts and have applied it to some hypothetical situations and to two real-life success cases in bringing peace out of conflict, the Colorado River Annual Operating Plan process and the cash register. We have seen seven mechanisms for promoting harmony at work in the various examples.

- *Improving participants' knowledge of each other's valuations.* This is the core of interest-based negotiation.
- *Improving participants' knowledge of the true effects of actions and the true valuation of states.* Lack of harmony, in the sense of unnecessarily long trajectories, can occur even with only one actor if that actor's knowledge is imperfect.
- *Reducing gaps between apparent and informed valuation.* Inaccurate valuations can not only produce unnecessary conflict, as in the last point, but also promote unstable harmony.
- *Excluding regions of the state space in which conflict is certain.* This is the guardrail idea, illustrated strikingly in the Colorado planning process.
- *Reducing the actions available to participants directly in favor of exogenous processes which participants can influence indirectly.* The less directly participants can oppose one another the less wasted action.
- *Altering the tactical valuation of states.* The cash register links making a record of sales to making change or giving a receipt and thus changes the tactical valuation of not recording a sale. Less subtly, one can use

one's own freedom of action to alter other participants' tactical valuations; effective use of threats in diplomacy works this way. A crucial and sometimes neglected part of this is communicating the tactical contingencies accurately to other participants, so that they know which courses of action will activate or avert the threat (Fisher, Kopelman, & Schneider, 1994).

- *Recruiting other participants whose available actions change the tactical valuation of states.* The cash register uses customers' valuations to enforce the tactical valuation of the proprietor.

We can use these observations to extend the coverage of coordination theory to situations in which disharmony results not from just from the complex logistics of working together but from the influence of divergent goals. Malone and Crowston (1994) outlined the scope of coordination theory in terms of types of dependencies between activities, such as shared resources and producer–consumer relationships. For each type of dependency they list example coordination processes for managing them. We can incorporate the methods for dealing with conflict that we have described into this framework if we can identify conflict with a particular kind of dependency between activities. We can then consider these methods for dealing with conflict to be coordination processes appropriate to this dependency type.

In fact, it seems quite natural to see many conflicts as dependencies between activities. If A and B are in conflict their actions will be strongly linked in opposition: Actions taken by A will likely evoke contrary actions by B and vice versa. Further, this linkage has clearly undesirable properties from the underlying coordination perspective. Accordingly we can propose the following new entry in the Malone and Crowston outline: *Dependency: Goal conflict, real or apparent.*

Examples of coordination processes for managing dependency: Increase communication of goals among participants, as in shift from positions to interests. Prune the allowable state space to bar regions of sharp conflict. Prune the available actions to reduce the possibility of direct opposition. Change side effects of A's actions (and/or B's) so as to increase agreement on the value of states, as in the cash register. Adjust the goals and actions of other participants so as to increase agreement between A and B on the values of states, as in the cash register with receipts.

4.2. Coordination Technology and Goal Conflict

Coordination theory is an applied theory, with one of its important applications being the design of technology to support coordination. We can ask what new technological opportunities are suggested by the examples we have discussed.

The AOP process uses little technology. Simulation models are used to support the discussions of alternative proposals in the AOP, and our own work (Reitsma, Zigurs, Lewis, Wilson, & Sloane, 1996; Zigurs, Wilson, Sloane, Reitsma, & Lewis, 1994) emphasizes the potential value of models in giving participants more accurate information about the consequences of possible actions. But this use of technology appears to be incidental to the success of the AOP process in bringing harmony out of conflict.

By contrast, technology is central to the cash register example. The example shows that introduction of an appropriately designed artifact can substantially transform participant's valuations of states and thereby profoundly reshape their behavior. The technology involved is not generic, in the way that a communication system or a scheduling system might be. Rather, a cash-register-like solution to a conflict seems to require a specific analysis of the goals and actions of participants in the conflict. Some of the general moves that are possible can be discerned, such as shaping a participant's behavior by making a desired action a side effect of some other action that will be reliably performed, or recruiting new participants whose goals and actions change the contingencies for the original participants. But much work is needed to develop a useful design approach from these beginnings.

The examples we have explored are ones in which conflict is at or near the surface. But we suggest that ideas about goal conflict may have relevance not only for these problems but also for problems that are within the current scope of coordination theory and technology. The argument is that conflict, and the control of conflict, are crucial in some applications of coordination that do not seem to involve conflict. Workflow systems provide an example.

Workflow systems (see surveys in Bussler, 1994; Ellis & Wainer, 1994) are coordination systems that manage the passing of task-related information, including the responsibility to perform a task, among workers in an organization. In principle, and sometimes in practice, a workflow system can streamline the distribution of work over the force of workers available to carry it forward.

A recurring problem with workflow systems is inflexibility. A system that represents the normal sequence of processing of tasks may get in the way of changes that are needed to handle special situations, such as the absence of some person who plays a key, bottleneck role. Left to themselves, human beings are adept at finding sensible variations of normal practice in such cases, but a workflow system may prevent them from doing so (Robinson & Bannon, 1991).

Ellis and Wainer (1994) argued that a sufficiently flexible workflow system should include a model of the goals of the participants in the process being managed. Such a representation allows alternate methods to be used as long as goals are satisfied.

In their proposal Ellis and Wainer note that goal conflicts can occur within the scope of a workflow system; they cite the example of a possible conflict between the goal of maximizing customer good feelings and maximizing the number of customers served per hour. In this conflict only the interests of the organization are at stake, because maximizing customer good feelings and expediting sales are both subgoals of the overarching goal of maximizing profit. But as the cash register and ticketing examples show, many business procedures are designed to manage conflicts between the interests of the organization and the interests of actors considered as individuals. This observation places an important limit on the desirable flexibility of a workflow system. It should allow alternative processes to be followed only as far as necessary checks on the goals of individual workers are preserved.

An illustration of this point is the management of contacts between purchasing agents and vendors. It is universally recognized that purchasing agents are vulnerable to improper influences from vendors, who may offer gifts and other inducements, hoping to gain favorable treatment of their products. Nearly all organizations have rules specifying what gifts, if any, purchasing agents may receive from vendors. Some go further and require that each purchasing agent handle only certain vendor accounts, and that the account assignments be changed frequently (Lee & Dobler, 1973). This policy reduces the value to vendors of offering inducements, as no long-term arrangement with a particular purchasing agent is possible. Further, it increases the likelihood that improper arrangements will be discovered, because a new purchasing agent would be able to see, for example, if supplies were contracted for at an uncompetitive price. In our analysis the policy alters the tactical value to both participants of entering into an improper relationship.

Now consider a workflow system charged with managing contacts between vendors and purchasing agents. A slavish implementation of the assignment shifting policy would mean that contact with a vendor would be blocked if the assigned agent were unavailable. An overly flexible system would give up control over vendor contacts altogether, and open the way for abuse. A system that incorporated the rationale for the assignment shifting policy would permit any agent who had not recently been assigned to that vendor to serve as a back-up contact, and could even permit an agent who had recently held the assignment to serve as back-up under exceptional conditions, meaning with very low frequency. These exceptions to the policy do not compromise its effectiveness.

Our argument here is that Ellis and Wainer are right in calling for workflow systems to incorporate representations of the goals of the organization and of actors within an organization. Further, the logic of policies and practices for controlling conflicts between the organization and individuals within it, like the use of cash registers, arrangements for ticketing, and assignment shifting in purchasing, should be represented in the system.

Bussler (1994) described a representation for the criteria that determine who is eligible to carry out particular activities in a work process. For example, Bussler's representation can specify that two particular tasks must be performed by two different people. But the representation does not capture why such a requirement is in place, and hence provides no help in deciding when violations of it might be acceptable. Representing such rationale is a tall order, on top of Ellis and Wainer's already ambitious proposal. Indeed, Robinson and Bannon would argue that this cannot be done. But it is hard to see how the needed balance of flexibility and control can be achieved otherwise.

4.3. Conclusion

We have argued that the coverage of coordination theory can usefully be extended beyond cooperation, where participants are presumed to share goals, to situations in which participants' goals are in sharp conflict. We have illustrated methods for handling conflicts so as to increase harmony: smooth and efficient working. We suggest that there are new opportunities for coordination technology that support these methods, including technology that acts by restructuring the situation in which participants must act. We also suggest that consideration of conflict and its management should influence the analysis of many coordination problems in which conflict may not appear to be a central concern.

ACKNOWLEDGMENTS

Preparation of the chapter was supported by the grant, "The impact of simulation modelling on group decision support system outcomes" under the NSF Coordination Theory and Collaboration initiative to CL, RR, and IZ, and by a Visiting Scientist award to CL from the National Center for Geographic Information and Analysis.

REFERENCES

Basar, T. and Olsder, G. J. (1982) *Dynamic Noncooperative Game Theory*. New York: Academic Press.

Braybrooke, D. and Lindblom, C. (1963) "A Strategy of Decision." Glencoe, NY: Free Press.

Brenner, M. J. (1973) *The Political Economy of America's Environmental Dilemma*. Lexington, MA: Lexington Books.

Bussler, C. J. (1994) Policy resolution in workflow management systems. *Digital Technical Journal, 6*, 26–49.

Ellis, C. A. and Wainer, J. (1994) Goal based models of collaboration. *Journal of Collaborative Computing, 1*.

Fisher, R., Kopelman, E. and Schneider, A. K. (1994) *Beyond Machiavelli: Tools for Coping with Conflict*. Cambridge, MA: Harvard University Press.

Fisher, R. and Ury, W. (1981) *Getting to yes*. Boston: Houghton-Mifflin.

Lee, L. and Dobler, D. W. (1973) *Purchasing and Materials Management*. New York: McGraw-Hill.

Lindblom, C. E. (1959) The science of muddling through. Public Administration Review, 19, pp. 79–88.

Lindblom, C. (1968) *The Policy Making Process*. Englewood Cliffs, NJ: Prentice Hall.

Luce, R. D. and Raiffa, H. (1957) *Games and Decisions*. New York: Wiley.

Malone, T. W. and Crowston, K. (1990) What is coordination theory and how can it help design cooperative work systems? In *Proceedings of the Third Conference on Computer-Supported Cooperative Work*. New York: ACM Press, pp. 375–387.

Malone, T. W. and Crowston, K. (1994) The interdisciplinary study of coordination. *ACM Computing Surveys, 26*, pp. 87–119.

Marcosson, I. F. (1945) *Wherever Men Trade*. New York: Dodd, Mead.

McKinney, M. (1992) Designing a dispute resolution system for water policy and management. *Negotiation Journal*, 153–163.

Reisner, M. (1987) *Cadillac Desert. The American West and its Disappearing Water*. Penguin Books.

Reitsma, R., Zigurs, I., Lewis, C., Wilson, V., and Sloane, A. (1996) Experiment with Simulation Models in Water Resources Negotiations. *ASCE Journal of Water Resources Planning and Management, 122*, 64–70.

Rich, E. and Knight, K. (1991) *Artificial Intelligence*. New York: McGraw-Hill.

Robinson, M. and Bannon, L. (1991) Questioning representations. In L. Bannon, M. Robinson & K. Schmidt (Eds.) *Proceedings of the Second European Conference on Computer-Supported Cooperative Work* (September 25–27, 1991), 219–233.

United States Bureau of Reclamation (1980) *Updating the Hoover Dam Documents*. Denver, Colorado: United States Bureau of Reclamation.

United States Bureau of Reclamation (1994) *Colorado River Annual Operating Plan Dossiers 1991–1994*. Denver, Colorado: United States Bureau of Reclamation.

Ury, W. L., Brett, J. M. and Goldberg, S. B. (1989) Dispute systems design: An introduction. *Negotiation Journal, 5*, 357–358.

Von Neumann, J. and Morgenstern, O. (1953) *Theory of Games and Economic Behavior*. Princeton: Princeton University Press.

Zigurs, I., Wilson, E. V., Sloane, A. M., Reitsma, R. F. and Lewis, C. (1994) Simulation models and group negotiation: Problems of task understanding and computer support. In R. Sprague and J. F. Nunamaker (Eds.), *Proceedings of the 27th Hawaii International Conference on System Sciences, Volume IV*. Los Alamitos, CA: IEEE Computer Society Press.

CHAPTER

23

Modeling Team Coordination and Decisions in a Distributed Dynamic Environment

Wei-Ping Wang
David L. Kleinman
Peter B. Luh
The University of Connecticut, Storrs

1. INTRODUCTION

1.1. Background

Distributed decision making is intrinsic to a variety of complex systems, for example, air traffic control, military command and control, and telemarketing networks. In such systems, human decisionmakers (DMs) who may be geographically separated, must coordinate to share their information and resources, and to sequence or synchronize their activities to attain common team goals in what is generally a dynamic and uncertain environment. Team coordination can be viewed as occurring along four dimensions: goals, resources, information, and tasks. Goal coordination involves goal selection and decomposition, and incentive strategy design in hierarchical or multilayer organizations [15, 17, 25]. Resource coordination is the allocation and management of limited–sharable resources among multiple DMs who are responsible for different activities [16, 18]. Information coordination involves dissemination and fusion of uncertain and incomplete information among distributed team members [20]. Finally, task–action coordination is the act of sequencing or synchronizing interrelated activities among DMs [15].

An essential characteristic of task–action coordination is that the tasks or subtasks to be carried out by individual team members are interdependent in time. Thus, team performance depends on sequenced or synchronized actions rather than on summed or aggregated responses. Performance on such tasks can be impaired, not because individuals within the team lack requisite abilities, but rather because the team as a whole fails to coordinate [5]. Steiner (1972) defined such coordination deficiency in teams as process loss [29]. Effective communication and coordination among team members appear to be vitally important, especially when tasks are characterized by high interdependency and high task complexity [24].

Our research addresses a task coordination problem in a distributed, dynamic, multitask context. Specifically, we study coordination within a hierarchical team of distributed DMs performing sequentially related task processing activities. The research has two constituent parts: empirical investigations to observe real human team behavior in a computer-mediated decision-making environment, and a modeling part to provide a conceptual framework and analytical models of team response. The empirical part, as reported in a previous paper [32], included a HIerarchical TEam Coordination (HITEC) experiment conducted with human subjects. The experiment has yielded significant findings on the effects of team communication structure, time pressure, and the role of a team coordinator on a number of team performance and team process measures.

This chapter presents the normative and normative–descriptive modeling part of our research, including the development of a structural framework for representing team coordination, and the mathematical modeling of the specific HITEC experimental conditions. Our purpose is to (a) analyze team coordination and decision-making processes in a formal framework, (b) mathematically model the decision-making problem the human teams faced in the experiment, (c) identify team coordination limitations and biases via model–data comparison, and (d) use the resulting normative–descriptive model as a simulation tool to examine the impact of communication on team performance.

1.2. Previous Related Work

In the study of team behavior in general, and team decision making in particular, it has been recognized that the central feature of a team lies in the interaction of its members [15, 17]. Since the early 1990s, researchers in different fields have addressed team decision making issues with respect to the impact of external factors on team performance [1, 5], effects of stress [34], utilization of communication [27], effects of telecommunication technology [15], and so forth. As a result, there have been a number of relevant empirical findings about team coordination, which provide both an underlying basis and a departure point for our research. For example:

- Team members often coordinate by sending communication messages to each other (called explicit coordination), and by exercising their mental predictions of each other's decisions (called implicit coordination) [3, 11].

- Team coordination strategies transition from explicit coordination under low task loading/tempo conditions to implicit coordination as load increases [11].
- As task uncertainty increases the ability of a team to coordinate implicitly is reduced. Under these conditions, explicit coordination via communications increases [7, 8, 11].
- The value of communications depends on the ability of the team to coordinate implicitly. Thus, if ample tools (e.g., centralized information displays or shared battle graphics) are provided to enhance implicit coordination, performance will be less sensitive to variations–limitations in the communication media [10, 26].
- Team members adapt their decision making and coordination strategies to changes in the communications media (delay, bandwidth, probability of message loss, and so on.) [10].
- Members of well-coordinated teams are often able to anticipate when teammates are going to need specific information for the completion of a task. They also provide such information proactively [19].

Although many empirical findings are important, close examination often reveals seemingly inconsistent and even controversial results [24, 30]. This is due in large part to the complexity of human team behavior, and the lack of encompassing theories. It is recognized that theories of team decision making need to be developed to integrate empirical results, to embody concepts, and to serve as a basis for future research [5, 21]. In response, some researchers have developed generalized theories of team behavior. As reviewed in [24], various formalized frameworks (conceptualizations) of human decision making have been developed. These frameworks describe the activities and processes of human decisionmaking from a psychological perspective or from a systems theoretic background. As an example of a psychologically oriented framework, Hackman's model represents a comprehensive conceptualization of group processes in an organizational environment [5]. Adopting Hackman–Morris' framework, Adelman et al. [1] presented a conceptual framework of distributed tactical decision making and conducted an experiment to validate it. This framework views the team decision making as a whole and represents it via an input–process–performance linkage to analyze factors affecting team decision making. These frameworks provide *qualitative* analysis and insight of team performance, but do not lead to quantitative predictions.

Frameworks developed from a systems theoretic background are more formalized or application oriented, such as the Optimal Control Model (OCM),

Human Operator Simulator (HOS), and Stimulus-Hypothesis-Option-Response (SHOR) models, as reviewed in [21]. These frameworks represent the logical (rational) decision-making processes from a systems point of view. Compared with the psychologically oriented frameworks, they can better serve the development of mathematical models and quantitative analysis, but they are weaker in explanations of human behavioral aspects. Moreover, the existing frameworks, mostly focusing on individual behavior, are not directly applicable to study team coordination.

People have realized that progress can be made in the study of teams by combining psychological and systems perspectives. Team coordination issues need to be addressed more vigorously via both modeling and empirical studies. In [30], Streufert et al. further argued that it would be nice if we could model, and consequently predict future team decisions on the basis of parameters generated by an understanding of the team's past decisions. It may be even better if decisions of individuals and teams could be accurately described by some mathematical model (e.g., one that could be simulated on a computer) [30]. This is what we pursue in our research, by following a normative–descriptive approach as outlined in [10].

1.3. Overview of the Chapter

The remaining chapter is organized into six sections. Section 2 develops a Coordination and Decision (CODE) framework to represent team coordination processes by integrating Wohl's SHOR model with the "shared mental model" construct. The latter is a recent construct that has gained considerable acceptance in the study of teams [3, 7, 23]. The framework then serves as a basis for the quantitative modeling of the hierarchical team coordination problem that was examined in the HITEC experiment [32]. Section 3 briefly describes the design and implementation of the experiment.

Section 4 presents the normative modeling of the HITEC experiment based on the CODE framework. A *distributed* model is developed by treating each team member as an individual decision entity who makes his or her own decisions and coordinates with teammates to optimize team performance. The model captures team coordination by evaluating potential coordination errors (decision conflicts in handling interdependencies) and determining communication needs and message usage. The model's algorithmic solution process is mapped onto the CODE framework, and analogies are drawn between mathematical procedures of the model solution process and human decision-making characteristics to give an intuitive "feel" for the model.

Section 5 develops the normative–descriptive model via an iterative process of model–data comparison. The normative model is first applied to solve a subset of the HITEC experimental cases. Model solutions are compared with empirical data from human teams. Consistent discrepancies are found and analyzed to show that human teams tend to overcommunicate in coordinating, especially under low time pressure; overcooperate on "team tasks" that involve multiple DMs; and reduce planning horizon and coordination activities as time pressure increases. These descriptive factors are quantified and incorporated into the model to develop a normative–descriptive model, which closely matches empirical results of human teams.

Section 6 presents an application of the normative–descriptive model, used in a predictive mode, to examine quantitatively the impact of communication on team performance. It is shown that the utilization of implicit coordination largely reduces the need for communication to maintain performance. However, satisfactory team performance depends on the appropriately integrated use of implicit and explicit coordination mechanisms (not just one). Concluding remarks are given in Section 7.

2. THE COORDINATION AND DECISION (CODE) FRAMEWORK

In a team context, humans make decisions through interactions with the environment–system they are attempting to control, and through interactions with their teammates. The environment refers to the decision-making context (e.g., a plant to be controlled or a jobshop to be managed). The environment is usually dynamic, and is subject to the effect of external factors, many of which are stochastic. In a task coordination problem, randomly arriving tasks (i.e., "things to do") of different types must be processed through concerted actions by multiple DMs. The DMs often have a limited amount of resource with which to process the tasks in such a manner as to attain a common team goal (e.g., maximize number of tasks completed, maximize total reward attained, and so on). Because some tasks require sequential processing by multiple DMs, the team members must coordinate with each other. Therefore, as shown in Fig. 23.1, any single DM is engaged in two types of interactions, one with the environment and the other with his or her teammates. A DM interacts with the environment as information is received from the environment (e.g., through observing the status of the various tasks), and makes decisions that change the environment (e.g., allocating resource to process a selected task). A DM interacts with his or her teammates via communication, informing one another of decisions already made, and of those being considered, and so on. At issue is the understanding of how a team member makes decisions and coordinates with others at the individual level, and how the team as a whole performs at the cooperative level.

We approach this problem by developing a COordination and DEcision (CODE) framework that combines Wohl's Stimulus–Hypothesis–Option–

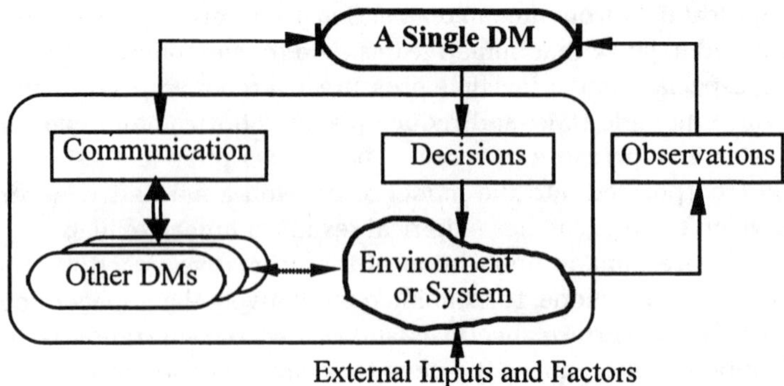

FIG. 23.1. Interhuman interaction in a team decision making context.

Response (SHOR) framework [33] with the mental model construct [3, 7, 8]. Although a number of frameworks (structural models or paradigms) have been developed to model or to represent the functional activities or processes in human decision making [10, 21, 22, 28], they mostly focus on a single human's interaction with the environment, and generally ignore the interactions among teammates (although teammates are sometimes treated as part of the environment). Thus, they are not appropriate nor adequate for studying team decisionmaking when coordination is a focal concern. In contrast, we develop the CODE framework with an emphasis on team coordination.

2.1. The SHOR Framework

The SHOR framework [33] represents human decision making as a four-stage iterative process: Stimulus, Hypothesis, Option, and Response (SHOR). In this model, data (stimulus) is obtained, and its relevance and trustworthiness examined. Hypotheses and inferences about underlying meanings are created and tested, and situation is assessed. Decision options are then identified and evaluated. The process is iterated with new hypotheses and options generated and evaluated, until a decision (response) is made. In a task coordination problem, a DM needs to observe the tasks to be processed, assess their status (e.g., which tasks have sufficient time or likelihood to be processed), generate options regarding when to process which tasks with what resources, evaluate the consequences, and make decisions.

Arguably, the SHOR framework depicts the mental activities involved in individual decisionmaking. It illustrates the informational interaction of a DM with the external environment, and emphasizes the iterative features of the human decisionmaking process. However, the interaction with teammates is not considered, and the mechanisms involved in the four stages of activities (S, H, O, and R) are not explicitly explained. Instead, Wohl mentions that the heart of the matter is the ability to derive information from data, and to use it to quickly assess likelihood of alternative hypotheses ("what is") and the consequences of the decision options ("what if") [33]. Such an ability, in our view, can be best explained by using the mental model construct.

2.2. Mental Model Construct

It is well known from control theory that optimal system performance cannot be achieved unless the controller is designed based on a good model of the system to be controlled [4, 28]. When a human being is put into the controller's position, research in cognitive engineering suggests that manual control of the system is based on a mental representation that the human has about the system behavior [22, 23]. Since the 1990s, researchers have used the internal model or mental model construct as a metaphor, analogy, or approximation to the internal representation a human holds about the external world [3, 7, 9, 28]. According to Rouse and Morris [23], a mental model can be defined as a "mechanism whereby humans generate descriptions of system purpose and form, explanations of system functioning and observed system states, and predictions of future system states" (p. 353).

Within a team context, a DM interacts with other teammates in addition to interacting with the environment. A "mutual/shared mental model" concept has thus been invoked by a number of researchers to explain how a DM interacts with teammates to reach coordinated decisions [2, 3, 35, 36]. *A mutual mental model refers to a DM's mental schema to anticipate the decision-making behavior and information needs of other DMs, based on their mutual understanding or shared viewpoint of the problem.* Bower et al. [3] suggests that effective team coordination may be the result of shared mental models of the team as well as of the tasks. The mutual mental model enables a DM to predict teammates' activities, anticipate potential coordination conflicts, and conduct coordination activities. The specifics (but not necessarily the structure) of the mental model depend on the problem context—that is, the level of detail for the cause-and-effect dynamics of the system under control, whether or not the team has local goals in addition to a global or team goal and what they are, a description of the team's information structure detailing any shared or common information, and so forth.

2.3. The CODE Framework

The SHOR framework describes the human decision-making process as a set of logical steps in reaching a decision. The mental model construct posits an underlying mechanism for describing human information processing, that is not explicit in the SHOR framework. In 1982, Athans [2] combined the mental model construct with the SHOR framework to provide both procedural and functional explanations of human decision-making. Furthermore, he applied the extended framework to a *team* context, and postulated that a well-trained team member must have a set of mutual expert (mental) models in addition to a mental model of the system. Each of the mutual mental models represents a suitably aggregated version of the mental model of each teammate. The extended framework, however, does not explain the team interaction process (i.e., team coordination).

To capture–model the coordination process, we believe that it is essential to distinguish between a DM's interaction with teammates and his interaction with the environment. These two interactions can be appropriately represented by integrating the SHOR framework and the mental model construct, and forms the basis of the CODE framework, as depicted in Fig. 23.2.

This framework treats a team member's coordination and decision-making processes as being supported by two channels of information flow: situation information and communication. Using the situation channel, a DM observes the environment, gathering such information as arrivals of new tasks, and time available for processing each task. Through the communication channel, messages related to task processing are exchanged among DMs. The acquired information is interpreted and processed using the mental model, which consists of two interrelated parts: the *primary* part representing the environment states and dynamics, and the *mutual* part reflecting teammates' anticipated behavior, such as their decision strategies and tendencies. The mental model, with an emphasis on the primary part, is then used to generate decision options and predict the consequences of the options (e.g., when

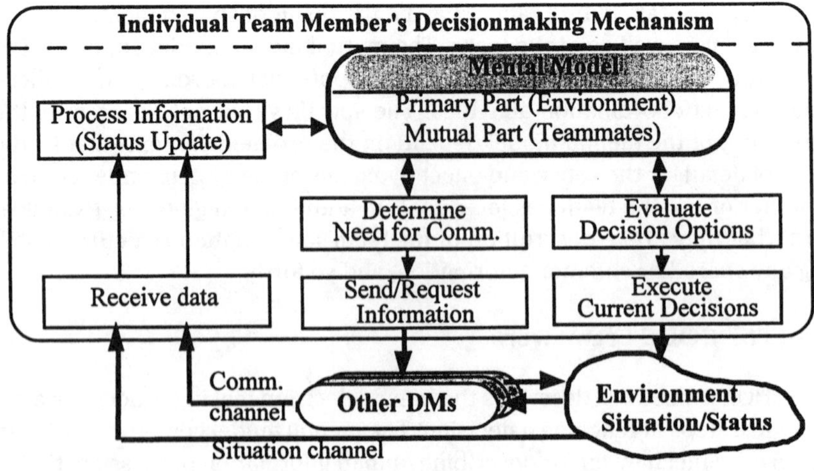

FIG. 23.2. Structure of the CODE framework.

to process a task and what the effects are on other tasks). The consequences are evaluated, and decisions are made and executed. Using the communication channel, the DM receives information from teammates about their decisions (e.g., whether a task is being processed, will be processed, or ignored). Such information may enable the mental model, mainly the mutual part, to further estimate teammates' likely decisions which are not communicated, and predict the decision consequences. Coordination needs are then evaluated and coordination activities conducted.

Coordination utilizes both the situation and the communication channels. Because all decisions affect the environment and may lead to changes in environment status, a DM can indirectly observe and potentially anticipate his teammates' decisions by monitoring such changes. The situation channel thus provides partial information about a teammate's behavior in addition to information about the environment. This enables the DMs to coordinate without communication. Coordination via the situation channel is referred to as "implicit coordination," as discussed in [11]. Implicit coordination is affected strongly by the team's information structure. With a highly decentralized information structure, DMs may have local information on separate parts of the environment, and thus make few observations about each other's behavior. In this case, teams rely less on implicit coordination than when the team members have more overlapping information [10].

The communication channel, on the other hand, provides a DM with direct information about others' decisions, and also enables the DM to tell others of his own decisions. Communication messages explicitly inform individual DMs about potential errors (e.g., when a teammate's decision appears different from what was anticipated), and coordination needs. Coordination via this channel corresponds to "explicit coordination" [11]. Explicit coordination is, however, costly in terms of time and effort [15, 29]. Communication, like any valuable resource to a team, requires team members to determine what and how much to communicate, to whom, and at what time, by evaluating coordination needs.

Coordination is usually a blend of implicit and explicit components, where the balance between them adapts to variations in the internal and external circumstances in which the team operates. As phrased by Salas et al. [24], the greater the degree of accuracy and overlap among team member mental models, the greater the likelihood that the team members will predict, adapt, and coordinate with one another successfully, even under stressful or novel conditions. At an extreme, if team members hold precise mental models of the environment and are capable of accurately predicting the decisions of their teammates, team coordination can be achieved without communication. This, however, is unlikely except for well-trained teams and in simple circumstances. Poor training, complex or novel situations, lack of a single team goal, and so forth, would cause mismatches in DMs' mental models, and communication would be needed to "fill in the gaps," thereby reducing the uncertainty that team members have about each other's actions. Kahan et al. [8] postulated that the major purpose of communication lies in the sharing of mental models, ensuring that people are "reading off the same sheet of music." Communications thus plays a very important role when team members cannot maintain harmonious mental models via the situation channel alone. In other words, the value of communications increases as the team's capability to coordinate implicitly is decreased [3].

In the remaining chapter we demonstrate that the CODE framework can provide a structure for developing mathematical models for particular coordination problems. Specifically, a normative and a normative–descriptive model are developed for the specific task coordination problem operationalized in the HITEC experiment.

3. HIERARCHICAL TEAM COORDINATION EXPERIMENT (HITEC)

The HITEC experiment was designed as a laboratory abstraction of an environment in which noncollocated team members must coordinate to process various randomly arriving "tasks" that have precedence (sequential processing) requirements, and deadlines, inherent in their operations. The DMs have a limited amount of resource, implying that a DM can attend to only a small number of tasks simultaneously. Thus, dynamic scheduling and coordination are paramount in such applications. Examples include Joint military operations involving intelligence gathering and close-air support for a number of on-going ground activities; maintenance and repair of parts coordinated across technicians at operational, intermediate, and depot levels of maintenance; manufacturing of a stream of parts that require different machine operations in various orders.

The HITEC experiment and its concomitant empirical findings may be found in a previous paper [32]. Therefore, we give only a brief description of the experiment to provide a context for our analytical modeling.

3.1. The Task Coordination Problem

The experiment considers a hierarchical team of one coordinator or leader and three subordinates working on separate but interconnected workstations in a laboratory environment. Each subordinate is provided with two units of a renewable resource and needs to coprocess randomly arriving generic "tasks." A task may be one of four types: small individual task (SIT), large individual task (LIT), 2-operation task (2OT), and 3-operation task (3OT). An SIT (requiring one unit of resource) or an LIT (requiring two units of resource) involves only one processing operation, and comes preassigned to a specific DM upon its arrival. A 2OT or 3OT, on the other hand, involves two or three operations, respectively, and requires sequential processing by two or three DMs with one unit of resource from each. We refer to the 2OTs and 3OTs as "team" tasks (TTs). The subordinates thus need to decide which tasks to process and when, and must coordinate with each other on team tasks. The coordinator, having no resource of his own, is responsible for aiding team coordination in processing team tasks. In addition, the task coordination problem is designed with the following features:

1. Tasks have different values: 10 points for SIT, 20 for LIT, 25 for 2OT, and 40 for 3OT.
2. The team has a limited time to process a task after its arrival (same for all task types).
3. Processing an operation of a task takes a fixed amount of time (same for all task types).
4. Resources are not transferable among the DMs.

The value of a task is proportional to the coordination effort required, and thus is proportional to the processing difficulty. The team's objective or goal is to maximize total task value by successfully processing tasks before their deadlines. This experiment scenario thus presents a dynamic environment having tasks of different processing difficulties, coordination requirements, and processing incentives.

3.2. HITEC Experiment Setup

The experiment apparatus consists of four computer workstations connected via an ethernet, as depicted in Fig. 23.3. Each workstation displays information on tasks and resources, and establishes communication links among the DMs.

Figure 23.3 shows a typical screen display for a DM, here DM2. Tasks, represented by icons, arrive randomly at the top of the screen. As time elapses, the task icons move down the screen toward a deadline. All tasks move at the same speed, and have the same initial time available for processing. Icons of different shapes denote tasks of different types (e.g., the icon near the upper right corner with a "2" inside denotes an individual task for DM2). The icon near the upper left corner of the screen denotes a team task that DM2 must process first, followed by DM1 and then DM3; it has a task id #05 and a value of 40. Task T-05 has its first operation highlighted, implying that its first operation is not yet finished. All team tasks arrive with the first operation highlighted.

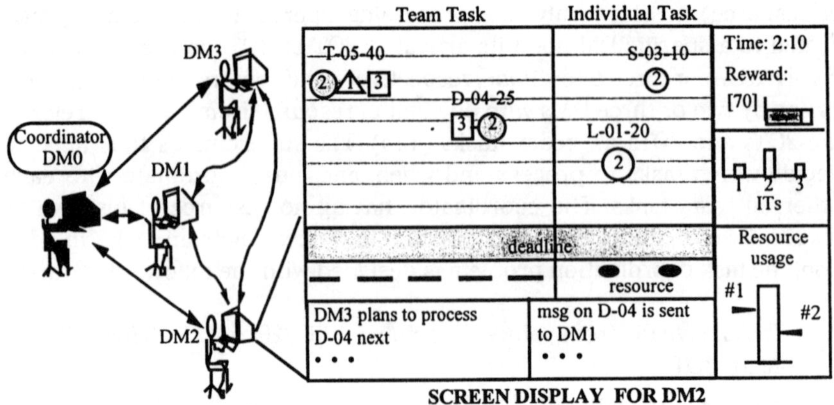

FIG. 23.3. HITEC configuration and typical display.

As shown in Fig. 23.3, DM2 has access to two units of resource, displayed as resource icons. Through simple mouse operations, DM2 can allocate these resources to process tasks–operations of his responsibility. Thus, at any time a DM can be simultaneously processing two tasks at most. In a window in the lower right of the screen, DM2 sees the amount of time remaining before a tied-up resource will be free to use again. DM2, however, has no direct information on the status of DM1's or DM3's resources.

The team has a decentralized but overlapped information structure (i.e., a DM does not see all of the team's information). As shown in Fig. 23.3, DM2 sees all icons of current team tasks (A current task is an arrived task which is not completely processed and its deadline is not yet passed). He also sees his own current individual tasks (ITs). However, DM2 does not see the icons of others' ITs. He is only presented the total value of ITs that each DM has.

Once DM2 finishes an operation on a team task, and if there are subsequent operations, he can change the highlighted part of the task icon to the next operation to inform others of the task status (which operations have been finished). This is called "task status update." The task status update informs others via the display media what a DM has done and signals the processing opportunity of a subsequent operation. Moreover, it indirectly reveals one's decision characteristics and helps other DMs to coordinate implicitly. For example, the team task at the upper left corner of the screen display in Fig. 23.3 is a 3OT, which requires DM2 to process first, followed by DM1 and DM3. When DM2 finishes the first operation of the task and updates the status, the second operation will be highlighted, informing DM1 for the next operation. By knowing that DM2 has finished the first operation of the task, DM3 can better predict the likely decision of DM1.

The experiment apparatus provides communication links among the team members, through which a DM can send formatted messages to inform other DMs as to which tasks he is processing, and which tasks he plans to process or ignore. A DM can also request information from other DMs. Specifically, the following messages can be used on a task-by-task basis:

"Ignore":	I plan to ignore this task;
"Processing":	I am processing this task;
"Plan":	I plan to process this task next; and
"Request":	Please send information about this task.

The coordinator has a display screen similar to those of his subordinates. One difference is that the coordinator can monitor all the DMs' resources, and their usage. Also, the coordinator's screen displays no ITs on a task-by-task basis; he sees only the total IT value each DM has on his display. Depending on the experiment conditions [32], the coordinator is allowed to use different coordination mechanisms, such as sending instructional messages, setting operation deadlines, or directly processing team tasks, corresponding to our manipulation of coordinator "role" as an independent variable.

The experiment setup, if viewed from the perspective of the CODE framework, provides a scenario for implicit and explicit coordination. The team members, because of the decentralized information structure, have partial observations of each other's decisions from the displayed task information. Task status update leads to task display changes which enable DMs to anticipate the (likely) decisions of their teammates, and coordinate implicitly. Team members can also communicate with each other by using formatted messages, and thus can explicitly coordinate their task processing activities, if they choose to do so.

3.3. Experiment Design and Measurement

The experiment implemented a full factorial design across three independent variables: four coordinator's roles, two communication structures, and two levels of time pressure. There were $4 \times 2 \times 2 = 16$ different conditions that are detailed in [32], and described in Section 5 with the model development. In the experiment, each condition was run twice with different task arrival scenarios. Therefore, there were 32 trials in total, with each trial lasting 12 minutes during which time the team was presented with a number of different team and individual tasks. Four teams, each with four subjects, participated in the experiment. A number of dependent variables were collected to measure team behavior, the primary ones being:

- *Team reward*: percentage of task value obtained (from the total task value presented).
- *Percentage of each type of tasks processed* (reflecting task processing patterns and coordination strategy).
- *Average slack time in task processing*: the average residual time between a task's completion time and its deadline (reflecting timeliness in task processing).
- *Coordination failure*: started but unfinished team tasks as a percentage of the total number of team tasks presented (reflecting failed effort in coordination).
- *Number of messages used and composition of message types* (reflecting communication pattern).

As the experiment and results are discussed fully in a previous paper [32], only the major results related to our normative modeling effort are presented here.

4. A DISTRIBUTED NORMATIVE MODEL

The basic tenet of our normative–descriptive modeling approach is that human decisionmakers strive for optimality, but are constrained by their inherent limitations and biases [10]. Thus, a normative–descriptive model attempts to bring into harmony what humans "should do" with what humans are actually observed to do—and attributes consistent differences to human biases and cognitive limitations. Based on the CODE framework, we first formulate normative submodels for individual DMs in the HITEC context, and proceed to develop a distributed model of the team by incorporating team coordination among the submodels.

4.1. Submodel Formulation for An Individual DM

In the HITEC experiment, each DM needs to decide the times at which to begin processing those operations under his responsibility. Because of the sequential requirement inherent in processing team tasks, decisions of different DMs are interrelated. Consequently, a DM cannot make effective decisions without considering other DMs' actual decisions, or their likely decisions. Inasmuch as the team has a common goal to maximize team reward, the best decisions for individual DMs are decisions that lead to the optimal *team* performance. Our modeling approach first formulates an *idealized* model for a generic DM, and then tailors this model to suit each individual DM by incorporating various HITEC peculiarities, such as uncertainties about other DM's ITs.

The team problem is to determine which DM is to process which operations, and when. Without considering (uncertain) future task arrivals, this problem can be formulated as a series of static scheduling problems and solved by using a moving–rolling window technique, as follows. At a decision time, k, we take a snapshot of the dynamic environment and assume that one attempts to schedule the tasks in the snapshot. Let (i, j) denote operation j of task i (an individual task has only one operation), and let T be the set of all task operations within the current snapshot. The objective is to determine the processing begin time b_{ij} for each operation so as to maximize the team reward J (total value of tasks completed by their deadlines):

$$J = \sum_{(i,N_i)\in T} v_i \, u(d_i - c_i), \tag{1}$$

where N_i is the last operation of task i, and v_i is the value of task i. If task i is completed by its deadline, $c_i < d_i$, the task value is obtained, $u(d_i - c_i) = 1$. Otherwise, the task value is lost, $u(d_i - c_i) = 0$. Considering the limited resource available to each DM, and the sequential requirement indigenous in processing the multiple operations of team tasks, the scheduling problem is subject to the following constraints:

Resource constraints: The number of resource units used by each DM cannot exceed the number available at any time k, that is,

$$\sum_{(i,j)\in T_p} r_{ij}\delta_{ijk} \le R_{pk}, \quad p = 1, 2, 3, \tag{2}$$

where T_p is the current set of task operations under DMp's responsibility, r_{ij} is the number of resources required by operation (i, j), δ_{ijk} is an index that equals one if operation (i, j) is under processing at decision time k and zero otherwise, and R_{pk} is the number of resource units available to DMp at time k.

Precedence constraints: An operation cannot be started until its preceding operation is finished, that is,

$$b_{i,j+1} > c_{ij}, \quad \text{for any } (i, j) \in T, \text{ and } j < N_i, \tag{3}$$

where $b_{i,j+1}$ is the begin time to process operation (i, j+1), and c_{ij} the completion time of operation (i, j). The completion time c_{ij} can be calculated from the begin time b_{ij}, i.e., $c_{ij} = b_{ij} + t_r$, where t_r is the time required to process the operation. (Note t_r is the same for all operations.) The precedence constraints (3) thus reflect the interdependencies among DMs' decisions.

Boundary constraints: To obtain the value of task i, the begin time b_{ij} of operation (i, j) must be within a range specified by the earliest allowable time e_{ij} and the latest possible time l_{ij}, that is,

$$e_{ij} \le b_{ij} \le l_{ij}, \quad (i, j) \in T. \tag{4}$$

This set of constraints is actually implicit in the formulation (1)–(3). It is made explicit here for later analysis of the *human* decision-making process. In the inequality (4), the e_{ij} and l_{ij} can be determined from the task arrival time a_i (or deadline d_i), the operation number j, and the last operation N_i of task i:

$$e_{ij} = a_i + (j-1) * t_r, \quad l_{ij} = d_i - (N_i - j + 1) * t, \quad (i, j) \in T. \tag{5}$$

The team problem can now be formulated as selecting the begin times $\{b_{ij}\}$ to maximize the team reward J, subject to the resource constraints (2), precedence constraints (3), and boundary constraints (4). Once the problem is solved, tasks can be processed according to the task processing schedule, which is optimal for the current snapshot. Once there is a new task arrival, the task processing schedule is obsolete. A new snapshot is taken, and the team problem is re-solved to generate updated schedules. The entire dynamic task processing problem is thus solved on a snapshot-by-snapshot basis (i.e., in a rolling–moving window fashion).

For each particular snapshot, the statistics of future task arrivals are not considered. A typical snapshot commonly involves four to six tasks for each DM. The problem solution thus involves a planning horizon of four to six decision steps. Whether the future task arrivals are considered or not has little impact on the resulting decisions (as shown in solutions in Section 5), due in large part to the fact that the task processing times required are short relative to the planning window, and future arrivals can only be estimated statistically.

4.2. A Decomposition–Coordination Solution Approach

In the earlier formulation, decisions of different DMs are coupled through the precedence constraints (3). These precedence constraints can be relaxed by using Lagrange multipliers to decouple the interdependencies among DMs' decisions. The problem can then be solved iteratively by generating decision options for different DMs independently, checking the constraint violations, evaluating the consequences of these violations, and regenerating (refining) the decisions.

Specifically, we introduce Lagrange multiplier λ_{ij} to relax the constraint between operation (i, j) and operation (i, j+1). The resulting Lagrangian to be optimized is

$$L = \sum_{(i,N_i)\in T} v_i\, u(d_i - c_i) + \sum_{\substack{(i,j)\in T\\ j<N_i}} \lambda_{ij}(b_{i,j+1} - c_{ij}). \tag{6}$$

The first summation in (6) is the total task value that can be obtained by processing tasks within their time window. The second summation reflects penalties caused by constraint violations. If a precedence constraint is violated, e.g., $b_{i,j+1} - c_{ij} < 0$, the resulting multiplier will be positive, $\lambda_{ij} > 0$. The violation of a precedence constraint consequently decreases the Lagrangian L. Intuitively, the Lagrangian L is a composite criterion reflecting the gains obtained by timely processing of tasks minus the losses resulting from constraint violations.

With L as a criterion, decisions b_{ij} of different DMs can be made separately as the precedence constraints are no longer considered as hard restrictions. While it is easy to find b_{ij} for each DM, the precedence constraints are usually not maintained. Indirectly, the Lagrange multipliers $\{\lambda_{ij}\}$ penalize the violations and reinforce the constraints. Now the problem involves two aspects: selecting the begin times $\{b_{ij}\}$ to maximize gain *and* determining multipliers $\{\lambda_{ij}\}$ to minimize constraint violations. Mathematically, this leads to the following problem

$$\{\lambda_{ij}^*, b_{ij}^*\} = \arg \min_{\lambda_{ij}} \max_{b_{ij}} L. \tag{7}$$

Substituting $c_{ij} = b_{ij} + t_r$ into the expression for L in (6) results in

$$L = \sum_{(i,N_i)\in T} v_i\, u(d_i - b_{i,N_i} - t_r) + \sum_{\substack{(i,j)\in T\\ j<N_i}} \lambda_{ij}(b_{i,j+1} - b_{ij} - t_r). \tag{8}$$

Let T_p denote the subset of task operations under the responsibility of DMp, p = 1, 2, 3. The total task operation set T is the union of the subsets, $T = T_1 \cup T_2 \cup T_3$. Through simple manipulation, the decision variables $\{b_{ij}\}$ in the Lagrangian L can be grouped according to the subsets, and decisions of different DMs become "separated" or decoupled, that is,

$$L = \sum_{p=1}^{3} \{ \sum_{\substack{(i,j)\in T_p\\ j<N_i}} \lambda_{ij}(-t_r) + L_p \}, \tag{9}$$

where

$$\begin{aligned} L_p = &\sum_{(i,N_i)\in T_p} \{ v_i\, u(d_i - b_{i,N_i} - t_r) + \lambda_{i,N_i-1} b_{i,N_i} \} + \\ &\sum_{\substack{(i,j)\in T_p\\ 1<j<N_i}} (\lambda_{i,j-1} - \lambda_{ij})\, b_{ij} - \sum_{(i,1)\in T_p} \lambda_{i1}\, b_{i1}. \end{aligned} \tag{10}$$

The expression L_p involves only the decisions of DMp. Because all decisions $\{b_{ij}\}$ are grouped into subsets, the maximization of L with respect to $\{b_{ij}\}$ can be performed separately on each of the L_p. Consequently, via (9), the problem (7) becomes

$$\{\lambda_{ij}^*, b_{ij}^*\} = \arg \min_{\lambda_{ij}} \sum_{p=1}^{3} \{ \sum_{\substack{(i,j) \in T_p \\ j < N_i}} \lambda_{ij}(-t_r) + \max_{b_{ij}} L_p \}. \tag{11}$$

The structure of Eq. (11) suggests an iterative solution procedure. Given a set of beginning times $\{b_{ij}\}$, the Lagrange multipliers $\{\lambda_{ij}\}$ can be determined to minimize L. Then given the $\{\lambda_{ij}\}$, new/revised decisions $\{b_{ij}\}$ of each DM can be made to maximize the decomposed objective L_p, p = 1, 2, 3. Mathematically, this procedure is expressed by the following bilevel scheme:

high level: $\{\lambda_{ij}^*\} = \arg \min_{\{\lambda_{ij}\}} L,$

low level: $\{b_{ij}^*\} = \arg \max_{\{b_{ij}\}} L_p, \quad p = 1, 2, 3,$ subject to (2) and (4).

The high-level problem can be solved by using the subgradient method which updates the multipliers according to the degree of constraint violations [6]. Each low-level problem is subject to the resource availability constraints (2) and boundary constraints (4), and can be solved by using the method of decision trees [13].

This solution process shows that decision options for individual DMs can be generated separately by solving the individual problems at the low level. Although these decision options are optimal with respect to the decomposed objective L_p, the global consequence has to be evaluated by considering these options together at the high level. There is an iterative process between the two levels, which suggests—albeit normatively—that the team decision-making process involves internal iterations (option generation, evaluation, and adjustment based on the current information set). This is consistent with our CODE framework as well as with Klein's mental model simulation conception [9], and Rasmussen's discussion on the iterative characteristics of human decision making [22].

4.3. Models With Local Information

If all DMs had the *same* global information of the environment (status of tasks and resources) and solved the *same* team problem in the same way (e.g., as above), they would all reach the *same* team solution. Team members would have accurate predictions of each other's decisions, and their decisions would be coordinated perfectly. When DMs do not have global information nor sufficient capability to reach a unique optimal solution, they will not be able to predict each other's decisions precisely, and the model-produced decisions for different DMs will differ in detail.

As described in Subsection 3.2, DM1 can observe the icons of team tasks (TTs) and his own individual tasks (ITs), but only knows the aggregated value of the other DMs' individual tasks. DM1 thus has uncertainty about the precise state of others' ITs, rendering DM1's submodel different from those of DM2 and/or DM3. The distinction among DMs' submodels is further elaborated in Section 5, where descriptive factors are introduced into the normative model.

Connecting the submodels for individual DMs with coordination links leads to a *distributed* model of the team (also called a distributed model, for short). Figure 23.4 illustrates the distributed model structure.

As shown in Fig. 23.4, the team as a whole receives information about the task environment as its input, and makes decisions to process the tasks as its output. The team members, including the coordinator, are modeled as different submodels with different local information and different responsibilities in decision making. The submodels interrelate via *coordination*. The coordination links among the submodels involve both implicit and explicit mechanisms. Because each DM's submodel predicts other DMs' decisions via solution of the team problem, the distributed model of the team contains a certain degree of implicit coordination (no inter-DM communication). The degree of implicit coordination depends on the amount of information available to the individual submodels to solve the team problem. The uncertainty a submodel has about other DMs' individual tasks affects its predictions of others' decisions. Consequently, implicit coordination is degraded, and explicit coordination is needed. The distributed submodels can send messages to each other to announce their decisions $\{b_{ij}\}$, thus helping to coordinate the decisions of the team. Now, the challenge is to bring intrateam communication into the above modeling framework, including a way to determine communication needs and to represent formatted messages.

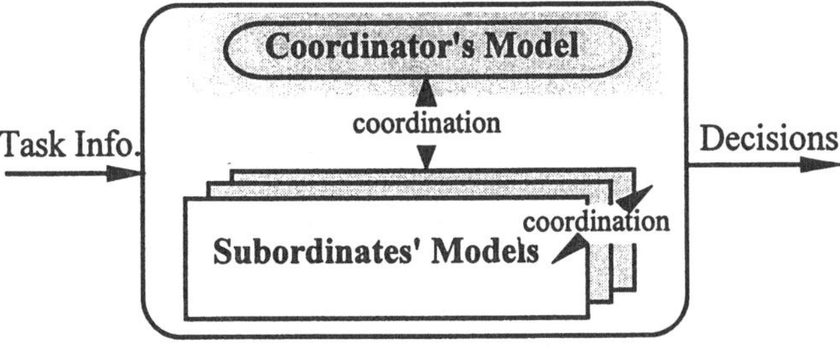

FIG. 23.4. Distributed model structure for team decision making.

4.4. Modeling Communication in the HITEC Experiment

For a given snapshot, the submodel for each DM solves the team problem based on its locally available information. As discussed in [31], the value of a Lagrange multiplier reflects the tightness of the corresponding constraint of the task in question. A large multiplier value implies a high sensitivity of team performance to the constraint, and a large performance degradation will incur if the constraint is violated. If communication can be used to avoid the violation, a large Lagrange multiplier value implies large potential benefit of communication on that particular task. It is thus reasonable to assume that if a limited amount of coordination effort is available to reduce constraint violations, the effort should be allocated to handle constraints with high multiplier values. Therefore, the multiplier values can be used to provide a rank-ordering as to which task operations have the tightest time windows, and are likely to benefit most from communications.

Communication can be treated as the exchange of decision information among DMs on a task-by-task basis. For example, the submodel of DM1 will solve the team problem based on the decentralized information DM1 has, and it can "inform" the submodels of other DMs about its decisions $\{b_{ij}^1\}$. The communicated b_{ij}^1 for operation j of Task i may be a processing decision DM1 just implemented ($b_{ij}^1 < 0$), or plans to implement right away ($b_{ij}^1 \approx 0$). This corresponds to sending a "Processing" message to other DMs as described in Section 3. Alternatively, the communicated b_{ij}^1 may relate to a decision planned for in the future ($b_{ij}^1 > 0$), which corresponds to a "Plan" message. When a task operation cannot be processed (not enough time available), the task will be ignored by the corresponding model (setting $b_{ij} > d_i$) and an "ignore" message will be sent. The "Request" message is not incorporated in our modeling as it was rarely used by human teams in the experiment, (well-trained DMs in a team will anticipate needs of other DMs, and hence unsolicited information transfers dominate [11]). By interpreting the communication messages in the ways given earlier, the model is able to incorporate the use of different message types.

A second modeling issue is the determination of to whom the messages should be sent. The experiment showed that communication messages were sent mostly from DMs responsible for preceding operations of team tasks to DMs responsible for subsequent operations (forward flow), as negotiation was not feasible. We thus assume that communication messages are sent in a forward flow, that is, the submodel of DM1 sends the message on b_{ij}^1 to the submodel of the DM responsible for the subsequent operation (i, j+1).

The received messages will be used by a submodel to adjust its decisions. A "processing" message ($b_{ij} = 0$ or $b_{ij} \approx 0$) indicates that operation (i, j) is being processed or will be processed immediately, and cannot be rescheduled. The submodel will then set the earliest allowable time to process the subsequent operation to be one operation processing time later, $e_{i,j+1} = t_r$. If a "plan" message ($b_{ij} > 0$) is received, the submodel will use the communicated b_{ij} in place of its estimated b_{ij} for processing operation (i, j). If an "ignore" message ($b_{ij} > d_i$) is received, the submodel will consequently discard task i (negotiation is not considered). By virtue of the communicated information from other DMs, a submodel is able to adjust some of its decision variables which had been previously estimated in isolation. Therefore, communication should lead to more highly coordinated decisions among the submodels when they have diverse solutions (e.g., caused by different local information at the DMs).

The model does not resolve the problem within a snapshot after receiving communication messages. In other words, the model does not iterate internally on communication. This is because (a) as time passes, communication affects future decisions rather than current ones (which are implemented right away), (b) any decisions to be implemented in the future will be re-evaluated (with the communication messages considered) in the next snapshot, because the model employs a moving window technique, and updates its solutions at each new snapshot.

4.5. DM1's Submodel as Viewed via the CODE Framework

The decomposition–coordination approach to solve the task coordination problem can be mapped onto the CODE framework to establish a correspondence between the quantitative and conceptual representations of human coordination and decision activities. Using DM1 as an example, Fig. 23.5 shows the CODE framework with mathematical variables mapped onto related functional activities.

Figure 23.5 shows that DM1 receives information about the environment (e.g., numbers of different tasks, task status) via the situation channel, and receives communication messages (about b_{ij}^0's) from *other* DMs through the communication channel. The information is processed to generate *approximate* operation completion time $\boldsymbol{c}_{ij}^0$ and begin time $\boldsymbol{b}_{ij}^0$ of *other* DMs' operations of the team tasks from the messages, and to estimate the earliest time e_{ij} and latest time l_{ij} to process an operation. With such information, DM1 solves the *team* problem iteratively using his mental model to determine the need for communication (based on the multipliers $\{\lambda_{ij}\}$), and makes his own decisions $\{b_{ij}^1\}$. DM1 is assumed to have limited communication capability, and only sends a message on an operation when the associated multiplier is positive. Then DM1 takes actions to communicate with other DMs, and to execute his task processing decisions. This decision-making process continues from one snapshot to the next.

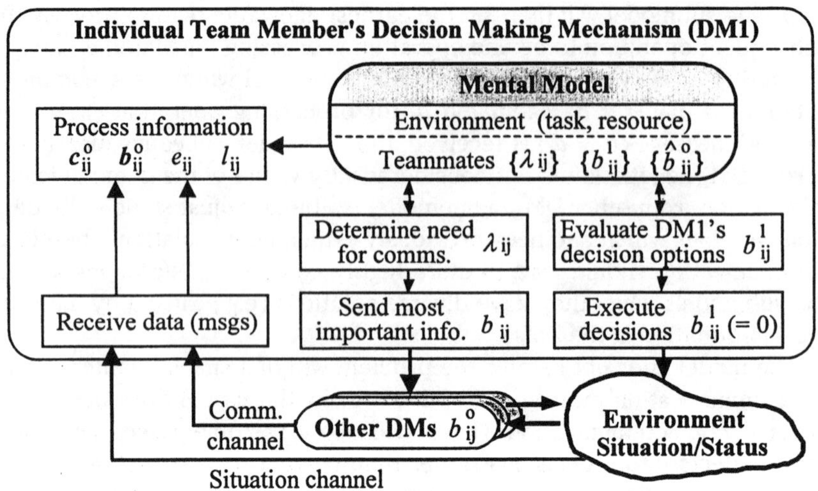

FIG. 23.5. DM1's submodel as mapped onto the CODE framework.

4.6. Relation to the HITEC Experiment

With respect to the HITEC experiment, the distributed model captures the following variations in coordinator's role, communication structure and time pressure.

Coordinator's Role. The distributed model captures two of the four coordinator's roles examined in the experiment (i.e., the Observer and the Advisor cases [32]). When acting as an observer, the coordinator is not involved in online decision making, so that the distributed team model only includes submodels for subordinates. In the Advisor case, the coordinator can send (formatted) messages to subordinates as regards their processing of team tasks. The distributed model thus contains a submodel for the coordinator–similar to those of the subordinates–that also solves the team problem based on its local information, as noted in Subsection 3.2. However, no tasks are actually processed by the coordinator.

The benefit of communicating with the coordinator lies in the unification of team members' decisions. Communication among the subordinates is based on individual submodel solutions. Communication from the coordinator is based on the solutions of the single coordinator submodel. Therefore, communication among the subordinate nodes tends to be more diverse than that from the coordinator. Better coordination may ensue if the submodels adjust their decisions according to communications from the coordinator as opposed to lateral communications from subordinates.

Communication Structure. Subordinates' communication to the coordinator affects the coordinator's model solutions, and in turn those of the subordinates themselves. Two communication structures were examined in the experiment: the Coordinator-Centered (CC) and the Fully-Connected (FC). These particular communications structures are often referred to in the organizational literature as "star versus completely connected," "centralized versus decentralized," and so on. In CC, subordinates can only communicate with the coordinator so that the distributed model does not allow information exchange among subordinate DMs. Messages regarding the subordinates' decisions $\{b_{ij}^{s}\}$ are only sent to the submodel of the coordinator, which in turn can send its recommended decisions $\{b_{ij}^{c}\}$ to the subordinates. In FC, all team members can communicate among themselves. In this case, the submodel of each subordinate also communicates with other subordinate nodes, in addition to the coordinator's node. Empirically, it was found that in the FC structure about one half of the subordinates' messages were sent to the coordinator. In the model, a particular communication message from a subordinate is sent randomly to either the submodel of (1) the coordinator, or (2) the appropriate subordinate, with equal probability. Clearly, a more refined modeling of interlevel communications is a topic for further study.

Time Pressure. Two levels of time pressure were created in the experiment by changing the task tempo. Under low time pressure, tasks arrived less frequently (arrival rate $a_r = 4.4$ tasks/min), had long initial time available ($T_a = 160$ sec), and took a longer time to process ($t_r = 35$ sec). Under high time pressure, the experiment has a faster tempo ($a_r = 6$ tasks/min, $T_a = 115$ sec, and $t_r = 25$ sec).

The distributed model is implemented for the actual experimental scenarios across the three independent variables comprising $2 \times 2 \times 2 = 8$ conditions. The model uses exactly the same data with the same task arrival sequence as in the experiment. For each experimental condition, there are two replications corresponding to slightly different task scenarios (generated via different random seeds). For both model and data the two replications are averaged to get results for each condition.

5. THE NORMATIVE–DESCRIPTIVE MODEL

The development of a normative–descriptive model involves an iterative process of model–data comparison, identification and quantification of human limitations and biases as descriptive factors, and their incorporation within the model. The process is carried out in two phases. The first phase considers basic relevant human cognitive limitations, which are known from previous research. The second phase reveals additional team coordination and decisionmaking trends or biases, and develops a normative–descriptive model of the team.

5.1. Incorporation of Basic Human Cognitive Limitations

The distributed team model is first implemented under the assumption that all DMs have perfect mental models, with global information and sufficient capability to solve the optimization problem (Eqs. 1–4). Under these conditions, all submodels of individual DMs generate the same schedule for processing a task, or they ignore the same tasks when necessary. There is no need for communication as no constraint will be violated, even though some may be tight with positive multipliers.

In general, this model showed significantly better performance than human teams, with higher team reward (92% for the model vs. 79% for human teams), fewer coordination failures (1.1% vs. 8.8%), and longer slack time (63 sec vs. 49.8 sec). This is primarily attributed to the unrealistic assumption of perfect mental models. According to our experiment observations and research on human cognition [10, 12, 32], the following factors need to be considered:

1. In the experiment, the team had a decentralized information structure. Each DM had access to detailed information on all arrived team tasks and his own individual tasks, but only saw the total value (i.e., aggregated information) of the other DM's individual tasks. Consequently, there was uncertainty about the arrival times $\{a_i\}$ and deadlines $\{d_i\}$ of those ITs. This uncertainty can be accommodated by assuming that the submodel of a DM has "noisy" data for the arrival times $a_i' = a_i + w_1$ and deadlines $d_i' = d_i + w_2$ of the ITs of other DMs, where w_1 and w_2 are random variables.

2. The earliest and latest times to process an operation of a team task could be calculated from the task arrival time, operation number, and processing time required as in Eq. (5). To do so, a human DM would need to memorize and manipulate the numerical values for each task. Given the dynamic multitask environment, one might not be able to do that precisely. This inability can be represented by an uncertainty in estimating e_{ij} and l_{ij}, viz. the submodel of each DM uses noisy estimates $e_{ij}' = e_{ij} + w_3$, and $l_{ij}' = l_{ij} + w_4$, where w_3 and w_4 are random variables.

3. A formatted communication message, as described in Subsection 3.2, only conveys information about a DM's task processing order (now, next, etc.) rather than the exact task processing time b_{ij}. The communicated information thus carries with it uncertainty about the actual b_{ij}. Thus, we model information exchange among submodels as conveying noisy begin times b_{ij}'

$= b_{ij} + w_5$, where w_5 is a random noise. As a DM's communication commonly occurs some short time after a decision is made, w_5 is assumed to be positive.

4. Typically, a DM would not start an operation of a team task until he received verification that the preceding operation was completed, as indicated by a change in the displayed task status. In the experiment, the status update was subject to random delays as a human DM could not monitor each task processing closely, nor update the task's status immediately after an operation was completed. Therefore, each submodel is only informed of the completion time of a team task operation after some random delay (i.e., $c_{ij}' = c_{ij} + w_6$, where w_6 is a positive random variable). Random delays in status update cause random delays in processing subsequent operations.

For simplicity, the random variables $\{w_i\}$ are assumed to be independent and uniformly distributed. The noise levels are selected based on extensive model testing after incorporating these random factors. Table 23.1 shows the selected noise levels, which are held constant over all experiment conditions. Table 23.2 shows the averaged team reward, slack time and interoperation slack time of the experimental data and the model solutions over the eight experimental conditions. Table 23.2 shows that the model solutions now more closely match experimental results in team reward and timing measures on average.

TABLE 23.1
Selected Random Parameters (Seconds)

w_1, w_2	w_3, w_4	w_5	w_6
[-70, 70]	[-10, 10]	[0, 10]	[0, 5]

TABLE 23.2
Model-Data Comparisons on Averaged Measures

	Team Reward	*Slack Time*	*Inter-Op Time*
Experiment	78.8	49.8 sec	10.9 sec
Model	81.7	55.5 sec	9.1 sec

5.2. Identification and Incorporation of Team Coordination Biases and Adaptation

When model results are compared to experimentally derived measures involving communication and task processing strategy across both levels of time pressure, a number of consistent discrepancies emerge:

1. Human teams sent more communication messages than did the model, especially "Processing" messages (related to current decisions). The average communication rate for the team (excluding observer under CC communication structure) was about 1.1 msgs per minute for each DM. In the model, a message is sent on an operation only if the operation has a tight window (associated with a positive multiplier). The model solution shows about 0.3 msgs per minute, about 70% less than that of human teams! The model solution also shows a message composition with much lower percentage of "processing" messages than that of the human teams, especially under low time pressure. This discrepancy suggests an "overcommunication" trend of human teams, as also discussed in [8, 14, 27].

2. Human teams processed significantly more 3-operation tasks (3OTs) but less large individual tasks (LITs) than the model as shown in Fig. 23.6(a). Human teams show a tendency to "overcooperate" on team tasks [18, 27].

3. Human team's planning horizon seems to decrease as time pressure increases. Figure 23.6(b) compares the experimental team reward with the solutions of two models: the first model (MDL1) having 3-stage planning horizon and the second model (MDL2) having 2-stage planning horizon. A decision stage is defined as a period where one decision will be implemented. The MDL1 solution matches the experimental result more closely than MDL2 solution under low time pressure, but the situation is reversed under high time pressure. This pattern was also reflected in other dependent variables. This "reduction of planning horizon" as an adaptation to time pressure, unlike the foregoing two coordination biases, appears not only in team coordination but also in single human decision making [26]. It was also manifested through analysis of team communication patterns in the empirical data [32].

The next step in our modeling is to incorporate the identified descriptive factors into the distributed model. This serves two purposes: to validate the identified descriptive factors through the extent to which they improve model–data comparisons, and to develop the normative–descriptive model. The descriptive factors are quantified and incorporated as follows.

1. Overcommunication—The model's communication rate (number of messages per unit time) under each condition is set equal to the level used by human teams. In the experiment, the average communication rate of each

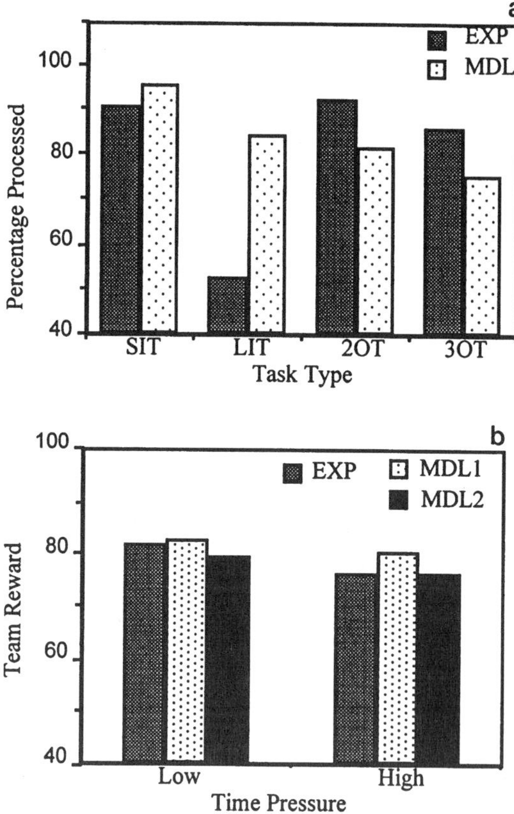

FIG. 23.6. Model–data comparison: (a) distribution of task types processed, (b) effect of time pressure on team reward.

subordinate was 1.0 and 1.3 message per minute under low and high time pressure conditions, respectively, and the rate did not change much with coordinator's role and communication structure. The rate of coordinator's communication was about 2.5 messages per minute, almost invariant across experimental conditions. According to the empirical communication rate, each submodel is assigned a fixed number of messages to send. When the assigned number of messages is not more than that indicated by the positive multipliers, the model will communicate based on the rank-ordering of the multipliers. Otherwise, the model will send messages on constraints with positive multipliers, and also send the extra messages (zero multiplier values) with priority on the most immediate decisions. The *types* of communication messages are determined by the value of the communicated $\{b_{ij}\}$. For example, if the model sends a message on a near zero b_{ij}, the message is interpreted as a "processing" message; when $b_{ij} > 0$ the associated message is one of "plan to process." Note that as a consequence of using the data-derived communication rate in our model, we can only examine model–data comparison with respect to the *relative* (%) use of different message types, as opposed to total message traffic.

2. Overcooperation–The model is modified to overvalue each 3-operation task by 5 points and undervalue each large individual task by 5 points. When the model has multiple solutions for a snapshot, it always chooses the one with team tasks scheduled earliest.

3. Planning horizon reduction–The model's planning horizon is fixed at 3 stages for low time pressure conditions and 2 stages for high time pressure conditions.

5.3. Results of the Normative-Descriptive Model

After incorporating the foregoing descriptive factors, the team model is again applied to solve the eight experimental conditions (across the three independent variables). The model solutions now agree closely with the empirical data across all the measures. Table 23.3 shows the model–data comparison in terms of five measures averaged over the eight experimental conditions.

The model solutions also match empirical data in various patterns, such as the composition of task types processed and the composition of communication messages used, as shown in Fig. 23.7. The composition of tasks processed is a measure of team task processing strategy, whereas the composition of messages used reflects strategy of explicit team coordination. The model–data matching in pattern as per Fig. 23.7 implies that the model not only reflects what the team did (performance measures), but *how* it was done (process measures).

The model results replicate the empirical data on a case-by-case basis, and thus exhibit the same variations to the independent variables as did the human teams. Figure 23.8 shows the model–data comparison across four

TABLE 23.3
Model-Data Comparison on Averaged Measures

	Team Reward	*Task Proc.*	*Coord. Failure*	*Slack Time*	*Inter-Op Time*
Experiment	78.8%	78.5%	8.8%	43.5 sec	10.9 sec
Model	79.1%	78.6%	10.1%	44.9 sec	10.2 sec

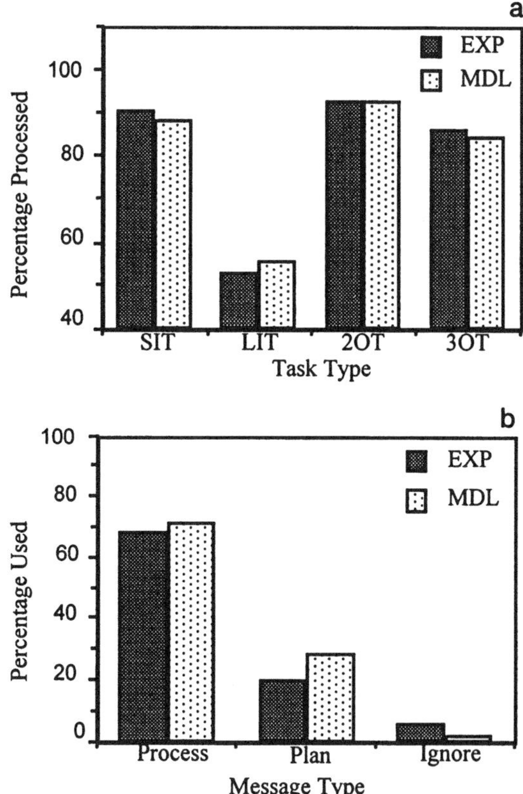

FIG. 23.7. Model–data comparison of process measures: (a) composition of tasks processed, (b) composition of messages used.

major measures: team reward, percentage of tasks processed, coordination failure, and slack time. In the figure, the cases are coded by a 3-character string XYZ with X = L or H, standing for Low or High time pressure; Y = O or A, for Observer or Advisor of coordinator's role; and Z = C or F, for CC or FC communication structure.

The earlier results can be averaged across different independent variables to analyze the effects of coordinator's role, communication structure, and time pressure in the same way as in the analysis of the experimental data [32]. Take team reward as an example. The model solution shows that team reward in the Advisor case (81%) is higher than that in the Observer case (77%). This indicates the benefit of having a coordinator to communicate with subordinates. The change of communication structure does not show much effect in team reward (about 1% change). This is attributed to the exercise of mutual mental models which enables each DM to anticipate

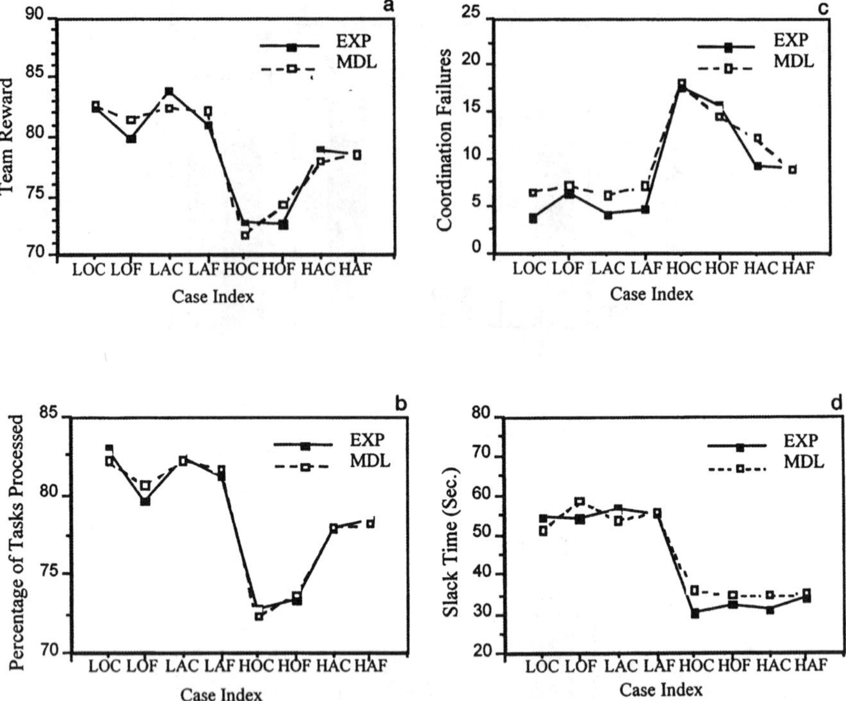

FIG. 23.8. Case-by-case model–data comparison: (a) comparison of team reward, (b) comparison of task processing, (c) comparison of coordination failure, (d) comparison of slack time.

others' decisions, and thus to coordinate implicitly. As time pressure increases from low to high, team reward reduces from about 82% to 76%. This is mainly attributed to a reduction in planning horizon as discussed earlier. These results are consistent with the experimental data as analyzed in [32]. Similar analyses can be made on other measures.

6. AN APPLICATION OF THE NORMATIVE–DESCRIPTIVE MODEL

The characteristics of implicit and explicit coordination have been discussed earlier in this chapter, as well as in other research [2, 3, 8, 10]. It is, however, difficult to observe empirically the mechanisms of implicit coordination as no effective methods exist with which to measure or to evaluate mental models upon which implicit coordination is based [3]. Nor is it easy in an experiment to control the mix of implicit and explicit coordination.

This, instead, can be achieved by using a model-based approach. Using our normative–descriptive model as a predictive computational tool, this section examines the two questions intrinsic to team coordination.

- Can a team achieve a reasonable performance by using only implicit coordination or only explicit coordination, or is it necessary to have both?
- What is the incremental effect of explicit coordination on team performance with respect to the existence of an implicit coordination mechanism?

Two simulation studies are conducted by changing the implicit versus explicit coordination conditions in the normative–descriptive model. The model implementation is otherwise kept the same (e.g., the noise levels). For each coordination condition, the model is applied to generate predictions for all eight experimental cases that were subsets of the HITEC experiment. The results for each coordination condition are then obtained by averaging the results of the eight cases.

6.1. Study 1: Effects of Implicit and Explicit Coordination

The first simulation study exercises the model at four coordination levels: "individual" (INDV), "communication" (COMM), "mental model" (MMDL), and "full combination" (FULL). At the INDV level, the submodel of each DM solves only his individual/local problem by assuming the most favorable conditions for its own decisions. For example, consider a DM who is responsible for the second operation of a three-operation task. This DM assumes a priori that the first operation will be processed at the earliest time and the third operation will be processed right before the deadline so that he has the maximum freedom to schedule the second operation. Decisions are made by scheduling task operations within resource constraints (Eq. 2) and boundary constraints (Eq. 4). Each submodel does not communicate with any other. If a submodel schedules an operation to be processed before its precedent is finished, the processing will be carried out immediately after the precedent is completed. This is equivalent to the use of task status update to keep all submodels informed as to when an operation of an team task is finished. The INDV level model achieves a team reward of about 62%, as shown in Fig. 23.9.

The model for the second level of coordination (COMM) augments the INDV level with communication capability. The submodel of each DM makes decisions as in the INDV level, but can communicate with others based on the local solutions. Because the submodel does not predict others' decisions, communication is conducted with priorities on "ignore" and "process-

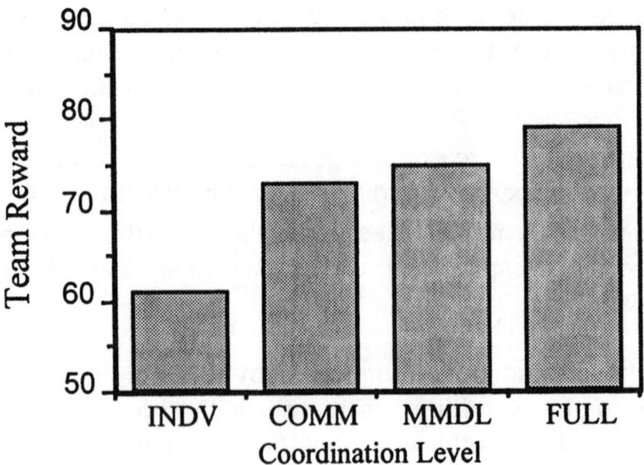

FIG. 23.9. Effect of coordination level.

ing" messages over "plan" messages, similar to the communication pattern of human teams [32]. Also the communication is limited at the empirical communication rate (about 4.2 msg./min). For example, if three decisions, one scheduled at Time zero and two at some time later, need to be communicated but only one message can be sent, the one scheduled at Time zero will be communicated (corresponding to a processing message). The team reward obtained in this case reaches 73%.

The MMDL level is the same as the Observer case in the CC communication structure, where the submodels, however, do not communicate with each other. Here the submodel of each DM predicts teammates' decisions and makes its own decisions by solving the team problem based on its local information. This case emulates a coordination condition with implicit mechanisms only. Team reward improves significantly to about 75%. The FULL level is the same as the Advisor case in the FC communication structure. Compared to the MMDL level, the FULL level adds explicit coordination capability. Each submodel solves the team problem to predict others' decisions (implicit coordination), and also uses communication with other submodels (explicit coordination). The advantage of communication is demonstrated by a small increase in team reward, reaching about 79%.

These simulation results show that team performance improves significantly (from about 62% to 75%) by adding either team communication or mental model predictions to an INDV model. Combining them generated a less significant improvement (from 75% to 79%). Therefore, a team may reach a reasonable performance by using either implicit or explicit coordination alone in the task coordination problem. It is, however, their combination that brings the team reward up to the experimental level (79%).

6.2. Study 2: The Effects of Communication Rate on Team Performance

The second simulation study examines in more detail the relationship between implicit and explicit coordination mechanisms. In the first study, the MMDL and the INDV levels had no communication, whereas the FULL and the COMM levels had communications at the experimental rate (1.1 msg./min per DM). This study examines two more cases, namely COMM* and FULL*, obtained by limiting the communication rate to 0.4 msg./min in the COMM and FULL cases, respectively. Figure 23.10 shows the results for the six simulation cases. The MMDL, FULL*, and FULL levels show the result of progressively increasing communication rate when the model has mutual prediction capability (solving the team problem with implicit coordination: w/ IC). At the INDV, COMM*, and COMM levels, submodels do not predict the decisions of each other (and there is no implicit coordination: w/o IC). With implicit coordination, the team performance does not degrade when communication rate is reduced from 1.1 msg./min to 0.4 msg./min. With no implicit coordination, limiting of communications causes a significant decrease in team reward.

This study shows that implicit coordination largely reduces the need for communications to maintain performance. The marginal benefit of having more communication depends on how much communication capability the team already has. When the team members do not utilize implicit coordination, due to lack of training or information, more communication capability would lead to better team performance (as long as the DMs are not overloaded).

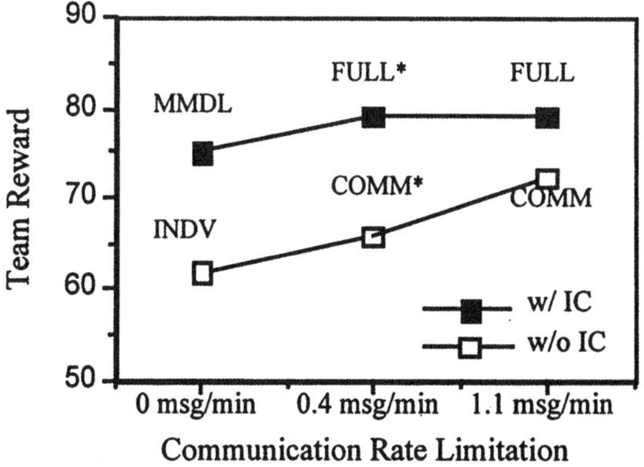

FIG. 23.10. Interaction of communication rate.

7. SUMMARY

Coordination has long been recognized as a key issue when studying distributed systems in general, and team decision making in particular [15, 18]. We believe that team decision making cannot be thoroughly understood without a knowledge of team coordination mechanisms, as it is coordination that makes a team different from a collection of individuals. With this in mind, we addressed the team coordination problem more directly than in previous research, and conducted a normative–descriptive study using a distributed task coordination problem within a hierarchical team. This chapter presented the analytical–normative and normative–descriptive parts of this study, and made the following four contributions.

1. A conceptual framework was developed to provide a structural format for team coordination and decision making. The CODE framework integrated the SHOR model [2, 33], the (mutual) mental model construct [3, 7], and the coordination mechanisms inherent in an individual's decision-making process in a team context. Team coordination was depicted as a mix of implicit and explicit mechanisms, where the balance between them shifts according to variations in the external and internal conditions. The strength of the CODE framework lies in its capability to organize existing results and draw new insights and inferences about team behavior. With its direct treatment of coordination, we believe that the CODE framework can help integrate empirical results in a systematic way to obtain consistent and insightful findings about team decision making, and provide as an axiom-like basis to generate hypotheses amenable for future testing.

2. The CODE framework was used as a foundation for our mathematical modeling of the HITEC experiment. The CODE framework guided the model development, provided a "human-like" view of the mathematical procedures, and gave an intuitive feel to the quantitative variables. The resulting distributed model captured implicit team coordination as mutual predictions of decisions, and explicit team coordination as decision information exchanges, as well as the actual distributed decision making of the team in its task processing. Thus, CODE provides a structure—rooted in human engineering—for computational models of team decision processes employing distributed intelligent "agents." Submodels for individual agents may be based on a dynamic programming formulation, such as ours, or use various decision rules such as in the work of Levitt et al. [35] or Carley and Prietula [36], or use a Petri net formalism as in Levis [37].

3. Two team coordination biases (overcommunication and overcooperation), and an adaptation mechanism to time pressure (reduced planning horizon) were identified as descriptive factors via model–data comparison.

The identification of the coordination biases and adaptation mechanism was a result of comparing empirical results (what human teams actually did) with normative model solutions (what should be done). These factors were quantified and incorporated into the normative model to yield a normative–descriptive model, that generated consistent data-matching results on a case-by-case basis.

4. Team implicit and explicit coordination were quantitatively analyzed by using the resulting normative–descriptive model as a simulation–computational tool. It was shown that having mutual mental models was crucial for a team to reach coordinated decisions and maintain performance when communication was limited, and that satisfactory team performance depended on the appropriately integrated use of implicit and explicit coordination mechanisms. Although these results have been discussed in the literature as inference, implication, or postulate [2, 3, 8, 10, 27], they are quantitatively demonstrated here for the first time. Such results find application to models that explicitly treat or simulate interagent coordination mechanisms, such as in the Virtual Design Team (VDT) simulation model of Levitt et al. [35] where communication messages are exchanged among intelligent (and hence "implicitly coordinating") agents via a choice of media.

There are a quite a number of areas in which the results of this chapter can be expanded (or strengthened) as topics for future work. One is to consider the impact of team versus individual goals on team performance and process measures. The current effort assumes that individual DMs have no self-centered interests, and that there are no conflicts between individual and team payoffs. A normative–descriptive study of individual versus team rewards was conducted by Shi, Luh, and Kleinman [25] using a variant of the HITEC environment. Basically, they found that under individual rewards there was an *increase* in explicit coordination, which was explained by the fact that a DM could not as accurately predict the likely decisions of his teammates (through the mutual mental model; i.e., implicit coordination was less effective).

An issue that plagues most laboratory research involving human teams is one of scale. It becomes extremely difficult, if not prohibitive, to conduct controlled laboratory experiments (on complex problems that stress coordination) with teams of size much greater than six. In order to make the leap to larger size teams (and organizations) we would build models that are validated on small teams and postulate that the predictive capability of these models extends to larger teams. Alternatively, for organizations that are inherently hierarchical (such as in the military), a model for a generic four-person hierarchy will often find itself repeated at higher and lower levels of aggregation throughout the organization. Thus, the issue is how to aggregate these generic modeling "units." Some work in this direction appears in Pete, Pattipati, and Kleinman [20] for distributed detection problems.

ACKNOWLEDGMENTS

This work was supported in part by the National Science Foundation under CTCT grant IRI-8902755, and by the Office of Naval Research under contract N00014-90-J-1753.

The authors would like to thank Mr. Daniel Serfaty from APTIMA, Inc. Woburn, MA and Professor Shi-Chung Chang from National Taiwan University, Taiwan for valuable discussions on the modeling and interpretation of implicit coordination.

REFERENCES

[1] L. Adelman, D. A. Zirk, P. E. Lehner, R. J. Moffett, and R. Hal, "Distributed Tactical Decision-Making: Conceptual Framework and Empirical Results," *IEEE Transactions on Systems, Man, and Cybernetics*, SMC-16 (6), 1986, pp. 794–805.

[2] M. Athans, "The Expert Team of Experts Approach to Command-and-Control (C2) Organizations," *Control Systems Magazine*, Sept. 1982, pp. 30–38.

[3] J. A. Cannon-Bowers, and E. Salas, "Cognitive psychology and Team Training: Shared Mental Models in Complex Systems," Symposium Address presented at the *Annual Meeting of the Society for Industrial and Organizational Psychology*, Miami, FL, April, 1990.

[4] R. Conant, and W. R. Ashby, "Every Good Regulator of A System Must Be A Model of That System," *International Journal of Systems Science*, Vol. 1, 1970, pp. 89–91.

[5] J. R. Hackman, and C. G. Morris, "Group Tasks, Group Interaction Processes, and Group Performance Effectiveness: A Review and Proposed Integration," in L. Berkowitz (ed.), *Advances in Experimental Social Psychology*, Vol. 8, pp. 45–99. New York: Academic Press, 1975.

[6] D. J. Hoitomt, P. B. Luh, E. Max, and K. R. Pattipati (1990), "Scheduling Jobs with Simple Precedence Constraints on Parallel Machines," *Control Systems Magazine*, Vol. 10, No. 2, Feb. 1990, pp. 639–645.

[7] P. Johnson-Laird, *Mental Models*, Cambridge, MA: Harvard University Press, 1983.

[8] J. P. Kahan, D. R. Worley, and C. Stasz, *Understanding Commanders' Information Needs*, RAND/R-3761-A, RAND: Arroyo Center, Santa Monica, CA, 1989.

[9] G. A. Klein, "Recognition-primed Decisions," in W. B. Rouse (ed.), *Advances in Man-Machine Systems Research*, Vol. 5, pp. 47–92, Greenwich, CT: JAI Press, 1989.

[10] D. L. Kleinman, P. B. Luh, K. R. Pattipati, and D. Serfaty, "Mathematical Models of Team Distributed Decisionmaking," in R. W. Swezey and E. Salas (eds.), *Teams: Their Training and Performance*, Norwood, NJ: Ablex, 1992, pp. 177–218.

[11] D. L. Kleinman, and D. Serfaty, "Team Performance Assessment in Distributed Decision-making," *Proceedings of Interactive Networked Simulation for Training Conference*, Orlando, FL. April, 1989.

[12] P. H. Lindsay, and D. A. Norman, *Human Information Processing*, London: Academic Press, 1977.

[13] D. G. Luenberger, *Linear and Nonlinear Programming*, Reading, MA: Addison-Wiley, 1989.
[14] K. R. MacCrimmon, "Descriptive Aspects of Team Theory: Observation, Communication and Decision Heuristics in Information Systems," *Management Science*, Vol. 20, No. 10, June, 1974, pp. 1323–1334.
[15] T. W. Malone, and K. Crowston, "Toward an Interdisciplinary Theory of Coordination," *MIT Technical Report*, CCS TR# 120, April 1991.
[16] J. Marschak, and R. Radner, *Economic Theory of Teams*, New Haven, CT: Yale University Press, 1972.
[17] J. E. McGrath, *Groups: Interaction and Performance*, Englewood Cliffs, NJ, Prentice-Hall, 1984.
[18] X. Y. Miao, P. B. Luh, D. L. Kleinman, and D. A. Castanon, "A Normative-Descriptive Approach to Hierarchical Team Resource Allocation," *IEEE Trans. on Systems, Man, and Cybernetics*, Vol. 22, No. 3, May/June 1992, pp. 482–497.
[19] B. B. Morgan, A. S. Glickman, E. A. Woodard, A. S. Blaiwes, and E. Salas, *Measurement of Team Behaviors in a Navy Environment* (NTSC-TR-86-014), Orlando, FL: Navy Training Systems Center, 1986.
[20] A. Pete, K. R. Pattipati, and D. L. Kleinman, "Distributed Detection in Teams with Partial Information: A Normative-Descriptive Model," *IEEE Trans. on Systems, Man and Cybernetics*, Vol. 23, No. 6, 1993, pp. 1626–1648.
[21] R. W. Pew, and S. Baron, "Perspectives on Human Performance Modelling," *Automatica*, Vol. 19, No. 6, 1983, pp. 663–676.
[22] J. Rasmussen, *Information Processing and Human-Machine Interaction: An Approach to Cognitive Engineering*, New York: North-Holland, 1986.
[23] W. B. Rouse, and N. M. Morris, "On Looking into the Black Box: Prospects and Limits in the Search for Mental Models," *Psychological Bulletin*, Vol. 100, 1986, pp. 349–363.
[24] E. Salas, T. L. Dickinson, S. A. Converse, and S. I. Tannenbaum, "Toward an Understanding of Team Performance and Training," in R. W. Swezey and E. Salas (ed.), *Teams: Their Training and Performance*, Norwood, NJ: Ablex, 1992, pp. 3–30.
[25] P. Shi, P. B. Luh, and D. L. Kleinman, "Team Coordination Under Individual and Team Goals," in K. M. Carley and M. J. Prietula (eds.), *Computational Organization Theory*, Hillsdale, NJ: Lawrence Erlbaum Associates, 1994, pp. 263–288.
[26] H. A. Simon, *Models of Bounded Rationality: Behavioral Economics and Business Organization*, Cambridge, MA: The MIT Press, 1982.
[27] M. E. Shaw, *Group Dynamics: The Psychology of Small Group Behavior*, New York: McGraw-Hill, 1976.
[28] H. G. Stassen, G. Johannsen, and N. Moray, "Internal Representation, Internal Model, Human Performance Model and Mental Workload," *Automatica*, Vol. 26, No. 4, 1990, pp. 811–820.
[29] I. D. Steiner, *Group Processes and Productivity*. New York: Academic Press, 1972.
[30] S. Streufert, and G. Nogami, "Cognitive Complexity and Team Decision Making," in R. W. Swezey and E. Salas (eds.), *Teams: Their Training and Performance*, Norwood, NJ: Ablex, 1992, pp. 127–152.
[31] W. P. Wang, and P. B. Luh, D. L. Kleinman, and S. C. Chang, "Coordination Mechanisms: A View from Dual Variables," *Proceedings of the 30th IEEE Conference on Decision and Control*, Brighton, UK, Dec. 1991.
[32] W. P. Wang, P. B. Luh, D. L. Kleinman, D. Serfaty, "Hierarchical Team Coordination under Time Pressure: Coordinator's Role and Communication Structure," submitted to *IEEE Transactions on Systems, Man, and Cybernetics*.
[33] J. G. Wohl, "Force Management Decision Requirements for Air Force Tactical Command and Control," *IEEE trans. on Systems, Man, and Cybernetics*, Vol. SMC-11, No. 9, September, 1981, pp. 618–639.

[34] D. Zakay, and S. Wooler, "Time Pressure, Training, and Decision Effectiveness," *Ergonomics*, Vol. 27, No. 3, March 1984, pp. 273–284.

[35] R. E. Levitt, G. P. Cohen, J. C. Kunz, C. I. Nass, T. Christiansen, and Y. Lin, "The Virtual Design Team: Simulating How Organization Structure and Information Processing Tools Affect Team Performance," in K. M. Carley and M. J. Prietula (eds.), *Computational Organization Theory*, Hillsdale, NJ: Lawrence Erlbaum Associates, 1994, pp. 1–18.

[36] K. M. Carley, and M. J. Prietula, "ACTS Theory: Extending the Model of Bounded Rationality," in K. M. Carley and M. J. Prietula (eds.), *Computational Organization Theory*, Hillsdale, NJ: Lawrence Erlbaum Associates, 1994, pp. 55–88.

[37] A. H. Levis, "Colored Petri Net Model of Command and Control Nodes," in C. Jones (ed.), *Toward a Science of Command, Control and Communications*, Washington DC: AIAA Press, 1993, pp. 181–192.

PART

V

COLLABORATORIES

CHAPTER

24

Social Theoretical Issues in the Design of Collaboratories: Customized Software for Community Support Versus Large-Scale Infrastructure

Geoffrey C. Bowker
Susan Leigh Star
University of California at San Diego

The same factors which have thus coalesced into the exactness and minute precision of the form of life have coalesced into a structure of the highest impersonality; on the other hand, they have promoted a highly personal subjectivity.

–Simmel (1960, p. 413)

1. INTRODUCTION: THE PROBLEM OF ELECTRONIC COMMUNITY

- *I live on the net.*
- *The Internet is a new nation.*
- *The laboratory of the 21st century has no walls and no boundaries, but is a virtual community.*
- *We are all Netizens now.*
- *Electronic communication has revolutionized the way science is done.*

Those of us studying the use of electronic media are often faced with statements such as these. The popular media often confound daily life and routine work and practice, electronic communication such as email, and that which transpires "over the net," with the concept of "community." There is a substantial elision of experience, material conditions, structural positions in particular social networks, communication, and location in discussions of "the net," and "the web."

As social scientists, this worries and intrigues us. We have been involved in the development and evaluation of several software systems for use by scientists. Whatever is happening with the scientists for whom the software was designed, it is clear that neither custom software efforts, nor the larger electronic environment are *literally* places where people live full time, nor even work full time. It does not provide either face-to-face local community nor full working infrastructure, as those concepts might plausibly be applied to close-knit collegial networks or to occupational communities and labor pools.

Early sociologists struggled along similar lines with the concept of community as it was affected by another large-scale technological shift, the industrial revolution. They used the term *gemeinschaft* to refer to tribal and village life, the sort one is born into, where everyone knows who you are by virtue of family and station. At first glance, it seemed that this sort of life was being threatened or even destroyed by cities and factory work. *Gesellschaft* referred to its opposite: the world of the industrialized city, marked by commerce, where who you are reflects your place in a more distanced, formally commercial and secular order. There were many arguments about whether urbanization had destroyed *gemeinschaft*, both among social scientists and in the general public sphere. Since their use during this time, the terms have been generalized more loosely to refer to intimate versus distanced relationships. (As well, the early sense of the disappearance of community has been modified and complexified.)[1]

During the infrastructural shift that is occurring with the building and integration of global electronic networks, some of the past lessons from sociological studies of communities and networks are useful. With the interest in terms such as *electronic community* today, the intimate versus distanced distinctions are again important. We seek here to clarify some senses in which *both* apply to the development of collaboratories. We are learning, as did early sociologists, that online community is not a choice between familiar locale and alienated metropolis, but that elements of both are important for design and analysis (Bishop et al., in press).

The work of doing science still takes place substantially off line, even though electronic communication and data sharing aspects are becoming increasingly more important. Even the parts of the work that may be isolated as "information work" are not necessarily conducted via electronic media:

---

[1]This section owes a great deal to discussions with Alaina Kanfer, and draws extensively on an earlier paper coauthored by Star and Kanfer, "Virtual Gemeinschaft or Electronic Gesellschaft?: Analyzing an Electronic Community System for Scientists," presented at the Society for the Social Study of Science (4S), Purdue University, November, 1994. Her consent to use this analysis is gratefully acknowledged.

People talk to each other, run down the hallway, write things by hand in notebooks and on labels, and also FAX and telephone each other constantly. Further, one is not "born" into the scientific "community," but one's sponsorship and apprenticeship occur over a long period of time "offline" for the most part, in graduate school and via long-standing collegial and friendship networks. At the same time, electronic tools are of growing importance, and elements of nature are being tested, taught, and modified in virtual space.

Bowker (1994a, 1994b) has used the concept "infrastructural inversion" to describe a conceptual shift in the social studies of technology, especially in history of technology. He implies that a figure-ground gestalt shift has occurred: decentering individuals, single artifacts, or even social movements as causal factors in large-scale scientific change. Instead, when infrastructural change is treated as the primary phenomenon, collective processes of transformation are more richly explained. Changes in infrastructural networks such as transportation, information, and domestic technologies explain a great deal about other forms of social change and social relationships—they are not simply substrate, but substance (Bowker & Star, 1999; Star, 1999). If this is true, then the substantive changes effected by (among many others) the National Information Infrastructure Initiative, the Collaboratory efforts, and the Digital Library initiatives have significance both for science and far beyond it. We now have a chance to observe this phenomenon as it unfolds. It is a moment that will not recur, and which requires extraordinary effect from social, information and computer scientists. One democratic concern here is that the social inequities and distributions of information resources will become somehow frozen or reified in the infrastructural changes. This begins with the simple notion of "information rich" and "information poor," but extends more complexly as more of life's business is conducted electronically. The digital divide has become omnipresent.

2. ON THE CONCEPT OF COMMUNITY: LESSONS FROM HISTORY

Infrastructural shifts on the scale of global electronic networking are not all that common in human history. They tend to generate extensive discussion of "basics": values, concepts, moral directions. During the great shifts of the 18th and 19th centuries from rural to urban, agricultural to industrial, and to large-scale organized capitalism, some basic questions were raised about community that echo those found today in *Science* magazine's articles on the global electronic laboratory and very large databases.

Distinctions between types of human bonding—and the troublesome notion of community—indeed informed the founding of the discipline of sociology. Nineteenth-century sociologists worried a great deal about the forces, or nature of the links that hold people together (e.g., Durkheim, 1984; Marx, 1970; Simmel, 1950; Tönnies, 1957), which seemed to be undergoing massive transformation throughout the Industrial Revolution. Did movement from the village, farm, and tribe to city, factory, and contracts change us, body and soul? Did what held us together in small, rural groupings differ radically from that which held us together in large urban conglomerates? If so, how?

Volumes, if not libraries, have been written on the contrast between *gemeinschaft* and *gesellschaft*, including the authors who find no essential change in human organization and bonding between country and city, farm and factory. The concept of *community* and all it might entail is one of the most contested in the history of social sciences. Some social scientists, such as Simmel (1950), held with confidence that the metropolis has spawned a new "mental life." In his classic essay on the topic, he claims that: "There is perhaps no psychic phenomenon, which has been so unconditionally reserved to the metropolis as has the blasé attitude" (p. 413).

Others went on to investigate the notion in rural societies in less-developed countries, such as Redfield (1947). As time went on, their claims were modified and challenged by other social scientists such as Lewis (1949) who found plenty of evidence for conflict and arms'-length relationships in the village, and Willmott and Young (1960) who found plenty of *gemeinschaft* in the close-knit working class neighborhoods of urban London's East End. It seems that community is not such an easy notion to place, nor such an easy one to dispense with.

Social scientists need concepts to describe how it is that people "stick together" within groups. But as with other fundamental concepts, such as "species" in biology or "culture" in anthropology (Clifford & Marcus, 1986), ironically it becomes both the glue that binds and the thing *least* agreed upon. (Perhaps it is just that, as Simmel noted long ago, conflict itself is "socializing," and the agreement to disagree is what binds these disciplines together.) Stacey (1969), in a magisterial review of the decades of arguments about the term *community*, notes that "It is doubtful whether the concept 'community' refers to a useful abstraction. Certainly, confusion continues to reign over the uses of the term" (p. 134).

Like "power" or "profession," the term community clearly points to a phenomenon of key interest for understanding large-scale change—but exactly what, or why, remains elusive. Stacey goes on to note that while one author deplores the romanticism of the notion, another claims it as the framework in which humans are introduced to civilization itself:

> This is so vague as to be nonsense: there is no such thing as community which does this. Various agencies are involved in this process of introduction, perhaps neighbors, almost certainly parents' kind and friends (which may live next door or miles away). These institutions may, or may not, be locally based.

> They may, or may not, be inter-related. If they are locality-based *and* inter-related then there may well be a local social system worth studying, but one would hesitate to call this a community. Nor is there any less lack of confusion in earlier usages of the term. (p. 135)

The conflation and generalization of these terms continue to this day. *Communities* seem to be everywhere in the media: the diplomatic community, the international community, the women's communication, the African-American community, the high-tech community, the bird-watching community. Perhaps our favorite of the season has been the "heterosexual community." What is the concept that joins such disparate collections of allegiances and heterogeneities?

In the world of science, the notion of "scientific community" (and its cousin, "invisible college") has been equaled only by the term *paradigm* in the amount of disputed terrain contained within it. Methodological divergences in how one would measure a community, where its boundaries are, whether it's a meaningful unit of analysis, and so on, have enriched and confused the world of social scientific work about science (STS, or science, technology, and society). Alternative notions have been proposed to emphasize one dimension or another of the social relations under scrutiny: communities of practice (Lave & Wenger, 1991); social worlds (Clarke, 1991; Clarke & Montini, 1993; Strauss, 1978); relevant social groups (Bijker, 1995), and actor networks (Callon, Law, & Rip, 1986), to name just a few.

The development of large-scale electronic infrastructures have given a new life to the battered notion of community, and have direct relevance to collaboratory research and its descendents, such as studies of cooperative work on the web and related CSCW (computer-supported cooperative work) projects. Early on, these events had two basic foci: *custom software projects* (such as the NSF collaboratories) which remotely link research already joined by common interests or heritage; and *tools for browsing* the extant internet resources in order to discover useful information or possible colleagues.

The collaboratory concept emerged in the late 1980s from a top-down initiative from the National Science Foundation in Washington. Dr. William Wulf, then director of the NSF Directorate for Computer and Information Science and Engineering wrote a foundational white paper: "The proposal, then, is to undertake a major, coordinated program of research and development leading to an electronic 'collaboratory' a 'center without walls,' in which the nation's researchers can perform their research without regard to geographical location, interacting with colleagues, accessing instrumentation, sharing data and computational resources, accessing information in digital libraries" (Lederberg & Uncapher, 1989, p. 19). Wulf's paper recalls Vannevar Bush's canonical *Science—The Endless Frontier*, which led to the foundation of the NSF. Bush had also called for improvements to scientific information flow. Bush's logic had been government through big science will give citizens health, wealth, and security—his clarion call opened with the words: "The Government should accept new responsibilities for promoting the flow of new scientific knowledge and the development of scientific talent in our youth. These responsibilities are the proper concern of Government, for they vitally affect our health, our jobs, and our national security" (Bush, 1990/1945, p. 8).

Wulf's logic, along similar lines, was that government through distributed science will give the nation technology, which leads to economic and military stature and competitiveness—in the opening words of his paper: "The health of the United States, economically and militarily, depends on its technology base. The technology base depends on the number, quality, and productivity of the nation's research scientists and engineers" (Lederberg & Uncapher, 1989, p. 19). Several important historical developments have occurred between the time of Bush and that of Wulf, of course. Most notably, has been inserted as a major mediator between science and nature (through simulations and advanced instrumentation). A new kind of information technology has become an essential support for scientific work, which has important implications for the practice of science as well as the notion of community.

Wulf's paper led to a workshop held at Rockefeller University in March 1989 (Lederberg & Uncapher, 1989, p. i). The workshop report found several needs for a collaboratory. Instruments, it was noted, were often to be found in environments hostile or inaccessible to people. Further, people themselves were inconveniently distributed, so that remote interaction with colleagues was necessary "whenever the appropriate mix of talents to address an interdisciplinary problem is not collocated anywhere." Finally, not only people and instruments, but also data were distributed—remote interaction was needed when: "the data are too vast to be replicated and managed at a single location," for example with the global seismic database. Accordingly, the goal was to build: "no less than a distributed intelligence, fully and seamlessly networked, with fully supported computational assistance designed to accelerate the pace and quality of discourse, and a broadening of the awareness of discovery: in a word, a Collaboratory." Here then is one defining reading of the word: collaboratories are about distribution in every sense of the word—distribution of things, people (thus Gallo formed a distributed college without walls—a "dream team" to fight AIDS) and information. This gives a great deal of scientific and theoretical power to computer and information scientists—who have developed theories of distributed databases and long-range communication networks; it allows a translation between government imperatives and new tools being developed within computer and information science: "The Collaboratory is much more than just a set of tools. It is a national computer-based infrastructure for scientific research."

The phenomenal growth of the web scarcely needs any review in this venue; the number of users grows exponentially. At the same time, there is considerable concern about the lack of good indexing and sorting tools, as well as a need for better means of ascertaining data quality. Thus the distinctions between custom projects and the development of the web are not absolute, bur rather foci that may blur into each other over time.

Even custom projects interface with the larger networks through email and links with databases (and increasingly this is the case for multimedia as well); browsing tools when adopted and extensively used in local sites come to form a *de facto* custom package over time.

With the advent of the Web, the repertoire of social science tools for its analysis has also vastly expanded, to include social studies of structural and nascent communities; web-based social networks (Kiesler & Sproull, 1996); online/offline "ecologies"; digital libraries (Bishop et al., in press; Weedman, 1992), and the use of advanced modeling techniques including visualization and VR.

3. HOW CAN ELECTRONIC NETWORKS SUPPORT A "COMMUNITY"?

In spite of all the controversy associated with exact definitions of community, there is general agreement that the sense of community rests on nontrivial, ongoing relations among people; some degree of shared knowledge, understandings, material objects, or conventional practices; and the idea that these two are not independent. Initial research on computer-mediated collaboration, or electronic communication systems showed some interesting effects in terms of the social relations, or role differentiation among members (Sproull & Kiesler, 1996). This in turn affected shared understandings, or consensus formation in decision making. A common finding in this research was that technologically mediated communication creates less role differentiation among group members that did face-to-face communication. This was attributed to the fact of less visible differentiation between group members when communication occurs electronically (you can't see someone's race or gender, for example; you couldn't hear their voice; you can't impute social cues about power or position by looking at their dress or posture). Consequently, concluded these researchers, there tends to be more uninhibited communication, more (vertical) communication between members of different status, and more equal participation in groups communicating via electronic mail (Kiesler, Siegel, & McGuire, 1984; Rice & Rogers, 1984; Siegel, Dubrovsky, Kiesler, & McGuire, 1986).

Researchers argued that the nature of decisions and agreements in such computer mediated groups may be affected, in part, by the decreased role differentiation that occurs in come computer mediated groups. Some researchers have found that less role differentiation allows group members to generate more ideas in problem-solving situations (Connolly, Jessup, & Valacich, 1990; Jessup & Tansik, 1991). When there are more ideas to choose from, group members may have a harder time deciding on a solution creating a longer time to reach consensus, or a point of action. This is obviously a relative notion, depending on small, identifiable groups with co-generated histories. Whether these ideas scale up to larger electronic groups is highly debated both about whether the distinction is too simplistic, or about whether other forms of social cues emerge over time. The larger and more distributed the groups, the more difficult status-role differentiation is to analyze. Baym (1995, 2000) argued that emergent groups on the net, such as Usenet groups, develop strong cues within the email messages themselves, including differentiation, leadership, and novel semantic conventions based on practice.

A linked finding was that groups within organizations communicating with computer mediation seemed to take longer to reach consensus than groups communicating face-to-face. Without traditional social cues to inform decision making, the process become more open, less reified or controlled by traditional lines of authority. Siegel et al. (1986) reached the same conclusion after observing greater choice shift and inefficient communication among group members communicating electronically than among group members trying to reach consensus in face-to-face settings.

On the other hand, Galegher and Kraut (1990) suggested that decreased role differentiation has the opposite effect on consensus formation. They focus on the diffuse responsibility and joint ownership that results from electronically mediated joint production. With less individual identification with the product, they argue, there will be a greater tendency toward conformity thus speeding up the consensus formation process.

In science, technological mediation—or electronic community systems—are becoming routine parts of scientific teamwork, both locally and at a distance. Modern, "big" science consists of scientists addressing problems so large they cannot be solved by a lone scientist. Such large problems require the combined efforts of scientific team members. Historically, one of the primary determinants of scientific collaboration has been physical proximity. However as the scope of scientific endeavors grows and members of the scientific community are more mobile, scientists working on the same problem often are not co-located. Physicists have a particularly well-developed infrastructure to support international collaboration of this sort (Traweek, 1988). Therefore, the benefits of productive collaborations afforded by proximity must be achieved by other means. It was claimed and hoped that electronic community systems will provide the means for frequent interactions, and joint access to tools and information for scientists collaborating long-distance (Kraut, Egido, & Galegher, 1990; Lederberg & Uncapher, 1989; Schatz, 1992). Since the mid-1990s, most of these tools operate via or alongside the Web.

One feature often integrated with electronic community systems is, of course, email. Early studies, partly in dialogue with the organization decision support studies of electronic "rooms" and local electronic messaging, tried to show how email would affect role differentiation and consensus formation in scientific collaborations. The findings were somewhat inconclusive. Tombaugh (1984) argued that greater role differentiation would have facilitated the international communication in an international asynchronous messaging, or conference system. Scientists in his study felt the need for more leadership. Hiltz (1983) studied 103 scientists communicating asynchronously over the net. This technologically mediated communication resulted in greater perceived understanding of other scientists' interests or theories, thereby affecting problem solving and decision making. Although this early research did not take place in anything like the Internet environment, it is useful in identifying problems in the design of electronic community systems for large, geographically dispersed scientific communities, and for illuminating some of the conceptual problems addressed earlier in this chapter.

Electronic infrastructural developments have made it possible to include in electronic community systems a variety of functions in addition to electronic mail (e.g., information sharing, document editing and collaborative writing tools, and data visualization techniques and collaborative tools). Although the emergent functionalities of a community system will depend on how community members use it, there are two fundamental functionalities for which such systems are designed:

1. An electronic system is designed as a quicker means for existing communications and social relations that compose a community. For instance, in a scientific community, journal articles can be viewed as a mode of communication of ideas in science—and electronic journals and preprints can provide the same function, more quickly.

2. The electronic medium can be used to support new activities. Different things are possible on electronic systems and the notion of scientific community can be changed. For instance, traditionally by keeping all information about an area available online, with annotations by and dialogues among experienced professionals, the training of newcomers can become an activity supported by the electronic system.

The degree to which these capacities of electronic community systems may lead to changes in the scientific community itself are only beginning to be analyzed. The first capability may lead to quicker spread of information or diffusion among a relatively well-defined group of scientists. The second approach may make it easier for new people to come into a specialty, and more difficult to maintain boundaries. In other words, electronic community systems may have the effect of reducing the gatekeeping roles of interpersonal relations (this is one hope of public policy advocates of such systems). However, if large resource differences continue to stratify electronic infrastructures (e.g., with respect to advanced multimedia) they may reinforce extant disparities.

These are some of the things that might be considered by designers of electronic community systems for scientists. An electronic system can be developed for a specific scientific community by community members or by outsiders. In addition, a "generic" electronic community system can be developed to support all types of general activity. When a scientific community adopts a generic electronic community system, its members can adapt some of the systems features for their specific use. Schatz, for example, proposed migrating the *c.elegans* WCS (discussed next) collaboratory system to other scientific communities, and this has been implemented for drosophila and yeast, among others.[2]

4. THE WORM COMMUNITY SYSTEM (WCS)

Scientists have, of course, been remotely operating scientific equipment with computer mediation for more than 20 years (e.g., the space program; see Olson & Atkins, 1990 for a discussion of this point). New to the collaboratory was a suite of communication and collaboration tools that allow distributed scientists to work together on data. This novelty can be seen in the Worm Community System (WCS), a customized piece of software designed to support the collaborative work of biologists sequencing the gene structure, and studying other aspects of the genetics, behavior and biology of *c.elegans*, a tiny nematode (Schatz, 1991).[3] It is a distributed "hyperlibrary," affording informal and formal communication and data access across many sites. It incorporates graphical representations of the physical structure of the organism; a periodically updated genetic map; formal and informal research annotations (and in this way constitutes an electronic publishing medium); directories of scientists in the community; a thesaurus of terms

[2]Compare Rader (1994) and Kohler (1995) for the lives of rats and drosophila in scientific networks. Kohler in particular, discusses the survival strategies the drosophila employ to protect this highly rarefied niche.

[3]A description and representation of WCS can be found at http://www.canis.uiuc.edu, along with a description of the Illinois Digital Library Project and the ongoing Interspace Project.

linked with a directory of those interested in the particular subtopic, and a quarterly newsletter–the *Worm Breeder's Gazette*. It also incorporates a database independently developed in Europe designed for the community, *acedb*. Many parts of the system are hypertext-linked with each other.

WCS was developed in 1990–1993 by Bruce Schatz and Sam Ward at the University of Arizona (after which it moved to the University of Illinois, and parts of its core programming were adapted in the Illinois Digital Library Project, 1994–1998, and in the ongoing Interspace Project). WCS was designed for a particular group with the idea of eventually migrating the structures of the software to other groups. Like the Sequoia 2000 project which deals with global change, this project was seen as being interesting both for its domain specific support and the nature of the computer science involved-meeting the information needs of scientists as well as providing a challenge for basic computer science research. (Some of the complexities and difficulties of this relationship are explored in Star & Ruhleder, 1996; and Weedman, 1992.)

Star and Ruhleder (1996) worked as ethnographers on the project, considering potential sociological effects and dynamics within the system as a whole. They traveled to worm labs across the United States and Canada, interviewed and observed the use of computing and other features of "worm work," including aspects of routine work and communication. As well, they asked questions about other features of the work, such as scientific careers in biology, competition, routine information-sharing tasks, and how computing infrastructure is managed. They visited more than 30 labs and interviewed more than 100 biologists during a 3-year period.

The worm community (their term for themselves, by the way!) consists of more than 1,400 scientists distributed around the world in more than 120 laboratories. They are a close-knit community and are very friendly. Until recently, most people were first or second generation of the field's founders. After the choice of *c.elegans* as the "model organism" for the Human Genome Initiative, some of this has changed (with increased resources, visibility, and competitiveness). Model organism means both that the actual findings from doing the worm biology and genetics will be directly of interest to human geneticists–for example, when homologues are found between oncogenes (cancer-causing genes) in the worm and in the human (although worms do not get cancer as such, there are developmental homologues) and that tools and techniques developed in the *c.elegans* mapping effort are put to use in the human project.

The worm itself is remarkable both as an organism, and as a component of a complex pattern of information transfer integral to the biologists' work. It is microscopic and transparent, with the surprising and convenient capability of being able to be frozen, mailed to other labs via parcel service, thawed out and retrieved live for observation. Worms and parts of worms travel from one lab to another as researchers share specimens. Worm strains with particular characteristics, such as mutation, may be mailed from a central Stock Center to labs requesting specimens. Tracking the location and characteristics of organisms thus is an important part of record-keeping and information retrieval. Two points emerge immediately here. First, both the worm and the scientist become part of a single distributed community. The worm biologists travel a virtual network and their community only exists at their set of nodes; their subjects travel a mail network, and live only at the nodes. Second, and most significantly, the worms and the scientists can only travel (really and virtually in turn) if there is a common set of standards shared across the network. Protocols must be in place to ensure that a given set of electronic signals means a contribution to a distributed database, and will be understood as such at each point along the way. Equally, there must be protocols to ensure that a given package of worm tissue means a standard mutation in each lab in the node. Berg (1997) calls this the need to discipline local practice, and he notes that his is a paradoxical feature of the attempt to create a transparent, flexible infrastructure.

Usage patterns in WCS reveal the sometimes competing nature of custom versus global emphases in information systems design. Many potential users of WCS moved to simpler, less functional web tools such as Gopher, Usenet, or simple email (and after the Web, migrated there). Star and Ruhleder (1995) analyze this in part as an unfamiliarity with some of the infrastructural tools, such as the Unix operating system, as well as other aspects of local infrastructure and support systems.

5. THE COLLABORATORY AND THE NATURE OF WORK

Ruhleder (1995) has written about the ways in which classical Greek scholarship changed with the introduction of the *Thesaurus Linguae Graecae*. This complete canon of classical Greek literature on database was made available online, during the 1970s with updates since. Tracking down the occurrence of a single word throughout that canon, with a view to uncovering its modalities, used to be a lobar involving sensuality (the feel and smell of the book so beautifully rendered by Charles Lamb), prodigious memory, and a goodly set of notes. It was not something one did at the start of one's career. One learned, though apprenticeship over the years, how and what and where. Now this work can be done with the touch of a button by a graduate student embarking on a PhD. Is it the same work in those two instances? Or, like Borges' two Don Quixotes, one written by Cervantes and one by a later academic, does the work itself change with its context, in this case its infrastructural support? We have so far looked at theories of work practice informing the development of collaborative infrastructure; in this section we explore how what it is to be a scientist is being affected by the development of high speed networked information infrastructures.

Steven Hawking speculated that by the turn of the century theoretical physics would be the province of the computer; the role of the human being would be to attempt to understand and appreciate discoveries made elsewhere. Although this seems unlikely, there are two basic ways in which the new information infrastructure is radically changing the nature of scientific work: the nature of representation and the nature of the scientific product.

The *nature of representation* is changing in the sense that theoretical work is increasingly being delegated to the intelligent instrument—which works through terabits of data streaming in and decides (by one of a number of algorithms) which data is interesting and which is not; and then represents the interesting data graphically according to another set of algorithms. The interpretive work is deliberately partially delegated to the machine, in order to cope with information retrieval. It is of course true that the appropriate algorithm can be changed, but one suspects that once this act of delegation is made and ramified (as one infrastructure submerges into another) then the attached algorithms will be naturalized (in the anthropological sense). (A relevant robust finding from library science is that patrons will use a convenient electronic source they know to be incomplete in preference over a card catalog that they know to be complete.) There will literally be no other way to see the world.

The nature of the scientific product is therefore changing in several ways. The scientific paper is arguably no longer the *terminus ad quem*. It is an archival document of use to people in other disciplines, argued one researchers (*Science*, 3/24/95, p. 1764). It is certainly increasingly the case the publication is proceeding online. This means more than the mere transposition of linear texts onto the screen. The new information infrastructure is just as significant as Eisenstein (1979) has persuasively argued that the book was for the presentation of scientific data. Information is not being presented here in linear form, with the word as the center of attention—rather the representation becomes the thing, with linear argument as secondary. At the limit, the scientific product becomes itself a library—the human genome for example—which is to be consulted as a huge interactive database created collaboratively by an array of henceforth anonymous authors.

6. THE UNUSUAL ROLE OF THEORY IN ELECTRONIC COLLABORATION

In computer and information science there is a unique relationship between theory and practice, fact and artifact, word and thing. The word (in the form of a computer program) *is* the thing (the instrument, the tool, the communication medium, the simulator); just as in a fully distributed, computer-mediated work environment the map *is* the territory. So many things that we as social scientists have been trying to prove for years-the inscription of theories in technical objects, the theory–ladenness of observation and so forth–are suddenly literal truths. We need to develop new theoretical sensibilities in order to move around in this brash new world.

There is a strand in science and technology studies that argues that social theory and values play a central role in engineering design (Star, 1999; Winner, 1980). In a classic article on the electric car, Callon (1989) argued that the "socio-engineers" designing the vehicle were at the same time betting on a theory of society in which the car itself became inevitable. Bowker (1994a) looking at *Schlumberger*'s scientific work argued that the geophysical company engineered work practices and social life around the oil well in such a way that their own science became first possible then inevitable. With the collaboratory–conceived here as the deliberate creation of a new information infrastructure for science–there is a multiple interpenetration of social theory and work practice.

At the broadest level there is the network architecture of the national information infrastructure itself. As is well-known, this architecture originated in the United States in the late 1960s in the need felt by the military for linking ARPA (the Advanced Research Projects Agency) projects–at the same time France was developing the CYCLADES network. This early connection with the military meant that much scientific development in the new information infrastructure has been physics-led. Thus, physicists developed the electronic preprint service that for many scientists has replaced the reading of journals (currently to be found at http://xxx.lanl.gov); the World Wide Web was first developed at the CERN laboratory.

In a brilliant paper, Abbate (1994) discussed the theoretical understanding by the main players of the nature of information networking–and how this played out in a series of relatively irreversible technical choices. There has been over the past few decades a conflict between two major protocols (X.25 and TCP/IP) describing the ways in which computers can talk to each other. The ARPA model (TCP/IP) assumed that the network itself should have low-level structure–this allowed greater heterogeneity among the laboratories being interconnected; although at the same time it entailed a greater degree of computing sophistication on the part of the labs themselves. The alternative protocol (X.25) grew out of a CCITT (Comité Consultatif International Télégraphique et Téléphonique) initiative. Drawing on the model of the telephone, the federated PTT's involved chose instead to make the network itself well-structured–so that at the other end there could be unsophisticated dumb users, just like clients of telephone companies. ARPA offered complexity with the advantage of control (Abbate, 1994, pp. 202–203); X.25 usability but little flexibility. ARPA modeled communication as being between well-equipped laboratories with their being a premium on speed and redundancy of communication—traditional military values; CCIT put the premium on volume and usability.

These differences have had very practical consequences for the practice of scientific work and for scientific communication. It was the flexibility offered by ARPANET that allowed the Internet to develop in such a distributed, anarchistic fashion—the efflorescence and rapid propagation of new programs and standards from a huge array of sources, since each laboratory in the military web was assumed to have an interest in maximal cooperation. The success of this model is most clearly demonstrated by the development of NCSA Mosaic in the early 1990s. Mosaic revolutionized the World Wide Web (developed at CERN); its HTML standard created a new kind of usability and transparency. Within this distributed model, the interactive sharing of information has been difficult technically (so many possible standards and protocols need to be taken into account simultaneously in order to create a transparent system). Recognizing this, ARPA concentrated work in the early 1980s on ways of translating email messages between incompatible systems: "The result has been that electronic mail is the only form of connection that has been fully achieved between diverse networks. Thus the communication aspect of networking has been emphasized, encouraging new uses of computers that stress interaction rather than calculation" (Abbate, 1994, p. 207). Typical of the complexities of the information infrastructure environment has been that this battle between the systems of X.25 and TCP/IP has not resulted in the death of one in favor of the other. Rather, X.25 is generally used, but only that subset of it that supports TCP/IP (Abbate, 1994, p. 206). In computer-mediated work, these forms of level shift are frequent. (For a fuller account of these transformations, see Abbate, 1999.)

The ARPA theory of a computer network as a set of connections between "centers of calculation" (Latour, 1987) has, then, led to a degree of local autonomy unusual in the history of large technical systems (e.g., compare the story of electricity networks as told by Thomas Hughes [1983]); and has led to an email-driven version of scientific community. There is no necessary paradox between military centralism and the democratization of Internet development. The key vision is that of the center of calculation being the node; and the question then is only who controls the nodes (and for a long period in post-World War II America, the military effectively controlled most significant high-tech laboratories).

However, it is not only at the level of network architecture that the theory of community with which one is working comes into play; on the contrary, in general one can say that with information infrastructure development of the order of scientific collaboratories and now digital libraries that it is theory all the way down. Another level of theory comes when one is trying to design an infrastructural tool that will actually get used by scientific researchers. To do this, one needs a model of what it is that scientists do, and then a suite of programs that will permit them to do the same better and faster.

Picture as a thought experiment an information systems designer assuming the truth of Merton's norms for the scientific community (cf. McClure et al., 1991, p. 93) for a discussion of what might happen to scientific norms with the introduction of electronic research networks). In the past, these norms may well have been a very useful part of the discourse of scientists: A positive self-image that demarcates science from business and projects an image of the scientist as the fair-minded arbiter of truth. But when it comes to developing an information infrastructure such as a collaboratory with which scientists will work to share and shape their experiments, then whether or not the norms represent working reality will make a difference. Thus, when Star as sociologist on the design team looked at the community of worm biologists, she found that these latter certainly did not want to share all information with rival labs on an ongoing basis, contra Merton's norm of communism: indeed, particularly early in their careers (as ambitious postdoctoral students carving out their own part of the genome), these biologists placed a great premium on secrecy. Scientists would not use a system that permitted no room for privacy: Working practice had to be made explicit in order to design a usable product, and that practice had to be informed by sociological theory. Star and Ruhleder (1996) noted that the WCS was designed to support tight long distance collaborations among the many researchers involved in the project; co-ordinate this scientific work; and allow the rapid involvement of new scientists by way of online recruitment and training.

In order to meet these goals, the infrastructural collaboratory had to reasonably reflect working practice in order to gain initial acceptance—although one assumes, of course, that a series of workarounds developed over time will increasingly allow for affordances between theory of practice inscribed in the infrastructure and practice itself.

7. HANDS-ON VERSUS AUTOMATED WORK

In the Internet, properties are constantly being swapped between humans and nonhumans—such that what constitutes mind, memory, intelligence, and scientific work are being redefined by the new infrastructure. It also impacts efficiency. Hiltz and Turoff's classic work *The Network Nation*, first published in 1978, makes the claim that: "Although a crucial endeavor to the maintenance of our society as we know it, research is a highly inefficient process when compared to other institutional functions" (p. 212). This passage reminds us that efficiency has long been a problem and a goal in electronic communication. This goal has been there, indeed, since the origin of computing: Babbages's original 1832 design for his calculating engine was based in part on his admiration for Prony's method of calculating logarithms—itself an application of the factory principle of the division of labor (Bowker, 1994b).

Hiltz and Turoff (1993) described a working computer conferencing system (CCS) that operated within an electronic information exchange system (EIES) as:

> Another capability being incorporated into EIES indicates the role a CCS can play in the area of resource sharing. A fairly sophisticated microprocessor with its own computer-controlled telephone dialer has been programmed to engage in the conference system as a full-fledged member, with the same powers of interaction as any human member (Hal Zilog, as it/she/he is referred to). This entity may perform any of the following tasks:
>
> 1. It may enter EIES and receive or send messages or retrieve and enter items into the other components of the system.
> 2. It may exercise certain analysis routines or generate display graphics from data provided by other EIES members, and return the results to them.
> 3. It may phone other computers and select data from existing data bases or obtain the results of a model to send back to any designated group of EIES users.
> 4. It may drop off and pick up communication items from other conference and message systems. (pp. 25–26)

This new member of the network was a full equal of any human members. Further, human members of the CCS were themselves transformed by the process in the sense that their disembodied intelligence would be free to act to its fullest capabilities: "computer based teleconferencing acts as a filter, filtering out irrelevant and irrational interpersonal 'noise' and enhances the communication of highly-informed 'pure reason'—a quest of philosophers since ancient times" (p. 28, citing Johansen, Vallee, & Collins, 1977).[4] Sociological studies of computer conferencing systems have tended to disconfirm these claims of enhanced filtering (Baym, 1995; Yates & Orlikowski, 1992); and indeed work in organization theory—notably inspired by Janis' classic article on Groupthink—has opened the question of the value of cooperative work (Kraut et al., 1990, p. 152).

However, the dream remains alive, as foreshadowed in the report of the 1993 workshop on collaboratories cited earlier, which aimed at creating "a distributed intelligence, fully and seamlessly networked." A scientific instru-

---

[4]It is only fair to note here that Hiltz and Turoff also point out that the authors themselves question the operation of this filtering.

ment in this view no longer a passive intermediary between the mind of the scientist and nature: "Incorporation of intelligence into the instruments allows the possibility of 'self-directed' data gathering, with the instrument itself deciding when data is significant and should be transmitted, setting parameters based on local feedback, and doing preliminary data reduction. This can lead to both reduction in communications and archiving requirements and better scientific data" (pp. 13–14). A formal model of information flow here can no longer have the structure subject+verb+object = scientist+instrumental action+nature; just as likely is instrument–instrumental action–nature, with the information systems designer and not the scientist as the *deus ex machina*.

So we have on the one hand the pure human mind and on the other the artificial mind of the intelligent information retrieval system: each made possible by the development of a seamless infrastructure. The human and the intelligent agent meet in the infrastructural database—thus the famous Los Alamos e-print archive referred to earlier (http://xxx.lanl.gov) in 1997 had a welcome to humans but a warning to nonhumans to be on good behavior: "ROBOTS BEWARE: indiscriminate automated downloads from this site are not permitted." Further exploration recovers the following message, topped by a picture of a no entry sign superimposed on a photograph of Commander Data from Star Trek the Next Generation:

> This www server has been under all-too-frequent attack from "intelligent agents" (a.k.a. "robots") that mindlessly download every link encountered, ultimately trying to access the entire database through the listings links. In most cases, these processes are run by well-intentioned but thoughtless neophytes, ignorant of common sense guidelines.
>
> (Very few of these same robotrunners would ever dream of downloading entire databases via anonymous ftp, but for some reason conceptualize www sites as somehow associated only to small and limited databases. This mentality must change—large databases such as this one [which has over 100,000 distinct URL's that lead to gigabytes of data] are likely to grow ever more commonly exported via www.)
>
> Following a proposed standard for robot exclusion, this site maintains a file /robots.txt that specifies those URL's that are off-limits to robots (note that the title/author listings for all archives remain available for remote indexing). Continued rapid-fire requests from any site after access has been denied will be interpreted as a network attack, and the automated response will be decidedly unfriendly. (Click *here* to initiate automated "seek-and-destroy" against your site.)

The point here is that as far as the *computer database* is concerned, there is very little difference between humans and nonhumans; just as for the scientific instrument there is very little difference between its own directive intelligence and that of the scientist.

The collaborative infrastructure is being designed precisely in the context of collapsing the human–nonhuman divide. The work of creating a seamless intelligent network is at present posited squarely on the possibility of rendering humans and nonhumans interchangeable. Impelling the collaboratory effort is a central focus on information as product and commodity. Notoriously, in any information-centered vision of the world, it matters little formally where the information is being held or processed (its container): The only thing that is important is that it circulate flawlessly and be analyzed thoroughly. Early work on the nature of information science after World War II instantiate this claim. One example is Wiener's early, outrageous conjecture that people might be sent down a variety of telephone wires as code, and restored physically at the other end: after all, we were just information (Wiener, 1957, p. 23). Another is Turing's famous demonstration that his abstract logic machine (an infinite roll of tape, and a mechanism for moving and marking) was equivalent to any real logic machine—whether this be lodged in the human brain or in a scientific instrument (see Bowker, 1994b for a further exploration of these issues).

Sociological and philosophical theory is getting literally encoded into the infrastructure of collaborative scientific work on the net. It becomes an active resource drawn on by engineers and designers as they create a new system. Thus any given theory—if encoded into successful software—can be truer now than it was before. Winograd and Flores' Coordinator, for example, was one of the early and most influential groupwork programs; it is one of several such programs that utilizes Searle's speech-act theory (Rodden, 1992, p. 5; Winograd & Flores, 1987). The program structures office communication into assertives, directives, commissives, expressives, and declarations; and any future researcher analyzing collaborative work using this system will find these naturalized categories structuring all computer communication and having ramifications for noncomputer mediated work. One could say that the infrastructure can only work if the theory that everything is information is true; a preferable statement would be that it can only work if it can make the theory that everything is information true—change the world in such a way that this is a fair description of the nature of things (see Suchman, 1994 for a critique of Winograd and Flores on these grounds, for example).

This is a somewhat pessimistic view of the collaboratory as architect of humans as vessels of pure reason, computers as same, and computer networks as reason distribution engines. There is of course another way of reading the collapse of the human/nonhuman divide—as represented by the works of Haraway (1985, 1997), Star (1991, 1999) and Latour (1993). According to this reading, categories that were assumed to inhere in the head (such as "memory," "cognition," and "learning" can themselves be understood as spatially and temporally distributed). Cicourel (1990), for example, pointed to a unity between social analysis and infrastructural development: "The idea of socially distributed cognition refers to the fact that participants in collaborative work relationships are likely to vary in the knowledge they possess, and must therefore engage each other in dialogues that allow them to pool resources and negotiate their differences to accomplish their tasks. The notion of socially distributed cognition is analogous to the idea of distributed computing" (p. 223). Or again, following historically on the lead of Maurice Halbwachs, an influential group of workers within the world of computer supported cooperative work (CSCW) have argued that memory is invariably a social phenomenon, which is both spatially and temporally distributed (Middleton & Edwards, 1990). Work in distributed artificial intelligence also speaks of "composite systems" of humans and machines.

8. CONCLUSIONS

Rather than indulge in an intellectually vacuous exercise of determining "where is the boundary" between online work and offline work, or the exact distinction between "electronic communities" and "scientific communities," we offer some findings and cautions about the visions of collaboratories. The community metaphor is a powerful one, but one whose heritage is so fraught that it is almost useless to try to retrieve it intact (see Jones, 1998 for excellent discussions of the matter in cyberspace). (Yet, the sheer level of use of the term demonstrates that we are using it for *something* important to us.) Rather, we would like to make the following observations.

Collaboratories contain inherently competing goals (as do all large systems). This is why they are communicative systems. With the growth of big science, for instance with *c.elegans* a designated model for the human genome initiative, an electronic community system is designed with the following goals in mind: to support long-distance collaborations among the many researchers in the large scientific effort; to help coordinate the large scientific effort; to allow the rapid involvement of new scientists by way of online recruitment and training. The worm researchers, however, were explicit in that they did not want to lose that informal, close-knit community feeling. A more structured scientific effort may impose formals ties and weaken the informal ties upon which the community has been built. The availability of online training, and reduced need for mentorship MAY indeed decrease the boundary definition and intimacy of the community, although this is by no means clear as yet. Therefore, the goals of the system are antithetical to the feelings of the existing scientific community. Therefore, the goals of the system are antithetical to the feelings of the existing scientific community. Indeed the goals of the system are in conflict with each other in precisely this way. Simultaneous attempts to build *gemeinschaft* and *gesellschaft*; to blue locale and global reach; to preserve intimacy *and* extend community infinitely will not work without careful attention to the distribution between hands-on and automated work, between *gemeinschaft* and *gesellschaft.*

In scientific communities like *c.elegans*, the scientists valued the close-knit collaborative working environment and were open to an electronic community system that supported this. An electronic system without a formal structure of information and communication links might best support this closeness. However, users of an electronic system get frustrated without some structured access to information, and the desire to use the system for training suggests a system with a more arms' length set of relationships and structures. These two requirements of an electronic scientific community system create an inherent design conflict. The solution to this conflict may come from a more "organized" system, that evolves in response to the community evolution, or perhaps from newly evolving forms and conventions that we cannot yet imagine.

The notion of collaboratory itself is a moving target. However, key elements are an orientation to information flow—between instruments, people, and documents—embedded in an integrated information infrastructure. It is assumed that within this infrastructure the map will become the territory. Just like Huysmans (1981) in *A Rebours* deciding not to visit London because he had already in a quayside restaurant in Calais experienced all the sensations that the visit itself would produce; so do the new scientists not need to see each other, their instruments, or the world in order to do their valuable work of theory production. At the same time, theories of situated action and workplace studies (Hutchins 1995; Lave, 1988; Star, 1995; Suchman, 1987) show us that without attention to the local contingencies and differences in hands-on, craft aspects of even formal work, systems and knowledge risk irrelevance and rigidity.

We see the important of vase, dense electronic networks that scientists use as an opportunity not to engage in boundary disputes, but rather to use the conceptual tools from different parts of the social sciences to understand the phenomenon empirically and theoretically. One thing is clear: Media hype is not helpful in this enterprise, nor is extending the inherited clutter and entropy associated with the concept of community.

However, we hope that perhaps a real opportunity to combine the empirical work from ethnography and situated studies in analyzing new forms of communication, media for work practices, and affiliations, if not communities, may help shed some light on this old problem.

There is nothing new about scientific collaboration being distributed in time and place—the correspondence circles of 17th-century scientists; Darwin's enormous range of correspondents; the large-scale collaborations during World War II leading to the development of the atomic bomb. What is new and interesting is the embedding of specific forms of collaboration into an information infrastructure that impacts the very nature of scientific work. We have argued that as the information infrastructure becomes ever more deeply engrained, then the successful theories inscribed into it will be naturalized. They will come to seem true and unproblematic. However, it should be noted that this is not equivalent to saying that the best theory will win. The history of standards and infrastructures makes it very plain that a series of contingencies mean that often the second best (or even the worst) will triumph. The Lotus 123 spreadsheet, the DOS operating system, and VHS format are (in)famous examples. Nor does it mean that the theory which becomes naturalized will give the best possible description of scientific work and practice. After all, Merton's norms were long naturalized in the scientific community; but they certainly did not describe the ways in which scientists acted. But this naturalization does count for something. The new truth becomes the problematic in terms of which theory—critical and otherwise—is defined.

Social theorists have taken on a very active role in the development of collaboratories. Much good sociological analysis has been written by authors involved in the design of systems. Where the field of science studies has in the past called attention to the sophistication of the actors' own perspective and served as spokespeople for the actors, the shoe is now firmly on the other foot. The designers of the new infrastructure are calling attention to the sophistication of sociology's views of information and work, and are serving to represent these views within their programs (Bowker, Gasser, Star, & Turner, 1997). A fearful, but quite pleasing, symmetry.

ACKNOWLEDGMENTS

WCS was partially funded by NSF under grants IRI-90-15047, IRI-92-57252, and BIR-93-19844. The Interspace project is currently housed within the Community Systems Laboratory (CSL), headed by Bruce Schatz, affiliated with the Graduate School of Library and Information Science and the National Center for Supercomputing Applications at the University of Illinois, Urbana-Champaign. Additional support was provided by the University of Arizona and the University of Illinois. Co-PIs Bruce Schatz and Sam Ward, and developers Terry Friedman and Ed Grossman were extremely generous with their time, comments, and access to data and meetings; we also thank our anonymous respondents for their time and insight. Additional thanks to Karen Ruhleder and Bill Turner.

REFERENCES

Abbate, Janet. 1994. "The Internet Challenge: Conflict and Compromise in Computer Networking." In J. Summerton (ed.), *Changing Large Technical Systems* (pp. 193–210). Boulder, CO: Westview Press.

Abbate, Janet. 1999. *Inventing the Internet.* Cambridge, MA: MIT Press.

Ackoff, Russell L., Thomas A. Cowan, Peter Davis, Martin C. J. Elton, James C. Emergy, Maybeth L. Meditz, and Wladimer M. Sachs. 1976. *Designing a National Scientific and Technological Communications System.* Philadelphia: University of Pennsylvania Press.

Baym, Nancy K. 1995. "From Practice to Culture on Usenet." In S. L. Star (ed.), *The Cultures of Computing* (pp. 29–52). Oxford, UK: Blackwell.

Baym, Nancy K. 2000. *Tune In, Log On: Soaps, Fandom, and Online Community.* Thousand Oaks, CA: SAGE.

Berg, Marc. 1997. *Rationalizing Medical Work—Decision Support Techniques and Medical Problems.* Cambridge, MA: MIT Press.

Bijker, Wiebe E. 1995. *Of Bicycles, Bakelite, and Bulbs: Toward a Theory of Sociotechnical Change.* Cambridge, MA: MIT Press.

Bijker, Wiebe E., Thomas P. Hughes, and Trevor Pinch (eds.). 1987. *The Social Construction of Technological Systems: New Directions in the Sociology and History of Technology.* Cambridge, MA: MIT Press.

Bishop, Ann, Laura Neumann, Susan Leigh Star, Cecelia Merkel, Emily Ignacio, and Robert Sandusky. In press. "Digital Libraries: Situating Use In Changing Information Infrastructure." *Journal of the American Society for Information Science, 51.*

Bowker, Geoffrey C. 1993. 'How to be Universal: Some Cybernetic Strategies.' *Social Studies of Science, 23,* 107–127.

Bowker, Geoffrey C. 1994a. *Science on the Run: Information Management and Industrial Geophysics at Schlumberger, 1920–1940.* Cambridge, MA: MIT Press.

Bowker, Geoffrey. 1994b. "Information Mythology and Infrastructure." In L. Bud-Frierman, ed. *Information Acumen: The Understanding and Use of Knowledge in Modern Business* (pp. 231–247). London: Routledge.

Bowker, Geoffrey and Susan Leigh Star. 1994. "Knowledge and Infrastructure in International Information Management: Problems of Classification and Coding." In L. Bud, ed. *Information Acumen: the Understanding and Use of Knowledge in Modern Business* (pp. 187–213). London: Routledge.

Bowker, Geoffrey C., Les Gasser, Susan Leigh Star, and William Turner (eds.). 1997. *Social Science, Technical Systems and Cooperative Work: Beyond the Great Divide.* Mahwah, NJ: Lawrence Erlbaum Associates.

Bowker, Geoffrey and Star, Susan Leigh. 1999. *Sorting Things Out: Classification and its Consequences.* Cambridge, MA: MIT Press.

Bush, Vannevar. 1990/1945. *Science—The Endless Frontier: A Report To The President on a Program for Postwar Scientific Research.* Washington, DC: National Science Foundation.

Callon, Michel. 1989. "Society in the Making: The Study of Technology as a Tool for Sociological Analysis." In W. E. Bijker, T. P. Hughes, and T. Pinch (eds.), *The Social Construction of Technological System* (pp. 83–105). Cambridge, MA: MIT Press.

Callon, Michel, John Law, and Arie Rip (eds.). 1986. *Mapping the Dynamics of Science and Technology.* London: Macmillan.

Cicourel, Aaron V. 1990. "The Integration of Distributed Knowledge in Collaborative Medical Diagnosis." In J. Galegher, Robert E. Kraut, and Carmen Egido (eds.), *Intellectual Teamwork: Social And Technological Foundations Of Cooperative Work* (pp. 221–242). Hillsdale, NJ: Lawrence Erlbaum Associates.

Clarke, Adele E. 1991. Social Worlds/Arenas Theory as Organizational Theory. In D. Maines (ed.), *Social Organization and Social Process: Essays in Honor of Anselm Strauss* (pp. 119–158). New York: Aldine de Gruyter.

Clarke, Adele E. and Theresa Montini. 1993. "The Many Faces of RU486: Tales of Situated Knowledges and Technological Contestations" *Science, Technology and Human Values, 18,* 42–78.

Clifford, James and George E. Marcus. 1986. *Writing Culture: The Poetics and Politics of Ethnography.* Berkeley: University of California Press.

Conolly, T., L. M. Jessup, & J. S. Valacich. 1990. "Effects of Anonymity and Evaluative Tone on Idea Generation in Computer-Mediated Groups. *Management Science, 36*, 689–703.

Durkheim, Emile. 1984. *The Division of Labor in Society*. Translated by W. D. Halls. New York: Free Press.

Eisenstein, Elizabeth L. 1979. *The Printing Press as an Agent of Change: Communications and Cultural Transformations in Early Modern Europe*. Cambridge, England: Cambridge University Press.

Galegher, Jolene, Robert E. Kraut, and Carmen Egido (eds.). 1990. *Intellectual Teamwork: Social and Technological Foundations of Cooperative Work*. Hillsdale, NJ: Lawrence Erlbaum Associates.

Groupe Géode. 1995. *Planifier l'émergence: la formation d'une stratégie dans une économie des compétences et des savoirs*, Paris: CERESI/CNRS, May.

Haraway, Donna. 1985. "A Manifesto for Cyborgs: Science, Technology, and Socialist Feminism in the 1980s." *Socialist Review, 80*, 65–107.

Haraway, Donna. 1997. *Modest-Witness@Second-Millennium. FemaleMan-Meets-OncoMouse: Feminism and Technoscience*. New York: Routledge.

Hiltz, Starr Roxanne and Murray Turoff. 1993/1978. *The Network Nation: Human Communication Via Computer* (rev.ed.). Cambridge, MA: MIT Press.

Hutchins, E. 1995. *Cognition in the Wild*. Cambridge, MA: MIT Press.

Huysmans, J. K. 1981. *A rebours*. Paris: Imprimerie Nationale.

Jessup, L. M. and D. A. Tansik. 1991. "Decision Making in an Automated Environment: The effects of Anonymity and Proximity with a Group Decision Support System." *Decision Sciences, 22*, 226–279.

Jones, Steven G. (ed.). 1998. *CyberSociety 2.0: Revisiting Computer-Mediated Communication and Community*. Thousand Oaks, CA: SAGE.

Kiesler, S., J. Siegel and T. McGuire. 1984. Social Psychological Aspects of Computer-Mediated Communication. *American Psychologist, 39*, 1123–1134.

Kiesler, Sara (ed.). 1998. *Cultures of the Internet*. Mahwah, NJ: Lawrence Erlbaum Associates.

Kohler, Robert E. 1994. *Lords of the Fly: Drosophila Genetics and the Experimental Life*. Chicago: University of Chicago Press.

Kraut, Robert, Carmen Egido, and Jolene Galegher. 1990. "Patterns of Contact and Communication in Scientific Collaborations." In J. Galegher, Robert E. Kraut, and Carmen Egido (eds.), *Intellectual Teamwork: Social And Technological Foundations of Cooperative Work* (pp. 149–172). Hillsdale, NJ: Lawrence Erlbaum Associates.

Latour, Bruno. 1987. *Science in Action: How to Follow Scientists and Engineers Through Society*. Cambridge, MA: Harvard University Press.

Latour, Bruno. 1993. *We Have Never Been Modern*. Translated by Catherine Porter. Cambridge, MA: Harvard University Press.

Lave, Jean and Etienne Wenger. 1991. *Situated Learning: Legitimate Peripheral Participation*. Cambridge, England: Cambridge University Press.

Lave, Jean. 1988. *Cognition in Practice: Mind, Mathematics, and Culture in Everyday Life*. New York: Cambridge University Press.

Lederberg, Joshua and Keith Uncapher. 1989. *Towards a National Collaboratory: Report of an Invitational Workshop at the Rockefeller University*, March 17–18.

Lewis, Oscar, 1951. *Life in a Mexican Village: Tepoztlán Restudied*. Urbana, University of Illinois Press.

Marx, Karl. 1970. *Capital, Vol. 1*. London: Lawrence and Wishart.

McClure, Charles, et al. 1991. *The National Research and Education Network (NREN): Research and Policy Perspectives*. Norwood, NJ: Ablex.

Middleton, D. S. and D. Edwards (eds.). 1990. *Collective Remembering: Memory in Society*. London: SAGE.

Olson, Gary M. and Daniel E. Atkins. 1990. "Supporting Collaboration with Advanced Multimedia Electronic Mail: the NSF EXPRESS Project." In J. Galegher, Robert E. Kraut, and Carmen Egido (eds.), *Intellectual Teamwork: Social and Technological Foundations of Cooperative Work* (pp. 429–451). Hillsdale, NJ: Lawrence Erlbaum Associates.

Olson, Gary, Ray Levitt, and Laurence Rosenberg. 1993. *Introduction, Coordination Theory and Collaboration Technology Workshop*, NSF, July 8–10.

Rader, Karen. 1994. "The Production, Distribution and Uses of Genetically-Standardized Mice for Research, 1909–1962. In D. Barkin (ed.), *Ideas, Instruments and Innovation*. Pasadena, CA: CalTech Workshop Conference.

Redfield, Robert. 1947. *Tepoztlán: A Mexican Village*. Chicago: University of Chicago Press.

Rice, R. E. and Rogers, E. M. 1984. "New Methods and Data for the Study of New Media." In R. E. Rise & Associates (eds)., *The New Media: Communication, Research, and Technology*. Beverly Hills: Sage.

Rodden, Tom. 1993. "Technological Support for Cooperation." In D. Diaper and Colston Sanger (eds.), *CSCW in Practice: An Introduction And Case Studies* (pp. 1–22). Berlin: Springer-Verlag.

Ruhleder, Karen. 1995. "Reconstructing Artifacts, Reconstructing Work: From Textual Edition to On-line Databank" *Science, Technology and Human Values, 20*, 39–64.

Schatz, B. 1991. Building an electronic community system. *Journal of Management Information Systems, 8*, 87–107.

Science Policy Study, Background Report No. 5. 1986. *The Impact of Information Technology on Science*. Report prepared by the Congressional Research Service, Library of Congress, transmitted to the Task Force on Science Policy; Committee on Science and Technology, U.S. House of Representatives, 99th Congress, Second Session, Serial T, September.

Siegel, J., V. Dubrovsky, S. Kiesler, and T. W. McGuire. 1986. Group Processes in Computer-Mediated Communication. *Organizational Behavior and Human Decision-Processes, 37*, 157–187.

Simmel, Georg. 1950/1908. "The Stranger." In Kurt Wolff (ed.). *The Sociology of George Simmel* (pp. 402–408). Glencoe, IL: Free Press.

Kiesler, Sara and Lee Sproull. 1996. *Connections: New Ways of Working in the Networked Organization*. Cambridge, MA: MIT Press.

Stacey, Margaret. 1969. "The Myth of Community Studies." *British Journal of Sociology, 29*, 134–147.

Star, Susan Leigh. 1989. *Regions of the Mind: Brain Research and the Quest for Scientific Certainty*. Stanford, CA: Stanford University Press.

Star, Susan Leigh. 1991. "Power, Technologies and the Phenomenology of Standards: On Being Allergic to Onions." In J. Law (ed.), *A Sociology of Monsters? Power, Technology and the Modern World: Sociological Review Monograph 38*. Oxford: Basil Blackwell, 27–57.

Star, Susan Leigh (ed.). 1995. The Cultures of Computing. *Sociological Review Monograph Series*. Oxford: Basil Blackwell.

Susan Leigh Star. 1999. "The Ethnography of Infrastructure." *American Behavioral Scientist, 43*, 377–391.

Star, Susan Leigh and Karen Ruhleder. 1996. "Steps toward an Ecology of Infrastructure: Design and Access for Large Information Spaces." *Information Systems Research, 7*, 111–134.

Star, Susan Leigh and Alaina Kanfer. 1993. *Virtual Gemeinschaft or Electronic Gesellschaft?: Analyzing an Electronic Community System for Scientists*. Paper presented at the Annual Meetings of the Society for the Social Study of Science (4S), Purdue University, West Lafayette, Indiana.

Strauss, Anselm. 1978. "A Social World Perspective." *Studies in Symbolic Interaction, 1*, 119–128.

Suchman, Lucy. 1987. *Plans and Situated Action*. Cambridge, England: Cambridge University Press.

Tombaugh, J. W. 1984. "Evaluation of an International Scientific Computer-Based Conference. *Journal of Social Issues, 40*, 129–144.

Tönnies, Ferdinand. 1957. *Community and Society (Gemeinschaft und Gesellschaft)*. Translated and edited by Charles P. Loomis. East Lansing, MI: Michigan State University Press.

Traweek, Sharon. 1988. *Beamtimes and Lifetimes: The World of High Energy Physicists*. Cambridge, MA: Harvard University Press.

Weedman, Judy, 1992. *Origins of Multi-Sector Scientific Collaboration: A Report on Research in Progress*. Paper presented at the Annual Conference of the International Network for Social Network Analysis, Dallas, TX, June.

Wiener, Norbert. 1948. *Cybernetics; or, Control and Communication in the Animal and the Machine*. New York: Wiley.

Young, Michael Dunlop and Peter Willmott. 1957. *Family and Kinship in East London*. London: Routledge and Kegan Paul.

Winner, Langdon. 1980. Do Artifacts Have Politics? *Daedalus, 19\09*, 121–136.

Winograd, Terry and Fernando Flores. 1987. *Understanding Computers and Cognition*. Norwood, NJ: Ablex.

Yates, JoAnne and Wanda J. Orlikowski. 1992. "Genres of Organizational Communication: A Structurational Approach to Studying Communication and Media." *Academy of Management Review, 17*, 299–326.

CHAPTER

25

A Path to Concept-Based Information Access: From National Collaboratories to Digital Libraries

Hsinchun Chen
University of Arizona

Bruce R. Schatz
University of Illinois

1. INTRODUCTION

Despite the usefulness of database technologies, users of online information retrieval systems are often overwhelmed by the amount of current information, the subject and system knowledge required to access this information, and the constant influx of new information [7]. The result is termed *information overload* [3]. A second difficulty associated with information retrieval and information sharing is the classical *vocabulary problem*, which is a consequence of diversity of expertise and backgrounds of system users [6, 21, 22]. Previous research in information science and in human–computer interactions has shown that people tend to use different terms (vocabularies) to describe a similar concept—the chance of two people using the same term to describe an object or concept is less than 20% [22]. The "fluidity" of concepts and vocabularies, especially in the scientific and engineering domains, further complicates the retrieval issue [6, 14, 20]. A scientific or engineering concept may be perceived differently by different researchers and it may also convey different meanings at different times. To address the information overload and the vocabulary problem in a large information space that is used by searchers of varying backgrounds a more proactive search aid is needed.

The problems of information overload and vocabulary difference have become more pressing with the emergence of the increasingly popular internet resource discovery services and digital libraries [16, 19, 25]. Retrieval difficulties, we believe, will worsen as the amount of online information increases at an accelerating pace under the National Information Infrastructure (NII). Although Internet protocols and World Wide Web (WWW) software support significantly easier importation of online information sources, their use is accompanied by the adverse problem of users not being able to explore and find what they want in an enormous information space [2, 4, 30].

The main information retrieval mechanisms provided by the prevailing resource discovery software and other information retrieval systems are either based on "keyword search" (inverted index or full text) or "user browsing." Keyword search often causes low *precision* (the proportion of the retrieved documents that are judged relevant) and poor recall (the proportion of the relevant documents that are retrieved) due to the limitations of controlled language-based interfaces (the vocabulary problem) and the inability of searchers themselves to fully articulate their needs. Furthermore, browsing allows users to explore only a very small portion of a large and unfamiliar information space, which, in the first place, was constructed based on the system designer's view of the world. A large information space organized based on hypertext-like browsing can also potentially confuse and disorient its user, giving rise to the "embedded digression problem"; and can cause the user to spend a great deal of time while learning nothing specific, the "art museum phenomenon" [5, 18]. This research aims to provide a semantic, concept-based retrieval option that could supplement existing information retrieval options.

Our proposed approach is based on textual analysis of a large corpus of domain-specific documents in order to generate a large set of subject vocabularies. By adopting cluster analysis techniques to analyze the co-occurrence probabilities of the subject vocabularies, a similarity (relevance) matrix of vocabularies can be built to represent the important concepts and their weighted "relevance" relationships in the subject domain [9, 17, 29]. To create a network of concepts, which we refer to as the "concept space" for the subject domain (to distinguish it from its underlying "information/object space"), we propose to develop general AI-based graph traversal algorithms (e.g., serial, optimal branch-and-bound search algorithms or parallel, Hopfield net like algorithms) and graph matching algorithms (for intersecting concept spaces in related domains) to automatically translate a searcher's preferred vocabularies into a set of the most semantically relevant terms in the database's underlying subject domain. By providing a more understandable, system-generated, semantics-rich concept space (as an abstraction of the enormously complex information space) plus algorithms to assist in concept/information spaces traversal, we believe we can greatly alleviate both information overload and the vocabulary problem.

In this chapter, we first review our concept space approach and the associated algorithms in Section 2. In Section 3, we describe our experience in using such an approach. In Section 4, we summarize our research findings and our plan for building a semantics-rich *Interspace* for the Illinois Digital Library project.

2. THE CONCEPT SPACE APPROACH AND THE ALGORITHMS

To alleviate information overload and the vocabulary problem in information retrieval, researchers in human–computer interactions and information science have suggested expanding the vocabularies for objects and linking vocabularies of similar meanings. For example, Furnas et al. [21, 22] proposed "unlimited aliasing," which creates multiple identities for the same underlying object. In information science, Bates [1] proposed using a domain-specific dictionary to expand user vocabularies in order to allow users to "dock" onto the system more easily. The general idea of creating rich vocabularies and linking similar ones together is sound and its usefulness has been verified in previous research as well as in many real-life information retrieval environments (e.g., reference librarians often consult a domain-specific thesaurus to help users in online subject search). However, the bottleneck for such techniques is often the manual process of creating vocabularies (aliases) and linking similar or synonymous ones (e.g., the effort involved in creating an up-to-date, complete, and subject-specific thesaurus is often overwhelming and the resulting thesaurus may quickly become obsolete for lack of consistent maintenance).

Based on our experiences in dealing with several business, intelligence, and scientific textual database applications, we have developed an algorithmic and automatic approach to creating a vocabulary-rich dictionary/thesaurus, which we call the *concept space*. In our design, we generate such a concept space by first automatically extracting concepts (terms) from texts in domain-specific databases. Similar concepts are then linked together by using several elaborate versions of co-occurrence analysis of concepts in texts. Finally, through generating concept spaces of different (but somewhat related) domains, intersecting common concepts, and providing graph traversal algorithms to lead concepts from a searcher's domain (queries expressed in his or her own vocabulary) to the target database domain, the concept space approach allows a searcher to explore a large information space more effectively. We present a blueprint of this approach next. Selected algorithms and examples are given for illustration.

A. Concept Identification. The first task for concept space generation is to identify the vocabularies used in the textual documents. AI-based Natural Language Processing (NLP) techniques have been used for generating detailed, unambiguous internal representation of English statements [28, 32]. However, such techniques are either too computationally intensive or are domain-dependent and therefore inappropriate for identifying content descriptors (terms, vocabularies) from texts in diverse domains. An alternative method for concept identification that is simple and domain-independent is the automatic indexing method, often used in information science for indexing literature [29]. Automatic indexing typically includes dictionary look-up, stop-wording (removing function words), and term-phrase formation. Another technique (often called "object filtering") which could supplement the automatic indexing technique involves using existing domain-specific keyword lists (e.g., a list of company names, gene names, researchers' names, etc.) to help identify specific vocabularies used in texts.

In our previous Worm Community System (WCS) project [13], we incorporated several thousand worm biology abstracts to generate a worm concept space. A sample entry is shown in Fig. 25.1. The indexing results using automatic indexing and object filtering for this entry are shown in Fig. 25.2. The parentheses indicate the number of occurrences of the specific term. (For algorithmic details, please see [13].)

B. Concept Space Generation. Although automatic indexing and object filtering identify vocabularies used in texts, the relative importance of each term for representing concepts in a document may vary. That is, some of the vocabularies used may be more important than others in conveying meanings. The vector space model in information retrieval [29] associates with each term a weight to represent its descriptive power (a measure of importance). Based on cluster analysis techniques, the vector space model

Journal Abstracts

```
Lit-type: "Journal"
Reference: "3"
Author: "Abdulkader N;Bruin JL"
Title: "Induction, detection and isolation of temperature-sensitive
lethal and/or sterile mutants in nematodes. 1. The free-living
nematode Caenorhabditis elegans"
Date: "1978"
Journal: "Rev. Nematol"
Abstract: "Applying a series of techniques intended to induce, detect
and isolate lethal and/or sterile temperature-sensitive mutants,
specific to the self-fertilizing hermaphrodite nematode C. elegans,
Bergerac strain (Abdulkader et Bruin, 1976), 25 such mutants were
found. Optimal conditions for the application of mutagenic treatment
and the detection of such mutations are discussed."
Source: "Rev. Nematol 1978 1(1): 27-38"
```

FIG. 25.1. A sample journal abstract used in concept space generation.

REFERENCE: "3"
DATE: "1978"
AUTHOR:
"ABDULKADER, N."
"BRUN, J. L."
TITLE:
"TEMPERATURE-SENSITIVE LETHAL" (1)
"TEMPERATURE-SENSITIVE" (1)
"MUTANT" (1)
"LETHAL" (1)
"ISOLATION" (1)
"STERILE MUTANT" (1)
"STERILE" (1)
"NEMATODE CAENORHABDITIS ELEGAN" (1)
"NEMATODE CAENORHABDITIS" (1)
"NEMATODE" (1)
"INDUCTION" (1)
"FREE-LIVING NEMATODE CAENORHABDITIS" (1)
"FREE-LIVING NEMATODE" (1)
"FREE-LIVING" (1)
"ELEGAN" (1)
"DETECTION" (1)
"CAENORHABDITIS ELEGAN" (1)
"CAENORHABDITIS" (1)
ABSTRACT:
"MUTANT" (2)
"TEMPERATURE-SENSITIVE MUTANT" (1)
"TEMPERATURE-SENSITIVE" (1)
"MUTATION" (1)
"LETHAL" (1)
"HERMAPHRODITE" (1)
"TREATMENT" (1)
"TECHNIQUE INTEND" (1)
"TECHNIQUE" (1)
"STRAIN" (1)
"STERILE TEMPERATURE-SENSITIVE MUTANT" (1)
"STERILE TEMPERATURE-SENSITIVE" (1)
"STERILE" (1)
"SERIES" (1)
"SELF-FERTILIZING HERMAPHRODITE NEMATODE" (1)
"SELF-FERTILIZING HERMAPHRODITE" (1)
"SELF-FERTILIZING" (1)
"OPTIMAL CONDITION" (1)
"OPTIMAL" (1)
"NEMATODE C. ELEGAN" (1)
"NEMATODE C." (1)
"NEMATODE" (1)
"MUTAGENIC TREATMENT" (1)
"MUTAGENIC" (1)
"ISOLATE LETHAL" (1)
"ISOLATE" (1)
"INTEND" (1)
"INDUCE" (1)
"HERMAPHRODITE NEMATODE C." (1)
"HERMAPHRODITE NEMATODE" (1)
"FOUND" (1)
"ELEGAN" (1)
"DISCUSS" (1)
"DETECTION" (1)
"DETECT" (1)
"CONDITION" (1)
"C. ELEGAN" (1)
"BRUN" (1)
"BERGERAC STRAIN" (1)
"BERGERAC" (1)
"APPLY" (1)
"APPLICATE" (1)
"ABDULKADER ET BRUN" (1)
"ABDULKADER ET" (1)
"ABDULKADER" (1)

FIG. 25.2. Indexed terms generated for a sample journal abstract.

could be extended for concept space generation, where the main objective is to convert raw data (i.e., terms and weights) into a matrix of "similarity" measures between any pair of terms [17, 27]. The similarity measure computation is mainly based on the probabilities of terms co-occurring in the texts.

After terms were identified in each document in the WCS project, we first computed the term frequency and the document frequency for each term in a document. Term frequency, tf_{ij}, represents the number of occurrences of Term j in Document i. Document frequency, df_j, represents the number of documents in a collection of n documents in which Term j occurs.

We then computed the combined weight of Term j in Document i, d_{ij}, based on the product of *term frequency* and *inverse document frequency* as follows:

$$d_{ij} = tf_{ij} \times \log(\frac{N}{df_j} \times w_j)$$

where N represents the total number of documents in WCS and w_j represents the number of words in Descriptor j. Multiple-word terms were assigned heavier weights than single-word terms because multiple-word terms usually conveyed more precise semantic meaning than single-word terms.

We then performed term co-occurrence analysis based on the asymmetric "Cluster Function" developed by Chen and Lynch [9].

$$W_{jk} = \frac{\sum_{i=1}^{n} d_{ijk}}{\sum_{i=1}^{n} d_{ij}} \times \textit{Weighting Factor}(k)$$

W_{jk} indicates the similarity weights from Term j to Term k. d_{ij} was calculated based on the equation in the previous step. d_{ijk} represents the combined weight of both Descriptors j and k in Document i. d_{ijk} is defined similarly as follows:

$$d_{ijk} = tf_{ijk} \times \log(\frac{N}{df_{jk}} \times w_j)$$

where tf_{ijk} represents the number of occurrences of both Term j and Term k in Document i (the smaller number of occurrences between the terms was chosen). df_{jk} represents the number of documents (in a collection of N documents) in which Terms j and k occur together. w_j represents the number of words of Descriptor j.

In order to *penalize* general terms (terms that appeared in many places) in the co-occurrence analysis, we developed the following weighting scheme which is similar to the *inverse document frequency* function:

$$Weighting\ Factor(k) = \frac{\log \frac{N}{df_k}}{\log N}$$

Terms with a higher df_k value (more general terms) had a smaller weighting factor value, which caused the co-occurrence probability to become smaller. In effect, general terms were *pushed* down in the co-occurrence table (terms in the co-occurrence table were presented in reverse probabilistic order, with more relevant terms appearing first). Sample results from the cluster analysis procedure are shown in Fig. 25.3.

C. Intersecting and Traversing Multiple Concept Spaces. A fundamental problem in information retrieval is to link the vocabularies used by a searcher (those he or she considers most comfortable and natural to use to

1. WARD, S. : SPERM: 0.213660
2. WARD, S. : SPERMATOZOA: 0.185520
3. WARD, S. : MSP: 0.146670
4. WARD, S. : SPERMATOGENESIS: 0.142000
5. WARD, S. : PSEUDOPOD: 0.135020
6. WARD, S. : SPERMIOGENESIS: 0.131230

⋮

1. SCHATZ, B. : WORM COMMUNITY SYSTEM: 0.679110
2. SCHATZ, B. : WORM COMMUNITY: 0.679110
3. SCHATZ, B. : COMMUNITY SYSTEM: 0.679110
4. SCHATZ, B. : POWELL, K.: 0.679070
5. SCHATZ, B. : PETERSON, L.: 0.679070
6. SCHATZ, B. : SOFTWARE: 0.652560

⋮

1. CED-9 : CED-4: 0.301500
2. CED-9 : CED-3: 0.289330
3. CED-9 : CELL DEATH: 0.275170
4. CED-9 : CED-9(LF): 0.262330
5. CED-9 : DEATH: 0.244440
6. CED-9 : PROGRAMMED CELL: 0.234000

⋮

1. CELL DEATH : DEATH: 0.434510
2. CELL DEATH : PROGRAMMED CELL DEATH: 0.368510
3. CELL DEATH : CED-3: 0.262800
4. CELL DEATH : PROGRAMMED: 0.213700
5. CELL DEATH : CED-4: 0.206270
6. CELL DEATH : PROGRAMMED CELL: 0.201770

⋮

FIG. 25.3. Sample results from worm concept space generation.

express his or her own information need) with the vocabularies used by a system (i.e., indexes of the underlying database). By creating a target concept space using the texts of the underlying database (e.g., a *C. elegans* worm database) and another concept space from texts representative of the searcher's reference discipline (e.g., human genome, fly genome) and intersecting and traversing the two concept spaces algorithmically, we believe we will be able to create a knowledgeable online search aide that is capable of bridging vocabulary differences between a searcher and a target database, thereby helping alleviate the information overload problem in a large information space. In previous research we have tested a serial branch-and-bound search algorithm and a parallel Hopfield-like neural network algorithm for multiple-thesauri consultation [10, 11]. The Hopfield algorithm, in particular, has been shown to be suitable for concept-based information retrieval.

The Hopfield net [23] was initially introduced as a neural network that can be used as a content-addressable memory. Knowledge and information can be stored in single-layered, interconnected neurons (nodes) and weighted synapses (links) and can be retrieved based on the Hopfield network's *parallel relaxation* and *convergence* methods. The Hopfield net has been used successfully in such applications as image classification, character recognition, and robotics [24, 31]. Each term in the network-like thesaurus can be treated as a neuron and the asymmetric weight between any two terms is taken as the unidirectional, weighted connection between neurons. Using user-supplied terms as input patterns, the Hopfield algorithm activates their neighbors (i.e., strongly associated terms), combines weights from all associated neighbors (by adding collective association strengths), and repeats this process until convergence. During the process, the algorithm causes a *damping effect*, in which terms farther away from the initial terms receive gradually decreasing activation weights and activation eventually "dies out." This phenomenon is consistent with the human memory *spreading activation* process.

The Hopfield net algorithm relies on an activation and iteration process, where

$$\mu_j(t+1) = f_s[\sum_{i=0}^{n-1} W_{ij}\mu_i(t)],\ 0 \le j \le n-1$$

$\mu_j(t+1)$ is the activation value of neuron (Term) j at iteration $t+1$, W_{ij} is the co-occurrence weight from neuron i to neuron j, and f_s is the continuous SIGMOID transformation function, which normalizes any given value to a value between 0 and 1 [15, 24]. This formula shows the *parallel relaxation* property of the Hopfield net. (Readers are referred to [11] for algorithmic detail.)

In conclusion, by acquiring vocabularies from texts directly (instead of from human experts), either in incremental mode or by periodic batch processing, and by creating concept spaces for the target databases and other related subject disciplines (i.e., preprocessing selected source textual documents), it is possible for a system to help searchers articulate their needs and to retrieve semantically (conceptually) relevant information.

3. RESULTS FROM PREVIOUS RESEARCH

We have tested the proposed techniques in several domains, most recently in the context of the Worm Community System.

• *Russian computing:* In [9, 10], we generated a Russian computing concept space based on an asymmetric similarity function we had developed. Using the indexes extracted from about 40,000 documents (200 MBs) and several weeks of CPU time on a VAX VMS minicomputer, we were able to generate a domain-specific Russian computing thesaurus that contained about 20,000 concepts (countries, institutions, researchers' names, and subject areas) and 280,000 weighted relationships.

We performed a memory-association experiment, comparing the (concept) recall and precision levels of the concept space and those of four East-bloc computing experts in associating concepts (for 50 randomly generated Russian computing terms). *Concept recall* is defined as the proportion of the relevant concepts which are retrieved and *concept precision* is defined as the proportion of the retrieved concepts which are judged relevant. The concept space outperformed all four human subjects in concept recall. Using the concept space as concept articulation aids, human subjects' concept recall performance improved significantly. Their concept precision performance became worse, however.

• *Electronic meeting systems:* In [6, 8], we tested selected algorithms in an electronic meeting environment where electronic brainstorming (EBS) comments caused information overload and (meeting) idea convergence problems. By extracting concepts in individual EBS comments, linking similar vocabularies together, and clustering related concepts, we were able to help meeting participants generate a consensus list of important topics from a large number of diverse EBS comments.

In an experiment involving four human meeting facilitators, we found that our system performed at the same level as two facilitators in both concept recall and concept precision. Our system, which ran on a 486 PC (MS Window), accomplished the concept categorization task in significantly less time (system vs. facilitators = 4 minutes vs. 50 minutes) and was able to trace the comments which supported the concluded topics.

• *Worm concept space generation:* In a recent NSF-funded project, we built a (*C. elegans*) worm concept space using the literature stored in the Worm

Community System (WCS) [13]. It took about 4 hours of CPU time on a DEC Alpha 3000/600 workstation to analyze 5,000 worm abstracts and the resulting worm thesaurus contained 845 gene names, 2,095 researchers' names, and 4,691 subject descriptors.

We tested the worm thesaurus in an experiment with six worm biologists of varying degrees of expertise and background. The biologists were asked to suggest terms relevant to a list of 16 previously selected worm-specific concepts (one term at a time). The worm thesaurus-suggested terms were then compared with those generated by the biologists. The experiment showed that the worm thesaurus was able to help suggest more terms for retrieval (on an average, from 6.2 terms to 8.5 terms). The worm thesaurus was significantly better than the subjects in concept recall, but inferior to the subjects in concept precision. We also found that the worm thesaurus was an excellent memory-jogging tool and that it supported learning and serendipity browsing.

• *Fly concept space generation:* As an extension of the worm thesaurus project and in an attempt to examine the vocabulary problem across different biology domains, we recently generated a fly thesaurus using 7,000 abstracts extracted from Medline and Biosis and literature from FlyBase, a database currently in use by molecular biologists in the *Drosophila melanogaster*-related research community [12]. The resulting fly thesaurus included about 18,000 terms (researchers' names, gene names, function names, and subject descriptors) and their weighted relationships.

In a similar fly thesaurus evaluation experiment (using 10 pre-selected fly-specific concepts) involving six fly researchers at the University of Arizona, we confirmed the findings of the worm experiment. The fly thesaurus was found to be a useful tool to suggest relevant concepts, improve concept recall, and to help articulate searchers' queries. However, fly subjects were better in concept precision than the fly concept space.

• *Fly-worm concept space traversal:* Our structural comparison of the fly and worm thesauri revealed a significant overlap of common vocabularies across the two domains. However, each thesaurus maintains its unique organism-specific functions, structures, proteins, and so on. Table 25.1 shows the numbers of terms in the worm and fly thesauri. These include the number of author terms, number of gene terms, number of subject terms, number of function terms (fly thesaurus only), and number of method terms (worm thesaurus only). The last three columns report the number of terms appearing in both thesauri and the respective proportion of each thesaurus that overlapping terms represent. It is not surprising that no overlap exists in gene names: the naming conventions for the two domains are extremely different. Furthermore, it is noteworthy that 252 author names appear in both thesauri. The format for author names is last name and first initial,

TABLE 25.1
Structural Comparison of the Fly and Worm Thesauri

	Worm Terms	*Fly Terms*	*Overlapping Terms*	*Percentage of Worm Terms*	*Percentage of Fly Terms*
Authors	2095	7221	252	12.0	3.4
Genes	845	4875	0	—	—
Subjects	4691	5821	1503	32.0	25.8
Functions	n/a	182	n/a	—	—
Methods	12	n/a	n/a	—	—
Total	7657	18101	2203	28.8	12.2

which could present some ambiguity. Still it is likely that some authors have published in both domains. The extent of overlap for the subject descriptors was 25.8% for the fly thesaurus and 32% for the worm thesaurus. With this much overlap, the likelihood of finding intermediate terms for concept space traversal is promising.

We believe that by intersecting concepts derived from the two domain-specific concept spaces and by providing AI search methods we will be able to bridge the vocabulary differences between a searcher's (e.g., a fly biologist's) domain and the target database's (e.g., the worm database's) subject area. We are in the process of testing and fine-tuning several search algorithms [11] and we also plan to expand our subject coverage to other model organisms including e. coli, yeast, rat, and human in the near future.

We have incorporated a worm thesaurus and a fly thesaurus into the WCS Release 2. An X-Windows thesaurus-browsing interface which can accept multiple terms, identify other relevant terms by means of the thesaurus, combine the weights associated with terms, and rank terms in order, has been developed, as shown in Fig. 25.4 (the thesaurus component is shown on the right side of the screen). Searchers can use the Thesaurus Window to elicit suggested terms from the thesaurus.

In a recent *C. elegans* meeting held at the University of Wisconsin at Madison (with about 650 participants), the WCS and the worm thesaurus were used extensively and perceived favorably by the worm biologists during the 3-day live demo sessions. They were able to consult the worm thesaurus whenever they wished to explore other topics relevant to their initial queries. Many graduate students and postdoctoral researchers, in particular, expressed great interest in the WCS and the thesaurus, especially for their potential value to help them quickly enter a new and dynamic research

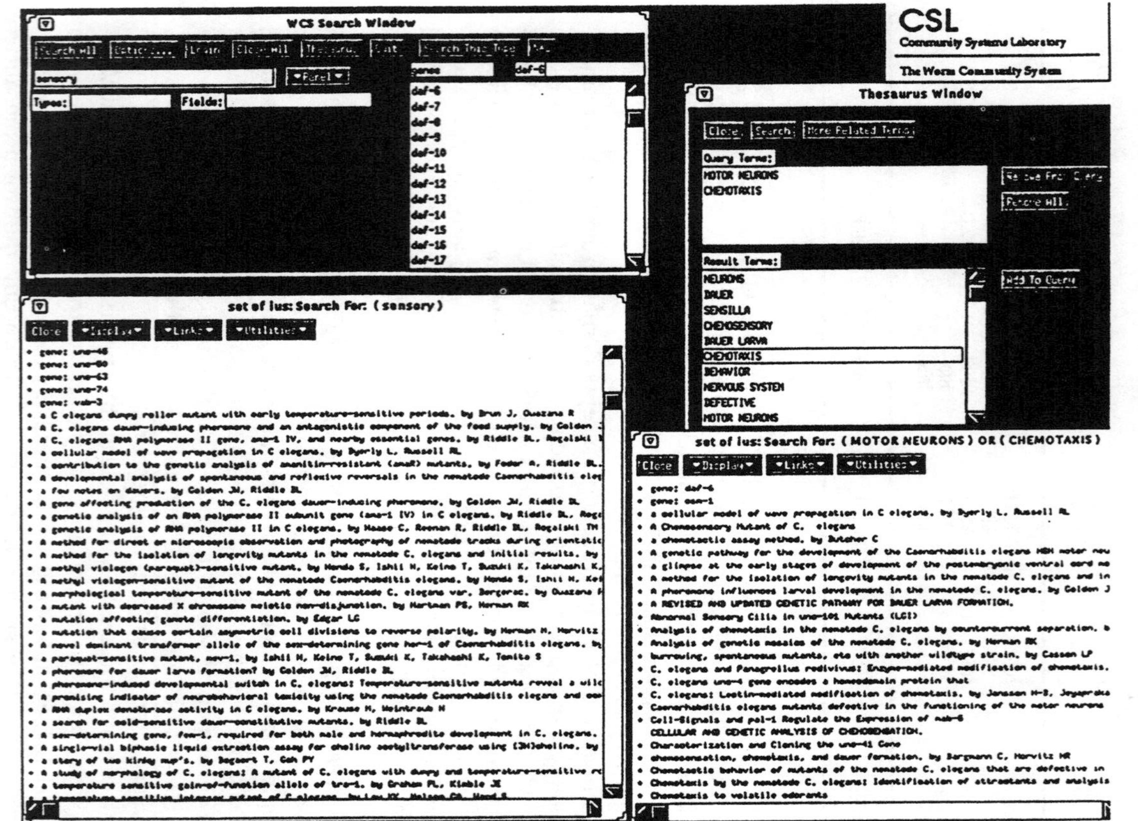

FIG. 25.4. Concept thesaurus in Worm Community System.

area. Many viewed the WCS as a comprehensive, tightly integrated digital library with an online reference librarian (i.e., the thesaurus and its browsing interface).

4. SEMANTIC RETRIEVAL ON INTERNET/WWW SERVERS AND DIGITAL LIBRARIES

The concept space approach to supporting semantic retrieval has recently been extended from the National Collaboratory domain to Internet and Digital Library applications. We highlight the status of our research and future directions next.

4.1. Building a WWW Server with Semantic Retrieval Capability

The WCS was created using proprietary GUI software and suffers from its poor portability. Recently, we have migrated part of the WCS design to a more portable and popular interface, the NCSA (National Center for Supercomputing Applications) Mosaic/WWW internet resource discovery software [30]. The prototype, called *BioQuest*, exhibits full-text searching capability through WAIS indexing and searching and Mosaic's form-capable browser. In addition, it provides semantic retrieval capability through a thesaurus component and a thesaurus browsing interface. *BioQuest* consists of about 4,000 worm documents (e.g., Worm Breeders' Gazette, conference proceedings abstracts, etc.), a 7,000-term worm thesaurus, and a 18,000-term fly thesaurus. Readers are encouraged to access the *BioQuest* URL at the following address: http://bpaosf.ba.arizona.edu:8000/cgi-bin/BioQuest

The following sequence of screendumps illustrates the semantic retrieval process supported by the thesaurus component. In a pilot study involving a junior worm biologist, the subject expressed an interest in searching "worm genes which determine sex, especially those that cause feminization." The user first entered "sex determination" in the *BioQuest* main search screen, as shown in Fig. 25.5. The option she chose was to search "Worm Document" (as displayed in the middle of Fig. 25.5). The system searched the worm database, which was indexed using the WAIS inverted indexing scheme, and displayed 40 top-ranked documents. Each document was assigned a document id (e.g., 3838.txt and the scoring scheme was based on WAIS, with 1000 being the highest document score). For example, Document 15 ("4635.txt") is shown in Fig. 25.6.

After browsing these retrieved documents, the user did not find any abstracts of relevance to feminization and decided to invoke the system's thesaurus component, as shown in the middle of Fig. 25.7 (search "Worm-Fly

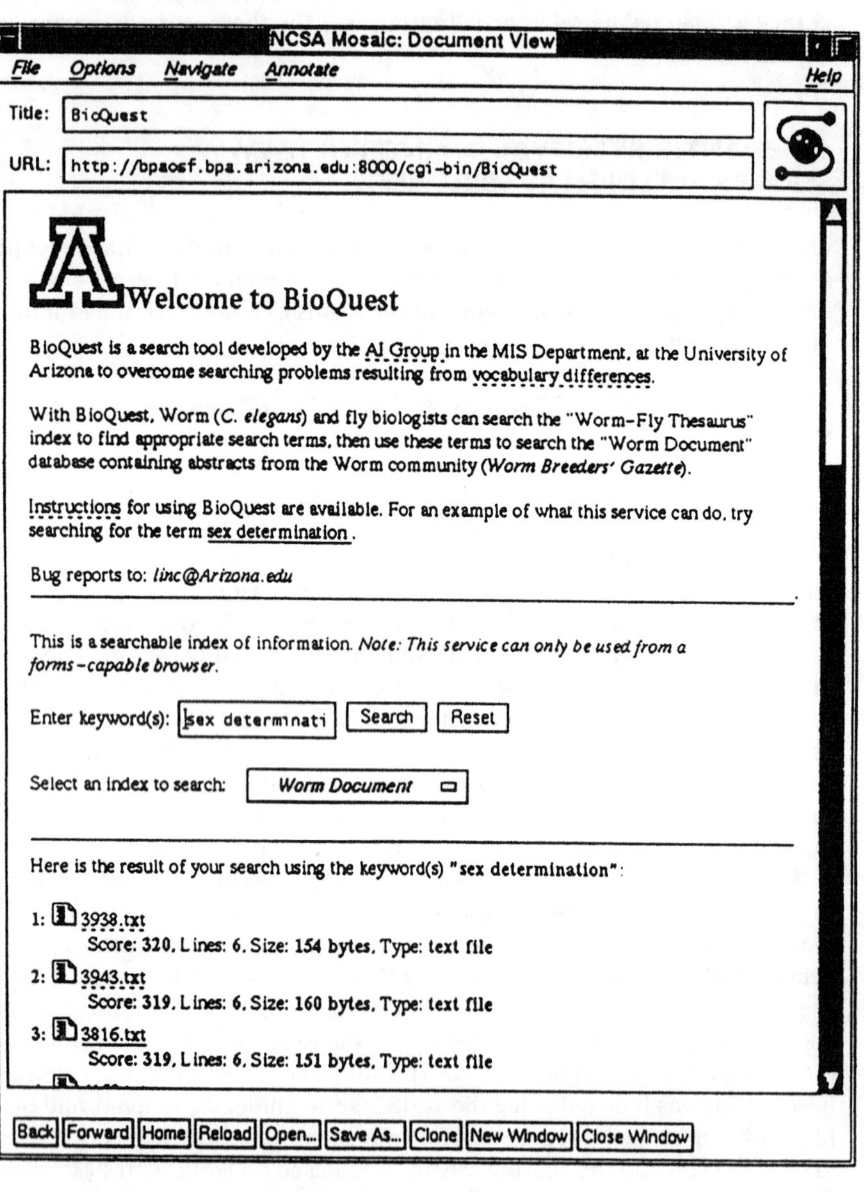

FIG. 25.5. System response when "sex determination" entered in the BioQuest main search screen.

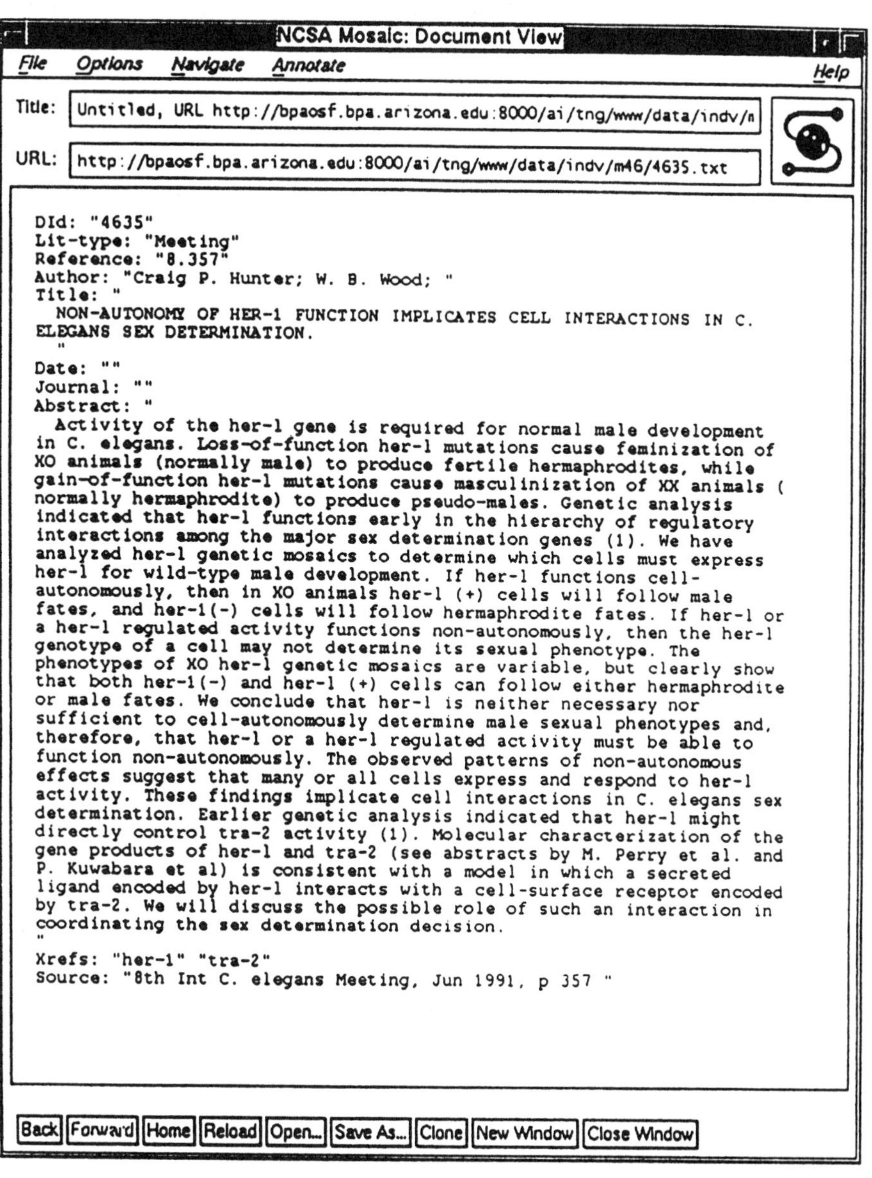

NCSA Mosaic: Document View

File Options Navigate Annotate Help

Title: Untitled, URL http://bpaosf.bpa.arizona.edu:8000/ai/tng/www/data/indv/n

URL: http://bpaosf.bpa.arizona.edu:8000/ai/tng/www/data/indv/m46/4635.txt

DId: "4635"
Lit-type: "Meeting"
Reference: "8.357"
Author: "Craig P. Hunter; W. B. Wood; "
Title: "
NON-AUTONOMY OF HER-1 FUNCTION IMPLICATES CELL INTERACTIONS IN C. ELEGANS SEX DETERMINATION.
"
Date: ""
Journal: ""
Abstract: "
Activity of the her-1 gene is required for normal male development in C. elegans. Loss-of-function her-1 mutations cause feminization of XO animals (normally male) to produce fertile hermaphrodites, while gain-of-function her-1 mutations cause masculinization of XX animals (normally hermaphrodite) to produce pseudo-males. Genetic analysis indicated that her-1 functions early in the hierarchy of regulatory interactions among the major sex determination genes (1). We have analyzed her-1 genetic mosaics to determine which cells must express her-1 for wild-type male development. If her-1 functions cell-autonomously, then in XO animals her-1 (+) cells will follow male fates, and her-1(-) cells will follow hermaphrodite fates. If her-1 or a her-1 regulated activity functions non-autonomously, then the her-1 genotype of a cell may not determine its sexual phenotype. The phenotypes of XO her-1 genetic mosaics are variable, but clearly show that both her-1(-) and her-1 (+) cells can follow either hermaphrodite or male fates. We conclude that her-1 is neither necessary nor sufficient to cell-autonomously determine male sexual phenotypes and, therefore, that her-1 or a her-1 regulated activity must be able to function non-autonomously. The observed patterns of non-autonomous effects suggest that many or all cells express and respond to her-1 activity. These findings implicate cell interactions in C. elegans sex determination. Earlier genetic analysis indicated that her-1 might directly control tra-2 activity (1). Molecular characterization of the gene products of her-1 and tra-2 (see abstracts by M. Perry et al. and P. Kuwabara et al) is consistent with a model in which a secreted ligand encoded by her-1 interacts with a cell-surface receptor encoded by tra-2. We will discuss the possible role of such an interaction in coordinating the sex determination decision.
"
Xrefs: "her-1" "tra-2"
Source: "8th Int C. elegans Meeting, Jun 1991, p 357 "

FIG. 25.6. Example of document found as a result of using "sex determination" entry.

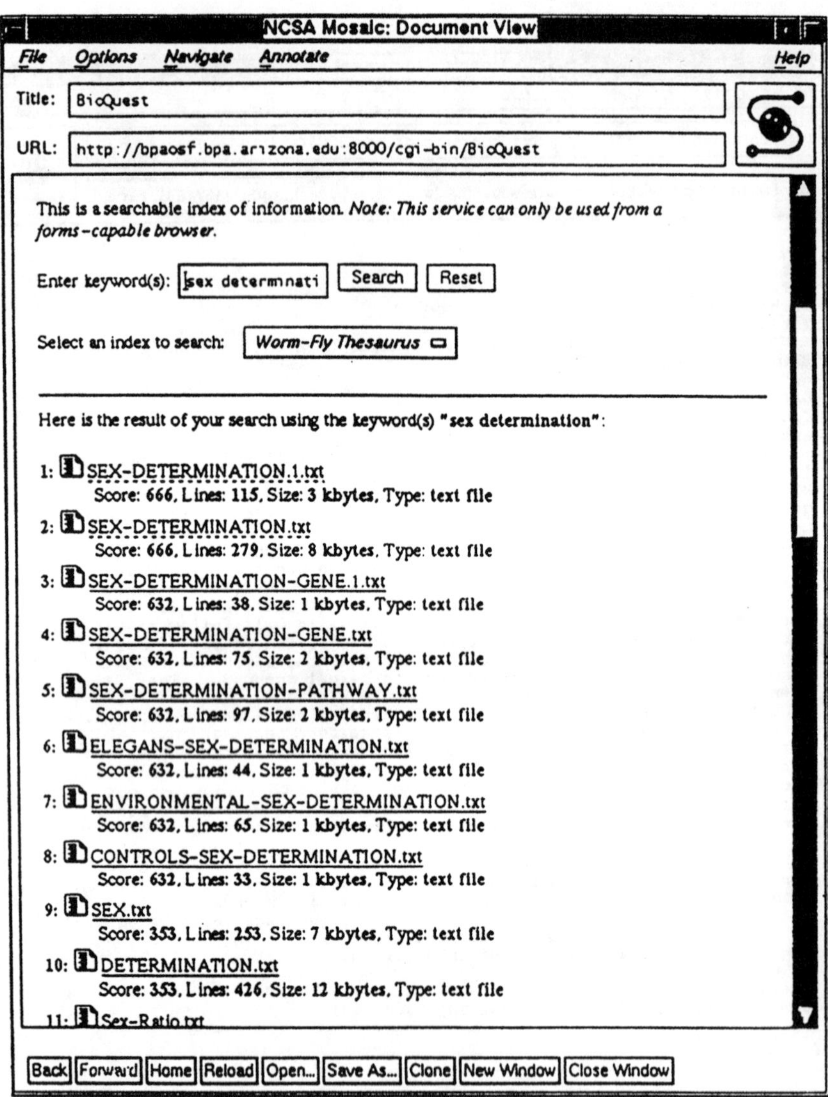

FIG. 25.7. Worm thesaurus invoked with user using "sex determination" entry.

Thesaurus"). Several thesaurus terms related to "sex determination" were retrieved, including "SEX-DETERMINATION-GENE." In WAIS indexing, hyphenation of a term was treated differently, for example, "sex-determination gene" was indexed as "SEX-DETERMINATION-GENE.1.txt" and "sex determination gene" (without hyphen) was indexed as "SEX-DETERMINATION. GENE.txt." Clicking on "SEX-DETERMINATION-GENE" produced specific terms (gene names) such as "FEM-1," "FEM-2," and "FEM-3" (genes which cause *fem*inization) as shown in Fig. 25.8. All related terms were ranked in reverse weighted order and the sources of these terms were indicated by "f" for fly thesaurus or "w" for worm thesaurus. For example, the thesaurus indicated that "FEM-1," "FEM-2," and "FEM-3" are worm terms only. By using the newly obtained terms, "FEM-1," "FEM-2," and "FEM-3," to search the worm database, *BioQuest* retrieved many more documents which were relevant specifically to genes that cause feminization, as shown in Fig. 25.9. The user browsed a few documents and was satisfied with the search results.

4.2. Status and Research Plan for the Illinois Digital Library Project

The Illinois Digital Library Initiative (DLI) project entitled: "Building the Interspace: Digital Library Infrastructure for a University Engineering Community," is one of six projects funded recently by NSF/ARPA/NASA [26]. The goal of the project is to evolve the Internet into the *Interspace*, in particular by bringing professional and semantic search and display of structured documents to the Net. To accomplish this, we are constructing a large-scale digital library testbed of SGML journal articles in the engineering domain while concurrently performing the underlying research to provide effective interaction across networks with such a library [30].

The semantic retrieval component of the Illinois project aims to create graphs of domain-specific concepts (terms) and their weighted co-occurrence relationships for all major engineering domains. Merging these concept spaces and providing traversal paths across different concept spaces could potentially help alleviate the *vocabulary (difference) problem* evident in large-scale information retrieval.

In order to address the scalability issue related to large-scale information retrieval and analysis for the current Illinois DLI project, we recently proceeded to experiment with using the concept space approach on several parallel supercomputers. Our initial test collection was 2+ GBs of computer science and electrical engineering abstracts extracted from the INSPEC database and the concept space approach called for extensive textual and statistical analysis based on *automatic indexing* and *co-occurrence analysis* algorithms. Initial testing results using a 512-node (Thinking Machine) CM-5 and a 16-processor SGI Power Challenge supercomputer were promising. The user-friendly shared-memory microprocessor-based SGI Power Challenge (a cluster of SGI workstations), in particular, is appropriate for the memory-intense digital library analysis and was later selected to generate a large-scale computer engineering concept space of about 270,000 terms and 4,000,000+ links using 24.5 hours of CPU time. Preliminary results have been posted at the *CSQuest* WWW server at: http://ai.bpa.arizona.edu/html/csquest/

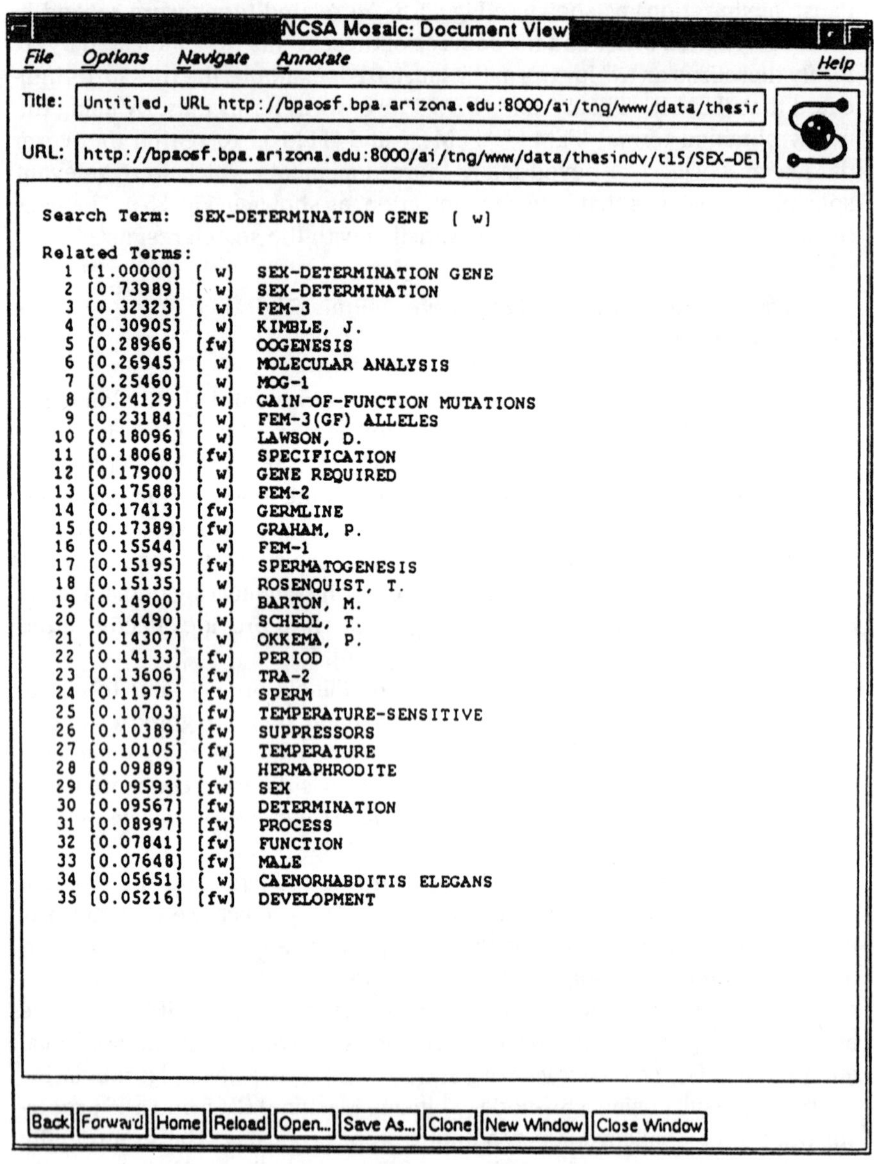

FIG. 25.8. Worm-thesaurus suggested terms which are relevant to "sex determination gene."

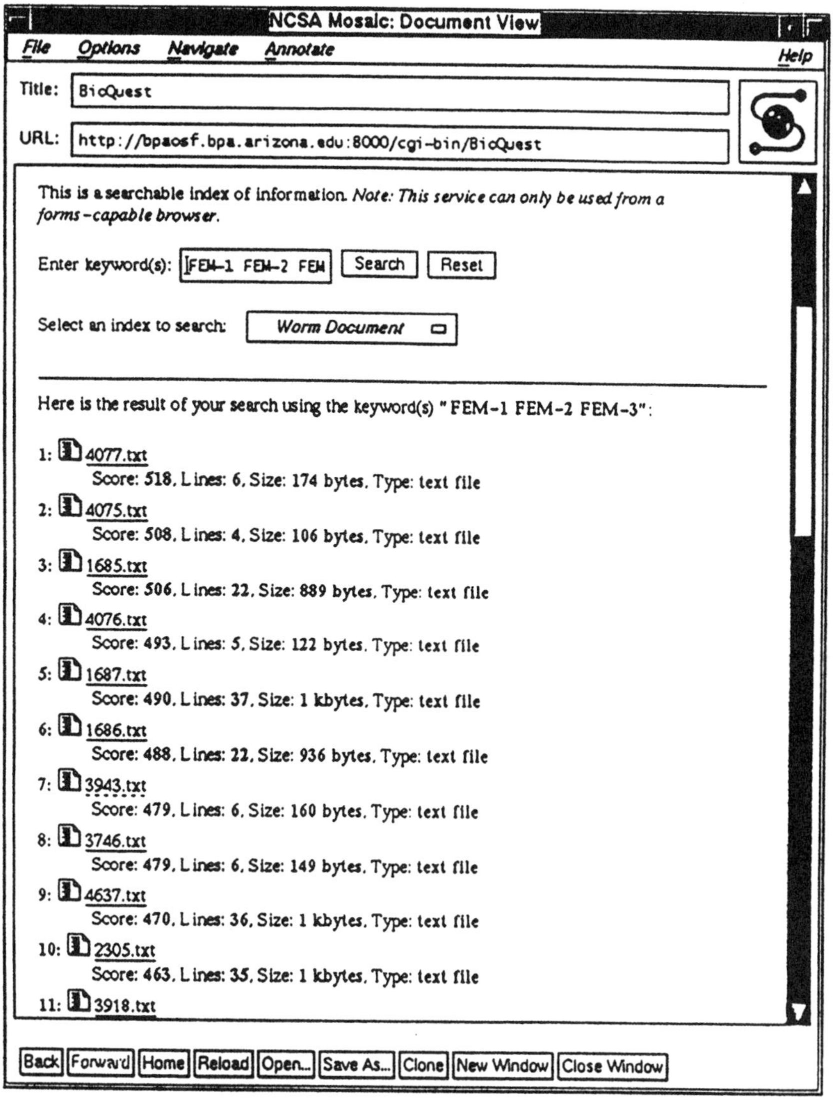

FIG. 25.9. Documents identified as relevant to FEM-1, FEM-2, and FEM-3.

Our recent system evaluation of term association involving 12 knowledgeable subjects revealed that the automatically created computer engineering concept space generated significantly higher *concept recall* than the human-generated INSPEC thesaurus (concept space : INSPEC thesaurus = 69.08% : 17.71%). However, the INSPEC thesaurus was more precise than the automatic concept space (concept space : INSPEC thesaurus = 59.50% : 68.22%).

Using the INSPEC thesaurus as the benchmark for comparison, we believe the computer engineering concept space has demonstrated its robustness and potential usefulness for suggesting relevant terms for search. However, we are convinced that multiple interfaces and multiple vocabulary search aids are necessary for effective concept-based search across multiple large-scale repositories and domains.

Our current work mainly involves: (1) creating concept spaces for other major engineering domains (in roughly the following order: chemical, materials, systems and industrial manufacturing, mechanical, aerospace, automatic, civil, agricultural and biosystems, geological and mining, marine, and nuclear and energy) using the 48-processor SGI Power Challenge Array, 16-processor Cray CS6400, and 64-processor Convex Exemplar (all accounts already have been set up with NCSA); and (2) developing robust graph matching and traversal algorithms for cross-domain, concept-based retrieval.

Future work also will include generating individualized concept spaces for assisting in user-specific concept-based information retrieval and developing genetic algorithm-based search agents for users, based on the Java language. Results from our research will be incorporated into an operational SGML search interface for the Illinois DLI engineering testbed. We are also investigating methods by which this semantic retrieval capability might be extended and scaled up to large distributed repositories (the Net or the NII).

5. ACKNOWLEDGMENTS

This research was mainly supported by the following grants:

- NSF/ARPA/NASA Digital Library Initiative, IRI-9411318, 1994–1998 (B. Schatz, H. Chen, et. al, “Building the Interspace: Digital Library Infrastructure for a University Engineering Community”),
- NSF CISE, IRI-9525790, 1995–1998 (H. Chen, “Concept-based Categorization and Search on Internet: A Machine Learning, Parallel Computing Approach”),
- NSF CISE Research Initiation Award, IRI-9211418, 1992–1994 (H. Chen, “Building a Concept Space for an Electronic Community System”),
- NSF CISE Special Initiative on Coordination Theory and Collaboration Technology, IRI-9015407, 1990–1993 (B. Schatz, “Building a National Collaboratory Testbed”),
- AT&T Foundation Special Purpose Grants in Science and Engineering, 1994–1995 (H. Chen), and
- National Center for Supercomputing Applications (NCSA), High-performance Computing Resources Grants, IRI950003N, 1994–1996 (H. Chen).

Most of these projects were made possible through the support and vision of late Dr. Larry Rosenberg of the National Science Foundation.

REFERENCES

[1] M. J. Bates. Subject access in online catalogs: a design model. *Journal of the American Society for Information Science*, 37(6):357–376, November 1986.

[2] T. Berners-Lee, R. Cailliau, A. Luotonen, H. F. Nielsen, and A. Secret. The World-Wide Web. *Communications of the ACM*, 37(8):76–82, August 1994.

[3] D. C. Blair and M. E. Maron. An evaluation of retrieval effectiveness for a full-text document-retrieval system. *Communications of the ACM*, 28(3):289–299, 1985.

[4] C. M. Bowman, P. B. Danzig, U. Manber, and F. Schwartz. Scalable internet resource discovery: research problems and approaches. *Communications of the ACM*, 37(8):98–107, August 1994.

[5] E. Carmel, S. Crawford, and H. Chen. Browsing in hypertext: A cognitive study. *IEEE Transactions on Systems, Man and Cybernetics*, 22(5):865–884, September/October 1992.

[6] H. Chen. Collaborative systems: solving the vocabulary problem. *IEEE COMPUTER*, 27(5):58–66, Special Issue on Computer-Supported Cooperative Work (CSCW), May 1994.

[7] H. Chen and V. Dhar. User misconceptions of online information retrieval systems. *International Journal of Man-Machine Studies*, 32(6):673–692, June 1990.

[8] H. Chen, P. Hsu, R. Orwig, L. Hoopes, and J. F. Nunamaker. Automatic concept classification of text from electronic meetings. *Communications of the ACM*, 37(10):56–73, October 1994.

[9] H. Chen and K. J. Lynch. Automatic construction of networks of concepts characterizing document databases. *IEEE Transactions on Systems, Man and Cybernetics*, 22(5):885–902, September/October 1992.

[10] H. Chen, K. J. Lynch, K. Basu, and D. T. Ng. Generating, integrating, and activating thesauri for concept-based document retrieval. *IEEE EXPERT, Special Series on Artificial Intelligence in Text-based Information Systems*, 8(2):25–34, April 1993.

[11] H. Chen and D. T. Ng. An algorithmic approach to concept exploration in a large knowledge network (automatic thesaurus consultation): symbolic branch-and-bound vs. connectionist Hopfield net activation. *Journal of the American Society for Information Science*, 46(5):348–369, June 1995.

[12] H. Chen, B. R. Schatz, J. Martinez, and D. T. Ng. Generating a domain-specific thesaurus automatically: An experiment on FlyBase. In *Center for Management of Information, College of Business and Public Administration, University of Arizona, Working Paper, CMI-WPS 94-02*, 1994.

[13] H. Chen, B. R. Schatz, T. Yim, and D. Fye. Automatic thesaurus generation for an electronic community system. *Journal of the American Society for Information Science*, 46(3):175–193, April 1995.

[14] J. Courteau. Genome databases. *Science*, 254:201–207, October 11, 1991.

[15] J. Dalton and A. Deshmane. Artificial neural networks. *IEEE Potentials*, 10(2):33–36, April 1991.

[16] O. Etzioni and D. Weld. A softbot-based interface to the Internet. *Communications of the ACM*, 37(7):72–79, July 1994.

[17] B. Everitt. *Cluster Analysis*. Second Edition, Heinemann Educational Books, London, England, 1980.

[18] C. L. Foss. Tools for reading and browsing hypertext. *Information Processing and Management*, 25(4):407–418, 1989.

[19] E. A. Fox, R. M. Akscyn, R. K. Furuta, and J. L. Leggett. Digital libraries: introduction. *Communications of the ACM*, 38(4):22–18, April 1995.

[20] K. A. Frenkel. The human genome project and informatics. *Communications of the ACM*, 34(11):41–51, November 1991.

[21] G. W. Furnas. Statistical semantics: How can a computer use what people name things to guess what things people mean when they name things. In *Proceedings of the Human Factors in Computer Systems Conference*, pages 251–253, Gaithersburg, MD, Association for Computing Machinery, March 1982.

[22] G. W. Furnas, T. K. Landauer, L. M. Gomez, and S. T. Dumais. The vocabulary problem in human-system communication. *Communications of the ACM*, 30(11):964–971, November 1987.

[23] J. J. Hopfield. Neural network and physical systems with collective computational abilities. *Proceedings of the National Academy of Science, USA*, 79(4):2554–2558, 1982.

[24] K. Knight. Connectionist ideas and algorithms. *Communications of the ACM*, 33(11):59–74, November 1990.

[25] K. Obraczka, P. B. Danzig, and S. Li. Internet resource discovery services. *IEEE COMPUTER*, 26(9):8–24, September 1993.

[26] R. Pool. Turning an info-glut into a library. *Science*, 266:20–23, 7 October 1994.

[27] E. Rasmussen. Clustering algorithms. In *Information Retrieval: Data Structures and Algorithms*, eds., W. B. Frakes and R. Baeza-Yates, Prentice Hall, Englewood Cliffs, NJ, 1992.

[28] N. Sager. *Natural Language Information Processing: A Computer Grammar of English and Its Applications*. Addison-Wesley, Reading, MA, 1981.

[29] G. Salton. *Automatic Text Processing*. Addison-Wesley Publishing Company, Inc., Reading, MA, 1989.

[30] B. R. Schatz and J. B. Hardin. NSCA Mosaic and the World Wide Web: global hypermedia protocols for the internet. *Science*, 265:895–901, 12 August 1994.

[31] D. W. Tank and J. J. Hopfield. Collective computation in neuronlike circuits. *Scientific American*, 257(6):104–114, December 1987.

[32] W. A. Woods. An experimental parsing system for transition network grammars. In *Natural Language Processing*, pages 113–154, ed. R. Rustin, Algorithmics Press, New York, NY, 1972.

CHAPTER

26

Technology to Support Distributed Team Science: The First Phase of the Upper Atmospheric Research Collaboratory (UARC)

Gary M. Olson
Daniel E. Atkins
Robert Clauer
Terry Weymouth
Thomas A. Finholt
Atul Prakash
Craig Rasmussen
Farnam Jahanian
University of Michigan

The Upper Atmospheric Research Collaboratory (UARC) is a project to provide upper atmospheric physicists with networked computer technology to support the practice of their science. UARC is an instance of a collaboratory, the "... combination of technology, tools and infrastructure that allow scientists to work with remote facilities and each other as if they were co-located ..." (Wulf, 1989, p. 6). A National Research Council (1993) report defines a collaboratory as a "... center without walls, in which the nation's researchers can perform their research without regard to geographical location–interacting with colleagues, accessing instrumentation, sharing data and computational resources [and] accessing information in digital libraries" (p. 7). Put simply, a collaboratory is the use of computing and communication technology to carry out geographically distributed scientific activity. For more background on collaboratories, see Finholt and Olson (1997).

Collaboratories provide scientists with access to each other, with access to information bases (digital libraries), and with access to remote facilities (see Fig. 26.1). Throughout the history of UARC the focus has been on the synchronous communication for the people-to-people and people-to-facilities components of the collaboratory. There have been two broad phases to the project. From its inception in 1993 until about 1996 the space scientists who were the testbed users in this project were all users of ground-based instruments at the Sondrestrom Upper Atmospheric Research Facility in Kangerlussuaq, Greenland. We provided them with real-time access to data from these instruments as well as conferencing capabilities so they could interact with each other over the data they were observing. The collaboratory tools were all built and deployed in the NeXTStep programming environment. Around 1996 the project entered a second phase. The user technology base shifted to Java-applets accessed from a Web browser, which enabled a considerable expansion of the user population. The science shifted from a single ground-based site to include multiple data sources, both land-based and satellite, covering much of the northern hemisphere. Real-time access to model outputs was also added. The present chapter focuses on the first phase of UARC; the second phase is still in progress.

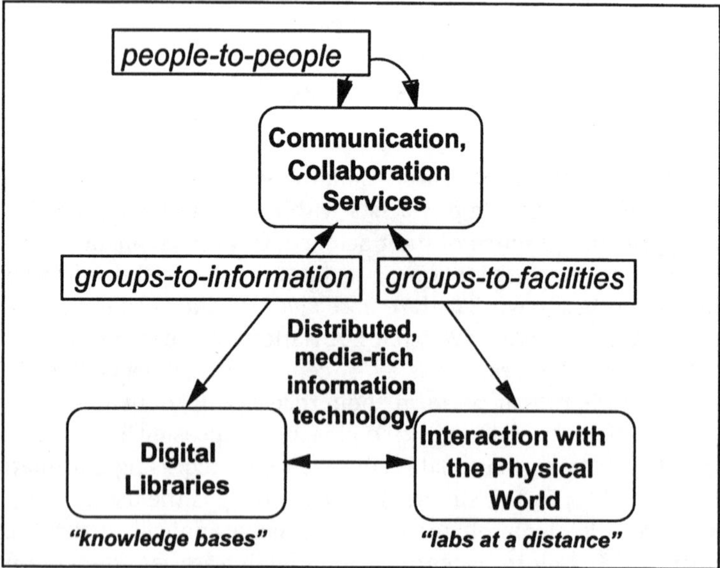

FIG. 26.1. A summary of the main relationships in the concept of a collaboratory.

PROJECT GOALS

The UARC project has a series of interrelated research goals:

Design methods: To discover systematic and detailed approaches to the design of effective team-science support systems; to verify these designs through the analysis of real use of prototypes based on user-centered, object-oriented principles.

Architectures for collaboration: To discover the supporting architecture required by a closely cooperating group of scientists with complementary expertise and goals who need to examine multiple instruments with specialized data displays; to implement this architecture to allow operations over a wide span of time zones via networks with low bandwidth and possibilities for failures; to implement an architecture that allows expansion of the numbers and types of instruments and users.

Behavioral changes in science due to new technology: To understand the effects of the introduction of collaboration technology on the patterns of scientific collaboration over the 9-year duration of this project.

Impact on upper atmospheric physics: To provide support for upper atmospheric physicists in performing timely and coordinated observations using a variety of ground based instruments; to use the UARC system to increase understanding of solar influences on the Earth's highly conducting upper atmosphere and the coupling of these influences to lower atmospheric layers.

These goals have required the tight synergy of a research team comprised of computer scientists and engineers, behavioral scientists, and upper atmospheric physicists. The project has been paced by rapid cycles of software development to support the physicists: creation of new software versions, deployment for conducting space science experiments, systematic evaluation of actual use, and subsequent modification of new versions based on users' experiences. Since the spring of 1993, the UARC testbed has gone through numerous cycles of development, approximately 5 months per cycle. UARC 5.3 was the final version of the initial round of software development in the NeXTStep software environment, whereas starting in 1996 the UARC software migrated to a series of distributed servers accessed through Java applets activated via a World Wide Web browser.

THE USERS

Upper atmospheric physicists study the interactions among the earth's upper atmosphere, the earth's magnetic field, and the solar wind. A common manifestation of this interaction in the aurora borealis, or "northern lights."

The physicists develop models based on observations from ground-based instruments, satellites, and rockets. The UARC project initially focused on a community of upper atmospheric physicists who used ground-based instruments in Greenland. The Sondrestrom Upper Atmospheric Research Facility has as its core instrument an incoherent scatter radar that is supported jointly by the National Science Foundation and the Danish Meteorological Institute. SRI International in Menlo Park, California, provides overall management for the facility. In addition, there are a number of other instruments at the site that are managed by a variety of principal investigators. Figure 26.2 shows a view of the Sondrestrom facility.

The radar is the most complex and expensive instrument at the site. It operates about 150 hours per month, and must be attended by the local staff. Its operation is usually scheduled in advance by making requests to SRI. There are many modes in which the radar operates, and some of them require extensive real-time decision-making depending on ionospheric conditions.

Other instruments vary in their complexity and need for interaction. Some, such as the imaging riometer (IRIS), run 24 hours a day, 365 days a year, and have no settings that can be varied. Others, such as optical instru-

FIG. 26.2. The observatory in Greenland. This picture highlights the radar and the buildings in which additional observational equipment is housed.

ments like the all sky camera, are used during darkness, which at Kangerlussuaq is abundant during the winter months but scarce in the summer. Some have different modes of operation or adjustable parameters. For example, various optical filters that can be set on the all sky camera.

In the past, most data collection required the physicists to be in Greenland to operate the instruments and monitor ionospheric conditions. If multiple instruments were involved, several scientists might arrange to be in Greenland at the same time. The physicists call such coordinated activity a data campaign. A campaign usually has a particular scientific focus and may involve simultaneous observations using several instruments. Campaigns are usually scheduled to take advantage of particular viewing conditions (e.g., moonless nights) or to coincide with other data collection events (e.g., a satellite passing overhead). Within a campaign period observations often take place only when relevant conditions are present. Campaigns involving the coordination of the radar with optical instruments are particularly frequent during the winter months.

In 1990 NASA installed in a 56 Kb data link to the Sondrestrom facility. This enabled access to data on local discs over the network, and opened the door to the possibility of remote interactions with the instruments.

The initial set of UARC users came from five sites: the Danish Meteorological Institute in Copenhagen, the University of Maryland, the University of Michigan, SRI International in Menlo Park, California, and Lockheed Palo Alto, also in California. During the early years several new sites were added: Cornell University, the University of Alaska, the University of New Hampshire, Phillips Laboratory, Florida Institute of Technology, and the High Altitude Observatory in Boulder, Colorado. Thus, even by the end of the early phase of UARC the user community had grown considerably.

PROJECT HISTORY

Discussions about the possibility of using the network connection to Sondrestrom to develop a collaboratory project began at the University of Michigan in 1991. In October of 1991 a workshop sponsored by the National Science Foundation provided an occasion for all of the principals to gather and discuss the feasibility of such a project. This led to the definition of the overall project goals described earlier. The participants in the workshop submitted a formal proposal for a collaboratory project to NSF, and it was funded as a cooperative agreement in September of 1992. Subcontracts were arranged for SRI, DMI, Maryland, and Lockheed.

The project was formally launched with a workshop of all key participants in late 1992. Project goals were reviewed and detailed plans were made. In addition, extensive work was done on gathering information about the practices of the physicists and developing user scenarios to be used in designing the early versions of the software.

During the early months of the project further observations were made of the upper atmospheric research community, both to develop specifications for the software and to document the practices of the community prior to the introduction of new technology. These observations included regular visits to the labs of participating scientists. In addition, an extended observation was made of a campaign team in Greenland over a 10-day period in March 1993. This was just prior to the introduction of the initial versions of the UARC software.

In parallel with early observations of the scientists, programming staff was assembled, and a prototype of the radar viewing software was developed. An early project decision was to develop software using the NeXTStep programming environment, with distributed objects written in Objective C. The rapid prototyping capability of this software development environment was an extremely important feature, as it facilitated the evolution of the software in response to how the scientists actually used it. The initial version of the UARC application allowed users to access radar data in real time, and provided a simple public chat window for communication. All messages exchanged through the chat window and all user actions were time stamped and saved in log files These data (which we continue to collect) have provided important information about whether new UARC designs meet the needs of physicists as they conduct observations.

The decision to use a homogeneous computing environment for the entire project was possible because of the small number of sites. This of course simplified interoperability. The project equipped each site with a NeXT workstation. Subsequent expansion of the project to additional sites used NeXTStep running on Intel 486 platforms. As mentioned, this phase of the project ended in 1996 when UARC software development shifted to a new architecture and a Web-based user environment. The NeXTStep version of the software was available after 1996, and a few users continued to use it.

The initial version of the software was first used in a scientific campaign in April of 1993. A senior space physicist was in Greenland, and his graduate student participated from Ann Arbor, Michigan. A member of the development group observed this campaign from Greenland. The campaign provided valuable user performance data, and extensive revisions were made in the UARC software. In June of 1993 this revised version of the software was used in another campaign with the same scientific focus, but with the same senior physicist in Ann Arbor and the same student in Greenland.

Based on the June campaign, further extensive revisions to the software were made. In addition, two new instruments, the imaging riometer and the magnetometer, were added. By the fall of 1993 campaigns using these three instruments were supported.

In December of 1993 the second annual project workshop was held. Prototype versions of new collaboration capabilities, an annotation feature and the ability to share windows, were demonstrated. Shortly after this workshop NSF held an external review of the project and approved plans for the remaining years of the project.

During 1994 the UARC software developed amidst extensive experience with users. By the annual workshop in Ann Arbor in December of 1994 the basic design of UARC 5.0 was set. UARC 5.3 was the final version of the software built using the NeXTStep environment.

On the basis of experience gained during the first 3 years of the project, the technical goal shifted to develop a more generic toolkit to support a broader range of collaboratories across multiple platforms. This toolkit was called the Collaboratory Builders Environment (CBE). The UARC software itself was rebuilt during 1995–1996 into a series of modules that capture the key functionality and interface clients that allow the UARC displays to be shown on any platform from a Web browser. This has allowed for considerable expansion of users and data sources, allowing UARC functionality to extend to other ground-based facilities, satellite data, and model outputs. Additional information about CBE is described in Lee, Prakash, Jaeger, and Wu (1996).

DESIGN METHODS

As mentioned earlier, the UARC project has been committed to a user-centered, iterative, rapid-prototyping design strategy, employing object-oriented methods. Although various textbooks on object-oriented analysis and design describe development methods (e.g., Coad & Yourdan, 1991a, 1991b; Jacobson, Christerson, Jonsson, & Overgaard, 1992), the methods are presented at a fairly abstract level, and it can be difficult to know exactly how to proceed. Therefore, we devoted considerable attention to the development of concrete design methods. These methods, described in more detail in McDaniel, Olson, and Olson (1994), used ideas from object-oriented analysis and design, business process reengineering, and human–computer interaction. A detailed set of steps were worked out, consisting of:

- collection and distillation of use cases, essentially user scenarios for how they do their work
- specification of which aspects of the work should be automated or supported, and what priority should be put on these functions in the development schedule
- design of software modules that implement these specifications

- application of interface analysis techniques from human–computer interaction
- rapid prototyping of the software
- analysis of user tests of the prototypes
- iteration through the entire sequence again as a result of user testing

This strategy has resulted in useful and usable software for our user community.

THE USER INTERFACE

Figures 26.3 and 26.4 show screen dumps of the final NeXTStep version of the UARC application. Figure 26.3 shows (clockwise from the upper left corner): the main menu, two radar data displays, the radar status window (in the center), the IRIS image window, an All Sky Camera image window, a Fabry-Perot interferometer data display, a display of three time-varying data streams

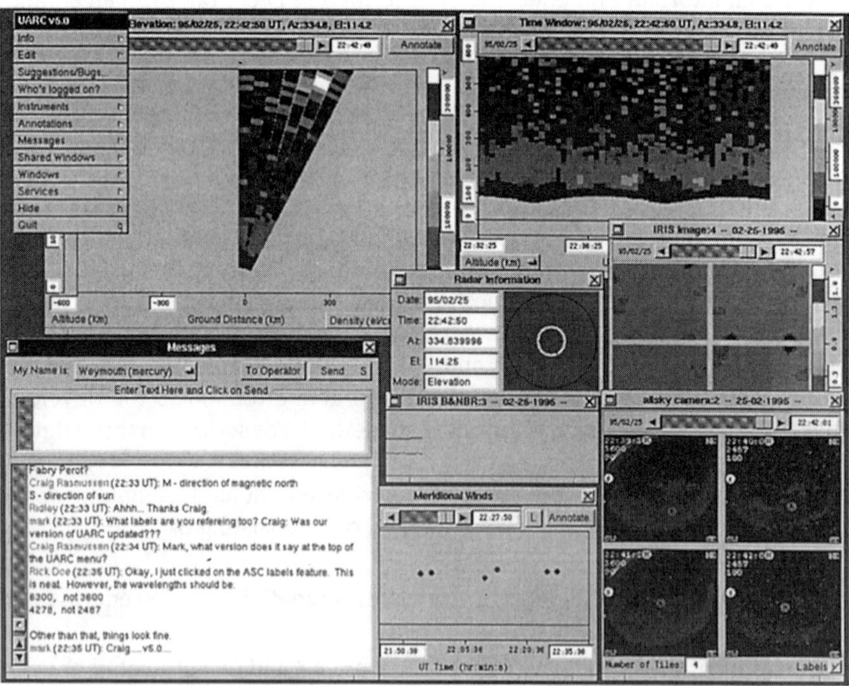

FIG. 26.3. A screen dump from UARC5.2 during an observational campaign in February of 1995. Several instrument data displays and status displays are shown.

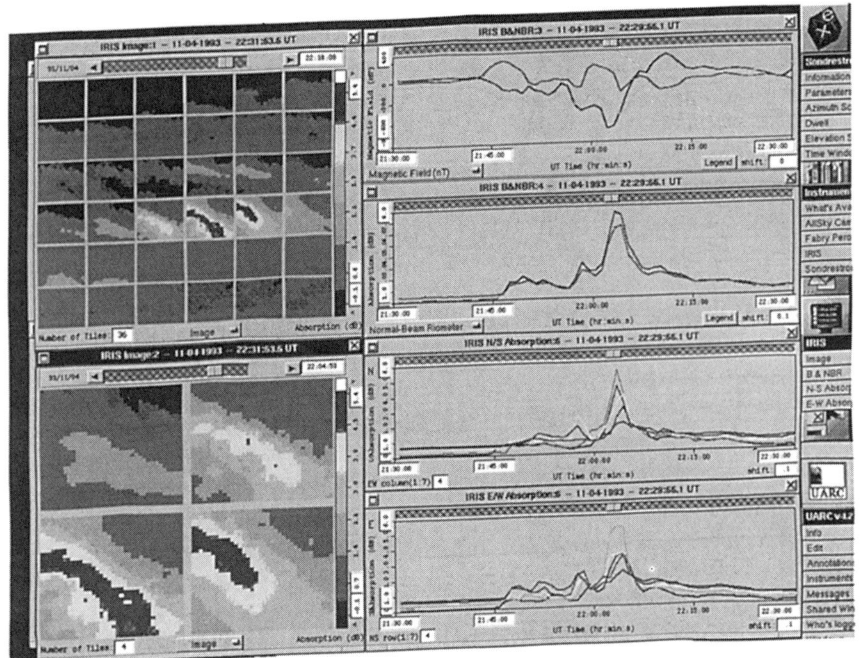

FIG. 26.4. Shows a screen dump with several displays depicting substorm activity during a campaign in early November of 1993.

from a magnetometer, and the UARC message window (the "chat window"). Figure 26.4 shows an array of IRIS displays depicting interesting features during an event which is called a magnetospheric substorm and is usually associated with very activity aurora near midnight local time.

THE UARC SYSTEM ARCHITECTURE

In this chapter we focus on the architecture of the most mature version of the NeXTStep system. This system had a number of good properties, but it did not scale well as we attempted to expand the number of users and data sources. The CBE architecture and subequent experience with the Web-based versions of UARC were intended to solve these problems.

UARC 5.3 was a system of servers and clients. To view data and collaborate the servers needed to be present. The total set of servers and clients consisted of a connected set of instruments, instrument servers, a data transport server, an annotation server, a shared window server, and a number of clients (see Fig. 26.5). The path of data from the instrument to the

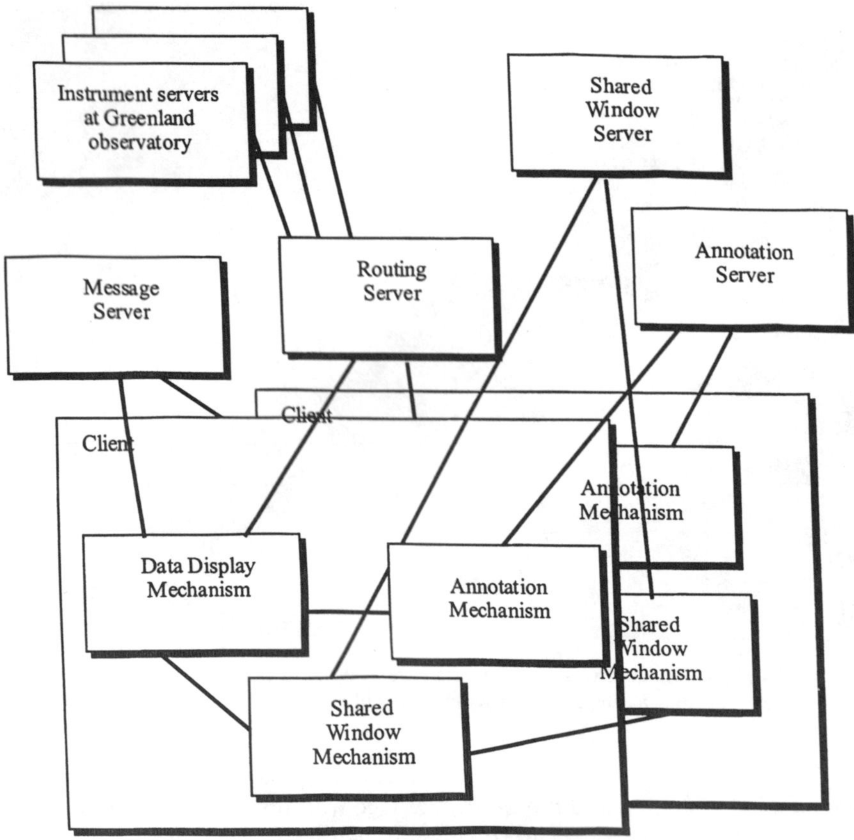

FIG. 26.5. Overview of the architecture.

client's display was as follows. Data was packaged into a "quick look" format at a computer (usually an IBM clone) attached to the instrument itself. An instrument's computer was usually connected, via Ethernet by TCP/IP sockets to a data transport machine, where data was packaged for the UARC system into an internal representation, a data "object." These data objects were then broadcast to all the clients, where they were "opened" and the data was formatted and displayed. Instrument data flowed from the instrument, to a central routing server, to the client, to the client display.

Collaboration among clients was achieved by a flow of data from client to client. In the case of the message window, data flowed through the routing server. In the case of annotations data flowed through the annotation server. And, in the case of the shared windows the request for connection flowed through a shared window server, after which the connection was between the clients. Hence, collaboration was supported by client to client communication.

The system was based on a set of interacting objects. For example, in the flow of data from instrument to view, there were objects representing: the instrument course, the data package, the client instrument connection, the instrument display manager, and the particular views of the data. The overview of the architecture shown in Fig. 26.5 depicts the major objects and the connections of data flow among them.

In actuality, there were a number of client–server relations in UARC. A breakdown of the details of the servers is as follows:

Instrument Data Server: each instrument had a task or task-set which gathered data from the instrument, packaged it for delivery on the net and supplied it to the central instrument-data server, the Routing Server.

Routing Server: The routing server maintained the list of all user applications that were using the system. It had four functions: (1) it maintained a list of clients who were currently running; a client could register or un-register, and this placed the client on the user application list or took them off; all clients were sent a copy of the user application list anytime it was updated; (2) it maintained a list of all instrument data servers currently providing data; all clients were given the current list of instruments whenever that list changed; (3) it routed any objects sent to it to all the user application clients in the user application list; and (4) it kept the current location of the annotation and the shared window servers, and sent these to clients that requested them.

Message Server: The message window took formatted rich-text messages, from individual users that were sent from the message window, time stamped them, and sent them to all current application clients. The Message Server was actually a part of the Routing Server.

Annotation Server: The annotation server took any annotation sent by a user application, and routed it to all the user application clients. The annotation server was also a specialized client of the routine server, such that any changes in the user application client list were passed on to the annotation server.

Shared Window Server: The shared window server made connections between clients who requested shared window services. The shared window server actually ran in the user application; there was one shared window server for each user in the system.

Figure 26.6 shows both the individual data rates and the combined data rate for the instrument data servers. The data rate was well below the total carrying capacity of the satellite link to Greenland (which was about 30K Bytes/sec). This data rate was a result of the design decision to send only

	Quick Look Data (bytes)	Kbytes/sec
Incoherent Scatter Radar	13K every 10 sec	1.3
AllSky Camera	5K every 20 sec (JPEG)	0.25
IRIS (Imaging Riometer)	50 every 1 sec	0.050
Fabry-Perot Interferometer	10 every 10 sec	0.001
Magnetometer	6 every 20 sec	0.0003
	Total Rate (approx.)	1.7 Kbytes/sec

FIG. 26.6. Data rates for the principle instruments in Greenland.

"summary" or "quick look" data for the high data volume instruments, the incoherent scatter radar and the all sky camera. In the case of the radar the data sent was that needed to generate a rough sketch display just like the display which was on site at the operator console in Greenland. The image from the all sky camera was compressed using JPEG, a standard for "lossy" compression. The full data from the radar and all sky camera were recorded locally in Greenland for later transfer via ftp or the shipment of backup media.

These instruments were handled by instrument data servers. In all cases, the packaging of the data was done through NextStep objects. First the data were parsed into an instrument-specific object for the graph controller object and data view object of the User Client Application (see the following). Then it was "wrapped" in a generic data object called a "stream" so that NextStep could take care of serializing the data using a read and write method for each type of object (which is defined when the object is implemented). NextStep streams could be "sent" to remote objects as arguments in distributed-object methods. In this way the implementation of communication between parts of the system was done at the object level without concern as to whether the objects are running on the same machine or not.

The user client consisted of a central controller dispatcher, instrument stand-in monitors for each instrument, multiple instrument displays, the message window monitor, a shared window monitor, and an annotations monitor. It served as a client for the Routing Server, the Message Server, the Annotation Server, and the Shared Window Server. It contained an instrument proxy for each instrument type that unpacked the instrument data into a data object that was used as the source for data display. Lists of instrument data objects were passed to the graph controller that generated the intermediate information and layout for the data displays. The data views object then generated the actual display, presented the user interface, and passed the results of user actions.

The annotation server received annotations from user clients, created unique identifiers for them, created an object for each annotation, and sent out appropriate information about each annotation to all active user clients. The annotation object kept the following information for each annotation: an integer id that identified each annotation uniquely; the creator of the annotation; an optional subject field; the instrument for which this annotation was made; the mode in which this instrument was being operated; and the time and date of the data stream for which the annotation was attached. A storage object kept track of the name of the user, the text entered, and the time it was entered for each annotation or amendment made by users.

On the client side an Annotation Coordinator in the user client communicated with the Annotation Server, kept a local copy of the annotation object list, and displayed and maintained the Annotation Browser and Annotation Windows. The Annotation Coordinator was connected to one Annotation Manager for each instrument. These Managers performed the instrument specific coordinate conversions to display the new annotation in the displays. An Annotation Interface object responded to mouse downs and button clicks, changed the cursor to the annotation cursor, and drew annotation icons. The Annotation Interface objects of each instrument talked to the instrument specific Annotation Manager.

Annotations were not saved beyond a session unless users specifically save them, although a plausible extension would have been to keep the annotations in a database that would allow them to persist beyond a session and would give users the full range of search and retrieval capabilities.

The shared window capability was based on a prototype implementation of DistView (Prakash & Shim, 1994), a toolkit that provided a shared window server, shared window manager, application object manager, export window manager, and import window manager. The shared window server of DistView played the role of the bookkeeper for exported windows. It was responsible for creating export and import window managers when requested by the application in which it was created. An application object manager supported the application object replication and state transfer operations. An export window manager provided several primitives for the membership and interface object replication and state synchronization services. The export window manager recursively followed the connections between the interface objects of the exported window retrieving the type, size, location, and state information and sent the acquired information to each client importing the window. An import window manager handled requests for the importing of windows and requested the export window manager to export the window to the requesting client. It also coordinated the sending of user actions on a shared window to all clients that share the window. Upon receiving the operation, the import window manager updated the state of the corresponding interface object and triggered a local processing that simulates the specified user-action.

The views of exported and imported windows were synchronized at the semantic, user-action level of abstraction. However, we found that the telepointing capability was more effectively and efficiently achieved by communicating low-level events so that smooth traces of the cursor movements were produced on exported windows. In order to prevent the applications from being blocked due to the telepointing facility, we adapted a nonblocking protocol for telepointing messages in which a message was dropped if it could not be immediately sent. This scheme may temporarily have left the views of shared windows out of synchronization. However, the number of messages for the cursor movements was large enough that the synchronization was often quickly restored. In practice, we found that the overall quality of the regenerated traces of the cursor on imported windows did not significantly suffer even if some messages were dropped.

As mentioned, this system architecture worked well in the early period of UARC, when the number of users and instruments was modest. We found that as the number of active users grew beyond ten and the number of instruments increased beyond five performance with the system seriously degraded. High network traffic loads increased the severity of the problem. This led to the design of the CBE architecture and its subsequent implementation in the Web phase of UARC. These issues are discussed in more detail in Hall, Mathur, Jahanian, Prakash, and Rasmussen (1996) and Lee, Prakash, Jaeger, and Wu (1996).

OBSERVATION OF THE USE OF THE SYSTEM

The NeXTStep version of the UARC software was used extensively from April 1993 until the spring of 1996. We captured the behavior of our users in several ways. First, all user actions with the software were recorded and time stamped in an action log. Second, the contents of the message window were saved by the message server for later analysis. Third, we hired behavioral observers in each of the major sites, and they directly observed the physicists using the software. The observers often asked questions about the software or made notes about how the scientists used it. Sometimes they videotaped these sessions for later analysis. Fourth, users themselves volunteered their reactions to the software, often via email. Starting in the fall of 1994 the software itself had a feature where users could report bugs and suggestions directly within the application to make this even easier, and it was used extensively.

We focused our behavioral observations on campaigns. As noted earlier, the early campaigns in 1993 focused on looking for convection boundary reversals. Only radar data were available over the network. By the fall of 1993 the IRIS and magnetometer data were available, and in the early winter of 1994 engineering data from the Fabry-Perot Interferometer were available. During the winter campaign season in 1993–1994 the UARC software was used extensively. Some particularly noteworthy events were a January 1994 campaign with a number of significant events that led to the conduct of a replay campaign in March 1994 (a specific description of this follows). In February 1994 two space scientists from outside the UARC sites came to Michigan to conduct a campaign rather than go to Greenland. One of these scientists was a theoretician who had never before seen data collection in progress in real time. Throughout this time monthly World Days, when the Greenland radar operates in a standard, predefined mode, were observed by scientists throughout the UARC network. In May of 1994 another convection boundary reversal experiment was done.

In the summer and fall of 1994 further extensive revisions of the software were made. A full complement of Fabry–Perot Interferometer data displays were added, the all sky camera was brought on line, a separate operator's window to support the Greenland site crew was added, the annotation and shared window capabilities were added, and numerous small fixes and additions were made to make the client application more useful and usable and to make the server more reliable.

To give an impression of what these campaigns were like, we include some data obtained between April 1993 and November 1995, during the use of the NeXTStep system for access to the Greenland facility. More recent campaigns using the Java-based implementation and a much wider range of users and data feeds have not been thoroughly analyzed yet. The first set of data are based on analyses of the message window files. We coded the content of the messages using a five-category coding scheme:

- Science—space science phenomena, data, methods
- Session—scheduling, timing, planning
- Technology—UARC system, NeXT, network
- Display—orienting to data displays
- Socializing—greeting, jokes, personal matters

This scheme was developed from earlier experiences with coding conversations while people used collaborative technology (e.g., Olson, Olson, Storrøsten, & Carter, 1993). Coders were trained so they had acceptable reliability in the coding of the messages.

Figure 26.7 shows the distribution of messages by these categories for four different classes of users, summed over all campaigns between April 1993 and November 1994. It is encouraging that for the scientists themselves the most frequent communications were about the science itself. This suggests that the UARC software was serving a useful purpose in the conduct of their science, a suggestion confirmed by detailed observations of their work and discussions with them during and after campaigns. The huge amount of discussion of the Technology by the Others is because these are the pro-

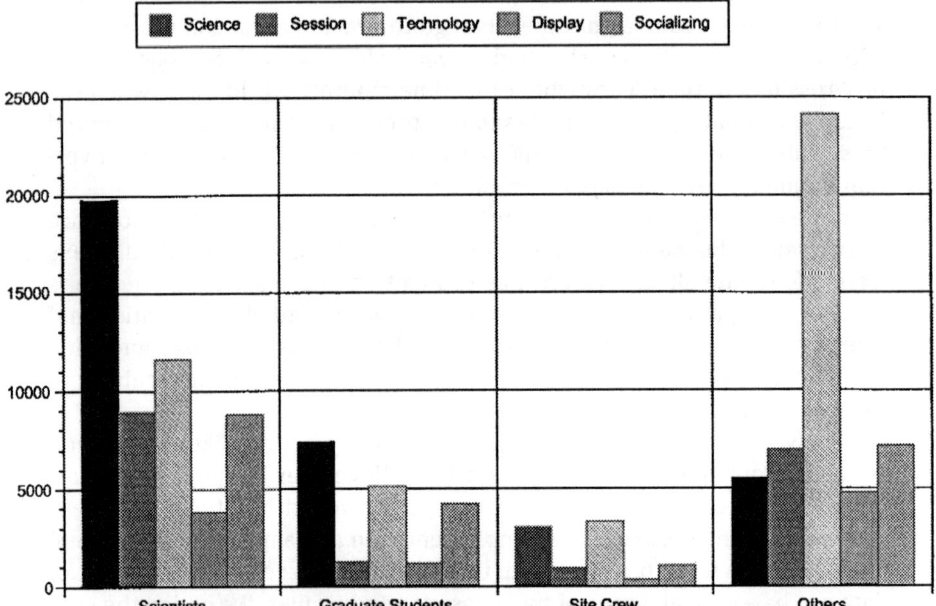

FIG. 26.7. Messages classified by category of Usage over four different classes of user, summarized over all the major campaigns, 1993–1994.

grammers and the behavioral scientists concerned with the development of the software itself, who often used the message window to query users online about the functionality and usability of the software. Indeed, analyses of the content of these Technology discussions has played a major role in the iterative development of the software.

Figure 26.8 shows the three convection boundary reversal experiments mentioned earlier. This shows only the data for the scientists. The distribution of message types is quite constant over this 13-month period, with Science messages dominating throughout. This is with three different versions of the software.

Figure 26.9 shows data for a number of other campaigns carried out during this period. We discuss the replay campaign shortly in more detail.

How do these electronic conversations compare with earlier face-to-face ones? We made such a comparison by using transcripts of face-to-face conversations made at the Sondrestrom site in March of 1993 with a selection of episodes from electronic conversations using the UARC chat facility. The episodes selected for both the face-to-face and electronic conversations

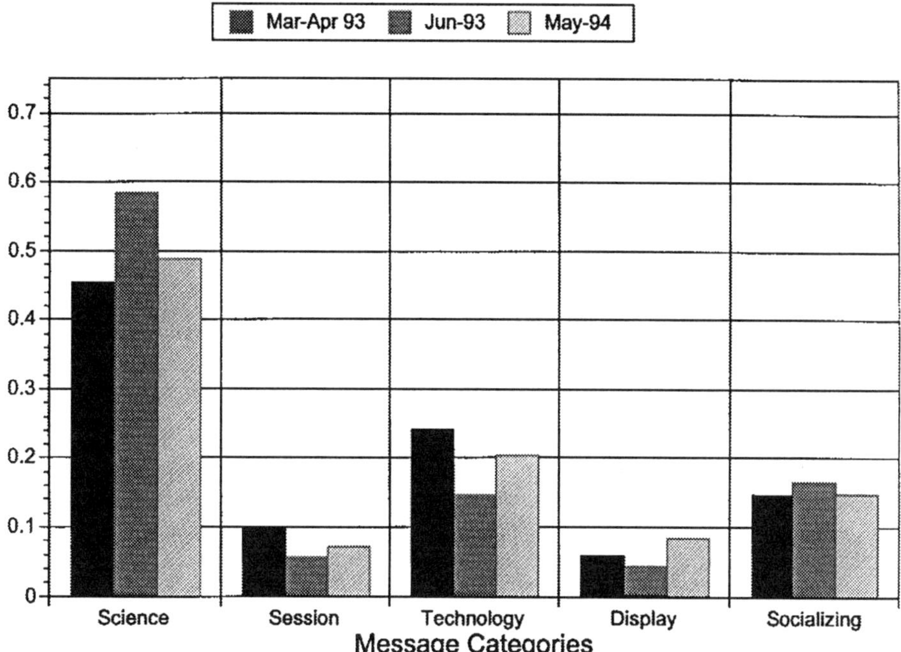

FIG. 26.8. Messages by category in three convection boundary reversal experiments. Note: this involved three different versions of the software.

were from campaigns that involved similar science goals. The conversations focused primarily on the real-time data from the radar. In the case of the face-to-face conversations the data were displayed on a bank of monitors along a wall, whereas in the UARC case they were in windows on the individual participants workstations.

Figure 26.10 shows the relative amounts of conversation in the five coding categories. Both kinds of conversation are dominated by science talk, particularly when interesting things were happening in the displays. During the times when upper atmospheric activity was limited, the face-to-face groups tended to socialize, whereas the UARC users tended to talk about the technology. Such talk was about improvements, bugs, problems, and wish lists of added functionality. Interestingly, there was also socializing in the UARC chat window. Most of it was greetings and goodbyes as participants came and went. But there were periods of jokes, teasing, weather discussions, and even a discussion of an ongoing NCAA tournament basketball game. The ele-

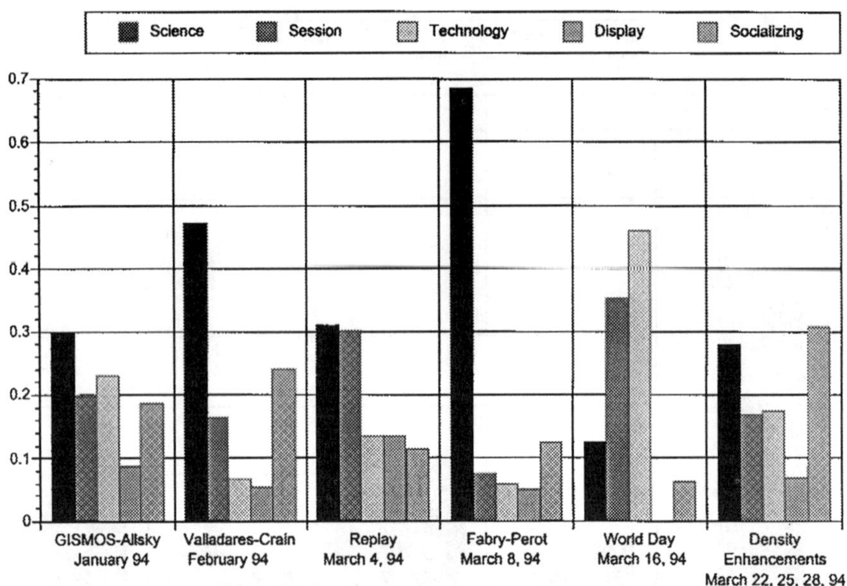

FIG. 26.9. Messages by category for additional campaigns, 1993–1994.

vated levels of display and session coordination in UARC are due to the greater difficulty of coordination using the technology. However, there is an interesting amount of display coordination in the face-to-face setting, reflecting the need to coordinate what people were looking at as they talked about data in front of a large bank of monitors.

Overall, the conversations in the two situations were quite similar. This indicated to us that the technology did not significantly interfere with the object of the scientists' work. The technology clearly got in the way from time-to-time, reflecting in part its prototype status. But the overall pattern of conversation in the electronic medium is surprisingly similar to the in-person interactions. For more details about these two conversational situations see McDaniel, Olson, and Magee (1996).

There has been considerable interest in the literature as to whether computer-mediated communication, with its reduced social cues, equalizes the participation among participants (e.g., Sproull & Kiesler, 1991). We found no evidence of this when we compared patterns of participation between face-to-face and UARC-based conversations. Figure 26.11 shows data for the same set of transcripts that we analyzed in Fig. 26.10. The participation patterns

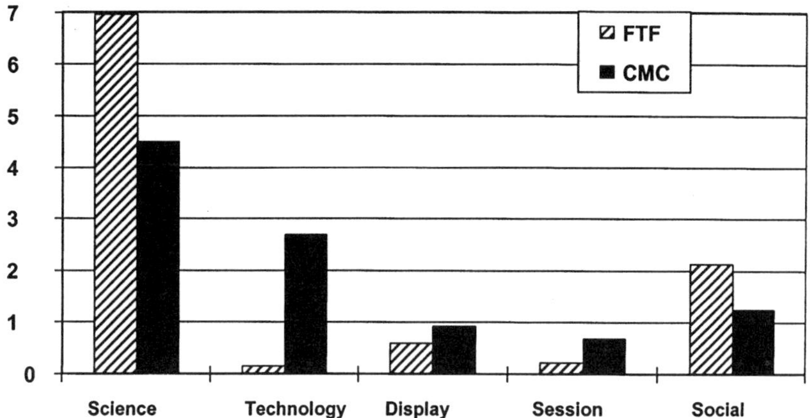

FIG. 26.10. Comparison of content for face-to-face (FTF) and computer-mediated (CMC) conversations.

are very similar for the two kinds of conversations, though significantly there is a much longer tail in the case of UARC, indicating that the technology allowed a large number of "lurkers," people who observed but did not participate very much. This long tail is of course quite important, as it shows how it is possible for the technology to bring the real-time practice of science to a much broader community.

The UARC software has also turned out to be useful between campaigns. Figure 26.12 shows the extent of use of the software between campaigns for the six most active users during the first several years of UARC. The seasonal nature of the science is clear from the periodicity of these data. This between-campaign usage focused, of course, on instruments other than the radar, such as the IRIS, the magnetometer, and the Fabry–Perot. UARC was also used for testing and engineering of the instruments. Some interesting episodes were observed, such as the day that a caribou walked through the field of radio receivers of the IRIS, disrupting the data. The site crew took a photo, digitized it, and sent it via NeXT mail the PI in Copenhagen.

The Replay Campaign of March 1994

As mentioned, there was a campaign in January 1994 with a number of events of great interest to the scientists. Because the data for this session were archived at Michigan for other purposes, several of the scientists asked if it would be possible to replay the 2 days in question so the phenomena that passed by in real time could be examined more carefully. The Michigan programmers set up a replay campaign for this purpose. The archived data were replayed, under hand control of a programmer in Ann

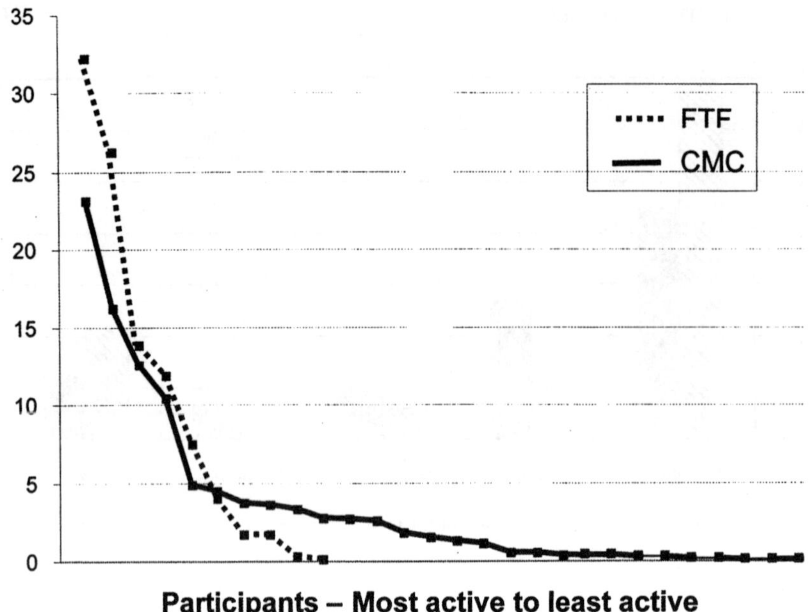

FIG. 26.11. Percentage of time taken up by different participants, ranked by frequency.

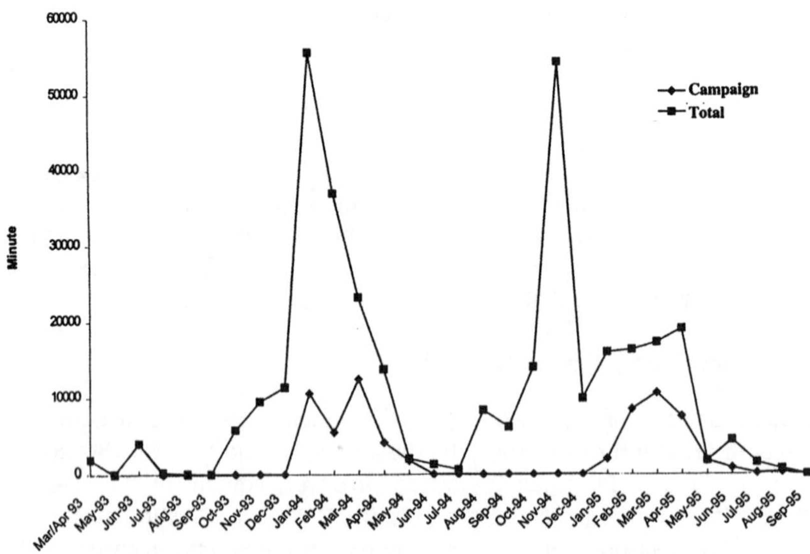

FIG. 26.12. Use of the UARC software by the six most active users, 1993–1995.

Arbor. The principal participants were in Copenhagen, Boston, and Menlo Park. The participants reported that it was extremely valuable to re-examine the session, being able to fast forward over quiet periods, pause or replay interesting periods, and converse through the message window about the phenomena.

This mode of operation had not been anticipated. However, the scientists have reported that this kind of replay campaign is useful both for the science itself and for the training of students and young scientists. We decided not to explicitly support this capability in the current NeXTStep-based versions of the UARC software. This capability is allowed for in the new CBE architecture, but has not yet been implemented.

Use of UARC for Graduate Student Mentoring

One feature of the UARC software that is potentially very important is its role in the training of graduate students. Previously, when data were collected by means of trips to Greenland graduate students would rarely be able to participate in data collection. But with this phase of the science available online students can participate in any campaign, even if only as an observer. This allows students to observe the interactions among a wider range of scientists than is available in their home laboratory, and indeed we have seen episodes of intense interaction between a student in one site and a senior scientist in a different site. Some of our recent extensions of UARC software to new sites will enhance and elaborate the its use for student training.

Summary of Use of UARC Software

The early UARC software was used extensively by a growing community of scientists for real-time data acquisition from Greenland. This provided a foundation for expanding the community of UARC users, making similar capabilities available for other sites where space scientists collect data, and making UARC available for the examination and analysis of archived data. Thus, the early phase of UARC represented a strong beginning for transforming the practice of science.

The technical and social vision of UARC were of course overtaken by the explosive growth of the World Wide Web in the 1994–1995 time period, leading to new phase in the project. The change to a Web-based system also enabled much wider access. Indeed, many of the space physics sites—both ground-based and satellite-based—on their own began providing real-time data feeds over the World Wide Web, which made it easier for UARC to incorporate a wide range of inputs within a unified framework. This enhanced the functionality of UARC and made it useful to an even broader community of users. Early indications are that this broader scope will bring about even more dramatic changes in science practice. But this more recent story is still in progress, and will require further experience and analysis before we understand the full significance of the later period of UARC development.

ACKNOWLEDGMENTS

The UARC project is supported by a Cooperative Agreement from the National Science Foundation. Many people have been involved in the development, testing, and deployment of the UARC software and the longitudinal study of UARC users, including Susan McDaniel, Eric Heldman, Stephanie Mackie-Lewis, Michael Gallo, Torben Elgaard Jensen, Efrat Elron, Joe Magee, Katrina Wade, Galye Farbman, Bill Mott, Bill, Shim, Ramani, Bob Sitar, and Aaron Ridley. We are deeply indebted to a number of people at the National Science Foundation for their stewardship of the project. We owe a special debt to Larry Rosenberg, who was responsible for funding and managing the NSF side of the UARC Cooperative Agreement during its early years. Subsequently Su-Shing Chen and Les Gasser have served in this role. Y. T. Chien also provided advice and counsel throughout the project.

REFERENCES

Coad, P., & Yourdan, E. (1991a) *Object-oriented analysis*. Englewood Cliffs, NJ: Yourdan Press.

Coad, P., & Yourdan, E. (1991b) *Object-oriented design*. Englewood Cliffs, NJ: Yourdan Press.

Finholt, T. A., & Olson, G. M. (1997) From laboratories to collaboratories: A new organizational form for scientific collaboration. *Psychological Science*, 8, 28–36.

Hall, R. W., Mathur, A., Jahanian, F., Prakash, A., & Rasmussen, C. (1996) Corona: A communication service for scalable, reliable group collaboration systems. In *Proceedings of CSCW '96* (Nov. 16–20, Boston, MA). ACM, New York, pp. 140–149.

Jacobson, I., Christerson, M., Jonsson, P., & Overgaard, G. (1992). *Object-oriented software engineering: A use case driven approach*. Reading, MA: Addison-Wesley.

Lee, J. H., Prakash, A., Jaeger, T., & Wu, G. (1996) Supporting multi-user, multi-applet workspaces in CBE. In *Proceedings of CSCW '96* (Nov. 16–20, Boston, MA). ACM, New York, pp. 344–353.

McDaniel, S. E., Olson, G. M., & McGee, J. (1996) Identifying and analyzing multiple threads in computer-mediated and face-to-face conversations. In *Proceedings of CSCW '96* (Nov. 16–20, Boston, MA). ACM, New York, pp. 39–47.

McDaniel, S. E., Olson, G. M., & Olson, J. S. (1994) Methods in search of methodology—Combining HCI and object orientation. In *Proceedings of CHI '94*, ACM, New York, pp. 145–151.

National Research Council. (1993) *National collaboratories: Applying information technology for scientific research*. Washington, DC: National Academy Press.

Olson, J. S., Olson, G. M., Storrøsten, M., & Carter, M. (1993). Groupwork close up: A comparison of the group design process with and without a simple group editor. *ACM Transactions of Information Systems, 11*, 321–348.

Prakash, A., & Shim, H. S. (1994) DistView: Support for building efficient collaborative applications using replicated active objects. In *Proceedings of CSCW '94*, ACM, New York, pp. 153–164.

Sproull, L., & Kiesler, S. (1991) *Connections: New ways of working in the networked organization.* Cambridge, MA: MIT Press.

Wulf, W. A. (1989) The national collaboratory—a white paper. Appendix A in *Towards a national collaboratory.* Unpublished report of an invitational workshop at Rockefeller University, March 17–18, 1989.

Author Index

C

D

Subject Index

N

O

P

R

S

T

U

V

W

X